THE DRINK THAT MADE WISCONSIN FAMOUS

**ALSO BY DOUG HOVERSON
PUBLISHED BY THE
UNIVERSITY OF MINNESOTA PRESS**

Land of Amber Waters:
The History of Brewing in Minnesota

The Drink That Made Wisconsin Famous

Beer and Brewing in the Badger State

DOUG HOVERSON

UNIVERSITY OF MINNESOTA PRESS

MINNEAPOLIS : LONDON

"Beer Cans and Breweriana" is adapted from Doug Hoverson, "Art, Beer, and Collecting: The ABCs of Breweriana," *ABA Journal*, Museum Commemorative Edition (June 2008). Special thanks to Dave Wendl, who provided access to the North Star Chapter archives.

Unless otherwise credited, all contemporary photography in this book, including objects from collections, is by Robert Fogt.

Copyright 2019 by Doug Hoverson

All rights reserved. No part of this publication may be reproduced, stored in a retrieval system, or transmitted, in any form or by any means, electronic, mechanical, photocopying, recording, or otherwise, without the prior written permission of the publisher.

Published by the University of Minnesota Press
111 Third Avenue South, Suite 290
Minneapolis, MN 55401-2520
http://www.upress.umn.edu

Book design and composition by Anders Hanson
Photographs prepared for printing by color specialist Timothy Meegan

ISBN 978-0-8166-6991-2 (hc)

A Cataloging-in-Publication record for this book is available from the Library of Congress.

Printed in China on acid-free paper

The University of Minnesota is an equal-opportunity educator and employer.

25 24 23 22 21 20 19   10 9 8 7 6 5 4 3 2 1

A tour guide at Pabst Brewing Co. in Milwaukee poses in a keg storage room (ca. 1953–54). COLLECTION OF JOHN STEINER.

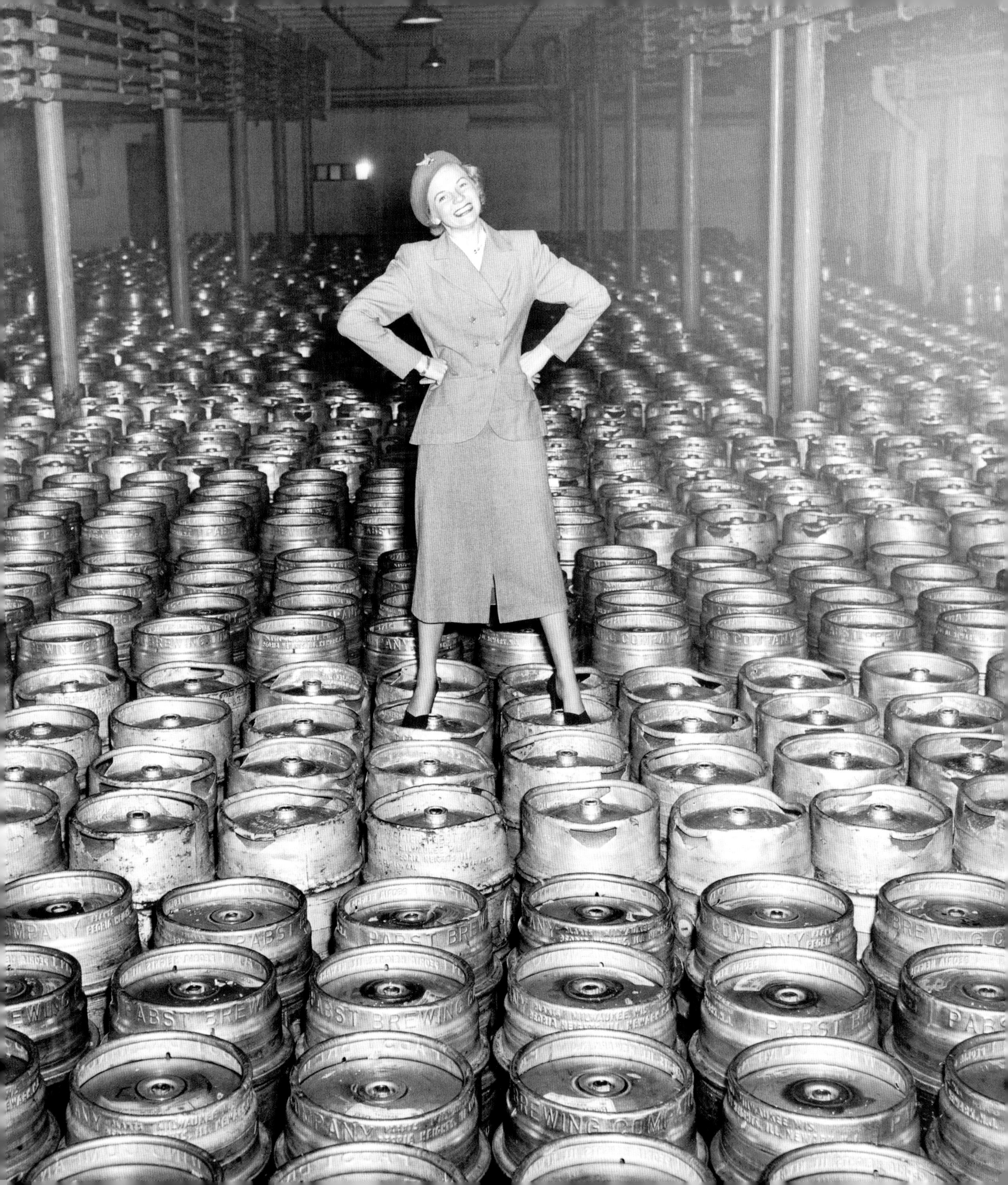
PABST BREWING
COMPANY
PABST BREWING
COMPANY

Table of

On Wisconsin! 1

Acknowledgments 7

1
From Barley to Barstool
The Art and Science of Beer 15

Thoughts on Enjoying Beer Properly 29

2
Pioneer Brewing
1835–1860 33

Becoming a Brewer 48

Charles Hottelmann 54

3
Encouraging Home Industry
1855–1915 61

Signs of the Times 70

4
The Leading Industry
1860–1920 93

Steam Breweries 111

5
Milwaukee–Queen of Lager
1865–1915 121

Sealing the Deal: Bottle Closures 134

Exhibitionists 155

6
Oasis in the Dry Years
1840–1932 169

Homebrewing 202

CONTENTS

7
BACK TO WORK, OFF TO WAR
1932–1955   207

WORKING IN A MID-SIZED BREWERY   221

8
THE AMERICAN WAY OF BEER
1945–1975   245

BERLIN BREWING COMPANY   273

9
ONE LITE ON, OTHER LIGHTS OUT
1970–2015   279

BEER CANS AND BREWERIANA   288

10
RETURN OF THE LOCAL
1965–2018   311

WHAT IS A CRAFT BREWERY?   329

RETURN TO POTOSI   352

WISCONSIN BREWERIES *and Brewpubs*   355

NOTES   677
INDEX   704

Leinenkugel's
Museum
Brewery
Tours
Chippewa Falls - 29 E. to 124 N.
COLLINS

ON WISCONSIN!

IT SEEMS UNNECESSARY TO JUSTIFY THE IMPORTANCE OF WISCONSIN IN THE WORLD of beer. After all, Milwaukee's baseball team is called the Brewers! There's a tavern at every intersection! But Wisconsin's claim to be the state that made beer famous is not obvious. New York, Pennsylvania, and Ohio all had more breweries in their histories in the period prior to the craft-brewing explosion, and California, Colorado, and eleven other states had more in operation at the end of 2016. Wisconsin's statewide production did not pass that of New York until 1949. While Pabst was the first American brewery to produce one million barrels per year, St. Louis's Anheuser-Busch (now AB InBev) has been the largest brewing company in the country since Dwight Eisenhower was president.

Beer came to Wisconsin with early settlers who brewed it for themselves, though for several decades it was a local product of no particular celebrity. The argument that Wisconsin beer became famous when brewers rushed to the aid of Chicago in the aftermath of the devastating 1871 fire is not convincing. Several Wisconsin brewers had been in the Chicago market years before, and the relief effort was unlikely to have spread the fame of Milwaukee or Wisconsin throughout the world. But by the 1880s, Wisconsin lager was in demand around the globe—a fact celebrated in the Schlitz logo. For well over a century, at least one Badger State brewing company has been among the five largest in the nation—sometimes as many as three at a time. Wisconsin's leadership of the industry makes the state worthy of study.

But there is much more to Wisconsin beer than just the Milwaukee and La Crosse giants. Milwaukee beer became famous through consistent quality and relentless promotion, but the smaller brewers of the Badger State built their reputations by jealously defending their local markets and building a sense of place for their products. German immigrants brought their craft and thirst with them to their new home, and provided the vast majority of the workers (and many of the customers). While it's not quite true that "every little town had a brewery," many did: Wisconsin's nearly eight hundred commercial breweries since 1835 have been spread out through nearly three hundred cities, villages, and townships. These breweries proved remarkably resistant to consolidation and contraction—in the decades after Prohibition ended in 1933, Wisconsin usually had more small-town breweries than any other state (except sometimes the much more populous Pennsylvania). Even before beer tourism became popular under that name, hunters, anglers, and other travelers purchased and enjoyed beer from small cities like Rice Lake, Stevens Point, and Chippewa Falls.

This diversity makes Wisconsin an excellent case study of America's brewing industry. The Miller Brewing Company (MillerCoors) is one of only three American breweries that grew from a family business in the mid-nineteenth century and survived Prohibition, consolidation, and market pressures to remain an international brewer today. Pabst, Schlitz, and Blatz led the growth of national brewers before Prohibition became federal law in 1920 and helped make bottled beer an important consumer product. Breweries in cities like Madison, Manitowoc, Racine, and Sheboygan gained a regional reputation, and the three big breweries of La Crosse earned a market well beyond the Midwest. But Wisconsin's hundreds of small family breweries demonstrated another facet of the industry that represented the vast majority of businesses. Some lasted for mere months, but the Leinenkugel family has just celebrated 150 years of brewing. A combination of dedicated ownership, relative geographic isolation, and local pride kept many of these businesses open long beyond what economics and business theory would suggest was possible. Wisconsin is arguably unique in its combination of

Despite its proximity to much larger breweries in La Crosse, the Fountain City Brewing Co. remained open until 1965. This "high profile"–style cone-top can dates to the early 1950s.
COLLECTION OF DAVID WENDL.

breweries that had the power to help determine market conditions and those that could only adapt to them. Its variety of breweries of all sizes and all durations makes Wisconsin more instructive and interesting to study than most other states.

Wisconsin offers other fields of analysis important to the brewing industry possessed by few other states. The importance of brewing to the state and its economy meant that beer was a frequent topic of legislation in state and local government. Wisconsin was (and is) home to dozens of important businesses that have supplied everything from refrigeration equipment to labels. The advertising campaigns undertaken on behalf of Wisconsin's breweries have been among the most memorable of those for any product. From the Blue Ribbon to the Miller Lite All-Stars, from "When you're out of Schlitz, you're out of beer" to "When you're out of Point, you're out of town," beer has been the welcoming face of Wisconsin to the nation. Wisconsin's brewery workers were part of the union movement that brought improved conditions to many workplaces, but they were also involved in several significant strikes that changed the balance of power in the industry. Wisconsin has given the world several important craft breweries, some of which have helped pioneer new models of operating breweries.

Wisconsin's brewers have been able to capitalize on the soil and climate of their home for many of the ingredients for their beer. Brewers were able to obtain much of their barley from local sources—especially rural pioneer breweries, which provided a lucrative market for this crop. The region centered on Sauk County was an important hop-growing district during the 1860s and 1870s, though most hops have been imported from other states and countries. The local water was ideal for brewing, and, just as important, it froze during the winter, so it could be harvested as ice. Wisconsin's geology and topography made possible the caves that were essential to developing lager beer in the days before refrigeration. Wisconsin's brewers used convenient lake, river, and rail transportation to ship their beer to a waiting world. Wisconsin's tavern culture has also played a role in making beer the ubiquitous host beverage of the state. Throughout the post-Prohibition period, Wisconsin led the nation in the percentage of beer sold on draught. Liberal laws also meant that beer could be purchased for consumption off the premises ("off-sale") in taverns, grocery stores, and even gas stations.

In short, Wisconsin took advantage of favorable resources, the presence of skilled and thirsty German workers, and good timing to become the state that represented lager beer to most Americans for more than a century. The social and political climate of Wisconsin encouraged craft brewers to establish new breweries and lead the way into the twenty-first century.

But Wisconsin also offers a counterpoint to the dominance of the beer barons. Reformers decried

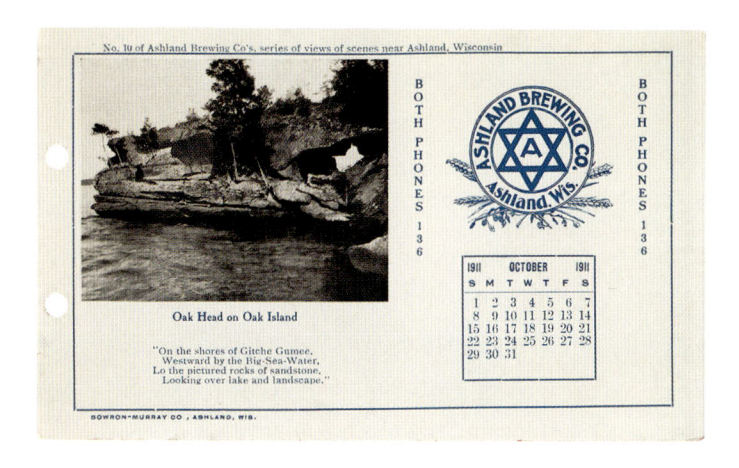

My interest in this 1911 calendar page from Ashland Brewing Co. increased dramatically when I noticed that it was printed by Bowron-Murray Co. of Ashland—in which my great-grandfather David Murray was a partner. COLLECTION OF DAVID WENDL.

the power of "lager beer" and the saloons, and the state was among the leaders in the temperance movement. Frances Willard helped found the Woman's Christian Temperance Union and became something of a cult heroine for women testing their political power. Temperance societies flourished in Wisconsin, and reform-minded politicians supported their efforts to improve society. While Wisconsin's politicians were relatively quick to adopt prohibition, the reaction of citizens to the law was much less enthusiastic. Their proximity to Chicago involved several Wisconsin cities in mob-related brewing activity, though outsiders were hardly required to encourage Wisconsinites of all walks of life to make their own beer.

While New York, Pennsylvania, Ohio, Missouri, and California all share many of these characteristics, no other state brings them all together, and no other state celebrates them so enthusiastically and almost effortlessly.

Even though I have been a lifelong Minnesota resident, Wisconsin has always been a special place for me. One of my first trips out of Minnesota was to visit my great-aunt in Ashland. Our visits to family in Ontario included a drive along U.S. Highway 8, which crossed Wisconsin at its widest point.

On those long trips I looked for license plates from different states, and the bright yellow "cheese" or "butter" license plates proclaiming the state as "America's Dairyland" were mobile calling cards for the "Cheeseheads." Little did I know in the 1970s that I later would spend nearly a decade

Memorable ad campaigns helped make Wisconsin beers a part of everyday life. Many people can still sing along with Pabst's "What'll you have?," which was introduced in 1951. COLLECTION OF JOHN STEINER.

4   THE DRINK THAT MADE WISCONSIN FAMOUS

researching another product for which Wisconsin was even more famous.

My first exposure to the beers of Wisconsin was probably through advertising. I have memories of television ads for Old Style proclaiming that it was "Pure Brewed in God's Country" and extolling the krausening process—whatever that was. The old Schlitz Malt Liquor commercials kept viewers wondering when the bull was going to burst through a wall. The Miller Lite All-Stars were unforgettable, and jingles for Blue Ribbon, High Life, and other brands, including Löwenbräu, provided entertaining breaks during football telecasts. (I never disliked the Packers, perhaps because I read Jerry Kramer's book *Instant Replay* at a young age, or maybe because I first started to follow football around 1973—a dark time for the Green and Gold.)

My Dad was at a stage where the most important factor in his beer-buying decision was price. We had Old Style and Special Export around the house on occasion, but only if they were on sale. I wasn't really aware of brands beyond the nationally advertised leaders until I went over to my friend Jeff Helgemoe's house in 1980 and saw his wall-to-wall collection of beer cans. I was sixteen at the time and thoroughly indoctrinated against drinking, but the colors, designs, and varieties of the cans made a lasting impression. As a nineteen-year-old college student, stopping in Wisconsin (drinking age: eighteen) to pick up some beer on the way back to the University of Michigan (drinking age: twenty-one) became a

While the more famous Paul Bunyan statues are in Minnesota, the legendary lumberjack is celebrated throughout the North woods. Weber Waukesha Brewing Co. canned Paul Bunyan beer during the late 1950s. COLLECTION OF DAVID WENDL.

ON WISCONSIN! 5

regular occurrence. Because I had fallen in with members of the Michigan Men's Glee Club who favored quality beer to cheap swill, I chose the legendary regional brands—Leinenkugel and Point.

When craft beers (then called microbrews) began to appear in the Twin Cities, a few Wisconsin brands like Sprecher were on the shelves next to Summit, Schell's, and Sierra Nevada. I was particularly fond of the Hibernia products, especially the Dunkel Weizen, a style I had not tried before. Each spring brought the competition between the Wisconsin bock beers—which was the best among Leinie, Point, or Huber? Usually Leinie's, but Point earned extra points for rarity, in much the same way that today a rare, limited-release beer tastes better because of the quest (and sometimes to justify the price).

When I completed my first book, *Land of Amber Waters: The History of Brewing in Minnesota*, I was interested in writing another book, but not necessarily on beer. However, my then-editor, Todd Orjala, insisted that I look east and take on the daunting task of writing about the heritage of a state identified with beer like few other places on Earth. Luckily, the people I had met and the things I learned during the earlier project helped make up for the fact that Wisconsin had nearly three times as many breweries during its history as Minnesota had. In addition, there were already several books on breweries in the Badger State to guide my early searches. This was neutralized by the fact that the Wisconsin Historical Society library was a four-hour drive from home (compared to a half-hour bike ride to the Minnesota Historical Society). It was fortunate that the vast expansion in the number of historic newspapers available online occurred during my research, and that many important Wisconsin papers were included in these holdings. (Unfortunately, Google News Archive Search temporarily removed the *Milwaukee Journal* and *Sentinel* a few months before I was done researching.) I was able to revisit places like the National Archives depository in Chicago, the Beer Institute, and the Library of Congress. I learned about the R. G. Dun & Company credit reports held in the Baker Library at Harvard University, which became a good excuse for a few working vacations to the East Coast.

Back in 2009, I was interviewed about my budding project by a radio host in Platteville and asked for the first time, "Why should a Minnesotan get to write a book about Wisconsin beer?" Aside from the fact that I had already deposited the advance check, there were several reasons. But sometimes it takes an outsider to appreciate the uniqueness of a culture and to explain to others what is self-evident to someone immersed in that way of life. And beer is not just another product or source of employment in Wisconsin: it's a way of life.

Tasting a variety of beers with like-minded investigators was an essential part of the research. In this tin sign "The House Committee on Refreshments" reported: "Beer may be right and not be Gund's, but it can't be Gund's and not be right" (sign ca. 1911). COLLECTION OF RICHARD YAHR.

Acknowledgments

"Are you writing another beer book? Can I help this time?" While most of the offers were to help taste the products of the breweries, hundreds of people helped expand my knowledge of Wisconsin's brewing history and its present industry. Many responded graciously to my requests for information or images; some sought me out and offered the fruits of their many years of painstaking research.

The brewers must be thanked first, because without them there is no product, and because they often had the least time to spare. To all of those who spoke with me while cleaning the brewhouse, adjusting the bottling line, or waiting for the boil to finish, thank you. Several brewers deserve special mention for the time they spent with me (some have moved to other breweries or retired since I spoke with them): in no particular order, Deb and Dan Carey of New Glarus Brewing Company, Randy Sprecher of Sprecher Brewing, Russ and Jim Klisch of Lakefront Brewery, Dick Leinenkugel of Jacob Leinenkugel Brewing

Company, Rob LoBreglio of Great Dane Pub and Brewery, Kirby Nelson (then of Capital Brewery), Marc Buttera of O'So Brewing, Tom Porter of Lake Louie Brewing, and Jim Wiesender and Todd Krueger of Sand Creek Brewing Company all went beyond the call of duty to tell me about their breweries and the business. Bo Bélanger of South Shore Brewery was the first to offer his assistance—at a book-signing event for *Land of Amber Waters* before this book was even under way. Others who offered me tours of their breweries (and products) or significant research assistance include Kevin Eichelberger of Red Eye Brewing Company, Paul Graham of Central Waters Brewing, Grant Pauly of 3 Sheeps Brewing, Bill Summers of Tribute Brewing Company, David Knuth of Knuth Brewing, Jamie (Martin) Baertsch of Wisconsin Dells Brewing Company, Hathaway Dilba of Ale Asylum, Jon Martens of Copper State Brewing,

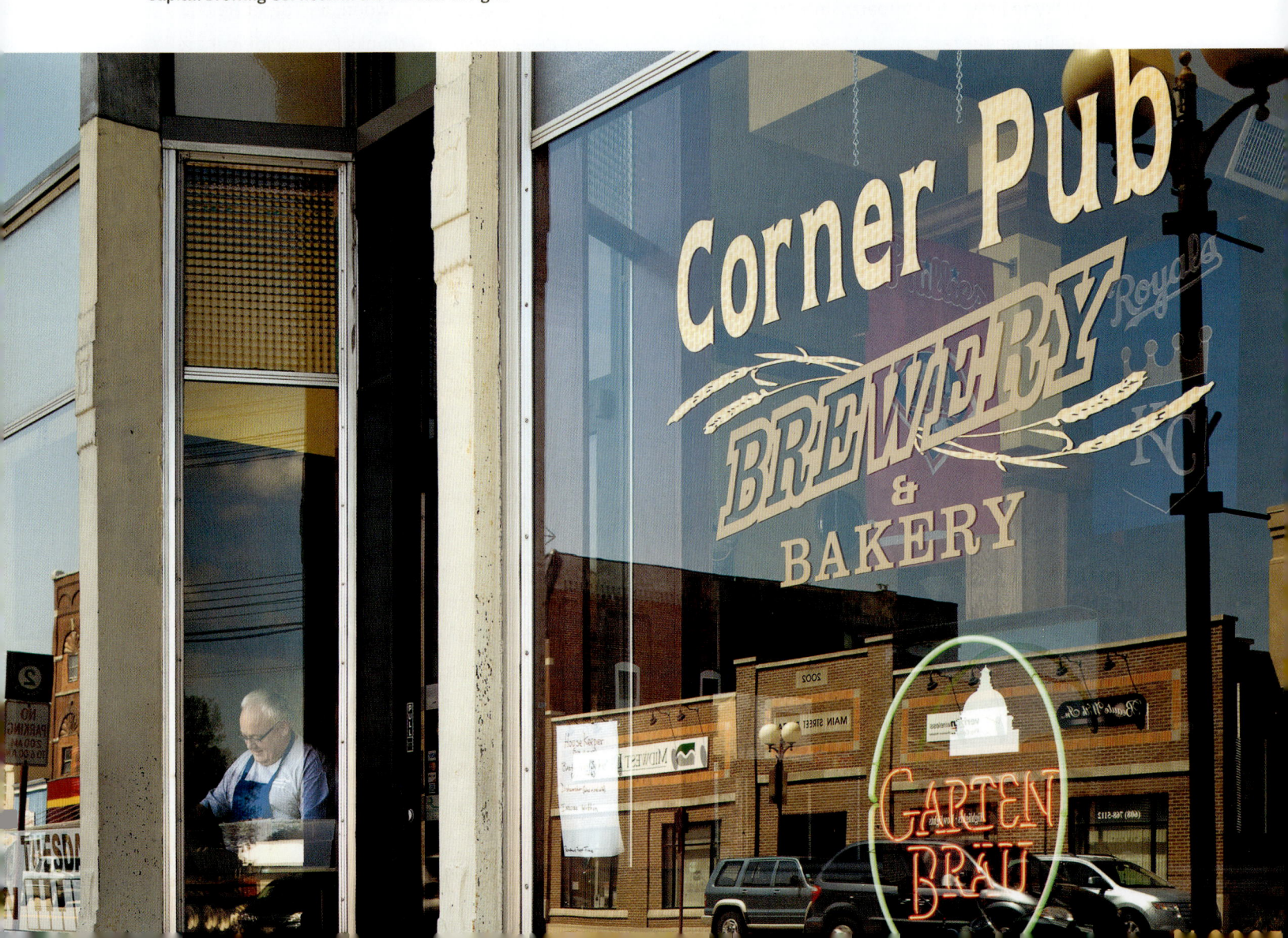

Brewer Pete Peterson made burgers in 2011 in the front window of the Corner Pub in Reedsburg. Note the early Capital Brewing Co. neon in the window at right.

Zach Kubichek of Sawmill Brewing, Robert Wilbers (then of Das Bierhaus), Page Buchanan of House of Brews, Christie Forrer of Rocky Reef Brewing, Trevor Easton of Alt Brew, Jason Rasmussen of Angry Minnow, Jim Stirn of Brewster Bros. Brewing Company, Dave Anderson of Dave's BrewFarm, Dan Stolt of Bloomer Brewing Company, Robert Flemming of Delafield Brewhaus, Leos Frank of Lazy Monk Brewery, Ed Rogers of Northwoods Brew Pub, Jim Goronson of Parched Eagle Brewhaus, Eric Hansen of 8th Street Ale Haus, Randy Lee of Valkyrie Brewing Company, and Kris Konyn of Railhouse Restaurant and Brewery. Tim and Toni Eichinger of Black Husky Brewing earn extra points for talking with me while I got to play with a couple of their dogs at the Pembine town picnic. Rob Larson and Stacey Schraufnagel of Tyranena Brewing Company, Nick Calaway of Ahnapee Brewery, Will Glass of the Brewing Projekt, John Zappa of Stevens Point Brewery, Roger and Cindy Miller of MoonRidge Brewpub, Steve Lonsway of Stone Arch Brewpub, David Oldenburg of Titletown Brewing, Michael Varnes-Epstein and Chris Balistreri of Driftless Brewing Company, Gordon Lane of Biloba Brewing Company, Andrew Fabry of Badger State Brewing Company, Patrick Rowland of Rowland's Calumet Brewery, and Richard Stueven all offered rich information via interviews or correspondence. Many more took time out at beer festivals to share their experiences. Brewery and taproom employees contributed their insights and helped guide my tasting sessions. Homebrewers and beer judges in Minnesota and Wisconsin also provided guidance on beer and brewing.

Obtaining the photographs of the many stunning brewery artifacts shown in these pages would not have been possible without the talent of photographer Robert Fogt and the patience of Bob and the collectors whose houses we took over—sometimes for several days at a time. Most grateful thanks to Tye Schwalbe, John Steiner, and Dave Wendl for allowing us to photograph their collections and for telling the stories behind the items. Tye helped facilitate our photo session at the ABA National Brewery Museum in Potosi, along with Herb Page, Larry Bowden, and Scott Reich. Scott deserves special thanks for providing more than one hundred images from his collection of Wisconsin craft beer labels and ephemera, as well as for introducing me to several breweries in the greater Madison area and keeping me up to date on events in the Wisconsin craft beer world. Herb and Helen Haydock helped coordinate a photography session at the 2010 NABA convention in Stevens Point and offered items from their collection for photographing, as did several other NABA members. Others who provided illustrations are credited throughout the book.

The organizations of brewery historians and artifact collectors create a valuable and friendly context that made my research much easier and more fulfilling. The American Breweriana Association (ABA), National Association of Brewery Advertising (NABA), Brewery Collectibles Club of America (BCCA) and the North Star, Packer, Badger Bunch, and Port of Potosi chapters thereof perform a great service in bringing together those who collect and research the history of breweries old and new, large and small. Collectors (and friends) who gave special assistance include Reino and Liisa Ojala, Barry Travis, Steve Ketcham, Del Worden, Jim Rowley, Jon Huntington, Pete Stark, Jerry Strebel, Herb Page, Jim Massey, Larry Bowden, Jeff Scholz, and Len Chylack. Peter Fauerbach and Nancy Moore Gettelman contributed information on their families' brewery. Extra special thanks to Tom Curran, who arranged an interview with his father, Patrick, who was president of the Berlin Brewing Company in its last years. Jerry and Sherry Janiszewski helped me with the Milwaukee brewing scene, and Lowell Peterson kept me current on La Crosse area breweries.

Several collectors who helped me have also written about brewery history, and their work, whether published or unpublished, made my work easier and the end result better. Other beer writers came to this subject by other paths but were equally gracious with their time and results. John Dutcher shared his research on breweries of southwestern Wisconsin, took me to several brewery sites, and introduced me to others who could help. Leonard Jurgensen has done more detailed research on the historic breweries of Milwaukee than anyone else and helped me separate history from myth for many of the earliest businesses. Richard Rossin Jr. generously made available the results of his archival research on breweries from Eau Claire to Sauk City to Cazenovia. Lee Reiherzer offered newly unearthed information about historic breweries on the north and west sides of Lake Winnebago and maintains the *Oshkosh Beer* blog, which chronicles the modern breweries of the region. Brian Zenefski was an expert guide to the breweries of Appleton, but his most valuable contribution to brewery history has been his passion for tracking down former employees of the Geo. Walter Brewing Company of Appleton and collecting their stories for posterity. Dave and Judy Eulberg shared their research on the Eulberg Brewing Company of Portage. Kevin Knitt's research on the breweries of Weyauwega helped untangle that complicated history and also assisted with research on breweries in Stevens Point. Robert Bier offered valuable help on the complicated history of the breweries of Janesville and publishes new research as he finds it on his "Janesville Breweries" Facebook page. Larry Bowden provided detailed information on the brewery in Platteville. John Robert Kurth shared his research on his family's brewery in Columbus and served Bob Fogt and me the tastiest one-dollar draught I've had in many years. Tony Dierckins shared drafts of his work on the breweries of Superior and provided continued advice as we debated the histories of the brewers of the Twin Ports. Randy Carlson's indexes to the major brewing journals made working with them much easier. Carl Miller gave me copies of early brewing directories. Otto Tiegs provided information about the breweries of Slinger and Watertown and wrote detailed articles about other breweries for *American Breweriana Journal*. Several of these articles were written with Bob Pirie, who has been a fountain of information about the current craft brewing scene as well as many historic breweries. Tim Wolter shared his work on the lesser-known breweries of Chippewa Falls and some of the remaining brewery caves of western Wisconsin (many chronicled at his blog *Detritus of Empire*). Michael R. Reilly's research, published on the Sussex–Lisbon Area Historical Society website, is especially helpful when researching Schlitz and the small breweries of Waukesha County. And while Rich Wagner, Donald Roussin, and Kevin Kious all specialize in other states, they helped with research ideas and engaged in the debate of who really made the first lager beer in America. Many others helped answer questions I had about various breweries.

Many other writers and historians provided essential help. Robin Shepard wrote the first true guidebook to the operating breweries of Wisconsin and was always willing to answer questions. Bob Paolino's work in *Great Lakes Brewing News* (later supplemented by Brad Bryan and Josh Johnson) was essential to keeping track of current events in Wisconsin beer, and he also engaged with questions on the relationship of government, law, and beer. Michael Agnew wrote an excellent guide to the breweries of "the Heartland" and has contributed advice through his blog *A Perfect Pint* and our frequent conversations at beer events. Paul Bialas shared photographs from his books and invited me to join him when he was photographing items in the Leinenkugel archives. Jana Weiß, a German scholar of American breweries, shared her research and insights. Wayne Kroll's research on the farm breweries of the state is an essential starting point for anyone studying Wisconsin's smaller breweries. Steven R. Libbey of the MrBottles.com website deserves special recognition for cataloging the bottles found by collectors and archaeologists. While not a brewing historian, attorney Richard T. Thomson offered useful insights on law and the brewing industry and provided searches of legal databases. The work of many others is cited throughout the text.

Susan Appel contributed the vast majority of the information on brewery architecture contained in this book and was always available to answer perplexing and trivial questions about brewery buildings. Tim Holian allowed me to use his collection of brewery publications as well as his oral histories of important brewery figures of the post-Prohibition period. These two also served as reviewers of chapters 1–10. Their thorough readings and careful comments and criticisms made this a more accurate, informative, and readable book.

Several museums and archives allowed access to their files for research or use of illustrations. Special thanks to Erik Brooks and Dan Scholzen of MillerCoors for tracking down dozens of pictures in a range of subjects and for fact-checking the sections on the breweries connected to the Miller family. Thanks to Erik for taking me on a tour of the warehouse where the Miller historic artifacts are stored. The staff of the Beer Institute in Washington, D.C., granted me access to its research library. Archivists at the Milwaukee County Historical Society assisted me with their collection and brought me books and artifacts seldom seen by the public. The Wisconsin Historical Society Library and Archives is a national treasure—but I wish the newspaper collection were organized by city and not by acquisition date. A significant portion of its map collection was placed online during the course of my research, which saved me considerable time, effort, and cost. Several of the Area Research Centers provided assistance, but the most important was Kathryn Otto and her staff at University of Wisconsin–River Falls. Since River Falls was the closest ARC to my home, they facilitated my many and voluminous requests from the archival collections.

My partners at the University of Minnesota Press have made another book possible, and their professionalism and patience have been remarkable. Todd Orjala left the Press a few years into this project (though not because the book took so long), and he was the one who insisted that I take on this daunting topic. Erik Anderson took over, providing essential support and guidance. Kristian Tvedten took care of many of the logistical and production issues; Caitlin Newman and later Molly Fuller and Eric Lundgren worked on outreach and development; and Erik Hane helped edit an early draft of the book. Laura Westlund shepherded the project through the process, Daniel Ochsner oversaw production, and Mary Byers provided thorough and sensitive copyediting.

Even with the involvement of so many people, this book is still incomplete and doubtless has inaccuracies. Some facts about the breweries may never be known. Some information may be known but was not available to me during the course of my research. And some information was omitted so that this book would be light enough to carry. At times I came to different conclusions than did others who studied the same sources, and for these instances I take responsibility. I hope this book will serve as a new baseline for the study of Wisconsin's breweries, a new start to the continuing discussion.

Finally, to those who supported me beyond the actual writing and research . . . My friends and colleagues at Saint Thomas Academy, as well as the students and their families, were just as supportive for this project as they were for *Land of Amber Waters,* which was even more appreciated since I did not have the benefit of a sabbatical this time.

Several longtime friends deserve thanks. Jeff Helgemoe got this started when he showed me his breweriana collection back in high school. Brad Peterson has been foremost among those who had to put up with my shoptalk in a taproom or brewpub when he was just trying to enjoy a beer. Lance Jones provided a bed and fellowship on trips to Milwaukee, and with his wife, Sandra, gave wonderful meals to a weary traveler. Mark Ahlstrom became a welcome companion at beer festivals and taproom visits. The second bass section of the Plymouth Congregational Church choir (Jim Bohn, Ray Martin, Ned McCraine, and Dan Dougherty) were a constant source of inspiration and a frequent source of beer.

So how does one write half a million words on the beer of one state and then try to thank his family in a few hundred words? Inadequately. My mother, Connie Murray, facilitated my first attempts at archival research many years ago and has been supportive ever since. She has a talent for finding obscure yet affordable books about beer and brewing online. My father, Burt Hoverson,

Many brewpubs have made special efforts to make their establishments family friendly. The cups, antlers, and activity placemats are from Moosejaw Pizza Company/Dells Brewing Co. in Wisconsin Dells, Great Dane Pub & Brewing in Madison, and Northwoods Brewpub in Eau Claire. AUTHOR'S COLLECTION.

shared a love of history and beer and, after I was able to convert him from the cheap stuff, has joined in many beer adventures and takes pride in sharing a name with Burton Ale. His wife, Sandy, continues to discover brewery artifacts on their frequent trips and encourages the project. My in-laws and extended family have all been enthusiastic about my work, as well as respectfully hesitant in asking how it has been coming along—my answer changed only by small degrees until recently. Thank you so much.

The biggest personal difference between this book and the last has been the growth of my children. Daughter Claire has grown from being appalled at my choice of research topics to insisting we go to good local taprooms with sour beers on the menu. Although she will not admit it, I half suspect that she chose to attend Illinois Wesleyan University because there was a Destihl brewpub near campus where I could take her to dinner when visiting. Son Alex has now survived, with no evident trauma, several years of having me as a teacher and coach, but he still claims to his author father that he doesn't like to read. Even when they tried to schedule vacations in places where they thought beer would not be a factor (as I promised them in the last dedication), it still was.

My wife, Kerry, probably has the most ambivalent view of this enterprise. At the beginning of *Land of Amber Waters* I wrote, "at least it's done." Or not. There were many things we could not have predicted about the reception of *Land of Amber Waters,* such as when friends and neighbors would introduce her as "the beer guy's wife." Watching while I held impromptu book signings at the kids' concerts probably wasn't part of the deal, nor was acting as a courier for work colleagues who wanted their copies of a four-pound book signed. Writing about Wisconsin has entailed much more travel and many more nights in my office. I still probably haven't helped you clean up the kitchen as much as I should—especially since my beer glasses have taken over more shelf space than you consider appropriate for any normal person. Yet you still put up with the disruptions and stay calm and caring. I love you, and this time I will make no speculative assurances that the beer writing is done.

A shaft of light illuminates the blow-off bucket at Sand Creek Brewing Company in Black River Falls. Excess carbon dioxide is released through the bucket while preventing oxygen from contaminating the fermenting brew.

CHAPTER 1

FROM *Barley* TO BARSTOOL

THE ART & SCIENCE OF BEER

A Sauk Co. farmer named Mathias Schmelzkopf fed a cow malt and hops, and a bit of a yeast cake, and claimed to have a cow that gave beer instead of milk!

Milwaukee Daily Journal, 1 NOVEMBER 1883

BEER IS A WONDERFUL COMBINATION OF SIMPLICITY AND COMPLEXITY. IT IS SO simple that illiterate peasants made it for centuries with only the ingredients at hand. Its complexity inspired some of the greatest minds of modern chemistry to help solve the problems of brewing. In lands from ancient Mesopotamia and Egypt to colonial America, individuals and governments recorded their attempts to brew, drink, and tax a beverage fermented from local grain. A few scientifically minded brewers even left their recipes.[1]

The term *beer* encompasses many beverages: it can be any fermented beverage with a grain base. (Sake, the Japanese drink, sometimes erroneously called rice wine, is actually part of beer's extended family.) The terms *ale* and *beer* are nearly interchangeable, but not quite. While ale is beer, not all beers are ales. In England during the Middle Ages, the term *ale* was commonly used for traditional fermented beverages, and *beer* was used to distinguish a new drink that was bittered with hops. Today, the term *ale* refers to beers made with top-fermenting yeast strains. (Ironically, many of the ales today are much hoppier than other beers, in contrast to the early use of the term.)

THE INGREDIENTS

Beer has four basic ingredients: water, grain, hops, and yeast. These can be combined in nearly infinite variations to create different styles and flavors. The famous Bavarian purity law of 1516, the *Reinheitsgebot*, prohibited the inclusion of any ingredient other than pure barley malt, water, and hops (yeast had not been identified as a separate component of beer at that date). European Economic Community regulations no longer allow Germany to enforce this law as a way of keeping out foreign beers, but many brewers worldwide still tout their adherence to the *Reinheitsgebot* as a mark of quality. Brewers have developed new styles and flavors throughout history, sometimes by combinations of new ingredients and happy

In addition to describing the brewing process, this placemat from Titletown Brewing served as a guide to the ten-beer tasting flight. This version was used in 2008—many of the flagship beers remain the same. AUTHOR'S COLLECTION.

accident, sometimes by intentional experimentation and careful research.[2]

WATER

According to an old story, a Chicago resident once attempted to cash in on the Gettelman Brewing Company's guarantee that their beers were made exclusively from barley malt and hops. (A label showing the guarantee is in chapter 5.) His claim—there was water in them! Most beers are more than 90 percent water, so the chemical content of the water has a profound influence on the flavor of the beer. The water of Pilsen in the Czech Republic is low in minerals, and this soft water contributes to the clean flavor of the beer known as pilsner or pilsener—variations of which have become the best-selling style of beer in the world. In contrast, the hard water of Burton-on-Trent in the English Midlands contains minerals (calcium and gypsum in particular) that aid in extracting the bittering resins from the hops and thus contribute to the hoppy character of English pale ales and India pale ales. Modern chemical processes allow international brewers (and even homebrewers) to reproduce the water chemistry of any region and brew style from all over the world with their own local water. The biggest difficulty that new multiplant brewing companies had to overcome in the mid-twentieth century was to make beer brewed at different plants taste the same. The success of the chemists allowed Schlitz, Pabst, Miller, and other companies to make beer of remarkable consistency.

Wisconsin brewers took evident pride in the quality of their water sources. Several Wisconsin breweries have featured the quality of their water in advertising campaigns, either directly or indirectly. The earliest known reference to brewing water was in an 1843 advertisement announcing the sale of William Miller's Brewery in Milwaukee, which touted "a never-failing stream of soft water which is introduced into the top of the brewery."[3] John Roethinger of Janesville advertised in 1872 that "his Ale and Beer are made from Pure Spring Water! and not from the water of the Rock River—the natural sewer of filth from a great extent of the country." Insinuations that his rivals were using tainted water were countered by a later article that described the process by which John Buob collected water from a distant spring and shipped it to his brewery by boat.[4] Early settlers in the village of Kiel claimed that Dimler's beer was better than Gutheil's because he used softer water.[5] In many cases the depth of a brewer's well was considered proof that it ran a modern, well-equipped brewery. Rudolph Heger's City Brewery in Jefferson claimed that the major reason its beer won a prize for purity at the St. Louis World's Fair

Many breweries advertised the purity of their water and some, like the Hortonville Brewing Co., bottled and sold their water. This sign is from the early 1900s. COURTESY OF NATIONAL BREWERY MUSEUM.

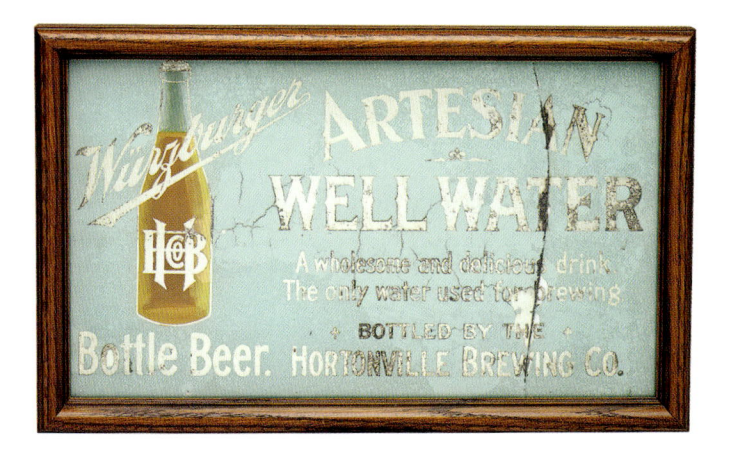

FROM BARLEY TO BARSTOOL   17

in 1904 was that the water was "obtained from a well six hundred and seventy feet deep cut out of St. Peter's sandstone."[6] Not all local water was suitable for brewing—a well dug in the 1850s by the Binz brothers in Sheboygan produced water with a high iron content and the beer made from it had to be dumped.[7]

As Wisconsin's cities developed modern infrastructure, many brewers found it convenient to use city water. Several Milwaukee breweries were using city water as early as the 1870s, for which they were originally charged at a rate per barrel of beer produced. Cities such as Eau Claire adopted similar rate schemes.[8] Of course, relying on city water made the brewers and city administrators both dependent on and at odds with each other. When beer production was revived in 1933, it was estimated that this would increase revenue for Milwaukee's water department by $50,000 per year.[9] On the other hand, an increase in water rates meant added expenses for breweries and threatened to put them at a competitive disadvantage. In 2010 MillerCoors protested a change in rate structure that would have increased its water bill (which was $1.2 million in 2009) by nearly 50 percent and threatened to shift production to other breweries around the country.[10] When cities began to fluoridate their water supplies in the 1950s, breweries needed to examine the effects of the changed chemistry on the brewing process. (Early studies disagreed on whether there was any significant effect.)[11] Roles even reversed in a few cases, with breweries providing water for the city. The first public water in Jefferson was provided by the brewery, and in Bangor the city owned the mains, but the Hussa Brewing Co. owned the wells and the pumps and collected the revenue.[12]

Barley's importance in brewing made it a lucrative crop for farmers. COURTESY OF MILLERCOORS BREWING CO.

GRAIN

The color, sweetness, and much of the flavor and nutrient value in beer comes from the mix of grain in the recipe. While nearly any grain can contribute fermentable sugars, the traditional source of these sugars in beer is malted barley. Barley grows best in temperate regions; early English settlers in the warmer southern colonies complained that they could not grow barley suitable for brewing ale. Wisconsin is on the edge of one of the most important barley-growing regions in the world, an

Although many pre-Prohibition breweries had their own maltings, most malt today comes from specialized producers such as Rahr Malting. Here are the germination compartments, in which the enzymes are activated and the complex starches are broken down into simpler sugars—a process that takes about four days. COURTESY OF RAHR CORPORATION.

area that stretches roughly from Lake Michigan to the Canadian Rockies. There are many varieties of barley, but most are categorized as two-row or six-row, depending on the arrangement of the kernels.

To produce fermentable sugars from barley, it first must be malted. To malt barley, the grain is first moistened and allowed to sprout. In this early stage of germination, the kernel produces starches to provide energy for the new plant as well as enzymes necessary for their conversion. To retain the maximum amount of starch in each kernel, the maltster stops the germination by drying the grain. The malt then may be roasted or smoked to give it unique color and flavor characteristics.

In the nineteenth century, many breweries of all sizes malted their own barley. These breweries

Ignatz Roehrl works in the testing area of the malt house of John Gund Brewing Co. of La Crosse in 1900. COURTESY OF MURPHY LIBRARY SPECIAL COLLECTIONS, UNIVERSITY OF WISCONSIN–LA CROSSE.

FROM BARLEY TO BARSTOOL 19

were important customers for farmers in the region. Breweries advertised that farmers could sell their barley for cash, and inland breweries sometimes offered to pay "Milwaukee prices."[13] The large quantities required led breweries to compete against each other for crops. John Knipschilt of Monroe attempted to lure Green County farmers to keep their barley at home, reminding them, "You can get your cash here as well as at Janesville, and at the same prices."[14] While slightly over half of Wisconsin's breweries malted their own barley just after the Civil War, this percentage declined slowly through the years until Prohibition began in 1920 as small rural breweries closed and others elected to buy their supplies from other maltsters. Even so, nearly half of Wisconsin's breweries still made their own malt, and some, such as the Kurth Company in Columbus and William Rahr Sons in Manitowoc, ultimately became more important as maltsters than as brewers.[15] Wisconsin malt was also in demand

Kurth Malting Co. of Columbus provided samples of their malt to brewers in these cans (ca. 1950s). COLLECTION OF TYE SCHWALBE.

Rahr Malting Co. sent this circular to Wisconsin farmers in the 1930s, encouraging them to grow Oderbrucker barley because of its desirable characteristics for malting. AUTHOR'S COLLECTION.

throughout the country. Brewers from Rhode Island to Alaska made a special point of advertising their use of Wisconsin malt in their beers.[16]

Wisconsin's maltsters worked with farmers to encourage cultivation of particular varieties of barley, often with the support of educational institutions and state government. When Prohibition lifted in 1933, the Chilton Malting Company reminded farmers to "bear in mind that Oderbrucker and Wisconsin No. 38 are the best suited for this territory and bring premium prices."[17] In 1935 farmers in Sheboygan County were invited to "Barley School" at Plymouth High School, where speakers from the malting industry and the University of Wisconsin Extension Service spoke about the commercial angle of raising barley. (Women and children who did not wish to attend the meeting were invited to a free show at the Plymouth Theater.)[18] Buffalo County held a county barley contest, in which samples brought to the local county agent's office would be judged by buyers from breweries in the area.[19] The actions of politicians in Madison often combined encouragement of barley farmers with interference in the brewing industry. In the immediate aftermath of Prohibition, some lawmakers attempted unsuccessfully to regulate the minimum portion of barley that could be used in each batch of beer, on the flimsy grounds that "the brewers' chemists might find a way to avoid use of barley and thereby take away the farmers' interest in beer."[20] In 1935 Governor Philip La Follette signed a bill requiring brewers and maltsters to file quarterly reports showing the sources of their barley. John Cashman, a Progressive Party state senator from Denmark, claimed farmers had a right to know where the barley was coming from and warned, "'If we find brewers who are using imported barley we will tell them to sell their beer where they buy their barley.'"[21]

In fact, the demands of the recipes meant Wisconsin breweries imported barley from domestic and foreign sources. Richard Owens, Milwaukee's pioneer ale brewer, had to travel to Michigan City, Indiana, to purchase the barley for his first batch. As the American West became cultivated, brewers tried the new varieties. A pre-Prohibition label for Pabst's Kaiser claimed that it contained exclusively Montana barley, and in 1873 Schlitz brought malt from Utah to make a Vienna-style lager.[22] Canadian malt could be brought in cheaply by boat through the Great Lakes and was popular both before and after Prohibition.[23] Modern

Sacks of malt await milling (in the machine in the rear of the malt room) at New Glarus Brewing Co. Malt from German and American producers is visible, hinting at the variety of inputs used by modern craft brewers. COURTESY OF NEW GLARUS BREWING CO.

breweries purchase their barley from all over the world, depending on the needs of their beer, but in recent years craft brewers have shown interest in using local ingredients in their beers.

To convert the starches in the malt to sugars that can be fermented by yeast, the grain must be mashed. The grain is first milled to separate the husk from the seed and to crack the seed just enough to expose the starches. The grain is then mixed with water to form a porridge-like mixture. By carefully controlling the temperature of the liquid in the mash kettle (or tun), the brewer can encourage different enzymes to work on the grains and break the large starch molecules into smaller sugar molecules that the yeast can digest. After the necessary sugars have been produced (usually requiring one to three hours), the sugars are rinsed from the grain in a process called sparging. This may be done in a separate vessel called a *lauter* tun, which has a strainer-like false bottom and rotating blades to help rinse the grain evenly. The liquid resulting from this process is called wort (pronounced "wert"). Prior to the twentieth century, it was a common practice to create two separate batches of wort from the first and second halves of the sparge. The "second runnings" were lower in fermentable sugars, and the resulting beer would therefore be lower in alcohol. (This is comparable to making a second pot of coffee from the same grounds.) This was then sold at a lower price as "table beer," "small beer," or "present-use beer."[24] A few homebrewers and craft brewers have revived this tradition. The wort is transferred to the brew kettle for brewing, and the spent grains are recovered and are often sold or given to local farmers, who consider it a high-quality livestock feed.

Some beer styles include grains other than barley. Adjuncts are ingredients other than barley or hops that impart specific flavors, colors, or other characteristics to the beer. Wheat beer (weizen or weiss beer, from the German words for the grain and the color white) uses wheat for as much as

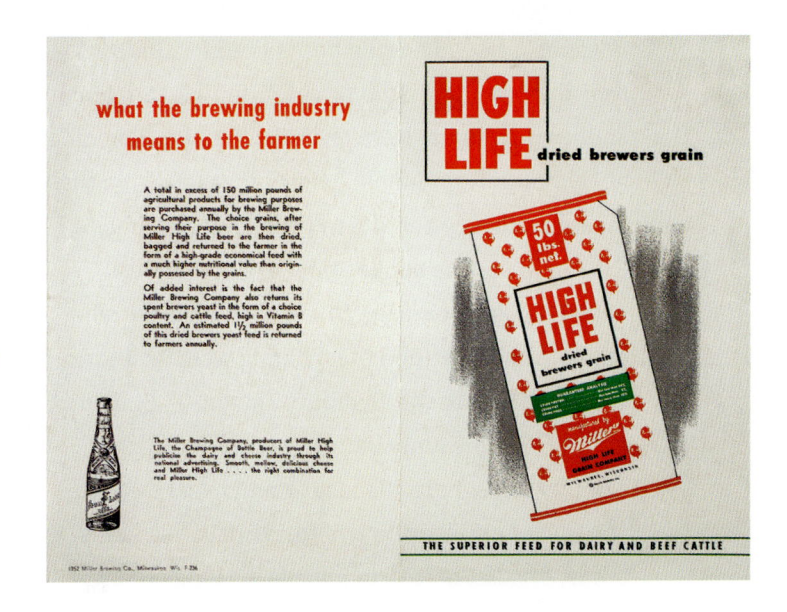

Wisconsin brewers have been disposing of their grain to livestock operations since the nineteenth century. Miller, like a few other large brewers, dried and packaged the grain for sale. Modern craft brewers seldom have facilities to dry the grain but save on solid waste disposal fees by allowing farmers to pick up the damp grain. COLLECTION OF JOHN STEINER.

half the grain bill. Wheat beers were considered a separate product and were exempt from the *Reinheitsgebot*. In fact, most of the world's most flavorful and best-selling beers (these are not the same) do not abide by the *Reinheitsgebot*. Many mass-market American beers include flaked corn (maize) or rice to lighten the color, provide flavor,

Beers containing coffee have become popular during the craft brewing era. The methods of introducing the coffee into the brew vary, as do the base styles of beer. Coffee is more commonly used in dark beers, with a few exceptions—such as Furthermore's Oscura, which was described as an amber lager. Many beers are named after the local roasters that provide the coffee. AUTHOR'S COLLECTION.

and improve head retention. Many of the flavorful beers of Belgium (and American brews inspired by them) add whole fruit, candi sugar, and syrups. Holiday beers from many nations are flavored with spices, and American craft brewers and brewpubs have become famous for their creative recipes.

HOPS

The wort resulting from the mashing process typically has a molasses-like consistency and a sticky sweetness. A beverage made simply by fermenting this would be nearly unpalatable, so some type of bittering agent must be added to balance the sweetness. Beer is intended to have a bitter component; those who complain about the bitterness in beer are ignoring its essential role in the complex flavor of a well-made beer. Throughout the history of brewing, many different herbs have been employed for this purpose. During the early Middle Ages, the most common bittering agent was *gruit,* a mixture of herbs about which there is still much speculation, but the primary ingredient seems to have been bog myrtle. The nobility of the period controlled the distribution and cost of gruit and made this *gruitrecht* into one of their major sources of income. Historians have suggested that the adoption of hops as a bittering agent was partly because of their superior qualities but also because using hops enabled brewers to evade the tax on gruit. American colonists used spruce tips as a common bittering agent where hops were not available.

Hops are small conelike flowers that come from the female hop plant (*Humulus lupulus*). Like beer itself, hops are both simple and complex. These vining perennials grow wild in many areas and can be easily cultivated at home in most regions; in fact, they can be difficult to eliminate once established. A handful of universities around

Hops climb the trellis at Dave's BrewFarm near Wilson. Increasing numbers of Wisconsin craft brewers are either growing some of their own hops or purchasing them from Wisconsin growers.

Entertainer Eddie Cantor (right) mugs for the camera while helping add hops to the brew kettle at Pabst Brewing Co. in 1946. COLLECTION OF JOHN STEINER.

the world have hop culture programs, and new varieties are introduced with some frequency. Hop varieties are selected for resistance to disease and yield as well as for their brewing characteristics.

The tiny yellow particles at the base of the flower contain resins and essential oils that serve different functions in making beer. The resins are the source of the alpha acids that provide the bitterness in beer. Hops can vary widely in the amount of alpha acids that are available to be isomerized and dissolved into the beer during the boiling stage, which is measured as a percentage. The noble hops of Germany and the Czech Republic are typically low in available alpha acids (around 4 to 6 percent), whereas many hops grown in the Pacific Northwest can have more than 10 percent available alpha acids. To impart bitterness to the beer, the hops must be boiled for at least sixty minutes. Hops may be added to the brew kettle either in their original whole-leaf form, more often as hop pellets, or occasionally as liquid hop extract. The resulting hoppiness of the beer is measured in International Bitterness Units (IBUs). Mass-market lagers are usually in the range of 8–25 IBUs, pale ales and stouts are often between 30 and 45 IBUs, and some craft brewers create exceptionally hoppy beers of around 100 IBUs.

The essential oils, on the other hand, primarily add flavor and aroma components to beer. These oils lose their potency if boiled or even if exposed to air for too long and therefore must be added to the brew very late in the boil so that the flavors and aromas are not literally boiled away. In a process called dry-hopping, some brewers add hops to the fermenter or aging vats to retain the maximum amount of flavor and aroma. Unfortunately, one group of essential oils contains sulfur, which reacts with light to produce the undesirable aroma known as skunkiness. Brewers, retailers, and marketers are thus sometimes placed in a difficult position: the safest way to package and store beer is in dark bottles or cans in closed boxes away from strong sources of light, but sometimes the best way to

Schlitz began advertising the virtue of its brown bottles before World War I and continued into the 1960s. The Brown Bottle hospitality centers at their breweries paid tribute to the importance of the campaign. AUTHOR'S COLLECTION.

FROM BARLEY TO BARSTOOL 25

draw attention to a brand is to package it in green or clear bottles in open carriers in a brightly lit display, which invites skunkiness.

YEAST

Yeast converts sugars into alcohol through the process of fermentation. For centuries the precise role of yeast in the brewing process was imperfectly understood. Monastic brewers in the Middle Ages are said to have called the fermentation process "God is Good," and brewers of the period observed semireligious rituals during fermentation. Wild yeasts present in the brewing environment were responsible for much of the fermentation in the premodern period; historians have speculated that some yeast was transferred from batch to batch on the surfaces of the brewing equipment. Not until after the development of the microscope and fundamental chemistry research by Joseph Priestley of England and Antoine-Laurent Lavoisier of France were the tools and knowledge available to understand yeast. The work of Louis Pasteur and

While not all craft breweries can afford a fully equipped lab such as this at New Glarus Brewing, the level of competition gives an advantage to those brewers who attend to quality control.

of Emil Christian Hansen of the Carlsberg Brewery in Copenhagen made it possible for brewers to isolate, breed, and maintain pure yeast strains. The purity of the yeast strain is critical for maintaining consistency of flavor, and modern brewers take great pains to protect their yeast from unwanted mutations.

While many different strains of yeast exist, most brewing yeasts can be divided into two classes (though some newly developed yeast strains blur the line between the two). Ale yeast, or top-fermenting yeast (*Saccharomyces cerevisiae*), generally ferments at higher temperatures, imparts more complex fruity aromas to the beer, and often remains on the top of the liquid after the process is complete. Lager yeast, or bottom-fermenting yeast (*Saccharomyces pastorianus*), typically requires cooler conditions, imparts fewer fruity esters to the beer, and settles to the bottom at the end of fermentation. Some beer styles, such as the German hefeweizen (wheat beer with yeast), are served with the yeast still in suspension in the beer, giving it a cloudy, but not unattractive, appearance.

In recent years, Wisconsin's craft brewers have shown increased interest in brewing sour beers, or in other words, beers that use lactobacillus, brettanomyces, or other less common organisms to create beers with a flavor that can range from a pleasing tartness to a mouth-puckering sour. Because these organisms carry the potential to infect the other yeast strains, brewers usually work with sour beers in a separate room from the rest of the brewery. New Glarus Brewing Company has converted its original brewery to a facility to brew its fruit and sour beers that is only half-jokingly referred to as "the Ebola room."

The fermentation process typically requires about a week. After fermentation is complete, what happens next depends on the type of beer. Cask-conditioned ales are moved directly into the vessels from which they will eventually be served and typically undergo secondary fermentation while in the cask. Most beers are filtered and moved to aging tanks. At this stage the beer is carbonated either by the forced addition of carbon dioxide gas or through natural processes. In the case of

The original New Glarus Brewing Co. building was dedicated to fruit and sour beers to minimize the risk of contaminating other brews.

FROM BARLEY TO BARSTOOL

lager beers (the word *lager* is from the German verb meaning "to store"), a longer period of aging is required to allow the beer to carbonate and to eliminate off-flavors from the finished product. Beer that has not aged long enough is called green beer; more than one American brewery has been doomed by attempting to shorten the lagering period. The most vivid example was Schlitz, which destroyed a century-old reputation in the late

Wisconsin's pride in its brewing industry was displayed at major fairs and trade shows, such as this one during the 1960s. COURTESY OF UNIVERSITY WISCONSIN–STEVENS POINT ARCHIVES.

1970s by attempting to do with chemistry what is best done with time.

After aging, the beer is ready for packaging in kegs, bottles, or cans and for shipping to the consumer. Brewers trust their distributors and retailers to ensure that beer is protected from damaging extremes in temperature and from rough handling that could make the beer undrinkable or unsuited for display in stores. After this, the taste of beer is up to the drinker.

A worker attends to a giant fermenter in the vast cellar at Pabst Brewing Co. in the 1950s. COLLECTION OF JOHN STEINER.

THE DRINK THAT MADE WISCONSIN FAMOUS

Thoughts on Enjoying Beer Properly

After taking into account that beer is best enjoyed safely and in moderation, a few simple steps will aid in appreciating the unique characteristics of each style.

Learn about the Different Styles of Beer

Broadly speaking, beer is divided into two main categories: ale and lager. Ales are made with top-fermenting yeast and are generally fermented at temperatures around 70°F. Ales tend to be fruitier in both aroma and taste than lagers. Lagers are made with bottom-fermenting yeast and require lower fermentation temperatures, around 50°F. There are also several varieties of hybrid beer, usually a beer using lager yeast fermented at ale temperatures, or the other way around.

Within these main categories exist infinite variations. The Beer Judge Certification Program 2015 Style Guidelines list thirty-four styles of beer, from "Standard American Beer" to "American Wild Ale," from "British Bitter" to "Smoked Beer." Within these styles there are almost 120 subcategories—and this doesn't even count subcategories for fruit and specialty beer, for which any brew could be its own subcategory. For example, style thirteen, Brown British Beer, has three subcategories: Dark Mild, British Brown Ale, and English Porter. Each subcategory has parameters for color, aroma, bitterness, flavor, and alcohol content. The style guidelines are useful, but brewers do not treat them as a straitjacket. The number of subcategories was seventy-eight as recently as 2004, testifying that some experimental styles have become so popular that they earned their own category designations (such as the six sub-subcategories of Specialty IPA). Many distinctive and flavorful beers do not fit clearly into any one category, and American craft brewers and homebrewers delight in pushing the boundaries of beer styles. The subcategory designation of "imperial" was borrowed from imperial stouts originally made by English brewers for the Russian market and is affixed to high-alcohol-content examples from any style.

It is important to remember that color has no relation to strength whatsoever. A golden Belgian-style ale can have upward of 10 percent alcohol by volume, whereas in Irish pubs draught Guinness Stout, which is nearly black in color, is around 4 percent alcohol by volume.

Serve Beer at the Proper Temperature

Most lagers should be served cool but not ice-cold. Ales can be served at cellar temperatures (around

50°F to 55°F). The common American myth that the English drink warm beer is not true; a pint of bitter is warm only in comparison to the near- or below-freezing temperatures at which American mass-market lager is typically served. Don't ice the beer mug—bacteria may be harbored in the ice. A rich and highly aromatic beer such as an old ale or a barleywine will be more enjoyable at room temperature or even warmed slightly by holding the glass in the palm.

Know the Alcohol Content of Your Beer

Drinking a large quantity of an extremely smooth beer only to discover that it was nearly 10 percent alcohol can cause anything from a severe hangover to a serious safety hazard. There is a good reason that many strong beers come in small bottles and are served in small glasses. For many years, the U.S. government required that alcohol in beer be measured by weight. The percent by volume is about 1.25 times the figure computed by weight, which encouraged the common myth that Canadian beer was stronger than American beer. American governments have finally joined brewers around the world and their counterparts in the wine industry, and refer to alcohol by volume.

Learn about the Brewing Process

Even the largest modern breweries emphasize the history and tradition of their brands and companies and want their patrons to know about them. Take a brewery tour, preferably at a small or mid-sized brewery. Tours of the massive breweries are interesting, but are often presented by tour guides who have not actually worked in the brewery, and the tours tend to focus on quantity, efficiency, and packaging. At smaller breweries, the tour is more likely to be given by a veteran brewery employee, perhaps even the brewmaster, who is more likely to discuss the differences in beer styles and how they are made.

Courtesy of MillerCoors Brewing Co.

COLLECTION OF JIM ROWLEY

Whenever Possible, Pour Beer into a Glass

Pouring beer into a glass lets excess carbon dioxide escape and allows the aromas to work with the flavors. While drinking straight from the can or bottle is sometimes unavoidable, it can create a feeling of excess gassiness. Pour the first two-thirds of the beer down the side of the glass, but pour the rest into the middle to raise a good head on the beer. This releases carbon dioxide and simply makes the beer look better.

European beer glasses are designed to contain a full legal measure of beer and still leave room for the type of head best suited for the beer (thick and creamy for a stout, big and frothy for a German hefeweizen). Pouring the entire beer down the side of a glass to minimize the head is primarily a North American habit designed to counter short-measure glasses or long lines at keg parties. In recent years, American craft brewers have been moving away from the "shaker pint," which is cheap and easy to clean and stack but does nothing to enhance the flavor or aroma of the beer. Some glasses represent cooperative efforts between brewers and glassmakers using the latest technology, but others would not have looked out of place in a bowling alley in the 1960s.

Understanding what beer is and how it is made is important for understanding how brewers and breweries have changed since Wisconsin's earliest European settlement to modern times, when people from all over the world come to Wisconsin to experience what beer has become. The story of Wisconsin is like beer: both simple and complicated at the same time.

FROM BARLEY TO BARSTOOL 31

The scene on this Pioneer Brew label from the early 1900s bears little resemblance to the process used in "the early days of brewing" on the Wisconsin frontier. While many early brewers used a large kettle to boil the wort, they probably did not brew on the edge of a cliff. The use of female Indian figures in advertising was common in the period, and they generally symbolized purity, though sometimes they were just used to add a colorful touch to the design. COLLECTION OF JOHN STEINER.

CHAPTER 2

Pioneer BREWING

1835–1860

The soil produces everything that grows in Germany, but with the difference that it produces more with less cultivation. . . . Everything here is still in the process of becoming, yet none can deny, that this land will soon be one of the most populous and wealthy of the free-states. . . . One would advise every poor and, in Germany, superfluous wage-earner to come to this country where most Germans quickly pay for their land by the labor of their hands and thus achieve an independent and care-free existence.

Franz Neukirch, WRITING TO HIS WIFE IN GERMANY, 1839

Beer came to Wisconsin before territorial status did. When European Americans began to expand the small existing settlements in present-day Wisconsin in the 1820s and '30s, the brewing industry was on the brink of the first major change in the nature of beer since the development of porter in the early 1700s. Up to this time, beer produced in America contained top-fermenting yeast strains because they were widely available (wild or self-cultured yeasts were generally used by households out of tradition and necessity) and less sensitive to change. Ale was easy to make. Top-fermenting yeast (*Saccharomyces cerevisiae*) tolerates warm temperatures, which was essential in the days before cold storage. If necessary, a variety of products that would produce a palatable beer could be substituted for barley malt and hops. Breweries were common features on the estates of landed gentlemen such as William Penn, George Washington, and Thomas Jefferson, and people of all income levels brewed beer for their own consumption. Even though several hundred commercial breweries existed during the eighteenth and early nineteenth centuries, many taverns and households continued to make their own ales.

It is likely that some of Wisconsin's earliest European settlers made some sort of ale at their fort, farmstead, or tavern, since this was one of the products a household was expected to produce. The *Young Woman's Companion & Instructor*, detailing everything an Englishwoman of 1806 needed to know about managing a household, contained twelve pages on brewing—everything from maintaining the brewing copper to inspecting the corks used for bottling.[1] This daily household activity was seldom recorded for posterity, but a few specific accounts of Wisconsin frontier homebrewing have survived. An English settler named Edwin Bottomley, who suffered from malaria in the 1840s, discovered that a few pints of beer a day reduced his attacks of "ague," and he proceeded to plant two acres of barley, writing to his father, "'I shall make my own malt and brew my own [beer].'" (Unfortunately, Bottomley died of complications from malaria despite his "pleasantly unique cure.")[2] Henry Sibley, a pioneer and representative of the American Fur Company in the western reaches of Wisconsin Territory (and later the first governor of the state of Minnesota), is known to have purchased hops for making ale, and other pioneer families may have done so as well.[3] Hannah Aldrich, a resident of Sylvan in Vernon County, wrote to her parents in 1857, "I make beer out of the roots that grow in the woods, of sarsaparilla, spignot, golden seal, hops anise, and other things. This is recommended to be very healthy to drink along in the spring and summer."[4] While Aldrich may have been describing something closer to modern root beer, she still referred to it as beer. Norwegians near Holmen in La Crosse County in the late 1860s customarily gave large parties before which "the most efficient cooks in the community were employed to prepare the food and to brew the homemade Öl or beer."[5]

It is unlikely that the Welsh or Cornish miners who led the European settlement of southwestern Wisconsin were prepared to go without ale for years at a time. Ale could have been brought into Wisconsin from established breweries elsewhere, but it was heavy and expensive to ship, and was easy to make at home. (St. Louis had a commercial brewery as early as 1809.)[6] There is some evidence of the presence of beer in Wisconsin before the arrival of commercial breweries, or before there was a brewery in a particular region. An order issued in 1835 at Fort Winnebago near Portage set the price of beer sold by the post sutler at 75 cents per gallon or twelve and one-half cents per pint—which raises the question of where the beer was coming from.[7] Likewise, an account of life in 1842 at the settlement of La Pointe on Madeline Island mentioned the presence of beer at this distant outpost with no obvious commercial source. It is likely that the beer at La Pointe was brewed at home, and even the beer at Fort Winnebago may have been brewed by the sutler, though the quantities available seem rather large for that.[8]

The opening of the Erie Canal through New York in 1825 made the Great Lakes easily accessible to settlers as well as merchants, and would drive the growth of Milwaukee and other lakeside cities, but lead mining once drew more people to Wisconsin than trapping or farming—over ten thousand to southwestern Wisconsin and northwestern Illinois by 1828. The miners were not as self-sufficient as the farmers, so they drew in merchants to supply their communities. The lead market was volatile, and prices sometimes dropped so that it took five thousand pounds of ore to buy a barrel of flour. Eventually this and the ending of the Black Hawk War in 1832, and the treaties that followed it, brought farmers to the area, and one of Wisconsin's first two federal land offices was established at Mineral Point (the other was at Green Bay).[9] With a permanent population, the beginnings of an agricultural hinterland, and a transportation system built for the mining industry, the conditions were ripe for the beginning of industrial brewing in the state.

Richard Unger has outlined six stages in the development of brewing. The homebrewing of Wisconsin's preterritorial era represents the first stage, household production for domestic consumption. Wisconsin skipped the second stage, that of household industry performed by specialists, largely because frontier life did not allow the sort of landed estates, such as those in Europe or on the Atlantic coast of North America, that could afford to keep a brewer among the domestic staff. The first commercial breweries in Wisconsin represented the third stage, individual workshops with some commercial activity.[10]

While the Wisconsin brewery story ultimately would be centered in Milwaukee, it did not begin there. Nor did it begin in or around Green Bay, despite that area's being home to so many firsts of European settlement in Wisconsin.[11] The first

H. S. Pritchard of Fort Atkinson had an extensive network of beer cellars under his brewery—large enough to drive a wagon in. The cellars were abandoned for a time and later used as storage space for the house that now occupies the brewery site.

commercial brewery designed to supply anyone other than guests of the house was John Phillips's brewery in Mineral Point, which was also the first manufacturing enterprise of any type in that booming community.[12] Very few stories about the Phillips brewery have been preserved. Aside from its beginnings in 1835 and fleeting newspaper references in various years until the early 1850s, documentation is scarce. An 1881 county history admitted that "as to the merit of the beer manufactured or the method employed, tradition is silent, but probably it was brewed in common kettles and was an indescribable tonic."[13]

The second brewery established in the state was also located in the lead district, about twenty miles from Mineral Point in Elk Grove, near the territorial capital of Belmont. The brewery of Henry Rablin and Thomas Bray, located at the site of Fort De Seelhorst starting in 1836, was described as a typical frontier structure: "made of hewn logs and rough rock." The brewery, like most others of its period, depended on horsepower to crush the barley. While the existing accounts do not provide the extent of the market for their beer, it was claimed that Rablin and Bray were able to demand an Eagle (ten-dollar gold coin) per barrel.[14] Elk Grove's brewery would exemplify the life story of many small-town businesses: a promising start, changing partnerships, intermittent closures, and vulnerability to fire and economic distress. Both Phillips and the successors of Rablin and Bray kept their businesses going until the 1850s, but by that point a new beer style had taken over, one better made in less primitive facilities.

The movement of brewing from the home or tavern to the commercial brewery accelerated largely because of the development in the 1820s of scientific lager brewing in Europe. The principal originators of the style were Gabriel Sedlmayr of Munich and Anton Dreher of Vienna. The beers of Munich were significantly darker than those of Vienna, but both were much clearer in appearance and mellower in taste than the beers that preceded them. During the 1840s, brewers in the Bohemian city of Pilsen (Plzeň) refined the style still further, using their extremely soft local water and distinctive Saaz hops to create an even lighter beer that soon was known worldwide as pilsner, or pilsener.

In 1840 John Wagner of Philadelphia brewed what historians have traditionally considered to be the first batch of lager beer in America, though this claim has been disputed. Unlike previous American brews, this recipe used a strain of yeast that precipitated to the bottom of the vessel as it fermented, a strain Wagner appears to have brought with him from Bavaria. The new lager beer had a lighter, more refreshing taste than American ales of the time, and the fact that the yeast dropped to the bottom of the fermenter instead of rising to the top like ale yeast allowed for a very bright beer with minimal sediment. The increasing availability of mass-produced glassware made a beverage that looked good even more appealing. The new style had two major drawbacks for existing producers, however. The bottom-fermenting yeast strains required significantly cooler temperatures to work. Unlike ale, making lager required brewers to find or create sufficiently cool cellar space to hold the beer while it aged. The need to dig

Pictures of Wisconsin's earliest breweries are very rare. Illustrations such as this usually appeared in city directories or other advertising matter. COURTESY OF MILWAUKEE PUBLIC LIBRARY.

It is not clear whether Ashland Brewing Co. brewed the London Porter under license from the Standard Brewing Co. of Rochester, New York, or if it simply served as the bottler. (The label from the 1890s is displayed on a later bottle.) COLLECTION OF JOHN STEINER.

caves, build cellars, or, later, install expensive refrigeration equipment meant that the shift to lager would favor large commercial brewers over smaller operations. This shift meant that the center of Wisconsin beer would move to the shores of Lake Michigan.

Quite a Profitable Business

Much of the history of the founding of Milwaukee and its brewing industry has blended with legend, and with each repetition of the legend, the historical record becomes harder to disentangle. Entrepreneurs such as Solomon Juneau and Byron Kilbourn laid the foundation for a thriving commercial town populated by a variety of merchants, speculators, and visionaries, all hoping to build their fortunes on the land or from each other. The nearly two thousand people in Milwaukee as of the 1840 census were primarily Anglo-Saxons (often called Yankees both in contemporary accounts and later histories) who had moved from the northeastern parts of America, many of them along the Erie Canal to the Great Lakes and then to the southeastern shore of Lake Michigan. Even after Germans flooded the city, the Yankees held on to most of the political and economic power.[15]

Reflecting both the tastes of the Anglo settlers and the scarcity of lager yeast, the brewery that has long (erroneously) been considered the first in the city that became synonymous with lager beer produced English-style ales. Richard G. Owens, William Pawlett, and John Davis established the Milwaukee Brewery in 1840 at 222 Huron Street (today Clybourne). Owens left his native Wales in 1832 at the age of twenty-one and moved to America. His story reads like many others of the nineteenth century: he worked in several different jobs in cities from Buffalo, New York, to St. Louis, Missouri, over an eight-year period. According to later accounts, when he came to Milwaukee in 1840, he formed the idea of a brewery almost immediately, and within a fortnight set off for Michigan City, Indiana, and came back on the sloop *Ranger* with 130 bushels of malt for his first batch of ale. He is reported to have used a wooden, copper-lined vat to make his earliest brews, but a wooden brew kettle would not have survived the fire necessary to heat the wort. It is possible that this vessel was the mash tun, to which boiling water was added, but these details were lost in the romance of the frontier story. That winter he upgraded his brewery with a twelve-barrel copper brew kettle brought overland from Chicago by oxen.[16] While these stories are not historically precise, Owens and his partners were undoubtedly working in primitive conditions with limited ingredients or equipment readily at hand.

Owens and his partners were among the exclusive ranks of pioneer businessmen whose enterprises were successful both in the short and long run. The firm was said to be a success from the start, replacing its primitive frame building with a stone structure, and in 1850 was the largest brewery by revenue (and tied for largest by volume) in a crowded market. Owens's business extended into the country behind Milwaukee right from the beginning. Pioneers near Mequon in Ozaukee County recalled a Fourth of July party in the early 1840s at which "sufficient money was raised to get a keg of Owen's best ale or beer from Milwaukee, and to hire a fiddler, who lived across the river."[17]

Newspaper ads of the mid-nineteenth century tended to pack a lot of basic information into a small space rather than trying to develop a unique brand identity. Jacob Muth's ad from 1859 made bolder claims to distinguish his beer.

Grateful for past patronage, he hopes by a strict personal attention to his business to merit a continuance of the same.
ULRICH SCHADEGG.
Burlington, Wis.   1y1

"No war, but peace in Burlington here, And nothing stronger than Muth's Lager Beer."

THE UNDERSIGNED begs leave to inform the trusty population of Burlington and vicinity, that he always keeps on hand the celebrated BUCK, LAGER, and COMMON BEER, and hereby recommends it for sale as a first rate remedy for the preservation of health. Do away with patent medicines, pills, &c., and drink MUTH'S BEER, and you will feel as well as a muskrat, as strong as a lion, and as happy as a man with the best feelings towards his fellow beings. Make once the experiment, and the second time you will need no persuasion. Facts are facts, and no humbug!
JACOB MUTH,
At the Burlington Brewery.
Burlington, Racine Co., Wis., June 1, 1859.

J. H. CONKEY & CO.,
HAVE JUST RECEIVED A NEW Stock of
DRY GOODS
AND
GROCERIES,

Even in 1860, after two decades of lager ascendency, Owens's brewery (now called the Lake Brewery) was still among the largest brewers in a city now ruled by Germans such as Schlitz, Best, Falk, and Blatz.[18] The Lake Brewery would continue to sell ale in the lager capital until 1880, when Owens closed the brewery and devoted his attention to his real estate business.[19]

The Spring Brewery, which produced from about 1856 until 1867 (much of that time as a branch of Sands' Ale Brewing Company of Chicago), outproduced the Lake Brewery for a few years. In 1862 it claimed to be the largest in the state and advertised throughout the region. The *Milwaukee Daily Sentinel* enthused that with the Sands brothers' purchase of the Spring Brewery there was no need to import Burton Ale or Barclay & Perkins Porter: "and now-a-days the old Uncle Toby's can drink a glass of cream ale over the evening fire and show a trifle of that English heartiness and sociability which seems to be inextricably associated with this sort of thing."[20] In fact, local commentators thought they detected a drop in "beer" (lager) consumption in Milwaukee the year after the Sandses took over the Spring Brewery, due to their success selling ale. The paper reassured its readers, "Lager, however, has probably suffered all it will by the competition, for that article will always be the favorite beverage with the German element of our population."[21] A few of the largest breweries in Milwaukee, Pabst in particular, would provide a porter or English-style ale as part of their portfolio, but after 1880 the ale specialists would be confined to a few English enclaves such as Janesville until the craft brewing era began in the 1980s.

The Munich of America

Much of Milwaukee's public image centers on its German heritage, and the rapid rise of lager beer culture cemented this early on for residents and

Even before they achieved national fame, brewers were respected members of the community. Governor Nelson Dewey named Philip [sic] Best a member of the honorary military company of Milwaukee Dragoons in 1850. COLLECTION OF JOHN STEINER.

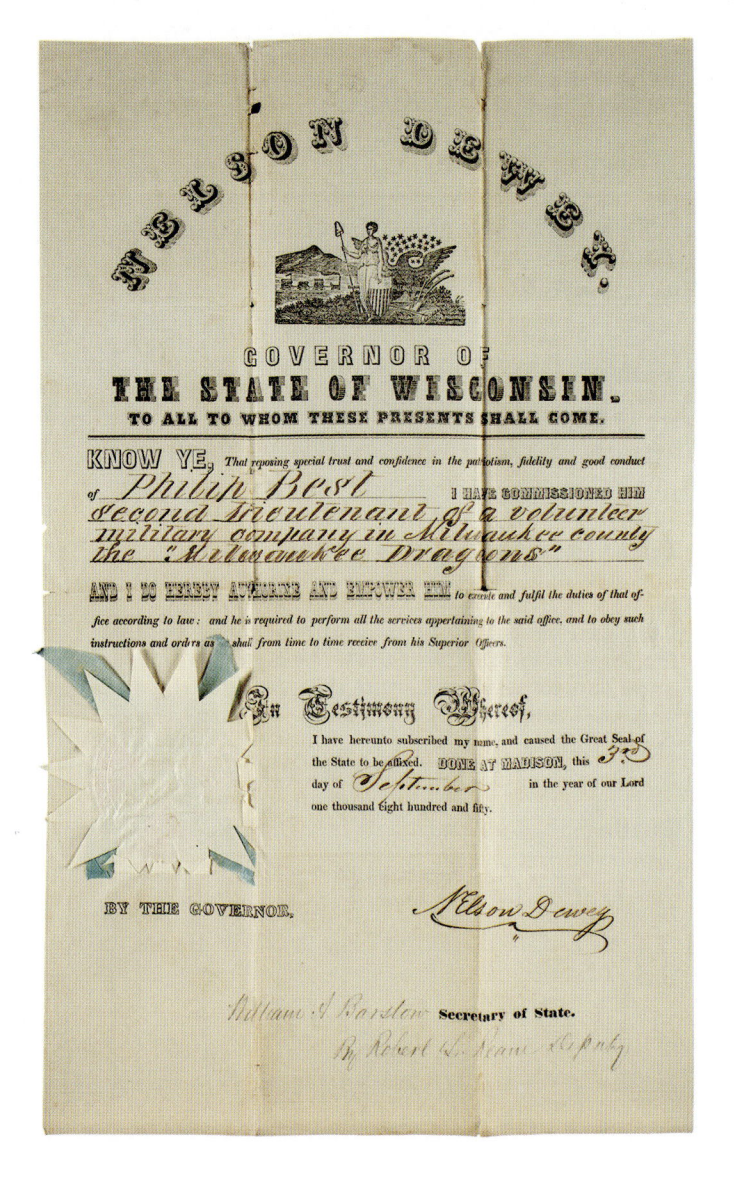

visitors alike. The Milwaukee Industrial Exposition of 1895 was an opportunity to celebrate the fiftieth anniversary of the drafting of the city's charter and the businesses that had grown with the city. One of the exhibits purported to be a reconstruction of the first brewery in the city. The model was not the Owens brewery, however; in fact, it was not even the first German brewery. It was the original Phillip Best brewery that had grown into the Pabst Brewing Company—the sponsor of the exhibit. The *Sentinel* published special features that attempted to explain the origins of the major industries and the ethnic groups that helped them grow. The descriptions help explain why the Owens brewery was sidelined: "The year 1841 is the year when the first German brewery was established here. There had been a so-called Lake brewery established by three Englishmen at the foot of Huron street, but the stuff which they manufactured was actually ale, and not beer."[22] By this point the kingdom of lager beer was well established, and ale was considered an entirely separate product.

The first German brewer in the city and state was Simon (or Herman) Reutelshofer (sometimes called Reuthlisberger), who was "a Wurtembergian and understood all about genuine beer," a claim that emphasized the contrast with the British ale brewers.[23] Research by Leonard Jurgensen argues that Reutelshofer was brewing before Owens, and that Owens embellished his claims to be the original brewer in the years that followed. Reutelshofer's primitive brewery at Walker's Point, at the corner of Virginia and Hanover, may not have made lager beer either, according to the much later reminiscences of Valentin Blatz. (It may have been a version of German "Alt" beer.) Reutelshofer was probably the first lager brewer in the state, but he was fated not to enjoy his position for long. He sought a mortgage from a baker named John B. Maier, but Maier somehow induced Reutelshofer to sell the brewery instead, and bodily threw him from the brewery when he refused to understand he no longer owned it.[24] It is not known if Maier was any better as a brewer, but he could at least pay the bills, and was eventually able to encourage his father-in-law, Franz Neukirch, to move to Milwaukee and take over the brewery in 1843. Neukirch stabilized the business, and soon brought in another son-in-law, Charles T. Melms, "who first started to brew along scientific lines" and set it on the road to being one of the most important breweries in the region.[25]

Reutelshofer, Maier, and their successors were not the only German brewers in town for long. While the precise starting dates are speculative, it seems that Conrad Muntzenberger was brewing by 1842 and that Wolfgang Weise started his brewery in 1843, passing it to David Gipfel later that year. But the most important of the first wave of firms was the Empire Brewery started by Jacob Best and his four sons. Best's brewery is the best documented of the early Milwaukee breweries in part because of the remarkable number of records that have survived from the pioneer era, and also because Phillip Best and later Frederick Pabst were relentless promoters of their brewery and earned frequent mention in the newspapers.

Of course, some of the feats of the business may not have happened exactly as the stories have been handed down. The landmark 1902 publication

100 Years of Brewing repeated the claim that Phillip Best made the first lager beer in Milwaukee. Although a treasure trove of information about early brewing, this was a promotional book, and submissions by the brewers were accepted uncritically. According to the story told by Best's brewmaster, Max Fueger, "a certain Wagner" had decided to experiment with bottom-fermenting yeast to make lager in Milwaukee for the first time, and therefore had ordered some from a brother who was a brewer in Bavaria. Wagner apparently had buyer's remorse, and offered it to Best if he would pay the freight charges. The account of the experiment provides a unique look at brewing practice in the antebellum period:

Finally the yeast came. It was packed in a strong wooden box about a foot and a half square. The yeast was packed in a sort of sawdust, around which were wound several folds of hop-sacking. The wrapping was carefully taken off, and to the astonishment of all of us, the yeast was found to be in good condition. We took it to the top of the main building and allowed it to dry out thoroughly. Then we dissolved the whole mass in a pail and allowed it to run through a sieve, which held the sawdust and permitted the yeast to pass into a proper receptacle below.

The capacity of our kettle in those days was just eighteen barrels, and we calculated that the yeast we had was just about enough for one brew. Neither Philip [sic] nor I slept very much while we were trying the new yeast, but it was a success, although we made better lager beer after six months than we did the first time.

Muntzenberger's brewery in Kenosha used this label sometime prior to 1884. COLLECTION OF JOHN STEINER.

THE DRINK THAT MADE WISCONSIN FAMOUS

One difficulty with the story is that Fueger claimed the first lager was not brewed until 1851. While both Fueger and Val Blatz may be correct that all the early beer was top-fermenting—technically classified as Alt beer—it is unlikely that Milwaukee's Germans were so late in adopting lager production. On the other hand, it is possible that early writers crediting Reutelshofer with the first lager may have been confusing German-style top-fermented beers with lager, and were simply contrasting the taste of these brews with their English counterparts.[26] However, advertisements in the *Wiskonsin-Banner* newspaper in early 1845 for Best & Company clearly mention *untergäbriges Bier,* or under (bottom)-fermenting beer, which seems to support an earlier date rather than a later one.[27]

Another intriguing question raised by Fueger's story is the identity of Mr. Wagner. The 1850 census and 1851 city directory identify a Lewis Wagner who had a brewery on Galena Street and who could match the description. However, another Wagner was in the area as well. In 1890, the *Milwaukee Journal* noted the passing of Ferdinand Wegner, who "established a brewery in Granville, where the first Milwaukee lager beer was made. He had been brewing such beer in his brewery in Philadelphia fifty years ago, and was the pioneer of that industry in this country."[28] It is possible that John Wagner of Philadelphia and Ferdinand Wagner of Milwaukee were different people, but confusion of names is also possible, and Wagner may have had both names and chosen to go by a different name in Wisconsin. He may also have been the Bavarian brother of Lewis Wagner referred to in Fueger's tale. Competing claims and imprecise memories make it unlikely that the first serving of true lager beer in Milwaukee will be definitely fixed at a point in place or time, but it is clear that shortly after its introduction, lager took over the efforts of the brewers and the hearts of the beer-drinking public.[29] By 1850 small family businesses had been formed under the names of Best, Krug, and Braun that would eventually become the breweries that brought the city fame: Pabst, Miller, Schlitz, and Blatz.

Filling the State

While Milwaukee had the necessary access to water, barley, and hops, as well as a population interested in making and consuming beer, so did many

While this Golden Glow coaster traced the birth of the brewery to the year of Wisconsin statehood, it most likely started brewing three years earlier. The view of the brewery is from the 1930s. COLLECTION OF TYE SCHWALBE.

PIONEER BREWING   43

cities in Wisconsin Territory. Other settlements on the shore of Lake Michigan presented evident advantages to the entrepreneur. Port Washington, about twenty-five miles north of Milwaukee, had an "early character" named John (or Leonard) Arnet, an Englishman "who had built a little cabin, and started on a small scale the manufacture of malt liquors." Arnet sold his beer for three cents a pint and "carried on quite a profitable business, and was very liberally patronized by the old settlers from all parts of the county, as his was the only establishment of the kind then known outside of Milwaukee."[30]

Southport, an unimaginatively named harbor town thirty-five miles south of Milwaukee, also figured into the brewing landscape. Spicer & Company announced in January 1843 that "the subscribers have now got the above establishment in full operation, and are prepared to supply Southport and the adjacent country with *Ale, Strong Beer,* and *Family Table Beer*: warranted equal to any made in the country." Like a number of other breweries of the era, they offered yeast for sale, though whether this was for homebrewing or baking was not made clear in the advertisement. More importantly for settlers, Spicer was the first Wisconsin brewer known to have advertised his purchase of barley from local farmers.[31] The brewery in Southport was an early example of a frontier brewery as a center of local agribusiness—buying and selling commodities and staple goods while producing a consumer product that was in local demand. Southport, soon to be renamed Kenosha, would be the first city in Wisconsin other than Milwaukee to support two breweries, when Conrad Muntzenberger left Milwaukee for the less crowded market to the south in 1847.

Somewhat surprisingly, the oldest European settlement on Lake Michigan's western shore, Green Bay, was among the last to have a brewery. Racine, Manitowoc, and Sheboygan were all on their way to being important brewing cities before

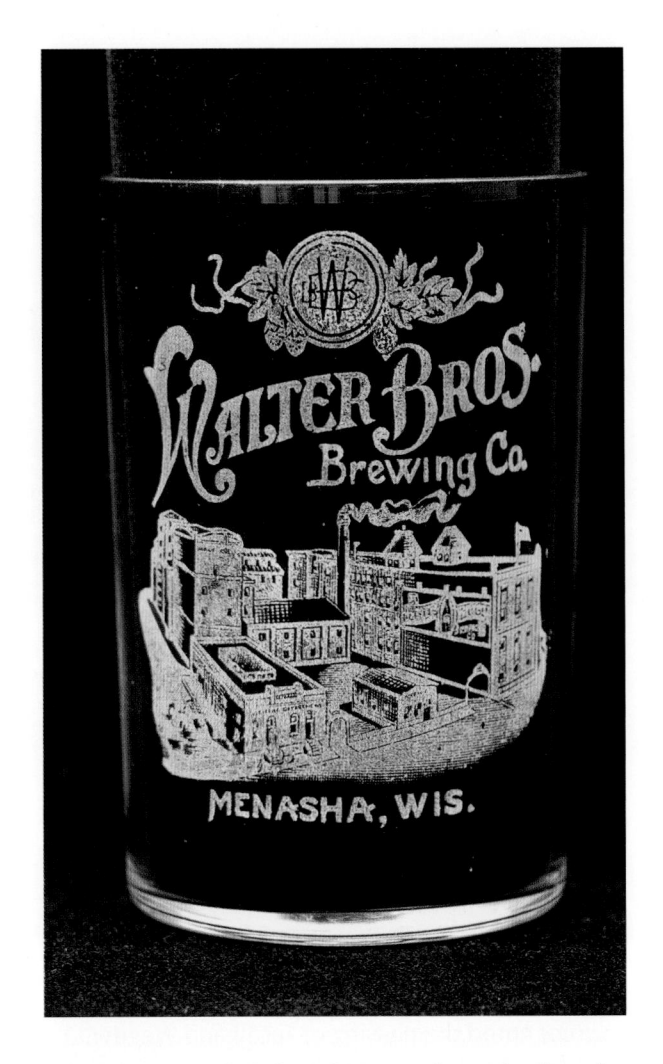

This Walter Bros. glass shows how many breweries throughout Wisconsin had grown into large industrial plants. The bottling department is in the front left, with the malt house behind it. The small building between the bottling house and the brewhouse is the office (ca. 1900). COLLECTION OF TYE SCHWALBE.

Francis Blesch started brewing sometime in 1850 or 1851.[32] Once established, Blesch brewed for nearly thirty years, and Green Bay would eventually host several important breweries that lasted into the twentieth century.

As breweries spread in from the shoreline, like most settlers they moved along the major rivers and branched out along their tributaries. Following the Milwaukee River inland, John B. Steinmetz established a brewery at Grafton in 1846, and Engels & Schaeffer branched off to locate in Cedarburg on Cedar Creek in 1848.[33] The Rock River proved to be popular for brewers, with breweries appearing in Janesville and Beloit and three breweries prior to 1850 in Watertown, farther upriver.

While Sauk City was on the Wisconsin River, it was founded less upon a particular set of geographic features or transportation advantages than where a particular speculator was able to purchase a land claim. Within a few years of settlement, Mathias Leinenkugel began to make beer using an iron pot. Historians of the Victorian period seldom allowed the lack of verifiable fact to interfere with description, and filled the gaps in evidence with florid prose:

> *How the product of this first process tasted, tradition saith not, but that it was welcome, and not discarded by any, may be well believed. But that it was up to the standard of the article manufactured here at present is not probable; yet when it came fresh from the old iron kettle, who can say that it was not as sweet and pleasant to take as any, and, withal, what better means of brewing the foaming beverage were in vogue a century or two ago anywhere.*[34]

Sauk City eventually became the jumping-off point for one of the great brewing dynasties of Wisconsin. The next generation of Leinenkugels started breweries in Eau Claire and Chippewa Falls, and the current generation has survived to see the family name on bottles, cans, and tap handles in every state of the Union.

Monroe, in Green County, was not near a major transportation route either. It was, however, the center of a large colony of Swiss immigrants, and a brewery was started there, perhaps as early as 1845, that flourished under the names of Hefty, Blumer, Huber, and Minhas. As the first brewery run by German speakers in the south-central part of the state, the brewery started by Mr. Bissinger was able to draw customers from a large radius, including some from Madison, who made a round trip of approximately ninety miles to bring kegs of beer home.[35] Shortly thereafter, entrepreneurs in Madison built their own breweries to satisfy those who came to the capital of the newly proclaimed state to make the laws and acquire a fortune from their passage.

By the time Congress confirmed Wisconsin's statehood in 1848, approximately forty breweries had commenced business and a few of them had already closed. Milwaukee had about a dozen of these, but the rest were spread along the lake and a mix of promising and unlikely spots on the interior. Given the highly speculative nature of business on the frontier and the mobile character of the population, it is not surprising that businesses came and went, and the failure rate of breweries cannot have been much different from that of similar businesses.

MAKING BEER, MAKING A LIVING

While a few farmers were able to treat brewing as a sideline to their main business, for most brewers selling beer was their primary or sole source of income. Their businesses were beset with problems that ranged from constructing suitable buildings and finding inputs to defending their businesses from political, economic, and even physical attacks.

While beer can be made nearly anywhere on a small scale, brewing for commercial purposes requires more and larger equipment and a building of sufficient size and sturdiness to contain it. Most of the early breweries for which descriptions exist were made at first of wood. The rustic nature of many of these early structures may have been exaggerated a bit by the Victorian-era historians who delighted in emphasizing the humble beginnings of leading citizens. John Gund's brewery in La Crosse "started in a small log house" and by 1881 was lauded as "one of the largest, best-furnished and thoroughly responsible corporations in the West."[36] Many of these breweries were constructed with logs, with some requiring cutting 150 trees. Other breweries made creative use of local materials. A correspondent to an eastern newspaper recounted the method that was used to build both a church and the brewery in Southport:

Frederick Miller is seated in the middle of the front row (with his hat in front of the blurry youth). While a few employees are shown holding brooms or other tools of their trades, most are simply enjoying a beer. Redington & Shaffer appear to have been itinerant photographers who were active in the mid-1870s and specialized in group pictures. COLLECTION OF JOHN STEINER.

A composition was made of sixteen parts gravel from the lake shore, and one part lime, the latter being slacked upon the gravel, and mixed directly with it. Two planks were then placed edgewise eight or twelve inches apart, and the space filled to a depth of eight inches. This was then suffered to stand till the next day, when it was sufficiently hardened to raise the planks and repeat the process. The walls were thus raised eight inches per day, and were as solid as stone.[37]

Even in the 1840s, some brewers on the frontier decorated their buildings to the extent they could. John Hettinger began work on what he called the Fort Winnebago Brewery in 1849, but local residents insisted on calling it the Old Red Brewery for its coat of red paint.

Very few buildings retained their primitive construction for long. Slightly more than a year after its founding in 1841, William Miller was advertising a "New Brick Brewery . . . with horse-mill attached for grinding all necessary grain."[38] Charles Haertel started brewing in a small building in 1852, but three years later demand forced him to build a three-story brick brewery, which had to be enlarged again in two years.[39] By 1860 new breweries on the frontier were often still made of wood, as were some in larger cities, but more and more began as modern industrial facilities. The *Kenosha Tribune and Telegraph* reported not only that Gunnerman and Gottfredson's brick building had "all the modern adaptations" but also that "its architecture is in the modern style." Conrad Muntzenberger's recent additions housed an eight-horsepower steam engine and machinery that was "in every respect complete."[40] Of course, there were some exceptions. The wooden brewery of Jacob Jussen in Columbus had been purchased by Alois Brauchle in 1849, and although he had rebuilt and made additions, an 1880 account saw little progress:

> The old Gambrinian temple still stands, though its beams are bent with the burden of time, and the walls within are odorous with age and the fumes of beer. . . . The general decay that pervades the premises must ultimately triumph in their destruction. The old maltster long since passed the meridian of life, and soon both he and his brewery must take places among the things that were.[41]

Esser's Best

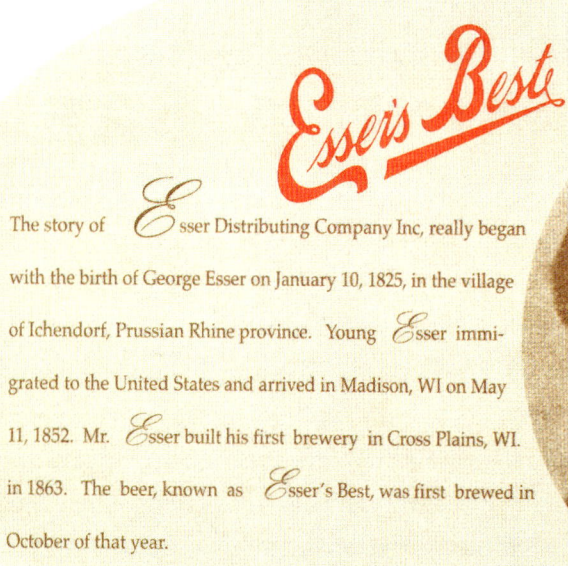

The story of Esser Distributing Company Inc, really began with the birth of George Esser on January 10, 1825, in the village of Ichendorf, Prussian Rhine province. Young Esser immigrated to the United States and arrived in Madison, WI on May 11, 1852. Mr. Esser built his first brewery in Cross Plains, WI. in 1863. The beer, known as Esser's Best, was first brewed in October of that year.

Pioneer brewer George Esser's descendants remained in the beer business as distributors after the brewery in Cross Plains closed in 1910. Wayne and Larry Esser, representing the fifth and sixth generations of the family in the business, brought back Esser's Best beer in 1995 (coaster ca. 2010). Author's collection.

The path of starting with rustic, temporary facilities and improving them as business improved would be retraced in later decades as new parts of the state were settled. But as time went on, new brewers would be trained in Milwaukee or some other

PIONEER BREWING 47

Becoming a Brewer

During the past two centuries, Wisconsin's brewers have learned their craft by apprenticeships and experience, formal training at an academy, or a combination of the two. In modern times, the term *brewmaster* is typically reserved for those who have successfully completed the required training in a formal brewing program; *head brewer* is commonly used for those with primarily informal training. In pre-Prohibition times, newspapers and histories were imprecise in their usage—sometimes designating nonbrewing proprietors as brewers while referring to highly trained brewmasters as foremen. Newspapers often took note of local businesses hiring "practical brewers," without clarifying what their training was. Employees other than brewmasters typically learned on the job—tasks such as shoveling grain or transporting kegs required little skill and could be picked up easily.

Many of these brewers had served as apprentices or brewers in their homelands, but most accounts are vague about where or how long they pursued their trade—though a few mention the cities in which they worked. In the early decades, those who ended up brewing in Wisconsin sometimes stopped first in older brewing centers such as New York, Philadelphia, Pittsburgh, St. Louis, or Cincinnati. By the late 1840s, Milwaukee had several breweries that served as training grounds. Prospective brewers acquired skills, experience, and connections they could use as they moved up the ladder within that brewery or when they set off to start their own business.

According to *One Hundred Years of Brewing*, schools specifically devoted to training brewers were not founded until the 1860s. The first such school in the United States was founded in New York in 1880. Two well-known academies were established in Chicago later that decade: the Siebel Institute of Technology and the American Brewing Academy.[1] (Milwaukee schools are covered in chapter 4.) The major brewing periodicals were often associated with schools, and the graduating class of each term was listed in those journals—to announce their achievement and to help them gain employment as well as to promote the school.

The brewers of the late nineteenth and early twentieth centuries needed training in the application of new scientific discoveries and technologies. Publications such as *Western Brewer* or the *Brewers Journal* kept industry members up to date (and in recognition of the origins of many brewers, several of these publications were printed in parallel German and English editions). Brewers also organized to share knowledge. The

---

1 *One Hundred Years of Brewing* (supplement to the *Western Brewer*) (repr.; New York: Arno Press, 1972), 152.

In the early years of a brewery, it was common for the proprietor to be the brewer as well. It was very uncommon for the brewer to be identified specifically on the label as William Spaeth was on this example (ca. 1910s). COLLECTION OF SCOTT REICH.

Master Brewers' Association of America (MBAA) was founded in 1887 and still serves the industry today. The Milwaukee District was one of the original districts, and nine Wisconsin brewers were among the one hundred in attendance at the first National Convention in Chicago.[2] (Brewers in the western part of the state may be members of the St. Paul–Minneapolis District, which was founded in 1907.)

In the twenty-first century, many of the same opportunities for learning the craft still exist, along with a few new paths. As of 2018, more than two dozen American colleges or universities offered training programs ranging from four weeks to four years. Some programs offer a portion of the instruction online. Brewers still attend MBAA conferences and local events, and since the mid-1980s the Brewers Association has presented the Craft Brewers Conference & BrewExpo America each spring. The Wisconsin Brewers Guild also sponsors technical conferences for its members. Some brewers got their start by volunteering in breweries and working their way up. One new path to brewing not generally followed prior to Prohibition was starting as a homebrewer and turning professional (see chapter 6 and individual breweries).

---

[2] *Communications* (MBAA) 23, no. 9, 10 (1962): 41, https://www.mbaa.com/about/history/HeritageChair/Pages/District-Milwaukee-Heritage.aspx.

PIONEER BREWING

city, dangers from attack would be less, and the economic system would be slightly more stable.

The early development of the brewing industry in Wisconsin took place in an era when increasing mechanization offered new, efficient laborsaving devices for those who could afford them. In looking back on the technological developments of the last

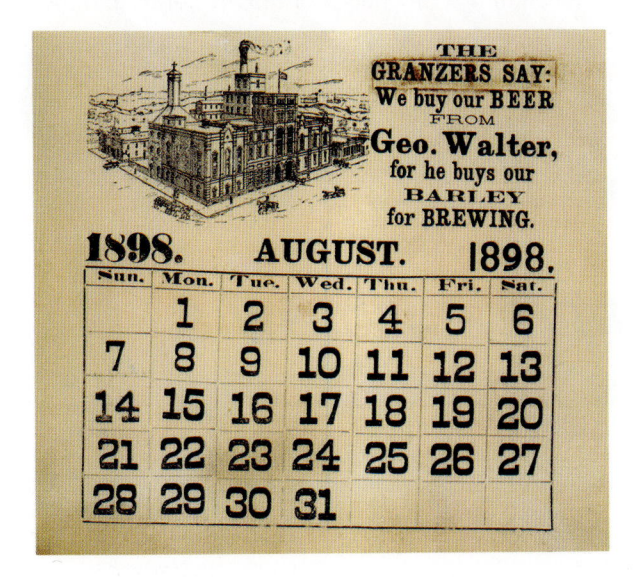

This calendar celebrates the mutually beneficial relationship between farmers and brewers. The section identifying the Granzer family is glued on, suggesting that it was covering an error in the original printing. COLLECTION OF BRIAN ZENEFSKI.

half of the nineteenth century, *One Hundred Years of Brewing* drew a contrast with the first half of the century:

> *The work required for the production of one brew of beer was exceedingly protracted and difficult. The hauling, dipping, pumping, breaking, stirring and boiling were tiresome work for the laborer, indeed requiring from fifteen to seventeen working hours every day, and making the brewers' occupation one of hard toil and of almost unbearable labor.*[42]

Valentin Blatz confirmed the tales of the hard and tedious work required in the antebellum years. He recalled in 1886 that production was low, in part because of the slow process: "Such things as pumps and hoses were unknown in those days, and the beer was drawn from the fermenting tubs in pails, and poured in the larger casks."[43] As soon as money and facilities allowed, brewers switched from hand power to horsepower, and later to steam power.

One of the reasons hand power persisted in breweries was that labor was usually readily available. While absence of advertising is only an indicator and not proof, an extensive survey of newspaper advertising during this period has turned up no examples of a brewer advertising for help, with the exception of an occasional plea for a skilled cooper. Brewers with very small operations could handle the task by themselves or with the help of family members.

Brewers in large cities, especially in Milwaukee, could count on a steady stream of immigrants to employ, some of them with prior experience. Many brewers came to America with training in their home country, though with the exception of a few like Frederick Miller, whose experience is well documented, little is known about the nature or duration of their experience.[44] Any training the brewers received was through an apprenticeship, since formal brewing schools did not start in Germany until the 1860s and in America until the 1880s.[45] Alois Brauchle of Columbus started as a brewer in his native Württemberg, then worked for Johann Braun in Milwaukee and at a brewery in Racine before moving to Columbus.[46] Carl Muench left his post as a foreman at a brewery in his native Würzburg and found a similar position with Schlitz in Milwaukee before buying a brewery in Appleton.[47] Not all German-trained brewers immediately found a permanent spot to follow their craft. Many worked in New York, Pennsylvania, or Ohio before arriving in Wisconsin. Several, like August Hochgreve, Balthasar Goetter, and Ulrich Oderbolz, were also trained as coopers and followed that trade before starting a brewery.

A number of brewers, in particular those who owned the brewery and hired a trained "practical brewer" or brewmaster, came to Wisconsin with no prior experience in brewing and sometimes no intent of starting such a business. George Esser began to study architecture in Germany, and when he immigrated to Madison after the revolution of 1848, he combined farming with building. By the mid-1850s he had made brewery architecture something of a specialty: building a cellar and "malt drier" for Frederic Sprecher in Madison. Sprecher then recommended him for similar projects at the breweries of Charles Haertel and John Hettinger in Portage. It was not until 1858 that Esser considered building and operating a brewery of his own, and even then he first bought and remodeled the brewery in Monroe before finally constructing his own in 1863 in Cross Plains.[48]

Wisconsin's pioneering breweries competed to secure ingredients just as they did to sell their beer. Whether in the major cities or in the countryside, breweries advertised regularly for barley, typically offering cash payment—which was welcome in a state that until 1852 prohibited banks and was therefore generally short of cash.[49] William Hodson of Janesville and William Anson of Watertown both had regular advertisements in their hometown newspapers seeking ten thousand bushels of barley. Editors drew attention in separate columns to the needs of the breweries and the benefit that such an expanding market would have for local farmers.[50] Indeed, in 1854, eight years after Hodson's request, his successor Arthur Brunster advertised an offer for twenty thousand bushels, suggesting that production had doubled to the dual benefit of drinkers and farmers.[51] Brewers sometimes claimed that they offered either "the best market price" or "Milwaukee prices" in an attempt to keep local barley from going to a rival brewer. Purchases of hops benefited merchants as well as growers. Even as Wisconsin's own production expanded, many brewers still sought hops from other regions, which created a competitive market in the cities.

Brewers also increased the local demand for other critical inputs, and therefore became an integral part of the village and city economy as well. Whether for making the beer or packaging it, brewers used an extraordinary amount of wood, and some photos of breweries display large woodpiles on the premises. Coal was scarce in Wisconsin's early days, and data from the 1850 Census of Industry suggest that the average small to mid-sized brewery used over one hundred cords of wood for fuel each year.[52] One brewery, Shepherd & Company of Racine, advertised that it would exchange ale for wood at its brewery near the shipyard.[53] Brewers often had their own cooperages to make barrels, and even businesses that didn't still needed a cooper on staff to repair damaged barrels and brewing vessels. Levi Blossom advertised for a cooper in 1847, adding, "None but men who understand their business need apply." Blossom also called for "50,000 staves and [barrel] heading," which suggests that his business was expanding rapidly.[54]

Brewers also created business for other local artisans, at least in villages or cities where such craftsmen existed. Robert Nesbit observed, "The German peasant in particular was apt to bring a tremendous kit, with the twin certainties that he was going into a wilderness and that Americans could never manufacture articles to suit his standards."[55] A large brewing copper would have been difficult and expensive to ship, however, even for German artisans, who generally came to America with more money than many other ethnic groups. One history of Columbia County records that "Henry Kurth came to Columbus with his family and a four-barrel brewer's boiler," but does not clarify whether he brought it all the way from home.[56] By 1844 Richard Owens was able to have his new kettle made in Milwaukee, but those in outlying areas still had transportation challenges. Otto Kerl was compelled to make two wagon trips to Milwaukee: one to order his kettle from C. H. Meyer (who specialized in steamboat work and so was used to large projects) and the other to pick up the finished product.[57] When Mathias Leinenkugel built his Eau Claire brewery in 1858, he took one of the kettles from his father's brewery in Sauk City to get started.[58] When local businesses were able to supply a local brewery with suitable equipment, the newspapers pointed to the transaction as evidence that their city was just as able to provide for the needs of their businessmen as Milwaukee or Chicago.

The most prominent engagement of a brewery with its community, of course, was the selling of beer. Nearly every early advertisement offered beer for sale at the brewery, and many firms offered to deliver beer anywhere in the city. Most of the breweries had a saloon, guestroom, or beer garden in which thirsty patrons could sample their wares in the freshest possible condition. While generally a scene of gemütlichkeit, there were occasional fracases or assaults, which made the life of a brewer even more grueling than it already was. Edward Mueller of Two Rivers was attacked when "he refused to give a gang of toughs beer," and although the perpetrator was convicted, he later escaped from jail.[59] John Shuler, who had a brewery at Castle Rock just south of Fountain City on the Mississippi River, was once forced to barricade his family in the brewery for protection against a group of American Indians who were angry at his decision to stop serving them beer.[60]

SECURING THE MARKET

As Wisconsin's brewers prospered, and thus were able to purchase more land or to improve that which they already owned, beer gardens became a common feature in city and country. In 1851 Charles and Lorenz Best of the Plank Road Brewery set up a beer hall at Market Square, so their older brothers, Jacob Jr. and Phillip, were pushed to begin retail sales of their beer in a similar manner.[61]

Across the state, beer gardens appeared wherever there were enough Germans to make the business a paying proposition. Fritz Diefenthaler started a beer garden near his Bluff Brewery in La Crosse, and a visitor in 1859 reported climbing the bluff to enjoy a drink of lager.[62] The opulent gardens of Milwaukee were important centers of entertainment as early as the mid-1850s. Charles Best & Company's "Summer Retreat" near their Plank Road Brewery was as lavish a pleasure palace as any in the Midwest at the time. The building held three hundred persons, and featured a brass band and "all kinds of cold eatables," including ice cream. Each Sunday afternoon two omnibuses left from the Market Square beer hall every hour, and a bus could be arranged on weekdays with advance notice. Best's lager was the featured beverage, but champagne, red and white wines, liquors, and coffee also were available.[63]

Wisconsin's brewers had a financial incentive to produce a high-quality product and to serve it in a congenial setting, because the competition was fierce, even in the interior of the state. While regular shipments from Milwaukee's port did not begin until 1852, occasional deliveries of beer within the state started several years earlier. During the years until Prohibition, breweries throughout the state claimed that their beer was "not inferior to the celebrated Milwaukee Lager Beer," or a similar boast. But Milwaukee was not the only source of competition. Advertisements by saloons and stores indicate that ale was being shipped in from Detroit during the 1840s, with J. L. Carew's amber, old stock, and pale and Burton ales specifically mentioned in an 1848 notice.[64] Detroit ale was available at least as far northwest as Oshkosh.[65] Chicago's ale brewers pushed into the Wisconsin market: the Sands' Columbia brewery acquired the Spring brewery in Milwaukee, and Lill & Diversy, one of the largest breweries in the country, leased the Bunster Brewery in Janesville to provide fresher beer to its customers.[66] British imports also appeared on the shelves of Wisconsin's providers. In 1847 William H. Hall of Milwaukee received a shipment of thirty dozen bottles of porter from the Robert B. Byass Brewery in London, which he placed on sale in addition to his existing stock of Tennent's strong ale from Glasgow and Philadelphia porter.[67] Other ads mentioned Burton ales (which was technically a category of ales from the city of Burton-on-Trent rather than a specific brewery) and porter from the well-known firm of Barclay, Perkins & Company. The prominence of individual brands in an era when most consumer products were sold as bulk commodities no doubt made an impression on Milwaukee's forward-looking brewers, as did the linkage of certain cities with entire beer styles.

A Common Table

For a large number of Wisconsinites, the brewery was a gathering place where functions of all sorts were held. Several breweries included dance halls, such as that of W. H. Austin, in Readstown, southeast of La Crosse, which unfortunately burned in 1858.[68] The Turners, the gymnastics-focused social club that was a feature of so many German communities in the United States, practiced for three years in the yard of John Gund's brewery in La Crosse.[69] Because the breweries often had some extra space and were well-known local landmarks,

Charles Hottelmann

Charles Hottelmann is believed to have begun brewing in Manitowoc around 1849. His brewery appears to have done well in the early days, though no precise figures are available until 1860, when he reported 1,200 barrels in that year's industrial census—the same as John Roeffs and more than William Rahr, his two most prominent local rivals. Like many other brewers, he obtained free publicity by donating kegs to the local newspapermen. The *Manitowoc Pilot* thanked him in 1859 for "a keg of excellent Lager Beer" and assured "Mr. H. that his kindness was duly remembered by some twenty or thirty staunch Democrats who met at the *Pilot* office and assisted in disposing of his gift."[1] Hottelmann was also highly regarded as a farmer—the *Pilot* made special mention in 1859 of an address he gave at the county fair to Germans about farming practices.[2]

Hottelmann sold his brewery around 1865 to Heinrich George Kunz, who had brewed previously in Branch and at Roeffs's brewery in Manitowoc. After several more ownership changes, this business eventually became the important Kunz-Bleser Co. and later a branch of Kingsbury Breweries.

---

1   *Manitowoc Pilot,* 28 October 1859, 3.
2   *Manitowoc Pilot,* 14 October 1859, 3.

Very few pieces of pre-Civil War Wisconsin breweriana are known. This Hottelmann receipt dates to 1859.
COLLECTION OF JOHN STEINER.

they were sometimes used for political meetings and quasi-civic purposes. In 1854, the inhabitants of the district represented by G. R. McLane gathered at the Fox River Brewery in Pewaukee to "consider whether he acted properly" by supporting the Kansas–Nebraska Act, which reopened the debate over the expansion of slavery in the territories. In one instance in 1856, the city of Sheboygan announced the building of a road and indicated that the contracting for the grading would be done at the brewery of Leonard Schlicht.[70] Of course, tavern customers often discussed politics outside the context of official meetings. One tale from territorial times holds that two of Milwaukee's principal lager brewers were divided over the proposed state constitution in the days when Wisconsin was applying for statehood. Apparently Jacob Best was in favor of the constitution, and Franz Neukirch was opposed. The story, as it has been handed down, claimed that

> *feeling was so bitter that the antis would not drink Best beer, any more than the constitutionalists would commit treason in drinking Neukirch's beer. The tavern-keepers, knowing the political views of their customers, were shrewd enough to take advantage of the situation. Although they kept only one kind of the two brews, i.e. Best's or Neukirch's, the saloonkeepers would inform the followers of both factions that they would serve either beer. And so the pros lined up on one end of the bar taunting their opponents by shouting "prosit Best," to which the antis would reply "prosit Neukirch." Little did they know it all came out of the same keg.*[71]

Throughout the 1850s, the patrons of the beer halls and beer gardens would be able to argue about banking, taxation, slavery, and even the legality of beer itself.

While Wisconsin's brewing industry was booming as a whole, each individual firm still faced the same difficulties common to other industrial concerns of the era. Most breweries were built near a source of water, and the spring, river, or lake could sometimes undermine the foundation and cause the collapse of a cellar or even the brewery itself. Part of Owens's Lake Brewery fell into Lake Michigan in 1858 after the foundation was eroded by the action of the waves over time. Fire was an ever-present danger for breweries. Breweries used fire for heating and light, and fires were fueled by barley, grain dust, straw, fodder, and manure in the stables, and large quantities of wood. William Hodson had the first brewery in Janesville, and suffered the first major fire in the city when his plant was struck by lightning. His fire was one of the disasters that compelled the businessmen of the city to organize a hook and ladder company in the early 1850s.[72]

A Temperance-Loving People

More dangerous to the brewing industry as a whole was a spiritual fire that swept through portions of antebellum society, stirring individual and political action to rid the growing republic of the scourge

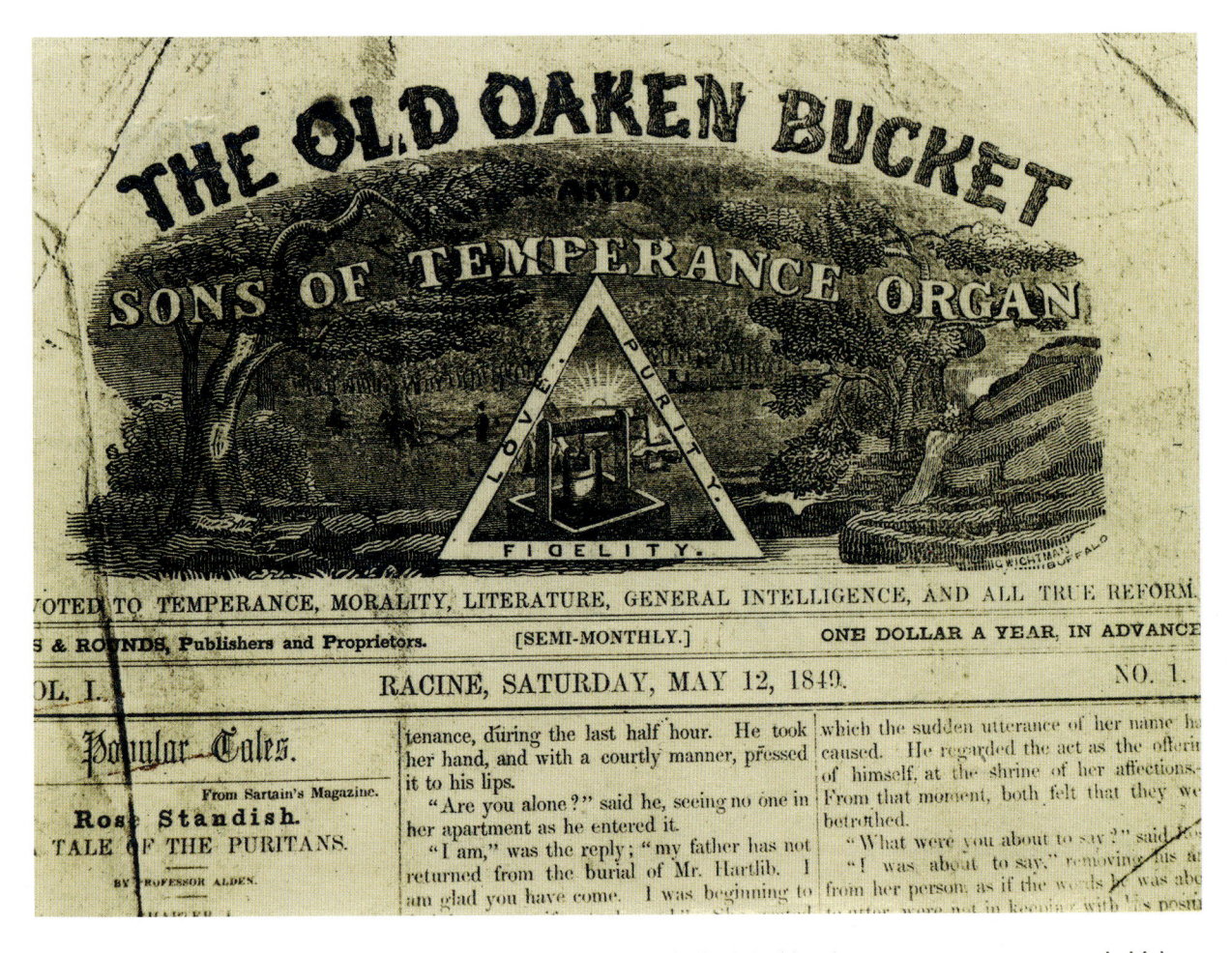

The "Old Oaken Bucket" was used to draw water from a well, and symbolized the idea that water was a strong enough drink for people of virtue. While numerous other temperance papers served Wisconsin readers, none had as elaborate a masthead. (Note the backward *D* in the word Fidelity.) COURTESY OF WISCONSIN HISTORICAL SOCIETY, WHI-67985.

of liquor. A significant number of Wisconsin's Yankee settlers were from the burned-over districts of New York and brought with them the zeal to create a perfect society. Scholars have labeled slavery and temperance the two most important issues in Wisconsin politics prior to the Civil War, though there were more subtle distinctions and shifting alignments concerning the liquor question. (Contrary to modern usage, in pre-Prohibition times the political and legal uses of the term *liquor* commonly included beer and wine.)

Politically conservative opponents of regulation were motivated by a libertarian objection to government interference in the private realm. Germans and other ethnic groups, whether politically conservative or liberal, sought to preserve their culture and resented the ethnically driven contempt of the Yankee elite. On the other hand, advocates of temperance legislation were divided by both the means and the scope of their proposed limitations. Groups such as the Washingtonians and Good Templars attempted to reduce drunkenness by making temperance an issue of personal morality. Sons of Temperance meetings were advertised in newspapers throughout the state, though occasionally the ads appeared next to those of the local breweries. Those who insisted on state action were divided on whether limited and heavily regulated use of alcohol was acceptable or whether the only moral option was a total ban on production and consumption.[73] The citizens of Southport were invited to a meeting in January 1846 at the Methodist church to form "a new Organization with a more rigid discipline than exists in the old Society."[74] Sometimes this dispute erupted into open warfare in the press. In 1850 the *Wisconsin Express* published some rather grudging praise of the newest brewery in Madison:

> *Although this is not an improvement which we can admire, or even approve, still, as such a thing must exist among us, we are happy to know that it is under the control of individuals who will conduct it with prudence, and that its evil tendencies will be as little felt, as could, under any circumstances, be expected from the existence of such an establishment among us. While we would wish that the wealth of our citizens might be expended in the construction of more worthy, or perhaps we should say, less deleterious improvements than breweries and distilleries, we still hope they will be so conducted as to not inflict an injury upon the habits of our citizens, or to cause this community to lose the good name which it of late has so fast acquired, of being a temperate, and a temperance loving people.*[75]

The rival *Wisconsin Free Democrat*, however, published a scathing retort the next week:

> *If the Company could only get a good pious Deacon to superintend the establishment, and a Temperance clergyman to invoke a blessing on each brewing, our friends of the Express would be delighted with the moral tone and tendencies of Messrs. Farwell & Co's brewery. What a consolation it would be to the parents of children bitten by mad dogs, to know that said dogs were owned and kept to run at large by prudent and excellent men, for their own pleasure.*[76]

Breweries fed this debate by declaring themselves temperance institutions, at least in contrast with distilled spirits. The *Stevens Point Pinery* editorialized in 1860 that "the Stevens Point Brewery is one of the best temperance institutions of the country, and is doing away with 'tanglefoot' whiskey permanently."[77] Brewers and their supporters made similar claims throughout the state and nation.

Political realities dictated compromise in the early days of the state, but in 1848 Wisconsin adopted an early version of what is now called the "dram shop law," under which sellers of liquor were required to post a bond and could be held liable for any damages suffered by the family of one of their customers. However, in 1851 Maine passed the nation's first prohibitory law, and Wisconsin activists saw their chance. They were able to place a referendum on the ballot for the November 1853 election, at least in part because the federal Compromise of 1850 had temporarily calmed the slavery question. Campaigning was vigorous, with supporters of the measure placing "ardent temperance women" at the polls for last-minute persuasion, while opponents, especially in Milwaukee, rolled out the barrels and offered liquid encouragement to vote wet. The measure passed by a narrow margin, but was ultimately vetoed by Governor William A. Barstow, who claimed the measure was both unconstitutional and filled with unwise exceptions. Attempts to place a second referendum on the ballot were rejected by the legislature, and the slavery question had heated up again with the debate over the Kansas–Nebraska Act, so temperance advocates were forced to fall back on more localized efforts until after the Civil War. In desperation, they claimed victories from acts of God. The *Fond du Lac Weekly Commonwealth* rejoiced in May 1860: "A ten thousand dollar Brewery was destroyed in Sheboygan by fire, a few days since. We accept it as another evidence of the fact that a good Providence reigns, and that he is still not unmindful of the true welfare of the Sheboyganders."[78] While editorial and religious opposition was unwavering, political steps would have to wait until the next wave of populist reform sentiment arrived in the 1870s.

By the end of the 1850s, Wisconsin's brewing industry had survived an attack on its very existence and was among the leading industries of the state. Production in Milwaukee alone had grown from about 20,000 barrels in 1850 to an estimated 100,000 barrels by 1857. Shipments of Milwaukee beer to other markets increased from 3,639 barrels in 1852 to nearly 30,000 five years later, helped in part by the completion of the Chicago and Northwestern Railway to Milwaukee. Cream City brewers reported shipments to New York as early as 1852.[79] While beer prices were volatile and varied from place to place, competition forced companies to keep their prices more or less in line, but the general trend was up, at least through 1857.[80] The Panic of 1857 brought an economic depression to the nation and a slow recovery to Wisconsin, but its effects on the brewing community were mixed.[81] The continued immigration of thirsty Germans may have buffered the industry from some of the effects of the Panic as well. One newspaper reported in separate but nearby paragraphs that a brewery was being started in the village of Montello and that one hundred Germans were planning to locate in and around Montello during the coming spring.[82] Breweries were also pushing into areas where temperance forces had previously excluded them. It was announced in 1858 that "a military company and a brewery are in the process of formation and construction at Appleton. The [Appleton] *Crescent* thinks the latter can depend on being well patronized as two-thirds of the population drink lager beer."[83] This was a mere three years after the *Crescent* had rejoiced that in the whole of Outagamie County "no Brewery or Whiskey Distillery vomits forth its stench upon the pure air of heaven."[84] Many cities viewed the expansion of their breweries as an indication of the health of their municipality and a vindication of their policies.

In 1859 Charles T. Melms remarked on the health of Milwaukee's brewing industry. He claimed that over $1,000,000 in capital was invested in the breweries of that city, and of the estimated 60,000 to 70,000 barrels produced, one-third was exported to Chicago, Iowa, Minnesota, and even more distant points. He also boasted, "I am shipping to New Orleans myself now."[85] Unfortunately, these exports would be cut off in two years, and the brewing industry and the country as a whole would have to adapt to the Civil War and its aftermath.

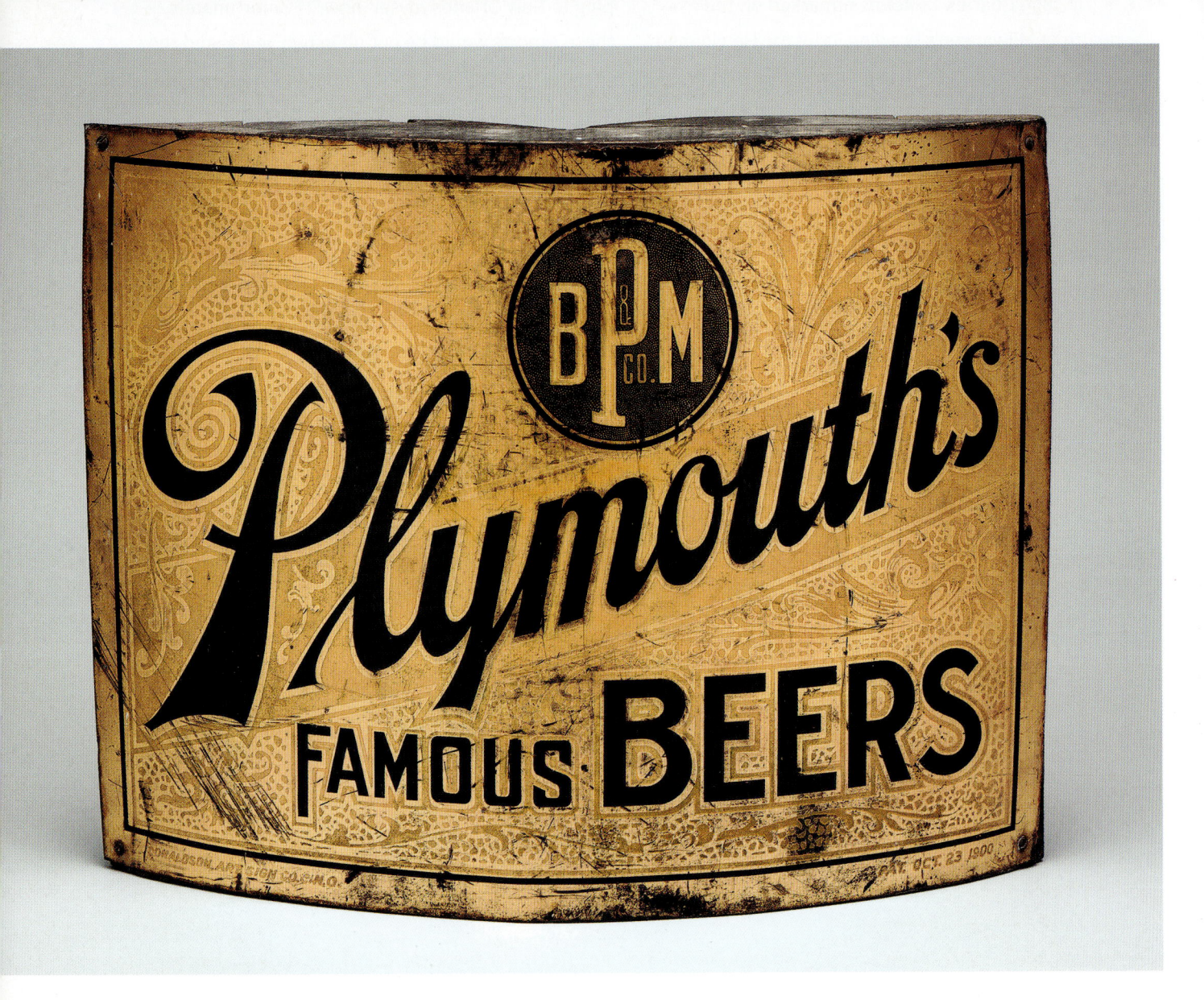

The apostrophe symbolizes the pride smaller cities took in the products of their local breweries. This corner sign dates to the period between 1913 and 1920, when the company was known as Plymouth Brewing & Malting Co. COURTESY OF NATIONAL BREWERY MUSEUM.

CHAPTER 3

ENCOURAGING HOME INDUSTRY

1855–1915

A brewery is an industry that the TIMES has advocated for the past four years. The amount of beer sent out by the four beer agents now in the city, will aproximate very nearly 10,000 barrels annually. This of itself is sufficient to maintain an extensive plant, give employment to a large number of men and keep within our own boundaries at least $60,000, which now finds its way into the hands of Milwaukee and other brewers. In addition, a brewery necessitates a malt house and creates a market for barley, for which there is now no regular established one. We hope that saloon owners and business men will give encouragement to the project. It will increase the population of the city, keep the money at home, and materially advance the farming interests. The establishment of flouring mills and . . . cheese factories has done this and a brewery will help.

Marshfield Times, 27 September 1889

THE FLOURISHING STATE OF WISCONSIN BREWING AT THE BEGINNING OF THE 1860S could be verified by a number of measures: the number of firms, the number of cities with their own breweries, or the production figures. While the Badger State was not yet a rival to New York, Pennsylvania, or Ohio, beer had proved to be a path to wealth for many families, and breweries had become important physical and social landmarks for many communities.

Despite the financial and political difficulties of the period from the Panic of 1857 until war broke out, the rate at which new breweries opened was greater than before the Panic. Some of these were in existing brewing centers such as Milwaukee or La Crosse, and some brought competition to cities like Oshkosh or Beaver Dam. But others expanded the reach of the brewing industry to areas that previously had to import their beer—sometimes from a great distance. In 1857 William Montmann started a brewery in Hudson on the western border of the state in an area where St. Paul was as much a competitor as Milwaukee or La Crosse. Anton Fischer brought brewing to the north shore of Lake Winnebago when he commenced operations in 1858 in Appleton. Oconto, Kewaunee, Marathon, Eau Claire, Juneau, Douglas, and Pierce Counties also gained their first breweries between 1857 and 1860. The advertisement of George Ruder's new brewery in Wausau was typical: "The superior facilities of fitting up, and the supply of pure water, and excellence of the stock on hand warrants Mr. Ruder in saying that he will furnish a better article of Beer than ever before manufactured in the Central part of the State."[1] The relative lack of breweries in the northwest made success seem likely for brewers like Louis Kiichli of Superior.

Cities within range of other brewing centers were often proud to have their own home enterprise. As Jacob Muth expanded his operation in Burlington, a local correspondent rejoiced that "as Canaan was found to be a land flowing with milk and honey, Burlington shall yet flow with good lager without the help of Fred Heck 'or any other man,'" referring to the most prominent brewer in Racine at the time.[2] George Esser, after helping build breweries in Madison and operating the Monroe brewery for a time, moved to Cross Plains near Madison and according to his own account quickly took the local business away from firms in Madison and Sauk City.[3]

Of course, individual financial hardships were common. While these were seldom detailed in newspaper or historical accounts, a few tales survive. Around the time of the Panic of 1857, one Christian Ernst Eckhardt of Sheboygan toiled for a shingle mill that had no cash to meet the payroll, so he was paid in shingles. "Having no use for them, he traded them to the brewery for beer, and, being so poor that he could not afford to consume that luxury, he sold it to the saloons for cash."[4]

DEATH AND TAXES

The outbreak of the Civil War slowed the pace of brewery creation and posed serious problems for some already in business. Investment capital became scarce, though a few firms managed to open or expand. The loss of brewery workers and construction laborers proved damaging and even fatal to some businesses. As the war dragged on, and additional forces needed to be raised, the *Milwaukee Sentinel* lamented:

> *The brewers . . . are suffering, or about to suffer, for hands. A great many men have been employed in the large breweries of this city, and a large proportion of them are enlisting. Mr. Melms, one of the largest brewers, lately received a notification from his men that he must employ other hands as they were about to enlist; and a few days ago all the workmen engaged on a new building at the brewery went off in a body, leaving their work unfinished.*[5]

While a big city firm as large as Melms could survive such a loss, small family operations, especially in rural areas, were much more vulnerable. Otto Kerl, who operated a small brewery at his farm in Dane County, was forced to cease brewing when all of his employees left "either because of free will or because of the draft."[6] George Esser was able to keep his brewery going by hiring a substitute to take his place in the army, but since he was not called until 1865, his substitute only served two months, never left Camp Randall, and Esser was out $800.[7] Germans were noted for their resistance to the draft, and draft riots occurred in both Washington and Ozaukee Counties. To add irony to injury, the location where the list of Second Ward draftees was posted was the Schlitz brewery.[8] On the other hand, a draft-opposing organization called the German Draft Association met at the "Third Ward Brewery" in Appleton in October 1863.

Brewery tokens are among the earliest surviving artifacts from Wisconsin's breweries. These tokens were nearly identical in size and shape to the new, smaller one-cent coin. Tokens like these were issued by many businesses in response to the coin shortage during the Civil War.
COLLECTION OF TYE SCHWALBE.

Breweries had served as centers of community and political life even before war broke out. The Republicans of Milwaukee's Sixth Ward met in 1860 at Simon Meister's brewery, and notices of similar events appeared in newspapers for the next few decades.[9] Although some German immigrants, most notably Carl Schurz and others of the "'48ers," had Republican leanings, others were Democrats. Charles Haertel, of the Portage brewery, earned

Breweries often portrayed their saloons as places where men from all walks of life could meet and discuss the issues of the day (Hausmann Brewing Co., Madison, ca. 1916). COURTESY OF NATIONAL BREWERY MUSEUM.

special mention in the *Sentinel* as an influential loyal German and anti-Copperhead despite his Democratic Party affiliation.[10] Whether Madison's Mathias Breckheimer was a Democrat or not, the Third Ward Democrats of his city met in 1864 at the former Sprecher Brewery, which he now operated.[11]

Some of the wartime meetings were less political and more destructive. In 1864 a group of soldiers in Madison, most from the Third Cavalry, went on a rampage at the Sprecher Brewery—apparently in a dispute over beer. One brewery employee attempted to fight back by tossing a ladle full of hot pitch on the soldiers, but missed and hit one of his fellow employees. During the "serious affray" one M. Smith, foreman of the brewery, had his skull crushed by an iron bar. In another case, however, beer mollified a rowdy group of soldiers: the Sixth Wisconsin, composed primarily of Germans and Irishmen, revolted against their food by breaking up the mess hall until their officers procured other food and "stood treat from their own purses for twenty kegs of beer."[12]

Alcohol use and abuse concerned troops and commanders throughout the war. While some

64 THE DRINK THAT MADE WISCONSIN FAMOUS

commanders believed an occasional drink had a positive effect on morale, most of the army was concerned about alcohol's effect on readiness. Commanders in the field were often distracted by the need to discipline soldiers for drunkenness. Ironically, the army seems to have had fewer problems with drunkenness during the War for Independence, when the soldiers had a daily ration of beer. The beer ration was replaced by a liquor ration early in the nineteenth century, probably because liquor was easier and cheaper to transport and because the army was doing most of its fighting on the frontier rather than near urban brewing areas. Secretary of War Lewis Cass prohibited the consumption of liquor at any military installation in 1832.[13]

RAISING FUNDS

In order to meet the desperate need for funds to conduct the war, the U.S. Congress passed a sweeping excise tax law in the summer of 1862. Income was taxed, as were luxury goods such as pianos, carriages, and gold watches. Business owners were required annually to obtain a license at a rate dependent on the type and size of the business. In addition, excise taxes were placed on the production of many goods, including beer. The Internal Revenue Act passed on 1 July 1862 established a license fee of $25 for brewers making fewer than five hundred barrels per year and a fee of $50 for larger brewers. Each barrel sold was subject to a $1 excise tax.[14] With an average price of $4–$7 per barrel before the tax, this amounted to a 15–25 percent increase in costs per barrel to the customer.

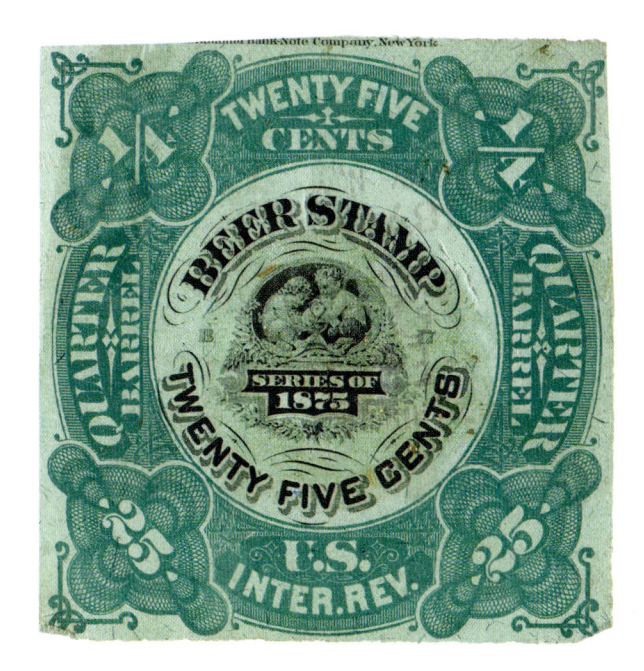

To prove payment of the excise tax, brewers were required to place revenue stamps over the bung of each keg. The stamps were destroyed when the keg was tapped and could not be reused. Stamp fraud was still common. AUTHOR'S COLLECTION.

Nationally, the new tax had some significant short-term side effects. While the Germans tended to be strong Free Soil advocates and many served in the military during the war, the brewers still saw parts of the law as unfair or impractical and wanted several changes made. A group of lager brewers in New York began to meet in 1862 and soon called for a national organization. These meetings led to what would soon become the United States Brewers' Association. While no Wisconsin brewers were represented at the first meeting of the USBA in New York, Charles Melms was appointed to a committee charged with drafting amendments to the tax bill. Milwaukee brewers attended the second conference, and by the third convention in Cincinnati, Joseph Schlitz was elected one of the secretaries of the organization. The fourth convention was held in September 1864 in Milwaukee, recognizing its importance to the industry in what were then still called the western states. The USBA was successful in making the excise tax more efficient and even succeeded in getting the tax lowered to sixty cents per barrel for thirteen months.[15] The tax eventually returned to a dollar, and became permanent after the war ended.

According to industry accounts, the close working relationship between the Internal Revenue Office and the USBA went both ways: the brewers claimed to be less prone to tax evasion than many other industries, and they usually accepted regulations that were both necessary and unavoidable without much complaint.[16] The records of the collectors themselves, however, indicate that many breweries paid a tax penalty at least once, and some breweries tested the vigilance of the revenue agents on a regular basis. A handful of Wisconsin breweries were seized by revenue agents for failure to comply with the law, and brewers were occasionally jailed for evasion. Some violations were more blatant than others. When the tax collector inspected Francis Blesch's brewery in Fort Howard he asked to see the grain book (which would show how much grain had been used and therefore how much beer had been made). "Blesch went and got it and handed it over with all the leaves cut out of it except the last page that was written upon. The cut on the stubs of the leaves was fresh and glistening and apparently just made." His brewery was seized immediately, and Blesch narrowly avoided being thrown in jail on the spot.[17] (More of these incidents are related in the histories of the individual breweries.)

Sometimes brewers were cleared of the charges, or at least were exonerated in the court of public opinion. When Fred Heck of Racine was arrested for stamp violations in 1875, the *Argus* contended an employee must have committed the offense, since Heck was "not that kind of a man."[18] Occasionally, it was the revenue officers themselves who abused the system. The same week Heck was arrested, the *Milwaukee Daily News* reported that a low-level revenue official named James White tried to bilk the Phillip Best Brewing Company out of money by falsely claiming to manager Frederick Pabst they had unstamped kegs of beer. Unfortunately for White, Pabst was not to be trifled with, and "the gallant captain responded by bouncing Mr. White with great promptness."[19]

In his definitive book on American brewing history, Stanley Baron suggested that the other side effect of the new tax was to force smaller or less financially sound breweries out of business—leaving their markets to be consolidated by larger producers. This was seldom the case in Wisconsin. Of the relatively few firms that apparently closed during the war after the imposition of the tax, most were in Milwaukee, and Baron's thesis may well apply to a few of them. But no contemporary accounts suggest that any particular brewery closed because of the tax. The effect may have been more pronounced in mature brewing centers like New York and Philadelphia.[20]

As the industry matured, the natural drift of proprietors in and out of the business seems to have resulted in more brewery closures than any particular historical event (other than Prohibition). Some probably stopped brewing because they failed to find a market, but others moved on to other, more lucrative businesses (though perhaps because they were unsuccessful as brewers). George Streng, who built the Whitewater brewery in 1859, was in the furniture business by 1861.[21] Thomas Young, who had established a flourishing brewery in Beaver Dam in the 1850s, opened a lime kiln east of the city in 1863, though "orders must be left at my old brewery."[22] Some brewers simply made a slight alteration, like Otto Zwietusch, who in 1864 closed his weiss beer brewery in Milwaukee and became a soda manufacturer and bottler. Zwietusch would, about fifteen years later, patent his "new process fermentation" and come back into the brewing business as a supplier.

Even before the war ended, the return of mustered out soldiers increased both the supply of and demand for beer. Captain Herman A. Meyer Jr. of Waukesha resigned from his position with the Twenty-Eighth Infantry regiment in February 1864, and by the end of the year he advertised that he had "again commenced to Brew" after seventeen months in the army.[23] Philip Eder of Fountain City spent more than a year in the fabled Iron Brigade before being invalided out in 1864, at which time he returned home to take up the brewing business again.[24] Esser specifically mentioned the return of soldiers as the primary reason he needed to expand his brewery.[25] The immediate postwar years certainly saw a boom in the number of breweries in the state. From a low of three breweries reliably known to have started in 1861, the pace accelerated to nearly sixty breweries whose first recorded mention was in 1867. While the rapid expansion slowed a bit from this frenzy, another thirty were founded by the end of the 1860s, and it was a rare year up to the nation's centennial in 1876 that did not see at least half a dozen new breweries in Wisconsin.[26]

FILLING THE STATE

As the nation and its economy returned to normal, German immigration and migration resumed, veterans and other settlers took up lands in sparsely populated parts of the state, and breweries multiplied to serve these residents' demand for fresh beer. Even though the number of breweries increased steadily, the total production fluctuated dramatically. While statewide output jumped first from almost 98,000 barrels in 1865 to over 136,000 the next year to over 200,000 in 1868, the next two years saw production fall back under 190,000 barrels before it began a steady climb that would be uninterrupted until 1894, by which point Wisconsin was brewing nearly three million barrels a year.[27] While the most dramatic contribution to that increase came from the Milwaukee breweries (covered in chapter 5), the expansion in the number of firms statewide played a part as well.

Many of the new breweries established during the fifteen years after the war would provide competition in growing cities. The Oshkosh brewing scene exploded after the war as Charles Rahr started a brewery in late 1865, Leonhardt Schwalm and August Horn partnered in a new business that began production in 1866, and in 1867 Franz Wahle built a brewery that he would lease two years later to John Glatz and Christian Elser. The latter two, along with Lorenz Kuenzl's brewery founded in 1875, would merge in 1894 into the Oshkosh Brewing Company.[28] Mathias Breckheimer moved into Madison in late 1865, completing the trio of Fauerbach, Hausmann, and Breckheimer that would compete against each other until Prohibition.

Brewers of this era, as in all other eras, knew the value of publicity, and Breckheimer gave tours to reporters who came out "confident of his producing a Capital City lager that can compete with the famed drink of Milwaukee or 'any other place.'"[29] Before the 1860s ended, Green Bay's Franz Hagemeister, Janesville's John G. Todd, Stevens Point's Adam Kuhl, and many others thought (mostly rightly) that their growing cities had room for another brewery. While these three in particular lasted several decades and became major competitors in their home markets, some smaller operations—often farm breweries—nestled in amongst their larger siblings. Barnard Gloeckler (or Gloeggler) left his brewery in Minneapolis during the war and moved to Portage, where he operated a small farm brewery near the much larger City and Fort Winnebago Breweries before eventually going into partnership at Fort Winnebago. Also in Portage, Stephen Fleck built his new Farmers' Brewery in 1869, whose market was described in the 1880 *History of Columbia County* as "entirely local."[30]

In some cases, existing brewers saw the expansion as a time to get out of the business and get a good price for their investment. Samuel Hocking of Janesville offered for sale in 1866 "the whole Fixtures for a small brewery"—everything from the 150-gallon brew kettle to his leftover porter bottles.[31] A few years later, Anson Rogers leased his Janesville brewery to John and Michael Buob so that he could spend most of the winter in Florida, anticipating the modern habit.[32] Many changes in

Many cities had several breweries of roughly similar size that competed for business. The three largest Madison breweries all had steins made by the same potter (ca. 1900). COLLECTION OF TYE SCHWALBE.

The Bender and Ruhland breweries were located about a block apart on the same side of Lynn Street. Breweries located within a city sometimes had more stylish architecture than the more utilitarian buildings in the countryside. The Ruhland Beer Hall was on the ground floor at right. Postcard, ca. 1900. COLLECTION OF JOHN STEINER.

ownership were simply a matter of the natural churn of business, rather than an indicator of trends in the industry. Business name changes were frequent until incorporation became widespread and replaced many family proprietorships.

More of the new breweries sought locations without an existing competitor in order to capture a market whose thirst was not yet slaked locally. The counties between Madison and the Mississippi River swelled with breweries during the decade after the war, in small villages such as Cazenovia and Wiota as well as larger cities like Platteville and Dodgeville. To the north, Manitowoc County added breweries in small settlements like Branch and Kossuth (Francis Creek), even with competition from the city of Manitowoc and other nearby brewing centers. The optimism of the times inspired breweries in cities that had abandoned brewing before the war, such as the Yankee stronghold of Beloit. Baraboo, which had a brewery in 1850 but a major bout of temperance activity in the middle of that decade, attracted not one but three new breweries during Andrew Johnson's brief presidency. This time brewing took root—the brewery George Bender started in 1868 lasted almost a century until 1966, and the George Ruhland brewery in Baraboo endured until 1915.

ENCOURAGING HOME INDUSTRY

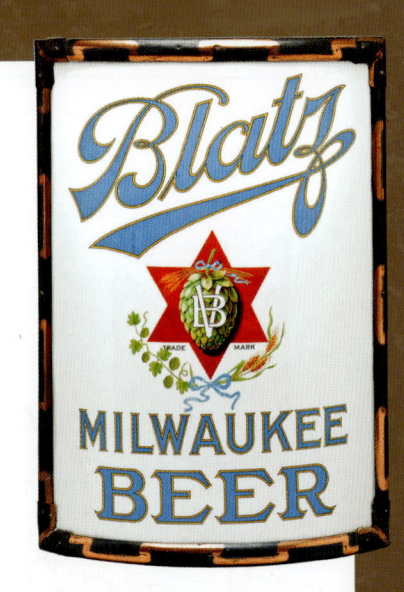

Signs of the Times

An article in the *Milwaukee Sentinel* claimed that beer signs were an American invention rather than an import from Germany (which seemed to ignore centuries of artistic British tavern signs). The earliest signs in Milwaukee were "bracket-like contrivances sawed out of wood and nailed against the door-post of the saloon like a wing" and featured a portrait of King Gambrinus "in profile with a wooden glass elevated as if about to propose the health of all within sight." These were replaced in the mid-1870s and early 1880s by wooden "bracket wings" with a dark background and the name of the brewery in gilt letters. Signs became more elaborate in the mid-1880s, as branding and securing lucrative saloon properties became more important. Next was the swinging sign, with (usually three) metal or wooden boards connected by iron rods or, occasionally, a wire mesh. The corner sign started to appear in the mid-1880s. At first it was usually just the brewery name along with "Lager Beer" and a hop trademark, but soon were added goblets, factory scenes, and other designs.[1] The tin corner sign of the nineteenth century lasted until Prohibition, but was joined by the much more colorful signs made of Vitrolite, a hard structural glass that made more detailed artwork possible.

Very few breweries created large or outdoor signs for their near beer products during the dry years, but after Prohibition beer signs returned. The new signs took advantage of electricity and neon to create some of the most memorable advertising pieces of the century.

---

1   *Milwaukee Sentinel,* 9 September 1888, 1.

Left: Corner sign, ca. 1890. The gold letters were painted with quartz dust. Collection of John Steiner.
Center: Porcelain and metal signs offered durability. Pre-1900. Collection of Richard Yahr.
Right: Vitrolite sign, ca. 1910s. Collection of David Wendl.

In at least one case, a village was founded because of a brewery. A 1904 history relates that "in 1866 the village of Centerville was given birth, largely from the fact of the erection of a brewery by C. Scheibe."[33]

The expanding market was not just satisfied by new firms—existing breweries across the state began to expand. In Janesville, which was the center of ale production, John Roethinger was compelled to expand his brewery "in consequence of the increasing demand." Like others with the opportunity to grow, Roethinger took advantage of the chance to improve his technology, in this case with "a Thirty Horse Power boiler, Steam Pump, and other necessities."[34]

New breweries found it even easier to start with new technology. In Janesville, where the competition among ale breweries was fierce, the elderly William Hodson reentered the business with a new brewery outfitted with innovative equipment. Less than a month later, an article reported that Hodson needed capital to expand, allegedly because of the high demand for the product, but an ad six weeks later seeking a partner for the brewery also noted that the brewery only had $300 cash to start operations. (A partner bringing in capital of $1,500 to $2,000 was promised a lofty 20 percent rate of return.)[35] Clearly the prospect of such large profits attracted businessmen with little brewing acumen or industry experience who were likely to fail in short order. Some may have simply had bad luck or picked a poor location. In several cases an investor with no brewing experience purchased a property and hired a brewer to improve chances of success.

Breweries provided significant economic benefits to their hometowns. The presence of a brewery in a new location was an encouragement to farmers to plant barley and sell it locally. Because of this, local newspapers were often vigorous advocates for breweries (unless their editors were temperance men). The *Marshfield Times* campaigned for several years to attract one to the city, claiming, "One of the finest openings in the Northwest for an extensive brewery is in this city" and a "home market for several thousand bushels of barley." Instead of seeking a comparison with Milwaukee, as so many boosters did, the paper pointed to nearby Spencer, noting that John Walter's brewery there "has proved a paying investment to the proprietors, a valuable acquisition to the town and put hundreds of dollars in the pockets of farmers in that vicinity." An appeal to local pride concluded that "thousands of dollars . . . yearly go out of the city for beer, and which should and would be distributed among laborers, farmers and merchants, were the supply manufactured at home."[36]

Brewers often ended up sending much of the barley back to farms or local residents who kept a few animals as livestock feed. The practice was so common that it was seldom noted in the press, but the *Oshkosh Daily Northwestern* could not overlook one instance:

> *A novel sight attracted the attention of the passer by in the vicinity of the [Horn & Schwalm's] Brooklyn Brewery yesterday afternoon. It was no less than 26 wheelbarrows filled with grain and manned by 26 stalwart women that caused the usual[ly] listless pedestrian to gaze with con-*

William Tetzlaff drove this wagon that picked up spent grains from Milwaukee breweries in the 1930s. COLLECTION OF JOHN STEINER.

siderable interest at the usual go-as-you-please race with grain for the sweepstakes. The women were those of the neighborhood wheeling malt and the refuse of the brewery house for their pigs.[37]

In most cases, the spent grain would have been picked up by men driving wagons, but households that had a few pigs in the yard would not need such quantities.

The many county history books of the late Victorian era emphasized the contributions of brewers to their communities—perhaps because they hoped to sell as many copies as they could to local businessmen. Ferdinand Effinger of Baraboo, for example, was described as a member of the Lutheran church and the Ancient Order of United Workmen. He was particularly lauded for his leadership in the Baraboo Männerchor, for which he "was one of the prime movers in its organization."[38] (Other examples are found in the second part of this book, "Wisconsin Breweries and Brewpubs.") More important, they also emphasized (often to the point of exaggeration) the relative merits of their breweries in the region and in the state. Of the Neillsville Brewery, the grandly titled *Clark County: The Garden of Wisconsin* enthused: "This brewery is one of the best properties of the kind in northern

Glasses like this one from the Neillsville Brewery were popular in the 1890s and early 1900s. They were most likely intended for home use since their fragile construction would not have held up to saloon use (ca. 1900). COLLECTION OF TYE SCHWALBE.

Wisconsin. . . . It consumes a large amount of barley, and gives a steady market for that kind of grain, which the soil here produces to perfection." To prove the importance of Neillsville to the entire country—and show that Milwaukee was not the only town that could sell beer—the authors noted, "The output of the brewery is sold along the Omaha and Central railroads, as well as supplying the home market." The ability to sell one's beer beyond the local market was not just a matter of prestige but also a positive balance of trade that improved the economic health of the community.[39]

These same county histories were decidedly "respecters of persons" and focused on citizens who held political office, which was yet another way in which brewers served their homes. Several were elected mayor, including Jacob Leinenkugel of Chippewa Falls, Charles Gillman of Mineral Point, William Rahr of Manitowoc, and Henry Bierbauer of New Lisbon, who earned special mention for being elected in a "Republican city" despite being a Democrat. The brewing family that supplied the most mayors to a city was the Knapstein clan of New London, where Theo (1881–82), brother Henry (1893–95), and Theo's son Mathias (1906–10) were all mayor at some point—Mathias took office at age twenty-seven and was dubbed "the kid mayor."[40] Other brewers elsewhere served as aldermen, city treasurers, or in other offices. A select group were even elected to the state legislature, including Theo Knapstein and Nicholas Schmidt of Marathon (City). A list of occupations held by members of the 1897 senate shows as many brewers as bankers, though the number in both cases was one.[41]

Of course, the presence of brewers in city and state politics brought forth charges that these men were using their offices to pursue legislation or ordinances that would benefit their industry, as some likely were. Allegations of misdeeds by the "brewery interests" increased over time as prohibitionist sentiment grew. Many if not most brewers, however, were also motivated by a sense of civic duty and concern for the town that was

ENCOURAGING HOME INDUSTRY

also their home market. In 1882 forces in La Crosse were trying to enforce the Sunday closing laws and elected Mayor H. F. Smiley, who was opposed by Charles Michel, whom the *Milwaukee Sentinel* called the "proprietor of the largest brewery in the state outside Milwaukee."[42] When Jacob Leinenkugel was elected mayor of Chippewa Falls in 1884, the *Sentinel* noted that while he was inclined toward less regulation of saloons, he did not run on that issue.[43] Many others were praised for their dedicated service, though again, many of these accounts came from books that were unlikely to print anything less than praise.

The brewers were sometimes accused of buying votes with beer—a practice not confined to Milwaukee. Ezra Williams, a Republican operative in Appleton, recalled how in 1904,

> Every day at about 4 p.m. I'd take my buckboard down to the old Appleton brewery and pick up a quarter barrel of beer. Then I'd throw a blanket over it and take it down to the old Fourth Ward, an all-Democrat area. The ward voted Republican in the election of 1904.[44]

Allegations of conspiracy reached even into the halls of the Wisconsin Senate. The *Stevens Point Journal* reported in June 1913 that "one member of the senate received signals from a brewery lobbyist who occupied a seat in the gallery."[45]

Brewers encountered allegations of unclean politics, but also of creating unpleasant or even toxic physical environments. Although Milwaukee brewers bore the brunt of these accusations (see chapter 5), other cities had to contend with environmental harm caused by breweries. Madison's *Wisconsin State Journal* reported in 1870, "Some residents of the First Ward complain bitterly of a nuisance caused by the emptying into the street of the cesspool of Maus' brewery, at the corner of State and Gilman streets. Were it not for the extreme cold, they say, the stench would be intolerable."[46] Breweries with steam whistles sometimes disturbed the neighbors, as was the case in 1883 when the whistle at the Schreier plant in Sheboygan went off at 2:00 a.m. and roused the fire department and nearly everyone in town. It turned out to be a false alarm compounded by a watchman who did not know how to operate the equipment.[47] But occasionally, what was once just noise becomes a cherished link to the past. In 2015 residents of Bangor voted to continue sounding four times a day the village siren that once summoned Hussa Brewing Company workers to their shifts.[48]

In many other ways, however, breweries were an economic boon to a community. The Lutz brothers of Stevens Point were lauded for making improvements to all their properties, and were praised as "bricks to improve things around them." Even citizens who were less than thrilled about the prospect of alcohol being manufactured nearby sometimes reluctantly admitted the benefits. When Henry Kaufman of Milwaukee announced in 1882 that he was planning to purchase and reopen the brewery in Wrightstown, between Green Bay and Appleton, the *Milwaukee Daily Republican Sentinel* claimed, "Although a number of the Wrightstown people do not approve of the business itself, they think that Mr. Kaufman's enterprise will largely add to the industry and business of the town."[49] In addition to providing fresh beer, breweries offered jobs and work for building trades, and brought in business by river, road, and rail. Although most breweries were established near transportation routes in the first place, expanding breweries demanded increased road improvements and rail connections. The Northwestern Railroad was authorized to build a new spur to Ernest Klinkert's City Brewery in Racine in 1890, in part to accommodate Klinkert's growing export trade to the south.[50] Breweries on significant waterways continued shipping by boat even after rail had reached most of the state. For example, in 1891 Hagemeister's Sturgeon Bay branch received permission from the state legislature to build a pier for the brewery.[51] These infrastructure improvements sometimes benefited other businesses directly. In Whitewater, Nicholas Klinger's brewery shared a "tramway" that brought ice from the lake with a local produce merchant. Some in the city found this arrangement ironic because the senior partner of the produce company was a staunch prohibitionist and had been "one of Klinger's liveliest antagonists in times past."[52]

The most popular bit of infrastructure was the brewery itself. While the majestic factories of Milwaukee drew the most attention from travelers and the media, evidence suggests that breweries in other cities encouraged visits and offered tours to interested groups. In July 1892 the *Milwaukee Journal* noted that two groups were planning excursions: the "Ernest Klinkert Friends" club of Milwaukee was headed south to Racine to visit the holy shrine of their faith, and the Glee Club of Milwaukee was venturing north to Port Washington and Cedarburg, "where many will accept an invitation to inspect the brewery."[53] A less common but still logical tour was reported in 1911 when "a number of boy delegates from the senior physics class visited the Polish Brewery [in Stevens Point] a short time ago and while making a tour of inspection were able to prove many of the laws of physics in regard to the steam engine, condenser, etc."[54]

Brewers with the proper license were entitled to have a saloon associated with the brewery (which in the twenty-first century would be called a taproom) that often welcomed more than just neighbors. Henry Bierbauer of New Lisbon

In addition to being taxed for operating a brewery, brewers who wished to sell their beer on the premises were required to pay a special tax to act as a "retail dealer in malt liquors." Alma Brewing Co. received this tax stamp for its twenty dollars per year payment in 1916. COLLECTION OF JOHN STEINER.

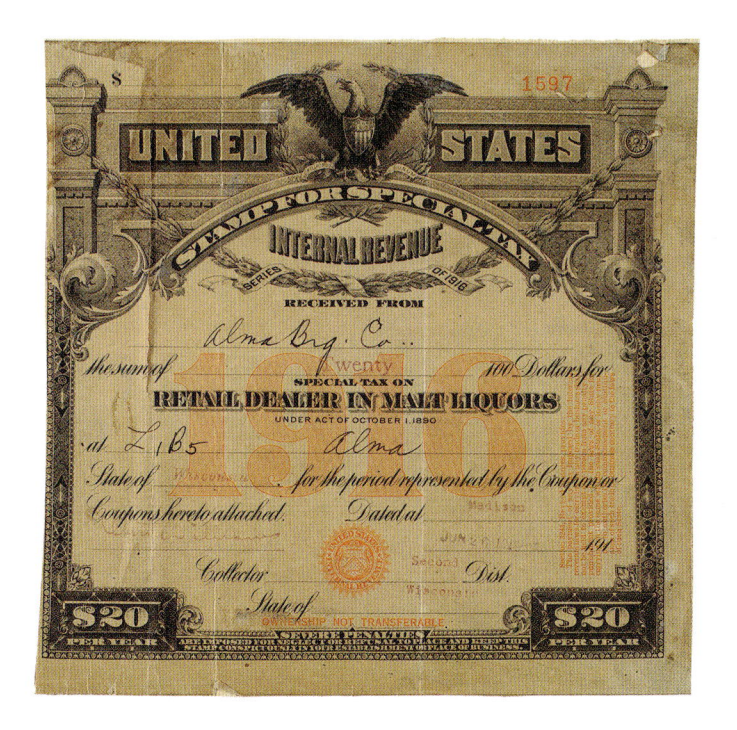

advertised in the early 1880s: "Gentlemen will find my brewery open at all lawful hours and are cordially invited to give me a call when in New Lisbon."[55] Nineteenth- and twenty-first-century breweries shared the need to build cash flow while they worked to develop other accounts. Breweries with sufficiently large halls could hold dances. Klinger's establishment in Whitewater apparently was popular enough in 1877 to feature a full orchestra (whatever size was meant by that) every night.[56]

UNWANTED ATTENTION

Brewers sometimes had to contend with malicious attacks on their property and profits. While acts of minor vandalism were probably more common than records show, a few incidents drew statewide newspaper attention. In 1874 the *Sentinel* printed a report from Prescott that "some person entered the brewery of N. P. Hustings in the night, and bored a beer tun, spilling about twenty barrels of the vital fluid." The writer then editorialized, "That is mean. Whoever did that would set fire to a house, or stab a man in the back."[57] Occasionally the vandalism took the form of defiling the beer. In 1870 the *Janesville Gazette* reported, "Some malicious chap has been playing havoc with the manufacturing of lager beer at Matt. Leinenkugal's brewery [in Eau Claire], by depositing gum Arabic in the cooler of that establishment."[58] Gum arabic has a thickening effect and would have destroyed the beer and clogged the equipment. In one incident in 1891, soap was thrown into a vat of beer at the Arcadia brewery, "but the mischief was discovered before the spoiled liquid had been mixed with that in other vats." Another soap incident was reported in 1892 at Schreiner's brewery in Plymouth, though this time the culprits put soap in four tanks.[59]

While vandalism was rare, robberies were more common. Some breweries were apparently more vulnerable than others—an 1882 report of a burglary at Hess and Lohrer's brewery in Madison noted, "This makes several times."[60] A large robbery took place in 1871 at Haertel's brewery in Portage, in which $500 was removed from the safe. The sum was larger than usual because Haertel often held money for other local businesses that were unable to make deposits after the banks closed.[61] While most breweries appear to have

Brewers typically used their profits to build homes suited to their status as business leaders of the community. The house Ulrich Oderbolz built in 1869 still stands across the street from what is now the Sand Creek Brewing Co. in Black River Falls.

owned safes, that did not prevent safecrackers from plying their trade. The safe of the Storck brewery in Schleisingerville (Slinger) was blasted in 1889, and the bandits got away with $500 in cash and $464 in notes.[62] Of course, if the safe proved unfruitful, there were other things to take from a brewery. When the new Rhinelander brewery was broken into in 1895, the burglars found the safe empty, so they settled for a keg and a few bottles of beer.[63]

Breweries were likely targets of crime because most were thriving local businesses with cash on hand. And while pre-Prohibition profit figures are difficult to find, especially for smaller family firms, the rate at which brewers were building fine houses for their families and erecting ever more monumental breweries suggests that business was good for many firms. Sometimes breweries even survived economic downturns better than other businesses. During the Panic of 1893, the *Wisconsin State Register* of Portage reported that "Epstein's brewery is well underway, and will be completed on contract-time. Brewing does not seem to suffer from stringency in money and the general trades depression."[64]

Speculation and Competition

With opportunities came speculation, and with speculation came rumors. As breweries moved from craft to industry over the course of the Gilded Age, more capital was required to start or update a brewery, which increased the stakes for cities trying to lure breweries or otherwise boost their prospects. Rumors of breweries coming to town appeared in newspapers with regularity—and the more distant the investors, the more excited the reports. A correspondent from Medford reported in 1885, "A gentleman from St. Paul is here with a view of starting a brewery," though it would be four years before one would be built. Even better was to hint that a famous name was allegedly behind the project. The *Oshkosh Daily Northwestern* invoked one of the most storied of all in reporting, "A man claiming to be a cousin of Phil. Best, the Milwaukee brewer, looked over Antigo and said he intended to start a brewery if he could find suitable property."[65] No brewery would open in that city until 1890, and that would be the work of local residents.

Jealousy crept into occasional news reports of pending breweries. The *Marshfield Times*, ever begging for fresh local beer, lamented, "We understand that a movement is being made to erect a brewery in the town of Lincoln, about two miles from Marshfield. We do not see why a good brewery would not pay here."[66] The brewery in Lincoln never materialized, like many other proposed breweries then and now. Some rumors were bigger than others—the *Chicago Herald* printed a report in 1891 that "Racine is on the eve of a gigantic boom. . . . An immense tract of land west of the city has been purchased by an eastern syndicate for the purpose of erecting a brewery," which never came to pass.[67]

As competition from larger breweries grew more intense, some prospective brewers sought distinctive market niches to set their businesses apart. One case, which may have been a century ahead of its time, was a proposed brewery near Appleton. In 1896 a report from Appleton

Vogl's Independent Brewing Co. proudly proclaimed it was "Not in Any Trust" on this label (ca. 1906). The declaration was an early example of the pride many modern craft brewers take in their independence from large multinational brewers. COLLECTION OF TYE SCHWALBE.

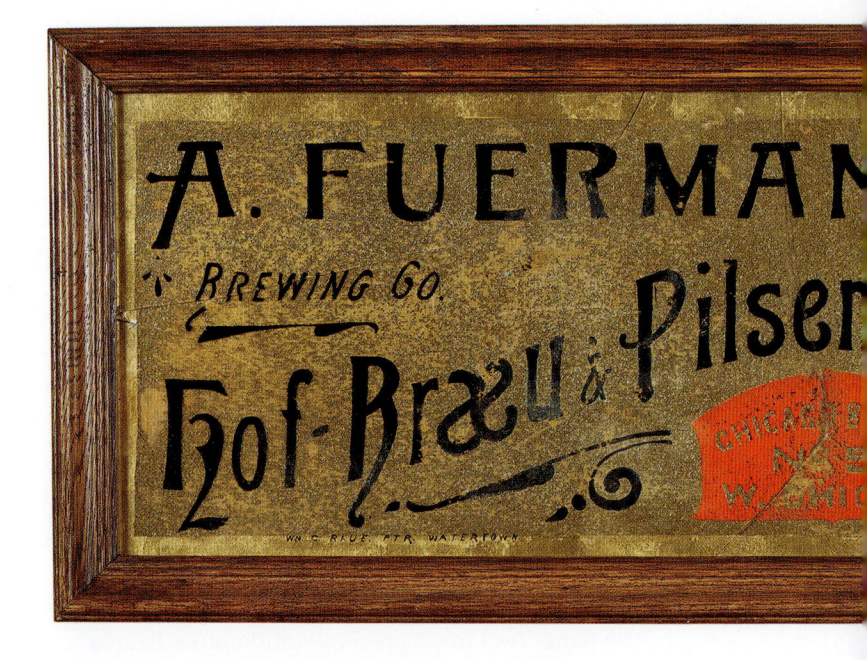

Watertown's A. Fuermann Brewing Co. was reported to have been taken over by a British syndicate in 1889, but no subsequent accounts confirmed this sale. This rare reverse-on-glass sign lists the company's Chicago Branch at No. 9 Ohio Street and may have been made for the Chicago market (ca. 1885). COURTESY OF NATIONAL BREWERY MUSEUM.

announced, "A brewery for the manufacture of Belgian beer, which is made entirely from hops and barley and contains no chemicals, is being built at Little Chute in this county." Despite considerable research, no completed brewery has been found that meets this description, so it is likely that funding was hard to come by for a new product with an untested ability to compete against lager beer.[68]

The wave of corporate mergers and trust building of the late Gilded Age spread to breweries as it did to nearly every other industry. An additional threat to local ownership was the prospect of purchase by British investors. While many Americans saw foreign ownership of U.S. firms as a threat to sovereignty, some stockholders found the high prices offered by these syndicates irresistible.

Although relatively few breweries passed into English hands, some companies combined in the 1890s as a defense against hostile takeovers. Massive mergers of as many as twenty breweries in Baltimore and Pittsburgh changed the landscape of the brewing industry and provided stiffer competition to the Milwaukee giants. Milwaukee breweries were constantly mentioned in syndicate rumors, owing to their worldwide prominence. One account claimed that an agent of "twenty million of dollars of British gold" wanted to purchase a controlling interest in all the big breweries in Milwaukee. Pabst was allegedly offered $9 million just for his brewery.[69] Ultimately, Blatz was the only major brewer in Milwaukee to follow the merger path. After much speculation, a deal was confirmed in February

CONTENTS 12 FLUID OZ. **THE BREWERY'S OWN BOTTLING**

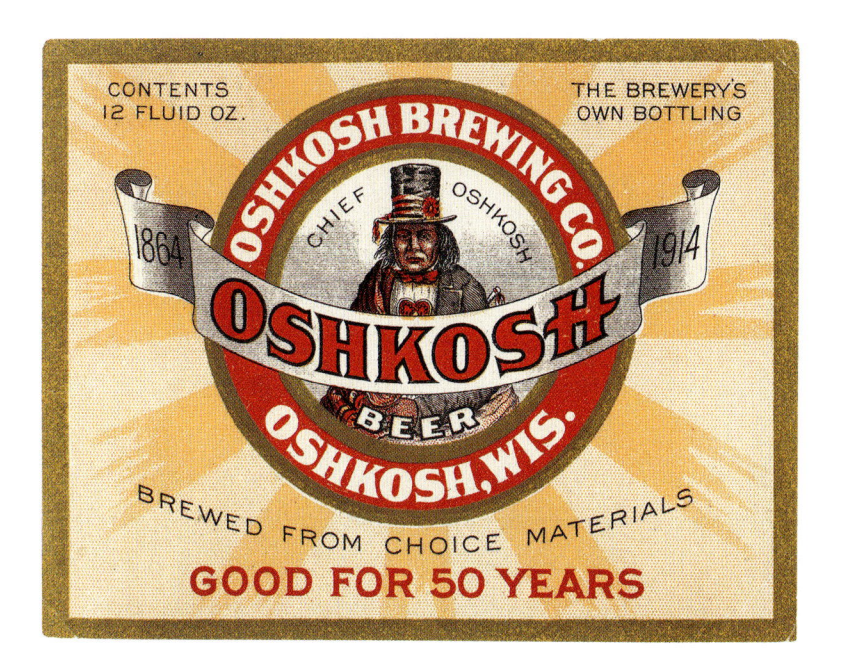

OSHKOSH BREWING CO.
1864 — 1914
CHIEF OSHKOSH
OSHKOSH BEER
OSHKOSH, WIS.
BREWED FROM CHOICE MATERIALS
GOOD FOR 50 YEARS

This label claimed the Oshkosh Brewing Co. was founded in 1864, even though none of the three breweries that combined to form it began that year. Earlier letterheads gave a date of 1866, which was when Horn & Schwalm's Brooklyn Brewery opened. The 1864 date persisted and was used to mark the company's ninetieth anniversary in 1954. COLLECTION OF JOHN STEINER.

1891 in which the Milwaukee and Chicago Brewing Company was formed with Val Blatz as president, including his brewery and five Chicago breweries. Blatz sought to defuse any public concern about another trust by explaining it was not a trust because the public could own stock.[70]

The most notable merger outside of Milwaukee took place in Oshkosh, where the local breweries had been hurt by business closures caused by the Panic of 1893. Temperance forces in the city were successful in enacting Sunday laws, which closed the saloons. To make matters worse, out-of-town breweries were using Oshkosh as their base to move into northern Wisconsin. Schlitz, Pabst, and Miller had bottling works in town and other Milwaukee brewers had agents, along with Anheuser-Busch and Cincinnati's Christian Moerlein.

While Charles Rahr's smaller brewery had a tight network of tied houses and modest ambitions, the three slightly larger breweries in town felt the outside pressure more keenly. In May 1893, August Horn of the Brooklyn Brewery (named after the neighborhood in Oshkosh), John Glatz of the Union Brewery, and Lorenz Kuenzl of the Gambrinus Brewery met to agree on prices and trade practices. Even this was not sufficient to support their businesses, so in March 1894 the three breweries pooled their plants and resources into a single company—the Oshkosh Brewing Company. The new firm claimed that it was formed in self-defense against outside breweries, but that would not be effective without selling off excess facilities, which none of the families was anxious to do at first. A new combined brewery would not be built until 1911. The three firms did begin to unify their brands, however, and by the end of 1894 they had begun using the image of Chief Oshkosh in a top hat, which remained the symbol of the company well into the twentieth century.[71]

A much larger combination was proposed in 1901 for northeastern Wisconsin under the unimaginative but comprehensive name of Wisconsin Brewing Company. Newspapers around the region reported the plan, and an article in the *Milwaukee Journal* listed Oshkosh Brewing, Oconto Brewing, Walter Bros. Brewing of Menasha, the Van Dycke and Hagemeister firms in Green Bay, Geo. Walter's Star Brewery in Appleton, and the Appleton Brewing and Malting Company as potential parties to the deal. The prospectus, said to have originated at Schlitz headquarters, had been sent to all breweries, but the reception was lukewarm at best. While both Frank Fries and Henry Schmitz of Appleton acknowledged that local competition was so heavy they could not get a "fair price" for their beer and predicted large profits for a combination, they saw pitfalls in the proposed scheme. Fries, of Appleton Brewing and Malting, allowed: "If this is a good thing, I am in it, heart and soul. But I will not allow anyone to come in here and dictate to me how my own business should be run. I should not allow my employes to be removed in order to make room for people from Milwaukee." Schmitz, speaking for the Star Brewery, warned, in what would be a precursor of the defense of local craft beer in the early twenty-first century, "We do not know whether it would be a good proposition to be implicated in this concern. The local people supply the demand for our beer and they are naturally prejudiced to trusts and this looks very like a trust." Other brewers quoted were equally dismissive, and thus another moneymaking scheme was thwarted by fiercely independent brewers.[72]

Despite the occasional rhetoric of reformers about the dangers of the "beer trust," trusts were comparatively unsuccessful in taking over the brewing industry on a national level. Financiers used to assembling combinations of railroads, oil refineries, or steel mills seldom understood the subtleties of making and selling beer. Smaller brewers usually held on to enough of the home market to prevent a trust from achieving monopoly status. Too much of the sales volume happened in too many small saloons for trusts to be able to buy enough outlets to corner the market. Local tastes differed, and local brewers often built a sentimental attachment to their beer in a way that makers of kerosene or steel could not. At this point, brewing science had not advanced to the point where a beer brewed in one location could be duplicated elsewhere. Furthermore, as Thomas Cochran pointed out in his history of Pabst, the economics of starting and expanding breweries were different from many industries dominated by trusts. The larger breweries were already so big that there were few more economies of scale to be gained, especially once shipping costs were added. Moreover, the cost of starting a new brewery was relatively low compared to other industries, and in the nineteenth century there were plenty of would-be brewery owners with the necessary skill and capital, or associates who could make up their deficiencies.

Despite the failure to establish massive combinations in Wisconsin, competition was decreasing in many cities, and prices were increasing for saloonkeepers. While closing dates for breweries are often even harder to pin down than openings, it is clear that while annual openings generally decreased during the period from 1880 to Prohibition, annual brewery closings held steady at a level above openings. What is more striking is that beginning in 1878, a large number of the closings each year were of breweries that had been open twelve or more years—many more than twenty years—rather than new firms that failed to get a foothold.

The effects on saloon owners were mixed. The majority of saloons sold only one company's beer on draught, so brewers were in constant competition to secure the loyalty of saloons through either favors or outright ownership. Well-established custom held that a glass of beer in a saloon should cost a nickel, so proprietors could not raise prices without a dramatic drop in business. Tied-house saloons in cities with little competition saw costs increase and profits diminish. Independent saloons sometimes were able to use their leverage to provoke price wars among the breweries. In the

Charles Van Schaick photographed these men and boys outside a saloon in Black River Falls around 1880. A sign advertising Hartig & Manz Watertown lager beer is featured prominently on the front. A collection of Van Schaick's photography was later used in Michael Lesy's 1973 book *Wisconsin Death Trip*. COURTESY OF WISCONSIN HISTORICAL SOCIETY, WHI-1905.

ENCOURAGING HOME INDUSTRY 81

early 1890s prices fell as low as four dollars a barrel for a time in some cities, not even enough for the breweries to cover costs. Saloonkeepers also played the brewers off against each other to receive cash inducements, favorable credit terms, or free beer—which large shipping brewers could meet more easily than local businesses.[73] Occasionally, small brewers engaged in similar tactics. Early in 1893, the *Journal* reported:

The village of Thorp in Clark county is passing through a merry war in which beer is the prime factor. A local brewery is in competition with foreign concerns. The Marshfield brewer gives each customer a free barrel for a starter, and the home institution [Leinenkugel of Chippewa Falls] furnishes ice free to each saloon-keeper during the season. The odds seem to be largely in favor of home industry.[74]

Farmers Brewing Co. produced Our Favorite near beer during Prohibition. This label depicts vigorous outdoor activities, and the baseball player seems to be inspired by the baseball cards of the 1910s. COLLECTION OF JOHN STEINER.

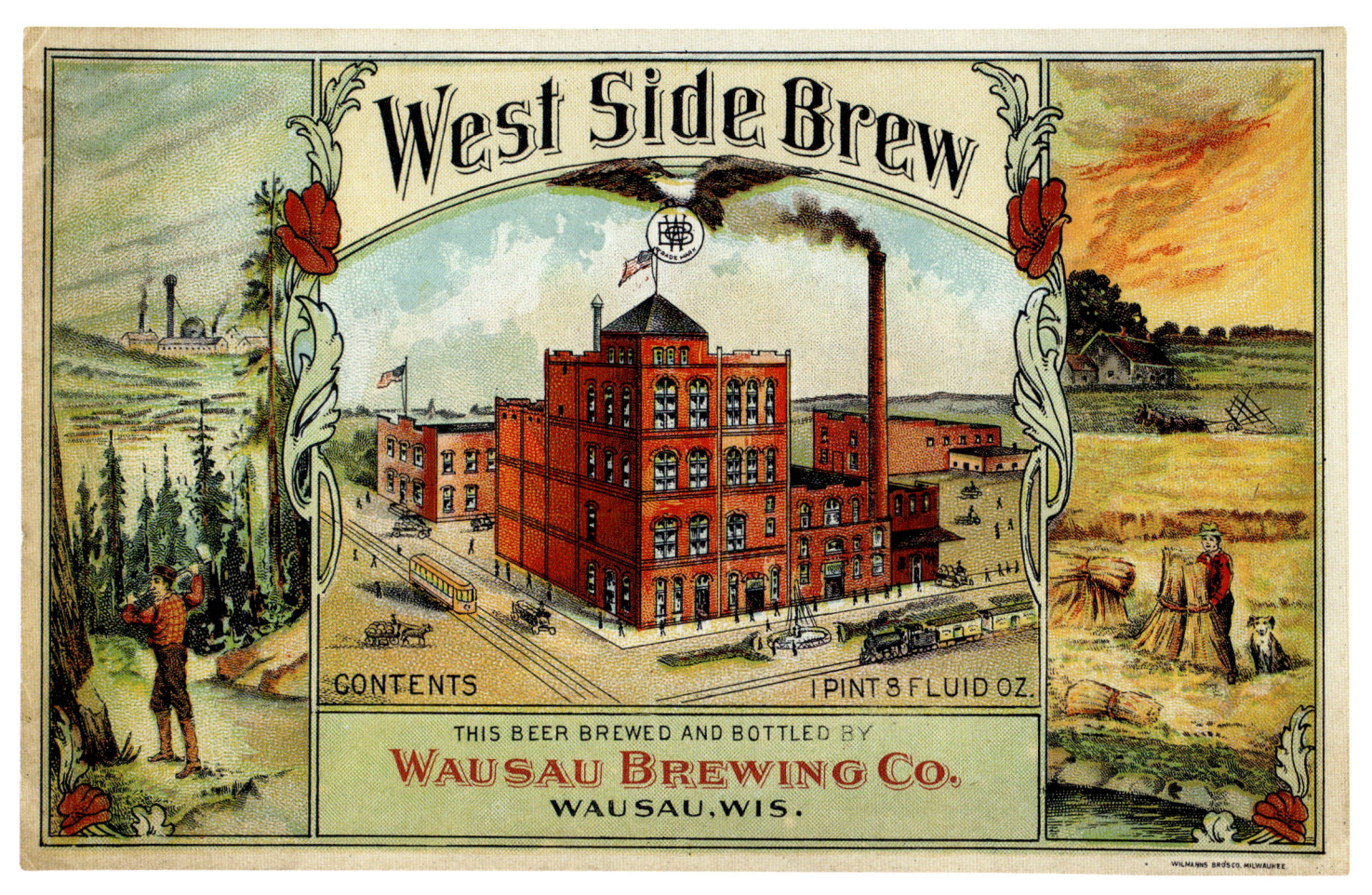

This triptych-style label used on twenty-four-ounce bottles celebrates the industry and agriculture of central Wisconsin—with the brand-new Wausau Brewing Co. at the center of it all (ca. 1915). COLLECTION OF JOHN STEINER.

But just as often, especially in an age when antitrust legislation was either inconceivable or ineffective, the brewers reached agreements to hold the price of beer up and avoided the price wars, thus squeezing the saloonkeepers.

Taking Stock

To fight back, some saloon owners banded together to make their own beer at a price they assumed would be cheaper than the marked-up rates offered by the shipping brewers. A few other breweries, even if not primarily owned by saloonkeepers, were owned by large groups of local shareholders with the goal of providing some competition to the dominant firm. One of the earliest of these, even before the Independent Milwaukee Brewery, was Citizens Brewing Company of Antigo, which was founded in 1899 and began production the next year. While Antigo was small, the prosperous lumber industry in the surrounding countryside may have made it appear a likely location for a second brewery, and in fact both survived until Prohibition. A group of Polish investors, including one who had been involved in founding Citizens Brewing, started the aptly named Polish Brewing Company in 1907 in Stevens Point, which had a

ENCOURAGING HOME INDUSTRY

considerable Polish population. The prevalence of Poles and other Eastern Europeans here and in the Milwaukee Brewing Company founded in 1893 suggests a desire to make their own way in an industry dominated by Germans.

The situation in Shawano was an interesting example of investors seeking to challenge an established business. By 1913 the Emil T. Raddant Brewing Company had a well-established market in Shawano County, but a new brewery was still being founded. Like several other new breweries of the time, Farmers Brewing Company sought to raise support from local investors. At the first stockholders' meeting more than seventy-five people attended, representing $50,000 worth of stock, so most of them must have had investments of less than $1,000. In response, Raddant offered stock of its own to investors looking for as little as one share. According to the advertisement, the offering was intended to raise funds for new storage tanks, which not only gave Farmers competition for funds but also served as a warning that a new brewery would face an uphill climb.[75]

The competitive nature of the Oshkosh market inspired one of the most important examples of the cooperative brewery idea. Joseph Nigl and Reinhold Thom, two saloon owners who had become irritated by Oshkosh Brewing Company's growing number of competing tied houses, and William Kargus, a disgruntled former employee of Oshkosh Brewing, formed a group of investors to build their own brewery to lower their cost of doing business. To emphasize the nature of what was first called the Cooperative Brewing Company, local saloon owners were encouraged to invest as much as they could, and no single shareholder could

This ad from an Appleton city directory around 1900, just after the death of George Walter, is one of the rare breweriana items noting that the brewery was owned and operated by the estate of the deceased. COLLECTION OF BRIAN ZENEFSKI.

own a majority of the stock. They eventually broke ground for their new brewery in March 1912, on a site just across South Main Street from the new plant of Oshkosh Brewing. Despite a campaign by the older firm to disparage the business plan of the upstart, the renamed Peoples Brewing Company had its beer on draught at twenty-five saloons and built a reputation that would carry it through Prohibition.[76]

Oshkosh was able to build a saloonkeepers' brewery with only local investors, but Wausau saloonkeepers in 1909 were being solicited for interest in creating a brewery that would be backed by a Minneapolis promoter. Ultimately the Minneapolis investor gave up and a brewery was built in 1913 with mostly local money, but the Wausau Brewing Company would feature out-of-town investors for much of its life.[77]

The Family Business

As the industry matured, so did its founders. While some firms simply went out of business when the founder died, in many cases the brewery remained in the family. Sixteen breweries had the word *estate* in the official brewery name for some period after the death of the proprietor. The average duration for these titles was three to four years, though for the Estate of Ulrich Oderbolz in Black River Falls it was less than two years. At the other extreme was the Henry Bierbauer brewery in New Lisbon, which went under the name of Henry Bierbauer Estate, New Lisbon Brewery for nearly ten years.

About forty women were listed as the principal owners of breweries at some point prior to Prohibition. Most of them took over active

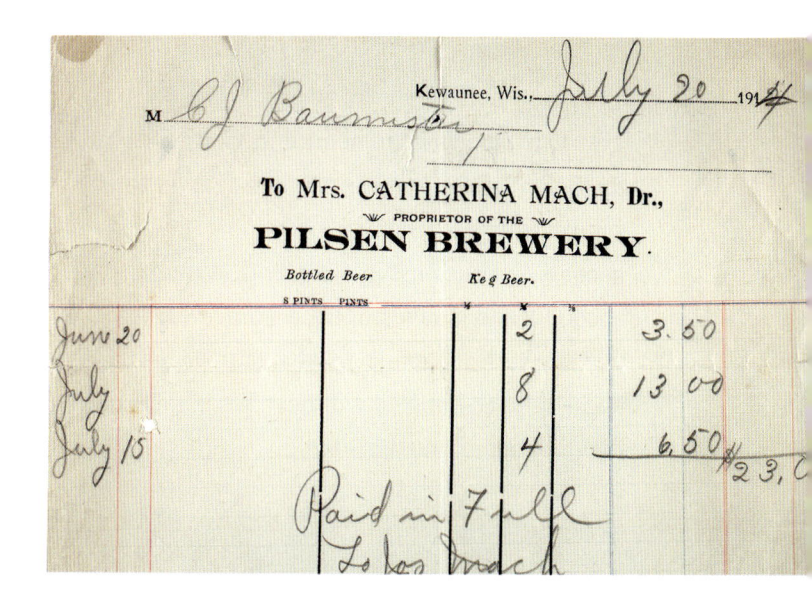

Catherina Mach was proprietor of the Pilsen Brewery in Kewaunee from 1909 to 1916. Wisconsin breweriana items featuring female brewery proprietors are extremely rare.
COLLECTION OF JOHN STEINER.

management after the deaths of their husbands. Johanna Heileman ran the largest of these, the City Brewery of La Crosse, which was under her name from 1878 to 1890. Even after it was incorporated in 1890, Johanna remained very much in charge, controlling the stock of the company and directing a period of sustained expansion. Johanna did not remarry and depended heavily on her sons-in-law to manage day-to-day operations, especially after her only son took his life at the age of twenty-eight.[78] Other widows operated the brewery but married a new brewmaster or manager themselves. After the death of Carl Muench in 1880, his widow, Wallie, took control of the brewery, but she married Mathew Heid in 1884, an event that earned mention in the *Milwaukee Sentinel,* in which the bride was described as "the wealthy proprietoress of the Muench brewery."[79] Octavia Van Dycke of Green Bay had her name on a brewery longer than any other woman: she took over operation in 1878 and

ENCOURAGING HOME INDUSTRY 85

even when it was later incorporated, it remained the O. Van Dycke Brewing Company rather than simply using her surname—a name it retained until going out of business in 1908. Both contemporary accounts and circumstantial evidence suggest that women were capable managers of their breweries and often had important direct roles in determining the direction of the business.

Sometimes a business operated under a woman's name even if her husband was alive, well, and running the brewery. Records of the credit evaluators for R. G. Dun & Company noted in 1862 that Jacob Melchoir of Trempealeau put the brewery property in the name of his wife, Wilhelmina, so that he could avoid paying a local tax that he considered unjust, though his wife paid it anyway. Later entries suggest the brewery

In many small breweries, family members held most or all of the stock. This 1916 certificate attested to Sophie List's ownership of four hundred shares in her family's brewery. COLLECTION OF TYE SCHWALBE.

may also have been in her name because most of the money behind the brewery came from her family.[80] George Schenck of Beloit put the brewery in the name of his wife, Augustina, for a few years, apparently to avoid being held responsible for some of the debts.[81]

In very rare cases, we have examples of women performing manual labor in the brewhouse rather than confining themselves to office work. Local accounts from Sauk City claim that Nic Drossen's wife, Anna, "also tended the kettle, sold the beer and distributed liquor as well."[82] An article looking back on the Liebscher brewery in Milwaukee recalled, "Those were the days also when men and women worked hard. . . . In rush times Mrs. Liebscher left her household duties and went to the brewery and helped stir the masses of mash with the huge ladles, or assisted in putting the amber fluid in bottles for delivery."[83]

Incorporating the brewery, even if all the stockholders were still family members, would make the transition smoother and allow businesses to bring in new members without changing the actual structure of the business. While emerging giants Pabst and Schlitz incorporated in the early 1870s, smaller family firms were generally slower to adopt this practice. Eventually many saw the wisdom of being able to pass the business on to the next generation without the inconvenience of probate hearings. Whether shares were held entirely by family members or not, many breweries simply added the word *Company* to the name of the founder or most important proprietor. However, about forty breweries from Alma to Whitewater changed the name to that of the home city—in many cases to represent or encourage wider ownership of stock. (Some of these changes were not at the first incorporation.) The case of Fountain City Brewing Company is illustrative—it was incorporated relatively early (in 1885), and county histories from both 1888 and 1919 noted prominent residents who were stockholders in the brewery even though their primary business interests were unrelated to beer, such as Andrew Dressendoerfer, a garage proprietor and creamery cofounder.[84]

A careful reading of the articles of incorporation for these firms reveals that some saw opportunities beyond the brewing of beer. Fountain City Brewing Company's 1885 articles were among the more limited: the company was formed for the business "of manufacturing beer, of buying and selling the same and of dealing generally in beer, barley, hops and other materials necessary or convenient for the manufacture, storage and sale of beer and similar beverages."[85] Home Brewing Company of Washburn, in addition to actually brewing, was allowed "to purchase, acquire, hold, lease, mortgage, sell and convey property, both real and personal; to acquire, hold and operate saloons and other places for the sale of malt and other liquors at retail; to loan money upon real estate and other security and to discount, purchase, hold and deal in commercial paper," which may have reflected their recent battles for retail outlets in the area.[86] Several other brewing companies also gave themselves the power to operate saloons and deal in real estate. Among the most unusual were the articles of Mauston Brewing Company, which included among its purposes "to establish, operate or acquire interests in Breweries, Ice Plants,

Like members of many other unions, members of the brewery workers' unions had elaborate ribbons they wore for parades and special occasions. Many ribbons were reversible and had a black side for use at funerals. Both the black Green Bay local ribbon and the Milwaukee maltsters' union ribbon at right are printed in German. The slogan "Einigkeit macht Stark" on the maltsters pinback top translates as "Unity makes strength." COLLECTION OF JOHN STEINER.

Lumber Yards, Mineral Mines or Manufactories of any sort."[87] Such language seems to indicate investors who were not interested in breweries per se but in any possible moneymaking opportunity.

ORGANIZING THE LABOR FORCE

Although organized labor was often more adversarial in Milwaukee than elsewhere in the state (or the nation, for that matter), strikes and boycotts affected other cities as well. In the late nineteenth century, the power of a union at even the larger breweries outside Milwaukee was nowhere near guaranteed. In 1891 union members in Sheboygan struck both the Schreier and Gutsch breweries, demanding an eight-hour day and a closed shop (where only union members would be employed). While a report in the *Milwaukee Journal* claimed that a boycott of these breweries' beers was working and that "Milwaukee beer is in demand by the carload," long-term success was limited since most of the saloons in the city were tied houses.[88] Mindful of violence during other strikes of the period, the *Journal* made a special point of reporting that "with the exception of one case, the strikers have maintained their position without molesting the men who have taken their place, but as a precaution several additional policemen have been appointed."[89] Schreier at least was able to break the union after a few days by offering five dollars more a month as long as workers left the union.[90] Gutsch fired all its union employees, which provoked a resolution from the Federated Trades Council condemning the action.[91]

Over time, however, unions gained greater leverage. Organizers based in Eau Claire were successful in unionizing not only Henry Michel's brewery there but also the eighteen workers at Leinenkugel's brewery in Chippewa Falls.[92] A boycott of beer from Klinkert's brewery in Racine (including by Milwaukee's Federated Trades Council) resulted in the unionization of that plant.[93] While not always successful, the solidarity among unions meant that boycotts by a majority of a city's workers could cause serious harm to a brewer who fell afoul of organized labor. The "intense union feeling, which exists throughout the city" led the combined unions of Marshfield to boycott the local brewery after the foreman "discharged a union man." Newspaper reports claimed, "Saloonkeepers

The "Ladies of the G. Heileman Brewery Co. Workers' Union" were photographed after the 1910 Labor Day Parade. COURTESY OF MURPHY LIBRARY SPECIAL COLLECTIONS, UNIVERSITY OF WISCONSIN–LA CROSSE.

have cancelled their orders with the home brewery, and [are] ordering the Milwaukee and St. Louis product."[94] The number of breweries willing to ship beer to cities in conflict made boycotts more likely to succeed, especially as breweries recognized unions in order to take advantage of such opportunities.

Occasionally, the strike was brief, as was the case in Oshkosh in April 1912, when a strike idled both breweries and five bottling works, but only for an hour. The workers obtained an extra dollar a week and a reduction to a nine-hour day.[95] Significantly longer was the strike two years earlier in Appleton and Menasha, which took a week to get thirty-five brewery workers a raise: $1.50 a week more for drivers and $1.00 for "inside workers."[96]

The most important brewing center outside Milwaukee was La Crosse, with three major breweries and several smaller ones. In the early 1880s the Michel, Gund, and Heileman firms extended their territory to the west along the railroads that crossed the Mississippi River at their city, leading to a period of rapid growth. This expansion brought a need for additional labor and eventually labor troubles. Over a twenty-year period from 1894 to 1913, the status of the unions in this city went

ENCOURAGING HOME INDUSTRY

from beleaguered to entrenched. A dispute flared up with the coopers' union in 1894, during which the union called for a boycott on Heileman beer since the company bought kegs made in a factory rather than by hand. The brewers called this boycott "unfair" since the union would not allow employees of the keg factory to join. As a response, "every brewery in the county" signed an agreement refusing to buy local kegs, which meant "a war on the union to which the brewers are not averse."[97] Three years later, in an article raising the possibility that disgruntled union members had started a disastrous fire at the Gund brewery (a theory Gund himself discounted), it was declared that "the union is not strong in La Crosse."[98] However, when a 1913 strike threatened to close five La Crosse breweries, the unions did so with the support of Milwaukee organizers and the confidence from the fact that "the plants are now all highly unionized and working on an eight-hour day."[99]

Of course the best way for workers to control their conditions would be to own the brewery themselves. Although no union ever actually ran a brewery in Wisconsin itself, the idea was proposed more than once. In addition to a discussion in Milwaukee in 1888 (see

Breweries have sponsored teams of various sorts for many years. The Kurth Co. Brewers of Columbus were among the most famous brewery baseball teams—one of their players eventually had several successful seasons with the Chicago White Sox. The 1907 team was noteworthy because of first baseman J. Williams—a rare African American player on an otherwise all-white team (second row, left). COLLECTION OF JOHN STEINER.

chapter 5), the possibility came up at the same time as the 1894 strike in La Crosse. Newspapers reported in September that the La Crosse Knights of Labor were buying the shuttered brewery in nearby Onalaska and planned to restart it. Unfortunately, none of the press accounts was specific about the Knights' connection or motivation, and at any rate, the brewery was not reopened.[100]

It is difficult to make sweeping generalizations about the state of brewing outside Milwaukee in the years between the Civil War and Prohibition. Most large cities hosted clusters of thriving breweries, yet many tiny villages supported "home industry" in spite of attempts by shipping brewers to conquer their markets. Other breweries failed during this period for a variety of reasons that defy easy analysis. Competition was surely a factor for many, though sometimes the death of the proprietor meant the end of the line. However, unless a brewery was so isolated in such a small town as to make it unprofitable for larger brewers to move in, those brewers that survived had most likely made the necessary upgrades in technology and packaging to compete with brewers down the road, in Milwaukee, and around the nation.

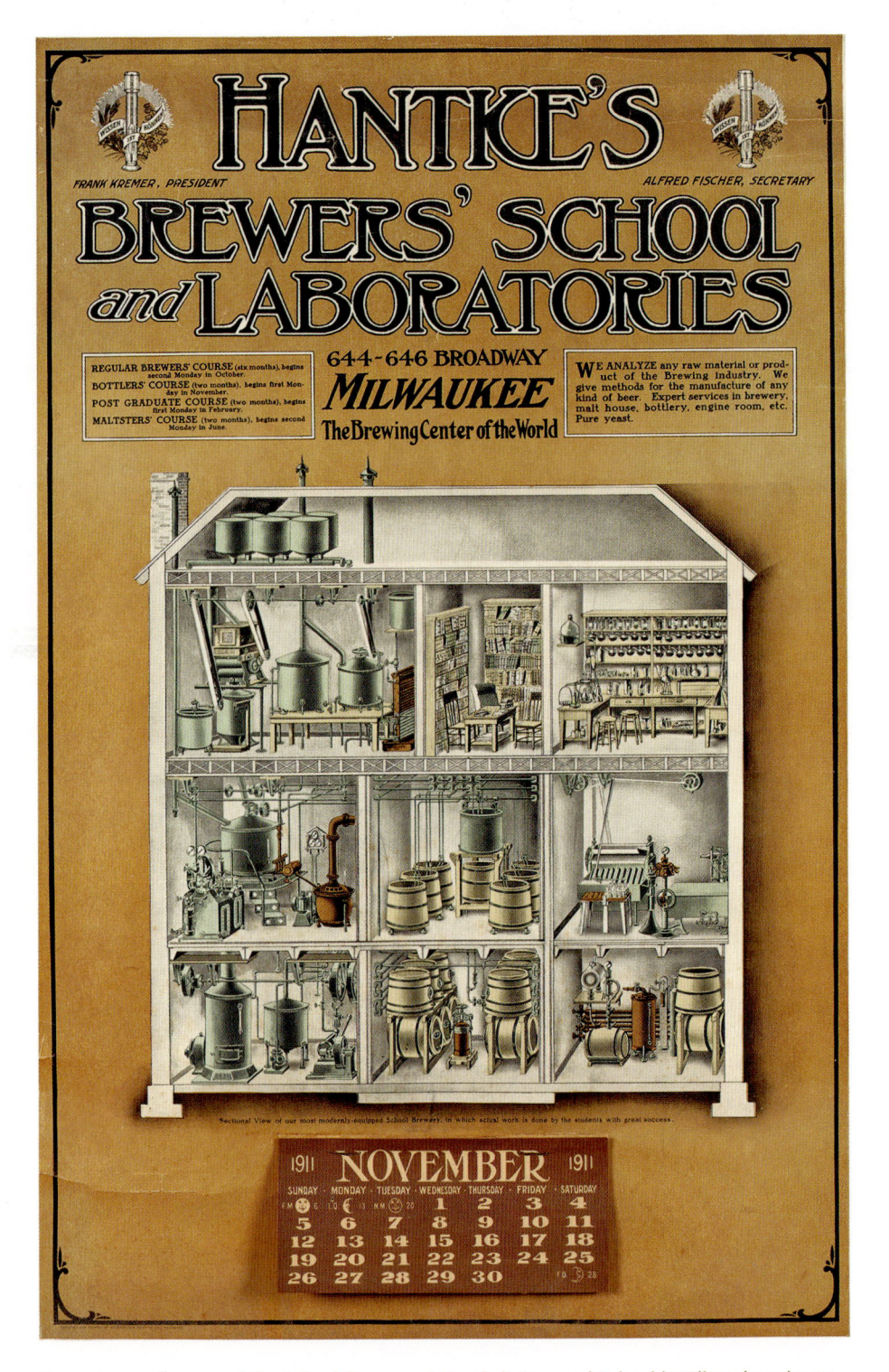

The cutaway diagram of the School Brewery at Hantke's Brewers' School in Milwaukee shows all of the equipment on which students practiced their craft. The library and laboratory are at the upper right. Calendar, 1911. COLLECTION OF JOHN STEINER.

CHAPTER 4

The LEADING INDUSTRY

1860–1920

The maple-sugar crop in Wisconsin has failed, but the increased beer crop more than makes up for the loss.

Daily Picayune (New Orleans), 21 May 1899

As the number and size of breweries in the Badger State grew, their business needs grew along with the market and the competition. Even if the most primitive farm brewer grew all his own barley and hops, he would still need either a cooper or a supplier of barrels as well as brewing equipment. Even the smallest brewer required power to grind the grain and some sort of sturdy structure to house the equipment. Of course, brewers with ambitions beyond their neighbors' tables required many more inputs and machines to produce a product ready to take to market. Furthermore, getting the beer into the mugs of customers would take just as much investment. As such, Wisconsin's breweries would inspire new industries, encourage existing ones, and even push for changes to the laws to make brewing more efficient and profitable.

Malt Shops

Wisconsin's barley crop expanded in the years after the Civil War until 1901, when its nearly 500,000 acres of barley yielded over thirteen million bushels—more than any state except California and Minnesota, and nearly as much as the entire nation produced in 1860.[1] But barley is not useful for brewing until it has been malted. Wisconsin's bountiful barley crops led to the logical conclusion that malting would be a profitable way to add value to Wisconsin's agriculture. As early as 1844, Wisconsin Iron Works of Milwaukie (as it was spelled at the time) was offering iron malt rollers for sale, suggesting local demand for equipment existed.[2] While it is not clear exactly how many antebellum brewers malted their own barley, it is clear that brewers of all sizes did so. In fact, some of Wisconsin's largest maltsters grew out of operations tied to a brewery. By the turn of the twentieth century, brewing had taken a backseat to one malting operation, and with the advent of Prohibition the Rahr Malting Company of Manitowoc abandoned brewing for good and eventually became one of the largest maltsters in the world. The Kurth Company, of Columbus, returned to brewing after Prohibition, but its malt business was more significant.

Malt house workers used wooden shovels when turning or shoveling grain to avoid creating sparks against the metal malting floor, which could cause a fire or explosion. This shovel was most likely used at the Oconto Brewing Co. prior to Prohibition. COLLECTION OF JOHN STEINER.

In 1949 Kurth ceased brewing but continued as an important malt producer. Although not as prominent in later years, the Portz Brothers Malt and Grain Company of Hartford and Schneider Brothers of Plymouth also were important malt suppliers in 1900 that had started attached to breweries.

Maltsters who did not also brew appeared first in New York in the 1820s, when John G. White of Albany used his experience and the city's location on transportation routes to build a lucrative business. This business model took a few decades to move to the Midwest, but by the time there were enough farmers to supply grain and enough brewers to buy the malt there were entrepreneurs ready to build. M. H. Pettit & Company, proprietors of the Kenosha Malt House, in 1857 became the first on Lake Michigan to start and remain an independent maltster.[3] A newspaper described Pettit's malting process, which, like brewing itself, used gravity as much as possible in the four-story structure. Pettit produced four hundred bushels each day, and was so highly regarded in the community that he was elected to the Wisconsin Senate. The article concluded: "If Mr. Pettit succeeds as well the coming winter in making laws for the people as he does in making malt for the brewers, we may expect good results from his coming term."[4] Another early maltster that remained prominent well into the twentieth century was Froedtert Malting Co., which started in 1867 in Milwaukee on Seventh and Cherry Streets. The company grew from making fifty bushels a day to operating "the biggest doggone malting plant in the world" after World War II.[5]

Unlike the breweries of Wisconsin, the malt houses were the subjects of numerous mergers and combinations. The Asmuth Malt and Grain Company combined with the Zinn Malting Company to form the Milwaukee Malt and Grain Company, which in 1897 became one of thirty-eight maltings to join the American Malting Company. This firm was based in New York City, but had plants throughout the Northeast and Midwest. The trust had great plans of "centralizing the manufacture and putting a stop to the competitive buying of barley," and predicted an annual profit of $1 million on the production of twenty-five million bushels of malt. However, a "maltsters from an interior part of the state" predicted a "flat failure" for the combine, and indeed, dozens of maltsters outside the combine thrived.[6] In fact, several new corporations were formed and new facilities built in the five years after the formation of American

During Prohibition, Rahr Malting Co. changed its name to Cereal Products Co. The company still uses the slogan "Malt of Reputation," though it is now headquartered in Shakopee, Minnesota. COLLECTION OF JOHN STEINER.

Malting. Among these was Chilton Malting Co., founded in 1902, which was an ancestor of the modern Briess Malting Company of Chilton.[7] Chilton was one of the few small-town maltings to attain the success and longevity of their small-town independent brewery compatriots. Others, such as

Milwaukee-Western, with a capacity of one million bushels per year, was just one of seven independent maltsters in Milwaukee in 1910, around the time this paperweight was given to customers. COLLECTION OF JOHN STEINER.

Lytle-Stoppenbach Company of Jefferson Junction, moved their main office to Milwaukee in 1902, ten years after starting business, though the plant remained in Jefferson County.[8]

The *Milwaukee Journal* presented a snapshot of the pre-Prohibition malting business in a special issue in June 1899. With a mix of Victorian understatement and exuberance, the headline proclaimed, "Malting Industry Very Extensive." The feature detailed the well over 7 million bushels of malt made the previous year—5.4 million bushels made by the "commercial maltsters" and 2.1 million made by brewery maltings. The value of the product was $3,640,000, and the industry contributed $151,800 to the economy through the employment of 260 men.[9]

THE HOP CRAZE

The hop trade began in Wisconsin almost as soon as brewing started. Although it is not clear exactly when hop culture shifted from crop to craze, it was well under way by the end of the Civil War. In 1865 farmers in Sauk County, the center of Wisconsin hop culture, were earning $800–$1,200 per acre, which was sometimes enough to pay for the land and all necessary improvements in a year. Sauk farmers earned a combined $2 million in 1867, of which $1.5 million was profit. In that year, an estimated nine thousand acres were growing in Sauk County, and farmers in Juneau and Monroe Counties shipped forty-three thousand pounds of "hop roots" (rhizomes), enough to plant two thousand acres more. By 1868 Wisconsin produced eleven million pounds of hops. Four million came from Sauk County alone—which amounted to about 20 percent of the entire nation's crop.[10] Production of this magnitude made Wisconsin farmers significant factors in world markets. Milwaukee newspapers reported world hop prices from London, and local newspapers from Shawano and Stevens Point to Sparta and Janesville carried articles on the best ways to plant, harvest, and process hops for the benefit of their many rural readers.[11]

Hops were a risky proposition for farmers. Many varieties do not produce a crop in the first year after planting, and the window during which the hops must be picked to maximize bitterness, flavor, and aroma is narrow—sometimes a matter of a week. Harvesting hops was very labor intensive, and attempts to develop mechanical hop pickers were not successful until the mid-twentieth century. As a consequence, thousands of workers had to be rushed to the "hop-pole district" to bring in the crop. Most of the hop pickers were young women, and railroads ran short of cars to bring the 20,000 to 40,000 workers into the sparsely populated hop districts.

In addition to the pickers, there were jobs for "box tenders," "pole pullers," and carpenters to build hop houses in which the crop would be dried. Harvesttime became a major festival in many communities, and, with all the female workers present, giant "hop dances" were common in the countryside.[12] Wisconsin's hop pickers were regarded highly in the trade, though apparently Wisconsin baling practices were not as good as those of more experienced processors in New York.[13] A certain amount of fraud may have occurred at times: one hop buyer in 1876 at Stevens Point reported finding a total of sixty pounds of small oak sticks in the centers of twenty-one bales purchased from one grower.[14]

But as with any agricultural crop, hops were (and are) subject to wild fluctuations in price. In 1868 one correspondent wrote glowingly of the activity and "pure plethora of prosperity" near Kilbourn City (Wisconsin Dells), but then predicted that within two years either the hop louse or a collapse of prices would cause a crash and that "more than nine-tenths of the ten millions of hop poles . . . will be used for firewood, fencing and the like."[15] In fact, 1868 ended with a substantial drop in hop prices, though the business recovered until another crash in the mid-1870s (perhaps related to the financial Panic of 1873) and the arrival of the hop louse brought to an end Wisconsin's prominence in the worldwide hop market.[16] An article in the *Reedsburg Free Press* also blamed farmers for pricing their crops too high and brewers for turning to imported hops. An advertisement on the same page of that issue, seeking an experienced hop farmer to lease a hop yard in Monterey County,

A group of female hop pickers (along with a few men) pose with garlands of hops in 1879, probably on the farm of Knut Heimdal in Deerfield Township, Dane County. The shadow of the photographer, Andreas Larsen Dahl, can be seen in the foreground. COURTESY OF WISCONSIN HISTORICAL SOCIETY, WHI-1955.

THE LEADING INDUSTRY 97

California, hinted at the eventual dominance of the American hop market by growers on the West Coast.[17]

As for beer's other key ingredient, yeast, most early brewers cultivated their own cultures and tended to be secretive about it, so there are few stories about its procurement. One of the few surviving tales describes the method by which the Kurth brewery got its yeast in early days.[18] One man would travel on foot from Columbus to Watertown to pick up an eighth barrel of yeast (from an unnamed source), but would then have to bear this burden back to the brewery—still on foot.[19] After the first propagation of pure yeast cultures by the Danish chemist E. C. Hansen in the 1880s, the technique was introduced to the United States by William Uihlein of Schlitz, who had studied with Hansen. Pabst was among the first breweries to adopt the new method, which promised much more consistent flavor and appearance for its beers.

ICE OF THE PUREST KIND

The other brewing input subject to the vagaries of weather and market conditions was ice. Ice was critical to conditioning lager beer, even in caves, and icehouses were prominent features on the footprint of nearly every brewery. In 1873 Phillip Best had four icehouses that held 10,500 tons of ice, of which 4,500 were used for cooling lager, the other presumably for chilling beer to be exported.[20] The massive volume and weight of the ice necessitated heavy construction but also spurred the search for more efficient ways to use ice and to ultimately replace it.[21]

Blatz's Hop Tea was a pre-Prohibition product that was more of a patent medicine than a substitute for beer. The product was nonetheless described as a "refreshing beverage." COLLECTION OF TYE SCHWALBE.

The addition of new icehouses at a brewery was a frequent topic in news updates on local businesses, though occasionally the icehouses were in the news because they caught fire. (While the idea of a fire in an icehouse is seemingly counterintuitive, the large amounts of straw or sawdust used to insulate the ice were potential fuel, as were the wood frame structures themselves.) The state of the annual ice crop was just as important a topic as any other crop. The *Sentinel* published a

PEWAUKEE ICE HOUSES.

The massive icehouses of the Phillip Best Brewing Co. show the infrastructure necessary to conduct the ice business (engraving from a souvenir booklet ca. 1880s). AUTHOR'S COLLECTION.

list of the Milwaukee-area ice harvests by brewery in February 1882, in which Best was reported to have stored 40,000 tons of ice. Best had almost three hundred men engaged in the harvest, Schlitz topped that with four hundred workers, and even the mid-sized J. Obermann Brewing Company had eighty-two men employed in this capacity.[22] Stanley Baron contended that ready access to cheap natural ice was one of the most important factors in propelling Milwaukee and Wisconsin to the lead of lager brewing in America.[23] The many breweries, especially the great shipping firms of Milwaukee, had their own ice facilities on inland lakes, often in Waukesha County, to process tens of thousands of tons of ice each year. The Gettelman Brewing Company of Milwaukee in 1882 built a dam on a river and by closing the gates just before freeze-up produced a large ice field.[24]

Ice harvesting brought physical danger as well. Most of the workers were younger men, since the work was often backbreaking and done in harsh winter conditions. Sometimes ice cutters and their teams of horses fell into the icy waters. Workers who simply guided the ice around earned about one dollar a day for a ten-to-twelve-hour day, while the more skilled packers could earn up to $1.75 per day. An article in the *Milwaukee Sentinel* in 1895 concluded, "The hours are long and the work disagreeable, and no one who can get anything else to do cares to engage in the ice harvest."[25]

Ice was needed not just for lagering but also for keeping beer cool during shipping and at its final destination. Breweries built icehouses at key shipping points, and local agents such as Julius Krost and Joseph Ziegler in New Orleans made a special point in 1875 of advertising "Milwaukee Lager Beer from the Celebrated Brewery of Joseph Schlitz . . . Imported in Ice, Fresh on Draught."[26] Shipping beer long distances, especially during the summer and in warmer climates, required the development and use of refrigerated railcars. While Anheuser-Busch is credited with being the first to make a substantial investment in these units after they were introduced at the Centennial Exposition in Philadelphia in 1876, Wisconsin's large breweries soon adopted "reefers."[27] The shortage of refrigerator cars in their early years was so severe that at one point Pabst considered establishing a factory to build his own.[28]

As with most other commodities in the late nineteenth century, enterprising businessmen sought to establish an "ice trust" to control the market and keep prices high. Rumors of trusts were rampant in the summer of 1890, when a trust allegedly controlled by the mayor of Minneapolis was reported in Minnesota and a Chicago trust was supposedly keeping prices artificially high.[29] (The profitability of any putative ice trust would decline with each passing year as artificial refrigeration became more common.) But even more disruptive to the ice business than collusion was weather. In several years, warm weather affected not just the supply of ice but its quality as well. Ice that was full of air bubbles was suitable only for industrial cooling, not for placing in drinks or other consumption. One particularly bad year was 1906, when "the continued smiles of Old Sol" led to an "ice famine which threatens to send the price of congealed moisture up like a runaway balloon."[30] In addition to the needs of local brewers and other merchants, the ice of northern lakes and rivers was expected to supply the needs of the entire country, so a warm winter would have effects well beyond the brewing districts and for many months.

For brewers the surest way to beat the ice trust and the weather, as well as to save valuable space in storage cellars, was to install artificial refrigeration. The first successful installations of "ice machines" in breweries came in the 1870s, and by

Large brewing companies required extensive networks of icehouses and depots throughout their sales territory. This Pabst icehouse in Rhinelander was photographed in the 1890s. COLLECTION OF JOHN STEINER.

1880 the idea had spread to Wisconsin. Phillip Best Brewing Company installed its first machine in that year, at a cost of $12,500. Frederick Pabst had been reluctant to adopt the expensive and unproven technology at first, finding cheap natural ice readily available. The equipment soon proved to be a success, however. Not only was the company able to eliminate purchases of ice for the brewery itself by 1888, it also eliminated the need for "dozens of ice cutters and handlers" and allowed for more precise temperature control as well as freeing up space in cellars for more beer.[31]

The Vilter Manufacturing Co. was best known for its refrigerating machinery, but also supplied bottling and other brewing equipment. The company also manufactured equipment for other industries. This letter describes mashing equipment being fabricated for the Milwaukee Brewery Co. in 1906. COLLECTION OF JOHN STEINER.

THE CREEDIEST ELEMENT

Other than prohibition, fire was the biggest single danger to breweries. The constant threat of fire from the combustible mix of flame and fuel had diminished little from pioneer days, and the growing size of breweries only made the losses more catastrophic. When Mathias Leinenkugel's brewery in Eau Claire was hit by lightning in August 1874, the *Milwaukee Sentinel* referred to the strike as "Heaven's Artillery."[32]

Sometimes the artillery was fired from inside the brewery. The coating of the inside of kegs with hot pitch was a hot and dangerous job, and the pitch house was a frequent source of brewery fires. One old-timer from Manitowoc recalled standing "around fascinated watching the men pitch the beer kegs. . . . This would cause a gas to form which was sufficiently strong to blow out the wooden bungs and it was as good as a Fourth of July celebration to just watch and listen."[33]

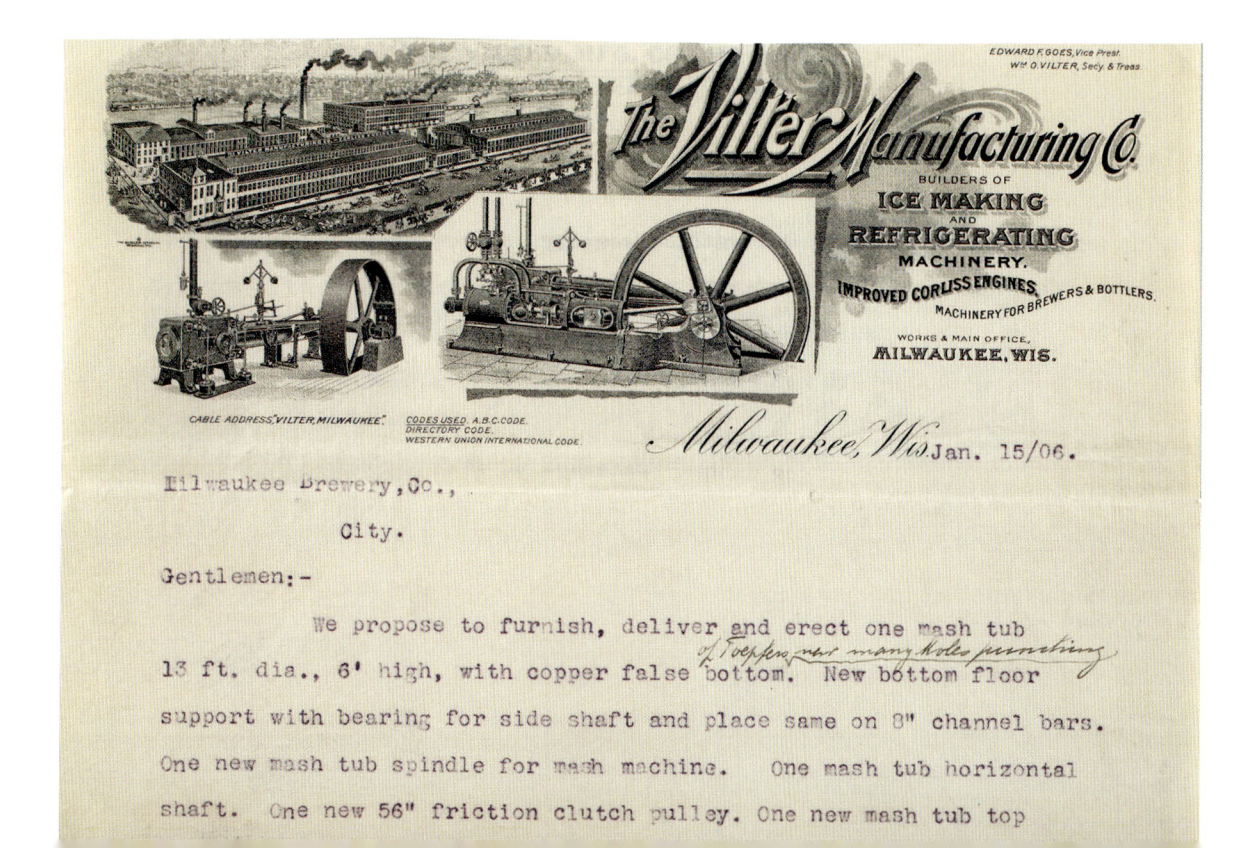

Fred Bandlow's brewery in Theresa was badly damaged by fire in 1901. He rebuilt and remained in business until 1910.
COLLECTION OF JOHN STEINER.

Milwaukee's breweries were prey for the Red Demon of fire as well. Several of the most catastrophic fires in the Cream City during the nineteenth century consumed major breweries. Best suffered two significant fires in the month of February 1872 alone: the first did $25,000 in damage at the Empire Brewery to the cooperage and stables, and a boiler fire caused $20,000 in damage to the brewhouse at the South Side facility.[34] The press may have become conditioned to massive amounts of damage—a year later the *Sentinel* reported on a minor fire at Best where damage "did not amount to more than about $25,000," which was corrected the next day to $25.[35] Blatz was victimized in 1873 by the most destructive brewery fire to date: it inflicted $400,000 in damage and reportedly could be seen from Racine, twenty-five miles away. Showing a sense of comradeship, Frederick Pabst and Emil Schandein offered Blatz the use of two cellars at the Empire Brewery to store salvaged beer while Blatz sorted out the damage.[36]

While claims of arson by burned-out brewers were common, occasionally there was substantial evidence that malicious human agents were at work. The *Sentinel* reported in August 1866:

> An attempt was made to fire Stoltz's brewery. . . . The incendiaries had piled hay, rags, and shavings in the rear of the building, saturated them with kerosene oil, and set fire to them. . . .

The object of the perpetrator in attempting the destruction of the brewery is unknown.[37]

While this report claimed the motive was unknown, it is tempting to speculate that it had something to do with an item in the city council minutes five months earlier, which reported that "a petition was read from residents of the First ward in regard to an alleged nuisance from the refuse water at Stolz's brewery."[38]

Fires continued to bedevil the breweries of Milwaukee for the rest of the century. After the Falk, Jung & Borchert Company burned for a second time in 1892, the *Journal* philosophized on the meaning of such a fire at the peak of the Industrial Revolution:

But perhaps after all, leaving the loss of human life aside, the most sober thoughts are likely to be aroused by the sight of some great manufacturing plant that has fallen a victim to the greediest and most destructive of all the elements.

A great factory is like the human body in all its intricate perfection. Nothing is missing and yet each detail is so dependent upon all the others that one being checked for a moment all are likely to stand still. The various machines and engines in a great plant are its heart, lungs and brain; they all work in perfect harmony together and each is necessary to the eventual result. There is, indeed, nothing in our intricate and complicated modern life more wonderful than a large manufacturing establishment, and to see one on fire cannot but arouse thoughts of a most depressing nature.[39]

Phillip Best Brewing Co. celebrated the rebuilding of the Empire Brewery after the catastrophic fire of December 1879 with this trifold card offering New Year's greetings for 1881. COLLECTION OF JOHN STEINER.

The disasters of the early 1870s drove brewers to adopt significant fire control measures, taking advantage of new technologies and building methods when possible. Pabst purchased a chemical fire engine called "Modoc" in 1876 for use by Best & Company's own fire department.[40] When Milwaukee adopted fire call boxes in the mid-1870s, Blatz and Best acquired alarm boxes number 52 and number 216, respectively.[41] Since stables were a fire risk with their bedding, fodder, and waste, Best built a "fire-proof, sky-light" barn at the Empire facility in 1877.[42] Despite all these measures, fire still struck the Empire Brewery just before Christmas in 1879, destroying the old malt

THE LEADING INDUSTRY 103

house, part of the new malt house, office, elevator, and barn.

When breweries were destroyed by fire, the owners still needed to keep cash flowing while they rebuilt. When Ferdinand Effinger's brewery in Baraboo burned in 1884, he "handled Milwaukee Beer" until his new brewery was completed.[43] Losses were especially hard to bear when stocks of beer were also destroyed in the fire, though sometimes the cellars were deep enough that the beer was saved. Beer bottlers also had to scramble to find a replacement supply when their source of beer dried up. When Eau Claire's Dells Brewery burned, bottler Louis Arnoldt had to bring in beer from Cream City Brewing Company in Milwaukee to replace beer that came from across the street.[44]

The one silver lining for burned-out brewers was the possibility of rebuilding with a more substantial structure containing up-to-date equipment. Brewers who would have been hesitant to interrupt their revenue streams to replace a brewhouse or make other significant changes could take advantage of their forced idleness and whatever insurance payments they received to start over with new technology and a more efficient layout. When the Muench Brewing Company of Appleton was destroyed in 1894, rebuilding began as soon as insurance was settled, "and they now have one of the best-equipped breweries in this part of the State, fitted, as it is, with all the latest improvements in machinery."[45] Occasionally one gets the sense that fires were almost literally heaven-sent opportunities. When the Schumann & Menges brewery of Prairie du Chien burned in 1872, construction on a new brewery began "a few weeks after the fire," suggesting that rebuilding plans were already in the works.[46]

The members of the Phillip Best Brewing Co. fire department pose in the studio of photographer Harry S. Sutter in 1883. COLLECTION OF JOHN STEINER.

EQUIPPED WITH THE LATEST AND MOST MODERN MACHINERY

As the aspirations of Wisconsin's brewers grew, so did the need to upgrade their plants with a variety of laborsaving devices, most advertised in the national journals that were enhancing the professionalism of brewing. While many of the related industries were based in the long-established brewing centers of New York and Philadelphia, Chicago was a major destination for brewers seeking machinery. The growing concentration of prominent breweries in Milwaukee and elsewhere in Wisconsin eventually drew entrepreneurs in several fields to the Cream City to supply the needs of the expanding firms. The drive for pure beer and efficient brewhouses inspired brewers to work out their own technical solutions to problems, and a few brewers ultimately became better known for their innovations than for their beer. Otto Zwietusch had a small weiss beer brewery in Milwaukee from 1858 to 1864, but later devoted his time to improving the brewing process. He became superintendent of New Process Fermentation Co. and held the patents for their products. He also developed "Otto Zwietusch's Patent Automatic Beer Preserver," which advertisements called "A Most Ingenious Invention for Preserving Beer by Means of Pure Carbonic Gas" and which won a medal at the 1876 Centennial Exposition.[47] Kenosha brewer Adolph Muntzenberger invented a barrel washer that was installed in the most prominent breweries of Milwaukee, Chicago, and other cities.[48]

But most of the supporting industries in the state were not founded by ex-brewers. The suppliers located in Milwaukee ranged from printers to manufacturers of heavy machinery. Modern breweries required large power plants, and Wenzel Toepfer and his sons Frank and Peter specialized in ironwork for the massive boilers as well as malt kilns and other equipment—often appearing as the only entry in the Milwaukee city directories under the rather specific heading "Brewers Iron Work." Vilter Manufacturing Company was founded in Milwaukee in 1867, quickly became an industry leader with its refrigeration equipment,

The Toepfer & Son iron boiler door was made around 1880 and was still in use at Pabst Brewing Co. a century later. A chain was attached to the two hooks on either side to lift the door. COLLECTION OF JOHN STEINER.

and had branch offices from coast to coast. (As of this writing the company is still in existence as a division of Emerson Climate Technologies.)[49] Edward P. Allis & Company (later Allis-Chalmers) produced brewery equipment ranging from pumps to grinding mills—some powered by the "Improved Corliss Engine." In 1893 the Milwaukee-based Nordberg Manufacturing Company created a new bottle washer that had a capacity of ten thousand bottles a day.[50] Each of these firms had clients around the country and helped spread the reputation of Milwaukee as an engineering center. The city also excelled in the production of less showy but equally important products, such as Winding & Gezelschap's asphalt floors.

As brewers expanded their territory and competition increased, so did the need for breweries to advertise their product and present a professional image. Milwaukee's lithographic firms printed everything from labels and letterhead to posters and brewery scenes. The Milwaukee Lithographic Company, founded in 1853, had customers all over the country for its labels and other paper products. It also specialized in large brewery lithographs ranging in size from 18 by 32 inches to 36 by 48 inches, which are prized by modern breweriana collectors.[51] Rival Gugler Lithographic Company was not founded until 1878, but built a large trade on the reputation of Henry Gugler, who had created one of the most famous posthumous portraits of Abraham Lincoln.[52] Gugler's offerings also included posters for bock beer, which could be customized for each brewery.[53]

Milwaukee had a variety of companies that attracted business from brewers near and far. In early days, the trip to purchase supplies in the city was a major undertaking. One account of the Kurth brewery in Columbus recounted the story of purchasing a new malt wagon from a wagon builder in Milwaukee. The man had to take two horses with a buggy on the two-day trip to the metropolis,

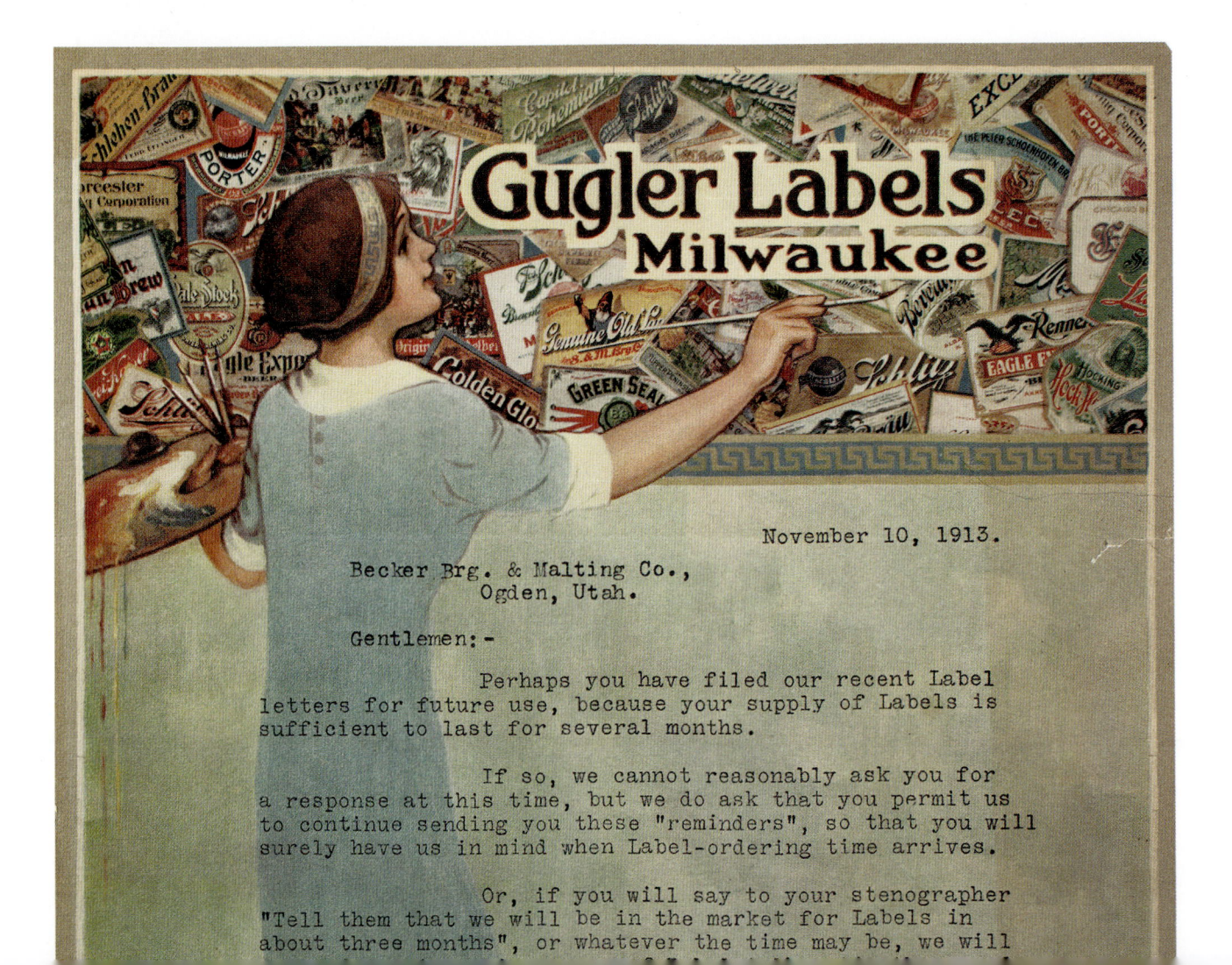

The spectacular letterhead for Gugler Labels from 1913 depicts dozens of actual labels. Several different Schlitz labels are visible, along with one from the Ferd. Effinger Brewing Co. in Baraboo (upper left). COLLECTION OF JOHN STEINER.

hitch the team to the new wagon, attach the buggy behind the wagon, and travel two days back.[54]

A Practical Brewer

Thomas Cochran contended that the period after the Civil War, especially from about 1873 to 1893, saw the greatest changes in the industry in the entire history of brewing, owing to the application of science and the introduction of new machinery. Using all the new procedures and equipment to make a more consistent beer required a brewer trained in their application. Many master brewers came from Europe already having been trained at schools in Berlin, Bavaria, or elsewhere. New brewing schools in America also formed to meet the need. Even with expert training available, most brewmasters still worked their way through the ranks at a large brewery before taking over their own establishment. The term *practical brewer* was sometimes used in the press to describe a brewer with formal training, though other articles and the schools themselves used it for a brewer with on-the-job experience.

Another of the firms founded after the Civil War that earned national renown was the Dunck Tank Works, manufacturer of fermentation tanks and other large vessels. Modern readers may better recognize the homonym dunk tank—popular at parties and fairs (letterhead from 1912). COLLECTION OF JOHN STEINER.

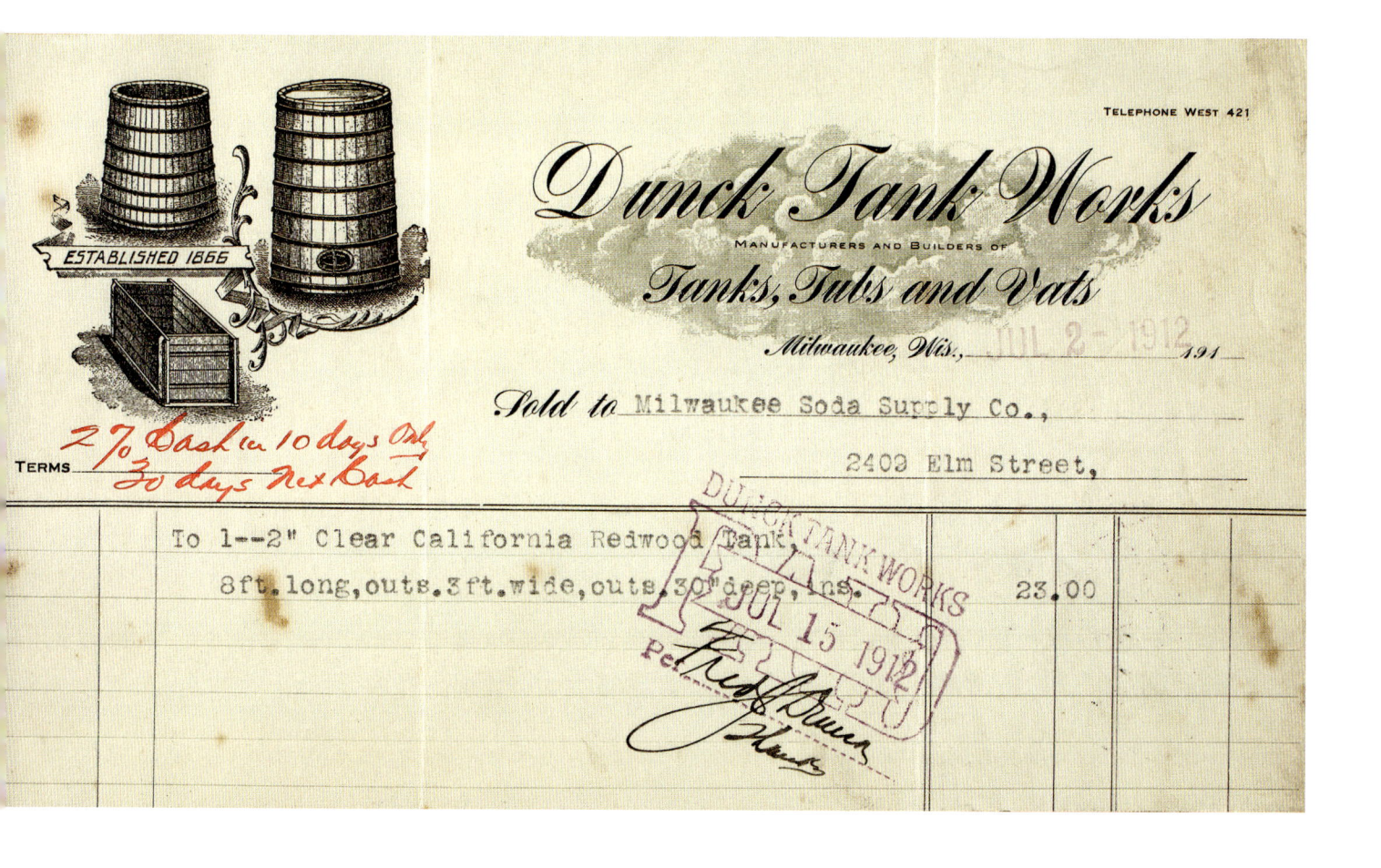

THE LEADING INDUSTRY

This ornate hydrometer and its wooden case were presented to Emil Schandein in 1878. Hydrometers are used to measure the specific gravity of a liquid. COLLECTION OF JOHN STEINER.

Hantke's Brewers' School provided instruction in bottling as well as brewing. This label (ca. 1915) indicates that students learned about beer styles other than lager. The school's motto, "Wissen ist Können," translates as "Knowledge is ability." COLLECTION OF JOHN STEINER.

Many midwestern brewers went to Chicago to study at the Wahl-Henius Institute of Fermentology, which was formed in 1886. The institute offered classes in brewing, general engineering, and mechanical refrigeration, and in 1900 added a course specifically designed for beer bottlers.[55] But Milwaukee also seemed like an obvious place for a brewing school, "because Milwaukee has always been a place of attraction for brewers, and to live in Milwaukee is pleasant and cheap." In 1898 Ernst Hantke, who had been a brewing chemist at Blatz, established the school that bore his name. From 1901 to 1916 the school also published *Letters on Brewing,* which provided technical and chemical articles in both English and German, and contained ads from a wide variety of suppliers. (There was, in addition, a short-lived Milwaukee Brewing Academy, which Hantke operated with Alfred Lasche.)[56] The most unusual suggestion may have been made when the Milwaukee public school system was updating its industrial training in 1887: "Perhaps in time, a brewing school might be added to the list of branches, and some first class brewery rented for the purpose of practical instruction."[57]

Of Stables, Wagons, Horses, and Sleighs

The process of delivering beer efficiently to customers also changed dramatically from 1865 to 1920. The horses that drew the brewery wagons were among the businesses' most prized assets. The Clydesdales, Normans, and Percherons preferred by brewers were sometimes raised in Wisconsin by breeders like Henry Brown of Grove Farm, near Augusta.[58] An 1882 article in the *Milwaukee Daily Republican-Sentinel* reported that the average cost of a team of horses was $500. The Normans used by Schlitz at the time weighed 2,800 pounds and could pull 10,000 pounds. Milwaukee breweries apparently did not own many Clydesdales at that point, but those in service had been raised near Janesville.[59] The Milwaukee breweries had by far the largest establishments, and nearly every brewery had a noteworthy team of horses—or many more. Horses were often cited in newspaper articles and county histories as a measure of a brewer's prosperity. Jacob Helf "constantly employs six men and three teams of horses to deliver his beer in the city of Kaukauna."[60] Kurth's Columbus brewery had barns to house four driving horses, eighteen draft horses, and six mules. These latter were used with a special wagon drawn by three mules that made a daily trip to neighboring Sun Prairie with kegs of beer.[61]

Experienced horses seem to have been just as important as experienced workers. A runaway incident involving several teams, including one from the Gutsch brewery in Sheboygan, was blamed on the fact that "both the horses [of the Gutsch team] are young and have not been in use on the brewery wagon long, having recently been purchased."[62]

Horses were also essential for power during the days before affordable steam plants, and sometimes longer for brewers who delayed updating. The Schlenk brewery of Beloit operated with horsepower at least through 1902. Oderbolz of Black River Falls was powered by horse into the 1890s, Mach and Langer of Kewaunee still in 1898. Even some breweries in larger cities like Sheboygan and Racine depended on horsepower into the 1890s. While the horsepower was often outside, some breweries had the horsepower enclosed in a structure and sometimes used the space above for other purposes. Edward Becker's brewery in New London had sleeping rooms above the horsepower,

A four-horse team from Boub's South Side Brewery in Janesville, ca. 1900. The flags and other decorations suggest the picture was taken the Fourth of July. COLLECTION OF JOHN STEINER.

and the Star Brewery in Appleton had a cooler on top of the horsepower building.[63]

Horses occasionally landed breweries in the news for accidents that ranged from the inconvenient to the tragic. The teams of Konrad Schreier Company of Sheboygan encountered newsworthy accidents twice in three months: first in late 1913 when a team ran away with the wagon and then in March 1914 when a horse got a shoe caught between a "frog" on the streetcar track (but somehow avoided breaking its leg).[64] A more disturbing incident was reported in Racine in 1879 when one of Fred Heck's horses "took fright" and threw its driver, though the driver was "beating him in a shameful manner."[65] Horses were frequent victims of brewery fires, though in the case of the 1872 fire at Phillip Best's Empire Brewery, forty horses were saved from a fire that destroyed the stables and cooperage.[66] The seven horses that died when lightning struck the West Bend Brewing Company in July 1893 and many others were not so lucky.[67]

Horses also sometimes pulled vehicles other than wagons, or "brewery rolls" as they were often called. During the winter, some breweries employed sleighs in place of wagons to deliver the beer across snow-covered terrain, and did so well into the twentieth century. Unfortunately, sleighs were no less subject to accidents than wagons. In February 1916 the Stevens Point Brewery team ran away, but the damage was limited to one case of beer falling off the sleigh.[68] In January 1918 the delivery sleigh of one of the Sheboygan breweries broke a runner and several kegs plunged into a nearby snowbank.[69]

Horses were not the only beasts of burden to transport beer to thirsty customers. Mules were sometimes employed, though they conveyed less prestige than a fine team of horses. Some "mule skinners," however, became beloved symbols of their breweries. Mathias Skarda, driver of a four-mule team for the Kunz brewery in Branch, Manitowoc County, reportedly "could crack a blacksnake whip with such proficiency the sound was heard for half a mile," though the storyteller granted "the wind would have to be favorable and the air clear."[70] To celebrate the release of bock beer during the spring, some breweries had special small wagons pulled by goats—the traditional symbol of bock.

Oxen were also sometimes called upon to pull the brewery rolls. According to local accounts, Joseph Osthelder, a veteran of the Fourth Wisconsin Cavalry during the Civil War, used to deliver beer for his family's brewery in the area around Sheboygan, "and it was oftentimes possible only with two teams of oxen." Osthelder also carried a gun for protection from both wolves and robbers.[71] Sometimes oxen were used if disease had incapacitated the local horses, though this was not always a smooth transition. When a brewery driver in Madison unfamiliar with oxen first drove a team into Capitol Square the animals got out of control and knocked over a stonecutter who was working near the street.[72]

Horses had problems besides running away and falling prey to disease. As one observer pointed out, "A circumstance that particularly unfits the horse for brewery work is the fact that the peak season of the brewery's business comes at a time

Steam Breweries

One of the most important developments in brewing technology was the move from horse and hand power to steam. Steam also replaced direct fire as the method by which the wort was boiled during the brewing process. Numerous breweries around the state identified themselves as "Steam" breweries to emphasize their technology in an era when the latest processes were considered the guarantee of quality. (This use of the term *steam* did not mean that they made "steam" beer. This was largely a California product in this era and was not as important then as Anchor Steam was in the early craft beer period.)

PROPERTY of JOHN BOETHINGER

Though it misspelled the proprietor's name, this sketch on an 1860s map of Janesville, Wisconsin, prominently displayed the Steam Brewery portion of the name as well as the essential smokestack. COURTESY OF BRUCE MONSON.

As breweries grew and prospered, they improved their equipment with the latest technology. In the late 1850s Conrad Muntzenberger of Kenosha added an eight-horsepower steam engine for "mashing malt, grinding, pumping water &c."[1] When Anson Rogers built a new brewery in Janesville, the *Janesville Gazette* noted that the power was all by steam—including steam elevators for lifting grain and hoisting kegs.[2] As brewers added their own bottling houses, they added steam power in these buildings as well, as Leinenkugel & Miller of Chippewa Falls did in 1881.

When brewers switched from direct-fired brewing coppers to steam, they had two choices. Brewers who did not want to change their brewing kettles could heat the wort by inserting steam-heated coils into the kettle. When brewers invested in new coppers, they generally added vessels with double bottoms that were simpler, more practical, and easier to clean.[3] After the 1887 explosion at the Rahr brewery in Green Bay, the company was forced to revert to the steam coil method while waiting for its new brewing copper to be repaired.[4]

For many breweries, adding steam power meant erecting a new building for the boilers. This was generally viewed as an important measure of industrial prowess—the annual Wisconsin state industry reports in the late 1800s and early 1900s reported the number of boilers and their horsepower as equally important to the number of buildings and number of employees. Of course, the increase in steam power meant that fewer men were required to do the work—and fewer horses as well. In 1887, after he upgraded to steam, William Weber of Waukesha advertised "a horse power [unit] for sale . . . cheap. A good opportunity for any one wanting such a machine."[5]

In time, more and more breweries switched to more efficient electric power. Even into the twentieth century, however, breweries with steam power were advertised as "modern" when put up for sale.[6]

1 *Kenosha Tribune and Telegraph,* 27 May 1858, 3.
2 *Janesville Gazette,* 1 December 1873, 4.
3 *One Hundred Years of Brewing* (supplement to the *Western Brewer*) (repr.; New York: Arno Press, 1972), 89.
4 *Oshkosh Daily Northwestern,* 29 August 1887, 3.
5 *Waukesha Freeman,* 29 September 1887, 1.
6 *American Brewers' Review,* November 1904, 524.

To celebrate the release of bock beer, many breweries held parades featuring goats, sometimes pulling miniature brewery wagons (ca. post-Prohibition). COLLECTION OF OTTO TIEGS.

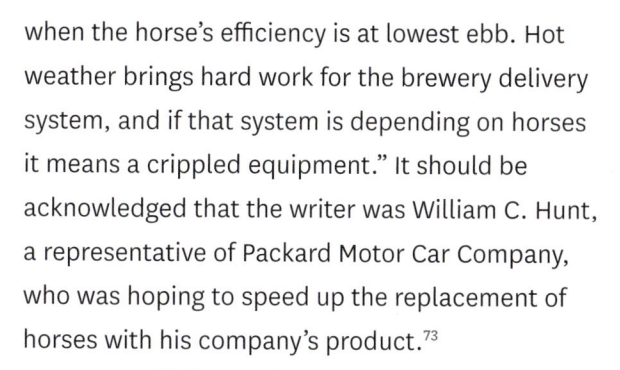

The procession in front of the Oshkosh Brewing Company in 1915 shows a transitional phase in brewery deliveries—a mix of trucks and horse-drawn drays. COLLECTION OF LEE REIHERZER.

when the horse's efficiency is at lowest ebb. Hot weather brings hard work for the brewery delivery system, and if that system is depending on horses it means a crippled equipment." It should be acknowledged that the writer was William C. Hunt, a representative of Packard Motor Car Company, who was hoping to speed up the replacement of horses with his company's product.[73]

Eventually breweries began to use motor trucks for delivery, and Wisconsin's breweries seem to have adopted these vehicles as the opportunity presented itself. Pabst purchased a Pierce-Arrow truck in 1911, and by the advent of Prohibition operated more than twenty of the same vehicle.[74] Miller purchased a Kissel truck for delivery in 1916.[75] Trucks were just as important to branch offices as they were in the brewery's hometown. The Lorain, Ohio, branch office of Pabst obtained a 1,500-pound Ford delivery truck in 1916, and "a five-ton Pierce-Arrow takes care of a very large portion of the distance delivery of the Chicago branch of the Schlitz Brewing Co."[76] However, some breweries may have been hesitant to invest too much money in an unproven technology with the prohibition movement gaining traction across the country.

One Milwaukee firm that epitomized the transition from horse to horseless was the Charles Abresch Company. Abresch began making beer and other delivery wagons "upon a small scale" in 1871, but his designs and a wealth of products to deliver in the Cream City enabled him to expand and become one of the "leading manufacturers in the United States of special wagons." Abresch made both keg and bottled beer wagons, and a list of his customers from 1896 includes breweries from New York to Vancouver as well as his hometown.[77] In 1891 he received an order for six beer

THE LEADING INDUSTRY   113

wagons from Australia.[78] An example of Abresch's work for Schlitz was described by the *Milwaukee Journal* in 1891:

> *Each wagon weighs 2,100 pounds, and has a capacity of thirty-six boxes or cases. The wagon is entirely enclosed and protected from the weather. The side and end panels, three and a half feet in height, are of heavy plate glass, with an ebony hue as background, on which highly-colored trade marks, various artistic letters, etc., are artistically painted. Each wagon is drawn by a pair of heavy blacks, and the three elegant turnouts represent an outlay of $3,600.*

In 1909 Robert Cramer, formerly an engineer with local machinery manufacturer Allis-Chalmers, suggested a partnership to build delivery trucks. The new Abresch-Cramer Auto Truck Company began selling trucks to breweries in 1910, but only remained in this business until Abresch's death in 1912, though they continued to make delivery truck bodies for other chassis through Prohibition (and later made sidecars for Harley-Davidson motorcycles).[79]

The move from horses to trucks required several changes for breweries and their personnel. Stables needed to be converted to garages (though Sanborn Fire Insurance maps were not published at frequent enough intervals to pinpoint when the changeovers happened, and the conversions do not seem to have been covered in the popular or industry press). Purchases of hay were displaced by those of gasoline, oil, and replacement parts. In addition, teamsters used to driving horses had to be taught how to drive and maintain trucks.[80]

Once the transition was in progress, however, the advantages for trucks seemed impressive. While the figures

One of Miller's new delivery trucks outside the Miller Café at Water and Mason Streets (ca. 1905). COURTESY OF MILLERCOORS BREWING CO.

114   THE DRINK THAT MADE WISCONSIN FAMOUS

Railroad freight cars provided another opportunity for breweries to advertise their product. Such ads were prohibited in the 1930s. This car was photographed around 1905. COLLECTION OF JOHN STEINER.

were being offered by truck companies, it was estimated that one truck could do the work of anywhere between four and eight horses. Trucks had a much greater range than horses, so smaller breweries were able to sell in territories previously out of reach. Early cost analysis also suggested trucks were significantly cheaper to operate than horses. Breweries claimed to need less space for garages than for stables, freeing up valuable land for other uses. As in America at large, there was some debate over whether gasoline or electricity was the preferred power source, but brewery trucks mostly would be sidelined before gasoline-powered trucks won the battle.[81] It was pointed out, however, that "the horse has reached the highest stage in its evolution. Its individual possibilities are incapable of further expansion. In striking contrast is the motor truck with its countless possibilities—some known but poorly developed and others yet to be discovered."[82]

Breweries near navigable water sometimes delivered their beer and retrieved their kegs via boat. The Potosi Brewing Company sent beer down the Mississippi River to Dubuque on the steamboat *Potosi*, and Oshkosh breweries shipped on Lake Winnebago. The *Potosi* made additional sales along the route to local farmers, who would call out an order, retrieve the floating keg tossed from the boat, and give back the keg, along with the payment, on a return trip.[83] The water trade was not without its own hazards, however. In 1888 a steamboat returning kegs to Horn & Schwalm's brewery in Oshkosh "became stuck and the captain was obliged to dump the kegs overboard and float them to shore."[84]

Delivered at the Depot

It is likely that contemporary chroniclers of brewery activities paid little attention to railroad shipments because, like the use of horses, using the railways was a natural part of doing business. Many breweries were located near railroads—both to bring raw materials in and to ship finished goods out. The limited mentions in newspapers or county histories indicate that breweries of all sizes in all parts of the state made at least some shipments by rail. In 1866 the Hope Brewery of Racine delivered shipments to railroad depots free of charge.[85] The Superior City Brewery announced it would deliver beer along the Northern Pacific Railroad route (which stretched about one hundred miles into Minnesota).[86] Kenosha's New Era Brewing Company shipped its beer as far as Georgia in the late 1880s.[87] Some medium-sized breweries were important enough for railroads to extend a spur to their plant, such as Shawano's Emil T. Raddant Brewing Company in 1912.[88]

Rail shipment also entailed costs beyond freight charges (which were a constant concern for breweries, as they were for all other businesses). Only larger breweries could afford to build and supply depots near the railroad stations in distant cities, though many Wisconsin breweries were in a position to make such an investment, including Klinkert of Racine, Gutsch of Sheboygan, the Green Bay breweries, and the largest of the La Crosse firms. (Milwaukee shipping is covered in chapter 5.)

Designed for a Brewery

Most pioneer breweries performed all of their tasks in one or two rooms, so the layout of the factory was not complicated. As brewing became more sophisticated, and as gains from economies of scale made larger breweries desirable, brewery design became more important. Smooth operation of the plant could save space, time, and money. Design and location of the brewery and all the related buildings became a science as well as a craft, and a generation of architects who specialized in brewery constructions rose to meet the challenge. Prior to

The ornate architecture of the Schlitz brewery was displayed in full color on this tray. While the tray is not dated, the image is identical to that used on company letterhead in the early 1880s, and the brewery's capacity in the mid-1880s was 600,000 barrels. COLLECTION OF TYE SCHWALBE.

the 1870s, most of those employed to erect Wisconsin's breweries were referred to in the press as builders rather than architects, at least in part because trained architects were rare outside the major cities.[89]

The larger and more prosperous breweries were able to hire professional architects who, even if not able to add to the brewer's ideas of how to arrange the inner workings, could at least create an exterior that would allow the building to claim its rightful spot in the cityscape. Milwaukee architect Leonard Schmidtner, most famous for his work on churches and government buildings, designed expansions for Franz Falk in Milwaukee and for Charles Haertel in Portage.[90]

The Portage brewery was built in 1865 with local brick and "together with the new courthouse and high school building will make a great addition to the better class of edifices in Portage within the past year."[91] While Milwaukee and Wisconsin in general were settled later than their rivals in Ohio or Missouri, the style and size of their breweries caught up quickly with those of their neighbors.[92]

The dominant architectural style for midwestern lager breweries for the decades after the Civil War was a German variant of Romanesque Revival known as *Rundbogenstil,* or "round-arched style." Susan K. Appel has written that the style symbolized the German background of the lager beer brewers but was also readily adaptable to buildings of different types. As new buildings were built for specialized uses, they could be given a shape and size appropriate for their function but could still be tied to the rest of the brewery campus through the design of the windows and doors.[93]

In 1880 Phillip Best & Company hired as its principal architect Fred W. Wolf of Chicago, who was part of the first generation of architects to

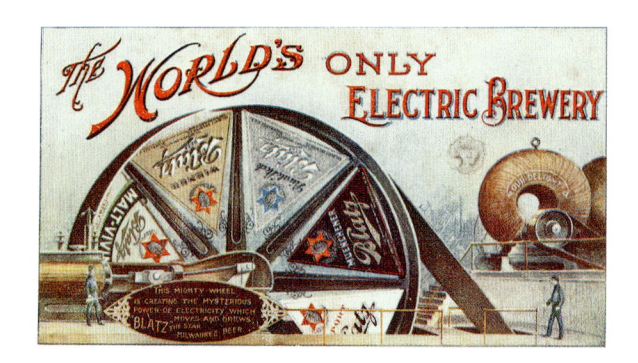

Blatz announced the electrification of its brewery with the souvenir card that featured the distinctive triangular labels superimposed on the flywheel (ca. 1893). COLLECTION OF LARRY BOWDEN.

THE LEADING INDUSTRY 117

specialize in brewery design. In 1879 Wolf designed an icehouse for Schlitz that was noteworthy not only for its size but also for its recognition that dependence on underground cellars for lagering and storing beer placed limits on how large breweries could grow. During the next decade Wolf helped lead the way to what became known as stock houses—in which the fermenting and aging of beer happened in an environment where the temperature was controlled by mechanical refrigeration rather than expensive and space-hogging ice. The need for controlled temperatures drove architects to design stock houses with fewer windows, or sometimes none at all, though they avoided blank walls by adding "bricked-in" windows or shallow arches to mimic the style of adjacent buildings.[94]

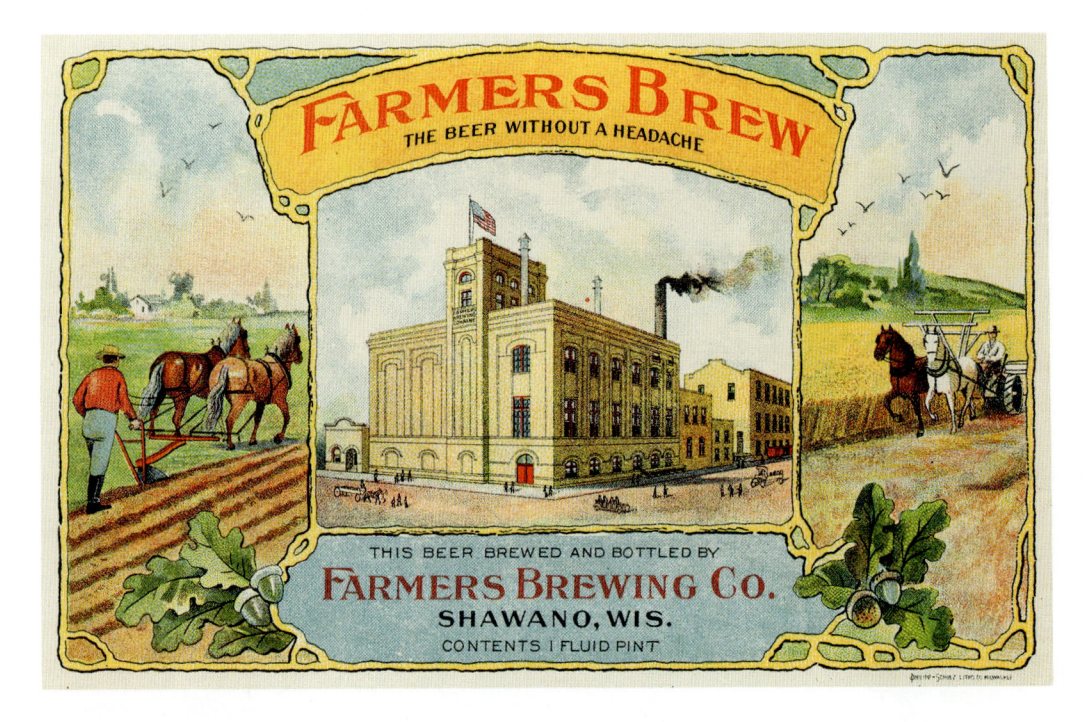

The new plant of Farmers Brewing Co. was typical of breweries built in the 1910s that had to start relatively large in order to be competitive. Farmers Brew made the dubious claim that it was "The Beer without a Headache" (ca. 1915). COLLECTION OF TYE SCHWALBE.

Some of the developments in brewery architecture in the 1880s and 1890s were possible because of the increasing adoption of electric light and power in breweries. In 1882 the malt house and engine room of Best's Empire Brewery were among the first structures in the entire city to be wired for electric light.[95] Falk's brewery was at least partially powered by electricity, since its dynamos also powered the electric lights in National Park, which went out when the brewery burned in 1889.[96] The adoption of electric power required its own modifications to the brewery complex. During the early 1890s remodeling of Blatz Brewing by Chicago-based architect August Maritzen, another brewery specialist, among the important new structures was a powerhouse with room for twenty-eight dynamos.[97] The next year Blatz laid claim to be "the only brewery run by electric power in the country," and later advertisements claimed, "The Nineteenth Century boasts of a Twentieth Century Brewery."[98]

Twentieth-century breweries had to account for numerous variables. A paper presented in 1911 by Chicago-based brewery architect Louis Lehle, a former partner of Wolf, laid out the details to

The bottling and pasteurizing operations at West Bend Lithia Brewing Co. The metal baskets were used to contain the bottles when they passed through the pasteurizer (the large unit in the left rear of the photo) (ca. 1912). COLLECTION OF JOHN STEINER.

A few breweries actually produced a Vacuum Bräu to celebrate the advanced technology of their brewhouse. This label appears to have been a stock label with the name of the Gutsch Brewing Co. added at lower right (ca. 1900). COLLECTION OF TYE SCHWALBE.

be considered. The location had to allow for easy delivery of fuel and raw materials and efficient shipping of finished beer. Railroad tracks had to be arranged so that parking a car in front of one building did not tie up traffic elsewhere in the complex. Furthermore, the layout of the buildings and their relation to each other should be designed to make expansion convenient without needing to shut down other parts of the brewery. The floors for many of the buildings were a particular problem. Some needed to be sanitary, others fireproof, others watertight. Roofs had to resist condensation, which would result in unwelcome drips inside. Cold-storage buildings required insulation, and there were several different types of insulation to choose from. With all of this, the weight of the materials and their cost still had to be considered, and fireproof materials were recommended wherever possible, because the construction of the building would also determine the cost of the insurance premiums.[99]

Most of the technical and scientific advances of the post–Civil War period were adopted by breweries throughout the state, not just the Milwaukee and La Crosse giants. Advertisements by equipment manufacturers in brewery trade journals trumpeted the variety of breweries that purchased their products, showing that modern brewing equipment was within the reach of smaller breweries and that industry suppliers solicited their business. It was the Milwaukee breweries with national markets that took the best advantage of these technological developments, however, and that would make Milwaukee the most important center of lager beer in the nation.

THE LEADING INDUSTRY

Two- or three-part hanging signs such as this were common in the late 1870s and early 1880s in front of saloons, though surviving specimens are extremely rare. COLLECTION OF JOHN STEINER.

CHAPTER 5

MILWAUKEE
Queen of Lager
1865–1915

The handsomest buildings in the city are devoted to the brewing of Milwaukee's celebrated beverage, the handsomest horses in the city are engaged in the work of delivering this beer to the various saloons. The best painting in the city is shown in the thousand and more signs that ornament the doorways where beer is sold and the finest turnouts with liveried coachmen and gold mounted harness are owned by the proprietors of the various breweries. It is said that strangers frequently take Best's south side brewery for some magnificent cathedral.

Oshkosh Daily Northwestern, 2 December 1875

THAT MILWAUKEE IS INEXTRICABLY LINKED IN THE AMERICAN CONSCIOUSNESS WITH lager beer is a triumph of craft and energy, but also of marketing—especially during the period between the Civil War and World War I, often called the Gilded Age. In only a few years had beer become the largest industry in the city by value of output, but it took many decades after the industry was started to catch up with the established brewing centers of New York, Brooklyn, Philadelphia, Boston, Cincinnati, Chicago, and St. Louis. The city ranked seventh in the nation in 1879, but had risen to fourth by 1890.[1] Despite the city's not being the leader in volume, by the 1890s the *Milwaukee Sentinel* was able to claim without blushing that "Milwaukee is today the acknowledged queen of the world in lager beer, the name being familiar in every country, civilized or uncivilized; and her sway universally acknowledged."[2] Milwaukee had other famed industries, but it was always to the breweries that visitors flocked—in part because a free taste of fresh lager would be more refreshing than samples from a tannery or machine shop. Other cities had great breweries, but it was Milwaukee's name that came to exemplify lager beer and had to be protected by lawsuits. Milwaukee's leading breweries did a better job of penetrating distant markets than any company other than Anheuser-Busch and were able to dominate the culture of their home city.

The Cambrinian Army

The brewing industry was largely stagnant during the Civil War, and several Milwaukee breweries saw their sales decline.[3] As the city and the nation emerged from the war and renewed civilian industry, this pattern was reversed dramatically. While identifying a single cause is impossible, the resumption of immigration to the United States, a postwar economic boom that provided workingmen with more disposable income, and a growing taste for lager beer combined with improved practices to push production to new heights. In 1866 Blatz led the city's brewers by producing 18,139 barrels. Six years later, they had more than doubled that output with 41,224 barrels. The growth of Schlitz was even more dramatic: their 3,882 barrels of 1866 put them in the middle of a large group, but a more than eightfold increase to 32,000 barrels in 1872 moved the company into third place well ahead of their nearest follower.[4] This increase was made possible by the construction of a new brewery in the late 1860s to replace the brewery August Krug erected in 1849 to commence business. The new brewhouse was forty feet high and included a large brew kettle with a capacity of 125 barrels, a twenty-five-horsepower engine, and a cement piping system to bring in water from the spring at the corner of Fifth and Sherman.[5]

By 1870 many of the twenty-five breweries located in the city had already moved beyond the small-family-business stage. Both Val Blatz and Phillip Best reported paying $50,000 in wages in the 1870 Census of Industry, and while they were far and away the leading employers, five other breweries paid more than $5,000 to their employees that year. A survey of newspapers and industry journals from this period reveals a constant stream of improvements throughout the Gilded Age. The most noticeable were the construction of new brewhouses, malt houses, and storage and other buildings. Philip Altpeter built an all-new weiss beer brewery in 1873, but many of the projects noted in the press were expansions of existing facilities or new buildings adapting to changes in the industry.[6] Best & Company built a new malt elevator in 1873 at a cost of $30,000—this helped boost their capacity to 150,000 barrels per year. The press also drew attention to new stables, icehouses, warehouses, caves, and brewing kettles, all fueling the rapid increase in production.[7]

The most important brewery expansion in the decade after the Civil War was the acquisition of Charles Melms's brewery by Phillip Best &

This view was one of sixteen included in a souvenir booklet published by Phillip Best Brewing in 1877. The accompanying text was provided in French, German, and English, suggesting the diversity of visitors to the brewery. The steamboat at lower left is the *Comet*, which was under the command of Captain Frederick Pabst before he retired to join the brewery. AUTHOR'S COLLECTION.

MILWAUKEE 123

Company. After Melms's death in 1869, the brewery, once the largest in the city and at that moment the third largest, was sold to pay the accumulated debts. Best finally secured Melms's brewery, which doubled Best's capacity and made it by far the largest brewing firm in the city. Best's original plant was known as the Empire Brewery (a name that had already been in use for several years), and the new acquisition was called the South Side Brewery. The new capacity allowed the company to boost annual production to over 100,000 barrels by 1874, making it the largest brewing company in the country (though because it was operating two plants, the largest single brewery remained that of Conrad Seipp in Chicago).[8]

Despite the rapid expansion of a few firms, growing beer sales allowed room for a large number of profitable breweries of all sizes. Blatz and Best both sold more than 18,000 barrels in 1867 and Melms exceeded 13,000. Schlitz and Falk were both over 5,550, five others were above or near 3,000, and four more sold at least 1,000 barrels. This distribution of production represented an industry with a fairly low level of concentration and one in which there was considerable room for movement up and down the list.[9] The jump of Schlitz to the top tier was one example. Miller and Falk were both well behind the leaders in

This rare label shows both Phillip Best breweries, the original Empire Brewery at left and the former Melms South Side Brewery at right. The *Comet* appears again, as it did in many Best and Pabst promotional materials (ca. late 1870s).
COLLECTION OF JOHN STEINER.

the early 1870s, but would become nationally known businesses in the next decade. However, the overall number of breweries began to decline gradually after the war as some smaller operators left the business, and individuals who entered the market in this era generally did so by purchasing an existing brewery, rather than establishing a new business.

The increasing prominence of Milwaukee on the national stage was aided by an increase in sales outside the state of Wisconsin. As noted earlier, Melms had been shipping to New Orleans prior to the Civil War, and Cochran cites examples of Best and other Milwaukee beer being praised as far away as Mexico.[10] After the war the city's brewers stepped up their exports, at least in part because their production was outstripping the growth of the city and the Wisconsin countryside. By 1871 Milwaukee's brewers produced 146,000 barrels,

Best's South Side Depot in Chicago was equipped with an icehouse, stables, and a spacious office. Railcars are visible to the right of the depot. AUTHOR'S COLLECTION.

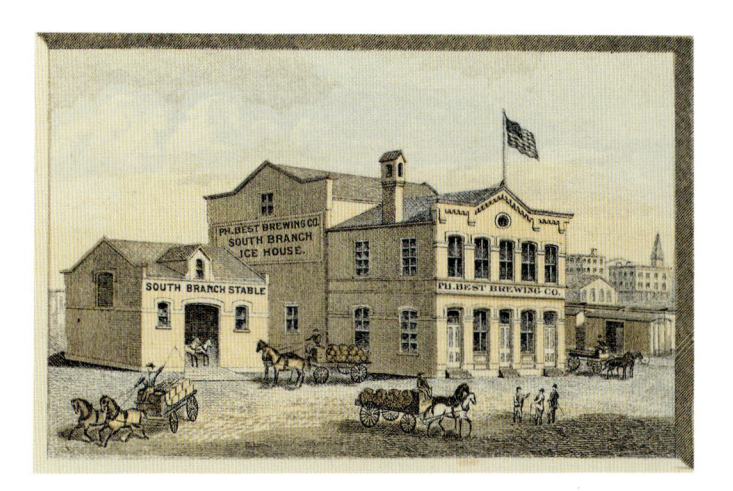

about two barrels for every inhabitant of the city. Although some local residents no doubt did their part, brewers of the Cream City were forced to once again increase their exports.

Their market increased significantly due to a neighbor's misfortune. The Chicago fire of October 1871 did not wipe out all the city's breweries, but nineteen were destroyed or heavily damaged, and only a few of these returned to business. Milwaukee's breweries were perfectly positioned to fill the shortage, especially since several already had offices in the Windy City. Edward G. Uihlein, the local agent for Schlitz, witnessed the fire and spent much of the evening dodging the advancing flames to return home safely. Milwaukee brewers not only sold beer in Chicago but also took advantage of the city's position as a railroad hub to expand their shipments across the nation.[11] The *Sentinel* reported that 1871 production was up 42,000 barrels from the previous year, and credited the growth to just two months of shipments south.[12]

Exclusive Agents

As breweries began to deliver beer farther from home, they needed to solve several technical and business problems. They had to ship beer in a way that would maintain its character and flavor over time and distance, and had to develop strategies for efficiently managing a far-flung business empire. Milwaukee breweries had offices in Chicago as early as 1854, but shipment of beer to and communication with that city was relatively easy given the short distance involved. By 1858 the city was shipping about 20 percent of its production out of

At least fourteen wagons and teams were lined up to deliver cases of bottled Pabst to New York–area customers from the branch office on West Forty-Ninth Street. The stable was located through the arch at the right of the building (ca. 1890). COLLECTION OF JOHN STEINER.

the region, but the destinations are not recorded. Little is known about the details of the shipping activities prior to the 1870s. It is not clear whether the breweries had traveling salesmen on the road, whether orders were sent in by merchants who had heard good things about Milwaukee lager, or by some other method. In general, the published accounts were more interested in proclaiming the growth than explaining how it came about.

As they sought wider markets, brewers had to develop a formal sales organization to satisfy existing customers and cultivate new ones. By the late 1870s Best & Company's dynamic tandem of Frederick Pabst and Emil Schandein had adopted a three-track system of representatives to sell their beer in distant markets. The least important of these (for brewers, anyway) was nonetheless an iconic figure in American business for several generations: the traveling salesman. A traveling man could serve a large region containing a number of relatively small accounts, though he was sometimes expensive to keep on the road, in part because of the expectation that he would visit saloons and buy a round for the patrons. Local agents were more important to building business than traveling men. A connection with Pabst or someone in the home office helped an agent get selected, but occasionally the company would try to attract an agent from another brewery with promises of better rates, better product, and even cash or gifts. The agent was responsible for providing storage (usually including an icehouse), but the brewery paid for a delivery wagon and horse or mule. A brewery, whether Best/Pabst or any shipping business, had to make careful calculations as to whether a particular market was worthy of an agency or just the regular attentions of a salesman.[13]

Even more critical was the transportation method itself. Earlier exports had been by boat, but this was generally slower and effectively limited the reach of shipping breweries to port cities and river towns. However, the completion of the transcontinental railroad and the railroad fever that followed the war gave breweries the opportunity they needed. Thomas Cochran concluded, "Bottled lager beer was a by-product of the railroads, and the beginning of nationwide sales followed closely upon the completion of a railroad network."[14] Milwaukee was a rail center and was also close to Chicago, which was the hub of all train traffic in the trans-Appalachian West. Cream City brewers therefore would be able to compete on similar terms to

Gustave J. Ramlack was the Pabst agent in Pittsburgh in the late 1800s and early 1900s. This bottle was produced after the invention of the crown cap in 1892. Note also the spelling of Pittsburg—it occasionally was spelled without the final *h* at the time. AUTHOR'S COLLECTION.

breweries in St. Louis, Chicago, and Cincinnati—their biggest rivals in the Midwest. Shipping breweries purchased or rented depots on railroad sidings near cities large and small to store and deliver their beer. These shipping breweries either set up branch offices with salaried employees or engaged local agents who worked on commission to handle their beer. While some of the expansions were to distant cities like New York or Pittsburgh, most were in the Upper Midwest.

While Miller was a bit behind its fellows in national expansion, it was the only Milwaukee firm to expand by building a branch brewery. However, the struggles of the Bismarck, Dakota Territory, brewery in the 1880s must have discouraged further attempts. The brewery, which one newspaper account reported as costing $100,000 to establish, was beset by bad water and inefficient

KANSAS CITY BRANCH, KANSAS CITY, MO.

Phillip Best Brewing Co. established its Kansas City office in 1879—at the time, its westernmost branch. This illustration is from a souvenir booklet published in 1884. AUTHOR'S COLLECTION.

MILWAUKEE 127

workers and management. Furthermore, when North Dakota became a state in 1889 it wrote a prohibition provision into the state constitution, so Frederick J. Miller decided to cut his losses and end the experiment.[15]

The Brewery's Own Bottling

Prior to the late 1870s, the vast majority of lager beer was shipped in kegs and served on draft. While bottled ale was common enough, bottled lager was virtually unheard of until the mid-1870s. Lager was consumed fresh from the keg even at home, except in those cases in which the quantity required was so small that even a "pony" keg would result in much waste. Bottled beer was too expensive for most retailers and customers, especially if it was likely to sit on the shelf for a prolonged period. Ales were less perishable and less dependent on high carbonation than lager, so a steady if not spectacular market for bottled ale persisted throughout the nineteenth century. It is likely that some private bottlers had a small trade in lager, but very little documentation exists to show the extent. Demand was starting to grow for bottled lager in the 1870s, however, and when local bottlers did not exist brewers would have to take matters into their own hands.

The first problem to be solved was that of the bottles themselves. A 1949 Blatz publication depicted what was reputed to be the first lager bottle, a ten-sided stoneware product that looked little like a typical beer bottle and was unlikely to have been designed for large-scale lager bottling.[16] It is most likely that brewers experimenting with bottling lager simply borrowed stoneware bottles already used for weiss beer or soda and put them to a new purpose. Because of the high carbonation of lager, bottles with strong walls and a firm closure were required, and weiss beer's effervescence provided adequate proof of a bottle's strength. But within a few years glass manufacturers began to offer bottles specifically for lager, so the appearance became more standardized.

Delivering a palatable bottled lager beer to customers, especially those at some distance from the brewery, required overcoming numerous technological and marketing hurdles. The work of Louis Pasteur was well known by 1880, but equipment to heat the bottles to a sufficient temperature to kill the offending microorganisms without unduly slowing packaging and shipping was not developed until later that decade. A further obstacle was the need to heat the bottles slowly so they did

John T. Schulkamp was a beer and soda bottler in Madison in the 1880s. This stoneware bottle appears to be marked H & J Schulkamp, which probably refers to Henry Schulkamp, a soda manufacturer. While stoneware bottles were still in use in the 1880s, their weight made them inconvenient and expensive to ship.
COLLECTION OF TYE SCHWALBE.

128   THE DRINK THAT MADE WISCONSIN FAMOUS

not crack or blow their corks. The best solutions ultimately involved putting bottles in a basket or on a conveyor that took them through stages of heating and cooling.[17]

Actually packaging the beer in bottles was filled with regulatory and technical hurdles. Until 1890 all beer first had to be racked into kegs, and then transported across a public road because brewing and bottling were not allowed to take place in the same building. The reason was taxation—beer was assessed by tax stamps on barrels, and therefore into barrels it went. But each additional packaging step increased the possibility of lost beer through spillage or of damage through oxidation or infection. Brewmasters must have been reluctant to have the company name attached to a product that could go bad once out of their sight, especially when bottling was done in a distant agency under conditions they could not control. Even the small weiss or "white" beer breweries were required in 1875 to comply with the same laws as lager and ale breweries, which was especially inconvenient since white beer required bottle conditioning and was therefore exclusively a bottled product.[18]

Given the bragging rights at stake, it is interesting that no other Cream City firm challenged Blatz's advertising campaign proclaiming it "Milwaukee's First Bottled Beer." Of course, Blatz's claim is inaccurate anyway because Blossom's Eagle Brewery was bottling at least as early as 1847. Cochran contended that Best experimented with bottling beer at the South Side plant in 1875, the same year Blatz claimed for its first bottles. Pabst historian John Steiner suggested that the Milwaukee Brewing Association, established in the former Kargleder brewery, was created to give Phillip Best & Company a way to continue experiments with bottled beer without putting the company name on the line (much as Miller did with Lite Beer in the 1970s). The presence of Best's Emil Schandein as president indicates at least that Best & Company had significant interest in the operations.[19]

EXCLUSIVE BOTTLERS

What was traditionally regarded as the first bottled lager in Milwaukee was produced by independent bottlers who contracted with a brewery. Blatz's first bottling was done by Samuel F. Rindskoff (or Rindskopf), though it appears he may not have been able to meet all the demand since the 1877–78 Milwaukee city directory also includes ads for Torchiani & Kremer. John Kremer was married to Val Blatz's adopted daughter Louise, which may have given the son-in-law an inside track on securing the lion's share of the business. Both companies continued bottling for Blatz for a few years, but eventually Torchiani & Kremer took over the business to such an extent that most histories report that they were the first bottlers.[20] Best farmed out its experiment to Stamm & Meyer, Franz Falk's beer was bottled by Arthur Gunther & Company, and Schlitz employed Voechting & Shape. Miller's first bottled beers were apparently produced without the company's direct cooperation by a small operator named Charles Henning, who had previously been employed by Voechting & Shape. Henning was not the only one to leave an existing bottler to start his own company—Norman Root started as the bookkeeper in Best's small

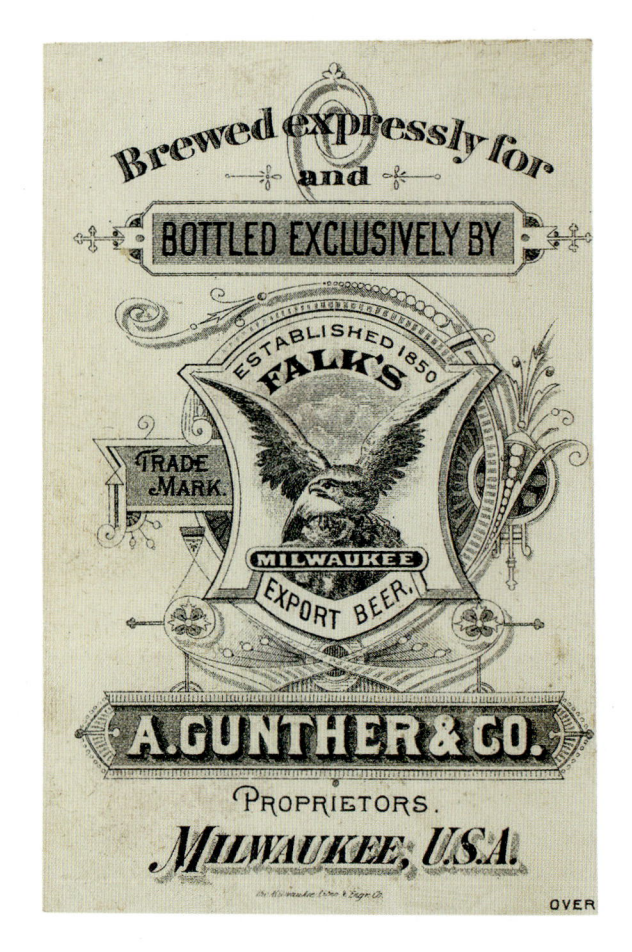

During the late 1880s, many businesses used ornate business (or trade) cards to advertise their products. In this era, Export Beer generally meant a beer that was brewed to be more stable and thus survive bottling and shipment, though Falk and Gunther also had Spanish-language versions of these cards for use in their Caribbean markets. COLLECTION OF JOHN STEINER.

operation, moved with it to Stamm & Meyer, and then founded N. A. Root Company, which bottled for Borchert and later Jung & Borchert.[21]

Starting a bottling operation required very little equipment, so nearly anyone with a building and available labor, such as Henning, could bottle beer. All that was needed was a supply of bottles, corks, foil wrappers to keep the corks in, cases or kegs to ship the bottles, and, of course, beer.[22] Barriers to entry were so low that Adam Dillmann was able to sell his saloon in March 1882 and in just over a month start the firm Dillmann & Morawetz, which became the bottler for Cream City Brewing Company on May 1.[23] Early bottles had rather plain labels by modern standards, but at this point the label was not designed for advertising, merely to identify the bottle as the property of the bottling company.

Reusing bottles was essential to running a profitable business, but this meant they had to

130   THE DRINK THAT MADE WISCONSIN FAMOUS

be cleaned. An account of early beer bottling in La Crosse reported, "When brewers began to turn out bottled beer a small quantity of lead shot was placed in each bottle, which was shaken by hand for the purpose of loosening any particles of dirt in the bottle. Subsequently they were rinsed out in water in the same crude way."[24]

A combination of good timing and active promotion made bottled Milwaukee lager an instant success. The 1878 Milwaukee city directory had full-page ads from Stamm & Meyer, Torchiani & Kremer, Gunther & Company, and Voechting, Shape & Company—all for a product that didn't exist three years earlier. The ad for Stamm & Meyer included engravings of the company's exhibits at the Centennial Exposition in 1876 and the Paris Exposition of 1878, while Torchiani & Kremer's page touted the fact that they produced "the only Milwaukee Bottled Export Lager Beer receiving a Premium at the Centennial Exhibition."[25] Agencies in far-flung cities continued to bottle using labels of their own or blanks provided by the home brewery—a practice that would extend into the twentieth century. Voechting & Shape even took control of distant bottling for a brief period. An ad from San Francisco in 1877 proclaimed that a local business, Richards & Harrison, were "Sole Agents, by appointment of Voechting & Shape, the only authorized bottlers of the celebrated Schlitz's Milwaukee Lager Beer."[26]

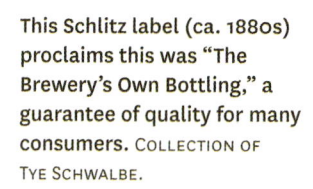

Blatz designed this elaborate display of its bottled beer for the World's Industrial and Cotton Centennial held in 1884–85 in New Orleans. The six-hundred-gallon barrel in the middle of the display had a window through which visitors could view a panorama inside. COLLECTION OF JOHN STEINER.

This Schlitz label (ca. 1880s) proclaims this was "The Brewery's Own Bottling," a guarantee of quality for many consumers. COLLECTION OF TYE SCHWALBE.

MILWAUKEE 131

Fred Miller's brewery was known as the Menomonee Valley Brewery from 1873 until 1888. Miller was among the first to have a bottling department under the brewery's own name (label ca. 1880). COLLECTION OF JOHN STEINER.

As bottled beer became firmly established, breweries sought to maintain both financial and quality control by either establishing their own bottling departments or buying out their former contractors. Pabst bought out Stamm & Meyer after Meyer's death in 1880, and Schlitz absorbed the operations of Voechting & Shape after Gustav Shape's passing in 1886. Torchiani & Kremer officially became the Blatz Bottling Department in 1881, though the firm remained in city directories under its original name until the late 1880s.[27] By the mid-1880s bottled beer was such a large part

These workers at Pabst are packing bottled beer into barrels for shipment. The bottles were wrapped in paper, and straw was packed around the bottles to protect them (ca. 1900). COLLECTION OF JOHN STEINER.

132 THE DRINK THAT MADE WISCONSIN FAMOUS

Although shipping cases were durable, they still could be damaged with heavy use. Pabst had an entire division of its carpenter shop devoted to repairing cases (ca. 1900). COLLECTION OF JOHN STEINER.

of the trade that the regulations prohibiting beer from being bottled directly from the aging tanks caused ever more profit-reducing inefficiencies. Despite this, those rules were to remain in place until the end of the decade.

Even once the beer was safely bottled, headaches remained. The bottles had to be packed in such a way that they would not break or explode during shipping, and would also retain an acceptable retail appearance. Although cases were quickly adopted by the industry, some breweries, including Best/Pabst, shipped at least a portion of their beer by cask, typically with six dozen pints or three dozen quarts wrapped in paper and packed in straw. Cases saved space but were subject to breakage if handled too roughly.

Furthermore, brewers often struggled with seasonal shortages of refrigerated railroad cars and fought railroad operators who wanted to minimize the amount of ice used to keep the beer fresh. Ice also had to be shipped to southern depots to supply the icehouses, though this was more important with kegged beer. The more stable bottled product improved shelf life, and by the 1890s brewers of all sizes advertised that their bottled beers were "warranted to keep in any climate." Bottled beer was often sent to southern or western states where demand was not great enough to have branch offices but too large to be totally overlooked. In 1888

Sealing the Deal: Bottle Closures

Bottling beer created a need to coordinate many new inputs, whether to physically contain the beer or to spread the fame of the brand.[1] As early as 1880, Voechting and Shape filled 275,000 dozen bottles for Schlitz, which required importing bottles from Germany and purchasing $20,000 worth of corks. In 1890 Pabst purchased eighteen million corks, at a cost of $80,000. Most of the corks came from Spain, and the international nature of this trade made the job of a brewery's purchasing department just that much more complicated.[2]

For centuries, corks had been the preferred bottle or jug closure, even though pounding the cork in probably resulted in many broken bottles. But unlike wine, beer bottling required the cork to be tied or wired down or wrapped with metal foil to prevent the cork from being expelled by the force of the carbonated beverage, and these extra steps took extra time and material. (A bottle fitted with a Putnam wired cork retainer is pictured in the entry for John Berg's Milwaukee brewery in the second part of this book.) Corks were a single-use product, although for breweries concerned about lower-quality beer being sold under their name at

This sturdy corkscrew distributed by the Gund Brewing Co. of La Crosse announced the gold medal it earned at the St. Louis World's Fair of 1904. COLLECTION OF TYE SCHWALBE.

Henry W. Putnam advertised his "Lightning" stopper in 1878 with much more emphasis on the patents he owned than on the virtues of the device. COLLECTION OF SUMMIT BREWING CO.

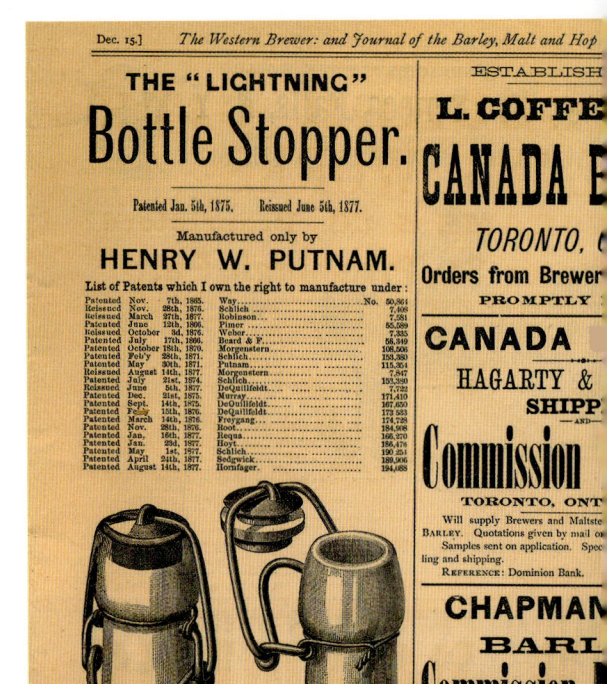

---

1 Material in this section was drawn from a variety of sources, but the most useful single source was the Historic Glass Bottle Identification & Information Website hosted by the Society for Historical Archaeology (https://sha.org/bottle/index.htm). Bottle collector and historian Steve Ketcham provided useful guidance.
2 *Milwaukee Daily Sentinel*, 8 January 1880, 5; *Sentinel*, 16 November 1890, 15.

a premium price, the presence of a fresh cork with the brand name was considered a guarantee of genuineness. For years brewery ads urged customers to "See that 'Blatz' is on the cork" or some similar phrase.

The search for the ideal bottle closure lasted several decades. The most common replacement for corks from the late 1870s through the end of the century was one of the variants of the "swing-top" closure: either the Lightning or Hutter variants. Both of these used an apparatus whereby moving a lever wire released a bail wire that held a stopper with a rubber gasket (metal for Lightning stoppers, porcelain for the Hutter style). The apparatus was attached to the bottleneck by a tie wire. (A example is the Pabst bock bottle later in this chapter.) William Painter, a machinist and inventor, created a lined rubber seal that was inserted into a groove in the neck of the bottle and was removed with a tool. This device found some popularity during the late 1880s and 1890s, but was quickly supplanted by Painter's most famous invention.

Painter led a group that incorporated Crown Cork & Seal Co. in 1893 to develop and sell a new closure he had patented the previous year: the crown cap. The new seal was inexpensive, airtight, easy to remove, and—most important for bottlers—it was applied by machine. It took a few years for the new closure to be widely adopted, since it required new bottles and most bottlers chose to use their existing stock as long as possible. Pabst did not switch to crowns until 1906, and Schlitz ads indicate that they were using both corks and crowns as late as 1912. But by the early twentieth century many brewers had adopted the crown cap, and after Prohibition it was used almost exclusively (except for a few swing tops or other closures on "picnic" bottles). A few European breweries still use Hutter stoppers, though modern ones are usually made of plastic rather than porcelain.

William Painter spent a significant portion of his career trying to develop the ideal bottle closure (as well as the ideal device to remove his closures). This patent illustration shows his design for an early crown cap remover.
COURTESY OF U.S. PATENT AND TRADEMARK OFFICE.

Pabst shipped no kegged beer at all to Alabama, Georgia, Idaho, Mississippi, North Carolina, South Carolina, or Wyoming Territory, but shipped hundreds or even a few thousand casks of bottles to those states.[28]

Bottling made it easier for breweries to offer more varieties of lager to their customers. Prior to the 1870s, if a brewery offered more than one style of beer, it was usually one or more ales and one lager. As bottling grew in popularity, however, brewers began offering styles beyond a simple lager called Export. Darker or more flavorful varieties such as Münchener, Kulmbacher, Wiener (Vienna), or Dortmunder began to appear regularly in advertisements and on trade cards. These styles were never more than a small percentage of a brewer's sales, but they offered a special product for elegant consumers and kept old-timers happy who were dissatisfied with the move to lighter beers.

Pabst had five bottled products in 1889, including Pabst Select in the unique tapered bottle—and sporting the blue ribbon that would later make it famous. The malt tonic, in the distinctive bottle used by most breweries for this beverage, was the subject of a wide-ranging promotion campaign in the 1890s by the company's advertising manager, A. Cressy Morrison. Tonics were usually sold in drugstores, which required breweries to establish additional sales and marketing channels. AUTHOR'S COLLECTION.

136 THE DRINK THAT MADE WISCONSIN FAMOUS

Finally, bottled beer made it easier for brewers to penetrate a critical market—urban households. While a large farm family with a number of laborers boarding may have been able to finish a keg of lager before it became flat and stale, ordering even a small barrel would have been uneconomical for a city family. Being able to order a case of bottles meant that the family could have beer on hand, but worry less about it going to waste. This emerging market also led to changes in advertising in which considerable effort was expended to persuade housewives to buy a case of bottled beer along with the rest of the household provisions.

As the need to ship ever more bottled beer increased, so did the mechanization of the plants. Even so, bottling shops remained a mix of hand labor and mechanization well into the twentieth century, especially at smaller breweries. A Milwaukee journalist touring an unidentified "Mammoth Brewery" gazed in wonder at the work under way:

Pabst distributed these "yard-long" calendars for several years in the early 1900s. This striking design for 1908 includes the birthstones for each month and their supposed symbolism. COLLECTION OF HERBERT AND HELEN HAYDOCK.

The bottling process is really the most interesting in many respects. There is no end of dash, crash, slop and pop about it—regular hurrah business. Old bottles are first unwired by a troop of boisterous kids; then soaked, washed and rinsed by a squadron of women in pattens; thereupon they are filled, corked and steamed by a skirmish line of men, and finally wired, labeled and packed by a platoon of girls. The automatic washer is a very ingenious contrivance; as the bottle's neck is pressed over the horizontal swab, this suddenly emits a spray of water and at the same time swirls around its bristles; all of which requires only that the bottle be firmly held in hand and directed against the swab as may be needed.[29]

MILWAUKEE 137

INTERIOR OF BOTTLING DEPARTMENT.

The bottling department of Pabst Brewing Co. as depicted in the Grand Army of the Republic souvenir booklet of 1889 was a marvel of industry. The engraver took special pains to emphasize the machinery that aided the entire process. Bottles are shown being packed into both barrels and cases. At lower left, several well-dressed visitors admire the efficiency of the plant. The engraving also shows the large number of women employed to label and wrap the bottles (and to attach a length of blue ribbon). AUTHOR'S COLLECTION.

While the engravings of bottle shops of the major brewers emphasize mechanization, the reality was that many of the tasks were still performed by hand, and typically by young women or children of both sexes.

The employment of women and youth was a cost saver for the breweries, and a much-needed source of revenue for poor immigrant families. In 1895 Schlitz paid young girls (the precise age range was not given) from $2.25 to $2.75 per week, and young boys $2.25. Older boys earned from $2.50 to $7.50 a week, compared with adult pay of $8.50 to $12.00 a week. At this time Schlitz employed about forty girls under age seventeen, and about fifty between the ages of eighteen and twenty-five.[30] At the same time, this labor was a source of concern and outrage for progressive reformers. Wisconsin had compulsory education laws and age requirements for workers in place by the 1880s, but these were routinely ignored by families desperate for income and employers in search of cheaper labor.[31] In June 1895 U.S. Labor Bureau special agent Ethelbert Stewart conducted an investigation of Milwaukee's breweries looking for violations. Schlitz claimed that it required certificates signed by the parents that their child was at least fourteen

This photograph of the bottle labeling area at Blatz depicts the youth of many of the men and women employed there. Much of the machinery resembles that in the Pabst engraving, though not on the same scale (ca. 1900). COLLECTION OF JOHN STEINER.

years old, and the company further assuaged the fears of moral crusaders by assuring them that boys and girls had separate meal breaks and that beer rations were strictly limited to two glasses for boys and one for girls.[32] Pabst had a similar policy about requiring a sworn statement from parents, though the company acknowledged that a few false statements had been made.[33] Pabst felt confident enough about its employment practices to feature three hundred girls from their bottling department in a parade celebrating the 1895 Milwaukee Industrial Exposition that same October.[34]

"AS TROUBLE WAS THREATENED"

The increasing industrialization of Milwaukee's breweries paralleled that of other manufacturing sectors of the American economy. While numerous small shops remained, breweries with employees numbering in the hundreds were leading the industry, and the concentration of more tasks within the companies suggested that increased vertical integration was the path successful firms would take. But whereas a small family brewery could set tasks and hours as the brewing cycle demanded with little difficulty, a major shipping brewery needed to demand much of its employees and to regiment their work patterns more. This led to increasing discontent in the workforce.

The rise of brewery unions also paralleled the rise of labor unions in the country at large, but Milwaukee's relative tardiness to organize is also indicative of the fact that the city's breweries were still generally smaller than rivals in Chicago, Cincinnati, or farther east. In 1860 census figures reported that no brewery in Wisconsin had more than eleven employees, and only three had as many as ten. In 1870 Phillip Best had one hundred employees, but that was a significant exception as the next largest, Blatz, had only thirty-five, and after that forces dropped to ten at Schlitz, Miller, and Falk. Outside of Milwaukee, only Rodermund of Madison and Haertel of Columbia had ten or more workers (though La Crosse figures were not available and at least two of those breweries were likely to be in this group). Firms of this size were still essentially small family businesses, and there would have been little demand for labor to organize. Many of the workers in these smaller businesses were either relatives or hands whose role was much more like that of an apprentice—learning the trade so they could later start or manage their own business.

Best led the growth, and the company also experienced labor difficulties first. The first known strike at a Milwaukee brewery took place at Best's Empire Brewery in May 1873. An article in the *Daily Sentinel* did not specify which workers went on strike, but reported, "The places of the strikers have been filled, and no interruption of business will occur." It also noted that "as trouble was threatened, a squad of police were detailed to preserve order," though no violence occurred.[35] Unfortunately for organized labor, the Panic of 1873 created massive unemployment, which made any attempt to improve wages or conditions a risky proposition with so much ready labor available to replace striking workers. The first attempt to organize workers beyond the city level, the National Labor Union, collapsed, and it would be several years before brewers in general and particularly in Milwaukee reorganized. In part, this was because brewery workers were generally much better paid than those in most other fields—from ten to thirteen dollars a week—when very few other skilled workers were making more than ten dollars a week.[36]

But, as Cochran and other historians note, wages were not everything. Up through the 1880s employees often worked fourteen-hour days, sometimes longer if a batch of beer did not finish on schedule. Multiple accounts report that a typical workday began at 4:00 a.m. Employees worked for two hours or more until their breakfast break, resumed until a 9:00 a.m. break, were back at it until their one-hour break at noon, and finished their day at 6:00 p.m. The early hours of some workers were dictated by saloons that wanted morning delivery of beer.[37] When looking back at this period from the 1930s, Fred Pabst Jr. remarked, "I often wondered why these men going home at night after six didn't meet themselves coming back at four in the morning."[38]

While many brewery workers lived to ripe old ages, they were at risk of a variety of workplace hazards. Especially at smaller breweries, employees often had to move from extremely hot conditions in the brewhouse or malt kiln rooms to very cool conditions in the cellar—which was blamed for a high incidence of rheumatism and respiratory problems among brewers.[39] More horrifying, and more newsworthy, were the numerous ways that brewery workers could be maimed or killed on the job. Employees could be crushed by falling grain or ice, scalded by falling into mash or brew kettles, or drawn into machinery. Workers could be burned while pitching barrels or in the occasional fires that broke out. The size of the brewery made no difference in the risk to which employees were subjected. There were two notable accidents involving employees of Liebscher & Berg's small weiss beer brewery within five months in 1871: a boy working at the brewery was drawn into the gears of the horsepower and suffered a mangled leg, and one of the company's drivers had a leg crushed when he collided with another team of horses.[40]

Nationally, brewery workers began to organize in earnest in 1879 in Cincinnati, and shortly thereafter in New York and elsewhere. Chief among their demands was the eight-hour day, which had become an important rallying cry for laborers in all industries. Milwaukee's brewery workers did not organize until 1886, when they formed Local 7953 of the Gambrinus Assembly of the rapidly expanding Knights of Labor.[41] The Knights had formed in 1869, but had remained a small secret society until 1879, when the organization became public and the new grand master workman, Terence V. Powderly, began to increase the scope of the union. From about 5,000 workers spread thinly across the country in seven hundred locals in 1879, membership exploded to over 700,000 members by 1886, with over two-thirds of that growth happening in that pivotal year for the Knights and American labor.[42]

Labor Fever

Labor troubles began early in 1886. Recognizing the threat, three breweries, Best, Schlitz, and Jung & Borchert, all agreed to lower the standard workday from thirteen to ten hours. However, the malt house workers of the city organized in March and began to pressure breweries for concessions. Pabst, who Cochran claims was "mildly sympathetic" to unions at this point, recognized the union and granted malt workers a six-day week with Sundays off.[43] At Blatz the maltsters went on strike at the end of March. The *Milwaukee Sentinel* reported that the strike was because the maltsters spokesman was discharged, but there were conflicting reports of the reason. The spokesman claimed it was because he complained workers had been given "stale beer" to drink, but the company held that it was because he "demanded their morning allowance half an hour earlier than usual."[44]

These were minor disputes compared to the conflict that exploded in May. The Knights and other trade unions called for strikes and parades on May 1 to push for the eight-hour day. While this call applied to workers in any industry, it provided special leverage for the brewery workers since it was during the season in which brewers were working full blast preparing for summer sales. The brewers attempted to forestall the strike by offering an increase in wages, but the unions rejected the proposals and walked out at all large Milwaukee brewers except Falk. Approximately 1,700 brewery workers joined nearly 14,000 other Cream City laborers on strike and constituted the single largest group other than garment workers. But the composition of the striking workers was fluid throughout the week.[45] The brewers did not attempt to hire strikebreakers, hoping the strike would be over quickly. It was critical, however, to return the firemen in charge of the boilers and the engineers to work as soon as possible so that refrigeration equipment could be operated and beer in the cellars would not spoil. To that end, Pabst and Charles Best met the demands of these workers on the first day for both the eight-hour day and higher wages.[46] On the other hand, pressure by union members forced workers at Falk to join the walkout after three days, even though they had expressed the desire to remain at work. Beer driver-salesmen, called peddlers in the term of the era, tried to continue deliveries, though by the third day they encountered rock-throwing mobs or were otherwise forced to return to the brewery. But later that day, Schlitz, Blatz, and Jung & Borchert had settled with their workers and were back in production, and Best had an agreement in principle that the union accepted by the end of the day. (The union insisted that Pabst fire about twenty workers who had continued to work through the strike and he refused to do so, but the union ultimately gave in.)[47] As a result, the *Journal* rejoiced, "The beer wagons are seen on the street again."[48]

Despite the settlements at the breweries, the city was still in a state of turmoil. Militia called out to keep the peace fired into a group of workers at the Bay View Roller Mills and killed at least six marchers (some sources say seven), a toll exceeded only by the Haymarket Affair in Chicago a day later.[49] The *Sentinel* reported that Pabst had prepared for an attack on the brewery by ordering the coopers to make two or three hundred oak clubs out of barrel staves, which were then placed at strategic locations around the buildings. To repel attackers, hoses were attached to vats of boiling water and one to the ammonia tank.[50] The *Daily Journal* added that Best employees were provided with rations in case they could not leave the building, and that "similar preparations were made in other breweries, the men being determined to resist outside intervention."[51] Even though most brewery workers did not gain an eight-hour day at this point, brewery workers tended to be more satisfied with their lot than other trades, at least in part because they were so much better paid in comparison.[52]

FROM KNIGHTS TO AFL

Many members of the public, including some sympathetic to labor's complaints, were appalled by the strikes and the violence that resulted. Condemnation of the Knights was widespread and marked the beginning of the organization's decline. The rituals of the order, which early twentieth-century socialist labor writer Hermann Schlüter called "nonsensical to a high degree," were not appealing to "sober and intelligent elements of the working class."[53] The Knights alienated brewery workers further by including a temperance clause in their constitution and even issuing an executive order banning beer at union picnics. The Gambrinus Lodge cut its ties with the Knights in 1887 and joined Local 9 of the National Union of United Brewery Workers of the new American Federation of Labor.[54] This began a period when struggles within the ranks of union laborers were just as problematic as conflicts between labor and management. In November 1887 workers at independent malt houses (called commission malt houses in contemporary accounts, in other words, those not part of a brewery) went on strike, seeking a wage increase of five dollars a week to bring their pay into line with that of maltsters at the brewery facilities. Their places were filled almost immediately, and an attempt to get Gettelman, Miller, and Cream City to boycott malt from these houses was rejected. The next step of the union was to declare a boycott of Milwaukee beer by members of Local 9, which also included the people making the beer. The brewers responded by announcing they would no longer recognize the union, though union workers were allowed to remain on the job.[55]

The national leadership of the unions may have overplayed their hands at this juncture. Both the Knights of Labor and the AFL called for nationwide boycotts of Milwaukee beer. While Schlüter's partisan account holds that sales "decreased enormously," Cochran's analysis of Best's sales shows little more than seasonal variation. Cochran also claims that some citizens resented union activities and may have made it a point to buy boycotted beer.[56] The last straw for the Milwaukee owners was when out-of-town beer was served at the Brewery Workers' Masked Ball in January 1888. A few days later, the proprietors announced that they would lock out members of Local 9 and no longer employ union men. Current workers who gave up their union membership could keep their jobs. The owners held most of the cards, since winter was a slow season and they could tolerate several weeks without production if necessary. Furthermore, the illogic of the brewery workers boycotting the very products that kept them employed was becoming more obvious. Finally, Milwaukee residents of all sympathies suspected that the national boycott was supported by breweries in New York and St. Louis, which stood to gain from Milwaukee's strife. On 25 January the union held a mass meeting in which nearly one thousand workers voted to stand with the union despite the threat of the lockout. That night, however, a *Sentinel* reporter interviewed Pabst "through the closed door of his residence on Chestnut street" and "the Captain" remained confident that most workers would choose their jobs over their union. His confidence was justified, since the workers at nearly every brewery overwhelmingly rejected the union.[57] The union was broken, and while the lockout left some lingering tensions, those passed quickly. A plan for a cooperative brewery to employ laid-off workers quickly foundered, and a series of small explosions at Blatz, which some accounts sensationalized as revenge, were probably caused by grain dust.[58]

For the next few years, Milwaukee beer was a nonunion product. Some national boycotts on Schlitz and Pabst were maintained (the only two with enough of a national market for such action to be effective), and a few smaller Wisconsin breweries such as Klinkert of Racine gained a bit of market share by advertising their union ties. But according to Cochran, the national shipping breweries made their peace with the unions in the early 1890s so that the race between Pabst and Anheuser-Busch for the top spot among the nation's breweries could not be manipulated by the unions. A new Local 9 was formed, and the AFL boycott was lifted.[59] By the early twentieth century Milwaukee's brewers were prepared to grant workers the eight-hour day, and in general relationships between labor and management were better in Milwaukee than in many other brewing centers. Jurisdictional clashes continued, but occasional disputes between the different trades covered by union contracts were overcome by general improvements in conditions and wages. In 1912, the brewers recognized a local for women working in the bottling houses, covering one of the last nonunionized groups in the breweries (foremen were not part of the union). Other than a few short strikes, labor relations were generally harmonious until Prohibition.[60]

FRINGE BENEFITS

Working at one of the world's leading breweries during this era had its compensations beyond the higher pay. Employees were often offered room and board in dormitories near the brewery, though it was also common for workers at much smaller breweries to live on the premises as well. This was probably welcome for newly landed immigrants or itinerant workers, though Schlüter claimed that these arrangements were often poor housing used to control the workers, who were too tired from their day's work to demand better.[61]

The popularity of their product and the sheer number of workers created opportunities for amusement not shared by all trades. The Brewers' Masked Ball was an important event on the Milwaukee winter social calendar, with the awarding of cash prizes a welcome attraction (along with the presence of beer).[62] At major parades, brewery floats accompanied by employees attracted considerable admiration (as well as giving workers a welcome day off). For the parade capping Milwaukee's Semi-Centennial Exposition in 1895, the entire first division of the parade consisted of brewery displays. Miller's float had an Egyptian theme, Schlitz had several floats, and Blatz, Gettelman, Milwaukee Brewing, Waukesha Spring Brewing, and the Graf and Hustings white beer breweries were represented, along with Froedtert Malting Company. Pabst made the biggest impression with one thousand workers, eleven delivery wagons, and three hundred girls from the bottling department; "a squad of big walking bottles created amusement."[63] Occasionally there were opportunities for recreation on-site, as was the case with Miller, which, fittingly enough for Milwaukee, included a bowling alley in the brewery complex.[64]

Brewery workers also enjoyed a certain amount of prestige, often associated with the gemütlichkeit of lager beer. During the 1880s there were contests at parish fund-raisers to determine the "most popular brewery foreman." It is difficult to imagine a similar contest between foundry foremen, especially if the winner was supposed to treat those assembled to its product. Brewery deliverymen and salesmen were welcomed in saloons by patrons and proprietors alike because of the imminent flow of free beer. A brewery salesman was especially important during slow times—and a good one could provide significant economic stimulus on his own. The *Sentinel* described the method of one brewery agent:

It was during these wet days . . . that men like Jack Zummach had extraordinary opportunities for displaying their talents. One seeing Jack empty schooner after schooner could not help admiring him. At every saloon he visited, he would order herring for the whole crowd, then beer would begin to flow. Having partaken of the herring and tasted a schooner or two of the free beer that Jack paid for, each of the hardy Tenth warders would immediately send up the boy or girl with a pitcher, and the lucky saloon-keeper, thanks to Jack, had his barrel of beer empty. In this manner Jack worked his way from saloon to saloon, emptying the schooners behind his shirt collar when his capacity was exhausted, and keeping up the record for his employers.[65]

Of all the brewery employees, the drivers of the delivery wagons seemed to elicit the most awe from the public and the press. They certainly presented an impressive appearance, high atop elegant wagons in control of the finest horses found in the city. In a wonderful example of Victorian overstatement, one journalist offered the following praise:

> *The giants who drive the beer wagons—the modern Anakim—are the instruments favored by destiny with the task of carrying forward an ancient industry, and one which has been carried on since the time treated of in the book of Leviticus. Under the influence of beer, heroes sprang up like the knights of the dragon's teeth and fulfilled their destiny. The drivers of the beer wagons are a race of modern knights, who sit on wagons and guide stolid Percheron or Clydesdale draught horses instead of prancing on war steeds. In all sorts of weather they are seen making their rounds, or standing in front of their customers' places of business in the act of lifting down the heavy half barrels or tossing up the empty kegs.*[66]

The praise of these teamsters was often justified: the *Wisconsin State Journal* wrote after an unusually large spring blizzard that had stopped trains and all other transportation: "One peculiar fact to be noted on the streets is that the first persons to break a road are the drivers of brewery teams, who rush in where milkmen fear to tread and butchers stand back in mute admiration."[67]

Of course, the fringe benefit most commonly associated with brewery work is free beer. Accounts differ as to whether consumption was unlimited or not, but there seem to have been at least some restrictions. In 1888, the *Sentinel* reported that during the 9:00 a.m. lunch break at the Best bottling works, "each one is allowed to take a pint bottle of beer—girls and all."[68] Since companies had to keep records of all beer produced and consumed for tax purposes, accounts exist of employee consumption, and these were often reported with amazement in the press. In 1881 the *Sentinel* noted, "It is said the employees in Miller's brewery consume fifteen kegs of beer every week," though it is possible that these were smaller kegs than full-size barrels.[69] In 1893 it was claimed that the average employee of Pabst drank between twenty-five and fifty glasses per day, though these glasses were probably a "Schnitt," which was closer to six ounces rather than a full pint.[70] (See the Riekes glass advertisement in chapter 1 for a comparison of glass sizes.) Even when limits were imposed, they were generous and not always universally adopted. In 1890 Pabst limited its employees to three bottles a day, as opposed to the previous policy under which "some of the brewery hands would consume forty to fifty glasses a day without a struggle."[71] Even with smaller glasses, this was a prodigious quantity, and the amounts were likely exaggerated. Some labor activists welcomed any reduction in free beer, since they saw the practice as a way by which employers not only avoided paying higher wages but also kept their workers docile and under control.[72]

But the employees couldn't drink all the output, and neither could all of Milwaukee, though it was not for lack of trying. Real estate transactions by breweries were sometimes significant enough to move out of legal notices and into feature articles. Under the headline "Prominent Places," the *Milwaukee Sentinel* reported in 1884, "The sales during the week include a large amount of property which has been purchased by brewery firms, and in the course of time all of it will be occupied by saloons."[73] A report of businesses in Milwaukee at the start of 1885 numbered the saloons in the Cream City at 1,100.[74] While legislation and economic conditions caused this total to fluctuate, the general trend was to grow with the city's population. The vast majority of beer sold in 1892 in Milwaukee's 1,400 saloons was Milwaukee beer, "while a few saloon keepers deal exclusively in Chicago, Racine, Kenosha or Sheboygan beer." The largest single retailer was the Schlitz Hotel, even before the Palm Garden opened (the second-largest was one of the few survivors of the short-lived "egg-house" craze, a type of saloon that gave away a free egg with each beer purchased). Even the consumption of three-quarters of a million barrels of beer each year in Milwaukee was not enough to absorb the output of Pabst's one million barrels, to say nothing of the more than two million total produced by the city's eight significant lager breweries.[75]

The Schlitz Palm Garden, at Third Street and Grand Avenue (the modern-day Wisconsin Avenue), opened in 1896 and closed in March 1921 after attempting to survive Prohibition. This postcard is part of a souvenir booklet ca. 1910. AUTHOR'S COLLECTION.

146 THE DRINK THAT MADE WISCONSIN FAMOUS

A Much Advertised Article

In order to keep pace with the competition, the brewers needed to search ever farther afield for markets. Pabst and Schlitz in particular saw the world as their market, and the Schlitz logo featuring Atlas holding up the globe was no coincidence. The great Milwaukee breweries left no stone unturned in the search to find a way to get their names before the public and their beers in the glass.

The most impressive way to attract customers was to welcome visitors to the brewery. It seemed that every individual or group traveling to the Cream City made "the customary visit to a brewery," whether as humble as the aldermen of Grand Rapids, Michigan, or as exalted as the delegates of the Pan-American Congress of 1889—who not only toured Pabst but were also driven past Schlitz and Blatz and stayed at the Schlitz Hotel.[76] In 1893 the number of guests at Best averaged between three hundred and five hundred each day, and the three full-time guides employed were often not enough to handle the throngs. Visitors to the brewery would be shown around the facilities, sometimes by a designated guide (Best had a well-known "one-armed" guide in the late 1880s), sometimes by one of the officers of the company. Guests were able to see all the functions from brewing to bottling and to gaze in wonder at decorative touches such as the eight-by-nine-foot stained glass window in the Pabst brewhouse depicting King Gambrinus.[77] Of course, a highlight of the tour was the ability to sample the freshest beer available, and in 1887 visitors to Milwaukee breweries enjoyed more than one thousand barrels of beer.[78] The most famous brewery guest of the Gilded Age was President Grover Cleveland, who toured Best while in town for the Milwaukee Industrial Exposition in 1887. After visiting Schlitz Park, the president and his party were escorted through the brewery by Pabst himself. At the end of the tour,

Captain Pabst inquired whether Mr. Cleveland would take a glass of beer. "With pleasure," was the response, and but a moment elapsed before the chief magistrate of the greatest republic on earth, held in his hand a glass filled with the foaming beverage that has done much toward making Milwaukee famous, "fresh from the wood."[79]

A newspaper in Janesville, home to several prominent prohibitionists, lamented that "President Cleveland, after being taken to a brewery by a republican mayor of Milwaukee, saw fit to drink a glass of beer. This terrible crime should be laid up against the president as altogether too heinous to be forgiven."[80]

As breweries expanded their markets, however, they needed to be able to offer their saloon customers more gadgets, artwork, and even furniture to keep the proprietors from trying a different brand of beer. Likewise, for households that could choose between multiple brands of local and imported bottled beer, the gift of a calendar, set of glasses, or bottle opener could be an attractive inducement. The amazing variety of advertising pieces seen on these pages and in the many extensive public and private collections testifies to the efforts made by brewers to place their names on customers' walls or in their pockets.

While brewers began their advertising with little general publicity, occasional newspaper articles about promotional items began to appear in the late 1870s. It is noteworthy that Best kept no general ledger detailing advertising expenses until 1878.[81] The *Daily Sentinel* noted that Blatz had published a book with a view of the city and its brewery in 1879.[82] Holiday greeting items were popular, and the Best trifold card celebrating the company's recovery from the 1879 fire was an early example of the genre (see chapter 4). By the 1890s picture postcards gained popularity—with the added advantage that the sender helped the brewery reach even more potential customers. By 1884 Best was spending about $11,000 a year on "signs, show cards, etc.," an amount that would climb to nearly $50,000 just seven years later.[83]

Some items were clearly intended for saloon or other retailer use. A two-by-three-foot lithograph of the brewery complex was unlikely to adorn the wall of a Victorian home, yet would be a perfect device for the wall of a high-class saloon. On the other hand, a souvenir spoon issued by Pabst in 1891 would have done little to advertise the brand in a saloon setting, but could be an attractive ornament to a family's china cabinet. Many of the small engraved glasses were evidently designed for household use since they would never have stood up to rough saloon use, and these glasses are conspicuously absent from the thousands of surviving saloon photographs.[84]

Like modern advertisers, breweries were apt to draw on important events for advertising material as well as the artistic styles of the day. After Benjamin Harrison won the presidential election of 1888,

> Gen. Harrison received a present yesterday that is not likely to be placed among his collection of gifts. It was an advertising sign from a Milwaukee brewery, giving in bright colors a view of Gen. Harrison and Grover Cleveland sitting at a table drinking overflowing glasses of beer served to them by a female in scant dress, with an outline of the White house in the background. It was sent to the president-elect by express by the audacious advertisers.[85]

The surprisingly quick and decisive victory in the Spanish-American War was celebrated by brewers along with most other Americans. Pabst issued its "Popular Men and a Popular Beverage" print, and both Pabst and Schlitz trumpeted the claim that their beer was the one preferred by American troops in the Caribbean and in the Philippines. Blatz joined in by noting in a small promotional pamphlet, "Complaints against the quality of Blatz are as scarce as Spanish victories in the Yankee-Spankee war."[86]

While women were not welcomed in many saloon settings, they were often present in artistic forms. (More information about women and saloons is found in chapter 6.) The first instance of brewers using advertisements depicting an attractive female to sell beer cannot be determined with certainty, but such images were commonplace by the 1880s. One example, noteworthy because it depicted a real woman, was the offer

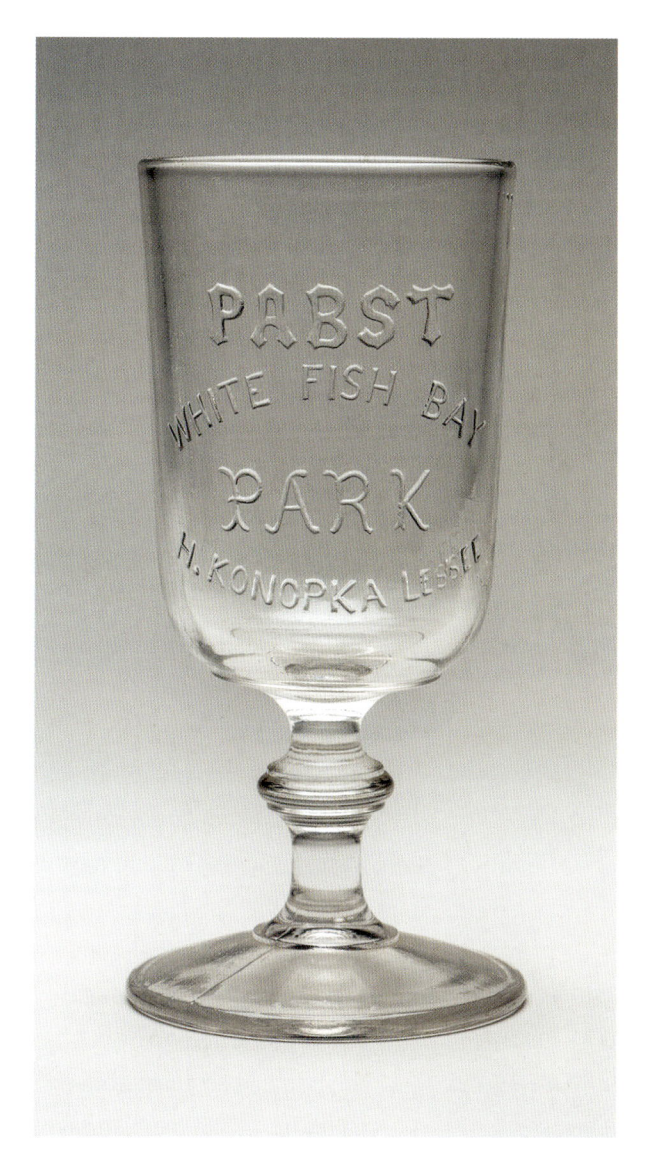

To emphasize the opulence of their establishments, the major brewers designed special glassware. Henry Konopka, a Russian immigrant, managed the Whitefish Bay Resort for Pabst Brewing from 1894 to 1904. Konopka installed a ten-car Ferris wheel in 1895 and for a brief period presented movies on an outdoor screen. COLLECTION OF JOHN STEINER.

The embossing on the shoulder of this bottle indicates that it was from Pabst's Boston agency. The tradition of depicting goats on bock labels has continued to the present (ca. 1890). COLLECTION OF TYE SCHWALBE.

MILWAUKEE 149

The "Popular Men and a Popular Beverage" posters were shipped to Pabst agents all over the world. Their China agents, Mustard & Co., advertised in the English-language Shanghai Mercury that they had received copies of the poster. While the officers are not labeled on the poster, they appear to be (back row) Commodore Winfield Scott Schley, Major General John Rutter Brooke, Major General Fitzhugh Lee; (front row) Major General Wesley Merritt, Major General Nelson Miles, Rear Admiral William T. Sampson, Commodore George Dewey.
COLLECTION OF RICHARD YAHR.

by Best of a nineteen-by-twenty-five-inch poster of First Lady Frances Folsom Cleveland, the young bride (twenty-one at the time of her marriage to President Grover Cleveland), in exchange for twelve coupons found on bottles of Best Tonic. Women were depicted either as the ideal female type of the era, the Gibson Girl, for example, or as exotic foreigners, such as members of a harem. Breweries generally avoided more explicit depictions, since women were becoming more important as customers, though a few prints included artistic nudes, usually mythical figures like "Die Lorelei."[87] (Examples of women in advertising can be found among the individual brewery histories in the second part of the book.)

One promotional item that could have been used either in the saloon or in the home was an attractive calendar. While most surviving examples are from the first decades of the twentieth century, as early as 1889 Blatz issued a calendar featuring "bearded hobgoblins" enjoying beer. Women also featured prominently on

150 THE DRINK THAT MADE WISCONSIN FAMOUS

The portrait of "Mrs. President Cleveland" was included on this small card advertising the much larger poster version. AUTHOR'S COLLECTION.

The small dish from Pabst's Harlem restaurant and the creamer from the Hotel Blatz in Milwaukee both date from around 1900. They indicate the degree to which breweries emphasized their brands in all their properties. COLLECTION OF JOHN STEINER.

calendars, but again, they were generally depicted as stylish rather than seductive.

There is little definite documentary evidence of brand loyalty among beer drinkers in the pre-Prohibition era, since formal market research did not yet exist, and the types of comments that would indicate strong preference for one beer over another are rare and not always reliable. The common preference for a local beer over outside brands would not have been as relevant in Milwaukee, where the national brands were brewed just down the street. Saloon patrons generally picked their watering hole for its location, the offerings in its free lunch, or the fellowship of like-minded patrons), rather than for the beer served.[88] The occasional accounts of preferences for Swabian beer or Munich beer found in the antebellum period were less important as Milwaukee's ethnic mix became more polyglot and as the beer itself became more homogeneous. Of course, employees of a particular brewery could be expected to drink the beer they made, but otherwise brand loyalty based on a particular image of who would drink a beer would be a characteristic of the mid-twentieth century. Given this, it is likely that signs on a tavern advertising the beer of a particular brewery were more an indication of quality and reliability rather than a beacon to those in search of a particular brand. (See the sidebar in chapter 3.)

MILWAUKEE   151

WHITE FISH BAY PARK of the PABST BREWING CO.

Pabst's vast Whitefish Bay resort was accessible by road, rail, and water. This illustration is from the G.A.R. souvenir booklet of 1889. AUTHOR'S COLLECTION.

While tied-house saloons retained their place as an essential outlet for brewery sales, the major brewers began to link their names and prestige to more elite establishments as well. Several breweries built or acquired hotels in the 1890s. Blatz took over the old Grand Central across from both city hall and the Pabst Theater in the 1890s and made the Hotel Blatz famous around the region for its annual game dinners.[89] Schlitz had not only a prominent Milwaukee establishment featuring the opulent Palm Garden but also other Midwest lodgings, including a hotel just west in Waukesha that opened in 1898, one in Winona, Minnesota, that opened in 1892, and yet another in Madison that was constructed in 1904.[90] Farther abroad, Schlitz purchased a hotel in Carlsbad (then called Eddy), New Mexico, at the same time it established a sugar beet factory in the area.[91] To the east there was a Schlitz Hotel on Staten Island, and another in Atlantic City, New Jersey. Sometimes the hotel proprietor was also the local agent for Schlitz beer, as was the case with Philip Kalkbrenner, who ran the chalet-styled Schlitz Hotel and rathskeller in Albany, New York, starting in 1897.[92] Pabst created the magnificent Whitefish Bay Resort, with its own hotel as well as an elegant pavilion and extensive garden.[93] Advertising through "famous places," as Cochran called it, not only drew attention to the Milwaukee brewers' brands but also did so in settings that associated them with high quality, fine dining, and a desirable lifestyle.[94]

Pabst moved into New York in force. According to a later account, Pabst "decided to show New York how beer should be drunk" despite the fact that New York produced even more beer than Milwaukee. The Captain (as the press delighted in calling him) established three spacious beer gardens: the Circle at 58th Street, the Harlem at 125th Street, and one in what was then called the Longacre Triangle but is today Times Square. The Harlem was at the time the largest restaurant in the country, with a seating capacity of fourteen hundred guests. Pabst sought to bring some of the Milwaukee style to Gotham by staffing the gardens "with Milwaukee experts at the tap," and backed up his investment with heavy advertising, pasting banners on curbs, walls, and wagons. Schlitz sought customers through "high class periodicals, including the widely circulated monthly magazines and famous weeklies like *Puck, Judge,* and others."[95] Ads for the Milwaukee shipping breweries could be found in newspapers all over the country and around the world.[96]

Despite the fierce competition, brewers sometimes worked together when it was in their mutual interest. One of the earliest recorded examples in Wisconsin of what could be called a "beer festival" was held in Milwaukee's Quentin's Park in September 1878 to raise funds to contribute to yellow fever relief in the southern states. (Quentin's Park later became Schlitz Park and then Lapham Park. In the twenty-first century, Carver Park occupies some of what was Quentin's Park.) The city proclaimed a holiday from work, and President Rutherford B. Hayes was in attendance. For this event, breweries contributed kegs in rough proportion to their size. Best and Schlitz donated twenty kegs each; Blatz, fifteen; Falk, ten; Miller, eight; Gettelman and Borchert, five each; and Obermann, four. In addition Liebscher and Meeske & Hoch each donated five cases of weiss beer, and the firms of Zwietusch, Werrbach, Wolf, and Graf & Madlener each contributed soda water.[97]

Brewers also cooperated in financial matters. In 1868 Jacob Obermann and Joseph Schlitz helped found Brewers' Protective Insurance Company of the West, which in 1871 became Brewers' Fire Insurance Company. While the company remained in existence until 1880, it does not seem to have conducted much business after the death of Joseph Schlitz in 1875, and the defunct company's records eventually went up in smoke during a fire at the Second Ward Savings Bank.[98] This bank was

The Pabst Loop Hotel at Coney Island was destroyed by a fire in July 1908 that threatened Luna Park and other nearby attractions. This picture shows the hotel in the late 1890s. The name came from the loop that the Brooklyn Rapid Transit tracks made around the building to head back to Brooklyn. COLLECTION OF JOHN STEINER.

also a cooperative project of the brewers, popularly known as the "Brewers' Bank," and grew to be one of the largest and most stable banks in the region. It was one of the few Milwaukee banks to survive the Panic of 1893, largely because president and principal stockholder August Uihlein of Schlitz personally guaranteed the approximately $9 million in deposits. In 1965 the building was donated to the Milwaukee County Historical Society, and it now serves as the society's headquarters and museum.[99] Milwaukee brewers also occasionally cooperated on production matters. In the 1890s Schlitz and Pabst jointly owned forty-two thousand acres of oak timber land along the Tallahatchie River in Mississippi. August Uihlein boasted that "all the Milwaukee breweries could not use it up in staves in 150 years."[100]

Cooperation on matters of mutual interest seldom extended to retail sales, since brewers continued to seek exclusive sales arrangements. In 1895 Pabst secured exclusive rights at the Wisconsin State Fair when beer returned to the fairgrounds for the first time in many years. The *Journal* noted with some irony that every county fair could sell beer, but until that year the state fair could not.[101] However, since it was hard to satisfy all beer drinkers with one brewery, some events ended up with multiple brewery sponsors. Both Pabst and Schlitz created commemorative booklets for the Knights of Pythias in 1890.[102] Pabst acquired nearly exclusive rights for sales at one of the most celebrated events of the nineteenth century—the World's Columbian Exposition of 1893. Visitors thirsty from riding the original Ferris wheel or other attractions on the original Midway could walk through the gleaming White City lit by the first significant use of alternating current electrical power to one of Pabst's eighty-seven beer stands. The contract was estimated to be worth $400,000 if fifty thousand barrels were sold, and "the counters over which it will be handed out will be more than two miles in length." But even here, Pabst had to share the limelight with a fellow Cream City firm. Miller got the contract to serve beer at the restaurant connected with the "captive balloon" exhibition on the fairgrounds. The balloon could carry twenty people at a time to an altitude of fifteen hundred feet—and as for the restaurant, "it is expected that two carloads of beer will be consumed in it daily."[103]

It was at the beer judging in 1893 in Chicago that one of the most famous disputes in American brewing history took place. Despite the pleas of the chair of the Committee on Awards to conduct a blind tasting and keep their scores secret, the individual judges decided to publish their scores and include twenty points for commercial importance, which meant that the tastings could not be blind. Scores started to leak out in the last week of October, and even though there was no official first prize, Adolphus Busch quickly claimed the honor for his company. However, a debate over tests administered by Harvey Wiley, chief chemist of the Department of Agriculture, resulted in the highest score being awarded to Pabst, and then Busch's claim that the tests were faulty gave points back to Budweiser. Newspaper reports could not agree on the reasons for the change: some reported that Pabst had been unfairly docked for the presence of salt, and Budweiser was said to have given a

A bottle made of bottles was the centerpiece of Phillip Best's exhibit at the Milwaukee Industrial Exposition of 1882. A display of the products of Otto Zwietusch is just visible at right rear of this stereoscopic view. COLLECTION OF JOHN STEINER.

Exhibitionists

THE GREAT FAIRS AND EXHIBITIONS OF THE LATE NINETEENTH AND EARLY TWENTIETH CENTURIES WERE opportunities for manufacturers of all kinds to show off their technology and quality in front of a worldwide audience. For breweries there were three major attractions: the opportunity to serve beer, the space to exhibit a lavish display, and the chance of winning one or more medals in a juried competition.

Even before major brewers got their own pavilions at fairs, they created elaborate exhibitions of bottled beer to demonstrate their technological capability and artistic skill. A few displays were preserved by photography, and a few more survive through written accounts. Blatz sent an exhibition to the 1885 World's Fair in New Orleans that featured a gigantic bottle pyramid and a "panorama in a [600 gallon] beer barrel."[1] The exhibitions at the 1893 Columbian Exposition were particularly lavish. Schlitz's $20,000 creation

---
1   *Milwaukee Sentinel,* 11 December 1884, 3.

was "a pavilion formed by two immense beer tuns" surrounded by four figures holding up an enormous version of the Schlitz globe trademark. The four figures in the corners symbolized that "Schlitz beer is being drunk in all parts of the world." The pavilion took advantage of the electrical theme of the fair as well: "The belt [of the globe] will be composed of glass jewels through which electric lights will shine and produce a brilliant effect." Among the souvenirs given out was a globe-shaped booklet "containing a dozen comic views to show the extent to which Schlitz beer is drunk." Not to be outdone, Pabst commissioned a thirteen-by-thirteen-foot model of the entire brewing plant done in solid gold (so the papers claimed; really it was gold-plated), estimated to cost $100,000. The model was housed in a lavish Beaux-Arts pavilion, which was brought north after the fair and attached to the Pabst family's new mansion on Grand Avenue (the modern-day West Wisconsin Avenue). The gold model made another appearance at the 1895 Milwaukee Industrial Exposition, this time housed in a replica of the original Phillip Best brewery, "with all of its quaint exterior appearance." Friezes on the interior walls of this structure depicted the entire history of brewing up to the emergence of Pabst; the cost of the exhibition was estimated at $100,000.[2]

The ornate pavilion that contained the Pabst exhibition at the Columbian Exposition now is attached to the Pabst Mansion. COURTESY OF CAPTAIN FREDERICK PABST MANSION, MILWAUKEE.

Some of the expenses of such exhibitions could be recouped through increased sales, especially if the brewery earned one or more medals for the quality of its beer. The elaborate advertisements of the period were decorated with detailed replicas of medals earned by the company at exhibitions, especially those of international events, which could be viewed as more prestigious. While flavor was usually a component of the judging, promoters interested in showing the advance of science based the majority of the score instead on chemical analysis and "purity" (though the judges at the World's Columbian Exposition included twenty out of one hundred points for "commercial importance," a trick that was alleged to give Pabst, Schlitz, and Anheuser-Busch an automatic twenty points). Expositions had no incentive to be overselective in awarding medals—the success of an event was largely dependent on the number of exhibitors, and breweries would

---

2   *Milwaukee Journal*, 1 April 1893, 2; *Milwaukee Sentinel*, 22 September 1895, 17; *Yenowine's Illustrated News*, 12 October 1895, n.p.; John C. Eastberg, *The Captain Frederick Pabst Mansion: An Illustrated History* (Milwaukee: Captain Frederick Pabst Mansion, 2009), 84–85.

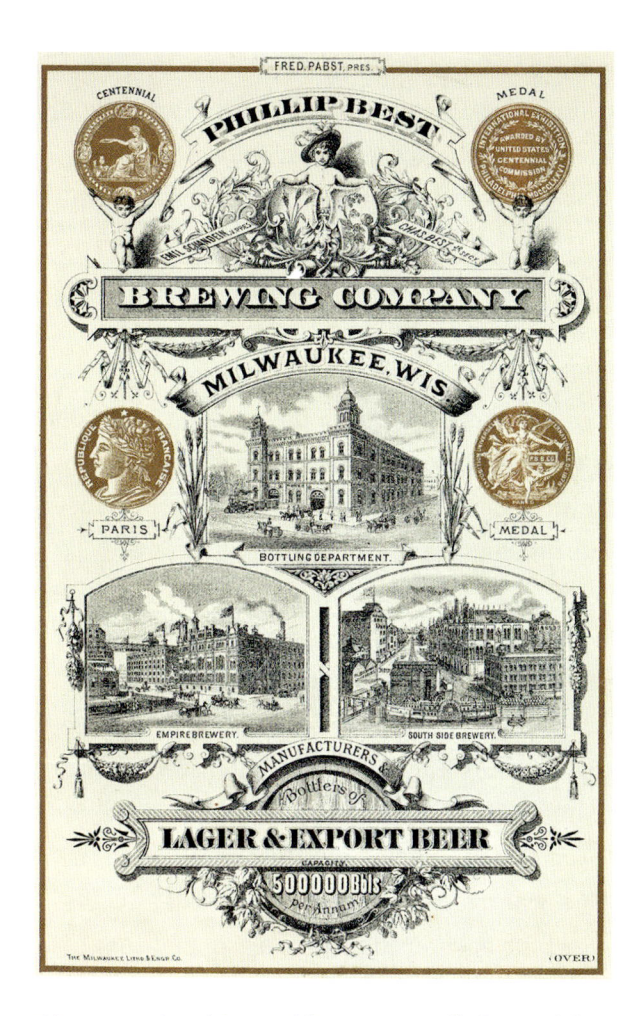

This ornate advertising card from 1881 proudly featured the medals earned at the recent Philadelphia (1876) and Paris (1878) expositions. COLLECTION OF TYE SCHWALBE.

John Gund Brewing Co. of La Crosse was awarded this medal at the Parisian Exposition Universelle in 1900. The medals were featured on a sign issued by the brewery shortly afterward. The medal on cans of Campbell's Soup is the same design and was earned at the same exposition. COLLECTION OF TYE SCHWALBE.

be more reluctant to incur the expense of creating and shipping an exhibit if there was little chance of a payoff. At the World's Columbian Exposition, every beer that earned more than 80 percent of the points earned a medal. (The story of the dispute between Pabst and Anheuser-Busch over the highest award is told in the main text.) The extent to which awards boosted sales is difficult to determine, especially since the 1876 Centennial Exposition in Philadelphia and the World's Columbian Exposition occurred during significant economic depressions. The awards may have meant more to smaller breweries, which could claim their beers were equal in quality to the most famous brands in the world.[3]

---

3   *Milwaukee Sentinel*, 28 October 1893, 1; Thomas Cochran, *The Pabst Brewing Company: The History of an American Business* (New York: New York University Press, 1948), 136–38; Maureen Ogle, *Ambitious Brew: The Story of American Beer* (Orlando, Fla.: Harcourt, 2006), 127–28.

MILWAUKEE   157

false positive result for salicylic acid. Politics were undoubtedly part of the cause for the swings, since four of the judges had ties with one side or the other. Busch pursued the fifth judge throughout Europe attempting to persuade him to change his score, and although he did so, the fair's executive committee had decided to stand by the scores, which made Pabst the winner.[104]

Ironies abounded in the whole affair. First, there was no official ranking—every beer scoring 80 percent or better was supposed to be awarded the same prize. While often represented as a battle between Blue Ribbon and Budweiser, some of the score claims were apparently based on an average of a brewery's entries, rather than the flagship beer. Furthermore, the only beverage to score a perfect 100 was Best Tonic, and Guinness Stout outscored the American lagers with a 98. Meanwhile, Schlitz declared itself the winner because its samples had the highest average on the purity score and made sure this claim reached the press. All brewers involved celebrated their largely illusory win in style. The employees at Pabst were given a holiday and each received a five-dollar gold piece. The "jubilant people of Milwaukee," perhaps mindful of the rivalry with St. Louis, planned a torchlight procession to honor the two breweries, followed by "a general jubilee at the two places," where it must be assumed that beer played a part. Pabst decorated the brewery with blue ribbons and particularly celebrated the Best Tonic's top overall score. The final irony is that while Pabst has implicitly linked the Blue Ribbon brand to this Columbian Exposition triumph, the company was tying blue ribbons around their bottles of Select beer as early as 1882, and by 1892 they were buying three hundred thousand yards of silk ribbon annually. So while the device turned into a brilliant marketing scheme, there was really no connection between the ribbon and the 1893 prize.[105]

Protecting the fame of Milwaukee beer sometimes required taking action against breweries other than the archrivals from New York or St. Louis. At least two smaller brewers, the Schroeder Brewing Company of Perham, Minnesota, and Stevens Point Brewing, adopted a rhomboid label with graphics that did not copy but certainly resembled the layout of a Schlitz label—Schroeder in particular. It was an advertising slogan on each label that caused the problems, however. In the case of Schroeder, the beer was billed as "The Beer That Makes Milwaukee Jealous" and Stevens Point promoted Pink's Crystal as "The Beer That Makes Milwaukee Furious"—both obvious references to "The Beer that Made Milwaukee Famous." Schlitz sued both and forced them to discontinue use of the labels. Milwaukee lawyer Theodore Kronshage, a specialist in trademark law, was retained by Schlitz, Pabst, and the Milwaukee Brewers' Association to litigate these and similar issues, and he was responsible for stopping all other brewers from using the term *Milwaukee* on any beer not produced in the city.[106]

Free from Poisons

Claims that adulterated beer was being produced either by particular breweries or by the industry in general posed even more danger to Milwaukee's reputation. It was seldom clear whether such claims were launched by prohibitionists, rival

The label that made Milwaukee litigate—Pink's Crystal (ca. 1905). COLLECTION OF JOHN STEINER.

brewers, disgruntled workers, or journalists in search of a sensational story. One that was most likely advanced by rival brewers was a story in 1874 published in New York newspapers claiming that Milwaukee brewers were using water from a tainted city well.[107] In January 1879 the *Milwaukee Daily News* published an extensive article producing evidence that several of the large shipping breweries were using rice and corn in their beer, which was indeed true.[108] Best's brewmaster Philipp Jung had been experimenting with rice since 1874, and brewmasters throughout the country were using different ratios of rice or corn to produce a lighter-bodied and lighter-colored beer.[109] Brewers claimed that this trend was responding to public tastes. Val Blatz further claimed that rice "costs more and cannot be said to be an adulteration."[110] The 1879 report argued, however, that "the amount of corn and rice which is used is dictated solely by the price of the barley market," and would be consistent with Martin Stack's claims that breweries took specific action to develop consumer preferences for products that were less expensive to make.[111] The *Daily News* reporter conflated cheaper with dangerous: "It will be observed that only one of the Brewing companies represented compounds its beer without the aid of deleterious compounds, that of Mr. Franz Falk. The other three still continue to impose their nauseating and health destroying manufacture upon a long suffering public."

The investigator's conclusion was based on month-by-month reports of corn and rice usage and differences between Best and Blatz, which may indeed have resulted from changing market prices, but the brewmasters still may have been experimenting with the grain bill, and different amounts of lighter and fuller beers were made in particular months. The *Daily News* reporter concluded by advocating for a beer inspection law, but such a law was unlikely to have banned beers containing corn or rice, and customers seemed to be embracing the "degenerate" beer.[112]

As consistency and shelf life of bottled beer became more important, breweries experimented with using additives or fining particles that would absorb suspended yeast and other particles to

MILWAUKEE 159

prevent secondary fermentation. Nearly all of these components were filtered out of the final product and were (and are) not harmful to health, but the press continued to stoke public concern.

Allegations concerning adulterated beer continued through Prohibition. Gettelman became one of several American brewers to advertise a $1,000 reward for anyone who could find anything in the beer other than malt and hops. This was reminiscent of Val Blatz's far more macabre offering of a $1,000 reward in 1865:

To my greatest surprise I learn that it is rumored that a man had met with an accident by falling into a fermenting or mashing tub in my brewery. Hearing the report, at first I thought it not worth while to pay any attention to such an absurd or malicious production; but learning that certain persons are making capital of this rumor, which was at first considered a bad joke, I declare said rumor an absolute falsehood, and offer ONE THOUSAND DOLLARS to any person, my workmen

Not only did this label for Gettelman's Lager Beer announce the $1,000 reward for anyone who could find impurities in the beer, it also advised customers to drink the beer at "a moderate temperature" and "never on ice." COLLECTION OF TYE SCHWALBE.

included, who will prove that any person has met with any such accident in my establishment.[113]

GOVERNMENT RELATIONS

Milwaukee's brewers tried to maintain good relations with all government entities but also used their important place in the city as an employer and source of revenue to shape elections and policy. This seems to indicate that breweries (especially the largest ones) were not mere production entities that responded to price and demand signals, but were active in shaping the political, social, and economic environment for their product, and not necessarily to the benefit of the consumer.[114]

Perhaps the most obvious way in which the great brewers sought to influence politics was through encouraging bloc voting by their employees. As early as 1867, the *Semi-Weekly Wisconsin* claimed that Val Blatz had the power to determine an election. According to the losing Democrats, "Blatz, the brewery man, went back on them. He promised to have his men at the polls early, but he kept putting it off until it was time to close the polls." The "indignant" Democrats debated whether or not to boycott Blatz beer in protest (but the papers did not report the result of those deliberations).[115] The *Daily Republican Sentinel* blamed the 1882 Republican loss on the brewery vote, claiming that most of the twenty-four hundred brewery workers were Republicans but the owners found it in their interest to vote Democrat, so "the brewers, at the late election, marched their men to the polls in platoons and voted them solid for the Democratic ticket."

Implicit in the account was the common accusation of political reformers—that bosses controlled the votes of their employees with either financial rewards or threat of dismissal.[116] This assumption was faulty in at least one incident four years later when "the People's party appeared to have their own way in the Sixth ward. At noon the employes of Schlitz's brewery marched to the polls in a body and voted the Labor ticket almost without exception."[117] It is extremely unlikely after the strikes and violence of 1886 that the Uihleins would have encouraged their employees to vote for a party with a distinct socialist slant. While newspaper accounts of similar bloc voting do not exist for later years, given the intensity of political organization in Milwaukee, it is likely that bloc voting by workers continued whether it was directed by the proprietors or not.

Another facet of the standard interpretation of political corruption in the Gilded Age is the influence of "ward bosses" in delivering the vote for the candidate who best obtains their loyalty. This practice was also present in Milwaukee; brewery officials were involved, as well as the ubiquitous saloonkeepers. While specific examples of brewery money taking this path to candidates are understandably absent from the records, political reformers and prohibitionists continued to make this link into the twentieth century (see the next chapter).

Although most brewery interactions with government were on the local or state level, the federal excise tax brought brewers into regular contact with the agents of Washington, and occasionally the brewers sought changes in federal law. The most important of these was the 1890 law that Pabst pushed to allow bottling to be done directly from designated tanks rather than from kegs. Pabst enlisted the help of Wisconsin's U.S. senators Philetus Sawyer and John C. Spooner and Third District congressman Robert M. La Follette Sr. to guide the bill through Congress. Since Pabst employees had developed a new pipeline and bottling system with a gauge that would guarantee accurate readings, the government agreed to the new rule over the objections of revenue officials who were reluctant to adopt any change. The new procedure still required a revenue official to be present while beer was running through the pipeline to the tanks in the bottling house, but it not only saved time and effort (and cooperage) but also protected the beer from temperature changes and exposure to the air.[118]

The constant expansion of the Cream City's breweries made brewers regular applicants for building permits and other requests of municipal government, a practice that literally transformed the city. Extending the railroad network had the potential to make brewery operations more efficient and profitable, but also to alter traffic patterns and complicate life for others. The "Beer Line," a six-mile stretch of the Chicago, Milwaukee and St. Paul Railway, served several brewers, including Pabst and Schlitz, and was one of the most congested rail lines in the state. In December 1890 the *Sentinel* reported a proposal by Pabst for a seven-block-long electric railway to link the brewery with the "Beer Line" at Third Street. The reaction of the paper to this scheme offers a hint of how brewing was perceived by the public: "The vast brewery is closely identified with the progress of the city, and any objections to this necessary improvement of the great plant, it is thought, will be overcome."[119] Interestingly enough, the rail link seemed at first to have been a newspaper creation, since the *Journal* published a report later the same day in which Pabst denied any such project existed.[120] Nonetheless, the next month Pabst obtained an estimate for building the electrified line, though the project never came to pass.[121] Pabst considered several other rail extensions over the next decades, but none were completed.[122] Getting the product from the brewery to the depot continued to be a problem for companies other than Pabst. Gettelman had to send five wagons of beer a day to the depot, which also required "a load of Ice in the summer time and one good load of hot manure in the Winter" to maintain the proper temperature.[123]

A critical part of running a profitable business is keeping costs down, and when those costs were from use of city services the brewers found themselves again in the political arena. Brewing is very water intensive, both in making the beer and in cleaning and disposing of waste products. Milwaukee had an advanced municipal water facility, but increasing fees for city water in 1879 drove Best to dig a new well at least in part to avoid these fees.[124] Later that year, the city health commissioner requested several brewers to appear before a meeting and answer questions about river pollution. Emil Schandein of Best reassured the commissioner that no chemicals were discharged into the river, only barrel, tub, and floor washings (which could also change the chemistry of the river, but this was less well understood at the time).[125] River pollution continued to be an issue in Milwaukee, though to be fair to brewers, manufacturing plants, mills, and tanneries also contributed to the problem. In 1891 pollution of the Menomonee River resulted in all three of the Wauwatosa-area brewers—Miller, Gettelman, and Falk, Jung & Borchert—being investigated and asked to clean up their operations.[126] By 1894 Gettelman remained one of the few businesses on the river that had not yet installed a sewage plant.[127] On the other hand, the always-innovative Gettelmans were among the early adopters of the low-smoke Orvis Steel Arch Furnace, which was touted as a "smoke consumer."[128]

Smoke and soot were a constant irritant in industrial cities, but the belching chimneys were also recognized and lauded as symbols of industrial development and economic progress. In an article headlined "Abate Smoke Nuisance," the writer lamented, "In all the city there is but one respectable chimney. That is the one that rises 100 feet over the plant which furnishes light to the Pabst brewery."[129] The writer was apparently referring to the recently completed 225-foot chimney to evacuate the smoke from twenty-four boilers of twenty-four hundred horsepower each.[130] Citation of such numbers was common as cities and their journalists sought to inspire civic pride and to attract still more businesses. An article titled "Spires of Milwaukee" listed the Pabst smokestack along with the peaks of city hall and several churches as the most notable features of the Milwaukee skyline.[131] When these authors or a visiting journalist from New England referred to "the belching chimneys of still another brewery," it was high praise for the industrious nature of the city rather than a complaint about the atmosphere.[132]

The prosperity of the brewers and their businesses was tolerated and even celebrated because of the jobs, revenue, and celebrity they brought to Milwaukee, but also the brewers were generally what would later be called good corporate citizens. The same New England writer who admired the "belching chimneys" also noted, "When contributions are needed for any object under the sun in Milwaukee, the brewers are first applied to."[133] The most noteworthy of these civic causes was the Twenty-Third National Encampment of the Grand Army of the Republic, hosted by Milwaukee in late August 1889. This annual gathering of veterans of the Union Army was a grand affair, and Milwaukee was not to be outdone by other cities. The hosts planned a mock naval battle on the lake and a grand fireworks exhibition (along with the obligatory brewery tours), and Pabst pitched in with the necessary $12,000 himself, on the condition that members of the Grand Army of the Republic and their families were seated first. Grateful veterans paraded past the brewery and were reported to have demanded Pabst beer at saloons of competitors and walked out if it was not available.[134] Throughout the era, breweries erected ceremonial arches, participated in parades, donated to charitable causes, and generally did their best to make Milwaukee a festive city.

However, occasionally the civic-mindedness of the brewers was alleged to conflict with their desire to profit from the gemütlichkeit of the city. In 1890

Milwaukee mayor George W. Peck announced plans to expand the park system and to build pavilions in city parks for a series of concerts.[135] During the planning stages a Chicago newspaper published the claim that brewers were aiming to defeat the public park plan in order to preserve their own private beer gardens.[136] Political rivals may have made the accusations, but during this period throughout the country brewery-owned beer gardens declined in popularity and city parks grew more important.

THE BEER BARONS

The result of all this technological advancement and advertising ingenuity was spectacular growth and expansion for the brands and great wealth for the proprietors. In 1867 the Cream City breweries combined produced eighty-three thousand barrels of beer—in 1893 Pabst alone produced that much in an average month.[137] The fame of Milwaukee beer had been spreading worldwide since the 1870s; an 1877 publication claimed that orders for the city's lager had been received from Australia and "other Pacific islands."[138] The promotional materials

Pabst Brewing Co. issued a thirty-two-page souvenir booklet to honor the G.A.R. encampment in 1889 in Milwaukee. The booklet included proclamations from politicians, information about the G.A.R., an artist's conception of the mock naval battle, and promotions for the Pabst brewery and its beers. AUTHOR'S COLLECTION.

and favorable articles in the press touted each brewery's distant markets as proof of quality and sound business management. Falk's shipments as of 1885 included about twenty thousand barrels of bottled beer delivered to Mexico, the Sandwich Islands (Hawai'i), and Central America.[139] In 1889 Pabst's bottled beer was "sent direct to Central and South America, to the Australian Colonies, to the East Indies, to Chili [sic], Japan and the far north colonies."[140] A *Milwaukee Sentinel* article in 1890 proclaimed that reports from American consuls abroad showed Milwaukee beer was popular in Mexico and Brazil. "At Trinidad, the only American beer known is from Milwaukee."[141] Cuba generally preferred Milwaukee beer, but it sold at a premium compared to English ales, which were considered inferior to Milwaukee lager but kept longer without ice. The article concluded in a patriotic vein that Milwaukee beer was selling much better at these locations than St. Louis beer.[142]

The wealth of the Milwaukee beer barons was often converted into opulent mansions. The Pabst family moved in 1892 from a three-story Italianate residence on Chestnut Street, near the brewery they had built in 1877, to a stunning mansion on Grand (now Wisconsin).[143] So many members of Schlitz's Uihlein family built mansions in the neighborhood north and west of the brewery that the area became known as Uihlein Hill.[144] Val Blatz, Fred Miller, and others built homes suitable for their station in society.

The letterhead for Schlitz Park in the 1890s proudly proclaimed its accommodations for twenty thousand guests at a time. Amenities included four bowling alleys, concerts during the summer, and, of course, opportunities to enjoy Schlitz beer at the restaurant or bar. COLLECTION OF JOHN STEINER.

Despite intermittent labor discontent, brewery workers occasionally gave celebrations for the beer barons more reminiscent of German royalty rather than republican businessmen. When August Uihlein returned from a lengthy vacation in October 1890, he was feted with a torchlight parade of employees.[145] Captain Pabst's return from an eleven-month voyage to Europe and the Holy Land was similarly celebrated in the community and the press.[146]

Even though the giant international brewers were what most people thought of when Milwaukee beer was mentioned, the Cream City was still able to support several smaller breweries. Cream City Brewing Company, A. Gettelman, and J. Obermann (which in 1896 became Philip Jung Brewing Company) all remained from the mid-1850s and were still popular and profitable.

More significantly, there were a number of new firms that tried to capitalize on the thirst of residents and the fame of the local product—some were successful, some never got beyond the planning stages. The Milwaukee Brewing Company was founded in 1893 and survived the financial crisis of that year and stayed in business until Prohibition. Milwaukee Brewing was noteworthy because it was founded in part by Polish American investors—the company bylaws were printed in English, German, and Polish. The Independent Milwaukee Brewery, famous for its Braumeister brand, was founded in 1901 and continued in business until 1963. A few weiss beer breweries also opened during the last decades before Prohibition, and other companies filed articles of incorporation, selected sites, and appeared in the city directories for a year or two. Some of these, including Mutual Brewing Company

The profits brought in by his brewery allowed Frederick Pabst and his family to live in luxury. The Pabst residence at the modern-day 2000 West Wisconsin Street featured elaborate interior and exterior designs. The Pabst pavilion from the 1893 Columbian Exposition was brought to Milwaukee after the fair closed and used as a conservatory for the mansion. COURTESY OF CAPTAIN FREDERICK PABST MANSION, MILWAUKEE.

A few new breweries managed to gain a toehold in Milwaukee's crowded beer market and carve out a profitable business. The Independent Milwaukee Brewery began operation in 1901. This photograph depicts revelers at the opening festivities. COLLECTION OF JOHN STEINER.

and the Home Brewery, never went into production. However, the confidence necessary even to plan a new brewery in Milwaukee testifies both to the American entrepreneurial spirit and to the possibilities of the Queen City of Lager. (More on these individual businesses is found in the second part of the book.)

There were clouds on the horizon for Milwaukee's beer barons, however. As the leaders of the industry, they felt more keenly any effect on beer caused by economic downturns, and the increased efficiencies and more affordable equipment they pioneered allowed smaller regional breweries to compete with their trade in bottled beer, which was no longer an exotic imported item.[147] Financial panics sapped consumers' buying power, and premium-priced national brands often suffered as a result. Increasing taxes threatened profit margins, even if not necessarily brewery survival as their owners predicted. A proposed federal tax increase led one member of the Milwaukee Brewers' Association (not to be confused with the brewery of that name) to predict the bankruptcy of every brewery in Milwaukee.[148]

But the most significant danger to brewers was from rising concern about the evils of the saloon and the power of the men who made the beer for them. The prominence of Milwaukee companies would make them among the most visible targets of the reformers who sought to abolish their business.

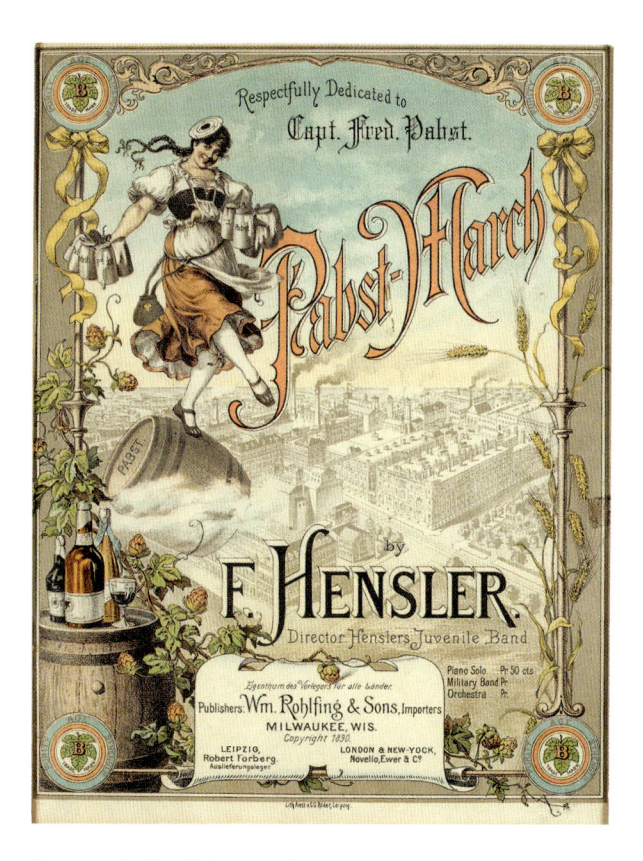

The popularity of the great brewers was sometimes celebrated in music. The "Pabst-March," published in 1890, could be purchased in arrangements for orchestra, military band, and solo piano. COLLECTION OF JOHN STEINER.

Look closer! It's actually Miller's Prohibition-era near beer product. This stunning tin-over-cardboard sign advertised "A pure tonic beverage" made by Miller High Life Co. rather than Miller Brewing Co. The well-known Girl in the Moon advertising figure brought only minimal success to the product. COLLECTION OF DAVID WENDL.

CHAPTER 6

OASIS
IN THE
DRY YEARS

1840–1932

The question is: Shall the many have food, especially our own soldier boys who are laying their lives and all upon their countries altar, or shall the few have drink? . . . During 1916 brewers used 3,556,103,596 pounds of foodstuffs. . . . This the nation cannot afford to lose by drink at this time, and its destruction and waste is traitorous. . . . All the grain used to feed horses and mules used in the liquor industry would be released for legitimate use on farm and factory production of war necessities. The 62,790 workmen now employed in making beer and whiskey will be released for needed trench, farm and factory work. Every brewery wagon, horse, harness, automobile, refrigerator car and train can be used to transfer food, fuel and munitions of war to their required destination.

J. L. Seder, Anti-Saloon League,
Stevens Point Journal, 29 December 1917

SINCE THE TIME OF WISCONSIN'S FOUNDING, INDIVIDUALS AND GOVERNMENTS tried to limit drinking and the alcohol trade. While Wisconsin became known worldwide for its beer, its temperance advocates attained nearly equal fame. Alcohol pitted ethnic groups against each other for social influence, a fact magnified by the diversity of Wisconsin's settlers. Temperance (the moderate, controlled use of alcohol) and prohibition (banning the manufacture and sale of alcohol) determined political behavior and were the subjects of more speeches, articles, meetings, dramas, and songs than perhaps any other crusade of Wisconsin's first century. Milwaukee's beer barons were held up as the epitome of evil, especially when anti-German sentiment flared during the Great War. Wisconsin adopted prohibition because of internal pressures as much as from external demands. Wisconsin's diversity and tradition, however, made prohibition impossible to enforce.[1]

The Growth of Temperance Ideals

Despite the modern connotations of the term *puritan*, ale was an indispensable part of the diet of the earliest English settlers. From early settlement well into the nineteenth century, supplies of fresh water were unreliable, and any drink boiled in the making was quite simply safer and more healthful. Ale and cider were common products of household manufacture in the colonies, and molasses and its distillate, rum, were among the most common imports to the colonies. Corn, rye, and other grain crops grew in importance as the settlers moved west, so the various members of the whiskey family became increasingly popular. As a side business, making whiskey was a lucrative way to use up excess farm production and to make some additional money. Distilled spirits had advantages over ale in addition to potency (if that is an advantage): they were less perishable and often improved with age. Transporting a barrel of whiskey to market rather than a barrel of ale would bring greater profits, and the whiskey would last longer at the saloon.

In the colonial period, the main target of reformers was drunkenness. While drinking alcohol was a part of everyday life for many, drunkenness was harshly punished by civil means such as fines, a term in the stocks, or social exclusion. In

Massachusetts, a scarlet *D* served to mark habitual drunkards and separate them from civil society. Ale was seldom mentioned as a cause of drunkenness—rather, it was advocated as an alternative to hard liquor. James Oglethorpe banned spirits from his new colony of Georgia in the 1730s but encouraged the use of sound English ale. This fit with the English belief (displayed in the famous engravings by Hogarth) that ale led to prosperity while liquor (specifically gin in Hogarth's depictions) would ruin civilization.

The foundation of the modern temperance movement was laid in the years following the Revolution. Among the educated elites, the general spirit of the time emphasized civic virtue and a sense of collective order and stability. This idea of republicanism saw liberty as something resting more in the ordered community rather than in the individual. The drunkenness of the disorderly rabble in the tavern was at least as much of a threat to civic virtue as it was a danger to bystanders. The single work that best set the tone for temperance reformers was *An Inquiry into the Effects of Ardent Spirits on the Human Mind and Body,* published in 1784 by Benjamin Rush. Rush was one of the heroes of the Revolutionary period—a signer of the Declaration of Independence, surgeon general to the Continental Army, and a famous politician and doctor—and therefore commanded attention. Rush's *Inquiry* was probably the first American work to treat drunkenness as a disease and to examine the effects of liquor on health. Rush believed that sound beer and wine had potential health benefits if consumed in limited quantities. He was among the first prominent Americans to call for a coordinated program of laws and treatment facilities to remedy drunkenness.

Rush was a politician and a physician; most of the early leaders of the temperance movement

Few breweries went as far as Kurth to market a product to temperance advocates. The inclusion of "directions" for use indicate this brew was being marketed as a tonic. Suggesting users consume "a glass full 3 times a day before or with meals" would encourage volume consumption if these guidelines were followed (label ca. 1900). COLLECTION OF JOHN STEINER.

were religious figures. Many Protestant denominations—Quakers, Methodists, Presbyterians, and some Baptists in particular—made sobriety an essential facet of the Godly life and viewed drunkenness as a sin for which conversion was the best solution. The first national temperance organization, the American Society for the Promotion of Temperance, founded in 1826, was largely an extension of religious leaders already active in pursuing this cause. The American Temperance Society (as it was usually called) proposed abstaining from ardent spirits and held that use of nondistilled beverages would help prevent many of the evils associated with hard drink. During the 1830s, however, many organizations and societies shifted their focus from temperance to total abstinence. Because many of the pioneering ministers and teachers in Wisconsin came from this Protestant tradition, they were able to ensure a solid following for temperance among the educated classes of the state.

Wisconsin lands were ripe for settlement when the huge migrations of the Irish and Germans arrived in America in the late 1840s. These settlers had strong traditions of social drinking in their home countries. Irish immigrants sometimes resorted to drinking as a defense mechanism against a new society that was frequently hostile to them and in which they often struggled to succeed. The fact that many of these new immigrants were Catholic was a major cause of concern for the established Protestant elite, and the drinking habits of the newcomers only magnified the threat posed to the carefully structured republican order.[2] While the peak period of anti-Irish violence in the 1840s primarily affected eastern states, some migrants to Wisconsin brought the stereotype of the drunken Irishman with them. The Know-Nothing Party and its nativist adherents were present in Wisconsin, but not as much as to the East.[3] Because many Catholic parishes were organized along lines of nationality rather than geography, this made both the Celtic Irish and the Teutonic Germans appear unwilling to assimilate and adopt the American Protestant republican social order. Some observers, however, made a distinction between the drinking of whiskey by the Irish and beer by the Germans and "characterized the latter as not half so bad as the former."[4]

Targeting Beer

For some temperance advocates, beer was a source of concern from the beginning. A Methodist report in 1832 worried that beer was being offered as a safe alternative and questioned whether "a man can indulge . . . at all and be considered temperate."[5] Ironically, the fact that lager beer invigorated America's limited brewing industry increased the attention temperance advocates paid to beer. Social reformers used the high-volume public consumption by the new immigrants as evidence of un-American behavior, and the reformers' position began slowly to displace the idea that ale or lager used in moderation was healthful. For many workers in the industrial and service sectors, and to some degree in agriculture, Sunday was the only day of rest each week. The spread of beer gardens across the state brought Germans, who viewed their day off as cause for celebration with song and drink, into conflict with many Protestants, who considered the Sabbath to be a day of sober worship. While antipathy to hard liquor was always present in the temperance movement, the increasing importance of lager beer and its German brewers, many of whom continued to conduct their business in the German language into the twentieth century, made beer a target in the eyes of reformers eager to form society according to their vision.

One group of women in Baraboo anticipated Carry Nation's demolition tactics by nearly half a century. In May 1854, fifty or sixty women marched from a hotel to a grocery to a saloon, destroying liquor and assaulting the owner of the saloon, who was known as French Pete. Six of the ringleaders were sued for damages, and were fined thirty dollars each.[6] Despite occasional flare-ups like this, there was little in the way of sustained protest by women until the 1870s.

Taking the Pledge

The early decades of large-scale European settlement in Wisconsin coincided with the emergence of the first significant fraternal organizations focused on temperance. The Washingtonians were founded in 1840 by six "drunkards" in Baltimore who sought to achieve abstinence and persuade others to follow their path. While they officially claimed no political or evangelical goals, some of the members went beyond moral suasion into fiery preaching and political advocacy.[7] The Sons of Temperance were founded in New York in 1842, and two years later formed a national organization.[8] The

Members of the Band of Hope took the "Triple Pledge": no alcohol, no tobacco, and no swearing. There were twenty reasons to pledge, several of which had little basis in science, such as number 17: "The use of tobacco leads to an appetite for drink."
COURTESY OF WISCONSIN HISTORICAL SOCIETY.

OASIS IN THE DRY YEARS   173

The Independent Order of Good Templars issued "traveling cards" to members for identification at other lodges. This one belonged to U. P. Olin of Waukesha and was issued in February 1858. COURTESY OF WISCONSIN HISTORICAL SOCIETY.

Independent Order of Good Templars (IOGT) arose somewhat later, in 1852, also in New York. These organizations adopted many of the trappings of secret societies such as lodges and rituals in order to build a sense of unity and support for those struggling with "King Alcohol."

Wisconsin settlers established local branches of national societies early on, especially in the centers of New England Yankee settlement. The "Friends of Temperance" were meeting in Janesville as early as 1839.[9] Sons of Temperance lodges began to appear in southern Wisconsin in the late 1840s. The Good Templar lodges arrived about a decade later, mostly in the late 1850s.[10] Wisconsinites started an order of their own in 1872—the Ancient Order of the Mendotas, founded on the shores of Lake Mendota.[11] Societies named after Saint Joseph and Saint Jerome provided similar refuges for Catholics in need of support in their struggles against drink. Frontier settlements often depended on traveling lecturers: Clinton, in Rock County, hosted its first temperance lecture in 1845, but had no lodge of any organization until 1863.[12] While some of the nineteenth-century histories may have overstated their influence, it is clear that thousands of Wisconsinites were at one time members of one of these societies.

Temperance societies often established libraries and sponsored social events for the edification of their communities. The Columbus IOGT organized a sleigh ride to Beaver Dam, and dances and concerts were common around the state. The Templars also had uniforms they wore to important events. An invitation to the 1895 Easter service in Ashland summoned members to "appear at the Asylum (meeting hall) . . . when the lines will be formed by the Captain General, preparatory to marching to the church. . . . Templar Uniform, Without Sword." The quasi-military organization, including ranks such as eminent commander and generalissimo, was presumably attractive to those who needed regimentation to prevent returning to drink.[13]

While initially enthusiastic, organizational disputes and cooling ardor caused many temperance

The Sons of Temperance also issued withdrawal cards, though the reason is not clear. COURTESY OF WISCONSIN HISTORICAL SOCIETY.

lodges to have relatively short lives compared to other fraternal orders. (Some divisions over tactics were recounted in chapter 1.) The Columbus lodge of the Sons of Temperance fell afoul of the national Grand Lodge in the 1850s when it allowed women to vote on an issue of importance. Threatened with revocation by the national body, the "liberal-minded cold-water champions of Columbus" surrendered their charter and all joined the local Good Templars instead.[14] Despite the national exclusion of women from active roles, "the ladies of the village" were critical to the early temperance movement in addition to their symbolic role as the keeper of the pure and virtuous home. The IOGT lodge established in 1855 in Oregon, Dane County, collapsed when everyone went to war, though the "lady members worked heroically to sustain it until their brothers should return, but without avail."[15] In addition, the problem of diminishing fervor and membership was common throughout the state both before and after the war. Many members eventually felt the organization was becoming less relevant to their lives, and others wished to save the money spent on membership dues.

Beyond the Pledge

Part of the reason some slid back into intemperance was the climate of temptation around them. The only way to remedy this was to eliminate alcoholic beverages, so temperance advocates became prohibition advocates and sought to use politics to bring about through law what could not be achieved through individual commitments. While all levels of Wisconsin government would be involved in regulation, eventually the federal government would have the final word.

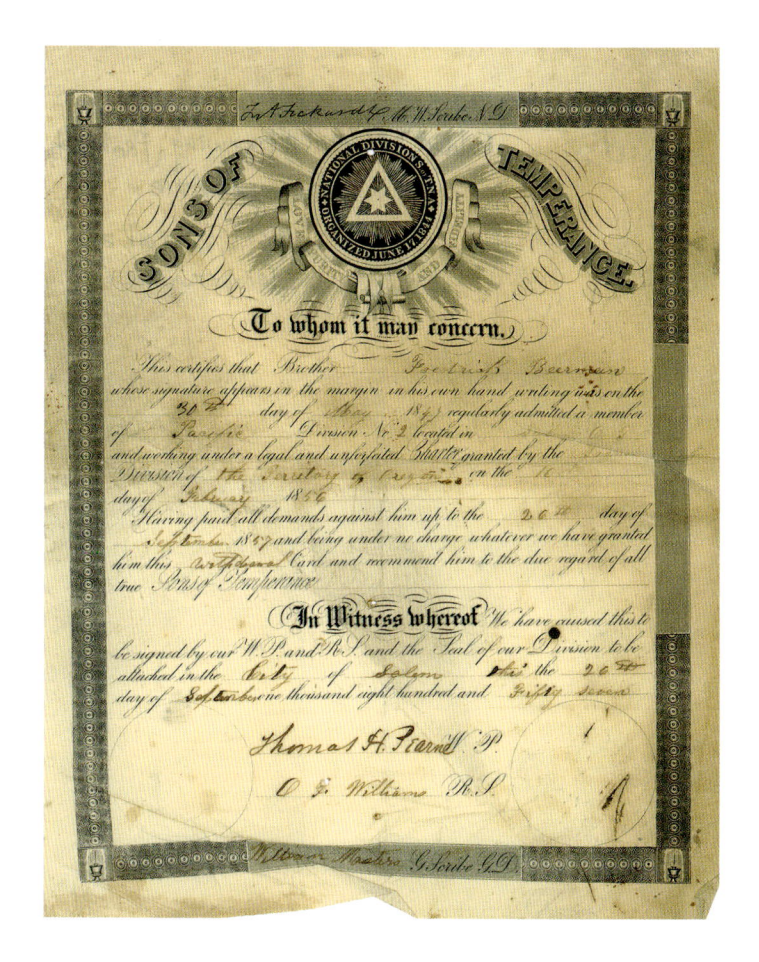

At the local level, ethnicity and purpose for settlement were the most important determinants of a community's attitude toward alcohol and the laws it would adopt and enforce. Colonel Samuel F. Phoenix started a "Temperance Colony Claim" in the mid-1830s, and he named both the county, Walworth, and one of its prominent villages, Delevan, after important New York temperance leaders. But Robert C. Nesbit concluded that

OASIS IN THE DRY YEARS 175

"the temperance crusade was not all moral fervor but held strong overtones of nativism, of rural versus urban, of American Protestantism versus Catholicism."[16] In small, homogeneous municipalities, civic leaders generally found little organized resistance to sumptuary laws (those that limited consumption of legal items) or to outright prohibition. For example, in Green County it was argued, "The leading citizens of Albany have always opposed the liquor traffic, and have thus kept up a continual battle with the demon alcohol."[17]

Most settlements, however, especially larger cities, were not as unified, as the alcohol business was considered good for the economy and breweries a point of pride for towns. But many newspaper editors were of Yankee stock and brought their opinions to the openly partisan newspapers of the nineteenth century. While the tirades against drink were sometimes local (see the exchange over Farwell's brewery in Madison in chapter 2), editors pressed for time and news often reprinted items from other papers to prove their points. In 1858 the *Baraboo Republic*, located in one of the most militant temperance cities in the state, printed an exchange between two other newspapers on the value of beer and breweries to the state. The editor of the *La Crosse Republican* had recently toured the brewery of C. & J. Michel in that city and reported:

> *We were much pleased with the neatness and general arrangement of the institution. Doctors disagree in regard to the effects of beer upon the system. Our experience proves that it is more safe than whisky, or any spirituous liquors, and we would advise all topers to eschew intoxicating drinks and take to Beer, until they can reform entirely.*

However, the response came from the *Mirror*:

> *Of course "doctors disagree"; for, while perhaps a majority of them make swill-tubs of themselves by toping beer, we are happy to know that a part of them have common sense and honesty enough to state the truth "in regard to the effects of beer upon the system." Your "experience," Mr. Editor . . . The fact is, we believe beer is to-day doing as much mischief in Wisconsin as any kind of intoxicating liquors; . . . it* will *intoxicate, and that it makes the most loathsome intoxication of all the black list of liquors. . . . Thus, by this talk of editors and doctors and ministers in its favor, it is gradually sweeping into the drunkard's road all who are not already there; so that we believe that of the next generation of drunkards there will be very few who did not make beer the stepping stone to their ruin.*[18]

The practice of reprinting articles from other temperance advocates became even easier when temperance lecturers wrote columns for newspapers, and when dry organizations began providing ready-made columns to be distributed nationwide.

Newspapers were not above castigating their own neighbors if they strayed from the true path. The *Wisconsin Chief* of Fort Atkinson had a very strong temperance position, as indicated by its motto "Advocate of Temperance and Human Freedom"—which put the cause even ahead of abolition. When rumors arose in 1863 that a third brewery was to be built in the city, it lamented:

> **The Demand Increases! The stomachs of our topers are so distended by practice that two breweries cannot supply their wants. Deacon Wells has sold a lot to Husher, and a third brewery is to be put in operation. Where was once the family altar, will soon be the mash-tub; where prayer once went up, beer will be poured down, and curses sandwich the seidles. What a change, Deacon!**[19]

Since no third brewery appears in the excise records until the 1870s, the rumors were premature, but public censure may have forced the proprietors to reconsider and delay the project.

Occasionally, a newspaper attacked the claim that breweries brought prosperity to a town. The *Wisconsin State Journal* lauded the progress made in the village of Clinton: "A few years ago liquor was sold from almost every other door and a brewery was running at full blast. Now the brewery has been converted into a dwelling house, not a drop of liquor can be purchased anywhere in the village. . . . The result of the whole matter is that business was never half so prosperous in Clinton before."[20] Newspapers such as the *Chief* or the *Old Oaken Bucket* of Racine served to get the word out, report victories, and urge steadfastness in defeat, but they alone could not win the war.

LOCAL OPTION

Generations of American politicians have held that the best government is that which is closest to the people. Whatever its truth regarding the millions of tasks governments have either undertaken or been charged with, in the case of alcohol policy it has a ring of truth, and alcohol may have more local variation than any other field of regulation. Hours of sale for on-premise and off-premise consumption, who may sell and purchase alcohol, container size, if and how it may be advertised, and dozens of other details all vary from town to town. Sometimes different parts of the same municipality will have different rules. The same was true in the mid-nineteenth century. While local ordinances were sometimes superseded by state or federal law, there was still plenty of scope for city councils and for citizen action.

Two particular categories of sumptuary laws had the most impact: Sunday laws and license regulation. While an 1859 state law prohibited alcohol sales on Sunday (and on the day and place of town meetings), enforcement was variable, especially in German communities. An unusual case occurred in Madison, whose diverse population and status as the capital meant that temperance clashes were both frequent and well publicized. In 1873, while Mayor Jared Comstock Gregory was out of town, the acting mayor, Chandler P. Chapman, began enforcing the Sunday closing law. He sent notices of intent only to saloons, however, and not to other regulated businesses. When Gregory returned two weeks later, the order was modified, but the angry reaction to the sudden enforcement may have contributed to the electoral polarization of the era.[21]

More important in the transition from temperance to total prohibition were the actions related to issuance of liquor licenses. Communities could choose not to issue licenses at all, a stance called "no license." Of course, this itself did not ban alcohol from a town. In October 1884 George Sarbecker was arrested for selling kegs of beer directly to households in Stoughton, which was a no-license city. The Wisconsin Supreme Court subsequently ruled that the sales were legal since the actual transaction happened when the kegs were loaded on the train in Janesville, not in Stoughton itself.[22] A no-license vote did not necessarily close a brewery: in 1874 Whitewater voted for no license by a margin of 174 votes, but Nicholas Klinger remained in business, though production dropped from 1,274 barrels in 1874 to 950 the next year.[23]

Once a municipality decided to issue licenses, the government could still hinder the sale of alcohol. The regime known as "high license" was most popular, because the local government received more revenue from each license, and temperance forces viewed the high price of a license (sometimes as much as $1,000 a year) as a likely deterrent against opening a saloon at all. Ethnic makeup was often decisive in determining how a city would vote on the question. In 1885 Milwaukee defeated a high license proposal of $500, leaving the license fee at $200.[24] The next year, however, Beloit, a Yankee stronghold, increased the total license charge to $700, not including state license and bond fees.[25]

The license question was sometimes the most important issue in local political campaigns. Temperance activists were frequent candidates for government positions, but brewers sought political office as well. While many of them no doubt had a sense of civic duty, they were unquestionably concerned with keeping their licenses affordable. In 1884 brewer Charles Gezelschap was nominated by the Democratic Party for the post of alderman in the first ward of Janesville. This triggered an angry response in the *Janesville Gazette* that all the Democrats were interested in was a low license ordinance.[26] The same year, Jacob Leinenkugel was elected mayor of Chippewa Falls along with seven Democratic aldermen "consisting primarily of saloon keepers." While observers expected the new administration to lower licenses from $200 to $100, it was noted that Leinenkugel had made no particular effort to campaign on that issue.[27]

Sometimes communities were founded specifically as dry havens in a wet world. While some of these remained true to the vision of their founders, a few strayed from the fold. Such was the case with Antigo, the moistening of which in 1891 was publicized outside Wisconsin:

> *The advent of a brewery into Antigo is like the proverbial last straw on the camel's back to the temperance zealots on Piety Flat, but their remonstrances are of no avail and the armorial bearings on an Antigo shield showing a bock beer glass pendant and goat rampant will soon adorn the saloons tributary to the city and help to spread the story of its debasement.*[28]

Financial considerations, whether private or public, continued to be a factor as governments weighed the merits of a wet or dry regime. Moving back and forth from dry to wet as Antigo did was not uncommon.

GRAHAM CRACKED

The presence of newspapers like the *Chief* that aspired to statewide influence, as well as the statewide fraternal organizations, laid the groundwork for resuming the campaign to dry up Wisconsin after the slavery issue was settled. Proposals for new laws continued, and, as Nesbit put it, "members of the legislature could always be found who would introduce temperance legislation."[29] Most of these laws were attempts by the Yankee power holders to legislate the behavior of other ethnic groups, and they clearly were perceived as such by the targets. The most significant of these, in terms of political fallout, was the Graham Law. Passed in 1872 and signed by Governor C. C. Washburn, it revived the old dram shop law with a $2,000 bond required of retailers, high fines for selling to drunkards, and new protections against circumvention. Despite a legal challenge, the Wisconsin Supreme Court upheld the right of the legislature to regulate liquor sales. The German voters, usually opportunistic in their voting rather than loyal to party, shifted their allegiance back to the Democratic Party or to the new Reform Party, which was financed by beer and liquor interests. As a result, Washburn and the dry Republicans were driven from office in the election of 1873. While railroad regulation received the most attention during the campaign, the deciding margins were cast in heavily German areas.[30]

Other sumptuary laws had less political import, but were just as irritating to advocates of personal liberty. The Anti-Treat Law, passed in 1881, made it a misdemeanor to buy a drink for another person in a bar and set a fine of ten dollars. Failing to buy a drink for the group in turn or to join in a round purchased by someone else was a violation of working-class ethics. But in a large group, going all the way around could lead to consuming many more drinks than an individual would buy for himself. According to Nesbit, legislators "treated

The bar of Hausmann Brewing Co. in Madison was similar to many other such establishments, though it had fewer items on the walls than most others with existing photographs. Note the number of spittoons on the floor near the bar.
COURTESY OF WISCONSIN HISTORICAL SOCIETY, WHI-3054.

the bill as a joke, but passed it, and it became law." In fact, the law that the anti-treating provision was supposed to amend had been repealed the previous year.[31] While the treating ban was repealed shortly thereafter, the proposal continued to reappear as late as 1913, 1915, and 1917. These were defeated, in part by the argument that it would prohibit a man buying his wife or daughter a drink. Of course, proponents of the bills argued,

OASIS IN THE DRY YEARS 179

"she would be better off anyway if she did not get liquor."[32]

"Home Protection"

Despite the disdain of the Sons of Temperance, women were vitally important to the dry movement. At first denied formal power, they normally used moral suasion to advance their cause.

In December 1873 and the first few months of 1874, a movement ignited by Eliza Jane Trimble Thompson of Hillsboro, Ohio, spread throughout the Midwest and northeastern states. "Mother" Thompson and her followers established prayer vigils outside liquor retailers, and occasionally inside as well. It is difficult to measure precisely the impact of the "crusade" in Wisconsin, especially since it coincided with a major legislative initiative, but it was credited with supporting several no-license votes around the state. Louis Schade, publisher of brewing industry journals and directories, claimed that 79 out of 280 breweries in Wisconsin closed because of the crusade and related temperance legislation.[33] (Schade had access to excellent data, but his numbers seem much too high based on known closing dates for breweries. Some may have closed temporarily. He may have been trying to galvanize action by brewers with dramatic figures.) Whatever the results, the months of activism inspired more permanent groups that would move beyond the sidewalks and into the halls of power.

In addition to being the center of ale brewing in Wisconsin, Janesville was home to Frances Willard, the dominant force in the Woman's Christian Temperance Union (WCTU). Senator Albert J. Beveridge called her "the greatest organizer of sweetness and light that ever blessed mankind" and "the Bismarck of the forces of righteousness in modern society."[34] Inspired by the crusade, Willard was part of the group that founded the national WCTU in 1874; she became its president in 1879 and remained in that post until her death

Visits to the home of Frances Willard became something of a pilgrimage for temperance supporters. The Loyal Temperance Legion of Wisconsin took a field trip to Willard's home for its eighteenth annual convention in 1909. Courtesy of Wisconsin Historical Society, WHi-56323.

in 1898. Under her leadership, the WCTU became more involved in politics and began to advocate specifically for the vote for women—especially on matters relating to liquor.[35] Wisconsin cities and villages were quick to form their own local "Unions." Janesville had a union of what was then called the Ladies Temperance Union even before the national organization was formed, and the Yankee stronghold of Beloit was one of several to found a union in the WCTU's inaugural year.[36] The organizational statement of the Baraboo Union was typical:

> *We, the undersigned, believing that the use of intoxicating liquors is the cause of much crime, pauperism and degradation, and that woman has a special duty and interest in the promotion of purity and good morals do agree to abstain from the use of all intoxicating liquors, including wine, beer and cider, and do form ourselves into a society for the purpose of disseminating the principles of total abstinence, and will hold ourselves in readiness at all times to carry out such measures, as shall, by us, be deemed wise to the end that the manufacture, traffic in and use of alcohol as a beverage may be forever abolished, trusting that the Divine Ruler of the universe will aid us in every good work.*[37]

In contrast to the societies that focused solely on the reclamation of the individual drinker, Willard went beyond the banner of "Home Protection" and embraced the philosophy "Do Everything." By the time of Willard's death, the WCTU "prosecute[d] over 40 departments of work" but each local union could decide in which fields to specialize. In the case of the Baraboo Union, they selected fourteen departments, ranging from "Sunday school work" and "County Fair work" to "Lumberman's work" and "Jail and prison" work. Two of the departments Baraboo chose likely had a major effect on laying the groundwork for a generation that would support prohibition: "press department" and "scientific temperance instruction."[38] Newspapers throughout Wisconsin and the nation featured weekly columns from the WCTU—a welcome feature for local editors with space to fill and scant time to write themselves. But according to William Jennings Bryan, the "scientific temperance instruction" campaign "did more than any other one thing" to gain the passage of prohibition. Led nationally by Mary Hanchett Hunt, this department coerced local school boards (and later state legislatures) to establish curricula that claimed, among other things, that alcohol burned the skin of the throat and that the majority of beer drinkers died of dropsy. Ultimately, about half the nation's schoolbooks bore the approval of Mary Hunt, and the WCTU locals sent members to the schools to make sure the curricula were being followed. Hunt's tactics, including shoddy science and shakedowns of publishers, eventually caused a breach with Willard, but by that time Hunt's movement had a life of its own.[39]

The WCTU lost its national driving force after Willard's death in 1898, but her legacy (including the fact that her birthday was a school holiday in four states, Wisconsin among them) lived on, and a new group had already taken the reins and was urging the movement forward.[40]

"'Tis the Saloon"

Although the saloon became the ultimate target of prohibitionists, to the point that even in the twenty-first century the term is seldom used, it played an important role in many communities as a meeting place for people of all walks of life, the "church of the poor," where "one did not even have to have respectability to enter."[41] The freedom of

The Loyal Temperance Legion focused on temperance education of children. Members here in are procession at their second annual convention in 1892 at Delavan. Note the wooden sidewalk in front of the post office. COURTESY OF WISCONSIN HISTORICAL SOCIETY, WHI-56327.

the saloon offered the chance to escape the regimented life of a worker in the Gilded Age. Elizabeth Jozwiak pointed out that workers

> *enjoyed the fact that the saloon was a place where men could meet in an informal, unscheduled setting. At work, bosses scheduled their time and dictated their activities. Reformers' saloon substitutes, such as settlement houses, therefore, did not compete well, because they tended to try to uplift and moralize and, perhaps most importantly, schedule workers' time. The saloon offered a haven where workers had some control over their lives.*[42]

The "workingman's living room" was particularly important in urban settings, where laborers were

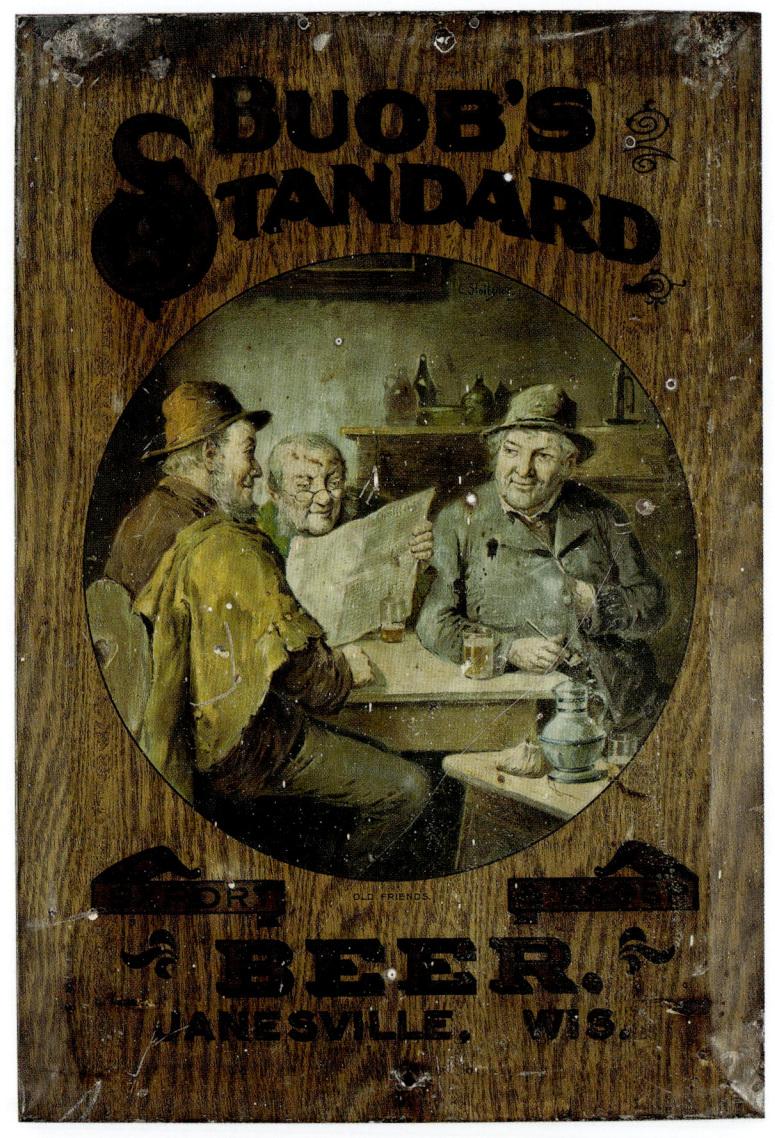

Many brewery advertising pieces portrayed the saloon as a place of relaxation and camaraderie. This stock Meyercord tin sign, titled "Old Friends," depicts lower-class laboring men who still enjoy reading the newspaper over a beer (ca. 1900). COURTESY OF NATIONAL BREWERY MUSEUM.

packed together in tenements and had little or no space in their homes for relaxation.

The pre-Prohibition saloon was a bastion of masculinity where female customers were generally not welcome. Some establishments had a side door that led to a back room where men could bring their wives or girlfriends, or some unaccompanied working-class women could participate in bar life.[43] Very few women in working-class saloons were prostitutes, who mostly kept to the dives of the slum districts.[44]

Aside from serving the community by providing a place to gather for relaxation, saloons often served purposes that were more civic in nature. Men shared neighborhood news, had access to newspapers to read about other topics, and could discuss politics. Even more importantly, saloons provided meeting places for organizations of all stripes that could not afford their own halls or that were prohibited from using public buildings. In Milwaukee, labor unions often met in saloons because they were located conveniently near the factories. In addition, the Social Democratic Party met in saloons, taking advantage of the natural inclination of men to talk about politics in that setting. As a consequence, some of the attacks on saloons used class differences and the specter of radical politics as a reason to close the saloons. The Socialists responded that these attacks were led by capitalist oppressors. The links between politics and saloons were clear to even casual observers: in 1902, a third of Milwaukee's forty-six alderman were saloonkeepers, and saloonkeepers held city office all over the state.[45] A saloonkeeper's name recognition and popularity were a big help at election time, as was the ability to lubricate the electoral machine with liquid incentive.

However, the benefits of fellowship, democracy, and civil society were neutralized and possibly outweighed by the vice, crime, and degradation found in many saloons. Some of the foulness came from the practice of spitting tobacco juice and the general inability of men to hit the spittoon. The saloon at the Fauerbach brewery minimized this problem by installing a granite trough along the base of the bar which could be flushed with water as needed, a device used by other saloons around the country. Unfortunately, the flushing feature proved even more necessary as some men chose to relieve themselves in the trough.[46] But spitting was a small concern compared to prostitution and gambling, which were common at saloons

Pabst's Gargoyle saloon in Milwaukee was an example of a tied-house saloon that catered to downtown businessmen. Note the absence of spittoons on the floor (a prominent feature in most other saloons of the era). The Gargoyle opened in 1906 and is pictured here in 1910. COLLECTION OF JOHN STEINER.

throughout the state. About half of Madison's saloons were reputed to have rooms at the disposal of prostitutes, and hundreds of slot machines tempted men to part with their earnings.[47]

In addition to corrupting men and women, saloons threatened to corrupt children through the common practice of "rushing the growler." A growler was a pail or bucket, often metal, which was taken to a saloon, often by one of a family's children, to bring back beer for the household.

Some accounts claim that the pails were sometimes smeared with lard in order to keep the foam down and allow for more beer.[48] Condemnation of this activity was under way at least as early as 1873, when Emma May Alexander Reinertsen, writing under the name "Gale Forest," began her campaign against "that crime against childhood and the state."[49]

While breweries attempted to distance themselves from the saloons when possible, their case was hard to make since the breweries owned so many of the establishments. The prevalence of tied houses made it easy to attribute any iniquities of the saloon to the brewers, even in cases when whiskey or other spirits were the cause of crime

There are no reliable accounts of how the metal beer buckets came to be called growlers. One story holds that the carbonation of the beer rattled the lids on containers such as the one shown here, creating a growling sound. Other versions claim that the growling was done either by the customers or the bartenders about the fairness of the measure of beer in the growler. The use of children—especially girls—to fetch beer (as shown in this photograph from 1908) was of great concern to anti-saloon crusaders. COURTESY OF MILLERCOORS BREWING CO.

or disorderly conduct. The brewery name was on signs by the door, and sometimes in the terra-cotta of the building itself. Newspaper headlines about saloon problems sometimes used the term "brewery rule" or blamed the breweries for any opposition to saloon regulation. During state investigations of prostitution in Wisconsin in 1913 and 1914, saloons came in for special criticism as breeders of what was then called the "white slave trade" and appeared to be trying to link specific breweries to the problem by asking what brands of beer were served at brothels that were separate from saloons.[50]

There were laws on the books to regulate saloons, but enforcement was inconsistent at best. Many thought the power of the brewers was ever present and insurmountable. Mary D. Bradford, who became superintendent of Kenosha's schools in 1910, recalled the situation when she took office:

> *The office of mayor was occupied by a man, who as a handsome, promising boy of a good German family, I well remembered. He now was the agent for Miller's High Life Beer of Milwaukee. Besides being the political boss of Kenosha, he represented Kenosha in the State Assembly at Madison. His palatial saloon was a popular place, advantageously located in the factory district of the city, its door diagonally across from the gate of the American Brass Mill, one of our largest industries. It is not an exaggeration to state that at that time the Milwaukee breweries ruled Kenosha through the hundred saloons that then flourished here.*[51]

For many reformers, eliminating the saloon in its entirety seemed like the only solution to the persistent problems—but given the political power of the brewers and publicans, was it possible?

WAYNE'S WORLD

Howard Hyde Russell, a fiery temperance preacher, founded the Anti-Saloon League in 1893 in Oberlin, Ohio, and soon positioned it as the clear leader of the prohibition movement. The ASL identified itself with the slogan "The Church in Action Against the Saloon," and was able to use its network of clergy and other activists to get the word out to tens of thousands of church members when action was required. But membership was not why the ASL replaced the WCTU in the temperance vanguard, but rather its focus on the single issue of the saloon. The WCTU call to "do everything" often created distractions from temperance activities, but the ASL declined to take stands on any issue not contained in its name. Aside from this laser-like focus, the other principle that Daniel Okrent identified as critical to the success of the ASL was intimidation. Okrent grants that the term *intimidation* seems harsh for a legitimate use of democratic political power, "but as practiced by the ASL, democracy was a form of coercion. Russell was direct about this: 'The Anti-Saloon League,' he said, 'is formed for the purpose of administering political retribution.'"[52] The ASL was among the first special interest lobbying groups to support candidates regardless of political party, a contrast to the popular politics of the Gilded Age, in which many causes resulted in the formation of single-issue political parties. The Prohibition Party was notably unsuccessful on the national scene, seldom getting more than 1 or 2 percent in presidential elections and only electing one member of Congress.[53] The ASL did not need to spend energy on party-building activities—only on supporting existing candidates who would vote with the league on the one issue that mattered.

The single person most responsible for the success of the ASL was Wayne B. Wheeler. Under his leadership as the group's general counsel, the organization grew, and by 1908 only four states were without a state league organization. The league thus was able to pressure politicians at all levels of government from every part of the country. Wheeler estimated in 1926 that the league had spent at least $35 million on efforts to influence public opinion.[54] Federal policy grew dryer and dryer. The passage of the Sixteenth Amendment authorizing an income tax gave Washington a source of income to replace alcohol taxes. The Webb-Kenyon Act of 1913 prohibited importing alcohol into a dry state, and was passed over President William Howard Taft's veto. This measure hit Wisconsin brewers especially hard, as their shipping breweries had supplied many of the dry states. The outbreak of war in Europe led to rising concern for military preparedness, so in 1914 Secretary of the Navy Josephus Daniels banned alcohol from all ships and naval installations. Several months apart at the end of 1913 and the start of 1914, prohibition amendments were presented to Congress, as they had been every year since 1876, but for the first time they were passed out of committee.[55]

The Schlitz Saloon in Madison was located at the northwest corner of King and East Doty Streets. It was just one of many tied-house saloons owned by the brewery. As of this writing, the building is still in existence and is located across Doty from the Great Dane Pub & Brewing Co. (though the arch is no longer extant) (photo from 1905). COURTESY OF WISCONSIN HISTORICAL SOCIETY, WHI-95620.

"PURE BEER IS PURE FOOD"

Several other political currents flowed together to make state and national prohibition a reality. The increasing power of reformers pursuing pure food and drug laws also put pressure on the brewing industry. Brewers had been accused of adulterating beer for many years, though most of the claims were wild rumors, misunderstandings of the brewing process, or chemically impossible (see chapter 5). In general, brewers worked with the agriculture department on legislation to maintain a good

186 THE DRINK THAT MADE WISCONSIN FAMOUS

We Go to Bohemia for Hops

We send our own buyers there every year to get the best that are grown, and we pay for them twice what common hops cost.

A partner in our business buys our barley, and selects the best from all.

We get our water from six wells, bored to rock.

Our yeast is all developed from the original mother cells which helped make Schlitz Beer famous.

We even filter air

All the air that touches Schlitz Beer comes to it through air filters.

And the beer itself is filtered through white wood pulp.

Then we age it for months, until it can't cause biliousness. We sterilize every bottle.

Yet Schlitz Beer costs only common beer prices

Ask for the brewery bottling.

THE BEER THAT MADE MILWAUKEE FAMOUS.

Schlitz went beyond any other brewery in emphasizing the purity of its beer. The increasing confidence during the era in the ability of science and industry to solve problems was exemplified by the appeals to the soundness of the brewing process as a guarantee of quality and purity. AUTHOR'S COLLECTION.

reputation with both regulators and the public. While the first actions to establish pure food regulation took place before the turn of the century, the process was accelerated by the publication in 1906 of Upton Sinclair's novel *The Jungle*. As part of the response to the public outcry, brewers were subject to new labeling rules, which required a statement of compliance with the 1906 Pure Food and Drug Act and an accurate volume measurement.[56] Brewers responded to these attacks with vigorous claims for the purity of their products. Schlitz in particular emphasized wholesomeness in their newspaper advertising, with slogans such as "Pure Beer Is Pure Food" and "Pure Beer Is Healthful—Schlitz Beer Is Pure."[57] Breweries large and small included statements on their labels that the beer was stored in glass tanks for purity, that it was a "wholesome beer for family use," or sometimes, more defensively, that the beer was "pure and without drugs or poison."

Some breweries made more aggressive health claims for their beer, though this practice started even before the Pure Food and Drug Act was signed into law. The breweries in Waukesha made much of the quality of the water from the nearby

OASIS IN THE DRY YEARS 187

springs, with the Milwaukee Waukesha Brewing Company going so far as to call one of its products "Health Beer." However, claims that beer was good for one's nerves paled against the claims and clear evidence of drunkenness and damage to health that bombarded the public.

The campaign to grant women the right to vote was a historical turning point in its own right, but was inextricably linked with the temperance movement. Susan B. Anthony and many other suffragists entered public life as temperance advocates and sought political answers when it became clear that social work alone would not do. While Frances Willard naturally was willing to "do everything," those who were otherwise single-minded prohibitionists and suffragists realized that an alliance was the best path to meeting both their goals. The brewers recognized the danger and mounted a condescending and often secret campaign against granting women the franchise, but their tactics backfired and created more sympathy for the women's cause.[58] The stars were aligning for the prohibitionists, but even the most optimistic still predicted many more years of struggle. However, the conflict that was engulfing Europe and the waters of the Atlantic handed the dry forces a weapon that would bring on nationwide prohibition within the current presidential administration.

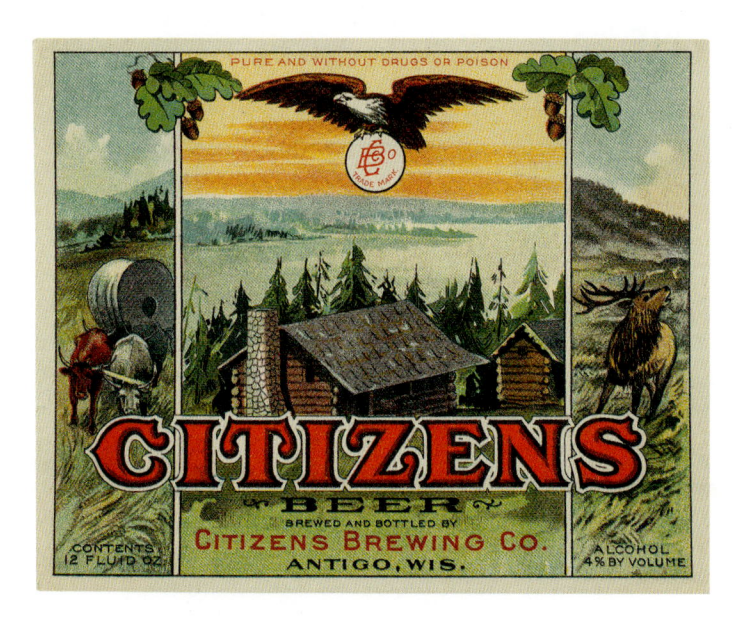

The passage of the Pure Food and Drug Act in 1906 encouraged breweries to trade on the purity of their products. Citizens Brewing Co. of Antigo emphasized that its beer was "pure and without drugs or poison" at the top of the label. Some antialcohol campaigners claimed that brewers released beer with arsenic—a poor way to encourage repeat business. COLLECTION OF JOHN STEINER.

The Waukesha breweries emphasized the health-giving qualities of their famous springwater. When William Weber took over the family brewery, he renamed it the Bethesda Brewery, after the pool with health-giving properties described in the fifth chapter of the Gospel of John (receipt from 1896). COLLECTION OF JOHN STEINER.

Where Disloyalty Chiefly Centers

During the late 1800s, the Germans were considered to be one of the most successful immigrant groups in America. German styles dominated classical music and were common in much popular and dance music, and German choral groups flourished across the nation. The German education model was adopted everywhere from kindergartens to leading universities. The Turner gymnastic clubs became popular centers for recreation. Immigrants such as sometime Wisconsin resident Carl Schurz became nationally known political figures. German advances in science and engineering helped

The Milwaukee Waukesha Brewing Co. was quite direct about the healthy properties of its brown beer. This label also claims that beer of 2¾ percent alcohol by weight was nonintoxicating—a common assertion at the time. After Prohibition, Fox Head Waukesha Corp. reused leftover Health Beer labels by printing over the word *Health* and any health claims on them (label ca. 1918). COLLECTION OF JOHN STEINER.

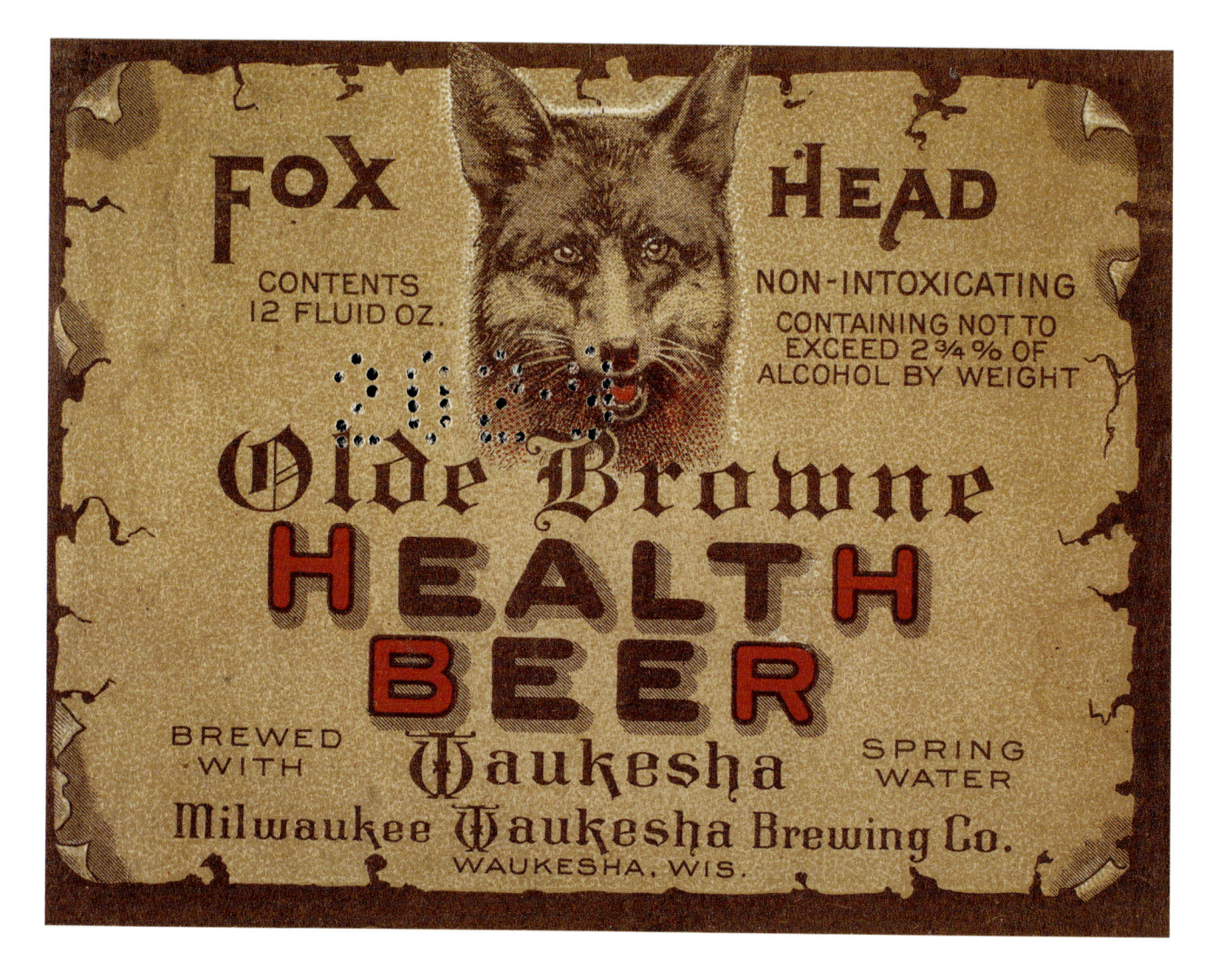

OASIS IN THE DRY YEARS 189

Erinnerung an das dritte Sänger-Fest des Sänger-Bundes des Nord-Westens.

Scene in Quentin's Park, Milwaukie, 29. Juni 1868.

Best & Co. sent a large traveling keg (with several taps) to the Third Sänger-Fest of the Sänger-Bund (Singer Union) of the Northwest, held in June 1868 in Milwaukee's Quentin's Park. Gatherings of German cultural organizations invariably featured beer gardens or other opportunities to enjoy cool lager beer. COLLECTION OF JOHN STEINER.

develop fields from transportation to communications. But the rising military threat of Kaiser Wilhelm II's empire eventually overshadowed these accomplishments and provided the impetus for the final moves toward national prohibition.

While there was some initial support among immigrants for Germany and the other central powers, the use of unrestricted submarine warfare turned most American citizens against the kaiser and put German Americans on the defensive. After the revelation of the Zimmermann Telegram (containing a proposal for a German–Mexican alliance) and the declaration of war on Germany, the campaign against perceived German sympathizers was institutionalized. As with the fight against women's suffrage, attempts by the brewers or groups funded by them to advocate their position on cultural or civil libertarian grounds backfired and even drew charges of treason. The National German–American Alliance was founded to advance culture, but then became the counterweight to the prohibitionists. After America entered the war, the alliance became a lightning rod for many attacks, but so did the brewers themselves. Milwaukee was referred to as "Schlitzville on the lake," the center of the production of "Kaiser Brew."[59] A leaflet distributed by the Wisconsin ASL titled "The Enemy in Our Midst" attacked the brewers for using barley, coal, and railroad cars that could have been diverted to the war effort, and urged a dry vote as the best way to win the war against Germany.[60] Former Wisconsin lieutenant governor John Strange was more direct and personal in his attack in early 1918:

> *We have German enemies across the water. We have German enemies in this country, too. And the worst of all our German enemies, the most treacherous, the most menacing, are Pabst, Schlitz, Blatz and Miller. They are the worst Germans who ever afflicted themselves on a long-suffering people. No Germans in the war are conspiring against the peace and happiness of the United States more than Pabst, Schlitz, Blatz, Miller and others of their kind.*[61]

Some brewers did not seem to perceive the direction of the political winds and continued business as usual. Appleton Brewing Company bought a saloon in Middlebury in May 1918—a point when brewers should probably have been selling off saloons rather than acquiring more.[62] This sanguine view of the situation was widely shared by Wisconsin's brewers. When the Wisconsin Brewers Association met in December 1917, its members "expressed confidence that defeat is in sight for advocates of prohibition" and that the "dry wave" had passed its peak.[63]

Although they were overstated for propaganda purposes, legitimate wartime needs began to limit brewing even before prohibition arrived. Grain was considered an essential war material, and its use for brewing purposes was severely limited by the Lever Food and Fuel Control Act of August 1917. Shortly thereafter, by executive order, President Woodrow Wilson limited the strength of malt beverages to 2.75 percent to conserve grain. This had an immediate effect on Wisconsin's brewers. Perhaps the most dramatic consequence was in Appleton, where Walter Brewing and Appleton Brewing were directed by Treasury Secretary William Gibbs McAdoo to combine their operations to save food and fuel.[64] A few other breweries combined, and nearly all had to alter their business.

Ultimately, the Food Administration issued an order prohibiting the manufacture of malt liquors after 1 December 1918. The counsel for the Milwaukee Brewers' Association, William H. Austin, estimated the supply of beer would last for about two months after that date, and cautioned that the stilled breweries would be of little use for military production.[65] Practically speaking, most brewing came to a halt before prohibition became official because material shortages, high input prices, the shortage of labor, and patriotic fervor forced many breweries to close well before their product was banned outright. By the end of October 1919, all of Wisconsin's breweries had ceased production.[66] Wartime prohibition (which was passed over President Wilson's veto) was challenged in court, but the U.S. Supreme Court ruled that the armistice did not end the war powers of the federal government, and the law stayed in force.[67]

The official beginning of national prohibition was established by the Eighteenth Amendment and its enabling legislation, the National Prohibition Act. The actual wording of the constitutional provision was short and simple, with most of the detail left to "appropriate" state and federal legislation: "After one year from the ratification of this article the manufacture, sale, or transportation of intoxicating liquors within, the importation thereof into, or the exportation thereof from the United States and all territory subject to the jurisdiction thereof for beverage purposes is hereby prohibited." Enforcement and the definition of intoxicating liquors were left to what became known as the Volstead Act, named after the progressive Minnesota congressman who drafted the bill with input from Wayne Wheeler. The critical clause was section 1 of Title II, which set the definition of intoxicating liquors "by whatever name called" as anything more than 0.5 percent alcohol by volume.[68] There was some question whether this provision would apply in Wisconsin, since states were given concurrent jurisdiction, and Wisconsin's legislature passed the Mulberger Act in June 1919 allowing beer of 2.5 percent.[69] As late as December 1919, brewers had been hoping for a court ruling that would allow beer at the wartime strength of 2.75 percent. But no such ruling was forthcoming, and brewers and customers began to make plans for the new dry era. It was no coincidence that the train that brought a symbolic corpse of John Barleycorn to a mock funeral service staged on the day Prohibition started in Norfolk, Virginia, by preacher Billy Sunday began its journey in Milwaukee.[70]

JOHN BARLEYCORN IS DEAD

Customers, retailers, and brewers had several months' warning before prohibition became complete, and all parties began to make plans for a dry future. Because the Volstead Act did not actually outlaw the consumption of alcohol, many households (and some saloons that were about to become speakeasies) laid in a supply to last as long as they could manage. In northern Wisconsin, it was "estimated that there is enough whisky stored away in Hurley and Ironwood [Michigan] and other towns on the range to float a battleship."[71] But for the breweries, the survival of their business and the welfare of their workers were at stake. Skilled brewmasters sometimes were able to move to other countries—Fred Blust of Gutsch Brewing Company may have gone farther than anyone else when he left Sheboygan in 1919 to accept a job with Cezejaria Brahma in Rio de Janeiro, Brazil.[72] Less-skilled workers had to hope that their employers could find another business for the company.

Obviously, the easiest conversion for a brewery was to make near beer or other malt and hop products. This had the added benefit of giving the brewmaster and other skilled workers some incentive to stay with the company and ride out the drought, as well as some relief for owners reluctant

Pabst Brewing Co. designed this unusual vehicle to promote its Pablo near beer—advertised as "The Happy HOPPY Drink" (photograph ca. 1926). COLLECTION OF JOHN STEINER.

Brewers like Weber Brewing Co. of Waukesha, which once touted its "Old Fashioned Beer," adapted during Prohibition to sell "New Fashion Brew," though the company continued to promote its product as ideal for enjoying with food and fellowship. This bottle contained the unusual amount of 12½ fluid ounces (bottle ca. early 1920s). COLLECTION OF JOHN STEINER.

to lay off longtime employees.[73] The process for making near beer required making beer first, and then dealcoholizing it through a process that boils off the alcohol—almost the opposite of distillation. At least fifty-six breweries are known to have made near beer during Prohibition, though few made much of a profit on it. Most of the brand names ended with the letter *o*. Some used the brewery's name, such as Leinenkugel's Leino, Klinkert's Klinko, or Shawano's Shano. Some were slight variations, like Pabst's Pablo or Schlitz's Famo (as in "The Beer That Made Milwaukee Famous"). A few were cleverer, such as Grafton's Camel or Cream City's Pilsnear (though Cream City stretched credibility by also offering "Stout" and "Extra Stout" near beers).

Despite attempts to market these brews as a "refreshing temperance beverage" or some similar phrase, there was little market for such a drink. As the old joke went, "Whoever called it near beer was a poor judge of distance." Near beers came and went, and the successful ones were judged mostly on how they tasted when they were "spiked"—had alcohol added to them. Few breweries went so far as Heileman, which actually marketed a product called Spike, and it

OASIS IN THE DRY YEARS

SPIKE

BREWED FROM CHOICEST HOPS AND MALT

MIN. CONTENTS 12 FLUID OZ

"IT'S A HIT EVERY TIME"

G. HEILEMAN BREWING CO., MFGRS. LA CROSSE, WISCONSIN

ALCOHOLIC CONTENT LESS THAN ½ OF 1% BY VOLUME   PERMIT No. W.L.88

Spiking near beer with alcohol was a common practice during Prohibition, but breweries seldom called attention to the practice in the way that G. Heileman of La Crosse did with Spike. The pretense that the beverage was a tribute to railroad workers was rather thin. At lower right is the L-permit number issued to Heileman. Each brewery licensed to manufacture near beer during Prohibition was assigned a unique number (label ca. 1930). COLLECTION OF JOHN STEINER.

was difficult to advertise this product's virtue in a way that would avoid complaints or prosecution. (More information on the Prohibition-era activities of individual breweries may be found in the second part of the book.)

Since making near beer required making beer first, it was a simple matter to skip the dealcoholization step and release a batch or more of real beer. There is no record of any of the Milwaukee giants being busted by what newspapers sometimes called "the sponge squad," but many small and mid-sized breweries succumbed to the temptation to keep their business alive with occasional lucrative shipments of real beer. Prohibition's first spring had hardly arrived before Ziegler's brewery in Beaver Dam was shuttered for making beer in excess of 3 percent alcohol.[74] Klinkert Brewing in Racine was closed because it had "for sale and is keeping for sale large quantities of intoxicating beer"—large meaning "several thousand bottles."[75] Often, repeated fines and closures failed to deter illicit brewing, and some breweries suffered multiple and increasingly severe sanctions. Five years into Prohibition, twelve Wisconsin breweries had been "padlocked" both literally and legally, meaning they were closed to all business activity.[76]

Hagemeister Brewing of Green Bay introduced Cameo Beverage even before Prohibition began. Newspaper advertisements offered conflicting claims for the product, touting is as the perfect tonic for curing "Spring Fever" while also claiming it was "Ideal as a Party Beverage." Cameo was offered in 12-ounce and 7-ounce bottles (the latter pictured here, ca. 1920). COLLECTION OF JOHN STEINER.

In contrast to the New Fashion Brew pictured earlier in this chapter, some brewers maintained that their near beer was little different from the previous product (label ca. 1927–28). COLLECTION OF JOHN STEINER.

The illicit brewing activity persisted because some of the government officials responsible for stopping it turned a blind eye—usually at a substantial price. In 1926 the former prohibition director for Wisconsin, Clark M. Perry, was sentenced to three years at Leavenworth prison for allowing the illegal withdrawal of real beer, and for accepting kickbacks of four dollars per barrel shipped from the Calumet Brewing Co. in Chilton.[77]

While most of the illegal beer was made by the pre-Prohibition brewery owners in an attempt to stay solvent, mobsters were active as well, especially in southeastern Wisconsin. In September 1924 headlines shouted "Sponge Squad Mops Up Ft. Atkinson Brewery" as fourteen truckloads of beer bound for Chicago were seized. Less than three months later, another raid resulted in twenty arrests, among them Tom O'Donnell, described as "a notorious beer runner and Chicago gangster," and John L. White of the Cassville Brewery.[78] Perhaps the most notorious of all was the Oconomowoc brewery, which was sold in 1919 to Andrew X. Fischer, who had begun brewing in Chicago and prior to his arrival in Oconomowoc had been a brewmaster at the Leinenkugel brewery in Chippewa Falls. In 1921 Fischer was arrested for selling beer that ranged from .91 percent to 1.7 percent—pretty weak stuff, but still over the legal limit. While he was jailed briefly for this offense, his local political influence resulted in an early release

OASIS IN THE DRY YEARS

and dismissal of the charges. (Fischer's local popularity was so great that he was elected to serve as mayor of Oconomowoc from 1932 to 1934.)

The brewery was sold in 1922 to George Sipple of Illinois, who resold it in 1924 to Walter A. Ross, a reputed mobster from Chicago. Ross was arrested in February 1925, after a truckload full of real beer tipped over on a road outside town. While Ross insisted it was near beer, the driver admitted to becoming intoxicated after drinking the product. Ross was raided again in June, when the value of the beer dumped was estimated at $51,000—a huge sum at the time. Ross was subject to several additional inspections and raids during the next few years. One local account holds that Ross avoided arrest on some occasions by having kegs with dividers in them: the top half containing near beer that could be discovered during a raid, with the full-strength beer in the bottom half. When the Ross operation was raided again in 1930, agents discovered a large distillery hidden in the brewery. Ross left town, and after Prohibition had turned over a new leaf running a restaurant in Minneapolis, but was arrested in 1936 when he visited Oconomowoc and was jailed yet again.[79]

Even when not making real beer, old breweries made appealing sites for other alcohol production. The abandoned Mequon and Mishicot breweries and the former Winz brewery in Menasha were found to have contained distilling operations, though when the Menasha brewery was raided again in 1931, it had reverted to beer.[80]

The desire to stay in the beer business even during Prohibition was stoked by the occasional rumors of legislation that would somehow make

This rare Kellermeister label was one of the few to bear the name of Walter A. Ross, target of several raids during Prohibition (label ca. 1926). COLLECTION OF JOHN STEINER.

Andrew Fischer was an experienced brewmaster who took over the Binzel Brewery in Oconomowoc just before Prohibition became law. Grape Smash was one of the brewery's nonalcoholic products (label ca. 1920). COLLECTION OF JOHN STEINER.

beer legal again in some way. As early as 1921, articles appeared claiming that the government would modify the Volstead Act to allow real beer to be sold as a tonic (at a rate of one pint every ten days).[81] The possibility of repeal was an issue in the 1926 Republican primary campaign for U.S. Senate between incumbent Irvine Lenroot and challenger John J. Blaine. Blaine's stance in favor of repeal earned him the derision of his opponents as a tool of the brewers, but even Lenroot supported heavily regulated beer.[82]

Brewing Company to "Products Company"

Many companies gave up brewing entirely but stayed in the agricultural products business. Antigo Brewing was purchased by the Langlade County Creamery and produced cheese under the Kraft Foods Company of Wisconsin label. By 1937 this plant claimed to be the largest producer of Swiss cheese in the world.[83] The large tanks in the brewery made dairy business a logical move for many firms, and the Storck, Effinger, Potosi, and several other breweries made and distributed popular dairy products. The Hussa Brewing Co. in Bangor converted its facility into a pickle factory. The Sturgeon Bay Brewery put everything into the one basket of a new, patented process for preserving eggs.[84] Many more, however, turned over at least part of their factories to cold-storage uses, since the brewhouse equipment was ill suited to any purpose except making beer or related products. The one bright spot was that bottling equipment could be used to package nonalcoholic drinks such as sodas, and more than twenty breweries took advantage of their name recognition and existing distribution channels to market a variety of flavors of soft drinks (a number that is tellingly less than half the number that made near beer).

Milwaukee's two international giants, Pabst and Schlitz, were much more aggressive in their attempts to create new businesses in the wreckage of prohibition. None went further than Schlitz, which built an all-new, state-of-the-art chocolate factory

This root beer bottle from Gutsch Brewing of Sheboygan is unusual for its hexagonal base. This design was used in the late 1800s to add extra strength to bottles designed for containing highly carbonated beverages, but such bottles were less common in the twentieth century, especially with a top designed for a crown cap. While stronger, the bottles were heavier and more expensive to ship (ca. early 1920s).
COLLECTION OF JOHN STEINER.

Schlitz produced a variety of different candies under the Eline brand. In addition to the Chocolate Covered Cherries in front, the orange can contained hard candies, and the large black box held Purity Village Chocolates (ca. early 1920s). According to a promotional booklet produced by the company: "This model plant was builded by Eline's to produce Chocolate, Cocoa and other food products to help develop for this great nation strong, healthy and contented men and women." COLLECTION OF JOHN STEINER.

in Milwaukee named Eline (after the phonetic spelling of the Schlitz owners' surname, Uihlein). The complex featured several buildings modeled after notable examples of English architecture and its own power plant, which used a new process that would burn coal without smoke or cinders that could taint the product.[85] Unfortunately, the brand, which was intended to rival Hershey, never gained much traction, and the business was closed in 1928 after causing the Uihleins a loss estimated between $15 million and $17 million.[86] The Uihleins had mixed results with other investments, but were able to hang on to the brewery and kept the Schlitz name in the public eye with Famo and other beverages.

Pabst's strategy for survival combined a number of small revenue-producing efforts with a few major product launches. Even before prohibition became official, Pabst was renting out idle sections of its plant to a shoe factory and a motorcycle shop. The company made a few ventures in metal manufacturing, perhaps because Milwaukee was already an important center for that industry.[87] The most ironic business located in the Pabst complex was a padlock factory, whose products were reported to "adorn swinging doors of once popular places in Milwaukee." At one point, a shipment of 147,600 locks worth $65,000 was sent to New York City, where the demand was even greater than in the Cream City.[88]

But it was cheese that made Pabst stand out among other dormant breweries during Prohibition. Fred Pabst Jr., who had taken charge of the manufacturing side of the business in 1921, had been experimenting for several years with cheese production on his Pabst Holstein Farms in Oconomowoc. In 1923 the cheese-making

Pabst offered bottled water by the case during Prohibition. The tag around the neck notes that the "new shorter bottle fits the ice box"—recognizing the increasing importance of in-home refrigeration in American homes (bottle ca. 1923). COLLECTION OF JOHN STEINER.

equipment was moved to the brewery, and production under the Pabst label began in earnest. Pabst Wonder Process Cheese came in five varieties: American, Pimento, Swiss, and Brick, all available in quarter-pound, half-pound, and five-pound packages, and the odiferous Limburger, sold only by the quarter-pound. Pabst-ett was, according to a description on the package from 1929, a "pleasing combination of cheese, milk protein, milk sugar [and] milk minerals." In seemingly unrelated claims, Pabst lauded its "zippy aged-in tang" and claimed "children digest it as easily as milk." In 1930 Pabst-ett introduced new Pimento, Swiss, and Brick flavors, and the company sold more than nine million pounds from 1926 through 1930.[89] Kraft Cheese successfully sued Pabst in 1927 for patent infringement, and Pabst paid a royalty to Kraft for several years but sold the cheese line to Kraft upon repeal.[90]

A number of breweries, especially larger ones with a wide pre-Prohibition market, turned to making products for homebrewing. Most of the large Milwaukee breweries offered one or more malt syrups, as did larger breweries outside the metropolis such as Oshkosh Brewing and G. Heileman of La Crosse. While the products were allegedly sold for baking and candy making, these claims were undercut by the existence of hopped malt syrup, which would have made unpleasant brownies or caramels but perfectly acceptable beer. Furthermore, an ad for Braumeister Malt Syrup claimed, "Folks know their malts in Milwaukee," and added, "To get the Purest, STRONGEST, Best Malt Syrup . . . demand Braumeister."[91] Why a cook would need the "strongest" malt syrup for making caramels is unclear.

By a loophole in the Volstead Act, it was not actually illegal to make beer at home for household consumption, and thousands of Wisconsinites bought ingredients or improvised their own and made homebrew. Stories abound of personal brewing: one of this author's relatives brewed in the Milwaukee suburb of Shorewood during Prohibition, though not everything went perfectly. He occasionally filtered the beer by using a freshly

OASIS IN THE DRY YEARS

A sampling of Pabst and Pabst-ett cheese products. COLLECTION OF JOHN STEINER.

washed diaper from the clothesline, though one day the diaper he selected had only been rinsed, and not fully washed. His wife, who was not pleased with his homebrewing, never told him that he had used a dirty diaper.[92] Accounts that claim "it is harder to find a family that didn't partake in the activity than to find one that did" may overstate the case. But while there were certainly regional variations, it is clear that homebrewing was fairly common, and beer was easy to come by. One remembrance from an unnamed resident of Bloomer claimed, "But everyone made home brew. So, of course we had to make it, too. We bought a five gallon Red Wing jar and some malt sugar and yeast. Now we were in business."[93] Many citizens made beer for their own use and shared it with friends, but those whose names made the local newspapers went into "business" to make money. These "wildcat breweries" sprang up in nearly every part of the state, and hardly a week went by without news of a raid somewhere in Wisconsin.

While many raids involved spirits rather than beer, the number of breweries raided was extremely high compared with neighboring Minnesota—suggesting that while making alcohol was a priority, in many cases local cultural tradition demanded beer over liquor.

The economic hardships that afflicted many Americans during Prohibition, even before the Great Crash of 1929, forced otherwise law-abiding citizens to try their hand at brewing. In 1923, the home of Frederick Bloesing near Eau Claire was raided, and his basement "was fitted up in what authorities declared a most perfect plant for the manufacture of beer." Bloesing had more background than many homebrewers because he had been formerly employed by the John Walter Brewing Co. (whose barrels he was using for his homebrew). His wages, however, had dropped from $300 a month to $150 and he claimed he needed the extra income to provide for his wife and seven children.[94]

Homebrewing drove citizens and suppliers to greater innovations, and drove police and lawmakers to frustration. In 1931, the Brewery Malt Company offered a product called Beah (with the name printed over a keg) and boasted, "No fermenting, No Sugar, No Bottling, No Boiling, No Yeast. Add to Water, It Is Made Instantly," without ever saying what "It" actually was.[95] In 1929 Senator Howard Teasdale (R-Sparta) proposed a bill to ban malt syrup to deprive homebrewers of their key ingredient. (Teasdale was also the chair of the committee investigating prostitution cited earlier.) During the debate it was pointed out that malt syrup was also used to manufacture candy, cereals, graham crackers, and even window shades and cloth. The committee chairman sarcastically asked Teasdale if it would have made more sense to prohibit growing barley instead.[96]

The accounts in newspapers following raids indicate that wildcat breweries were sometimes large ventures—some much larger than the "nanobreweries" of the early twenty-first century. One operation discovered in 1926 on a farm in Rochester, west of Racine, had two brew kettles with a capacity of one hundred gallons (just over three barrels) and twelve fermenters capable of holding six thousand gallons (almost two hundred barrels).[97] A 1929 raid on an outfit in Waupun yielded 43,200 bottle caps, among other supplies.[98] The degree to which the press had to change its descriptions of wildcat breweries was exemplified by a 1931 account referring to a brewery with three fifteen-barrel brewing coppers as "miniature."[99] While many of the larger operations were in the countryside, a few were in the heart of major cities. Federal agents uncovered one such brewery,

G. Heileman Brewing of La Crosse was one of many breweries that packaged malt syrup during the dry years. Several, like Heileman, tied the malt syrup to their flagship beer brand—Heileman employed the familiar grenadier to advertise Old Style malt. Heileman also retained the "Brewing Co." name during Prohibition, rather than calling itself "Products Co." or a similar name. COLLECTION OF TYE SCHWALBE.

Blatz sold hops in small boxes suitable for home use, though many homebrewers opted for hop-flavored malt syrup. AUTHOR'S COLLECTION.

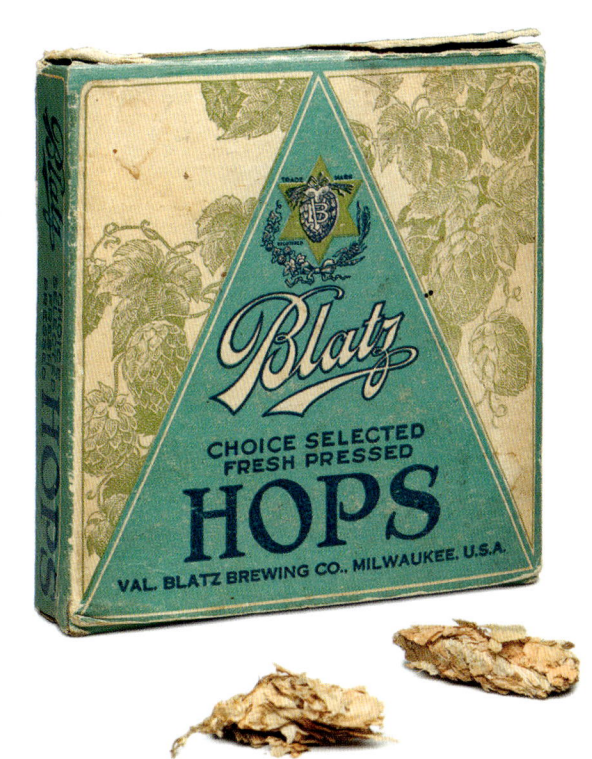

OASIS IN THE DRY YEARS   201

Homebrewing

Homebrewing was a regular part of housekeeping for some of the earliest European settlers in Wisconsin. As professional brewers proliferated, the need for households to brew their own beer diminished—though some probably continued to brew out of habit or remoteness. These primitive brewers needed to find their own ingredients, as malt syrups were not widely available until the approach of Prohibition.

Prohibition created the conditions for an explosion of homebrewing. Professionally made beer was illegal (though not nonexistent), and providing an adequate substitute was a simple matter of mixing ingredients and waiting. An important development was the appearance of retail outlets for malt and hops. Nearly every major Wisconsin city had at least one such business, though none came close to the more than one hundred that carried on the trade in Milwaukee. When real beer returned in 1933, the vast majority of these stores closed as customers returned to inexpensive, well-made commercial beer. Due to an oversight by Congress, home winemaking was permitted after repeal, but homebrewing remained illegal.

Despite the outlaw nature of homebrewing, a few enthusiasts continued to make their own beer, though they often were forced to do so without fresh ingredients or much scientific insight into the brewing process. A few hardy brewers, mostly on the West Coast, began to organize in the early 1970s. Portland's Fred Eckhardt published his *Treatise on Lager Beers* in 1970, a forty-eight-page volume that challenged would-be brewers to make beers more flavorful than those offered in taverns or on store shelves.[1] America's first homebrewing club, the Maltose Falcons, was founded in suburban Los Angeles in 1974.[2] Between formal and informal meetings and

---

1 Tom Acitelli, *The Audacity of Hops: The History of America's Craft Beer Revolution* (Chicago: Chicago Review Press, 2013), 20–21.
2 Acitelli, *The Audacity of Hops*, 32.

Tasting glasses from the 2011 and 2010 editions of the Great Taste of the Midwest in front of the program book from 2011. Tasting glasses at Wisconsin beer festivals tend to be larger than those in many other states. AUTHOR'S COLLECTION.

publications, brewers began to refine their recipes and techniques. A few winemaking stores began to carry ingredients for beer, and while it was still illegal, there was no record of anyone being arrested for homebrewing or selling beer supplies.[3]

Shortly after legislation legalizing homebrewing was signed in 1978, Charlie Papazian and Charlie Matzen founded the American Homebrewers Association (AHA) in Boulder, Colorado, and began publication of *Zymurgy* magazine. Wisconsin's first organized homebrewing club was the Kenosha Bidal Society, which was founded in 1979. The Madison Homebrewers and Tasters Guild, founded in 1983, gained particular fame by hosting the Great Taste of the Midwest since 1987.

After some initial reluctance, suppliers have embraced the homebrewing movement, and the retail infrastructure is much more elaborate than it was during Prohibition. Wisconsin's Briess Malting Co. was the first malting company to provide smaller quantities of malt to homebrewers. Homebrew shops expanded the variety of ingredients and equipment available, and the number of books on homebrewing techniques and recipes fills many shelves.

Wisconsin's homebrewers have still had occasional legal problems. In 2011, the Wisconsin Department of Revenue changed its interpretation of existing regulations and concluded that providing samples at homebrew shops and tasting beer at homebrew competitions fell outside the law. Home Brew Island, a popular feature of the Great Lakes Brew Fest in Racine where local homebrew clubs offered samples of their beers, was canceled in 2011 because of uncertainty over the law. (Home Brew Island has since been reinstated.)[4] As of 2018, there were more than eighty homebrewing clubs in Wisconsin registered with the AHA. Many of the clubs sponsor homebrewing contests and encourage their members to become educated beer judges through the Beer Judge Certification Program.

---

3   Acitelli, *The Audacity of Hops*, 58.
4   Bob Paolino, *Great Lakes Brewing News*, June/July 2011, 16, 24.

OASIS IN THE DRY YEARS   203

Herman M. Brandt's brewing supply shop at 1258 National Avenue, pictured here in 1928, was only one of more than one hundred such establishments listed in that year's Milwaukee city directory. While most businesses simply had the proprietor's name, others left no doubt as to the purpose of the supplies, such as Copper Kettle Malt Products, Home Beverage Malt & Hops Co., and the Hop Shop. Brandt's primary brand appears to have been Braumeister Malt Syrup from Independent Milwaukee Brewing Co., but signs advertising Schlitz malt syrup are visible next to the door. Brandt also displayed fifty-gallon barrels for sale for $2.50 each, suggesting that some of his customers were producing large quantities of homebrew. COLLECTION OF JOHN STEINER.

located in a house owned by "an attractive 35-year old woman" on North Sixth Street in La Crosse, in April 1932. Agents discovered a trapdoor in the garage leading to a series of tunnels "big enough for a man to walk through" and equipped with an elaborate alarm system. The brewery in the basement consisted of two mash tuns of 500 gallons each, four fermenters of 450 gallons each, an electric refrigeration machine, two bottling machines, a capping machine, and other equipment. Neighbors were apparently well aware of the construction of the facility, and informed inquiring reporters that the tunnel excavations had been completed the previous August.[100]

Of course, breweries capable of brewing fifteen-barrel batches were not producing for family use, but for sale to speakeasies either directly or through gangsters. The reality of the situation was portrayed in a long article in the *Sheboygan Press* in February 1929, through which the editors responded to a claim by Mrs. H. L. Van Allen, head of the Wisconsin WCTU, that the saloon was essentially dead and that Wisconsin was an "arid" state. The *Press* investigated Fond du Lac (not to "besmirch" that city but because it was Mrs. Van Allen's home) and found as many as two hundred establishments licensed as "soft drink parlors" that were known wet retreats, including "distinguished (?)" locations called the Bucket of Blood, the Broken Knuckle, and the Rats' Nest—hardly names that suggested patrons enjoying Coca-Cola or a root beer float. In answer to her claim that "we have seen no evidence of widespread home brewing," the newspaper suggested that "Mrs. Van Allen evidently does not do much calling," and then became positively indignant in cataloging the counterevidence:

204   THE DRINK THAT MADE WISCONSIN FAMOUS

When prohibition closed the breweries it put in the place of every brewery thousands of home breweries. Why do hardware stores and other establishments, including department stores, carry the machinery for home brewing if it is not with the idea of selling it? . . .

It is hardly possible that a violator of the law is advertising his business. . . . But if she wants to get at the facts, let her inquire of some of the meter readers for the gas and electric companies, and they will give her a pretty clear conception of the increased revenue as a result of cellar activities. Inquire of some of your grocery men, and if they are honest they will tell you they are selling increased quantities of Eagle lye.[101]

In the words of longtime *Green Bay Press-Gazette* columnist Jack Rudolph, Wisconsin was "usually wetter than a spaniel in a thunderstorm." Wildcat brewers, bootleggers, and speakeasy operators made good money, which was important as the Great Depression took hold in the late 1920s, and suffered little if any loss of prestige in their community if arrested.[102] In fact, there is little evidence that Wisconsin's brewing families lost any of their social standing or importance to the community during Prohibition. Obituaries for brewers often took a wistful tone remembering the old times. References in newspaper society pages continued to treat brewery owners and their families as the pillars of the community that they had been in wetter days, and those businesses still in operation often continued to sponsor community teams and events as before.[103] Surviving companies continued to make charitable donations: Gutsch Brewing of Sheboygan in 1923 donated $100 to a local fund devoted to relief of starving children in Germany.[104] (See the individual brewery sections for examples of these activities.)

Wisconsinites continued to fight against prohibition with the ballot as well as with the barrel. In 1926 a referendum to call on Congress to modify the Volstead Act to allow 2.75 percent beer passed in the state by extraordinary margins in places such as Milwaukee, where the preliminary count estimated a seven to one margin in favor of beer.[105] In April 1929 a statewide referendum opposed continued enforcement of the Severson Act, which provided for state enforcement of prohibition, and Governor Walter J. Kohler Sr. signed the bill repealing the act, claiming that prohibition "has created a national situation which has become intolerable."[106]

The continued inability or unwillingness to enforce prohibition finally compelled the Hoover administration to investigate the situation. The formation of the Wickersham Commission in 1929 gave hope to brewers that the Volstead Act might be modified. Pabst announced $800,000 in improvements in anticipation of the return of real beer.[107] Prohibition, ratified with great speed and by great margins just over a decade before, had indeed been a "noble experiment," but one incompatible with the traditional cultures of many of Wisconsin's prominent ethnic groups.

Introduced in 1938, the label for Denmark Brewing Co.'s 20th Century Pale Beer captured the spirit of the technological achievements of the era. An ocean liner, a streamlined train, an airliner, and an airship all suggest the modern world that had modern tastes for which this beer was brewed. The statement "Internal Revenue Tax Paid" was included on labels from the 1930s until 1950. COLLECTION OF TYE SCHWALBE.

CHAPTER 7

BACK TO WORK, OFF TO WAR

1932–1955

"He got a glass of beer. Ain't he the lucky guy?"

Milwaukee Journal, 7 APRIL 1933

MANY WISCONSINITES OF THE 1920S CONTINUED TO BELIEVE THAT LEGAL BEER would return soon. The members of Sheboygan's Brewery Workers Local 277 were still meeting on the second and fourth Mondays of each month—some were still employed making near beer.[1] Rumors and proposals seemed more legitimate every year. The board of directors of Effinger Brewing Company actually hired renowned Chicago brewery architect Richard Griesser to draw up plans to renovate their plant.[2] Brewers were buoyed even more by the popularity of Democratic presidential candidate Franklin D. Roosevelt and the party platform plank to repeal Prohibition. The possibility of repeal may have been a factor for many who voted for Roosevelt in 1932.[3] Even before the new president took office in March 1933, the slumbering industry began to rouse. Breweries from Kenosha to Superior began to prepare for the foamy flood.

While many in Wisconsin saw the return of beer as a cultural landmark, for Roosevelt and his administration the return of beer was a way to increase tax revenue and eliminate the drain on the public purse from the costly and ineffectual enforcement of Prohibition. While total repeal of the Eighteenth Amendment was in the uncertain future, the first steps to return legal beer were taken quickly. Roosevelt's message to Congress was simple:

> *I recommend to the Congress the passage of legislation for the immediate modification of the Volstead Act, in order to legalize the manufacture and sale of beer and other beverages of such alcoholic strength as is permissible under the Constitution; and to provide through such manufacture and sale, by substantial taxes, a proper and much needed revenue for the Government.*
>
> *I deem action at this time to be of the highest importance.*[4]

The Cullen Bill, passed almost immediately after Roosevelt's inauguration, modified the Volstead Act to define beer of 3.2 percent alcohol by weight as nonintoxicating and allowed its sale in any state that did not have conflicting prohibition laws. The 3.2 percent alcohol level was selected rather than the prewar 2.75 percent level because a higher level of alcohol was considered chemically necessary to make a better-tasting beer.[5] The city of Milwaukee agreed with Roosevelt's assessment, passing a resolution of appreciation to the president that read in part:

> *The benefits Milwaukee will derive from the passage of this amendment are incalculable, thousands of operatives in the brewing industry and allied trades will resume work, the value of taxable property will increase, thousands of dollars will pour into the city treasury, and property and homeowners will obtain substantial relief from the burden of taxes they are now carrying.*[6]

With the political barriers mostly removed, it was time to make beer.

Removing the Padlocks

For those breweries that produced near beer throughout Prohibition (of which there were 164 nationwide), switching to beer was as simple as eliminating the dealcoholizing step. For Pabst, Schlitz, Miller, and Heileman, brewery renovations were more a matter of making sure they had enough capacity to meet the demand for real beer; the cost estimates for these renovations made the day after Roosevelt's election ranged from $1 million to $2 million.[7] Less expensive improvements were required at the much smaller Cream City Brewery and Independent Milwaukee Brewing Company.[8]

Some breweries had more to repair than others. Effinger's plant was in bad shape in 1931: "Within the year past most of the insulation in the cold storage rooms having dry rotten and fallen away, the ceiling and floor over the old keg beer racking room having fallen in and considerable of the cooling machinery had badly deteriorated on account of non-use." Unfortunately, the condition of the building lowered its value, giving the firm fewer assets against which to borrow money for repairs.[9] Breweries that had been mothballed or converted to other uses became scenes of frantic activity. This flurry of building was most welcome to tradesmen unemployed during the Depression. In Ripon, Wisconsin,

> *a large crew of men are employed . . . and many trades are represented in the work. Electricians are re-wiring the place, boilers and tanks are being reconditioned, and the bottling apparatus*

Fauerbach Brewing of Madison was among the many breweries that ordered new equipment to meet the demand for newly legalized beer. These new tanks ordered from the Heil Co. of Milwaukee were delivered in April 1934. COURTESY OF WISCONSIN HISTORICAL SOCIETY, WHI-16688.

is being brought up to date. An addition to the present bottling plant is to be built later.[10]

In some cases, the improvements were even more fundamental. In the small village of Arcadia, Wisconsin, a crew was employed connecting a power line to the brewery, which apparently disconnected their power during Prohibition.[11] Other breweries needed to install all-new equipment, or at least claimed they did in articles and advertisements. Rhinelander Brewing essentially started from scratch, enlarging the old building and putting in all-new equipment.[12]

Sometimes there were literal government constraints to cut through. In Shawano it was announced:

> *Federal Judge F. A. Geiger will hear arguments Saturday on the petition of the Farmers' Brewing company, Shawano, for removal of a padlock affixed on the brewery January 19 as the result of a raid Aug. 12, 1932. . . . The brewery asserted "grounds for the alleged nuisance have been removed by action of congress in legalizing 3.2 per cent beer."*[13]

Few single actions better symbolized the end of the long dry spell than cutting through the lock before starting to brew again.

BACK TO WORK

While temporary jobs for local craftsmen were important, the prospect of good, long-term

As brewing returned, brewmasters, bottlers, and other skilled brewery personnel needed to keep up with the latest trends in the industry. Milwaukee hosted the Master Brewers' Association of America's annual convention in 1937. Conventions like this enabled brewers to see (and possibly order) the latest in brewing equipment. AUTHOR'S COLLECTION.

brewery jobs was even more important during the Great Depression. Fred Pabst Jr. announced, "The day legal beer arrives we will raise our force from 600 to 2,000 employees." Miller projected an increase from 400 to 1,500 at the brewery, and more than 3,000 more in sales and other divisions. Independent Milwaukee Brewing planned to employ "several hundred more," and even Cream City planned to increase from twelve to about seventy-five men.[14] When a brewery was one of the

210 THE DRINK THAT MADE WISCONSIN FAMOUS

major employers in a smaller city, the jobs provided were even more important to the community. While Milwaukee hired the most brewery workers, estimates claimed that several thousand men would be employed directly by breweries in other parts of the state, with even more employed by industries that supported the breweries.

Businesses critical to the operation of breweries were under just as much pressure as the breweries to meet orders, and with similar promise of profits. Imperial Lithographing of Milwaukee had orders for 278 million beer labels.[15] The George J. Meyer Manufacturing Company had $1.2 million in orders for bottling machinery. After the Cullen Bill was passed and signed, the president of Meyer announced a $5,000 contribution to the Democratic National Committee because "at least one political party kept its pre-election promises." (This was newsworthy because neither Milwaukee nor Wisconsin was a stronghold for the Democrats at the time.)[16] Factories whose products were complementary to the enjoyment of beer were also busy. Furniture makers in Sheboygan were busy making more chairs and wooden bar games, and therefore Sheboygan's Jenkins Machine Company was filling orders for woodworking machines. Milwaukee firms swamped with new business included makers of barrels, boxes, pretzels, malt, pumping equipment, beer mugs, steel tanks, and insulating mats for breweries.[17] But as much interest as there was in job creation, the immediate anticipation was focused on the amber nectar soon to be flowing from bottles and taps and how to get it to thirsty customers.

New Beer's Day

The excitement surrounding the return of legal beer bordered on frenzy. The *Sheboygan Press* enthused, "Independence day without the firecrackers!

On 26 March 1933, the *Milwaukee Journal* carried a press release thinly disguised as an interview with Gustave Pabst touting the virtues of steel beer kegs. Breweries felt the need to prepare customers for this innovation because traditional coopers were still prevalent in Wisconsin. Indeed, an amendment was offered to the state bill legalizing beer that would have outlawed metal kegs in Wisconsin (it was ultimately defeated). Some Wisconsin breweries used wooden kegs for several decades; the last traditional cooperage, Frank J. Hess and Sons Cooperage in Madison, remained open until 1966. The Pressed Steel Tank Corp. created this early steel keg for Cream City Brewing in 1933.
COLLECTION OF JOHN STEINER.

Armistice day with the return of beer instead of soldiers!" Radio stations, still experimenting with live journalism, offered a variety of programs. In Sheboygan, WHBL planned to broadcast the arrival of a plane carrying Blatz beer from Milwaukee via a microphone placed outside the studio.[18] WTMJ of Milwaukee planned several hours of coverage, including interviews with brewery personnel, accounts of the entire delivery process, and the arrival of the first keg at Mader's German restaurant.[19] Some Wisconsin cities delayed their formal celebration, either because the local brewery wasn't ready yet or, as in Oshkosh, where the official event was scheduled for the day after Easter, "because of a desire not to interrupt the observance of the Lenten season."[20]

Breathless promotion was hardly needed. Crowds numbering in the thousands gathered outside more than twenty Wisconsin breweries. Brewery personnel were allowed to load brewery trucks and railcars before midnight in anticipation of the great moment. The *Milwaukee Journal* described the scene:

> *But there was a peculiar hush hanging over it all. The throngs ambled here and there—men and women, boys and girls, arm in arm—aimlessly, curiously, grinning, expectantly.*
>
> *And then . . .*
>
> *With a whoop the whole picture changed. Brewery doors flung open. Motors roared. Traffic whistles blew. . . .*

The first legal bottle of Pabst Blue Ribbon Beer after Prohibition came off the line on 27 March 1933. The label was signed by the inspector from the U.S. Department of the Treasury.
COLLECTION OF JOHN STEINER.

The crowds let loose. People slapped one another on the back. They danced. They leaped. They broke into cheers that swept out from the Blatz brewery spectators, the Schlitz crowd, the Pabst crowd, reverberating. . . .

For 10 minutes the factory whistles kept blowing. And for 10 minutes the spontaneous outburst of the crowd kept up.[21]

Traffic moved only through careful management of cars and trucks that had arrived many hours earlier from all points of the compass. In Sheboygan, an observer spotted vehicles from Wisconsin, Illinois, Iowa, Minnesota, Missouri, and Michigan. Except for the largest Milwaukee firms, the breweries themselves had few delivery vehicles. To make up this deficit, every restaurant, tavern, and household that could sent a vehicle to ensure they got some of the first available beer.[22]

The competition for the first keg or case was often heated. In Stevens Point the leading hotel sent a car to the local brewery five hours in advance, only to have a man from a country tavern escape with the first keg of Point Special. Two mixed cases of Milwaukee beer were taken to the airport, put on a waiting plane, and flown to the nation's capital, where they were presented to President Roosevelt. Deliveries in central Wisconsin were made more dramatic by a storm that coated roads with snow and ice. However, the snowbanks allowed those who had somehow purloined a bottle of beer from a passing case a chance to chill the beer quickly before savoring its contents.[23]

With so few breweries open around the nation, Wisconsin's firms had the task of supplying the thirsty in a wide radius. G. Heileman of La Crosse reported orders from Los Angeles, Winnipeg, and the West Indies. A Boston dealer was particularly persistent, demanding fifty carloads of beer.[24] Smaller breweries sought distant markets as well, aided by the fact that they needed less to supply their hometowns. West Bend Lithia, Chilton's Calumet, and Monroe's Blumer were among those supplying markets all over the country.[25] Despite the interest in distant markets, brewers assured

Schlitz employees and members of the public celebrate the first train to leave the Schlitz brewery yards on 7 April 1933.
COURTESY OF WISCONSIN HISTORICAL SOCIETY, WHI-1929.

local residents that they would be taken care of before orders were filled abroad.

Despite the enthusiasm, problems on the first day were rare. In Milwaukee one man was killed when he was run over by a beer truck after falling off a refrigerator car at Schlitz. At Blatz, a series of loud bangs followed by a flash and sirens was taken at first as an attack by hijackers, but it turned out to be a truck backfiring.[26] The hijacking fear was not totally unfounded, since gangsters were not going to let their major source of revenue go without a fight. A Pabst truck carrying four hundred cases of beer to Chicago was stopped on the Waukegan Road by four armed men. In one of the friendlier instances of gang activity, the hijackers drove the deliverymen around in a car for five hours and then gave them their empty truck back after the beer had been unloaded.[27] As late as June, a load of eighty barrels from the Kewaunee Brewing Co. was hijacked en route to Chicago.[28]

Aside from a few dire and desperate warnings from the WCTU and other drys, the return of beer was met with much rejoicing. Songwriter Irving Berlin observed the return of legal beer and announced: "What it amounts to . . . is that our public again will become singers. Now they are definitely listeners."[29] Most accounts included descriptions of

A truck loaded with cases of Blatz beer in 1933. The improvements in truck transportation since the pre-Prohibition years encouraged brewers to ship less by rail and more by truck. COLLECTION OF JOHN STEINER.

Patrons pack the barroom of the Fauerbach Brewing Co. for a taste of legal beer on 7 April 1933. The crowd was mostly men, but a few women were present. Behind the bar, a portrait of President Franklin D. Roosevelt and banners praising the New Deal show the gratitude many felt for the president's role in bringing beer back. COURTESY OF WISCONSIN HISTORICAL SOCIETY, WHI-1956.

singing by reveleres, with "Sweet Adeline" among the favorites, though one *Journal* account noted its relative absence and suggested, "Perhaps the flow of beer was not in sufficient quantity to intone the old song properly."[30]

A RIGHT TO BE GLAD

Those whose jobs depended on brewing and related industries were even more enthusiastic about the return of beer than consumers. In a special section of the *Milwaukee Journal,* a wide variety of businesses congratulated the city on the return of beer. Some ads celebrated traditional ties to beer: the Northern Pacific Railway welcomed back beer and the business it would bring the company, with early estimates at 150 carloads daily. As a reminder of old tavern lunches, another ad offered customers Jack Sprat brand pickled pigs' feet packed in beer steins (just in case they had disposed of their drinking vessels in the previous fourteen years). Other ads in the supplement illustrated the changing world that the brewers were reentering. An ad touting Phillips 66 gasoline showed how much the automobile and delivery truck had changed transportation and shipping since 1920. Another, offering home refrigerators by General Electric, signaled to brewers that the importance of home consumption of beer would increase in the years after Prohibition. Government officials joined in the celebration and the analysis. Wisconsin governor Albert G. Schmedeman reassured those who feared the return of beer would decrease milk consumption and hurt dairy farmers, "We are encouraged by the knowledge that cheese has always been the boon companion of beer and the demand for Wisconsin cheese . . . will see a marked increase."[31] Milwaukee officials estimated that the return of brewing would increase revenues from use of city water by more than $50,000 per year.[32]

For the most part, the euphoria over economic stimulus was well founded. *Brewery Age* estimated that $10 million in excise taxes had been collected in the first few days of legal sales.[33] Over the next few years, more than forty thousand people found employment in the nation's breweries, and many thousands more were employed supplying the breweries or selling their products. Many of the suppliers represented the most important industries of the Upper Midwest. The lumber industry,

After the return of beer, Blatz issued a series of coasters that celebrated the contributions of the brewing industry to the national economy. Another coaster in this series proclaimed that brewers paid $1 million in taxes per day to federal, state, and local governments—$500 a minute to the federal government. AUTHOR'S COLLECTION.

farmers, and malting companies in Wisconsin and surrounding states all benefited and grew.

PRODUCTS, PLACES, PEOPLE

The spectacle of the early days of legal beer, with its celebrations and seemingly unquenchable demand for any and all beer, masked the underlying difficulties facing businesses trying to earn a steady profit. Beer had been gone for thirteen years, and American society had changed, along with drinking tastes. Beer was returning during the worst economic crisis in the nation's history—which affected everything from financing to labor to demand for the product itself.

The vast majority of breweries after Prohibition were companies that had been in business before, and with a very few exceptions they were family firms that still bore the founder's name and in which stock was still closely held by his descendants. They had survived Prohibition in part because they had little debt and were able to keep enough cash flowing to pay the bills. Most returning breweries had developed a following in their home region and were able, at least at first, to trade on this loyalty after reopening. Leinenkugel in Chippewa Falls, Walter Brewing in nearby Eau Claire, and many other breweries were able to recover much of their market despite not being ready on New Beer's Day. The Berlin Brewing Company was not ready in time, so it distributed Manitowoc Products beer for a few weeks until it was ready, hoping to retain its local accounts.[34] The George Walter Brewing Company of Appleton published an ad that attempted to convert its delay into virtue: "With but a limited time elapsing between the passage of the beer bill and the time

After beer became legal again, beer signs reappeared on taverns and restaurants throughout the state. This two-sided hanging sign dates from the 1930s. COLLECTION OF MARTIN SCHRYVER.

While ales were much less popular than lager beers, a few breweries continued to make ale, and some taverns, such as the Ale House, continued to feature it (matchbook cover ca. 1940). COLLECTION OF TYE SCHWALBE.

when beer may actually be sold, we decided not to rush production at the risk of disappointing our patrons."[35]

What Ales Thee

Most returning breweries regained their loyal customers by bringing back favorite old brands, but deciding what type of beer to make was not always self-evident. Lager was the clear favorite in Wisconsin as in most of America west of the Appalachians, but a few large breweries, notably Pabst, Miller, and Blatz, also included an ale in their portfolios. Ten smaller breweries experimented with ale styles as a way of filling a gap in the market, but demand was weak. Most of these labels did not survive more than a few years after World War II. The boldest move was made by tiny Mayville Brewing Company, which hired a Swedish brewmaster from Chicago who proposed to make Swedish-style dark ales and to market them in Chicago—a venture that proved unsuccessful.[36]

In contrast to the tepid demand for ale, the release of bock beer each spring was always a highlight of the beer year, and was frequently a cause for parades and other celebrations. Nearly two-thirds of Wisconsin's post-Prohibition breweries made bock beer for at least a few years, from the smallest village lager brewery to the mighty giants of Milwaukee.[37] West Bend Lithia Brewing Company felt so confident about its ability to supply customers with lager in 1933 that it also prepared bock for its traditional Easter-time

Ogren's Swedish Porter (and Stout, which had a nearly identical label) failed to gain a profitable market, and Mayville Brewing Co. soon went out of business. These beers were sold in eleven-ounce bottles (label from 1935–36). COLLECTION OF TYE SCHWALBE.

release.[38] But they were among the very few—for most breweries, bock beer waited until 1934. With the loss of tied-house saloons due to post-Prohibition regulations, brewers raced each other to get their bock in the taverns and restaurants, most of which were not willing to commit more than one draught line to a seasonal specialty. The American Brewers' Association proposed a uniform date for bock release, often 17 March, and encouraged its members to cooperate, "providing all other associations and members of the brewing industry will do likewise."[39] Despite these efforts, brewers often complained that their rivals were releasing bock early and getting an unfair advantage.[40]

Calumet Brewing Co. produced this label for "High Power Bock" before the federal government outlawed such claims in 1935. The "High Power" and "Bock" labels appear to be overprinted along with the box intended to cover the word *not* in the statement of alcohol content. The U-permits were issued to breweries in 1933, but these statements were also removed from labels in 1935 on the grounds that they could provide the mistaken impression that the federal government inspected or approved the contents of the package.
COLLECTION OF TYE SCHWALBE.

HOMETOWN SUDS (SUD BY SUDWEST)

While it was a common boast that "every little Wisconsin village had a brewery," some communities truly seemed to believe that a local brewery was an essential public service, rather than just a traditional ethnic business. In the village of Mayville, a number of townsmen "agreed that [the mill] should be converted into a brewery, because Mayville is entitled to a suds manufacturing plant."[41] In some small cities, like Arcadia, Rice Lake, and Fountain City, the brewery had a public tap where the locals could draw themselves a foaming mug of fresh beer.[42] Arcadia Brewing ran afoul of Wisconsin officials when it was found that 14 percent of its output was being dispensed free of taxation in this way.[43] Even in the much larger city of Superior, the Northern Brewing Company had "no bar but [we] let each person help themselves to a reasonable quantity."[44] For some people, the brewery taproom was just as important to community life as a tavern or restaurant, though the amount consumed by patrons probably was inflated through distant memories. The taproom or rathskeller was an important goodwill effort by the brewery, and failure to accommodate local residents could result in diminished support for the brewery.[45]

This perception that every city could support a brewery—encouraged by the initial success of legal beer—led new investors to seek profits by reopening a defunct brewery or building an all-new plant. Investors even sought to open new companies in four municipalities in Wisconsin that had never before hosted a brewery. Only those in Denmark and Westfield went into production, and they only survived thirteen and nine years, respectively.[46] Out-of-state investors were common. Chicago investors were already familiar with Wisconsin's breweries from Prohibition-era operations, and were looking into purchases from New Glarus to Sturgeon Bay. Investors from St. Paul built the Capitol Brewing Company of Milwaukee in 1933, and another group of St. Paulites restarted the Bloomer Brewery in 1934.[47] The strong socialist community in Milwaukee attempted to start a cooperative brewery, but the proposed Cream City location never produced any beer, and they moved the business to Grafton.[48] The Milwaukee-Shawano Brewing Company holds the dubious distinction of being the first Wisconsin brewery to close after Prohibition: it began brewing in late 1933 and shut down in May 1934.[49]

The newly reopened breweries faced immediate shortages, in particular of bottles and kegs. In the rush to obtain kegs, brewers incurred greater transportation expense. Some cooperages did not dry their wood thoroughly in the hurry to meet the demand, making the kegs heavier, and the German kegs imported to fill the gap were of heavier workmanship to begin with. The American Brewers' Association launched a program to have brewers report the lower actual weight of their cooperage in an attempt to forestall a railroad rate increase in 1937.[50]

Several employees of the Geo. Walter Brewing Co. of Appleton gather in the brewery taproom (ca. 1970). Left to right: Matt Rossmeissl, Bill Ashman, Tom Ashman, Marlin "Tex" Behnke, and Robert "Cookie" Hauser. The tap is the device at far right. COLLECTION OF BRIAN ZENEFSKI.

The Wisconsin Co-operative Brewery operated from 1935 until 1941. COLLECTION OF TYE SCHWALBE.

BACK TO WORK, OFF TO WAR 219

MEN AT WORK

There was no shortage of labor for the breweries. Because the specter of Prohibition remained until after World War II, breweries frequently publicized their contributions to the community. The most important, given the catastrophic unemployment during the Great Depression, was the number of jobs created directly and indirectly by the resumption of business.

The biggest Milwaukee breweries had payrolls numbering in the thousands. A list of brewery job descriptions compiled in the late 1930s described more than three dozen distinct positions available at a large brewery. Most of these jobs did not require previous experience and so were eagerly sought as entry-level jobs. In a large brewery, most positions offered opportunities for promotion, so the majority of year-round employees expected to make a career out of their work in the brewery. Working conditions in the breweries were considered "as ideal as the work will allow." The breweries were "clean, well ventilated and well lighted." Hazards were considered "negligible," in comparison to many other industries.[51]

Small breweries sometimes had trouble retaining brewmasters and other key personnel. The local-interest columns of the *Winona (Minn.) Republican-Herald* chronicled the movements of nearby Arcadia Brewing Company's brewers: Peter Kronschnabl left for Germantown; Joseph Hartel came to Arcadia from Jackson, Michigan, but soon left for Eulberg Brewing in Portage. Ernest Maier arrived from Chicago and resigned a year later, Albin Bill went from Arcadia to Reedsburg, and Harold Hoover went to an unnamed brewery in Milwaukee. Even bookkeeper Irene Brandt left to take a job in Milwaukee.[52]

The brewery workforce was not diverse by modern standards. With the exception of a few office workers, the workforce was exclusively male. While some women were employed in bottling prior to Prohibition, social norms during the Depression reserved most jobs for the male breadwinner of the family. The Rhinelander Brewing Company made a special point of hiring "chiefly married men who have lived here some years."[53] In addition, brewery workers were usually of German descent or from other nations with a brewing heritage. Many employees were hired based on recommendations from friends or neighbors, creating a largely closed society.

TAP A CAN

A large brewery with healthy cash flow and strong credit was in a better position to take advantage of technological improvements, especially in packaging, than was a small brewery with limited access to capital. The single most important advance in the

Early advertisements for canned beer sought to develop customer acceptance. The list of advantages included several that were unique to flat-top cans, including the space-saving features. The advantage of disposability would be less appealing to many twenty-first-century consumers. AUTHOR'S COLLECTION.

Working in a Mid-sized Brewery

Working in the local brewery was a good, steady job. The pay was usually more than for similar jobs elsewhere, especially at the many unionized breweries. There was a certain amount of celebrity attached to working at the brewery, plus the free beer. However, hours were often long, the work could be dangerous, and all employees needed to work together and sometimes cover for each other to get the beer moved around from tank to tavern.

The Geo. Walter Brewing Company of Appleton provides a good example of a typical brewery workforce. Several families had multiple members and generations employed at the brewery, and many jobs passed from father to son. The changing nature of brewing and the daily realities of promotions, absences, and helping out in other departments meant that a given employee could have multiple titles during his career.

Adler Brau historian Brian Zenefski spent several years tracking down employees of Geo. Walter Brewing or their descendants to assemble a list of the men who made and sold Adler Brau in the period between 1933 and 1972, when the brewery closed. Zenefski undertook his ambitious project to pay tribute to the many unsung workers who made it possible for everyone else to enjoy his or her beer. Through his work, it is possible to get some idea of the community of a post-Prohibition brewery.

Meet Some of the Geo. Walter Beer Guys (1930s through 1972)

- **Alex Knaus:** Alex senior was one of the early brewmasters in the years after Prohibition.
- **Alex A. Knaus:** Son of Alex senior, Alex was brewmaster from 1949 until the brewery closed in 1972. He also held the title of plant superintendent.
- **John Haug, Sig Ligelbach, George Blessing:** These three also were brewmasters in the early days after the return of real beer. Blessing's brewing notes were discovered by Brian Zenefski and provided to Stone Arch Brewery, where they became the basis for the version of Adler Brau that has been brewed off and on in recent years.
- **Jerome Linskins:** Jerry was an assistant brewmaster for many years.
- **Ervin La Budde:** As chief engineer and head of maintenance, Erv was perhaps even more important to getting the brewery running again after Prohibition than the brewmaster. His duties included being head brewery mechanic and repairing delivery trucks when needed. He was also the first president of the brewery workers' union.

Front row: Leo Toonen, assistant office manager; Nic Dohr, office manager; Alex Knaus, brewmaster; Erv La Budde, chief engineer; Art Winz, driver.

Second row: Frank Fries, salesman; Rolland Marx, office accountant; Henry Rossmeissl, office help and truck driver; Tony Popp, fermenting cellar; Rudy Fischer, driver; Andy Janssen, driver; Joe Stilp, driver; Ed Martens, fireman; Bill Drexler, bottling department; Al "Tiny" Stilp, driver; Alex Knaus Jr., apprentice brewer; Frank Stilp, fireman; Bill Stilp, driver.

Third row: Wilbur Popp, fermenting cellar; Bill Spilski, driver; Ed Zeininger, driver (floater); George Niles, driver; Andy Pekel, bottler; Leon "Tuffy" Toonen, floater; John E. Walter, brewhouse; Oscar Dohr, racking room; George E. Walter Jr., finishing cellar. (John E. and George E. Walter were both grandsons of the brewery founder.) COLLECTION OF BRIAN ZENEFKSI.

- **CLARENCE "DUTCH" VAN HANDEL:** Dutch was originally hired as an assistant brewmaster, but when Dutch and Alex Knaus disagreed about certain aspects of the brewhouse, Dutch was made a goodwill man. A goodwill man (sometimes called salesman or field man) would visit drinking establishments and buy the patrons a round of Adler Brau to drum up business for the brewery.

foreman and took over his father's job when Erv retired. He also

generation of La Buddes to work at the brewery. He worked in the
driver.

a supervisor in the bottle house. Later, he became a field man. Field
unts and worked to build up new business for the brewery.
d in the bottle house. He ran the bottle cleaner and unpacked empty
ing line.
ck driver for many years, and then became a goodwill man.
Bill worked in the bottle house and was a goodwill man. He was active
elpful to Brian in gathering the information included in this list.
rewhouse and drove a delivery truck. He retired after fifty years of service to the brewery, and was honored with a gold watch.

BACK TO WORK, OFF TO WAR   223

- **Kenneth Merkes:** Kenneth took over the delivery route of Joe Stilp. His weekly schedule gives an idea of the variety of accounts. Monday and Thursday: accounts in Brillion (east of Appleton). Tuesday: grocery stores. Wednesday: Marion distributor (northwest of Appleton). Friday: home deliveries.
- **Earl Muenchow:** Earl was a truck driver who also worked in the brewhouse when needed.
- **James "Jim" Weisgerber:** Jim was another employee who switched off between the brewhouse and delivery trips.
- **Matthias "Matt" Rossmeissl:** Matt was the son of Henry Rossmeissl, who was brewery president in the 1960s. Matt took over for Jim Weisgerber in the brewhouse when Jim was making deliveries. Matt also helped out on Friday, which was cleanup day at the brewery. Instead of brewing, employees would flush the system with caustic cleaner. Matt was also heavily involved with the union, much to the consternation of his father.
- **Harrison Coons:** Harrison was a brewhouse assistant who took over the brew kettle when Matt Rossmeissl was on vacation.
- **Joseph Glasheen:** One of Joe's jobs in the bottle house was to look through the inspection glass to check fill levels and find impurities in the bottles. While most of this work was eliminated when Geo. Walter Brewing acquired the second RCA inspection machine in Wisconsin, he still used the inspection glass when the RCA machine was being serviced. He took over for Tuffy Toonen in the bottle house when Tuffy was out on deliveries.
- **Norman Wettstein:** Norm was a fireman, which in breweries meant taking care of the boilers and keeping them fired up. The difficult part of this job was shoveling all the coal necessary to maintain the fires. Norm also served as a watchman in the brewery.
- **Martin "Spec" Hubers:** Spec had one of the least glamorous jobs in the brewery—stacking cases in the bottle house. But someone had to do it.

This label was for a bottle containing "12 fluid ounces or less," suggesting it was intended for underfilled bottles ("short fills") that would be given to employees instead of being destroyed. AUTHOR'S COLLECTION.

- **Marlin "Tex" Behnke:** Tex worked in the brewhouse filtering the beer, pumping it to the bottle house, and filling ("racking") kegs.
- **James Lenz:** James sometimes worked in the brewhouse, but mostly worked in the bottle house operating the bottle washer and pasteurizer.
- **Leroy Stierman:** Leroy was another employee with many tasks. He operated the bottle filler and the case packer. He also filled in on the inspection glass when the RCA inspector was being repaired.
- **Carl Kettner:** Carl worked in the brewhouse, but also worked in the bottle house making sure labels were on correctly. He also had the Chilton delivery route.
- **Robert "Cookie" Hauser:** Cookie worked in the fermentation cellar. He was the only man known to have died on the job at the brewery. He was overcome by fumes while cleaning out one of the fermenters in 1971.
- **Tom Ashman:** Tom was a true jack-of-all-trades in a business where multiple jobs and titles were common. During his years at Adler Brau, he worked on the mash tun, cooler, and filter and cleaned the brew kettle. He pumped beer to the bottle house, washed and pitched kegs, and worked in the bottle house when needed. He also delivered beer on Fridays.
- **Bill Ashman:** Bill washed kegs, helped pitch kegs, and stacked full kegs. He also helped clean empty beer tanks.
- **Rolland Marx:** Rollie was general manager of the brewery during the later years of the business. He negotiated union contracts, worked with the federal government to get approval for labels, and ran the day-to-day business of the brewery. He earned the respect of employees and fellow businesspeople in Appleton. When the property was sold after the brewery closed, Rollie handled this as well.
- **Don and Mike Marx:** Rollie's sons helped out in the brewery as boys, assembling beer cases and doing other light work.
- **William Selle:** Bill was the office manager for twenty-two years.
- **Joe Ebenhoe:** "Little Joe" worked in the office for ten years and became office manager when Bill Selle left for a position outside the brewery.

There were at least forty other men who worked at the brewery at various times after Prohibition. Some worked only as summer help, but sometimes a summer job became a full-time position. Charles Rundquist was a local high school teacher who worked for Adler Brau during the summer when he was not teaching. He worked in the bottle house, delivered beer, and helped wherever he was needed. After he had done this during the summers of 1962 and 1963, school authorities told him that he had to choose between teaching or the beer business, since they thought it set a bad example for a teacher to be seen in a beer truck and then in the classroom.

Geo. Walter Brewing never employed women, which was somewhat unusual, since many breweries employed women in clerical positions.[1]

---

[1] Information from Brian Zenefski, "Employees of the George Walter Brewing Co., Appleton, WI" (unpublished manuscript and accompanying correspondence, 2016).

Many of the earliest flat-top cans included opening instructions on the sides. An original "church key" opener was often given away in each case of canned beer. The first opening instructions showed only one hole, but later versions recommended making two holes so that air could enter the can and allow the beer to flow out faster. COLLECTION OF DAVID WENDL.

years after legalization was the introduction of canned beer. First introduced by American Can Company and G. Krueger Brewing of Newark, New Jersey, in January 1935, canned beer exceeded all early sales projections. Convinced by the early reaction, Premier-Pabst (as it was known during the mid-1930s) signed on with American Can and became the second company to market beer in cans. Krueger and Premier-Pabst both used American Can's flat top, which could be filled faster and saved space but required new equipment. Rival manufacturer Continental Can Company challenged American's monopoly with the so-called cone top, which could be filled on existing bottling lines. In addition, cone tops could be opened with bottle openers that customers already owned, whereas flat tops required new tools (the so-called church key openers) and instructions.

Premier-Pabst's first newspaper ads in the summer of 1935 touted the advantages of the "Keglined TapaCan": the beer was protected from light, there were no bottle deposits to pay and no empties to save or return, the cans took up less space in the refrigerator, and—important in an era when many retailers were not allowed to sell cold beer—the cans chilled faster than bottles. Opening the flat-top can was no problem either, since an opener was given away with the purchase of three or more TapaCans.[54] While Premier-Pabst launched the cans on a nationwide basis almost immediately,

226 THE DRINK THAT MADE WISCONSIN FAMOUS

the company may have been hesitant to risk the name of their flagship Blue Ribbon on a canned product at first and instead brought back the brand name Export for the canned brew. (The Blue Ribbon name had been given to bottled and draught Blue Ribbon Ale in 1934, but the canned ale was Old Tankard.)[55]

By the end of the first year of canned beer, *Fortune* magazine opined, "One feels that the brewer must either adopt both containers or shut up shop and go out of business." While customer acceptance was critical to the long-term success of the beer can, the economics of the bottle house were also important. A thousand bottles, including labels and crowns, cost $21.83; a thousand cans cost at least $24, more if crowns were needed. Since cans were lighter and took up less space, they offered a significant transportation cost savings. This factor would be outweighed, however, for most brewers by the cost of having to buy new cans for every shipment.

The extent to which the calculations of brewing companies was changed was dramatically outlined by *Fortune*:

This cardboard point-of-sale advertisement for the early Schlitz cone-top cans attempted to build consumer acceptance for canned beer by emphasizing its similarity to bottled beer. This type of cone-top can is known as an inverted-rib low-profile can. COLLECTION OF DAVID WENDL.

Cone-top cans offered advantages to both brewers and customers. The brewers could fill the cans with slight alterations to their bottling equipment. Customers could use openers they already had. Cone-top manufacturers also claimed that the crown protected the spout and enabled customers to drink straight from the can. This crown from the Weber Waukesha Brewing Co. emphasizes this feature. COLLECTION OF TYE SCHWALBE.

BACK TO WORK, OFF TO WAR

The beer business is no longer simple. It is tangled in technology and higher economics. It is deviled by freight rates, the science of plastics, the rent of floor space, the price of steel, the properties of sunlight. Its lexicon bristles with terms like one-trip container, metal turbidity, nonrefillable, flash pasteurization, dealer resistance. Bottle washing and the dimensions of a refrigerator shelf suddenly become slide rule problems. The beer business finds itself rudely thrust under the microscopes of expensive laboratories, onto the desks of investment counselors, across the drafting boards of advertising men; and toted from door to door by canvassers in dead-earnest surveys. The beer business did not bring this on itself. It was brought by the tin can.[56]

Crowntainers were two-piece cans introduced in 1940 by Crown Cork & Seal Co. They proved popular and remained in use through the 1950s. COLLECTION OF DAVID WENDL.

RED TAPE AND REVENUE STAMPS

While brewers were overjoyed to be back in business, their joy was tempered by the maze of regulations with which they had to comply. Much of the regulation was designed to make sure the practices that motivated prohibition could not be repeated. The laws passed by federal and state governments to prevent breweries from gaining undue influence over individual retail establishments proved particularly tricky for brewers to negotiate. (The law governing Wisconsin was created by the Leidiger Beer Bill of 1933, sponsored by brewer and assemblyman Louis G. Leidiger of Merrill.)[57] Most of these strictly regulated the dollar value of merchandise or service that a brewery could provide to a retail store, restaurant, or tavern—in some cases prohibiting it completely. These were intended in part to protect cash-strapped local breweries from national breweries, which had more money to lavish on their customers. The uncertainty led to frequent appeals to Wisconsin's Division of Beverage and Cigarette Taxes (BTD) agents to clarify the rules.

In addition to helping with local questions, the state

228 THE DRINK THAT MADE WISCONSIN FAMOUS

agency helped the Wisconsin brewers challenge out-of-state breweries (called "foreign" even if located in the United States) that were using unfair or deceptive trade practices. The biggest problems were with breweries from Illinois. Chicago was the headquarters for several of the most prominent bootlegging gangs during Prohibition, and it was alleged that many legal breweries in Illinois and several in Wisconsin were under direct or indirect mob control.[58] The BTD sent numerous reprimands to the Prima Brewing Company and Manhattan Brewing Company, both of Chicago. In addition to frequent mishandling of stamps, Prima was charged with using labels without sufficient identification of the brewery name and location for several brands, including the ironically named Pride of Wisconsin.[59] Wisconsin Brewing of Kenosha, located near the Illinois border, was investigated for illegally transferring Wisconsin tax stamps to the Manhattan Brewing Company, which then laundered them to other Chicago breweries. The element of danger present in working for the BTD in this era is suggested by its considerable correspondence with Smith & Wesson about maintenance of the division's firearms.[60]

Other regulations were proposed by politicians who were not opposed to the return of brewing but wanted to ensure their constituents were neither harmed by nor placed in a position to benefit from the economic engine that was beer. Large and small breweries alike were threatened by legislation proposed by lawmakers who did not understand the brewing industry or process. In addition to the attempted ban on steel kegs in Wisconsin, an assemblyman who was concerned that "brewers' chemists might find a way to avoid use of barley and thereby take away the farmers' interest in beer" proposed a requirement that all beer have at least 66 percent barley malt. Luckily for brewers catering to American tastes for beer with substantial amounts of corn or rice, the rule was defeated by one vote. In 1937 a congressman from Iowa proposed a bill that would have imposed an extra tax of fifty cents per gallon on any beer made with agricultural commodities not grown in the United States. Such a bill would have made it nearly impossible to maintain the consistency of brands made with imported hops (not to mention nearly double the cost of beer), but the American Brewers' Association believed (rightly) that it was unlikely to become law.[61]

The largest breweries, such as Pabst, Schlitz, and Miller, had their own legal departments that handled tax and compliance issues and were available to deal with problems encountered by their distributors and customers as well. Smaller brewers depended on industry organizations like the American Brewers' Association for legal advice.

Guidance from the ABA was critical for smaller brewers trying to negotiate the programs of Roosevelt's New Deal, which marked the largest expansion of federal government activity in American history. All businesses with eight or more employees were required to participate in the new Social Security pension scheme and to file all the necessary paperwork with the relevant agencies to demonstrate compliance. In these and other similar cases, the ABA sent monthly circulars to its members explaining the new regulations.[62] The National Recovery Administration caused another major compliance headache for the brewers. The NRA wage and price standards were designed to allow for fair profits and wages without triggering inflation in the recovering economy. While theoretically voluntary, the administration put heavy pressure on all businesses to fall in line. Like other industries, brewers that adopted NRA codes placed the NRA eagle prominently in their advertisements and sometimes on their packaging materials. But the NRA was ruled unconstitutional in 1935, largely because smaller producers resented the fact that large businesses had written the codes with government in a way that would benefit larger firms.[63] Another New Deal program, the Civilian Conservation Corps, benefited brewers, since beer was sold at the camp canteens.[64]

This label from a La Crosse Breweries sixty-four-ounce "picnic" bottle bears the NRA eagle along with the U-permit statement. It is also noteworthy since it has the word *volume* in the alcohol content statement crossed out and replaced with the word *weight* (ca. 1934). COLLECTION OF TYE SCHWALBE.

FEDERAL, STATE, AND LOCAL

The American federal system, with its web of concurrent powers shared by state and federal governments, created many of the greatest headaches for brewers of all sizes. Even government officials ruefully admitted that "a nation-wide business must constantly keep its lawyer on one side and its accountant on the other."[65] Prior to repeal, states had not imposed excise taxes on alcohol—leaving this revenue source to the federal government. But with the federal government, forty-eight states, and more than 175,000 smaller government units all seeking to fund essential operations during a national crisis, alcohol taxes became tempting targets. Moreover, politicians preferred raising such "sin" taxes rather than politically unpopular income or sales taxes. Policy makers recognized the importance of the overlapping alcohol taxes to all governments, as well as the entrenched nature of local interests, and grudgingly conceded that these taxes could not be streamlined.[66]

All units of government clung to their ability to tax alcohol because of the regulatory functions the tax and its administration served. States that sought to discourage alcohol often raised taxes to high levels—especially if there were no breweries in the state and the tax would be borne largely by parties who could not vote on the policy. State excise tax rates changed frequently and varied widely—in 1948 amounts ranged from sixty-two cents per barrel in Missouri and California to ten dollars in Louisiana.[67]

Wisconsin required stamps on all bulk beer packages, and each brewer had to purchase stamps in advance from the Beverage Tax Division. While many other states also used stamps, about a dozen adopted a system of special crown caps and can lids.[68] Because the states using tax-paid crowns and lids were primarily in the southern and eastern parts of the country, the burden of purchasing these items and keeping them straight in the bottle house fell primarily on a few large brewers, including Blatz, Miller, Pabst, and Schlitz.

These breweries typically had compliance offices that dealt with the tangle of regulations, but large and small brewers alike frequently fell afoul of government agencies.

The government agencies were at least efficient and responded to questions or disputes quickly. Of the hundreds of questions put to either the BTD or the IRS, most were answered on the next business day. This does not mean the answer was always what the brewery hoped to hear. In general, state agencies seemed more willing than the federal government to work with the brewers. It may have been because of the shorter chain of command, or because the state government had more incentive to keep breweries operating profitably and maintain their local revenue sources.

Ohio used tax-paid crown caps to collect beverage taxes. Most tax crowns featured either the state seal or another easily recognizable emblem. Few smaller brewers exported to states with crown requirements, although the Independent Milwaukee Brewery shipped to Michigan. Even the sophisticated bottle houses of the giant brewers had all they could do to keep up with the changing requirements. Not only did the tax rate change every few years, rendering older crowns void, but several states, such as Kansas, required the package size to be indicated on the crowns. To make matters worse, Minnesota required crowns of different colors for 3.2 percent beer and "strong" beer. A brewery might need as many as forty different crowns to distribute a flagship brand like Schlitz throughout the country—not to mention a similar number for each premium and "popular price" brand. COLLECTION OF TYE SCHWALBE.

BEING LABELED

Wisconsin was one of many states that adopted the federal label standards contained in federal Regulation 7 for local use. Among other things, Regulation 7 specifically prohibited any strength or health claims on beer labels. While the list changed throughout the period, the forbidden words and phrases included "strong," "full strength," "extra strength," "full old-time alcoholic strength," "tonic," "healthy," "vitamins," "non-fattening," "stimulating," and many others, but with the proviso "except where required by law."[69] One of those places was neighboring Minnesota, which required the word

BACK TO WORK, OFF TO WAR   231

"strong" on any beer of 5 percent or greater alcohol by volume. Nebraska and North Dakota required that the alcohol content be printed on their labels, but Nebraska required alcohol by weight and North Dakota alcohol by volume. In addition, North Dakota did not accept the commonly used "does not exceed [a given percent]" wording, and required a precise measurement—which could not vary by more than .2 percent.[70]

Since the federal government regulations normally took precedence over any conflicting state regulations, the situation with beer labels was most unusual. A single national standard would have been much easier for brewers to follow, but the states jealously guarded their prerogatives to regulate and tax alcohol. A number of brewers tried to simplify their compliance by using different neck labels in different states, but that only solved the problems of the office staff—not of the bottle house employees responsible for operating the label machines.

Meeting federal requirements meant following some seemingly arbitrary, if not silly, standards. Section 8 of the labeling regulations required that a twenty-four-ounce package must be labeled as a three-fourths quart. Alcohol content could not appear in print larger than 6-point boldface capitals, unless local regulations required otherwise.

Fox Head Waukesha may have been trying to attract more customers with this unusual method of measuring the strength of their beer, but 10 percent proof is the same as 5 percent alcohol by volume—so this was really just a standard lager beer (label ca. 1934). COLLECTION OF TYE SCHWALBE.

The tap knobs of the immediate post-Prohibition era were much smaller than the tap handles of the craft beer era, but they were intended more to identify the tap for the bartender rather than to promote the beer to the customer. The Bonded Pilsner Beer knob in the center is one of the few known artifacts from the Old Lager Brewing Co. of Milwaukee, which existed from 1934 to 1938. (All knobs are from the 1930s.) COLLECTION OF JOHN STEINER.

232   THE DRINK THAT MADE WISCONSIN FAMOUS

Protecting All Parties

While seemingly absurd, the various requirements were intended to protect the brewers from unfair competition as well as to protect the public from fraud. During the 1930s the states adopted their own requirements for labeling tap handles in retail establishments. In Wisconsin each tap needed to have a sign on or near the tap indicating the manufacturer and type of beer that was visible for a distance of ten feet. Some tavern keepers objected to the signs because they got in the way of business, and "the customers take them off the bar as souvenirs, and, in some places we have had to replace them a half dozen times." The BTD argued that the law reduced the substitution of cheaper beers for more expensive brands, which apparently occurred with some frequency.[71] In one case, the Oshkosh Brewing Company appealed to the BTD for assistance because local taverns were pouring other supposedly inferior beers under Oshkosh tap signs. The company was reluctant to take the matter to the local district attorney "because if we did, we probably would be black-listed by the tavern-keepers' association."[72]

Irrational Exuberance

The excitement of drinking real beer again and the attractions of being able to supply the seemingly endless demand encouraged more breweries to open than were needed to meet the long-term demand. In more than twenty cases, a company either filed incorporation papers or made other serious moves to establish the business, but never produced any beer.[73] As more and more breweries finished reconditioning and started production, Wisconsin's number of breweries grew until eighty-eight were in production in March 1936.[74] A few breweries had already closed, however, including Milwaukee's Banner Brewing Company, an all-new brewery that went out of business the previous month. Breweries in Medford and Kenosha had also closed after very short terms of operation (though Medford would open again in 1940). The list of breweries began to dwindle and the number of businesses dropped to seventy-four in September 1938. Two closed because of low demand for their style of beer: Mayville Brewing, mentioned earlier, and Milwaukee's new Fischbach Brewing Company. Fischbach was probably doomed by its decision to focus on wheat beers, which were popular before

Gettelman Brewing Co. of Milwaukee celebrated the return of nickel beer with this spinner token. The raised dot in the middle of the 5¢ beer side elevated the token so that it could be spun on a table. The arrow pointed to the person selected to buy the next round of beers. COLLECTION OF TYE SCHWALBE.

Prohibition but found little favor after and were largely supplanted by soft drinks. Several other breweries closed for reasons that were never specifically reported, but were almost certainly financial, especially since 1937 saw a return of unemployment and a sharp decline in the health of the economy. While a few of the casualties were formed after repeal, like Riverview Brewing of Manitowoc, most were venerable firms that had been in business before 1870. Among these were the Fox Lake Brewing Co., which was founded in 1856, and Milwaukee's Cream City Brewery, which could trace its lineage back to the West Hill Brewery of 1853.

Matters got so bad for the brewing industry that the Wisconsin legislature demanded an investigation of the BTD to determine why tax revenues had declined so much. The responses from the brewers surveyed agreed that the economy was solely to blame. Miller went into more detail, noting, "A large portion of beer tax revenue is derived from so-called draught beer, which is sold in large quantities in establishments near large industrial plants. The fact that such plants have been partially closed, or at least operating on a restricted schedule, is reflected in greatly decreased sales of such establishments so located."[75]

The small brewhouse of the Banner Brewing Co. and its apparently hand-built equipment had much in common with the start-up breweries of the early craft brewing period. Unfortunately, Banner was not able to gain a share of the competitive Milwaukee beer market (photograph from 1935). COLLECTION OF JOHN STEINER.

Fischbach Brewing used this neck label on bottles of its Weiss Beer (ca. 1934). COLLECTION OF TYE SCHWALBE.

Another factor in the struggle of Wisconsin breweries to survive in the years after Prohibition was the vigorous competition from out-of-state breweries. In July 1934, twenty-three such breweries purchased revenue stamps to sell their beer in Wisconsin. Most were from the border states of Illinois, Minnesota, and Michigan, but three Indiana breweries were also included in the list. A few of the breweries in cities just over the Wisconsin border, such as Winona and Red Wing, Minnesota, had only a token presence, but four breweries bought more than $1,500 worth of stamps. These purchases by Prima of Chicago, Theo. Hamm of St. Paul, Fitger Brewing of Duluth, and Menominee-Marinette Brewing of Menominee, Michigan, were more than stamps bought by forty-seven of the eighty-eight Wisconsin breweries that month.[76] Before World War II began, breweries from Adam Scheidt Brewing of Norristown, Pennsylvania, to Olympia Brewing of Tumwater, Washington, to Cervecería Cuauhtémoc of Monterrey, Mexico, would apply for permission to ship their beer into the state.[77] More than fifty breweries, including Anheuser-Busch and Falstaff of St. Louis, were registered with the state treasury by 1940.[78]

"The Army Calls for Beer"

It is possible that breweries were in better shape for the rigors of wartime regulation than many other businesses since they were already used to documenting every purchase, sale, and action. Nonetheless, many new restrictions were placed on breweries (and all other businesses) in the name of the war effort. Nearly everything from grain to labels to space in railcars was in short supply. As millions of men were mobilized into the armed forces, labor became scarce as well. Imported hops from Germany were no longer available, so brewers had to adjust their recipes or,

as in the case of Pabst's recently launched Andeker, discontinue brands altogether.[79]

Tinplate was reserved for military uses, so canned beer for civilian use was discontinued for the duration of the war. Of course, one of the military uses was to provide 3.2 percent beer for

Donors to Pabst's war bond drive in 1943 sign a replica bomb to symbolize their contribution. While the identifications listed on the back of the photograph are not all legible, these signers appear to be, from left to right, Everett Glenn, Viola Murphy, Eugene Palecki, Al Kinville, and (illegible but looks like) Coyo Patcuda. COLLECTION OF JOHN STEINER.

armed services personnel—each brewery, no matter the size, was required to sell 15 percent of its output to the government. Cans that were to be shipped into combat zones were painted olive drab instead of their usual bright colors so they would not glint in the light and give away the location of troops or their bases. Smaller breweries generally supplied camps near the breweries rather than overseas bases. Some breweries, including Weber Waukesha and Carl Ebner Brewing of Fort Atkinson, supplied beer for captured Germans in POW camps in Wisconsin.[80] Breweries that had not previously had government contracts needed to learn new procedures, but the BTD and brewers' organizations guided them through these mazes as well.

Brewers were concerned about calls for the return of prohibition in the name of the war effort, and dry forces did indeed seize the moment and attempt to limit sales on and around military posts. Most military leaders, however, were against this move and claimed that 3.2 percent beer was critical for morale. Dry advocates ended up on the wrong side of public opinion when they inaccurately blamed drunken sailors for the disaster at Pearl Harbor and sounded too much like the Axis leaders, who blamed American decadence for the war.[81] There were occasional rumors that particular breweries had Nazi symbols on their labels,

Schlitz was proud to announce that it exceeded the requirement that 15 percent of its production be sold to the government. Providing beer to the armed forces built goodwill that likely helped build brand loyalty after the war. AUTHOR'S COLLECTION.

Some beer intended for consumption by military personnel was exempt from taxation. This beer had special labels so that brewers and revenue officials could make sure the proper tax was paid. COLLECTION OF TYE SCHWALBE.

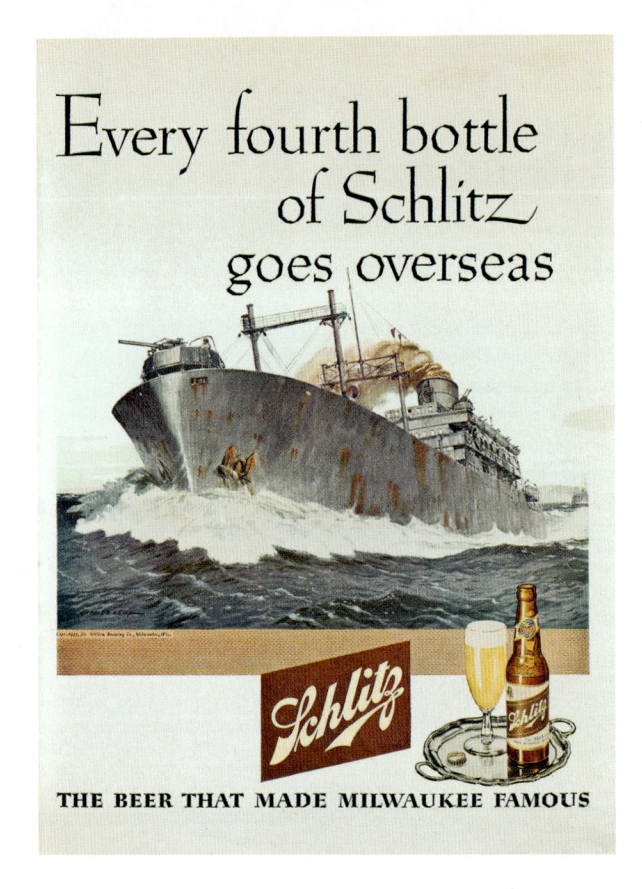

though Kingsbury had removed the swastika on its labels earlier. Rumors spread in 1941 about Goebel Brewing Company of Detroit having Nazi sympathies may have been started by Wisconsin brewers angry about Goebel's price-cutting tactics.[82]

While they did not have to give up production, the brewers and their employees made numerous sacrifices in all aspects of business. The United States Brewers' Association recommended that its members forgo making bock beer starting in 1944 to reduce grain use and save on packaging material.[83] Vehicles and fuel were diverted to the war effort, and businesses were informed of the latest changes in rationing and other measures through monthly bulletins from the Office of Price Administration (OPA). When the Stevens Point Beverage Company sought to replace a worn-out 1933 delivery truck (which had been driven 313,000 miles already), the request was denied on the grounds that "it has not been shown . . . that the service for which the new vehicle is requested is necessary to the war effort or to the maintenance of essential civilian economy."[84] Workers were encouraged to carpool, and each business was required to submit a monthly "car occupancy report" to the OPA.[85]

Because of fears of wartime inflation, the OPA also set ceiling prices for nearly every consumer good, including beer. These ceilings continued for some time after the war ended, and were reinstated during the Korean War. The lists showed a

In addition to cutting down on their own use of critical wartime supplies, breweries used their facilities to assist scrap metal drives and other home front efforts. This picture is labeled "Tin for Uncle Sam, Aug. 28, 1942." COLLECTION OF JOHN STEINER.

The Kingsbury Pale near beer label from the early 1930s featured a swastika, which was considered a symbol of good fortune in many cultures. The device was removed from the labels after it became associated with the Nazi Party in Hitler's Germany. COLLECTION OF TYE SCHWALBE.

BACK TO WORK, OFF TO WAR 237

clear hierarchy of value, and put on paper for all to see what were considered "cheap" beers. One list, published in 1946 for the counties in northeastern Wisconsin, showed prices ranging from 10½ cents per twelve-ounce bottle for Marshfield Lager, Point Special, and Mathie-Ruder's Red Ribbon up to 16 cents for Ballantine Ale, one of a handful of non-Wisconsin brands. (Schlitz was the most expensive Wisconsin label at 15 cents.)

Breweries joined other businesses and civic organizations in contributing to the war effort on the home front. Breweries sponsored war bond drives and included the exhortation to buy bonds on nearly every piece of advertising or packaging. However, a plan by Capitol Brewing of Milwaukee to give customers defense stamps (a way to save up for defense bonds 10, 25, 50 cents or a dollar at a time) for buying beer was ruled illegal.[86] Breweries were also active participants in scrap metal drives, at least in part because they needed some of the scrap metal themselves.

Bottle caps became central to brewery conservation drives. The tinplate used in the caps was critical to the defense industry, and brewers were required to reduce use of crowns by 30 percent. Every effort was made to reduce the use of caps and to reuse those that were necessary. When possible, retailers were urged to switch to draught beer. At one point, the BTD suggested that Pabst and other brewers promote this shift with the slogan "Pull the tap and save a cap to kill a Jap." Customers were asked to switch from twelve-ounce bottles to thirty-two-ounce bottles to make one cap do the work of several.[87] Breweries could also recondition the caps, but whether done by hand or with a reclaiming machine invented by Albert J. Bates of G. Heileman Brewing, the process still cost more than buying new caps. However, since

As breweries scrambled for supplies, they were willing to try almost anything to keep production going. Oshkosh Brewing offered defense stamps in return for bottle caps. When Calumet Brewing closed, Denmark Brewing tried to secure Calumet's cap allocation on the grounds that it was now "performing their duties in that vicinity." Other breweries sought solutions from the past: La Crosse Breweries asked permission to use old porcelain stoppers (of which they had several thousand cases remaining), and Oconto Brewing sought (unsuccessfully) to provide reusable rubber stoppers on their half-gallon containers. COURTESY OF WISCONSIN HISTORICAL SOCIETY.

Defender Beer appealed to the patriotic spirits of Americans during World War II (label ca. 1942).
COLLECTION OF TYE SCHWALBE.

breweries were ordered to cut their use of new caps by 30 percent, there was little choice.[88]

The essential raw materials for beer were limited as well. In order to divert more malt to the production of industrial alcohol, small brewers were not allowed to exceed their 1942 malt usage in 1943, and large brewers had to make a 7 percent cut. At the same time, brewers were expected to increase production in order to meet the government contracts and to relieve the nationwide beer shortage. The War Production Board made clear the government position in early 1942, declaring, "Experience in other countries has indicated that [beer and wine] have a value in sustaining morale both to civilians and to the armed forces," and established that breweries should produce an amount equal to about two-thirds of the 1941 barrelage for civilian consumption (in addition to the government set-asides) despite the shortages.[89]

The restrictions on malt forced brewers to experiment with other grains in an attempt to keep production up while still creating a palatable beer. The substitute brewing materials included the common adjuncts yellow corn, unmalted barley, and wheat, but also ranged as far as oats, rye, mandioca (cassava), and even potatoes. All of these "filled the gap between the demand for beer and the curtailment of malt."[90] Some of the new formulas were unmemorable, but Gluek Brewing Company of Minneapolis developed a more successful brew that the company patented and marketed as Sparkling Stite—the first patented malt liquor. (Grand Valley Brewing Company of Ionia, Michigan, brewed Clix Malt Liquor in 1937, but did not patent the recipe.)[91] Malt liquor was slow to catch on in Wisconsin (Gettelman's University Club was one of the few early examples), but Stite was later acquired by G. Heileman Brewing, and the formula would become a moneymaker for state breweries in later years.[92]

Another tactic to get more malt was to purchase another brewing company, close it down, and take its malt allocation. Although few Wisconsin breweries were transferred during the war for these purposes (the purchase of Merrill's Leidiger Brewing Company by Bloomer Brewing Company is a rare example), the trend concerned some industry officials, who feared that otherwise healthy breweries would be driven out of business, and there would then be less competition after the war was over.[93]

Equally frustrating to shipping brewers were the transportation restrictions. In the spring of 1943, the government limited rail shipments of beer to less than the previous year's amount, yet in the same announcement brewers were urged to try to gain transport savings without depriving any region of the country of beer. A few months later, brewers were urged to make additional conservation

Breweries eagerly joined patriotic campaigns to support the war effort at home. Heileman Brewing placed the "Keep Pitching America" logo on matchbooks and fold-tab buttons (both 1942). COLLECTION OF TYE SCHWALBE.

Members of the rack room (kegging) and cellar crews at Pabst sign up for a blood drive in 1944. COLLECTION OF JOHN STEINER.

plans, and at the same time to find ways to meet the nationwide beer shortage. As the War Food Administration noted, "Many brewers have already withdrawn from distant markets and are pushing sales in areas nearer their plants in order to save transportation."[94] The large Milwaukee breweries and Heileman were hit especially hard since they were among the major suppliers of some of the most sparsely populated areas of the country.

While some brewery employees were considered essential to the war effort and exempt from service, many others were called into active duty. Even brewery officials not in the armed forces helped the war effort. James G. Shakman, vice president of Pabst, toured liberated Europe as the technical adviser to a special unit that reconditioned damaged breweries in liberated territories and prepared them to produce beer for the occupation forces.[95] Breweries of all sizes pointed with pride to their workers serving on the front lines and joined in the sorrow when an employee made the ultimate sacrifice. The loss of workers to the war sometimes caused problems for the breweries. After being cited for improper stamp cancellation, Blatz blamed the problem on "a very large turnover on help in the last few months due to the boys leaving for the army and also for defense work."[96] Wausau Brewing Company had record-keeping problems since both their bookkeeper and a key bottle shop employee had left for military service.[97] Women filled many vacancies. Instead of being relegated to the bottle house, as they were before Prohibition, some held highly skilled positions—often places vacated by their husbands. Nationally, more than seven thousand members of the brewery workers' union were in the armed forces, and more than two hundred were killed in action.[98] Wisconsin had its share of the fallen, among them two killed in Germany: John E. Giverson, a tank driver who had worked for Fountain City Brewing, and Waukesha's Harold Hughlett, a Fox Head employee who was with the Eighty-Third Infantry.[99]

Hardship Cases

At the end of the war, the brewing industry took several years to return to normal. Material restrictions were lifted only gradually: canned beer was not available for civilian purchase until the spring of 1947. Grain restrictions were increased in 1946 so that food could be sent to starving nations in Europe, then were lifted just in time to be reimposed for the Korean War. In 1946 a coal shortage threatened breweries' ability to continue production, though Wisconsin breweries typically reported having enough coal on hand.[100] Many of the wartime changes became permanent parts of the American beer scene: cardboard cases replaced wood, and the lighter, thinner beers of wartime remained even after malt restrictions were lifted.

It is often difficult to declare precisely why a brewery closed, but wartime economic challenges certainly played a part. Seven breweries closed in 1942, and two more in 1943. Interestingly, no breweries failed in 1944, 1945, or 1946, which suggests that the most vulnerable had been weeded out and those remaining were able to profit from the increased wartime demand. But sometimes the vulnerable were among the venerable. Of the eight pre-Prohibition breweries that closed for good during World War II, the youngest was the Binzel Brewing Company of Oconomowoc, which had been founded in 1868; four were founded in the 1850s.

The 30 percent cut in grain imposed on 1 March 1946 caused a shortage of beer around the country and a flurry of purchases of Wisconsin breweries. Louis Ziegler Brewing of Beaver Dam and Carl Ebner Brewing of Fort Atkinson were both sold to Crescent Commercial Corporation, a wholesale liquor firm in Los Angeles. The Reedsburg Brewery, Denmark Brewing, and Eulberg Brewing of Portage were all sold to investors from Chicago. W. R. Hansen of Birmingham, Alabama, purchased the Electric City Brewing Company of Kaukauna. Elsewhere in the country, breweries often were purchased for their grain allocations, but Wisconsin firms were usually acquired to brew beer for shipment elsewhere. Crescent planned to increase shipments to the West Coast from its two breweries, but Electric City had already been selling most of its beer in the South, so that transaction would not significantly change the brewery's local business.[101] These actions, however, were not enough to save all the breweries: Electric City and Denmark both closed in 1947 and Ebner, now under the Ziegler name, ceased production for eighteen months shortly after the sale.

A few tavern keepers resurrected the idea of cooperative breweries to guarantee a cheap supply of beer, despite the poor track record of such businesses. The Wisconsin Tavern Keepers Association proposed buying the Capitol Brewing Company of Milwaukee in 1946. Previously, most of its output had been going to Texas and eastern cities—of the more than 27,000 barrels produced in 1945, only 372 were sold in Wisconsin.[102] The sale did not go through, however, and the brewery closed in 1948, right before the brewery workers' strike in Milwaukee. The Fort Atkinson brewery was reopened by a group of fifteen southern Wisconsin tavern keepers in 1948 under the name Ziegler Old Tap Brewing Company. Despite the new lease on life, it closed for good in 1950.[103]

National figures show a rapid decline in the number of breweries from a high of more than 750 in the mid-1930s to fewer than 500 by 1943. Many of these businesses were conceived with more optimism than resources. If a brewery made it past the early business shocks of World War II, it was likely to survive until the 1950s. But Wisconsin, with more breweries to start with, had more to lose. The results of 1951 were typical of the gains and losses for Wisconsin's brewing industry. The state produced 1,045,804 more barrels in 1951 than in 1950, but only eighteen of the state's forty-nine breweries shared in the increase. Three breweries closed for good (Reedsburg and the two plants of Ziegler in Beaver Dam and La Crosse), and many others saw declines in sales.[104] Altogether, fifteen breweries closed between 1947 and 1953, leaving the state with roughly forty brewing companies, half of which were producing fewer than 25,000 barrels. Both large and small breweries would have to fight harder to defend their Wisconsin markets, but breweries seeking to grow would have to win the battle through territorial expansion.

"SHOWING OFF THE NEW POWER MOWER" by Fred Siebel. Number 108 in the series "Home Life in America"

Now that summer's in the air—

What makes a glass of beer taste so good?

Malted barley and other grains carefully selected from our country's choicest crops. The tangy hops that give beer its distinctive taste are harvested only when their flavor is at its best.

Pure clear water—pure as the finest spring water—and brewing equipment kept absolutely spotless to maintain that purity.

Important minerals—including certain basic elements our bodies use up every day—are among the natural ingredients of beer.

The way it "belongs" with the friendly informality that's so much a part of American life. No wonder beer and ale are traditionally considered *beverages of moderation*.

Beer Belongs — Enjoy It! America's Beverage of Moderation

By 1955, the United States Brewers Foundation had already published 105 different paintings in the series "Home Life in America," which sought to demonstrate that beer was a natural part of everyday life. "Showing Off the New Power Mower," by Fred Siebel, captured the new American ideal of a house in the suburbs with a backyard so large a power mower was necessary. The USBF was careful to show the beer poured into a glass rather than being consumed directly from a bottle or can. This showed off the clarity, rich color, and fine head to the best effect. AUTHOR'S COLLECTION.

CHAPTER 8

THE *American* WAY OF BEER

1945–1975

I've tried them all. . . . And regardless of what label or slogan you choose, it all tastes as if the secret brewing process involves running it through a horse. Oh, there may be a few small, obscure breweries tucked away in remote corners of Wisconsin, making beer that is more than sour-tasting fizz water, but their products don't get to our liquor stores or into the bars. The waitresses don't mention those names in their routine recitations of the available brands. . . . It wasn't always this way. . . . But something happened. Maybe it was Prohibition. . . . More likely it was the postwar drift to mass production, bigness, mergers, packaging efficiency, and the substitution of advertising for reality. Our national shame is that we make the world's worst beer!

Mike Royko, CHICAGO DAILY NEWS, 1973

AS WISCONSIN'S BREWERS BEGAN TO SHAKE OFF WARTIME RESTRICTIONS, approaches to the next decades would vary depending on the sizes of the companies and the reach of their brands. Years' worth of remodeling, expansion, product development, and territory extension that had been delayed by the war burst forth in an explosion of activity that was visible to almost everyone in the country. At the same time, this aggressive expansion led to struggles over market share that would see overall industry production increase dramatically but would witness the loss of over 80 percent of the nation's breweries. Although Wisconsin was a relative island of safety in these frothy storms, the changes would still cost the state the majority of its breweries—from tiny village firms to nationally known brands.

The New Beer Culture

Entering the 1950s, the brewing industry needed to adjust to operating under a new set of conditions, some of which had been developing since repeal, but which combined after the Korean War to make the beer business significantly different from before. The most beneficial change for the brewing industry was that beer was beginning to reestablish the respected place it held in American social life that had been damaged around the turn of the century. The restored position of beer in family life resulted from technological and commercial developments. While home refrigeration first became affordable in the 1920s, by the 1950s a refrigerator could be found in nearly every home. The convenience of being able simply to go to the kitchen and grab a beer (or, as some popular depictions of the time suggested, to have one's wife deliver a cold beer) made it less critical to go down to the neighborhood tavern. This made it possible for brewers to separate beer itself from the evils of the saloon to a much greater extent than was possible before Prohibition, and to present beer as a wholesome product to be enjoyed by everyone.

In order to cement this impression in the public mind, both the national brewing organizations and individual breweries began advertising campaigns based on family life themes. The United States Brewers Foundation launched a series of national ads known as the "Home Life in America" series. By depicting beer as a virtuous source of refreshment in the pages of *Life, Look, Collier's, McCall's,* and *Woman's Home Companion,* brewers were largely successful in positioning beer in the mainstream of

American social life.[1] So successful, in fact, that legislation targeting these ads was introduced in Congress by Representative Laurie Battle of Alabama. His unsuccessful bill proposed to ban all sorts of "misleading" advertising, including anything that suggested beer "would increase social or business prestige, or is traditional in American family life or a part of the atmosphere of the American home."[2]

Beer advertising had entered a new phase in the postwar period. As noted previously, brewers were very cautious in the immediate post-Prohibition period, sometimes because state laws forced them to be restrained. An article by Reginald Clough reprinted in *Brewers Digest* in April 1952 divided the development of print advertising for beer into four stages. Immediately after repeal, brewers were simply trying to establish their business and their name. In some states, beer advertising prohibited any product claims other than the fact that beer existed and that it was on sale in a certain location. In the second phase after repeal, brewers built their brands and emphasized the

Number 114 in the "Home Life in America" series—"We Won!," by Haddon Sundblom—depicts football fans returning home for a party after the big game. Both canned beer (in flat-top cans) and bottled beer are shown ready for serving in tall pilsner glasses. Most of the paintings in the series depicted young people in affluent settings, implying that beer was found in the best modern homes (1955). PHOTOGRAPH BY CHARLES WALBRIDGE. AUTHOR'S COLLECTION

THE AMERICAN WAY OF BEER 247

With home consumption of beer increasing, taverns needed to offer an inviting and colorful atmosphere. These striking bar lights, sometimes called "cab lights," were introduced in the 1930s but remained popular for many years. COURTESY OF NATIONAL BREWERY MUSEUM.

This modern couple enjoys the convenience of a six-pack of half-quart cans (tin sign from 1956). COLLECTION OF DAVID WENDL.

responsibility of (and economic benefits from) the industry. The phase during World War II promoted wartime morale while still keeping the brand name before the public. The final phase, reached at the end of wartime material shortages, emphasized the trend toward home consumption, and therefore the advertising focused largely on packaging and convenience.[3] A large portion of the advertising for beer in the late 1940s and 1950s focused on the fact that beer could be purchased at the local store, and introduced a variety of different convenient packages in which to bring it home. The six-pack, borrowed from the soft drink industry, was introduced in California in 1947 and spread quickly to the Midwest and throughout the country. Soon innovation seemed to focus less on trying to make a better-tasting beer and more on making the most creative six-pack holder.

Sending beer home with the consumer became even more important as America's dining habits changed during the baby boom generation. An article in *Brewers Digest* noted that television was keeping people at home more often and there was an increasing trend toward "casual entertaining at home." Part of this was motivated by another factor: the increasing number of families—especially young families with multiple children. The cost of going out now included the cost of a babysitter. As more restaurants began to offer take-out meals (resulting ultimately in the advent of the store-bought "TV dinner"), brewers prepared their advertising to position beer as the logical accompaniment.[4]

"Just the Kiss of the Hops"

Americans' tastes were changing along with their habits. Some of the changes may have been caused by the increasing popularity of soft drinks, or by the rise of mixed drinks during Prohibition. Frank C. Verbest, president of Blatz Brewing, analyzed the situation in 1955:

> This is the way we reason: Beer reached its peak in popularity during the period of unrestricted immigration just before World War I. Since that date the people have changed and their tastes have changed. For instance, the trend has been from bitter to sweet chocolate, from strong Turkish cigarettes to mild Virginia ones, from strong cheeses to mild processed ones, from salty to mild butter. But while tastes have been changing, beer has remained largely the same. There has been a trend to the use of less hops, which give the sharp or bitter taste to beer, but otherwise the changing has been in the packaging.[5]

These seven- and eight-ounce bottles appeared almost immediately after repeal and remained popular for several decades. They were especially popular at bowling alleys and taverns throughout Wisconsin. Of note in this set are the two bock labels and Chesterton Ale—one of the few ales to appear in this size package. The Pioneer Lager bottle is of particular interest: it claimed to be bottled by De Pere Brewing Co., but the U-permit of the brewer was that of the Menominee-Marinette Brewing Co. of Menominee, Michigan. De Pere Brewing is not known ever to have brewed its own beer. COLLECTION OF JOHN STEINER.

THE AMERICAN WAY OF BEER

This was not just the opinion of a struggling Milwaukee brewery; it was held throughout the industry. A *Brewers Digest* editorial in 1946 opined:

We must always emphasize the fact that our brews should be designed not to please ourselves nor even a few conventional connoisseurs but to satisfy the masses of consumers and potential consumers. . . . The general public today is looking for beer with a delicate flavor—not too pronounced a flavor. They want a beverage which they can enjoy and which will refresh them and which they can consume congenially and without unpleasant effects of any kind.[6]

Brewers looking for more customers and new markets were forced to make sure that their flagship beers would not offend anyone rather than trying to brew a unique product. Many breweries continued to release bock beer in the spring, especially the smaller firms, but as these companies closed bock became less common. The large breweries sometimes included an "old-world style" product in their line, but the homogenization of American beer was nearly complete. The president of Minnesota-based rival Grain Belt Brewing summed up the situation:

"The big successes among regional beers in the Western United States are Coors, Olympia, and Grain Belt. The big thing they have in common is that they are milder than competing beers. Young people, those between 21 and 35, represent the biggest consumers of beer by far." As they come of beer drinking age after a young lifetime of milkshakes, Cokes and candy bars, *"there is a much easier transition to our type of product than to a bitter beer."*[7]

Blatz seems to have had some reservations about the potential of Tempo. The brand was available only in bottles and cans (not on draught), it was test-marketed in southern cities, and there were no plans at first to sell it in Milwaukee or elsewhere in Wisconsin. AUTHOR'S COLLECTION.

While the brewers were competing on nearly every possible front, there were very few attempts to compete on flavor, except to claim that one beer was milder or more drinkable than any other.

The quest for smoothness without noticeable beer flavors led brewers to attempt new products. "Maybe Blatz has come up with the answer." Frank Verbest's analysis, quoted earlier, was connected to the launch of a new Blatz product: Tempo. Blatz made bold claims for the new beer, notably that it was the first beer the company could discover that used fresh rather than dried hops in the brewing process. While this may seem enticing to a modern craft beer drinker, this was not a "fresh hop" beer designed to emphasize hop flavor and aroma, but instead used an extract made from fresh hops designed to minimize hop presence. But despite the "hundreds of thousands of dollars" spent in researching and marketing it, Tempo lasted only a couple of years before going the way of most "innovative" products—which are often, in fact, less distinctive than their predecessors.

Despite the poor track record of beers designed for people who don't like beer, brewers continued to search for the magic elixir that would bring them the lion's share of this elusive market. In 1969 Schlitz introduced Encore, which was positioned as "something special," a beer "brewed better than it has to be." Newspaper ads claimed, "Encore was never meant to be sold. It was our brewmaster's own private recipe. Something he brewed just for his friends." In reality, the secret wasn't so much the recipe as it was longer lagering times. The clear bottles had a gold tint and "mirror-like finish" (which contradicted Schlitz's decades-long insistence on brown bottles). The television ads, in a nod to Frank Sinatra's hit "It Was a Very Good Year," proclaimed "It's a Very Good Year, for Beer." But while Encore lasted more than a year, it was not a particularly good year, and the product quickly disappeared from shelves.[8]

Attempts to extend the market were not restricted strictly to classic beer styles, nor were they all done by the Milwaukee giants. An early venture into the world of what would later be tagged "malternatives" appeared at the end of 1956 with the launch of "Sassy Brew—The Drink That Never Tells on You." It possessed "the

The warning "NOT to be sold to minors!" emphasized the problems brewers had when attempting to make a flavored alcoholic beverage that would almost certainly attract younger drinkers. The cola flavor bottle at left has a Pennsylvania beverage tax crown. COLLECTION OF JOHN STEINER.

characteristics of beer, except for taste, and its consumption involves no after-breath"—apparently the source of the claim in the slogan. Like beer, it developed a head when poured, but it was designed to be served over ice. It was available in three flavors—Cola, Punch, and Collins—the result of "extensive surveys" by "an outstanding national research group" that discovered "the need for a new taste." Among the important discoveries was that 70 percent of women approved of the taste. While "the Most Revolutionary Development in Alcoholic Beverages of the Century" was developed at Wahl-Henius Institute of Chicago and owned by Sassy International Inc., it was brewed at Weber Waukesha. Sassy International planned to license up to ten other facilities around the country, but the drink never met expectations—nor was it the long-term salvation for Weber Waukesha, which merged with neighboring Fox Head Brewing in 1958.[9]

The advertisements of the post–World War II era display a reluctance to describe flavor as anything other than mild or smooth (which really are not flavors). Schlitz's series of television ads during the 1950s–1970s epitomized the reluctance to claim bold flavor in a beer. Schlitz beer had "just the kiss of the hops" in "a great light beer." In the late 1960s, a TV commercial parody of *My Fair Lady* emphasized the brand had "absolutely no trace of beer bite." Print ads added "no bitterness" or "no harsh bitterness" to the "kiss" text. Apparently Schlitz had some concern that its flagship product might also be viewed as too light, even watery, so the company sought a counterbalance that could imply a "bold" product without actually discussing

Pabst emphasized the consistency of Blue Ribbon that came from blending "33 Fine Brews . . . into One Great Beer." The Blue Ribbon Town ads—in which all the people were made of blue ribbons—ran during World War II and usually contained some message about wartime conservation or morale. The 33 into One slogan was still present, but by this time it was so well known that it could be relegated to a corner. PHOTOGRAPH BY CHARLES WALBRIDGE. AUTHOR'S COLLECTION.

252 THE DRINK THAT MADE WISCONSIN FAMOUS

strong flavors. The term *gusto,* borrowed from an Italian (or Spanish) word for vigorous enjoyment of eating or drinking, seemed to be strong enough to appeal to men without having any particular meaning.

The biggest media change as it related to beer advertising in the 1950s was the development of commercial television. Television ads had the potential to combine the strong visual effects of a large newspaper ad with radio's spoken text or jingles. TV also added attractive moving pictures to the mix—views of the brewing process, scenes of swiftly flowing streams of water, or the irresistible image of a glass being filled from a tap, bottle, or can. Early television ads were not an art form, but beer commercials would help make them so. Some industry analysts saw TV ads as a moving, talking, point-of-sale promotion—just the thing to convince the bar patron watching the ball game to order another beer. Other observers believed that television advertising fit well with the general advertising approach of the breweries and with the shift of beer consumption to the home. Spending on television spots by brewers was nonexistent at the end of World War II, but by 1951 it exceeded $5.2 million per year, and its rate of expansion would only increase as money spent on print ads (and, to a lesser extent, radio) decreased dramatically. However, network television and radio advertising was expensive, and thus worthwhile only for the largest national brewers: Anheuser-Busch, Pabst, Blatz, Schlitz, Miller, and Ballantine.

One of the difficulties in attempting to analyze breweries based on difference in size is categorizing them properly. The most useful division was outlined by William O. Baldwin in his study of Wisconsin breweries from the mid-1960s: very small (less than 75,000 barrels per year), small (75,000–250,000), medium (250,000–750,000) large (750,000–3 million), and giant (more than 3 million).[10] With this division a striking feature of Wisconsin's brewing landscape becomes evident: the state's breweries tended to the extremes in size. In 1964 Wisconsin had three of America's seven giant breweries, half of the nation's thirty-eight very small breweries (neighboring Minnesota had six of the remaining nineteen), but very few small, medium, or large breweries. Statistics from the early 1950s to the early 1970s tell a story that was playing out in the brewing industry as well as the rest of society. Big firms with nationally advertised brands were pulling market share from regional and local firms, and products became more homogeneous. The market left for mid-sized breweries was shrinking quickly, as were their numbers. When World War II ended, there were almost 500 breweries in the United States, but by 1961 there were only 229, as an average of seventeen breweries closed every year. By 1972 there were fewer than 150 breweries operating in the United States, and most of these belonged to companies that operated in multiple locations.[11] Of course, the industrial analysis usually left out the very small producers, since their share of the national market was too small to be measured. Their small size may have saved them from the predations of Wisconsin's giant breweries, who had more to gain from knocking bigger breweries out of larger distant cities rather than gaining a few thousand barrels and considerable ill will closer to home.[12]

Go West, Old Brewery!

The American way of life after World War II featured mobility undreamed of by previous generations. Population began to shift south and southwest, first as wartime industries drew workers, but then as air-conditioning and water projects made hot and arid regions bearable. The interstate highway system made driving more efficient, and increasing disposable income made the family road trip a regular event. The growing ease of commercial air travel brought even far-flung destinations within easy reach. Selling beer to Americans on the move would lead to important decisions by brewery marketing departments and would help separate the successful breweries from the losers.

As competition increased, breweries needed to cut costs and increase production. For breweries in a national market, transportation costs cut into competitiveness and profitability. Breweries trumpeted "Local Prices" (or "Popular Prices" or

Pabst distributors could have their pictures taken with a giant bottle at a convention, preparing them for the 1950 sales campaign. COLLECTION OF DAVID WENDL.

254 THE DRINK THAT MADE WISCONSIN FAMOUS

"Western Prices") in their advertising to gain an advantage over Budweiser, Pabst, and Schlitz. Since matching this tactic by price-cutting risked cheapening their brand's image, the best long-term way for the largest brewers to respond was to develop breweries nearer to their distant markets. Brewing companies had operated multiple plants before. Most were near their home markets and were acquired to expand capacity, as when Best acquired the Melms brewery in 1870. The most distant expansion was that of Miller to Bismarck, North Dakota, in 1885. Green Bay's Hagemeister purchased the former Leidiger brewery in Sturgeon Bay in 1887. Brewers were concerned, however, that differences in water chemistry would cause the same beer at branch locations to taste different—a fatal flaw in a product that equated consistency with quality. While Pabst brewed Blue Ribbon in both Milwaukee and Peoria, malt was shipped from the Milwaukee plant and water chemistry was carefully adjusted at Peoria to match that of the home brewery.[13]

The palm trees in this promotional book from 1956 depicting Schlitz's gleaming new Van Nuys brewery emphasize the differences from the Milwaukee plant, as does the beach house look of the Brown Bottle hospitality center. AUTHOR'S COLLECTION.

Among Schlitz's export markets in the 1970s was Israel, for which it produced this sixteen-ounce can labeled in Hebrew. COLLECTION OF DAVID WENDL.

The success of Pabst at Peoria, along with the expansion of St. Louis–based Falstaff to Omaha and New Orleans in the 1930s, convinced brewers that nationwide manufacturing was both possible and essential.[14] Pabst made the first move after World War II with its purchase of the Hoffman Beverage Company in Newark, New Jersey, in December 1945. Hoffman was best known for soft drinks, but had added a brand-new brewery in 1934 to capitalize on the return of beer. Pabst's technical staff made the necessary alterations, and by 1946 fresh, Newark-brewed Blue Ribbon was being distributed through Hoffman's extensive network in the Northeast. Pabst's national market share jumped by more than a full point from 1945 to 1949, from 3.6 percent to 4.7 percent.[15]

The race was on. While Schlitz and Anheuser-Busch were planning their eastern moves, Pabst moved west by purchasing the 700,000-barrel plant of the Los Angeles Brewing Company in 1948. At first this facility remained an autonomous subsidiary and continued to produce its flagship Eastside beer. It wasn't until five years later that the brewery was updated to produce Blue Ribbon. Newspaper ads in November 1953 heralded Pabst's creation of the first "Atlantic to Pacific Chain of Breweries."[16] Meanwhile, the Geo. Ehret Brewery in Brooklyn, which was the largest brewery in the nation in the 1870s, once again became part of the country's largest brewer when Schlitz purchased it in 1949.[17] Erwin C. Uihlein cited the "vast growth and development" of California when Schlitz invested $20 million in a new brewery in the northwest Los Angeles suburb of Van Nuys.[18] Press coverage stressed both the modernity of the facility and the provisions for visitors and community groups in the Brown Bottle hospitality center.[19]

Shown here in 2013, Miller's Fort Worth brewery has easy access to both highways and railroads for shipment. COURTESY OF MILLERCOORS BREWING CO.

THE DRINK THAT MADE WISCONSIN FAMOUS

Responding to continuing shifts in population distribution, Schlitz acquired breweries in Kansas City and Honolulu and built new breweries in four southern states between 1956 and 1972. The growth of Schlitz was symbolized in the evolution of the copyright statement at the end of the company's television commercials. In the early 1960s it listed each city, by 1970 it read "Milwaukee and Other Great Cities," and by the end of the decade it was "Schlitz. Milwaukee and the world."[20] Miller was a relative latecomer to national plant expansion, purchasing the brewery of General Brewing Company of Azusa, California, in April 1966 and a failed Carling Breweries facility in Fort Worth, Texas, a few months later.[21] Pabst consolidated its production and did not make a further expansion until its new plant near Perry, Georgia, opened in October 1971.[22]

Expansion, however, was expensive. Although companies did not always disclose the purchase price, Schlitz was reported to have paid $13 million for Burgermeister Brewing Co. of San Francisco (with production of 693,000 barrels in 1960). This was still cheaper than a new brewery—Schlitz spent $20 million on its new Tampa branch a few years earlier. Of course, for the extra money Schlitz got a brewery built to its specifications (and with a first-year production target of 800,000 barrels) rather than an old facility that would require extensive retrofitting.[23] When Miller purchased the former Carling brewery in Fort Worth, the cost of the plant was approximately $5.5 million, but the expense of renovating the brewery (which was only two years old at the time of the sale) was well over $7.5 million.[24] Only a brewery with a sound financial position could undertake such moves.

The purchase of regional brewers by Milwaukee and St. Louis firms meant that the dramatic increases in production from the late 1950s to the early 1970s came from just a handful of brewing companies. In 1956 Schlitz led the nation with 5.9 million barrels produced at its four plants. Schlitz's new facilities in Winston-Salem and Memphis each had a capacity of 4.4 million barrels.[25] It was little wonder that industrial scholars and business journalists treated beer as just another oligopoly— an industry with only a handful of leading firms— similar to steel, autos, or laundry detergent. In fact, the trend of rapid consolidation was evident throughout American industry. Venerable automobile brands like Studebaker, Packard, Hudson, and Nash met their ends as American production concentrated in the Big Three. All sorts of local consumer products, from soft drinks to candy bars, were pushed out of business by national brands. However, most scholarly analyses made generalizations that oversimplified the brewing industry— hardly anyone goes on vacation and is excited to find a laundry detergent they can't buy at home.

The increasing concentration of market share in fewer firms attracted the attention of the Federal Trade Commission to the brewing industry. As national breweries gained control of more plants in more markets, federal regulators stepped in to limit the control any one brewery would have in a given market.

The first Wisconsin merger to come under scrutiny was between two of the most venerable names in Milwaukee beer. In July 1958, Pabst announced it was acquiring the Blatz Brewing Company for $16.5 million. The plans for consolidation became clear as the old Blatz brewery was taken off-line and plans were made to produce Blatz at all four of Pabst's breweries.[26] However, the Justice Department challenged the merger in October 1959 on the grounds that the merger "eliminated competition between them and also tended to substantially lessen competition in the whole beer field."[27] Pabst was prohibited from using Blatz assets or giving rights to distribute Blatz to any Pabst distributor until the case was settled.[28] As is typical with antitrust litigation, the case dragged on for years, even affecting Washington politics. Political columnist Drew Pearson claimed the official leading the suit, Robert Bicks, was blocked from being confirmed by the Senate as head of the Antitrust Division in retaliation for his moves against the Pabst-Blatz merger.[29] The case was dismissed by the district court in Milwaukee in 1965 but was reinstated by the U.S. Supreme Court. Pabst was ultimately forced to divest itself of the Blatz holdings, which were then put up for sale again.[30]

Schlitz's expansion into California also fell afoul of antitrust regulators. The 1960 attempt to purchase Burgermeister was first blocked by Miller, and later by other breweries with California plants.[31] Schlitz was found in violation of Section 7 of the Clayton Act and ordered to divest itself of Burgermeister and Labatt shares and was prohibited from exercising any control over any California brewery (other than its own plant) and from acquiring any other brewery anywhere for ten years.[32] Complications like this ended attempts by Pabst and Schlitz to buy other brewers and forced them to expand capacity by building their own breweries.

Pabst oasis at Shriner's New York convention was a popular spot. Jim Adams (l), Dick DesVerney are Pabst's hosts to Chicago's Sunny Barret and the Medina Lodge of New York, potentate, C. Dargans.

Floyd Smith, buffet attendant on C. & N. W. crack "Twin Cities 400" gets call from Jim Adams at the Chicago terminal. This is only one of the many fine trains that Adams services in the Chicago area.

At the Sleeping Car Porters Brotherhood New York convention, organization official Ashley Totten is "surrounded" by Pabst men, William (Bill) Hall and DesVerney during a break between meetings.

Pabst sought out talented African American sales representatives several years before the civil rights movement began. The salesmen shown here in 1952 represented the company at national conventions and handled accounts in major urban areas. AUTHOR'S COLLECTION.

SAY IT LOUD . . .

Breweries were swept along with many of the broader cultural currents of the nuclear age. Sometimes they were able to ride the waves of social developments in the 1960s and '70s to greater success, other times they were tossed dangerously close to the rocks. Just as television, migration, and industrial consolidation forced brewers to adapt, so did the civil rights movement.

As with the broader civil rights movement, the first steps toward recognizing the role of African Americans in consuming beer and respecting that buying power with employment started before the dramatic events of the 1950s and 1960s. In 1938 Pabst, deeply engaged in the post-repeal scramble for new markets, decided to gamble on hiring William (Bill) Graham. According to one enthusiastic account, "For the first time since Egyptians started making beer 3,000 years ago, the industry had a Negro salesman." He was first assigned to Cleveland, which the company considered a friendly town, but he proved his worth by selling six thousand cases of Pabst to an Elks convention in St. Louis—the heart of enemy territory. Pabst continued to add African Americans to its sales force; by 1952 the company had thirty black sales representatives.[33]

During the summer of 1969, Black Pride Inc. was founded by a group of about sixty-five investors as an attempt to give blacks in Chicago and elsewhere "some control over the economics of the communities in which they live and thus to be able to shoulder a greater amount of responsibility for what those communities are." Concerned about the flight of dollars from black urban consumers to

Black Pride was available in bottles and these striking cans.
COLLECTION OF DAVID WENDL.

white suburban entrepreneurs, President Edward J. McClellan hoped to keep some of the millions of dollars spent annually by African Americans in their communities. Although the hope was that Black Pride Inc. would eventually encompass many economic activities, the first product the company became involved with was beer. The reasoning was simple: expenditures for alcoholic beverages were higher per capita in predominantly black areas than in predominantly white areas, and 70 percent of the sales went to three large national breweries, so it seemed like there was room in the market for a product targeted specifically to these customers. In addition, in Illinois beer was sold on a cash exchange basis, so money would not be tied up in inventory for a long time.

While the company eventually hoped to own and operate its own brewery, Black Pride Inc. first contracted with West Bend Lithia Brewing to produce Black Pride beer. McClellan compared West Bend's role to that of Branch Rickey, the Dodgers' general manager who gave Jackie Robinson his chance in Major League Baseball. Unlike some attempts to reach the African American market, Black Pride did not have any special formulation, since the founders were "convinced that blacks have no unique product characteristic preferences beyond that of high quality." Black Pride would later become a distributor for G. Heileman Brewing, ostensibly "positioning itself for continuing stable growth," but more likely to provide an alternative source of revenue if sales of Black Pride–branded products floundered, which they did.[34]

Meanwhile, a Milwaukee-based group, United Black Enterprises, had a more ambitious dream. It was formed in July 1968 to attempt to purchase the Blatz brewery when Pabst was forced to sell it due to the antitrust decision. When this attempt was unsuccessful, UBE turned its sights on smaller breweries more within its means. A candidate was found in the struggling Peoples Brewing of Oshkosh. UBE president Theodore (Ted) Mack Sr., a Milwaukee entrepreneur and a former employee of Pabst, began negotiations to obtain financing and secured the brewery in April 1970. There were troubles almost immediately, as UBE attorney Harold B. Jackson Jr. had reportedly said that if the organization acquired a brewery, management positions would be filled by blacks and the policy would be to hire blacks. Mack immediately refuted the rumor and insisted that all the current employees would be retained. At a meeting with the media and area officials shortly after the purchase, Mack claimed, "We're not making any black beer" and "I didn't buy this brewery for black power. . . . There is only one kind of power in this country and that's green power—money." He expressed concern about the reputation of Oshkosh as a bigoted city but confirmed his plan to move to the city and assured citizens: "I don't scare easily."[35]

At first Peoples held its own, was the subject of a feature story in the *New York Times,* and even bought struggling crosstown rival Oshkosh Brewing and took over production of its brands.[36] Peoples was sold in the pubs on many University of Wisconsin campuses, and in 1971 it was accepted for sale in Milwaukee's County Stadium.[37] Sales in

Peoples Brewing Co. used ads featuring African Americans to market their beer in Milwaukee. They were used primarily in establishments frequented by African Americans to avoid sparking backlash from white customers unwilling to purchase a "black" beer. COLLECTION OF LEE REIHERZER.

Compare this mechanized bottling house of the 1930s to those shown in chapter 5. The worker at left is preparing the bottles for the filler in the center; the capper is on the right. Many brewery jobs were much less laborious after Prohibition than before, but they still presented dangers to workers. COLLECTION OF JOHN STEINER.

Norman Steiner started at Miller Brewing Co. in 1946 and worked there for thirty-four years. He drilled the hole so that he could carry his employee badge on a key chain (ca. 1950s). COLLECTION OF JOHN STEINER.

the Milwaukee market did not go as well as planned outside the inner city, however. Mack claimed, "Our salesmen, black and white, have been told in these places that they were not going to sell any n——r beer." He further admitted, "Our best sales market is still in the Fox River Valley," where Peoples had regained all but two of the accounts that originally dropped the beer because it was black-owned. An attempt to move into Gary, Indiana, was delayed when Indiana state troopers and tax officials impounded the first shipment of beer when it was brought across state lines.[38]

As progress slowed, Mack became increasingly frustrated and found resistance everywhere. He blamed the African American community for not supporting the brand, though his target consumers complained that the premium-priced beer was too expensive. At one point, Mack threatened to move operations to his home state of Alabama, despite the fact that brewing was not legal there.[39] Finally, in November 1972 the company sued the Department of Defense, alleging that Peoples "had not been given a fair chance to get large government orders for beer for the armed services," and demanded $100 million in damages from Defense and the Small Business Administration.[40] A few weeks later Peoples suspended production "until it could secure larger contracts," but never reopened.[41] The company filed for bankruptcy the following March.[42]

THE AMERICAN WAY OF BEER   261

TAKE THIS JOB AND SAVE IT

As national breweries pressed their capacity to the limit, and as small brewers struggled to survive, the fates of their workers were at stake as well. The smallest breweries generally did not have unionized workforces, but most medium and large breweries did. A few small breweries, like Potosi Brewing, had aspirations to ship into heavily unionized markets such as Chicago and organized their employees into unions at least in part so that they could put the Union Made slogan on their labels.[43]

Large breweries by this point had well-established unions, so the bloody organizing drives of the 1880s were far in the past. Management at these breweries typically had smoothly functioning agreements with their various unions, though there were occasional flare-ups. Since the workforce was often larger than a thousand, companies like Schlitz and Heileman sought to prevent problems with detailed employee handbooks, which had extensive lists of offenses for which employees could be dismissed. Both also included items designed to keep the workers in a loyal frame of mind. The Schlitz handbook concluded: "Work With Us . . . Not Just For Us."[44] Heileman's guide, "A Two-Way Street," ended with "Ten Points," which included sayings like "You cannot lift the wage-earner by pulling down the wage-payer." The paternalism expressed in these sections might have been possible in a small family brewery, but was less likely in a multimillion-dollar corporation.[45]

But small size did not protect a brewery from costly or bitter strikes. The workers of Oconto

This unusual advertising piece was designed to be mounted above a car or truck license plate (ca. 1950s). COLLECTION OF TYE SCHWALBE.

Brewery workers walk a picket line, most likely at Pabst. While the date is not marked on the photograph, one of the striking workers carries a picket sign reading "Big League Wages for a Big League City." Since the Milwaukee Braves of the National League arrived in 1953, it is most likely that the picture was taken during the seventy-six-day strike of that year. COLLECTION OF JOHN STEINER.

Brewing Company went on strike in May 1961 over wages and their insurance and health benefits. The three-week strike was marred by violence: a delivery truck was given a police escort to Beloit after the brake hoses were slashed by a group of workers.[46] Most strikes at breweries both large and small were less dramatic, however.

As breweries sought cost savings to be more competitive, jobs were increasingly at risk. In 1955 the struggling La Crosse Breweries Inc. switched to a local distributor rather than use its own trucks for deliveries in the city. Local 81 went on strike, demanding the reinstatement of the union crews on the delivery trucks. The demand was met two weeks later, but in the meantime the company received a temporary injunction against picketing by the striking workers.[47]

As G. Heileman Brewing grew in both size and importance, it became a bigger target for strikes. Workers at the Kingsbury branch in Sheboygan went on strike for the first time in their history in 1971 over wages, benefits, and conditions. Two weeks after the strike began, Heileman's president, Russell Cleary, announced that the brewery was to be closed, but claimed it was an economic issue unrelated to the strike.[48] As the strike continued, Sheboygan's mayor, Roger D. Schneider, appealed to Heileman to reverse the decision. After Local 277 voted to continue the strike, Cleary charged that Brewery Workers representative Ray Tiechmann wanted the Sheboygan plant closed to benefit Milwaukee union members.[49] The strike was over in twenty-four days, but the brewery would close for good shortly thereafter.

The strikes that had the biggest effect on the industry were those in Milwaukee. Sometimes the strikes were over very specific work issues. Milwaukee's Local 9 struck Schlitz and Pabst in April 1960 over a dispute on how high cases of empties would be stacked on pallets—management wanted them stacked seven high, workers demanded six. While only a few workers were directly affected, more than 1,800 employees walked off at Schlitz and 1,400 at Pabst for a few days.[50]

The strike of 1953 had long-term effects that probably doomed several breweries and changed the industry for the next two decades. On 15 May, about 7,500 workers walked off the job and established picket lines around Pabst, Schlitz, Miller, Blatz, Gettelman, and Independent Milwaukee Brewery. The members of Local 9 had approved the strike by the overwhelming tally of 6,652 to 108. Labor's major demands were a decrease in the workweek from forty to thirty-five hours and a twenty-five-cent increase in the hourly wage.[51] For several weeks, both sides attacked the other in full-page newspaper ads as negotiations stalled. At the end of the first week, the Wisconsin State CIO Council asked Milwaukeeans to "drink as much beer as humanly possible" to exhaust the stockpiles and put pressure on management. State CIO president Charles Schultz proclaimed, "'When present stocks of Milwaukee beer are gone the way of all good, union-made beer, there won't be any more.'"[52]

Brewery strikes were different from coal strikes or automobile strikes. Beer was difficult to stockpile in advance because it tastes best when fresh. The widely dispersed production of beer meant that there was usually an unaffected brewery ready to make up the deficit. Schlitz and Pabst each had breweries in other states that were not affected by the strike, and Pabst's Peoria plant was just over two hundred miles from Milwaukee. In addition, the union charged that some companies were attempting to brew beer elsewhere and sell it under the same brand name—citing an alleged deal between Blatz and Chicago's Canadian Ace brewery.[53] Such efforts pitted the breweries possessing multiple sites against those that did not. Near the end of the strike Blatz took out full-page ads reminding drinkers that Blatz was made only in Milwaukee and was therefore superior to "carbon copies" made in "Peoria, or Brooklyn, or Newark."[54]

Breweries outside Milwaukee took advantage of the crisis to pick up the slack and move into new territories. The Cream City was responsible for producing 15 percent of the country's beer, and a strike that affected production and shipments during the peak summer season left many drinkers and their suppliers thirsty for alternatives. Stroh, Carling, and Falstaff picked up some of the lost business in their territories, and Hamm solidified its already noticeable presence in Wisconsin. Anheuser-Busch passed the wounded Schlitz and took over first place among American breweries in 1957—a position it would never relinquish.[55] The higher wages won by the union led directly to higher prices for Milwaukee premium beers, which gave the other national brewers and larger regional producers a chance to consolidate their gains.[56] As a state, Wisconsin lost its first-place spot in total beer production, and would not gain it back until 1956 (though Wisconsin and New York had been

Edna Ann Vistart, a union steward at the Miller Brewing Co., holds up a button with the slogan "Beer, Let's Make It." The buttons were part of a campaign sponsored by Local 9 of the United Brewery Workers of America to boost sales in 1959 (*Milwaukee Journal* photograph). COURTESY OF WISCONSIN HISTORICAL SOCIETY, WHi-66826.

trading off for some years and would for a few years longer).[57]

What was an opportunity for the larger rivals of Milwaukee was a veritable lifeline for smaller Wisconsin brewers. Some literally owed their survival to the strike. The Burlington Brewing Company, which had gone into receivership the previous October, was now in the black because of the demand to replace the lost Milwaukee beer.[58] Fox Head Brewing, in nearby Waukesha, reported demand four times greater than it could meet. Fox Head had anticipated the walkout and hired sixty extra workers to double production in April so that beer would be ready during the strike. Wausau Brewing was another company that planned ahead and was ready to meet the increased demand. As the strike ended, Wausau's manager, James P. Fernock, was optimistic that the company could "consolidate a lot of the gains we made in sales, especially in Wisconsin and northern Illinois."[59] With varying amounts of optimism, executives hoped to keep their newfound gains. A few breweries saw little influence of the strike on their business, like G. Heileman of La Crosse and Leinenkugel Brewing in Chippewa Falls, which were either already at full capacity or attributed the increase in sales to warm weather rather than the strike.[60]

For the most part, gains by smaller brewers were in their home territories, but a few reached out to new markets they hoped to keep even after the strike.[61] Later analysis estimated that breweries outside Milwaukee had doubled production and that more than fifty different non-Wisconsin brands were imported by the city.[62] The final resolution of the dispute came in late July and was pushed off the lead of many Wisconsin papers only by the news that a truce had been signed that day in Korea. The seventy-six-day strike had shaken up the leaderboard, given hope to struggling firms, and changed the strategy of many executives. The decision by Pabst to begin brewing Blue Ribbon in Los Angeles came shortly after the end of the strike, and may well have been a move to guarantee the supply of the company's flagship brand in the event of another crippling strike. Heileman not only refused to raise its prices but also reemphasized its bond with workers and credited a cooperative union with helping the company make a profit and provide job security for its workers.[63]

Other labor disputes were addressed by litigation rather than by strikes. In 1965 Virginia Murphy, Veronika Monostori, and Catherine Pelot, all laboratory employees of Miller Brewing, filed the first complaint with the Wisconsin Industrial Commission concerning sex discrimination in employment. They alleged that they were paid seventy cents an hour less than men who did the

Two Rivers Beverage Company was one of about a dozen breweries around the country to make Brewers' Best Pilsener. Brewers' Best was intended to give small and regional brewers a label with national brand recognition and to help them save money by using mass-produced marketing pieces. Customers appeared to be unwilling to develop loyalty to a generic-sounding product, however, and the experiment only lasted from 1947 to 1951. AUTHOR'S COLLECTION.

same work.[64] The commission ruled in favor of the women and awarded them back pay.[65]

The Cream City avoided another major strike until 1969, when 4,500 workers at Milwaukee's breweries (now just Schlitz, Miller-Gettelman, and Pabst-Blatz) went out in early June. While the city was indeed out of Schlitz, it was not really out of beer. But this time, there were fewer breweries in existence to take up the slack, and few of them were able to supply much additional beer. Several days of protests at Schlitz resulted in more than thirty arrests, and Students for a Democratic Society visited the picket line to distribute pamphlets and talk to picketers. However, the union disavowed any link and rejected offers of support from SDS, calling them a "revolution oriented" Marxist group.[66]

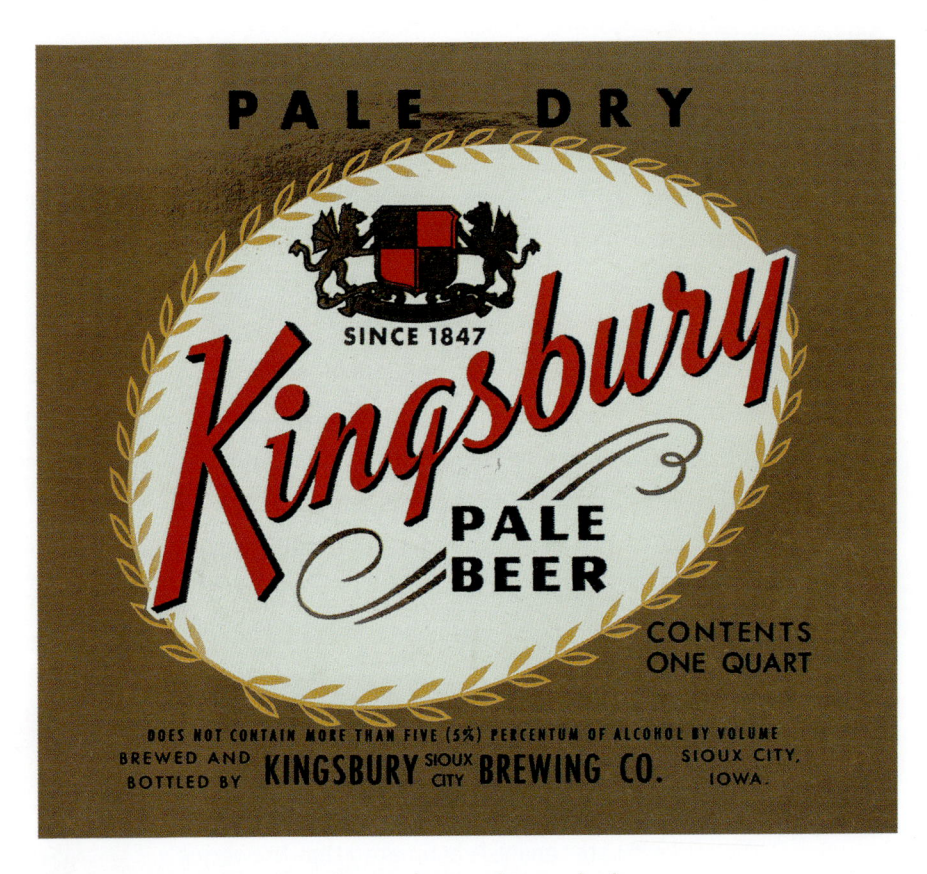

Kingsbury operated the Sioux City Brewing Co. after purchasing it in 1959 until the plant was closed the next year. COLLECTION OF JOHN STEINER.

The 1969 strike lasted thirty-six days—a heat wave following a mild start to the summer was credited with speeding up negotiations to get the supply of beer flowing again.[67] However, the option of the company simply to close any plant affected by a strike would become the unpleasant reality for brewery employees.

PREDATORS AND PREY

A brewery in a small town has a distinctive place in the life of the village and its citizens. The smokestack and other structures of the brewery tower over the rest of the town, and it often functions as a center for communal life, a source of pride for an otherwise anonymous town, and driver of the local economy. When a small town loses its brewery, it loses part of its life as well as a large portion of its livelihood.[68]

Wisconsin's smaller breweries put up a valiant fight for survival, a struggle that shows the difficulties in generalizing about an industry. The state was home to three of the oligopolists (and eventually a fourth when Heileman joined the top ranks). It is true that the general decline in the number of breweries in operation was also reflected in Wisconsin, but loyal drinkers of local beer

266   THE DRINK THAT MADE WISCONSIN FAMOUS

These six- and eight-ounce bottles featuring painted labels were used during the 1930s and 1940s. Green bottles, rare in Wisconsin during this period, were sometimes used for ale. COLLECTION OF JOHN STEINER.

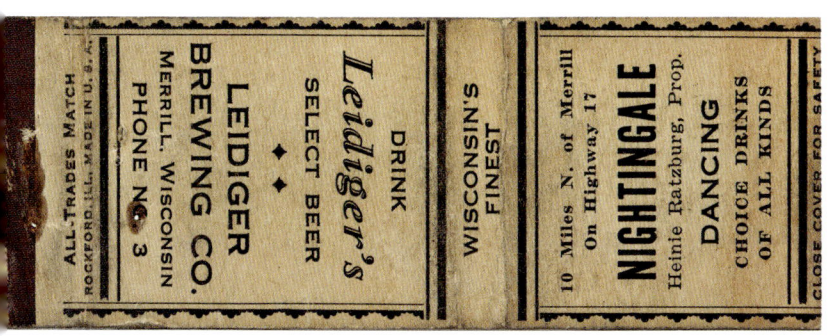

Wisconsin's smaller breweries were able to survive longer than their counterparts in many other states because of the state's tavern culture and high consumption of draught beer. The Nightingale, ten miles north of Merrill, proudly offered Leidiger's beer to patrons who needed a break from dancing (matchbook ca. 1940). COLLECTION OF TYE SCHWALBE.

kept small-town breweries open longer than their counterparts elsewhere.

To stay afloat, many of Wisconsin's small breweries copied the tactics of their bigger rivals, though on a more limited scale. Kingsbury Breweries became the first Wisconsin firm outside Milwaukee to operate a brewery in another state in 1959 when it purchased Sioux City Brewing, which was then Iowa's largest brewery. The move was intended to help expand the western periphery of Kingsbury's market into Nebraska and the Dakotas, helping it to fifth place in state sales. G. Heileman

THE AMERICAN WAY OF BEER 267

Brewing was mired in thirty-ninth place among America's breweries in 1957, but in 1959 it began an expansion program that started in Wisconsin with the purchase of a controlling share of Kingsbury. It stayed within the region for the next several years, purchasing the breweries and brands of Fox Head of Waukesha, the Independent Milwaukee Brewery, and Gluek Brewing of Minneapolis. Heileman was generally more interested in the brands than the breweries, though most of these were losing popularity (which is often why the breweries were for sale in the first place). Kingsbury's popular-price beer helped round out Heileman's brand portfolio.[69] Only the Kingsbury plant in Sheboygan remained open after Heileman acquired the company. Roy Kumm, Heileman's president, made a bolder move to expand the company's reach in 1967, when he purchased two breweries in Kentucky, the large George Wiedemann Brewing Company in Newport and the smaller Oertel Brewing of Louisville. The Newport plant remained in production and pushed Heileman's total capacity to over two million barrels.[70] (The story of Heileman's continued expansion and growth is covered in the next chapter.)

The persistence of the small-town bar or rural tavern in Wisconsin contributed to the survival of small breweries in a way their counterparts in other states could not take advantage of.[71] Small brewers were able to compete better with their giant rivals in draught beer sales in taverns than by matching the variety of different packages that the large shipping brewers were able to offer because of economies of scale. While sales for on-premises consumption generally declined nationwide, and most states consumed about 10–15 percent of their beer on draught, Wisconsin's share of beer sold on draught was usually closer to 40 percent.[72]

Small breweries had to work hard to maintain their draught accounts in taverns. Effinger Brewing Company of Baraboo published a newsletter for taverns that provided

Small knives were among the useful tools breweries gave away as promotional items. They often included a bottle opener or a can opener among their tools (sometimes both). These knives date from the 1950s. COLLECTION OF DAVID WENDL.

hints "to help you sell more beer." This was especially important for Effinger, since over 80 percent of its production was in keg beer, a high ratio even for Wisconsin. Effinger also suggested ways for its accounts to sell more of its bottled beer, much of which would be sold in bars but consumed off the premises.[73] While small and mid-sized breweries were generally unable to match the range of package sizes of the large breweries, the seven-ounce bottle was adopted by breweries of all sizes and became a favorite in bowling alleys and other gathering places.[74] The bottle was known by many names: Nip, Shorty, and Cub were typical, as were variations on the brewery's regular brand. These packages were sometimes promoted heavily by the brewery—Rhinelander produced well over one hundred cartoon ads for its Shorty bottles.[75]

While internal migration and tourism helped spread demand for national brands, Wisconsin's attractions may have helped sustain the tavern culture. Wisconsin Dells has been a family vacation spot for generations, but Wisconsin also attracted hunters, anglers, campers, and cabin dwellers—sometimes as families, but often in all-male groups. Instead of being dragged by their children to a family restaurant, the men would patronize the local tavern and often make their brand decisions based on price.

Small breweries capitalized on outdoor tourism in a way that large breweries did not need to, selling local beer in stores and gas stations on the way to lakes or hunting camps. Labels, especially those from the northern breweries, were decorated with pine trees or lake scenes. The Effinger Brewing Company proclaimed on its labels that it

A few breweries borrowed a tactic from other businesses. Kingsbury, West Bend Lithia, and Knapstein were among the companies in the mid-1950s that offered customers points for each purchase that could be redeemed for a variety of household items and toys. Even though the sled, utensil, or fishing pole did not have the brewery name on it, the desire to keep accumulating points encouraged repeat business. Kingsbury distributed the items through their local dealers, which built loyalty to particular establishments. AUTHOR'S COLLECTION.

THE AMERICAN WAY OF BEER

was brewed "in the Devil's Lake-Dells Region."[76] Local breweries often sponsored hunting and fishing contests, and some offered the facilities of their distributors for weighing the catch. Oshkosh Brewing was particularly active in the 1960s, sponsoring both deer hunting and sturgeon-spearing contests. Prizes always included cases of Chief Oshkosh beer along with other useful items, such as insulated underwear. Newspaper photos of contest winners brought the brewery free and favorable publicity.[77]

Breweries also kept their brands in the public eye—and in their pockets, and garages, and kitchens—with a staggering array of glassware and gadgets. Some items, such as ashtrays, may well have started in taverns but migrated home with customers. Thermometers, paperweights, ice picks, key rings, and, of course, openers all reminded customers of the helpfulness of the company and the refreshment of the brands. The most obvious reminders were glasses, mugs, and pitchers emblazoned with the brand name. Many breweries came out with new shapes or designs on a regular basis, and some offered glasses for special occasions. Walter Brewing Company of Eau Claire advertised a set of eight beer tumblers with the brewery name and some decorative holly sprigs during the 1967 and 1968 Christmas seasons: "A $2.49 value only $1 with coupon."[78]

For some businesses, diversification was a possible answer to financial crisis. Several breweries became distributors for other brands of

Punchboards were a popular form of gambling in bars for many years. Customers punched a hole with a stylus and pushed through a piece of paper with a number that corresponded to a particular prize (in this case, Potosi beer). Punchboards were most popular in the late 1930s but maintained limited popularity for a few years after World War II. COLLECTION OF DAVID WENDL.

These Old Milwaukee cans are from the period before Schlitz launched the major advertising campaign to support the brand. Left to right: ca. 1950s, ca. 1960, ca. 1941. COLLECTION OF DAVID WENDL.

beer, including Berlin Brewing (for Schlitz), Effinger (Miller), and J. Figi of Marshfield (Grain Belt). In the case of Figi, the brewery itself was a diversification, since John Figi already ran the world's largest mail-order gift cheese business from Marshfield.[79] Operating a distributorship enabled a closing brewery to retain at least some of the drivers and warehouse employees. In a few cases, such as Effinger, adding another line of beer was seen as a way to shore up profits rather than as a replacement for the local beer, but in time the popular brands drove the original inhabitants out of the nest. Effinger's request to the federal Alcohol and Tobacco Tax Division for permission to store Miller on brewery premises was made because "we need this new business enterprise," namely, to sell Miller "in an area in which we are very weak with our own brand." Unfortunately, since that area was the one that surrounded the brewery, this betrayed little hope for Effinger's Badger Brew.[80]

Despite their best attempts, Wisconsin breweries went out of business at a depressing rate from the early 1950s to the early 1970s. Newspapers often noted the overall decline when announcing another closure: the *Marshfield News-Herald* noted that when John Figi bought the Marshfield brewery in 1965 it was one of twenty-four breweries in the state, but when it closed a mere two years later there were only fifteen left.[81] While it is sometimes tempting to point to a particular event as the most important cause of a brewery's final end, in most cases, it was simply a combination of factors that added up over time. Sometimes there was not even a particular straw that broke the camel's back, just the accumulated effects of age, costs, and relative inefficiency.

Sometimes the answer was simple profitability. The closure of Northern Brewing Company in Superior was announced with the headline "High Costs Blamed for Brewery Fate."[82] Rahr Brewing in Oshkosh was caught between a sales slump and increasing wage demands in the mid-1950s. Brewmaster "Chuck" Rahr also refused to abandon the older, more time-consuming brewing methods, so the company was unable to cut costs.[83] When Fox Head Brewing of Waukesha was closed and its assets were sold to G. Heileman Brewing Company, Fox Head's parent company, Noramco Inc., decided "to get out of the business because Fox Head was not operating at a profit."[84]

The margin of error was often very small. When it closed in 1966, Marathon Brewery was the smallest in the state, with production of just over four thousand barrels the year before. With such numbers, any market was important, and when the brewery could not "get the type of bottles wanted by area supermarkets" it combined with a general lack of public interest to hasten the end. As was often the case, "the closing of the Marathon brewery went almost unnoticed, except for concerned residents of the Marathon area," which must not have been many other than the twelve employees. The brands were sold to the Figi Brewing Company in nearby Marshfield, which itself closed a year later.[85]

In some instances, owners and employees saw the closures as temporary measures. When Fountain City Brewing ceased production in June 1965, brewmaster Karl Grabner claimed, "There is a good future for this brewery. It can certainly go places. It's a shame the place has had to suspend operations. I hope it is only temporary."[86] Unfortunately, it was permanent.

This does not mean that brewers and industry observers did not attempt to assign blame. Large breweries clearly had a marketing advantage over their smaller cousins. When the Potosi Brewing Company closed in 1972, president Adolph Schumacher lamented, "We used to give away blackboards with our beer name on top but then the big breweries started giving away big fancy ones and none of the tavern owners wanted ours anymore."[87] One small brewer, writing in *Brewers Digest*, blamed the small breweries for fighting the wrong battle:

> *Due to the fact that a light bodied pilsener type beer is more stable and lends itself more easily to mass production and longer shelf life, it has become the only well known product of the brewer's art. The small brewer has been inclined to follow the trend in the mistaken belief that if he can successfully copy the products of his competitors his beer will be accepted. Herein lies his*

BERLIN BREWING COMPANY

THE STORY OF THE BERLIN BREWING COMPANY FOR THE YEARS AFTER PATRICK J. CURRAN BOUGHT A controlling interest in 1956 until it closed in 1964 was typical of many similar small breweries in small towns. The brewery had a skilled and loyal workforce and a solid local trade, but money was always in short supply, and the struggle to keep customers (and find new ones) meant that the margin for error was very thin.

As the last remaining union shop in Berlin after the Carnation condensed milk factory was destroyed in 1956, wages for the brewery employees were among the best in the city. Pat Curran recalled that "no one got overpaid," but no one quit either. The brewery normally paid workers in cash, and once paid employees in two-dollar bills so that as the bills circulated the community could see how important the company was to the local economy. Employees had to pitch in wherever needed. Many employees helped repair the brewery or fix the trucks; bottle house labelers had delivery routes on Fridays.

Small and mid-sized breweries were sometimes successful in expanding their markets by brewing special beers for particular bars, restaurants, or package stores. The label for the beer Berlin Brewing Co. brewed for the Sportsman's Bar in the 1950s was essentially a negative image of the label for their own brand. COLLECTION OF SCOTT REICH.

Building community relations ranged from buying rounds for customers in taverns to supporting area businesses. The brewery helped sponsor the local Mardi Gras and fall festivals and generally emphasized selling beer at sporting and civic events. It built a mobile cooler on a trailer, which may have been the first in the state (and was an ancestor of the mobile serving units used by craft brewers in the early twenty-first century). The brewery sampling room had copper mugs for the use of guests—though the mugs had a tendency to disappear. Since the

THE AMERICAN WAY OF BEER

brewery was right across from the city swimming pool, younger customers would often come over after a swim, sit on old kegs, and enjoy fresh local beer.

It was essential to secure the home trade, but Berlin Brewing could not have survived without expanding its market. In the immediate area, Redgranite was a particularly good territory, and Berlin beer sold well in New London. Milwaukee was right on the edge of Berlin's distribution radius of about one hundred miles, and the brewery had several accounts in the Cream City. The most distant locations where Berlin beer could be found were La Crosse and Fountain City, along the Mississippi River. Berlin Brewing also made about fifty different private labels for stores, bars, and restaurants, such as the Silver Crisp and Nelson's Tomahawk.

Like many small breweries, Berlin Brewing Company was not able to spend a lot of money to support its products. The company did a little advertising on area television stations and had some point-of-sale promotions. The brewery could not afford many of the usual promotional items such as coasters, glasses, or trays. Peoples of Oshkosh was a significant competitor, though Berlin felt little pressure from area brewers such as Geo. Walter of Appleton, Stevens Point Brewery, or Oshkosh Brewing Company. According to Curran, the biggest competition was from St. Paul's Theo. Hamm Brewing Company, which had a strong presence in Wisconsin.

While Berlin Brewing Company continued to pay its suppliers, meet payroll, and make a bit of money, it was not enough "to make us think we were going to be around forever." Ultimately, Curran decided to close the company while it was still profitable rather than waiting until it was unable to meet its obligations.[1]

---

1   All information in this section comes from Patrick J. Curran, interview by author, 23 July 2017.

first mistake, for he has placed himself in direct competition with the large national brewers. He is offering a product which is so similar that it cannot be expected to enjoy a superior position in the face of the large scale advertising which he cannot afford.[88]

One problem that was very real was the price war initiated by the big brewers, Schlitz in particular. The major national brewers all had a "popular price" beer: for Anheuser-Busch it was Busch Bavarian (later just Busch), for Schlitz it was Old Milwaukee, and for Pabst it was Red White and Blue. (Pabst also advertised Blatz at "local prices" during the early 1960s.)[89] Part of the reason they were able to sell these at a lower price was that the breweries spent very little money on advertising to support the brands. Advertising was generally limited to point-of-sale displays or price listings in a local retailer's ads. In the mid-1960s, however, Schlitz began a nationwide advertising campaign for Old Milwaukee, including a long series of television commercials. Local breweries were able to compete against national premium brands on price, but not against a national low-price brand.

The biggest villain for the smaller brewers was cut-price promotions. While direct evidence was hard to come by, the circumstantial evidence was striking when sales by the big three went up by much more than the industry total. The Brewers' Association of America, which primarily represented smaller breweries, alleged that Anheuser-Busch and Schlitz were targeting the territories of small breweries and cutting prices to the point where sales of the local beer nearly dried up for several months.[90] The organization collected examples of "unfair trade practices," including coupons given by Schlitz to consumers entitling them to a free beer at a bowling alley or bar, with payments to tavern keepers upon redemption. In response, the BAA created an Unfair Trade Practices Fund to help with the lobbying and litigation expenses. Unfortunately, the brewers most in need of this support were in such bad shape they were unable to contribute to the fund.[91] The situation for Potosi Brewing was typical, as the declining volume caused by "the large breweries' secondary beers at low prices" made it impossible to invest in the new equipment that would make Potosi efficient enough to compete in any meaningful way.[92]

While the Federal Trade Commission proceeded to build a case against Schlitz, sometimes a brewery reluctantly conceded that factors other than predatory pricing resulted in closure. In response to an inquiry from the FTC, Fred J. Effinger found four reasons for the end of his family's brewery: the reopening of an ammunition plant nearby, which caused a labor shortage and increased wages beyond what the brewery could afford; "inability to keep up with the packaging parade"; its location in a small community with a large influx of tourists aware of national brands but not Effinger's; and Schlitz sponsorship of and donations to Circus World Museum productions, which built goodwill in the museum's Baraboo home. Effinger minimized the effects of Old Milwaukee on the demise of his company's Badger Brew.[93]

Occasionally advocates of small breweries appealed to patriotism. In an editorial focused on the decline of breweries in Wisconsin, the author warned:

> *If—the trend continues—there will only be a handful of Brewing Companies left. Which means—that imported Beers will come into Wisconsin (and all other states) to take up the slack. There will be Beer sold in the State of Wisconsin—which will have been Brewed in Asia by cheap foreign labor. Wisconsin Brewers who fought—and bled—for our country—may well ask themselves the question—"who won the war anyhow?" Did the United States of America win a war so that all Small Brewers will be put out of business—and so that Beer from Asian Breweries can take the place of that produced by the American Small Breweries?*[94]

Despite these concerns, the big threat was from just down the highway, rather than from overseas.

The impact on the community of a brewery closure was significant, and nearly catastrophic in the case of a small town. When Fountain City Brewing Company closed in 1965, brewmaster Grabner emphasized, "The brewery was important to the community because of the men it employed. . . . The employees in a small plant work harder than in a large plant because they have pride in their hometown business. The employees were cooperative and did everything they could to keep the brewery open."[95] Whether the closing was prolonged or sudden, the effect on the community was the same. Berlin Brewing, founded before the Civil War, saw production rise over 20,000 barrels in the aftermath of World War II, but it declined and settled in around 10,000 barrels for most of the 1950s and early 1960s. The threat of closure in 1956 from declining profitability led the city to launch a "community-wide effort" to save the brewery by selling 450 shares of brewery stock to local residents. It was estimated that a 3,000-barrel-per-year increase was all that was needed to return to the break-even point, and that community support would help reach that target. The effort saved the brewery for a few more years, and the Berlin brewery–sponsored softball team continued to lead its league. In 1961, however, the city raised its water and sewer rates to a level that put the brewery's cost at ten times that of some of its rivals. When Berlin ceased brewing in 1964, the city lost not only several jobs but also the revenues from water and sewer fees.[96] Likewise, when Walter Bros. Brewing Company in Menasha closed, it removed $150,000 in taxable property from the city assessment lists. Municipalities, charities, and other businesses dependent on the breweries suffered as well as the families of the laid-off workers.[97]

Case Study on the River

The Potosi Brewing Company had remained profitable through the early seventies despite the difficulties. However, the cost of improving the brewery to keep pace with its rivals proved an insurmountable hurdle. Advances such as the "pop-top" can required older breweries to purchase new equipment and made existing supplies obsolete. The market as a whole was shifting to nonreturnable bottles, which required either new packing equipment or costly alterations to existing machines as well as the constant purchase of new bottles. New or even secondhand equipment could be much more expensive than a brewery could afford. In 1972 the Schumacher family estimated that it would take nearly $1 million to properly equip the plant for the next quarter century. The company did not have the cash on hand, and since production and market were both shrinking, banks were uninterested in making a loan likely to end in default.[98]

In addition, in a circumstance repeated elsewhere in the state, time was running out for members of the Schumacher family and other key employees. President Adolph Schumacher was eighty-one, cousin Rudolph had returned to run the bottling plant after having been retired for ten years, and all the other Schumachers were over seventy. The next generation had little to no interest in continuing the business—Rudolph had returned because his son had left to take a job with John Deere in Dubuque, Iowa.[99] Replacing long-time brewmasters became harder as a generation of German brewers retired and small companies were confronted not just by a lack of qualified individuals but also by the difficulty of finding brewmasters willing to work in a small town for lower wages than they could get at a major brewer or for a company in another field.[100] While the brewery was still making a small profit, it was clear that there was no future for the company. "It is hard to think that a business that never lost money should be closing," Rudolph Schumacher lamented. "I guess you could say that old age is creeping up on the Schumachers. And when you are old, you have to give up and quit."[101]

The closing of the brewery cast a pall over the village. PBC was the only industry in town, and residents feared not just unemployment for many of the forty-five remaining workers but also loss of the tax base as well as water and sewer receipts for the village.[102] The ripple effects were felt throughout the community. With the brewery gone, railroad business at the depot dropped significantly. Local businesses that supplied the brewery and its workers closed, forcing residents to leave town to fulfill many needs.[103] Even with these more urgent concerns, residents were also distressed about the loss of a local product. One employee of a tavern and beer depot complained, "While we will still be able to get it [Holiday was purchased by Huber Brewing Co. in Monroe], it just won't be the same. It won't be a local beer."[104]

Potosi was one of four breweries to close in 1972, along with Peoples, West Bend Lithia, and Geo. Walter Brewing of Appleton. When Heileman finally closed the former Kingsbury plant in 1974, and Rice Lake Brewing Company ceased to brew the same year, Wisconsin's brewing industry had been reduced to eight breweries—the lowest number since the early 1840s. The good news was that the four remaining smaller breweries seemed stable, and the four giants were continuing to dominate the nation's brewing landscape. But the signs in the taverns and the dusty beer cans on shelves in basements around the nation served as reminders of the diversity of Wisconsin's beer only a few years earlier.

"Everything You've Always Wanted in an Ad Campaign . . . and Less." More than one hundred commercials starred members of the Miller Lite All-Stars—one of the best-loved advertising campaigns of the latter part of the twentieth century. The collection of athletes, tough guys, funny men, and "the Doll" helped move Lite from a curiosity to one of the best-selling brands in the country. PHOTOGRAPH BY JOE KENNEDY; COPYRIGHT 1985 LOS ANGELES TIMES–WASHINGTON POST NEWS SERVICE. COLLECTION OF OTTO TIEGS.

CHAPTER 9

ONE LITE ON, OTHER LIGHTS OUT

1970–2015

"In the beer business, if a company loses its resources and money, but retains its reputation, it can always be rebuilt. But if it loses its reputation, no amount of money and resources will bring it back."

Ted Rosenak, CITED IN *ADVERTISING AGE,* 20 APRIL 1981

When America celebrated its Bicentennial in 1976, Wisconsin had a quartet of nationally famous breweries that had been influential for nearly two-thirds of the nation's history. But just because a business makes it through 130 years doesn't mean it will make it to 140. By the turn of the twenty-first century, two of the four Wisconsin breweries that had once been in the top five producers in the nation were closed for good, and the other two were operating under significantly different management. With the exception of Miller, which was compelled to merge with competitors, the iconic labels that once dominated store shelves and tap handles were mostly consigned to "retro" status. The story of the big four is a study of business conditions and marketing more than brewing tradition or flavor, but it still demonstrates Wisconsin's central role in the global brewing industry.

The House of Heileman had many rooms in 1982. Its ten breweries from Seattle to Auburndale, Florida, from Baltimore to Phoenix brewed two dozen major labels—most of them once regional favorites. Tuborg Beer (lower left) was a faux Danish import beer. Malt Duck (lower right) was a fruit-and-beer hybrid that was popular with some drinkers during the 1980s and 1990s. The lineup included an ale, two cream ales, two malt liquors, and a near beer. COURTESY OF MURPHY LIBRARY SPECIAL COLLECTIONS, UNIVERSITY OF WISCONSIN–LA CROSSE.

By the 1970s the vast majority of beer sold in America was brewed by just a few large companies. However, more brands were available on the shelves than there were breweries. As the large breweries gobbled up their smaller rivals they kept the labels alive if they had any sort of local following. Thus, when Heileman purchased the Gluek Brewing Company of Minneapolis, the former continued to brew Stite—among the first beers to be called a "malt liquor" and infamous among drinkers for causing hangovers. In fact, Heileman purchased more breweries and more labels than any other American brewery and kept some of the local brands alive as long as they were profitable.

Despite the variety of labels, the beers were mostly the same liquid in different packages. Most of the local brands had little advertising support, and they generally competed on price rather than on their reputation for flavor or quality and often were phased out.

Of the Milwaukee breweries, Schlitz and Pabst both preferred to expand by building their own breweries, and at any rate they were largely precluded from purchasing other breweries by the likelihood of antitrust action from the Justice Department. Miller Brewing Co. was smaller, however, and less likely to incur the wrath of federal regulators. In addition, Miller, which had clung to a single brand for so long, was about to lead the charge in what businesses call line extensions.

For Wisconsin's big four, and their rivals in St. Louis and elsewhere, sales volume was critical. Large breweries have extremely high fixed costs, including labor, maintenance, and depreciation, so selling enough beer to cover them is essential. Once past that threshold, though, the profit is significant. One industry analyst estimated in 1980 that "the majors make $20 or more on the last barrel they ship. So you see how important that volume really is." Throughout the last decades of the twentieth century, the major brewers would fight a battle against profit-sapping overcapacity, which

ONE LITE ON, OTHER LIGHTS OUT 281

Fred C. Miller points with pride as the last of ninety new fermenters is hoisted into place in 1950. The tanks were part of a $15 million expansion program (between $122 million and $230 million in 2016 dollars). A real live "girl in the moon" rode the fermenter as it was raised. COURTESY OF MILLERCOORS BREWING CO.

was especially important to companies for which profit was not just a matter of pride but of income to shareholders who demanded immediate return on investment rather than long-term growth.[1]

LEAVING THE FAMILY

A significant step on the path to the corporatization of many of America's breweries was the loss of family ownership and management. The dread combination of debt and death forced many breweries, both large and small, to look outside the family for gold and guidance. While Blatz was well ahead of the trend by giving up control to a nonfamily corporation in the 1890s, others followed in time. Heileman passed from family control just after repeal. Not only was the second generation of the family aging, but the firm needed a significant infusion of new capital and the family's finances had been drained by thirteen years of Prohibition. In July 1933, the G. Heileman Brewing Company was incorporated in Delaware, with directors from the La Crosse and Chicago areas. (A few Heileman descendants retained stock in the firm or served as officers, but none owned more than 5 percent of the stock.)[2]

Miller remained a closely held family firm through the 1950s. But the 1954 death of Frederick C. Miller and his son Fred Jr. in a plane crash marked the beginning of a slow transition. New president Norman Klug was a most able manager though not a family member. The remaining third-generation descendants, Louise Mulberger and Harry John Jr., were growing less interested in purveying alcohol and, especially in John's case, more interested in their work through Catholic foundations. Mulberger sold her majority interest of Miller stock to W. R. Grace & Company in 1966, and John followed three years later. The Miller family was no longer part of the firm that bore their name.[3]

THE LITE DAWNS

Contrary to many accounts, the story of low-calorie beer begins well before Lite Beer from Miller appeared in 1973, and even before Rheingold introduced Gablinger's in 1966. As early as

1939, Schmidt's of Detroit and Sterling Pilsner of Evansville, Indiana, were advertised as low-calorie beers that claimed to be no more fattening than "a good-sized orange" or "3 little graham crackers."[4] Schmidt's crosstown rival Pfeiffer chimed in by announcing, "Pfeiffer's is a low-calorie beer, you know. It's kind to folks who are concerned about extra poundage."[5] Ads of this type disappeared as World War II intensified, but as the Korean War was winding down, a handful of brewers around the country began testing the market for low-calorie beers. Dawson's, of New Bedford, Massachusetts, may have been the first when it advertised its "calorie controlled" lager in 1952.[6] Recognizing regional tastes, they also introduced "calorie controlled" ale in 1953. Ballantine threw a cooler full of ice water on these accelerating claims by noting, "It is only fair to say that practically all of today's beers are lower in calories than they used to be. All are starch-free, none has more than a negligible trace of sugar."[7] They still asserted, however, that "laboratory tests show Ballantine has fewer calories than any other leading beer. But Ballantine not only watches your belt-line. It brews to the American taste as well as the American figure."[8] These beers were not specially designed light beers—the brewers simply made dietary claims for their regular products.

The first beer specifically designed to be lower in calories appears to have been Southern Select Superlite, a short-lived beer introduced in 1954 by Galveston-Houston Breweries. Superlite was intended to appeal to women, and was released in tandem with Southern Special, which was a heavier beer aimed at men. Superlite was not a success, and promoting beers based on their calorie content was largely dropped as a sales tactic (except for Kingsbury Near Beer).

It was not until 1961 that Piel Brothers of New York resurrected the old Trommer's brand it had purchased a decade earlier for the name of its foray into low-calorie beer. Trommer's Red Letter claimed to have only fifty calories per six-ounce glass, stemming from "a genuine new discovery, which has taken us several years to develop in our laboratories."[9] (It should be noted that while all these beers were sold in twelve-ounce packages, the calories were counted per six- or eight-ounce serving.) What the company still hadn't discovered was how to sell a light beer. What press attention Red Letter got was mostly derisive: nationally syndicated columnist Bob Considine sarcastically exulted, "Russia may be able to put men in space, but what has it done about low calorie beer?" He concluded his comments by reminding readers of near beer and the quip he attributed to Bugs Baer: "'Whoever named it Near-Beer was just a bad judge of distance.'"[10]

The era in which there was always a low-calorie beer on the market began in late 1966, when Brooklyn's venerable Rheingold brewery began shipping Gablinger's. One sign that public tastes were changing was the appearance of a second reduced-calorie beer at almost the same time, Meister Bräu's Lite. A few other breweries experimented with similar beers on a local level, but Gablinger's and Meister Bräu were the only two to attempt anything resembling national distribution. Neither was a spectacular success, but both lasted for several years. One problem was that low-calorie

| 1967 | 1972 | 1974 | 1989 | 1990 | 1992 | 1994 | 1996 | 1998 | 1999 | 2003 |

The classic Lite can was almost unchanged for its first two decades. During the 1990s the Miller name became more prominent and the sheaves of grain disappeared. The twenty-first century brought a total makeover of the can, but Miller returned to a version of the original design to celebrate the fortieth anniversary of the brand. The cans at the far left are the original Meister Bräu designs. COURTESY OF MILLERCOORS BREWING CO.

beer was sometimes treated as a generic product by retailers: Ben's Beverage Mart in Waunakee announced "We Now Carry Low Calorie Beer" without mentioning a brand.[11]

Lite had no particular reason to be any more successful than similar beer brands. It became one of the labels acquired in 1972 by Miller when the assets of Chicago's Meister Bräu were split up between Miller and Huber. Lite was originally an afterthought in the deal, but Miller's new management believed there might be a niche market worth pursuing. After adjusting the formula so it would taste more like a typical beer, the company began test-marketing the "Fine Pilsner Beer" with the name Lite Beer from Miller (to protect the name of the flagship beer from being dragged down if Lite flopped).

Miller's advertising agency, McCann-Erickson, was working on the problem of how to avoid the poor performance of Gablinger's, which suffered from an advertising campaign that was at best uninspiring and that some industry analysts interpreted as suggesting beer drinkers were overweight and should drink less.[12] McCann-Erickson's Bob Lenz and Pacey Markham came up with an unbeatable combination for Lite: a great tag line—"Everything you've always wanted in a beer . . . and less"—and undeniably manly characters to say it. Ironically, the first athlete to pitch Lite on television, retired New York Jets running back Matt Snell, had been asked to endorse Gablinger's when he was working for Rheingold, and retorted that it tasted like "frozen ice water."[13]

TASTES GREAT, SELLS BETTER

As Lite proved worthy of continued marketing support, the commercials took a broad view of stardom, including actors and drummer Buddy Rich, but the best known of the early pitchmen was author Mickey Spillane, whose hard-edged private eye and sometime alter ego Mike Hammer brought an indisputably masculine flavor to the television ads, especially when paired with "the Doll," buxom actress Lee Meredith. Nonathletes continued to appear—most notably comedian Rodney Dangerfield, on his continuing quest for respect. But the sports theme eventually took over, and the "Miller Lite All-Stars" became some of the most popular pitchmen of the era. The debate between "tastes great" and "less filling" first argued by Celtics coach Tommy Heinsohn and referee Mendy Rudolph was repeated not just in commercials but also in spontaneous real-life situations. Lines such as Bubba Smith's "I also like the easy opening can" and Bob Uecker's "I must be in the front row!" were common catchphrases at the time and were repeated for decades by those who remembered the ads fondly—to the bewilderment of those who didn't. Ultimately there were more than one hundred commercials in the series, which was named by *Advertising Age* magazine the eighth-best advertising campaign of the century because it took "a single beer brand and transformed it into an industry-wide segment."[14]

Lite had launched the most important change in the brewing industry since Prohibition. Every brewer now needed a light beer in its lineup to remain competitive. Like Miller, Anheuser-Busch was hesitant to make a light version of the flagship Budweiser at first (opting instead to offer Anheuser-Busch Natural Light), but most other breweries attached "Light" to the name of at least one of their beers. Schlitz was the first of the large brewers to do so, but the others followed in due course. But Lite's unique spelling and advertising muscle set it apart from most of the contenders, and when patrons asked for a Lite, it was Miller they wanted, and Miller they usually received.

Unlike many product launches, Miller Lite was a financial success almost overnight. Part of this was because Miller was spending almost three dollars per barrel on advertising in 1976, nearly three times the industry average—much of which was used to acquire exclusive advertising rights for most of the significant sporting events in the United States. But the numbers told the story: in the first year of the national launch, Miller sold almost thirteen million barrels of beer (including High Life and other products). In the second full year of Lite, the company topped eighteen million barrels, and volume exceeded twenty-four million the next year—nearly doubling in two years. Lite was so popular that it had to be rationed so that distributors would have enough to supply all markets. Revenues likewise reached new heights: $1.328 billion in 1977. Miller jumped from fourth

The vast forest of fermenters of Miller's new Irwindale, California, brewery, under construction (ca. 1977). COURTESY OF MILLERCOORS BREWING CO.

place in production into the second spot in the same two-year period.[15]

The unimaginable popularity of Lite forced Miller to expand much faster than earlier plans dictated. Miller had been operating around the clock even before the national launch of Lite, so existing breweries were expanded; new breweries under construction in Fulton, New York, and Eden, North Carolina, were scaled up during the building process; and more breweries were constructed in Irwindale, California, and Albany, Georgia.[16] Miller built yet another plant in Trenton, Ohio, though this plant was mothballed upon completion in 1984 and not opened until 1991, as the company had built to the point of overcapacity.[17] The new breweries were able to install the latest technologies and also spread the company's footprint around the country to save on shipping costs. The frenetic pace also strained supplies of inputs, so the company built a new bottle plant to supply the Fulton brewery and a can factory for Eden.[18]

Miller's place as the country's number-two brewery was uncontested, and the only question was whether or not it would be able to challenge Anheuser-Busch for the top spot. In 1978 Miller's president, John Murphy, was optimistic that the gap between A-B's 25.6 percent of the domestic beer market and Miller's 18.8 percent would be closed in a matter of a few years. Murphy, an aggressive competitor and a bit of a showman, had a rug with the Anheuser-Busch logo made for his office so he could walk upon and roll his chair over it, and even had a voodoo doll of August Busch III.[19] The battle for number one would be played out less in the brewhouse and in the warehouse than in the courthouse and on the airwaves, however. Saturation advertising, which Philip Morris brought to Miller, drove many smaller breweries out of business since they could not even approach Miller's (and A-B's) spending per barrel.[20] But as brewing became a two-horse race, some of the most legendary names in Milwaukee fell off the pace.

PRECIPITATING A CRISIS

The last brewery other than Anheuser-Busch to occupy the top spot among American breweries was Schlitz, which held that title in 1956. While it would never regain that lofty perch, Schlitz had still grown from 5.77 million barrels in 1961 to 15.12

This Schlitz flashlight (ca. 1970s) was one of the author's first pieces of breweriana. AUTHOR'S COLLECTION.

million barrels in 1970 through successful product launches for Schlitz Malt Liquor and the reintroduced Old Milwaukee.[21] On the other hand, a series of failed investments—some of them breweries, but also South American fishing fleets and a duck farm—left the company with a lot of unaccustomed debt. In addition, the Uihlein family members, who controlled 75 percent of the company's stock, appeared unwilling to put their dividends at risk to make meaningful acquisitions or to increase the advertising budget enough to compete with Bud and Miller. A leadership vacuum in several key positions below the level of chairman meant that the brewing, marketing, and finance divisions were not communicating well. Chairman Robert Uihlein, who was more comfortable with finance than other operations, sought to increase profit by cutting costs wherever possible.[22]

Schlitz had been cutting costs by using cheaper ingredients since the early 1960s, though the use of less barley malt and hops resulted in a lighter beer with less aftertaste, which appealed to a broader, more refreshment-oriented customer base. Schlitz developed a new fermentation process, introduced at the Milwaukee plant in 1974, called "accelerated batch fermentation" (ABF). While this allowed each brewery to churn out more beer in the same amount of time, and to cut costs dramatically, it created a public relations problem when competitors claimed that Schlitz was selling "green" or unfinished beer. Schlitz defended the process and changed the name to "accurate balanced fermentation" to highlight brewing consistency. But explaining a complex process seldom makes matters better. One frustrated director muttered, "'In the brewing business, if you say you use the same process your ancestors used in 1700, people think that's good, but if you say you use the same transportation your ancestors used in 1700, people question your sanity.'"[23]

The ABF problems were soon amplified by a quality-control problem even nonexperts could see just by grabbing a bottle. Faced with a government proposal requiring ingredient listings on all products, Schlitz's legal team recommended that the company eliminate any compounds that might look unappetizing or scary on a label. Most worrisome was a seaweed-derived silica gel with enzymes designed to precipitate out unwanted proteins and make the beer more stable to prolong shelf life. So at the beginning of 1976 the silica gel was replaced with a different product that filtered out before packaging and that therefore would not have to be listed. Unfortunately, the new Chill-garde, which was supposed to prevent chill haze, did not interact well with the foam stabilizer and created a haze of tiny flakes that got more pronounced as the beer aged. Some overseas shipments developed a thick haze almost right away. One former Schlitz employee remembered, "If you turned a thirty-two-ounce bottle over it looked like a snow globe."[24] While it took several months to figure out exactly what the problem was, the first solution attempted actually made matters much worse. The foam stabilizer was simply removed, and the resulting beer was almost completely flat due to the lack of proteins once provided by malt and hops. While the problem was solved by the fall, millions of loyal consumers had been driven away from a beer that looked awful, despite being perfectly safe. Schlitz

Beer Cans and Breweriana

Although people have saved brewery items since the nineteenth century, the beginning of modern breweriana collecting probably began with the legendary "Uncle" Ernie Oest. He began collecting shortly after repeal, and he made it his quest to visit every brewery in America. The photographs he took during his travels became an important part of the historic record. For many, beer items were a subset of antique collecting. But the rapid decline in the number of breweries during the years after World War II brought increasing attention to everyday objects that were now "collectors' items."

During the 1960s, a few specialists in beer items began to write about their collections and started organizations to facilitate buying, selling, and trading. Collector and author Will Anderson coined the term *breweriana* (pronounced brewery-anna) around 1969 as a catchall term for any item bearing

This wall of cases and bottles only hints at the range of breweriana that can be collected. Nearly everything in this picture dates between 1933 and the late 1950s. (Most of the bottles in the cases are actually soft drink bottles, but that is a topic for another book.) Of special note is the De Pere Brewing Corp. case (fourth from left, second row from bottom). De Pere never actually received its brewing permit, so its beer was brewed at Menominee-Marinette Brewing Co. in Michigan. COLLECTION OF JOHN STEINER.

Celluloid beer combs (or foam scrapers) were popular in the decades following repeal. They were used by bartenders to scrape the foam off the top of a freshly poured glass of beer. They fell from favor in the late 1950s and early 1960s when bartenders and patrons realized the potential for contamination resulting from the combs being left in cups full of increasingly murky water. COLLECTION OF TYE SCHWALBE.

a brewery's name. The next year, the Beer Can Collectors of America (BCCA) and the Eastern Coast Breweriana Association were founded, and several other national and regional organizations followed in the next decade.

Much of the surge in breweriana collecting was due to beer can collectors, many of them young. Some junior high schools even had beer can collecting clubs. To encourage collectors, many regional and local breweries made colorful cans for festivals and local retailers, as well as numerous variations of their flagship cans. The early bylaws of the BCCA prohibited buying and selling cans at club events and established a guide for trade values based on broad categories (for example, cone tops and current gallon cans were both worth eight points, in contrast with foreign cans, which were worth two points). While this kept values from inflating, it was a barrier to new collectors who had nothing to trade. The major national breweries appealed to collectors with variations on their regular products but also created series of collectible steins

Many of the breweries that survived into or through the 1970s capitalized on the beer can collecting craze. By packaging a popular-price beer in different cans for civic events or local retailers, they could guarantee at least some sales to customers who wanted the new can and were willing to buy large quantities to have traders available. PHOTOGRAPH BY CHARLES WALBRIDGE. AUTHOR'S COLLECTION.

ONE LITE ON, OTHER LIGHTS OUT 289

When breweriana collectors meet, they usually enjoy beer along with the artifacts. Sometimes a local brewery will create a special beer for the event or will package one of its regular beers with a commemorative label. Viking Brewing Co. of Dallas (as it was then known) brewed Unconventional for the Seventeenth Annual Meeting of the American Breweriana Association in 1998. COLLECTION OF SCOTT REICH.

The Packer Chapter's membership primarily hails from northeastern Wisconsin. Each April the chapter hosts Trade-A-Thon (TAT) in Green Bay, where collectors can meet and see what new finds their friends have discovered. COLLECTION OF DAVID WENDL.

and sold items previously available only to distributors or retailers at the well-stocked gift shops at their breweries.

Although beer can fever declined during the 1980s, the rise of microbreweries offered a new source of variety for collectors. Micro or craft cans were rare until the mid-2000s, when breweries could afford the equipment, so collectors focused on bottles, crowns, coasters, and glassware. As the number of U.S. breweries has surpassed six thousand, the opportunities for collectors of all types of items are limitless.

Collecting breweriana is much more than a way to count how many beers one has had. Collecting brings people together to share a common interest despite other differences. Breweriana illustrates advances in technology and changing economic patterns. It shows changes in society, design, and consumer preferences. Breweriana keeps family names alive and celebrates the enterprising spirit of people around the world. Some anthropologists contend that civilization started because of beer—and the community of collectors certainly did.

secretly recalled the bad beer, and over one million bottles were crushed and buried with a front-end loader at the Memphis plant, and more at Tampa.[25]

Schlitz brought on the flaky beer crisis by trying to avoid federal regulations, but the company incurred even more federal wrath by challenging the government over illegal sales practices. The Justice Department pursued charges against Schlitz, which then suspended and later fired several key marketing and sales professionals, perhaps attempting to avoid penalties. During all of this, Chairman Bob Uihlein was diagnosed with acute leukemia and died in November 1976. The new leadership team had virtually no experience selling beer and was not ready for the task ahead. In March 1978 the Justice Department handed down a 747-count indictment against the company that included charges of tax fraud and conspiracy in addition to the 743 charges of illegal sales practices.[26]

Don't Care Where It's Made

Schlitz's troubles were masked briefly by a three-month strike at Anheuser-Busch in 1976, which pushed Schlitz to record volumes of 24.16 million barrels, but the flagship beer was declining and about to crash. Market research that showed consumers thought Schlitz tasted "terrible" was countered with a succession of ad campaigns that either flopped or hurt the brand more. The latter was exemplified by the attempt to bring back the gusto theme with ads in which an off-camera voice threatened to take away a drinker's gusto and the drinker retaliated. Viewers generally missed any humor in the ads, and the campaign became known as "Drink Schlitz or I'll kill you."[27] Another questionable ad campaign paid actor James Coburn $500,000 just to say two words—"Schlitz Light."[28]

The company hired Frank Sellinger away from Anheuser-Busch to return Schlitz to its previous glory, but efforts to reformulate the beer and restore consistency to the marketing plan were

The Schlitz "Send a Child to Camp" program began in 1966 in Chicago and spread across the nation by 1969. Several thousand urban youth were sent to summer camps, sponsored by local taverns that met sales quotas to trigger sponsorships by Schlitz and its local wholesalers (coaster from 1970). AUTHOR'S COLLECTION.

unable to lure drinkers back to the brand consistently. By 1980 production was down to fifteen million barrels, though the company's earlier expansions left it with capacity for more than twenty-five million barrels, even after shedding the new Syracuse brewery and the older, smaller Honolulu brewery.[29] An ad campaign featuring live blind taste tests (including one during the 1981 Super Bowl) showed that many customers preferred Schlitz to their regular beer, but persuaded few drinkers to switch.[30] The next year, Schlitz workers went on strike in June over wages, but rumors swirled that the company might use the strike as an excuse to close the large but inefficient brewery. At the end of July, with a purchase bid by Heileman pending, Schlitz shocked Milwaukee's economy and psyche by closing its landmark brewery on Galena Street, putting more than seven hundred union employees out of work.[31] As with many such closures, politicians became involved but were able to do little good. Governor Lee Dreyfus attempted to land a trade deal with China that would send Wisconsin beer to the most populous country in the world (and that was allegedly experiencing a beer shortage at the time), though nothing came of it. Congressman Henry Reuss urged Milwaukee mayor Henry Maier to refuse a demolition permit (though none had yet been requested), on the grounds that it would "sabotage" attempts by others to purchase and run the plant.[32]

Although the sale to Heileman was blocked by antitrust regulators, Schlitz's continued vulnerability made it ripe for takeover, and in 1982 Detroit-based Stroh's, then the seventh-ranked brewery in the country, launched a bid for the larger, fourth-ranked Schlitz. Though Schlitz at first sought to block the sale, Stroh's was eventually successful, and local ownership of "the beer that

Pabst attempted to increase market share by offering canned beer in three different size containers. The full quart can was available only for a few years in the mid-1950s. It was sold in a two-can carrier called the "Big Twin" and included opening instructions on the can. The twelve-ounce can at right is unusual for the 1950s in that it included the contents measured in centiliters, suggesting it was intended for foreign markets. COLLECTION OF DAVID WENDL.

made Milwaukee famous" came to an end after 133 years.[33] The revolving billboard over the Cream City's downtown that once promoted Schlitz now advertised Budweiser—the ultimate insult to the proud tradition of the city.[34]

FADING BLUE RIBBON

Just a few blocks away, another icon of more than a century of Cream City brewing was sliding rather than crashing. Pabst's expansion of the 1960s and 1970s also left it with more capacity than it needed. This was especially true after sales peaked in 1976 with over 17 million barrels and then began to slide, sometimes by a million barrels a year. While it is less easy to point to a single cause of Pabst's decline, many analysts blamed the decision by the company to reposition Blue Ribbon as a "popular price" brand. While the process may have started as early as the 1960s in some markets, the trend accelerated in the 1970s. In the short run, the numbers looked good: Blue Ribbon sold 15.2 million barrels in 1977 and dominated its price category. By 1984, however, sales were less than half that total, and crosstown rival Old Milwaukee had passed Blue Ribbon's once mighty brand in the category.[35] The most important trait of a "popular price" beer is that is has less marketing behind it, which makes it counterproductive to arrest a plunge by increasing advertising. What advertising was done did little to counteract the public perception that PBR was now a cheap brand.

The response of the company seems to have been more about buying market share than earning it. Through a series of complicated mergers, spinoffs, and trades, starting with the purchase of Portland, Oregon's Blitz-Weinhard Brewing Company in 1979, by the end of 1983 Pabst ended up with venerable labels such as Olympia and Hamm's as well as the successful Olde English 800 malt liquor. But with the labels and the expected markets and market share they would bring, the company also ended up with even more excess capacity than before. Company pronouncements lauded deals with Weinhard, Olympia, and Heileman as extending the reach of Pabst into new markets, ignoring the fact that Blue Ribbon was once a national brand even without the support of a brewery in each region.[36]

The last thing Pabst needed while trying to recover was to fall prey to the corporate raiding that transformed much of American and international business during the 1980s. Minneapolis-based investor Irwin Jacobs began a proxy fight in December 1981 that lasted until early 1983. Ultimately, new president William F. Smith Jr. and the company board resorted to a "scorched-earth" strategy through which Heileman, which had a competing bid for Pabst on the table, ended up with Pabst's gleaming new plant in Perry, Georgia, and two other breweries. While Pabst may have won the battle, it was poised to lose the war, since the fight and declining sales left it with so much debt that it would have to sell to one of the two persistent suitors: either Heileman or Jacobs's acquisition partner, Paul Kalmanovitz of California.[37] Heileman thought it had a deal in late 1984, but Stroh and C. Schmidt & Sons of Philadelphia asked for an injunction against the sale on the grounds that it would give Heileman too large a market share in Wisconsin and eleven other states. With the sale stalled, Heileman relented, and by the end of February 1985, Kalmanovitz had full control of Pabst.[38]

The methods of most corporate raiders of the era were to buy a company, often through a leveraged buyout, and then pay back the debt incurred by selling off assets and cutting costs dramatically. Kalmanovitz, a "reclusive multimillionaire" who had a reputation in the brewing industry for cutting costs at Falstaff and California's General Brewing Company, immediately began to swing the ax. Within a month, one hundred sales employees were let go—prompting angry reactions from area distributors and a loss of business. The advertising budget was dramatically reduced, just after the company had undertaken a relative splurge to launch Hamm's and Olympia as national brands.[39]

But "New Pabst's" empire of eighteen brands was built on shaky foundations. The support for Hamm's and Olympia only cannibalized customers from Blue Ribbon.[40] Despite claims that tough economic times were causing consumers to be more price conscious, the popular-price category continued to slump.

The Milwaukee brewery was aging, and even a $7 million upgrade in 1983 was nowhere near enough to make the plant competitive with newer facilities elsewhere. Nearly all the equipment was old, and old equipment in the bottling or racking (kegging) operations was not just inefficient but could even reduce the shelf life of the beer. Pabst also suffered from the gradual shift from drinking in taverns to consumption at home. In its heyday, the Milwaukee plant was the largest draught beer operation in the world, shipping seven to eight thousand kegs a day. Even in the 1980s, it was still shipping about three thousand half barrels and a thousand quarter barrels each day. Some operations were still labor intensive. For instance, Pabst kegs were still sealed by hand with wooden bungs, whereas Miller, which had relatively less draught business before, was able to switch to bungless kegs. Pabst was seeking a lot of small

Jacob Best Premium Light was Pabst's attempt to define the "premium light" category. Introduced in 1982, it was still available on shelves well into the 2010s—though by that point it was sold as a low-price beer rather than a premium product (coaster ca. mid-1980s). AUTHOR'S COLLECTION.

niche markets, which Smith called "work[ing] the seams." Pabst even offered Olde English 800 malt liquor, a product normally consumed directly from the bottle, on draught. All this had to be done on a dwindling budget with a skilled but expensive workforce.[41]

While there were occasional glimpses of progress, including ad campaigns that claimed "It's what's inside that counts" or demanded "PBR Me ASAP!," the decline was irreversible. Hopes that Blue Ribbon could be repositioned as a premium beer were for naught—once a beer has been labeled a low-price beer, it is nearly impossible to get consumers to pay top dollar again. Ad campaigns targeting older drinkers brought only brief bumps in sales. According to industry consultant and brewmaster Joe Owades, Pabst's strategy seemed to be to simply rely on its loyal customers to "drink its beer 'until they died.'" Meanwhile, the brewery in Milwaukee continued to age, and the company's financial position deteriorated. Part of this was an unintended consequence of the struggle against Jacobs. Smith noted back in 1983 that enough "'shark repellants have been built into the company's structure to ward off another Jacobs-type raid,'" but anything that made the company unattractive to investors would also be a drain on the business itself.[42]

"We Love Milwaukee, but We've Got to Make Money"

There had been rumors that the Milwaukee brewery would close as early as 1984, but in 1995 the rumors gained new credence as Pabst finally moved about two-thirds of its production to Heileman's in La Crosse, laying off 70 percent of its workers. Concern heightened as management rescinded health and death benefits for retired employees a few months later. Milwaukeeans, especially union members, began to boycott Pabst—which management claimed, perhaps rightly, would only make the problem worse. Local 9 offered $5 million in wage and benefit concessions to try to keep the brewery open. But on 17 October, management announced it was closing the brewery for good.[43] Political leaders were outraged, calling the move "deplorable . . . and just plain cruel to the workers," but were unable to alter events. The closing had ripple effects on Miller, which would be liable for about $35 million to cover an unfunded liability in the Milwaukee Brewery Workers' Pension Plan.[44]

William Bitting, cotrustee of S&P Company, the foundation through which Kalmanovitz and his successors managed Pabst, lamented, "We love Milwaukee, but we've got to make money." When it closed, the Milwaukee brewery was producing only 30,000 barrels a month, less than it produced a century before and only about 6 percent of capacity. Of Pabst's 6.3 million barrels sold in 1995, only about a third was made in Milwaukee, and the rest came from the old Olympia brewery in Tumwater, Washington, from the old Pearl brewery in San Antonio, or was brewed under contract by Stroh or Heileman.[45]

While Pabst's decline was not as precipitous as Schlitz's, the causes were still evident. A six-million-barrel brewery was simply too large to be a niche market producer, and the upgrades to make it an efficient competitor with breweries that were less than ten years old would have been too expensive to justify. The industry was plagued by overcapacity, and had been since the 1970s. At a Milwaukee event in the mid-1970s, a reporter remarked to a Schlitz executive, "'They're drinking it faster than you can brew it.'" The exec surveyed the crowd and lamented, "'No they're not.'"[46] Many Milwaukeeans pointed the finger of blame at poor management. Other analysts noted that successful brewers created successful new products each generation, and Pabst neglected to do so. Furthermore, the new products it attempted, especially the numerous light beers, never took off.

But even with Miller still in town, the closing of Pabst hit Milwaukee hard. One Pabst worker observed ruefully, "'Beer means to Milwaukee what casinos meant to Las Vegas . . . if they took away beer, I just don't know what else Milwaukee would be famous for.'"[47] Upon closing the Milwaukee brewery, Pabst relocated its corporate headquarters to San Antonio, where the former Pearl Brewing plant was located, but five years later this 115-year-old brewery also was shuttered. More than 300 more workers lost their brewery jobs, though about 110 administrative employees remained—for a while.[48] When Pabst's brewery in Fogelsville, Lehigh County, Pennsylvania, closed in September 2001, 380 more jobs were lost and the roughly two million barrels brewed there were contracted to Miller plants.[49] Pabst, which had grown from the Empire Brewery into a worldwide empire, was now simply a beer marketing company, rather than a brewing company.[50] The headquarters of this company, now called the Kalmanovitz Charitable Foundation, moved to suburban Chicago in 2006.

In 2010, after the IRS ordered Kalmanovitz to divest based on a rule that prohibited charities from owning for-profit businesses for more than five years, the company was purchased by C. Dean Metropoulos.

By this time, PBR had experienced something of a renaissance as the preferred beer of urban hipsters, supported by low-key marketing targeted to festivals where young urban residents congregated. Pabst actually outpaced the rest of the beer category in 2010, growing at a 4.3 percent clip. The Metropoulous family moved the offices to Los Angeles and began to advertise the brand, which threatened its credibility with the hipster market.[51] In the fall of 2014 Pabst was purchased by Oasis Beverages, a Cyprus-based company that was then the largest independent brewery in Russia, though Russian-born CEO Eugene Kashper came to the United States at age six and was an American citizen. While some newspaper headlines made the sale seem like the greatest catastrophe in the U.S.–Russian rivalry since *Sputnik,* Kashper was a beer person rather than a corporate raider and began to reinvigorate not only Pabst but also the other labels owned by the company.[52] By 2017 Pabst had brought back Old Tankard Ale (reportedly brewed according to the 1937 recipe) and reintroduced Ballantine Ale on a limited basis. Pabst also opened a pilot brewery and brewpub in an old church on the brewery campus that the company purchased in the nineteenth century.

Ice Dry Light Domestic NA Premium Import Brand Beer

The Harvard University economist Joseph Schumpeter outlined in the 1940s the theory of "creative destruction," through which new innovations promote economic growth but drive out existing products and businesses that ruled the old order. While the most common examples given are typically things like digital cameras driving out film or online news supplanting print newspapers, it sometimes seemed during the last decades

In the last decades of the twentieth century, national breweries attempted to attract attention with packaging. Introducing a new label, bottle, or can would guarantee mention in industry publications and may have inspired additional purchases by curious customers. The differently shaped bottles probably had little sustained effect on sales—especially for Old Style, which was already a successful brand. The St. Patrick's Day edition Lite bottle is the latest of this set (ca. 1990). AUTHOR'S COLLECTION.

ONE LITE ON, OTHER LIGHTS OUT 297

of the twentieth century that the beer business was facing similar turmoil. While most of the new products were still essentially beer, the quest for a new product that would capture market share and lead to industry dominance remained fierce. "Microbrewers" were beginning to attract the attention of the national brewers but were not seen as a serious threat. Much of the creation was of line extensions that would appeal to large national audiences and steal drinkers from rival brewers. Rather than reviving existing brands, the search for the "next big thing" required formulas and brewing processes that either were new or could be presented as new.

The success of Lite and its many imitators suggested to brewing executives that new products could be the path to fame and fortune in the brewing industry. The major breweries, unwilling to be caught unprepared for a hot trend as they were when Lite struck it big, were much quicker to jump on any new product that showed any promise. Unfortunately, few of the products had any particular selling point other than being new and different, and none of the new styles of the 1980s or 1990s had any lasting impact other than requiring beer can collectors to install more shelves.

Tonight, Let It Be Litigated!

The first battlefield for new products was the superpremium category. While several breweries had made a draught-only "old world" product intermittently since Prohibition (most notably Pabst's Andeker), Anheuser-Busch's Michelob (with a sale of about nine million barrels a year by the late 1970s) had essentially had the bottled market to itself since the early 1960s. In 1975 Miller began producing an American version of Munich's Löwenbräu—American in that it included corn and was not aged as long as the original. A-B filed a complaint with the Federal Trade Commission that Miller's ads implied the beer was made in Germany when it was in fact made in such stereotypically American locations as Fort Worth. Miller was forced to change its advertising to emphasize the brew's American origins, but the beer continued to grow in popularity through 1982, after which sales declined and Miller let the brand go to Labatt USA in 1999.[53]

Milwaukee's other brewers saw potential in the category, and may have sensed an opportunity with Miller's difficulties. Schlitz's superpremium Erlanger was an all-malt beer in contrast to Miller's Löwenbräu, which had 28 percent corn grits. Schlitz also hoped that positive reviews for Erlanger would help boost the image of the entire product line. Introduced in test markets in 1979, it was distributed nationally the next year and achieved some modest success.[54]

Pabst, perhaps typically, decided to send multiple horses into the superpremium stakes. The company was proud of pointing out that it had been brewing Andeker since 1939, but it was not until 1980 that it decided to challenge Michelob and Löwenbräu on a national basis with bottled beer.[55] However, the company was simultaneously launching two other products that competed for the same customers. In the western states, the company expanded distribution of Henry Weinhard's Private Reserve, acquired with the

Several large Wisconsin breweries sought to one-up their competitors or cash in on line extensions. Pabst offered Extra Light to those for whom mere light was not enough. Old Style had one of many Dry beers that hit the shelves in the late 1980s. Most of the "draft" beers had light version, and most of their labels used the same gold-and-black color scheme. A tiny Old Style shield above the word *Classic* is all that indicates this is not the better-known Miller or Michelob version. PHOTOGRAPH BY CHARLES WALBRIDGE. AUTHOR'S COLLECTION.

Blitz-Weinhard Brewing Company the year before, to seven states beyond Oregon and California. Meanwhile, it also launched Pabst Special Dark, described as "the lighter dark beer."[56] Descriptions in the press suggested that this was essentially a somewhat lighter version of Pabst bock, and was targeted at the same drinkers as Andeker. Ad campaigns urged, "Don't be afraid of the dark," and emphasized the lightness of its taste (and depicted a bottle that was shaped suspiciously like Michelob's). Miller answered back with a short-lived test marketing of Clipper, "the dark light beer," which was actually a lower-calorie beer, unlike Special Dark. Despite some initial interest in the Pabst product, the dark light or light dark beers failed to find a customer base large enough to sustain production.[57]

COLD-FILTERED

Ten years after Miller struck it rich with Lite, the company struck gold again, and put it on the labels. Miller Genuine Draft used filtering technology acquired from Sapporo Breweries in Japan rather than pasteurization to remove any microorganisms that could reduce the beer's shelf life. While debate continues among brewing experts whether pasteurization significantly harms flavor (craft brewers generally do not pasteurize), the promise of "fresher" beer was appealing to many drinkers. MGD's clear bottle, black-and-gold label, and appealing advertising made the beer a hit among younger drinkers, and catapulted the label into the top ten sellers in the country within four years. Nearly every major brewer quickly attached "Draft" to one or more of their beers, most notably Michelob Golden Draft, which not only borrowed Miller's color scheme but appropriated the MGD handle as well.[58]

WHY MAKE DRY?

One trend Miller shunned was the second major Japanese-inspired product: dry beer. Asahi Super Dry had become an immediate hit in Japan in

ONE LITE ON, OTHER LIGHTS OUT   299

Rodney Northern, brand manager for Icehouse, shows off a case of the new beer in November 1993. COURTESY OF MILLERCOORS BREWING CO.

1987, and several American brewers introduced their own versions as soon as they could brew and market them—though the American brands were lower in alcohol. A-B led the way into this category for a change, and Heileman brought out dry beers in each of its regions—staging a hasty midnight release of Old Style Dry in Chicago to beat Michelob Dry into that critical beer market. By mid-1989 Heileman had no fewer than five dry labels in different markets, ranging from Rainier Special Dry to Lone Star Dry. The most important selling proposition was the lack of any "aftertaste," which brewing professionals rephrased as "having no extreme flavor characteristics that might alienate sections of the populace."[59] Despite hopes that dry beer would be the magic key that would unlock the market of female drinkers, consumers never quite understood what "dry" beer was. Miller's reluctance was shrewd, as the category became irrelevant by the mid-1990s.[60]

The final mainstream style to captivate the country (briefly) was "ice beer." Fittingly enough, this concept swept south like an arctic blast from Canada, where Labatt had pioneered the style. Unlike dry beer, ice beer was a readily understandable concept, especially for those Canadians who had discovered how to set their beer outside in the cold, fish out the ice that formed and thereby increase the alcohol concentration of their drink. Unlike the Canadian versions, which indeed removed a substantial amount of the ice and approached 7 percent alcohol by volume (ABV), the American brands allowed most of the ice to melt back into the beer to remain around 5.5 percent ABV. (A-B ice beers allowed all the ice to melt back.)[61] Even if consumers didn't understand the process, "ice" at least sounded cold and refreshing, which was what beer was supposed to be.

Miller had actually opened the category in 1993 by importing Molson Ice through their just-acquired Molson USA unit. While Miller claimed that its own Icehouse, marketed under the Plank Road Brewery name, was the first ice beer, it actually debuted the same day as Budweiser Ice Draft. The name sounded refreshing, even if anglers actually occupying icehouses often sought beverages with warming qualities. Tested in the fall of 1993, it was so successful that national rollout was accelerated to the beginning of 1994. The beer replication process was now well advanced, and within months most major breweries had an "ice" version of many of their beers: around thirty-five were on the shelves within a year after Icehouse first appeared. Miller's big bet on ice beers helped the company increase sales in 1994, despite flat or declining sales for High Life, Lite, MGD, and Milwaukee's Best. While many analysts predicted a demise for ice beer similar to that for dry, as of 2014 the category still had four of the top thirty-five brands in the United States and occupied about 4 percent of the market.[62]

Less and More

Two somewhat contrary new products blossomed in the 1980s—both focusing on alcohol content rather than taste or process. Low-alcohol beers, or LAs, were intended to respond to increasing concerns over both drunken driving and health and fitness. Of further concern was legislation that would withhold highway funds from states,

Mickey's Malt Liquor was most famous for its "Big Mouth" bottles. The African American model suggests the target market for the brand (plastic sign from 1978). Collection of David Wendl.

"Don't Say Beer, Say Bull!" Schlitz Malt Liquor was the only malt liquor supported by a sustained national advertising campaign. The television commercials from the late 1970s and early 1980s featured actors ranging from Don Adams (*Get Smart*) to Richard Roundtree (*Shaft*) and musicians from the Platters and Kool and the Gang (in the same commercial) to 38 Special and the Marshall Tucker Band (also in the same commercial). While this plastic sign is not dated, the model's jacket and long collar date it to the late 1970s. Collection of David Wendl.

ONE LITE ON, OTHER LIGHTS OUT

Wisconsin among them, that did not increase their legal drinking age to twenty-one. Brewers were anxious to find a product that would make up for the loss of an estimated five to nine million barrels.

Though the first example of the style was Pace, by Hudepohl Brewing Co. of Cincinnati, Anheuser-Busch was the first national brewer to enter the category with LA, another beer taking the name of the category.[63] Heileman was among the many who followed with LAs of their own, and also may have had the most—applying the tag to Blatz, Old Style, Black Label, Rainier, and Lone Star products. Anheuser-Busch quickly filed suit against Heileman (and other breweries) for using the LA designation. But even though Heileman, Miller, and others were cleared of copyright infringement and unfair competition, by the time the decision was handed down, the category had become insignificant.[64]

In contrast, the malt liquor category was well established, dating back to the material shortages of World War II. (Confusingly, some state laws required any beer with an ABV over a certain level, usually 5 percent, to be labeled as malt liquor whether it was representative of the category or not—which included most imports.) Most malt liquors, noticeably stronger than premium beers, were either regional specialties, like Goetz Country Club, or made by smaller companies, like National's Colt 45. Most major brewers had a label—Miller even attached the company name to a malt liquor for a few years in the early 1970s, but in general these brands got little marketing support and were primarily purchased by customers in urban areas. As the 1980s dawned, Wisconsin firms controlled the majority of malt liquor brands, most through recent acquisitions. Pabst had acquired Olde English 800, which sold much better than its own Big Cat. Heileman's family of brands now included Colt 45 as well as its own Mickey's Malt Liquor. But as the decade advanced, the major brewers jumped back into a market that had previously been dominated by Schlitz. Rather than presenting a demure image, such as Miller's old University Club, the new brews subtly or not so subtly touted their alcoholic strength to their often poor and minority customers.

By the early 1990s appeals to minority customers by competing labels were even more overt. Pabst had already begun marketing Olde English 800 with the slogan "It's the Power" and also had ads in Spanish with the parallel claim "Es la Fuerza." Heileman made a more blatant appeal during the summer of 1991 with a new malt liquor called PowerMaster, which, according to the label, was a stronger version of Colt 45. The initial label approval granted by the Bureau of Alcohol, Tobacco and Firearms was rescinded after ATF officials saw the brand's advertising, which was perceived as being targeted at young black drinkers. U.S. Surgeon General Antonia Novello asked the company to change the name, since African American males had higher rates of cirrhosis of the liver. Activists also protested the name. Chicago ministers Rev. Michael Pfleger and Rev. George Clements came to La Crosse to meet with then-Heileman president Thomas Rattigan and were arrested for trespassing when they did not leave after being denied the meeting. (Pfleger was also on trial at the time for painting over alcohol and tobacco billboards aimed at inner-city minorities.) Within weeks, federal regulators officially "pulled the plug" on PowerMaster, much to the disappointment of Heileman, though the beer reappeared a year later as Colt 45 Premium.[65]

A rival to PowerMaster, St. Ides, was also brewed in La Crosse, though the brand was actually owned by McKenzie River Brewing Company. When Stroh Brewery Company purchased Heileman in 1996, most of the country's malt liquors were manufactured by the same brewery.[66] St. Ides, popularized by rapper Ice Cube in the movie *Boyz n the Hood,* was accused of using gang imagery in its advertising and of glamorizing gang activity. Numerous public interest groups protested the ads, which also claimed St. Ides would improve sexual prowess and made disparaging remarks about Olde English 800. Rapper Chuck D of the group Public Enemy also protested against the advertising in the song "1 Million Bottlebags." These ads were changed, but the focus on the urban black market continued.

The last straw for many activists followed in 1992 when Hornell Brewing Company, a beer marketer based in New York, contracted with Heileman to brew Crazy Horse malt liquor. While Hornell officials claimed they were honoring the warrior who led the defeat of General Custer at the Little Bighorn (known to the Lakota people as Battle of the Greasy Grass), American Indian activists, South Dakota politicians, and Surgeon General Novello all argued that the name was insulting.[67] South Dakota congressman Tim Johnson proclaimed, "'It is particularly repugnant to see the name of Crazy Horse identified with a product which has been the cause of untold suffering and pain for thousands of Native American families and individuals,'" and that using Crazy Horse to sell high-alcohol beer "'simply adds insult to injury.'" The problem was made worse by the product and packaging, which was a distinctly whiskey-colored liquid in a whiskey-bottle-shaped container. As concern and protests increased, several states, including Washington, Nebraska, and Minnesota, acted to ban the product.[68] In fact, Congress passed a law banning use of the name, which was later overturned on First Amendment grounds.[69] In 2001, three years after Stroh's left brewing, John Stroh III made a formal apology to the Lakota nation and made a peace offering to

Built in 1969 and painted with the Old Style design in 1970, each tank in the "World's Largest Six-Pack" held 22,000 barrels. According to the company, drinking a twelve-ounce beer every hour of every day would empty all the beer in one tank in 120 years. The four most visible cans were wrapped with the design of La Croix Lager cans in 2003. PHOTOGRAPH BY CAROL M. HIGHSMIGH, COURTESY LIBRARY OF CONGRESS.

descendants of Crazy Horse, though Hornell was still fighting a battle to keep using the name and did so for several years.[70]

House of Heileman– Lots of Rooms, Shaky Foundation

While Heileman had been the main target of malt liquor protests, most of the publicity the company earned from the late 1960s through the 1980s was positive. When Roy Kumm took over as president of the company in 1957, Heileman was a "troubled regional brewer," and without a new strategy, the company would have most likely become the target of a larger brewer.[71] Kumm led the expansion in the Midwest, both by careful management of Heileman products and by acquiring smaller breweries. Starting with the acquisition of Wiedemann Brewing Company of Newport, Kentucky, in 1967, Heileman began the steady climb from a ranking in the midtwenties. Kumm's innovative strategy would be imitated by other companies, but with less success. The larger financial world was taking notice, as publications from *Barron's* to *Dow Digest* chronicled the path of the upstart from La Crosse.[72] Even though Heileman's stock was listed only on the Chicago Stock Exchange, it was still a publicly traded company, and as such was under more pressure to turn a regular profit than a family firm.

Kumm set ambitious goals for his company, first to be in the top ten by 1970, and then to be in the top five by 1975. The first step was the purchase of the Blatz brands from Pabst in 1969. In order to meet the demand for Blatz, employment and capacity were increased at La Crosse and Sheboygan, and three hundred thousand barrels had to be brewed at Pabst. Kumm's strategy of buying capacity instead of building new breweries enabled the company to expand at about three to four dollars per barrel, instead of estimated costs of thirty-five to forty dollars per barrel. Unfortunately, while undergoing surgery for an ulcer in 1970, Kumm was discovered to have stomach cancer, and he died in March 1971.[73]

Fortunately for the shareholders, employees, and customers of G. Heileman Brewing, Kumm's son-in-law, Russell Cleary, had been groomed to take over leadership, and he proved to be every bit as dynamic a leader as Kumm. Cleary believed that Heileman had to rank in the top five of U.S. breweries in order to survive, and he launched an ambitious expansion program to reach that goal. In 1972 Heileman purchased the western plants of Associated Brewing, which, although based in Detroit, owned breweries in Evansville and South Bend, Indiana, and St. Paul, Minnesota.[74] The company also acquired several popular brands, including Sterling, Drewrys, and Schmidt (not to be confused with Schmidt's of Philadelphia). While the U.S. Justice Department originally sought to block the deal, it was eventually approved, boosting Heileman from fifteenth to eighth among breweries. As a condition of the deal, Heileman was prohibited from purchasing additional breweries in the Upper Midwest for ten years without the approval of the Justice Department.[75] The enhanced status of G. Heileman Brewing enabled the company to list its stock on the New York Stock Exchange in 1973 (it remained on the Chicago exchange as well).[76]

Swift reaction to industry trends also helped Heileman grow. When Schlitz stumbled and Anheuser-Busch suffered a strike, Cleary pushed Old Style in Chicago and gained the top spot in that coveted market with a 30 percent share. Constrained in the Upper Midwest, Heileman purchased Rainier Brewing Company of Seattle, along with several popular brands and more than one hundred wholesalers.[77] The Rainier purchase gave Heileman a presence in forty-six states, though the vast majority of the company's beer was sold in just twenty states, from Pennsylvania to the Great Plains; this region consumed half the beer sold in America.[78]

In 1979, Heileman made a purchase that gave it a true national presence. In March it announced the agreement to purchase Carling National Breweries, which had four breweries, the most important of which was in Baltimore. Carling was available to Heileman after Pabst was prevented from buying it on antitrust grounds. This deal brought not only four million barrels of desperately needed capacity but also Colt 45 Malt Liquor and Carling Black Label, which had nearly national distribution. The move pushed Heileman to sixth nationally, with the sliding Pabst and Schlitz within striking distance, and Coors possibly in range, especially with the brewery Heileman acquired in Phoenix, in the heart of Coors territory. By the end of the decade, Heileman was undertaking major expansions in La Crosse, Newport, and St. Paul, as well as a new corporate headquarters in La Crosse. Heileman was credited with being the pioneer of the "multi-regional brewer" model and was considered "the best managed and fastest growing

Originally brewed as a malt liquor, Special Export was later repositioned as a premium beer. This striking design was used in the late 1980s. AUTHOR'S COLLECTION.

brewery in the industry."[79] Continued growth and the successful acquisition of Pabst brands noted earlier moved the company into fourth place behind Coors. The new Val. Blatz Brewing Company plant in Milwaukee also created new possibilities for the company.

In the mid-1980s several clouds appeared on the horizon. Expansion into southern markets did not go as well as planned, and Coors began expanding east of the Mississippi for the first time and made a big push into Chicago. Nevertheless, Heileman stock was still doing well, and the company continued to pay a dividend each year. Then, in September 1987, Australian financier and brewery owner Alan Bond flew to La Crosse and informed Russell Cleary of his plan to take over the company. Cleary fought the move for several weeks, and state and national lawmakers sought legislation to protect the company. Governor Tommy Thompson called the legislature into special session, and a bill was passed toughening the state's antitakeover laws. All this did, however, was force Bond to increase his offer from $38 to $40.75 a share, at which point Cleary, facing shareholder lawsuits, agreed to a merger rather than a takeover, and the deal was done. Cleary was offered a place on the board of Bond Corporation Holdings Ltd. and was placed in charge of all North American brewing operations. The $1.3 billion total paid for Heileman turned out to create a debt that Bond was unable to pay.[80]

The stock market crash of October 1987 shook the foundations of many corporations that had been built by leveraged buyouts, and Bond may have been forced to sell assets even faster than was typical in such cases. Perhaps the most important development was the retirement of Russell Cleary in January 1989. Analysts downgraded their assessment of the company even more, arguing, "'Without Cleary, it just isn't like it used to be.'" In the midst of swirling rumors about mergers with Stroh, Coors, or possibly both, Alan Bond's financial empire collapsed in the biggest failure to date in Australian history. Heileman sold the St. Paul brewery to local investors and declared Chapter 11 bankruptcy in 1991, and began selling off property in La Crosse in 1992. Unfortunately, continuing pressure from debt and competition prevented Heileman from restoring a solid financial

G. Heileman Brewing presented steins to employees and distributors from 1979 through 1996. This stein, from 1980, pictures eight of the nine Heileman plants (Belleville, Illinois, is missing), each of which brought new local or regional labels to the House of Heileman. While the slogan "We don't aim to make the most beer, only the best" is wrapped around the base, the company was definitely trying to make more beer. PHOTOGRAPH BY CHARLES WALBRIDGE. AUTHOR'S COLLECTION.

position. In 1996 new owners struck a deal with Stroh Brewery Company, a longtime rival for plants, brands, and market share, to take Heileman into bankruptcy and then sell it to Stroh. After 137 years, G. Heileman Brewing Company ceased to exist as an independent entity in July 1996.

The Stroh purchase resulted in brewery closings in San Antonio, Perry, and Baltimore. The La Crosse brewery, however, was producing at near capacity, and workers were pulling extra shifts to keep up. But the price wars between Busch and Miller were having the same effect on Stroh as they had on Pabst. Stroh's market share continued to slip, and the $291 million in debt it incurred in the Heileman purchase dragged the company down further.[81] In 1999 most of its assets were sold to Pabst—the company that Heileman had been trying to purchase for years—with a few labels, including Hamm's, Mickey's, and Olde English 800, going to Miller. Unfortunately for its many longtime brewery employees, the La Crosse plant was not included in the deal and was closed at the end of July.[82]

Miller Clear was the result of fourteen months of innovation at the Milwaukee brewery. The most critical part of the process was "ultrafiltration," which required new equipment. The sales failed to live up to the hard work of several different teams at the brewery (photograph ca. 1993). COURTESY OF MILLERCOORS BREWING CO.

From the moment they learned the La Crosse brewery was in jeopardy, community leaders and politicians worked to find a buyer for it. In 1999, just before the scheduled closure, a local buyer emerged to save the brewery. James J. Strupp and John D. Mazzuto's purchase provided the brewery time to get going again, this time under the name City Brewing Company, which harked back to its earliest days.[83] While City's own brands were generally well regarded, they didn't sell

ONE LITE ON, OTHER LIGHTS OUT 307

well, so the company turned its attention to contract brewing, which proved very successful. The company was so successful that in 2006 it purchased the former Latrobe Brewing Company of Pennsylvania (makers of Rolling Rock beer), from Anheuser-Busch in order to increase capacity. By 2010 the company did not own any of its own brands, but had contracts with about two dozen other businesses to brew beer and manufacture other drinks, ranging from AriZona teas to "malternative" beverages such as Smirnoff Ice.[84] Employment reached over five hundred and was approaching its peak in the glory days of the House of Heileman. Continued demand led City to purchase the former Coors brewery (built by Schlitz) in Memphis in 2011, bringing the total capacity of all three breweries to approximately ten million barrels. This purchase returned City to the lofty fourth-place perch that Heileman briefly occupied during the Cleary era, though without the prestige of having a brand like Old Style that could be identified with the company.[85]

City Brewing took a small step toward regaining its local presence in 2016 with the introduction of Old Style Oktoberfest. While the label was still owned by Pabst, the beer was brewed and packaged in La Crosse under the direction of longtime City brewmaster Randy Hughes and Pabst brewmaster Greg Deuhs, who was an assistant under Hughes in the 1990s.[86] Even with the diminished brand identification, the World's Largest Six-Pack still remains decorated with the La Crosse Lager can designs that were applied in 2003, and the statue of King Gambrinus across the street still raises his flagon to greet travelers and revelers.

For those who thought Lite still had too many calories, Miller released Miller 64. The product is still on the shelves as of this writing. AUTHOR'S COLLECTION.

SAB Story

Meanwhile, across the interstate from the gleaming new Miller Park baseball stadium, the namesake company was in trouble. Between 1993 and 1996, the company had introduced sixteen new products, bringing the total up to forty-three, several of which performed adequately at best, such as Red Dog, another product bearing the Plank Road label. The Plank Road operation gave Miller a chance to experiment with new beers without a direct association with the flagship brand. This would minimize the damage of a failed product, and might encourage people who would not otherwise drink a Miller beer to try a new product.[87] Most of them ranged from dismal to disastrous, including Miller Clear—an attempt to cash in on an apparent trend in clear products ranging from colas to deodorant to gasoline. Miller was losing ground to Anheuser-Busch, dropping to less than 20 percent market share in the United States for the first time in years. Perhaps more embarrassingly, beer was now listed as "Other" in graphs showing Philip Morris's sources of income.[88] The Miller Lite All-Stars had been retired, and subsequent campaigns never captured the public imagination. By 2000 Lite was mired in third place among light beers, trailing both Bud Light and Coors Light. The biggest financial disaster was caused by the launch of Miller beer. Planned as a direct rival to Budweiser, it lacked an identity and was quickly labeled "Miller Miller." The crash of the brand cost $70 million and seven hundred jobs.[89]

In 2002, a relative unknown in the American brewing scene, South African Breweries (which, despite its name, was based in London), purchased 64 percent of Miller from Philip Morris (now known as Altria Group). SAB was looking for a much bigger U.S. presence, and for more sales in harder currencies. For Miller, the deal promised more attention to the beer business, since SAB was first and foremost a brewery operation.[90] The brewing world was further rocked in late 2007 by the news that SABMiller and Molson Coors signed an agreement to create a joint venture called MillerCoors. This combination of the second- and third-largest breweries in the country received antitrust approval since rival Anheuser-Busch (soon to be bought out by Dutch-based InBev) still held 48 percent of the market. Fears that the headquarters of the new venture would move to a "neutral site" were realized when the company opened a new headquarters building in downtown Chicago.[91] The merger mania was not over. In 2015 AB InBev offered $110 billion for SABMiller. However, antitrust regulators refused to agree to the merger unless the new company divested itself of the North American operations of MillerCoors to another company. In October 2016 Molson Coors acquired SABMiller's stake in MillerCoors and all of the Miller brands. Molson Coors became the world's third-largest brewer (by enterprise value) and as of 2017 had not closed any of its breweries.[92]

The new company faced a declining beer market with changing demographics. As early as 2007, Miller introduced Miller Chill, a beer with hints of lime and salt, to appeal to the Hispanic market. MGD 64, later rebranded as Miller 64, was designed to appeal to consumers counting not just calories but now carbohydrates.[93]

But even with all the new line extensions, the old flagships were in trouble, and their companies were too. It would have come as a shock to a visitor from the 1970s that the Wisconsin-owned brands in the 2010s most closely associated with the state's beer culture were from breweries in small cities seemingly left behind by the consolidation of the industry. The styles of beers made in New Glarus, Lake Mills, Amherst, and other places—even more shocking.

This sample of craft beer cans only hints at the diversity of Wisconsin's modern brewing industry. Canned craft beer was rare until the early 2010s. Some breweries could not afford canning equipment; others preferred to use bottles or believed that customers would prefer bottles to cans. As canning equipment became less expensive and leading breweries introduced cans, the number of canned beers on the shelves exploded. PHOTOGRAPH BY CHARLES WALBRIDGE. AUTHOR'S COLLECTION.

CHAPTER 10

Return of The Local

1965–2018

Drinking a fresh, full-bodied beer "is like tasting butter for the first time after eating margarine all your life."

Alan S. Ditky, of Hibernia Brewing Ltd.,
in Business Week, 20 January 1986

WISCONSIN'S BEER DRINKERS HAVE BEEN NOTED FOR THEIR BRAND LOYALTY. The flip side of this often was the lack of a sense of adventure. While devotion to old favorites helped keep several local breweries alive into the 1970s, it may have also prevented the state from being among the leaders of the trend toward new "specialty beers," as they were often called in the mid-1980s. Mass-market lager had taken root, the signs were already up on the taverns, the taps were on the bar inside, and the drinkers of the state took comfort in the familiar light golden liquid in their pitchers and mugs.

Still Famous

By the early 1980s, the brewing industry had shrunk to about sixty breweries nationwide, and several of those were owned by major multiplant brewing companies—meaning the number of independent companies was closer to fifty. However, unlike their neighbors Minnesota, where the brewing industry was dwindling, or Iowa and Illinois, where it had all but vanished, Wisconsin occupied the commanding heights of the industry. In 1975, a year before the first American "microbrewery" was founded, Wisconsin was home to the second-, third-, and fourth-largest breweries in America. Six years later, four of the five largest brewing companies in the country were headquartered in Wisconsin. On the other end of the spectrum, Wisconsin also contained four of the nation's

During the 1970s and early 1980s, bock beer was the only regular seasonal beer brewed in America. Each year, bock lovers eagerly awaited the new batch and compared the merits of each brand. All of these labels still bear the traditional symbol of bock beer—the goat. Because bock was made only for a limited time each year, cans are much scarcer and therefore prized by collectors. AUTHOR'S COLLECTION.

nineteen breweries that produced less than three hundred thousand barrels that year—more than any other state.[1] What little variety existed in style could also be found in the Badger State, since its smaller breweries continued to produce bock beer after most of the larger breweries had discontinued it as unprofitable. It is possible that Wisconsinites felt less longing for a resurrection of brewing since the industry was still so prominent both on the local landscape and in the ledger.

The return to traditional dining that inspired some of the craft beer movement was perhaps less important in Wisconsin, since local restaurants were still more of a presence there than in many other states. Supper clubs, family restaurants that often had been area fixtures for more than half a century, remained more prevalent in Wisconsin than anywhere else. Food writer David McAninch said of them, "People go back to these places again and again over the span of decades—not for gastronomic discovery but for comfort, for that peculiar sense of well-being experienced when eating food that is delicious in precisely the same way it was when you were a child."[2] That sense of comfort likely extended to beer choices as well, which may well have limited acceptance of new brands or styles.

Wisconsin is not simply a time capsule, however, but also a modern, industrial, and cosmopolitan state that responds to economic and cultural trends. During the Reagan administration, the relatively strong dollar made it cheaper for Americans to travel to Europe and sample the historic styles of traditional brewing centers. The strong dollar made European beers cheaper to

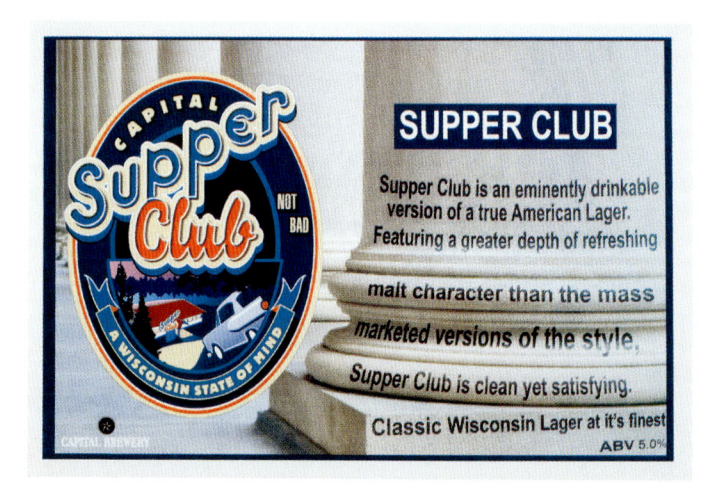

Capital's Supper Club lager was introduced in 2010 and was an immediate success. It was designed as an easy-drinking, old-fashioned American lager to go with old-fashioned American food. AUTHOR'S COLLECTION.

import as well. The prosperity of the upper-middle and upper classes during the Reagan years created the "yuppie," whose willingness to spend heavily on luxury items helped create the market for more expensive beers. Philip Van Munching (whose family's company used to import Heineken) explained how this trend spread through society: the average person couldn't afford the BMW or the Armani wardrobe, but "imported beer is a badge, a status symbol. And it is an affordable one." Bottled beer was a better badge than draught beer because it was easier for everyone to see who had chosen the most expensive beer, and who therefore must have the best taste (or the most disposable income).[3]

Another trend inspired at least in part by the willingness to spend a little more, but more dependent on the environmental movement, was the turn toward locally produced goods. For about a century after the Civil War, Americans had been conditioned by advertising to think that national brands were higher quality, more consistent, and more prestigious than local products. This rationale often applied to beer as well. Small-town breweries were often caught between the gratitude of the local population for jobs and the reluctance to buy their beer because "it isn't any good," or "it gives you gas," or any of the other complaints about the local product. (Most of the problems attributed to local beer were due to the quantities consumed rather than the product itself, especially because its lower price made it popular with youth and heavy drinkers.) Of course, in Wisconsin, the national product was also a local product. But by the 1970s, Americans became concerned about the disappearance of the family farm, the corner drugstore, the ma-and-pa grocery, and other institutions that were seen as an essential part of America's culture and heritage. At the same time, quality-control problems in the American auto industry and other fields made consumers reevaluate the relative value placed on efficiency compared to craftsmanship, leading people back to local producers.

Part of the reason craft beer has flourished in Wisconsin has been the success of brewers at building local markets and restoring the idea that communities should support their local brewers (bumper sticker from 2017). AUTHOR'S COLLECTION.

Some individuals and groups with a sense of history sought to revive traditional methods and products that were disappearing as the secrets of their creation went to the grave with the passing generation. Bringing back seasonal and regional beer varieties echos the goals of the Slow Food movement, which seeks to stem the loss of traditional flavors and ingredients as tastes and production became more homogenized. American beer lovers visiting Britain were inspired by the Campaign for Real Ale, which was created in reaction to the consolidation of British breweries and the disappearance of cask-conditioned ales in favor of the cheaper force-carbonated "keg bitter." The relatively small number of Americans who cherished distinctive beers began to inspire a veritable Noah's ark of vanishing beer styles.

As with so many reactions to mass-produced popular American culture, what has since come to be called the craft brewing movement started on the Pacific Coast. The craft brewing revolution was led by three different types of breweries: small community breweries that had survived the consolidation and developed unique and different beer styles, new microbreweries, and brewpubs. In addition, some breweries became "contract brewers," using spare capacity to brew beer for other companies. Some of these contractors were restaurants that wanted a house beer, some were beer marketing companies that had no plant of their own, and some were microbrewers who needed packaging facilities or extra capacity.

The Survivors

In 1965 Fritz Maytag (of the appliance family) learned that the San Francisco brewery that made his favorite beer, Anchor Steam, was about to close. The company had survived multiple fires and relocations since its founding in 1896, but the same pressures that were forcing smaller breweries across the country to close were about to take their toll on Anchor and its draught-only business. Despite having no brewing background, Maytag purchased a controlling interest in the brewery and by 1969 owned it outright. Not only did Maytag continue production of the brewery's signature Steam beer, but by 1975 he had introduced other traditional styles such as porter, pale ale, barleywine, and an annual Christmas beer with different artistic labels every year. Maytag began bottling in 1971 and started shipping beer outside California in 1975. Anchor beers were priced the same as imported brands but were not supported by any advertising beyond word of mouth.[4] Maytag's slow but steady growth at Anchor demonstrated to other brewers the potential in seeking new markets instead of trying to compete directly with the national brewers and their mainstream lagers.

The stories of the four small Wisconsin breweries that survived into the era of specialty, micro, and craft beers are as varied as the stories of those that failed. The individual variation contains elements of forward thinking, luck, timing, and financial stability. Even that was not always enough, since one of the four succumbed to financial pressures after a few years of being one of the most innovative breweries in the nation.

From Oldsters to Youngsters

By the 1970s the Jos. Huber Brewing Company was the second-oldest surviving brewery in Wisconsin (Pabst preceded it by a year). Alone among its small-town competitors, Huber grew not just steadily but significantly in the years after the Korean War. From a low of 11,000 barrels in 1952, production expanded tenfold by 1964, and ten years later topped 250,000 barrels. Why Huber so dramatically bucked the trend of other small Wisconsin breweries appears to be a combination of factors, including aggressive and well-timed expansion decisions.

Despite the goal of a group of Green County tavern owners who acquired majority control of the stock in 1948 to focus on the "home market," Huber began to expand its sales territory in the late 1950s, and the increased orders required more capacity. The company installed new aging tanks, bottling equipment, and equipment to fill flat-top cans.[5] Flat-top cans were less common among smaller breweries because the equipment was more expensive, but the cans were easier to fill and cheaper and easier to ship and store. The *Monroe Evening Times* editorialized:

> *This product will put the Huber brewery in better position to compete in the market with the larger firms and will insure continued and expanded employment for Monroeites. . . . That decision by its stockholders took a good deal of courage*

since this is an era when small breweries are fast disappearing as major beer producing firms capture more and more of the market. We believe the Monroe community owes a grateful salute to the owners of the Huber company for their willingness to expand and their confidence in the Huber product's ability to win wider acceptance in defiance of a modern trend.[6]

The sales department sought out far-flung markets such as Kansas, Colorado, Texas, and California for its increased production of canned beer. Most of the product remained in the Upper Midwest, however; this created some challenges for the brewery, which still shipped directly to many retailers. Some establishments would take Huber beer only if they could have it on an exclusive basis in the region, which "cut down the number of markets into which the beer could be introduced." In order to get around this barrier, Huber began to add more labels to its existing Huber's, Golden Glow, and Hi Brau brands. The multiple-label strategy has continued to the present day, though names have changed and the number has expanded and contracted several times. By 1975 the company offered thirteen different brands in cans, making them a favorite with beer can collectors. At first, Huber honored requests for sample cans for no charge. As requests ballooned to 800–1,000 each month, however, the company started charging a dollar per can in an attempt "to cool the fever."[7]

Huber's acquired many of their labels by purchasing the assets of defunct breweries. While Huber was neither the first nor the most prolific of the label scavengers, its success rate was high compared to many who followed similar strategies. When the Rhinelander Brewing Company closed in 1967, Huber purchased the Rhinelander brand, which was still popular in the cabin and resort country of north-central Wisconsin. In 1972, Huber purchased the assets of Potosi Brewing, located about sixty miles to the west, which included the Good Old Potosi, Holiday, and Alpine labels.[8]

The next year Huber felt confident enough to buy and operate an entire brewery. The former Peter Hand brewery in Chicago, being operated by Meister Bräu Inc., went bankrupt in August 1972. The next April Huber purchased the seventeen buildings on more than five acres and prepared to reopen the brewery to brew Old Chicago beer. The Hand brewery operated for about five years before closing in 1978, resulting in financial and tax disputes that carried on for another year.

Among Huber's acquisitions was an obscure label from the Potosi assets that was to make the brewery famous around the world. The Augsburger beer made in Monroe bore little resemblance to that made in Potosi, or previously by the Van Merritt Brewing Company of Chicago. Brewmaster David Radzanowski related, "'We picked the label first . . . because it was the name we wanted for our super premium beer. Then we blended the beer to suit it.'"[9] Small-town breweries generally had little interest in the category because of the cost and competition from major breweries, but Huber was willing to take a chance, and by 1979 Augsburger was responsible for most of the company's growth.[10] "Augie," as it was popularly known, was lagered for eight weeks, instead of the much shorter times of mass-market lagers.

The brand won several awards and was perfectly positioned to take advantage of the interest in more flavorful beers that exploded in the 1980s.[11] By 1987 Augsburger accounted for more than 50 percent of Huber's production and was the major reason Huber had a presence in forty states. Huber officials attributed the strong sales in markets like Denver to an "'upscale, yuppie type of thing.'"[12] The fame of the brand extended to Germany, where company president Fred Huber was awarded the key to the city of Augsburg. In the first year, Augsburger sold 16,000 cases; in 1985, 1.5 million cases went to thirsty patrons.[13]

The popularity of Augie made it a legitimate competitor in the superpremium category, so Huber was forced to back the brand with advertising in a way unusual for small-town breweries. The brewery, which had done no advertising other than small newspaper ads or point-of-sale promotions until 1979, initiated a series of popular radio advertisements featuring brewmaster Hans Kestler touting the virtues of Augie in a strong German accent. An even bigger leap was television—Augsburger was the first beer to be advertised on Chicago's public television station, WTTW.[14] Huber's advertising budget was $750,000 in 1983, which was a staggering figure for the brewery, but during the same year Miller spent $44 million just to advertise Lite.[15]

Huber had numerous contracts to brew beer under other labels, which had varying degrees of success. One of those contract brews ended up becoming the face of the company. By 1985 Fred Huber was burned out and looking for relief. The holding company that bought his brewery sold the Augsburger label to Stroh to pay down the debt and actually closed the plant in 1988. In the search for new buyers, one favorite emerged: Fred Huber. After months of negotiations with the company as well as the union, Huber regained possession of his old company. But the label that accounted for more than half its production and well over half its profits was gone, and it was in need of a new flagship brand.

Augsburger Dark appealed to drinkers looking for a different experience. Augsburger brands were responsible for much of Huber's growth in the 1980s. AUTHOR'S COLLECTION. PHOTOGRAPH BY CHARLES WALBRIDGE. AUTHOR'S COLLECTION.

RETURN OF THE LOCAL 317

Since 1966 Huber had been brewing the house beer of the famous Berghoff Restaurant in Chicago. By the late 1980s Huber was shipping about three thousand barrels to the restaurant each year, and in 1986 began bottling the beer for sale in the Chicago area.[16] Fred Huber believed Berghoff was the flagship brand the business needed. To emphasize the importance of the label, the company that formed to purchase the brewery was called Berghoff-Huber Brewing. The name reverted to Huber Brewing in 1991, but by that point the Berghoff brands, which now included several seasonals, were more than a third of the company's production.[17]

Over the next several years, Huber expanded into a number of foreign markets. In 1992 the brewery started producing beer for the Compañía Cervecera Victoria Brewery of Nicaragua (based on a connection made a decade earlier when a Nicaraguan brewery technician worked at Huber as part of an industrial exchange program).[18] The brewery also used its own labels to move overseas: exporting Old Chicago to Britain, Paraguay, and Argentina, and Wisconsin Club to Brazil, Panama, England, Russia, and France.[19]

Despite the expansion, Huber experienced financial difficulties. After a loss of almost $600,000 in 1994, the firm entered Chapter 11 bankruptcy

The relatively large capacity of the Monroe brewery made Jos. Huber and later Minhas Craft Brewery a logical plant for contract brewing. Huber was among the brewers that cashed in on the beer can collecting mania of the 1970s and 1980s by making special beers for festivals and gatherings. Wau-na-beer was produced for the First National Gathering of Scrimshanders (artists who carve whalebone). Dempseys Ale was a Huber label rather than a contract brand. AUTHOR'S COLLECTION.

318 THE DRINK THAT MADE WISCONSIN FAMOUS

during the summer of 1995. Huber was taken over by General Beer Distributors of Madison, which a year earlier had purchased the Berghoff brand through its Wisconsin Brewery subsidiary. General Beer pledged $2 million to help pay creditors and update the brewery yet again. Old Chicago found new markets in Japan and Russia.[20] But as the brewery expanded, it broke one important link with the past. By 2003 Huber was forced to eliminate the returnable twelve-ounce bottle from its package mix. Too few customers were returning the bottles to make their use economical, and glass manufacturers stopped producing them.[21]

The same year the returnable longnecks disappeared, a new contract brew arrived that would change the company's future. The brother-and-sister team of Ravinder and Manjit Minhas, children of immigrants from India to Canada and both in their twenties, had introduced Mountain Crest Classic Lager in their home province of Alberta. Their beer was first brewed in 2002 at Minnesota Brewing Company in St. Paul, but it soon moved to Stevens Point Brewery and City Brewery in La Crosse. By the summer of 2003, the brand was brewed at Huber, and it quickly became the engine of increased production—by 2005 it was 85 percent of the brewery's output. Eventually, the Minhas family decided to purchase the brewery, and in October 2006 they closed the deal and renamed the company Minhas Craft Brewery. The "youngest brewery owners in the world" invested $6 million in the brewery, and by 2009 the expansion program was completed and production again approached 200,000 barrels. About 80 percent of the beer was exported to Canada, and another 10 percent of the volume was brews made under contract for other companies.[22] Minhas also introduced several new craft labels and new flavors under the revitalized Rhinelander name, including some that the old Rhinelander brewers never could have imagined, such as Chocolate Bunny, a stout brewed with cocoa powder.[23] By 2016 Minhas ranked ninth in the country among craft brewers, with 274,454 barrels produced.[24]

WHEN YOU'RE OUT OF POINT . . .

The survival story for another century-old brewery, Stevens Point Brewery, was dramatically different from the national and international ventures of Huber. Even as late as 1989, Stevens Point beer was seldom available more than fifty miles from the brewery.[25] Point made only one brand (not counting the bock beer released each spring), and until the late 1990s had no excess capacity to engage in contract brewing or buy defunct labels. The company's conservative business model and defense of its local market was most likely the secret of its success.

During the years after World War II, Point's production was steady if not spectacular. Under the guidance of the Korfmann family of Milwaukee, the brewery maintained a modest profile in its home market, sponsoring a popular golf tournament and numerous other civic events, and running regular advertisements in local newspapers most Fridays. Innovations were few and conservative. The big news of 1962 was the introduction of an eight-pack bottle package, and in 1966 Point adopted the pull-tab can.[26] While not spectacularly profitable, the company had paid a dividend every year since 1945.[27]

The dedication of Point to its longtime customers would be sorely tested during the mid-1970s, all due to one newspaper column. Mike Royko, the acerbic, Pulitzer Prize–winning Chicago syndicated columnist, hosted an unscientific beer tasting in the summer of 1973. While several national brands finished at the bottom of the twenty-two tasted, Point Special ended up second, tied with Bass Ale, just behind the German import Würzburger and far ahead of any other American brands.[28] Requests came immediately from Chicago distributors hoping to handle the brand, and eventually agents from as far away as India and Hong Kong sought exclusive rights to bring Point Special to their markets.[29]

But the national recognition took the brewery by surprise and, as President Felix (Phil) Shibilski lamented, "We're not geared up for this."[30] The company's equipment could not handle high-speed operations, so the brewery was able to increase production to only around 50,000 barrels, and then only by asking more of its employees.[31] The next year, Point Bock sold out in a month, twice as fast as usual. In 1975 Trans World Airlines called, requesting two hundred cases a month to sell on its flights. This request also had to be refused, since the Shibilski family (who now controlled the brewery after the death of Calvin Korfmann in 1974) refused to neglect their loyal accounts in central Wisconsin.[32] The only way Point Special or Bock made it out of the area was in the trunks of tourists who took some home to the Twin Cities, Chicago, or other destinations.

Point's bright-blue can was easy to spot on store shelves and was a beacon to travelers looking for this distinctive local beer. Spud Premier Beer, brewed with potato starch, was a predecessor of many brews during the craft beer era that would use fermentable ingredients other than traditional grains. PHOTOGRAPH BY CHARLES WALBRIDGE. AUTHOR'S COLLECTION.

Production stayed around 50,000 barrels for a few years, but began to drop steadily through the 1980s, reaching a low of less than 27,000 barrels by 1992. During these years, Point tried a few short-lived line extensions, such as Eagle Premium Pilsner and Special Edition. More unusual was Spud Premier Beer, which was brewed with potato starch and introduced as a fund-raiser at the first home football game of 1989 for the University of Wisconsin–Stevens Point, a game known as the Spud Bowl.[33] Spud was brought back for a few more years, but the novelty faded, as seemed to be the case for the whole brewery. In general, Point had bucked industry trends, in particular by not offering a "light" beer until 1988. The company now had extra capacity, and in 1989 it signed an agreement to bottle the beers of Capital Brewing Company of Middleton.[34] Loss of some of its local market, due to a combination of increasing competition and the increase of the legal drinking age to twenty-one, forced Point to expand its reach, and in 1990 it shipped their first beer to Minnesota.[35] Point had survived into the 1990s, but the outlook for the future was uncertain at best.

The partner Point chose for its long-awaited move into Chicago, Barton Beers Ltd., turned out to have the answer. Barton purchased the

Point's recent beers include many varieties that are dramatic departures from Point Special. The Whole Hog series of higher-alcohol beers included a Raspberry Saison and a Pumpkin Ale as well as Russian Imperial Stout and barleywine. Nude Beach was a popular summer seasonal, and Winter Spice was one of several winter beers. PHOTOGRAPH BY CHARLES WALBRIDGE. AUTHOR'S COLLECTION.

brewery in 1992 from the Shibilski family and drew upon their resources to invest almost $3 million into upgrading the brewery. Barton's demand for craft beer labels led to the introduction of Classic Amber, Maple Wheat, Winterfest Spice, and Pale Ale. While Point Special was still the biggest seller, the repositioning of Point as a craft brewer rather than a struggling local lager brewer was well on the way. Under Barton, the company began to increase capacity, which was up to 70,000 barrels by 1996. Thus equipped, Point was able to devote more effort to the new specialty brands, as well as to contract brewing, which was at that point about 15 percent of revenue.[36]

The Barton era ended in 2002, when Jim Wiechmann of Milwaukee, through his company SPB LLC, purchased the brewery.[37] The same year, Point returned to making soft drinks with the introduction of Point Premium Root Beer. Point kept pace with other craft brewers by bringing out a series of limited edition, higher-alcohol beers. The Whole Hog Limited series, including bold styles such as Russian Imperial Stout and Raspberry Saison, were sold in four-packs and would have been nearly unrecognizable to the company's brewers of a century earlier.[38] By 2014 Stevens Point Brewery had expanded capacity to 120,000 barrels per year and continued to engage in contract brewing for clients in Wisconsin and all over the country. Growing markets led to even more expansions of the brewery. In 2013 Point launched its fourth expansion in four years, and this one included a second brew kettle as well as additional fermenting capacity. This boosted capacity from 120,000 to 150,000 barrels per year.[39] Point beers were distributed in more than half the states in the Union, but the majority of business remained in Wisconsin—true to the company's local roots. (Additional information about Point's recent history is found in the second part of this book.)

A STRATEGIC PARTNERSHIP

Leinenkugel emerged from World War II in an enviable position for a small-town brewer. It was one of the largest breweries in the state outside Milwaukee, trailing only Heileman, Kingsbury, and Fox Head Waukesha, and its production was more consistent than the latter two. Production exceeded 90,000 barrels in both 1949 and 1953, and even though output leveled off just above 70,000 starting in the mid-1950s, production was consistent at this level for the next fifteen years and was enough to surpass all the small-town breweries except the resurgent Huber Brewing Company.[40] While significant modernizations were few, the brewery kept up with packaging trends and followed the industry leaders to flat-top cans in 1958. Longtime employees credited survival to maintaining close relationships with distributors and tavern owners in their "sovereign territory"—an area of about 5,200 square miles within about 100 miles of Chippewa Falls. Relations with customers were also enhanced when the brewery hired its first official tour guides during its centennial year of 1967.

Despite a firm foothold in northwestern Wisconsin and a strong following in the Twin Cities, production dropped again into the 60,000-barrel range in the early 1970s, just as William Leinenkugel took over as president of the firm.[41] To reverse the trend, Leinenkugel decided to expand

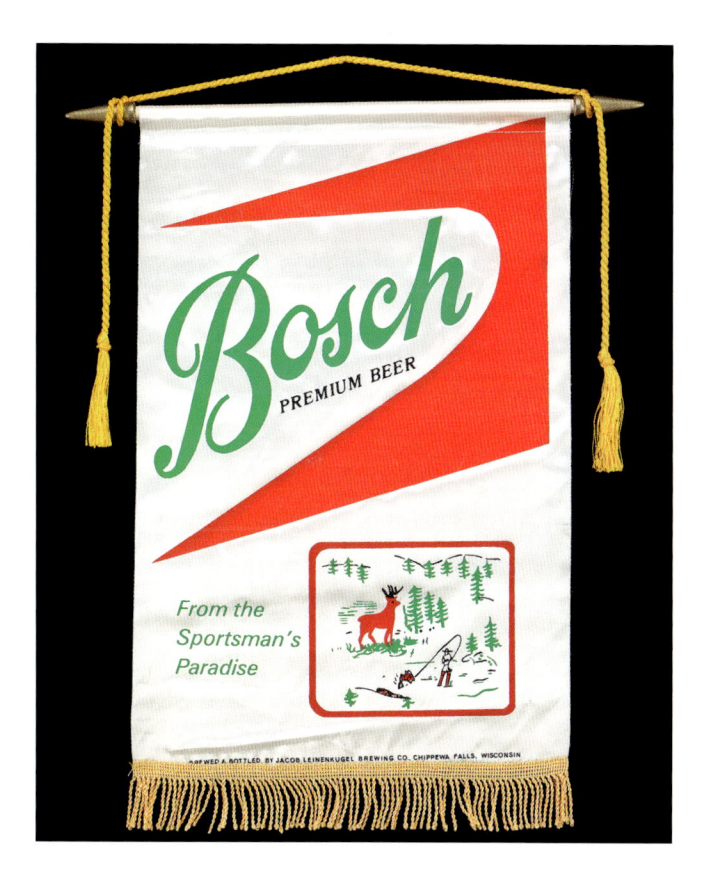

Leinenkugel Brewing Co. produced this pennant during the mid-1970s, shortly after it purchased the Bosch brand. COLLECTION OF BOB POST.

the brewery's territory. In October 1973 Leinenkugel purchased the assets of Bosch Brewing Company of Houghton and Lake Linden, Michigan. Chippewa Falls took over production of Bosch products, but more importantly, Leinenkugel gained access to Bosch's twenty distributors in northern Wisconsin and Michigan's Upper Peninsula.[42]

Although the Bosch purchase helped, Bill Leinenkugel also decided that, rather than trying to compete with the Milwaukee brands on price, he would price the beer so that the brewery could make a profit, rather than simply focusing on sales volume. Leinenkugel also decided that the expansion had to be supported by more aggressive marketing, as well as an important line extension.

By this time, Miller Lite had appeared on the scene, and, as Leinenkugel observed, "it was time to take some guidance from their customers." At first, Chippewa Pride was reformulated and positioned as the "light" brand, but the link to the light style was not strong enough. To give their distributors a competitive brand, the company introduced Leinie's Light, which later became Leinenkugel's Light and lasted under that name until the 1990s.[43] Despite these changes, and other adaptations such as building a Hospitality Center in 1979, sales were inconsistent, and production dropped under 60,000 barrels in 1985. While not yet in desperate straits, the company needed financial and marketing support to make a comeback.

Late in 1987 the management of Miller Brewing Company reached out to Leinenkugel regarding a joint marketing agreement, looking for a way to move credibly into the craft beer market and to trade on the mythic image of a small brewery in the north woods. Fans of the brewery, as well as residents of the Chippewa Falls area, viewed the proposal with trepidation, worrying in that era of corporate raiders that Miller simply wanted the labels and the magic and had no interest in the brewery or the community. Miller assured the existing management that it would still be in charge of the brewery, and the sale became official 1 March 1988.

The gains in sales were immediate. In 1988 production was just over 90,000 barrels—more than it had been in thirty-five years. By 1993 output had nearly doubled and was over 250,000 barrels by 1998. While the growth was spectacular, there were growing pains along the way. In the first few years, a number of midlevel managers and support staff descended on Chippewa Falls, all trying to make alterations that would enable them to claim credit for the changes. Jake Leinenkugel worked with the top brass at Miller to clear away the would-be advisers, and was allowed to run the brewery the way that made it successful in the first place. John Leinenkugel, marketing assistant during the mid-1990s, affirmed, "'There's always this fear that we'd get "Millerized.' . . . It's still a family brewery and it's important to me that we keep it that way.'"[44]

The introduction of Red in 1993 was the first major new product, one that Miller executives saw as key to competing with Coors's popular Killian's Irish Red, but it was merely the first of an cascade of new beers to flow from the north woods. Leinenkugel adopted a two-prong strategy: offer small-batch labels designed to appeal to the dedicated craft brewer while trying more accessible products to spread the brand to new drinkers. Among the former was Big Butt Doppelbock, a heavier dark lager introduced in 1996 as a spring seasonal.[45] The other category was best exemplified by Leinenkugel's Honey Weiss, a sweeter, lighter wheat beer that first appeared as a summer seasonal in 1995, but which proved so popular that it went year-round almost immediately, and ultimately became the label that was the spearhead for the national expansion. By 1998 Honey Weiss was absorbing 75 percent of Leinenkugel's advertising budget, but the results bore out the wisdom of the decision.[46]

As the brewery entered the second decade of Miller ownership, the two-prong strategy accelerated and produced beers that were critically acclaimed and big sellers, though not always at the same time. Honey Weiss was joined by Berry Weiss and Sunset Wheat, which was the company's answer to the popularity of Coors's Blue Moon. Leinenkugel was among the first to bring bottled shandies to American drinkers in 2007, with the introduction of Summer Shandy. *Shandy* is an English term for a beer mixed with fruit juice, traditionally lemonade, similar to the German Radler. By 2012 Summer Shandy, despite only being available half the year, was the top-selling label for the brewery, and was the beer

Leinie's Red Ice combined two beer trends of the 1990s: "red" beers and ice beers. This beer was released only in Michigan (label ca. 1994). COLLECTION OF SCOTT REICH.

By 2011 the Leinenkugel product line included beers ranging from the refreshing Weiss beers to the rich beers of the Big Eddy series. Leinenkugel Limited was first released in 1986 as a fall seasonal, but by 1991 was a year-round brew. It was later retired. AUTHOR'S COLLECTION.

that finally made Leinenkugel products available in all fifty states. Meanwhile, on the other end of the spectrum, the Big Eddy series appeared in 2007 with an Imperial IPA followed by Russian Imperial Stout. The series, which numbered six by 2013, all had an ABV in excess of 8 percent, and the Ryewine introduced that year weighed in at 10 percent.

Through all the expansion and product development, Leinenkugel strove to maintain the north woods cachet that had helped keep the brewery alive during the lean years of the 1970s and '80s. The most visible nod to this tradition was the opening of the Leinie Lodge in 2003. This visitor center, which served as the starting point for tours and a gathering place for sampling beer, also housed a gift shop with a wide range of clothing, bar items, and novelties. More important, the brewery continued to make Leinenkugel Original, though distribution was limited to Wisconsin and neighboring states.[47]

BEER THAT IS DIFFERENT

The last survivor of the Walter family breweries, the Walter Brewing Company, endured into the 1980s by trying to maintain its local market and acquiring a few labels from defunct breweries in Wisconsin and Minnesota. During the late 1950s and 1960s, Walter typically produced just over 30,000 barrels per year, about half of what rival Leinenkugel produced in nearby (but smaller) Chippewa Falls. The slogan "Beer That Is Beer," used for several decades, was circular but catchy.

One point of differentiation from other breweries was that Walter offered a Holiday beer each winter from the early 1950s. It appears that the company's advertising budget was limited, since each ad appeared only a few times, and the 1967 Holiday ad was identical to the 1966 one—a problem since both ads claimed it was the thirteenth year for Holiday Beer. The purchase in 1969 of brands from Bub Brewing Company in Winona, Minnesota, propelled production to approximately 50,000 barrels for the next decade, but it then began to drop again, reaching a low of about 21,000 barrels in 1984.[48] The brewery was then operating only one day a week and was on the verge of closing when a new owner brought a change in direction.[49]

Michael Healy was the son of a Chicago tavern owner who developed a taste for German beers and beer gardens during his military service in Germany. He worked for a bank note printer for a while, but decided to switch to brewing, which was anything but a license to print money. In 1983 he became intrigued by the growing market for "import quality domestic beer." After working with Chicago-area beer expert Alan Dikty to find a site in Chicago, they decided to purchase the struggling Walter business rather than spend additional money to build from the ground up. Another reason to select the Eau Claire location was the possibility of establishing what Healy called "an on-premise retail outlet"—in other words, a beer garden.[50] Healy kept most of the existing employees, including brewmaster John J. Walter, expanded employment to thirty, and began to develop beers that would match those he had enjoyed in Germany.

Healy's first beer was different from what most other American microbreweries tried for their early offerings and a significant departure from the old Walter's products. Hibernia's Dunkel Weizen combined two features then rare in American beer: dark and wheat. Although wheat beers were common prior to Prohibition, they fell from favor, and the few examples available in America were imported German brands. Hibernia's Dunkel Weizen tasted different from nearly any other American beer, largely because of the distinctive taste produced by the yeast used for wheat beers.

Hibernia helped reintroduce German-style all-malt and seasonal beers to Upper Midwest drinkers in the late 1980s. AUTHOR'S COLLECTION.

The bold move paid immediate dividends when Dunkel Weizen earned second place (Samuel Adams Boston Lager was first) out of more than one hundred beers at the 1985 Great American Beer Festival (GABF). Hibernia eventually filled out its lineup of seasonal specialties with Bock in the spring, Oktoberfest in the fall, and Winter Brau, a German Alt beer, during the winter (Dunkel Weizen was the summer seasonal). But immediately after the success with Dunkel Weizen, Hibernia established its flagship beer, Eau Claire All Malt Lager, which was a modified version of the old pre-Prohibition Walter recipe.[51]

It was unusual for a new brewer to offer only German styles—the vast majority of the new brands were variations on English-style ales. Most microbreweries found ale recipes to be more forgiving, and few had the tank space to accommodate the longer time required by the lager beer cycle. Hibernia, however, had an experienced brewmaster and an established plant with a capacity of 100,000 barrels, which provided the skill and space to age lager-style beers. Production began to creep up again and was almost 25,000 barrels in 1986—far more than any start-up microbrewer could imagine in its second year.

After weathering some initial shortages caused by high demand, Healy and Dikty began to ship their products to other markets. The Chicago area accounted for nearly a third of Hibernia's sales by 1987, and the Minneapolis–St. Paul area absorbed a large share as well. Even distant markets such as Columbus, Ohio, and Portland, Oregon, were able to provide Hibernia brews to curious beer lovers.[52] Hibernia used some of its considerable excess capacity to brew specialty beers for other companies on contract, including Portland Lager for a company in Maine and Vienna All Malt for Vienna Brewing Company of Milwaukee, a business headed by award-winning homebrewer Gary Bauer.

In a move that seems more revolutionary in retrospect than it did at the time, Hibernia offered Eau Claire All Malt in cans as early as 1986, which appears to give it the title of the first "craft" beer to be canned in the United States. (The only possible challenger might be Augsburger, but that was generally classified as a superpremium beer rather than a craft beer.) Healy claimed early on that "it may seem strange when you are working 20-hour days, but so far we are having fun." Dikty added, "Where else but in America could an Irishman and a Pole employ Scandinavians to make a German product in a city with a French name?"[53]

But one Hibernia canned product may have contributed to the company's problems. In 1987 the company agreed to brew and package Treaty Beer for an organization in northern Wisconsin opposed to spearfishing by local Native American groups. Hibernia made about 700,000 cans before ceasing production. While the brewery claimed that the beer was profitable, it was discontinued due primarily to a boycott of the brewery's other products and taverns and liquor stores that sold them.[54]

Hibernia had a few scattered successes in the late 1980s. Dunkel Weizen won another medal at the GABF in 1987 (the first year entries were judged in categories rather than by consumer preference), and a new product called Hibernia Master Brew won silver in the European Amber category in 1988. But Healy had offered another, more ominous toast in 1985: "Where else but in America could the son of an immigrant end up owing a million dollars?"[55] Ultimately, the load of debt, increased cost of insurance, and decreased sales due partially to the release of a bad batch of beer forced Hibernia to close its doors for good in 1989.[56]

New Brewers: Catching the Second Wave

Wisconsin was relatively late to join the parade of brand-new breweries. Brewing historians consider the period beginning with the opening of California's New Albion Brewing Company in 1976 to around 1980 to be the first wave. Fourteen states already had new brewing companies by the time Wisconsin acquired its first in 1986—the state that beer made famous was preceded by less traditional brewing centers such as Idaho and Arkansas.[57] Perhaps fitting for a state dominated by large breweries, in Wisconsin the first person to set up a new brewery was a former employee of a major brewery, rather than a pioneering homebrewer with a dream. Several homebrewers would indeed turn professional, but the first microbrewers or specialty brewers in Wisconsin had a professionalism found in few other states—which may have helped them survive in a cutthroat market. (More information on each of these breweries may be found in the second part of this book.)

From Pabst to Proprietor

Randy Sprecher fell in love with full-flavored beer when he served with the U.S. Army in Germany. He came back, settled in California, and started homebrewing while studying construction and engineering in order to build his own brewery someday. Unlike many who went directly down that path, Sprecher studied fermentation science at the University of California, Davis. He moved to Milwaukee to work for Pabst for sixteen years, rising to superintendent of brewing operations. After losing his job as Pabst contracted, he revisited his earlier dream. Seeking the opportunity to brew beers with more character, he and a partner converted an old tannery chemical factory in the Walker's Point area into the first new brewery in Milwaukee since the 1930s. Brewing commenced in late 1985, and the next January kegs of Special Amber and Black Bavarian began to ship to area accounts. Clearly Sprecher had found an untapped

Sprecher Brewing Co. has typically celebrated anniversaries with Belgian-style ales. The two twenty-two-ounce bottles both contained beers with fruit or fruit juice added (bottle at left, 1999; others, 2010). AUTHOR'S COLLECTION.

What Is a Craft Brewery?

During the 1970s, the newest breweries were generally referred to as small, though the need for specific terminology was not urgent since few people were referring to them at all. Stuart Harris, then a volunteer staff writer for the homebrewing magazine *Zymurgy,* has been credited with coining the term *microbrewery,* drawing on his experience in microcomputing.[1] The term was used in May 1981 in a seminar sponsored by the American Homebrewers Association and gradually became the accepted term for these new businesses.[2] Determining what "micro" or small actually meant would prove to be fraught with controversy: at first any brewery producing (or able to produce) 5,000 barrels per year or less was considered small. As the category grew, so did the threshold. At this writing the Brewers Association (BA), the leading national industry group for craft brewers, considers a microbrewery to be a brewery producing less than 15,000 barrels per year.[3]

Defining "craft brewer" also changed along with the industry—but again, not without controversy. The earliest definitions created by the predecessor of the BA, the Association of Brewers, were vague. In 2004 the newly organized BA defined an American craft brewery as *small* (annual production under 2,000,000 barrels); *independent* (less than 25 percent of the brewery is owned or controlled by a non–craft brewer alcohol company); and *traditional* (has an all-malt flagship or at least 50 percent of the volume is all-malt beers).[4] As some of the leading craft breweries continued to grow, the line for "small" was eventually raised to 6,000,000 barrels per year (a volume that took Schlitz 108 years to achieve).

The "traditional" label proved contentious. The requirement that the brewery focus on all-malt beers ruled out the two oldest small breweries in Wisconsin, Huber Brewing Company (as it was at the time) and Stevens Point Brewery. The BA changed the definition in 2014 to reflect the fact that using adjuncts (fermentable ingredients other than barley malt) is in fact traditional. The change allowed (the renamed) Minhas Craft Brewery and Stevens Point Brewery to join New Glarus Brewing Company among the twenty-five largest craft breweries in America. The BA defines breweries with production between 15,000 and 6,000,000 barrels per year as "regional" breweries.

---

1. Steve Hindy, *The Craft Beer Revolution* (New York: Palgrave Macmillan, 2014), 33.
2. Maureen Ogle, "First Draft Follies: Early History of the American Homebrewers Association and the Brewers Association, Part 2," 6 April 2009, http://www.maureenogle.com/maureen-ogle/2009/04/07/first-draft-follies-early-history-of-the-american-homebrewers-association-and-the-brewers-association-part-2.
3. Hindy, *The Craft Beer Revolution,* 33–34.
4. Hindy, *The Craft Beer Revolution,* 192–93.

Around 2007 a new subdivision emerged: nanobreweries. At the moment, there is no precise definition for the term. Some attempts measure batch size (upper limits can be set anywhere from three to seven barrels per batch) and others consider yearly output. By any measure, nanobreweries are very small and have a very limited distribution range.

As of 2018 the Wisconsin Brewers Guild had more than one hundred brewery members and over two dozen affiliate members. It supports its member brewers by sponsoring festivals and through political lobbying (sticker circa 2017). AUTHOR'S COLLECTION.

market, since by August his beers were available in sixty bars in Milwaukee and a few in Madison.[58]

Sprecher's financial situation was also unusual among the new breed of brewers. He was able to finance much of the start-up with savings, and was able to avoid the large debts that doomed many of his compatriots. By the summer of 1988, Sprecher was offering three brewery tours every Friday and Saturday, employing twelve people during peak times, and expanding his lineup to most major German beer styles.[59] The most notable was Black Bavarian, a schwarzbier that, despite its dark color, was relatively mild. Sprecher was also among the first to bring back Mai Bock and Oktoberfest styles with their traditional rich flavors.[60]

Less than a decade after opening, Sprecher's original location was unable to keep up with demand, and the old building was becoming structurally unsound.[61] The brewery was so pressed for capacity that some draught beer production was contracted to Capital Brewery in Middleton.[62] In 1994 Sprecher moved to a former elevator car factory in the northern Milwaukee suburb of Glendale. During the industry slowdown in the late 1990s, the company developed an important source of revenue with a new line of soft drinks. Its root beer became a big seller and was followed by other flavors, including a dramatiginger ale with a dramatic ginger flavor. In 1996 Sprecher sold more soft drinks than beer, but beer remained the focus of the business.[63]

#1 RATED

Madison seemed like a logical place to locate a small brewery. The presence of a major university attracted students on voyages of discovery (both academic and otherwise), as well as professors and employees of high-tech companies with disposable income and refined tastes. State government also drew people who could be interested in a fine libation. Madison had been without a brewery of its own since Fauerbach closed in 1966, but it had the necessary combination of population and interest to be attractive for what was still a risky venture.

Serious discussion of a brewery for the Madison area went public in 1984 when a group of investors led by Ed Janus began raising money. Janus, former general manager of the Madison Muskies Minor League Baseball team, believed that "Madison is one of those places where you can actually succeed making an honest product."[64] Capital Brewery Inc. purchased equipment from an old German brewhouse and hired Austrian brewer Michael Braitinger to serve as a consultant. Braitinger held that American brewers had done for beer what McDonald's did for the hamburger and Wonder did for bread, and promised special tastes for each season.[65] Governor Anthony Earl helped open the formal sale of shares to the public at an event in late October 1984. Recognizing the importance of price to consumers, Janus told prospective investors that the beer would sell for about four dollars a six-pack—about a dollar more than "superpremium" beers but a dollar less than imports. He also hinted at the variety of beers in the future Garten Bräu line: one of the beers was to have an alcohol content of 8.5 percent, and Janus joked with Governor Earl, "You have to have a letter from your mother to drink this stuff."[66]

Capital Brewery's Wild Rice beer was one of the first commercial beers to use that grain (label ca. 1990). AUTHOR'S COLLECTION.

Brewmaster Kirby Nelson and his team created many distinctive beers, including Blonde Doppelbock and Autumnal Fire, which took its name from the caption of a photograph in the *Milwaukee Journal-Sentinel* of Nelson admiring a pint of the deep-amber lager. Eisphyre was a version of Autumnal Fire that was frozen and some of the resulting ice removed to create an even more concentrated doppelbock at 9.8 percent ABV (bottles ca. 2011). AUTHOR'S COLLECTION.

As with many firms proposed during the emergence of the microbrewery, few things went quite as planned. While Capital's founders preferred a location in downtown Madison, they settled for the former Mazo Egg & Produce building in Middleton, on the city's western border. The original plans also called for a restaurant attached to the brewery, which would have made it the first brewpub in the state. As happened with most other breweries, the original plans for capacity and speed of growth were behind schedule. The industry journal *New Brewer* reported that Capital was planned as a 50,000-barrel brewery, which the company would not reach for decades.[67] Sixteen years after opening, Capital reached 15,931 barrels in 2002, after a 2,000-barrel jump from the year before. That was enough to move it from "microbrewery" to "regional brewery" status according to the terms used at the time.[68] Finally, the initial beers may have been a bit bold for the market. Garten Bräu Lager was introduced to appeal to those who found Garten Bräu Special and Dark too heavy.[69]

Despite the fits and starts, Capital endured and became not only profitable but a leader in the industry. In 1998 the Beverage Testing Institute ranked Capital Brewing the seventh-best brewery in the world and the highest-rated among American brewers. The company incorporated this honor into its packaging, putting it prominently on cases and six-pack holders.[70]

ON THE LAKEFRONT

Wisconsin's first homebrewers to take the plunge into a larger brew kettle were the Klisch brothers of Milwaukee. A friendly sibling rivalry drove Russ and Jim to improve their beers, and praise from friends and winning Best of the Fair at the Wisconsin State Fair inspired them to start their own brewery. They started small, originally planning to brew part-time at their home in the Riverwest neighborhood, but they eventually located in a former bakery at 818A East Chambers Street. Like the other new Wisconsin breweries, Lakefront Brewery began with German-style lager beers, including Klisch Pilsner (the State Fair champion) and Riverwest Stein Beer, and did not consider an ale until what Jim called the "fourth formulation."[71]

Once the brothers decided to move beyond traditional German styles, Lakefront did so with innovations seldom before seen in the industry. Their Pumpkin Lager was the second pumpkin beer brewed in the United States, and Lakefront Cherry Lager may have been the first bottled fruit beer since Prohibition. Before its first decade was over, Lakefront became the first USDA-certified organic brewery in the country and launched Organic ESB (Extra Special Bitter).[72]

Lakefront was also developing a reputation for entertaining brewery tours. Unlike many tours, where the tour and explanation came first and the beer afterward, guests were encouraged to take a beer along on the tour. Another attraction was the brewery's unique collection of equipment—either converted from various other purposes or hammered together by the brewers to serve their needs. One food critic referred to the ill-fitting menagerie as a "Frankenstein operation," a term that since has been applied to several other breweries made up of scavenged equipment.[73]

The search for more space led to a former power plant for the Milwaukee Electric Railway Company located at 1872 North Commerce Street,

Lakefront joined the growing number of brewers making a Christmas or winter beer with its Spiced Lager. Most spiced holiday beers to this point had been English-style ales, so brewing a lager was unusual. COLLECTION OF SCOTT REICH.

where Lakefront moved in 1998. The additional space allowed for several new features to attract guests to the brewery. The brothers' interest in historic preservation led them to acquire Bernie Brewer's Chalet, which had been in the old Milwaukee County Stadium until it was torn down and replaced with Miller Park. For several years, guests were allowed to go down the slide (though not into a beer mug as at the stadium) for a small

Bernie Brewer's Chalet at Lakefront Brewery. This photograph is from 2011, after the slide was removed.

donation to charity. The upper level was turned into a beer hall called the Palm Garden (a tribute to the old Schlitz landmark), with decorative lights that once hung in the Plankinton Hotel. And, of course, tour guests could still tour the brewery with a beer in hand, and see the old dairy fermenters with Larry, Moe, and Curly of the Three Stooges painted on the ends.[74]

DRINK INDIGENOUS

In 1993 Wisconsin native Deb Carey decided to channel her entrepreneurial spirit and start a brewery of her own as a present to her husband, Dan, who had studied brewing at UC Davis and served as a production supervisor for Anheuser-Busch. After looking at several locations, they picked the small city of New Glarus in the far south of the state. Some of the residents were a bit skeptical about the Careys' project, but over time Deb's community-centered attitude and the extraordinary beer made by Dan won over the town.[75]

In a short time, their beer won over the world. While Dan started by brewing authentic German lagers (Edel-Pils was the first regular beer), he soon started experimenting with other styles, including Belgian-style fruit beers. Wisconsin Belgian Red, an ale brewed with a pound of Door County Montmorency cherries per bottle, won the gold medal in the specialty category of the 1996 Brewing Industry International Awards, beating out long-established Belgian breweries such as Hoegaarden and Belle-Vue.[76] Soon rumors of unusual and hard-to-find beers available only in Wisconsin began to circulate, and travelers began bringing home collections of Uff-da Bock, Apple Ale, and, of course, Wisconsin Belgian Red in its wax-dipped, 750-milliliter bottles.

In 1997 the brew that became inextricably linked with New Glarus Brewing first appeared. Spotted Cow was described as a Wisconsin Farmhouse Ale, brewed with local malts, flaked barley, and "a little hint of corn," to honor Wisconsin corn growers and create a unique flavor. The slightly sweet and fruity beer quickly became a hit, and the cow imagery captured the spirit of Wisconsin to such an extent that Spotted Cow became a cult beer for many outside Wisconsin. More importantly, its popularity could not be

Spotted Cow and Belgian Red may be the most famous of New Glarus's beers. AUTHOR'S COLLECTION.

ignored by restaurants or taverns, so Spotted Cow often became the first craft beer tap handle in many establishments that had until then served only mass-market lagers.

The rapid increase in local demand led to a need for both expansion and contraction. New Glarus experimented with exporting to the Chicago area, but ultimately decided that the headaches of shipping out of state were not worth either the effort or the attention that was drawn away from the local markets in Wisconsin, which continued to demand more beer. The company turned a profit each year of operation by not expanding beyond what the market could absorb, though that turned out to be quite a lot. As Deb Carey marveled, "We wanted to brew world-class beer for our friends in Wisconsin. We just didn't know we had so many friends."[77]

Historians of the craft beer movement generally place the end of the second wave of microbrewery openings around 1996, when new breweries began to engage in public stock offerings and became targets of buyouts by major corporate investors (though not in Wisconsin).[78] By that year, microbreweries had spread to the four corners of Wisconsin and much of the middle of the state. Some of these businesses would survive the industry shakeout of the late 1990s; some did not even make it that far. In the meantime, more breweries were opening, this time in places where thirsty patrons could also get a burger or a sandwich to go with their beer.

RISE OF THE BREWPUB

While industry definitions have changed over time, in the simplest terms a brewpub is a restaurant that brews its own beer for service on the premises. In 1982 Washington's Bert Grant challenged the existing laws (or lack thereof) and opened Yakima Brewing and Malting Company, which brewed and sold its own beers on the premises.[79] Prior to

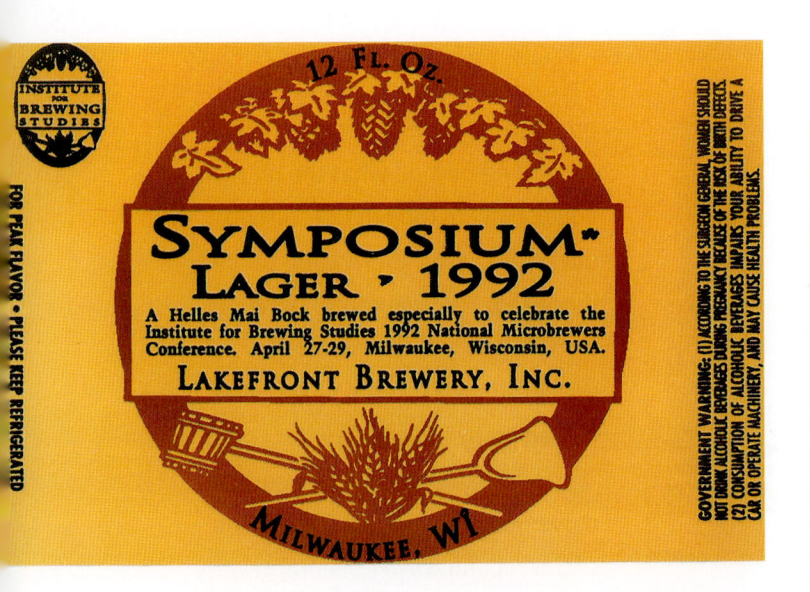

Craft brewers have been meeting since the mid-1980s to exchange ideas, examine new technology and ingredients, and enjoy each other's beer. Lakefront brewed a Mai Bock for the 1992 National Microbreweries Conference in Milwaukee. When the event returned to the Cream City, New Glarus Brewing made a special Eisbock for the (renamed) 2000 National Craft Brewers Conference and Brew Expo America. COLLECTION OF SCOTT REICH.

Prohibition, many breweries had a saloon at or very near the brewery, but afterward the three-tier system appeared to outlaw a brewery's ability to own a bar. Breweries could have a hospitality room, but could only give away samples, not sell their beer either by the glass or package. In Wisconsin's pro-tavern climate, there were few legal barriers to brewpubs but several logistical challenges, shared with similar businesses around the nation.

Brewing systems suitable for use in a restaurant were essentially unknown, so brewers were obliged to piece together their own equipment—basically larger homebrewing systems. In addition, brewpubs combine all the complexities of a brewery with all the risks and rewards of the restaurant business. Restaurants are dependent on the endurance of the proprietor, sometimes on the pleasure of the landlord, and always on the reputation of the food and service. If the location is poor or customer satisfaction is low, a brewpub is likely to close no matter how good the beer is. In most cases, the management's respect for quality beer carried over to the menu and created an establishment people visited regularly even if they were not very interested in craft beer. In the second decade of the twenty-first century, some states allowed breweries to call themselves brewpubs even if they served little or no food, but Wisconsin laws require a food component. Wisconsin is one of the many states that allow brewpubs to sell growlers or bottles for off-premises consumption, and is one of a smaller number that allow brewpubs to distribute bottles and cans to other retail establishments.

BIDAL TO BREWPUB

The first brewpub in the Upper Midwest (and sixteenth in the nation) was founded in Kenosha—not Milwaukee, Madison, or Chicago. This was not as unusual as it may seem, since Wisconsin's first homebrewing club, the Kenosha Bidal Society, was founded there in 1979—just after President Jimmy Carter signed H.R. 1337, which legalized homebrewing at the federal level. One of the local homebrewers, Jerry Rezny, teamed up with Jerry Gretzinger to open Brewmasters Pub Restaurant and Brewery in 1987, in a barn-shaped structure that had previously served as a tannery and part of a monastery. Over the course of the next sixteen years, a number of different brewers directed the brewhouse, most of them veterans of the local homebrewing community. Brewmasters became known for an eclectic mix of styles—often the result when those who are homebrewers at heart are given the freedom to brew nearly anything they think patrons may enjoy drinking. Styles ranged from their attempt at an "ice beer" and a highly regarded pilsner to several Belgian and English varieties. In 1996 Rezny and company expanded to a second location on the north side of Kenosha. Each location had its own brewing system and brewing team, but they coordinated brewing operations so that most of the beers were the same at both locations. Both locations closed in 2004, but Brewmasters had already shown that the brewpub model was viable in Wisconsin.

Although Brewmasters was first, a pair of Milwaukee establishments opened within the year. Unfortunately, Century Brewing Company was destroyed by arson less than a year after opening, but Water Street Brewery became a fixture in downtown Milwaukee and later added three suburban locations. Water Street remains the longest-serving brewpub in Wisconsin, and one of the oldest in the nation.[80] Cherryland Brewing in Sturgeon Bay was the final brewpub to open during 1987.

After the initial flurry of openings in 1987, brewpub expansion slowed for the next several years. A few of the early businesses stretched the definition of brewpub. John and Phyllis Junger's Appleton Brewing Company provided beer to multiple restaurants in the Between the Locks Mall, rather than being a single entity. (Cherryland had a similar relationship to its associated restaurant.) Bob and Bonita Rowland's Calumet Brewing Company, in Chilton, was really more of a tavern that brewed their own beer than a full brewpub, since they had

Brewmasters' Pub bottled some of its beers during the mid-1990s. Southport was the original name of Kenosha.
COLLECTION OF SCOTT REICH.

Water Street Brewery has issued a series of commemorative coasters for major anniversaries. The twenty-fifth anniversary edition was inspired by the classic Braumeister label from the Independent Milwaukee Brewery. COLLECTION OF SCOTT REICH.

a limited bar food menu. Both these businesses had strong links to local brewery history: the Rowlands adopted the name of the previous brewery in Chilton, and Between the Locks Mall occupied a portion of the former Appleton Brewing & Malting complex.

FURTHER OPENINGS

Seven years after brewpubs arrived in the state, the capital finally got its own, and in grand fashion. New Yorkers Rob LoBreglio and Eliot Butler purchased the historic Fess Hotel building near the capitol, and after spending about $800,000 on remodeling, they opened the Great Dane Pub and Brewery on 14 November 1994. While most new restaurants and breweries enjoy a brief honeymoon period, Great Dane's start was extraordinary. The 170 barrels sold in about three weeks was a pace that would add up to 3,000 barrels a year and make the brewpub one of the biggest in the country in their first yeaer of operation. While it did not maintain that pace, LoBreglio's beers helped establish Great Dane as one of the leading breweries in the state.[81]

The opening of Great Dane was the vanguard of a flurry of brewpub openings all over the state. From 1995 to 1999, an average of six new brewpubs opened each year, in regional centers, vacation country, and other locations. Green Bay, Oshkosh, and Superior saw brewing return for the first time

The brewery in the former Appleton Brewing & Malting building has gone by several names. It was known as the Stone Cellar Brewpub from 2005 to 2017 (coaster ca. 2007). AUTHOR'S COLLECTION.

A bartender draws a pint of Black Watch Scotch Ale from a cask at Great Dane Brewery and Pub. While several brewpubs offer cask beers pulled by beer engines, very few serve beers directly from the firkin (10.8 gallons) or pin (5.4 gallons) except on special occasions

in decades, though on a much smaller scale. Cabin owners and resort visitors could now have a fresh local beer when they went "into town" in Marinette or Minocqua. Travelers to the iconic Wisconsin tourist magnets of Door County and Wisconsin Dells could find a brewpub when they wanted a break from the fish boils or chain restaurants. The majority of these new brewpubs have survived to the present—through ownership changes, contraction in the brewing industry, rising input prices, and a few catastrophic fires.

The identities of the brewpubs were as different as their locales and proprietors. The EndeHouse Brewery and Restaurant occupied a historic Victorian-era residence in Reedsburg. Several other brewpubs took advantage of existing structures, including the landmark railroad depots that became the home of Titletown Brewing Company in Green Bay and the first location of South Shore Brewery in Ashland. Brewery Creek, in the historic city of Mineral Point, combined a bed and breakfast with its brewpub and brought back the idea of a frontier tavern where travelers could have a glass of the house ale before retiring upstairs for the night. Of course, some owners wanted to create all-new buildings designed to show off the brewery to their restaurant patrons. Most were in suburban locations, as was the case for Northwoods Brewpub, located in a shopping mall on the edge of Eau Claire, and the Delafield Brewhaus, visible south of Interstate 94 west of Milwaukee.

The late 1990s also brought the advent of the brewpub chain, which, like other craft brewing trends, arrived in Wisconsin somewhat later than in other states. The Rock Bottom Brewery chain opened its first location in downtown Denver in 1991 and had already expanded to eleven other cities when it established the Milwaukee restaurant, its thirteenth, along the riverfront in 1997.[82] A few years later, Wisconsin would develop its own native brewpub families. The Legends group of restaurants began with a location on the edge of Green Bay in 1998, and expanded to De Pere in 2001 and to Ashwaubenon in 2004. The restaurants were somewhere between a sports bar and a supper club, and each had a small brewing system operated by a brewer who traveled between restaurants. Milwaukee Ale House led the charge to the northern periphery of the Milwaukee metropolitan area with a branch in Grafton that opened in 2007. The original Milwaukee brewpub, Water Street Brewery, opened a branch to the west in Delafield in 2000,

The Ende family residence in Reedsburg became Pete Peterson's first brewpub in 1996. The restaurant occupying the space today still features a sign advertising EndeHouse Gold Ribbon Ale (photograph from 2011).

In contrast to the historic surroundings of the downtown Madison brewery, Great Dane's Fitchburg location was built as a brewpub from the start (photograph from 2011).

its own Grafton location in 2011, and another to the south in Oak Creek in 2015. Great Dane opened its second location in Fitchburg in 2002, and a third in 2006 on the west side of Madison. The company purchased the bankrupt Hereford & Hops brewpub in Wausau in 2009 and converted it to the Great Dane brand, and opened a branch on the east side of Madison in 2011, which served Great Dane beers, but did not brew at that location. It took a change in the law to allow brewing at the Hilldale location, since previous law limited a brewpub to two branches. The 2007 change, known sometimes as the "Great Dane Bill," was seen by some as detrimental to smaller operations, and by others as an unnecessarily complicated answer to the problem of brewpub growth.[83]

THE SHAKEOUT

Industry analysts have referred to the nationwide drop in microbrewery and brewpub openings from 1996 to 2000 as a "shakeout," when poorly planned or capitalized businesses and operations that made poor beer closed due to the workings of the "invisible hand" of the marketplace. More breweries closed than opened in 1999—the first time that had happened since the craft beer boom began two decades earlier.[84] Again, Wisconsin was a few years behind the national trend. Openings of new breweries and brewpubs remained strong through 1999, but then began to taper off. Breweries and brewpubs opening in 1996 suffered the highest mortality of any year in Wisconsin's craft brewing history: of the twelve to open that year, only three remain (all brewpubs), and more than half closed within five years.

Industry analysts disagreed on the causes for the shakeout. Partially to blame was a glut of beer on the shelves, some of which was not well made. While it is difficult to pinpoint the cause of any particular brewery failure, many of the new breweries were operating with a hodgepodge of equipment, sometimes unsuited for brewing, and quality-control problems sometimes resulted in bad beer leaving the brewery or beer going bad from sitting on store shelves. The very public feud between global breweries, some craft breweries, and contract brewers exacerbated the quality debate.[85] Many of the labels overcrowding the shelves were introduced by "beer marketers" who may or may not have had a particular recipe in mind, but who had a branding idea and a desire to cash in on the apparently endless willingness of American craft beer consumers to buy anything once as long as it had a colorful label or an amusing name. The lack of repeat purchases often left the contract brewers stuck with piles of unused labels and equally high piles of unpaid bills.[86]

In general, brewpubs fared better than microbreweries during the late 1990s and early 2000s, since they served a very limited local market and did not need to worry about fighting for shelf space or tap lines with larger or better-established rivals. However, some new microbreweries were able to gain a foothold during the period. Tyranena

Rob Larson of Tyranena Brewing Co. in Lake Mills was one of the first Wisconsin craft brewers to become most famous for aggressively hopped beers. The popular Bitter Woman IPA inspired several variations in the Brewers Gone Wild! series that experimented with different ingredients (bottles ca. 2007–11). AUTHOR'S COLLECTION.

Brewing Company in Lake Mills began operations with a brewing system acquired from a shakeout casualty, Ambleside Brewing in Minneapolis. Central Waters Brewing Company began brewing in Junction City in 1998 but grew steadily and was forced to move to a new site in Amherst in 2007 to meet the demand and to gain space for its burgeoning barrel-aging program.

THE NEW WAVE: NANOS AND NEW IDEAS

As the industry uncertainty of the early 2000s shifted toward renewed enthusiasm, brewery openings increased again and held a steady pace.

The tailrace still flows from the former Cedarburg Mill and marks the entrance to Silver Creek Brewing.

Black Husky beers were first packaged in twelve-ounce bottles, each with one of Toni and Tim Eichinger's rescue sled dogs featured on the label (bottles from 2010). AUTHOR'S COLLECTION.

At the same time, Wisconsin's breweries ceased to be a few years behind national trends, and some of the new businesses were among the pioneers in new ways of organizing a brewery.

Among the new breweries that began the resurgence in 2004 were two that introduced new business models. Brewing returned to the historic city of Cedarburg for the first time since Prohibition when Silver Creek Brewing opened in a historic gristmill dating to the 1850s—with the millrace still flowing vigorously. But Silver Creek was a bit different. It did not bottle beer on a regular basis for retail sale, so it was not a microbrewery. Silver Creek did not have a kitchen, so it was not a brewpub. While the term had not yet come into common usage, it was among the first brewery taprooms in the nation—a brewery that served its beer only on-site.

The other pioneer of 2004 had the word in its name. The Pioneer Haus was also known as the University of Wisconsin–Platteville Dining Services Brewpub. At the time, it was the only college or university to have its own brewpub. Much of the work was done by students as part of their biology courses. While university administrators were skeptical, shortly after opening the house brews were outselling Miller Lite by a two-to-one margin.[87] Since then, other colleges around the country have created their own breweries, often to serve as labs for certificate or degree programs.

The term *nanobrewery* first started to be used around 2007. While the precise definition continues to evolve, a batch size of five barrels or less would describe most breweries in the category. In essence, many of these breweries were simply large-scale homebrewers who obtained the necessary permits to sell their beer.[88] The first in Wisconsin to adopt the description appears to have been Black Husky Brewing, founded in 2010 in Pembine, in the far northeastern part of the state. The brewhouse was located in a log cabin built by owners Toni and Tim Eichinger. While Black Husky's distribution was at first limited to the immediate community, demand for their "Rarely Balanced, Never Boring!" beers encouraged the Eichingers to distribute to a limited number of stores and restaurants as far south as Milwaukee and Kenosha.[89] Other breweries followed that claimed the title of nanobrewery—One Barrel Brewing Company emphasized its lack of size right in the name.

Although also categorized as a nano, Dave's BrewFarm was most noteworthy for what its name implies, the first true farm brewery to be opened in Wisconsin since the nineteenth century. In the rolling hills near the village of Wilson, "Farmer Dave" Anderson grew hops and other botanicals for use in the creative recipes brewed on the small system in the farmhouse. Power for the brewery came from the landmark windmill that towers above the property. A pair of popular beers, BrewFarm Select and Matacabras, were brewed and packaged briefly under contract, but the range of beers available at the taproom reflected the variety of ingredients available to modern brewers.

A rustic sign guides guests to the taproom at Dave's Brew-Farm. The twenty-kilowatt wind generator (named Jake) is visible in the background.

DECISIONS, DECISIONS

Modern brewers need to be creative—about their beer recipes, about their distribution channels, and about their sources of funding. While most beer is still sold through wholesalers and retailers, and most breweries are still funded through bank loans or private funds, the era of online communities brought new opportunities for breweries. House of Brews in Madison was a typical brewery in some respects: it had a taproom, did some contract brewing for even smaller operations, and participated in collaboration projects with other breweries. But owner Page Buchanan also experimented with a "Community-Supported Brewery"

MobCraft Beer's logo on this early sticker (ca. 2013) suggests how online discussions can combine to produce a successful beer. COLLECTION OF SCOTT REICH.

along the lines of the more widespread community-supported agriculture (CSA) model. Customers subscribed in advance for a six-month or one-year portion of brewery production, and later received a set amount of beer when it was produced.

Even more emblematic of the internet era is MobCraft Beer. Taking advantage of the younger generation's interest in online communities and social media, MobCraft founders Giotto Troia, Andrew Gierczak, and Henry Schwartz decided to "crowdsource" their recipes. Beer enthusiasts were encouraged to submit recipes online, MobCraft selected a short list of finalists that had the promise to be both commercially and technically successful, and potential customers could then vote for their favorites by placing preorders for the beers of their choice. The finalist with the most preorders was then brewed (at House of Brews) and shipped to the preordering customers, with the rest sold at select bars or retailers in the area.[90] Some of the early winners represented minor variations in common recipes (Hazelnut Amber, Black Vanilla IPA); others were significant flights of brewing fancy, including Rabbit's Bounty Carrot Cake Ale and Mayan Chocolate Chili Ale.[91]

Wisconsin's craft breweries have mirrored the times in ways beyond social media and eclectic flavors. Some of the new breweries, especially those designed from the ground up, have made environmental concerns an important part of their operations. For example, Central Waters Brewery in Amherst was built to use solar power to provide both hot water and electricity, and to be as efficient in using both as possible.[92] Central Waters became the first brewery recognized in Wisconsin's Green Tier program of environmentally friendly businesses, and the first in the Green Masters program.[93]

The locavore movement to emphasize locally grown products has also been embraced by Wisconsin's craft brewers. In particular, participation in the Midwest Hops and Barley Co-op, inspired at least in part by rising hop prices in the late 2000s, helped renew the cultivation of hops and malting barley in the state. The ability to tout local ingredients used in their beers added what South Shore's Bo Bélanger described as an important way to set products apart in a crowded market of craft beers.[94] The six hop growers in the co-op harvested more than eleven hundred pounds of hops in 2011, with varieties ranging from

Even before Wisconsinite, Lakefront brewed Local Acre, which used 100 percent Wisconsin-grown six-row barley and Wisconsin-grown Cascade hops. The label also includes the vital statistics of the beer and Lakefront's meters showing the balance between characteristics for drinkers not familiar with the other measures (label ca. 2009). COLLECTION OF SCOTT REICH.

classic European types like Tettnang and Golding to powerful West Coast varieties like Cascade and Magnum.[95] Lakefront Brewery took the local ingredient quest to its logical conclusion with Wisconsinite, a wheat beer made with 100 percent Wisconsin-grown barley, wheat, and hops, along with the first-known yeast strain to be developed in the state.[96]

CREATING THE CRAFT

Anyone planning to start a brewery in the craft brewing environment of the late 2010s was faced with a host of choices about the nature of their proposed business.[97] The first decision, of course, is where to locate the brewery. While some founders have an idea and seek a particular location to make it work, most brewery owners had a vision to bring a new brewery to their hometown. Founders then need to decide whether to settle on a downtown location, a site in the suburbs, or even a farmstead or other rural setting. Sometimes the choice reflects the vision of the owners about the type of image they want to develop—an urban meeting place, a family friendly beer garden, or a strictly industrial facility. More often, the choice of building is based on what is available in the founders' price range. The local population or business density appears to be less important, since breweries have been able to draw visitors to remote rural destinations as well as recovering urban neighborhoods.

Breweries have joined or led the redevelopment of blocks or even entire neighborhoods.

Several Milwaukee neighborhoods are home to multiple breweries, and in places like Walker's Point and Riverwest breweries draw in visitors and provide local residents with a center of recreation and entertainment.

The availability of funds often determines the type of equipment the brewery will start with. The rapid pace of brewery expansion has created a market for hand-me-down brewing equipment, so a new brewer can acquire high-quality used equipment that was simply unavailable to a start-up thirty years ago. Some brewers with ready funds are able to capitalize on the demand for craft-brewery-sized equipment and start with an all-new brewhouse custom built for their space. Others, whether because of lack of funds or a do-it-yourself ethic, still cobble together a system out of whatever equipment is at hand. Used dairy tanks and other improvised equipment still are found in some Wisconsin breweries.

Modern craft brewers are able to draw on both traditional and modern sources of funding. They may be able to acquire loans from banks or government entities, raise money from family and friends, or use their own assets. One brewer in northern Wisconsin sold her car in order to buy a pilot brewing system. But today's brewers are also able to raise money through Kickstarter or other "crowdfunding" sources that were unimaginable prior to the internet era. In addition, modern craft brewers may be able to keep their "day job" and operate the brewery a few days each week. While some farm brewers of the pre-Prohibition era treated brewing as a sideline, the vast majority of earlier brewers had no option but to make their brewery a full-time business.

A significant difference between the modern industry and that of previous eras is that many craft brewers started their business as a second career. Many came from related occupations such as bartender or restaurant manager, or elsewhere in the brewing world; others left careers as salespeople, engineers, or even doctors to follow the path of King Gambrinus. Although there were many nonbrewers who ended up as brewery proprietors in the nineteenth century, they generally purchased a share in an existing brewery for the possibility of profit, rather than following the dream of making their own beer and watching paying customers enjoy it.

The brewhouse of Potosi Brewing Co. is typical of many modern craft breweries. Here, new equipment was wedged into a small space in an old building.

WELCOMING CUSTOMERS

For the majority of production breweries that elect to serve beer to customers on the premises the next question is about the ambience of the taproom. Some breweries are family friendly, some are dog friendly, and some are both. Many modern breweries are located in repurposed industrial buildings that feature high ceilings and lots of space. Those in downtown storefronts often have less space to spread out, but have a more intimate feel. Most brewers have a sense of history, so locating in a restored building is an attractive proposition—especially if it has lots of exposed brick and massive wooden beams to provide atmosphere.

Exposing all that history requires hundreds if not thousands of hours of work, often provided by the founders, their families, and friends. While the lengthy build-out process may take more than a year, it saves money and creates a deep sense of ownership that can be an attractive part of the brewery's story. At Appleton Beer Factory, the crew spent more than twenty-five thousand hours at night and on weekends converting their former auto parts supply store into a brewpub.[98] Visitors to Sawmill Brewing Company in Merrill can peruse a leaflet describing the local artisans who helped create the taproom.

Perhaps the decision most evident to customers is the type of beer offered. With so many

The taproom of Appleton Beer Factory shows off the fruits of years of work. Much of the wood in the taproom was repurposed from elsewhere in the building. The building's original boiler was fabricated in the 1930s. COURTESY OF APPLETON BEER FACTORY.

Building a portfolio of barrel-aged beers requires infinite patience as well as a substantial investment in cooperage. The barrel cellar at Central Waters Brewing Co. contained approximately forty-five hundred barrels as of July 2017. Their location in a rural area means that land and warehouse space are relatively inexpensive, which allows beer to be stored in barrels for up to three years. Barrel aging requires careful monitoring of the beer to make sure it is racked or bottled when the desired flavor profile is achieved. COURTESY OF CENTRAL WATERS BREWING CO.

RETURN OF THE LOCAL   347

Since its introduction in 2013 by Oskar Blues Brewing of Longmont, Colorado, the aluminum "crowler" has become a popular package among craft beer customers. Oskar Blues partnered with Wisconsin Aluminum Foundry of Manitowoc to design the cap-sealing machines. Crowlers and their glass cousins (called "howlers," "meowlers," or other brewery-specific names) may be used by customers who do not want a full half gallon of a beer. Breweries will sometimes offer rare or high-alcohol beers only in the smaller containers. PHOTOGRAPH BY CHARLES WALBRIDGE. AUTHOR'S COLLECTION.

breweries in the state, a new brewery in a crowded region will have to distinguish itself with high-quality beer that is different from beer already available nearby. Most brewers insist that they are making beers they enjoy drinking, though an entire lineup of "extreme beers" would be expensive to make and might not generate enough regular business to pay the bills. A market like Madison has been able to support breweries specializing in gluten-free and in Belgian-style gueuze. A brewery located in a small city, however, will likely have to offer a broad-based lineup of familiar styles to build a steady business to support any experimental beers. A further constraint on beer variety is the fermenter space available. A brewer with only a few fermenters is unlikely to brew many lagers, since they tie up the tanks for much longer than most ales. Brewers need to be aware of trends in the brewing world—in order to draw attention from craft beer aficionados and the websites they frequent, a brewer may wish to offer barrel-aged beers, sour beers, and beers to fit each season. Selling a small number of wax-dipped bottles of a limited edition beer creates an instant collectible and inspires publicity for the event. Brewers need to be careful, however, that they are not distracted by "the next shiny object" and avoid investing time, effort, and reputation in a dead-end style.

Once the beer is made, it needs to be brought to consumers. Even breweries that do not bottle or can their beer for off-premises sales have many more package options than even a few years ago. While the sixty-four-ounce growler has been in Wisconsin since Capital Brewery filled the first one in 1992, a modern brewery can package fresh beer in thirty-two-ounce glass "howlers," thirty-two-ounce aluminum "crowlers," and a variety of other glass packages. Craft breweries also share credit for the renewed popularity of the sixteen-ounce "tallboy" cans.

WHAT'S IN A NAME?

With the astounding increase in brewers in Wisconsin and nationwide, it has become much more difficult to find a name for a brewery, and especially a name for a beer, that has not already been taken. The founders of Badger State Brewing Company were surprised to discover that name was still available—and filed their paperwork to claim it the next day. Contrary to the pre-Prohibition practice, very few brewers have taken the name of their founders—since 2010 only Brenner Brewing, Stillmank Brewing, and Knuth Brewing have been added to the list of eponymous breweries (though a few others, such as Kozy Yak, 'Vik'ing Brewpub, and Barley John's, incorporated the owner's name in some way). Slightly more common have been breweries named after a city or county: about a dozen fit this description if Bobtown Brewhouse & Grill (located in Roberts) counts. Besides these classic nomenclatures, brewery names can come from many sources: local landmarks, dogs, or in the case of Turtle Stack Brewery, a reference from a Dr. Seuss story. The selection of a name and any artwork or branding that goes with it may be designed to attract a certain type of drinker. Somerset's Oliphant Brewing, for example, created a quirky backstory for the name and artwork, and has attracted customers interested in their experimental beers.

If picking a brewery name is sometimes difficult, selecting a beer name is even more complicated. Unless the brewery is simply using style names for the beers (porter, IPA, milk stout), it needs to perform due diligence to make sure the name is not already in use or be subject to possible legal action. For a beer offered only at the brewery taproom, it might be possible to get away with using a name already in use. But the farther the beer is shipped from the brewery, the higher the risk of a clash. In 2015, O'So Brewing changed the

Collaborations between brewers have become a popular way to experiment with recipes and build bonds locally and internationally. Dubbel Czech was a collaboration between Badger State Brewing Co. and MobCraft Beer. Released in December 2014, it was described as "a double blond ale with the spirit of a Czech lager," but fermented with a Belgian ale yeast. Dirk Naudts of De Proefbrouwerij in Belgium invited Dan Carey of New Glarus to partner on an abbey-style ale. Because De Proef products were imported by Artisanal Imports, a distributor with a national presence, this became one of the very few New Glarus beers that could be purchased legally outside Wisconsin. PHOTOGRAPH BY CHARLES WALBRIDGE. AUTHOR'S COLLECTION.

name of Night Train porter to Night Rain in order to retain the ability to ship beyond Wisconsin and Illinois. The most noteworthy example of multiple beers with the same name arose in 2016, when three different beers named Bubbler were offered by Plymouth Brewing, Next Door Brewing, and New Glarus Brewing. The three were able to avoid lawsuits, but this case illustrates the difficulty of finding a name that has never been used before.[99]

Breweries sometimes cooperated in the past, but there are many more opportunities to do so in the modern craft era. Many taprooms have one or more beers from other nearby breweries to cross-promote businesses that are viewed more as collaborators than competitors. In fact, collaboration beers have become very popular in Wisconsin. Starting in 2012, Madison-area breweries joined together to make a beer called "Common Thread" using a different style each year, and the project went statewide in 2017. The Belgian tripel brewed in 2015 was the creation of a group of women brewers. The breweries of Green Bay have banded together to create a "Locals Only" beer since 2014. Numerous other brewers have produced smaller-scale partnership beers. Cooperation also extends to brewers sharing equipment—several small brewers share canning lines to save on the considerable expense of purchasing their own line. Finally, nearly every new brewer has a story to tell about some industry veteran who helped with advice about equipment, brewery design, or recipes, or who just sat down for a few beers and listened.

Collaboration with other businesses is also critical to brewery survival. Taprooms without their own kitchens depend on neighborhood restaurants or food trucks to provide sustenance for their customers. Brewery taprooms also are hesitant to provide direct competition to area bars and restaurants—hoping some of them will also carry their beer. Many breweries have elected to open just a few days each week and close earlier each night, which not only limits their direct competition but also eliminates the problem of rowdy late-night revelers.

SAME AS IT EVER WAS

Many of the conditions faced by craft brewers in 2017 are similar to those faced by Wisconsin brewers since territorial times. Brewers need to comply with government regulations, pay their taxes, and make good beer. Partnerships form and dissolve—often amicably, sometimes not. Breweries lose valued employees who leave to found their own breweries or take a senior position elsewhere. Brewery founders need to hire more employees as they grow and sometimes hand over brewing duties to someone else. Growth leads to expansion of existing facilities and sometimes requires moving to a new location.

New Glarus Brewing launched its Employee Stock Option Program in 2015. About half of the original investors sold some or all of their stock to create the ESOP. New Glarus Brewing was also among the first craft brewers to provide health care coverage for their workers. AUTHOR'S COLLECTION.

While many breweries have no plans to expand much beyond their neighborhood, others want to bring their beer to thirsty customers all over the state or region. This sometimes forces the owners and brewers to confront an awkward question: what happens when you become the big brewer you used to complain about? While growing so big that your brewery is purchased by a global corporation for a king's ransom would be viewed as successful by most in the business world, the craft brewing world places a premium on intangible characteristics, for good or for ill. The quest among some beer seekers for the next big thing values newness and scarcity above all—sometimes at the expense of quality. At this writing, none of Wisconsin's new craft breweries have been purchased by international brewers or larger craft brewers. Whether because there are few Badger State breweries large enough to be of interest or whether the proprietors have resisted any offers, there have been no polarizing transactions like the sale of Chicago's Goose Island Brewing to Anheuser-Busch InBev.

As breweries reach their third or fourth decades of operation, they face a question shared with their predecessors: will the brewery outlast the involvement of the founders? So far, the number of Wisconsin breweries being operated by someone other than the founder is relatively low. A few brewpubs have been sold to new owners, but more have closed than transferred owners. It is difficult to make comparisons between brewery closures in the nineteenth century and the modern era since such a small percentage have closed. Of the approximately 200 breweries and brewpubs that have opened since 1986, about 150 are still open.

Tapping the Legacy

Eighteen decades after John Phillips first brewed in Mineral Point, seventeen decades after Phillip Best launched his empire, five decades after Lite changed the beer world, and three decades after the first microbrewers risked their savings, Wisconsin's brewing scene represents a diversity of scale not seen since the nineteenth century, and a diversity of flavors unimaginable at any previous point in history. A start-up like Ale Asylum grew to the point that it needed to build its dream brewery simply to supply increased demand, and new companies like Wisconsin Brewing in Verona (not to be confused with other businesses that once used the name) could build spectacular facilities right from the start. Landlocked breweries like Capital and Lakefront considered branch breweries to increase capacity, and even brewpubs like Titletown were compelled to find new space to brew the beer sought by a thirsty populace. With all the expansion, the sense of community and place that permeates the state encouraged small brewers to take a chance that their products would be welcomed. Some hoped to grow and challenge the established businesses, others simply wanted a small place to show off their passion for flavorful beer. The forest of tap handles at taverns rivals the forests of the north woods in scope, without the sameness of a stand of pine trees. Wisconsin beer is still famous, and many more names have made it so.

Return to Potosi

After nearly four decades as one of the leading small breweries in the Upper Midwest, the Potosi Brewing Company closed in 1972. (The closing is covered in chapter 8 and the second part of this book.) For many years, local residents clung to a forlorn hope that something could be done with the old brewery buildings. Talk of locating a restaurant and museum within the brewery began a few years after its closing, with speculation serious enough to be mentioned in regional newspaper articles as early as 1981.[1] The discussions languished, however, and so did the property, which grew more dilapidated with each passing year. Eventually, it looked "like a bombed out structure in a war-torn country."[2] The buildings were open to trespassers and the elements, but most of the damage was caused by time and erosion. Years passed, and optimism faded. Even the placement of the Potosi Brewing Company buildings on the National Register of Historic Places did little to promote the site, and that designation is also no guarantee of preservation.

The dilapidated buildings of the Potosi Brewing Co. as they appeared in August 2004, before restoration began. The portion to the front left now houses the brewpub; the main brewhouse to the rear contains the museums. PHOTOGRAPH BY THE AUTHOR.

In 1995 Potosi resident Gary David purchased the bottling house across the street and began to restore it. His success generated new interested in the brewhouse itself. David purchased the building at the county auction, then enlisted his friend Rick Tobin, his cousin Denis David, and Denis's wife, Madonna, to build support for the restoration. They established the Potosi Brewery Foundation in 2000 and acquired the brewery by donation the next year. Seeking a partner in the creative reuse of the building, they made a presentation to the American Breweriana Association, a national organization dedicated to brewery history and artifact collection, which in 2004 decided to locate its National Brewery Museum and Library in the brewery after restoration. The $7 million restoration project was completed in less than four years—on time and very close to on budget.[3]

---

1. Ron Seely, "Potosi Brewery Reminder of Bygone Days," *Wisconsin State Journal*, 1 February 1981, sec. 4, 1.
2. Frank Fiorenza, e-mail to author, 26 June 2013.
3. Tom Rejmaniak and Doug Hoverson, "Museum Goal Becoming Reality," *American Breweriana Journal,* September–October 2004, 20–22; Len Chylack, "The National Brewery Museum & Research Library," *American Breweriana Journal,* Museum Commemorative Edition, June 2008, 23, 27–28.

While the museum occupied most of the building, the most important revenue stream came from the Potosi Brewing Company brewpub on the premises. The first two beers at the brewpub were Good Old Potosi Golden Ale and Cave Ale Amber Ale. From there, however, the brewers branched out and developed several highly regarded beers, including Snake Hollow IPA, named after the snakes that were sometimes found in the original brewery in the old days. The most popular brews were also brewed for packaging under contract at Stevens Point Brewery—with all proceeds donated to the Potosi Brewery Foundation.

Demand for Potosi beers increased, and soon it was clear that a production brewery in Potosi offered the advantages of drawing even more people to the region and providing more space for the expanding barrel-aging program. In January 2015 Potosi Brewing opened its new $5.5 million brewery, featuring a forty-barrel brewhouse and state-of-the-art equipment from the centrifuge to the canning line.

As of 2018 Potosi Brewing offered five "core brews," seven bottled seasonals, three canned seasonals, and six barrel-aged specialties. Potosi beer has returned to many of its former markets in Wisconsin, Illinois, and Iowa. The brewery is also brewing and packaging beers for other businesses under contract. The brewery has helped drive economic growth in Grant County. The Potosi Brewing Company employs about thirty full-time staff and another thirty part-time workers. In one twelve-month period, visitors to the museum came from all fifty states and thirty-five countries.[4]

The exhibits in the ABA National Brewery Museum and the Potosi Brewing Company Transportation Museum remind visitors of the diversity of Wisconsin's brewing history. The products on tap just a few steps away are proof that the present of Wisconsin beer is just as diverse and even more flavorful. Potosi Brewing Company, both the past and the present versions, typifies the potential for beer and brewing to bring communities together and to represent those communities to the rest of the world.

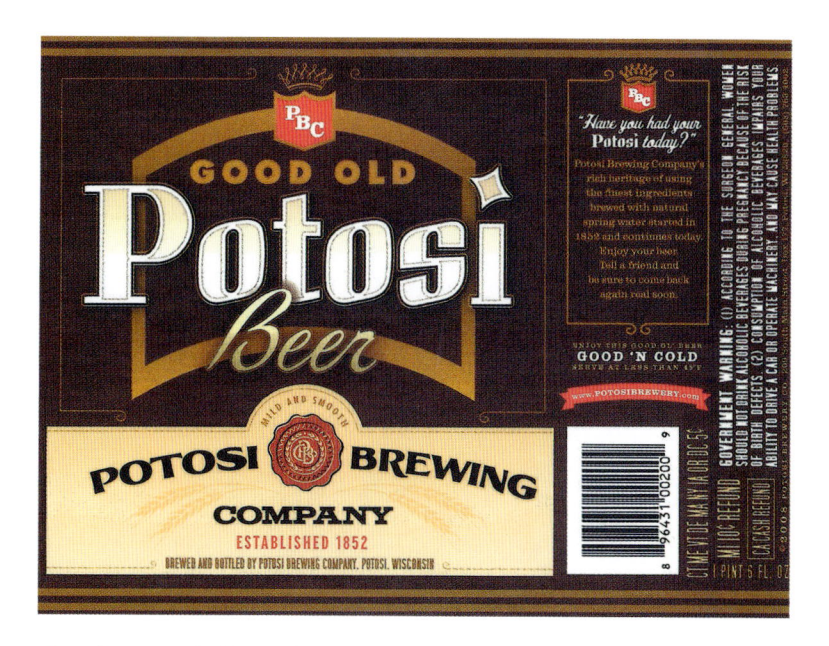

The reborn Good Old Potosi Beer was a light ale, rather than a lager like the original. COLLECTION OF SCOTT REICH.

---

4 Mary Glindinning, "The Craft: Small-Town Brewing Makes a Comeback," *Dubuque Telegraph Herald,* 4 February 2016, http://www.telegraphherald.com/biztimes/articles/article_ab54e150-ab41-56e1-b0bd-06c1985a5d5d.html.

While brewers reluctantly accepted taxes and regulations, voluminous government records are a boon for brewery historians. This tax stamp was issued to Hemmings Ale Brewery in Janesville. COLLECTION OF JOHN STEINER.

Wisconsin Breweries *and Brewpubs*

ASSEMBLING THE STORY OF A PARTICULAR BREWERY CAN BE A DIFFICULT AND frustrating task, though the reason for the difficulty varies. For many of the Milwaukee and La Crosse giants, a wealth of information is available—the goal is to tell the story without getting bogged down in every minor plant improvement or change of corporate officers. For other breweries, the challenge is in finding any reliable information at all. In a few cases all I had to go on was a single reference in a gazetteer or nineteenth-century county history (though further evidence may exist unknown to me). For brevity, these breweries are simply listed with no attempt to weave a story from minimal data.

Not only is the existing information often scarce, but sometimes the data may be contradictory. Different spellings of names might be reconciled, but occasionally the combination of variable spelling, illegible handwriting, and poor interpretations of foreign names render it nearly impossible to determine if two references are actually to the same person or not. To address confusing references, I used first printed (as opposed to manuscript) local sources (usually contemporary newspapers), followed by government documents or other financial records. Some questions were resolved by the spelling on the brewers' tombstones (usually found through findagrave.com).

The dates on which a brewery began operation, changed ownership, or closed can also be sources of confusion. Popular histories written even a decade or two after the event are often based on imprecise recollections of long-time residents or are written to praise those business owners who will be buying the book rather than to inform future investigators. Contemporary newspapers might resolve conflicting dates, but newspapers are not always available—and even when they are, they didn't always cover brewery news. Newspapers in large cities seldom covered small businesses historically, except a few retailers who advertised in their pages. Some newspapers did not cover brewery happenings because of temperance leanings or lack of interest. Newspapers sometimes reported proposed openings and business changes as actual occurrences, and rarely published corrections or addenda. Some brewers encouraged editorial interest by dropping off a keg at the newspaper office on special occasions. The opening of a business is generally more newsworthy than the closing of any but the largest firms—and in many cases, it is not clear if a business closes for good or just temporarily.

In the brewery listings, I included question marks by dates of opening, closing, or proprietor change unless I had a reliable contemporary source (or multiple less-reliable sources). For those breweries for which the earliest listing is in city or state directories, it is likely that it was open during the year prior to publication of the directory, if not earlier. These publications required time to compile and probably reflect data from the previous year. Businesses were listed when the company was formed, even if they were not yet brewing (or never brewed). Occasionally a business that was a beer distributor or brewery supply company was erroneously listed among the breweries. While brewing industry journals and directories should be more accurate, they were sometimes as much as two years behind in updating business changes.

Government data are often very specific and useful, especially the censuses of industry published in 1850, 1860, 1870, and 1880. Yet these may be incomplete; entire counties are missing for some years, and only businesses with more than five hundred dollars of financial activity in the previous twelve months were included. The population census is valuable for identifying those who were brewers by profession (though not all were brewery owners), and some brewers were listed under another occupation, usually farming. Excise tax records exist for the years 1867–1874, with scattered entries after this period; these are in Record Group 58, Records of the Internal Revenue Service (Wisconsin portions are located at the National Archives in Chicago). While these records are very accurate in documenting the existence of a brewery and production figures, they often confuse names and show different parties responsible for the tax when no change of ownership occurred.

Other primary sources such as land records, court records, and business records can provide valuable information. Land records are less definitive than they could be, since many brewers operated without owning the land underneath. The records of R. G. Dun and Company, dating from the late 1840s through 1884 (accessible at Baker Library, Harvard Business School), provide generally reliable information about ownership changes and the financial health of a business—and even sometimes comment on the quality of the beer and the drinking habits of the proprietor.

Speaking of proprietors, clearing up brewery history is further made difficult by the fact that the proprietor was often not the brewer, and existing records used different names interchangeably. Although I have been able to identify a number of "practical brewers" and brewmasters, I will not attempt to list all the known brewers at any particular brewery. These lists would be badly out of date for many modern craft breweries and could be tedious reading for defunct breweries. Some information has been left "on the cutting room floor," but I would be happy to provide what I have for researchers interested in a particular brewery.

Throughout this book, I attempted to do as much as I could to confirm the dates of business changes (while still actually completing the book at some point). In the "brewery biographies" I did my best to label what is speculation and state which sources informed those inferences. Readers will likely have information I was unable to find or access during my nine years of active research. I welcome updates and plan to create a public site where these will be published, shared, and discussed. History is never really final: new information and interpretations mean that there is no "one true version" of what happened, except for raw details of chronology and identity.

Journals such as *The Western Brewer* are a treasure trove of brewing history, even if some information in these publications was out of date. COLLECTION OF SUMMIT BREWING CO.

A Note on Sources

To maintain the narrative line in this section, I typically will not list the most common directories each time they are used unless there is an important disagreement with other sources. The 1857–58 Wisconsin State Directory (essentially duplicated in 1858–59) is the source of most brewery openings listed as 1856?. For production data in 1850, 1860, and 1870, the source is almost always the U.S. Census of Industry; presence in these records most likely indicates that the brewery was open at some point during the previous year. I referred to the industry directories *American Brewers' Guide 1873* (for 1871 and 1872 data); Louis Schade's *Brewers' Hand-Book for 1876* (1874 and 1875); F. W. Salem's lists in *Beer: Its History and Its Economic Value as a National Beverage* (1878 and 1879). Although most of these figures use a fiscal year beginning May 1 or June 1, I sometimes identified the period by calendar year unless it made a difference in interpreting the history of the business. The Wisconsin industrial censuses of 1885 and 1895 provided production figures by city, which was useful for locations with only one brewery.

Later industry directories generally listed capacity rather than production, and few breweries ever produced at the stated capacity. I used the directories *Tovey's Brewers' and Maltsters' Directory* of 1882 and 1891; *Wing's Brewers' Annual* of 1884 and 1887; *The Brewers Hand Book* of 1900, 1905, 1912, and 1916. Thanks to Randy Carlson, Carl Miller, Reino Ojala, and Kevin Knitt for use of their directories.

After 1935, the figures are drawn primarily from the Wisconsin Department of Revenue figures, researched and provided by Tim Holian, or from documents in the Wisconsin State Archives, Register of the Wisconsin Division of Beverage and Cigarette Taxes. Modern production figures are either from the Department of Revenue numbers, the brewers themselves, or from annual figures published in *The New Brewer*.

Any figures from newspaper articles or other periodicals are usually cited in the text. Thanks to Randy Carlson and The Beer Institute for access to their collections of brewing industry publications, and especially to Randy for his exhaustive indexes of many of these journals. Several years of these journals are now available online through Google Books or HathiTrust Digital Library, and the American Breweriana Association is currently digitizing the entire existing collection of *Western Brewer*. Full disclosure: your author has been a financial contributor to this endeavor.

The newspapers used in this research were viewed on microfilm at numerous libraries, online through several searchable databases, and occasionally the original printed copies. No effort was made to separate which electronic database or source was used, because the same paper may have been viewed in different formats at different times. All newspapers are cited in simple newspaper format.

A Note on Quantities

The brewing industry measures beer production by 31-gallon barrels. This converts to approximately 248 pints or 330 twelve-ounce bottles or cans. Some early

Keg loss continues to be a problem for brewers. This pre-Prohibition token represented the 50-cent deposit paid on an 1/8 barrel keg to the Hussa Brewing Co. of Bangor. COLLECTION OF TYE SCHWALBE.

"Steinie" bottles were released in the mid-1930s and were popular until World War II. Casino Special (right) was first brewed for the Blue Ribbon Casino at the Century of Progress exhibition in Chicago. Saxon Brewing Co. of Jefferson never obtained a brewing permit, so Saxon Elixir malt tonic is the only product known from this brewery. Beer Depot Special was a store brand brewed by Capitol Brewing Co. of Milwaukee. COLLECTION OF JOHN STEINER.

censuses reported production in bottles without specifying the size; the twelve-ounce bottle did not become the standard size until the twentieth century. Quarts remained common through Prohibition, and a survey of the labels pictured in this book reveal a wide range of volumes. Other figures apparently used a smaller size keg for their measure, since the reported production is way out of line with what is known about the brewery. Government figures usually indicate tax paid withdrawals, which does not include beer given away on the brewery premises.

Playing cards while drinking beer remains popular, and breweries still offer playing cards to advertise their brands. The Gund specimen at far right is circa 1900; the others date between 1933 and 1960. COLLECTION OF TYE SCHWALBE.

A Note on Prices and Wages

Converting prices and wages from historic periods to current dollars is imprecise at best. Beer and its inputs are essentially commodities and can be converted with fair accuracy through consumer price indices. Wages and income may be better measured through an index that relies heavily on purchasing power parity: what a given amount could have purchased in different periods (or locations). For the conversions included in this book, I based my figures on data obtained from MeasuringWorth.com.

A Note on Notes

In order to keep this book a manageable length, footnotes are not included in this section. Readers interested in sources may refer to a fully annotated, unillustrated online version of the individual histories available at https://www.upress.umn.edu/book-division/books/the-drink-that-made-wisconsin-famous.

WISCONSIN BREWERIES AND BREWPUBS

ALCOMA (Ahnapee)
(Kewaunee County)

Joseph Hipler (?) (ca. 1860)
John Powell (ca. 1861)
Mathias Simon & George Laux (ca. 1865–67)
George Laux & Co. (1867–69)
Wyta Stransky/Stransky & Swaty, Ahnapee Brewery (1869–1875)
Ahnapee Brewing Co. (1875–1884)
Henry Schmilling, Ahnapee Brewery (1884-85)
John Skala, Ahnapee Brewery (1886–1890)
Pytlik Klogner, Ahnapee Brewery (1890-93?)
(Modern) 115 Navarino Street

The early years of Ahnapee's first brewery are known only from indirect references. Joseph Hipler is listed as a brewer in the 1860 census. A county history from the early 1920s reported that in 1867 Louis Bruemmer purchased an interest in a brewery "operated theretofore by John Powell and others," but he soon went into the hotel business. According to local historian Virginia Feld Johnson, Powell probably died after the battle of Perryville in 1862, so he could not have owned it for long. (Powell owned property on Block 15 between Steele and Clark and Third and Fourth, which may have been the site of this brewery.) Johnson also holds that Bruemmer bought his interest from Mathias Simon, and ran it with Simon's former partner, George Laux. Simon was included in the R. G. Dun & Co. records from 1865 until 1867, and was also listed as the owner of a general store. Laux appears in the excise tax records in 1867, sometimes under the name of George Laux & Co.

The *Kewaunee County Enterprize* provides a clear link between the Laux and Stransky businesses. It reported in February 1869 that Wyta Stransky of Kewaunee and Herman Seidemann [sic] of Sturgeon Bay had purchased the Ahnapee brewery from Laux. Seidelman apparently didn't stay long, since Franz Swaty became Stransky's partner in the business soon after the purchase.

In the fall of 1869, Stransky and Swaty built a new brewery on Block 2 of Young and Steele's Plat, between what was then South Water Street and the Ahnapee River. The brewery was praised as the first substantial brick building in the county. By 1874, Stransky had completed a new dock behind the brewery, and beer was shipped by water to customers north of town, sometimes in the sloop *Whiskey Pete*. The local newspapers quoted locals and visitors who claimed that Ahnapee lager beer was just as good as Milwaukee lager.

Henry Schmilling purchased the brewery in 1879, and began to make repairs and upgrades. By 1884 the malt facilities were expanded so that they could supply all of the brewery's needs and the brewery had a reported capacity of 2,000 barrels per year. One unusual feature of the brewery (which predated Schmilling's improvements) was the windmill on the roof used to provide power for grinding malt and pumping liquids. Schmilling also added an icehouse and a malt house, and sank a new well in front of the brewery.

John Skala and J. B. Orth leased the brewery in 1885, but encountered a run of bad luck. A fire that year caused minimal damage, but one the next year left the upper floor badly damaged. At first Skala planned to rebuild, but later that year he moved the brewing equipment to Menominee, Michigan.

After Skala left, the property changed hands several times, eventually winding up with Edward Decker. Accounts differ as to whether Decker simply held the property or continued the brewery. The *Enterprize* reported in June 1889 that Pytlik Klogner was planning to lease the brewery and *American Breweries II* lists "Klogner & Ptilik" [sic] as running the business until 1893, but the firm does not appear in the state business directory of 1891 or in other records. The 1894 Sanborn Insurance Map shows the building still owned by Edward Decker, but indicated that a family lived in the premises and did not include the capacity of the brewery, which was common on these maps—so it is most likely that the brewery had not been in business since Skala left.

Several companies used the building for manufacturing and storage during the twentieth century until Dr. Charles W. Stiehl purchased it and started Von Stiehl Winery in 1968. The building was named to the National Register of Historic Places in 1994. Henry Schmilling was the great-great-great-great uncle of Aric and Brad Schmiling [modern spelling], who purchased the business in 2003 and are the owners as of 2017.

This illustration from an 1872 county atlas showed the brewery windmill above the daily hustle and bustle around the brewery. Courtesy of Wisconsin Historical Society, WHi-101201.

Ahnapee Brewery (2013–present)
105 Navarino Street

Brewing returned to Algoma in 2013 when Aric and Brad Schmiling of Von Stiehl Winery opened a brewery taproom in a small building next to the historic brewery. The brewing is done in the former Carnival Guernsey Dairy northwest of the city. Head brewer Nick Calaway previously served as general manager of Titletown Brewing Co. in Green Bay, and moved to Von Stiehl for a job that demanded less time than the restaurant business. In 2017, Calaway fulfilled the original plan by purchasing the brewery from the Schmilings.

In keeping with the German heritage of the brewery, the original beers were traditional German styles such as Vienna lager, Bavarian dunkel and Munich helles. Even the English-style Noble IPA used German malts and hops. Calaway soon introduced creative special releases such as the Hobo series. The first was a Belgian-style quadruple abbey ale released in

The first 12-ounce bottles from Ahnapee Brewery featured Two Stall chocolate milk stout and Little Soldier, an American amber ale named in honor of Civil War veteran (and pioneer Ahnapee brewer) Henry Schmilling. COURTESY OF AHNAPEE BREWERY.

2014, which was followed by several barrel-aged beers. Some of these were bottled for sale at the taproom (usually a limited release of 500 bottles), but bottling for distribution throughout northeastern Wisconsin began in 2016. The bottling plant was installed in a building across the street from the taproom.

ALMA *(Buffalo County)*

John Hemrich, Union Brewery (1855–1862)
John A. Hunner, Union Brewery (1862–64)
Rissler & Jung, Union Brewery (1865–68)
Rissler & Hemrich, Union Brewery (1868–1871)
John Hemrich, Union Brewery (1871–1888)
William & Alvin Hemrich, Union Brewery (1888–1890)
Henry Huber & Fred Hemrich, Union Brewery (1890–91)
Alma Brewing Co. (1891–1919)
EAST SIDE OF MAIN, NORTH OF WATER STREET (MODERN 800 BLOCK OF SOUTH MAIN)

The Union Brewery is usually credited with being the first industry in Alma—taking advantage of the surrounding farm country that supplied raw materials for producing lager beer. John Hemrich (Hemmrich) arrived in 1855 and built a log brewery to take advantage of the traffic from the nearby steamboat landing. According to local tradition, John Spany built the brewery, but supposedly forgot to put in openings for windows. L. Kessinger, writing in the 1888 *History of Buffalo County, Wisconsin* speculated: "it can readily be imagined that there must have been, and there still is, a considerable demand for their product." Indeed, the 1860 Census of Industry listed Hemrich with a production of 1,800 barrels of beer in the past year with a value of $7,000—more than the breweries in La Crosse or any other city in the western part of the state. The *Buffalo County Journal* claimed, "He has facilities for manufacturing a Better Article of Beer than any other brewery in Northwestern Wisconsin."

In 1862, Hemrich rented his brewery to John A. Hunner, who then went "to La Crosse or Dubuque to engage a brewer." He was evidently successful, because later ads reported he had engaged "the services of one of the best and most skillful brewers in the western country" and operated the brewery for about two years. In February 1863, Hunner went through the ice crossing the Mississippi River with a pair of horses and a wagon (though the account did not confirm that it was a brewery wagon). By 1864, Hunner had purchased the Wisconsin House and was preparing to start his own brewery (see next entry).

Rissler and Jung operated the brewery for the next few years. Hemrich moved back into the business with William Rissler during 1868,

The Alma Brewing Co. letterhead from the early 1900s featured a Gambrinus-like figure. COLLECTION OF JOHN STEINER.

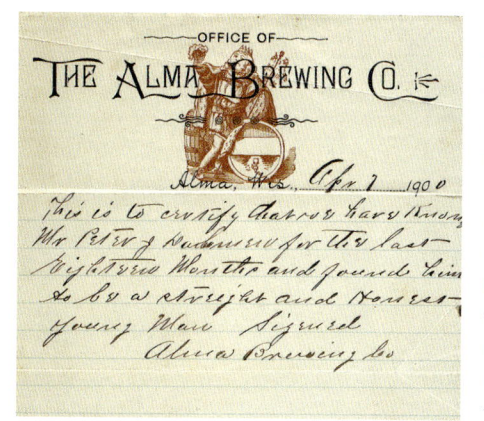

a date confirmed by ads in October that listed Hemrich & Rissler at the top and Rissler & Jung at the bottom. By the summer of 1871 Hemrich was once more sole proprietor, but production had declined since the heady days of 1860 to about 400 barrels a year in the early 1870s, perhaps because of increased competition. Most of the sales were in Alma and the surrounding farm towns. Hemrich expanded the brewery over the next two decades by adding a brick malt house in 1876 and a stone icehouse in 1880. By the late 1880s the brewery was the least impressive of the structures, so Hemrich replaced the original log structure with a new frame structure containing a new steam engine and other fixtures acquired from a local mill. The brewery made a lager beer that was known as Alma Bride due to a label misprint (intended to be Alma Pride) and a bock beer each spring. Despite the progress, Hemrich had his share of bad luck as well. The brewery cellar was flooded in June 1880 and he lost most of his beer. The next year his fifteen-year old son drowned while swimming near the brewery. By 1888 Hemrich was now in his mid-60s, and apparently tired of the business, so he leased the brewery to his sons William and Alvin and moved west to Washington.

The two brothers only held the business for two years. In 1890, area newspapers announced that the brewery was to be sold at auction in April, and later that "parties from California," had taken over the brewery. Henry Huber and Fred Hemrich brought in Christ Carisch from Fountain City to take over management of the brewery, and later they changed the name to Alma Brewing Co. after the other firm of that name closed in 1891. While popular as brewmaster, Carisch was perhaps more famous for having a son, George, who signed a contract to pitch for Cap Anson's Chicago White Stockings of the National League (though he never reached the majors). In 1907 the brewery was sold to a new management team of Charles Huth, A. W. Hofer, and William Ulrich, who continued the business until Prohibition in 1919. The building stayed in the Ulrich family until it was razed in 1937.

John A. Hunner (1864–66)

William Briggeboos, Alma Brewery (1866–1888 or 1891?)

215 SOUTH MAIN STREET

According to the 1888 county history, J. A. "Squire" Hunner started this brewery in "the old Wisconsin House," but sold it to old settler and Hunner's former business partner William Briggeboos in 1866. In 1871, Briggeboos (various spellings) set about building a new brewery across the street from the original location. Production fluctuated during the 1870s from just over 300 barrels to more than 600. By the late 1880s industry directories listed his capacity at more than 2,000 barrels—though he probably never produced at full capacity. Several sources claim that the brewery closed during 1888, which is supported by an article in the *Winona Daily Republican* suggesting Briggeboos was planning to reopen it. The article enthused over his cellars and claimed "Many an old pioneer of this county who blew foam off Briggeboos's beer back in the sixties would be pleased to do so again just for luck and to remind them of ye good old days." One local history claims Briggeboos retired in 1891, but this may have been from his milling business. The family continued to live in the brewery after his death in 1893. The building was razed in 1924, but the caves were later used for growing mushrooms and even as a natural air conditioner for a filling station later located on the site.

Charles Zengel (1869–1870)

"ABOVE THE LIME KILN"

Charles Zengel's brewery was derided in the 1888 county history as a "feeble attempt." However in 1870 he produced enough to be included among firms that did at least $500 worth of business during the year—producing fifty barrels that were sold at the prevailing local rate of $10 each. By far the smallest of Alma's breweries, he may have found the competition difficult to overcome. Excise records from January 1871 note that Zengel had ceased brewing on the previous June 30th and had "no beer on hand."

AMHERST (Portage County)

Central Waters Brewing Company (2007–present)

351 ALLEN STREET

Central Waters moved to their new location in January 2007, and at first the brewhouse was a "frankenbrewery" affair. The bottle filler was a 1968 model from Germany; the case erector (which prepares cartons for filling) was of 1950s vintage from the old Rainier brewery in Washington, and the bottle labelers came from the Stevens Point Brewery just a few miles away. Within a few years the brewhouse, cellar, packaging hall, lab, and barrel warehouse all featured state of the art equipment which enabled Central Waters to embark on brewing projects that have earned them national acclaim. Its Shine On red ale celebrates a partnership with the Midwest Renewable Energy Association. In 2009, the brewery added one thousand square feet of solar collectors which, when combined with a radiant floor heating system and other energy efficient systems, made the brewery Wisconsin's "first Green Powered Brewery." The brewery was able to double production from three thousand barrels to six thousand barrels in 2010 without any increase in energy consumption. The brewery is also one of several which has made commitments to buy local ingredients from the Midwest Hops & Barley Co-op.

For many craft beer lovers, the most important addition to the brewery is the barrel warehouse added in 2010 and expanded many times since. Several thousand oak barrels are used to age some of the brewery's beers, including imperial stout and barleywine. The oak adds a variety of flavors including vanilla and coconut to the already rich beers. Central Waters has also launched a sour aged beer program with sixty-four barrels, though as of 2016 Exodus has been the only beer released in this series. With experimental projects there are risks and occasional setbacks. In 2012, Central Waters recalled that year's edition of Peruvian Morning barrel-aged coffee stout because it was taking on undesirable flavors for the style. However, the vast majority of the barrel projects yielded excellent results and earned medals at national and international competitions. In several states, the barrel-aged brews are the only Central Waters products available. Paul Graham noted that since the local nature of craft beer is very important to consumers, the flagship beers are less relevant to distant customers, so the specialty products are more viable.

ANTIGO (Langlade County)

Frank (John?) Chalupsky (1890–92)

John Benishek (1892–93)

(John) Benishek & (Albert) Fisch (1893–94)

Frank Hanzal (1894–95)

Antigo Brewing Company (1896–1920)

EDISON STREET AND NINTH

The town of Antigo was first started as an oasis of temperance, but the residents soon overturned the wishes of the founder and voted to grant liquor licenses. The establishment of a brewery in the town was noted with some irony by the *Chicago Herald,* which claimed it would "make a good market for all the barley raised in Langlade County," but that it was "like the proverbial last straw on the camels [sic] back to the temperance zealots on Piety Flat." Despite being founded relatively late, sources still

Two early barrel-aged beers. More recent labels did not include the vintages. AUTHOR'S COLLECTION.

362 THE DRINK THAT MADE WISCONSIN FAMOUS

This tray (ca. 1910) featured a stock image titled "Good Friends." Brewery trays often featured women, but horses (sometimes joining women) were also common. COLLECTION OF HERBERT AND HELEN HAYDOCK.

show some confusion over the early years of Antigo's first brewery. The name of the founder is given variously as Frank or John Chalupsky.

By November 1893, Albert Fisch (Fish) had joined John Benishek, and the company was registered as a brewer of more than 500 barrels, though figures in 1895 show output closer to 200 barrels. In September 1896, ten businessmen reorganized the business as Antigo Brewing Company. The brewery continued through Prohibition, during which they produced near beer for a short time.

The products of the building found a much wider market in its later years: The building was purchased by the Langlade County Creamery and produced cheese under the Kraft Foods Co. of Wisconsin label. In 1937, this plant claimed to be the largest producer of Swiss cheese in the world.

Citizens Brewing Company (1899–1920)
(SUPERIOR STREET) EDISON STREET AND 9TH

In September 1899, a group of Langlade county residents formed the new Citizens Brewing Co. to compete with Antigo Brewing Co. In 1913, the name of the firm was changed to Northern Manufacturing Company, though it continued in the beer business. Shortly after the advent of Prohibition, the plant was sold to the Langlade Farmer's Cooperative and converted into a warehouse.

As the end of Prohibition neared, Antigo residents hoped to build a new brewery, and twenty local businessmen met to plan a brewery that would employ forty men, though Northern Lakes Brewing Co. never got past the planning stages. (A label from Citizens Brewing Company is found in chapter 6.)

APPLETON *(Outagamie County)*

Anton Fisher (1858–1860)
Carl (Charles) Muench (1860–1882)
Mrs. Wallie Muench (1882–84)
Muench Brewing Company (1884–1893)
Mrs. Wallie Heid, Muench Brewery (1893–99)
Appleton Brewing & Malting Co. (1899–1917)
George Walter Brewing Co. (1918–1920)
1004 SOUTH [OLDE] ONEIDA ROAD

Appleton's founders intended it to be a virtuous university city. A laudatory passage in a county history claimed: "their previous religious training and the influence of the University raised the morals of this community to a high standard. Groggeries, doggeries or saloons were not permitted to locate here." When gaps in enforcement appeared, alcohol was branded as a foreign contaminant. The *Appleton Crescent* of 15 July 1854 bemoaned "Heretofore there have been sundry places where Menasha beer was bought and drank." However, strong liquor was a bigger menace, and by 1860 the *Crescent* reluctantly admitted "Most of the [whiskey] dealers have decided henceforth to sell nothing but beer and ale so that some good has been accomplished."

By this point, Appleton no longer needed to import beer from outside. Anton (John) Fisher started a brewery "on the old Menasha road, above the old canal." After two years (one source claims the sale was in 1859), Fisher sold to Charles Muench (or Carl, even listed as Joseph), who had previously worked as a foreman in the Schlitz brewery. He began to improve and expand the brewery. In 1863 he built a "Summer House" in the beer garden of what was now often called the "Fourth Ward Brewery." The brewery grew under Muench's guidance and sold more than 1,900 barrels in 1879. However, Muench died on 20 May 1880, while construction of a new brewhouse was underway. His widow Wallie took over management of the brewery and appears to have run the business well: *Western Brewer* praised the new brewery and said it "speaks volumes for the enterprise and business ability of Mrs. Muench." When she married brewery employee Math. Heid she was identified in newspaper accounts as "the wealthy proprietoress of the Muench brewery." (City directory ads in 1887 listed Mr. Heid as the proprietor.)

The brewery continued under the Muench name and became a joint stock company in 1891 with Mrs. Heid remaining in charge as president. Son William Muench was now an important member of the firm, and in 1893 he was sent to Chicago to buy new equipment, including a refrigeration plant. The brewery was destroyed in a devastating fire in 1894, but rebuilt with "all the latest improvements in machinery." The family sold the brewery in 1899 and the new owners formed Appleton Brewing & Malting Company. Among the officers was the brewmaster, John Haug, and Frank Fries, son of a former owner of the rival Star brewery. By 1910 the brewery was selling 19,000 barrels per year, most of it the Mellow Brau and Prime brands. Like many breweries of its size, it did its own malting and bottling, but it also

An Appleton delivery truck loaded with kegs, ca. 1910. COLLECTION OF BRIAN ZENEFSKI.

WISCONSIN BREWERIES AND BREWPUBS 363

boasted that it used "home barley exclusively," which was less common. The firm claimed a delivery radius (by wagon) of twenty miles and a workforce of twenty men.

The shortages brought on by American involvement in the First World War forced Appleton Brewing and Malting to combine with Geo. Walter Brewing Co. in 1918 in order to save fuel and other materials. The building was used mostly for storage after it closed in 1920, though the Wonder Instant Heat Co. proposed to use it to manufacture chemical heating and cooling products. (This company disappeared shortly thereafter and was suspected of fraud.) The Appleton Brewing & Malting site later became the location of the Stone Cellar/Arch brewpub.

George Muench (1862–68)
George Mayer (1868–1870?)
Mayer & Unmuth (1870?)
Louis Unmuth (1870)
Fries & Unmuth (1870–?)
Michael Fries (1871?–1876)
Susan and Elizabeth Kohl (1876–1877?)
Winz & Fries (1877?–1880)
Walter & Fries (1880–85?)
George Walter Brewery, aka Star Brewery (1885–1899)
Geo. Walter's Estate (1899–1903)
Geo. Walter Brewing Co. (1903–1920)
Geo. Walter Brewing Co. (1933–1972)

CORNER OF WALNUT & LAWRENCE (200/220 WALNUT)

The exact origins of Appleton's longest-lived brewery are not clear. The Geo. Walter Brewing Co. claimed an establishment date of 1862, but little has been found about George Muench's years as proprietor except a listing in an 1865 business directory. Muench himself was listed as a brewer in the 1860 census, but was probably working at Carl's brewery.

The "Third Ward Brewery" was an important meeting place for the local German community: in 1863 the German Draft Association met there to tell men how "to avail themselves of this opportunity to protect themselves against the Draft" into the Union army. Adler Brau historian Brian Zenefski has compiled the most complete research on the post-Muench years and has clarified the numerous changes in ownership. One county history claims that Michael Fries took over the business in 1869, though the records of R. G. Dun & Co. indicate that Louis Unmuth was the proprietor in 1870, and by the beginning of 1871 Unmuth and Fries were partners. *American Brewers' Gazette* showed that Fries produced no beer in 1871–72, which makes sense if he was not yet sole proprietor. When Fries died in 1876, ownership apparently passed to his two daughters, who later sold their interest to Werner Winz (often listed in sources as Wing). In 1880, George Walter, brewery foreman at the Carl Muench brewery, purchased a half interest in the brewery. Winz retired in 1885, after which Walter bought the remaining interest of Fries' descendants and changed the name to the Star Brewery. Walter had been trained as a brewer in Germany and had worked for Phillip Best and at Klinger's brewery in Whitewater prior to coming to Appleton. Through the expenditure of about $40,000, this "hustling, wide-awake" businessman built the capacity of the Star Brewery to 30,000 barrels and employed twelve men all year. Refrigeration equipment was added in 1896 (if not earlier) as part of another large expansion project.

During Prohibition, Geo. Walter Brewing Co. stayed in business making "'kickless brew" and soft drinks. Zenefski confirms that, like so many others, Bravo near beer was not popular, and the brewery stopped production and rented space to other businesses.

Like most breweries, Geo. Walter Brewing experienced a mix of success and frustration when beer came back on the market. Walter was not ready to sell on "New Beers Day," but chose to make a virtue out of the delay in newspaper ads that proclaimed: "We feel, however, that we could not risk producing a beer made under makeshift conditions. After all, the name of Adler Brau is synonymous with QUALITY." Nonetheless, there were occasional quality control problems: in 1938, state regulators ordered the company to adjust the bottling line because it was underfilling the bottles which put them at risk of prosecution.

Like many Wisconsin breweries, Geo. Walter was in good shape to take advantage of the wartime beer shortage, and increased production in the few years after the war. Walter joined other brewers in offering a smaller bottle (the Little Adler) and an annual bock, with dark malt purchased from Chilton Malting Co. (now Briess Malting). The brewery also produced Holiday Special during the winter. Longtime brewmaster Alex Knaus recounted that Holiday Special used imported hops and more grain, resulting in an alcohol content of about 4 percent, as opposed to Adler Brau which was 3.5 percent. The company only made three or four brews of Holiday Special each year, and it was only offered in bottles and cans. Sold for the same price as Adler Brau, it was made as a holiday gift to the customers.

Geo. Walter Brewing continued to emphasize their local roots in an attempt to head off competition from national brands. Full-page newspaper ads proclaimed that the brewery employed forty-six Fox Cities people,

The different window styles on each section reveal that the Geo. Walter Brewing Co. was built in stages. The bottle on the left section was almost ten feet tall and weighed 165 pounds. After the brewery closed, the bottle was removed and sold to Albers' Bar in Hilbert. (The bottle no longer exists; photograph from late 1960s.) COLLECTION OF BRIAN ZENEFSKI.

had a payroll of $224,000 and paid taxes of $385,000. (See sidebar in chapter 7.) The beer was "Made in Appleton, Especially for Fox Cities Tastes." Even while leaning heavily on tradition, Adler Brau was also a beer for the modern era because it was "Electronically Inspected." The brewery supported local charities: one ad featured a photo of a brewery truck driver distributing March of Dimes canisters.

However, sales continued to slip in the decades immediately after the war. By 1968 production was less than half the 54,000-barrel peak in 1947, and well below the 39,000 barrels sold in the resurgence of the early 1960s. As the struggles continued, a group headed by George M. Walter of Eau Claire's Walter Brewing Company purchased the Appleton brewery and promised to "take a more aggressive stance." Remodeling and repairs were started, and old-fashioned Adler Brau was slated to return in earlier packaging. However, the brewery's stockholders rejected the new arrangement, and the brewery closed for good at the end of April 1972.

Mors & Becker (1867?–?)
Becker & Bayer (1870?–1871?)
FOURTH WARD

The 1867 excise records list Mors & Becker of Appleton as a brewery of less than 500 barrels. *American Breweries II* includes an L. Becker operating in the 1870s: this is probably Edward Becker, who in 1870 was a 43-year-old Prussian living in the fourth ward. He shared lodgings with Anton Beyer, a 42-year-old countryman who was apparently a partner in the brewery. Neither of the two owned any real estate, so they may have been leasing their brewery. Becker and "Beir" appear in the 1872 state business directory, though by this time they had begun a partnership with Theodore Knapstein in nearby Hortonia Township, just southeast of New London.

Krefertz & Wing (1877–79)

The R. G. Dun records list Krefertz & Wing as brewers from 1877 to 1879. They indicate that the two "formerly worked in a Brewer [sic] here and started from what they saved from their wages." This account seems to indicate they started their own small brewery, but the presence of Wing (or Winz) leaves open the possibility that they took over another brewery for a brief period. They were not listed separately in Salem's 1880 records, but if they were out of business by that point they would not have responded to his survey.

Nicholas Kirsch (1896–97)
PACIFIC & BATEMAN

It is possible that Kirsch succeeded George Dambruch, who was listed as a brewer on Pacific Avenue in the 1895 city directory, but was later listed as a soda water manufacturer. There is also a possibility that Kirsch or Dambruch were simply agents for another brewer—agents were sometimes listed in directories as breweries. The other mystery brewer of Appleton, Joseph Dethier, was not linked with this address.

Appleton Brewing Co.
Dos Bandidos (1989–1997)
Adler Brau Pub & Restaurant (1997–2005)
Stone Cellar Brewpub (2005–2017)
Stone Arch Brewery (2012–present)
Stone Arch Brewpub (2017–present)
1004 SOUTH OLDE ONEIDA STREET

The site of Appleton's oldest brewery seemed like a logical spot to create Appleton's first brewery in almost two decades. John and Phyllis Jungers opened Appleton Brewing Co. in 1989 in what was once Appleton Brewing & Malting Co. and was by then Between the Locks Mall. John Jungers worked with Gary Bauer to develop methods and recipes and hired Bill Gilbert to be the first head brewer, though eventually Jungers took over most of the brewing himself. Most beers were sold under the Adler Brau label, though they bore little resemblance to the old Walter product. (The Adler Brau label became unregistered after seven years of non-use.) Appleton Brewing produced about four hundred barrels its first year.

While usually classified as a brewpub, Appleton Brewing Co. supplied more than one restaurant in the complex so it went slightly beyond the original brewpub model. At first their beers were served in Skyline Haus as well as the Mexican restaurant Dos Bandidos (which is often listed as the name of the brewpub during this era). Adler Brau was also available at Johnny O's pizza place until it closed in 1994. In 1997 Dos Bandidos closed and the space was converted to Adler Brau Pub and Restaurant—a name which placed more emphasis on the beer.

Jungers also went well beyond most early brewpubs in his production for markets outside Between the Locks. While the biggest project was brewing beer for games of the Wisconsin Timber Rattlers minor league baseball team, he also brewed beers for local festivals like Greenville Catfish Races or Omro Oktoberfest, or even large family celebrations. He brewed Republican Ale for a festival in Ripon, which claims to be the birthplace of the Republican party. He also developed beers containing ginseng and another that tasted like shiitake mushrooms. When selling beer at baseball games, production was around 1,000 barrels per year.

In 2004, Jungers retired and the father and son team of Tom and Steve Lonsway purchased the company. Steve had previously operated Homebrew Market in Appleton, and was a brewer for Fox River Brewing Co. (at both locations). The next year they changed the name of the business to Stone Cellar Brewpub and built a reputation with several award-winning beers. In their first year, Stone Cellar brewed less than 500 barrels, but they began steadily to increase production. From the beginning, the Lonsways operated a small bottling line and shipped kegs of beer to other restaurants in the area. Ultimately, demand became so strong that they expanded the brewery and created a new entity, Stone Arch Brew House, to supply the market with bottled and draught beers for consumption elsewhere. (A Stone Cellar coaster is pictured in chapter 10.)

In 2012, the Lonsways expanded the brewery in order to sell more bottled beer in outside retail outlets. However, they discovered the Stone Cellar name was already trademarked by a winery, so they renamed the brewery and the bottled beer Stone Arch, emphasizing a feature of the underground portion of the old brewery made from locally harvested fieldstone. By 2013, Stone Arch beer was already available in over 200 off-premises accounts. (As of 2017, about 21 percent of the annual production was bottled beer.) Stone Arch continued to brew beer for local festivals, such as the Mile of Music festival in Appleton and the similar Electric City Experience in Kaukauna. The same year the Lonsways bought the nearby Riverview Gardens event center to host larger events than the brewpub could hold, including buffets for Easter, Mothers' Day and Fathers' Day. In 2017 the Lonsways decided to consolidate the brewery, brewpub and event center under the Stone Arch name to eliminate confusion and create a stronger identity for the business and brand.

Fox Classic Brewing Co. (1991–92)
318 West College Avenue

Former high school English teacher Todd Hanson began planning the Fox Classic Brewing Co. in 1989. A homebrewer since the mid-1970s, he became one of the earliest to "go pro." His investors were primarily family and friends. The brewery was located in an "entertainment complex" in the Park Central building. Unusually for an early microbrewery, Hanson specialized in lagers. The brewery had some striking silver foil labels and named beers after famous local figures such as Father Jacques Marquette and Harry Houdini. The beers were released in kegs and 12-ounce bottles, but Hanson's expectations for sales were probably beyond what the market could then support.

Fox River Brewing II (1997–2007)
Fratello's Restaurant & Brewery (2007–2012)
Fox River Brewing Company (2012–present)
4301 West Wisconsin Avenue (Fox River Mall)

Opened as a branch of Fox River Brewing of Oshkosh in 1997, the brewery built a strong business in the Grand Chute neighborhood. The name change to Fratello's in 2007 represented no change of ownership or management. The establishment changed its name again to Fox River Brewing Company in 2012. The beers brewed at Appleton and Oshkosh were the same, but some included Appleton heritage in their names such as Houdini Honey Ale and Paper City Pilsner. Fox River Brewing installed a bottling line at the Appleton location in 2015, after which production jumped to over 1,100 barrels. (See Oshkosh for more information about Fox River Brewing.)

Appleton Beer Factory (2013–present)
603 West College Avenue

Appleton Beer Factory represents the fruits of a multi-year renovation of the former Schreiter Auto Supply building in the historic downtown. Many of the furnishings were built from material reclaimed from the shop or the apartments upstairs. Most of the labor was done by the father-son team of Jeff and Ben Fogle and their wives Leah and Mairi—they estimated that about 25,000 hours of work went into preparing the space and fabricating the brewing equipment. Appleton Beer Factory opened in November 2013 and quickly established its credentials as a favorite location for beer lovers. The styles have all been ales which first bore the style name, though they acquired more colorful names later. After becoming established, they have made experiments with barrel-aging.

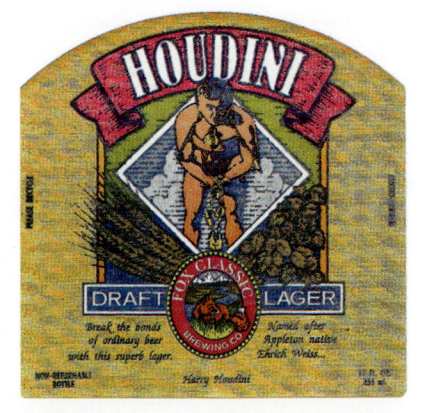

Appealing to the local market, Fox Classic beers were named for famous area residents. Erich Weiss gained worldwide fame as escape artist Harry Houdini. Collection of Scott Reich.

Arcadia (Trempealeau County)

Bills & Mergener (1872–75)
Nick Mergener & Co. (1875–76)
C. Wolf & Bion (1876)
Shebert & Bion (1876–77)
John Bion (1877–78)
John N. Fertig (1878–1883)
Fugina Bros. & Fertig (1883–86)
John Bion (1886–1890)
Courtney & Fricker (1890–92)
William Fricker (aka Hohmann & Fricker) (1892–97)
Fricker & Hugn (1897–98)
William Fricker (1898–1900)
Arcadia Brewing Co. (1900–1909)
Arcadia Brewery, Peter Kronschnabel (1909–1920)
Arcadia Brewing Co. (1934–1949)
Corner of 3rd and Main (101/109 North 3rd Street)

According to the 1917 county history, "The Arcadia Brewery has long occupied a leading position in Arcadia business life." It could be nothing less in a village where St. Joseph's Catholic Congregation was licensed as a retail malt liquor dealer. While some sources have Nick Mergener starting the brewery in 1872, he was still part of Kasper Neher & Co. in Augusta at this time, so a starting date around 1875 seems more likely. Arcadia's brewery went through a rapid succession of owners and lessees before finally settling down. In 1876 it was destroyed by fire, but Bion & Co. built "an imposing structure" which served as part of the brewery for several decades. Unlike many of their contemporaries, their loss was covered fully by insurance. When the Bradstreet Company assessed the creditworthiness of Wisconsin firms at the beginning of 1884, they noted that Fugina Bros. & Fertig ran a general store as well as the brewery (and gave them a "very good" credit rating—the highest they could have at their level of wealth). Christian Bion joined his brother in the business in 1887.

The Arcadia brewery suffered an unusual misfortune in 1891, when a vandal dumped

This post-Prohibition Arcadia sign included an uncommon feature: a thermometer. COLLECTION OF TYE SCHWALBE.

soap into a vat of beer—luckily the "mischief" was discovered before the bad beer reached the public. A single bad batch would have been a notable setback for a brewery only producing about 1,000 barrels per year in the 1890s and which was still dependent on horsepower.

At the end of the century, William Fricker gave up ownership to the newly formed Arcadia Brewing Co., but stayed on as brewmaster. The officers of the company were all leading businessmen, including vice president Napoleon Cramolini, a publisher who was described in a contemporary account as a "cultivated and educated typo" (the word typo was actually the typographical error). In 1909, brewmaster Peter Kronschnabl leased the brewery from the company and managed it until Prohibition. Perhaps even more mobile than other brewers of his era, he had worked at least eight different breweries around the Upper Midwest before arriving at Arcadia.

During Prohibition, the company reorganized under Kronschanbl's son-in-law Ralph Haines as the Arcadia Bottling Works, but did not entirely give up the old product. Federal agents raided the former brewery in October 1931 and broke up brewing equipment and dumped a quantity of homebrew so great that residents downstream on the Trempealeau River reported smelling the beer as it flowed by.

Like many undercapitalized breweries, Arcadia had trouble preparing for legal beer, and was not ready for market until July 1934. Under the direction of Kronschnabl and Joseph Weiter, an investor living in Mexico, new machinery and fermenters were installed to double capacity to 20,000 barrels. By 1936 they had added bottled beer to their line-up and were expanding sales. In 1937 Weiter retired, and local businessmen purchased the brewery.

After Prohibition, Arcadia fit the romantic picture of a classic small Wisconsin brewery—making sure locals had plenty of free beer. This, however, stood the company in poor stead with the state authorities (as noted in chapter 7). The brewery had numerous other problems as well. The BTD was suspicious of the high rate of loss and waste reported by Arcadia, but an investigator found that the brewery was using pre-Prohibition bottling equipment that filled only ten bottles at a time and could only cap one bottle at a time, so which broke more than the usual number of bottles in the process. Even small misfortunes were magnified. One of their distributors in Ellsworth reported that mice or rats had eaten the revenue stamps on eighty-five cases of Arcadia beer, which could not then be sold. Like several other small Wisconsin brewers, production peaked in the mid-1940s, but the precipitous drop from 17,000 barrels in 1946 to 2,000 in 1947 showed that the end was near. the brewery closed for good in 1949.

ARENA (Iowa County)

Lake Louie Brewing Co. LLC (2000–present)
7556 PINE ROAD

Lake Louie isn't really much of a lake—really a quarter-acre pond. Tom Porter left his engineering career to start a brewery with his 401k savings, and liked the local water, which was nearly identical to that of Burton-on-Trent. While the water supply was excellent, the rural location meant there were no public sewers, so wastewater was first treated on site and later put into holding tanks and trucked out for treatment. As a consequence, Lake Louie uses much less water per barrel of beer than most breweries (about a five to one ratio). The obvious first beer, a porter, required some experimentation, but reached the market in January 2000 and soon became popular in its limited distribution area around Madison.

The original three-barrel system was soon too small to keep up with demand, and Porter was compelled to expand to a fifteen-barrel system within two years. In 2005 they introduced six packs, which helped expand their market beyond what could be reached by draft accounts or growler sales. By 2007 capacity was 2,000 barrels, but that doubled by 2011 and distribution was expanded statewide. The brewery's offerings cover the full range of ales, and have been notable for including several different scotch ales—in fact, the Warped Speed Scotch Ale has become the flagship beer.

In 2014, Lake Louie introduced three new series: Hop-A-Louie, Session, and Dark Shadows. Several of the new beers, such as Bunny Green Toe IPA were named after movie or television references. One of the session beers, 10-81, refers to the police code for a breathalyzer request. In an interview, Porter claimed the new beers were partially about preventing boredom but also argued "'I feel that with trends right now that any small brewer sitting on their laurels and saying "I've got a flagship and my bills are paid" has a mindset that is going to get them to become a former brewery . . .'" After fifteen years of brewing, Lake Louie finally released its first traditional lager,

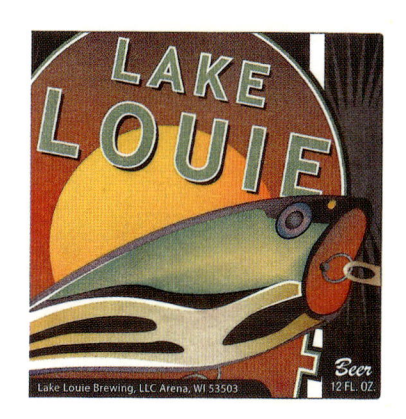

Lake Louie labels, ca. 2012. The specific beer is indicated on a neck label. COLLECTION OF SCOTT REICH.

WISCONSIN BREWERIES AND BREWPUBS 367

an Octoberfest. Since then, their Pilsner has joined the regular lineup.

ASHLAND (Ashland County)

Bay City Brewery (late 1850s?)
The exhaustive and reasonably reliable *History of Northern Wisconsin* published in 1881 reported: "The first brewery [in Ashland] was built in Bay City, but was discontinued after a short time." Bay City was on the eastern end of pioneer Ashland, and was vacated in 1860. This suggests a date in the late 1850s for the brewery.

Frank X. Schottmueller, Ashland Brewery (1872–1885)
Philip Becker, Ashland Brewery (1885–1892)
900 EAST 2ND STREET
Frank (or Francis) X. Schottmueller left his brewery in Taylors Falls, Minnesota, to establish what was described as "a large stone brewery" in the growing port city of Ashland in 1872." He first appears in the excise records in November of that year. Production records indicate his output was usually around 200 barrels a year, though when the Ashland Union brewery opened his sales dropped to 79 barrels in 1875—whether this was from competition or other factors is not clear. Schottmueller remained in Ashland as a grocer after leaving the brewery, though he also resumed ownership of his former brewery in Minnesota.

Philip Becker took over the brewery in 1885—another stop on his brewing odyssey around the state. One industry journal reported in 1887 that he had a partner named Dutean. The brewery closed with no fanfare in 1892 as Becker focused his attentions on his Hurley brewery.

Goeltz & Miller, Ashland Union Brewing Co. (1874–1876?)
ELLIS DIVISION ON BAY CITY CREEK
The *Milwaukee Sentinel* noted that a second brewery was being built in Ashland, and the *Ashland Press* of 8 August 1874 provided a complete description of the plant. It reported it was "one of what is known as the new process breweries," though the description was typical of other breweries of the era. It claimed a starting capacity of forty barrels a day, but it was "only being run to meet present demand." Ashland Union produced 254 barrels in its first year of operation, but did not survive more than a few years. It is not included in Salem's list or business directories after 1876. Adam Goeltz later built and operated a saloon and boarding house.

Miller & Co. (1888–1899)
Ashland Brewing & Malting (1891–1901)
Ashland Brewing Co. (1901–1920)
Ashland Brewing Co. (1934–37)
100 BLOCK, 10TH AVENUE EAST
In summer 1887, the *Milwaukee Daily Journal* reported that Miller & Co. were planning to erect a brewery in Ashland. It was operational by 1888, and while it was called Miller & Co. for a decade, city directory entries listing it as Ashland Brewing Co. appeared as early as 1891.

By 1913, Ashland Brewing Co. was selling 20,000 barrels per year in a fifty-mile radius around the city while employing about 30 men. F. W. Miller was still the president of the firm, though it does not appear that he took a regular role in management. The firm was outspoken on the prohibition question. The manager of the brewery participated in a local option meeting at an area church, and the directors published a resolution against the proposed laws. As municipalities in northern Wisconsin went dry in the 1910s, Ashland Brewing sought to capitalize by offering to ship beer by the keg, case, or an early example of a six-pack to residents of surrounding towns. The ad urged customers "Because your town has gone "DRY" do not become a whiskey drinker. We will be glad to assist you in being truly temperate, by furnishing you "ASHLAND," the Beer of Purity." Among the products offered was their version of Standard Porter from Rochester, New York, but it is not clear whether they were brewing it or simply bottling it. (An image of the bottle is in chapter 2.)

By 1919, plans were underway to convert the brewery into a malted milk factory. The Ashland Brewing Co. returned to brewing after Prohibition, but was slow to commence production. Mr. C. Scott claimed that the plant would be ready by July 1933, but production did not actually start until May 1934, and was by then under the ownership of Theodore Oudenhaven, who was also president of the Electric City Brewing Co. in Kaukauna. Production was never more than a few hundred barrels per month, and from the middle of 1936 it dropped precipitously from 440 barrels in July to a paltry 6.75 barrels in February 1937. By May of that year, Edward B. Johnson, receiver of the bankrupt company, informed the Beverage Tax Division that he was selling the last few cases of White Ribbon Beer—"The Ace of Taste"— and wrapping up the business.

South Shore Brewing Co. (1995–present)
SOO LINE DEPOT, THIRD AVENUE WEST AT FOURTH STREET (1995–2000); 808 WEST MAIN STREET (2001–PRESENT)
Eugene "Bo" Bélanger established South Shore Brewing Co. in 1995 in the old Soo Line Depot. The companion business Railyard (Brew)Pub was located in the same building. They started

South Shore bottles from 2000 to 2010. The early six-pack box is from when the brewery was located in the Soo Line depot pictured on the side. After the fire, labels read "Hand Crafted in the Historic Downtown District." The labels depict Ashland's historic ore dock, at one time the largest in the world). AUTHOR'S COLLECTION.

bottling later in 1995, during which two people hand-filled and hand-labeled 22-ounce bomber bottles at what Bélanger described as "the breakneck speed of ten cases per hour." However, the brewery suffered from the same "Red Demon" which bedeviled many earlier breweries. In the spring of 1997, there was a fire on the restaurant side that left the brewhouse intact. However, a disastrous fire on 1 April 2000 gutted the historic depot and forced the brewery to look for a new home. South Shore relocated a few blocks away in the old L. C. Wilmarth #1 building (in which this author's ancestors once operated a printing company) and reopened in May 2001. Once again, South Shore was associated with an independently owned restaurant, Deep Water Grille.

Bélanger and South Shore have been among the leading Wisconsin brewers in using locally grown ingredients. They were one of six founding members of the Midwest Hops and Barley Co-op, and in 2008, Belanger and a neighbor grew 140,000 bushels of barley—enough to supply the brewery's base malt needs for the next year. Bélanger's interest in "grain to glass" brewing was inspired by his maternal grandfather, who owned a farm in Indiana on which Bo and his family helped with harvests.

South Shore was an early proponent of creative beers: in 2007 Bo brewed Applefest Ale with locally pressed cider and released the first version of Bourbon Barrel Coffee Mint Stout—and a barrel-aged version of the brew that was often one of the most talked about offerings at beer festivals of the era. However, most of South Shore's beers are on the lower end of the alcohol range and designed for repeat drinking. For six years, Bélanger commuted to brew for Olde Hayward Eatery & Brewpub (Muskie Capital) in which he was a co-owner.

Ashwaubenon *(Brown County)*

Legends of Ashwaubenon (2003–2013?)
940 Waube Lane
Opened as a branch of Legends of Green Bay in 2003, this sports bar had a slightly different feel than the other locations, but similar menu items and beers.

Augusta *(Eau Claire County)*

Kaspar Neher (& Co.) (1870–78)
Neher's first appearance in the excise records at Augusta was in February 1870, and he and his neighbor Nicholas Mergener were listed as brewers in the 1870 census. Along with partner Jacob Haskett, the small company produced fewer than 100 barrels in its first year, but increased to more than 180 barrels by 1875. The editor of the *Augusta Herald* thought highly of their product and praised it in print several times, as well as insinuating that he should get a complimentary keg upon the birth of Neher's son. Records of production exist through 1875, but credit reports of R. G. Dun & Co. noted in October 1876 that Neher's Augusta brewery was mortgaged (at that point he was part of the Huber and Neher partnership brewing in Chippewa Falls). The *Eau Claire Daily Free Press* reported (perhaps belatedly) in June 1878 that the Augusta brewery had been closed up and advocated converting it into a cheese factory.

Avon Center *(Rock County)*

James Lane (1871)
James Lane made a brief appearance in the excise records in 1871. He produced for three months during the spring—though never more than two barrels in a month.

Aztalan *(Jefferson County)*

Foster & Danner (1860?–1867)
George Foster (1867–1873)
Leissegger & Burns (1874–75)
George Foster (1876?–1878)
Charles Baireuther (1882–89)
Johnson Creek Road
George Foster and Henry Danner began brewing north of Aztalan sometime in the early 1860s. Danner left the partnership in 1867, and Foster hired eighteen-year-old Rudolph Heger to work in the brewery. George Foster's brewery produced just under 500 barrels a year at its peak in the early 1870s. Like many small breweries, it was taxed on nearly twice as much beer during the early summer months as during the rest of the year. The brewery narrowly avoided destruction by fire in 1871 when the nearby marsh caught fire. Foster was not able to escape an $800 fine in 1871 for violation of revenue laws—a substantial sum equivalent to the revenue from about one hundred kegs of beer. According to Schade, the new ownership of Leissegger & Burns just missed the 500-barrel mark, selling 499 during 1874. Leissegger and Burns may have been leasing the brewery from Foster, since he was reported to be the owner of the "Marsh Brewery Farm" again when he injured his hand in the malt mill at his brewery. Ironically, a similar accident occurred during his previous tenure in 1873 when a boy "got [his] wrist mangled in some machinery. Foster died a year later, and the obituary noted that the business "was unprofitable & his wealth dwindled away."

The brewery apparently remained vacant for four years, until Charles Baireuther traded his horse and lot for the old Foster brewery. It is possible that Baireuther did not start brewing right away, because an 1888 *Jefferson Banner* article reported that "Baireuther now has his brewery running full blast, & his beer wagon is seen on the streets every morning." Unfortunately, Baireuther suffered two catastrophic fires almost exactly a year apart. After the May 1889 fire he rebuilt quickly, but when the brewery burned again in May 1890 the rebuilding process dragged out over several years. It is unclear whether Baireuther ever brewed in the new facility, but in 1894 Hugo Graf, an employee of Pabst, purchased it. Graf next appeared in local accounts is as the local agent for Pabst, so it is likely that he did not brew his own beer. Graf moved to Burlington in 1896 and the brewery appears to have been abandoned, though a 1975 *Banner* article included photos of the cellar from the old brewery.

Baileys Harbor *(Door County)*

Door County Brewing Co. (2013–present)
2434 County Road F
Despite the importance of tourism in Door County, the area had been without a

production brewery since before World War II. But in 2013, John and Angie McMahon and their sons Danny and Ben started production at their small brewery in Baileys Harbor. At first, some of their beer was produced under contract at Sand Creek Brewing in Black River Falls, but over time, production moved to the Baileys Harbor facility. The first brewery tap room opened in 2014. Door County's beers exhibited a strong Belgian influence, both from the Belgian heritage of the region and because of the brewers' tastes. Among their more noteworthy beers were a series of farmhouse ales for each season. In July 2017 Door County Brewing opened a new tap room at 2088 Highway 57.

BALDWIN (St. Croix County)

John P. Mueller (1873?–1875)
"East of Town"

The *Milwaukee Sentinel* also noted in September 1873 "At Baldwin they are building a brewery and circulating a petition for a Good Templars Lodge." The *Baldwin Bulletin* added that the proprietor was John P. Mueller. It is likely this was not his first brewery building, since the *Bulletin* noted in January 1874 "Mr. M. has heretofore been unable to supply the demand, and when we consider the quality of that manufactured by him, in comparison with the impure stuff made in St. Paul, we are not surprised that every dealer prefers Baldwin beer." By September, Mueller was already adding to his brewery. Unfortunately, one of Mueller's sons was injured while working at the grain mill, which forced the partial amputation of several fingers. Mueller produced 957 barrels in 1874, which was more than many established breweries in larger cities, however production dropped precipitously to 161 barrels in 1875—which suggests that he may not have operated for the full year.

It is possible that Mueller used at least some local hops, since they were grown in the area and were reported still to be clinging to a fence at the Hopyard School in the 1930s.

BANGOR (La Crosse County)

Joseph Hussa (1862?–1891)
Estate of Joseph Hussa (1891–95)
Hussa Brewing Company (1895–1920)
West End of Commercial Street (West of Modern Seventeenth Street)

When Joseph Hussa started his brewery in Bangor is in some question. *100 Years of Brewing* claimed 1858, but the 1860 population census places both Joseph and brother John in Fox Lake, boarding with and probably junior partners of Frank Liebenstein. In some records, ownership of the Bangor firm was listed as J. & J. Hussa in the late 1860s and early 1870s. Despite being so close to the major brewing center of La Crosse, the brewery thrived on a small scale for several decades: typically producing between 400 and 1,000 barrels each year. Following Joseph's death, his heirs undertook significant expansions. *100 Years* reported that a malt house was added in 1893 and a bottling plant in 1896. These improvements helped push sales from 650 barrels in 1885 to 4,760 in 1895 and to 8,500 barrels in 1902.

The Hussa brewery suffered many of the typical industry disasters. The plant caught fire on 15 February 1911 and suffered a loss close to $50,000. The damage was higher than it might have been, for though fire crews arrived from La Crosse, mud in the water clogged the fire engine and made it impossible to pump. This may have been the motivation for creating an unusual and possibly unique municipal water arrangement. By 1916, the city of Bangor owned 6,100 feet of water mains, but the Hussa brewery owned the wells, the pumps, and the water—and collected the revenue. The city had a contract with the brewery for hydrant service, fire protection and public fountain service. When restrictions on fuel use were imposed after entry into World War I, the Hussa Brewing Company was ordered to close in February 1918 for violating the Monday closing order designed to conserve fuel. However, the brewery successfully appealed the order by claiming the brewery was responsible for heating and furnishing water for the village.

The approach of Prohibition encouraged the company to act quickly rather than hope beer still would be allowed. By mid-1919, the brewery already had been converted to a pickle factory under the same management.

Kinky Kabin Brewing Co. (2012–13)
105 16th Avenue North

The first brewery in Bangor since Prohibition started production in a former garage in October 2012. Owner and brewer Jeff Steidl used modified dairy equipment to produce his Apricot Naughty Wheat beer, which was sold in bottles and on draught. Steidl hoped to brew 200 barrels his first year, but only produced fifty. The brewery closed in December 2013.

BARABOO (Portage County)

H. A. McCartny (1850–1851?)

H. A. McCartny began advertising in the *Sauk County Standard* of Baraboo in July 1850, proclaiming "Citizens supplied at their door." McCartny does not appear in the 1850 census. An article in the Sauk County Standard of 5 October 1853 specifically notes that there was no

The view of the brewery on this tray does not match Sanborn insurance map depictions. The bottle house at lower left is rotated 180°; the wagon house at far right rear is missing a chicken house; and the building between the wagon house and residence does not appear on any maps between 1892 and 1922. Collection of Gary Schultz.

brewery in Baraboo, so he must have closed prior to that time. A note in the 1880 county history claiming "[T]he first brewery in the place was located on the north side of the river, and was burned down, with other property, at an early day" may have referred to McCartny's brewery.

M. Schu (1860?)

M. Schu and his younger brother (?) Jacob were listed as brewers in the 1860 population census. They owned substantial property, so it is likely though not certain they operated a brewery at least for a while.

George Ruhland (1866?–1902)
Ruhland Brewing Company (1902–1918?)
235 Lynn Street

While *100 Years of Brewing* claims that Ruhland founded his brewery in 1867, the 1880 History of Sauk County claims he started in 1866. He does not appear in tax records until 1871. In the 1870s Ruhland's was among the smaller breweries in the region but showed the growth typical of similar breweries at the time, selling 241 barrels in 1874 and expanding to 470 by 1879. The 1880 history explained: "capacity . . . has been increased from time to time to accommodate local custom." With the approach of Prohibition the financial position of the brewery deteriorated, and by mid-1918 the firm was in bankruptcy court, though some sources suggest the brewery ceased production in 1915. (It was still listed in a 1916 industry directory, though these had a tendency to lag behind events.) In 1918 residents of Baraboo voted the city dry, and the brewery's fate was sealed.

Parrish & Brother (1867–68)
Parrish & Bow (1868–1870)
412 Oak Street

Loomis and Caleb Parrish had both lived in Baraboo for a time, but Caleb then moved to Oregon and Loomis became involved with a brewery in Sparta. In November 1866 they returned to Baraboo and purchased a building which they quickly converted to a brewery. The ale brewery of Parrish (or Parish) and Brother first appears in tax records in January 1867, though local papers indicated that the first brewing did not take place until February. In 1868, Loomis sold his share to Edwin R. Bow, who carried on the business with Caleb Parrish, though they put the brewery up for sale in June of that year and did not brew during the period when the brewery was on the market. Parrish & Bow seem to have been more interested in their feed store than the brewery, but appear to have brewed on and off until 1870, when, according to the 1880 county history, "the business was suspended." Loomis Parrish moved to Eau Claire and managed a brewery there for several years.

Bender & Miller (1867–1870)
George Bender (1870–74)
Anna Bender (1874–1880)
Bender & Effinger, Baraboo City Brewery (1880–1881?)
Ferdinand Effinger (1881?–1911)
F. Effinger Brewing Co. (1911–1920)
The Effinger Co. (1933–1949)
Effinger Brewing Co. (1949–1966)
331/335 Lynn Street

The 1880 county history reported that George Bender and Frank Miller founded Baraboo's third brewery of 1867, but that Miller withdrew shortly after the founding—circumstances borne out by tax records. Bender appears to have had trouble making money at first. The R. G. Dun & Co. records note that "When he was running his brewery without retailing, he was pretty hard up, but he now keeps a Saloon in his brewery + is making money. Was consid[ered] rich before he built the brewery, invested all he had prob[ably]." Bender provides a nineteenth-century example of how a brewery taproom was essential to build the brand and cash flow—a method adopted by many twenty-first century craft breweries.

George Bender died in 1874 but left his widow Anna with few debts, and she carried on the business with great vigor—even adding a two-story hotel to the complex at the corner of Bridge Street. With the help of her oldest son Robert, Mrs. Bender's brewery became the largest in town, passing the 500-barrel mark in 1879. At the end of 1879, Ferdinand Effinger arrived in town, and took over as superintendent of the brewery. The next year Effinger rented the brewery with Adolph Bender, and around 1881 he bought out Bender and ran the business on his own. The brewery was destroyed by fire in July 1884, but Effinger held his customers by distributing Milwaukee beer until his new brewery was completed. The brewery installed a bottling operation in 1896, and with the work of five employees could produce 5,000 barrels a year. Effinger purchased one of the first trucks in Baraboo in 1908, but could only use it for city deliveries because the roads in the surrounding country were so bad. A large expansion in 1913 featured an artificial refrigeration plant, allowing the brewery to discontinue using ice.

When Prohibition arrived, Effinger switched to producing near beer and soft drinks. The first name chosen for the near beer was Nearo, but Effinger cancelled that plan upon discovering that the name was already owned by Dick Bros. Brewing Co. of Quincy, Illinois. In addition, they launched a line of ice cream that was so popular that dairy giant Borden purchased it in 1931. The same year, the directors of the company sensed that there was "much agitation for the return of manufacture of beer and deem it advisable at this time to place the plant in usable condition . . ." Unfortunately, the brewery was in bad shape. The insulation in the cold storage rooms had

A tin sign (ca. 1900s) titled "A Good Judge." The center is slightly convex. COURTESY OF NATIONAL BREWERY MUSEUM.

rotted and decayed, the ceiling and floor of the keg racking room had fallen in, and much of the machinery had deteriorated from lack of use and maintenance. Effinger hired the eminent brewery architect Richard Griesser to draw plans for remodeling. The record is not clear on whether Effinger had beer ready on "New Beers' Day," but they certainly had beer on the market shortly after 7 April 1933.

The 1930s and 40s brought change to the brewery but also some degree of success. Like other breweries, Effinger had to adjust to new regulations and market realities. In 1935, the directors noted "the public in general seems to be inclined to favor the milder fermented beverage," and amended their production to increase the amount of 3.2 percent beer—a move that would also save the company money by using less grain. Increased sales enabled the company to buy new equipment and expand their range, though in 1943 they closed the wholesale office in Madison. The brewery had a particularly good year in 1944, profit per barrel and case was up, and the company increased the annual Christmas bonus to the employees to $25 (compared to $10 in the previous three years).

Like several other local breweries, Effinger reached peak production of about 18,000 barrels in the years immediately after World War II. But like many of their counterparts, business began to slide thereafter. The company undertook several initiatives to boost sales. They started a newsletter directed at customers (mostly taverns selling the beer at retail)

Advertising a darker beer by suggesting it would go well with a cigar was common; showing the beer in a wine glass was less so (ca. 1910). COLLECTION OF JOHN STEINER.

"to help you sell more beer." In 1952 newsletters promoted the 7-ounce bottle but also noted that Effinger "consistently sold over 80 percent of our production in draft beer."

Effinger tried to make the most of its location in the center of a popular tourist area by introducing labels in 1954 that advertised "In the Devil's Lake—Dells Region." The *Wisconsin Teamster* proclaimed in 1960 that the brewery employed twenty-two workers and used seven trucks to serve a fifty-mile radius, and noted that some of the flagship Badger Brew went to other large cities. But these numbers did not reveal the underlying weakness of the company. From 1956 to 1959 the brewery incurred an average loss of $20,000 a year, and started to distribute Miller products to increase income. In 1960, production dipped below 10,000 barrels and never recovered. Effinger attempted to distribute Badger Brew in Milwaukee, but lost sales when their major account went out of business and when the brewery was forced to raise the price of the beer. Competition from national brands and local wage and price conditions doomed the business. Ultimately, the company elected to sell the Badger Brew name and all remaining packaging, labels and cooperage to the Oshkosh Brewing Co. in March 1966. (More on the reasons for the final closing of Effinger is found in chapter 8.)

Conway Pub & Brewing Co. (2003–?)
215 SOUTH BOULEVARD
This brewpub opened in 2003 but had little time to get established.

BEAVER DAM *(Dodge County)*

Mike Biersach, Beaver Dam Brewery (1853–55)
Biersach & Liebenstein (1855–56)
Goeggerle & Patzlsberger (1856–1863)
John Goeggerle (1863–1901)
J. Goeggerle Brewing Co. (1901–2)
Julia Goeggerle (1902–4)
Louis Ziegler (1905–1920)
Louis Ziegler Brewing Co. (1933–1953)
516 MADISON AV.

Michael Biersach (Biersack) built a brewery in Beaver Dam in 1853 for, as a city history put it, "the purpose of making his native brew." However, *100 Years of Brewing* claims that the first beer was "top fermentation beer" or ale, which was unlikely to be the lager familiar to German immigrants. Around 1855 Frank Liebenstein became a partner in the business, but in 1856 they sold the business and Liebenstein moved to nearby Fox Lake to start a brewery there. The new owners were John Goeggerle, and John and Joseph Patzlsberger, the last of whom had been employed by a brewery in Madison. In 1860 the Beaver Dam Brewery was the smallest of the three in town, but still produced 800 barrels. After Joseph died in 1862, Goeggerle bought out the remaining shares the next year and ran the brewery by himself

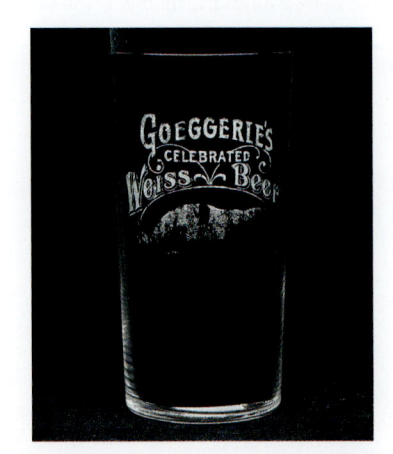

Very few pieces of breweriana from Goeggerle's brewery are known. The object under the name is badly worn but may have been a badger or another rodent. COLLECTION OF TYE SCHWALBE.

for the next four decades. During the Civil War, Goeggerle launched an additional product, a distilled liquor made from local fruit (called whiskey by one historian but more likely a form of schnapps). This drink became a feature of New Year's Eve celebrations at the brewery for many years. Goeggerle appears to have improved the brewery gradually over the years—building its capacity to more than 2,000 barrels by the mid-1880s and taking over as the largest brewery in Beaver Dam. By the time of Goeggerle's death in 1902, the brewery was making lager and weiss beer and was bottling at least some of the production. Frank Goeggerle took over operation of the brewery for two years, but he passed away in 1904. (The brewery was sometimes listed in directories under the name of John's widow Julia.)

Louis Ziegler, already proprietor of a brewery in Mayville, purchased the brewery at the beginning of 1905 and renamed the firm the Louis Ziegler Brewery. He built a new and larger brewery in 1906, a new bottling house in 1916, and other improvements along the way. The original brewhouse was razed in 1912.

During Prohibition, Ziegler produced near beer and malt syrup that was used to make home brew, which the Beaver Dam centennial history reported without any sense of surprise. However, in April 1920, Ziegler was arrested on charges of selling full-strength beer. Louis Ziegler died in 1927, and his wife Anna took over the business. As the repeal of Prohibition approached, the directors reorganized the company and began to prepare for legal beer. Local demand in Beaver Dam had to be met by imported beer for several weeks, but by the end of April the brewery was reopened. It was difficult for Ziegler Brewing Co. to establish their business in the years after repeal because of rapid changes in ownership. Louis Ziegler Jr. died in 1933, and the business changed hands several times until the Hutter Construction Company of Fond du Lac purchased the brewery. (The Hutters were related by marriage to the Zieglers.) The centennial history claimed that production was 50,000 barrels a year, but actual production figures were closer to 15,000 barrels per year. However, production spiked to approximately 36,000 barrels in 1946, which made the brewery an attractive purchase.

Robert D. Hamilton, a beer distributor in Los Angeles, was looking for breweries that could produce inexpensive beer for his West Coast accounts. He purchased Ziegler in 1946, and shortly thereafter added the former Ebner brewery in Fort Atkinson and the Kunz brewery in La Crosse to his holdings. After a brief surge in production to 38,000 barrels in 1949 (which may represent the production of all three plants—the records are not clear), sales dropped dramatically, though the brewery had a combination bottling and canning line by 1952, and offered Ziegler Old Fashioned Lager in cone-top cans. In 1953 only 2,000 barrels were made in the few months before closure.

Charles Schutte, Farmer's Brewery (1857–59)
Schutte & Aman (1859–1864)
Charles Schutte (1864–66)
(J.) Philip Binzel (1866–1898)
Binzel & Baum (1898–99)
J. Philip Binzel (1899–1902)
Louisa Binzel (1902–4)
J. Ph. Binzel Co., Binzel Brewery (1904–1920)
510 Madison Street

The centennial history of Beaver Dam boldly proclaims "All old histories tell us that the Farmers' Brewery, the second establishment of its kind in Beaver Dam, was built by Charles Schutte in 1857," though various spellings of Schutte appear and he is even called George in some accounts. Schutte took on George Aman as a partner in 1859, and they appear together in the 1860 census of industry. The partnership was dissolved in 1864 and Schutte continued alone. When John Philip Binzel's brewery in Waupun burned in 1866, he moved south in search of less-charred pastures, and purchased the Farmer's Brewery. Binzel had trained in Milwaukee with Schlitz and Blatz, and his reputation helped the

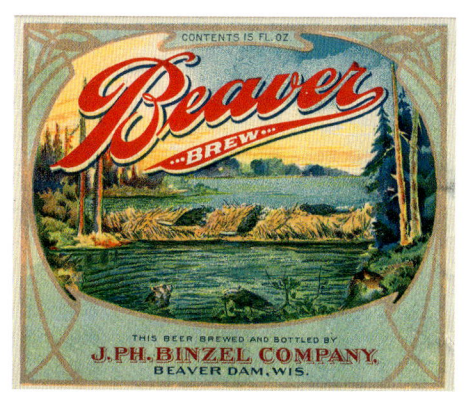

It was inevitable a Beaver Dam brewery would produce a label depicting a beaver dam. The contents of this bottle were listed as 15 ounces—an unusual volume, but many pre-Prohibition bottles contained amounts other than 12 ounces. COLLECTION OF JOHN STEINER.

brewery expand production. By the early 1880s, Binzel had the largest of the three breweries in town.

Increased demand forced Binzel to expand, and in 1892 the wooden brewery and malt house were torn down and replaced with brick structures. Visitors to the brewery could enjoy not just a mug of beer, but also fresh caraway rye bread baked by Philip's wife, Louisa, in a giant oven near the brewery. The brewery suffered a fire in 1894, but recovered quickly and continued to build its market through Philip's death in 1902. For four years, Louisa ran things

The Farmer's Brewery was typical of many early breweries: a small structure that could not be identified as a brewery without the barrels outside and the sign on the building. Engraving ca. 1860. COURTESY OF WISCONSIN HISTORICAL SOCIETY, WHI-97779.

with the help of sons Edward and Alvin, but in 1906, son Rudolph bought the brewery from his mother. Rudolph had attended Hantke's Brewer's School in Milwaukee and served as brewmaster at Kiewel's in Little Falls, Minnesota as well as helping in his father's brewery; he put his training to use by installing new equipment including a modern bottling line.

When Prohibition arrived, Binzel joined with his cousin Philip to organize the Oconomowoc Canning Company, and he later continued in the canning business in Marshfield. In 1936 the buildings were sold to the neighboring Louis Ziegler Brewing Co. for use as storage. After being used for a variety of storage and light industrial purposes, the buildings were razed with the rest of the Ziegler complex in 1984.

Thomas Young (mid-1850s–at least 1860)

Considering the reported size of Thomas Young's brewery, it is remarkable that so little is recorded of it. The industrial and population reports of the 1860 census report that he sold 1,000 barrels of beer during the census year, and employed four brewery laborers who boarded with his family. The fact that Young and three of his employees were from England suggests that at least part of his output was English-style ales. It is possible this business became the Steil brewery, with Niehoff owning it during the transition.

Joseph Miller (ca. 1860)

Joseph Miller was listed as a brewer in the 1860 population census.

Bernard Niehoff (ca. 1860)

Niehoff's brewery is listed in *American Breweries II*, but it is unclear whether Niehoff briefly operated one of the other known breweries in Beaver Dam, or if he was a separate firm.

George Aman (1864–66)
Berthold & Schmidt (1866)
ADJACENT LOTS WEST OF GOEGGERLE BREWERY ON PRESENT MADISON STREET

After selling his interest in Farmer's Brewery to Charles Schutte, George Aman went into business for himself in the summer of 1864. He purchased two empty lots just west of Goeggerle's brewery (and slightly farther down the street from his former partner), bought an old sash factory building and moved it onto the lots and converted it into a brewery. He sold this business in July 1866 to Bertholdt and Schmidt (first names not recorded) for $5,000. Unfortunately, the brewery burned that September, and was a total loss.

Pfestel & Steil, New Brewery (1868–1870)
Frank X. Steil New Brewery (1870–1884)
SPRING STREET

The New Brewery of Pfestel & Steil first appears in tax records in November 1868. It was built on the site of the Aman brewery which had been destroyed by fire two years earlier. By the next entry in 1870, F. Steil appears alone. Frank Xavier Steil also ran a saloon in connection with the brewery, and in some records is listed as a saloonkeeper rather than a brewery owner. It is likely that he brewed mostly for his own trade. The 225 barrels he produced in 1870 was less than one third as much as his two neighbors, and by 1878 his 112 barrels was one tenth the production of Goeggerle and Binzel. Despite the small size of the operation, Wing's 1884 directory lists Steil as producing ale and porter, doing his own malting, and selling bottled beer.

Unfortunately, tragedy struck the family through the second brewery fire at that location. On 29 June 1885, a fire broke out in the residence (the report in the *Milwaukee Sentinel* claimed that the brewery and saloon wing had not been in use for a time). Frank was able to jump from the second-floor window and his wife Frances was able to drop their infant child to him and then escape by a ladder. Their eleven-year-old son and eight- and six-year-old daughters slept in a different part of the house and were not able to escape. The brewery was not rebuilt, and the tragedy was still vivid many years later for those who witnessed it.

BELOIT *(Rock County)*

William Shovenfelter & S. M. Hamlin (ca. 1850)

Shovenfelter and Hamlin were both listed in the 1850 population census as brewers. They were listed in close proximity in the census and may have worked together.

Bernard Cunningham, Beloit City Brewery (1857?–1862?)
NORTH SIDE OF LIBERTY NEAR 4TH

Bernard Cunningham's Beloit City Brewery appears in both the 1858 and 1862 city directories.

Church & Kenworthy (1867)

Beloit's character as a religious college town hindered the survival of many of its breweries. Church and Kenworthy appear to have operated for only a few months during 1867 according to excise records.

Montayne & Wheat, Steam Brewery (1865?–66)
Richardson & Barrett, Beloit Steam Brewery (1866–68)
NORTH END OF THIRD STREET

R. D. L. Montayne had a steam (powered) brewery at least by 1866, and probably earlier. Richardson & Barrett purchased the brewery during the fall of 1866. However, their brewery was destroyed by fire at the end of the month. The newspaper reports claimed "[t[he fire originated in the office, in the north-east part of the building, and is thought to be the work of some villainous incendiary, as there was no fire used in that part of the brewery . . ." The loss was recorded at $14,000, which suggests that their brewery was fairly large compared with others of the time, and also suggests that Montayne started before 1866. Richardson still appears in 1868 tax records, but with the notation that he was not brewing.

George Schlenk, Beloit Brewery (1875?–1878)
Schlenk & Co. (1878–1880?)
Augustina Schlenk (1880–1898)
Frank Schlenk (1898–1915)
134 STATE STREET

In November 1869, the *Janesville Gazette* reported: "Beloiters are becoming bibulous again. Beer-bibbers around here are soon to have a brewery of their own, and then 'won't we all be joy-joy-e full when Johnny comes 'straggling' home' bloated, bleared, and brutalized by the brewing of our own bummers."

However, it would be several more years before Beloit had its own brewery again.

George J. Schlenk had been brewing in Rockford, Illinois, since at least 1863, but by

1873 he was shipping beer across state lines to Beloit. The precise date he moved his brewery to Beloit is not clear. His Beloit ads in late 1873 no longer list his address as Rockford, but there are no records of production in 1874. An 1879 county history claims Schlenk started in 1875 and that he made lager as well as ale (and small beer).

Beloit's Yankee heritage suggests that for the relatively few beer drinkers there, ale was more popular than lager. Wing's indicates that Schlenk's brewery specialized in ale and porter, and was bottling it, and *100 Years of Brewing* supports this description of the product line.

Like most brewers, Schlenk started small, producing only a few hundred barrels a year, but like most Wisconsin ale breweries, Schlenk's never got particularly big—*100 Years of Brewing* claims that its output at the turn of the century was only about 1,500 barrels per year, quite small for the largest brewery in a mid-sized city. But he apparently had wide distribution—the earlier county history claims his goods were shipped to "Racine, Milwaukee, and other places." The brewery was damaged by fire in January 1880, but in December 1890 the brewery was gutted by a fire "supposed to have been set . . . by unknown persons."

George Schlenk was in financial trouble by the early 1880s, and the brewery was placed in the name of his wife Augustina. (Some sources claim the proprietor was August Schlenk, but there does not appear to have been such a person in the family.) The eldest son, William, worked in the brewery, but when Augustina disposed of the brewery around 1898 it was to her younger son, Frank. Frank had been running the operation since at least 1891, when he made the news for selling beer without a license. (He was acquitted on the grounds that the prosecution could not prove that the bottles contained beer.) The brewery closed around 1915.

BT McClintic Beer Company (1997–2001)
136 West Grand Avenue #245
BT McClintic Beer Company was founded by brothers Brian and Tony McClintic in the mid-1990s, and their beer reached the market in May 1996. The first batches were brewed at Cold Spring Brewing Co. in Minnesota until they opened their Beloit location in 1997. McClintock Pilsner and Amber both earned medals at major beer competitions, and increased demand led the brothers to begin a contract brewing arrangement with Roundhouse Brewing of Aurora, Illinois, to brew and bottle the most popular beers.

In 1999, the McClintics received help from a small business development program to add a brewpub in the Reardon Building in the historic Chester Square complex. The next year they began selling their beer at Beloit Snappers baseball games. They also distributed some beer in Northern Illinois. Despite the expansion, the company went out of business in 2001.

Bergen Township *(Stoddard) (Vernon County)*

Rudolph Weile (1866?–1870)
Rudolph Weile started brewing on his farm in rural Vernon County sometime prior to 1867. Weile's production was typically quite small: just 4.5 barrels in June and July of 1867 combined. Weile's last appearance in tax records was in August 1870. Shortly thereafter he moved to Albert Lea, Minnesota, where he started a larger brewery and operated it for more than a decade.

Berlin *(Green Lake County)*

Oscar B. Caswell (prior to 1856–58?)
William H. Cottrell (1858–59)
Henry Smith (1859?–1860?)
John Sporer (1868–69)
Northeast Corner of North Wisconsin and East Liberty Streets
A *Milwaukee Daily Sentinel* account of Berlin in 1856 mentioned a brewery among the industries in town. A city history from 1998 claimed that Caswell started his brewery in 1850. However, this date is not yet supported by other data, and may have been a misinterpretation of the date in *American Breweries II,* since it claims Caswell sold it "soon," but Caswell was still in possession around 1858. An 1853 ad in the *Marquette Mercury* indicated that Caswell had a saloon, but mentioned nothing about brewing. Evidence suggests that Caswell sold the brewery to William H. Cottrell, who was listed in the 1858 city directory as the proprietor of a brewery on the same block. Cottrell appears to have sold the brewery to his employee Henry Smith, who was listed as a brewer living in the city of Berlin in the 1860 population census. Smith was an English immigrant who appears to have employed elderly countryman William Ford (72 years of age) at the brewery.

It is not yet clear how long Smith continued the brewery, but he was not listed in excise records or other sources by 1867. In April 1868 John Sporer appears in the excise records for the first time, apparently at the same site on Wisconsin near Liberty. However, his brewery burned in February 1869, and he did not rebuild.

Joseph Beck (1858?–59)
August Buhler (1859?–1875)
Schmidt & Schunk (1875–79)
Louis Schunk (1879–1896)
Jacobina Schunk (1896–1901)
Berlin Brewing Co. (1901–1920)
Berlin Products Co. (1920–1933)
Berlin Brewing Co. (1933–1964)
Near Modern Ripon Road and Whiteridge Road (to 1867); 277/283 Broadway (1867–1964)
The first appearance of August Buhler as a brewer is in the 1860 population census. According to the local history *Home Town Ties,* Buhler and his brother Edward built their first brewery on a spring near what later became the Conservation Club. However, the location of the brewery appears to match the brewery sold at public auction in September 1859 by Joseph Beck, who defaulted on a lien taken out a year earlier. It is possible that the Buhlers built a new brewery, but they may also have taken over Beck's "wooden brewery building." In 1867 they built a new brewery in the city on Broadway. The brick used for the brewery was made from the clay dug out to make the cellar. His modest brewery appears to have averaged less

than ten barrels per month. Around 1875 the Buhlers apparently closed the brewery and the property was purchased by H. S. Sacket. In October 1877 he sold the brewery to the partnership of Schmidt and Schunk, both of Milwaukee. The *Milwaukee Sentinel* approved of the investment, claiming "There is not a town in the State the size of Berlin without one or more breweries in successful operation." After a few years Louis (or Ludwig) Schunk bought out Schmidt and ran the brewery until his death. Even as late as 1887, Louis Schunk was producing less than 500 barrels per year.

In 1901 Charles Kulnick, who had been with the Schreihart brewery in Manitowoc, purchased the brewery from Jacobina Schunk and began a massive improvement program. Most of the old brewery was torn down and a new brick structure was erected, and the first batches of the new Berliner and Eagle Special were sold in 1902. In 1911 the company built a "sampling house" on the southwest corner of West Huron and South Capron streets, which served the unlikely combinations of public bath house, barbershop, and tap room for the brewery. The brewery also sold Berliner Tonic—one of several small-town breweries to include this product in their lineup.

During Prohibition, the brewery made a short-lived attempt at producing near beer, but had little success. The brewery made some real beer during the dry years, though by careful concealment they were able to avoid trouble with the law. Charlie Kulnick moved back to Manitowoc to run Manitowoc Products. He would later become president of Walter Bros. Brewing Co. in Menasha before his death in 1938. James Kulnick took over the brewery in 1933, and Berlin Brewing Co. began to produce real beer again. (They distributed Manitowoc Products beer for a few months until Berliner was ready.) In the years after Prohibition, Berlin Brewing Co. established itself as a viable regional brewery, with 90 percent of its production consumed in the Fox River Valley. They offered bock beer in the spring and a Christmas or holiday beer in the winter. Berlin beer was not necessarily regarded as a "cheap" beer: An Office of Price Administration list of maximum beer prices for 1946 listed Berlin Export at 12¢ per bottle—above the average for a small town brewery on this list. The brewery reached peak production of 23,000 barrels in 1945, but sales dropped to 8,000 within six years.

The brewery was sold to J. T. Savage in 1949, but sales remained low under the new management. James Kulnick remained as general manager and brewmaster until the beginning of 1955. The brewery was still using wooden kegs as late as the 1950s, since in April 1953 there was an explosion at the brewery, apparently caused by a fire in the barrel pitching room, which injured three firemen and a pitch room employee.

The brewery was an important part of the community for more than just the championship softball teams sponsored by the company. During the 1956 tornado that devastated the city, Berlin Brewing Co. supplied the hospital with water from its artesian well. After the big Carnation foods plant was destroyed in the storm, Berlin Brewing became the only union shop in town. When the brewery was in danger of closing during the summer of 1956, the Berlin Industrial Development Corporation launched a "community-wide effort" to save the brewery. The group hoped that local residents would buy a total of 450 shares in the brewery, and they estimated could reach the break-even point with a 3,000-barrel increase in sales. Local trucking executive Patrick J. Curran became the new president of the company. He set about stabilizing the business, which at that point didn't even have spare tires for the delivery truck. To compound the problems, the brewery smokestack collapsed in the first year of the new management, but this gave Curran and his team the opportunity to switch to gas power, which they had hoped to do at some point anyway. (This also made the city happier, since the old smokestack was right by the city swimming pool.)

During the next few years the brewery was profitable again, and had accounts as far away as Milwaukee. Despite this, Berlin Brewing focused on its local market. The company purchased everything they could in Berlin to support local vendors, but most brewing materials came in by rail to a siding half a mile from the brewery. Berlin did not have a nearby truck rental business, so the brewery often let local residents borrow the brewery trucks when not in use (and provided free beer when the truck was returned).

Berlin Brewing Co. competed primarily on price, and made about fifty different private labels for stores or restaurants. (Labels from this period are pictured in chapter 8.) While Berlin never canned beer, they had considered including cans and were able to use a variety of bottles to save money. Berlin Brewing purchased the labels of New London's Knapstein Brewing when the latter closed, and continued to supply some of the Knapstein markets. However, the brewery was feeling competition from Milwaukee brands, and when the city of Berlin raised sewer and water rates, the brewery's prices became less competitive. The brewery offered to reduce sewage outflow instead of paying higher rates, but nothing came of the proposal. The brewery closed in 1964, and the company began to distribute Schlitz beer to its old accounts. Curran emphasized that the business did not fail—that all suppliers and employees were paid in full. The plant was torn down in July 1966 and replaced with a grocery store. However, the Berlin Brewery softball team reformed and was still successful for many years. Berlin Brewing Co. is still incorporated in the state of Wisconsin as of 2017.

Berry Township
(Dane County)

Otto Kerl (1853–1861)
Section 27, Berry Township

Otto Kerl began production in his farmstead brewery around 1853 by his own account, though published sources offer dates ranging from 1851 to 1856. He brewed two or three times each week, and shipped beer as far away as Dodgeville. Kerl's partner Carl Ludwig left after about five years to start his own brewery in Hillsborough (as it was spelled at the time). Kerl stopped brewing in favor of farming when his employees left to fight in the Civil War. Additional information on the founding and operation of Kerl's brewery is in chapter 2.

Big Bend *(Waukesha County)*

Longnecks Brew Pub and Restaurant (2006–8)
S68 W22665 NATIONAL AVENUE

This suburban brewpub opened in 2006 but suffered from a difficult economy and lukewarm reception for their beers. The address is sometimes reported as being in Vernon, Wisconsin.

Black Creek *(Outagamie County)*

Eclipse Brewing (1997)
910 APPLE CREEK ROAD/N 4524 STATE HIGHWAY 47

Located in a small town north of Appleton, this brewery was credited in various online sources with a capacity of 1,200 barrels per year. Brewer Bill Stevens released a few brands, including der Schatten Special (Schatten means shadow, and Stevens had also considered going into the window shade business).

Black River Falls
(Jackson County)

Ulrich Oderbolz, Black River Falls Brewery (1856–1900)
Ulrich Oderbolz Estate (1900–1)
Anna Oderbolz, BRFB (1901–7)
Oderbolz Brewing Co. (1907–1913)
Badger Brewing Co. (1913–1920)
Badger Products Co. (1920–1933)
320 PIERCE STREET

Swiss immigrant Ulrich Oderbolz came to America in 1852 and wandered around the Midwest for several years, working at a brewery in Canton, Ohio and as a cooper in La Crosse among other occupations. Upon moving to Jackson County, he selected a site up the hill from the Black River to establish his brewery. The brewery prospered, typically producing more than 500 barrels each year, with a peak of 832 in 1875. In 1885 Wisconsin census figures reported sales of 400 barrels, and an 1891 industry directory listed capacity as under 500 barrels. The 1892 Sanborn maps depict a relatively primitive brewery for the time, still dependent on horsepower and candles for light. However, by 1895 the total tripled to 1,200 barrels, likely the result of a considerable upgrade. The 1902 Sanborn map shows a much more modern facility, with steam power, and additions to the building. By this time, the brewery had its own bottling works across the street from the brewery next to the two-story Oderbolz residence in the Italianate style which still stands across the street from the brewery. (See photo in chapter 3)

While the patriarch himself survived to lead the brewery for almost half a century, not all members of his family were so lucky. The first tragedy to strike the Oderbolz family was a gruesome one. On February 15, 1888, Charley Oderbolz fell into the mash kettle. The eighteen-year-old kept his head above mash and climbed out, but was horribly burned and attempts to remove his clothing only made matters worse. He died the next morning after an agonizing night. Ulrich died at age 80 in 1900, and his son Frank took over operation of the brewery. Frank was a well-known banker and local office holder, and had success with the brewery for a decade. However, on May 21, 1911, Frank drowned after the boat he was in went over a dam on the Black River that he had helped build. Shortly after Frank's death, Ulrich's widow Anna sold the brewery to a

A stein advertising Oderbolz's brewery, ca. 1890s.
COLLECTION OF TYE SCHWALBE.

group of local businessmen who renamed the company Badger Brewing Co. Several of the new owners were independent saloonkeepers who hoped to make their own beer to keep costs down. The brewery suffered a minor fire in February 1917, but escaped with only $2,000 damage.

When Prohibition arrived, the brewery offered New Style Temperance Drink, a short-lived near beer. The building was eventually sold to the Miller-Rose poultry company. (Premature newspaper reports had the building being converted to a vegetable canning plant or cold storage in 1919.) The building suffered a massive fire in 1932, which destroyed the second and third floors. The second floor was rebuilt, and the building was used as a soft drink bottling plant. The building was used on and off for various purposes until a new brewery took over the premises in 1997 and fresh local beer returned to Black River Falls.

Pioneer Brewing Co. (1995–2004)
Sand Creek Brewing Co. (2004–present)
320 PIERCE STREET

Only a few pre-Prohibition Wisconsin breweries were restored to their former uses after more than a few decades had passed. One of these was the old Oderbolz brewery, which became the home of Pioneer Brewing Co. in 1995. Dave and Jim Hellman, who had been successful beer distributors in central Wisconsin, bought the building, which still had feathers in it from its days as a turkey processing facility, and hired Todd Krueger as brewmaster. It took some time to renovate the building, but the first beer reached the market in June 1997. (See Chapters 1 and 10 for photographs showing how the old building was adapted to fit modern brewing equipment.) In 1998, Pioneer acquired the Wisconsin Brewing Co. of Wauwatosa, which had been devastated by two floods. The brands and a couple of employees moved to Black River Falls. The brewery made both Pioneer and Wisconsin Brewing Co. brands for several years, but after 2005 the Wisconsin Brewing Co. names were phased out though some of the beers remained (Wood Duck Wheat became Woody's Wheat,

The taproom of Sand Creek Brewing Co. features a rare neon from the era of the Pioneer Brewing Co. 2011.

for example). The brewery gained a reputation for quality across a variety of styles: Krueger won gold awards at the 2000 World Beer Cup for Oscar's Chocolate Oatmeal Stout and Pioneer Black River Red Märzen, and in 2002 for Oderbolz Bock.

In 2004, the Hellmans moved back into distribution, and the brewery was sold to a partnership of the Sand Creek Brewing Co. owners headed by Jim Wiesender and brewmaster Todd Krueger. (See the entry under Downing.) In the last decade, Sand Creek has developed a solid reputation for its own brands and has become a respected contract brewer—brewing and bottling beers for companies from Wisconsin and Minnesota and as far away as Kentucky. Among the noteworthy contract projects was BluCreek (originally called BluBrew) a beer containing juice from Maine blueberries that was sold in the Madison area but was also marketed in Japan by HMS WorldSupply. During the Pioneer era, the brewery made house beers for the Black Rose Brewpub in La Crosse. In several cases, Sand Creek's contract operations served as an incubator for breweries that needed to get beer on the market to build a revenue stream in order to get their own brewery built, such as Fulton Beer of Minneapolis and Lift Bridge Brewing Co. of Stillwater, Minnesota. Sand Creek also brewed the creative Furthermore Brewing Co. beers including Thermo Refur: An ale brewed with organic red beets and black pepper.

In 2015, Sand Creek Brewing purchased Furthermore Brewing Co. and Cross Plains Brewing Co., makers of Esser's Best beers. All of the brands were already brewed at Sand Creek, and Wayne and Larry Esser of Cross Plains and Aran Madden of Furthermore stayed on to serve as representatives of their brands for Sand Creek. Two years later, Sand Creek was happy with the continued incremental growth of these labels. Increased growth of their own labels and their recent acquisitions meant that by 2017 only about 5 percent of production was contract-brewed brands, though this included the new Lombardi Golden Ale and Lombardi Lager, brewed for a grandson of the famous coach.

To date, Sand Creek continued to produce fine examples of craft beer favorites, including barrel-aged beers and SMaSH ales (single-malt, single hop). Distribution range has varied, but Sand Creek beers have been shipped to parts of Minnesota, Iowa, and Illinois, though as of 2017 distribution has been limited to Wisconsin and a few locations in the Twin Cities.

Sand Creek also has brewed three varieties of hard lemonade, as well as special fruit versions and occasional barrel-aged editions. Sand Creek Hard Lemonade became available in cans for the first time in late 2016.

Bloomer *(Chippewa County)*

Wendland & Adler (1872–75)
John Wendland (& Co.) (1875–1890)
Liehe & Koepp (1890–93)
Charles Liehe (1893–99)
Bloomer Brewing Co. (1899–1920)
Bloomer Beverage Co. (1933–35)
Bloomer Brewery (aka Bloomer Brewing Corp.) (1935–1947)

Grove Street north of 17th

Started in what was previously called Vanville, John Wendland's brewery at Bloomer and High streets built a steady, if limited, business in the northwest region of Wisconsin. Wendland and his partner Fred Adler appear in the excise records for the first time in October 1872 and reported selling three barrels of beer in November and fourteen in December. They expanded production quickly and by 1875 sold 513 barrels, which made them a "large" brewery by excise tax standards. A local history by Tina Susedik recounted that Adler sold his half of the brewery to Wendland in 1882, getting out just before a series of fires struck the brewery. Wendland rebuilt after the 1883 fire and was brewing in a much larger brewery by 1886, only to have the brewhouse burn down again in July of 1888 with a heavy financial loss, of which less than half was covered by insurance. Most of the other structures were saved, so Wendland rebuilt yet again. The local newspaper account claimed that at the time of the fire it "was becoming one of the best paying breweries in this section and Mr. Windlandt [sic] was beginning to reap a benefit from the manufacture and sale of excellent beer."

Wendland decided to leave the beer business in 1890 and sold the brewery to J. F. Koepp of Bloomer and Charles Leihe of nearby Eagleton for just over $10,000. (Leihe's residence in Eagleton was reported as the brewery's location in a few state directories, leading some sources inaccurately to list Eagleton as having its own brewery.) Neither Leihe nor Koepp were brewers by trade, so they hired A. Mueller from Pabst to run the operation. In 1898, they sold the brewery to Charles Althans and Valentine Schoen, who changed the name to Bloomer Brewing Co. They embarked on an ambitious program of improvements that included fireproofing the brewhouse and adding steam power. According to Susedik, the brewery used wind power prior to that time with horse power available for windless days, but it is likely that the windmill only served the malt kiln on which it was located since the Sanborn map of 1893 listed the source of power as wood. Althans used his background as a tinsmith to fabricate much of the copper equipment for the brewery, as well as mugs for the brewery saloon. Althans and Schoen sold the business to Cornelius Schwartz of Chicago in 1912, who then sold to the Breunig family in

The Bloomer Brewing Co., ca. 1915. The painted logo at left was a figure seated in a crescent moon, which bore a slight resemblance to the Miller Girl in the Moon logo. Much of the brewery remains as pictured here, though a larger office was added just to the left of the center portion after Prohibition. COLLECTION OF JOHN STEINER.

March 1915. Jacob Breunig owned the brewery through Prohibition, though he leased the building at least once. Unfortunately the lessees used the equipment for distilling and were raided by federal agents in March 1928.

Breunig later sold the brewery to A. L. Lipschulz of St. Paul, who prepared to bring local beer back to Bloomer. The renamed Bloomer Beverage Co. reentered the market with Yankee Special in December 1933, and promotion continued the next year with a float in the Fourth of July parade shaped like a giant beer barrel. Lipschulz sought markets beyond the local area—shipping beer to Minnesota and the Dakotas. Lipschulz experienced financial difficulties, and sold the brewery to the Tankenoff family in 1935. M. B. Tankenoff became company president, and Al Tankenoff became the new manager. (Tankenoff's obituary reported he took over the brewery in 1937.) Tankenoff changed the name back to Bloomer Brewery, and soon changed the lineup of beers to feature Al's Ale and Al's Lager. He later changed the names to less personal labels such as Wisconsin Pilsner and Buckingham Ale. It is noteworthy that Tankenoff continued to offer ale as a standard product, since it was generally less popular in the Upper Midwest than in the Northeastern states.

Bloomer is located in the heart of Wisconsin's "cabin country," and Tankenoff recognized the importance of Twin Cities customers to his business. He was originally from St. Paul, and company letterhead from the late 1930s included the address for the office and warehouse in St. Paul.

In 1938 the Bloomer Brewery was authorized to offer 250 shares of stock for sale, but the City of Bloomer was told it could not accept stock in return for providing city water. During World War II, Bloomer had contracts to supply beer to the armed forces, so thousands of Americans who otherwise never would have heard of Bloomer were introduced to it with a welcome bottle of beer.

The end of World War II brought the end of the brewery as well. Susedik's account claims that "Bloomer residents were not happy having a Jewish businessman in town and they boycotted him, so he gave the beer away. In 1947, after losing beer contracts with the war department he bottled what beer was left in vats and shipped it to England." Other historians of the Bloomer brewery reject the idea that business suffered from anti-Semitism, and it was unlikely to have slowed Tankenoff, who was a leader in the Anti-Defamation League. Tankenoff switched to developing shopping centers and other financial businesses, and died in 2006 at the age of 101.

The U-Permit notation indicates that this label was from 1935, the first year of Al Tankenoff's ownership. The "strong" descriptor would be outlawed the next year. COLLECTION OF TYE SCHWALBE.

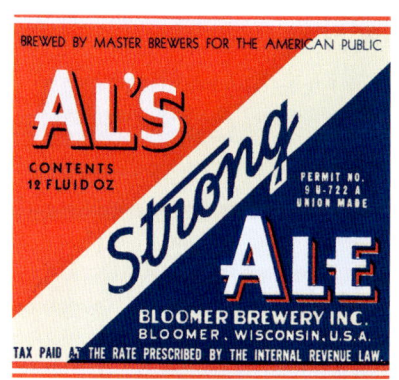

Bloomer Brewing Co. (2013–present)
1526 MARTIN ROAD

The second coming of Bloomer Brewing Co. began as a nanobrewery occupying some of the old brewery caves. Sicne 1985, Dan Stolt had rented a portion of the old brewery for his business, Stolt Excavating & Trucking. Inspired by homebrewing experiences with his son, he began homebrewing in part of the old brewery. His first beers were brewed for the local Good Friday fish fry. After experimenting with recipes for about five years, he settled on brews that became Bloomer Beer, Duncan Spring Blonde Ale, and Town Brown. In April 2013, he opened a taproom in the brewery and began serving his beers one or two nights a week.

By 2016, Bloomer Brewing beers had become so popular that Stolt upgraded his brewhouse to a seven-barrel system and planned eventually to add a bottling line. Water for the beer comes from the same well used by the earlier Bloomer brewery. Stolt hired a sales representative in 2017 to help service the twenty-two draught accounts and to help build toward the goal of around forty. As of July 2017, Blooming Brewing typically has eight beers on draught in the taproom—which is decorated with photographs of and artifacts from the earlier brewery.

BONDUEL *(Shawano County)*

Slab City Brewing Co. (1995–2006)
W3590 PIT LANE

The Slab City Brewing Co. was an early example of a small rural brewery of the type that would become common in Wisconsin a decade later. Owner Bill Winsand cobbled together a small brewing system on an old farm and began to brew a variety of ales and a seasonal bock. After a few years, the brewery outgrew the original farm milkhouse and Winsand installed a larger brewhouse in an adjacent building. Several of the beers were well received, in particular the Esker Alt and the Milkhouse Stout. Over the next several years Winsand expanded both the brewery and distribution range, and products which once had been available only in growlers and a few local draught accounts

WISCONSIN BREWERIES AND BREWPUBS

starting in 2002 were available in six packs throughout much of the state. The brewery closed in 2006.

BOSCOBEL (Grant County)

Ziegelmaier & Bielerman (1866?–67)
George Ziegelmaier (1867–1884?)
Frank Wunderle? (1883?–84?)
William Brewer (Bruer) (1884–87?)
George Reiner (1887–88)
Schuler & Dobler, Boscobel Brewing Co. (1895–1908)
Joseph A. Dobler, Boscobel Brewing Co. (1908–1912)
Dobler Brewery (1912–13)
Boscobel Brewing Co. (1913–1920)
Boscobel Brewing Co. (1920–1942)
WISCONSIN AVENUE, NEAR MADISON STREET

The firm of Ziegelmaier and Bielerman first appeared in the existing excise records in May 1867. The 1881 county history reported that George Ziegelmaier returned to Boscobel in 1866 after bouncing back and forth between that village and MacGregor, Iowa and "bought out the first brewery." While it is indeed possible that Bielerman or another party had started the brewery much earlier, this phrase in a generally ungrammatical paragraph may also simply mean that Ziegelmaier bought out Bielerman's interest. However, an article from September 1867 refers to "cleaning up and refitting the entire establishment," which should not have been necessary if the brewery was only a year old. Ziegelmaier, who was a baker by trade, hired F. Rabenstein to be his brewer. The brewery suffered a major fire in 1868, but rebuilding started almost immediately. In 1873, Ziegelmaier was prosecuted for allegedly selling beer on Sunday at his brewery, but he was found not guilty.

At some point during 1884, William Brewer took charge of the brewery (perhaps after a short period of management by Frank Wunderle), and Brewer ran it for about three years. During this period the brewery had its own malting facilities, and sometime between 1884 and 1887 added a bottling facility. Despite the expansions, production was usually about 300 or 400 barrels per year. The brewery George Reiner took over sometime in 1887 or 1888 was a prosperous concern, which unfortunately drew the attention of the criminal element. In August 1888, Reiner was assaulted with a four-foot sled stake and robbed of about $300 and his gold watch and chain. Reiner was apparently unable to return to work for some time, since it was later reported that a brewer from Milwaukee bought 300 barrels of beer from the Boscobel brewery at a sheriff's sale for one dollar each—a price which suggests the beer was not fresh (and that he may have been more interested in the cooperage). The Boscobel brewery disappeared from lists of brewers for several years.

Around 1895, Frank Schuler and Joseph Dobler formed Boscobel Brewing Co. After more than a decade together, Dobler took over the company on his own. In the 1912 *Brewers' Hand Book,* Dobler listed his son Carl as the brewmaster, but because Carl was thirteen years old at the time, Joseph was probably having a bit of fun with the survey. By 1916, John Blass was listed in directories as the president of the Boscobel Brewing Co., and remained so through Prohibition.

Boscobel Brewing Co. was not in operation during Prohibition, but became one of many small town breweries to return after the dry spell. Boscobel was not ready in April,

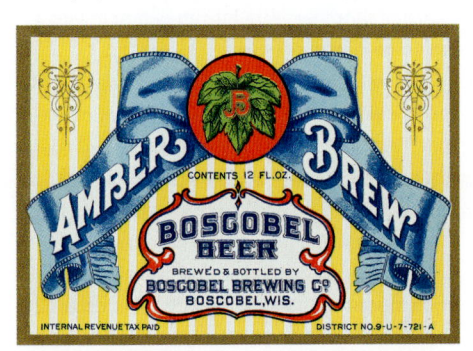

Pabst viewed Boscobel Brewing's first label after Prohibition as trademark infringement. The blue ribbon logo with a B superimposed on a hop in a red circle was very close to that of Pabst. Boscobel agreed to change the label and replaced it with a stylish Art Deco design. Pabst helped pay for the redesign rather than suing. COLLECTION OF TYE SCHWALBE.

but by September John Blass had received his permit and was ready to brew. The years after Prohibition did not go smoothly for Boscobel. Premier-Pabst (as it was at the time) threatened the company over the blue ribbon on its label but the dispute was solved when Boscobel agreed to redesign the Amber Brew graphics. Premier-Pabst need not have worried much about the competition, since Boscobel never produced more than a few hundred barrels a year, with all but a few barrels sold in the immediate area. The company went out of business in November 1937, but was reorganized in 1938 under the receivership of George Doll, who replaced the Amber Brew brand with Eagle Brew and Boscobel's Pride. Continuing financial problems led to the brewery being auctioned at a sheriff's sale in 1939, but the only bidder was the existing mortgage holder. Starting in the summer of 1939, the brewery was operated by Joseph Doll and Harry Geisler, but from 1939 to 1941 Boscobel produced less beer than any other Wisconsin brewery open during those years. The period of intermittent shutdowns ended when the Boscobel brewery closed its doors for good in June 1942. The building was razed in 1999 and the stone was used for other projects.

Franz Liske (1869–1872?)

For a brief period, the small village of Boscobel had two breweries. Liske's firm was much smaller than Ziegelmaier's—brewing about a third as much in the periods where data exists and apparently never more than one hundred barrels.

BOULDER JUNCTION (Vilas County)

Big Bear Eatery & Brewery (1996–98)
10490 WEST MAIN

BRANCH (Manitowoc County)

Gottfried Kunz (1858–1872?)
Elizabeth Kunz (1872?–1882)
Peter Herman (1882–83)
SECTION 5, MANITOWOC RAPIDS TOWNSHIP

According to local and family accounts, Gottfried Kunz arrived in the tiny hamlet of

Branch in 1858 and began building a brewery with the help of his sister Elizabeth and his cousin Heinrich George, who also became Gottfried's brother-in-law when he married Elizabeth. H. George was the head brewer in Branch until 1860 when he went to Manitowoc to work in breweries there. Elizabeth apparently played an important role in managing the brewery, since by the 1870s the business was conducted in her name, even though Gottfried lived until 1877. Gottfried also owned a hotel, and may have focused his time on that endeavor. The brewery grew until it produced 1,629 barrels in 1879—more than any brewery in the city of Manitowoc other than William Rahr's. An atlas from 1878 includes an illustration of a prosperous looking brewery next to a handsome residence, indicating this was much more than a simple farm brewery.

Sometime around 1882 the brewery passed into the hands of Peter Herman who owned the local mill and other businesses. In early 1883 the brewery burned, and the *Lake Shore Times* noted that Herman did not intend to rebuild "at present, but will turn his attention exclusively to farming." Later in the same column, the Branch correspondent reported: "Mr. Peter Herman treated us to a glass of Rahr's Bock Beer to-day. It was fine, but if our Bock had not got scorched so bad, we could have had some of our own."

D. B. Pierce (1871?–1872?)

The brewer that historian Wayne Kroll identified as DeWitt B. Pierce is in the 1872 state business directory. He appears in no industry publications nor excise records.

BRITISH HOLLOW
(Grant County)

Thomas C. Jones (1839?–1845?)
NEAR MODERN U.S. HIGHWAY 61

Research by local historian John Dutcher has identified a brewery extant in 1840 mentioned in passing by an 1844 account as that of Thomas C. Jones. Jones was apparently not popular in the area and was involved in several lawsuits during his few years in British Hollow. Very little is known about Jones' brewing, but it is known that he moved west after a divorce and a flurry of lawsuits in 1850. The brewery may have stayed in operation after Jones departed, since descendants of the other British Hollow brewers remember older relatives pointing to the former Jones property and being told "that's where the competition was"—a state which was only possible if brewing continued after 1850. It may have continued as an informal farm brewery, since it appears in no other official records.

Joseph Udelhofen (1856?–1859?)
Miller & Mohrenberg (1859?–1867?)
Stephens & Mohrenberg (1868–1871)
Mohrenberg & Macke (1871–72)
Henry Macke (1872–1882)
Joseph Vogelberg (1882–1890?)
NEAR MODERN U.S. HIGHWAY 61 AND BRITISH HOLLOW ROAD

Sometime in the mid-1850s, Joseph Udelhofen began brewing in British Hollow. While he was still listed in the 1860 population census as a brewer, the brewery is listed in the census of industry under the name Miller & Mohrenberg, who were also listed in the population census as brewers. Udelhofen may still have owned the brewery at this point, since he is the only one of the three listed as owning any real estate. The 1860 production was about 500 barrels, which sold for $6 each.

By 1868, Samuel Stephens had replaced Mathias Miller, and in 1871 Henry Macke would become William Mohrenberg's partner. Macke bought out Mohrenberg in 1872 and ran the business without a partner for the next decade. British Hollow was a very small community, so the brewery was clearly built to supply the surrounding countryside. The proprietors built caves in the hillside near modern Hippy Hollow Road to age and store their lager. In the early 1870s Macke was producing between 1,000 and 1,200 barrels per year with the help of three employees in his horse-powered brewery, about the same as the brewery in the much larger community of Potosi a few miles to the south. The capacity under Joseph Vogelberg's direction was 2,000 barrels per year, according to *Wing's 1887 Annual*. Adam Schumacher, later the owner of the Potosi brewery, worked at the brewery for a few years during Vogelberg's proprietorship. Vogelberg may also have had a partner named Frammel[?] for a year or so at the beginning of his proprietorship. Local historian John Dutcher holds that Vogelberg may have stayed in operation as late as 1890, but industry documents do not provide evidence for a specific date.

BROOKFIELD *(Waukesha County)*

Biloba Brewing Co. (2014–present)
18720 Pleasant Street (2014–17)
2910 N. BROOKFIELD ROAD (2017–PRESENT)

The husband and wife team of Gordon and Jean Lane opened Biloba Brewing Co. in Brookfield to bring craft beer and a comfortable gathering place to their hometown. In addition to a long career at Briess Malting Co., Gordon is also a licensed cheesemaker. He began homebrewing in 1974—five years before it was legal.

The city of Brookfield was trying to revitalize its downtown area, and was very helpful to the Lanes as they developed the business. The taproom was modeled on similar facilities on the West Coast, with no televisions to distract from conversations. The beer menu emphasized Belgian styles and included several barrel-aged products. Gordon taught daughter Kristen how

Biloba Brewing takes its name from the ginkgo biloba tree, an ancient tree common in Asia and later introduced to other continents. AUTHOR'S COLLECTION. PHOTOGRAPH BY CHARLES WALBRIDGE.

to brew and she soon took over brewing duties. Daughter Kathryn manages the tasting room and handles marketing and social media.

The popularity of the beer and the taproom forced the Lanes to look for a new site, which they found just around the block from their original location. They moved to the new location early in 2017. The new facility allowed them to expand the brewhouse to a ten-barrel system and provided additional storage space for the barrel-aging project.

Buffalo *(Buffalo County)*

John Schuler (1863–1871)
CASTLE ROCK, TWO MILES SOUTH OF FOUNTAIN CITY ON HIGHWAY 35.

According to an article in the *Winona Republican-Herald* from 1936, John Schuler had been having hard luck attempting to farm his land, but discovered seven large springs near the large bluffs along the Mississippi River. Schuler had worked in a brewery in Johnstown, Pennsylvania for two years prior to coming to Wisconsin, so he decided to try his hand at brewing in his new home. The brewery was a fairly simple structure, with a cellar below and a second floor used as a tavern and living quarters that were reached by an outside stairway.

Census and industry records indicate that Schuler's production was quite small—seldom much over 100 barrels a year and often less—but similar to that of many other farm breweries. However, accounts claimed that Schuler occasionally took deliveries to the farmers on the ridge above the river, and sometimes even took the ferry across the river to Minnesota City to sell surplus beer.

While Schuler was proud of his beer, his brewery was better known for the clientele of the tavern. The brewery was on the stage line between La Crosse and St. Paul, and was a lodging and refreshment stop for travelers. Occasionally the travelers were unsavory, as was the case with a mysterious well-dressed duo, who announced upon departure that they were the locally notorious Williams brothers. They paid for their breakfast by tossing Mrs. Schuler a gold coin, but took their leave on the river in Schuler's skiff. Schuler also had a reputation for serving beer to the remnants of the local Indian population. While Schuler relented and sold "fire water" to them, he insisted that they drink it elsewhere. On one occasion, Indians desperate for more beer besieged Schuler's brewery, and the family barricaded themselves inside with whatever improvised weapons they could find until the Indians decided to leave. After a few years, competition from the growing breweries in Fountain City and Winona forced Schuler out of business.

Mr. Charles Schacttler (Schaettle) (1858–1862?)
Ackerman & Co. (1859–1860?)
G. W. Ackermann, Spring Lake Brewery (1862?–63?)
SPRING LAKE

Kessinger's *History of Buffalo County* claims that the Buffalo City brewery was built in 1858. The Dun Credit Report volumes identify the proprietor as Charles Schacttler (Kessinger spelled it Schaettle), a former leather dealer from Cincinnati. In 1859 he sold a half interest in the brewery to pay his debts, and shortly after sold out entirely and went into the lumber business. The brewery must have been reasonably substantial, since a half share sold for $2,000 and it was listed as employing two workers and made 200 barrels of beer worth $1,600 in the 1860 industrial census. The new owners were Ackerman & Co. The population census suggests G. W. Ackermann (spelled differently) was a recent arrival in Wisconsin, and that Ackermann's neighbor, Xaver Stofer, worked at the brewery as well. Kessinger's history later refers to "a shooting match at Mr. Schaettle's place . . . where he had a brewery at the time," so it is possible that he took the brewery back for a short time, though the account may have been imprecise about ownership. Starting in late 1862 and running through September 1863, the *Buffalo County Republican*, a German-language newspaper, carried ads for Ackermann's brewery, now called the Spring Lake Brewery, offering "*gutes Schenk und Lagerbier*."

Burlington *(Racine County)*

Jacob Muth, Sr. (1852–1872)
109 NORTH MAIN STREET

Jacob Muth, a brother-in-law of Jacob Best, started the first manufacturing enterprise in Burlington when he began brewing in 1852. Details about his first years in business are scarce, but by 1860 he ran the second largest brewery in Racine County, producing about 500 barrels a year. Muth was quite proud of his beer, as indicated by his 1859 advertisement in the *Burlington Gazette*:

> *No war, but peace in Burlington here, and nothing stronger than Muth's Lager Beer.*
>
> *The undersigned begs leave to inform the trusty population of Burlington and vicinity that he always keeps on hand the celebrated Buck, Lager, and Common Beer, and hereby recommends it for sale as a first rate remedy for the preservation of health. Do away with patent medicines, pills &c., and drink Muth's Beer, and you will feel as well as a muskrat, as strong as a lion, and as happy as a man with the best feelings towards his fellow beings. Make once the experiment, and the second time you will need no persuasion. Facts are facts, and no humbug!*

The most dramatic event at the brewery occurred in May 1864, when an arsonist started a fire in a wagon of hay at the brewery. When Jacob Muth went out to fight the fire, the intruder entered the house and threw vitriol (sulphuric acid) at Mrs. Muth—no motive was known for the crime.

Muth continued in the brewing business until 1872, when converted his brewery to a malt house. According to R. G. Dun & Co. records, business started well, but by 1877 he was out of business. When the malt house was put up for sale in 1877, it was advertised as having a capacity of 75,000 bushels per year. The plant was purchased by the Finke-Uhen Brewing Company and used as both a malt house and brewery. The building was purchased (for payment of $859 of back taxes) by the Haylofter theater group in 1943 and converted into a theater. They presented the first show on the new stage in 1954, and the Haylofters still occupy the building as of this writing.

J. Smith (1862?–1870?)

Smith's brewery is known only through the R. G. Dun & Co. credit reports. An entry in 1863 noted that he was doing a large business and making money, but the only other entry, from February 1874, reported that he had gone bankrupt and departed four years earlier.

Anton Finke (1858?–1873)
William J. Finke (1873–1884)
W. J. Finke & Co. (1884–1897)
Finke-Uhen Brewing Co. (1897–1922)
Burlington Cereal Products (1920?–1933)
Burlington Brewing Co. (1933–1953)
Van Merritt Brewing Co. (1953–54)
Wisconsin Brewing Co. (1954–55)
425 McHenry St.

While some accounts have this business starting in 1865, census and R. G. Dun & Co. records indicate that Anton Finke started brewing in Burlington closer to 1858. The existing records suggest a modestly successful business during the early years. Dun & Co. reported that Finke was "inclined to drink his own product as most brewers are," but that it did not interfere with his attention to business and that he was "well liked in the place." In 1866, he was burned in an accident while pitching a barrel, but recovered. Anton Finke died in 1873, and while the business was carried on under his name for a time, his widow Catharine and son William soon changed the name of the company. They acquired the former Muth malt house, added a bottling facility during the 1880s and continued to expand the plant throughout the next decade to push capacity to around 5,000 barrels a year.

When the company was incorporated in 1896, John Uhen was brought into the business as president. The brewery was the scene of a tragedy in 1899 when William J. Tulif, a night watchman for the company, was found murdered in the office. The brewery continued to grow over the next two decades, especially after a new brewhouse was built in 1903 which quadrupled capacity. In 1910 the brewery produced and shipped about 15,000 barrels of beer, and the brewery employed about two dozen men, making it the fifth-largest manufacturing employer in the city. Both Finke and Uhen drew praise for being "among Burlington's most progressive and public spirited men."

During Prohibition, the plant stayed in business making wort, first under the Finke-Uhen name, and then as Burlington Cereal Products. Burlington's proximity to Chicago made it an appealing location for production of illicit beer, and the brewery was raided at least twice and discovered to be in violation of the Prohibition Act. Finke-Uhen was one of six breweries in 1922 that was not only fined but also assessed thousands of dollars in back taxes.

After Prohibition, the Burlington brewery was purchased by what the papers called "a Chicago concern . . . seeking control of several Wisconsin breweries" or "Chicago men," terms which, intentionally or not, seemed to imply bootlegger connections. In the case of Burlington, the bootlegger connections were not simply suspicions, since one of those concerned was George "Dutch" Vogel, who was what one paper called "a beer baron of the prohibition era." Vogel had been linked to jewel robberies, spent time in Joliet State Prison, and was acquitted of murdering a police office with the famed Clarence Darrow on his defense team. Vogel was officially the "chief shipping clerk" of the new Burlington Brewing Co., but he was known to have a significant financial stake in the firm as well. Documents of the Beverage Tax Division continued to allege that Burlington was "a gangster outfit" for several years. Despite the out-of-town ownership (though Vogel himself moved to a home on nearby Browns Lake), Burlington stressed its heritage in early advertisements: "Burlington Brew is made in the old Finke-Uhen Brewery in Burlington by Michael Deubig, formerly brewmaster for the Finke-Uhen Brewery. This in itself should be a recommendation for Burlington Beer."

Burlington added several brands to its lineup in the years after repeal, including Chesterton Ale and the beer the company became most famous for, Van Merritt beer. Brewed at Burlington "with exclusive permission of de Sleutel Brewery" of Dordrecht, Holland, Van Merritt anticipated Löwenbräu and other licensed versions of imported brands by several decades. Van Merritt was advertised as a superpremium beer: "You can taste the difference. You're glad to pay the little extra it costs." (Though it was often more than a little extra—a Chicago area liquor store advertised it at $4.40 a case in 1946, nearly twice as much as Chicago's Prima or Prager and exceeded only by Gluek's Stite malt liquor from Minneapolis.) Van Merritt was shipped well beyond Chicago—correspondence shows that Burlington products were exported to Los Angeles and Las Vegas by the early 1940s and newspaper ads offered it for sale in Reno. (Sales in Nevada during this period were not necessarily due to mob connections. Wisconsin beer was in demand around the country and smaller breweries sought sales opportunities wherever they could find them.) Burlington was one of several smaller Wisconsin breweries to sell much more of their product outside the state rather than for home consumption: in January 1938, for example, it sold 342 barrels in Wisconsin but exported 1,132 barrels.

After a minor corporate reorganization in 1937, the company continued in business, though records show it was losing money at rate faster than any other Wisconsin brewery at some points—more than $80,000 combined in 1940 and 1941. The war brought additional difficulties, as it did for all breweries. In 1942, the brewery proposed cooperating with the City of Burlington on a trash collection program, since the brewery had authorization to salvage tin cans of size No. 10 or larger to reclaim for bottle crowns. The city rejected the plan, since its trucks would have to make the same rounds twice, but allowed the brewery to have "the privilege of picking out what cans it can use, at the city dump, paying for them at the federal rate of $6 a ton." On the other hand, employees of the brewery were noteworthy for their patriotism. Not only were they the first firm in the city to have 100 percent

Two versions of Burlington's Van Merritt cans, both from the 1950s. COLLECTION OF DAVID WENDL.

participation in the payroll allotment program for purchasing war bonds, they doubled their original pledges in July 1942 as other businesses caught up.

During the war years, Burlington's production rose as high as 50,000 barrels, which spurred the company to build a new bottling plant that would double capacity to bottle thirty-eight barrels per hour. But in the early 1950s, sales dropped precipitously. Van Merritt's availability in two sizes of bottles as well as cans did little to increase its popularity. Vogel died in 1951, but that August the brewery redoubled its newspaper campaign for Van Merritt, pledging to continue it indefinitely if it bore fruit. However, it was almost completely unsuccessful, and even with the Milwaukee brewers' strike of 1952 the Burlington brewery closed in October of that year, leaving forty-five employees without a job. The following July, Maurice Frank of Chicago purchased the brewery and started to reinvigorate the plant and the Van Merritt brand. He assured all former employees of their jobs, and pledged to use the seventy salesmen of his Chicago liquor distribution business to push sales nationwide. In an echo of the Brewers' Best scheme (see Two Rivers and Chapter 8), Frank announced plans to license other breweries around the country to make Van Merritt, claiming that demand was outpacing supply and arguing that the new distribution plan would make better use of a national advertising campaign and cut costs. The company was renamed Van Merritt Brewing Co. in August, and brought in new management to oversee the expansion. Despite the excited announcement in March 1954 that sales were up 700 percent from the previous year (not difficult since the brewery was closed for most of the year), in April the brewery was sold to Weber Waukesha Brewing Co., which used it for the production of soft drinks. The Van Merritt brand was sold separately to Chicago-based partners of Frank, who continued it for a few years at other breweries (including Oconto).

F. G. Klein & Co. (1891?–1901?)
PINE AND MILL STREETS

Francis G. Klein, a native of Alsace, was known much better for businesses other than brewing. He was credited with making the "first cow-fender ever put on a locomotive" while in Pennsylvania, and after moving to Racine he was one of the earliest employees of J. I. Case's threshing machine factory. Klein stayed in this line of work when he moved to Burlington and set up a machine shop in his new home. Klein began manufacturing carbonated beverages with J. H. Bower & Co. in the mid-1880s. In 1889 Klein's son Otto purchased Bower's share and the firm became F. G. Klein & Co. Around 1891 they included beer in their product line. The 1900 population census specifically lists Klein as a manufacturer of weiss beer, and a 1900 industry directory shows a product line including ale, porter and weiss beer. The company soon dropped beer and specialized in soft drinks for many years until declaring bankruptcy in 1937.

BURR OAK *(Farmington Township) (La Crosse County)*

Johnathan Teisch? (1868?–1870?)

Excise records reveal the tiny nature of this brewery. During the period from August 1869 to February 1870, only once did Teisch produce more than one barrel of beer per month. While it is possible he produced intermittently in other years, there is no record of his operations.

BUTTE DES MORTS *(Winnebago County)*

Christoph Klenk (1857–1862)
Louis Schwalm (1862–65)
Frederick Bogk (1865–1873?)
WASHINGTON STREET BETWEEN ONTARIO AND MAIN

The research of Lee Reiherzer in Winnebago County land records has added much to the previously scant information about the small brewery on the north side of Lake Butte des Morts. Christoph Klenk purchased two lots from Butte des Morts pioneer Augustin Grignon in 1857 and began to build a brewery. The land sloped toward the lake and was convenient both for digging a beer cellar and hauling ice from the lake. By 1860, Klenk and his two employees were producing 250 barrels of beer a year with horse power and perhaps some steam power, since the census of industry lists a boiler among the equipment.

In 1862, Klenk sold the brewery to Louis Schwalm of Oshkosh, and eventually became a brewer in Buffalo, NY. Louis' younger brother Leonhardt would soon form the Horn & Schwalm Brooklyn Brewery in Oshkosh. It is not clear if Leonhardt served as the brewer or was active at Butte des Mortes, since he was also involved with the Lake Brewery in Oshkosh. Leonhardt purchased the brewery from Louis in November 1865, but sold it a month later to German-trained brewer Frederick Bogk.

Bogk appears to have expanded the brewery since he purchased two adjacent plots of land. Articles published in the mid-twentieth century claimed the "big red building was a landmark for many years afterward and could be seen for miles from up or down the river." While the brewery may have been bigger, production was not. The 1870 census of industry reported sales of 200 barrels, and industry figures listed no production in 1870-1 and only eighty-two barrels in 1871-2. The later articles claim that the brewery burned at some point, but do not specify when—so it is possible that the fire happened sometime in 1870 and interrupted production for several months. The last known reference to Bogk's production was a tax penalty paid in February 1873, and the brewery disappears from the records. Bogk was most likely driven out of business by competition from breweries in nearby Oshkosh. Bradstreet's credit reports of 1884 list Bogk as a vinegar manufacturer, and he passed away in 1886. The brewery site is now residential property.

CADIZ TOWNSHIP
(Green County)

Peter Ede (1859?–1860?)
Prior to his longer stay at Wiota, Peter Ede started a brewery in Cadiz Township that was large enough to appear in the 1860 Census of Industry. In the year ending May 1860, the forty-eight-year-old English immigrant produced one hundred barrels of ale, which sold for $6 per barrel.

CALUMET TOWNSHIP
(Fond du Lac County)

Mathias Aigner (1868?–1876?)
SOUTH EDGE OF SECTION 6
Aigner appears in existing excise records or industry directories intermittently between 1868 and 1872. Total production in the years ending May 1871 and 1872 was twenty-three and twenty-two barrels respectively. Aigner was listed as a farmer in the 1870 census, so it is likely that he brewed only occasionally to supplement his income.

CALVARY (Village)
(Fond du Lac County)

Philip Becker & William Wolff (1871?–72?)
Becker & Wolff (sometimes listed as Wolf & Becker) appeared in excise records and other records in 1871 and 1872, when they produced 111 barrels and 340 barrels respectively. Wayne Kroll holds that this firm and the later Mt. Calvary business of Matthias Bourgeois and successors are the same brewery (see Mt. Calvary).

CARLTON TOWNSHIP
(Kewaunee County)

Wenzel Havliceck & Wenzel Holub (1865–67?)
Wenzel Holub (1867–1872?)
Anton Langenkamp & Bro. (1874?–1898)
Walecka & Kulhanek (1898–1901)
SOUTH EDGE OF SECTION 32,
CARLTON TOWNSHIP
Wenzel Havliceck and Wenzel Holub appear to have begun brewing in Carlton Township near Tisch Mills in 1865, though Havliceck's first appearance in the excise records is not until 1867. Havlicek apparently left the partnership in late 1867, and Holub continued on his own. By 1870, Holub employed three men and made 160 barrels of beer, which he sold for $10 per barrel. Holub remains in the excise records through November 1872.

Anton Langenkamp was in possession of the brewery at least by June 1874, when he was first listed in the R. G. Dun & Co. credit reports. (This account claimed he had been in business eight years at that point, which is clearly not true at this location.) While his production was generally small, he made money and generally paid his bills in cash. He made about 200 barrels per year during the late 1870s, but increased to more than 450 barrels by 1882. The operations of the brewery after this point can only be pieced together from industry directories. The capacity of the brewery seems to have increased during the mid-1880s, and sometime prior to 1891 he built a malt house. In the early 1880s Langenkamp switched his mailing address to the Tisch Mills post office, though this does not seem to represent a change in the location of the brewery. (This brewery is often known as the Tisch Mills brewery, and the rare breweriana from this business use the Tisch Mills location.)

In the last years of the brewery, it was operated by Walecka and Kulhanek, but there is little information about their operations.

The names Frank Lufter and James Lodel were listed in state business directories in the late 1880s and early 1890s as being brewers in Tisch Mills, but there is nothing in the industry directories that confirms they had their own breweries.

CASSVILLE (Grant County)

Schmitz & Co. (1854?–59?)
Andrew Ortscheid (1859–1860?)
Schmitz & Weisse (1860?–62)
Schmitz & Ortscheid (1862–?)
DU CHEIN STREET NEAR BLUFF STREET
(BLOCK 51 LOT 6)
Schmitz & Scherer (1867?–1873)
F. Scherer & Co. (1874–78)
Scherer & Alrath (1878–79)
Schmitz & Grimm (1879–1880)
Aloys Grimm (1880–88)
Derichs Bros. (1889–1891)
Mathias Lorscheter (1891–95)
Cassville Brewery
Habermann & Lorscheter (1895–99)
George Scheibl (1899–1904)
Mrs. Mary Scheibl (1904–7)
Andrew J. Lindner (1907–1920)
Cassville Brewing Co. (1933–38)
BREWERY AVENUE
The history of Cassville's brewery is confused by a number of seemingly contradictory records. While a 1976 history of the city reports (without specific documentation) that William Schmitz started the brewery in 1854, the older 1881 history of Grant County claims that Schmitz did not move from Galena, Illinois to Cassville until 1855, and that his first business there was a hardware store. However, the state business directories of the late 1850s list Seitz & Co. as the Cassville brewers, and an entry in the R. G. Dun Company credit reports list Voltz & Sitz as the brewers in July 1858. Sitz and Seitz may well be interpretations of Schmitz, but there is also the possibility that Schmitz may have leased the brewery to other parties.

By the time of the 1860 Census of Industry, the Cassville brewery was operated by Andrew Ortscheid with the help of his son, Andrew, and Michael Faltz. Since the population census reported that Ortscheid owned $1,500 in property, he may have purchased the brewery. The brewery's production was quite small— only fifty barrels in the year ending May 1860, which sold for $6 a barrel. The brewery next appears in records in 1862, when the firm of Schmitz & Weisse dissolved. Weisse took the tin shop they had owned, and Schmitz took the brewery, now in partnership with Andrew Ortscheid, who may have remained as the brewmaster during the previous partnership.

The best evidence suggests that a new brewery was built in the late 1860s, apparently across the creek from the first structure. By 1867 (if not earlier) William Schmitz was back in business, and with new partner Franz Scherer (or Scherr). While apparently too small to be included in the 1870 census of industry, by 1871 the brewery produced 330 barrels and nearly doubled production to 630 the next year. In 1873 Schmitz sold his half to Scherr for $7,300, but by the end of the decade, production was back in the 200-barrel range and the company was in financial difficulty. The brewery was sold at foreclosure sale in 1878, and Schmitz returned from the saloon business to take charge of the brewery again, this time with financial partner Henry Abrath. This arrangement lasted only briefly, and by late 1879 Schmitz was in business with Hugo Grimm. Schmitz again sold out in 1880 (this time for $7,850, so the value of the property was at least holding steady). Grimm's brother Aloys was also associated with the property during the 1880s, but the fact that the Cassville brewery is not listed in most industry directories during this decade suggests that the brewery was not in production for much of that time. This hypothesis is supported by an article announcing the reopening of the brewery by the Derichs brothers in late 1888. Aloys Grimm may have kept a financial stake in the property for several more years since Tovey's Brewers' Directory still lists him as the owner as late as 1891.

This tapping system is not original to the Cassville Brewing keg but was typical of many pre-Prohibition taps. Post-Prohibition tap handles were required to have a tap knob identifying the brewery and the brand. COLLECTION OF TYE SCHWALBE.

From this point, the Cassville brewery changed hands several more times, but often from one family member to another. Mathias Lorscheter operated the brewery alone for about five years, but when he took on a partner, it was his brother-in-law John Habermann. New owner George Scheibl added a bottling line to the brewery during his term, and the company continued to malt at least some of its own barley. When Scheibl died in 1904, the business was carried on by son-in-law William Grimm (under the name of Scheibl's widow Mary) until it was purchased by another son-in-law, Andrew J. Lindner.

Lindner was by far the most accomplished brewer to own the Cassville plant, and his leadership stabilized the company for the next several decades. Linder had worked for several other Midwestern breweries, including Anheuser-Busch, and took formal training in 1903 in Chicago. The company continued to operate until Prohibition temporarily closed its doors. The brewery was reopened in 1923 by J. L. White, allegedly to produce a product "in every way conforming to the Volstead Act." However the brewery was raided shortly thereafter and White, Lindner and two others were prosecuted in 1924 for violating the Act.

Despite the setbacks of the Prohibition years, Lindner maintained control of the brewery and began to make preparations to re-open the brewery in the Spring of 1933. The *La Crosse Tribune and Leader Press* reported that "A force of mechanics was at work" installing new refrigeration equipment, repairing casks and repairing and redecorating the office. After three months of work, the brewery resumed brewing in July, and further benefitted the community by employing thirty men. Even with the modern refrigeration equipment, Cassville still advertised that its beer was "Aged in a Cave" on labels and other advertising. (A sign from this era claims the year 1854 as the start of the brewery.) The company was shipping beer to Madison (where it sponsored a bowling team in the Arcade Ladies League), and as far as Cedar Rapids, Iowa.

Unfortunately, the small brewery was having trouble staying afloat, and by December 1938, the company had ceased operations. Lindner was still trying to reopen the brewery in 1940, but had no success.

The Cassville Brewery had one last attempt at new life in 1946, when the Louis Ziegler Brewing Co. of Beaver Dam showed interest in purchasing the brewery, at least in part to secure an additional grain allocation during the period of input restrictions. Even though the brewery had not operated during the previous twelve months, an allocation was granted and a contract was drawn up. However, Ziegler pulled out of the deal in December and the Cassville brewery was left to decay. The brewery was razed in 1967.

CAZENOVIA *(Westford Township)* *(Richland County)*

Alois Fix (1867?–1874)
Schott, Saltzenberger & Co. (1874–77)
Joseph Justin (1877–79)

In 1864, Alois Fix moved north from Richland City and purchased a store in Cazenovia. He established a new brewery near Cazenovia in Westford Township. Excise records suggest that a Zelley Mahler may have leased or operated the brewery for a few months in early 1868. (There was a Cecelia Mahler who owned land near Fix's, and this may be the same person.) Recorded production of the brewery was seldom more than ten barrels a month and usually much less—during the year ending May 1871 Fix brewed a mere thirty-three barrels. R. G. Dun Company records report that Fix was an "honest German" but starting in the 1870s he apparently indulged in his own product to the detriment of business. By 1875 the property was in his wife Dorothy's name.

Excise records and industry directories seem to indicate that Fix leased or rented the brewery starting in December 1874. The firm of Schott, Saltzenberger (or Solchenberger) & Co. operated the brewery for a few years, followed by Joseph Justin. Neither of these new operators did much to expand the business. Schott and Saltzenberger brewed eighty-four barrels in 1875 and under Justin production dropped from eighty-eight barrels in 1878 to nineteen in 1879—probably marking the end of the brewery. In 1879 Dorothy Fix put the brewery up for sale along with a house and nine acres of land. Alois was still listed as a brewer in the 1880 population census, but he apparently ceased brewing well before then.

Cecil *(Shawano County)*

E. W. (William) Buche, Cecil Brewery (1893–1906?)
Between modern WI-22 and South Warrington Avenue northeast of Lake Drive

William Buche began brewing in Cecil, on the east end of Shawano Lake, around 1893. His brewery was a large one for a small village even though it had no bottling facilities and no malt house. Buche built a large two-story residence, which still stood in 2015. In 1905, the brewery was absorbed by a stock company that also took over the Raddant brewery of nearby Shawano at the same time. The new firm did not continue the Cecil operations very long, and the Sanborn map of 1907 shows the brewery buildings as vacant. William Buche later became brewmaster at Raddant Brewing Co.

Cedarburg *(Ozaukee County)*

Engels & Schaeffer (1844?–1850)
August Runge (1850?–1860?)
Dr. Theodore Fricke & Co. (1866?–1874)
Cedarburg Brewery, John Weber (1874–1920)
NE corner of Riveredge & Water Streets

The precise year in which Charles Engels and Lewis Schaeffer began to brew is in dispute. The 1881 county history says 1848, other sources claim 1844. It is also unclear exactly when Engels and Schaeffer gave up the brewery. The 1850 census still has the two as brewers in Cedarburg (along with two brewery employees). By the 1860 census year, Runge's brewery was producing 560 barrels a year, making it one of the largest breweries in the county. One local source claims Dr. Theodore Fricke and John Weber, a stonemason by trade, took over the brewery in 1862 (though this source also claims that Fricke died in 1865, when in fact he lived well beyond then). The 1881 county history claims that the pair purchased the business in 1869, though this is contradicted by multiple sources. Dr. Fricke was a practicing physician, so his role was to own the property and provide the capital, while Weber managed the brewery. By the early 1870s the brewery was selling more than 1,100 barrels a year, which ranked them among the largest breweries in the state outside Milwaukee. Weber took over the brewery himself around 1874, added steam power in the late 1870s, and boosted production to around 1,500 barrels a year. By the mid-1880s the R. G. Dun & Co. credit reports indicate that Weber was "doing very well" and "has the monopoly in this line" in Cedarburg. The 1895 Wisconsin census of industry reported Weber had produced 2,600 barrels the previous year, all of it draft beer. Even as late as 1916, industry directories recorded no bottling operations at Cedarburg, and no bottling house appeared on insurance maps. (Dr. Fricke is known to have packaged beer in stoneware bottles, and a few exist in private collections.) With the arrival of Prohibition, the company moved briefly into soda water, but the lack of a bottling plant made this difficult and the company went out of business.

After Prohibition ended, there were rumors that the brewery would reopen. The *Port Washington Pilot* reported that three Port Washington men and a Cedarburg man were negotiating to buy the Cedarburg brewery, but the brewery never produced again. Since 1970 the building has served as a center for local artists.

Henry Bender (1860?)

Henry Bender appears as a brewer in the 1860 population census. These records indicate that he owned his own property, which suggests that he did not work at August Runge's brewery, but is not conclusive.

Sliver Creek Brewing (2004–present)
N57 W6172 Portland Road at Columbia Road

Silver Creek Brewing Company was founded in 1999 by Steve Venturini, Steve Roensch and Todd Schneeberger—all members of a local homebrewers club. In 2002 they began serving beers at their pub in the historic Cedarburg Mill, and in 2004 they began to brew at the site. While sometimes listed as a brewpub, Silver Creek is more correctly classified as a taproom since it does not have its own kitchen or restaurant. (Original plans called for a limited menu of sandwiches and other simple items.) Guests in the beer garden can gaze at the nearby creek and waterfall, while those inside can watch as the original mill race streams through the bar. In addition to their numerous beers, Silver Creek has become famous for its blonde root beer. (Silver Creek Brewing is pictured in chapter 10.)

The Fermentorium (2016–present)
7481 Highway 60

The Fermentorium opened its doors to the public in 2016 at a location just outside of Cedarburg.

The Fermentorium features five different series of brews: Traditional, Hop Wheel, Brewer's Reserve, Barrel, and the Pilot Series, through which any brewery employee can try out a ten-gallon batch. Several of the Pilot beers, such as the IPAs Juice Packets and Rainbows & Lollipops, have been added to the regular lineup. As of 2017, several Fermentorium beers were available throughout Wisconsin in bottles.

Cedar Creek *(Polk Township)* *(Washington County)*

Jacob Pfeil (1860?–61?)

The only evidence of Pfeil's brewery is his presence in the population census of 1860. Some evidence suggests that Cedar Creek supported two breweries, so his may have been separate from that of Lehner's (listed under Slinger). This brewery could also be the same as one of the numerous other breweries in that part of the county during the 1860s.

John Hellenschmidt (prior to 1867?–1872)

The first recorded mention of John M. Hellenschmidt's brewery was in the excise tax reports of December 1867, when he sold five barrels of beer. He appears in the tax records through 1871, but his brewery burned in February 1872, and he did not rebuild.

Cedar Falls *(Dunn County)*

Hans von Kessel (1881?–1882?)

The *Milwaukee Daily Sentinel* reported in March 1882: "Hans von Kessel, a former reporter of the Herold and Freie Presse, is at present the proprietor of a brewery in Cedar Falls, Wis." The brewery is not listed in industry publications of the time.

Centerville Township *(also known as Cleveland and Hika)* *(Manitowoc County)*

Simon Krause (1857–1866?)
Christian Scheibe, Centerville Brewery or Centerville Brewing Co. (1866?–1888)
Centerville Brewing Co. (1890–98?)
Hoffman & Mill? (1893?)
Gartzke Bros. Brewing Co. aka Centerville Brewing Co. (1898?–1911)
Centerville Brewing Co. (1911–17)

Simon Krause is credited with brewing the first beer in the township in 1857. Krause appears in various state directories as late as 1880, though no local or industry sources have him there after 1866. Sources differ on when Christian Scheibe left the former Hottleman brewery in Manitowoc and purchased the Centerville business. Some local histories claim 1866, but others report 1867 and excise records do not include production prior to May 1867. As early as 1870, he was producing 450 barrels eight months of operation with three employees. Production jumped to almost 1,000 barrels by 1875, and after twenty years of brewing, Scheibe had built a substantial market in the region, since *Wing's* annual lists his capacity as approximately 6,000 barrels. A county newspaper boasted in 1886, "The Centerville Brewing Co. . . . sell large quantities of their product at different points along the railway." Scheibe also added malting and bottling operations sometime between 1884 and 1887.

Unfortunately, the brewery suffered a disastrous fire in November 1888, which inflicted a loss of $40,000 with insurance on less than half that amount. In the wake of the fire, both the Rahr and Kunz & Bleser breweries of Manitowoc offered to sell Scheibe beer with which to supply his accounts until he could rebuild. Rumors swirled about the rebuilding plans—a month after the fire Milwaukee papers claimed that Christian Scheibe would continue to farm in Centerville but his son, newly-elected Assembly member Emil, would build a new brewery at Brillion, to the northwest in Calumet County. But a few days later, new reports placed Emil at the head of a $35,000 stock company that planned to rebuild in Centerville.

While the Centerville Brewing Co. was indeed rebuilt, the Scheibe family decided to focus on brewing in Marshfield and Grand Rapids. The new Centerville firm was incorporated in 1890 by Allis Kraus, Henry F. Gutsch, and Gustav A. Scheibe. However, it was managed by the Gartzke brothers, Emil and Otto, who would run the brewery for the next two decades and eventually become officers, bringing other family members in as they came of age. (The Hoffman & Mill reference contained in *AB2* is not yet confirmed by local sources.) The

An attractive glass sign from the later years of the brewery. Note that the location was given as Cleveland. COLLECTION OF TYE SCHWALBE.

company made the newspapers several times, but other than a series of advertisements in 1913 in the *Sheboygan Press*, it was usually for bad news. Their safe was broken into in 1899, and they had a team of horses stolen in 1908. In 1902, the brothers were arrested and fined several hundred dollars for reusing revenue stamps. In 1907 Edward Gartzke was badly injured when the elevator in which he was transporting eight kegs of beer slipped and crashed. The most interesting news item was published in 1912, when the Centerville brewery was rumored to be a pawn in a local price war—the retail liquor dealers of Manitowoc proposed taking stock in the Centerville concern and using it to produce beer for less than the increased prices demanded by Manitowoc companies.

While the 1913 advertisements proclaimed that "Our Special '20th Century'" was "The Beer Everybody Wants," not enough people wanted it to keep the company on sound footing. By 1915, the Rahr company of Manitowoc held the mortgage for the brewery and had to defend their property against claims ranging from $500 in wages to over $5,000 in unpaid bills for ice machinery. The brewery appears to have continued in business to some extent after it was sold to meet the demands of creditors because an article in September 1917 claimed the brewery had closed "a few months ago."

CHILTON *(Calumet County)*

John Paulus (1857?–1872)
Arlen & Gut (1859?)
Ulbrich Gut (1859–?)
Philip Becker (1875–1885)
Gutheil Bros. (1883?–1888?)
NORTH OF MODERN W. MAIN, WEST OF HEIMANN STREET

J. Paulus is listed as a brewer in Chilton as early as the 1858 state business directory but may not have brewed regularly. He appears to have transferred the brewery to other operators on occasion, since the *Chilton Times* published a notice of the dissolution of the brewing firm of Arlen & Gut in 1859. While Paulus was listed as a brewer in the 1870 census, he was identified as a farmer in 1860, and this along with his absence from industry directories and excise records suggest he might have brewed off and on during his earlier years. The one known figure from the Paulus era was fiscal 1870, when he brewed 280 barrels, which sold for $8 per barrel. Paulus died in 1872, and the brewery lay dormant.

Philip Becker took over in 1875 and suffered a major fire almost immediately. His rebuilt brewery was much larger, and by 1878 it was producing over 1,000 barrels per year—more than three times as much as local rival Gutheil. While Becker was in debt for several years, he had a solid reputation for business and continued to improve his position into the 1880s. By 1882 his output was over 1,400 barrels. A bird's eye map of 1878 includes an inset illustration of Becker's large plant and the adjacent "Summer Garden" complete with pavilion.

In early 1884, the Milwaukee brewery of Jung & Borcherdt leased the brewery for $1,100 a year for four years to gain additional capacity. Becker was retained to be superintendent, but the arrangement soon collapsed and Becker moved to Ashland to take over the Schottmueller brewery. The brewery was then converted to a malt house for the Milwaukee firm. The 1891 Sanborn map shows the facility still in use, but by 1898 it was no longer used as a malt house and use was limited to a depot for Pabst, which had purchased the assets of the Jung & Borcherdt.

Some sources, including Wing's directories, list this brewery as being operated by Gutheil Bros. from 1883–1888, but local evidence about their proprietorship is lacking. They may have operated it for Jung & Borcherdt, or it may be a directory error since the same firm was also listed in Kiel (and is better documented there).

Fred R. Gutheil (& Co.) (1866–1882)
Jaeckels & Thomas (1882–83)
Nicholas Thomas (1883–88)
Thomas & Freyer (1888–1890)
Albert Freyer (1890–91)
Freyer & Hoch (1891–93)
Gierow & Hoch (1893–1901)
Gierow & Hoch Brewing Co. (1901–7)
Chilton Brewery (Kroenke & Landgraf) (1907–1910)
Calumet Brewing Co. (1911–1920)
Calumet Brewing Co. (1933–37)
Henry Rahr Brewing Co. (1937)
Calumet Brewing Co. (1937–1942)
125 EAST COMMERCE

Fred Gutheil moved from Kiel to establish a new brewery in Chilton in 1866. (Accounts that he began brewing here in 1853 are refuted by local reports.) His brewery remained a relatively small operation through its first few decades. During the early 1870s he was producing a steady 200-plus barrels a year, and finally crossed the 300-barrel threshold before the end of the decade. Gutheil had a strong reputation as a businessman—the R. G. Dun & Co. credit evaluator reported in 1873 that Gutheil was "Good as the Bank of England."

Gutheil's production was down to 162 barrels in fiscal 1882, and soon sold his brewery and went to Gunnison, Colorado to look over the prospects for a brewery there. New owners Jacob Jaeckels and Nicholas Thomas were a saloon owner and a blacksmith respectively. Jaeckels sold his share to Thomas in 1883. As Thomas was not a brewer, he was forced to hire trained brewers to supervise production. One of these, Erhardt Kick, died in February 1888 when he fell off a board placed across a vat filled with hot water. However, it appears that Thomas and his successor made substantial expansions, since several sources report that capacity (and sometimes production) in the 1890s was more than 3,000 barrels.

Stability arrived with the partnership of Herman Gierow and John Hoch in 1893. Albert Freyer sold out and was considering a move to Jefferson, and Gierow took his place and joined Hoch for the next fourteen years. Gierow retired in 1906, and the next year John Landgraf first became associated with the firm he would guide even after Prohibition. He soon gave the brewery the name of the county in which it operated.

While the Calumet Brewing Co. was seldom in the news in the years before Prohibition, the company grabbed frequent headlines in its last two decades. The Prohibition-era company, Calumet Sales Corporation, was padlocked in 1925 for violations of the dry laws. The brewery was the subject of more praiseworthy headlines starting in 1932 when the Calumet Brewing Company bought Calumet Products Company and proposed to manufacture "Canadian King" liquid malt. This was merely a prelude to the excitement that followed the election of Roosevelt in 1932. The *Sheboygan Press* announced that Calumet Brewing Co. was preparing for legal beer, and planning to spend $65,000. The excitement was heightened in this small city by the news that "offers have been made by outside capital in Menasha, Milwaukee, Philadelphia and other places to operate the brewery." Newspapers also lauded the fact that fifteen men would obtain work at the brewery during desperate economic times.

The widespread interest in Chilton's brewery seems to have been more than local boosterism. While the officers of the company included no-one from farther away than Milwaukee, when the brewery shipped its first beer in early May 1933, a carload a day was destined for Minnesota, Iowa, North Dakota, Nebraska, and 2,000 cases a day to Los Angeles. The revived Badger Brand was drawing attention around the country. However, Secretary O. W. McCarty reassured Chilton residents at the official launch celebration for Badger Beer that "Calumet County will receive first attention from the Calumet Brewing Co." Indeed, the company supported the local community by sponsoring a basketball team called the Badger Brands "with a strong line-up of the best basketball players in this territory." It also sponsored the Badger Boys, a piano duo which played a regular fifteen-minute program on WIBL radio (Sheboygan).

Unfortunately, Calumet Brewing Co. was also receiving first attention from government officials in Madison, Milwaukee and Chicago. In April 1934, federal authorities in Milwaukee heard arguments on a motion to revoke the company's brewing permit—reported to be the first such action since repeal. On 1 June, the brewery was seized by a team of deputies and federal agents led by the U.S. marshal. The plant was idled except for running the refrigerating plant to keep the existing beer from spoiling. The raid was said to be either the first of its kind in the United States or the first such act in forty years. A review of the books at the brewery led Wisconsin's revenue auditors to conclude "that there was juggling going on." Based on the counts of barrels and discrepancies between state and federal revenue stamps, Wisconsin inspectors reported ". . . it is evident that either state, Minnesota or Wisconsin, has been defrauded of its revenue." While the company challenged the seizure, federal judge F. A. Geiger upheld the action, though he ruled that certain personal articles "such as a picture of President Roosevelt" might be excluded from the seizure. By fall, the remaining beer was sold to meet obligations, and the brewery was purchased by another group of mostly Chilton residents led by Edward Bonk.

For the next few years, the brewery struggled to make a consistent profit. In February 1937, Calumet Brewing Co. was sold to Henry C. Rahr Brewing Co. of Green Bay. This arrangement was short-lived, and by July the Calumet name was back on the company. While production hovered around 10,000 barrels for the next several years, the company was in a precarious financial position. When war broke out in 1941, increasing taxes and high material costs, in part because of the small brewery's inability to purchase at favorable rates compared to larger firms, pushed the company to the brink. While management claimed the brewery "had been selling enough . . . to have operated at a profit under ordinary conditions," in March 1942 Calumet Brewing Co. closed its doors for good and dumped 9,000 gallons of beer into the Manitowoc River rather than pay the license fees and taxes required to sell the beer.

Rowland's Calumet Brewing Co., Inc.
(1990–present)
25 N. Madison Street (1990–present);
57 School Street (production brewery)
(2000–present)

Located in a classic Wisconsin corner tavern, Rowland's Calumet Brewing Co. was among Wisconsin's pioneering brewpubs. In 1983, Bob and Bonita Rowland bought a tavern located in a nineteenth-century building that had been home to Chilton's first fire station and housed city hall for a period before becoming a tavern in 1937. They renamed the establishment the Roll-In. A few years later business was slowing when Bob read a magazine article about brewpubs. Bob already had some experience homebrewing (learned from his father in the hills of West Virginia), and decided to try "the craziest idea I've ever had." Rather than starting with scavenged brewing equipment, Rowland purchased a new three-barrel system from JV Northwest of Oregon. The rest of the equipment was purchased locally and local contractors completed the extensive remodeling of the tavern to accommodate the brewhouse—very much like new breweries of the nineteenth century. The first beer went on tap in September 1990, and in the next two years the business was attracting regulars from around the region and travelers from all over the world to visit what Rowland claimed was then the smallest city in the nation to have a brewery. During the first year he produced a mere eighty barrels, but pushed the total over one hundred barrels the next year.

It was during that second year of operation that Bob Rowland had the idea hold a craft beer festival in Chilton—one of the first such

This stunning light is a rare example of an "infinity sign." Although about only eight inches deep, it gave the impression of being much deeper. COLLECTION OF JOHN STEINER.

Growler from Rowland's Calumet Brewing Co., acquired in 2008. AUTHOR'S COLLECTION.

events to be held outside a major city. Eight different breweries attended the first year (pouring a mere sixteen beers), but the Wisconsin Micro Brewers Beer Festival soon grew to around thirty breweries—which was all that could fit comfortably in the Calumet County Fairgrounds.

Rowland's Calumet Brewing continued to grow within its modest capacity, and by 1997 production was over 300 barrels. The increased demand led them to purchase new building that year. They purchased a seven-barrel brewing system and by 2000 they were brewing in the new School Street location. In 2005, Bob and Bonita celebrated fifteen years as a brewpub and production of their 5,000th barrel. Rowland's Calumet Pilsner was based on the recipe handed down from Bob's father, who said "'he needed it a little thicker and heavier to wash the coal dust out of his throat."

For many years the Rowlands operated a pilot brewery for Briess Malting Co. of Chilton—brewing nearly seventy batches that were sent all over the world to showcase Briess products. Bob Rowland dedicated his 1,876th barrel of beer to Briess (that being the year they were founded).

Tragedy struck when Bob Rowland died at age fifty-five in May 2006—just four days before the fifteenth annual Beer Festival. The festival went on that year "as a celebration of Bob, a celebration of life, a celebration of beer," as Bonita put it, and has continued to be a successful festival. The Rowlands' son Pat took over brewing duties. Both Bob and Pat were active in local community groups and served terms as president of the local Chamber of Commerce. One flavorful contribution to civic affairs is the apple-pumpkin beer brewed for the Crafty Apple Festival.

As of 2017, Rowland's beer was available in about forty retail accounts around northeastern Wisconsin, as well as at the Roll-In Brew Pub in Chilton.

CHIPPEWA FALLS
(Chippewa County)

Francis X. Schmidmeyer (1855?–1876)
Herbert Mansen (1859?–1860?)
Huber & Neher (1876–79)
MODERN WEST RIVER STREET, WEST OF SUPERIOR STREET

Research by Wisconsin archaeologist Tim Wolter indicates that F. X. Schmidmeyer (various spellings) was brewing in Chippewa Falls as early as 1855. Schmidmeyer apparently leased or rented the brewery off and on, since it is Herbert Mansen who is listed in the 1860 census as the Chippewa Falls brewer. Its production was relatively large for a business so far out on the frontier—200 barrels were produced in fiscal 1860 with the help of two employees. The brewery burned in March 1865, and unfortunately the insurance had run out about a month earlier. Schmidmeyer began to rebuild, and by October 1866 was able to announce: "This Brewery has been recently completed and has all the modern appliances for making No. 1 Beer and Lager." Kasper Neher, later of Augusta, was the foreman/brewmaster "for a long time" until 1869, and may have leased the brewery at some point. Schmidmeyer's reputation seems to have been good in this era, since the *Chippewa Union & Times* referred to him as "owner of the best brewery in the Chippewa Valley" and claimed that "everybody knows you can't be beat at" brewing good beer. Unfortunately, he also incurred a hefty $500 fine for violations of the revenue law in 1871. Production jumped from 374 barrels in fiscal 1871 to 624 in fiscal 1872—not as much as the nearly 1,000 produced by Leinenkugel & Miller, but more than any other brewery in the surrounding counties.

Schmidmeyer's ownership story is complicated by the fact that he is reported in several sources to have taken as his second wife the widow of a brewer named Gebhard, who may have leased or purchased the brewery from Schmidmeyer. (An 1867 article in the *Semi-Weekly Wisconsin* reported that Gebhard ran the only brewery in town at that point.) Documents discovered by Wolter suggest that it was Amelia who actually owned the property and Schmidmeyer ran the brewery for her, but he was clearly responsible for the brewery several years before this marriage. Confusingly, a note in the *Chippewa Herald* reported that Schmidmeyer "resume[d] possession of the lower brewery, and hereafter will have charge of it." While the figures for 1874 and 1875 report no production, it is clear that Schimdmeyer was still in business, since he was listed as having made $5,000 of brewery improvements during 1873. During 1874 Schmidmeyer had a short-lived partnership with Mike Welton, which dissolved in August.

In 1876, Schmidmeyer got out of the brewing business for good when he leased the brewery to Huber and Neher. Their early reports in R. G. Dun & Co. reports suggested they were responsible and doing well. Production in 1878 was back to 1872 levels. However, by early 1879 they were rated as "irresponsible" and by the end of the year were out of business. The buildings remained for several years, and were used as temporary housing for three families of Russian refugees in 1882. A cave in Irvine Park is all that is known to remain of Schmidmeyer's business.

Leinenkugel and Miller, Spring Brewery (1867–1883)

Jacob Leinenkugel's Spring Brewery (1883–1898)

J. Leinenkugel Brewing Co. (1898–1920)

Jacob Leinenkugel Brewing Co. (1933–1987)

Jacob Leinenkugel Brewing Co. division of Miller Brewing Co. (1987–present)

124 EAST ELM STREET (FORMERLY JEFFERSON AVENUE)

Twenty-six-year-old Jacob Leinenkugel was the third member of his family to start a brewery in Wisconsin. He and his partner John Miller, a friend from his years in Sauk City, selected a location higher up the hill than their rival Schmidmeyer, and began production in 1867. While they seldom made news in the first year or two, by the 1870s the local and regional papers were full of news about the rapid expansion of the brewery and the quality of its product.

From the beginning, Leinenkugel & Miller devoted time and treasure to expanding their plant. Less than four years after opening, they had a cellar cut into the rock which a visitor from Madison described as "nearly as large as Rodermund's." Later that year, they embarked on a major building program which included new residences for the partners, an addition to the brewery, new machinery, and two noteworthy additions that showed how far they were ahead of most other breweries of their size and age. Among the new machinery was a new boiler, which made them one of the rare steam powered breweries outside of the major cities. In addition, the new malt house was built entirely of stone, indicating they already had sufficient funds to build a more permanent structure than the usual frame buildings. Just two years later, Leinenkugel & Miller were compelled to add a three-story "patent ice house, so that beer can be made in the summer just as well as in winter." This new building was designed with a short "underground railway track connecting it with the front cellar," which was a feature few country breweries could dream of. During 1873, the company spent $33,000 on improvements—a staggering sum for a small brewery in the 1870s: nearly as much as the total cost of the county courthouse then under construction and more than twice as much as the new First National Bank. The *Herald* concluded in 1879: "a year never passes but what these energetic citizens are erecting something." Even so, the brewery was still a small-town operation. An 1880 article praised the delivery wagon and its team of "dapple gray horses weighing sixteen hundred pounds each," but it was notable that they only had a single wagon and team.

The most significant expansion of the first few decades began in the summer of 1880, when the partners began to prepare to bottle their own beer. This move made them among the earliest smaller breweries to have their own bottling operation, and the *Herald* rejoiced: "there won't be any more necessity for importing Milwaukee or La Crosse bottled goods." By the next February the company advertised cases of twenty-four quarts or thirty-six pints, "Delivered to any part of the city, or at express office, or railroad depot, free of charge." The new filling and bottle washing equipment supported a capacity of 1,500 quart bottles per day. This capacity gave them a significant advantage over small local bottlers, however, such businesses did not disappear from the scene—in fact, local grocer John P. Mitchell also set up a bottling operation in the back of his store in 1880.

Like most breweries of the era, the Leinenkugel & Miller brewery functioned as something of an extended family. A dormitory provided housing for the many single men who worked at the brewery, and Jacob's first wife Josephine was responsible for the meals of up to twenty men, as well as her own household chores and caring for children. The company family lost a member in 1884 when Leinenkugel bought out the interest of founding partner John Miller. The company continued to prosper under Jacob's direction, and the Herald was able to report at the end of the decade Leinenkugel's beer had "stopped the demand for foreign importations" from Milwaukee. In fact, Leinenkugel was solidifying his own hold on other markets. He sent his son Matt to operate the depot in Eau Claire—right in the backyard of other Leinenkugel breweries. Advertisements from the late 1880s and 1890s show that Leinenkugel also produced porter and bock beer, offering his customers a full product line.

In addition to his duties at the brewery, Jacob Leinenkugel was an important political leader of the community. He was elected alderman in the first city election of 1869, and later served three terms as mayor in addition to several more terms on the city council. Jacob was a benefactor to the community in ways beyond politics. He was a major contributor to St. Charles Boromeo parish and donated altars for the new church. He also had a reputation for helping the needy with food from the grocery story and meat market that he ran along with the brewery. Jacob was also foresighted enough to realize the importance of protecting his business for his family. In 1898

This pre-Prohibition tray emphasized the health-giving properties of Leinenkugel High Grade Beers.
COLLECTION OF GARY SCHULTZ.

he incorporated the company with himself as president—and not a moment too soon, since he died the next year at age fifty-seven. The transition to the next generation was smooth: son Matt took over as president, daughter Rose's husband Henry Casper became general manager and younger daughter Susan's husband John Mayer became sales manager. Descendants of all three would remain with the company well into the twentieth century.

The Leinenkugel Brewing Co. of the early twentieth century was a flourishing business. Around thirty men were employed at the brewery, and the beer was distributed throughout Northern Wisconsin. The brewery employees were unionized in 1903, about the same time as their brethren in Eau Claire. The brewery campus of 1910 included a modern brewhouse, a sprawling malthouse adjacent to the cellars, a cooper shop, a carpentry shop, the bottling facility, a boarding house, stables and several storage and utility buildings.

Prohibition forced the brewery to adapt. Luckily, the brewery was in sound financial shape, and could survive the tepid reception given its near beer, Leino. Eventually, a popular soda water helped pay the bills and keep the company functional during the dry era.

Many repairs and upgrades were required before the brewery could reopen in 1933. The company also replaced the horse teams with trucks, though one horse team was kept on for city deliveries until after World War II. While members of the Leinenkugel, Mayer and Casper families remained in charge of the brewery, the brewmasters were equally important, starting after Prohibition with Cornils F. Schmidt. Elmer Baesemann took over in 1945 and oversaw the postwar wave of improvements. Some improvements were required by the state, such as the installation of sewage and waste disposal facilities in 1949–1950 to reduce pollution in the Chippewa River. The brewery kept one nod to tradition by maintaining horse-drawn deliveries to some city accounts through the early 1950s. The brewery continued to consolidate its business in northwestern Wisconsin, and even established an agency in Onalaska, on the doorstep of its rivals in La Crosse. Among Leinenkugel Brewing Company's many promotions were frequent sponsorships of horseracing prizes at fairs throughout northern Wisconsin.

As bars began to offer more beers on draught, breweries sought to make their tap handles stand out to encourage patrons to buy their beers. Leinenkugel's canoe tap handles from the early 2000s continued the northwoods theme of much of the company's marketing. COLLECTION OF JIM AND RUTH BEATON.

Like many smaller breweries, Leinenkugel was relatively late to adopt the beer can—only turning to the Crowntainer style in 1952 and replacing it with the flattop can in 1958. The company was in a good enough financial position to replace all its fermenters in 1964 with state of the art glass-lined tanks, and installed a new aging cellar in 1967.

The brewery remained a fixture in the region from its centennial into the next two decades, in part because of its expansion into Michigan's Upper Peninsula with the purchase of Bosch Brewing Co. in 1973 and a strong following in eastern Minnesota. But declining sales encouraged Leinenkugel to accept a purchase offer from Miller Brewing Co. in 1988. The move gave Leinenkugel marketing and sales resources unimaginable by most small town breweries, and Leinenkugel products eventually became available nationwide.

The new popularity of Leinenkugel products strained the capacity of a brewery designed to supply a regional market. The company moved some draught beer production to Miller's main brewery, and to the Heileman-owned

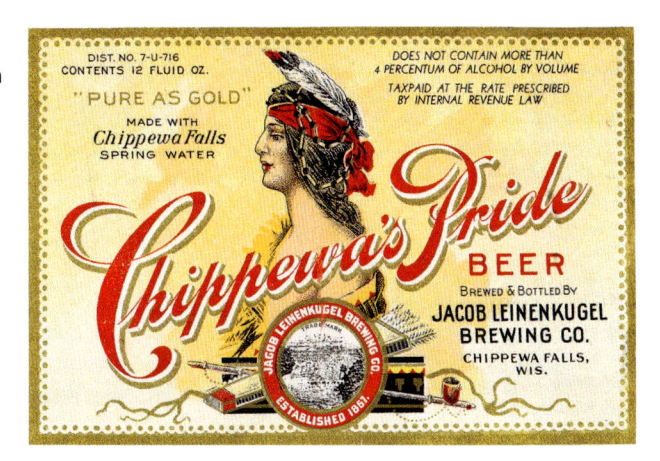

The classic post-Prohibition Chippewa's Pride label included a version of the pre-Prohibition logo as well as the Indian maiden featured on the label up until the present. COLLECTION OF TYE SCHWALBE.

WISCONSIN BREWERIES AND BREWPUBS 393

Blatz brewery in Milwaukee. This ran counter to an earlier pledge that all beers still would be made with water from the Big Eddy spring near the brewery. Leinenkugel's need for more production became so acute that in September, 1995, it purchased the Blatz facility from Heileman, which was in need of cash. After the formation of MillerCoors, this facility on Tenth Street provided part of the name for the company's Tenth and Blake division that focused on craft beers, imports, and other beers marketed in a similar manner. (The Blake portion came from Coors' Sandlot Brewery (later Blue Moon Brewing Company @ the Sandlot) located inside Coors Field on Blake Street in Denver.)

Even as the market expanded, Leinenkugel Brewing Co. continued to emphasize the small-town, family-owned nature of the business. The Leinie Lodge became a popular tourist destination, and the company celebrated its 150th anniversary in 2017 by enhancing the tour experience with new displays and features. (More on the period from 1950 through the present appears in chapter 10.)

Louis Busselman (1869?–1872?)
Union Brewery (1872)
Oehlschlager and Kuehn (1872–73)
Peter Mairet & Fred Schmidt (1873)
Schmidt & Son (1873–75)
SPRING STREET, ACROSS FROM DUNCAN CREEK

Louis Busselman, Adam Dearen, Adam Owener and Conrad Strosell are listed as brewers in the 1870 population census, and all lived in close proximity of each other. Busselman was the only one with measurable property holdings, so he may have been the senior partner of the business. However, when the Union Brewery appears in the excise records, the partners are listed as Busselman, John P. Mitchell and Mathew J. Cummings. The firm was dissolved in May 1872 when Busselman left the partnership. It is likely that Oehlschlager and Kuehn took over this brewery in 1872, since dates in the excise records fit and there is no evidence of a fourth brewery in the city. The same records suggest that Schmidt & Son had the brewery by December 1873, but statistics for 1874 and 1875 record no production. The *Chippewa Herald* has a few brief mentions of the brewery during the month when Mairet & Schmidt were in business, but provides no information other than the fact that beer was produced and the partnership broke up in December 1873. The assessment of the firm by the R. G. Dun & Co. researcher "Know little ab[ou]t the bus[isness]" applies as much to the brewery's history as it may have to the brewers' acumen.

Brewster Bros. Brewing Co. (2016 to present)
402 WEST RIVER STREET

Located near the location of the former Schmidmeyer brewery, Jim Stirn and Kurt Schneider opened their brewery and distillery in 2016—the first combination of its kind in the state. They designed the twenty-barrel brewing system to fit the space, which was a former video rental store (and which earned recognition for Best Adaptive Reuse Project in the 2016 Wisconsin Main Street Awards). The brewery and taproom have patios that overlook the Chippewa River valley. The 2,500-liter fractional distillation unit and a 100-liter developmental still are used to produce vodka, rum, gin, flavored whiskies and other spirits. The brewery side of the business offers a variety of ales along with occasional seasonal lagers.

CHRISTIANA TOWNSHIP
(Village of Clinton) (Dane County)

G. Lewis (1849?–1858?)
Geo. Hartwell (1860?–?)
Jacobson and Hartwell (1866?–67)
Ole Jacobson (1867–1872)
K. J. Gildenhaus (1872–73?)
Henry Mehls (Mehels) (?–1878)

The 1880 history of Dane County claims that a Mr. Lewis established a brewery few years after the settlement of the village of Clinton (modern Rockdale), which was around 1846. The 1850 census lists John Smith, a native of England, as a brewer, but since he owned no real estate is possible that Lewis hired him to make the beer. G. Lewis is still listed in the state business directory of 1858, but nothing else is known about him or his brewery.

George Hartwell appears in the 1860 census as a brewer, but like Smith, he appears to have been an employee rather than the proprietor. Excise records suggest that sometime before 1867 Hartwell formed a partnership with Norwegian immigrant Ole Jacobson. Hartwell apparently left the partnership that year and Jacobsen became sole proprietor. According to the 1870 census he had one employee, countryman Ole Olson. The excise records report that the capacity of Jacobson's brewery in 1870 was thirty barrels a week, though sales were typically closer to seven barrels a month. The 1880 history says that Jacobson also ran a distillery at the site. In 1872 Jacobson apparently turned the business over to K. J. Gildenhaus. Henry Mehls produced 166 barrels in 1878, but reported no production the next year and the brewery apparently closed. Wayne Kroll's research supports the supposition that the various businesses reported under the Christiana name were the same brewery.

The *Wisconsin State Journal* reported in January 1881 that the old brewery in Clinton had been converted to a temperance hall, which was dedicated with speeches from several regional heroes of the movement, including the headliner Jack Waburton—known for saving many souls. At some point the large building appears to have become a creamery, which was photographed around 1900. The size of the structure lends credence to the reports of the thirty-barrel capacity in the 1870s.

CLARKS MILLS
(Manitowoc County)

Nicholas Ball (1870?–72?)
Anton Baumann (1873?)
John Geo. Faatz (1874?–75)
Faatz & Schweitzer (1875?–78)

The brewery in Clarks Mills was most likely started by Nicholas Ball (Bool) around 1870. On an 1872 map of Manitowoc County, he appears in the Clarks Mills business directory as

Nicholas Ball. According to the 1873 excise collection records, the brewery was in the hands of Anton Baumann. The brewery sometimes listed as located in Cato and belonging to John Geo. Faatz was in fact the Clarks Mills business. Faatz was listed in the R. G. Dun & Co. records as the brewery owner in July 1875, and had brewed 141 barrels in the previous year. By the beginning of 1876 his property was in the hands of creditors, and it is possible that the Schweitzer who appears in the name of the business starting in 1876 was either a new investor or a major creditor. In July 1878 the firm was reported as out of business. Some sources list the brewery as late as 1880, but there is no production data to support this.

Clear Lake *(Polk County)*

William Kuether Brewing Co. (2004–6)
360 Fourth Street

William C. Kuether owned the Anheuser-Busch distributorship in the Twin Cities, and his son Billy decided to open a brewery in northwestern Wisconsin, hoping that name recognition in the beer community through his father's business would help gain a foothold with distributors and retailers. Kuether purchased the old Village Hall which had been slated to be razed, purchased equipment from a defunct brewery in Washington, and began the renovation process. The William Kuether Brewing Co. served its first beer, Blonde Ale, in late June 2004. The company brewed about half a dozen beers, most marketed under the 'Sconnie label (a slang term for Wisconsin). Brewer Richard Stueven reported that whatever the merits of Clear Lake were as a business location, the water there was "fantastic for brewing."

Local customers were not particularly interested in the 'Sconnie beers, which made marketing against Miller Lite and Leinenkugel a constant challenge. Bottles and kegs were shipped to the nearby Twin Cities, but this market was not as lucrative as they had hoped. Disappointing sales and higher than expected expenses led to the brewery's closure in 2006.

Cold Spring Township *(Jefferson County)*

Edward Roethe (1859?–1860)
"One mile north of Whitewater"

Edward Roethe was listed as a brewer in the 1860 population census, though not in the industrial census of that year, which probably means that he did not reach the $500 sales threshold required for inclusion. However, when the brewery burned in September 1860, Roethe's loss was given as between $3,000 and $4,000, a large sum for a year-old brewery, which suggests that Roethe may have been in business somewhat earlier than so far known. Roethe later went into the furniture business in Whitewater with George Streng. It is also possible that this brewery was started prior to 1856 by William Marshall (see Whitewater).

Columbus *(Columbia County)*

Jacob Jussen (1848?–49)
Alois Brauchle (1849–1886?)
Peter Brauchle (1886?–1897)
August Nothhelfer (1897–1900)
Agnes Brauchle (1900–1901)
City Brewing Co. (1901–3?)
Ludington Street

According to an 1880 county history, Jacob Jussen was "the pioneer brewer of Columbus." Apparently the brewery was situated in his house on the west bank of the Crawfish River. Jussen soon sold the brewery to Alois Brauchle (sometimes called Louis or A. Louis), who had trained as a brewer in Wurtemburg. He worked for Johann Braun in Milwaukee for two years, then went to a brewery in Racine before coming to Columbus to work for Jussen in 1848. There are few records of early production, since Brauchle was not included in either the 1850 or 1860 industry censuses. This is not surprising, given that even in the early 1870s Brauchle was still producing well under 100 barrels a year. In fact, in 1874, he only produced four barrels, but recovered to sixty-nine the next year, which put him at the lead of the city's three breweries, who seldom totaled 200 barrels until 1879. Brauchle also sold ice at his brewery, which in 1859 he sold for 1¢ per pound and which he claimed was "the purest kind, and was put up on purpose for family use, and for cooling drinks in saloons."

In the 1860s, Brauchle had a solid reputation, but in the mid-1870s he began to suffer financial reverses, and by 1880 was regarded as a poor credit risk. In 1884, Alois' son Peter took over the brewery. In 1886 he struck a new artesian well at the brewery, though this new well apparently reduced the flow of other wells in Columbus. Excise records show that Peter produced more than 500 barrels in 1894, but dropped back below that mark by 1896. Brauchle appears to have left brewing in 1897, even though his name is still found in the often-inaccurate state business directories as late as 1905. During August Nothhelfer's term the brewery suffered a major fire sometime after September 1898, just a day after the insurance had expired. However, the 1904 Sanborn map indicates that Brauchle was operating a small pop factory in one room of the old brewery, the rest of which was labeled vacant and "not kept in repairs." The proprietorships of Peter's wife Agnes and the later City Brewing Co. are not well documented and may have simply represented continued ownership of the property rather than an active brewery.

Henry Kurth (1859–1880)
John H. Kurth (1880–86)
John H. Kurth & Co. (1886–1904)
The Kurth Co. (1904–1920)
The Kurth Company (1933–1949)
Ludington Street, later Park Avenue

Henry Kurth clearly intended to make a career of brewing in Columbus, since a contemporary history claims that he arrived with "his family and a four-barrel brewer's boiler." In 1865 he had prospered enough from the "'creamy, dreamy beer'" to build a new brick brewery at a cost of $4,000, which he equipped over the course of the next year with new equipment. The new brewery had a capacity of sixty barrels per week, though local demand was seldom

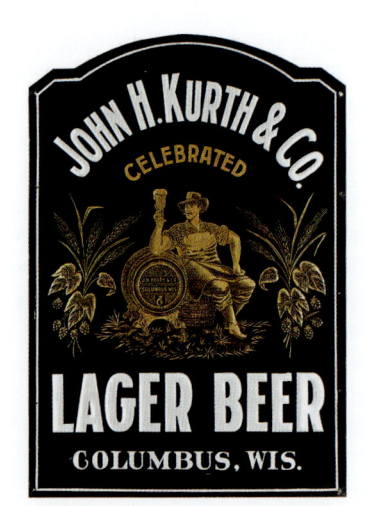

A striking tin sign (ca. 1895). Courtesy of National Brewery Museum.

more than 300 barrels per year through the 1870s. In 1880, Henry turned the company over to his son John Henry, whose brother Christian joined the newly named John H. Kurth & Co. in 1886. The second generation expanded the brewery over the next few decades: in the early years of the twentieth century they built a new five-story brewery, and added on to nearly every part of the brewery including the bottling department which had been started in 1895.

A modern account of the brewery history by John Robert Kurth claims that the "heyday" of the brewery was in the early 1910s. The plant had a capacity of 100 barrels a day and supplied three tied houses in Columbus and seventeen others throughout the area. The company offered six different beers during this period: Banner lager, the darker Luxemburg, Columbia, a bock, Xmas Brew, and a draught lager. The brewery had its own hop farm, and distribution warehouses in Luxemburg, Portage and Tomah.

Kurth became a union shop in 1903 with thirteen charter members, whose wages increased to $2.50 a week. Malt house workers also received one day off per month. Employment data compiled by the state of Wisconsin in 1908 showed that the company employed thirty men and one woman, but most of these worked in the malt house, which had become much more important than the brewery. This gap grew in 1916 when the brewery suffered a catastrophic fire. The brewery was rebuilt, but with the imminent onset of Prohibition, beer never had a chance to re-establish itself.

The Kurth Co. malting business expanded significantly in 1911 when it established a plant in Milwaukee on Burnham Street (an area that was the center of Milwaukee's malting district for much of the twentieth century). The new facility had a capacity of two million bushels, making it one of the largest in the country.

Kurth Co. made some soft drinks during Prohibition, and resumed brewing shortly after beer was re-legalized. Its post-Prohibition brewing capacity was a modest 25,000 barrels, but after 1940 production was an even more modest 1,000 barrels per year. The Banner and Luxemburg brands had a small local following, but the attention of the company was on the profitable malting business, and brewing ceased in June 1949. Most of the buildings were removed over the years, and as of this writing only the office building remains,

The semiprofessional baseball team of Kurth Brewers was well known prior to Prohibition. Pitcher Frank "Seagan" Lange had four successful seasons with the White Sox in the 1910s (Lange's name is misspelled on this 1911 Piedmont cigarette card). They also fielded an African American player, Johnnie Williams, during the early 1900s (see 1907 team photograph in chapter 3). AUTHOR'S COLLECTION.

which is operated as a part-time tavern by LauRetta and John Robert Kurth.

Stephen Fleck, Farmer's Brewery (1869–1880)
Hayden Bros. (1880–81)
LUDINGTON STREET

Stephen Fleck began brewing in Columbus in 1869. The brewery was a small one that supplied only the immediate area. The Farmer's Brewery name and the small production suggest that the brewery was a side business for Fleck. In none of the years with known production quantities did he make more than sixty barrels (though he did out-produce Henry Kurth for a few years in the mid-1870s). The Hayden brothers appear in some brewery lists, but without information about their business.

Hydro Street Brewing Co. (2011–15)
152 WEST JAMES STREET

Aaron and Sandye Adams began serving house-brewed beer at their small brewpub in downtown Columbus in late 2011, though the grand opening was not until January 2012. The brewhouse was essentially a small system of homebrewing equipment which had a capacity of about one barrel per batch. Initial reception by the community was favorable, and the mug club had over 300 members by 2013. Hydro Street bottled some of their beers, notable among these was Seven Sisters Scotch Ale, which was strong enough on draught at 8.5 percent, but the bottled version was 10.7 percent.

The building, while historic, made brewing operations difficult. Attempts to expand brewing capacity required significant upgrades to the building. Hydro Street received a significant loan from the city of Columbus in 2013 to expand the business, but in 2015 they defaulted on the loan and the business closed.

CORNELL *(Chippewa County)*

Moon Ridge Brewpub (2015–present)
501 BRIDGE STREET

After being inspired while on vacation by the success of a brewery on the island of Maui, Roger and Cindy Miller decided to start a brewpub at home in Chippewa County. Their business opened in November 2015 in a former

396   THE DRINK THAT MADE WISCONSIN FAMOUS

restaurant. Roger designs and brews the beers, and Cindy creates pizzas using dough made from spent brewing grain.

Response from the community was enthusiastic, and in 2017 the Millers began an expansion program to increase the space in the restaurant and brewhouse and to install larger brewing equipment.

CROSS PLAINS *(Dane County)*

Geo. Esser & Son (1863–1885)
Jacob Esser, Cross Plains Brewery (1885–1910)
END OF WEST BREWERY ROAD

George Esser was one of the relatively rare brewers to establish his business during the Civil War when manpower was scarce. By 1870 Esser's brewery was comparatively large for a rural brewery, producing in excess of 500 barrels per year and by the end of the decade production approached 1,000 barrels. George's son Jacob joined the firm in 1881. George rented the brewery to Jacob in 1885, and it was run under his name for the next quarter century. Like most other breweries of the era, they delivered beer to the surrounding communities themselves, with a barrel of beer priced at $7 while a case of thirty-six bottles cost $1.75.

Competition from larger brewers in Madison and Milwaukee eventually forced the family to become distributors for other breweries as well as making their own beer. However, the company mortgaged the brewery to Hausmann Brewing Co. of Madison for $12,000 in 1910, and stopped brewing in Cross Plains. The family name moved in 1912 to Janesville where the old Hemming brewery became the Geo. H. Esser Ale & Porter Brewery. The Cross Plains business distributed Hausmann's beer until Prohibition at which point their main product became Blatz's near beer. Family accounts suggest that they continued to sell significant amounts of real beer as well.

The company resumed distributing beer after Prohibition, specializing in Fauerbach and Heileman's Old Style, as well as Ballantine Ale. At this writing, the fifth and sixth generations of Esser's family are keeping the old family label alive. Esser's Best and Esser's Cross Plains Special were reintroduced in the mid-1990s by the father and son team of Wayne and Larry Esser and brewed under contract. (Additional information on the early years of George Esser's brewery is found in Chapters 2 and 3.)

DALLAS *(Barron County)*

Viking Brewing Co. (1994–2010)
Five Star Brewing Co. (2010–11)
Valkyrie Brewing Co (2011–present)
234 DALLAS STREET WEST

Randy and Ann Lee founded the first microbrewery in Northwest Wisconsin in 1994 in a former Ford dealership in the small town of Dallas. Viking Brewing Co. became best known for unusual beers, including Hot Chocolate, with cocoa and hot peppers, and their first-ever brew, Mjød, an interpretation of a braggot (or bracket)—a mix of mead and beer. Another early beer was Fiddler's Finest, brewed for the Fiddler's Inn tavern just across the street from the brewery. The brewing schedule was largely dependent on the temperature in the poorly insulated brewery—ales were brewed during the warmer summer months and lager in the winter. Viking started packaging their beer in 22 oz bottles, but switched to 12-ounce bottles in 2005. The bottling machine is extremely old, which makes bottling "painful," but they have no plans to spend the money necessary for a canning line.

In 2010, the Lees sold their U.S. trademark on the Viking name to an Icelandic brewery that wanted to ship its Viking beer to America. The brewery operated briefly as Five Star Brewing, with a plan to offer a more traditional line of beers in six-packs instead of four-packs. The Lees were able to return to their Viking identity with the new name of Valkyrie, and abandoned the plan to limit the varieties of beer. During the course of a typical year, between fifteen and twenty beers are available in bottles or on draft.

While Viking brands were distributed in Minnesota, Valkyrie beers have been distributed mostly in a five-county range near the brewery. (A few accounts come to the brewery to pick up beer.) Some of the old Viking beers returned as styles became popular again. Valkyrie War Hammer is a variation on the old Viking Whole Stein: a coffee, oatmeal milk porter. Most of the beers emphasize grain rather than hops, but Supernova, a "Royal Australian" (not "imperial") IPA reaches 90 IBU while balanced with complex malt character.

A small selection of the many styles brewed during the Viking era. Many brands had whimsical names and creative label designs. J. S. Bock had a few bars of music on the left side of the label. AUTHOR'S COLLECTION.

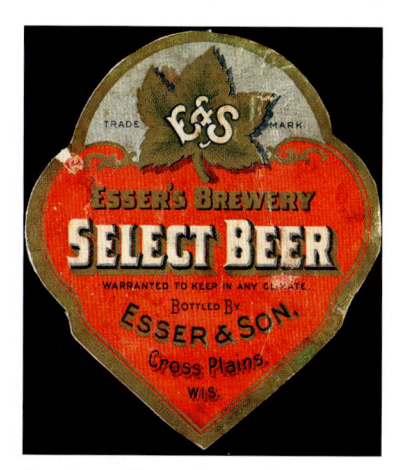

Very few pieces of breweriana are known from the early years of Esser's brewery. This label is from the early 1880s, when the company was still Esser & Son. COLLECTION OF TYE SCHWALBE.

WISCONSIN BREWERIES AND BREWPUBS 397

Valkyrie has continued its heritage of supporting community events from Morris Dancing to jazz combos. Their Oktoberfest has been popular for many years, especially the years when they cooked an extremely large bratwurst—often around 150 feet long. Continuing the tradition of brewers seeking political office, Randy planned a run for governor in 2002, and went so far as to start collecting signatures to get on the ballot.

DARLINGTON (Willow Springs Township) (Lafayette County)

Ashworth and Jackson (1867–1872?)
COLLINS & CHRIST (1872?–1877)
About one and one-half miles from Darlington on the banks of the West Pecatonia River

An early history of Lafayette County suggests that John Collins and John Chris [sic] started their brewery shortly after the Civil War, but the 1870 census does not list them as brewers. It is more likely that the brewery was started by Edmond Ashworth and Mr. Jackson. The excise records indicate that they started brewing in July 1867. Local historian John Dutcher contends that Ashworth and Jackson operated the brewery until around 1872, at which point Collins and Christ took over. Circumstantial evidence for this is found in the 1870 population census where Ashworth and Christ are near neighbors. Excise records for 1877 show Ignatius Collins as the party responsible for the tax. The brewery was struck by lightning and burned in 1877, thus "leaving the town free of this respectable nuisance."

DEERFIELD (Dane County)

Erik S. Hanhagen/Hauchung/Hanahaugh (1867–1870?)
John Writenberg (?) (1868)
E. Silperson (1870?–72?)
The inconsistent and often unreadable handwriting of those collecting data for directories, tax records, and the census adds confusion to the story of Deerfield's brewery. It appears that Erik S. Hanhagen or Hauchung began selling beer in November 1867. He may have leased the brewery to John Writenberg for several months in 1868 since Writenberg's name appears in the excise records. The 1872 state business directory claims the Deerfield brewery is run by E. Silperson, but it is likely that this is yet another misspelling of the original brewer's name (a contention supported by historian Wayne Kroll).

DELAFIELD TOWNSHIP (Waukesha County)

L. Wolff (1849?–1850?)
L. Wolff had a fairly substantial brewery in Waukesha county around 1850, since he reported production of over 300 barrels in the 1850 census of industry. While the industry census placed his brewery in Delafield, the population census of that year places him in Summit township. It is not clear how long he remained in business—the only possible clue was a notice of an 1859 sheriff's sale of land in Delafield that included brewery lots (though no owner was listed).

DELAFIELD (Waukesha County)

Joseph Dietrick, Delafield Brewery (1870?)
MILL STREET
The Delafield Brewery on Mill Street is noted in secondary sources, and Joseph Dietrick is listed as a brewer in the 1870 population census.

Delafield Brewhaus (1999–present)
3832 HILLSIDE DRIVE
The Delafield Brewhaus has developed a reputation for the variety and quality of its house beers. John Harrison, who has been with the Brewhaus since the beginning, and brewing chemist Dana Wolle established a disciplined process for making a wide variety of beer styles. Unlike many smaller breweries, Harrison and Wolle experimented with using as many as twenty different strains of yeast instead of one or two strains.

Founded originally by Mary Ann and Kim Witt and Cheryl and John Poweleit, Delafield Brewhaus was able to take advantage of a growing suburban region near major highways, and was one of the first brewpubs in Wisconsin to be located in a building built specifically for that business. Harrison selected a top of the line brewhouse, which is located right in the middle of the restaurant. The most notable features other than the brewing system are the giant fermenters that set off portions of the restaurant—brought in from Stevens Point brewery after they were withdrawn after one hundred years of service. Co-owner Bob Flemming has displayed a portion of his breweriana collection on the wall.

Water Street Brewery Lake Country (2000–present)
3191 GOLF ROAD
The first foray of Milwaukee's Water Street Brewery into the suburbs was to the west in Delafield. This restaurant opened in 2000, and featured a similar display of breweriana to the Milwaukee location.

DENMARK (Brown County)

Denmark Brewing Co. (1934–1947)
113 MAIN STREET
The Denmark Brewing Co. was one of the rare breweries to open after Prohibition in a city that had not hosted a brewery before the dry

The brewhouse divides the sections of the restaurant. The signs and posters displayed in the restaurant and bar represent breweries from around Wisconsin and all over the world. COURTESY OF DELAFIELD BREWHAUS.

years. The company was incorporated in 1933, and began production in 1934. Old Town Lager was the first brand, joined in 1938 by 20th Century Pale (pictured in chapter 7). The company built an addition in 1937, and production ranged between 12,000 and 20,000 barrels per year until the mid-1940s.

The end of the brewery was turbulent. In addition to rumored ties to Chicago gangsters, Alvin Bardin, a resident of Portage who was then president of the company, was accused by a stockholder of misappropriating about $400,000 of brewery funds, dealing in the black market, watering the beer and selling only eleven ounces of beer in the 12-ounce bottles. In addition, Lawrence P. Bardin, Alvin's brother, was still being paid $250 a week as general manager of the Denmark brewery even while working for another of Alvin's breweries (in Indianapolis). The black market allegations included evidence from a Florida distributor who had paid $2,400 above the wartime ceiling price for beer in 1946. In addition, the federal government had tax claims against the brewery totaling $259,191.29 for the years 1944–46 (as well as nearly $400,000 for the Eulberg Brewing Co.) Making matters worse, in 1948 Alvin Bardin allegedly dumped illegally between 30,000 and 40,000 gallons of beer into the Noshota River, poisoning hundreds of thousands of fish including freshly stocked trout. The river was cloudy for about four miles toward Lake Michigan, according to the area game warden. (The beer had to be dumped because it could not be sold due to the nonpayment of tax.) Alvin Bardin later faced a civil suit seeking $3,622 for killing game fish. The brewery closed in 1947, and the equipment was sold at auction in September 1948. The building still stands as of 2017.

Green Bay Brewing Co. (Hinterland Brewing) (1995–99)
5312 Steve's Cheese Road

Green Bay Brewing Co. was started by the husband and wife team of Bill and Michelle Tressler. Bill was a beer journalist who decided he wanted to create the beer instead of simply writing about it. The brewery was located in a former cheese plant (accounting for the unusual address). They tapped their first kegs of pale ale and amber ale on 9 November 1995 at the Cock & Bull Publick House in Green Bay. Their initial success compelled them to upgrade from a seven-barrel brewing system to a thirty-barrel system within a few months after opening. Tressler won several medals for his beers while brewing at this location, including a Gold at the 1997 World Beer Championships for his Bock. At least some of the syrup in the Maple Bock was harvested by the Tressler family. The beers were marketed under the Hinterland brand, though the company's official name was Green Bay Brewing.

Hinterland beers were bottled almost right away, and the brewery did occasional small contract brews to supplement their own label business. Their bottled beers were distributed as far away as Minnesota. The Tresslers fit the location to the name in 1999 when they moved to their new brewery in Green Bay. (See the listing under Green Bay.)

Denmark Brewing (1999–2008)
6000 Maribel Road

Longtime homebrewer Keith Gillaume went professional with his hobby in a two-story garage on his property. Most of the brewery was adapted or fabricated by Gillaume, and he had a capacity of about 300 barrels per year. The brewery offered a mix of styles, most of them ales. After the brewery closed, some of the equipment was purchased by O'So Brewing Co. of Plover and used in their first location.

Chatterhouse Brewery (2014–16)
5675 Maribel Road

Terry Taylor, a homebrewer who developed a taste for beer while living in Belgium, began setting up the brewhouse for Chatterhouse Brewery in September 2014. He received his brewing permit and started operation early in 2015. The brewery itself was not open to the public, but George Street Connection in De Pere served as a tasting room and retail outlet for the brewery. Chatterhouse beers were available on draft and in bottles, including No Sacrifice Ale, a gluten-free brew. In March 2016, the brewery announced that it was temporarily ceasing operations due to family issues, but has not restarted as of 2017.

DE PERE *(Brown County)*

Alexander P. Schmidt (1874–1905?)
Oneida Road, West De Pere (approximately modern 630 Grant Street)

After serving in the Civil War, Alexander Schmidt began to learn the brewing trade in Manitowoc. Excise tax records suggest that he ran a brewery with his father Martin in Manitowoc Rapids for several months in 1872. An 1895 county history claims he moved to Mazomanie where he ran a saloon and boarding house for a year, after which he returned to the north and started a brewery on land near De Pere. In 1874, De Pere newspapers reported that a party was looking for a brewery location on the west side of the river. By December, the *News* was able to report that Smith [sic] had commenced operations and "sometime in the latter part of January will afford the disciples of Gambrinus an opportunity to sample a quantity of native lager." The reception to Schmidt's product was enthusiastic, as the News rejoiced: "He has succeeded in making so good an article of lager beer that it will not require many days to wipe all foreign competition in the traffic of this article. We understand not a single keg of Milwaukee beer is now

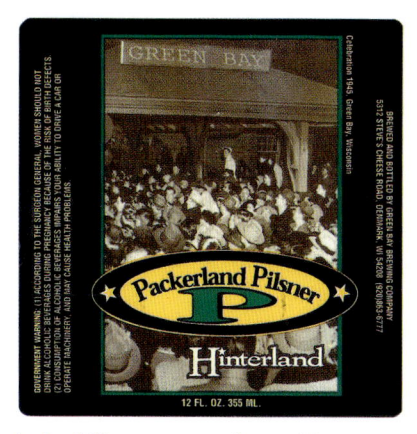

Packerland Pilsner was one of several beers to capitalize on the popularity of the NFL team. The label features a victory celebration in 1945. Collection of Scott Reich.

This business envelope from Schmidt's brewery was mailed in December 1886. It lists Schmidt's location as Nicolet rather than De Pere. COLLECTION OF JOHN STEINER.

brought to De Pere, and very little from Bellevue [Green Bay]."

Sanborn maps show a variety of facilities on the premises at various periods, including corn cribs, a straw stack, and a smoke house. The main building also included the Schmidt residence. The brewery was never large—sources agree that capacity was around 500 barrels per year—and the trade was all in the immediate area. In the late 1880s Schmidt advertised his business as brewer and malter, sometimes under the name of the Nicolet Brewery. There is no evidence that he ever bottled beer at the brewery. De Pere was a promising market, and Schmidt faced the possibility of local rivals twice: once in 1892 when Wallner & Deda of Kewaunee were exploring another location, and again in 1904 when a plan was publicized to turn the Transit House into a brewery at a cost of $50,000, but nothing came of either scheme. While some sources contend the brewery was in operation until 1908, the brewery is not included in the comprehensive lists of factory inspections undertaken by the State of Wisconsin in 1906, 1907 or 1908, and may have stopped brewing prior to that time.

Egan Brewing (1996–2001)
330 REID STREET

Egan Brewing started in 1996 to produce house brand bottled beers for Hansen's Dairy Store next door. In 1997 they added an account for Chuck's Deli stores, brewing Chuck's Famous Ales which were sold in unusual nine-packs of returnable bottles. The Egans added a bar in 1997 and a restaurant in 1998, which technically made them a brewpub. The restaurant may have actually hurt the business—some observers claimed that the bar was more popular with locals and some craft beer customers may have gone elsewhere. The brewery was without a head brewer for several months, during which local homebrewers and Green Bay Brewing Co. helped supply beer. The typical production of the brewery was about 200 barrels a year.

In April 2000, owner Nick Egan entered a partnership through which the restaurant became "Gallagher's of De Pere." The house label business dried up, and the relationship with Gallagher's did not meet expectations. The beers made by Greg Nash and Richard Steuven earned praise from Wisconsin beer writers, but the market for bottled craft beer in the Green Bay area was not well developed at this point, and the Egan family closed their brewery in September 2001.

Legends of De Pere (2001–present)
875 HERITAGE ROAD

The second of the Legends chain opened in 2001. These brewpubs are covered under the Howard location.

RockPere Brewing Co. (2014–present)
2284 LADDIE TRAIL

RockPere Brewing is a nanobrewery located on a hobby farm just south of De Pere in Rockland. Some of the hops for the beer are grown on the farm. A variety of ales are served at their "exclusive pourer," the Brickhouse in DePere.

DE SOTO *(Freeman Township) (Crawford County)*

George Eckhardt (1868–1882)
Charles Reiter (1882–84?)
Frederic Ponsloff (1884?)
Connelly, Kane & Co. (or Kane & Connelly) (1884?–86?)
MILL STREET

George Eckhardt began brewing in 1868 in a former store built by Cate & Co. ten years earlier. In 1870, he reported production of just under 300 barrels, but during the next few years he seldom sold more than ten barrels a month, even during the summer. By the end of the decade Eckhardt's production was back to around 250 barrels a year. Eckhardt ran a saloon in De Soto and another across the Mississippi River in Lansing, Iowa.

According to the county history, Charles Reiter took over the firm in 1882. At the time, his production was about 400 barrels per year, which was large for such a small river village. The last years of the brewery can only be pieced together through a few entries in industry and government publications. Frederic Ponsloff is listed as the owner of a brewery and saloon in De Soto in *Bradstreet's Reports* of 1884, and the Wisconsin industrial census of 1885 reported a brewery in Freeman producing 140 barrels of beer, presumably by the firm of Kane & Connelly listed in Wing's 1884 annual. The De Soto brewery is no longer listed in the 1887 annual.

DODGEVILLE *(Iowa County)*

Bichel & Trentzch (1867–68)
John G. Trentzch & Co. (1868–1872)
John G. Trentzch (1872–1880)

John Trentzch and J. F. Bichel (or Pischell) moved from Mineral Point to Dodgeville in 1867 and laid the foundations for what would soon be a stone brewery with a two-story wood superstructure. Trentzch had several partners during the first five years of business, including Bichel, John Rudersdorf and H. Zirfass. The excise records suggest he was on his own by the spring of 1872. The brewery had a capacity of about 400 barrels, though production was usually more like 200–300 barrels per year. The brewery burned to the ground in the spring of 1880 with a loss of $8,000, only $2,000 of which was covered by insurance. He did not rebuild, though portions of the cellar and icehouse still remain on private property.

DOWNING *(Dunn County)*

Sand Creek Brewing Co. (1999–2004)
SCHROEDER FARM, 1442 DUNN/ST. CROIX ROAD

Sand Creek Brewing Co. was an expansion of Cory Schroeder's homebrewing operation on the family farm. He partnered with Jim Wiesender and started brewing commercially with converted equipment in 1999—becoming one of three farmhouse breweries at the time in Wisconsin (the others were Lake Louie and Slab City). The "Frankenbrewery" nature of the business was best exemplified by the fifty-foot trailer that was used for conditioning and storage space. In late 2001 they purchased some equipment from the defunct Cherryland brewery to improve operations. Sand Creek Golden Ale and English Style Special Ale were only available on draft and in growlers within a limited area since the brewery's capacity was only 150 barrels per year. Despite brewing only two or three times a month, Sand Creek filled about 10,000 growlers during the five years of operation at the first location. Jim Wiesender described brewing at the cramped location as "fun, but tough." They attempted to expand in the Menomonie area, but instead took advantage of the availability of the Pioneer Brewing Co. brewery in Black River Falls. The rest of the story is covered with Pioneer/Sand Creek at the Black River Falls section.

Downsville (Dunn County)

John Sheibly (1866?–1867?)
Little is known about John Sheibly's brewery near Downsville, except that he produced fifty-six barrels during the summer of 1867. His brewery may have been acquired later by Valpon and Saile.

Vaplon? & Saile (1873?–1874?)
Vaplon & Saile first appear in the excise records in May 1873. Charles Saile had been brewing in Hastings, Minnesota until 1870, so could not have been part of this business prior to that date. Saile moved to Rice Lake to open a brewery in 1874, and it is not known if Vaplon continued on his own. A flood on the Red Cedar River in 1879 destroyed the brewery, though accounts suggest that the brewery had been empty for some time.

Dundas (Woodville Township) (Calumet County)

Valentine Schaeffer (1856?–58?)

Duplainville (Waukesha County)

J. Wertz (1856?–58?)
Wertz's brewery was included in the 1857 and 1858 state business directories. There was a J. A. Wirth who in 1861–1862 co-owned a parcel of land in the area with Jacob Goettelman, also a brewer in the area, and this is likely to be the same person.

Durand (Pepin County)

Harstoff & Stending (1863–66)
Lorenz & Jacoby (1866)
Philip Lorenz (1866–1890?)
Baur & Mertes (1890–91)
Baur & Breunig (1891–1908)
Durand Brewing Co. (1908–1920)
SOUTHEAST CORNER OF WEST WELLS STREET AND 9TH AVENUE WEST

Local histories disagree about the origin of this brewery. An account from 1891 claims that Harstoff & Stending (or Steiting) founded the brewery in 1863 and sold it to Lorenz; a 1919 history says that Lorenz founded it himself. The R. G. Dun credit reports indicate that Lorenz had a partner by the name of Jacoby for a few months in 1866, but that partnership was short-lived and dissolved in December 1866. By 1870, Lorenz was producing about 200 barrels a year in his hand-powered brewery. Production dropped in the early 1870s, but the biggest blow was a massive brewery fire in 1874, after which he rebuilt. (A different regional history claims that the fire was in 1874, but two pages later reports that it was in 1871.) County histories suggest that the brewery may have been closed at times during the 1880s, but it continued to appear in the normally reliable industry directories.

The next era began in 1890 when Frank Baur took over the business. Baur's first partner Nicholas H. (Nick) Mertes left the firm after about a year and was replaced by Jacob Breunig, who remained for the next twenty-four years. Throughout this period, the brewery was the largest industry in Durand and enlarged its capacity to more than 3,000 barrels, added a bottling line (prior to 1900), and expanded distribution in the region. The brewery's water came from a pure artesian well, though the brewery was built on top of a buried creek that flowed into the Chippewa River.

Breunig went to the Bloomer brewery in 1915. F. X. Warm replaced Bruenig as brewmaster, though Baur's son Anton had completed his brewmasters' training and was preparing to take over the brewery when Prohibition arrived and the brewery closed.

After the repeal of Prohibition, Durand's old brewery was one of several targeted by investors to resume production of legal beer. A group of investors from Minneapolis sought to reopen the brewery and expand its size to 45,000 barrels. These plans never were realized, and the equipment was sold off over the next ten years. In 1945, the former brewery buildings were used by the Hercules Powder Company, whose most notable line at the time was making whey from which penicillin was developed. Later on, Bauer Oil Co. took over the buildings for tire repair and retreading.

Alfred Calvert (1865?–1866)
Gustav Stending (1866–1876)
John Stringer (1876–79)
RIVER STREET

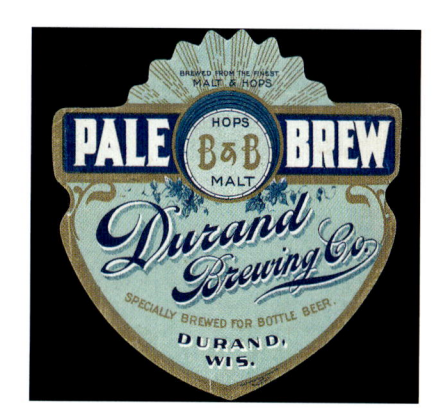

A very rare label from Durand Brewing Co., which kept the B & B logo for Baur & Breunig even after the name change. COLLECTION OF TYE SCHWALBE.

The River Street brewery was started by Alfred Calvert sometime prior to 1866. Articles in the *Durand Times* in September 1866 indicate that Calvert was building an addition to his brewery, which was possible in the first year of business but less likely.

Gustav Stending (or Steiting) moved over from the Wells Street brewery in late 1866, and "turned out his first 'brew' of ale" in December, which the *Times* proclaimed "sustains the high reputation that that institution had earned under its former proprietor." The R. G. Dun reports contained an evaluation of him as a "good man in his business" in 1866. The industrial census of 1870 shows Stending's production as around 200 barrels a year, similar to that of rival Lorenz, though Stending's brewery had at least some horsepower unlike Lorenz's hand-powered facility. In an 1873 industry directory, the ownership of this brewery was given as "Gustav Stending and wife" (Catherine). By this time his production had dropped to seventy-six barrels, a more precipitous drop than his crosstown rival. Stending appears to have transferred the brewery to John Stringer (sometimes given as Stimger) around 1876. Unfortunately, the brewery was destroyed by fire in January 1879 and was not rebuilt.

Eagle River *(Vilas County)*

Loaf & Stein Brewing (1997–99)
219 North Railroad Street
Brian & Andrea Smoko opened Loaf & Stein Brewing in a former American Legion Post in 1997. It remained in business for about two years, after which the brewing equipment was sold to Bull Falls Brewery of Wausau.

Tribute Brewing Co. (2012–present)
1106 North Bluebird Road
Bill Summers and Marc O'Brien founded Tribute Brewing Co. in 2012. They wanted a one-word name for the brewery, and actually started by looking at names of cars. The Mazda Tribute was one of the "finalists," and the name Tribute allowed them to name beers after local figures or landmarks, and to contribute to the community. (In addition, the middle letters of Tribute are IBU.) The taproom opened several months

This metal key fob dates from 2017. Author's collection.

before their own beer was available, which provided the advantage of allowing the owners to track which guest beers were popular and select their own brands accordingly.

The first packaged Tribute beers were sold in growlers at local grocery stores. But by January 2017, the first 16-ounce cans featuring Blueberry Train Wheat and 28 Lake Lager were on the shelves. A month later, Tribute celebrated its fourth anniversary with Vier, a Belgian-style quadrupel ale. The brewery has a barrel-aging program underway—one of the first projects features their popular White Legs pepper ale aged in tequila barrels.

East Troy Township *(Walworth County)*

John F. Schwartz (1847–1850)
Section 35, East Troy Township, near intersection of modern Miller Road and Honey Creek Road.
John F. Schwartz arrived in Wisconsin in 1841, when he bought eighty acres in East Troy Township (east of the village of that name). In 1847, he built a brewery, but only operated it for about three years until it burned down in 1850. He then gave up brewing for farming.

Eau Claire *(Eau Claire County)*

Anthony Schaefer & Mathias Leinenkugel (1858–1861)
Leinenkugel & Tobias Bullesbach (1861–62)
Mathias Leinenkugel, North Eau Claire Brewery (1862–1874)
Theresa Leinenkugel, Eagle Brewery (1874–1886)
Joseph M. Leinenkugel aka Leinenkugel Bros. (1886–88)
Henry Michel (1891–1904)

Michels Brewing Co. (1904–1912)
Northeast Corner of North Farwell & Madison
In the late 1850s, Eau Claire seemed like a promising site for settlers and therefore for would-be brewers. George Esser and John Hermann considered moving from Madison to start a brewery on the Chippewa River. However, they learned upon arrival in Eau Claire that Mathias Leinenkugel, whose father operated the Sauk City brewery, had already arrived with Anthony Schaefer to start their own brewery. While some accounts have this brewery starting in 1857 or as early as 1855, it is clear from local newspaper accounts that they did not have beer for sale until very late 1858 at the earliest. The 1860 Census of Industry put production for the previous year at 400 barrels, worth $2,800. Schaefer (or Shaefer) sold his share to Tobias Bullesbach in 1861, who then sold it to Leinenkugel for $1,000, $500 less than he paid for it. It is not clear whether the drop in value was due to the Civil War, concern about the future of the area, or another reason. Whatever the case, Mathias Leinenkugel found himself in sole possession of the North Eau Claire Brewery.

Leinenkugel continued to prosper, offering local residents bock beer in the spring, and by 1869 he was shipping beer to other cities to the east along the West Wisconsin rail line. During 1872 and 1873 he improved and expanded his brewery, and his production jumped from 341 barrels in 1872 to 562 the next year and an astounding 1,670 in 1874. Unfortunately, Mathias Leinenkugel did not live to see the results of this development—he died of kidney disease aggravated by fever at age 38 in October 1874. His wife Theresa inherited the brewery and proceeded to operate it for the next several years. While one business directory from 1874 calls this firm the Badger State Brewery, it was still called the North Eau Claire Brewery in all other sources until 1875, when the name Eagle Brewery was first used.

The brewery Theresa acquired was the largest in Eau Claire, and produced over 1,200 barrels most years. Soon Theresa's son Joseph was helping manage the brewery along with foreman Henry Koke, though Theresa was still listed as proprietor in all communications. She was held in high regard as a businessperson—the R. G. Dun & Co. credit reports state she was considered "very truthful" and "has been very successful." The reports further noted "The bus[iness] is managed by her son Jos.[eph] and he is of good ability. As with most breweries, they continued to make improvements as finances allowed. During a fire in 1881 the *Weekly Free Press* noted that the Eagle brewery had its own pump and hose, so the fire department was not needed that time. At some time prior to 1883 steam power was installed at the brewery, making fire less of a risk. In 1883, Joseph Leinenkugel purchased the Dells brewery, and in the next several city directories, Theresa Leinenkugel was listed as proprietor of both the Eagle and the renamed Empire breweries.

Theresa Leinenkugel passed away on the last day of 1885, and after that things went poorly for the family enterprises. Joseph and his brother Henry took over the breweries (while their sisters relinquished all rights to these properties). The sisters may have made a good decision, because whether the purchase of the Empire brewery was more than the finances could stand or the brewery improvements were not supported by increasing sales, Leinenkugel Bros. found themselves in debt. The company failed in the summer of 1888, and creditors seized the beer in the Eagle brewery (no mention was made of beer at the Empire brewery, so it may have ceased production earlier). The Leinenkugels won a lawsuit for damages since the beer was allowed to spoil before it could be sold, but this was not enough to restore the brewery to them, and the brewery was shuttered for approximately three years.

In October 1890, the *Eau Claire Weekly Leader* mused: "It is a wonder the old Leinenkugel brewery has lain idle so long. It is good property, and if the right man gets hold of it, it will pay well as there is no better stand in the Northwest." The right man was apparently staying at the Eau Claire House at that moment, since Henry Michel soon purchased the old Eagle brewery and began preparing the facility to brew once more. Michel (often spelled Michels) had worked at Philip Best for thirteen years, and after that ran his own breweries for about eight years—first at Mount Calvary, then at Neenah. With typical booster overstatement, the *Weekly Leader* gushed in June 1891, "The brewery now owned and conducted by Mr. Michels . . . career has not been one of success until this gentleman took hold of it . . . it hardly looks like the same place," despite the fact that Michels had only taken over the brewery five months earlier and ignoring the success of the brewery in the 1870s.

Michel's first decade seems to have been one of general progress. Newspaper ads noted the arrival of his bock beer each season and occasionally his "selebrated [sic] Extra Lager." In 1900 the brewery added a new bottling department and, since they could start with new machinery, used bottles with crown caps instead of corks. The brewery touted the relatively new device with ads showing a man laboring to pull a cork contrasted with a demure young woman easily popping the crown off her bottle.

The second decade of Michel's ownership was much more turbulent. A fire in 1902 caused $25,000 of damage, though the brewery was quickly rebuilt and more modern equipment was employed. About six hundred barrels of beer were saved from the fire, which allowed the firm to maintain some cash flow, though one sixty-barrel cask burned through "and let its amber contents foam all over the place." The rebuilt brewery became a union shop in December 1903, as the company signed an agreement with United Brewery Workers of America. Tragically, Henry Michel died suddenly of "catarrah of the throat" on May 15, 1905, and his son Henry Jr. was forced to take over the business. The family-owned company seemed to be in good shape until 1912, when the *Leader* suddenly announced that the company had been sold to "a large Milwaukee brewing firm," which was to enlarge the plant and keep Henry Jr. on with the new enterprise. However, within six months the brewery was being used as a warehouse and shop instead of beer, and Eau Claire was down to a single brewery.

Taylor & Son (1856?–1858?)

There was a John Taylor in Eau Claire who had a livery business in the late 1850s, and it is possible that his occupation was misread when compiling the 1857 state business directory.

Heyson & Son (1856?–1858?)

There was an Augustus Huysen in town at the time, but he was a merchant and lumber dealer and did not have sons of an age to be business partners. This may well be another misinterpretation on the part of the directory compilers.

Steiting and Winggen (1859–1861)
South end of block 40, R. F. Wilson's Addition (Half Moon later Oak Grove Township)

In December 1859, an ad in the *Eau Claire Daily Free Press* proclaimed "Steiting and Winggen have just completed their new Brewery . . . and are now manufacturing and will keep constantly on hand a superior article of Lager Beer, which we offer as low as can be bought in any market. The quality of our beer is the only recommend [sic] it needs. We will warrant it to be equal, if not superior, to any manufactured west of Milwaukee." Gustave Steiting and Peter Winggen apparently did not produce enough

The back of this advertising card reported that annual production was about 10,000 barrels and that Select Export and Standard Family Lager bottled beer were both offered. The church in the background is Sacred Heart Catholic Church.
COLLECTION OF TYE SCHWALBE.

WISCONSIN BREWERIES AND BREWPUBS   403

during their first few months to reach the $500 threshold necessary for inclusion in the 1860 Census of Industry, but seem to have remained in business through fall 1861. At this point their advertisements cease, and there are no further references to this brewery in Eau Claire. Steiting sold his share of the property to Winggen in 1863 and moved about thirty miles southwest to start a brewery in Durand.

Melchior Neher (1864–68)
John A. Hunner (1868–1873)
SOUTHEAST CORNER OF BROADWAY AND BARSTOW STREETS

In June of 1864 John Neher and his family were victims of a fire in a distillery that also served as their dwelling. Son Melchoir then bought a piece of property in North Eau Claire (about two blocks from Leinenkugel's Eagle Brewery) and erected what the papers called the "new" brewery in July of 1864.

His North Eau Claire business soon was in full production and a reporter from the *Daily Free Press* imagined that if all the beer were poured out "[it] would make a navigable stream on one of our streets." Interestingly, "Kneer's" beer was "pronounced to be equally as good as the celebrated La Crosse beer," rather than the more common comparison to Milwaukee lager. Neher joined Mathias Leinenkugel in donating beer to the local Catholic Festival in May 1865—where sales of beer brought in $70 for the cause."

John A. Hunner, a former hotelkeeper in Alma, purchased the land and brewery in 1868. By 1870 his horse-powered brewery was apparently large enough that he needed to employ two hands in the brewery, the brothers Louis and Henry Haffner. His production increased seemed to fluctuate between 250 and 500 barrels a year, though in 1873 he was reassessed a higher tax as a large brewer of more than 500 barrels. In 1872 Hunner built a brick addition to his brewery at a cost of $1,500, with "ample facilities for extinguishing, in case of a conflagration." Unfortunately, they seem not to have been ample enough, since the building was destroyed by fire in December 1873, with a loss of more than $10,000, including most of the brewing ingredients stored at the brewery. Hunner made no attempt to rebuild, and the Dun & Co. credit reports suggest that he turned to drink after the fire with the result that he had almost no assets remaining. The property was put up for auction—ironically the auctioneer was Loomis Parrish, a former rival brewer.

H. J. Leinenkugel & Son, City Brewery (1867–1875)
Caroline Leinenkugel, City Brewery (1876–78)
Frase & Lissack, City Brewery (1880–81)
Carstens & Hartwig, West Side Brewery (1881–84)
Eau Claire Brewing Co. (1884–85)
RANDALL STREET AT HEAD OF HALF MOON LAKE

The second Leinenkugel brewery of Eau Claire first appears in the excise records in November 1867, when Henry Joseph and his son Henry Joseph Jr. outsold their cousin Mathias twenty-one barrels to thirteen. While the brewery was clearly in business at this date, research by local brewery historian Richard D. Rossin Jr. shows that the Leinenkugel did not buy the property on Half Moon Lake until 1870. They may have been leasing a brewery, or perhaps brewing at another site. But by 1871, the father and son company was the largest brewery in Eau Claire (though Mathias would pass them in 1872). During a short period in the mid-1870s Eau Claire had three different breweries run by members of the Leinenkugel family. The local esteem in which the family was held was demonstrated in 1874 when the younger Henry Joseph was elected to the Eau Claire City Council from the 6th ward. But within two years he was dead—felled by typhoid fever contracted during a journey to Madison. Even though his father was alive he had retired from the business, so the new proprietor of the brewery was the younger H. J.'s widow, Caroline. This created a unique situation in Eau Claire in which the two Leinenkugel breweries and the Hantzsch brewery all had women listed as proprietors. However, the brewery had underlying financial problems. The R. G. Dun & Co. credit reports indicate in 1876 "their bus[iness] affairs were badly mixed up," and production dropped to 625 barrels in 1878 from a high of 1,450 in 1875. By November 1878 the brewery was shuttered and the Leinenkugels were looking for buyers.

In March, 1880, the *Eau Claire Argus* announced "Messrs. Frase & Lissack have purchased the Leinenkugel brewery on Half-Moon Lake, which they are placing in first-class condition for the manufacture of beer." August Frase (or Trase) and Ernest Lissack (or Lissaick) operated the brewery for less than a year, since the *Weekly Free Press* noted in February 1881 "The brewery of Frase & Lissack has quit brewing the foaming beverage of Gambrinus. There was not sufficient demand for the beer and the firm yielded to the inevitable." Rossin points out that this was a strange statement given that the Dells brewery had burned down only months before. It is likely that demand was lacking because the beer did not find favor in the local market.

Sometime in the summer of 1881, the City Brewery was purchased by Charles Carstens and Albert Hartwig and renamed the West Side Brewery. After operating under this name for more than two years, Carstens, Hartwig, and J. P. Fox formed a corporation called Eau Claire Brewing Co. with plans to enlarge the building and increase the brewery's capacity. However, in July 1885 the brewery burned with a loss of $10,000, only about half of which was insured. Despite the usual talk of rebuilding the plant, the brewery was allowed to decay and production never resumed.

Loomis Parrish & Co. (1869–1871)
E. Robert Hantzsch & Co. (1871–77)
Emilie M. Hantzsch (1877–79)
139–141 BARSTOW STREET

Ernest Robert Hantzsch had been a liquor dealer in Eau Claire since the 1850s. He also appears to have been something of an adventurer, since a county history claimed that he had been part of William Walker's 1855 private invasion of Nicaragua, as well as in charge of organizing the defense of Eau Claire in the Dakota War of 1862 (during which the Dakota never got within 170 miles of Eau Claire). Hantzsch's distillery was destroyed by fire early in 1870, and he appears to have switched from spirits to beer when rebuilding. Ads in the early 1870s proclaimed "I have connected with my store, a first class Brewery, under the superintendence of an experienced brewer . . . ." But who was that brewer? Some evidence suggests that it may have been former Sparta brewer Loomis Parrish, who was brewing in 1870 and 1871 at the site of Hantzsch's old distillery. Parrish was brewing somewhere in Eau Claire in 1869, since the 1870 Census of Industry indicates he had been in operation at a steam-powered brewery for all of the twelve months prior to May 1870. (While the data are not complete and possibly inaccurate, it appears that made in excess of 400 barrels in that year, though if the input figures are correct it was remarkably unhoppy beer.) The exact location of the old distillery does not match the Barstow address, but the ad may have been describing the site in general terms. Because Parrish never owned this property, and since in 1873 Hantzsch advertised for the return of kegs bearing either his name, Loomis' name or both, it seems that Loomis may have leased the brewery for a year before turning his attentions to other civic and business pursuits.

Hantzsch began running the brewery under his own name in 1871, and appears to have had some success according to the newspapers, though the few existing production figures show he lagged behind the other Eau Claire breweries. Unlike his local rivals, Hantzsch appears to have featured ale in his early years, though he also made lager and "pop beer" which may have been equivalent to white beer. One local account, possibly garbled, holds that Hantzsch had a beer vault on the south side of the Eau Claire River, and that he hauled beer in large vats to the top of the hill and poured it down a pipe into a vat in the vault to cool it. (If true, this would have created several interesting logistical problems as well as increasing the possibilities for contaminating the beer.) It is noteworthy that he was bottling beer as early as 1871, and the same ad requesting the return of kegs also urged those "in possession of stone bottles, quarts and pints with my name pressed in" to "deliver the same at my store. . . ." Hantzsch appears to have been distracted by his other business interests at time, including his store that sold a variety of items including "Glassware for Fitting up saloons." In December 1875, the *Daily Free Press* reported that Hatnzsch was "for the present giving his entire attention to his brewery," and again in January 1877 the paper mentioned he had "recently re-established himself in business at the old stand." While production continued to be in the two to three hundred barrel range, it continued to trail other city breweries, even though Hantzsch was the first in town to bottle lager beer. An 1875 entry for Ebner and Oliver in Schade's directory of brewers may represent another period when Hantzsch stepped back from active brewing and Edward Oliver was the responsible party (perhaps with the assistance of William Ebner, or perhaps the entry was an error and was supposed to be Edward Oliver).

These interruptions were likely caused by Hantzsch's need to dig out of the financial hole caused by rebuilding after the 1870 fire. By 1878 the brewery was in the name of his wife Emilie, probably in an attempt to shelter the property from creditors. At some point, he apparently borrowed $5,000 from John Meyer of Black River Falls and was unable to pay off the loan, so Meyer came into possession of the brewery and store which were disposed of at a foreclosure sale in September 1880. The brewery was used briefly as a factory, and in 1882 was turned into a depot for the bottled beer of Leinenkugel and Miller of Chippewa Falls.

Leinenkugel & Welter (1875–77)
Kohlenborn & Quick (1877–78)
Henry Sommermeyer & Co. Dells Brewery (1878–1882)
Frank Huebner, Dells Brewery (1882–83)
Theresa Leinenkugel, Dells Brewery (1883–85)
Theresa Leinenkugel, Empire Brewery (1885–88)
John Walter & Co., City Brewery (1889–1909)
John Walter & Co., City Brewery (1909–1915)
John Walter Brewing Co. (1915–1920)
Walter Brewing Co. (1933–1985)
Hibernia Brewing Co. (1985–89)
HOBART & ELM STREETS/318 ELM

In late 1874, Michael Welter (or Wetter), a former employee of Mathias Leinenkugel's North Eau Claire brewery, apparently went into business for himself and started building a new brewery, with Henry Joseph Leinenkugel as either a financial backer or a fellow brewer. While they brewed 108 barrels during their first year, their term did not last long, and the property passed through the hands of real estate agents to the Kohlenborn and Quick families. It is not clear if they brewed during their short ownership, but they soon sold the property to local businessman Henry Sommermeyer (various spellings), who brought in brewer John Ellenson to run what was now called the Dells Brewery.

While Sommermeyer increased production from 239 barrels in 1878 to 712 barrels in 1879, his time as owner was memorable for more dramatic reasons. In April 1879, the ice house next to the building collapsed under the weight of the ice—perhaps because the foundations were not set properly. In August 1880, there was a small fire that did only $75 worth of damage. However, in November 1880 the brewery was totally destroyed by a fire which the *Argus* claimed was "the work of a wicked incendiary—possibly one of the same kind of temperance reformers who have been operating in Ohio and elsewhere." Sommermeyer & Co. suffered a loss of about $20,000, though they had insurance of $15,000 through seven different companies, four of them Canadian. While there were erroneous reports that Sommermeyer would recover by buying the brewery on Half Moon Lake, the company instead rebuilt and the *Argus* reported in February 1881 "The top of Sommermeyer's brewery is again visible over the trees in North Eau Claire."

After the brewery was rebuilt, Sommermeyer sold the business to one of his employees, Frank Huebner, who had only slightly better luck. Huebner contracted with Louis Arnoldt to bottle his beer in 1882, but suffered another catastrophic fire in 1883. The *Daily Free Press* blamed the extent of the destruction on the fact that while the city had telephones there were none in that part of the city, and even though there were water and fire pumps available, the nearest water required two thousand feet of hose to reach the blaze. Early rebuilding speculation centered around a corporation which was supposed to hire Huebner back as brewer. However, Huebner instead sold the land to Joseph Leinenkugel, who began rebuilding what would be his family's second brewery in the city. By November forty men were at work on the building, which was in production the next year. For a few months, the brewery appears still to have been called the Dells brewery and occasionally the second Eagle brewery, but in 1885 city directories refer to the Leinenkugels as proprietors of their old Eagle and the new Empire brewery.

Unfortunately, this marked the beginning of a downturn in the Eau Claire Leinenkugel family fortunes. Theresa Leinenkugel died in December 1886, and it is possible that this plus the estimated $30,000 spent on the Empire brewery caused the family to go into debt. (See also the Eagle Brewery.) The Empire brewery was closed and its future was in doubt once more.

The *Eau Claire Daily Free Press* reported in December 1889 that negotiations for the sale of the old Sommermeyer brewery were pending, and the rumors had buyers coming from Chicago, Milwaukee, or England. The truth was much less dramatic—John Walter, who had indeed once worked at Best's Brewery in Milwaukee, had lost his brewery in Spencer and was looking for a new brewery that would not require building a new plant. By June 1890 Walter & Co. were advertising the availability of kegs for home delivery. Within a year the company built a new five-story malt house with all the most recent equipment from Toepfer of Milwaukee. Disaster struck soon into the new owners' term when fire destroyed most of the wooden portions of the building in February 1892. Rebuilding started immediately and within two years the brewery had added a bottle house and advertised bottled beer for the first time in 1894.

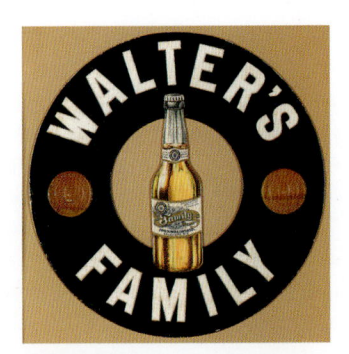

Many breweries claimed that their beers were brewed "for family use," but it was uncommon to produce a Family Beer brand. The bronze medal-like discs on either side of this die-cut cardboard sign are the brewery logo, not medals earned at expositions. COLLECTION OF MARTIN SCHRYVER.

Business grew so rapidly that by 1906 Walter & Co. was forced to consider a massive expansion. Chicago brewery architect Richard Griesser drew up the plans for the new brewhouse, which included more efficient electrical power systems and equipment to capture and reuse the carbon dioxide given off during fermentation. The new building was praised not just for its cleanliness and efficiency, but also for the additional jobs it brought and the confidence shown in the economy of Eau Claire. A new bottle house was put in operation in 1913, and the brewery did a solid business until prohibition. The company produced near beer briefly, but like most of these products, they sold poorly, and the plant sat idle for all but a year of the dry spell.

Like many brewers, John Walter passed away during Prohibition (in 1932), but there were numerous family members available to restart the business. His nephews Edgar, Martin and Charles (along with other investors) purchased the brewery from Walter's widow Linea. Martin, who had previously worked at the family brewery in West Bend, was named the president of the Eau Claire brewery and held this position for the next thirty-four years. While beer was not ready immediately upon legalization, the family's experience helped rebuild the brewery's reputation and distribution after Prohibition. By 1953, Walter's "Beer that is Beer" ranked eighth among Wisconsin breweries outside of Milwaukee. Unfortunately, Leinenkugel, which was twice the size of Walter, was within easy shipping distance, and Eau Claire was easily reachable for breweries in Milwaukee, La Crosse, and Minneapolis-St. Paul. Walter was able to hold on to some of its local market, but sales decreased steadily from over 60,000 barrels a year just after World War II to an average of about 30,000 barrels a year in the mid-1960s.

The company was able to nearly double production in the early 1970s as it picked up labels from three defunct breweries. The Bub Brewing Co. of Winona Minnesota (whose owner, Carlus Walter, was a distant cousin of the Wisconsin Walters) closed in 1969. West Bend Lithia, another Walter family firm, closed in 1972 and sent its Old Timers brand west to Eau Claire, and Walter's acquired the Breunig's brand in 1974 from Rice Lake Brewing Co. However, these breweries went out of business partly because the brands were no longer competitive, so acquiring labels with limited popularity was not a solid expansion strategy. The new brands were all sold in nondescript cans where the only difference in the design was the brand name at the top. Production began to decline again until it hit a low of about 23,000 barrels in 1983.

The big brewery on Hobart and Elm gained a new lease on life in 1983 when Chicago investor Michael Healy bought the plant and renamed it Hibernia Brewing Co. Despite the Irish name,

This small tip tray was presented to visitors at the opening of Walter's new brewery in 1907. It featured a stock image seen on trays of several other brewers. COLLECTION OF TYE SCHWALBE.

406   THE DRINK THAT MADE WISCONSIN FAMOUS

Hibernia brewed mostly German styles like Oktoberfest, Dunkel Weizen, and an all-malt lager. The brewery won several awards in the mid-1980s, but financial and quality control problems forced the brewery to shut down permanently in 1989. After years of neglect and decay, all the buildings were razed except the bottle house. The Walter's label was resuscitated by Eau Claire's Northwoods Brewpub in 2009 and brewed by them since (now at their location in Osseo). (Additional information about the Hibernia period is in chapter 10.)

George Lang (1870?–1872?)

George Lang appears in the Dun & Co. credit reports as a saloonkeeper and brewer in 1870. It is most likely that he had a very small operation to make beer for his own saloon, since he does not appear as a brewer in any other records. He was apparently in and out of business throughout the 1870s, and it is even less clear how often he brewed during this period. The Dun evaluators were not impressed by his credit record and warned "parties trusting him will surely get beat."

P. Lorenz (1877?–1880)

The R. G. Dun & Co. credit reports are the only source for P. Lorenz, who ran a small brewery in the late 1870s. The Dun reports claimed he did a "limited" or "small" business as a brewer, and while his character was good he was "not much of a business man." His property was foreclosed upon in 1880 and he apparently left brewing.

Alexander Zippemer (1883?–1884)

The Bradstreet credit directory of 1884 listed Alexander Zippemer as a manufacturer of beer and soda in Eau Claire. However the Eau Claire city directory of that year lists him only as a soda manufacturer and a bottler. He may have brewed weiss beer on a small scale for a few years.

Northwoods Brewpub (1997–2015)
3560 Oakwood Mall

Northwoods Brewpub was the first establishment of its kind in Northwest Wisconsin. Owner Jerry Bechard is also the owner of the locally famous Norske Nook bakery/restaurants, and Northwoods was a part of his

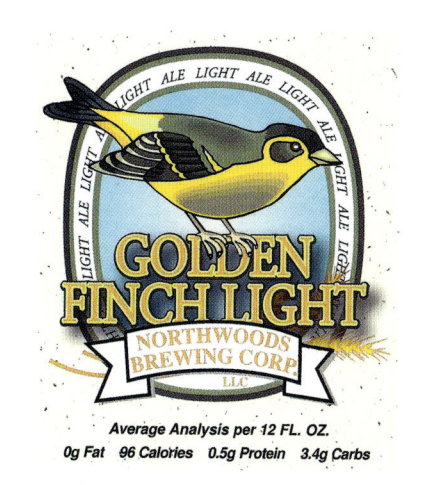

Most Northwoods beers are named after the flora or fauna of northern Wisconsin. Golden Finch Light was no longer among the regular beers in 2018. COLLECTION OF SCOTT REICH.

expansion of the restaurant business. In the rustic lodge-style restaurant near the Oakwood Mall, Bechard and brewmaster Tim Kelly produced a traditional lineup of beers including a couple of award-winners: Little Bandit Brown earned silver at the Great American Beer Festival and Floppin' Crappie Ale won an award less well known to craft beer aficionados—#1 Biker Beer at the Sturgis Brewfest in 2004. Northwoods was among the first Wisconsin brewpubs to offer their beer in 12-ounce bottles.

Northwoods undertook a brewing challenge in 2009 when they launched a re-creation of Walter's Beer—an Eau Claire tradition since before Prohibition. The beer quickly became a best-seller for Northwoods, though it inspired the usual divided opinions of most reintroduced labels—some old drinkers claimed that it was very close to the original, other swore that it was nothing like the old recipe.

In November 2015, Northwoods closed its Eau Claire location and moved to a new brewery in Osseo.

Lazy Monk Brewing Co. (2011–present)
320 Putnam Street #111 (2011–present); 97 West Madison Street (2016–present)

Leos Frank, an emigrant from what was then Czechoslovakia, had been a computer programmer (and other things) before starting Lazy Monk Brewing Co. in 2011. He viewed the brewery as his second chance at answering the question "What do you want to do when you grow up?" Frank selected a site in a former bakery in his home of Eau Claire, and began brewing with what was essentially a scaled-up homebrewing system. He hired an engineer from Menominee to fabricate the brewing and fermenting vessels, but did most of the wiring himself. Frank was able to self-finance the brewery, which meant that he had no loans and no pressure from the bank to release beer before it was ready.

Frank decided to brew lagers, based on his Central European background and a sense that a "guy with a funny accent should be brewing beers that sound like him." His first beer was a pilsner, followed by a Bohemian dark lager and several traditional German-inspired seasonal beers. When Frank had built enough of a market to start packaging his beer, he had additional decisions to make. In his first location he had very little storage space, so he had no room for a truckload of bottles or cans. He began selling beer in growlers at a number of area retail accounts, in addition to growler sales at his taproom. Reception for his beers was enthusiastic, and after just a few months it was clear that "Lazy Monk" did not reflect the nature of the business—it should have been named "Busy Monk."

As Lazy Monk expanded, Frank decided it was time to introduce cans, and in July 2013 the first four packs of 16-ounce cans appeared in stores. Eventually, Frank moved beyond lagers and offered some hoppy American styles such as a Rye IPA. By mid-summer 2017, Lazy Monk typically had eleven beers on tap at any given time, and released their first ever bottled beer—an Imperial Lager.

In 2015, Leos and his wife and co-owner Theresa decided it was time to find a larger facility, and purchased a former home furnishings showroom from the City of Eau Claire. The new location was not only much larger, but also located in downtown Eau Claire overlooking the Chippewa River. The new bier hall and central location exposed more drinkers to

The label at the top indicates this early Lazy Monk growler was filled with Bohemian Dark Lager. Frank found that growlers stood out in coolers from "six packs that yell at you with color." AUTHOR'S COLLECTION.

Lazy Monk beers, which also drove increased can sales. In 2017 Frank hired a salesperson to take care of outside accounts so he could devote more time to brewing. By 2018, the brewing equipment had been moved to the new location.

In addition to the traditional beer hall, the brewery continued to host the Oktoberfest that began at the first brewery, and added an annual Christkindlmarkt (Christmas Market) and Spring Market.

The Brewing Projekt (2015–present)
2000 North Oxford Avenue Building 3 (2015–18); 1807 North Oxford (2018–present)
The Brewing Projekt story is familiar to many who have attempted to start a business. Will Glass, who was the proprietor of the local craft beer bar the Fire House, got tired of talking about other peoples' beer and decided to start his own brewery. After signing the lease for a brewery site, the federal brewer's license was delayed because of the 2013 government shutdown. Unfortunately, this caused Glass to lose the first location. He was able to find a second location, but the revised federal application was not acted upon until Glass contacted members of the Wisconsin legislative delegation to expedite the paperwork. The company then had to contend with state laws, and finally was able to open the brewery and taproom in April 2015.

Brewing Projekt beers tend to be creative combinations of flavors rather than traditional interpretations of a style. IPZ was a mash up of a Bavarian unfiltered Zwickelbier and an IPA. Another interpretation of an IPA contains gunpowder green tea and citrus zest. The imperial stouts all include extra ingredients. The few styles that are truer to form are maltier styles like Scottish ale and Oktoberfest. While there are several lagers in the portfolio, Glass reflected that the demand for particular styles meant that the brewing philosophy was shifting from "whatever we wanted [to brew], to whatever we wanted that was hoppy."

As of July 2017, Brewing Projekt employed sixteen people, about half of them full time. Each employee of the brewery, whether they work in the brewhouse or not, is required to know how to operate the half-barrel pilot brewing system, in order to promote experimentation.

Glass always intended the first location to be temporary premises, and in 2017, Brewing Project got city approval to move to a larger location on Oxford Avenue. This move also involved protracted negotiations, this time with the Eau Claire Redevelopment Authority. The new facility opened in 2018.

K Point Brewing (2016–present)
4212 Southtowne Drive
The K Point (from the German *konstruktionspunkt*) is a term that indicates the steepest point of a ski jumping hill and was once used to calculate hill size. (It is still used to calculate points.) Longtime homebrewers Lon Blaser and Tom Breneman began thinking about the idea for K Point Brewing in 2014, and after many months of planning they were ready to open in May 2016. The brewery is located inside the Coffee Grounds—a popular coffee shop, bakery and retail outlet which is also known for its extensive selection of craft and import beers.

K Point brewing focuses on traditional styles, though Blaser and Breneman have not ruled out creating specialty beers in the future.

EGG HARBOR *(Door County)*

Shipwrecked Brew Pub (1997–present)
7791 Egg Harbor Road
One of two brewpub/hotel combinations in Wisconsin (the other is Brewery Creek in Mineral Point), Shipwrecked was established in 1997 by Bob and Noreen Pollman, owners of Door Peninsula Winery. For a time, their son Robert was brewmaster, but he was succeeded by in 2008 Rich Zielke.

Zielke's brews tend to be drinkable styles that appeal to the tourists who visit Door County. Shipwrecked had experimented with having some of its beers brewed and bottled under contract by other breweries, but in 2010 they installed their own small bottling line at the brewery—for visitors who wanted to take a souvenir home from Door County. In recent years, Zielke experimented with new beers such as a spruce IPA, and the brewery introduced the increasingly popular 32-ounce growler package for take home beer.

The building was built in 1882 as a saloon by George Barringer, and an expansion in 1904 added guest rooms and a dining room. However, the site became most notorious during the Prohibition area when Al Capone frequented the area and tunnels dating back to the nineteenth century were used for quick escapes. Local tradition holds that two revenue agents who crossed Capone disappeared in these tunnels. The brewery and inn are reputed to be haunted—most famously by Jason, who is said to have been an illegitimate son of Capone who either hanged himself or was murdered because he was about to turn Capone over to the authorities. Other spirits have also been reported in the building.

ELK GROVE *(Lafayette County)*

Rablin & Bray Brewery (1836–1850)
Emmanuel Whitham (1850–54?)
John Rablin (1854–55?)
Richard Brewer (?)
Peter Lauterbach (?–1857?)
The second commercial brewery in Wisconsin was on the site of old Fort De Seelhorst,

or Collettes Grove. Henry Rablin and Thomas Bray built the brewery out of logs and stones, and operated it together until 1842, when Bray moved to Wisconsin Rapids. Rablin advertised the brewery for sale in 1845, but apparently found no takers at that point. The brewery suffered a fire in 1848, and accounts suggest that the brewery was in and out of operation several times. Local accounts claim that Rablin (and sometimes still Bray) leased the brewery to "different parties" for the next several years. Research by John Dutcher has shown that these lessees or renters included Emmanuel Whitham (or Withorn) and possibly his son William, Richard Brewer, and Peter Lauterbach. The Dun credit reports indicate that a John Rablin was associated with the brewery in 1855 (though not operating it at the time), but this further complicates the name situation, since William Rablin is the only son of Henry that appeared in both the 1840 and 1850 censuses. While the closing date of the brewery is unclear, the 1881 county history claims both that it closed in 1856 and that it went down in "the wreck [Panic] of 1857."

ELLSWORTH (Pierce County)

Nicholas P. Husting (1893–97)
Ellsworth Brewing Co. (1897–1905?)
MAIN STREET, EAST OF DOWNTOWN

Ellsworth Brewing Co. was founded relatively late among the pre-Prohibition breweries. Surrounded by several larger brewing cities, including the Twin Cities, Hastings and Red Wing in Minnesota, Ellsworth had a difficult market. Nonetheless, Nicholas Husting, previously the brewer in nearby Prescott, tried to make the brewery in Ellsworth profitable. The brewery was in operation by 1893, though the malt house was still under construction according to the 1894 Sanborn map.

Around 1897, the firm changed hands, and F. B. Saxton headed the new Ellsworth Brewing Co. at least from then until 1900, though Julius Diebenow was mentioned as the proprietor in one account. The company continued to develop the plant, finishing the brewery and adding an office before 1900, as well as digging an E-shaped cellar forty feet into the bluffs on the south side of the brewery. The brewery appeared only occasionally in industry directories, and the Sanborn maps gave no indication of capacity, though in excise records it was recorded as a brewery of less than 500 barrels.

The 1900 Sanborn map placed the brewery on Main Street near the intersection of Pleasant Avenue, but the 1912 map showed the closed brewery closer to the intersection of Main and Wall Street.

ELROY (Juneau County)

J. Schorer (1879–1882?)
BLOCK 1, LOTS 4 & 5 (ORIGINAL PLAT) (MODERN STATE HIGHWAY 80 SOUTH OF CENTER STREET)

After several years in Sauk City, Joseph Schorer established a short-lived brewery in Elroy. Research by Richard D. Rossin Jr. has uncovered that Schorer was making deliveries by 1879, but the local newspaper was a temperance publication so they paid little attention to the brewery. While he appeared in the 1880 population census and a few industry publications, little is known other than the fact he made lager beer and operated a brewery of less than 500 barrels. A list of businesses in the city published in the spring of 1882 includes the brewery, but in October 1883 the paper reported a fire at the "old" brewery—suggesting that it had closed sometime before that date.

FARMERSVILLE (Dodge County)

Georg Schmid (1857–1892)
FARMERSVILLE AND DAIRY ROADS

Georg Schmid's brewery is sometimes listed in industry publications as being in Leroy, since records sometimes used a village, a township, or a nearby post office for the location rather than a precise address. According to the exhaustive research of Michael D. Benter, Georg Schmid had been trained in the brewery of his father in Regensburg, Germany, and moved to Farmersville in 1856. The brewery was officially the Farmersville Brewery and Saloon, though locals called it Greinerschimd's brewery—a compound of Schmid and his wife Anna Maria's maiden name. (Benter holds that this was less an indication of joint ownership and mostly came from a need to distinguish the many Schmids in the area.) Schmid grew and malted his own barley, and stored beer in caves excavated on the farm. While several industry directories list Schmid's brewery, he often did not report production, though the scant available data suggests that he usually brewed around 100 barrels per year for local consumption.

Schmid stopped brewing in 1892, likely because of a combination of health problems and increased competition from breweries both near and distant. He held on to the attached saloon until 1898, when he sold it and moved to Fond du Lac County. The saloon remained in use as a rural tavern into the twenty-first century.

(It is likely that the George Smith listed in the 1888 and 1891 state business directories as a brewer in Knowles is the same as this Georg Schmid.)

Jacob Lehner (1860?–69)
Michael Lepner (1876?)

The precise location of this brewery is unclear, and may not have been in Farmersville itself. Jacob Lehner was listed in the 1860 population census as a brewer and farmer in Le Roy, and may have had one or more partners in his venture. He appears in the 1869 excise records, though his business was listed at that time in Mayville. A state business directory from 1876 listed a Michael Lepner brewing in Farmersville, which may be a continuation of this firm.

FARMINGTON (Fillmore) (Washington County)

Ernst Klessig (Klessing) Farmington Brewery (1859?–1864)
Ernst W. Jaehnig, Farmington Brewery (1864–1875)
Liberta Jaehnig (1875–1881)
MODERN STATE HIGHWAY 84 EAST OF HWY M

While the 1881 county history claims that Ernst Klessig built his brewery in 1860, he probably was brewing prior to 1860, since he would have had trouble making 500 barrels in a new brewery by the time of the industrial census. Klessig had lived in Farmington for several years prior to opening his brewery, and was postmaster for the village for some time. A local history claims: "during an Indian scare, they let all the beer run away and were prepared to leave for St. Louis" (presumably the Dakota War in Minnesota in 1862). Klessig died in March, 1864, and his widow Liberta ran the business until the next year when she remarried Ernst Jaehnig, who took over the brewery. Jaehnig conducted the brewing operations and kept the brewery in the "large" category for several years, though production declined during the early 70s. The business was listed in Liberta's name starting in 1875, though Ernst lived until 1879.

The brewery appears to have been highly regarded in the area and was considered a reliable business. Their market included the county metropolis West Bend, where they were regular advertisers in the newspapers. At one point in 1876, a news item reported: "Our brewery is running with full force, but cannot make enough of the favorite beverage to fill all orders." Liberta's son H. John Jaehnig eventually took over management, but the company remained in Liberta's name in most records. Its output was back over 1,000 barrels in 1878, but it dropped by more than 300 barrels the next year, and by the end of 1881 the R. G. Dun & Co. credit reports indicated that the family had sold out and quit the business.

Fitchburg *(Dane County)*

Great Dane Pub & Brewing #2 (2002–present)
2980 Cahill Main

After Wisconsin law was changed in the so-called "Great Dane Bill," Great Dane opened its second location in the Madison suburb of Fitchburg. The new location was in a building built for Great Dane, so had a more modern feel than the downtown location. The beer list includes most of the standard beers from the downtown location, as well as specials specific to that location such as John Stoner's Oatmeal Stout, named after the first farmer in the area. (A photo of the location is found in chapter 10.) Production at this branch is typically just over 1,000 barrels per year.

In 2013, the Fitchburg pub was the first in Wisconsin to install set of self-service taps at select booths where customers could pour their own beer. The systems include a digital display to show what beers are on tap, and monitor sales by the ounce.

Florence *(Florence County)*

Nicolet Brewing Co. (1999–2011)
2299 Brewery Lane

Co-owners Art Lies and Deb Simons acquired hand-me-down brewing equipment from New Glarus and bottling equipment from Summit Brewing Co. in St. Paul, and began production in mid-1999. Bottled beer first appeared in 2000, and the company began to offer a variety of German-style beers. The company was subject of occasional closure rumors, and Lies was moved to respond in 2008 "Sorry to hear we closed last year, someone should have told me. Think of all the fishing I could have been doing." In 2011 Nicolet Brewing closed and the equipment was sold to Base Camp Brewing of Portland, Oregon.

Fond du Lac *(Fond du Lac County)*

Jacob & Charles Frey (1849–1881)
P. & N. Seresse (Frey Estate) (1881)
Southwest corner of Macy & West Division Streets

Brothers Jacob and Charles Frey began building the first brewery in Fond du Lac in 1848, and were in production the next year. As their business expanded they continued adding to their plant and built "an extensive trade" in the city and the surrounding area. By 1860 they had $10,000 invested in the brewery, which employed four hands and made 1,000 barrels of beer (which sold for $6 a barrel). Production surpassed 2,200 barrels by the early 1870s, and the business continued to prosper. Jacob Frey appears to have been a respected member of the community—he was appointed to a county committee that was part of a statewide initiative to encourage immigration. (The Frey brothers were also briefly owners of Melms' brewery in Milwaukee—see that entry.)

The end of the brewery was tragic. At the end of 1880, the business was booming and the Dun & Co. credit reports noted that they had "the largest saloon business here" (though total production was less than rival Bechaud) and that they were making money and owned valuable real estate. But Jacob Frey died in January 1881, and brother Charles took his own life in March of that year. The Seresse brothers took over the brewery for a short period—Nicholas Seresse was then a saloonkeeper who had been employed by Frey in the 1860s and early 1870s. Unfortunately, the plant was destroyed by fire in June 1881, and the oldest brewery in Fond du Lac never produced again.

Henry Rahte (1850?–1865)

Henry Rahte's brewing operations were apparently a side business for this wealthy wine and liquor merchant. In August 1850, Rahte advertised for "a number of hogs, to fatten," which were to be brought to "the Whiskey Distillery, (not the Brewery,) of Henry Rahte." The brewery may have operated only intermittently since mentions of the brewery are scant until 1865, when it was reported that his brewery "on the outskirts of the city of Fond du Lac" had been destroyed by fire. The loss was reported to be $4,000 above insurance, and apparently was not worth rebuilding.

Hauser & Dix? (1857?–1871?)
Hauser & Bechaud (1871?–72)
Paul Hauser (1872–77)
Anthony Vogt (1877–78)
Portland Street south of Division

Paul Hauser lived in Taycheedah, just east of Fond du Lac, at least by 1856, and numerous sources placed his brewery there from 1858 to the late 1860s. (The account of this brewery is covered under Taycheedah.)

Still, he had at least some operations in the city of Fond du Lac as early as 1857, when he and Richard Dix operated a lager beer saloon on the corner of Main and Sheboygan.

(They may or may not have brewed there at that time.) References in the R. G. Dun & Co. credit reports located Hauser (or Hauser & Dix) sometimes in Fond du Lac, sometimes Taycheedah, and sometimes both. A 1905 history of the county claims that the buildings taken over by the Harrison Postal Bag Rack Co. on Portland Street were built by Hauser & Dix "as a place to store and handle the beer." However, the same account also notes "the spring water at Taycheedah could not compete with the fountain water in Fond du Lac in making and selling beer." It seems that Hauser abandoned the Taycheedah site, perhaps after an 1872 fire, because an 1881 history described the Portland Street location as "the large brick building erected by Paul Hauser, for a brewery."

Hauser seems to have run into financial problems in the 1870s, perhaps because of the burning of his Taycheedah brewery and the expense required to build the Fond du Lac facility. The Dun Co. reports regress from "credit good" to "caution advised" to "[I]s strongly embarrassed" in 1877. At this point he had turned the property over to Anton Vogt, a former sales agent, as "a Cover." By the next year he had sold the brewery to Vogt, though the Dun Co. reports conclude "he would be perfectly honest man if his misfortunes had not driven him into a corner." A few months later Hauser was out of business entirely, and Vogt apparently did not continue brewing.

Andrew Schenkel, Weiss Beer Brewery (1867?–1875?)
46 GROVE STREET

Andrew Schenkel is known mostly from the excise records from 1867 through 1872. He is listed in the 1872 city directory (as Schankel) as a brewer living at 46 Grove. A newspaper account in May 1875 reported that the dwelling and brewery of John Shingle (apparently a garbled reading of Schenkel), on Grove Street, had burned. Another account claimed that Schussler's nearby West Hill brewery was the business that burned, but this does not fit with the continued presence of Schussler's company for several more years.

Adam Sander Brewery (1867?–1897)
Sander Bros. (1897–1920)
MILWAUKEE ROAD (ONE MILE SOUTH OF CITY LIMITS) (MODERN SOUTH MAIN STREET)

Adam Sander left his partnership with Andrew Schneider in a Plymouth brewery to start his own in Fond du Lac. The generally accepted date for the start of business is 1867, but an obituary for Adam's son Albert claims 1864. Sander built a steady business, but the 600 to 700 barrels he typically produced in the 1870s made his one of the smaller lager breweries in Fond du Lac. R. G. Dun & Co. investigators reported a decline in fortunes and reliability from the late 1860s to the early 1880s, but unlike other troubled firms Sander was able to turn things around. In the late 1890s Sander turned over control of the brewery to his sons (Adam died in 1901). Also during this period, the company added malting and bottling operations.

Since the brewery was located outside the city limits, Sander Bros. does not appear on Sanborn Insurance maps until 1902. At this point they had a bottling house located south of the brewery, but by 1915 the bottling operations were moved across Milwaukee Road.

During Prohibition the company incorporated to manufacture non-intoxicating beverages, though evidence of production is scant. The brothers appear to have gone into the bowling alley business, perhaps to diversify their holdings. When legal beer was on the horizon, the company made plans to reopen as Pioneer Brewing Co., but as with many other proposed post-Prohibition businesses, nothing came of the plans.

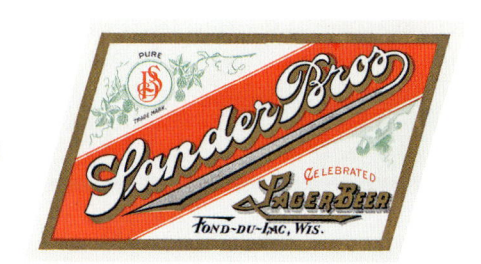

A pre-Prohibition Sander Bros. label (ca. 1900). COLLECTION OF TYE SCHWALBE.

A. G. Bechaud (1871–75)
A. G. Bechaud & Bros., Empire Brewery (1875–1891)
Bechaud Brewing Co., Empire Brewery (1891–1920)
A. B. Bechaud (1920–1933)
Adolph Bates Bechaud, Bechaud Brewery (1933–34)
Bechaud's, Inc. (1934–1941)
457/481 WEST 11TH STREET

The Bechaud family, including brothers Adolph, John, and Frank, arrived in central Wisconsin in 1852. During the Civil War, Adolph and John both enlisted in the Union forces—Adolph mustered out as a captain after four years in the Thirteenth Illinois Cavalry, and John served two years in the First Michigan Cavalry. After returning, John was a partner in the Taycheedah brewery for a few years until he joined his brothers in the family firm which Adolph started in 1871.

A rather effusive account from 1887 reported:

> From the very start they determined to succeed, and by producing a fine beverage and applying themselves unremittingly to its affairs, secured a good name and trade, and brought the Empire Brewery to a point of prominence in its line seldom, if ever, excelled. For sixteen years they have worked together with singular harmony and brotherly good feeling and have placed themselves above want and in good circumstances, not only owning this establishment but much other choice and valuable property.

The company expanded its plant in the late 1870s, only to have it destroyed by fire in January 1884. The brewery was quickly rebuilt and reoccupied its place as the largest brewery in the city. The brothers incorporated in 1891, and continued to expand—building a new brewhouse in the late 1890s. The company began offering bottled beer sometime in the late 1870s. At first the bottling was contracted to H. W. Eaton, but soon after they built what was referred to as a "steam bottling establishment," though the accounts do not clarify

Bechaud's brewery was pictured on this Perfecto Brew label (ca. 1912–14). This label indicated contents of 13 ounces, another example of nonstandard volumes. COLLECTION OF JOHN STEINER.

whether this was powered by steam or that the beer was pasteurized. The Sanborn Insurance Map of 1898 shows an "ice run" going to the brewery from the West Branch of the Fond du Lac River, and by 1902 they had constructed a separate coal conveyor from the railroad line to the brewery.

By 1912, the Empire Brewery employed forty men and did a business of $120,000 a year. The company owned a saloon and controlled a local brickyard for a while. While the decades before Prohibition were generally uneventful, the brewery sued the city in 1908 for damages over alleged odors from the sewer plant (and lost), but five years later was itself charged with creating a public nuisance by discharging waste into a depression in the old riverbed where it collected "and is offensive."

The years of Prohibition were not kind to the Bechaud family. The brewery was destroyed by fire in 1925, a padlock order for the brewery saloon was filed in 1928, and August R. Bechaud took his life in 1931 at age 56. Despite this, the family remained interested in brewing, and was prepared to begin when Prohibition waned. However, Adolph B. Bechaud made what may have been either the best or worst prediction about post-Prohibition industry. In 1932 he claimed that "old style lager probably will not return," arguing that near beer and its higher carbonation "probably has supplanted the older types of beer 'for good."

Bechaud Brewing Co. was one of several breweries ready with beer upon re-legalization. (Bechaud was part of a corporation called Pioneer Brewing Co. in 1933, but this entity never produced any beer.) The company was sold in 1937 to A. V. Orth of Milwaukee and Robert Bechaud of Hancock, Michigan, who was a nephew of Adolph. In 1939, Robert Bechaud purchased Hillsboro Brewing Co., a firm his uncle had reported to the Beverage Tax Division for noncompliant labels two years earllier. During its last years, production at Bechaud struggled to reach 10,000 barrels per year, and a bookkeeper was fired for embezzlement and poor record keeping (which resulted in a tax penalty for the company). Ultimately, Bechaud Brewing Co. shut down in January 1941, and Bleser Brewing of Manitowoc acquired the Empire label. The brewery building remained in use for several decades as a storage or garage facility.

As important as Adolph B. Bechaud was to Fond du Lac brewing, his career beyond the brewery was one of national importance. He served the Franklin Roosevelt administration for two years as part of a nine-member board that helped direct the National Recovery Administration. After leaving the brewing business, he moved to the Scientific Lighting Co. for two years, and then took charge of the Ben-Hur freezer company (which was a division of Schlitz). At Ben-Hur, Bechaud was responsible for the rapid growth of the company in the years after World War II and helped make the large home freezer a common household item.

Charles Bailey, Spruce Beer Brewery (1871–78?)
Charles Bailey appears in the excise records as a spruce beer brewer beginning in 1871. The R. G. Dun & Co. records also indicate that he was in operation in 1871, but listed his business as soda bottler, which was a common line of work for brewers of weiss and spruce beer. He appeared in the 1872 and 1875 city directories as a brewer of spruce and white beer, residing at 53 East Division (but the location of his business was not listed). The Dun records note that he was out of business by July 1878.

J. H. Lockwood, Spruce Beer Brewery (1871–72)
The 1872 city directory enthused that "millions of bottles" of "spruce—or pop—beer" were made annually in Fond du Lac. J. H. Lockwood was among the several listed as manufacturing spruce beer, though he only appeared in the excise records in 1871 and 1872, and in the 1872 city directory he was listed as owning a restaurant at 487 Main Street. He was still in the 1875 directory, but without an occupation, and disappeared from the directory the next year.

Louis Valentine & Co., Spruce Beer Brewery (1871–1872?)
Louis Valentine was another of the several spruce beer brewers operating in Fond du Lac during the early 1870s. Like most of the others, he was only in the excise record for two years, which suggests that spruce beer was something of a fad. Valentine ran a restaurant at 531 Main, and also manufactured "Valentines premium ginger and spruce beer."

Joseph Schussler, West Hill Brewery (1871–1884)
Schussler Bros. West Hill Brewery (1884–1891)
172 HICKORY STREET
The 1875 Fond du Lac directory reported that Joseph Schussler established the West Hill Brewery in 1871, though the same account also calls him Jacob at one point. While the business may have been established in 1871, it did not report any production until June 1872 (though excise records contain a note that tax assessed included months back to December 1871). The 1875 directory indicated that the business was run primarily by Joseph's son Charles. The original brewery burned in May 1875, but soon was rebuilt. By the end of the 1870s, production had increased to approximately 1,000 barrels per year. An 1881 history claimed "[Schussler's] method of brewing is different from others, and known only to himself." The brewery suffered another fire in December 1882, which the *Oshkosh Daily Northwestern* claimed was the third one.

By 1884, Joseph's sons Albert and Arthur

took possession of the business. Arthur was listed in the city directory as a "beer peddler" and Albert was a "malster" [sic], but Joseph was still named as brewer. The company was not always listed in industry directories of the era, so production may have been intermittent. The brewhouse was destroyed by fire in May 1891. While news accounts claimed that the brothers planned to rebuild, the insurance covered only about a quarter of the cost of the damage, and so the rebuilding plans were dropped. Arthur continued as a beer peddler, but as the local agent for Pabst.

Hiram W. Eaton, Spruce Beer Brewery (1864–1887)

20 NINTH STREET

H. W. Eaton began manufacturing soft drinks in 1854, and started the Fond du Lac Soda Bottling Works in 1864. It is not clear for how many years he included Spruce Beer in his lineup. He was more famous for soft drinks and for bottling Standard Nerve Food. Eaton bottled beer for Bechaud Bros. for a few years in the 1870s. By the 1890s, Eaton was chief of police in Fond du Lac and was no longer listed as a businessman.

Philip Stamm, Weiss Beer Brewery (1867?–1875?)

401 MAIN STREET, LATER 436 MAIN STREET

Philip Stamm established his restaurant around 1867, and sometime after that began brewing weiss beer. According to the 1872 city directory:

> ... *he manufactures a superior beer, which is becoming quite popular in this vicinity, because of its refreshing and stimulating qualities. It is known as 'Stamm's White Beer," and is said to be by many physicians, a valuable drink and is recommended by them to their patients. Persons desiring White Beer should ask for Stamm's, and see that they get it.*

Stamm only appears in the excise records in 1871, and then as part of the weiss beer firm Stamm & Severin of Taycheedah. It is possible that the brewing was being done at a location separate from the restaurant. Stamm moved his restaurant prior to 1875, but continued to offer his "white beer."

Almon W. Lockman, Spruce Beer Brewery (1880–1903)

JOHNSON STREET NEAR JUNEAU

James T. O'Halleran, Excelsior Spruce Beer Co. (1907–8)

Mrs. Mary O'Halleran, Excelsior Spruce Beer Co. (1908–1914)

O'Halleran & Finnegan, Excelsior Spruce Beer Co. (1914–18)

235 EAST 2ND STREET

FORT ATKINSON
(Jefferson County)

George Lewis (1850?–1851)

H. S. Pritchard (& Co.) (1851?–1879?)

A. Dalton & Co. (Dalton & Grassmuck's Brewery) (1879–1880)

WEST MILWAUKEE STREET

The earliest brewing in Fort Atkinson is mired in confused local accounts. A book published to celebrate the city's 150th anniversary claims that Pritchard started in 1845, but also lists Pritchard and Dalton as separate businesses. There is no brewer listed in the 1850 census, but that does not mean that no one was brewing. Wayne Kroll has identified the first brewer on this site as George Lewis, which is supported by the 1879 county history.

Henry S. Pritchard, Canadian by birth, took over the brewery in the early 1850s and began a gradual expansion program. In 1857, master mason William Romander was killed when part of a new cellar collapsed and buried him. By 1870, Pritchard's brewery was by far the largest such establishment in Fort Atkinson, employing eight men to produce 1,000 barrels per year in just seven months of operation. Production dropped more than 200 barrels in 1872, though it is not clear why. Pritchard had multiple partners during his ownership, D. S. Morrison at one time, David Snoven from 1870 to 1872, David Vandenburg briefly in 1870 and Norman F. Hopkins starting in 1873. Moses Woodward was also listed as a brewer in the 1860 census, and since there is no evidence of his own brewery, it is possible that he may have been a partner of Pritchard at this point. At some point in the 1870s Pritchard stopped brewing. The 1879 county history suggests that the brewery was still in full operation through the late 1870s, but also claims that Lewis and Morrison were both still associated with it.

In 1879, what was described as "Pritchard's old brewery" was purchased by A. Dalton of Chicago and William Grassmuck (or Grassmenck), who had been head brewer for Fuermann in nearby Watertown. The latter was clearly in charge of brewing operations, and the business was locally referred to as "Grassmuck's Brewery," but the name usually listed in official records was A. Dalton & Co. Andrew Dalton was a "malt manufacturer" according to the 1880 census, and may have provided capital for Grassmuck. Grassmuck managed to restart production and brew ninety-two barrels in 1879. Dalton had big plans, and proposed expanding the malting part of the business to provide malt for the Chicago market. However, about a year after purchase, the brewery was destroyed by fire, with insurance covering just over half of the $10,000 loss. Some lists have Dalton & Co. still in business in 1884, but the company does not appear in any industry directories after 1880. (A modern photograph of the brewery cave is in chapter 2.)

Martin Huscher (1860?–1860)

Louis Liebscher (1861–64)

M. Huscher (1867?–1873?)

John Christoph Reglein (1874–78)

Nicholas Klinger (branch of his Whitewater brewery) (1878?–1882)

SHERMAN STREET (FORMERLY GERMAN STREET)

Martin Huscher was listed as a brewer in the 1860 census (though spelled Kuscher). Huscher may have worked for Pritchard, but the census indicates that he owned real estate and personal property, which would have been less likely if he was an employee of another brewery. It is possible that Louis Liebscher took over this operation when he moved from Milwaukee to start brewing in Fort Atkinson in 1861. Liebscher decided that business would be better in Milwaukee, so he returned there in 1864.

Huscher apparently returned to his brewery in the mid-1860s and kept it going on a small scale. Huscher and his fifteen-year-old son Louis, who worked in the brewery, produced seventy barrels in the year prior to the 1870 industrial census.

According to a history of Waukesha County, Carl (or Charles) Hasslinger operated a brewery in Fort Atkinson from 1869 to 1872 before moving to Jefferson. However, excise records and both population and industrial census data place Hasslinger in Jefferson in 1869 and 1870, so while it is not impossible that Hasslinger had a role in the Fort Atkinson operation, census and excise records seem to indicate otherwise.

During the mid-1870s, John Christoph Reglein became proprietor of the brewery. He more than doubled production from 1874 to 1875, bringing the output over 800 barrels.

The brewery served as a branch of at least one other brewery. Nicholas Klinger of Whitewater controlled the brewery for a few years around 1880. It is also possible that this business was owned by Blatz in the mid-1880s, because a report from 6 September 1886 announced that "The brewery at Fort Atkinson, owned by Val Blatz, burned with a loss of $6,000." That December, the *Milwaukee Sentinel* reported that the "brewery and dwelling of Mrs. Hoosier [sic] burned." This wording suggests that Martin had died, and the relatively low amount of damage may indicate that there was no longer brewing equipment at this location.

Groh & Henschel (1868–1871)
This business is listed in *American Breweries II* as part of the Liebscher/Huscher brewery, but it is clear from the excise records that this business was operating separately at the same time as Martin Huscher. According to the 1870 industrial census there was one employee in addition to the two partners, and the business produced 500 barrels of beer (which sold for $8.00 each). This was about half the size of Pritchard's brewery, but much bigger than Martin Huscher's business.

William Spaeth (1883–86)
William Spaeth, City Brewery (1886–1920)
Carl Ebner Beverage Co. (1922–1933)
Carl Ebner Brewing Co. (1933–1946)
Louis Ziegler Brewing Co. (branch) (1946–48)
Ziegler's Old Tap Brewing Co. (1948–1950)
NORTH SIDE OF RIVER NEAR RAILROAD BRIDGE (1883–86); 26 SOUTH WATER STREET (1886–1950)

William Spaeth began brewing as soon as he arrived in Fort Atkinson, starting in a building on the north side of the river near the railroad bridge, and moving to his permanent location in 1886.

Spaeth continued to grow steadily in the years prior to prohibition. His production was given as 4,000 barrels in 1910, but six years later this had doubled. Despite this increase, Spaeth did not perform all the operations that most other breweries of this size usually had. He did not begin bottling until 1908, and according to industry journals never did his own malting. However, he did upgrade his brewery with a refrigeration plant in 1913.

Carl Ebner came from Chicago to take over the brewery and began setting up Carl Ebner Beverage Co. in 1922. In September 1924, the "Sponge Squad" raided the brewery, confiscated fourteen truckloads of beer bound for Chicago and arrested twenty people, including "notorious beer runner and Chicago gangster" Tom O'Donnell. Another raid in 1926 seized a load of unfermented wort, but Ebner appealed on the grounds that wort was not covered by the law. Federal Judge Claude Luse agreed, since wort had other uses and had to be combined with other ingredients to produce alcohol. This served as a test case for the rest of the country, and was critical for breweries trying to earn revenue during the dry era.

After Prohibition, Carl Ebner Brewing Co. resumed brewing, but Carl Ebner himself died in September 1933, and was unable to enjoy the return of legal beer. The company started well, but sales continued to slip despite shipments to Missouri (and likely other markets). The brewery had antiquated equipment, and as late as 1940 was still bottling from barrels rather than from conditioning tanks. Ebner Brewing was among the brewers that shipped beer to German P.O.W. camps in Wisconsin, though their attempt to have this beer considered tax-free was denied by state authorities.

In 1946, the plant was purchased by Robert D. Hamilton, a beer distributor in Los Angeles. At this time, acquiring a brewery not only netted the brands and equipment, but also the grain allocation and the stocks of other rationed materials. Given the outdated condition of the Ebner plant, the latter was probably more attractive to Hamilton than the brewery or brands. During the short period when it was operated as a branch of the Ziegler Brewing Co. of Beaver Dam, most of the production was shipped to California. The majority of the brewery lot was razed but the old brewery saloon remained as of 2017.

Philip Eckhart (1871?)
Philip Eckhart appears in the excise records in August 1871 with a note that he was a brewer of "small beer." He was listed as a cooper in the 1870 census, and may have briefly dabbled in brewing, or temporarily owned another brewery.

Henry Daniel (1872–1873?)
EAST WATER STREET
Henry Daniel first appears in the excise records in 1872, and was listed in the 1873 *American Brewers' Guide* directory as the producer of sixty-three barrels during the previous year. Given the dates of operation, it is possible that he briefly took over the brewery of either Groh &

Cut-out signs were common during the decade after Prohibition ended.
COLLECTION OF JOHN STEINER.

Henschel or Martin Huscher, especially since neither of them is in the 1873 list.

FOUNTAIN CITY *(Buffalo County)*

Alois Katler (1855?–57?)
Hoeflein & Herley (1857?–58?)
MAIN STREET

The 1888 county history makes a vague reference to "the first attempt" at a brewery in Fountain City, as having been located on the site of the machine shop of John Clarke (which was then just across from the Eagle Hotel on Main Street). According to Wayne Kroll, the first proprietor was Alois Katler, who was succeeded by Hoefelin & Herley, who appear in the 1857 and 1858 state directories. The county history suggests that the first site was only in operation for a few years, though Kroll links this business to the later Eagle Brewery (which does not appear to be the same location, and Dun records disagree with Kroll's timeline here). The site may have been used longer, since a 1919 county history claims vaguely that Philip Eder "engaged in the brewing business opposite the Eagle Hotel" for a short time before going to the Eagle Brewery. The same account has Eder building the Lion Brewery, which burned shortly thereafter, but that version claimed the Lion Brewery preceded the Fountain City Brewery, which is contradicted by excise records and industry directories.

Eder & Richter, Eagle Brewery (Richter & Co.) (1856–1863)
Eder & Brother (1863–65)
Xaver Erhardt (1865–66)
Ewe & Krieger (1867?–69)
Michael Pistorius (1869–1872?)
William Hoke? (1870–1871?)
Henry Behlmer and Henry Fiedler (1872–73?)
Mrs. Pistorius (1872–75?)
F. Moethwig & Co. (Koschitz & Moethwig) (1872?–73?)
John Koschitz, Eagle Brewery (1875?–1908)
John Koschitz Brewery (John Koschitz Estate) (1908–1915)
FRONT STREET, NORTH OF DOWNTOWN

According to the 1888 county history, Fred Richter and Valentine Eder started brewing in Fountain City around 1857. The brewery called Richter & Co. in the 1860 industrial census employed only those two men and produced 600 barrels of beer. In 1863 Richter left the partnership and was replaced by Valentine's brother Philip, just returned from service in the renowned Iron Brigade. The Eders sold out to Xaver Erhardt, a local saloonkeeper, who then sold the brewery just before he died to Louis Ewe and Mr. Krieger (both of La Crosse). The business was then operated by Ewe and Krieger for a few years, but taken over by Michael Pistorius in 1869. Pistorius first appears in the excise records in 1869, but the R. G. Dun & Co. reports claim that he did not take over from Ewe & Krieger (or Krueger) until 1870. The 1870 industry census lists Pistorius as the proprietor of what was the largest brewery in the county, with production of 500 barrels.

The overlapping of dates from different sources that confuses the picture of many breweries is especially evident in the case of the Eagle Brewery. The Dun & Co. records note that Pistorius was out of business by January 1874 and back in by mid-1876, but this could be referring to his saloon. William Hoke appears in the excise records during 1870 and 1871, and he fits better as a renter here than with the Lion Brewery. Confusing the records further is the presence in an 1873 industry directory of the firm of Behlmer & Fiedler, whose production was the same for the two years as Pistorius. The excise records could be read to support this, and Dun indicated that Fielder was renting the brewery he operated in 1875. Meanwhile, the same records have John Koschitz renting the brewery from Pistorius at least as early as 1875, and running it with Mrs. (Mary) Pistorius, who owned it at the time. Koschitz was an Austrian immigrant who seems to have taken over the brewery by himself by 1880. (Mary Pistorius was still in the population census in 1880, but Michael was not.) Schade's 1876 guide listsed Koschitz with a partner named Moethwig in 1874, and a low production of 123 barrels and none in 1875, which suggests that the brewery was going through difficult times. By the end of the decade Koschitz had

This embossed quart bottle from Fountain City's Eagle Brewery features a "Lightning"-type closure. Many breweries used bottles with the text "This bottle not to be sold," though this probably did little to prevent bottle loss. COLLECTION OF TYE SCHWALBE.

production up to around 280 barrels per year, and the Dun reports gave him a positive rating.

For the next several decades, the brewery did a small but steady business. Sanborn maps showed a small (500-barrel capacity), primitive brewery, which as late as 1910 still used horse power and candles for lighting. Industry directories claim that Eagle Brewery offered bottled beer as early as 1884, but no bottling works were identified on maps on the brewery premises. John Koschitz died in August 1908, but the brewery remained in operation for a few more years, despite the death of Jacob Koschitz while working alone at the brewery in 1911. August Nothhelfer came from Appleton, Minnesota to operate the brewery, but it finally ceased brewing in 1915. The brewery was razed in 1940, and the bricks were given away free to anyone who would come and pick them up.

George P. Ziegenfuss (1855?–1880)
Peter Oehlschlager (1871–72)
John S. Ziegenfuss (1878?–1881)

George Ziegenfuss came to Fountain City in 1855 from Galena, Illinois, where he had lived for three years after emigrating from Prussia. Sources differ on when he first brewed in Fountain City, placing the date somewhere between 1855 and 1857. The R. G. Dun & Co. credit reports indicate that during the mid-1860s he was not flourishing, but making an acceptable living. Production was typically small—fifty barrels in the 1870 census year. Around 1867 the name recorded for excise purposes was John S. Zigenfuss, though this person is not listed in the 1870 population census. (The first name is not given in that year's industrial census.) The Dun reports and excise records show that Ziegenfuss closed the brewery in January 1871, but then rented it to Peter Oehlschlager, an itinerant brewer who during his career worked at a half a dozen breweries in Wisconsin and Minnesota. Oehlschlager left in 1872, and Dun listed the brewery as out of business. However, the Ziegenfuss family resumed control in the mid-1870s, though the only known production was 268 barrels in 1878. Both George and John are listed as brewers in the 1880 census, but by 1882 they are no longer listed in industry directories. In 1884 John was listed as a butcher in Fountain City and the family was evidently out of the brewing business.

Eder & Richter, Lion Brewery (1868?–1870)
Eder & Bodmer (1870–72)
Eder & Lenhardt (1872–75)
Fiedler & Lenhardt (1875–77)
Henry Fiedler (1877–79)
MAIN STREET

Kessinger's 1888 county history reported that a new and "very large" brewery was built around 1870. This appears to fit the description of the Lion Brewery, which appeared under that name in the 1870 industry census with the proprietors Philip Eder and Frederick Richter. This pair earlier had been associated in the Eagle Brewery. The amount of capital invested was $14,000, which was significantly more than most other small town breweries. Since that year's census only showed production of 120 barrels, it is likely that it had not gotten to full production yet, but the partners first appeared in the excise records in 1868.

Otto Bodmer purchased Richter's share of the brewery in 1870, but sold it two years later to Michael Lenhardt. The R. G. Dun & Co. reports showed that Eder was no longer brewing in October 1875, but the brewery itself continued, since the firm of Fiedler and Lenhart [sic] reported production of 525 barrels that year. The ownership situation was apparently in flux, because when the brewery burned in April 1879, a newspaper account reported that it was still owned by Eder and Lenhardt, but operated by Henry Fiedler. The Lion Brewery was not rebuilt, but the site would later be used for the new Fountain City Brewing Co.

Fountain City Brewing Co. (1886–1920)
Fountain City Brewing Co., Inc. (1933–1965)
436/444 MAIN ST.

The Fountain City Brewing Co. was one of the first breweries in Wisconsin to be founded as a corporation, rather than growing out of an existing family business or partnership. In 1960, then-owner Marvin Witt related a traditional tale of the founding:

> There's a story that two men met at the Golden Frog—the oldest café in Fountain City. They said that to stimulate business in Fountain City, there should be a creamery and a brewery. One man said, 'You sell stock for a creamery and I'll sell stock for a brewery.' and that's the way the brewery was supposed to have been started.

The articles of incorporation from 1885 state that the company would be in the business of "manufacturing beer, of buying and selling the same and of dealing generally in beer, barley, hops and other materials necessary or convenient for the manufacture, storage and sale of beer and similar beverages." More than a dozen men were among the original directors of the company—most of them important local businessmen but few of whom had any experience in brewing.

Rumors of the new enterprise started early in 1885, and by May the company was soliciting bids from contractors for construction of the plant. Construction proceeded quickly, and machinery was delivered for installation in November. The first beer went on sale the next year, and the company was successful from the start. Henry Fiedler, formerly of the Lion Brewery in Fountain City, was elected secretary and agent of the company in 1889. Sanborn maps

This early post-Prohibition label indicated to which federal revenue district the brewery had paid its tax "at the rate prescribed by internal revenue law": District No. 9. COLLECTION OF TYE SCHWALBE.

show that capacity in the early years was about 4,000 barrels per year, and that a bottling works was added sometime in the mid-1890s. Despite having been built with numerous modern advances such as steam power, the company still used ice for cooling until Prohibition.

During Prohibition, Fountain City Brewing Co. was dissolved (the annual report filed with the State of Wisconsin in 1921 listed the nature of the company's business as "selling out.") Another local company, R-K-S, took over the near beer business for a short time. But as soon as the dry period ended, a new company, headed by Kurt Schellhas, part of a brewing family from nearby Winona, Minnesota, made plans to reopen the brewery. The building got a new roof, new floors, new plumbing and a paint job, and all new equipment was purchased, including a twenty-ton ice machine. The company bought a new truck and purchased six hundred new wood and steel barrels. The first beer was packaged in kegs, but a few picnic bottles were filled, and the bottling line was set up as soon as practical.

Fountain City Brewing Co. was a typical example of a small town brewery with a limited market. The sales area was between forty to fifty miles from the brewery, but this included the city of Winona on the Minnesota side of the Mississippi River. About half the brewery's output was shipped to markets outside Wisconsin, in fact at one point the Wisconsin Beverage Tax

Division allowed Fountain Brewing to modify their bookkeeping since "this brewery does most of its business in Minnesota." Fountain Brew was a popular local beer, and the company supported the brand by sponsoring a bowling team and a basketball team called the Fountain Brews. Kurt Schellhas was active in the Master Brewers' Association of America, and the brewery served as a social center for the community. In the early 1950s, Fountain Brew appeared in cans, relatively late for the industry overall but not atypical for smaller breweries that were short on capital for new equipment. (A picture of the Fountain Brew cans is in the preface.)

Unfortunately, like most other small and small town breweries, production surged briefly after the end of World War II, but the company could not sustain the growth. From annual production just under 5,000 barrels prior to the war, production jumped as high as 18,000 barrels in 1948, only to drop below 10,000 barrels for good in 1956. The brewery was sold to Marvin Witt of Winona in 1960, who retained most of the fifteen employees. A redoubled sales effort led to a slight increase for a few years, but nowhere near the 22,000-barrel capacity of the brewery. The company prematurely celebrated its 80th anniversary in 1963 by opening a new hospitality room, the Old Heidelberg Room, and introduced a premium brand called Fountain Club—but to no avail. In June 1965, the company announced it was going out of business. Brewmaster Karl Grabner hoped the shutdown was only temporary, but no buyers could be found to return the plant to operation.

Fox Lake *(Dodge County)*

Frank A. Liebenstein, Fox Lake Brewery
   (1856–1873?)
John Shleip, Fox Lake Brewery (1873?–79)
J. A. Williams, Fox Lake Brewery (1879–1880)
Catherine Liebenstein Fox Lake Brewery
   (1880–1892)
J. C. Williams, Fox Lake Brewery (1892-?)
Fox Lake Brewing Co., Frank (Franz) Ring
   (1902–1912)
Fox Lake Brewing Co., John C. Brodesser
   (1912–1920)
Fox Lake Brewing Co. (1933–37)
Mill and Trenton Streets

Frank Liebenstein left Beaver Dam and began brewing in Fox Lake in 1856. By 1860 the industrial census showed he had built annual production to 500 barrels a year with the help of four employees, two of whom were Joseph and John Hussa, who would later found their own brewery in Bangor.

The Fox Lake Brewery is yet another where different sources present different ownership data. Unfortunately the brewery does not appear in the R. G. Dun & Co. credit reports, and the excise records are complete only through 1873. Salem's table lists John Shleip as the responsible party (with production of only 91 barrels in 1878 and 150 the next year.) Salem's listing for John Regelein in Fox Lake probably should have been in Fort Atkinson. The Bradstreet credit report of 1884 lists both Mrs. F. Liebenstein and James A. Williams as brewers in Fox Lake, though there was never more than one brewery there. A newspaper report on an 1884 burglary at the brewery gives the owner as Frank Liebenstein, though it is possible others were running the brewery for him. F. A. Liebenstein appears in some directories as the proprietor as late as 1891, and did not die until 1917 at the age of ninety. Despite Frank's persistence, for most of the 1880s and early 1890s the brewery was listed in industry directories under the name of Catharine Liebenstein, most likely for tax or debt reasons.

In 1892, the *Milwaukee Sentinel* reported that J. C. Williams had purchased the brewery property of F. A. Liebenstein for $1,300, but provided no other information. However the brewery disappears from industry and Wisconsin business directories for the next decade, so it is not clear if Williams actually brewed in Fox Lake. The Sanborn map of 1892 indicated that the plant was used for storage and bottling of beer, but that the kettle was not in use, and the 1898 map indicated that everything was vacant except for the residence on the property.

Most Christmas beer labels, stock or otherwise, featured Santa Claus, holly leaves, or a winter scene. This post-Prohibition label with a knight is a less common design. COLLECTION OF TYE SCHWALBE.

In 1902, Frank Ring took over the brewery, and with his son Frank Jr. as brewmaster, began making beer again. They began bottling beer at some point after 1905, and a 1911 newspaper advertisement called special attention to the quality ingredients used in their bottled beer, and assured customers "Telephone Orders Promptly Delivered."

In 1912, Louis Ziegler and two Mayville saloon owners purchased the brewery from Ring, and shortly thereafter turned it over to Ziegler's son-in-law, John C. Brodesser, who ran the brewery until Prohibition.

Fox Lake Brewing Co. was not among the breweries ready on New Beers' Day, but the new company headed by Donald Stroh and brewmaster Andrew Fischer began production shortly thereafter. The regular beers included Vienna and Old Golden Brew, and the company also brewed bock and Christmas beers. Through 1935 production was typically around 600 barrels per month, which placed it in the middle of the pack among smaller Wisconsin breweries. In May and June 1936, the brewery produced more than 1,000 barrels to get ready for the summer beer-drinking season. However, the initial enthusiasm was short lived, and the company was unable to achieve similar figures the next year and production dropped to a paltry twenty-nine barrels in July 1937 as the brewery ramped down productions. The brewery ceased operations in August 1937.

FRANKLIN, HERMAN TOWNSHIP (Sheboygan County)

Claus Menke (1853–57)
Gustav Seideman, Shankler Brewery (1859?–1865?)
William Pfeil & Seideman (1865–68?)
William Pfeil (1868–1871)
C. Gataike (1870?)
Gustav Seideman (& Son) (1871–77)
Seideman & Koellner (Koemner) (1877–78)

The history of this brewery is made confusing by the fact that it was sometimes listed in Franklin, sometimes in Herman, and occasionally in Howards Grove (and it was once listed in Manitowoc County as well). The earliest known brewer was Claus Menke, who built a brewery in 1853. He operated it until 1857, when he "went into a brewery in Menasha." This enterprise apparently did not pan out, since he returned to Franklin, but this time as a toll keeper on the Calumet & Sheboygan plank road (though the 1860 census still listed him as a brewer). After Menke left, Gustav Seideman took over the brewery and had some involvement for most of the next two decades. As described in the 1860 census, the brewery represented an investment of $2,000, employed two, and produced 300 barrels of beer. (The name Shankler Brewery was in the 1860 industrial census, which suggests that Mr. Shankler leased it to Seideman, but is not conclusive.)

In 1861, there was a disastrous fire at the brewery, in which not only was the brewery destroyed, but when one Charles Mattes attempted to enter the brewery, he fell into the cellar "and was burned up."

Around 1865, William Pfeil joined the brewery, though sources disagree on how long he worked with Seideman. By 1870, the brewery was still powered by hand and only employed two, but Pfeil and employee Philipp Wolf still made 500 barrels of beer the preceding year. (The industrial census made a distinction between 400 barrels of beer and an additional 100 barrels of lager.) The excise records show a C. Gataike as the responsible tax paying member of the Franklin/Howards Grove brewery, but it is not clear what his status was in the business. The R. G. Dun & Co. credit records present a confused picture of Pfeil's credit, sometimes saying it was fine, but at one point in early 1872 described it as "Nix Gut." In 1872 Pfeil went to Sheboygan and opened a saloon, later started manufacturing soda water, and in 1880 was elected sheriff of Sheboygan County.

Seideman returned to the brewery in 1871, though the brewery may have been out of production for part of 1871 and 1872. He and his son Frank continued to operate the brewery through 1877. Gustav and his new partner A. Koellner reported producing 370 barrels in Salem's survey, but none the next year, and the brewery disappears from the records except for one reference to Seideman & Pfeil in the 1884 Bradstreet reports, which is the one that places them in Manitowoc County (and must be viewed with caution).

FRANKLIN (St. Martins) (Milwaukee County)

Godfred Gross (1859?–1867?)
Philip Gross (1867?–1894?)
NEAR MODERN 11765 WEST ST. MARTINS ROAD

A local history of St. Martins claims that the Gross brewery was built sometime in the 1850s. The 1860 industrial census listed Godfred Gross as a brewer in Franklin, with an output of 200 barrels. Gross is listed as a farmer in the population census, but his brother-in-law George Henry Engelhardt and employee Matthew Pilmire (Pilmiro) were both listed as brewers. (Engelhardt's brother, John Philip, was already brewing in Milwaukee [see Main Street Brewery]). Godfred's son Philip continued the business, beginning to run it in his name sometime in the mid-1860s. Philip Gross still appeared in the 1884 Bradstreet credit reports, and local accounts contend that the brewery continued to operate until around 1894 though it was not included in industry directories.

The Gross brewery is important because of its links to Miller Brewing Co. Godfred's daughter Elisabetha (Lisette) married Frederick Miller in 1860, and in 1876 Miller hired her cousin Heinrich Engelhardt to be foreman of the brewery in Wauwatosa. Local accounts contend that after the marriage of Frederick and Lisette most of the beer was actually shipped to the Miller brewery and that some kegs bore the combined names of Gross-Miller. Some also claim that the recipe for Miller High Life came from the Gross brewery, but this cannot be proved conclusively.

Jacob Cromaner (1875?–1876?)

FREISTADT (Ozaukee County)

Leonhardt Bodendorfer (1866?–1872?)
NEAR SWAN ROAD AND MEQUON ROAD

Leonard Bodendorfer had a brewery in the western part of Mequon township near the intersection of Swan and Mequon Roads, which could be consistent with a location in the village of Freistadt. The cellar was still evident in the late twentieth century. Kroll agrees that this brewery was separate from Zimmermann's in Mequon proper. Excise records place Bodendorfer in Mequon in 1867, but the 1870 population census has him living with Adolph Zimmermann in Mequon and working at Zimmermann's brewery. The 1872 directory lists him in Freistadt.

FUSSVILLE (Waukesha County)

J. Adolph Birkhauser (1849–1850)
Henry J. Fuss (1860s?)
Jacob Stolz (1871?)
John H. Fuss & Baines (1873?–74?)
Henry Stolz? (?)
SECTION 14, MENOMONEE TOWNSHIP (1850); EASTERN EDGE OF SECTION 24 ON MODERN STATE ROUTE 175 (1874)

According to a county history, Joducus Adolph Birkhauser had been a brewer in Cologne, Germany, before coming to Waukesha County in 1849. He started a brewery there, but died in 1850, and may not have produced any beer. There is a listing matching his description in the 1850 population census (though with a different spelling).

Wayne Kroll, the expert on Wisconsin's

small rural breweries, holds that the breweries operated by members of the Stolz and Fuss families were continuations of Birkhauser's brewery. The families that owned the brewery seemed stalked by ill fortune. In 1870, the *Daily Milwaukee News* reported a man missing:

> *Jacob Stultz [sic], who owns a brewery in Fussville, came to this city a week ago with a load of pork. He sold it and received his money, after which he went to the Fond du du Lac House and put up his team. He left the hotel soon after saying that he was to take dinner at another place. He never returned, and from that time his friends have been able to discover no trace of him. Mr. Stultz was a prominent citizen of Fussville, and his disappearance leave a wife and several children distressed at the dread uncertainty of his fate. He was a man of about 40 years of age, six feet high, and of rather a stout build... It is supposed that he has been foully dealt with for the purpose of obtaining the money he received from the sale of the pork....*

Just over three years later, Stolz's successors had a narrow escape:

> *At Fussville, Waukesha county, the family of John Fuss, brewer, had a narrow escape from death by the destruction of his residence Thursday night. The fire was discovered by the brother of the brewer, who managed to reach the place in time to save the slumberers. Fuss' residence and brewery were totally destroyed. Loss about $6,000.*

It is not clear when Henry Stolz rebuilt the brewery, or how long he produced at all. Some accounts of this brewery have been complicated by data on the brewery in Milwaukee that was owned at various points by members of the Fuss and Stolz families. There are also two locations given for breweries in Fussville at different times.

GALESVILLE (Trempealeau County)

Thamish & Melchoir (1868–69)
Leopold Melchoir (1869–1870?)

The brewery of Thamish and Melchoir first appears in excise records and Dun & Co. reports in 1868. The limited mentions in the excise records show that they were only producing two to four barrels per month, which was probably just enough to supply the saloon they ran. The Dun & Co. reports noted that they had "expended considerable money in excavating and erecting a brewery & saloon." The property was in the names of the wives of both men, and Melchoir's wife provided most of the money through her family in Bavaria. Problems with the partnership caused a breakup in 1869, and Melchoir continued alone. The excise records show the name Leopold Melchoir, which is supported by the 1870 population census. However, the Dun & Co. records give the name of Jacob Melchoir throughout the period. There was clearly a separate brewery in Galesville, rather than just confusion with the Melchoir brewery in Trempealeau, since a "Letter from Galesville" in the *Winona Daily Republican* from 1869 reported "A brewery supplies the social Teutons with their favorite beverage." A later history from the 1930s tells of a brewery in Galesville operated by Jacob's brother Leopold. No record of the brewery after 1870 has been found to this point.

GENEVA TOWNSHIP (Walworth County)

Absalom Shaw (1856?–1859?)

Absalom Shaw kept a grocery store in Geneva, and according to the 1857 and 1858 state business directories, was also a brewer. The Dun & Co. credit reports indicate that he was also a "watch tinker" but adds that the business was successful largely because of his "shrewd wife." These reports specifically mention that beer was stocked among the groceries, and that Shaw occasionally consumed a fair amount of his own stock. By 1860 Shaw was no longer in Geneva.

GERMANTOWN TOWNSHIP (Juneau County)

Henry Runkel (1858–1867)
Maria Runkel (1867)
NEAR MODERN COUNTY ROAD G

Historian Richard D. Rossin Jr. has discovered that Henry Runkel started construction of his brewery in 1858. In 1867, the excise records show that the business was now in the name of Maria, though Henry was still alive and well. Brewing continued until 1867, when the Runkels moved the brewery and equipment to Mauston. An obituary of Henry Runkel published in 1905 suggests that they moved the brewery because the prospects for growth in Germantown had collapsed, and Mauston was more promising.

Jacob Gundlach (1856?–1858?)

Jacob Gundlach was one of the founders of Germantown, and was listed as a physician in the 1860 census. He appears as a brewer in the 1857 state business directory, and may have been the same person who was a partner with William Gillman at the brewery in Highland a decade earlier.

William Hughes (1869?–1870)

When researching the Runkel brewery in Germantown, Richard D. Rossin Jr. came across references to a second brewery cave, which he located on the property of William Hughes. Hughes was listed as a saloon owner in 1860, but he appears in the 1869 and 1870 excise records as a brewer (and produced about thirty-eight barrels in the period between June 1869 and April 1870). He may have started brewing earlier to supply his saloon. Hughes switched careers and was listed as a ferryman in the 1870 census.

GERMANTOWN (Washington County)

George Frederick Roth (1849?–1860?)

George Frederick Roth was the first brewer in Germantown or the surrounding area comprising census district 48. He was in operation at least as early as 1849 and possibly earlier, since he had produced 520 barrels by the time of the 1850 industrial census—a near impossible task in the first few months of the year for a brand new brewery at that time. Despite competition from other brewers in the immediate vicinity, Roth's business continued to grow, and he produced 750 barrels by the 1860 census. Roth's brewery was a good starting place for brewers—Conrad Deininger went on to his own brewery in Sauk City and Bernhard Mautz or Mauz seems to be the same person who later had a brewery in Madison. Roth apparently went out of business sometime in the early 1860s, and never appeared in the excise records. He was not in the 1870 census, but by 1880 was keeping a hotel in Schliesingerville (Slinger) at age 72.

John Staats (1852?–1880)
John Staats Estate, Ph. G. Duerrwaechter, admin. (1880–82)
Valentine Staats & Brother (1882–?)
A. H. Reingrueber (1890–1904)
Milwaukee-Germantown Brewing Co. (1904–6)
Vogl's Independent Brewing (Brewery) Co. (1906–1916)
Germantown Spring Brewing & Soda Co.? (1916)
Milwaukee-Germantown Brewing Co. (1933–1941)

Northeast Corner of Fond du Lac and Freistadt Roads

According to an 1881 county history, John Staats founded a brewery in Germantown and ran it for twenty-eight years prior to his death. However, this source and the R. G. Dun & Co. records puts his death in 1880 (though the index of death records places it in 1881), which would suggest a starting date of 1852 rather than the traditional date of 1854 given in other sources. Possible support for an earlier date is provided by a claim on the Milwaukee-Germantown Brewing Co. letterhead from 1938 that "Germantown Beer has Quenched the Thirsty for 76 Years," but breweries have occasionally either made mistakes on the date of origin or claimed an earlier date for enhanced prestige. (And this claim only takes the brewery back to 1862, unless they were not counting the Prohibition years.)

By the 1860 Staats' brewery was well-established, producing 400 barrels with three employees. Staats was in the excise records from 1867 through 1872 though his absence from the 1870 census suggests his production was quite small some years. However, he maintained production over 300 barrels per year in the mid-1870s and by the end of the decade was selling more than 700 barrels per year.

After Staats' death, the brewery was run by Philip G. Duerrwaechter, but according to Dun the business was having trouble paying its debts. While some sources claim that John's eldest son Valentine took over the brewery with an unnamed brother, the brewery is not listed in any of the industry journals during the mid-1880s, so the brewery may have been mothballed during this period. By 1890, A. H. Reingrueber (or Reingraeber) had begun to bring the brewery back. The company (usually listed as located in South Germantown during the next few decades) remained relatively small. The brewery did not begin bottling beer until after 1900, and did not do its own malting. It employed five hands in 1910, which was much more in keeping with a small country brewery than one on the edge of Milwaukee. The company went into bankruptcy in 1906, and the new firm of H. Vogl's Independent Brewing Company took over (while the incorporators were all Vogls, they were Joseph, John and Louis—none with an H.) (A label from Vogl's Independent Brewing Co. is in chapter 3.)

In an interesting postscript to the pre-Prohibition era, *American Brewers' Review* published a note in June 1916 that Vogl's Independent Brewery had been succeeded by Germantown Spring Brewing & Soda Co., which had as its principals Selma E. Lomasky and Laura Engelhardt. This is confused by the fact that two other addresses have been given for this business, both of them closer to downtown Milwaukee, and with Arthur Warschauer as the contact in the 1916 city directory. Nothing further was published except a note in *Western Brewer* that the Germantown Spring Bottling and Soda Co. had closed. It would be interesting to know if these two women were entrepreneurs on their own or were acting for others.

The reformed Milwaukee-Germantown Brewing Co. was brewing by 1934, and while it brewed under its own name, it also brewed house labels for distributors. In fact, the distributing company at 1801 N. Marshall Street in Milwaukee (known at different times as Grant Distributing and Gesell Distributing) was part of the company and at least in 1938 all bottling was done at that address. The new company did not build a strong following, and production dipped from over 10,000 barrels in the mid-1930s to under 5,000 barrels in 1941, and the brewery closed that year.

John Schlict (1856?–1860?)
Charles Reidenbach (?–1870)

Goldendale Road, south of Freistadt Road

In his book *Wisconsin Farm Breweries,* Wayne Kroll reports that the Schlict and Reidenbach breweries are continuations of the same business. He also includes the Roth brewery with this business, which is possible, but in addition to his entry in the 1857 Wisconsin state business directory, Schlict is listed as a brewer in the 1860 population census with $2,000 of his own real estate, raising the possibility if not likelihood that this was a separate brewery. Since the three employees of Roth's brewery are already accounted for in the census, it is possible that Schlict had his own brewery.

George Regenfuss & Co. (1858–77)
John Sieben (1877–79)

Near Goldendale Road

The Regenfuss brewery in Germantown is sometimes listed under Meeker or Richfield, the post offices used in the 1860s and 1870s.

Hundreds of empty cases piled outside a rustic building, possibly a depot, around 1915. Like Vogl's labels, the cases announced that the brewery was "Not in Any Trust." COLLECTION OF JOHN STEINER.

420 THE DRINK THAT MADE WISCONSIN FAMOUS

George Regenfuss started brewing around 1858, but by 1860 had invested $4,000 in a brewery that produced 500 barrels of lager. (The prevailing price for a barrel of lager at that place and time was $5.) While this brewery is not in the 1870 industrial census, it is listed in the excise records, though in 1872 the name on the brewery is George Jr., one of the many Regenfuss children. George's brother Mathias was also listed as one of the "interested persons" in the 1873 industry directory. In 1871 the Regenfuss brewery produced an impressive 1,000 barrels of beer, but production dropped sharply to 425 barrels the next year. Sales were back up again the next few years, but according to the R. G. Dun & Co. credit records, the brewery was in financial trouble. The elder Regenfuss died in 1877, and the brewery was taken over by John Sieben, who may have been a creditor. Sieben was unable to get the brewery out of debt, and it was closed by 1879. The younger George Regenfuss went to Milwaukee to work in a brewery there (as did his brother Frank).

GLENDALE *(Milwaukee County)*

Sprecher Brewing Co. (1994–present)
701 WEST GLENDALE AVENUE

(The origins of Sprecher Brewing are covered under the Milwaukee entry and at some length in chapter 10.)

In 1994, Sprecher Brewing Co. moved from its original Milwaukee location to a former elevator car factory in suburban Glendale. This new facility continued to expand and a two-story addition was built in the early 2010s. Much of the equipment was designed and built by Randy Sprecher and his team, including the direct-fired kettle, but the newer parts of the brewery are fully automated.

The beers brewed by Sprecher have expanded to include nearly every known style. There have been several Belgian-style beers, especially for anniversaries, as well as German, English, and American styles. Sprecher was one of the few American breweries to experiment with African beer styles. Brewmaster Craig Burge developed the sorghum-based Shakparo Ale and the banana-based Mbege Ale in 2006. Shakparo was reformulated in 2007 to be gluten-free. In recent years, Sprecher has added some hoppier beers to its lineup, including the Whole Cone Hop Series, which featured offerings like CitraBomb—about as far away from Black Bavarian as one can get. Sprecher even had a light beer for a few years—Sprecher Light was sold on draught from 2005 to 2008 at restaurants that carried Sprecher beer. Sprecher did occasional contract brews, the most noteworthy being Mamma Mia! Pizza Beer, which was brewed with tomatoes, garlic, oregano and basil.

Chameleon Brewing Company was started in 2010 as a way for Sprecher to reach a wider range of drinkers—some of whom may have viewed Sprecher beers as too full-flavored. Chameleon beers tended to be lighter and were designed to be "easy-drinking" without actually using the term "session beer."

In 2013, Sprecher capitalized on its popular soda line with one of the first alcoholic sodas—Sprecher Hard Root Beer. While many other breweries followed the root beer trend, Sprecher added five other hard soda flavors in the next three years. Sprecher has also offered other products, including beer-flavored kettle chips and barbeque sauce.

As of 2017, Sprecher beer is distributed in twenty-five states—mostly east of the Mississippi River. The brewery produced over 25,000 barrels in 2015, continuing a trend of increasing sales. The Sprecher name also appears now on restaurants, as well as inside them. Starting in 2010, Kevin Lederer obtained a licensing agreement to use the brewery name (and feature their productions) on pubs in Madison, Wisconsin Dells, and Lake Geneva, Sheboygan, and Watertown. The brewery has no ownership stake in any of the restaurants.

Bavarian Bierhaus (2016–present)
700 WEST LEXINGTON BOULEVARD

The Bavarian Inn, which had been a gathering place for area Germans and lovers of German culture since 1968, closed in 2011. In 2015, Brauhaus Milwaukee began to remodel the site and opened the new Bavarian Bierhaus Brewpub and Beer Garden in April 2016. The new complex featured a large dining hall, a tap room, and a beer garden.

Brewers Nate Bahr and Mike Biddick use the fifteen-barrel system primarily for German-style beers befitting the establishment, but they also brew a few ales and some beers with additional ingredients for variety.

GRAFTON *(Ozaukee County)*

J. B. Steinmetz (1846–1870)
Charles Quenengasser (1870–76)
Klug & Co. (1878–1880)
Grafton Brewing Co. (various proprietors) (1880–84)
John Weber, Grafton Brewery (1884–1890)
William Weber Grafton Brewery (1890–1920)
Blessing Beverage Co. (1920–1933)
Grafton Brewing Co. (1933–35)
Wisconsin Cooperative Brewery, Inc. (1935–1941)
1230 12TH AVENUE

John B. Steinmetz is reported to have started his brewery in Grafton around 1846. Steinmetz produced 300 barrels in 1860, among the smallest in the county of those breweries included in the census. The opinion of his business as reported by the R. G. Dun & Co. agents was originally quite high, but by 1867 they reported that drink had gotten the better of him and reported that he was "generally 3 sheets in wind." Unfortunately, he did not attend to business and was in debt by the end of the decade.

The Grafton brewery is not included in the 1870 industry census, likely because it produced little or no beer during the preceding year. The brewery was not included in excise records during 1869, but in 1870 these records bore the name of the new owner, Charles Quenengasser. Quenengasser restarted production on a small scale, brewing 217 barrels in 1871 and 293 in 1872. However he disappeared from both excise records and industry directories after this point, and the R. G. Dun & Co. records indicate that he was in financial difficulty and facing a number of lawsuits.

Over the next few years, the brewery went through several ownership changes. Dun notes that the Grafton Brewery was under the direction of August Klug and Co. (the "Co." was Charles Schlegal) as of the beginning of 1878. Production statistics listed in Salem's table show production of 168 barrels in 1878 and 1,116 in 1879, but there is a good chance the latter number was a typographical error, since it would be more than the brewery's capacity several years later, and the company was still in financial trouble. By 1881 Kersting & Co. were the new operators of the brewery, but this lasted only about a year. The next owners were Peter Spehn and Henry Diedrich, but the Dun reports did not rate their business acumen highly. Spehn operated the brewery by himself in 1883, and Schlegal appears to have been involved in the business again, but by the beginning of the next year Dun's agent predicted that the brewery would "be taken over by someone else."

That someone else turned out to be John Weber, who owned the successful brewery in nearby Cedarburg. Weber placed his twenty-two-year-old son William in charge of the Grafton plant, and after a few years the brewery was operated in William's name. William soon started bottling his beer, and the company remained profitable under his direction through Prohibition.

As Prohibition approached, Weber decided to sell the brewery to George Blessing, who had previously been associated with Port Washington Brewing Co. Blessing made a couple of different brands of near beers including one called Camel, but not all of the product went through the dealcoholization step. The brewery was raided in July 1923, and revenue agents later claimed that Tommy O'Donnell, the gangster who operated the Fort Atkinson brewery, was also behind the illicit brewing at Grafton.

After Prohibition, the Grafton brewery housed one of the rare attempts to create a cooperative brewery that actually got off the ground. The Grafton Brewing Co. got underway under the management of George Blessing in late 1933, but he died shortly thereafter and the brewery was in need of new management. Meanwhile, the Wisconsin Co-operative Brewery had been incorporated but needed a plant. While Milwaukee tavern keepers were the primary constituency of the co-op, membership in the cooperative was "limited" to anyone who was "a consumer, producer, worker, wholesaler, importer, directly or indirectly interested in goods manufactured"—in other words, not really limited at all. Brewery workers would be allowed to work for their membership certificates, which otherwise cost $500. One news report noted: "Several leading socialists of Milwaukee county are among the organizers," including State Senator Walter Polakowski, and Edward Ihlenfeldt, a building contractor and would-be Democratic politician who was a proponent of other cooperatives and barter exchanges during the recovery period. While the founders selected a site at 20th Street and Morgan Avenue in Milwaukee and went as far as to launch a public contest to name their new beer, the Milwaukee brewery never materialized. Instead, they purchased the shuttered Grafton brewery and began production there in 1935. The new company did steady if unspectacular business for several years. Available production and sales figures indicate that the vast majority of the beer was sold in Wisconsin, and that sales of draught beer were significantly larger than bottled beer—both of which would make sense for a brewery founded by tavern keepers. In fact, one of the bottled brands was called Milwaukee Tavern Beer. They also made a few private label beers, as well as occasional bocks and holiday beers. However, the detailed financial reports filed with the State of Wisconsin showed that the cooperative was running a deficit each year, and by 1941 Wisconsin's cooperative brewery was dissolved.

Milwaukee Ale House (2008–present)
1208 Thirteenth Avenue
Milwaukee Ale House opened its first branch location in May 2008 in a Riverside location in Grafton.

Water Street Brewery (2011–present)
2615 Washington Street
The Water Street Brewery in Grafton, located just off I-43 and Washington Street, opened in 2011.

GRANVILLE *(Milwaukee County)*

Ferdinand Wagner (1843?–1880?)
Fond du Lac Road
Obituaries for Ferdinand Wagner declared that he came to Wisconsin from Philadelphia in 1843, and established a brewery in Granville where he brewed the first lager beer in the state. (The question of who really brewed the first lager in Wisconsin is covered in more detail in chapter 2.) According to the 1860 census he sold $1,200 worth of beer but the volume was unclear since he was "unable to state[,] no books." (The average price in Milwaukee at the time was between $5 and $6 per barrel and may have been higher in the countryside, so it is likely he produced slightly more than 200 barrels that year.) He had $2,000 worth of capital invested in the two-horse power brewery. He only reported one horsepower in the 1870 census, but was at least able to show production of 100 barrels of beer. It appears that as he got older he brewed less and less—the reported figures for 1871 and 1872 were twenty-five and twenty-four barrels, respectively.

Wagner's brewery appears to have been a gathering place for clubs and societies as well as a place to find a glass of lager beer. Wagner gave up brewing around 1880 and moved to Milwaukee to live with his daughter and son-in-law. One of Wisconsin's pioneer lager brewers died in June 1890 at the age of seventy.

The label for Grafton Finer Beer evoked the Budweiser label in both color and design. COLLECTION OF TYE SCHWALBE.

Jacob Stoltz (1866?–68?)
Fuss & Baines (1872?–73?)
John H. Fuss (1874?)
WEST GRANVILLE

The second brewery in Granville was started in the mid-1860s by Jacob Stoltz, who first appears in the excise records in 1867. The firm does not appear in the 1870 industrial census, and excise data is missing until 1872, but the industry directory of 1873 reported that this brewery produced 101 barrels in 1871 and 251 in 1872. John H. Fuss was listed as living in Menomonee, and is listed in the 1870 census as a farmer Monomonee township, Waukesha County. Thomas Baines is not readily located in the census. Fuss appears alone in the 1874 excise records.

GRAVESVILLE *(Calumet County)*

T. Sussenguth (1873?–1884?)

Theodore Sussenguth was listed in the 1880 census as a soda bottler, and appeared in that occupation in both the Bradstreet and Dun credit reports at various points between 1873 and 1884. (The Dun reports locate him at Chilton—the two cities are adjacent.) Nothing is mentioned about brewing in these limited references, though it is possible that he manufactured weiss beer or even brewed lager or ale for a short time.

GREEN BAY *(Brown County)*

Francis Blesch, Bay Brewery (1851–1879)
PEARL STREET BETWEEN WALNUT AND HUBBARD (NOW 500 BLOCK NORTH BROADWAY)

Green Bay went for a surprisingly long period between its founding and the establishment of its first brewery. Francis Blesch started brewing sometime around 1851 in the Fort Howard section of what is now Green Bay. (There were actually four men in greater Green Bay who were listed as brewers in the 1850 population census: Blesch, Alexander Alexis, Joseph Odholek, and Dominick Troyer, who would later establish a brewery in St. Paul. Blesch lived with Odholek, but there is no evidence that the other three were employed in their trade in Green Bay at that point.) Blesch built the first two-story stone structure in the city in 1856, and he was highly regarded for his industry.

Interestingly, the text of Blesch's newspapers ads changed in May 1857 to indicate that he was about to begin selling "Lager Beer"—he had previously just offered "Good Beer." This may have simply been a new point of emphasis in advertising, but the wording suggests that he had been producing German ales prior to this point. The change may have been spurred by a fire in August 1856 that destroyed the brewery—forcing Blesch to rebuild. In fact, Blesch's continued additions to the brewery were noted by a Ft. Howard correspondent as evidence that Green Bay was recovering from the Panic of 1857. The R. G. Dun & Co. credit reports lauded him in 1860: "He is a German of most industrious habit & we considered him one of the safest men in the County. He is a man's man." Figures from the 1860 census of industry support the assessment of his industry—Blesch operated the only steam-powered brewery in the state outside Milwaukee, and produced 1,000 barrels of beer with four employees. Blesch had his own cooperage and bought thousands of bushels of barley from area farmers. However, the Dun evaluator in 1861 reported there was no change "except that his beer is becoming unpopular." Unfortunately, no contemporary accounts provide any clues why that was the case.

By 1870, Blesch had significant competition for the thirsts of area residents. There were three other steam breweries in town, and while he was now making 2,000 barrels per year, this now ranked third in Green Bay. (For some reason, Green Bay breweries were omitted from industry directories in the early 1870s, so production figures after this point are missing.) In 1876, the brewery was seized by federal authorities for violation of revenue laws (more details are in chapter 3). Unfortunately, this was not the first time—the brewery had also been seized in 1865, though Blesch was able to settle the claims quickly. The brewery ceased production sometime prior to July 1879.

William Schmidternecht (1856?–1859?)

A list of businesses in Green Bay published in the *Green Bay Advocate* in 1856 includes an entry for a brewer named William Schmidternecht. He is mentioned nowhere else in several years of newspapers, but an article from early 1859 reports that there were "four or six" breweries in or within a short distance of Green Bay, and given the known dates of starting for other breweries, it is likely that Schmidternecht was still functioning.

Hochgreve & Rahr (H. Rahr & Co.) (1858–1868)
August Hochgreve, Bellevue Brewery (1868–1879)
Christian Kiel (1879–1882)
C. Hochgreve & Son Bellevue Brewery (1884–1893)
Caroline Hochgreve, Bellevue Brewery (1893–94)
Hochgreve Brewing Co. (1894–1920)
Hochgreve Brewing Co. (1933–1949)
RIVER ROAD OPPOSITE ALLOUEZ AVENUE

August Hochgreve established his brewery with partner Henry Rahr in the section of Green Bay which had just recently been renamed Bellevue (replacing the less appealing name of Shantytown). Hochgreve had trained as a brewer and cooper in Herzberg, Hanover, Germany, and Rahr had worked at his uncle's brewery in Manitowoc. Some of the early newspaper references for the brewery refer to the as H. Rahr & Co., "an enterprising firm from Manitowoc." Production apparently began late in 1858, and by 1859 they were advertising that they had "the means and apparatus to furnish [beer] in any quantity." Business was so good by the mid-1860s that the company built another brewery in Green Bay—a very early example of a branch brewery! After a few years of running the breweries together, they dissolved the partnership. Gus Hochgreve stayed at the Bellevue location and Rahr took charge of the East River Brewery (see the rest of the history of Rahr's plant under that location). Some accounts suggest the partnership dissolved earlier because of the existence of the new brewery, but contemporary sources show the dissolution did not occur until June 1868. Both firms were doing well by the 1870 census—Hochgreve had produced 1,500 barrels of beer in the preceding year, along with 2,000 barrels of "shenk" (table beer or small beer). The former sold for $10 per barrel, the latter $9.

Hochgreve built a new brewery starting in 1872, during which "the buildings that have heretofore done service are now being torn down" and a single new building was built that occupied the space of all the older detached buildings, at an estimated cost of $25,000. When Hochgreve died in 1877, his widow, Caroline, took over the business with the help of her sons Adolph and Christian. Production dropped a bit after Gus's death, averaging about 1,400 barrels in 1878 and 1879, and they fell well behind the Rahr and Hagemeister breweries. It is likely that the building project was a drain on the finances of the family and business: the R. G. Dun & Co. records expected that the estate would not be able to do much more than cover the existing debts. In some sources Christian Kiel is listed as being associated with this brewery as well as his own business in Kossuth. Kiel was the father of Hochgreve's widow Caroline, and the Dun reports confirm that he was managing the brewery for the estate. (In fact, none of the Hochgreves in the 1880 census were listed as involved with the brewery.) Some other sources suggest Kiel had his own brewery in Green Bay during the 1860s, but this is not supported by contemporary evidence. Despite the apparent break in ownership dates, it is clear that the Hochgreve family continued to control the brewery. Adolph was president for many years and was eventually succeeded by brother Chris.

Hochgreve remained the smallest of Green Bay's four breweries for many years, perhaps because they were the last to bottle their own beer, which they did not commence until between 1900 and 1905 when they established a small bottling room in the basement below the office just north of the brewery. A 1905 industry directory reported that Hochgreve included porter among their products, and while rival Rahr was making porter, it is not clear if there was enough local demand for two porter brewers.

Hochgreve started installing egg-processing

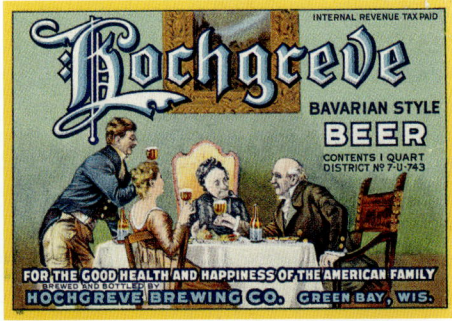

In the years immediately after Prohibition, brewers endeavored to place their product as a normal and positive part of everyday life. These two labels from Hochgreve Brewing Co. went further than most, depicting pleasant family scenes with virtuous Americans who enjoy healthful beer. Hochgreve's Bavarian was a premium product, and it may be no accident that the family enjoying it is clearly more affluent than the workingman who relished his lager. COLLECTION OF TYE SCHWALBE.

equipment when Prohibition appeared imminent, but it was one of two Green Bay breweries (along with Rahr) that produced 2.5 percent beer in the period after beer was theoretically outlawed, pending a final ruling on whether or not beer of that strength would be permitted. This experiment was soon ended, and Hochgreve Brewing Co. went mostly dry along with the rest of the nation. Mostly. In March 1924, three employees of the company were arrested while driving a truck filled with forty cases of real beer. Chris Hochgreve was also charged in the case, and later pled guilty and was sentenced to six months in jail. The brewery was closed, and its permit to make near beer revoked.

Hochgreve Brewing Co. was not ready to provide beer on 7 April 1933, but they were ready shortly thereafter. By 1935, business was good enough that the company announced a $50,000 addition to the plant. Hochgreve's advertisements emphasized tradition and heritage rather than modern techniques—one slogan from the late 1930s proclaimed Hochgreve Beer as "Aged in wood until it's BETTER than good!" Chris Hochgreve died of a heart attack in September 1939 (Adolph had passed away in 1932) but other family members were available to take over the business. They expanded during World War II, and continued to distribute throughout Northeastern Wisconsin. Production hovered between 25,000 and 32,000 barrels in the years before the war, but increased to nearly 50,000 barrels during the latter years of the war, which was the brewery's reported capacity. Unfortunately the increase was more than the brewery was authorized to brew, and Hochgreve was charged in 1946 with exceeding their grain quota during the previous year. Production dropped off sharply thereafter and in November 1949, the company announced that it was going out of business after more than ninety years of family operation. The company was solvent, but the prospects for the future were dim. The brewery was leased out for storage of food products.

Robert Charry & Joseph Gecman, Bay City Brewery (1857?–1860?)

CEDAR STREET

In January 1858, Joseph Gecman advertised *Green Bay Advocate* that he was

> prepared to furnish the citizens of Green Bay and vicinity with a good quality of BEER at his new brewery on Cedar street, immediately in the rear of Mrs. Irwin's residence. Also a good quality of yeast always on hand. I am determined to make my beer as good as any that comes into this market, and sell it at such prices as will make it to the interests of all to want to patronize me. Give me a call and try my Beer.

The use of a residence as a landmark indicates the low importance of formal addresses in pioneer communities.

424 THE DRINK THAT MADE WISCONSIN FAMOUS

The 1860 census suggests that Bohemian immigrants Charry and Gecman were partners and that Charry provided the capital and Gecman was the practical brewer, though both were listed as brewers in the census.

Charles Kitchen (1860–1877?)
WASHINGTON STREET

One of the more interesting small breweries in Wisconsin history is that of Charles Kitchen in Green Bay. He operated the only known combination brewery and bakery in the pre-Prohibition era, and specialized in English-style ales. An advertisement placed upon commencing business in 1860 proclaimed:

> *The subscriber has completed his arrangements to supply the public with what is called in England Pure Ale, or Ale made free from coloring or other pernicious ingredients said to be used by public Brewers. The only ingredients known to this are malt and hops. He flatters himself that after an experience of about 10 years in the manufacture of Malt and Ale, he can produce a purer article than has ever before been introduced into this section of the country. Those of weak constitutions, and heads of families, will find this life giving beverage just what they need.*

Kitchen appears to have continued brewing on and off in a small way for the better part of the next two decades. The R. G. Dun & Co. credit reports indicate that he was doing well for several years, but that trade was tapering off in the 1870s and he was out of business by 1877.

Philippe Flamon (Hannon/Annon) (1856?–1876)

When Xavier Martin traveled to the Belgian settlements of Brown County in 1857, he was struck by their love for two things—music and beer:

> *I found the people apparently very poor, but a more industrious crowd of men, women and children I have never seen. . . . many were making or brewing their own beer, . . .*
>
> *The Belgian settlers are great lovers of music; nearly every settlement has a brass and string band; they love to sing songs . . . Their favorite drink is beer, and Philip Hannon, one of the first settlers, built a brewery at which he made a peculiar kind of beer; when a Belgian had drunk sixty or seventy glasses of that beverage, he would begin to feel good, and then he would sing . . .*

While it is tempting to imagine Flamon brewing the rich Belgian abbey ales of the late twentieth and early twenty-first centuries, the comment about "sixty or seventy glasses" suggests it was "table beer" of much lower alcohol content.

Belgian immigrant Philippe Flamon appeared in the 1860 population census as a brewer, and his reported real estate holdings of $300 seems to indicate a very small brewery. The brewer of Wequiot listed in the 1857 state business directory as Philip Annon is most likely the same person. Flamon first appeared in the R. G. Dun & Co. records in 1869, which notes that he ran "a small concern but is quite a decent man." The 1870 census lists him as a farmer, which suggests that brewing was a part time business. He continued brewing at least occasionally through the 1870s, but was reported out of business by 1876.

Henry Rahr, East River Brewery (1864–1888)
Henry Rahr & Co., East River Brewery (1888–1891)
Henry Rahr's Sons (1891–1900)
Henry Rahr Sons Co. (1900–1913)
Rahr Brewing Co. (1913–1920)
Rahr Green Bay Brewing Co. (1933–1966)
1317/1343 MAIN STREET (1331 MAIN STREET AFTER PROHIBITION)

The East River Brewery was built in 1864 by August Hochgreve and Henry Rahr to meet the demand for beer that could not be satisfied by their Bellevue brewery. In 1868, they decided to split and each take one brewery; Rahr got the newer plant. Henry Rahr had worked at his uncle's brewery in Manitowoc prior to coming to Green Bay, and brought with him a reputation as a capable brewer. Rahr was bottling at least by 1882 and probably before that point.

The East River Brewery was the site of one of the worst industrial accidents to that point in Green Bay, and one of the worst brewery accidents of its era. On 3 August 1887, a vat containing seventy-five barrels of boiling liquid exploded, killing six and wounding seven others, a tragedy which the *Milwaukee Daily Journal* announced with the stunningly insensitive headline "Boiled in the Brew." The brewery replaced the old brew kettle with a steam fired apparatus in an attempt to avoid future catastrophes.

Rahr also purchased the former Nolden brewery in Escanaba, Michigan, and continued to operate the plant—producing 7,300 barrels in 1890, which was over 500 barrels more than at their Green Bay brewery. Henry Rahr died in April 1891 at fifty-six, and the firm was renamed to indicate that his sons had taken over the business.

The company was incorporated in 1901, but nearly all the directors were family members, with the exception of brewmaster George Groessel. Groessel moved around more often than most experienced brewers: He worked in Rahr's brewery on three different occasions, for his first brewing job in the late 1860s, again in the mid-1870s, and then finally for the last two decades before Prohibition. In between he worked for Franz Falk in Milwaukee, breweries in Chicago, Naperville, Illinois, La Porte, Indiana, and about twenty years in the Van Dycke brewery in Green Bay. While many brewers changed locations while younger in order to learn the business and advance, Groessel changed several times after being made foreman of significant regional breweries. The

Barley replaces the rays of the sun in this tray (ca. 1910), which advertises Rahr's Special Brew and Standard. COURTESY OF NATIONAL BREWERY MUSEUM.

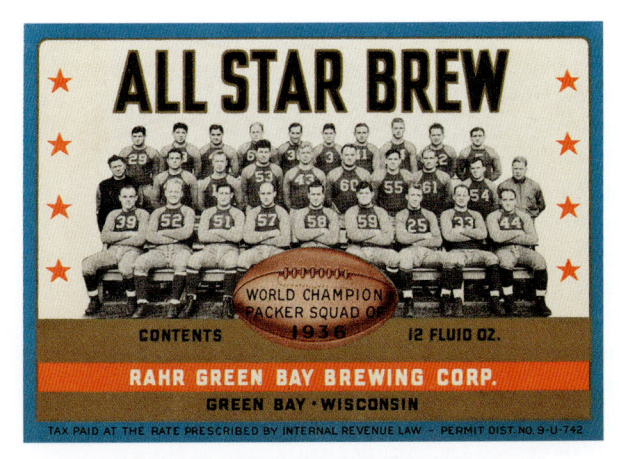

The Green Bay Packers of the 1930s were among the legendary franchises in American sports history. Five members of the 1936 championship team are enshrined in the Pro Football Hall of Fame: founder and coach Curly Lambeau (second row, far left); end/defensive back Don Hutson (back row, third from right, 14); halfback Johnny (Blood) McNally (second row, 55); fullback Clarke Hinkle (back row, 41); and quarterback Arnie Herber (back row, second from left, 38). Modern licensing restrictions generally prohibit recognizable players in beer advertising, so labels like this are extremely rare. COLLECTION OF TYE SCHWALBE.

company made many of the usual improvements that merited write-ups in the trade journals—for example a new office and bottling house project in 1909 worth $25,000 was mentioned prominently in *American Bottler*. Rahr took advantage of a new hydroelectric dam on the Peshtigo River and made the switch to electric power in 1910.

During Prohibition, the Green Bay Rahrs succumbed to the same temptation of many of their fellow brewers. In 1922 Fred A. Rahr was sentenced to eight months incarceration for manufacturing real beer, as well as being fined $7,600 himself and incurring a $15,000 fine on the company. However, the company known as Green Bay Products was able to make a smooth conversion back to beer and reformed itself as Rahr Green Bay Brewing Corporation in January 1933—though they did not have beer ready in April of that year. However, the new brewery was not controlled by the Rahr family, and in 1936 Otto Rahr announced that members of the family were planning a new brewery in Green Bay with a capacity of 60,000 barrels. (Nothing came of this plan.)

In February 1937, Henry Rahr Brewing Co. purchased the troubled Calumet Brewing Co. of Chilton and operated the plant as a branch for few months before selling it. (A label from this period is pictured in the Calumet story.) Other than this, for most of the next three decades the firm that would eventually be called Rahr Green Bay Brewing Co. led the life of a standard mid-sized brewery. The good years during and after World War II persuaded management to increase capacity from 50,000 barrels to 75,000 in the early 1950s. It generally had one flagship beer (first Old Imperial and, starting in 1952, Rahr's) with a few attempts at line extensions such as the Van Dyck brand introduced in 1949. Rahr's introduced canned beer in 1956 to keep pace with other mid-sized breweries. While Rahr experienced the same boom during the war years as most other Wisconsin breweries—it had later boomlets as well. Rahr was one of several smaller Wisconsin breweries to be helped by strikes in Milwaukee, and the company also was able to take some business from other breweries in the area that had closed. The brewery approached 50,000 barrels as late as 1960 and expanded its market to include Illinois, Minnesota and Michigan as well as Wisconsin. The company was forward looking enough to hire an advertising agency at the end of 1960 to compete with larger firms. But production dropped off dramatically during the early 1960s, and the last brewery in Green Bay succumbed to competitive pressures in 1966. The company was sold to Oshkosh Brewing Co., and production at the brewery ended just over one hundred years after it began. Oshkosh Brewing Co. planned to continue the brands and keep the Rahr sales and distribution staff, but Oshkosh was having its own problems and while they brewed Rahr beer for a few more years, it was not a solution for that company either.

Hagemeister & Co., Union Brewery (1866–1873)
F. H. Hagemeister, Union Brewery (1873–1882)
F. H. Hagemeister & Son, Union Brewery (1882–86)
Hagemeister Brewing Co. (1886–1926)
MANITOWOC ROAD (MODERN 1607 MAIN STREET)

Francis Henry Hagemeister worked at a meat market in Milwaukee prior to moving to Green Bay and starting a butcher shop there sometime prior to 1860. In 1866, he joined with Charles Fuller, Joshua Whitney and Herman Merz to found the Union Brewery, but by 1873 he had bought out their interests and controlled the brewery himself. He continued to run the butcher shop and was listed as a butcher in the 1870 census. (Merz was the only one listed as a brewer in the 1870 census, though Charles Rahr was listed as one of the employees of this brewery, rather than his own family's firm. Merz sold his share to Hagemeister in 1871.) By 1875 he finally left butchering to devote his full attention to the brewery. The Union Brewing Co. was the most heavily capitalized brewery in the Green Bay area in 1870, with $36,000 invested in the modern ten-horsepower steam brewery. At this point their

This early label dates prior to 1891, after which the brewery was no longer the East River Brewery. Porter brewing was rare outside southeastern Wisconsin. Porter is generally a showcase for roasted malt flavor, so the choice of hops to decorate the label is less fitting. COLLECTION OF JOHN STEINER.

426   THE DRINK THAT MADE WISCONSIN FAMOUS

production of about 1,400 barrels was still less than the other breweries in town, but they continued to grow. By 1879, Hagemeister was second only to Henry Rahr in Green Bay, and at nearly 2,700 barrels, was one of the largest breweries outside of Milwaukee. By 1884, Hagemeister's capacity had surpassed Rahr's, and both had begun bottling operations (Hagemeister's prior to 1883). Much of this growth has been attributed to the work of Frank's eldest son Henry, who worked in the brewery from an early age, and by 1886 became president of the reorganized company. Brother Albert was secretary and treasurer, and youngest brother Louis was manager of Sturgeon Bay branch and of the bottling department before his early passing in 1895 at the age of thirty. Louis had an elite brewing education: in addition to earning a diploma, he worked for the Voight brewery in Detroit, the Keeley brewery in Chicago, and the Dallas Brewing Co. in Texas before returning to Wisconsin.

In 1887, the Hagemeisters made a bold move by purchasing the former Leidiger Bros. brewery in Sturgeon Bay. Unfortunately, no records exist to show to what extent beer styles and recipes were coordinated between the two breweries. (The history of this plant is covered under Sturgeon Bay.) Hagemeister may well have needed additional capacity, since their production was nearly 19,000 barrels in 1890. The company was also incorporated that year, with a capital stock of $150,000 that put it among the largest breweries in the state at the time. The brewery continued to grow after Frank's death in 1892. However the operations were not compact: the 1894 Sanborn maps show the brewery office on North Adams between Main and Pine, and a coal shed on Cedar between Jackson and Van Buren in addition to the main brewery on what was then Manitowoc Road. Hagemeister had depots in other cities including Stevens Point, which was already well stocked with breweries and depots. In addition, in 1906, the company changed its charter to rename the business Hagemeister Brewing Co. of Green Bay and Iron Mountain, Michigan, demonstrating its reach into the Upper Peninsula. The company did not actually have a brewery there, simply an agency, but incorporating in Michigan allowed them to avoid additional taxes levied on "foreign breweries." At one point in 1907, Hagemesiter Brewing "shipped several barrels of bottled beer to Fort Worth, Texas" perhaps through a connection Louis made while in Dallas.

Henry Hagemeister was so highly regarded among his fellow brewers and fellow citizens that he served as president of the Wisconsin Brewers' Association for a time and was also a member of the Wisconsin State Assembly and the Wisconsin State Senate.

During the Prohibition years, Hagemeister Brewing Co. changed its name to Bellevue Products Co., and turned to other products, including a near beer called Cameo, which was introduced before Prohibition and was advertised as a top-shelf product available in both 7-ounce "nips" and 12-ounce sizes. (A photo of a Cameo bottle appears in chapter 6.) However, brewing of real beer continued, and in 1926 the company was charged with producing about $20,000 of "good beer." (The two directors who were sent to prison, Henry Herrick and Leon Patterson, were later pardoned by President Coolidge.) The company went out of business shortly thereafter, and was the only one of the three Green Bay breweries active just before Prohibition that did not return to production afterwards.

The greatest legacy of Hagemeister Brewing, however, may be colored green and gold. The Green Bay Packers played their first four seasons at Hagemeister Park along the East River, and their next two at Bellevue Park, which was bordered to the west by the Hagemeister/Bellevue bottling house.

Landwehr (& Baier), City Brewery (1873–76)
Louis Van Dycke (1876–78)
Octavia Van Dycke (1878–1884)
O. Van Dycke Brewing Co. (1884–1908)
CHICAGO AND SOUTH JACKSON STREETS

Landwehr & Baier (or Beyer) started work the City Brewery in the fall of 1872. The equipment arrived the next spring, and the "casks, kebs, tubs etc. for Landwehr's new brewery came down the river on a scow in tow of the tug *Ajax*" for delivery to the brewery site. A few years later Sebastian Landwehr sold it to a consortium headed by Louis Van Dycke. Van Dycke had been a shingle manufacturer in nearby Dyckesville before moving to Green Bay with his family. Van Dycke may have had little interest in the brewing part of the business, since he is listed in the 1880 census as a dry goods merchant, and former partner Michael Baier appears to have been retained as the head brewer. Louis died in 1881, and his widow Octavia took over the business with the help of her eldest son Emile (or Emil) (though the brewery had been in her name for three years already).

The Van Dycke brewery settled in to the middle of Green Bay's brewers, producing just over 6,500 barrels in 1890. They began to bottle their own beer sometime prior to 1887 in a facility on the Chicago Street side of the complex. The company was not in the papers often, except for when their safe was blown open in 1886 (with a loss of $148) and when a small building burned in 1892. Despite the earlier

This large cork-finished Hagemeister bottle is probably from around 1890. Export was generally a term for a brewery's bottled beer rather than a product to be shipped abroad, but the inclusion of U.S.A. on the label suggests that Hagemeister may have been seeking foreign markets. COLLECTION OF JOHN STEINER.

The employees of Van Dycke pose for a picture, ca. 1895. Several men in the back row are holding malt shovels. The group is framed by two corner signs in the front and two bock posters in the rear. At least two different bottled products are displayed on top of the cases: the taller bottles appear to be the Lager (the labels match the design on the signs). COURTESY OF NATIONAL BREWERY MUSEUM.

name change, the company was not incorporated until 1902, with Octavia, Emil, and Constanz F. Van Dycke as the officers.

The Van Dycke Brewing Co. closed in 1908 for reasons that are not clear. It is possible that a major improvement project in early 1906 placed a financial strain on the company and it was unable to recover. The building was sold to the Hochgreve Brewing Co., but Hochgreve then sold it again and it was no longer used for brewing.

Titletown Brewing Company (1996–present)
200 DOUSMAN STREET (1996–PRESENT); 320 NORTH BROADWAY (2014–PRESENT)

Titletown Brewing Company has perhaps the most majestic location of any of Wisconsin's brewpubs—the former Chicago and Northwestern Railroad Depot. Opened in 1899, the depot served regular passenger service until 1971 and other rail service until 1994. The Fox Valley & Western Railroad, the last owner, vacated the building that year, and the building remained vacant until Titletown Brewing took over the space in 1996. Trains still traverse the tracks, providing an authentic feel for diners on the patio of this National Register of Historic Places property. Artifacts of the railroad era decorate the walls.

Founder and president Brent Weycker decided to open a brewpub after reading about the concept in a magazine. Co-founder John Gustavson designed a business plan for a brewpub in his masters program in business management. These two Green Bay natives led the Titletown development group along with Denver's John Hickenlooper, then a developer of brewpubs including his Denver flagship Wynkoop Brewing Co. (and later governor of Colorado). In early proposals, the restaurant in the space was to be called the Railway Express Brewery and Pub. In 1996 Jim Olen was named the first head brewer, and the first batch of Railyard Ale was brewed in November 1996 to be ready for the December grand opening.

For most brewpubs, the story of the company's development is much less dramatic than for production breweries. Head brewers come and go, new beers are introduced, and good brewpubs such as Titletown win their share of brewing awards. The ability to expand is limited by the space available—which was definitely the case for Titletown and its historic structure. Titletown sponsored a charity beer fest during its first summer, opened its rooms to local events both public and private, and hosted live music performances. However, Titletown had larger dreams right from the beginning. Perhaps because of the influence

Titletown Brewing added a new entryway to the Larsen Co. cannery and remodeled the rest of the building to create a space that combines the historic and modern. COURTESY OF TITLETOWN BREWING CO.

of Hickenlooper and the idea that a company could operated multiple brewpubs (even if they were not truly a chain), Titletown proposed establishing a brewpub in downtown Wausau as early as August 1997. Nothing came of these plans when John Gustavson left the company in 1998, and Titletown appeared to settle in for a long run as an established restaurant and gathering place with its own beer.

However, after about fifteen years of operation, the popularity of the brewpub and demand for kegs from other restaurants and taverns forced the company to consider a major expansion. Luckily, an appropriate property was located right across Donald Driver Way. Titletown formed a partnership with Smet Construction Services called DDL Holdings to transform the former Larsen Company vegetable cannery into a new brewery and tap room. The first stages of the project were completed in October 2014 and Governor Scott Walker tapped a ceremonial keg to celebrate. This eventually became part of a much larger redevelopment project of the area called Larsen Green. In September 2015, the Roof Tap patio joined the existing Tap Room, and offered visitors unparalleled views along with their beer. The expanded guest space also allowed for more creative projects, such as commissioning an original theater show from Let Me Be Frank Productions called "Rahr's Beer and Titletown USA," a story about a small brewer struggling to survive competition from Milwaukee.

The new brewery, and its capacity of 35,000 barrels per year, made it possible to make a major commitment to producing bottled beer. The first two bottled products were Johnny Blood Red and Green 19 IPA, joined soon after by Boathouse Pilsner. Production, which had been creeping slowly toward 2,000 barrels in the cramped space behind the bar in the depot, jumped to nearly 4,000 barrels in 2015 and 5,555 barrels the next year.

In a throwback to an era when breweries sponsored teams, Titletown has sponsored softball teams in Green Bay leagues. In a departure from those years, in 2013 Titletown employed two female brewers—Krystine Engebos and Heather Ludwig. Throughout its existence, Titletown has functioned as a social center for downtown Green Bay—hosting public and private events of all kinds, and attracting visitors to an area that has been revitalized at least in part because of the company's efforts.

Green Bay Brewing Co. (Hinterland Brewing Co./Hinterland Brewery) (1999–present)
313 Dousman Street (1999–2017); 1001 Lombardi Avenue (2017–present)

Bill and Michelle Tressler decided to move their brewery to Green Bay in 1999 in part to expand and add a high-end "farm-to-table culinary experience," but also because Bill almost burned the Denmark brewery down. Their new location was directly across the street from Titletown Brewing, giving downtown Green Bay its own (small) brewpub district.

After the move from Denmark, Hinterland stopped bottling its beers for several years—partially to focus their efforts on building up the restaurant side of the business, and partially because the bottling equipment took up room they wanted for the restaurant. In 2005, they began to brew beer for bottling at Gray's Brewing Co. in Janesville and reinstituted distribution of Pale Ale and other brews in northeastern Wisconsin. Eventually bottling operations were brought back in house.

Once established in Green Bay, the Tresslers opened additional restaurants, at least in part to showcase the talented chefs developed in the Dousman Street kitchen. In 2003 they purchased the Whistling Swan in Door

The Amber Ale box and Maple Bock bottle are from the brewery's earlier location in Denmark. After starting bottling in Green Bay, Hinterland used the German-style half-liter bottles for several years for seasonal and special beers. As of 2018, Door County Cherry Wheat is sold in 12-ounce bottles. Author's collection.

County's Fish Creek, and four years later they opened the Hinterland Erie Street Gastropub in Milwaukee.

Looking back on the first ten years of the company, Bill Tressler admitted that Hinterland "was probably not the perfect model from the outset. The company was probably fairly under-funded...." He added, "[F]rom the day it was born I don't think six months went buy [sic] without making changes." As a result of the "hard knocks MBA" Tressler earned, Hinterland reestablished itself in the packaged beer market while maintaining its strong reputation as a gastropub. Beers such as Luna Stout (made with coffee from the local Luna Café) gained a strong following, and Packerland Pilsner reappeared in 2014 after being dropped shortly after the Packers' 1997 Super Bowl victory. Hinterland made the foray into canned beer in September 2013 with 16-ounce cans of White Cap IPA, followed in 2015 by 12-ounce cans of Packerland.

Hinterland's success created the opportunity to break ground on larger quarters in 2016 in the Titletown District near Lambeau Field. Tressler, head brewer Joe Karls, and their team brewed the last batch of beer on Dousman Street on the last day of February 2017—a blackberry Berliner weisse. Dousman Street

The new location of Hinterland is just across a parking lot from Lambeau Field. Courtesy of Hinterland Brewing Co.

closed in early April, and the new restaurant opened to the public on 12 April. (The Dousman Street location was soon purchased and transformed into Copper State Brewing Co.)

Rustic Rail Grill & Brewhouse (2005–7)
Black Forest Dining & Spirits (2009–2011)
1966 Velp Avenue

Rustic Rail Grill and Brewhouse opened in February 2005. The owners were Mike and Cindy Haverkorn, Rob Servais, Neal Van Boxtel and Greg Kamps. The restaurant was located in a brand-new log cabin-style lodge intended to highlight the region's connection to logging and rail transport. They started with four house-brewed beers: The Golden Rail, Northwoods Nut Brown, Honey Rail Pale, and Bearpaw Oatmeal Stout. The brewery was still participating in beer festivals in 2007, but ceased brewing shortly thereafter.

A second attempt to establish a brewpub in this building was Black Forest Dining & Spirits. This business only lasted about two years, and was replaced by the Harley-Davidson dealership that occupies the building as of July 2017.

Badger State Brewing Co. (2013–present)
990 Tony Canadeo Run

Homebrewing friends Andrew Fabry, Mike Servi, and Sam Yanda turned their passion into Badger State Brewing Co. in 2013. The three partners were looking for a name that would connect with a lot of people, and preferably one that was not limited to the Green Bay area that would limit future expansion. Amazingly enough, the Badger State name was available and had not been used since the Janesville brewery of that name closed in 1920—so they filed the necessary forms the next morning. The brewery is located in an industrial site in Lambeau Field Stadium District. (The street is named after a Green Bay Packers Hall of Famer from the 1940s and 1950s.)

The first beers, Bunyan Badger Brown Ale and Walloon Belgian Witbier, led a lineup that proved so popular that production jumped from under 300 barrels in 2014 to around 1,000 in 2016. As a result the brewery was forced to expand in 2014 and again in 2016. The latter expansion also included an event space

Many breweries offer sampling flights. Some flight trays are simple wooden boards, whle others have unique designs.
COURTESY OF BADGER STATE BREWING CO.

to host private parties. Badger State began canning beer in 2015, and several specialty beers appeared in 750 ml bottles.

Conscious of the energy-intensive nature of brewing, Badger State announced a partnership with Arcadia Power to purchase 100 percent of its power from Midwest wind farms. Fabry noted that the business plan for the brewery "had renewable energy as a focal point from the start." Badger State also wanted to offer unfiltered beers, but clean and stable beers, so they were one of the first breweries of their size to install a centrifuge to remove particulate matter from the finished beer.

Badger State has been an active collaborator with other breweries. Fabry said that sometimes the collaboration projects are simply based on "who you're sitting with at the bar talking about beer," but they have a special affinity for breweries founded at about the same time. In late 2014, they teamed up with MobCraft to brew Dubbel Czech, a hybrid Belgian and Czech beer with a label featuring the teams of MobCraft and Badger State and a football player with a resemblance to the Green Bay Packers quarterback of the era, Aaron Rodgers (who starred in commercials for State Farm Insurance touting their "Discount Double Check"). They also participated in a project with Titletown, Hinterland, and Stillmank called Locals Only! which used locally grown grain and hops.

Stillmank Brewing Company (2014–present)
215 NORTH HENRY STREET
Brad Stillmank is another homebrewer who was able to make a career out of a former hobby. Stillmank did not jump straight from the ranks of homebrewers to owning his own brewery, however. He worked for Ska Brewing in Durango, Colorado for a time, and earned a brewers' certificate from the highly regarded program at University of California—Davis. (He was also one of the very first Certified Cicerones (beer servers) in 2009.)

Stillmank Brewing Company started as a client brewer who made their flagship beer, Wisco Disco, at Milwaukee Brewing Company. Wisco Disco is an unusual hybrid beer—an English-style ESB with lactose added for smoother mouthfeel. In 2014 he purchased an old warehouse in Green Bay to establish his own production facility. In the new brewery, Stillmank numbered his four fermenting tanks 15, 4, 12, and 80—after Packers greats Bart Starr, Brett Favre, Aaron Rodgers and Donald Driver. Once open, Stillmank added new beers to the lineup, including an IPA called Super Kind and the Bee's Knees—a honey rye ale. These beers were released in 16-ounce cans almost immediately, and Wisco Disco was popular enough to be sold at Lambeau Field during Packers' games. During the first year of operations, Stillmank brought out a coffee beer, made its first lager, and brewed Double Disco, an imperial pale ale, for its first anniversary. Stillmank has also joined the list of breweries that are offering barrel-aged beers.

Leatherhead Brewing Co. (2015–17)
875 LOMBARDI AVENUE
Co-founders Amanda and Chad Sharon and Sheila and Ian Perks had been thinking about opening a brewery for three years, but were inspired to take action after tasting a stout brewed by Chad's cousin Jacob Sutrick (formerly brewer at Stonefly in Milwaukee). They acquired a defunct restaurant building and converted it into Leatherhead Brewing Co. By the summer of 2017 they had expanded their beer list to thirteen different draught beers, plus Forgotten Beard, a barrel-aged version of Full Beard Stout packaged in 22-ounce bottles.

Copper State Brewing Co.
313 DOUSMAN STREET (2017–PRESENT)
Copper State Brewing Co. took over the old Hinterland location and made significant changes to the pub and dining areas. However, co-owner and brewer Jon Martens was able to keep most of the Hinterland brewhouse intact. He also trained on the system with the Hinterland staff before taking over.

GREENFIELD *(Milwaukee County)*

The Explorium (2016–present)
5300 S 76TH ST UNIT 1450A
Mike and Joan Doble founded the Explorium in 2016 in suburban Greenfield. They were inspired by the first Doble family brewery, Tampa Bay Brewing Company in Ybor City, Florida. In keeping with the theme of exploration and discovery, most of the beers are named after explorers—including Patagonian Hitchhiker, named after the hypothesis that the first lager yeast originated in that region of South America.

GREENFIELD TOWNSHIP *(Barre Mills) (La Crosse County)*

Valentine Zimmerman (1867–1872?)
Valentine Zimmerman apparently operated his small farm brewery just east of La Crosse for about five years. He first appeared in the excise records in September 1867, having produced two barrels of beer the previous month. In the 1870 census he was listed as a farmer, so it is likely that brewing was a part-time occupation for him.

HAMMOND *(St. Croix County)*

(T. Frederick) Weyhe & Son (1873–79)
Hammond was regarded as a strong temperance village, but still hosted a brewery for about six years. Weyhe & Son appeared in excise records in April 1873, and he produced 121 and 157 barrels in 1874 and 1875. The R. G. Dun

& Co. credit evaluator took a dim view of T. F. Weyhe's financial position (going back to his time in Hudson) and continued: "to crown all he cannot retail any beer in Hammond during the present year, but must ship it all away and sell it wholesale."

HARTFORD (Washington County)

Nic Metzer (& Co.) (Whitman & Metzer)
    (1866?–1871?)
John Huels (1871?–73?)
Jacob Portz, Hartford City Brewery
    (1874–1890)
Jacob Portz Brewing & Malt Co. (1890–95)
Portz & Werner, Hartford City Brewery
    (1895–1900)
Geo. Portz, Hartford City Brewery
    (1900–1902)
Joseph Schwartz, Hartford City Brewery
    (1902–4)
Joseph Schwartz Brewing Co. (1904–1937)
200 East Wisconsin Street

Nicholas Metzer began brewing in Hartford sometime prior to May 1867, when existing excise records begin. While Nic appears in the excise records, it is George Metzer (most likely his brother) who appeared in the 1870 census as the principal, and probably the owner of the property as well. The Metzer brewery produced 400 barrels in 1870 with their horse and three employees, and if the industrial census is accurate, priced their beer at $7.50 per barrel, which was the cheapest in Washington County at the time.

In late 1871, John Huels, formerly a brewer at Huelsberg, purchased the Hartford brewery and ran it at least until early 1873 (he is still listed in the industry directory for that year). Production declined from 314 barrels in 1871 to 245 the next year which may have represented Huels' declining interest in the brewery. Huels decided to trade the Hartford brewery for the Kiefus House hotel (later the Gasper House) owned by Jacob Portz, and in 1874 Portz took over the brewery.

Portz expanded production quickly, from 94 barrels in 1874 (during which the brewery may not have been in operation the whole year) to 469 barrels in 1875, and to 700 barrels a year by the end of the decade. In 1876, Portz was charged by two of his workmen that he had failed to cancel tax stamps on the kegs. However, the account in the *West Bend Democrat* concluded that the workers "got their backs up" and "the whole affair was gotten up to injure an apparently innocent man" out of "personal malice." Portz rented the brewery to Stephen Mayer of West Bend for a short time in 1880, perhaps because Mayer needed extra capacity for his growing business.

Industry directories do not list any malting operations in the early 1880s, but Portz built a malt house in the mid-1880s and soon this business became just as important as the brewery. When the company was incorporated in 1890, this was indicated in the name of the business. Around 1895, the two businesses were split among Jacob Portz's sons: Louis and Andrew took the malting plant, and George operated the brewery. George partnered with William Werner for a few years, but later bought out Werner's interest and ran the brewery alone.

Joseph Schwartz purchased the brewery from Portz in 1901 for $34,000 and began to enlarge the plant and increase production. (The Portz family continued in the malting business.) Schwartz was another brewer who served in the Civil War, in his case, with the 1st Wisconsin Volunteers. In the mid-1910s, Joseph promoted his son Andrew to manager, and left most of the day-to-day operations in his hands. This was a wise decision since Joseph died in August 1917. Andrew was not the brewmaster, however, this position was held during the 1910s first by William Frank and after his death in 1914 by William Bauer. Among Joseph Schwartz's innovations was to purchase a delivery truck for the brewery. This particular two-ton KisselKar was the subject of an article in *Motor Truck* magazine in 1913. It plunged through a stone wall and over a ten-foot embankment into a mill pond, but was hoisted out with a derrick and turned out to have suffered so little damage it was able to make an eighteen-mile trip later that day. This was touted as evidence of KisselKar's durability as well as proof that the motorized truck could not only replace horse-drawn drays but improve upon them.

The Schwartz family diversified their business during Prohibition in a spectacular way. The company bought Hartford's Eagles Park, and began leasing the recreational facilities. In 1928, they built a large octagonal ballroom, which was reputed to be the largest dance hall in the state. "The Schwartz" hosted the bands of Guy Lombardo, Lawrence Welk, Woody Herman and the Dorsey Brothers among others. The era of big name acts continued until 1944, when the ballroom and park became Camp Hartford, a detention facility for German prisoners of war. (The ballroom has since been restored and as of 2017 was called the Chandelier Ballroom.)

It is unlikely that Joseph Schwartz Brewing Co. was ready to sell beer on the day when beer became legal since they do not seem to have had their license in time, but they began production again during 1933. Sales were never particularly high after Prohibition, typically only a few hundred barrels a month, but in 1937 sales were consistently under 100 barrels a month, and the brewery stopped producing that summer. The Schwartz company went

A post-Prohibition corner sign, made by Veribrite Signs of Chicago. Corner signs were much less common after Prohibition. COURTESY OF NATIONAL BREWERY MUSEUM.

bankrupt, and both the brewery and ballroom were turned over to creditors.

Baum & Eckel (1866?–1869?)
D. & J. Baum (1872?)

Baum & Eckel (later just Baum) are known mostly from excise records. A Jacob Baum boarded with Henry Eckel in 1870, though neither was listed as a brewer. Daniel Baum and his father John were farmers in Wayne Township. While listed in the 1872 directory, this was likely a very small farm brewery.

Red Brick Brewing Co./Rothaus Restaurant & Brewery (1995–2000)
4900 State Highway 175

Red Brick Brewing Co. and Rothaus Restaurant & Brewery was a short-lived brewpub in Hartford, featuring the beers of brewmaster Robert Wilbers.

HARTLAND, DELAFIELD TOWNSHIP (Waukesha County)

Christian Christianson (1867–1872?)
Kaeding & Krause, Bark River Brewery (1872?–77?)

Sometimes listed in excise records under the post offices in Hartland or Hawthorne, the brewery of Christian Christianson appears to have sold its first beer in November 1867. By 1870 he was selling about 100 barrels a year, which made his one of the smallest breweries in Waukesha County. Records of R. G. Dun & Co. show that Christianson was regarded as an honest man, though heavily in debt.

At some point, most likely in early 1872, Christianson sold the brewery to John H. Krause and Frederick Kaeding. The 1873 *Atlas of Waukesha County* includes an advertisement for John H. Krause as the proprietor of the Bark River Brewery, in which it was noted that he was also a wholesale and retail dealer of beer and liquor, but the atlas fails to locate the brewery on any of the maps. The brewery's production never seems to have been much more than 100 barrels, and the Dun records suggest that Krause was in and out of business over the next few years. He was probably out of business altogether by 1877 if not before.

HAYWARD (Sawyer County)

Angry Minnow (2004–present)
10440 Florida Avenue

Brothers Will and Jason Rasmussen started Angry Minnow in a building constructed in 1889 for lumber magnate Robert McCormick. Neither had any brewery or restaurant experience, but Jason was a homebrewer who gained experience by attending Siebel Institute and working as an apprentice at Great Dane in Madison. The brewpub quickly became popular with vacationers and cabin owners in the Hayward area, many of them from across the border in Minnesota. The brewery started bottling some of its beers in 2006 and self-distributed them in the local area. Around 2012, Angry Minnow added a small canning operation, which helped even out sales during the slower seasons. The canned beers were distributed as far north as Bayfield, and south to Hudson. The cans proved especially popular with customers who wanted to take home the beer they had on vacation. Over the last several years, production has grown gradually but steadily, approaching 1,000 barrels in 2016. Jason Rasmussen estimated that Angry Minnow could produce as much as 1,300 barrels "going flat out," but they had no plans to expand beyond existing capacity.

Oaky's Oatmeal Stout was one of the popular Angry Minnow beers bottled in the late 2000s. COLLECTION OF SCOTT REICH.

Old Hayward Eatery & Brewpub/Muskie Capital Brewery (2005–2010)
15546 Highway B

Muskie Capital Brewery was a sister brewery to Ashland's South Shore Brewery, and South Shore's Bo Belanger traveled from Ashland to Hayward (about sixty miles each way) three times a week to brew with Badger Colish and the rest of the brewing team. The fifteen-barrel system enabled Muskie Capital to handle the needs of Old Hayward Eatery and also produce some extra for South Shore. The economic downturn that started in 2008, along with changes in city policies in Hayward made operating two brewpubs impractical, and Muskie Capital closed in 2010.

HIGHLAND (Iowa County)

Jacob Gunlach & Phillip Gillman (1846?–47?)
Phillip Gillman (1847?–1860?)
Charles Gillman (1865?)

According to the county histories, Jacob Gunlach built a log structure that was the first brewery in Highland, and Phillip Gillman started brewing there the next year. It is possible that Gunlach was merely a builder and not a partner in the brewery, since county histories of the late nineteenth century often used that phrase to indicate erecting the structure rather than starting the business. He appeared in the 1850 census as a storekeeper, so may have had a financial stake in the business. The history of this brewery is also confused by the different names given to Gillman. There was a brewer named Philip Gillman *[sic]* in the 1850 census, but he was located in eastern Grant County, which was quite close to Highland in western Iowa County. But it was William Gillman who was listed as a brewer in Highland at that time (and boarded in the same establishment as Gunlock *[sic]*).

It is not clear how long this brewery was in operation. It appears in no excise records, industry journals or other records, and the 1865 state business directory lists Charles Gillman, who was brewing in Mineral Point at the time but may have taken control of the Highland establishment. The 1881 county history says only "Eventually the building was converted to other uses, until it burned in 1880."

Peter Seigut & Bros. (1855–1862)
Topp, Lampe & Imhoff (1863–67)
Schaffra & Lampe (1867–68)
Schaffra & Victor (1868–1870)
Schaffra & Meyer (1870–72)
John Schaffra (1872–1883?)
John A. Semrad (1887–1893)
John A. Semrad & Bros. (1893–1904)
Semrad Bros. & Pusch Brewing Co. (1904–1920)
Semrad-Pusch Brewing Co. (1933–1942)
FOOT OF BREWERY STREET

The 1881 county history reported that Peter Seigut and Bros. built this brewery in 1855, which they operated until it burned in 1862. The Seiguts left brewing after the fire, but John Topp, Anthony Imhoff, and the Lampe brothers built a new brewery. For the next few years, the Highland brewery went through the frequent ownership changes often suffered by a small town brewery with a limited market and limited capital. John Schaffra (or Schafer) took the place of Topp and Imhoff in 1867, but the Lampe family interests went to Victor and then to Meyer before Schaffra took the business on alone. (No one other than Schaffra was listed as a brewer in the 1870 population census.)

John Schaffra's time as owner met with mixed success. He had a reputation for brewing good beer, and produced nearly 400 barrels in 1870, but the R. G. Dun & Co. credit reports noted that he was personally reliable but was having a hard time resolving his debts. By 1883 he was out of business—although some sources list his term continuing until 1887, it is likely that the brewery lay dormant for at least part of this time since no Highland brewery appears in the industry directories.

In 1887, John V. Semrad, an immigrant from Bohemia, purchased the brewery with his sons John A., Frank and Joseph. In 1893, the elder Semrad retired and his sons took over the business. Anthony (Anton) Pusch, a refrigeration expert, bought a share of the brewery in 1904, and the company then took the rather

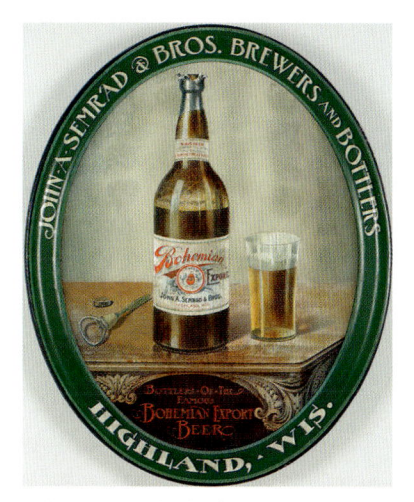

Semrad & Bros. emphasized its bottled beer on this pre-Prohibition tray. COLLECTION OF RICHARD YAHR

long name that would last for almost three decades. John A. Semrad sold his shares in 1912 and moved to a farm near Boscobel, so the remaining brothers carried on the business with Pusch. The company introduced a new flagship brand, Old Regulator, which would be revived after Prohbition.

The brewery suffered a fire in July 1901 that inflicted heavy damage, but unlike many smaller breweries, they appear to have had insurance adequate to cover most of the costs. The rebuilt brewery included five buildings, two of them over three stories, and employed fifteen men. Business continued to expland. The brewery's capacity was listed as 40,000 barrels and nearly forty men were employed just before beer production ceased in 1919.

The company was able to survive Prohibition by making near beer and bottling soft drinks. As a consequence, the Semrads and Pusch were ready to make a quick transition to making real beer again. However, one newspaper account claimed that the brewery had never shut down during Prohibition, but another report said that the plant had been shut down and the old plant was torn down and replaced by a new larger one. The plant wasn't quite ready in April 1933, but repairs and enlargements were made during the summer and the

newly incorporated and renamed Semrad-Pusch Brewing Co. was soon ready to reintroduce Old Regulator. Among the ways the brand was promoted was with a bowling team called the Old Regulator Beers in the Madison Businessmen's League. Just before the brewery closed, however, Old Regulator was phased out—the brewery letterhead from 1942 only mentions Bohemian Style Highland Beer. While the brewery had a capacity of 50,000 barrels it never approached that volume, and by the end of the decade sales were below 3,000 barrels a year. The brewery was strapped for cash, and could not afford to buy the required revenue stamps more than a day in advance. The brewery went into receivership in January 1942, and shut down shortly thereafter. According to a Semrad descendant, the story told by the family is that Blatz bought the bankrupt company because it needed the copper and could not get it through other means because of wartime restrictions. The brewery was later razed, and only remains of the loading dock are left as of this writing.

HILLSBORO *(Vernon County)*

Ludwig (& Landsinger) (1858–1874)
Frederick Schnell (1874–1890)
Joseph Bezucha (1890–1913)
Hillsboro Brewing Co. (1913–19)
Hutter Brewing Co. (1933–36)
Hillsboro Brewing Co. (1936–1943)
WOOD AVENUE, EDGE OF TOWN

Carl Ludwig left his brewing partnership with Otto Kerl in Berry and moved west to start his own brewery in Hillsborough (as it was then spelled) in 1858. The company's post-Prohibition letterhead proclaimed that their beer was "Enjoyed since 1852," but there is no evidence to support that early a date in Hillsboro. The first brewery was a small log building, but he later built a more modern structure. During at least part of this time, Joseph Landsinger was a partner in the business. Ludwig only sold ninety barrels of beer in 1870 in twelve months of operation, and known production records from the late 1860s and early

This postcard shows Bezucha's brewery, ca. 1910. Note the older spelling of Hillsborough painted on the wall. Six men, probably Bezucha and his crew, sit on kegs in the front center. COLLECTION OF JOHN STEINER.

1870s show similar small levels. The R. G. Dun & Co. credit reports confirmed his small scale, but noted in 1870 that business was down because "of want of patronage by reason of the hard times" though he was still worthy of credit. However he ultimately went out of business in 1874.

Frederick Schnell purchased the brewery that year, and either enlarged the plant or better used its existing capacity because he produced 364 barrels in 1875 and 590 in 1878. For the next several years, industry directories listed the brewery's capacity at 1,500 barrels, and in 1882 Schnell produced 1,300 barrels. In addition to brewing, Schnell also was a brick manufacturer for several years.

By 1890, the brewery was in new hands. Joseph Bezucha was a Bohemian immigrant who was also listed as a farmer in the 1900 census. During the 1890s his business was mostly draught beer shipped to saloons in the area, though he had competition from Hillsboro establishments that were importing Hausmann's lager from Madison, Reedsburg beer, or bottled brands from Milwaukee. He advertised "Special attention paid to family orders."

The Hillsboro Brewing Co. was incorporated in February 1911, mostly by Bohemians from Hillsboro, along with W. H.H. Cash from New Lisbon. Under the new management, the brewery became larger and more modern. The brewery made the switch from ice to refrigeration in 1911 with the installation of a sixteen-ton ice plant installed by the ever-present Vilter company of Milwaukee. A comparison of Sanborn maps from 1904 and 1914 shows that bottling facilities were added between those years (the only known paper label prior to Prohibition includes the post-1907 requirements, and the 1911 annual report confirms the existence of bottling operations). While Joseph Bezucha was among the original incorporators, he withdrew from an active role in the business. Oscar Ondracek was the brewmaster in 1912, but was succeeded by Edward Geisler in 1913. The brewery continued in operation until the government-ordered shutdown in 1919. The corporation disbanded and forfeit their incorporation at the beginning of 1922, and the property was sold in 1923.

After Prohibition, the Hillsboro brewery was reopened by a new corporation, the Hutter Brewing Co. The articles of incorporation allowed for operating a wholesale and retail ice business and left open the door to be a distributor for products of other breweries. The Hutter family lived in Fond du Lac and the only director with an address in Hillsboro was Edward Aman. Brewing began in 1934, but the company struggled. In August 1936, the brewery was reorganized as a new Hillsboro Brewing Co. The principals were all from La Crosse and two of them, G. W. and M. W. Heinrich, gave their name to the new flagship beer, Heinie's, introduced in 1938. The brewery also made Imperial Club and bock and holiday beers, as well as continuing Hutter's Hillsboro Pale. Some of the beer was shipped to Minnesota, but usually less than two hundred barrels per month. Hillsboro Brewing Co. had problems other than modest sales. The auditors of the Beverage Tax Division had reported in 1937 that the records of the company were in bad shape, and Bechaud's Inc. of Fond du Lac complained that Heinie's Strong Beer contained only 4.6 percent abv when the label advertised it as being more than 5 percent. (Hillsboro was allowed to continue using the labels after cutting off the top border that had the offending claim.) The company declared bankruptcy in January 1938, and remained out of business until late 1939. The new president of the brewery, Curt Pfeiffer, had been with Mathie-Ruder Brewing Co. in Wausau, and was expected to restore the fortunes of the brewery. Nearly all the employees were new and inexperienced, since those that were with the business before had left to find other jobs. the company produced more than 5,000 barrels in 1940 and approached 7,000 the next year. For some reason, perhaps in response to the declaration of war in December 1941, Hillsboro Brewing Co. decided to reintroduce a near beer brand in 1942, and Imperial Club was rebranded as "A Pure Cereal Beverage." This project was not a success, and the brewery went out of business in 1942.

Hillsboro Brewing Co. (2013–present)
815 WATER AVENUE

Snapper and Kim Verbsky purchased the property at 815 Water Avenue with the idea of turning it into a pizzeria. They decided to add a brewery because Snapper's dad, Joe, was an avid homebrewer. Just a few days after Joe brewed a batch of porter that he thought was his ideal brew in 2012, he was killed in a car accident. If anything, this made the Verbskys more serious about setting up a brewery in honor of Joe.

The restaurant opened in 2013, and brewing started in 2015. As of 2017, the flagship beers were Joe Beer, based on Joe's porter recipe, and Hillsboro Pale Ale. They also had six other regular beers and four seasonals. In addition to pizza, the restaurant also features a selection of sandwiches.

HORICON *(Dodge County)*

Paul Deierlein (1858–1882)
Charles H. Deierlein (1882–84)
John S. Deierlein (1884–1891)
HUBBARD STREET

In late August 1858, the *Horicon Argus*

434   THE DRINK THAT MADE WISCONSIN FAMOUS

announced: "We learn that two Germans have purchased brick and lumber and will soon commence building a brewery, on Hubbard street, near the Depot. It will be on a large scale, and will be a good investment." The *Argus* remained enthusiastic as the brewery approached its opening: "Paul [Deierlein] is an old brewer, and says he can make as good Lager as any men dare drink. Good for Paul, say we." While the praise for the quality of the beer may have been accurate, the expectation of a "large scale" brewery was not. The business was among the smallest breweries recorded in the 1860 industrial census, representing an investment of just $600 and producing just 150 barrels of beer (selling for $6 each). The brewery never grew very large: producing 175 barrels in 1870 and only seventy-six and seventy-three in 1878 and 1879.

The brewery continued to operate on a small scale through the 1880s under Paul's second son, Charles, and then his youngest son, John.

John Grosskopf (1864–66?)
Herman, Marquart & Co. (1866?–68)
John Grosskopf (1868–1870)
Grosskopf & Wolfram (1870–1872?)
Lawrence Wolfram (1872?–78?)
John Grosskopf (1878–1884)

John Grosskopf was the second brewer in Horicon, starting his business in 1864 according to the standard county histories. The excise records have Herman, Marquart & Co. for the 1867 license year, but it is not clear if they were leasing the brewery temporarily. (Grosskopf was not in the excise records during that year, so it is more likely that Herman, Marquart & Co. operated Grosskopf's brewery rather than starting a third brewery in Horicon.)

While Grosskopf's brewery had slightly more capital invested ($1,000) than his rival Deierlein, there was little difference in size. Grosskopf reported an identical 175 barrels in the 1870 industrial census, and nearly identical totals of seventy and seventy-five barrels in 1878 and 1879. Neither Horicon brewery produced much more than was necessary to satisfy local thirsts. The excise records show that Grosskopf had a partner for a few years named Lawrence Wolfram who was listed as a saloonkeeper in the 1870 census.

Grosskopf's brewery found its way into the newspapers twice for crimes committed on the premises, which suggests that his brewery may have attracted a rougher crowd than Deierlein's. In 1878, one Dan Crowley was killed in a fight at Grosskopf's brewery, and in 1884 the business was held up by four drunken railroad workers, though the marshal arrived in time to arrest the parties. Grosskopf's brewery disappeared from directories after 1884, and it is possible that the last incident persuaded him to leave the business.

HORTONVILLE, HORTONIA TOWNSHIP *(Outagamie County)*

Miller & Co. (1871?–1872?)

Miller & Co. were listed as brewers in the 1872 state business directory. They appear in no other sources, but John Miller appears in several records as a saloonkeeper in Hortonville. He may have brewed on a small scale, bottled beer for someone else, or simply been mislabeled in the directory.

Charles Hoier (1899)
Hortonville Brewing Co. (1900–1920)
NEW LISBON PLANK ROAD (MODERN WEST MAIN STREET/WI 15) NEAR BLACK OTTER CREEK

Charles Hoier was a blacksmith prior to opening a small brewery in Hortonville. His brewery began operations in April 1899, but was destroyed by a fire only three months later. When the brewery was rebuilt, it was under the auspices of the Hortonville Brewing Co. The new building was depicted in the 1901 Sanborn map as a small frame structure. The company added artificial refrigeration in 1907, and by 1909 the company had constructed a bottling house and a storage shed. Hortonville Brewing advertised in the 1910 Directory of Outagamie County, proclaiming: "Our Beer is a Wholesome and delicious Drink." Orders were "promptly filled" if customers called phone number twelve "with two rings." The company incorporated in Wisconsin in 1916, but aside from adding Inc. to the name, it had little affect on business. One of the original incorporators was

The Meek Company of Coshocton, Ohio, made tin plates called Dresden Art Plates, patterned after the porcelain of the German city. This stock plate depicts Ariadne, the mythological figure who helped Theseus slay the Minotaur and escape the Labyrinth. Hortonville's Wuerzburger Bottle Beer is advertised on the back. COURTESY OF NATIONAL BREWERY MUSEUM.

Joseph Borsche, who served both as president and brewmaster—a rare combination except in the smallest of breweries.

The brewery was in the news when a local drinker (a minor at the time of the episode in 1913) sued for $9,500 damages (perhaps $200,000 in 2018 dollars) because he "imbibed too much of the amber fluid dispensed at the brewery," collapsed after leaving on a frigid night and ended up having a leg and the other foot amputated due to frostbite. The company continued in business through Prohibition, but closed and was razed shortly thereafter.

HOWARD *(Brown County)*

Legends Brewhouse (1998–present)
2840 SHAWANO AVENUE

Couples Jay and Julie Gosser and Greg and Ann DeCleene started their first Legends Brewhouse in the Howard portion of Green Bay in 1998. Brewer Ken Novak created a number of different beer styles on the small brewing systems in each location. The other restaurants are the De Pere location and the now-closed Ashwaubenon site.

HUDSON (St. Croix County)

William Montmann (1857–1891?)
A. & J. Hochstein, Artesian Brewery (1891–1906?)
Henry M. Singleman Brewing Co. (1906–1910)
SECOND AND WALNUT STREETS (TO 1866);
SOUTH BANK OF LAKE MALLALIEU EAST OF 2ND STREET (AFTER 1866)

Hudson's first brewery was established in 1857, by William and Henry Montmann, as part of a store, bakery and hotel enterprise in the center of the city. Their property burned in the Great Fire of 1866, and they decided to rebuild on the south bank of Lake Mallalieu, which at the turn of the century was still called Willow River Mill Pond. The plant was run by hand but switched to horsepower sometime after 1870 and had a lagering cave and a saloon to serve patrons. In 1870, Montmann brewed 300 barrels, half as much as his rival Whye, but Montmann had other businesses to look after as well.

Sometime prior to July 1891 Anton and Joseph Hochstein purchased the brewery, and ran it until about 1906. Henry Singleman then took charge, and built capacity to 12,000 barrels per year (though production seems never to have approach that). Around 1910, it appears that Singleman sold out to rival Casanova Brewing Co., because the 1912 Sanborn maps label the building as Casanova Brewing Co. Plant No. 2 (though it was not in operation at the time).

J. F. Weyhe (1867?–1869)
R. A. Gridley (1869)
Gridley & Weyhe (1869–1871?)

The least known of Hudson's breweries started prior to 1867, when J. F. Weyhe (or Whye) began production. He appears as a brewer in the 1870 census, though Russell A. Gridley, his business partner, was listed as a (wealthy) farmer, and may have been the money behind Weyhe's brewing experience. An advertisement in 1869 proclaimed that R. A. Gridley had just purchased the City Brewery and had recommenced the manufacture of lager beer. The brewery was not particularly small for northwestern Wisconsin, brewing 600 barrels in 1870.

Some accounts list Weyhe as a predecessor of Louis Yoerg, but most histories claim the two were not the same business and the *Hudson Star & Times* included a new brewery built by Louis Yoerg among the buildings erected in 1870. The reason for the end of the brewery is not clear, but the R. G. Dun & Co. credit reports suggested that Weyhe was in financial difficulties. Weyhe may have moved to seek better prospects in nearby Hammond, or may have been trying to avoid creditors.

Louis Yoerg (1870–1890)
George Riedel, City Brewery (1890–96)
Joseph A. Casanova (1896–98)
Casanova Brewing Co. (1898–1920)
COULEE ROAD

Louis Yoerg was a son of Minnesota's pioneer brewer, Anthony Yoerg. Rather than stay in the family company, he decided to move east and start a brewery in 1870 in Hudson (even though the census listed him as living across the river in Stillwater, Minnesota at the time). His first brewery was destroyed by fire in 1873, but he rebuilt and equipped the new brewery with steam power in 1876. By the mid-1880s capacity was listed as more than 2,000 barrels per year—far more than his rival, Montmann.

After Yoerg's death the brewery was purchased by George Riedel, who operated it for a few years before selling it to Joseph A. Casanova. Casanova was a Swiss immigrant who had been employed at a brewery in Stillwater. The brewery was destroyed by fire in July 1898, and when it was rebuilt it operated as the Casanova Brewing Co., reflecting the presence of his brother Christopher in the firm. In 1910 the brothers bought out their crosstown competition when they purchased the Singlemann Brewing Co. for $16,500. While reports claimed that the two plants were to be consolidated, the Singleman plant was shuttered and all brewing took place at the Coulee Road facility. Casanova Brewing continued to operate until Prohibition, when it switched to a near beer called Caso and a line of popular soft drinks. The building still stands as of Summer 2017, and is occupied by a restaurant and liquor store. The brewery caves are used occasionally for special events.

Hudson Brewing Co./American Sky Brewing Co. (2012–15)
1510 SWASEY STREET

Greg Harris was an enthusiastic homebrewer who embraced the dream of taking his hobby to the next level. With business help from his wife and co-founder Molly, they began to plan Hudson Brewing Co. They wanted their brewery to stand for something more than just beer, so they decided to honor the service of their grandfathers in World War II and the Korean War by naming the brand American Sky and giving the beers names that paid tribute to military aviation. Tailgunner Gold was named after Molly's grandfather, who served as a tailgunner in Korea. Most beers featured American ingredients, but Dogfight had a mix of American and German malts, hence the name.

Hudson Brewing Co. opened its taproom, the Hangar, in September 2012. The taproom evoked an airplane hanger, the bar was shaped like an airplane wing and the tasting flight trays were shaped like propellers. The walls were decorated with aviation-related art and objects, as well as photos of military veterans—many brought in by patrons. Greg continued with the flagship brews but also introduced

Casanova Select label, ca. 1899. It is not clear what is meant by "Brewed especially for Select." Many beers were "warranted to keep in any climate," advertising their stability and longer shelf life.
COLLECTION OF JOHN STEINER.

flavorful specialty and seasonal beers, including a chocolate peanut butter stout that was released around Valentine's Day. The Hudson Brewing Co. name was soon dropped and the company took on the name of its beer brands.

In June 2015, the Harrises sold American Sky Brewing Co. to Lucid Brewing Co. Lucid (now North Loop BrewCo), was forced to close the taproom because of licensing issues, which was one of the reasons they were interested in the purchase in the first place. Lucid moved the brewing equipment from Hudson to its Inbound BrewCo taproom in the North Loop neighborhood of Minneapolis.

Pitchfork Brewing (2013–present)
709 Rodeo Circle

Mike Fredericksen was a long-time homebrewer and former employee of the Northern Brewer homebrew store in St. Paul. As president of the Sconnie Suds homebrewers club, he worked with the Wisconsin Homebrewing Alliance to help rewrite a law preventing homebrewers from taking their beer off the premises where it was made. Partially because of the attention generated by his testimony, he was encouraged to start Pitchfork Brewing Co., which opened with several co-founders in August 2013. Jeff Milleson joined the brewing staff as a volunteer apprentice in 2013, but by 2015 he had been promoted to Assistant Brewer.

The brewery, located in a small strip mall on the edge of Hudson, serves mostly ales and occasional lagers. A noteworthy beer is the occasional French Toast Ale, which is served with cinnamon sugar on the rim of the glass.

Huilsburg (Herman Township) (Dodge County)

John Huels (1850–1865)
August Thielke (1865–1871)
Eifert & Scharmann (1871–77)
Johann Heinrich Eifert Sr. (1877–1881)
Johann Heinrich Eifert Jr. (1881–87)
South Side of County Road S east of County Road P

John Huels (Hills) arrived in Herman Township in 1847 and began farming. In 1850, he started a brewery, and in 1858 added a general store—thus providing most of the commerce in the small village of Huelsburg (today Huilsberg). According to one county history, he was "a man of many attainments, being a homeopathic physician of exceptional skill besides doing a large mercantile business. In 1860, what was usually called the Herman Brewery produced an impressive 700 barrels of beer with three employees. He sold the brewery in 1865 to his brother-in-law August Thielke, who operated it for several years. Production declined through the 1860s, and in 1870 he reported sales of only forty barrels, though the brewery was only in operation for six months (and now employed only one).

Local historian Michael D. Benter has cleared up the previous confusing listings for this brewery. Thielke, probably overburdened by running multiple businesses and a farm, sold the brewery and its associated saloon to Johann Heinrich Eifert Sr. and Heinrich Scharmann Sr. In September 1871. Both were listed as farmers in the 1870 census, and may have had no experience brewing. Other than excise tax entries in 1871 and 1872, this brewery disappeared from the industry directories and only appeared in the 1876 state business directory and the 1884 Bradstreet credit reports, so it was probably run on an extremely small scale and did little more than supply the neighboring saloon. Eifert and Scharmann ran the brewery together until Scharmann sold his share in October 1877 (he died three months later, and may have sold out because of declining health). Eifert operated the brewery until 1881, when he died of a stroke, and his son Johann Jr. took over. He continued the brewery until 1887, when his son-in-law Charles Schott took over the saloon and elected to discontinue the brewery.

Humbird (Mentor Township) (Clark County)

Ignatz Gondrezick (1869)
Andrews & Gondrezick /Andrews, Hay & Co. (1869–1871)
Ernest Eilert (1871–1885)
East of Modern County Road F near East Fork of Halls Creek (Southern Border of Section 20, Mentor Township)

The 1881 history of Northern Wisconsin claims that Andrews and Gunderson erected the Humbird brewery in 1870. However, Gunderson was clearly a misinterpretation of Gondrezick, and excise records show he started production in 1869. Gondrezick is included in the 1870 industrial census as having operated for six months of the previous twelve. While no total number of barrels is recorded, information from the excise records and his total sales of $1,500 suggest that he produced about 150 barrels in that time (at a Clark County price of $10 per barrel). The brewery was destroyed by fire in September 1870, which may have encouraged Gondrezick to try elsewhere. The early business names appeared at different times in different sources, and seem to have been more differences in reporting than significant changes in ownership. The 1873 *American Brewers' Guide* directory indicates that George M. Andrews and Ernest Eilert owned the brewery together at that date, suggesting a more gradual transition than the 1881 history presents.

Ernest Eilert was trained as a brewer in Waukesha County by his father and in 1871 he moved to Humbird to take over management of the brewery (Gondrezick had started a new brewery in Tomah). Like many other brewers, Eilert held political office, serving as a town supervisor for several years. He stepped up production from 73 barrels in 1871 to an average of around 500 barrels a year in the late 1870s. By 1884, Wing listed his capacity at 2,500 barrels and indicated that he was bottling some of his beer. The R. G. Dun & Co. reports praised his business acumen and noted that he also owned a farm and other property in the county. They also reported rumors in 1883 that he was planning to buy the brewery in the county seat of Neillsville—rumors that proved well founded, but not until fate took a hand. Eilert's Humbird brewery burned in early 1885, and he moved to Neillsville a few months later.

HURLEY *(Iron County)*

Philip Becker, Hurley Brewery (1887–1895)
Gogebic Range Spring Brewery (1895–96)
M. E. Lennon, Gogebic Range Spring Brewery (1896–98)
McGeehan Bros. (1898)
WEST SIDE OF SIXTH AVENUE, NORTH OF GOLD STREET

Hurley was well known for consumption of alcohol, so it was fitting that there was an attempt to establish a home brewery to satisfy the local market. Philip Becker, who had previous brewing experience in Ashland, moved east to this thirsty city and excise records indicate that he started paying tax on beer in May 1887. The brewery depicted on the 1888 Sanborn map had a bottling works across the street right from the start. By 1891, the plant had a capacity of 3,000 barrels, and had added new icehouses and a keg washing building. The expansion continued in the mid-1890s with the construction of a new brewhouse, which was connected to the old building by a bridge, along with another new icehouse.

Becker suffered from the wild atmosphere in Hurley at least once, when one of his workers was killed soon after opening. Becker's biggest problem appears to have been financing. The rate of expansion seems to have been more than he could sustain, and the market for local lager beer may have been less than he expected. Hurley was a tempting market for large shipping brewers, who could have undercut Becker on price—the most important factor for the city's saloonkeepers. The Gogebic Range Spring Brewery (with or without Lennon's name in the business) was the first company to operate the brewery while it was in receivership.

The end for the brewery came in September 1898, when the brewery became what one headline called "Food for Flames." The loss was estimated between $35,000 and $40,000, which included five teams of horses that could not be rescued in time. McGeehan Bros., the receivers of the bankrupt brewery, had less than $10,000 insurance, and the building was not rebuilt.

Interestingly, there is one additional reference to a brewery in Hurley prior to Prohibition. The *Winona Republican Herald* reported that the president of the Badger Brewing Co. of Hurley had been indicted for liquor law violations, and included the information that fire had partially destroyed the Hurley brewery in December 1919. The fire marshal seized the brewery for the investigation, did not allow the beer to be removed, and after the Volstead Act took effect the next January, brought charges against the officers. This brewery does not appear in any industry publications, and the only known Badger Brewing Co. was in Black River Falls. The brewery may have been a wildcat operation—which would not have been out of character given Hurley's reputation.

HUSTISFORD *(Dodge County)*

R. Kamlich (1866?–1868?)

R. Kamlich appears in the excise records in 1867 and 1868. Wanye Kroll has him (spelled Kamlah) listed as the predecessor of Nic Metzer's brewery, but the two of them appear at the same time in the excise records in different cities, suggesting that they were separate businesses.

JANESVILLE *(Rock County)*

Hodson & Co. (1846?–1853?)
MAIN STREET NEAR MILWAUKEE

William Hodson, an important business leader of Janesville, built the first brewery in that city in 1846. As many other pioneer brewers discovered, having a brewery was only part of the process—he also needed to acquire the raw materials, and therefore advertised regularly in local newspapers for several thousand bushels of barley as well as for experienced coopers to make barrels to store and ship the product. Hodson advertised yeast for sale at his brewery as well as beer. While it was important as a business, Hodson's brewery was most famous for having been the victim of the first major fire in Janesville, in which the brewery was struck by lightning and destroyed. Hodson rebuilt immediately, and by 1850 the brewery of Hodson & Leach was the third largest in the state outside Milwaukee. It sold $6,500 of beer in 1850, and while the barrel total is not given, if it was sold at the prevailing Wisconsin rate of $4 to $5 a barrel, this would be at least 1,300 barrels. Leach was probably an absentee owner since he does not appear in the local census, but four brewers other than Hodson are listed: William Eggleston, Thomas Boyce, Jasper Sears and Leonard Lampson. None of these men were born in Germany, which is an indicator that English-style ales dominated the market in largely Yankee Rock County. When Hodson encountered financial troubles, his brewery and other properties were sold at a Sheriff's sale in 1853, but he would return to brewing in Janesville. The 1879 *History of Rock County* claims that Hodson sold out to the Bunster brothers, but subsequent research has called this into question.

John Buob (1853–54)
Boub & Rogers (1854–1868)
A. Rogers, Janesville Brewery (1868–1871)
John Buob & Bro. (1871–1882)
Gezelschap & Knipp, City Brewery (1882–86)
Knipp Bros., City Brewery (1886–88)
Louis F. Knipp, City Brewery (1888–1891)
Louis F. Knipp Brewing Co. (1891–93)
Louis F. Knipp (1893–1903)
Croak Brewing Co. (1903–1920)
Bower City Beverage Co. (1933–39)
500–520 NORTH RIVER STREET

John Buob probably began brewing in Janesville in 1853, though some sources place the date later. A later biography stated that he had been brewing in America since 1844. Buob was a native of Switzerland, so came from a lager beer tradition as opposed to the ale brewers who otherwise dominated Janesville. Buob sold a share in the brewery to Anson Rogers, who would soon serve two terms as mayor of the city. For some reason, the brewery was listed in the 1860 industrial census as Buob and Brunbolt, with a production of about 650 barrels of lager. Ads for Buob & Rogers in 1861 announced they were making both ale and lager, perhaps in deference to local tastes. However, they were also looking for a bigger market, since their ads also invited "Country

Dealers" (rural saloons and merchants) "to call at this Brewery before purchasing elsewhere as we are determined to deal in such an article and on such terms as cannot fail to be satisfactory." This partnership continued until 1868, when Buob sold his share and moved to Jefferson to build a flouring mill. Rogers ran the brewery on his own for four years, then Buob returned to Janesville and took control of the brewery again. Rogers planned to spend the coming winter in Florida with his daughter in hopes that her health would improve (making them very early "snowbirds").

This time, John Buob was joined in partnership with his brother Michael, twenty-one years his junior, who had remained at the brewery with Rogers. An article honoring Michael's retirement from brewing in 1913 claimed that he had started working at his brother's brewery in 1857, when he would have been about thirteen years old. Rogers continued to own the building, and the brothers leased the building but owned all the brewing equipment. This became a factor in 1873 when the brewery burned at the hands of a suspected arsonist. (Local residents heard a buggy stop for a moment at the gate about fifteen minutes before the alarm was given, and the fire started in an area distant from the brewkettle, which was the only fire in the establishment.) The insurance arrangements were complicated by the fact that Rogers had insurance on the building, but the Buob brothers had insurance on the contents. The new brewery was steam powered including the elevators for grain and keg transport. Fermentation took place in an open vessel (in German, *kuhlschiff*) in a room featuring windows on three sides that could be opened and closed. The brewery was constructed of brick and St. Peter sandstone, but the smokestack was made in Chicago and shipped to the site on two flatbed rail cars. Production at the new facility was among the largest in the state, especially outside Milwaukee. From 1,900 barrels in 1870, sales oscillated between around 1,500 and 2,500 barrels throughout the 1870s, topping 3,100 barrels in 1879. In general, the brewery had a good reputation for quality, honesty and stability, though the Buobs had a large mortgage on the property. John Buob was injured in an accident at the brewery when a large ice block slipped and crushed him at the bottom of a chute, but was able to return to work soon after.

In 1882, the Buob brothers left brewing (temporarily) and the brewery was rented to Charles H. Gezelschap and Louis (Lewis) F. Knipp for a ten-year term. These two had impeccable brewing credentials—Gezelschap had been a manager at Blatz and Knipp learned brewing at Miller and was most recently with the Milwaukee Brewing Association. Gezelschap stayed in Janesville only a few years, after which Knipp took over. He was joined briefly by his brother William Philip, who later went to a brewery in Huntington, Indiana. Despite the fact that the Dun & Co. evaluator considered the brewery old, small, and unsuccessful, the business prospered under Knipp's management: a newspaper account related that in 1888 Knipp sold $50,000 worth of beer, which required 19,000 bushels of barley and 12,500 pounds of hops, as well as 200,000 barrels of water (a rare report of water use). Knipp also made improvements to the brewery. He added an ice run to the river, but installed an ice machine in 1893. Knipp built a new fifty-barrel brewhouse in the mid-1890s, but the brewery still did not have its own bottling works. An 1896 souvenir publication on the businesses of Janesville reported "The brewery also makes a specialty of putting up fine brands of bottled beer," but this must have been done by an independent bottler since it could not have been done in an existing room of the brewery without violating federal law.

Knipp's more than two decades at the brewery ended in 1903 when the Croak brothers, William and Frank, formed the Croak Brewing Co. Their first major announcement was a half page ad for "special May brew," which was probably similar to bock. They claimed "every home where good robust health is valued should have in its cellar a small four gallon keg" which could be obtained for one dollar. Interestingly, they noted that it was "by far the most expensive brew that has ever left the Knipp brewery" and the beer itself was still called Knipp's beer. (Bottled beer was still not available.) The brewery continued to advertise Knipp's beer for at least two years. Finally, in 1906, the brothers installed bottling equipment and launched beers with the Croak brand, which they advertised heavily in the newspaper. In an unusual departure from tradition, when Croak released its bock in 1914, it was available in bottles only—it had long been a beer hall specialty and while many breweries bottled bock, very few if any others sold it exclusively by the case.

As prohibition approached, the Croak brewery debated what to do. As of 1918 they had not yet decided what to do with the buildings, and Frank Croak poured cold lager on any idea that the brewery could make enough beer before wartime prohibition took hold to last through the dry spell. The brewery stopped production on 30 November 1918, though some men remained employed to process the five-month supply of beer on hand. The company was reported to be considering making artificial ice, though a later article reported that Croak was now making near beer and Frank Croak stated "I have never even thought of manufacturing ice." The company jumped on the announcement that "war beer" of 2.75 percent strength could be made, though they refrained from actually restarting the brewery despite several notices in the newspaper that "[S]moke will soon be floating from the tall chimney at the Croak Brewing Company ." After the Volstead Act took force, there was debate in 1921 over making beer legal in Wisconsin, and Croak Brewing Co. again announced its interest in production. They expected to be issued a permit to brew—and Frank Croak went so far as to resign his position on the Janesville police and fire commission. However, these hopes were dashed, and the brewery was forced to stick to near beer.

After Prohibition, the Croaks reformed the brewery under the new name Bower City Beverage Co. While the company name had changed, the flagship beer was still marketed

Bock beer labels nearly always featured a goat, making this label from around 1934 quite unusual. Knapstein Brewing of New London used the same label. COLLECTION OF JOHN STEINER.

under the name Croak's Select. Sales in the first few years were about average for a smaller Wisconsin brewery, with some of the beer sold out of state (most likely in Illinois). Business began to decline in 1936, and the last sales were recorded in December 1938. Bower City Beverage sought bankruptcy protection in 1939, and the last remaining brewery in Janesville closed its doors for good.

Morshe & Wagoner, Black Hawk Brewery (1856–58?)
John Roethinger & Co. aka Rock River Brewery (1858?–1865)
John Roethinger, Phoenix Brewery/Janesville Steam Brewery/Cold Springs Brewery (1865–1878)
August Lutz & Co. (1872–74?)
C. Rosa & Co. aka Rosa & Bender (1878–1880)
W. J. Marshall (1880)
J. Haiga (1880–81)
Anna B. Roethinger (1881?–83?)
Nicholas Kramer (1883–84?)
John Buob, South Side Brewery (1885–1890)
Buob Bros., South Side Brewery (1890–97)
Michael Buob, South Side Brewery (1897–1904)
M. Boub Brewing Co. (1904–1915)
Badger State Brewing Co. (1915–18)
FOOT OF MAIN STREET & BELOIT ROAD

According to the 1879 *History of Rock County*, Morshe and Wagoner built the Black Hawk Brewery near the south end of Main Street. After a few years of "unsuccessful work" they sold "the implements" to John Roethinger who built "more commodious quarters hard by." (Even though this probably means the Black Hawk Brewery should be treated as an entirely separate business, local histories cover them together, perhaps because the new "quarters" were simply an addition.) An obituary for Roethinger related that he had worked at breweries in Pennsylvania and Illinois before coming to Janesville about 1857. It is possible that he worked for another firm (perhaps even Morshe and Wagoner) before starting his own business. Roethinger first appears in the 1859 city directory and in 1862 his business is identified as the Rock River Brewery. But in early November 1865, his brewery was destroyed by fire. The brewery at the time was rented to John Henry, who owned most of the contents of the destroyed brewery and attached dwelling. The family had to escape through a window, and a young boy was almost left behind. Roethinger rebuilt almost immediately, and like many other breweries that rose from the ashes, he named this the Phoenix Brewery. The new brewery employed steam power, so it was also sometimes called the Phoenix Steam Brewery or the Janesville Steam Brewery. (This is not to be confused with breweries that made "steam" beer, mostly in California at this time.) The engine was a twelve-horsepower unit that was only exceeded in size by a few breweries outside of Milwaukee.

Conscious of the diverse tastes of Janesville's tipplers, Roethinger offered a full range of beer styles. Because he was a German, he brewed lager, but he manufactured ale as well. An 1870 advertisement that announced the release of that year's "Buck Beer" (bock) also included "Stock Lager, Cream and Stock Ale at the rate of ten dollars per barrel." (An 1872 advertisement touted his Champagne Ale and Sparkling Stock.) This price was confirmed by the 1870 industrial census, which also recorded that he sold 2,000 barrels of beer and 500 barrels of ale (though a note in the *Gazette* said he made 2,000 barrels of lager and ale per year). Roethinger built a new ice house in late 1870 to help keep up with demand, but even this was not enough, so he embarked on a major expansion in the summer of 1871 in which he added a thirty-horsepower boiler and other modern equipment. Even while touting his modern equipment he also reminded customers that his brewery was the only brewery in the area located by and using water from a spring. His emphasis on the water source also resulted in the brewery being called the Spring Brewery or Spring Brook Brewery at various points. The Phoenix name was no longer in use in the early 1870s, but it could have been revived in 1872. In July of that year a fire started in the malt kiln, but the brewery employees had enough fire fighting equipment to douse the flames. However, the fire broke out again with more ferocity and consumed the entire brewery including the stables. The cellars were flooded and while some of the lager was saved, the ale casks were heavily damaged. Roethinger ordered lumber for a new brewery the day after the fire, traveled to Milwaukee to purchase a new brewing kettle and started again.

After rebuilding the brewery, Roethinger leased or rented the property to several tenants who did not share his brewing talents. Roethinger may also have needed money, since the repeated construction costs must have weighed on him, and the R. G. Dun & Co. credit reports indicate he had mortgages on the property, horses and beer. The first tenants were August Lutz & Co., (Joseph Walter was the "& Co."), who were not considered stable and were out of business by the middle of 1874. Roethinger apparently took the brewery back again, though production was now under 1,000 barrels a year. In 1878, the firm of Rosa & Bender took control, and the Dun investigator suspected that the brewery was "only a blind" for some other more nefarious business, and concluded: "the concern is in bad odor and should not be recommended for credit." (The sketchy reputation of the saloon at the brewery dated back at least to 1867, when a bartender was shot at by a drunken patron whom he was trying to evict.) This partnership continued through 1880, but went out of business and was succeeded by W. J. Marshall and then J. Haiga in quick succession. Meanwhile, John Roethinger had died in 1879 and the property passed to John's widow Anna B. Roethinger, who by 1882 produced only lager. Their son George was listed as a beer bottler in the 1880 city directory, and may have assisted with the brewery.

Nicholas Kramer became the manager of the brewery in September 1883 and made a final attempt to revitalize the Cold Springs brewery. He applied for a liquor license for the saloon at his brewery and began making beer. Unfortunately, the brewery burned for the third time in September 1884. The employees were on the second floor, and were unaware of the fire until alerted by a passing farmer. The loss of about $4,000 was not covered by insurance and the Roethinger family involvement came to an end.

After about two years away from brewing, the Buob brothers returned to the business at a new location. The *Daily Gazette* announced in November 1885: "The old brewery at the foot of Main street which burned some time ago, has been rebuilt, and to-day is running at its full capacity." John Buob was solely in charge of the brewery at this point, and Michael

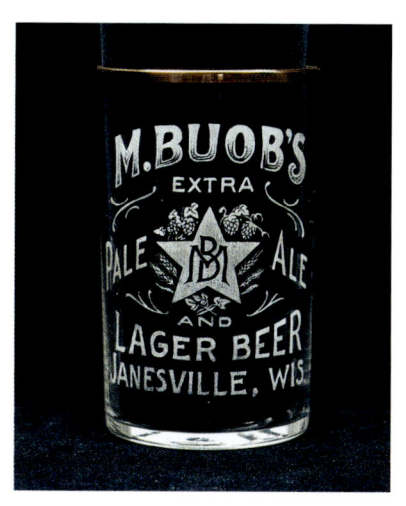

These glasses (ca. 1900) were not durable enough for saloon use and were probably given to residential customers. COLLECTION OF TYE SCHWALBE.

remained at the saloon on River Street. By 1888, Buob had production back up to 1,400 barrels per year and was the only brewer in Janesville with his own bottling works. The Buob brewery offered a full range of beers, including lager, ale and porter.

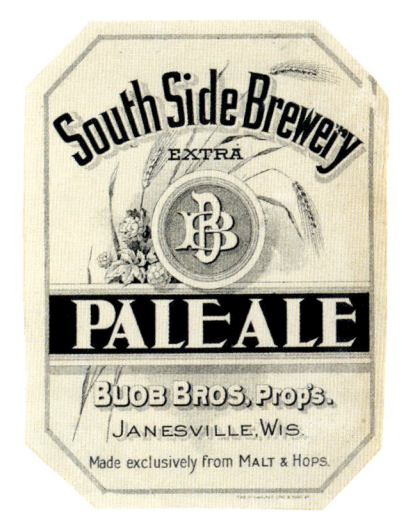

Aside from some name changes as the brewery passed from John to Michael, the Buob tenure was by far the least dramatic of any who occupied the block. There were no major fires or other disasters, and the Buobs were able to keep building their reputation and market. They expanded and improved the brewery campus on a regular basis: Adding new ice houses along with a slide from their own ice pond. In 1901, the employees of Buob's brewery (along with those of Knipp's brewery) met to form a union, but there was no significant conflict between labor and management recorded. After the formation of the M. Buob Brewing Co. In 1904, Michael retired from active involvement in the brewery and sold part of his interest in the brewery to his son William and to William Hart.

In keeping with the developing American reliance on scientific authority, Buob ran an advertisement in 1911 for their Golden Crown Beer that featured commentary by the brewery's chemist:

In the first place it may be a surprise to many of you to know that the brewery employs a chemist. My work is to test the water which we use, the malt, the hops, to test beers and also brewing, to see and know that just the proper chemical action takes place at a certain time and that certain other chemical actions are made impossible.

After the usual praise for their beer as a healthful tonic, he added this offer: "A case will be delivered to any responsible party in Janesville. After you have drunk three bottles if you are not perfectly satisfied that the beer is all I claim for it the Buob Brewing Co. will send a wagon for the remaining bottles and you won't owe a cent."

Will Buob continued to manage the brewery until his death in 1912, after which his widow, Mary, took over the firm as administratrix. A year later, the brewery was sold to Nicholas Schmidt, Leo Hucherheidt and Leo Stieher, all of Milwaukee. When Badger State Brewing Co. was organized and took over the brewery in April 1914, Leo Stieher remained general manager, but Peter Meer and Albert Blume were the two other principals. Original expansion plans included artificial refrigeration, but the 1915 Sanborn map only shows an expanded system of ice slides. In 1917 Badger State announced plans to increase capacity to 10,000 barrels a year, but this was ill-timed, with Prohibition looming on the horizon. The brewery went out of business before Prohibition actually arrived. (A photo of Buob's wagon and team is found in chapter 4, and a tin sign is pictured in chapter 6.)

Henry B. Bunster & Arthur W. Bunster (1854–55)

Lill & Diversy (branch) (1856–59)

EAST SIDE OF MAIN STREET BETWEEN NORTH FIRST AND NORTH SECOND

Based on the often vague locations given in city directories and early histories, some chronologies suggest that the Bunster (Brunster) brothers took over the brewery Hodson's brewery in 1854. However, the research of local historian Robert Biers seems to indicate that the Bunsters built a new brewery as part of Bunster's

This Buob Bros. Pale Ale label lacked bright color but had a clear design and an unusual octagon shape. COLLECTION OF TYE SCHWALBE.

WISCONSIN BREWERIES AND BREWPUBS 441

Block on the east side of Main Street between North First and Second Streets. Henry B. Bunster delegated management of the brewery to his brother Arthur who operated the brewery and a distillery. Bunster also advertised for barley—and because he needed it for two purposes he advertised for 20,000 bushels. Bunster stayed only a short time, and eventually moved to British Columbia where he became a member of Parliament. In August 1855 the *Janesville Gazette* reported that Bunster had sold out to A. W. Parker, who planned to use the building for a machine shop. However, Parker's plans must have fallen through, because in November 1856, the Lill & Diversy brewery of Chicago advertised that they had leased Bunster's brewery and malting establishment and would "keep constantly on hand Pale Amber, Brown Ales, Porter, Ale and Lager Bier." The earliest ads imply that the brewery was still in operation, but by 1858 the beer is advertised as the product of the Chicago brewery, though it appears they were still malting in Janesville because they were still soliciting barley. One ad listed prices for the various different grades of beer—which was extremely uncommon at that point in Wisconsin. Following the English system of letter grades indicating strength, barrels of XXX pale sparkling ale or cream ale were $7.50, and XX cream ale sold for $6.50. While they soon moved out of the brewery, the city was a promising market for a Chicago ale brewery seeking to expand its reach, so Lill maintained a branch in Janesville until 1870. An ad in the 1862 city directory announced "Cash paid for barley at the North Western Depot," which was one indicator of a shift in how American agribusiness was conducted. While most breweries bought their barley at the brewery, Lill & Diversy purchased it at the depot, perhaps in part because the barley was to be shipped to Chicago for malting, but also perhaps because more and more farmers were shipping their crops by rail, and this arrangement would be more convenient to both parties.

The Bunster brewery chronology is further confused by that fact that he appears to have built another brewery across the street which later became Govier & Harvey's Eagle Brewery. (See subsequent entry.)

Jacob Singer (1856?–1858?)
LOTS 5–8 CAULKIN'S ADDITION
Jacob Singer's small brewery was only in operation for a few years in the late 1850s. Singer lost his property at a Sheriff's sale in late 1858, which may have marked the end of his brewing.

A. W. Bunster (1858–1861?)
Govier & Harvey, Eagle Brewery (1862–1863?)
WEST SIDE OF MAIN STREET, "REAR OF BIG MILL"
The research of Robert Biers seems to have cleared up the apparent overlaps of the Lill & Diversy local offices, the various Hodson brewery sites, and who took over Bunster's brewery. It appears in 1858 that Bunster opened a new liquor store and brewery across Main Street from the earlier Bunster's Block. It is unclear how long he remained in the brewing business here before leaving for Canada.

In 1862 John Govier and George Harvey advertised that they were brewing "a very superior Ale, which for Purity and Delicacy of Flavor Cannot be excelled." The 1862 Janesville directory also mentioned porter among their products. They offered three different sizes of kegs, and solicited business from families and taverns alike, and accepted orders either at the renamed Eagle Brewery (which they specifically identified as "formerly Bunster's brewery") or at Harvey's liquor store. However, the new business lasted only a short time before the site was sold to Pixley, Kimball & Co. and was converted to a machine shop.

Samuel Hocking (1862–66)
WEST MAIN BETWEEN NORTH FIRST AND SECOND
On 8 November 1862, Samuel Hocking announced to "the citizens of Janesville and vicinity" that he had

> commenced the business of Brewing according to the method pursued in the old country, and upon the true and only true theory, that malt and hops are all that is necessary and proper to make good Beer or Porter. And having had thirty years experience in the business, in England, Canada and the United States, he feels confident that he can give entire satisfaction to all who may be pleased to favor him with a share of their patronage, to which end he will exert the utmost skill.

He offered a range of beers including ale, porter, "East India Ale," and a separate entry for "an excellent article of Ale and Porter for invalids." He also advertised "Table Beer made to order in any quantity desired." (To an Englishman of the time, table beer meant a low-gravity beer that would have an alcohol content of between 2.5–3.5 percent abv, intended to be consumed with a meal.) He concluded that he made "a superior article of bottled beer, kept constantly on hand." However, he needed help distributing his stock, since he also advertised for a "good beer peddler with team." His location was challenging, since he was located next-door to the Janesville agency of Chicago ale brewers Lill & Diversy.

Hocking's business apparently did not turn out has he had hoped, because in October 1866 he advertised for sale "[t}he whole fixtures for a small brewery" which included "one Copper Kettle, capacity about 150 gallons, as good as new; Mash tub, Cooler; under back well and work Pump; Barrels; Half and Quarter Barrels; Malt Mill, for hand or horse power; Fanning Mill, &c. Also a lot of Porter bottles, and Boxes to hold two dozen bottles, with partitions; one large bar room Mirror; one Ice Box, two large Stoves, Taps &c. &c."

Hocking asked that the items be removed before 16 November, apparently because there were other plans for the building.

William & Maria Hodson (1875–77)
69 NORTH MAIN STREET
William Hodson returned to brewing in Janesville in 1875. He built a new brewery, but needed a partner, one, according to an ad "that could be taught brewing in all its branches, upon the latest known principles of manufacture." This was important since the new brewery was built "upon the most modern, scientific plan, so as to save labor as well as to prevent acidity in Ales, caused through the influence of electro magnetism."

In a glowing feature, the *Janesville Gazette* described the new forty-horsepower boiler, the "patent refrigerator," and "the apparatus for extracting the fine flavor from the hops by giving the ale an infusion of them, instead of a decoction," and boasted, "We are told that the Hodson brewery is the only institution in the United States that has such a convenience." Less than a month later, another article reported that Hodson needed capital to expand, allegedly because of high demand for the product, but an ad six weeks later seeking a partner for the brewery also noted that the brewery only had $300 cash to start operations. (A partner bringing in capital of $1,500 to $2,000 was promised a lofty 20 percent rate of return.) The brewery went into operation in October, and he planned to "contest the field for the best ale, and being an experienced manufacturer, he will make a demand for his product." However, in December the brewery's advertisements proclaimed that Maria Hodson (who appears to have been William's daughter) was the proprietor of the brewery at 69 Main Street. William was still looking for a partner for two reasons: "for in two months since the first barrel of Hodson's Pale Ale went into the market, in Janesville alone twenty-two saloons are supplied, and over forty private families, with many orders from the country which, from the want of barrels, etc., cannot be filled. Another and more important reason is that the brewer and sole manager of the concern is in his seventieth year . . ." Yet another reason was exposed in a brutally honest advertisement—the firm needed money, since

> after paying the Government License, all the cash capital the Hodson Brewery had to start business with was $300, and without any additional help the brewery, with its financial fetters, coupled with the untiring opposition of wealthy brewers, can show the extent of its business and profits by government books and other records, to have been during the past four months upwards of five hundred dollars; had more capital been employed, the business would not have been confined to such a limited circle. . . . annual rental of $500 . . . for the brewery, saloon and residence . . .

It seems that no partner with the desired capital of $1,500 to $2,000 (or $5,000 worth of property) was ever found.

The Hodson brewery made a special point of the purity of their beer in advertising, emphasizing that no corn was used, because corn, "either yellow or white is an impure article, containing fusel oil which, as the United States dispensary says, is a violent poison. . . ."

Unfortunately for the Hodson's they were never able to solve their capital problems. Hodson had no property and the Dun & Co. report of early 1877 listed the ownership as "Maria Hodson and parties unknown." By the middle of that year, the firm was listed as out of business. There were rumors about "Chicago parties" buying the brewery and building it into "the largest brewery in Southern Wisconsin" but these plans never came to fruition.

John G. Todd (1868–1890)
Fardy & Robinson (1890–91)
N. B. Robinson & Co. (Robinson's Ale Brewery) (1891–98)
N. B. Robinson Brewing Co. (1898–1904)
POST OFFICE BLOCK (1 EAST MILWAUKEE OR 16 EAST MILWAUKEE)

In 1868, John George Todd purchased a former bakery located in the basement of the post office building. It was an attractive location for a brewery because cellars were already excavated, and "there was a splendid never failing spring of water, of a temperature so cold that in the summer, ice can be entirely dispensed with for cooling purposes." As a laudatory article in the *Daily Gazette* put it, Todd began "without capital, but understood the trade, and went in for success." He began brewing with a three-barrel brew kettle, which he soon replaced with a kettle double that size. With this system, he once produced nearly 1,100 barrels in a year, which meant a full brew every other day—a very high frequency for a brewery of that size.

Like his ale-brewing compatriots, Todd offered a variety of styles, including "Bitter Beer, Mild Ale, Old Stock and Brown Stout."

He guaranteed his product was "as pure as the best imported English ales." In some ways Todd seems to have anticipated the early twenty-first century brewery taprooms by offering special beers only available on site. At one point in August 1871, he had on draught Pale Stock Ale, XXX Porter, and "Old Stock Ale, brewed October 1869." Todd also brought his ale to local fairs: it was "on exhibition on the grounds of the Southern Wisconsin Fair of 1870" and in September 1873 he closed down his brewery saloon so that his one legally authorized retail outlet could be at the Rock County Fair. Mentions of Todd's Ale at fairs continue at least through 1883. The reputation of Todd's brewery had by this point extended beyond the borders of Wisconsin. The *Gazette* reported in 1873: "A firm at Marquette wants to contract with Todd to take all the ale his brewery is capable of manufacturing. Todd will probably not accept the offer as he cannot more than half supply his present list of customery [sic]." Perhaps the greatest (and most unusual) testimonial to Todd's ale was the claim that it had cured a ten-year-old boy of inflammatory rheumatism.

The 1881 county history made a point of relating that Todd's ale was made "mostly from Wisconsin hops," which was important to local boosters. In a biography of Todd in 1879, the *Gazette* reminded readers: "When we consider that the real wealth in a community is derived solely and directly from the producer and manufacturer, it must not be forgotten that the success of Todd's Ale and Porter Brewery whilst gratifying to the proprietor, has been proportionately beneficial to the city at large. Three-quarters of the ale manufactured at this brewery is shipped to points throughout this State, Illinois and Michigan."

Todd repaired and expanded his brewery in 1874, boosting weekly capacity from twenty-four barrels to 150 and was looking toward the Chicago market and proposed a depot there. It was therefore "a source of gratification" to Janesville that Todd was the only ale producer west of the Great Lakes who was showing an increase in sales, and that he was making two-thirds of all the ale in the state. The fulsome praise of Todd's ale continued, as the *Daily Gazette* proclaimed: "In many instances it has restored the invalid to perfect health and vigor. The proverbial beauty of the women of Janesville and the fine physique of many of the men, is much to be attributed to Todd's Ale and Porter."

Todd introduced a new beer in 1884—India Pale Ale. His IPA was "brewed on the same principle as the celebrated ales of Bass, Allsopp, and others of Burton-upon-Trent, England," and was "brewed entirely from the finest description of malt, and judicious blending of the hops of the Atlantic and Pacific states." There were very few advertisements of the time that mentioned the origin of the hops used in a beer, and it is interesting to speculate to what degree Todd anticipated the citrus and pine flavors of the "West Coast" IPAs of the early twenty-first century. Demand for Todd's beer was such that he apparently did not have to solicit orders—he was able to build a comfortable living on the orders which came in on their own, and even these kept the brewery at full production. A biographical sketch at the beginning of 1889 confirmed that "He has acquired sufficient means to carry him through life, and he is willing to let the remaining years pass as easily as possible." In fact, Todd retired in 1890, and sold the business to Norton B. Robinson and Matthew Fardy, who ran the Myers House Sample Room. Fardy, Robinson & Co. ran a liquor business in addition to the brewery, and after a few years Fardy took over the liquor part of the company and Robinson ran the brewery. At least early on, they seemed to have maintained much of Todd's market. A feature in the *Gazette* announced that Fardy & Robinson were producing India Pale Ale, XXXX Stock Ale, and London Porter, which were distributed in Michigan, Illinois, and Iowa as well as Wisconsin.

But business must have declined because in 1901 Robinson started a major newspaper advertising campaign to increase sales, during which Robinson's Ale cost 50¢ a "jug," could be ordered by mail or phone, and would be "[d]elivered in [a] private buggy direct from [the] brewery." He also introduced Robinson's Pure Scotch Ale, which was on sale at only twelve select saloons. However, patrons could order for home use an eight-gallon keg for $2.25 at any of these locations or from the brewery. Robinson hedged his bet on ale by becoming the southern Wisconsin distributor for John Gund's Peerless bottled lager. The company received an infusion of new capital in 1902 to add new machinery and establish a bottling plant in Milwaukee, with the funds coming from Chicago and Milwaukee investors, but by this point Robinson was no longer with the company. N. P. Robinson Brewing remained in the city directory through 1903, but in 1904 Frank P. Williams of the brewery advertised the company was for sale. The ad claimed it was the "chance of a life time" since "Nothing Pays as well as Brewing." No experience was necessary since a qualified superintendent was present, and the brewery was for sale only because Williams planned to move away since his wife had asthma. It appears there were no takers since the brewery disappeared from the newspapers and industry directories after 1904.

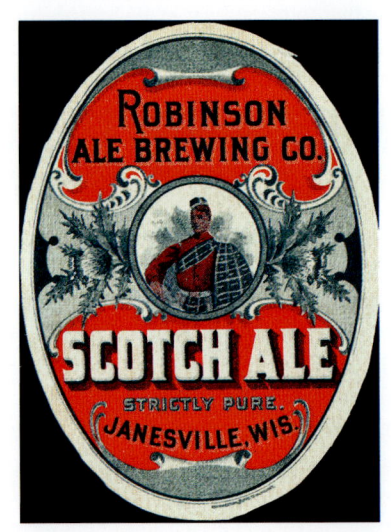

Scotch ales, which emphasize rich malt character over hoppiness, were uncommon in the Midwest in the decades before Prohibition. This label features thistles on either side of the Scotsman. COLLECTION OF TYE SCHWALBE.

William Hemming (1879–1883)
William Hemming & Son (1883–1901)
William Hemming's Sons (1901–1912)
Hemming's Ale Brewery, George Esser (1912–15)
Esser's Ale Brewery (1915–1921)
61 WEST MILWAUKEE STREET (1879–1882); 58 NORTH FRANKLIN STREET/106–110 NORTH FRANKLIN STREET (1883–1920)

William Hemming, a liquor dealer in Janesville, was bottling beer for several years before opening his own brewery. An advertisement in 1873 announced: "I am bottling [sic] a fine article of ale and porter, brewed at Todd's brewery especially for my use. The Quality I Will Guarantee Equal to any imported Scotch imported [sic] ale or porter. The Medical Fraternity can rely upon my bottled ale and porter being perfectly pure and well adapted for the use of invalids. The price I have put down low to bring the article within the reach of all. Orders from families, fishing and pic nic parties executed with promptness."

Hemming's "house brands" faced a crowded market in Janesville, and it is not clear how long he continued to offer it, or how long Todd was able to spare the brewing capacity to make a brand other than his own.

In 1879, the Englishman Hemming started brewing ale and porter himself. He had a liquor store on West Milwaukee Street, and it is possible that he was brewing there. (It is tempting to speculate that Hemming started in the former Hodson plant on North Main, but there is no conclusive proof.) Hemming found the existing premises too crowded (which seems to argue against Hodson's old plant), and in 1882 began contracting with local builders for a new brewery to be erected on Franklin Street at a cost of $3,500. The new facility was described as "a model for convenience and built to last," and the cleanliness of the plant was given special praise. As he opened the new brewery, Hemming brought his son, William J., in as a partner. They continued brewing ale and porter, though an 1889 account suggested "the brewery has not been ran at its fullest capacity." William Hemming died in 1896, but

William J. carried on, eventually taking brother John into the business.

In 1899, the property on which the brewery sat was sold to the Howe Brothers. Hemming leased the brewery building and continued to operate it without interruption. In 1912, William J. Hemming retired from brewing and sold the business to George H. Esser (of the Esser brewing family of Cross Plains), and Joseph Esser became the new brewmaster. The business was still run as Hemming's Ale Brewery through 1914, after which the Essers put their own brand on the company, and in 1915 they began to advertise Esser's Ale. The brewery continued making ale through Prohibition, after which the Essers briefly manufactured near beer. The brewery was sold in 1921 to Heibel Bottling Company of Madison, local bottlers of Coca-Cola and numerous other beverages, and George Esser became manager of the Janesville branch.

Gray Brewing Co. (1993–present)
2424 West Court Street

The modern Gray Brewing Co. claims a lineage dating back to 1856, when J. C. Gray started a soda water factory in Janesville. His son, C. C. Gray took over the business in the late 1870s, and by the turn of the twentieth century the company had a fine reputation for "ginger ale, soda water, champagne cider, seltzer and various other temperance beverages." However, there is scant evidence that the company ever made lager beer or ale during the nineteenth century. No city directory or industry publication lists them as a brewer, they do not appear in excise records (the taxes applied to weiss beer brewers) and the Sanborn maps from 1895 to 1915 show no evidence of a brew kettle. There is the possibility that they made weiss beer for a limited time, or that they bottled beer for a local brewer.

The modern incarnation of Gray Brewing Co. began production in 1993, and in a fitting nod to local tradition, was among the first of Wisconsin's new micro- or craft breweries to feature ales rather than lagers. Gray sold just under 2,000 barrels in their first year, which would have been an unheard of first-year total for J. C. Gray in 1856, but was a tiny part of the Wisconsin beer market in the 1990s. In the succeeding years, Gray's developed a following for their Oatmeal Stout and other English-style beers. In 1997, Gray Brewing was one of several breweries that came to the aid of Wisconsin Brewing Co. after the latter was flooded out: Gray offered their plant to Wisconsin Brewing to brew some batches until their equipment was repaired. Gray was one of the first Wisconsin breweries to offer a sample pack, which was one of the few eight packs on the market. In 1999, Gray Brewing began offering lager styles for the first time. Sales were uneven: over 4,000 barrels in 2000, but under 3,000 the next two years. By 2004, Gray had enough following (and enough capacity) to make winter seasonal beers a regular part of the line up, and they were shipping their beer to Connecticut and their sodas to California and Oregon. In addition to their own brands, Gray did contract brewing for several other beer companies, including Fauerbach Brewing Co. of Madison and Milwaukee Ale House.

In 2006, Gray Brewing Co. opened a lavish brewpub in the Madison suburb of Verona, called Gray's Tied House in a nod to the British tied house tradition. At first they were simply serving beer brewed in Janesville, but soon began to make beer on site.

JEFFERSON *(Jefferson County)*

Stephen Neuer (1852?–1874)
George Frommader (1870–71)
Christian Neuer (1874–78)
Neuer & Georgelein (1878–1880)
Christian Neuer (1880–82)
Berens & Stephan, Jefferson Brewery (1882–84)
Berens Bros., Jefferson Brewery (1885–86)
Joseph Berens, Jefferson Brewery (1886–88?)
South Side of East Racine Street opposite North Marion Avenue

Most accounts agree that Stephen Neuer established the first brewery in Jefferson. Neuer came to Wisconsin from Wurtemburg, and worked as a maltster for a short time before moving to Jefferson and starting his brewery. His brewery was not large enough to be listed in the 1860 industrial census, but by 1870 his horse-powered brewery made sixty barrels of beer—still the smallest in Jefferson and among the smallest recorded in the census. Early in 1870, Neuer leased his saloon and brewery to George Frommader, who held it for about a year. It appears that Frommader and his partners emphasized the saloon rather than the brewery, since no production was reported for 1871, and Neuer only produced thirty barrels after he resumed operation of the brewery in 1872. After Stephen Neuer died in 1874, his son Christian took over and increased production to over 200 barrels in 1874 and 1875.

In 1878, the younger Neuer took on John Georgelein (spelled a variety of ways) as a partner at least through 1880. However, Neuer's health was failing and he retired from active brewing in 1883 (and died in 1884). It is possible that he had leased the brewery during his illness since *Western Brewer* noted that Berens and Stephan had replaced Neuer in late 1883 and the *Jefferson Banner* reported that Stephan's brewery team had a brief runaway in February 1884.

The final ownership stage of this brewery began when the Berens brothers purchased the brewery from the Neuer estate in February 1885. Throughout the summer the *Banner* published several notes that the brothers were making improvements to the brewery including new structures. However, it is possible that the improvements were too big a financial strain for the company, because after an appearance by Joseph Berens in Wing's 1887 directory the brewery disappears from industry sources, and by 1890 the *Banner* was referring to construction projects by the "old Neuer brewery." The building remained until 1928 when it was razed.

Jacob Breunig (1855–1889)
Kiesling, Mattes & Heinz, lessees (1886–87?)
Jefferson Brewing Co. (1887–89)
Joseph Breunig (1889–1890)
Jefferson Brewing & Malting Co. (1894–1919)
Northeast Corner of Main and Racine Streets

Jacob Breunig built a small frame brewery in

1855, which by 1860 had grown to produce 400 barrels. Encouraged by this growth, Breunig razed the original brewery in 1863 and built a new brick brewery, along with a new residence, an icehouse, and a "hall for theatrical entertainments." The new brewery was one of the largest in the county and produced 1,000 barrels in 1870. Production dipped under 1,000 barrels during 1871 and 1872, but then recovered and was over 1,000 barrels for the rest of the decade.

Breunig's business was steady and uneventful for most of his ownership. Despite unfounded rumors that he planned to sell out, Breunig continued to upgrade the plant, and in 1884 it was reported he "has thrown away the old horsepower in his brewery and put in an eight hp steam engine which doubles his capacity." In 1886, he leased the brewery to a stock company comprised of three of his brewery employees: Christian Kiesling, F. Mattes and Hubert Heinz. They continued the business for a few years under the name of Jefferson Brewing Co. (not to be confused with the brewery of that name located on First Street). The brewery Breunig handed over had a capacity of 2,500 barrels of beer and 5,000 bushels of malt per year. Heinz left the partnership in April 1889 to take over the bakery and saloon of Adam Puerner, and shortly thereafter the brewery was sold. The purchaser was Joseph Bruenig, who was a cousin of Jacob and had worked as a brewer in Stillwater, Minnesota. Unfortunately, Joseph died within a year of purchasing the brewery and Jacob purchased the brewery back from the estate. Jacob did not return the brewery to production, and the estate had to sell off the remaining beer before the license expired in May 1890.

The brewery remained vacant for a few years, and the 1892 Sanborn map showed that the building was being used for storage. The Breunig Block was sold in 1892 to A. Puerner & Son, who made plans to restart the brewery. He consulted in 1892 with Albert Fryer of Chilton who was looking for a new location, but this deal fell through and Fryer remained in Chilton for another year. Puerner then turned to Joseph Beischel, Andrew Kippes and Rudolph Weckwerth to run the brewery. This group operated under the name Jefferson Brewing and Malting Co. and by the end of 1894 had the malt house up and running, and had their first beer on sale in April 1895.

The tenure of Jefferson Brewing & Malting Co. was generally uneventful except for steady improvement to the premises as practical. They installed a new thirty-five-barrel kettle in 1904, and artificial refrigeration in 1911. The refrigeration plant was hailed as a major innovation since it was a newer type using carbonic anhydride rather than ammonia, which eliminated many of the dangers involved with the latter compound. The system also saved the brewery from having to procure 1,200 tons of ice every year and doubled storage capacity. All this new equipment required upgrading the boiler from 40 hp to 80 hp to handle the load. Shortly thereafter, Beischel bought out Weckwerth's shares and continued the business under the existing name (Kippes had left the business earlier). The change in ownership was recognized the next year when the brewery released Beischel Beer. The brewery's bock beer was also sold under the Beischel name. Even though Beischel was the name identified with the brewery, the real estate was still owned by the A. Puerner & Son Co. The brewery continued until the approach of Prohibition in 1919, when Beischel retired. Beischel and Andrew Kippes died within a month of each other in 1938, two years before local beer returned to Jefferson.

Christian Illing (1856?–1860?)
Henry Lang (1860?–1873)
Danner & Heger, City Brewery (1873–1880)
Rudolph Heger, City Brewery (1880–1908)
R. Heger Malt & Brewing Co. (1908–1919)
Saxon Brewing Co. (1936–39)
Perplies Brewing Co. (1940–1953)
(THIRD STREET, CORNER OF MECHANIC) 114 NORTH CENTER AVENUE, LATER 1008 CENTER (AS PERPLIES)

While a few later histories focused on praising local businessmen credit Henry Danner and Rudolph Heger with starting the City Brewery, its true origins lay almost a quarter of a century earlier. Christian Illing was listed in the 1857 state business directory as a brewer, but may have been there earlier. *American Breweries II* lists Illing as continuing through 1862, but there was no sign of him in the 1860 census, whereas Henry Lang (Lange/Long) was present as a brewer with $1,000 of real estate, so it is likely that he had taken over by this point. Lang's output was not particularly large in 1870, only eighty-eight barrels, but it is possible that he was already exiting the business, since his entry for the annual brewery excise tax in May 1871 was deliberately crossed out, and there was no production record in the 1873 *American Brewers' Guide* for the previous two years.

The standard county histories claim that Henry Danner (Donner) and Rudolph Heger purchased the brewery from Lang in the fall of 1873. Their ownership gave the business an immediate boost, and production jumped from 245 barrels in 1874 to 438 the next year to 714 by 1879. By 1879, the *History of Jefferson County* reported: "four hands are employed in conjunction with the proprietors, who prepare their own malt, and turn out about one thousand barrels of foaming lager annually" (though the thousand barrel figure should be taken as an enthusiastic estimate compared with Salem's more reliable figures). The beer was shipped to nearby Cambridge, Johnson's

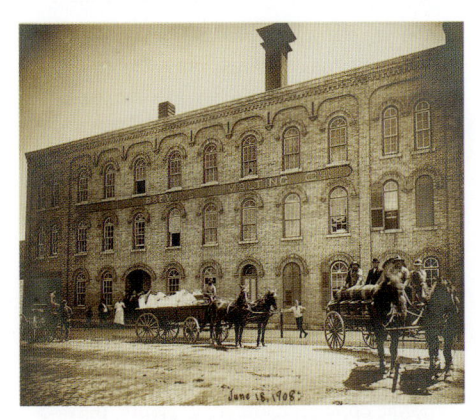

This picture of Jefferson Brewing & Malting Co. is dated June 18, 1908. The wagon at center carries blocks of ice. COLLECTION OF JOHN STEINER.

Creek and Fort Atkinson, as well as numerous accounts in Jefferson.

In 1880, Danner sold his share in the brewery to Heger, who continued with the brewery until his death in 1913, and whose name remained on the firm until Prohibition. Interestingly, despite Heger's Prussian origins, the industry directories list his brewery as producing ale and porter through the mid-1880s and do not list him as a lager brewer until 1887. Heger does not seem to have been an active brewer himself since several brewmasters or foremen were mentioned in the press and it is possible that the style of beer depended on the hired brewmaster. The most important of these was the brewmaster in 1887, Conrad Birkhofer, who was a lager brewer and would later gain fame as the brewmaster at Minneapolis Brewing Co. (later Grain Belt) and then at the Conrad Birkhofer Brewing Co. in Minneapolis. (A photo of Heger's Pioneer Brew label appears in chapter 2)

Heger's brewery was in the news more often than most breweries, and it was for a mix of positive innovations and unfortunate events. Heger built a new stone and brick brewery in 1887, which also brought favorable mention to the local craftsmen who provided the labor and material. Heger had one of the first two private telephones in the city in 1888, the other being in the county clerk's office. The beginning of the city water system dated to 1893 when Edward Mueller was awarded a franchise to construct a water pipe leading from Heger's brewery to other customers. The water was an important part of Heger's beer which won the second place award at the 1904 St. Louis World's Fair for purity. The company purchased one of the first delivery trucks in the area, and the Garford vehicle "was satisfactory to the Co."

Unfortunately, Heger Malt & Brewing Co. was also the site of several industrial accidents. Several workers caught limbs in machinery, John O'Conner fell down a flight of stairs and Peter Berens fell forty feet down an elevator shaft (but survived). The most ghastly of the accidents occurred when Fred Zobel was shellacking the inside of one of the large casks, and lit a candle after the electric light stopped working. The fumes ignited and badly burned Zobel and Marten Wagner, who tried to pull Zobel from the cask. Zobel died the next morning. Another fire in 1902 provided the trial run for the city's new fire whistle (which was said to be unusually shrill) when a fire started in the barrel pitching room. A less common environmental hazard (for breweries) was reported in 1891 when the "horrible stench from Heger's hog pen at the brewery" threatened to close the East side school.

Of course, the biggest threat to the brewery was the onset of Prohibition. Even before the 18th Amendment took effect, the brewery complex was turned into a plant to process dairy products, and the top floors of the brewhouse were removed.

Hopes for the return of local beer to Jefferson were evident as soon as beer was legalized. In June 1933, the *Banner* reported that George Held of Milwaukee was preparing to renovate the buildings and commence brewing. These plans fell through, and in in 1935, the city encouraged the St. Lawrence Distilling Co. to make use of the old Heger facility. This project failed to gain traction, either, and the buildings remained vacant. In 1936, Saxon Brewing Co. was incorporated in Jefferson County (though by Milwaukee area directors) to operate the brewery. While Saxon did produce a limited amount of malt tonic, there is no evidence they made any beer, and they never appeared in the state production or stamp sales figures. (A photo of the Saxon malt tonic bottle is at the end of the introduction to the brewery section.)

In 1940, Emil Perplies, formerly of the defunct Kenosha Brewing Co., succeeded in renovating the brewery and actually bringing beer to market. His draught beer appeared just before Thanksgiving that year, and bottled beer was available early the next year. Perplies announced that he would use local Ladish Malt exclusively, as well as the finest ingredients of all types. The company was still using wooden kegs at least through 1943, because there was

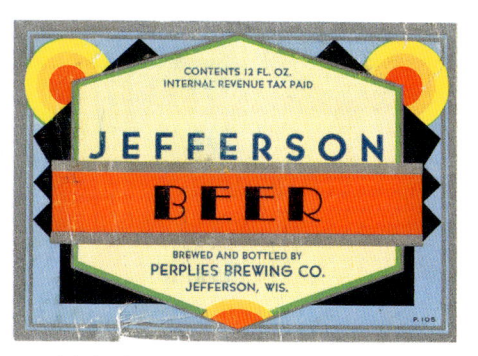

Beer labels often used popular typefaces and designs. The geometric shapes and the typeface for the word *beer* evoke the Art Deco style of the late 1930s. COLLECTION OF TYE SCHWALBE.

another fire in the pitch room that year. Production was low at first, but Perplies experienced the largest war-era increase by percentage, jumping from about 5,000 barrels in 1943 to nearly 20,000 by the end of the war. (The 20,000 figure is impressive, since capacity was listed in a 1944 brewery directory as 12,000 barrels.) Unfortunately, the company was charged with selling some of this increase at prices exceeding the maximum wartime limits, as well as increasing the price by eliminating quantity discounts and by reducing the quality of the beer.

The dramatic wartime surge gave the owners confidence to install new equipment in 1947 (the old equipment was shipped to a brewery in Rotterdam). However sales plummeted to pre-war levels almost immediately and the brewery was struggling. Things were made worse when Ernest Perplies was arrested in 1947 for larceny involving a complicated scheme of charging taverns desperate for any beer an advance and then failing to deliver the beer. A fire in August 1953 was the final straw for the company, which went out of business shortly thereafter. Emil Perplies applied in 1972 to open a small brewery at 114 Center Street, but this was an era when breweries were closing, not opening, and anyway his application was denied by the City Council. The old brewery, since converted into apartments, burned in 1973, and the remains were razed immediately thereafter.

WISCONSIN BREWERIES AND BREWPUBS

Ernst Swellingrade (1860?)

Ernst Swellingrade was listed as a brewer from the 1860 population census. He had $2,000 worth of real estate, so it is less likely he was merely an employee. His listing in the census was fairly close to that of Stephen Neuer, so it is possible they were partners briefly.

Chas. Hasslinger (Mick & Hasslinger) (1869–1870)

The firm of Mick(?) and Hasslinger appeared in excise records in August 1869, but by next May the business is under Charles Hasslinger alone. Hasslinger (as Hustinger) was included in the 1870 industrial census as a brewer of 150 barrels—which was not much, but still ranked third among Jefferson's five breweries.

F. J. Schatz (1866?–67)
John Kemeler (1867–1872?)
EAST RACINE STREET

While it is not clear when F. J. Schatz started brewing, it was after 1860 and prior to August 1867, when he sold his brewery to Bavarian native John Kemeler (or Kemmeter). Kemeler appears in the excise records from October 1867 until October 1872, but his brewery was too small to be included in the 1870 census of industry. The 1870 population census shows a brewer named Christoph Miller living very near Kemeler, but it is not clear if Miller was a partner of Kemeler, an employee, or if he had his own brewery (which is possible since he had $1,000 of real estate). Statistics in the 1873 industry directory suggest that Kemeler may have ceased production during 1872, since his production dropped from eighty-seven barrels in 1871 to twenty the next year. An obituary printed in 1900 claims he conducted the brewery for over twenty years, but since he was a saloonkeeper after the brewery disappeared from the records there is a chance he still brewed some beer for sale at his own saloon.

Schmidt & Co. aka Jefferson Brewing Co. (1892–95)
EAST SIDE OF FIRST STREET, NORTH OF DODGE AVENUE, ACROSS FROM THE RAIL DEPOT

The second company to do business as Jefferson Brewing Co. was started by Charles Baireuther (previously a brewer in nearby Aztalan), who had recently purchased the hotel across First Street from the Chicago & Northwestern depot. In 1891, he began "a large addition to the building, in order to have ample room for brewing." Construction continued through the next year, but when the brewery opened, it was under the management of Schimdt & Co. and called the Jefferson Brewing Co. (though it was often referred to as the Baireuther brewery). The *Banner* reported that the company was growing rapidly, but in September 1893, Adam Schmidt was badly injured in a runaway accident, and he apparently decided to retire from brewing. The brewery was sold to Hugo Graf of Milwaukee, who had been employed by Pabst. On taking charge of the plant he ceased brewing and made it the site of his Pabst distributorship.

JOHNSTOWN *(Rock County)*

M. D. Waters (1856?–1858?)

M. D. Waters is known only from the 1857 and 1858 Wisconsin state business directories. The 1857 Rock County gazetteer confirms there was such a person in Johnstown, but did not provide any information about whether he was a brewer or not.

JUNCTION CITY *(Portage County)*

Central Waters Brewing Co. (1998–2007)
701 MAIN STREET

Cofounders Jerome Ebel and Mike McElwain decided to make their homebrewing hobby a profession, and in 1996 purchased a building in Junction City. The site was selected at least in part because it was in the middle of their intended sales territory. In the early years, the capacity was 300 barrels a year, but the popularity of their early beers, especially Mud Puppy Porter, encouraged them to expand. The brewery began distribution in spring 1998 with draught beer, and then added 22-ounce "bomber" bottles. The first beer to be packaged in 12-ounce bottles was Y2K Catastrophe Ale, an American-style barleywine.

In 2001 the brewery was sold to Paul Graham and Clinton Schultz, both of whom had been working at the brewery. Central Waters began its highly regarded barrel program at this location in 2003, which started with a bourbon barrel stout and was crowned with a gold medal at the Great American Beer Festival for their Bourbon Barrel Cherry Stout in 2006. Central Waters also started an associated brewpub in Marshfield (see separate entry). In 2006 the company broke ground on a new brewery in Amherst, and began production there in 2007. (See Amherst for the history of Central Waters since 2007.)

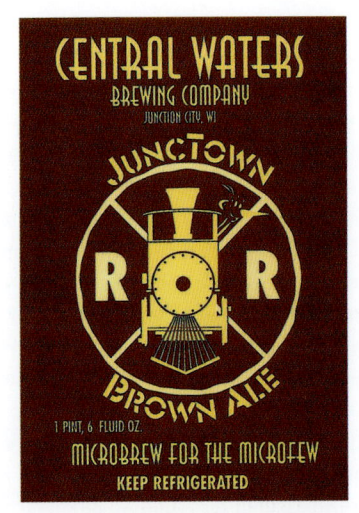

The JuncTown Brown Ale label paid tribute to the first home of Central Waters. This label was for a 22-ounce "bomber" bottle. COLLECTION OF SCOTT REICH.

KAUKAUNA *(Outagamie County)*

Peter Dedrich (1856?–58?)

Dedrich appears to have had a short-lived brewery in Kaukauna.

Michael Kline (188x?–86)
Helf Bros. (1886–1891)
Helf & Brill (1891–95)
Jacob Helf, Buchanan Brewery/Kaukauna Brewery (1895–97)
Helf Bros. Brewing Co. (1897–99)
Jacob Helf & Co., Kaukauna Brewery (1899–1908)
Jacob Helf Estate, Kaukauna Brewery (1908)
Katie (Mrs. Jacob) Helf, Kaukauna Brewery (1908–1912)
SOUTH SIDE OF 10TH STREET, TWO BLOCKS WEST OF HENDRICKS AVENUE SOUTH

The older of the two Helf family breweries in Kaukauna (Buchanan Township) was started by Michael Kline (probably Michael Jr., who was listed as a farmer in the 1880 census) sometime in the 1880s. Some sources list him in partnership with Adam Hilz for a short period. Around 1886, Peter and Jacob Helf moved from Fond du Lac to take over the small brewery. The brothers remained together for several years, but soon began the moves that make it difficult to untangle the history of the breweries. Sometime around 1891 the brothers split up and Jacob went into partnership with John Brill at the Tenth Street location. (The company was still named Helf Bros. on the December 1890 Sanborn map.) Helf and Brill continued through at least 1895, when their brewery was totally destroyed by fire. The brewery was rebuilt, and in 1897 a new company was formed, Helf Brothers Brewing Co. (this time Jacob and John C.) This partnership was dissolved in February 1899 and Jacob remained at this brewery and John moved to the North Kaukauna brewery "which for some time has been idle." The building was struck by fire again in 1898, and again was rebuilt. The 1900 Sanborn map shows a much smaller brewhouse complex, since the malt was made at the Desnoyer Street location, but a larger racking room for keg beer and a new bottling house in what had previously been labeled a pop manufactory. In 1906, the brewery had a capacity of 5,000 barrels per year. Jacob Helf died suddenly in January 1908, and the brewery continued only a short time under the administration of his widow, Katie. By 1913 the buildings were vacant, and were torn down shortly thereafter.

Helf & Ristau, City Brewery (1893-97)
Helf Bros. Brewing Co. (1902-6)
Regenfuss Brewing Co. (1906-1934)
Electric City Brewing Co. (1934-1947)
729 DESNOYER STREET

After the first Helf Bros. partnership in the Tenth Street brewery broke up, Peter Helf joined with Charles Ristau, a liquor dealer, to establish the City Brewery in the north part of Kaukauna. According to the 1894 Sanborn map, the brewery used a windmill to pump water, which was unusual at this late date. This partnership lasted for about five years, at which point Ristau went into the hotel business and the brewery apparently lay idle. When the second Helf Bros. partnership dissolved, John C. Helf moved to this location. The Sanborn map of 1900 indicates that this plant was used only for malting, but refers to it as Helf Bros. Brewing Co., which seems to indicate that the brothers had combined their efforts again. (It is also listed in the 1900 industry directory as Helf Bros.)

At some point prior to 1906, the brewery was put back into operation at a capacity of 3,000 barrels a year and a bottling house was added to this site. In 1906, John Regenfuss purchased the brewery and expanded its capacity to 8,000 barrels. (The 1911 county history says he bought the brewery from Peter Helf, which could mean either that he still owned the property from the 1890s, or that John and Peter were the Helf Brothers in this brewery, though *American Brewers' Review* of April 1906 states only that this was the former Peter Helf brewery. *Western Brewer* inaccurately reported that Regenfuss had purchased the Jacob Helf brewery in South Kaukauna.)

John Regenfuss was a trained brewer, and had worked at Walter Bros. Brewing Co. in Menasha prior to his arrival in Kaukauna. He made several improvements to the brewery including a new brew kettle in 1909 and a brick addition to the plant in 1910. An announcement of the expansion noted "Mr. Regenfuss is a great believer in home trade and has stated that all of the material used in the building will be purchase in Kaukauna and all the labor will be done by home contractors."

Later in the dry years, Regenfuss Brewing also acted as the local agent for Atlas Special Brew from the Atlas Brewing Co. of Chicago. John Regenfuss died in September 1932, so was unable to see his brewery return to operation a year later.

The brewery retained the name Regenfuss Brewing for a short time, but then changed to Electric City Brewing Co. There was still a Regenfuss presence at the brewery, however, since Leo Regenfuss was employed as an assistant brewer until the brewery closed. In addition, John's brother Jacob came to the brewery in 1906 and remained until 1945. The brewery returned to the Pearl Foam brand name from before Prohibition for a short time, but also sold Electric City lager and Pilsner Club. In 1938, they introduced a new flagship beer, Mellow Brew. Like most other Wisconsin breweries of the era, they made bock beer in the spring and offered a Winter Brew under different names. Electric City shipped a small amount of beer to Michigan in addition to their Primary Wisconsin market.

During the war years, Electric City continued to produce beer, but was charged in 1945 with violating wartime wage and price controls by granting an unauthorized wage increase to its employees. In 1946, the brewery was sold to W. R. Hansen of Birmingham, Alabama. His purpose in purchasing the brewery was not clear, though since it was announced that president Arthur Jones would continue as manager of the business and Hansen would "act as sales manager for the southern territory," it was likely that Hansen was trying to secure a supply of beer for Alabama during the postwar transition period. The brewery remained in operation until early 1948 when it closed for good.

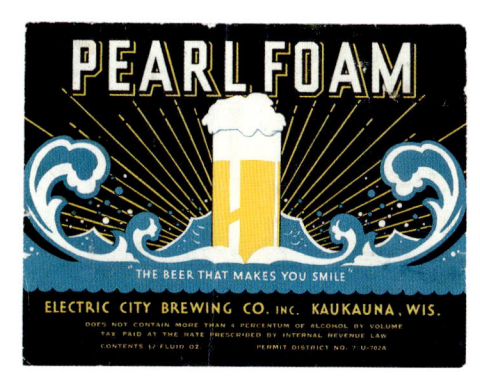

A glass of beer rising dramatically from the water adorns the Pearl Foam label. Kaukauna acquired the nickname Electric City after the first hydroelectric dam was completed there in 1882. COLLECTION OF TYE SCHWALBE.

Kenosha (Kenosha County)

Joseph Spicer, Southport Brewery (1842–1854)

J. M. Hughes (1854–1858?)

"On the bayou east of the Durkee House"

During the period before Southport became Kenosha, the Southport Brewery of Spicer & Co. began production in late 1842, and advertised the next January that they were prepared to sell ale, strong beer and family table beer. In addition to ale, they also sold yeast to households and paid cash for barley. By 1850 Spicer was producing 550 barrels a year, which sold locally at $5 per barrel. The brewery burned in March 1851, and the reports referred to it as the old brewery and claimed it was unoccupied.

In May 1854, Spicer sold his brewery for $3,100 to J. M. Hughes, who was described as "a wealthy and well known brewer and business man of Cleveland, Ohio." Hughes continued to operate the brewery long enough to listed in the 1857–58 Wisconsin business directory.

Conrad Muntzenberger (1847–1873)
Muntzenberger & Co./Engel & Muntzenberger (1873–75)
A. Muntzenberger (1875–1884)
Muntzenberger Brewing Co. (1884–85)
New Era Brewing Co., aka Milwaukee Malt Extract Co. (1885–89)
Griesbach Brewing Co. (1890–93?)
6 North Main and Water Streets

Conrad Muntzenberger left Milwaukee for what was then known as Southport in 1847 and started a new brewery, which was sometimes erroneously called the first brewery in the city (or even the first outside Milwaukee). It is possible that these accounts meant the first lager brewery outside Milwaukee, but even this is not certain. By 1850, his brewery produced more beer than any brewery outside of Milwaukee except for the Keyes brewery in Madison (which produced 3,000 barrels to Muntzenberger's 2,000). The company grew quickly, but then leveled off instead of following the trajectory of the Milwaukee firms that had grown at a similar rate during the period before the Civil War. Muntzenberger seemed satisfied with a steady level of production—as late as 1879 his production remained right around 2,000 barrels per year. Muntzenberger had an 8-hp steam engine in the mid-1850s, making his one of the first steam-powered breweries in the state, but technological advance did not necessarily mean constantly expanding capacity, at least in this case. The Muntzenberger family contributed to the advancing technology of the industry as well: Conrad's son Adolph invented a barrel washer which was patented in 1873 and adopted quickly by major brewers throughout the country.

In addition to his brewing enterprise, Conrad Muntzenberger was said to have "amassed a fortune" in real estate, was "considered the most influential Democrat in southern Wisconsin" and was a great booster of education. Muntzenberger scaled back his involvement in the brewery in 1875 when his son Adolph and William Engel took over the brewery (which carried on for a time as Muntzenberger & Co.) for the last few years of lager brewing, the firm went under Adolph's name. (A Muntzenberger label is shown in chapter 2.)

In 1885 a new era began for the brewery when the Milwaukee Malt Extract Co. bought the Muntzenberger plant to produce their patented New Era Beer. Headed by a group of Milwaukee brewery suppliers including Charles Kiewert and Otto Zwietusch, Milwaukee Malt Extract Co. was to manufacture the beer patented by Zwietusch and Dr. Charles H. Frings under the name of New Era Brewing Co. (so New Era owned the recipe and Milwaukee Malt Extract brewed it under license, but it was all the same people). Conrad Munztenberger was brought into the firm as a director, and his brewery was taken over by the new company and dedicated to making the new product. The company appears to have attempted to market the product in states that had enacted prohibition laws such as Iowa, but they ran into difficulties when the Chicago, Rock Island &

The prominence of three patent dates on this label (ca. 1887) testifies to the significance of invention and innovation for Americans during the Gilded Age. COLLECTION OF JOHN STEINER.

Pacific Railway refused to carry the product on the grounds that it violated Iowa liquor laws. Ultimately, the Iowa court agreed that it was a malt liquor and therefore contraband, and could not be carried by railroads in the state whether it was intoxicating or not. New Era Beer was sold as far away as Georgia, though it continued to result in prosecutions on the grounds that it was still beer. The company was reorganized in 1890 as the Griesbach Brewing Co. with an infusion of new capital and new directors, though Otto Zwietusch was still among them and its product was still New Era Beer.

The end of brewing in pre-Prohibition Kenosha came in 1893 when the Griesbach Brewing Co. building was destroyed by fire. Arson was suspected, especially given that the harnesses of the fire apparatus had been cut.

Gottfredson & Gunnerman (1858–1859?)
Jacob G. Gottfredson (1859?–1877)
J. G. Gottfredson & Son (1877–1889)
Main Street, foot of Union

Jacob G. Gottfredson conducted a variety of establishments during his varied business career in Kenosha. He started making vinegar, then ran a cigar store for a while, then started a brickyard (the latter two he continued to run during his brewing career). In 1856, he bought a share of a malt house, and in 1858 he opened his brewery on Main Street. The *Kenosha Tribune & Telegraph* praised the "large brick building erected last season by Messrs

Gunnerman & Gottfredson. Its architecture is in the modern style; the building is designed for a Brewrey [sic] and has all the modern adaptations for that purpose." In addition to confirming that Gottfredson had a partner in the early years of the brewery, the article also implies that some breweries occupied buildings not designed for that purpose. Apparently the first building was inadequate, since it was reported a few months later "Gottfredson & Gunnermann have removed their Brewery building, on the north side of the creek, and commenced the erection of a new one on the site of the old one."

While his volume data is missing from the 1860 census, the total revenue suggests Gottfredson sold around 1,000 barrels during the previous year. Like his near neighbor Conrad Muntzenberger, Gottfredson never grew much beyond the scale reached in the early 1860s. The highest known production level for the brewery was just under 1,300 barrels in 1874. The last time Gottfredson appeared in a brewing industry directory, his capacity was only 3,000 barrels, which would have been plenty to supply a small local market, but an anomaly for a large city located halfway between Chicago and Milwaukee. Gottfredson advertised ale during the mid-1860s, but by the 1870s he was listed in industry directories as a producer of lager only (though he may have continued a small ale trade without emphasizing it).

The brewery suffered a fire in 1876, but it did not touch the brewhouse itself, just the barn and the icehouse. Damage was reported as $1,000 and "two roast pigs," which indicated that, like many other breweries, the Gottfredsons kept livestock at the brewery. The brewery burned again in June 1889, and while the insurance covered the loss, it appears that this provided the Gottfredson family with the incentive to leave the brewing business. A portion of the building was later used for the local Pabst agency, which was managed by Frederick J. Gottfredson.

John Engelhardt (1860?)
John Engelhardt is listed in the 1860 population census as a brewer. It is possible that he worked for either Gottfredson or Muntzenberger (whom he lived relatively near) but the fact that he was listed as having $1,000 in real estate makes it a reasonable possibility that he operated his own brewery for a time. He also may have been a predecessor of N. A. Brown.

N. A. Brown (1860?–1866)
Montagne & Graff, aka Brown's Ale Brewery (1866–68)
Stanley & Griffin (1869)
Michael Griffin (1869–1870)
John Gunnerman (1870–72)
Harrington & Heitmann (1872–1873?)
BETWEEN MAIDEN AND LAKE

N. A. Brown was listed as a brewer in the 1860 census, though because he reportedly had no real estate he may have been employed at another brewery (perhaps Engelhardt?), or could have been the manager of a brewery he was leasing or renting. By the mid-1860s, R. G. Dun & Co. reported that he had slowly recovered from large debts and by 1866 was doing a large business. In 1866, he sold out to William Montagne. Even with the new ownership of Montagne and Graff, the old name Brown's Ale Brewery was sometimes still used in newspapers, and the name of John D. Montagne appeared in excise records.

During 1868, the brewery of Montagne & Graff (spelled here Montague and Groff) was seized by federal revenue officials on a charge of fraud, most likely improper handling of revenue stamps. the litigation produced an impressively long case title that was a typical inventory for a brewery of the period: "The United States of America against steam engine, boiler and gearing, seven large mash and workin [sic] tubs, copper still, warm and fire place, one pump, ale in tubs in brewery, one malt mill, one and one half bales of hops, ice house and contents, thirty-two barrels of ale in brewery, office and contents, furniture and safe, one double wagon, one single wagon, one hundred and twenty-five empty barrels, two horses, brewery building in the city of Kenosha, Wisconsin . . ."

According to a report, most of the fixtures were purchased by two former employees to restart the brewery, but they appear to have sold them again to other parties. Michael Griffin, a former soda water manufacturer, took over the brewery with a partner named Stanley, though Griffin's ownership was short and the Dun investigator was skeptical at best about his reliability, once calling him "an ugly customer."

The 1870 population census and excise records indicate that John Gunnerman (or Grunnerman) was the next owner of this brewery. (This Gunnerman may have been Gottfredson's founding partner.) His brewery burned in May 1871, and reports indicated that arson was suspected. The final known owners of this brewery were John Harrington and Clement Heitmann (or Hightman), who brewed 100 barrels in 1872, but disappear from the records after that.

William F. Martin (1900?–1905?)
William F. Martin was listed as a lager brewer in the 1900 and 1905 industry directories. These directories were sometimes out-of-date, but seldom if ever included a listing for a business that was not actually a brewery. However, William F. Martin was listed in the 1900 census and the 1903 city directory as a soda manufacturer, and a scan of Kenosha newspapers shows no evidence of lager brewing.

Wisconsin Brewing Co. (1933–36)
Kenosha Brewing Co. (1936)
The Wisconsin Brewing Co. was incorporated in April 1933, one of many businesses to be formed in the immediate wake of the legalization of beer. The articles of incorporation authorized the company to "make, manufacture, compound, brew and prepare bock beer, lager beer, schenk beer, Weiss beer, and all other kinds and varieties of beers or brewed liquors of an alcoholic content not to exceed 3.2 percent by weight, all in conformity with the laws of the United States of America. . . ." While most of the language was standard boilerplate, the presence of "schenk beer" indicates an interest in an older style which was lower in alcohol and therefore clearly under 3.2 percent.

Wisconsin Brewing may have applied for a trademark for Old Style Beer, as indicated on the label, but Heileman already had a lock on the name, so this brand was produced briefly only in 1933. COLLECTION OF JOHN STEINER.

Production started in October 1933, but they apparently never bottled anything other than lager. Known production was never more than 900 barrels a month, but there was a significant drop during the summer of 1935 and the company ceased production by November. The company also encountered legal difficulty with the State of Wisconsin, which discovered that Wisconsin Brewing Co. was illegally transferring revenue stamps to Manhattan Brewing Co. of Chicago, which was selling them to Best Brewing, also of Chicago. This was of particular concern to Wisconsin officials, since Manhattan Brewing was generally thought to be controlled by Chicago gangsters.

In 1936, Emil Perplies restarted the brewery as the Kenosha Brewing Co., and started to produce Old Kenosha Brew. Perplies hoped to expand his market beyond Kenosha, and to that end he advertised for Danish and Italian speakers to act as representatives in Racine. However the company encountered labor troubles in June 1936, when bottle house employees walked out in a dispute over hours and wages. The company announced that beer would be shipped to Milwaukee to be bottled in a union shop there, and then shipped back for distribution. However, the stress on the company caused it to close for good in August 1936.

Brewmasters Pub, Restaurant & Brewery (1987–2004)
4017 EIGHTIETH STREET
Brewmasters was the sixteenth brewpub to open in the United States, and the first in the Upper Midwest. Its story is told in more detail in chapter 10.

Brewmasters Pub—Parkside (1996–2004)
1170 TWENTY-SECOND AVENUE
Jerry Renzy opened the second Brewmasters Pub in a building that had formerly been the Pub and Grub bar and a barbeque restaurant. The Parkside location had a brewing system almost twice as large as the original location, but both had about the same number of beers on tap at any given time. The two locations generally coordinated their brewing and recipes, but had a few beers that varied by location.

Rustic Road Brewing Co. (2012–present)
510 FIFTY-SIXTH STREET
Greg York founded Rustic Road Brewing Co. in 2012 after more than ten years experience as a homebrewer. He selected Kenosha because he saw promise for the revitalization of the downtown area and wanted to be a part of the growth. The nanobrewery started with a small German brewing system and four fermenters. York selected Southport Wheat as his flagship beer to pay tribute to the earliest days of Kenosha and because of Wisconsin's historical importance as a wheat producing state. Most of the beer is consumed in the brewery taproom.

Public Craft Brewing Co. (2012–present)
716 FIFTY-EIGHTH STREET
Matt Geary was exposed to the craft brewing scene in Kenosha ten years before he started Public Craft Brewing Co.—his wedding reception was catered through Brewmasters Pub, the first brewpub in the Upper Midwest (see the Brewmasters entry). After graduating from Kenosha's Carthage College, he worked at various jobs in the area and homebrewed in his spare time. He eventually started putting together a business plan, took the Concise Course at Siebel Institute in Chicago, and eventually began brewing an American pale ale on 4 July 2012.

Public Craft introduced canned versions of flagships Bits & Pieces IPA and K-Town Brown in late 2016, and regularly releases firkins of special beers in their taproom and at beer festivals.

R'Noggin Brewing Co. (2016–present)
6521 120TH STREET
Brothers Kevin and Jeff Bridleman started as homebrewers. They opened R'Noggin in 2016.

KEWAUNEE (Kewaunee County)

William Blackwell (1856?–58?)
Adolph Ebel (1860–64)
William Blackwell appears as a brewer in Kewaunee in the 1857 state business directory. It is possible that his brewery was the predecessor of the Adolph Ebel brewery, because according to local papers Ebel does not fit into the Kewaunee Brewery timeline. Neither Blackwell nor Ebel are in local newspapers or the 1860 census, so the status of their brewery is uncertain.

The early history of brewing in Kewaunee is further confused by a report in the *Kewaunee County Enterprize [sic]* in 1860 that ". . . the large, new three story building built last season by Mr. Duchoslaw for a brewery and cabinet maker's shop, has recently been purchased by Mr. Metzner with the intention to put into operation a bakery . . . ." It is possible that

The label for the 1994 Anniversary ale offers little information about what style of beer was in the bottle. COLLECTION OF SCOTT REICH.

Metzner's plans did not go through, since the Kewaunee Brewery started up shortly thereafter. It is also possible that Ebel took over this building for a short time.

Berni & Zimmerman, Kewaunee Brewery (1859?–1860?)
Ulricker & Zimmerman, Kewaunee Brewery (1860?)
Arndt & Wenger, Kewaunee Brewery (1860?–62?)
Deda & Wenger (1862–64)
Deitloff & Wenger (1864–65?)
Brandes & Wenger (1865?–66)
Charles Brandes, Kewaunee Brewery (1866–1882)
Frank Nuhlicek, Kewaunee Brewery (1882–88)
Mach & Langer, Kewaunee Brewery (1890–1902)
Anton Mach, Pilsen Brewery (1902–7)
Anton Mach Estate, Pilsen Brewery (1907–9)
Mach's Pilsen Brewery, Mrs. Catherina Mach (1909–1916)
Pilsen Brewery, Raymond Rauch (1916–1920)
Kewaunee Brewing Co. (1933–1942)

SOUTHWEST CORNER OF ELLIS AND DODGE STREETS (324 ELLIS)

One history of Kewaunee County claims that the first brewery there was that of Stephen Berni, started in 1859. But not until June 1860 did Stephen Berni and Julius Zimmerman announce in a newspaper ad that their "brewery is now in complete operation, and that they are now prepared to furnish the best quality of Lager Beer, in any quantity at the lowest prices." Zimmerman was in the 1860 population census, but not Berni. Instead, Zimmerman's partner at the time of the census (which would have been very nearly the same as the ad) appears to have been Joseph Ulricker, who lived next door and owned an equal $1,000 of real estate. But a year later, it was "Messrs. Arndt & Wenger of the Kewaunee Brewery" who announced that their new cellar was now filled with "lager beer for the summer months." J. Peter Arndt (Arendt) purchased Zimmerman's share in the brewery late in 1860 and "Pete" received rave reviews from the editor of the *Kewaunee County Enterprize* for his lager.

Ownership of the Kewaunee Brewery continued to change rapidly. The *Enterprize* noted in March 1862 that the brewery had recently changed hands, and "Messrs. Deda and Winger [sic] . . . will be able to supply all demands with Ale and Beer not anywhere surpassed." It is interesting that ale was mentioned specifically, though it is possible since Kewaunee was a port city that some of the mariners preferred ale. Deda was also proprietor of the Wisconsin House, and sometime around early 1864 seems to have returned to the hotel business full time (for the moment). Wyta Stransky, another local businessman, stepped in to provide the capital for Wenger, though this arrangement was also short-lived. A few months later, the names in the Kewaunee Brewery ads are Deitloff & Wenger. Sometime in late 1865 or early 1866, hotel owner Charles Brandes (or Brandis) purchased Deitloff's share of the brewery. (The Robt. Jos. Binger listed in the R. G. Dun credit evaluations of 1865, is almost certainly a misinterpretation of Wenger.)

At this point, a business change occurred that confused most previous chronologies of Kewaunee breweries. In June 1866, Brandes sold the Steam Boat House hotel "to attend to his Brewery, Flouring and Lumbering business." A few days later, Joseph Wenger sold out and joined a partnership to build another brewery in the city (see the Bavaria Brewery).

Brandes was literally a survivor—he was one of only six to survive the 1852 wreck of the steamer *Atlantic* on Lake Erie. (Brandis had also served on the *Sea Bird* when it was commanded by Captain Frederick Pabst.) Near disasters followed Brandes on shore as well. The brewery suffered a freak accident in 1868 when lightning struck the cellar during a storm and about forty barrels of beer were burst open. As one newspaper lamented, "What a pity."

Brandes produced almost 500 barrels in 1870, which sold for $10 per barrel. His production remained between 400 and 500 barrels for the rest of the decade. In 1882, he sold his brewery to Frank Nuhlicek, who operated it for the next several years. In 1890, Nuhlicek sold the brewery to fellow Bohemian Anton

This tray dates from the 1930s. COURTESY OF NATIONAL BREWERY MUSEUM.

Mach for $7,500. Mach and his partner, Joseph Langer, continued the brewery until Langer sold his share around 1902, after which Mach renamed the brewery in honor of the brewing capital of his homeland. In 1906 Mach began to expand the brewery, planning to add a bottling house and steam power, but he died in 1907 and his widow Catherina (Katie) took over control of the brewery, assisted by her sons Anton Jr. and Joseph. The Mach family eventually sold the Pilsen Brewery to Raymond Rauch for $13,500. Rauch operated the brewery until Prohibition.

After Prohibition, the Kewaunee Brewing Co. was reformed, but using the old Pilsen Brewery site rather than the old Bavarian/Kewaunee Brewing Co. site (which has further confused some previous chronologies). They rehired Raymond Rauch to be brewmaster and got going as soon as possible, but they were still not ready for the first day of legal beer. To satisfy their customers, they imported beer from other cities. The first batch of their own beer was put on sale 5 May 1933—after the first eighth-barrel keg was delivered to the mayor of Kewaunee. The first beer was draught only and bottled product was not available until an all-new $20,000 bottling plant was completed. The brewery had trouble making all their equipment work in the early months of production—at one point the boiler failed and a "huge threshing machine" was moved in, and this contraption provided enough steam to run parts of the plant one at a time. The brewery eventually packaged beer in sizes ranging from both 6-ounce and 7-ounce up to 64-ounce "picnic" bottles. Hopp Brew, named after company president Charles Hopp (rather than any particular hoppy character, though the similarity of names was fortuitous), was available on draught in Kewaunee and surrounding counties.

Kewaunee Brewing Co. encountered many of the ups and downs typical to most small town breweries, or small town businesses in general. They supported community organizations by sponsoring the team and donating a set of new jackets for the Kewaunee entry in the county baseball league. The brewery had to appeal to the city council in 1936 to get chickens housed next to the brewery removed so their odor could not ruin the beer. Kewaunee Brewing closed for good 1 November 1942. The building was put to other uses including bottling soft drinks and remained largely intact through 2012, but was subsequently razed. (A photo of the Defender Beer label is in chapter 7)

Lutz & Wenger (1866–67)
Lutz, Lorenzo & Co. (1868)
Charles Deda, Bavaria Brewery (1868–1885)
Charles Deda & Son, Bavaria Brewery (1885–86)
Bergman & Deda, Bavaria Brewery (1886–89)
Wallner & Deda, Bavaria Brewery (1889–1893)
Wallner & Holniak (1893–95)
Kewaunee Brewing Co. (1895–1916)
Beardsley Street and River Road
While *American Breweries II* has Lutz & Trottman and a Mr. Ritter as the first proprietors of the Bavaria Brewery, the *Kewaunee County Enterprize* indicates clearly that Lutz and Wenger (Winger) started a new brewery in 1866.

This would fit with the records of R. G. Dun & Co., who have Wenger and Lutz first appearing in late 1866, but in 1867 Wenger died, and by 1868 the business was insolvent. The excise records indicate that a new firm called Lutz, Lorenzo & Co. commenced operations in February 1868, but they apparently only operated the brewery for a few months. Trottman was actually a brewer at Two Creeks, twelve miles south of Kewaunee.

Charles Deda returned to brewing when he acquired the brewery in 1868. He named it the Bavarian Brewery, even though he was listed as an Austrian in the 1870 census (and a Bohemian in 1880). He was not included in the 1870 industrial census, but his production in the 1870s slipped from 458 barrels in 1874 to under 300 barrels in 1878 and 1879, though he exceeded 500 barrels in 1882.

Charles Deda brought his son into partnership in 1885, which was fortunate since he died later that year. The younger Deda had brewing experience, but entered partnerships with experienced brewmasters. One of these was Fred C. Wallner, who came to Bavarian Brewery in 1887 and became a partner shortly thereafter. Wallner's travels were remarkable even for an occupation in which brewers trained in multiple breweries and moved around to get better situations. He trained as a brewer in Deggendorf, Bavaria, and started with Philip Best in 1881. After his time at Bavaria Brewery, he went to Bethesda Brewery in Waukesha, then to Walter Bros. in Menasha. However, his next move was to Cerverceria la Perla in Guadalajara, Mexico, then to Olympia Brewing Co. in Washington and by 1912 he arrived at Sacramento Brewing Co. in California.

Under Wallner's direction, the brewery started building a malt house in 1891, and upgraded some of their other buildings. In January 1892, the frame brewhouse was totally destroyed by fire, and the three employees who slept in the building had a narrow escape. After the fire, the Wallner and Deda considered building their new brewery in De Pere, but decided instead to rebuild in Kewaunee. The *Milwaukee Sentinel* noted in 1894 that William Willinger of Manitowoc had purchased an interest in the Bavarian Brewery, and he formed a new company with Wallner and Thomas Holinak. However, in November that same year, the *Sentinel* reported that the Bavarian Brewery, "which has been in financial straits for some time past," had failed. It was sold at a sheriff's sale for $5,300 the following April.

In 1895, Kewaunee Brewing Co. was reorganized and incorporated, with Charles Brandes Jr. (whose father was with the earlier Kewaunee Brewery) among the original incorporators. Prior to 1905, the malt house was converted into a bottling plant. Starting in 1906, the Bohman family took over ownership of the brewery, with Joseph, Barbara and Mary Bohman serving as officers of the company. Joseph's son Joseph J. Bohman was the brewmaster during most of this period.

In 1915, the Bohmans sold the brewery to out-of-town investors—Theodore Klett lived in East Troy and Emma and Louis Kretschmer were from Milwaukee. The evidence suggests that brewing ceased sometime in 1915, and that the brewery did not return to production. The Kewaunee Brewing Co. was dissolved, and the building lay vacant before being razed.

Kiel *(Schleswig) (Manitowoc County)*

Gutheil & Bro. (1858–1880)
Gutheil Bros. (1880–87)
Modern 23050 Highway 57
While accounts differ, it is likely that Bernhard and Ferdinand Gutheil established their brewery just outside of Kiel in 1858. According to one history, they delivered beer with a horse-drawn wagon to the nearby villages of Louis Corners, St. Nazianz, Millhome and St. Anna. In 1866 Ferdinand moved to Chilton to start a brewery there, and brother Louis, late of the 9th Wisconsin Infantry, was brought into the partnership. While they were not large enough to be included in the 1860 industry census, by 1870 they were making 250 barrels a year. Production dipped in the early 1870s, but by 1879 the Gutheils were making an impressive 670 barrels per year.

An account by long-time Kiel resident John Schroeder recounted "Neither of the two brothers did the brewing, but depended upon hired help. They used to have one braumeister who made excellent beer . . . but always they made the beer too good for the price they asked. There was never much profit left for the owners." Schroeder also provided valuable details about beer drinking in the 1880s:

"They used to have various-sized glasses, too. There was the largest size, called the Plattdeutscher Schmitt [schnitt], and the square Mecklenburger Schmitt. Five of the large ones was all I could drink...." There is no evidence that either of the breweries in Kiel malted their own barley.

According to Schroeder, the Gutheil brothers gave up the brewery when Louis was became County Clerk in 1887. (It was still listed in an 1891 state business directory, but those were often out of date.) There is a William Haak listed as a brewer in the 1888 state business directory who may have taken over the brewery for a short time, but this is the only reference to him, and he moved to Sheboygan shortly after, so even if he did take over the brewery, his term was brief. It is possible but less likely that he started his own brewery, or he may have been a distributor rather than a brewer.

John Dimler (Deumler) (1859?–1872)
Modern 28 East Fremont
John Duseler [sic] was listed as a brewer in Schleswig Township in the 1860 census. Since he had $2,000 of real estate it is likely that he was operating his own brewery at this point, though one history of Kiel claims he did not start brewing until 1869. (This is clearly inaccurate since R. G. Dun & Co. have him in their records in 1867.) An old resident, John Schroeder, remembered in 1927: "The beer that Dimmel [sic] made was the best that was ever had in this vicinity... It was better than the best that ever came from the Gutheil brewery. The reason for that was the water Dimmel used was softer." The 1870 industrial census reported production of 150 barrels, but this dropped sharply over the next few years: to seventy barrels in 1871 and thirty-seven barrels in his final year of operation. One local history recorded: "A few aged residents of our town remember coming in with their father to visit the Dimlers who then distributed samples of the old braumeister's art. However, competition of other breweries and the difficulties encountered in distribution made the Dimlers sell their building...." Schroeder claimed that "Henry" Dimler encountered financial trouble when he went into debt to build a new cellar. Dimler's brewery was also the site of a stabbing in April 1872, which may have been the final straw. The brewery was sold to Dr. Carl Dreher, who turned it into a medical office and drug store; it later became Riverside Grocery.

Kossuth *(Francis Creek)*
(Manitowoc County)

Joseph Kobes (1867?–1875?)
Adam Warm (1870?–1874)
Anna Warm (1874–77)
Wayne Kroll lists Joseph Kobes as the founder of this brewery. The R. G. Dun & Co. records first mention Kobes as a brewer in 1867, and continues to report on the brewery through 1875. The reports note that by July 1880 Kobes has moved out of the country and the brewery is run down entirely and abandoned. This data makes it difficult to state conclusively that the Kobes brewery and the Warm brewery are the same business, however it is possible that Kobes was the owner and Warm was the brewer. (Warm does not appear in Dun, which suggests he could have been an employee.)

Adam Warm is listed in the 1870 industrial census, though with only fifty barrels produced he was among the smallest brewers in the state. In the next years his production barely exceeded thirty barrels a year. Adam Warm died sometime around 1874, and his widow Anna operated the brewery for a short time. It remained a small operation, peaking at fifty-one barrels in 1875. After this point, she disappears from the industry records and is listed in the 1880 population census as retired.

Anton Chloupek (1867?–1880)
Mathias Dolegal (1874?–1876?)
Frank Jentsch? (1883–1884?)
Anton Chloupek owned a flour mill and feed business in addition to his brewery. He is first mentioned as a brewer in the R. G. Dun & Co. credit reports in 1867, but may have been brewing earlier. By 1870 he was brewing 300 barrels of beer, and was over 200 barrels the next two years. Dun claims that he sold out in 1874 to focus on his flour and feed business but does not name the purchaser. It was most likely Mathias Dolegal, as he was listed as a brewer in Kossuth in Schade's 1876 directory, though no production was recorded in 1874 or 1875 (which was not inconsistent with a purchase in late 1874). The brewery reportedly burned in December 1874, which means that Dolegal may have spent at least part of 1875 rebuilding. He is not in excise records or those of R. G. Dun & Co., and in the 1880 census he is listed as a farmer, but lived close to Anton Chloupek. It is possible that he was the one that took control of the brewery for a few years. Chloupek returned to the brewery late in the decade, though production was 192 barrels in 1878 and only 96 the next year. In 1880, Chloupek lost his business to a flood that washed away most of his buildings. Anton Chloupek died before the end of the year, and while his son Adolph took the property, there was no brewery to continue.

Frank Jentsch (Jeutsch) was listed by *Western Brewer* as a new brewer in December 1883. Wayne Kroll lists Jentsch as a continuation of Chloupek's firm, though that means he would have had to build a new brewery. Jentsch appears as Jeutsch in the Wing's 1884 directory (which would have been compiled in 1883). Jentsch also could have been another interpretation of Franz Rank.

Franz Rank (1879?–1880?)
Wayne Kroll lists Frank Rank as a brewer in Kossuth, but there is little information about his business. It is possible that he may have succeeded to the Kobes brewery, though the Kobes brewery had been reported as abandoned at that point. Franz Rank and Franz Jentsch may also have been different interpretations of the same name.

La Crosse *(La Crosse County)*

While La Crosse had the advantages of rivers, river bluffs with natural caves, rail links and lots of Germans, many other cities had these as well. What made this mid-sized city punch well above its weight class in the international brewing market was the presence of several talented brewers with enough capital to expand their breweries at the right time. The water in La Crosse was excellent brewing water, but other cities shared this as well. The La Crosse brewers were aggressive in expanding both their plants and their markets. The names Michel, Gund and Heileman were known throughout the Upper Midwest and beyond, and no city of similar size had so large a market. The home market was not trivial, either: in 1887, La Crosse granted licenses to 140 saloons. Throughout Western Wisconsin, Minnesota, Iowa and beyond, La Crosse beer was used as a comparison point in the same way as Milwaukee's. A brewery in Eau Claire was praised in 1865 with the compliment "the article that comes from his brewery is pronounced to be equally as good as the celebrated La Crosse beer."

By the late twentieth century, La Crosse-made beer was shipped around the world, and many regional favorite brands were owned and brewed by the G. Heileman Brewing Co. in a city where breweries had been among the largest employers since just after the Civil War. While Heileman (later City Brewing Co.) dominated the local industry as well as the skyline, in the twenty-first century new craft breweries have been attracting customers to their taprooms—some located just steps from where their nineteenth century ancestors were located.

Jacob Franz (France), Eagle Brewery (1850?–1862)
Franz & Mueller, Eagle Brewery (1862–67)
Kappes & Mueller, Eagle Brewery (1867–1870)
Geisler & Hagen (1868)
Kappes & Hofer, Eagle Brewery (1870–75)
John Hofer, Eagle Brewery (1875–78)
Franz Bartl (1886–1904)
Franz Bartl Brewing Co. (1904–1920)
George Kunz Company (1933–37)
Louis Ziegler Brewing Co. (1948)
Ziegler's Old Fashioned Brewery of La Crosse, Inc. (1948–1950)
1201–1217 La Crosse Street

Jacob Franz started the Eagle Brewery, the first in La Crosse, perhaps as early as 1850. Another local story holds that Franz, in partnership with Dr. Gustavus Nicholai, placed beer on the market in 1854, just ahead of John Gund, whose first batch of yeast failed to ferment. Very little is known about the earliest years, since La Crosse newspapers devoted very little space to local businesses other than advertisements. Production in 1860 was 150 barrels, more than anyone except Gund or Michel. By 1870 the Eagle Brewery was one of the smallest in La Crosse by production, and much smaller than the rest in terms of capital invested—only $1,600 compared to the tens of thousands of dollars sunk in by their rivals. This lack of capitalization was probably related, either as cause or effect, to the frequent changes in ownership. In 1862, Fred Mueller sold his butcher shop and joined Franz in the Eagle Brewery. Around 1867, Franz moved to Sioux City, Iowa and leased the brewery to Peter Kappes (Mueller remained at the brewery). The excise records include a single reference to Geisler and Hagen, who may have rented the brewery for a short time during this transition in late 1867. The Kappes and Mueller partnership lasted only two years, after which Mueller went into the retail liquor business. Kappes then took over, and was joined in 1871 by John Hofer, who appears to have been employed in the Zeisler brewery in 1870. Hofer and Kappes rented the brewery for a few years until they finally purchased it from Franz sometime in 1874. The next year Kappes left the firm and Hofer continued alone for a few more years. Neither Kappes nor Hofer had much capital available, and Hofer was apparently in substantial debt from buying the brewery. Sometime in 1878, Kappes went out of business and the Eagle Brewery was apparently vacant for some time, since it was absent from industry directories from 1879 to 1884.

The Eagle Brewery was resurrected by a veteran brewer, Franz Bartl. Like many other brewers, Bartl was well traveled: his first American brewery experience was in Ohio, he then went to Menasha, and then arrived in La Crosse. Even then, he kept moving around: he was foreman of Zeisler's brewery for five years, then he moved up to a similar position at Gund Brewing, and then went to the smaller Peter Bub Brewing Co. across the river in Winona, Minnesota. He returned to La Crosse in 1884 and for the first time became proprietor of a brewery. (There is some dispute as to which year Bartl actually started brewing at Eagle. It is possible that he bought the brewery in 1884 but did not have it ready for production until 1886.) Bartl quickly expanded the plant, and by 1890 the Eagle Brewery had a capacity of 10,000 barrels per year, about ten times what it had been. An industry directory claimed that he offered bottled beer as early as 1887, but no bottling works were confirmed in local sources until after 1896, when Bartl was one of the incorporators of Eagle Bottling works, which bottled Eagle Brewery beer. At one point, Bartl apparently considered purchasing the nearby Onalaska brewery and putting it back into

Both the main label and the neck label are featured on this tin sign (ca. 1900). COLLECTION OF HERB HANSON.

Despite appearances, the back of this small hand mirror (ca. 1900) is two-dimensional. COLLECTION OF TYE SCHWALBE.

commission. However, like most plans around the Onalaska site, it came to nothing.

By the beginning of the twentieth century, Bartl was well established and had a steady local trade. He offered two brands of bottled beer in 1907, Premium Brew and High Grade. Both of his sons were trained in the business: Joseph attended the Wahl-Henius Brewing Academy in Chicago, and Edward traveled to Bohemia to work at his uncle's large brewery there.

After Prohibition law, the Bartl family held on to the brewery, but leased it in 1931 to George Kunz to brew wort. Kunz already had a wort plant in his former brewery in Manitowoc, so he apparently found the wort business worth expanding. When Prohibition ended, Kunz converted the facility back to beer, received a brewing permit in October 1933, and began business as the George Kunz Company. Kunz used local labor to recondition the brewery, and signed an agreement with the local brewery workers' unions. Hourly wages ranged from 50¢ to 85¢ for a forty-hour week. At first only draught beer was available, but there were three brands: Hoffbrau, Dortmunder and Extra Pale. Eventually LaX Club lager and Alt Brau bottled beers reached the market. This venture only lasted until 1937. While the brewery was closed, the equipment was maintained just in case it could be reopened.

After remaining idle for several years, the facility still referred to locally as the Bartl Brewery gained a new lease on life in 1947, when it was purchased from Joseph A. Bartl and Edward Bartl by Robert D. Hamilton of Los Angeles, a beer distributor on the West Coast. He already owned the Ziegler breweries in Beaver Dam and Fort Atkinson, and immediately began renovations in La Crosse to brew beer for the western market. Among his planned additions was a new bottling plant, though these plans were delayed and ultimately shelved. Production started in September 1948, and employment increased from twelve to twenty-one hands in 1949, with a peak of twenty-eight during the busy summer season. The beer was sold under the Ziegler name, and used the same label designs as brews made at the other two breweries. While much of the beer was shipped to the West Coast, some of Ziegler's "Old Fashioned Lager Beer" was advertised and sold in the local market. However, the venture was not a financial success. The brewery ceased production in 1950, and the plant now known as Ziegler's Old Fashioned Brewery of La Crosse was sold at sheriff's sale in August 1951. (Labels for the La Crosse branch were essentially the same as those used by other branches of Ziegler Brewing.)

After the sale, the plant was used by Independence Bottling Co. The brewery remained standing until 1971, when it was demolished to make way for a gas station.

John Gund, La Crosse Brewery (1854–58)
Front and Division Streets

John Gund was the son of a hop and tobacco farmer in Baden, Germany, and was trained in the old country as a brewer and cooper. Prior to arriving in La Crosse, he was employed in the Dubuque brewery of Anton Heeb, and at two different breweries in nearby Galena, Illinois. In 1854, he moved to La Crosse and built a small log brewery and a home at the corner of Front and Division streets. Starting in December 1854, he advertised that he had "established at this place a BREWERY, for the manufacture of ALE and BEER which he shall keep on hand cheap for cash."

Even at this early date, the brewery served as a center for German culture: the Turners met for their gymnastics in the yard of the brewery. He operated this brewery for four years before partnering with Gottlieb Heileman to build the City Brewery on Third Street.

Charles & John Michel, La Crosse Brewery (1857–1882)
C. & J. Michel Brewing Co., La Crosse Brewery (1882–1920)
La Crosse Breweries, Inc. (1933–1956)
700 block of Third Street

According to local accounts, Charles Michel left Germany in the 1840s to avoid spending three years in the army. His brother John joined him shortly thereafter, and they started a business as builders in Philadelphia. They went to California during the Gold Rush, but as builders rather than miners. After returning east to be closer to the rest of their family, they then went to Chicago, and then to Davenport, Iowa. In early 1856, they decided to move up the river to St. Paul, but since the ice was not fully out, they were compelled to stay in La Crosse, and ultimately decided to remain there. They started as builders, but realizing that existing breweries were not able to meet the demand, they decided to enter the brewing trade.

By 1860, La Crosse Brewery was the largest in the city and one of the largest in the western part of the state. The Michels sold 1,200 barrels in 1860 and 3,000 barrels by 1870. Michel's steam plant produced fourteen horsepower—again, more than almost any brewery outside of Milwaukee. The Michel brewery was an important landmark and tourist attraction. An 1863 traveler recounted during a trip along the Mississippi River, "While enjoying this drive, we were taken to the brewery of the Messrs. Mitchell [sic], which partly supplies La Crosse with a finely flavored lager." The Michels used caves in Mormon Coulee to store their finished beer until they were able to dig cellars under the brewery. After the end of the Civil War, the Michels poured money into updating the brewery, investing the then enormous sum of $12,000 in 1866 alone.

A feature article from 1879 proclaimed the brewery had a capacity of 15,000 barrels per year, and was running at full production. Their hops were purchased "from California and Bangor, Wis., mostly from the latter place." Among the brewery equipment listed in the article were an eighty-six-barrel brew kettle, a sixty-eight barrel *kuhlschiff* (open cooler), fourteen seventy-eight barrel fermenters and 128 twenty-two-barrel conditioning vats in the cellar. The brewery used 3,000 tons of ice each year to cool the thousands of kegs resting in the cellar. The company had twenty-seven employees, twelve of whom were employed in the bottling room where they were at work "washing, filling, steaming, corking, cooling and labeling some fifteen barrels a day, 48,000 bottles a month." This passage is important because it shows not only that Michel was bottling at this early date, but also that the process included pasteurization (steaming) and all the modern features of the most advanced Milwaukee breweries. The article claimed that at this point the product of Michel and other La Crosse breweries "is shipped mostly to Minnesota, and westward." In addition, the Michel family home was one of the first in La Crosse to be heated by steam, since piping could be run easily from the brewery next door. The C. & J. Michel Brewing Co. was incorporated in April 1886, with a capital stock of $150,000, and C. F. Fischer joined the Michels as principal incorporators.

Like most breweries, Michel Brewing Co. was subject to fire, like the one in early 1897 that caused $8,000 of damage. Michel's financial situation was such that they were able to keep insurance payments up, so this loss was completely covered. However, the fire of September 1897 was so great that insurance of $150,000 was only enough to cover half the loss. Everything was destroyed except the office and part of the engine house, along with 5,000 bushels of barley and 12,000 barrels of beer. The disaster also put 150 employees out of work, though it is likely that some were employed to rebuild the brewery.

Michel Brewing Co. started exporting beer to Minnesota very early, and was distributed in South Dakota at least by 1885 if not earlier. The company had a sizeable presence in Southern Minnesota, where the railroads made shipping from La Crosse easy. Michel advertised regularly in Minnesota newspapers, though the ads were smaller and had less variety than those of Gund or Heileman. Most ads had simple sketches of people serving the beer in various settings with praise for the beer's delicate qualities. In 1900, ads for Michel's Perfection Beer claimed it was "Good Any Time . . . for Clubs, Hotel Bars, Buffets and Fastidious Families." When Elfenbrau was introduced to export markets in 1910, the company emphasized the cleanliness and modern washing equipment of the brewery, and claimed the brand was "Wholesome as Sunshine." With these ads Michel was consistent with most other brewers, who focused on health and sanitation to blunt the criticisms that had brought about the Pure Food and Drug Act in 1906.

Michel's established market was a reason it was one of the biggest prizes in the La Crosse brewery trust that was floated in 1899. In this scheme, the three largest breweries, Michel, Gund, and Heileman, would each brew either for home trade, export, or brew ale only, and the smaller breweries in the city (and Hussa Brewing Co. in Bangor) would be closed and used for storage. While articles of incorporation for a La Crosse Brewing Co. were filed with the Secretary of State of Wisconsin, the plans were dropped after about a year.

In 1907 the company built an all-new brewhouse across the street from the first location, and the original plant was used for office and storage space. Because construction started during the "Panic of 1907," funding could have been a problem, but twenty-seven year-old Carl Michel went to see banker Charles Dawes of Chicago (later famous for the "Dawes Plan" that helped stabilize European economies during the 1920s), who provided the necessary capital. The new brewery increased the company's capacity from 75,000 to 300,000 barrels per year, keeping Michel among the largest breweries in the region. The company was licensed to do business in Minnesota, South Dakota and Iowa, and in 1910 they expanded to Montana. Michel's regional importance was such that they were one of the breweries cited in a national ad campaign by Schlitz (Gund was another), in which Michel's use of a cardboard case cover to protect the beer from light was used as proof that Schlitz's brown bottles were superior.

Some later accounts claim Michel made near beer early in the dry years, but no labels are known. Even before Prohibition took full effect the company changed its name to La Crosse Refining Company, and switched to malt syrup products, which required new equipment for manufacturing and packaging. Since sugar prices had risen during World War I their original plan was to produce maltose syrup, which was more like table sugar. However, sugar prices dropped again after the war so they brewed a "straight malt syrup."

As the return of legal beer approached, La Crosse Refining prepared to reconvert the plant and president Carl Michel announced at the end of March 1933 that they would take immediate steps to prepare the brewery for making 3.2 percent beer. These steps included

Many women were among the employees of C & J Michel Brewing Company. The signs suggest this photograph dates from the 1890s. COURTESY OF MURPHY LIBRARY SPECIAL COLLECTIONS, UNIVERSITY OF WISCONSIN–LA CROSSE.

This simple brass bottle opener (ca. 1910) has only one tool, unlike many others of the period that may have included a cigar cutter or a square hole to adjust early automobile headlamps. Very few metal openers were colored. COLLECTION OF TYE SCHWALBE.

Backbar lights, designed to sit on a counter or ledge, were popular after Prohibition. A light on the bottom illuminated the translucent material on both the striking main sign as well as the small flange that wrapped around the shelf or counter. The artwork reflects the label redesign of 1954. COLLECTION OF TYE SCHWALBE.

new refrigeration equipment and expansions to the bottling line. The company planned to reintroduce two classic labels, the former Michel flagship Elfenbrau, and the famous Peerless beer formerly brewed by Gund Brewing Co. Luckily, the renamed La Crosse Breweries, Inc. was able to bring back former Michel brewmaster Ernst Chitel to recreate his old recipe, and to hire Louis Sliberschmidt, the former brewmaster at Gund, to supervise the return of Peerless. Brewing began later in 1933, and soon bottled Elfenbrau and Peerless were on sale again.

La Crosse Breweries tried to keep pace by updating equipment as possible. They added a canning line in 1948, and installed a new bottling line with capacity of 240 bottles per minute in 1949. The brewery sponsored the La Crosse Mohawks baseball team of the Western Wisconsin League and changed the name to the Peerless Mohawks in 1953. The company re-entered much of its former export market, and by 1954 Peerless was sold in Minnesota, Iowa, Illinois and North Dakota as well as Wisconsin. While the brewery produced over 63,000 barrels in 1953, this was not enough to run the brewery efficiently, and was a drop in the tankard compared to the half million barrels made a few blocks away at Heileman. Matters were made worse by a strike in June 1955 by workers at the brewery over the decision by management to save money by using a local distributor instead of delivering beer with its own union employees. The strike was settled after a few weeks when the brewery decided to self distribute again, but the brewery was in too precarious a position to suffer any economic shock. La Crosse Breweries finally succumbed to competition and declining sales in 1955. Potosi Brewing Co. acquired a license to brew and package Peerless beer. The 1907 brewhouse survived until 1997, when it was razed.

Gund & Heileman (1858–1872)
Gottlieb Heileman, City Brewery (1872–78)
Johanna Heileman, City Brewery (1878–1890)
G. Heileman Brewing Co. (1890–1999)
City Brewing Co. (1999–present)
1018 THIRD STREET

When Gottlieb Heileman first arrived in Wisconsin, he stopped first in Philadelphia, and then went to Milwaukee. While in the Cream City, Heileman was partner in a bakery, rather than a brewery. When he moved to La Crosse in 1857, he worked for a few months in Charles and John Michel's brewery before leaving to get married. He returned to La Crosse and joined with John Gund in his new brewery. The partnership of Gund and Heileman would help establish La Crosse as one of the leading brewing centers of the continent for generations.

The City Brewery brewed one thousand barrels in 1860, the first year for which figures are available—a good showing for a two-year-old brewery. While the 1870 industrial census is illegible in places, the entry that appears to be the Gund & Heileman brewery produced 2,600 barrels, among the largest in the state. The brewery had advanced from what was listed as "horse and hand" power in 1860 to a twelve horsepower steam engine a decade later. A few years later, Gund & Heileman produced over 4,100 barrels, a total which, if accurate, made them the largest brewery in the state outside Milwaukee. The brewery was so profitable that in 1870 Heileman was able to build his family a new residence reminiscent of an Italian villa. (The house remains on the brewery property as of 2017 and has been used for offices since 1960.) The brewery employed twelve men at this point, and while Gottlieb's wife Johanna served meals to the unmarried workers, as was typical at the time, she insisted that the wives of married workers take care of their own husbands.

In 1872, the partners decided to dissolve their partnership. The reasons why are not clear, but local legend holds that Gund and Heileman flipped a coin to divide the assets, which included the brewery and the International Hotel and Saloon. Heileman reportedly won, and took the brewery. Gund went on to start a new brewery, his third, and would soon outproduce his ex-partner. Production at Gottlieb Heileman's City Brewery was still among the best in the state, but he lost ground as Gund became established. The City Brewery suffered its biggest loss when Gottlieb Heileman died in 1878, at age fifty-four. Johanna Heileman took charge of the brewery, aided by several family members including her brother-in-law Reinhard Wacker and her son-in-law Emil T. Mueller. The business was stabilized under their able leadership and began to grow again. The brewery was not incorporated until 1890, and even then, Johanna was still very much in charge and her sons-in-law were the other major stockholders. (A second personal tragedy struck the Heileman family in August 1895 when Henry Heileman took his life after a period of poor health and depression at age twenty-six.)

G. Heileman Brewing expanded their market in the same way as most of their rivals—

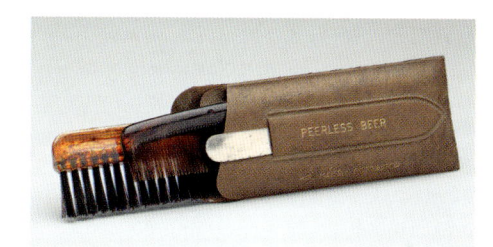

Searching for ways to keep Peerless Beer in the public eye, La Crosse Breweries distributed this beauty kit in the 1950s. COLLECTION OF DAVID WENDL.

A beautiful tray from 1900 or 1901, when Old Style Lager was still Old Times Lager. The Golden Leaf label was one of the most eye-catching and intricate die-cut labels ever produced. COLLECTION OF TYE SCHWALBE.

through the sale of bottled beer. The local German-language paper *Nord Stern* included a mention of bottled beer, the Weiner (Vienna) brand, which was a common brand or style for many breweries to bottle before Prohibition. The brewery also had an Export beer in bottles, though at this time it simply meant that it was shipped beyond the home market, rather than outside the United States. Heileman adopted the porcelain swing top bottle closure in 1887, and packaged Weiner in these new bottles. The company introduced Golden Leaf beer in 1899, and this remained the flagship beer until it was supplanted by Old Style Lager. Old Style was first known as Old Times Lager, but another brewery claimed the name infringed on their brand, and Heileman made the change that created a label famous for most of the century.

Heileman does not seem to have advertised widely or regularly until around 1905, when it launched regular campaigns in multiple markets. Old Style ads touted it as 'The Medalless Beer," a clear swipe at rival Gund who mentioned their 1904 medal in nearly every ad. (However, an ad campaign in 1907 used a device that looked suspiciously like a medal.) Like its rivals, Heileman also boasted of the health-giving properties of the beverage, claiming "There is more strength and nourishment in one pint bottle of Old Style Lager than there is in a quart of common beer. That is why it is called the beer with a "Snap" to it."

Heileman opened its first agency outside La Crosse in 1885, in Glencoe, Minnesota, about fifty miles west of Minneapolis. It soon had five agencies in South Dakota, one in North Dakota, ten more in Minnesota, and two in Illinois. But the success of Old Style led to significant expansion. Old Style could be found in nearly every state as well as in parts of Canada and the Caribbean, in part because beer could be shipped by rail to customers who were not served by a local distributor. However, there were agents for Heileman all over the country, including in some unlikely places. The company expanded its reach into the south, particularly Texas, where by 1916 they had distributors in Fort Worth, Austin, Beaumont and San Antonio. When Atlanta went dry in 1916 (though with many loopholes), Heileman advertised in the *Atlanta Constitution* that their "Georgia Patrons" could order their beer from wholesalers in Chattanooga, Memphis, Jacksonville, Pensacola, Tampa and New Orleans, as well as distant Key West. To the west, E. S. Allbritton's Old Style Lager Distributing Company was located in Salt Lake City (the Mormon prohibition of alcohol was not enforced strictly until 1921). Old Style was even available in St. Louis.

Old Style's national fame led to numerous imitators using old and style in the name (though some of those accused of copying the name probably arrived at their brand name independently). While the company sued for brand infringement in at least one case, in general they took the approach that imitation was the sincerest form of flattery. In a series of ads in 1914, Heileman claimed "there are 28 imitations of Heileman's famous Old Style Lager" and announced they had added a "crimson triangular corner" to the label as a guarantee of authenticity.

However, Heileman's national presence only increased the company's exposure to prohibitionist forces. As noted above, the onset of prohibition in markets like Atlanta limited possibilities for growth and created added costs to serve remaining markets. When Clay County, Minnesota, went dry, Heileman closed their agency in Moorhead, as did Gund, Blatz and several Minnesota breweries. However, the Moorhead depot supplied North Dakota and other points west, so this affected more than just northwestern Minnesota. As the reality of national prohibition grew, G. Heileman Brewing prepared to cut its losses. Newspaper advertising was cut back dramatically, and the company introduced "New Style Brew," which still had Old Style's "Snap." The remaining beer on hand was sold until 1 March, and then lager brewing operations stopped. Heileman and Bartl both made plans in 1921 to manufacture beer if laws were changed to allow light beer for medicinal purposes, but no such change in the Volstead Act was forthcoming.

G. Heileman Brewing Co. was among the most active manufacturers of alternative beverages during Prohibition. They produced a line of sodas all of which bore the Old Style name, continued sales of malt tonic, and malt syrup (which was actually manufactured by

The green label for Old Style was one of the most elaborate of its era. The scenes of brewing throughout history and a verse from a German drinking song left almost no room for the product name except on the sign above the tavern door (it was also prominent on the neck label). The unusual label wrapped all the way around the bottle. COLLECTION OF TYE SCHWALBE.

Blatz in Milwaukee). Their near beer products, including the suspiciously named Spike introduced in 1922 (pictured in chapter 6), sold moderately well at first and were distributed in fourteen states from Michigan to Wyoming. However, sales dropped to 20,000 barrels, a small fraction of the 140,000 barrels of non-alcoholic products sold in the pre-Prohibition year of 1917. To make matters worse, a 1931 fire destroyed three warehouses and damaged a fourth, causing $50,000 in damages that the struggling business could ill afford. Legal beer could not return soon enough for Heileman.

As one of the 218 breweries around the nation that had managed to continue making near beer through 1932, they were in an enviable position to resume production of real beer. Conversion of equipment began in November after the election of Franklin Roosevelt, and Heileman was among those whose plants were besieged at midnight on 7 April 1933 when shipments of Old Style could resume. Initial demand was overwhelming, with orders coming from as far away as Boston and Los Angeles and even the former markets in the Caribbean. The brewery was operating eighteen hours a day and still could not keep up with demand. Sales in the first three days alone were around 2,500 barrels, which made the brewery an attractive target for safecrackers, who struck the company about two weeks later and got away with almost $2,000 in cash and checks.

The rush exposed the fact that the brewery needed significant expansion and upgrading.

This Old Style light probably dates to the early 1940s. The shield logo just visible at left was from that period. COLLECTION OF TYE SCHWALBE.

However, the Heileman family was short of cash and the company needed a fresh infusion of capital. The family sold out and the Chicago brokerage house of Paul H. Davis and Co. turned the business into a public company with a mix of La Crosse and Chicago residents as directors. The Davis company remained the major stockholder at first and planned an expansion program to boost capacity from 150,000 to 250,000 barrels per year. The company was listed on the Chicago Stock Exchange, but the new owners pledged to employ only La Crosse residents.

The years after repeal brought two important new members to the Heileman family of products. The first was a new beer, which brewmaster Jake Gehring first made for a company picnic in 1934. This "special" (and stronger, at 6 percent) brew proved so popular that it was introduced to the public in the fall of 1934 as Special Export in brown bottles with yellow neck labels. The other new introduction was canned beer. Heileman was an early adopter of Continental Can's cone-top style can, but the company was not happy with the can lining or the amount of air that could be trapped in the cone, so they changed to flat top cans, though not until 1950. These products, and the continuing success of Old Style in packages from eight ounces to half-gallon picnic bottles, resulted in sales of 272,638 barrels of beer in 1935. Their market included thirty-seven states, but the home market was not neglected. Heileman built the Bier Stube in La Crosse, which was a tavern styled after a Dutch inn.

The pressures of World War II forced G. Heileman Brewing to cut back in several ways. The market shrank to eighteen states, mostly because of restrictions on transportation of anything other than military supplies. Limited

Many generations enjoyed smoking while drinking a beer. The image on the side is a replica of a mid-1930s bottle cap, likely dating the lighter to that period. COLLECTION OF TYE SCHWALBE.

access to raw materials forced the company to decrease the amount of hops in the beer, though this change proved popular and remained in place after the war. (Additional information about Heileman during the war is included in chapter 7.)

G. Heileman Brewing was one of the breweries in position to take advantage of the post–World War II building boom. In the years after the war, it doubled the capacity of the brewhouse, installed a new bottling line, and launched a $1.5 million project to build new storage cellars. The company's product line included dried grains and yeast as well as its famous beers, and provided work to more than 500 employees. There were occasional setbacks, such as a strike in 1948 and another warehouse fire in 1950, but in 1953, Heileman produced over half a million barrels of beer, which placed it far ahead of any non-Milwaukee brewery—the next largest was Fox Head in Waukesha, which barely topped 100,000 barrels. But the 1953 figures included a boost from increased sales due to the strike that year in Milwaukee, and production stagnated for the next few years. The directors of the company named Roy E. Kumm president in early 1957, a move that was to propel the company to new heights over the next decades.

While the rebranding of Old Style was important to Heileman's recovery and growth, the key was Kumm's plan to bring the company into the top five of American brewers by buying additional breweries for their capacity and brands. The first was the Kingsbury Brewing Co. with its three plants, but many more would follow. The new brands were typically acquired to fill holes in the low cost portions of the product line up, and eventually the House of Heileman (as it began to be called in 1963) would brew nearly 400 different labels during

This twelve-pack of flattop cans is from the mid-1950s.
COLLECTION OF DAVID WENDL.

the period from 1960–1999. Heileman supported the increased capacity with new sponsorships, particularly in the lucrative Chicago market where they sponsored broadcasts of the Cubs and Bears, and placed Old Style on sale in Wrigley Field.

Kumm and his successor, son-in-law Russell Cleary, also diversified the company by acquiring bakeries and manufacturing companies, several of which were purchased to keep the business in the La Crosse area. The company continued to buy bakeries and snack food companies until the late 1980s, and eventually became the fifth-largest baking company in the nation. G. Heileman company was very much a La Crosse company, and its local sponsorships demonstrated their commitment to the community. They were involved with everything from charitable events to curling bonspiels. Heileman also played a vital role in the development of La Crosse's famous Oktoberfest. Brewery tours were a regular feature of the Fest, and entertainment often featured national acts like the Louis Armstrong Orchestra.

Roy Kumm died in 1971, but he had prepared his son-in-law, Russell Cleary, to take over the business. Cleary embarked on a nationwide program of brewery acquisitions, which included Associated Brewing and its three breweries in 1972 for $17.5 million. The prize in this acquisition was the former Jacob Schmidt brewery in St. Paul, which quickly became the second most important brewery to the House of Heileman after the La Crosse plant. By this point, Heileman was the eighth-largest brewery in the country, and further acquisitions would push the company into the top five. The corporation moved from the Chicago Exchange to the New York Stock Exchange, but with that came increasing attention to growth and the bottom line, and the impatience of investors in a business that is not always steady or predictable. Thanks to expansions at the St. Paul and Newport, Kentucky breweries, by the end of the 1970s, sales were over eleven million barrels and the company moved into a new headquarters building.

Unfortunately Heileman, with its collection of aging breweries, was now competing on an international level in a cutthroat industry. However, while earnings were up, sales were essentially flat from 1984 to 1986, so the board of directors created a "poison pill" plan to discourage hostile takeovers. The brewery moved to take over the brands of the Christian Schmidt Brewing Co. in Philadelphia in 1987, continuing the strategy of growth by buying other labels, but this time did not include the Schimdt brewery in the deal, since the company already had enough capacity. G. Heileman Brewing Co. was acquired by Australian financier Alan Bond just before the October 1987 stock market crash. (The story of the takeover and collapse is told in more detail in chapter 9.)

As the company dealt with the debt, it began to shed assets. The Evansville brewery was closed in 1988, and most of the bakery holdings were sold off that year, along with the Machine Products division. The Belleville, Illinois brewery was closed in September of that year. Sales were declining, and in early 1989, the modern brewery in Perry, Georgia was closed. Brewery closings resulted in several hundred employees losing their jobs at each facility, but it was not enough to reverse the company's falling fortunes. The plant in St. Paul was closed down in January 1991, despite the fact that Heileman had invested more than $45 million in modernizations since 1972. The brewery was down to five plants (Seattle, Portland, San Antonio, Baltimore and La Crosse) and employment was down to about 2,500 workers.

In 1993, the banks that owned Heileman sold the company to a Dallas-based investment firm, Hicks, Muse, Tate & Furst, Incorporated. The new company, faced with the reality that sales had dropped from 17.5 million barrels in 1983 to 8.9 million, and that market share dropped from 10 percent to 4.5 percent, asked Russell Cleary to come back as an advisor. But by 1996 the company was bankrupt again, and was purchased by Stroh Brewing Co. of Detroit. Stroh operated the brewery for three years, but Pabst and Miller bought out Stroh in 1999, and the brewery in La Crosse was closed in August.

After a few false starts (covered in chapter 9), the brewery was saved by local investors and reopened for production before the end of the year as City Brewing, a tribute to its original name from the 1850s. Most of the brewery's brands bore the City name, with a few taking the name of the host city. The company also did a significant amount of contract brewing. Platinum Holdings ran into financial difficulties, and in September 2000, a new company was formed—CBC Acquisitions, which purchased the brewery with help from an employee ownership plan. In the first year after the CBC purchase, employment at the brewery jumped from a few dozen to 250. Over the next several years, employment climbed back to over 500 workers, about what it was during the 1990s. The contract business was so lucrative that City Brewing was able to purchase the old Rolling Rock brewery in Latrobe, Pennsylvania from Anheuser-Busch in 2006 and the former Schlitz plant in Memphis from Coors in 2011, which was renamed the Blues City Brewery. But the breweries own brands had trouble making headway in a crowded market, so over time the brewery shifted to brewing beers under contract almost exclusively. There were occasional attempts to offer their own brands, such as the Golden Leaf series in 2006-7 and the La Crosse Session Series Amber Lager in 2013, but these were typically a drop in the barrel compared to total production: in 2006 City's own brands represented 32,000 barrels out of a total of 1.6 million. However, in 2016 one of these contract brews returned a bit of the history to the La Crosse plant. Pabst Brewing Co., which by this point owned the Old Style brand, introduced Old Style Oktoberfest and had it produced in La Crosse, where the former Heileman brewmaster, Randy Hughes, was still employed. As of this writing, City Brewing Co. LLC employs about 500 in La Crosse, and has capacity to produce seven million barrels at the home plant.

Ignatz Furst (1856?–58?)

Ignatz Furst is so far only known from the Wisconsin business directories of 1857 and 1858 (and 1858 was mostly a reprint of the previous edition). He was not mentioned in any other sources. It is possible that he could have been a predecessor of either L. Betz or L. Schuster who are mentioned in the 1860 industrial census, but no link has been found to this point. He later started a brewery in nearby Sparta.

Gustavus Nicholai (1857?–1860?)
Near Southeast Corner of Second and Pearl Streets

According to local historians, Dr. Gustavus Nicholai, former partner of Jacob Franz, began brewing near the corner of Second and Pearl Streets. There is an entry in the 1860 industrial census for a brewer named Gustavus whose last name is illegible. This brewer produced 100 barrels with two men and a horse.

L. Schuster (1859?–1860?)

L. Schuster started brewing in La Crosse sometime prior to 1860. In that year's industrial census, he was shown to have brewed 100 barrels of beer with two hands in a horse-powered brewery.

L. Betz (1859?–1860?)

L. Betz is listed as a brewer in the 1860 industrial census. At that point he was one of the smallest breweries in La Crosse with production of 100 barrels per year. His brewery was powered by horse and employed two men.

Zeisler & Nagel, Plank Road Brewery (1867–69)
George Zeisler, Plank Road Brewery (1869–1890)
Geo. Zeisler & Sons, Plank Road Brewery (1890–1902)
718 North Third Street

One account claims that the Plank Road Brewery was started as early as 1861, but most sources place the date at 1867. The Hoffman article which put the date at 1861 conceded that the brewery was not fully complete until 1867, at which time its capacity was 1,500 barrels per year. Otto Nagel left the partnership in 1869, and Zeisler carried on alone.

In January 1874, Zeisler's brewery was destroyed by fire, with a loss of $18,000. He started rebuilding immediately, planning a grand reopening on July 4th, but the brewery was struck by lightning and suffered another fire that luckily only ruined part of the building and set back reconstruction plans.

While not as important nationally as some of its local rivals, the Plank Road Brewery was still a popular spot in La Crosse. It had a summer biergarten and dance hall that operated through the 1880s when Zeisler built his paper mill and turned the dance hall into a paper storage warehouse.

The Plank Road Brewery was victim of yet another fire, its fourth significant blaze, in December 1882, which did significant damage to the brewery and malt house. However, he rebuilt quickly, and the R. G. Dun & Co. continued to rate him as a good credit risk despite his losses. In 1893, saloon owners in La Crosse proposed starting a stock company to operate their own brewery, and it was rumored that the plan was to buy Zeisler's brewery rather than build a new one. While a few such saloonkeeper breweries were formed around the state, this one never got beyond the rumor stage.

After the brewery closed, it was purchased by the La Crosse Plow Company, which was later acquired by Allis-Chalmers. It was eventually converted into a tire warehouse.

This ad for Zeisler's brewery (ca. 1900) was in a German-language booklet commemorating the leading citizens and businesses of La Crosse. The reverse side described Georg Zeisler Sr. as "one of the most popular citizens and successful brewers of the beer-loving city of La Crosse." Collection of John Steiner.

John Gund, Empire Brewery (1873–1880)
John Gund Brewing Co. (1880–1920)
Ninth and Mormon Coulee Road (Modern South Ave/US Highway 61)

John Gund dissolved his partnership with Gottlieb Heileman in 1872, but his purpose was to run his own brewery, not to leave the beer business. The new brewery was farther from the center of the city, and Gund had several acres on which to build. The new Empire Brewery grew quickly—brewing over 1,500 barrels in its first full year. By the end of the 1870s it was over 6,000 barrels, second in the city only to Michel and twelfth largest in the state. Even as the brewery grew it continued some of the practices more common to smaller breweries in smaller cities. Gund raised turkeys on the premises, which made news in 1878 when one was struck by lightning and killed. John Gund Brewing Co. was among the first breweries in Wisconsin to incorporate, though it was still very much a family firm, with John Gund Sr. and sons George and Henry as the officers. George left the firm in 1882, and was replaced by John Jr.

To secure the market for their beer, John Gund Brewing Co. joined their rivals in establishing a system of icehouses and agencies throughout their expanding sales territory. An ad for an agent handling Gund in 1893 boasted: "More La Crosse Beer is sold in Northwestern Iowa than all other brands put together." Ads for Peerless, "the Beer of Good

Larger breweries offered stemware, often intended for their premium beers. This Gund glass featured an embossed image of King Gambrinus inside the letter G (ca. 1900). COLLECTION OF TYE SCHWALBE.

Cheer" appeared in newspapers in Illinois, Minnesota, South Dakota, Nebraska, and Montana as well as in Iowa and Wisconsin. While many of the cities Gund targeted either had no brewery or not enough capacity for the market, Gund had agents and even tied houses in major brewing centers such as Minneapolis. In 1908 Gund owned twenty-two saloons in Minneapolis, more than Pabst or Miller and more than twice as many as G. Heileman's nine. Distant customers were still able to obtain premiums from the brewery: in 1901 interested parties could order "a handsome lithograph booklet describing the brewery free on request"; the next year they could send 15¢ for a "pack of fine playing cards." Peerless was even available in Winnipeg, Manitoba, which indicates that Gund Brewing was willing to do the extra legal work to export to another country. Gund also made sure to control important saloon locations—in 1905 they snapped up the former John Walter saloon on Pearl Street for $6,000, a considerable amount for a small property but not for a prime location.

Gund's newspaper advertising was much more like the Milwaukee national giants than it was like that of a regional brewery. Rather than having a single small ad that repeated from issue to issue, or a handful of rotating ads, Gund produced major ad campaigns with as many as forty different ads emphasizing a particular theme. The 1906 campaign focused on health and purity—not a coincidence with the popular agitation for pure food and drug legislation at the time—with quotes from medical experts (many of them German) about how wholesome pure beer was. The next year the health claims continued, but focused on the quality of ingredients. An ad from 1908 included copy typical of the claims made for beer at the time: "Doctors all agree that for nursing mothers nothing equals the juices of barley and hops. A pure malt and hop beer produced healthy blood, stimulates the digestive organs and feeds the whole human organism.... [Peerless] It's alive with health and goodness, and deserves to be your home beer." Ads cited the awards won by the brewery, especially the Gold Medal earned for purity at the 1904 World's Fair in St. Louis. (The medal earned at the 1900 Paris Exposition is pictured in chapter 5.)

Two campaigns stood out for their scope and imagination. In 1905, the company ran a series of at least sixteen ads featuring

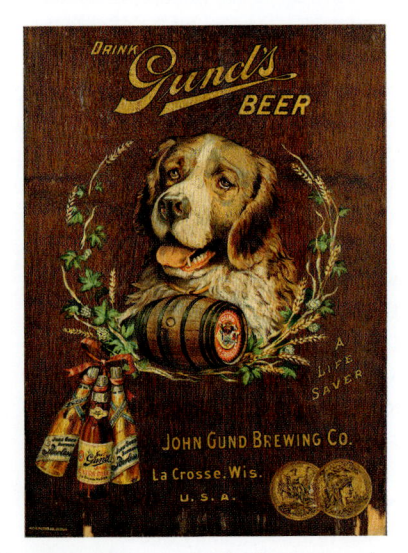

This sign, one of many made by the Meyercord Co. of Chicago, features the 1900 Paris Exposition medals at lower right. The logo on the side of the St. Bernard's keg matches the one on the goblet above. COLLECTION OF TYE SCHWALBE.

"peerless" figures in politics, industry, and war. Many were figures well known: Edison, Carnegie, Theodore Roosevelt. Others assumed readers were informed on national and world politics: Mayor John Weaver of Philadelphia, Governor Charles S. Deneen of Illinois and Premier Arthur Balfour of the United Kingdom. Much more unusually, two ads featured the Japanese heroes of the Russo-Japanese War. One boasted that "Field Marshall Oyama is a peerless strategist and John Gund is a peerless brewer.... Oyama has outclassed his foe in the art of war, John Gund has outclassed his rivals in the art of brewing." Oyama's sketch, and that of Admiral Togo, portrayed their features as much less oriental for Gund's midwestern audience. Even more elaborate was the series of ads that began in 1912 featuring a run of more than forty multi-panel cartoons featuring "Brur Badger" (sometimes spelled "Bre'r Badger") who engaged in a variety of exploits with his forest friends to promote Gund's Peerless beer. Readers were urged to "Clip these Peerless cartoons. You will want the entire series."

Increasing business meant frequent expansions for the brewery. In 1884 Gund added a third icehouse with capacity of 7,000 barrels, which at forty-two feet high and seventy-one by sixty-six feet in area, was bigger than the entire original brewery. Gund was also an early adopter of technological improvements—the brewery was equipped with the second telephone line in La Crosse. As one of the largest breweries in the region, Gund Brewing Co. was sometimes rumored to be involved in merger or trust combinations. In 1890, the press announced that Gund's brewery and John Orth Brewing Co. of Minneapolis had been purchased by English capitalists and were to be merged into "Minnesota and La Crosse Breweries Company, limited." This announcement was speculative at best, though later that year Orth combined with three other Minneapolis breweries to form Minneapolis Brewing and Malting Co. (later Grain Belt). Increasing production also required increases in staff of all kinds. In 1905 the *La Crosse Tribune* printed two very prominent help wanted ads placed by

This triptych was a souvenir of the opening of Gund's new brewery in 1898. The capacity of the new plant was listed as 300,000 barrels per year, consisting of draught beers Standard, Extra Pale, and Salvator and the bottled Extra Pale and Peerless. COLLECTION OF HERB HANSON.

Gund: one seeking a "Bright young man" and the other looking for "Girls for Bottling Works." Apparently they did not receive enough female applicants, because a week later the ad was amended to included boys and girls. The bottling works they would be employed in were among the most modern in the country. Designed by leading brewery architect Louis Lehle, the facility was powered by electricity rather than steam, and as a consequence could be laid out in an efficient manner without being limited by the need for belts driven by a central steam engine.

The brewery, now with a capacity approaching 100,000 barrels a year, was the victim of a spectacular fire in September 1897, which destroyed most of the brewery complex, partially due to inadequate water pressure from the city water works. The source of the fire was subject of much speculation, such as a blaze in one of the brew kettles, but was never definitely determined. John Gund had a team at work clearing debris only five hours after the fire was first discovered, and rebuilding plans were put in place the same day. Water continued to be a concern for the brewery and the city, especially as brewing capacity increased. In 1905, Gund Brewing finished a large water project which enabled the brewery to pump more than five million gallons per day, more than a million gallons above the needs of the entire city. This freed up millions of gallons of city water for other businesses and residences.

Like many other large breweries, Gund acquired saloons and depots throughout their territory. However, there were risks associated with holding more properties. For example, in April 1906, a hotel and saloon in Muscoda owned by Gund burned, causing a significant financial loss. Gund Brewing seems to have had limited success in following the example of their Milwaukee rivals in establishing a chain of hotels, though they did attempt to purchase a property in Janesville. Prohibition was a growing threat to Gund's property as well. Attempts to establish lucrative agencies or tied houses were dependent on the often-changing desires of local voters. In 1907, Gund Brewing spent $4,500 on a saloon in the small town of Hanska, Minnesota, only to have the town vote dry the next year.

John Gund Sr. had built an enviable reputation around the nation and in La Crosse. Upon his death in 1910 after a long illness, all the breweries and saloons in the city were closed on the day of his funeral. His sons were also respected members of the community. George was the first treasurer of the Board of Trade and was first president of the La Crosse Baseball Association in 1887. Henry was a member of the first Board of Park Commissioners. John Jr. was a city alderman, was a director of the United States Brewmasters'

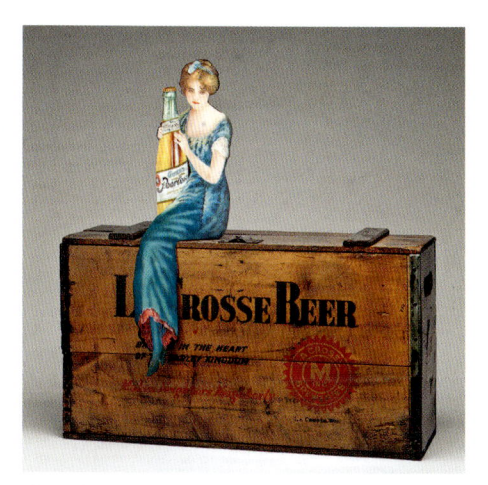

The painted metal figure that advertised Peerless beer in the 1900s is perched on a wooden case from the post-Prohibition Peerless–La Crosse Breweries. COLLECTION OF TYE SCHWALBE.

Association and director of the Inter-State Fair held in La Crosse.

While Gund Brewing kept making beer right up through Prohibition, the Gunds showed little interest in staying in business to make other products. While some sources claim they never made near beer, advertisements and artifacts exist for Peerless Brew, though ads only appeared for a few months in 1920, and the experiment was dropped quickly. After the brewery closed the plant was used for other purposes. Milwaukee Corrugating Company and Swift and Co. took over part of the facility,

The stables of the Gund Brewing Co. (ca. 1900) show the elaborate harnesses used with the brewery teams. COURTESY OF MURPHY LIBRARY SPECIAL COLLECTIONS, UNIVERSITY OF WISCONSIN–LA CROSSE.

while the stables were used as an armory by the 120th and 121st field artilleries until 1960. Some of the steel tanks were sold to La Crosse County and used for storage of road oil. The Gunds of La Crosse joined relatives located in Ohio, where, among other things, they operated another Gund Brewing Co. Later generations owned the Cleveland Barons NHL hockey team and Cleveland Cavaliers NBA basketball team as well as the San Jose Sharks NHL team. A few buildings remain as of 2017: the bottling works at 2130 South Avenue were converted into apartments and added to the National and State Registers of Historic Places in 2008. The stables across the street were added to the Registers in 2016.

G. F. Voegele & Bro., North La Crosse Brewery (1887–1898)

Voegele Bros., North La Crosse Brewery (1898–1900)

Jacob L. Erickson, North Side Brewery (1900–1901)

Jacob L. Erickson, Monitor Brewery (1901–1920)

210 MILL STREET

The press in Wisconsin took note in 1886 that "La Crosse is to have still another brewery." This turned out to be the North La Crosse Brewery, though the early reports claimed that the twenty-five barrel per day brewery would make weiss beer, when in fact the Voegele brothers are known to have made only lager. The machinery was reported to cost $3,000 and "the vats in the building used in the making of beer have a capacity of sixty barrels each," though this seems more likely to refer to fermentation or conditioning tanks rather than the brew kettle, which would have been rather large for such a brewery.

Jacob Erickson, who was in the lumber business, purchased the bankrupt brewery from the Voegele brothers in 1898. Soon after, he changed the name to Monitor Brewery, for the street that ran just south of the brewery. Erickson was not a brewer himself, but employed Georg Neukomm, a brewmaster with almost thirty years experience. Erickson expanded the territory of the brewery to include the surrounding area and southern Minnesota.

Erickson's Monitor Brewery produced little breweriana. Advertisements like this were often placed in local newspapers near the end of the year. COLLECTION OF TYE SCHWALBE.

As beer was about to return in March 1933, Walter Erickson, manager of the La Crosse Malt Company, announced plans to reopen eventually but these, like many such plans in the heady days after beer returned, never came to fruition.

Emil G. Kohn, South Side Brewery (1896–99?)

The South Side Brewery of Emil Kohn started operations in 1896. Shortly thereafter, a "low lived vandal" broke in and destroyed nearly $500 worth of beer. The intruder reportedly tampered with six vats of twelve barrels each, spoiling the contents in a way not specified in the papers. Kohn was not in the 1900 city directory, so it is likely he had moved by then, though La Crosse brewery historian Tye Schwalbe contends that he may still have been in business as late as 1900.

Warninger & Houthmaker, La Crosse Bottling Works and Berlin Weiss Beer Brewery (1896–1906?)

518–520 SOUTH THIRD STREET

La Crosse Bottling Works grew out of a small business started by Gust Carl in the late 1860s. He sold the business to Huelsch Brothers in 1890, and they in tern sold it to George H. Warninger in 1891. He and August Houthmaker operated the bottling works and a weiss beer brewery for about a decade a few blocks from Heileman's massive brewery. Their ads in the city directory announced they were "[M]anufacturers and importers of fine Belfast aromatic ginger ale, soda water, ciders, natural mineral waters, Weiss beer, Beasley's porter, etc." While they clearly were importers of porter, they appeared in the industry directory of 1900 as brewers of weiss beer, so they can be included in this list with confidence. In 1903 they dropped their names from the company and the firm was simply known as La Crosse Bottling Works. Houthmaker left for the Pacific Coast, but Warninger carried on for a few more years. By 1905 the company was no longer in brewers' directories, and the 1907 La Crosse city directory entry no longer included the Berlin Weiss Beer Brewery part of the business name. However the product list still included weiss beer, which they still may have made themselves since they already had the equipment and it was not an expensive product. By this point Warninger was still listed in the directory as the proprietor of the business, but under the firm's entry he was not listed among the officers. A few years later Warninger was manager of People's Ice & Fuel Co., though Houthmaker had returned and rejoined La Crosse Bottling. La Crosse Bottling continued in business for several more decades at the same location.

Black River Brewery & Pub (1995–96)

200 MAIN STREET

Black River Brewery & Pub occupied part of Historic Powell Place, a three-story Victorian commercial block in downtown La Crosse. It brewed its own house beers for a few years until the business was replaced by Doc Powell's. The new business needed more room, and the brewing equipment required modifications, so it was removed and Doc Powell's had its house beers brewed by Sioux Falls Brewing Co. in South Dakota.

Bodega Brew Pub (1996–98)

122 SOUTH FOURTH STREET

Located in the popular La Crosse night spot Bodega, the Brew Pub made some house beers on their half-barrel system for a few years. Pearl Street Brewing moved into Bodega in 1999 and brewed there for several years before moving to their current location.

Pearl Street Brewing Co. (1999–2004)
Pearl Street Brewing Co. (2006–present)
122 South Fourth Street (1999–2004); 1401 St. Andrew Street (2006–present)

Joe Katchever and his father, Tony, started Pearl Street Brewing Co. in the basement of Bodega Brew Pub in 1999, making it a true brewpub for several years. At first the vast majority of the beer brewed on the 6 ½ barrel system was sold at Bodega, but eventually Joe began selling extra kegs to other bars. The basement brewery proved too small for a true commercial operation, so the Katchevers began looking for a larger space, preferably in La Crosse. They ended up moving into the former La Crosse Footwear building. The company had been famous for rubber boots, which ended up providing the name for one of the popular beers, Rubber Mills Pils. The new brewery was ready to go in 2006, using equipment from New Belgium Brewing Co. in Colorado by way of Port Washington Brewing Co.

The new brewery has plenty of space for a taproom and events, and there are several major events each year. The brewery has made an effort to practice environmentally responsible brewing techniques, and regular events feature encourage cycling and recycling. The brewery also grows their own hops, features a public hop-picking each fall, and brews their Harvest Ale using only these hops.

These two beers show the range of Pearl Street beers. El Hefe is an easy-drinking hefeweizen, while Dankenstein is a bold double India Pale Ale. Author's collection.

The Downtown Brown Ale (now known as D.T.B. Brown Ale) was an early favorite at the Bodega location, but the new location has allowed Katchever and his team to brew lager styles and to offer around a dozen seasonal and limited release beers. Among the most notable are an Imperial IPA called Dankenstein and Smokin' Hemp Porter, made with cherrywood smoked malt and toasted Canadian hemp seeds, which is released only on draught every April 20. Other brews have explored sour styles, such as Pearl-iner Weisse, or 17-Up Anniversary Gose, based on the tart and salty beer of Goslar, Germany. The brewery started bottling in 2007, and their market has expanded to include Southern Minnesota as well as most of Wisconsin.

Turtle Stack Brewery (2015–present)
125 Second Street South

Turtle Stack Brewery opened in June 2015 with seven beers on tap in the tasting room. Brewer and part owner Brent Martinson was a homebrewer who also had previous experience at Water Street Brewery Delafield. The brewery is located in the former La Crosse Clock storefront, which was remodeled extensively for the brewery. The name came from the many turtles that may be seen on logs in the Mississippi River Valley, but also the Dr. Suess book *Yertle the Turtle*. When a turtle king orders his subjects to create a higher throne by stacking themselves into a tower, one brave turtle rebelled against authority and burped, which caused the throne to collapse. As the brewery's website proclaims:

> Without choice there is no freedom. By providing a variety of well-crafted beers we hope to empower the masses and invite people to join the ever-growing 'stack' of craft beer enthusiasts fighting for freedom of choice by demanding more flavorful beer options.

La Crosse (Campbell Township) (Sauk County)

Fritz Diefenthaler, Bluff Brewery (1856–1871?)
Highway 16 (Old Salem Road)

Fred Diefenthaler is reported to have started his brewery in Campbell Township, just outside of La Crosse, in 1856. He is listed as a farmer in the 1860 population census, so it is likely that for a time, at least, brewing was a side business. Diefenthaler apparently did not brew enough to qualify for the industrial census in either 1860 or 1870, and in the 1870 population census he was recorded as having the unusual circumstance of owning more personal property than real estate. In fact, one source referred to his brewery as being on the Hauser farm, so Diefentahler may never have owned much more than the brewery itself. Diefenthaler's beer garden, sometimes called "Deutsch Lager Beer Garden," was a popular spot where visitors could have dinner and fine views of the Mississippi River valley. Most sources claim that his brewery ceased production in 1870, and Diefenthaler purchased a farm elsewhere in the county. He advertised regularly in the German-language newspaper *Nord Stern* from 1857 to 1871, which seems mostly to agree with the other accounts. The records of R. G. Dun & Co. indicate that he was out of business by mid-1873, but they only surveyed businesses every year or so in that region, so he may have been out of business in early 1872. Portions of his brewery cave remain on what is now Wisconsin Highway 16. An account written many years later related that ". . . beer was made in the winter and hauled by sleighs to the bluffs along the Mormon Coulee road where large caves had been dug in the cliff side. Many a story was told of the days when large bob sleds carted great loads of beer kegs to these caves, overturning on the way to send the full kegs rolling merrily down the hill side."

Lake Delton (Sauk County)

Pumphouse Pizza (1998–2002)
19 West Monroe

Pumphouse Pizza was founded by three college roommates and originally featured local craft beer. However, they were homebrewers who wanted to be able to make larger batches of beer, so they began brewing at the restaurant in 1998. Mark Schmitz (who learned about the hospitality industry while working at Wisconsin Dells landmark Noah's Ark) became the

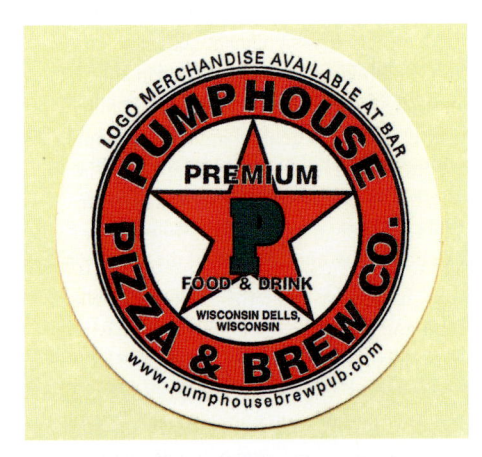

This coaster advertises the much more familiar Wisconsin Dells location rather than Lake Delton. COLLECTION OF SCOTT REICH.

primary owner in 1999, and the pumphouse theme came from his memories of hanging around a gas station as a youth in Iowa. After a few years at this location, Schmitz decided to expand his restaurant business, and opened the much larger Moosejaw Pizza/Dells Brewing Co. in Wisconsin Dells proper.

Lake Geneva *(Walworth County)*

Geneva Lake Brewing Co. (2012–present)
750 VETERANS DRIVE #107

Geneva Lake Brewing Co. was founded by Pat McIntosh, a long-time area resident, who was looking for a change from the corporate world. He brought on his son Jonathan, who had started as a home brewer and then studied at Siebel Institute in Chicago, as head brewer. The brewery, located in a small business park east of Geneva Lake, began production in Spring 2012 and the tap room opened that fall. By November, the brewery was selling 22-ounce bottles of their four regular beers: Cedar Point Amber Ale, No Wake IPA, Narrows Kölsch-style and Weekender Wheat. Geneva Lake beers were available on draught in seventy-seven Wisconsin locations before Thanksgiving of 2012.

As the brewery built a following, Jonathan was able to experiment with new styles of beer, though he brewed Halloween Pumpkin ale during the first few months of operation.

In 2013 he brewed a double IPA called Implosion, which was available in 22-ounce bottles in limited quantities at the tap room. Later that year Geneva Lake brewed Imperial Cherry Stout with juice from Door County, which was also offered in bottles. By May 2014, Geneva Lake entered the Illinois market, and that same month worked with Midwest Mobile Canning of Chicago to bring out No Wake and Cedar Point in cans (Boathouse followed a few months later).

Geneva Lake Brewing has continued to offer draught-only seasonals such as their Oktoberfest Ale.

Lake Mills *(Jefferson County)*

Tyranena Brewing Co. (1999–present)
1025 OWEN

Rob Larson founded Tyranena Brewing Co. in 1998. The company's name (pronounced tie-rah-NEE-nah) comes from the waters of nearby Rock Lake, which contain a number of underwater pyramids possibly built by a Mississippian culture of early people from a village at nearby Aztalan. One of the original beers, Stone Tepee Pale Ale, was named after these structures, and most of the brands are named after local landmarks, pioneers, or legends. Rocky's Revenge brown ale is named after a lake monster supposed to inhabit the depths of Rock Lake. Headless Man Amber Alt, the first brew made by the brewery, is named after an effigy mound built by native peoples centuries ago.

The best-known Tyranena beer, Bitter Woman IPA (named after a nineteenth-century Lake Mills spinster), exemplifies how Larson and his brewers diverged from the dominant theme of most early Wisconsin craft brewers—a focus on hop-forward aggressive beers. (Bitter Woman and variations on that theme are pictured in chapter 10.) One problem encountered by Tyranena and others focusing on hoppy beers was that the hop shortage of 2007-8 meant increased prices and inability to get certain hops that were key to their recipes. As the shortage eased in 2009, they were able to bring back hoppy specialty beers.

Another innovative beer was Rocky's Revenge: originally brewed as a schwarzbier (dark German lager), it was reintroduced as a brown ale with part of the batch aged in bourbon barrels, an early entry in what became a flood of barrel-aged beers during the next decade. Larson also launched a series of limited-release brews called "Brewers Gone Wild!" which was billed as "A Series of Big, Bold, Ballsy Beers." The first was "Who's Your Daddy," a barleywine-style ale. Despite its well-earned reputation for hoppy beers, Tyranena also offered well-made German seasonals like Maibock and Oktoberfest.

Despite recurring problems with equipment chronicled in the occasional e-newsletters, Tyranena showed steady growth as the hop heads of Wisconsin found the beers: from 811 barrels in their first full year of 2000, the brewery topped 1,000 barrels the next year. The brewery approached the 2,000-barrel mark five years later, and topped 3,000 barrels in 2009 as their market expanded in Minnesota and into Illinois. Production reached a new high of 5,392 barrels in 2014.

During its nearly two decades of operation, Tyranena has become a

These Tyranena bottles date from 2000 to 2011; Stone Tepee Pale Ale and Fighting Finches Mai Bock are no longer available in 2018. The label designs have remained much the same throughout the brewery's history. AUTHOR'S COLLECTION.

social center for Lake Mills and the surrounding area. The Oktoberfest Bike Ride, the Beer Run, the Dog Wash and other events draw large crowds, and the tasting room hosts live music many Saturday nights. The tasting room frequently features draught-only specialty beers. As of 2017, Tyranena employed four full-time and one part-time employees in the brewery, another four full-time staff members in sales and the office, and about twenty part-time workers in the tap room.

Lancaster *(Grant County)*

Charles B. Angus (1898–1904)
Charles B. Angus was a bottler in Lancaster, but local historian John Dutcher has discovered references that suggest he may have also brewed his own beer. It is possible that he, and possibly his successor N. J. Tiedemann, manufactured weiss beer, which some people did not consider as true beer and therefore did not report its makers as brewers.

Lawrence *(Westfield)* *(Marquette County)*

Dahlke Brewing Co. (1934–1943)
Otto Tiegs and Bob Pirie uncovered the history of this rare post-Prohibition brewery that did not start before the dry years. Gustav Dahlke got started in business by providing electrical power in Marquette County. In 1933, Dahlke feared that the poor economy might force businesses and households to cut back on their use of electricity, so the return of legal beer provided a different path to profit. While neither he nor anyone else in the family had any experience in brewing (and some members were teetotalers), he began construction on land near Lawrence owned by Dahlke that featured an artesian well to supply all the brewery's needs. (The brewery is typically listed at nearby Westfield, since Lawrence had no post office.) After a protracted construction period that included four injuries to workers (including Dahlke), the brewery was ready in early 1934.

Dahlke was unable to afford new equipment, so he attempted to buy a used brewhouse and other machines. Gustav's son Harvey was in charge of most of the purchasing and negotiation. After several deals fell through, the Dahlkes were able to purchase some of their needs from Kewaunee Brewing Co. Other equipment had to be purchased new. Finding a brewmaster was easier. Gustav Kuenzel, once owner of Stevens Point Brewery, was happy to move back to Wisconsin and take over the new business. Kuenzel was a highly regarded brewer, and his appointment gave the inexperienced firm credibility.

Production started in May 1934, but it was in many ways a very primitive operation. All packaging was done by hand, and in the early years Harvey Dahlke saved money by purchasing old bottles with metal fasteners instead of crown caps as well as whatever bottles he could scrounge. In an ad from 1936, Dahlke advertised "half gallons, pints, pony keg[s] or quarter barrel[s]," but no 12-ounce bottles. On the other hand, Dahlke spent enough on advertising to be competitive with the many other breweries of Central Wisconsin. The brewery ordered neon signs and metal signs for its retailers, and distributed foam scrapers, matchbooks and other items to customers.

Dahlke Brewing experienced some initial success. In 1936, Kuenzel brewed over 5,000 barrels of beer, though there was significant seasonal variation. He brewed over 700 barrels in July, and less than 300 in the winter months. Dahlke beer emphasized quality and purity, though eventually the federal government took issue with the "Pure and Wholesome" slogan and demanded a change. Dahlke launched a contest to create a new slogan, offering $25 to the best slogan written on the back of a Dahlke label and mailed to the company. The winner was "Best for Zest," which was first used in late 1937. However, sales had already begun to slip. In 1937, production dropped to about 3,000 barrels, and by 1939, it was just over 1,000 barrels. Much of the decline was due to the passing of Gustav Kuenzel in 1937. After his death, new brewmaster Wayne Dahlke changed the recipe and produced a cheaper, lighter beer. Dahlke started to lose accounts and distributors. In 1938, Harvey Dahlke began to bottle soft drinks, and in the early 1940s Dahlke began to increase the emphasis on these products and minimize the brewing part of the business. The final straw for the brewery came in early 1943, when several brewery workers left because of a labor dispute. Brewing was phased out during the summer of 1943 and came to an end in August. The building was used for soft drink bottling until 1966.

LeRoy *(Dodge County)*

Horace Barnes (1860?)
Horace Barnes was listed in the 1860 population census as "farmer and brewer." He lived in close proximity to Jacob Lehner, whose small farm brewery is covered in the Farmersville entry. It is possible that they shared a brewery, but they may each have had their own small operations.

William Kohl, Farmers Union Brewery (1867?–1872)

Anna Kohl (1872–1873?)

Nic. Weidig Farmers Brewery and Saloon (1877?–1886)

Michael Platzer (1888–1891)

Modern County Road Y, East of LeRoy
William Kohl started brewing sometime prior to May 1867, when he first appears in the excise

Marquette Beer was produced for Tony Berg of Milwaukee, who ran Tony's Pony, a local beer outlet. COLLECTION OF JOHN STEINER.

records. (According to the excise records, Kohl also owned a bowling alley.) Kohl operated the brewery intermittently until his death in July 1872. Anna Kohl was listed as proprietor of the brewery in the 1873 brewers directory, but no production was listed for her in 1871 or 1872. (Those figures may have represented the lack of production under her ownership, since excise records show production for William during that period.)

After Kohl's death the brewery lay idle for several years until Nic. Weidig restarted the brewery. The few known production figures range between 160 and 200 barrels per year, placing him among the smallest breweries in the state. Because there were so many other breweries nearby, it is likely that Weidig's brewery supplied a strictly local business. Weidig was also a farmer, shoemaker, and township official as well as a brewer. He closed the brewery in 1886, probably due to illness, since he died in April 1887.

A few years later, Michael Platzer leased the brewery from Weidig's widow Theresa, and began to repair and upgrade the facility in September 1888. In 1890, he enhanced his tavern with new furniture and a bowling alley. Local historian Michael D. Benter has speculated that all of these improvements were the result of a visit by a salesman from Brunswick-Balke & Collender Co., which had already been selling bar furnishing and had recently added bowling equipment to its wares. Benter noted that Platzer was mentioned in local newspapers more often than his predecessors—providing details like his styles of beer (Münchner Hofbrau and Wiener) and prices (75¢ for an eighth barrel and 5¢ for two glasses). Benter suggests that Platzer was a more experienced brewer than either Kohl or Weidig, so he may have been more used to advertising, but it also may have been a newspaperman who was more interested in beer than before. Platzer's brewery burned in April 1891, and was not rebuilt.

Peter Seifert (1892–93)
Historian Michael D. Benter has discovered that Peter Seifert, the brewer of Waupun, built a brewery in LeRoy after Platzer's brewery was burned. It is not clear where his brewery was, but Benter argues that it is likely that Seifert used the caves excavated by William Kohl. Seifert sold both of his breweries in 1893, but there is no evidence of the LeRoy brewery returning to production. New breweries were rumored to be in planning for LeRoy in 1897 and 1900, but there was no further mention of these projects.

LIMA TOWNSHIP *(Grant County)*

Charles Foast (Frost) (1893?)
Wayne Kroll lists Charles Foast as the operator of a small farm brewery in Lima Township, which is supported by John Dutcher. He is listed in *American Breweries II* as Frost.

LINCOLN *(Kewaunee County)*

George E. Laux (1875?–1880?)
John Eisenbeis & Co. (1881?–83?)
NEAR SILVER CREEK AND MODERN COUNTY ROAD P ALONG SOUTH BORDER OF SECTION 14, LINCOLN TOWNSHIP

Bavarian native George E. Laux started brewing at Lincoln sometime prior to 1876. (He sold his brewery in Algoma (then Ahnapee) in 1869). In 1878 he produced 138 barrels on his small farm brewery. He produced 166 the next year, and was still listed as a brewer in the 1880 population census. Sometime prior to 1883 John Eisenbeis & Co. took over the brewery, but the brewery was closed by revenue officials in April 1883, and it appears not to have reopened.

LINN TOWNSHIP
(P. O. Tirade) (Walworth County)

Hiram Downer (& Co.) (1856?–1870)
According to an 1857 map of Walworth County, Hiram Downer had a distillery on his two hundred acres in Linn Township, but there were other structures shown that could have been a brewery. The 1857 state business directory listed him as a brewer, and by the time of the 1860 census his fairly substantial business employed three workers and produced 1,000 barrels of beer. The population census of 1860 listed Downer as both farmer and brewer, but production of 1,000 barrels was more than just a side business. Downer continues to appear in the excise records through 1870, but the population census of that year listed him only as a farmer, and he was no longer in the industrial census.

LOCK HAVEN *(Vernon County)*

F. Davidson (1857?–1858?)

LOMIRA *(Dodge County)*

Star Brewing Co. (1912–1945)
Harold C. Johnson Brewing Co. (1945–1954)
PLEASANT HILL AVENUE

While several breweries decided to specialize in malting after brewing for many years, the Star Brewing Co. of Lomira was a rare contrast—the brewery was built as an accessory to the malt house. There were rumors of a brewery in Lomira as early as 1905, "for which a site has been secured by the Advancement Association." This proposal did not pan out, but in 1910 Albert, Rudolph, August and Edward Sterr built a malt house, and soon decided to add a brewery. The brewery began operations in 1912, and right from the beginning the labels for Star Lager and Star Bock announced that the beer was made by union labor. The Sterr brothers further diversified their business holdings when they started a

Star Brewing proudly announced its union workforce on this tin-over-cardboard sign (ca. 1940).
COLLECTION OF SCOTT BRISTOLL.

canning plant to take advantage of the peas grown in the area.

After Prohibition arrived, Albert Sterr bought the interests of his brothers, and, between the three family businesses and his other properties, Sterr became one of the largest property holders in the county. The brewery continued to make near beer and malt tonic during Prohibition, but the canning business helped the company survive through the dry years.

As brewing returned, Star Brewing made an early misstep: the company was convicted of using sodium sulfite in their beer in violation of pure food laws. However, the company rebounded and managed to survive the both the thinning of the herd that took place in the 1930s and the pressures of World War II. Albert Sterr died in 1938 and his fourth son, Roman, took over the business and guided it through World War II. Star Brewing continued to make Star Lager, introduced new brands such as Harvest and Muenchener, and brewed several labels for distributors and bottlers, including John Graf of Milwaukee.

In 1945, Harold C. Johnson purchased the brewery and renamed it after himself. He retained the Harvest brand, but also introduced Johnson's Premium and Malt Marrow. One of the advances made by Johnson in 1950 was to add canned beer to the lineup—making the brewery a relatively late adopter of cans. Only the Champagne Pilsner brand was canned, but this represented about 30 percent of production at the time. Keeping production near capacity was a constant struggle throughout the post-Prohibition periods under both owners. While capacity was listed at 50,000 barrels, production was often less than 10,000 barrels and never surpassed 18,000 barrels. The brewery closed in 1954, and the building was demolished over several years during the 1990s.

LOWELL (Dodge County)

George J. Schmieg & Co. (1856?-1880?)

George Schmieg is believed to have started brewing sometime around 1856. By 1860, Schmeig & Co. (the Co. part was presumably his boarder, brewer Peter Christman) were brewing 500 barrels of beer. (In excise records he appears as J. G. Schmieg.) In 1868 he built a new brewery, but apparently used most of his capital, since the R. G. Dun & Co. credit reports indicate that he was struggling financially, though continuing to pay his bills.

Joseph Golling, Brick House Brewery (1850?-1860?)

Joseph Golling appeared in the 1850 population census as a brewer, though he did not appear in the industrial census of that year. He appears to have brewed until at least 1860, even though he is not included in the industrial census of that year, because he is listed as "Proprietor of the Brewery" on a map from that year.

LYONS (Walworth County)

Casper Feser (1867?-1869?)

The first record of Casper Feser (Fezer) as a brewer was in the R. G. Dun & Co. records of 1867, though he may have been producing prior to that time. He first appeared in the excise records in 1868. Dun reported Feser was "doing a small bus[iness] in 1868, but by February of 1870 he was out of business.

MADISON (Dane County)

Frederic (Adam) Sprecher (1848-1859)
Breckheimer & Hausmann (1859-1864)
George Rockenbach (1864-68)
Peter Fauerbach (1868-1886)
Maria Fauerbach (1886-1890)
Fauerbach Brewing Co. (1890-1966)
651-653 WILLIAMSON

Frederic Sprecher was the first brewer in what was now the capital of the State of Wisconsin, starting there the same year as the territory was granted statehood. (It is not clear why some accounts give his name as Adam; the census, city directories and nineteenth-century histories all call him Frederic.) He brewed about 100 barrels in his first year, but in only two years S. Keyes & Co. passed Sprecher, who brewed a modest 230 barrels in 1850 in a hand-powered brewery with his assistant John Blossner. The brewery grew at a measured pace over the next decade, and by the 1860 industrial census Sprecher's brewery was now producing with the aid of horse power 1,800 barrels. Sprecher released a bock beer several years—in 1859 it was available for only one weekend in June. Unfortunately, Sprecher died in 1859 and the brewery appeared in the 1860 census under the name of his widow, Margaret.

Sometime soon after Frederic's death, Mathias Breckheimer and Joseph Hausmann leased the business from Margaret, though the brewery, a local landmark, continued to be referred to as Sprecher's brewery in the press. In fact, an ad for their bock release (in May, this time), identified the brewers as "Messrs. Houseman and Bruckheimer [sic] (at the well known Sprecher Brewery)," but added "The 'Sprecher Brewery' was always popular, but never more so than under its present gentlemanly managers." Hausmann and Breckheimer were so popular that they both soon acquired their own breweries: Hausmann purchased Voight's Capital Brewery and Breckheimer built a new plant on King Street.

In 1864, Margaret Sprecher remarried, and her new husband, George Rockenbach, became proprietor of the brewery. His time at the brewery was brief, though the R. G. Dun & Co. credit reports noted that he was honest and a good businessman even though he had no source of capital and the property remained in Margaret's name.

Peter Fauerbach (whose earlier career is covered in New Lisbon), moved to Madison in 1868 and leased the brewery. In 1880 he purchased the business, and ran it until his death in 1886 from stomach and liver problems. The *Wisconsin State Journal* mourned: "The deceased was a devoted husband, an indulgent parent, and a large-hearted, public spirited citizen, whose loss will cause wide-spread sorrow." The business was conducted in the name of his widow Maria for several years until the company was incorporated in 1890.

After incorporation, the brewery began to grow at a more rapid pace, jumping from

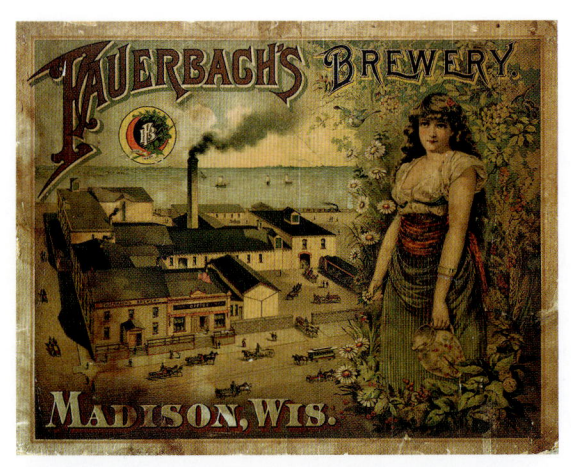

This striking bird's-eye view of Fauerbach's brewery shows the entire brewery complex ca. 1884. Several buildings were added during the next few decades. COURTESY OF THE WISCONSIN HISTORICAL SOCIETY, WHi-3489.

2,000 barrels in 1890 to 4,000 barrels in 1896. Fauerbach's location gave it an advantage over its rivals in the heart of the city, since it had more room for expansion. Their first bottling plant on the premises was built during the mid-1890s next to the brewery office on the Blount Street side. Subsequent Sanborn maps show the company filling in the block, expanding the capacity of the grain elevators to 40,000 bushels and adding new auxiliary buildings. The brewery's expansion was occasionally slowed by natural disaster, as in April 1899 when part of the roof was blown off by a tornado.

Sometime in the 1890s Fauerbach introduced a malt and hop tonic called Nectarine, which had nothing to do with the fruit (from nectar) and was advertised in the 1900 city directory as "The best tonic for the weak and overworked."

Fauerbach continued to grow through World War I, but with Prohibition imminent, Fauerbach began producing and selling alternative beverages. Even before the nation went legally dry, the company was advertising Fä-Bä, which claimed to have a hoppy taste and was "different from all other beverages because it [is] brewed right."

Because Fauerbach had been producing other beverages during Prohibition, it was a relatively easy transition back to beer. As a consequence, Fauerbach was one of the breweries open on 7 April. Observers of the festivities at Fauerbach's brewery reported that the hundreds of people crowding the premises were enthusiastic though orderly. The demand compelled Fauerbach to install new equipment almost immediately, especially for bottling, so they could attempt to fill orders that were arriving from as far away as Los Angeles. Even Milwaukee accounts were ordering more Fauerbach beer.

While initial sales were promising, Fauerbach was forced to struggle to survive against larger competitors, many located just to the east. Fauerbach introduced the Hostess Pack, a twelve-pack of bottles, and encouraged sales of this package by offering savings stamps for return of empty bottles and caps. The company advertised in 1937 that it was the only 100 percent union brewery and 100 percent union soft drink plant in Dane County. Since it was the only brewery, that was slight praise, but the ad also highlights that Fauerbach in 1936 became the Pepsi bottler for the area. World War II also tested the brewery. Like every other business and household, it was challenged by rationing—though it was able to procure permission to buy two new tires and two new tubes for its delivery trucks in August 1942.

The only remaining brewery in Madison during Prohibition had a product called Varsity to honor the Badgers football team. This 24-ounce bottle dates to the 1920s. COLLECTION OF JOHN STEINER.

Fauerbach attempted to expand its market in order to survive against increasing competition. The 100th anniversary of the brewery in 1948 was shared with the centennial of Wisconsin statehood, which gave the company an opportunity to harness the publicity and increase sales. They introduced a new beer, Centennial Brew (or "CB"), stepped up advertising in Madison, and distributed their bock in Milwaukee. At various times, the brewery distributed in Illinois, Minnesota, Nebraska, and both Dakotas, and had a fleet of seventy-five trucks to transport the product. Fauerbach Brewing sponsored a baseball team in the Madison Industrial League during the early 1950s, and was involved in many other community activities. In 1940 Fauerbach sponsored at least twelve different bowling teams, some named after different brands and others named after the department in the brewery for which the bowlers worked. In the 1960s, Fauerbach emphasized convenience in its advertising, citing the 6-pack, 8-pack, 12-pack and 24-pack packages of bottles in addition to the six-pack of cans. Hoping to appeal to the home market, many ads also emphasized the local ties of the brewery: "The Fauerbach Brewing Company of Madison and all of its employees, many of whom are your neighbors (all of whom are your friends), wish you an enjoyable Labor Day Weekend!" The convenience of the "thro-way" bottle was also a major selling point, since customers did not have to pay a deposit or collect the bottles for return. One of the more unusual promotional items was a pair of scorecards for customers to use in keeping track of the balloting at the 1952 Republican and Democratic national conventions.

In 1961, after a court battle over control of the company, sixty-seven-year-old Dr. Louis Fauerbach took over as president (and remained a practicing physician). Under his administration and that of master brewer Karl P. ("Prib") Fauerbach, the company continued to hold its own against major shipping brewers in

A Fauerbach-sponsored baseball team in Black Earth in June 1956. The CB patches on the sleeves are for Centennial Brew. COURTESY OF THE WISCONSIN HISTORICAL SOCIETY, WHI-92732.

the Madison market, and the Pepsi-Cola part of the business increased its revenue. Capacity of the brewery was 75,000 barrels per year, but except during the war years it never produced more than 50,000 barrels. Production generally remained above 30,000 barrels per year through 1962, but starting in 1959 there was a steady decline in sales. Competition finally drove the brewery out of business in 1966. There were rumors that G. Heileman Brewing Co. of La Crosse was interested in purchasing Fauerbach, but both sides denied any interest in a deal. Brewing ceased in June of that year.

After the brewery was closed, the complete interior of the brewery tavern including the Williamson street entry doors was sold to the Wagon Wheel Resort in Rockton, Illinois. The brewing equipment was removed, and Madison had no local beer for almost three decades. The brewery was torn down in 1967, but the land was vacant until 1980 when a condominium and apartment complex called the Fauerbach was built on the site.

In 2005, Fauerbach descendants brought back the Fauerbach brand in a version brewed under contract by Gray Brewing Co. in Janesville. The beer was well received, but contract difficulties forced discontinuation of the brand.

Tibbits & Gordon (1849?–1850?)
S. Keyes (1850?–52?)
T. H. White & Co. (1852?–54)
White & Rodermund (1854–55)
John Rodermund, Madison Brewery (1855–1875?)
Rodermund Brewing Co. (1875–1880)
YAHARI CANAL: SHERMAN AVENUE AND LODI ROAD

The Madison industrialists Tibbits and Gordon added a brewery to their mill complex sometime in 1849. By 1850, management of the brewery was in the hands of S. Keyes, who was referred to as John Keyes in one newspaper account. The business was sometimes called the Madison Brewery when it briefly was under the names of Tibbits, Gordon, and Keyes in 1850. It was the largest brewery in the state outside of Milwaukee, and not very far behind only three of those at 3,000 barrels. Keyes was involved with the brewery at least through 1852, when he was mentioned as being in control of "an extensive brewery" operating under water power. The water power was shared with Farwell's Mill, a large business owned by Farwell & Co. and the brewery was occasionally referred to by the Farwell name (Leonard J. Farwell was governor of Wisconsin from 1852–1854).

In approximately 1852, John Rodermund, an experienced brewer, took control of the brewery and continued to expand the plant. It is possible he was the head brewer in 1850, since he was the only other brewer in Madison at the time other than Adam Sprecher and his employee. According to one account, Farwell himself asked Rodermund to come to Madison. For a short time, Rodermund was joined by T. H. White, who apparently provided the capital for the two to buy the business from Tibbits and Gordon, since the business was under the name of T. H. White & Co. The two were "determined that the reputation of MADISON ALE shall not be excelled by any in the country. This ad also pointed out another unusual feature of this brewery: they had a store associated with the brewery with "a large and complete stock of Merchandize [sic], . . . which they will exchange with Farmers for their produce, on as good terms as any mercantile establishment west of the [Great] lakes." (Keyes had started the "dry goods and grocery store" the previous summer).

By the time of the 1860 industrial census, his 4,500 barrels of lager and ale were still the most outside of Milwaukee, and well ahead of the Gutsch brewery in Sheboygan. Rodermund was the only brewer outside of Milwaukee to employ as many as ten men, and his was one of only two in the state to claim water as their source of power (Jacob Konrad in Weyauwega was the other). Rodermund made the most of his location on Lake Mendota by establishing a landing that was used for regattas. There was also a tavern at the malt house that was a popular spot for many decades. Rodermund used ox teams to get kegs of beer to Madison establishments. The generous brewer also once shipped beer down the river, though without success:

While the Hook and Ladder company of this city [Madison] was trying to save one of the bridges from being carried away by the late raging flood, they had to witness a tantalizing passage. Mr. Rodermund, a wholesale brewer, cast from his brewery into the stream above the bridge, several kegs of lager, to refresh the firemen, and as they were seen

There are very few artifacts from Rodermund's brewery. The back of this copper token advertised that Rodermund manufactured stock and cream ale as well as lager. COLLECTION OF TYE SCHWALBE.

WISCONSIN BREWERIES AND BREWPUBS   473

bobbing in the stream the firemen endeavored to secure them but without success, the kegs making clear of every hook into the lake.

By 1870, Rodermund's brewery represented an investment of $25,000—by far the most of any brewery in the city and his annual production of over 3,000 barrels also led his Madison rivals. He offered his patrons Bavarian and Vienna lagers, Cream and Stock ales and "pale Malt" beer, as well as dealing in malt and hops. An even more significant sign of growth was the advertisement in the 1873 Madison city directory that announced Rodermund's depot at 13 Fourth Street in Chicago. Whether this was a response to the Chicago fire or just a natural expansion is not known but a later history suggests that Rodermund was successful in Chicago for at least a while. In October 1873, a fire described as the worst ever in Madison destroyed the original Farwell mill as well as Rodermund's brewery. The fire was blamed on a drunken mill employee, but there was no hard proof. While Rodermund had about $37,000 of insurance, his loss was close to twice that. Rodermund began rebuilding shortly thereafter, however, the momentum the business had earlier was gone. It took two years for the brewery to begin production again, and by this point, Rodermund had dropped to fourth place out of five capital city breweries. Rodermund himself went bankrupt and died in 1875, and Jacob Veidt, took over as superintendent of the brewery. The *Wisconsin State Journal* provided an unusual amount of detail about Veidt's beer in August 1875:

Mr. Jacob Veidt, the manager of the Rodermund Brewing Company, has purchased from Lodi some very choice new hops, of the Palmer's seedling variety, which have done very well this year. Mr. Veidt does not propose to let the reputation of the Rodermund beer and ale suffer in his hands, and uses the best of material, taking care to have it treated in the best manner.

Veidt earned praise for his cream ale in 1876, which was claimed "most beneficial as a tonic." In 1877, Veidt left Madison to take over the former John Beck brewery in Milwaukee, which in 1879 became Cream City Brewing Co.

By 1880 Rodermund's brewery was no longer listed in city or industry directories, nor in the 1880 industrial census. The property lay idle for several years, but was purchased by Joseph Hausmann in 1888 for $10,000 (though there were rumors that three former Des Moines brewers were negotiating for the property, and even earlier rumors that "Chicago men" were looking at converting it to a pork packing plant). The press speculated that Hausmann would use the new site to expand his business, but it appears that he never actually brewed there. However, he did use the malt house, which was closed in 1917. During Prohibition a speakeasy set up operations in the old malt house, which was converted into a tavern upon Repeal. The building was razed in 1948.

William Voight, Capital Brewery (1854–1864)
Joseph Hausmann, Capital Brewery
   (1864–1891)
Hausmann Brewing Co. (1891–1920)
333 State at Gorham

Carl William Voight (or Voigt) came from Saxony to Madison in 1854, where he set about establishing a small ale brewery with a four-barrel capacity per batch. In 1856, he decided to switch to lager to meet the increasing market for the German style. Voight quickly boosted production to 2,000 barrels in 1860, well behind Rodermund but well ahead of Sprecher. Voigt employed six men at this date, more than most other breweries in the state. The census also noted the unusual situation that his brewery was powered by both horse and fire. Voight may have been in a transition between power sources, since he advertised his old horse power for sale, which he offered to "exchange for a horse or sell cheap for cash." It is possible that some of Voight's ingredients came from his own eighty-acre farm, which included grapes, wheat, and barley, among other crops.

Voight's brewery was the site of one of the melees caused by Union troops massed at Camp Randall. Roaming soldiers broke into his brewery and stole whiskey, but Voight scared them off with a gun. Local sympathy was with the proprietor, and one newspaper affirmed: "Mr. Voight is a quiet and respectable German citizen and his saloon and brewery has been conducted for years with marked propriety." Voight began to advertise in newspapers in 1862, "inform[ing] his friends and the residents of Madison and Dane county, that he is now brewing at his Brewery, on State street," Porter, Pale Cream Ale, White and Lager Beer. The editor of the *Wisconsin Daily Patriot* added: "Mr. Voight's beer has been well liked in this city for several years past, and his skill and facilities for brewing warrant that the liquors he announces will be well and wholesomely brewed." He also brewed a bock beer, which the editor confirmed was "richly flavored and foaming." While the ads may have attracted attention, some of it was undesirable, such as the robber who stole about $13 from the till in August 1863. Production also dropped in fiscal 1863 to 782 barrels, which might have been caused by some of the wartime stress on his business.

In 1864, Voight left Madison and moved to Milwaukee where he spent two years as a grain shipper and owner of the schooner *Columbian*. He then moved to Detroit where he opened the Milwaukee Brewery (really!), which he sold to his son Edward in 1871. The new proprietor of the Capital Brewery was Joseph Hausmann, who had worked previously at the Yellow Creek Brewery in Freeport, Illinois, at Krug's (later Schlitz's) brewery in Milwaukee, at the Haertel brewery in Portage, and finally as proprietor of his own brewery in New Lisbon. Hausmann had served in the German army during the revolution of 1848, and wore a saber wound for the rest of his life. Soon after opening, Hausmann delighted the staff of the *Wisconsin Daily Patriot* by leaving them a couple of kegs—no doubt hoping for some free publicity. The editor responded: "Mr. Housman [sic], formerly chief brewer at the old Sprecher brewery, where he established a reputation as a first class brewer, is now proprietor of Mr. Wm. Voigt's Brewery, in the 1st Ward, and we can bear testimony to the superior quality of the beer

Part of Hausmann's Capital Brewery was built in the Italianate style popular in the mid-nineteenth century. COURTESY OF THE WISCONSIN HISTORICAL SOCIETY, WHI-11692.

manufactured by him in his new quarters. We wish him success."

And Hausmann was successful. His brewery produced around 1,500 barrels in 1870, nearly doubled that to just under 3,000 in each of the next two years, and by 1875 was closing in on 4,500 barrels. He remained around that total for a few years, but took another leap forward in 1879 when he produced over 5,800 barrels, good for twelfth-most in the state. In 1877, Hausmann began to sell bottled beer, but because of his cramped location, he did not yet have room for his own bottling plant. The *Wisconsin State Journal* explained:

> Madison has entered the lists in the manufacture of bottled beer, which has recently become so popular throughout the West. Joseph Hausmann has made a contract with Mauz & Little, our local bottling firm, and the article will hereafter be found in competition with Milwaukee brands. Hausmann's beer is already famous, and in this new form will meet with an extended trade all over the country.

Mauz & Little were short-lived, and by 1883 son Carl Hausmann had established a bottling works across the street to be the sole bottler of his father's beer. The business was definitely a family firm, since Carl's older brothers Otto and William were the clerk and foreman respectively. William had served as an apprentice first with the McAvoy brewery in Chicago and then, appropriately enough, at the Voigt brewery in Detroit (the name was generally spelled without the h in Detroit).

Hausmann expanded his brewery in 1883 by a method that would be much more common in later years—buying out one of his competitors. Hausmann took over the brewing apparatus and beer on hand of John Hess, who ran a smaller brewery about a block west of Hausmann on State Street at Gilman. Hausmann was in the midst of building a new brewhouse at that time, and the equipment would be useful in the new plant and the stock of beer could bridge the gap if the brewery was closed due to construction. The brewery's output continued to climb, reaching 12,000 barrels in fiscal 1890 and 18,500 in 1896.

In 1892, Joseph incorporated the business with his sons William, Carl, and Otto. This particular version of the corporation was dissolved in 1909, but a new version of Hausmann Brewing Co. was formed shortly afterwards. Hausmann Brewing Co. began bottling on their own premises sometime in 1892, though most of the bottled product was still consumed in Madison and Dane County. Unlike most of its rivals, Hausmann appears to have continued to brew ale at least intermittently through 1905, though the major brands were Export, Lager, and Hofbräu. The saloon at the brewery was a favorite of college students since it was close to campus. The saloon remained in operation despite an ordinance prohibiting saloons within a mile of campus by using some creative measurement to determine where the one-mile line was.

A lengthy evaluation of Madison's breweries published in 1897 reported that Joseph Hausmann was one of the wealthiest men in Madison, estimating his net worth around $500,000. It also had praise for his children and their work in developing the business, and attributed the success as much to them as to the springs on the property that provided pure brewing water. The brewery adopted artificial refrigeration in 1894 and added additional storage buildings soon after. In addition, Hausmann Brewing Co. was central to the first electric plant in Madison, since the first power and dynamos were set up in the brewery in 1888. Hausmann Brewing Co. followed some of their Wisconsin rivals in investing in hotel properties: the Carlton hotel in Edgerton, once one of the fanciest hotels in the state, was built by Hausmann in 1898 for $25,000.

Joseph Hausmann died in 1902, but his brewery continued to grow. An account published in 1928 claimed that the brewery was producing about 35,000 barrels of beer in the years before Prohibition, which required ten horses to distribute throughout the city. This Prohibition-era article also wryly noted, "Yes, beer was delivered in the day-time in those days." Hausmann's size made it the subject of merger speculation, even if unfounded. In 1907, Carl Hausmann denied rumors of a combination that would include breweries from St. Louis, various firms in Ohio, and Hausmann (as well as Klinkert's brewery in Racine). The Hausmann brewery also employed more men than either of the other breweries in Madison, a fact borne out at the 1908 city Labor Day picnic when there was a tug of war between the Hausman brewery workers and the combined Fauerbach and Breckheimer employees.

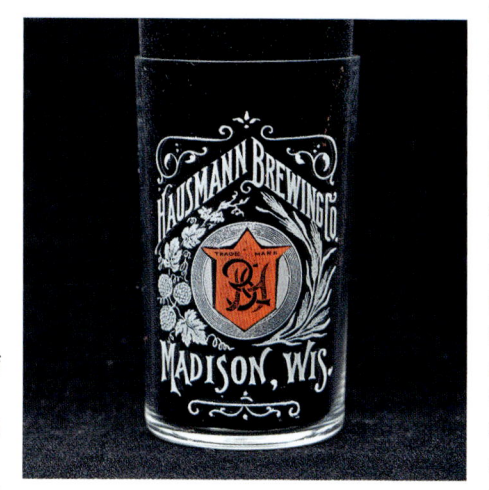

Etched glasses were common around 1900, but examples with color were rare. COLLECTION OF TYE SCHWALBE.

WISCONSIN BREWERIES AND BREWPUBS

Hausmann continued to be a successful brewery right up until Prohibition. The company altered its articles of incorporation to allow the manufacture of "drinks of all kinds, either with or without alcoholic content," and indeed began to produce near beer while leaving the door open should beer be re-legalized. However, the Hausmann brewery building burned in March 1923 in a spectacular fire that caused $100,000 of damage and put firefighters at risk when carbon dioxide and ammonia tanks exploded. The prime piece of undivided real estate on State Street was sold and the building was razed the following year. In 1924 the site was considered for a new City Hall, but 400 women protested the proposal, apparently because of its ties to alcohol. Hausmann Brewing Co. was dissolved in 1928. In 2005, Gray's Brewing Co. of Janesville introduced Hausmann's Pale Beer as a tribute to the long-defunct but once important brewery. Angelic Brewing Co. later occupied the site of Hausmann Brewing Co.

Mathias Breckheimer (1865–1901)
Breckheimer Brewing Co. (1901–1916)
215 King Street (between North Wilson and Clymer (modern Doty))

Mathias Breckheimer arrived in Milwaukee in 1849, where he worked for two years in Phillip Best's brewery. He moved to Madison in 1851 and worked for John Rodermund until 1859, when he and Joseph Hausmann leased the Sprecher brewery. In 1864, Mathias Breckheimer left the Sprecher Brewery and started in business by himself. The next year he purchased a building that was once a plow factory across from the City Hotel, and began the process of converting it into a brewery. As with many brewery projects, then and now, the build-out took months verging on years. In November 1865 he was almost done, and the *Wisconsin State Journal* reported on his progress:

> The new brewery on King street, opposite the City Hotel, is now partly in working order and by next week will be completely finished. We went through it yesterday, and saw the arched cellars deep underground and the smooth malt floors, the former lined with big casks, and the latter covered with grain. The malt kiln shows the latest improvements, as does all about the brewery. A horse was pumping water out of a 73 feet deep well containing an average of about 34 feet of the liquid that is as necessary to brewers as to total abstinence men. The hall in which the foaming lager will be served is large and lofty, and is fitted with an elegant counter and other substantial conveniences. There is a cooperage attached to the brewery in which all the casks and kegs are made. Mr. Breckheimer, the enterprising citizen who owns and built this brewery, thoroughly understands his business, and with the facilities he has, and his known skill as a brewer, we are confident of his producing a Capital City lager that can compete with the famed drink of Milwaukee 'or any other' place. We understand that the hall will be opened next Monday evening, with the music of the brass band, foaming lager, and a large and social gathering of Breckheimer's numerous friends.

Complete descriptions of breweries such as this are relatively rare, especially the details of the attached beer hall, though the precise dimensions of the well were common as a measure of technological advancement.

Having a landlocked downtown location placed restrictions on Breckheimer's growth. The 1885 Sanborn map shows an unusual shallow v-shaped building, dictated in part by the triangular lot on which it sat. Breckmeimer was not listed as having malting capacity anytime after 1880, and while malting facilities were mentioned in the above description, later Sanborn maps indicated that they were not in use. The company did not have its own bottling facilities until after 1900. Capacity was also limited—production was listed in 1897 as being around 2,000 to 3,000 barrels per year, which was now behind the rapidly growing Fauerbach. Mathias Breckheimer died in 1899, and his son Mathias took over the business.

Breckheimer Brewing Co. managed to continue until the United States entered World War I. However, financial difficulties forced the company to cease production at the end of June 1917. By the time Prohibition began, the Breckheimer Brewing Co. had been converted to the Breckheimer Seed Co.

Barnhard Mauz (Mautz) (1865?–1870)
Lang & Miller (1870–71)
Miller & Co. (Miller & Kaiser) (1871–72)
John Hess (1874–79)
Hess & Fairbanks (1876–77)
Hess & Moser (1880–81)
John Hess (1881–82)
Hess & Loeher (1882–83)
State and Gilman Streets (84 State Street)

Barnhard Mauz (both names spelled various ways) started a brewery in Madison sometime prior to his first appearance in the city directory in 1866. His brewery was among the smallest in Madison—producing 535 barrels in 1870—but still a respectable size compared to most other firms in the state. Mauz's brewery is not as well documented as some of his rivals, though there were a number of incidents at the brewery which made the news. In 1870, a worker named Wolfgang Anzinger suffered a gruesome accident in which his shirt got tangled in the malt mill and his hand was drawn into the mill. While he lost two fingers and a considerable amount of skin up to the elbow, he still survived. As noted in chapter 3, residents complained about the smell of the brewery waste in 1870, though these complaints were not limited to Mauz's tenure—a similar complaint came before the city council in 1872 after Miller & Co. took over.

It appears from excise records that Miller & Co. leased or rented Mauz's brewery in the fall of 1870, since the name first appears in October 1870. The R. G. Dun & Co. records claim that Mauz sold out to Lang and Miller in late 1870, which would be consistent with excise records. The name varies between Miller & Co. and Miller & Kaiser in this source, but Mathias Miller named the business the Empire Brewery, a designation that remained until it closed (it appeared in the 1877 city directory as the Imperial Brewery). Miller and Joseph Fuchs (the "& Co." as of 1872) nearly doubled production, jumping from 649 barrels in 1871 to 1,211 in 1872. Miller & Co's brewery (still called Mauz's brewery at times) was one of three Madison breweries (along with Hausmann and Brickheimer) to be decorated in 1871 for a parade of German Americans celebrating their homeland's victory in the Franco-Prussian War. However, the excise records suggest that Miller & Co. only produced for part of 1873, and they vanish from the records after that point.

The following year, John Hess left his brewery in Pheasant Branch and took over the Empire Brewery. With various partners, he continued to develop the brewery, boosting production to nearly 1,700 barrels by the end of the 1870s. While still powered by horse (unlike Hausmann and Fauerbach), his 1880 production was second in Madison only to Hausmann.

At the end of 1879, business was falling off, and Hess brought in Adolph Moser who, according to the Dun evaluator, "[brings] in no capital but has valuable experience in [the] brewery bus[iness]." Moser left at the end of 1880, and Hess was on his own until he brought in John Loeher in 1882. In 1883, Hess bought out Loeher, and a few days later sold the equipment and remaining beer to his rival a block to the east, Joseph Hausmann. Hess gave up brewing and devoted his attention to the livery business. It is possible that Hess tired of the business after having been burglarized "several times" in the early 1880s.

Frank Martin (1869)

Frank Martin owned a small business, and in early 1869 installed "a small Ale Brewery." He appeared once in the excise records, in May 1869. The R. G. Dun & Co. evaluator reported that Martin was considerably in debt but that he was "a very honest[,] industrious[,] energetic[,] and thrifty man" and had made a good start. Unfortunately, that virtue was not enough, and Martin was out of business in a few months.

Great Dane Pub & Brewing (1994–present)
123 East Doty

New Yorkers Rob LoBreglio and Eliot Butler opened Great Dane Pub & Brewing in the former Fess Hotel building in downtown Madison in 1994. Great Dane expanded to four other locations: Fitchburg in 2002, Hilldale in 2006, Wausau in 2009, and Eastside in 2010. The Eastside pub, located in Grandview Commons, is the only one without a brewery on site. Production at the downtown brewery is typically just under 2,000 barrels per year. (The origin and expansion of Great Dane is covered in more detail in chapter 10.) They released their first bottled beer in 2012, inaugurating the series with an imperial red ale (at 11.5 percent).

The first Great Dane location occupies three former businesses on the corner of King and East Doty. The center was the Fess Hotel; just to the right was the Central House hotel (which the Fess Hotel took over in the early 1900s). The building with the brewpub sign housed retail, including a paint store and a furniture store. At far left, a modern building stands on the site of the Breckheimer brewery. PHOTOGRAPH BY ROBERT FOGT.

Growler from Angelic Brewing Co. (ca. 2004). AUTHOR'S COLLECTION.

The downtown location of Great Dane was also the first brewpub in the area to offer the 32-ounce "crowler" package.

Angelic Brewing (1995–2005)
322 West Johnson Street

Angelic Brewing was located in a building that was once part of Hausmann Brewing Co., just off State Street in downtown Madison. Brewmaster Dean Coffey created multiple award-winning beers, all of which had names relating to angels, mythical deities, or various interpretations of the afterlife. In 2005 Coffey left to co-found Ale Asylum, and brewing ceased at the Johnson Street location, though the restaurant remained open until 2008 (often featuring beers made at Ale Asylum).

J. T. Whitney's Brewpub and Eatery (1996–2009)
674 South Whitney

J. T. Whitney's Brewpub and Eatery was founded in 1995 and began brewing in 1996, making it the third brewpub in Madison. Brewmaster Rich Becker's family came from Bamberg, Germany, and he brought the smoked beer (*rauchbier*) traditions of that city to some of his beers at J. T. Whitney's. (For a while, Becker did double duty as the brewer at Grumpy Troll in Mt. Horeb.) Later, he was one of the early craft brewers of sour beer styles in Wisconsin, introducing styles such as Berliner weisse and Flanders red. Whitney's opened another restaurant in Oregon, Wisconsin, in 2008, though all the brewing was done at the Madison brewery. Whitney's closed in early 2009 due to financial difficulties, and while Becker and Tom Volke tried to put a reorganization plan together, they were unsuccessful.

Vintage Brewing Co. was a project that grew out of Madison's Vintage Spirits & Grill. Brittany, Mark and Trent Kramer had discussed starting a brewpub, and they eventually brought brewer Scott Manning on board. They took over the recently vacated J. T. Whitney's space, opened the restaurant in January 2010, and served their first Vintage beers a month later.

WISCONSIN BREWERIES AND BREWPUBS   477

The beer lineup typically includes a range of common styles, along with creative versions of those styles and some cask-conditioned beers. Vintage was among the earliest American craft brewers to make a version of Sahti—a Finnish ale brewed with juniper berries. Several Vintage beers have won medals at Great American Beer Festival and World Beer Cup.

In 2013, Vintage opened Woodshed Ale House in Sauk City, which serves a menu of pizzas along with Vintage Brewing Co. beers. A new brewpub in Sauk City opened in 2018.

Ale Asylum (2006–present)
3698 Kinsman Boulevard (2006–2012); 2002 Pankratz Street (2012–present)

Ale Asylum was founded by Dean Coffey and Otto Dilba after Angelic Brewing closed. They first looked at a location in Fitchburg, but settled on a location near the Madison airport. Ale Asylum's first location was a hybrid between a brewpub and production brewery because the tap room served a selection of sandwiches, pizzas and salads, though there was no full kitchen.

Ale Asylum's brews met with immediate approval, finding a market with Wisconsin drinkers willing to choose hoppier and higher alcohol beers. The Kinsman Boulevard location limited possible growth, so they selected a new site approximately two miles to the west on the other side of the Madison airport. A chart published on the brewery website in 2011 made the case for expansion: The new facility would have 45,000 square feet as opposed to 8,000, maximum capacity would jump immediately from 11,000 to 50,000 with room to grow, the brewhouse system would be nearly three times as large and there would be room for a bottler capable of 277 bottles per minute instead of the 70 bottles per minute of the old 1972 system then in use.

The new brewery was built from the ground up at a cost of $8 million, and was ready to brew in 2012. Growth continued, and Ale Asylum expanded its market to Illinois in 2014. The new brewhouse and packaging plant had a mix of new and used equipment, but all was state of the art. The brewery also has its own lab, and incorporated energy-saving technology for heating and cooling.

The brewery's beers generally have names that play on the theme of "Fermented in Sanity," with brands such as Bedlam! and Demento or that emphasize strength and robust flavor such as Ballistic, Ambergeddon, and Napalm Bunny. Otto Dilba created the art work for the labels, and Dilba and his wife Hathaway work on the branding based on their combined more than two decades in marketing.

In December 2014, Ale Asylum Riverhouse opened on the Riverwalk in Milwaukee. Riverhouse is restaurant and bar that features Ale Asylum beers, but does not brew on site. Riverhouse is not owned by the brewery, but by restauranteur Tim Thompson, who also worked at Angelic Brewing Co.

Granite City Food & Brewery (2006–present)
72 West Towne Mall

The Madison location of the Granite City Food & Brewery opened in December 2006. It was the first (and still only) Wisconsin location of a brewpub chain that started in St. Cloud, Minnesota, in 1999. As of 2017, Granite City has thirty-six restaurants in fourteen states from Maryland to Kansas.

Beer writer Michael Agnew categorized the Granite City locations as "fermenteries" rather than true breweries, since the wort for all restaurants is produced at a single site in Ellsworth, Iowa and trucked to each establishment. The trademarked process, invented by Granite City founder Bill Burdick and called "Fermentus Interruptus," was designed to guarantee quality and consistency of the beers at all locations. Each restaurant finishes the fermentation process under the guidance of regional brewers and their teams.

Over time, Granite City has introduced more seasonal beers and more beers with higher alcohol content, including Batch 1000 Double IPA, with 7.8 percent alcohol and 76 IBU.

Great Dane #3—Hilldale (2007–present)
357 Price Place

As noted in chapter 10, operating a brewhouse at Great Dane's Hilldale location required a change in state law that allowed brewpubs to have more than two branch locations. So while the restaurant opened in 2006, the brewery was not operational until the end of 2007. The size of the Hilldale location allowed for more expansion to increase capacity, and Hilldale serves as the production site for most of the packaged beer. Production at this location is typically around 2,700 barrels per year. When Great Dane started canning beer in 2016, the mobile canning line was set up at Hilldale.

The Hilldale brewery brews most of the Great Dane beer sold at Madison Mallards' baseball games, including two brewed just for the games at Warner Park (aka "The Duck Pond"): Mallard's Ale and Big League Brown. Great Dane was one of the founding sponsors of the Mallards in 2001, and has a permanent presence with the Great Dane Duck Blind, an outfield seating area at Warner Park which was redesigned in 2017 using old shipping containers.

While all the Great Dane locations have the same basic beer and food menus, each location may have special beers or features. Bockfest, which brings together several area craft brewers and their bock beers each February, is unique to the Hilldale location.

House of Brews (2011–2017)
4539 Helgesen Drive

Most Ale Asylum beers emphasize hops and are at the high end of the alcohol content range for their style. The labels often feature the theme "Fermented Insanity" in their designs. AUTHOR'S COLLECTION.

Because the Community Supported Agriculture (CSA) movement started in the Madison area in the early 1990s, it was only fitting that Wisconsin's first Community Supported Brewery (CSB) would also call Madison home. Page Buchanan was inspired to try the concept with a brewery by a fellow Madison Homebrewers and Tasters Guild member who had a CSA farm. Subscribers were able to get a set amount of beer (typically a case of 22-ounce bottles) each month, as well as discounts and invitations to special events at the brewery. The format was tweaked over the years, but remainedpart of the business. While the CSB was the core of the business plan, House of Brews sold its first keg of beer (Prairie Rye Kölsch) in September 2011 at the Malt House—an institution in Madison among those who enjoy the brewed and distilled fruits of the grain.

In addition to tapping into part of the local culture, a CSB provided a different model both for raising capital to brew, and for delivering the product to customers. One advantage was being able to circumvent taverns and distributors reluctant to carry a beer that was unfamiliar. However, the more spontaneous nature of recipe creation meant that in the early years Buchanan was unable to brew any particularly hoppy beers because it was difficult to get some hops on the spot market. The standard beers in the House of Brews lineup tended to be maltier styles, such as an oatmeal stout and a Scotch ale.

Another less common brewing model provided at House of Brews was a Brew on Premises operation. In B.O.P., individuals or groups can use the brewery equipment to make and package a beer of their own. Buchanan described B.O.P. as less about the actual brewing and more as "being Captain of the Good Ship Lollipop,"—in other words, creating a fun event.

However, what House of Brews perhaps was best known for was its contract brewing operations, which became an incubator for other noteworthy breweries. Among those that got their start in House of Brews were MobCraft and Alt Brew—Wisconsin's first all-gluten-free brewery. House of Brews also provided capacity for brewpubs whose demand outstripped their capacity, such as Madison's One Barrel Brewing Company. In August 2017, Buchanan put the brewery up for sale, citing the challenges of the contract brewing market and of starting the brewery on his own, which left him undercapitalized.

One Barrel Brewing Co. (2012–present)
2001 Atwood Avenue

Madison's first "nanobrewery" of the modern craft era was the aptly named One Barrel Brewing Co., which opened in July 2012. Founder and brewer Peter Gentry created a brewery taproom with what was essentially a large homebrew system to brew beer one barrel at a time. The taproom served a limited menu of food from neighborhood restaurants and artisans.

While Gentry originally planned to stay small, the brews that he and his team crafted were so popular that they first had to contract out the brewing of some of their draught beers to House of Brews, and later One Barrel made the leap to bottled products. As of 2017, One Barrel Brewing brands were available in significant portions of Southern and Northeastern Wisconsin.

Karben4 Brewing Co. (2012–present)
3698 Kinsman Blvd.

Brothers Ryan and Zak Koga and their friend Alex Evans were all natives of Appleton, and after following separate paths, ended up in Madison. Ryan's path included brewing at Yellowstone Valley Brewing Co. in Billings, Montana, and Zak and Alex's discussions of business opportunities finally meshed with Ryan's career. They also brought in another friend of Zak and Alex, Tom Kowalke, to be the resident artist and to tend bar in the taproom. They moved into the former location of Ale Asylum and retained some of the old equipment, but completely remodeled the taproom and began serving beer the last weekend of 2012.

The name Karben4 was designed to be "a made-up name that did not already exist in any other capacity," to avoid a name that would limit the business in the future. It is based on the element carbon, which is essential to organic life, but with a phonetic spelling to differentiate their brand.

Ryan's first beers were generally inspired by English styles, though the first bottled beer, Fantasy Factory, was an IPA which, even though it still used English malts, indicated a definite

House of Brews beers were in enough demand that they were sold at local retailers in bottles and cans. Photograph by Charles Walbridge. Author's collection.

Most of One Barrel Brewing Company's bottled beers were produced under contract at other area breweries. Banjo Cat evokes OBBC's early penguin logo, often featured on cardboard coasters. Photograph by Charles Walbridge. Author's collection.

trend toward bigger, hoppier beers. The first bottles reached store shelves in October 2014, and from there Karben4 began to add additional bottled brands and soon expanded distribution to Milwaukee and the Appleton/Fox Cities area.

Next Door Brewery (2013–present)
2439 Atwood Avenue

Next Door brewery was founded by Pepper Stebbins, a former bartender at Great Dane-Hilldale, and Keith Symonds, who had brewing experience in the northeastern United States, along with Aric and Crystal Dieter. They planned a neighborhood restaurant that would focus on collaborations with "local tastemakers" and that could serve as a community gathering place. The restaurant located in a former appliance shop, opened in August 2013, with several of Symonds' beers on tap, including Wilbur, a cream ale with malted oats (the name was a reference to the 1960s TV show *Mister Ed*). Symonds left the brewhouse in 2014, and Bryan Kreiter took over brewing duties.

As Next Door beers grew in popularity, they were encouraged to bottle and distribute several of their year-round beers. Bottles were first introduced in 2015, and as of 2017 three year-round and two seasonal beers are available in six-packs in most of southern Wisconsin. In addition, Next Door has nine beers available in 22-ounce bomber bottles, five of which are only available at the brewery. The styles in the bomber bottles are typically dry-hopped beers, wood-aged beers, or sour beers.

Funk Factory Geuzeria (2014–present)
1604 Gilson Street

Levi Funk opened the first facility in the state designed exclusively to blend and age Belgian-style lambic ales. Funk purchases wort from other breweries (a relationship he began with O'So Brewing of Plover), brings it to his barrel warehouse, and then adds fruit or blends different batches to achieve the desired flavors, or sometimes whatever flavor develops. Due to the time and cost involved in the aging and blending process, Funk Factory beers were subject to very limited release at first.

In 2017 Funk opened a tasting room at the barrel warehouse. To celebrate, he introduced his first regular bottle release, the first meerts beer known to have been made commercially in the United States. Meerts (March, in Flemish, after the month they were typically released in Belgium) is typically low in alcohol with a citrusy sour character.

Greenview Brewing Co. LLC/Alt Brew (2016–present)
1808 Wright Street

When Trevor Easton's wife Maureen was diagnosed with celiac disease, they had to change how they enjoyed beer together. There were few gluten-free beers available in their area, and none of them craft beers. Trevor was an avid homebrewer, so he spent almost three years working on recipes to find some that would have craft beer flavor while not depending on traditional brewing grains. He decided that beers featuring Belgian yeast strains were best suited to gluten-free brewing, and the first beer became Rustic Badger, a farmhouse ale.

The Eastons began brewing their beers at House of Brews in a special room that used positive air pressure to make sure there was no cross contamination from other grains in the brewery. The first batches reached the market in May 2014, and sold very quickly. In 2015 they began planning their own brewery, and selected a site that happened to be on a bike trail that connected Karben4 and Ale Asylum. They began brewing at their new location in 2016, and their beers were soon available on draught at several restaurants and in bottles at several dozen stores—mostly in the Madison area. Their beers include several seasonal offerings, including an imperial pumpkin ale.

The brewery and taproom both employ precautions to avoid contamination of the brewhouse or the beers. The production facility uses positive pressure to keep unwanted organisms out, and the non-gluten free guest beers served in the taproom are served in disposable plastic cups to prevent contamination of glassware.

Rockhound Brewing Co. (2016–present)
444 South Park Street

Nate Warnke, a geology major from University of Wisconsin-Madison, decided in 2014 to leave his job in the insurance business and follow his dream of setting up a brewpub. Most of the beers have names dealing with geology in some way. For the first few months, the beers were made at either Great Dane or House of Brews until Warnke began brewing on his own system.

Lucky's 1313 Brewpub (2016–present)
1313 Regent Street

The building at 1313 Regent Street has been home to several businesses since the 1920s, most of them repaired vehicles. Many of the beers and food items have football-themed names to build on the brewpub's proximity to Camp Randall Stadium.

Maiden Rock (Pierce County)

Rush River Brewing Co. (2004–7)
W4001 120th Avenue

Rush River Brewing Co. was founded by a group of friends who met at the Bulldog pub in Minneapolis. Unable to find a suitable site in the Twin Cities, they decided to look across the river, and found a spot in scenic Maiden Rock.

The strong reception to their beers required more production than they could handle in the small Maiden Rock brewery, so they set about

This Next Door coaster (ca. 2013) is made of cork, rather than the more common paperboard for brewery coasters. COLLECTION OF SCOTT REICH.

This coaster is one of the few pieces of breweriana produced for the original Maiden Rock location. COLLECTION OF SCOTT REICH.

looking for a new location, and found one in an industrial park in River Falls.

Manitowoc *(Manitowoc County)*

William Rahr, Eagle Brewery (1847–1880)
Rahr & Rontauscher (1854?–55)
Wm. Rahr Sons, Eagle Brewery (1880–1893)
William Rahr Sons Co. (1893–1911)
William Rahr Sons Brewing Co. (1911–1920)
Cereal Products Co. (Cepro) (1920–1932)
WASHINGTON, BETWEEN SIXTH AND SEVENTH

William and Natalie Rahr emigrated from the Rhineland to America in 1847. The eloquent but romanticized version of the story told by eminent American artist and designer Rockwell Kent (who was a friend of the couple's grandson Guido Reinhardt Rahr) depicts the reluctance of Natalie to move to the frontier and her insistence on bringing her beloved piano. The family settled in the rough frontier village, which Natalie helped civilize by teaching French, English, and piano lessons. William started a brewery in the town that was still frequented by native peoples—some of whom allegedly enjoyed standing outside the Rahr home and listening to Natalie play the piano.

William began constructing a brewery almost immediately, though it is likely it was not in production until 1848. As one of the major agricultural businesses in the community, Rahr was an important buyer of barley and a provider of other staples, such as vinegar, which was "always on hand" at the brewery. While most brewers simply advertised the "highest market price," Rahr was much more specific in 1857, pledging to "pay 70 cents per bushel, one third in cash, one third in four months, and one third in six months, for which he will give approved notes drawing 10 per cent interest." Rahr's inability to pay the full amount in cash was probably related to the financial panic afflicting the nation at the time, and it is not recorded whether farmers were enticed by the possibility of earning interest rather than cash up front. For a brief period in the mid-1850s, Rahr had a partner named Rontauscher, but by the beginning of 1855 Rahr was sole proprietor again.

In June 1855, fire destroyed Rahr's brewery and home, despite the best efforts of the townsfolk to fight the fire. The *Manitowoc Tribune* praised their efforts: "The manner in which a number of ladies stepped into the line and assisted in passing buckets of water, would have been gratifying to the most enthusiastic advocate of Women's Rights, and their example was not lost on those of the stronger sex, who behaved with the cool steadiness of veteran firemen." Even though his insurance reportedly had just run out, Rahr's success to that point ensured he would have little difficulty raising capital to rebuild. Rahr's advertising in the early 1870s was more like that of a large Milwaukee firm than a country brewery. In 1871, he proclaimed he furnished "the several kinds of Beer of the Best Quality in any quantity, at the lowest price." While the "several kinds" were not listed, it still indicates a wide range of products, and the reference to low prices was unusual this early. Rahr was an early adopter of bottled beer—the 1878 atlas of Manitowoc County (probably compiled in 1877) listed him as "Brewer, Maltster, Manufacturer and Bottler of Export Beer." The distinction made here is interesting—implying that bottled beer was a manufactured product whereas draught beer was brewed. At the time, this would have been viewed as application of science and industry, rather than a abandonment of craft tradition.

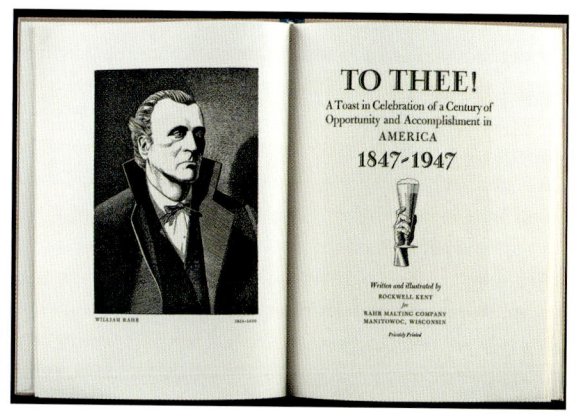

By the early 1880s, Rahr's brewery was by far the largest brewery in its area, brewing over 4,000 barrels a year. The company's ever-expanding malting operations were shipping to major breweries in St. Louis. But the company and family suffered a tragedy in 1880

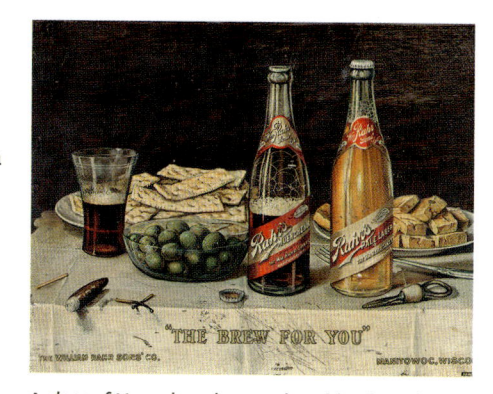

The title page of Rockwell Kent's *To Thee!* included a portrait of William Rahr at left. After *To Thee!* was published, Kent, a socialist, came under attack for his views; he won the Supreme Court case *Kent v. Dulles*, which restored his right to travel. Much of his writing celebrated America and freedom. AUTHOR'S COLLECTION.

A glass of Muenchner beer and a table of snacks are featured in this still life (ca. 1905). The bottle opener could also serve as a stopper. COURTESY OF NATIONAL BREWERY MUSEUM.

WISCONSIN BREWERIES AND BREWPUBS 481

when William Rahr fell into a brewkettle while inspecting the plant and suffered burns from which he never recovered. Rahr's sons William, Maximilian, and Reinhardt continued the brewery in his honor under the name William Rahr Sons (sometimes printed as William Rahr's Sons) and maintaining the Eagle Brewery name for the time being. They incorporated as the William Rahr Sons' Co. in 1893 with the three sons and Frank A. Miller as directors. While the brewery continued to operate, the malting part of the business became more important and was among the industry leaders in adopting new technology. The company was the first to install a scientific malt testing laboratory and in 1906 doubled capacity of the Manitowoc plant from one million to two million bushels per year. The company also acquired patents for roasted and caramel malts (caramel refers to the color) as well as for a malt coffee which became popular in France, and established a roasting department to create these products.

The factory continued to grow during the next decades, including a $250,000 addition in 1910 that occupied an entire block of Sixth Street. Rahr also added a sales office in New York and a large elevator in Minneapolis, the center of the nation's grain business. By 1913, the company had a capacity of five million bushels per year, offered specialty malts such as Black, Amber and Vienna in addition to their pale base malt, and shipped to breweries all over the country. The company did business under several different names during this period, including Manitowoc Malting Co. and Gould Grain Co. (in Minneapolis).

World War I forced the breweries of Manitowoc to reevaluate their position even before Prohibition arrived. In order to comply with wartime restrictions, William Rahr Sons' Brewing, Schreihart Brewing, and Kunz-Bleser Brewing merged into a single corporation that would be known as Manitowoc Breweries Co. The new firm included officers from each of the companies—Maximilian Rahr represented his company on the board. The new combination planned to close one of the breweries, two of the bottling houses, and eliminate other duplications that would create savings in fuel, ammonia, labor and grain. Since Rahr was already looking more to malt production, it made sense for that brewery to close. During Prohibition, the company changed its name to Cereal Products Co. (Cepro). With brewing illegal the value of the company and its assets was sharply lower.

In 1932, as many in the industry sensed that Prohibition's days were numbered, the company changed its name back to Rahr Malting Co. In 1934 the company added a major addition in Manitowoc, but in 1936 built "the most modern malthouse in America" in Shakopee, Minnesota. The Manitowoc facility continued to be operated by the family for nearly three decades and Rahr Malting remained an important corporate citizen for many years. In addition to employment and sponsorships, Rahr employees were recognized in experts in all their fields. At the 1939 Vocational Guidance Day at Lincoln High School, Rahr personnel represented the accounting and chemistry professions. Rahr Malting sold its plant in Manitowoc in 1961 to Anheuser-Busch, and moved its headquarters to the Shakopee plant.

Rahr Malting is one of the largest malt producers in the world, with malthouses in Shakopee and Alix, Alberta, as well as a 4,000,000-bushel elevator complex in Taft, North Dakota.

Charles Hottelman (1849–1865?)
H. George Kunz (1865?–1872)
Elizabeth Kunz (1872)
J. & P. Schreihart? (1872–73)
Frederick Pautz & Co. (1873?–1879)
Fred Pautz (1879–1883)
Grotch & Seidel (?)
Kunz, Bleser & Co. (1890–1913)
Kunz-Bleser Co. (1913–18)
Manitowoc Breweries Co. Plant B.
Manitowoc Products (1919–1933)
Kingsbury Breweries Co. (branch) (1933–1950)
902–910 MARSHALL

(The Hottelman era is covered in chapter 2.)

Heinrich George Kunz, who had previously been a brewer at his brother-in-law's plant in Branch and in Roeff's brewery in Manitowoc, purchased the brewery around 1865. Christian Scheibe was Kunz's partner for a few months before Scheibe moved to Centerville. Kunz came from a large family of brewers in Untergroeningen, Germany, and their Lammbrauerei (Lamb Brewery) is still in operation as of 2019. H. George Kunz died in 1872 at age 42, and his widow Elizabeth maintained the brewery for a short time. She sold the brewery to her brother (and H. George's cousin as well as brother-in-law) Gottfried Kunz, who still owned the brewery in Branch. Gottfried may have bought the brewery to help the family, but whatever the reason, he did not operate the brewery but instead sold it to Freidrich Pautz, a local teamster. The excise records list J. & P. Schreihart as the proprietors of this brewery, and while John Schreihart is known to have worked there in 1872, they are unlikely to have owned the property (though they may have rented it briefly). Pautz ran the brewery successfully for several years (with Schreihart as the "& Co.,"), making a dramatic jump in production from 926 barrels in 1878 to 1,345 the next year. But Schreihart left in 1879 to run his own brewery, and even though Pautz still produced almost a thousand barrels in 1882, by 1883 he was in financial trouble. The brewery was foreclosed, and Pautz went out of business.

Louis Kunz II followed his brother H. George to America and ended up in Manitowoc by way of New Orleans. (His traveling companions included the Eulberg brothers, later brewers in Portage.) After working for a time at his brother's brewery, he sought employment at Phillip Best Brewing Co. to advance his skills. About a year later he took over as brewmaster at the Kunz brewery in Branch, and then moved back into Manitowoc to work with John Schreihart at his new brewery. After about six years there (covered under that business), Kunz and Daniel Bleser purchased the former Pautz brewery, which had lain dormant for several years. One county history claims that Kunz and Bleser purchased a brewery from Grotch and Seidel, but the latter appear in no industry directories and may have been real estate brokers rather than brewers.

An early example of a resealable bottle cap.
COLLECTION OF TYE SCHWALBE.

The brewery suffered a fire in December 1895 that started in the machinery department and caused several thousand dollars loss, which was reportedly covered by insurance. This plant was rebuilt, but the company built an all-new brewery in 1905, and converted the old brewery into an expanded bottling house. The new brewery was powered by electricity as well as the usual "modern machinery and every convenience for the business." Among these machines was an "electric cleansing apparatus for use in currying and brushing horses," with battery-powered brushes which was supposed to supposed to remove dirt from the brewery's twenty-four horses in one tenth the time it would take by hand. This device was considered "in thorough keeping with the progressiveness of the institution." The company also opened depots around the region to distribute their beer more efficiently.

The prosperity of this brewery was demonstrated in 1902 when Daniel B. Bleser purchased one of the first two automobiles in Manitowoc, which had to be shipped from New York. The brewery also threw a grand picnic for all employees and friends of the brewery in 1910 to celebrate the twenty-fifth anniversary of the partnership.

During World War I, the Kunz, Bleser brewery became Manitowoc Breweries, Plant B, and remained in production until Prohibition took effect. Daniel Bleser died in 1921, having turned his interest in the company over to his sons. During the dry period, the company changed its name to Manitowoc Products, and began to produce near beer. The company developed one of the few commercially successful near beers—Kingsbury Pale, using a recipe acquired from the Winnipeg brewery Pelissier's Limited. The Cedar Rapids, Iowa distributor, "Heinie" Jensen, claimed to have sold nearly two million bottles of Pale in 1931 just in his territory. The product was so successful that Manitowoc Products was compelled to add capacity at both newly acquired Sheboygan plants as well as the Manitowoc facility—one of the rare brewery expansions during Prohibition. Kingsbury Pale was one of the few near beers to be distributed across the country, a fact that was to shape the goals of the company after beer returned.

Manitowoc Products breweries were among those that were able to provide beer on 7 April 1933, having made an easy transition from Kingsbury Pale Brew to Kingsbury Pale Beer. However, the company had much grander plans than simply supplying the region. During the summer of 1933, Daniel C. Bleser announced plans to expand the existing breweries in Sheboygan, exercise options on breweries in Pennsylvania and California, and change the name of the company to Kingsbury Breweries. This would be less limiting than a place name not widely known outside the Lake Michigan region. While the headquarters of the company would remain in Manitowoc (in an expanded office building) the reach of the new company would be national. Bleser took the unusual and newsworthy step of having the new incorporation documents flown to Madison and back so the company could begin operations under its new name on 1 July. Kingsbury listed its stock on the Boston, Chicago and New York stock exchanges—another bold move that emphasized the goal of being a truly national business. The idea of a west coast brewery seemed like the solution to the high cost of shipping beer to California (45¢ per case), and at one point Bleser was compelled to deny rumors that the company was preparing to build a $1 million brewery in Los Angeles.

However, the rapid expansion of Kingsbury Breweries largely left the Manitowoc plant on Ninth and Marshall behind. The brewery had little room to expand and, unlike the two Sheboygan facilities, was not located on a railroad spur, which increased the time and cost to prepare beer for shipment. At first, the Manitowoc brewery was essential for providing extra capacity for large orders such as the thirty-two rail cars of beer sent to Nebraska in August 1933, but the majority of production took place at the former Gutsch and Schreier plants. While there were no publicly released figures comparing production between Sheboygan and Manitowoc, all the expansion and effort was at the Sheboygan location. Sometime in early 1950 operations were shut down at the Manitowoc facility, though the offices remained there until 1963 when Kingsbury was purchased by Heileman. The brewery at Ninth and Marshall, which still bore signs of the Kunz-Bleser era, was razed later that year.

Manitowoc Products continued to make Banquet Tonic for a few years after Prohibition ended. It was unusual for malt tonic to be packaged in something other than the standard tonic bottle. This may have been a temporary solution to a bottle shortage.
COLLECTION OF JOHN STEINER.

Roeffs & Hagen (1854?–59)
John Roeffs (1859?–1866)
Albert Wittenberg? (1867?–1871?)
Frank Willinger? (1871?)
Charles Schirbe? (1871?–72?)
Thurm & Carl (1875?–76?)
J. Richter? (?–1878)

"Foot of Eighth Street" (modern site of Manitowoc Lincoln H. S.)

John Roeffs and George Hagen started their brewery in Manitowoc sometime prior to 1857, and one county history puts the date as early as 1854. In May 1859 the partners split and Roeffs continued the business until he died in 1866. His widow was left in debt, and most of the property was transferred to relatives in Germany who had been supporting the brewery. Mrs. Roeffs continued operating the brewery at least long enough to join Rahr and Kunz in advertising for the return of their empty kegs in September 1866.

The history of this particular site is not clear thereafter. *American Breweries II* lists Charles Schirbe as the next proprietor at this site, but there is no contemporary local confirmation. The successor was Albert Wittenberg, who appears in the excise records in September 1867 and the *Manitowoc Pilot* confirmed that Wittenberg had come from Two Creeks to take over the brewery. He was still in the 1870 population census as a brewer, as well as in the industrial census of that year, producing 460 barrels. Frank Willinger is offered as Wittenberg's successor in *AB2*, but there is no clear line of succession, and no date is given for Willinger's brewery in a 1904 county history. (Willinger was also a partner of Schreihart for a brief period much later and owner of a beer hall that became Courthouse Pub)

It is also possible that the Thurm and B. Carl listed in Schade's 1876 directory were associated with this site. J. Richter was listed as having brewed 589 barrels in 1878, but nothing the next year.

Lincoln High School was later built on the site of the brewery, which was known locally as Roeff's Hill.

William Fricke (1862–1870?)
Carl Fricke (1871?–79)
John Schreihart (1879–1884)
Schreihart & Kunz (1884–85)
Kunz & Bleser (1885–1890)
Schreihart Brewing Co. (1891–1918)
Manitowoc Breweries Co. Plant a (1918–19)

Tenth and Washington

William Fricke is credited with founding in 1862 the brewery that eventually became Schreihart Brewing Co. *One Hundred Years of Brewing* realistically claims that Fricke produced one hundred barrels in that first year. At some point the brewery passed to Carl (or Charles) Fricke, who was listed as proprietor in an 1872 map of the county. The Fricke brewery was the smallest in the city, producing only 143 barrels in 1871 and 268 the next year. Carl Fricke last appears in production records in 1878, when he produced 320 barrels. Both William and Charles were interested in other businesses as well, and these other businesses usually determined how they were listed in directories or credit reports.

In 1879, the brewery was acquired by John Schreihart, an experienced brewer who devoted more time to the business. By 1882 production was over 2,000 barrels, making him second only to Rahr in the area. When Louis Kunz II returned from Milwaukee and Branch, he rejoined Schreihart at his new brewery. In 1885, Schreihart left for an extended European trip, and leased the brewery to Kunz for the five years of his planned absence. Kunz brought in his friend Daniel B. Bleser to help run the business.

Upon Schreihart's return in 1890, he formed a new firm with Frank Willinger and Gustave Mueller, though Willinger left the firm the next year. In 1898, Schreihart advertised the brewery for sale in brewing journals, though he ended up retaining it. Schreihart and Mueller continued together until the firm was incorporated as Schreihart Brewing Co. in 1904, even though that name had been in use since 1890. In 1918, he built the Schreihart Block building at the corner of Tenth and Washington (which still exists as of 2017 and is recognizable by the heart on the upper façade of the building).

The brewery continued to upgrade its facilities, in particular by adding a 25-ton ice machine in 1900. In 1911, John Schreihart retired from active management and his son Henry J. and his son-in-law Charles Kulnick (who had purchased Mueller's shares) took over the business. Even as new generations of leadership took over, the founders were still fixtures at the brewery. John's older brother Peter continued to visit the office nearly every day to consult with the staff, even after his ninetieth birthday (he died in 1920 aged 95).

When the three Manitowoc breweries combined in 1918 (see the Rahr section), Schreihart Brewing Co. became Manitowoc Breweries, Plant A, and continued for the few remaining months of legal brewing. Charles Kulnick, formerly treasurer and manager of Schreihart, became president of the new company and Otto Senglaub became assistant secretary. When Prohibition arrived, the Schreihart brewery was converted to manufacture ice cream and soft drinks in the renamed Manitowoc Products Corp. The brewery did not return to beer production after Prohibition, since Manitowoc Products under its new Kingsbury Breweries name centered most of the brewing in its more efficient

Schreihart Brewing Company's logo, used on buildings as well as labels, was "Schrei-" inside a heart. Wiener or Vienna beer is an amber-colored lager that was produced by many Wisconsin breweries before Prohibition. Collection of John Steiner.

plants in Sheboygan. The Manitowoc Products name was retained by the new dairy subdivision of the company and the plant on Tenth and Washington continued to make ice cream.

Joseph Hoyer (1869?–1871?)

Joseph Hoyer was a saloon owner who appears to have operated a small brewery for a few years—probably at his saloon. (He was also listed as a pop manufacturer in the R. G. Dun & Co. records.) His brewery was certainly on a small scale, and he never appeared in the excise records. Entries for Hoyer in the Dun records have him as a saloonkeeper (and butcher) at other times.

Zinns & Schmidt (1872?–1873?)

John F. Zinns and Henry Schmidt so far are known only from their listing in the 1873 *American Brewers' Guide*. They produced 134 barrels in fiscal 1872.

Edward Hollander (1869?–1870?)
Christian Fick (& Co.) (1870?–72)
Fick & Hollander (1872–75)
Christian Fick (1875–76?)
Christian Dobert (1879–1880)
Engels Brewing Co. (1880–84?)

WASHINGTON NEAR 20TH OR 21ST STREETS

The origins of this brewery are obscure, but Edward Hollander was listed as a brewer in the 1870 population census (with real estate worth $3,000, so it is unlikely he was working for another brewer). Christian Fick (sometimes Frick) first appears in the Dun & Co. credit reports in 1870, and this source also records the change of names to Fick and Hollander and back again, though other sources only list Fick. This brewery increased production from 126 to 336 barrels from 1871 to 1872, and Fick maintained production just under 500 barrels in 1874 and 1875.

While no explicit proof has been found, locations given in city directories suggest that Engels Brewing Co. followed Fick. Christian Dobert was a tannery owner who provided much of the capital for Engels and was sometimes listed in industry directories as the proprietor. Engels only purchased enough stamps in 1881–82 to cover about one hundred barrels of beer, and apparently went out of business soon after. There is an obscure reference in the *Milwaukee Daily Journal* to an 1883 fire at "Schultz's brewery" in Manitowoc. Since no other Schultz brewery is known there, it is possible that Schultz was renting or leasing Engel's brewery at the time.

Peter Schwarzenbart, Weiss Beer Brewery (1899?–1901?)

FRANKLIN BETWEEN TENTH AND ELEVENTH

On the opposite side of the block from Schreihart Brewing Co., Peter Schwarzenbart ran a short-lived weiss beer brewery. Unlike many other weiss beer breweries, which used a no-boil method, Schwarzenbart had a weiss beer kettle that was shown on the Sanborn insurance maps. While he was listed as a weiss beer brewer on the 1900 map, by 1906 his business was listed only as a "Pop Factory" and the kettle was "not used." Schwarzenbart was listed as a weiss beer brewer in the 1900 industry directory, but not in 1905.

Riverview Brewing Co. (1933–37)

1100–1106 SOUTH WATER STREET

Riverview Brewing Co. was one of the rare post-Prohibition breweries not housed in an earlier brewery—Julius Graff and Theodore Fricke remodeled an old canning factory. The company had its Malt City beer on draught in taverns by the end of August, advertised as "just a little bit better than the beer you have thought to be the best." Riverview also emphasized that it was "employing all local men" and echoed the slogan of the National Recovery Administration that they would "'do our part' to help spread employment at fair wages."

The initial response encouraged the company to add more storage tanks in October to double capacity, as well as to offer a special holiday brew in December. Riverview also released their bock beer in March 1934. Bottled beer was not available until November 1934, when Malt City Pale made its debut. Two years later, the brewery advertised "3 Ways to a Merrier Christmas": Malt City Export (at $1.85 per case), and Malt City Regular Beer or Bock Beer (at $1.65 per case). While almost every brewery had a "regular" beer, it was very rare for it actually be named that. Bock beer was a spring tradition, so its appearance at Christmas suggests that Riverview may have been desperate to increase sales. That desperation was even more apparent the next February when the company offered two cases of Export for $2.85, but noted "All Sales made under this Offer are for Cash only." Riverview Brewing went into bankruptcy a few months later, and the property was sold at auction for a mere $200 to Ed Schreihart, who held the mortgage.

Bleser Brewing Co. (1937–1942)

1004 WASHINGTON STREET

The return of the Bleser family to brewing in Manitowoc was announced in late November 1936, with the formation of the Bleser Brewing Co. The new firm was to occupy the plant of the former Manitowoc Brewing Co. Plant A, previously Schreihart Brewing Co. and the brewery where president Daniel C. Bleser's father Daniel B. Bleser entered the business in 1885. The junior Bleser, who had been born in a house on the site of the brewery, had been president and manager of Kingsbury Breweries, but he retired from that company in 1934. Bleser hired his son-in-law Harold Alt as the brewmaster and immediately

The perforations on the label indicate that this bottle was filled May 14, 1935. Lightning stoppers were most popular before the development of the crown cap, but some breweries used them for picnic bottles after Prohibition. The closure helped maintain freshness if drinkers did not finish the beer at first serving. COURTESY OF NATIONAL BREWERY MUSEUM.

began remodeling operations that would create a brewery of 75,000 to 100,000 barrel capacity. Bleser lured former Kunz, Bleser Co. administrator Arthur H. Senglaub away from Kingsbury to manage the office. The brewery began distribution in June 1937, and the proposed reach of the company was signified by the presence of vice-president George Deegan, who specialized in sales and was to be stationed in Chicago to supervise the move into that potentially lucrative market. Bleser Brewing eventually shipped beer to Kansas, but it is not known if they had any success in the Windy City. The first beer was Bleser Better Beer, which came out first in draught and by July it was available in "Steinie" bottles. The beer was made with union labor, and the barley used was also malted by union members. Even before they began distributing beer, the company was offering to sell wet brewers' grains to farmers (as opposed to larger breweries which sold dried grains).

The Bleser family had been active in community affairs for decades, and Bleser Brewing joined many other brewers in sponsoring bowling teams and community events. The company's Arthur Senglaub represented the brewing trades during Vocational Guidance Day at Lincoln High School. They introduced Gold Coast Pale Beer in 1939 as a premium beer, and acquired the Empire label from the defunct Bechaud brewery in Fond du Lac. However the company was having some quality control problems and had to give refunds and dump beer due to "over-pasteurization and mishandling." Daniel C. Bleser died in November 1939, and the company's financial trouble resulted in a declaration of insolvency, but the brewery was allowed to continue operations. They hoped to secure additional markets for their beer in Nashville, Tennessee, but production continued to decline. In 1941, Bleser Brewing Co. offered a set of twenty "cookbooklets" which could be purchased for 10¢ and three Gold Coast bottle caps. During the early years of World War II, the brewery fell in line with wartime conservation measures by encouraging customers to buy the "Economy Size" 32-ounce bottles, which would save tin, steel and cork by using fewer crowns. Unfortunately, the brewery was still in shaky financial condition, and the pressures of the wartime economy forced the brewery to close in late summer 1942.

Courthouse Pub (2001–present)
1001 South Eighth Street

F. Willinger's Beer Hall was built around 1885 (some accounts claim as early as 1860) on a site near Manitowoc's historic county courthouse. (A large photo of the beer hall—featuring signs advertising the beer of both Wm. Rahr's Sons and Kunz, Bleser & Co.—decorates the wall behind the bar.) The current building was built in 2001, and maintained some of the feel of the Colonial Inn, one of the restaurants that occupied the space after Willinger closed due to Prohibition. Owner John Jagemann wanted to offer handcrafted beer to match the handcrafted food, so he brought in Brent Boldt to brew a variety of beers on the four-barrel extract system. The beer menu at Courthouse Pub changes regularly, so there really is no particular flagship beer. In deference to the history in Manitowoc, many of the Courthouse Pub beers have been lagers. Perhaps the most noteworthy beer was the project to brew a version of Two Rivers Beverage Company's White Cap beer in 2006. Courthouse Pub is known for its wine list, which has won numerous awards from *Wine Spectator* magazine.

Manitowoc Rapids
(Manitowoc County)

Schmidt & Son (1872–74)
Martin Schmidt, Silver Lake Brewery (1874–78)
Near Modern US Highway 151 near Silver Lake (NE quarter of SE quarter of Section 33, Manitowoc Rapids Township)

According to one account, Martin Schmidt and his son Alexander started a brewery near Silver Lake, in Manitowoc Rapids Township, in 1872, "where a profitable business was conducted for sixteen months. . . ." Business jumped from 115 barrels the first year to 670 two years later. The rest of Alexander's story is covered under De Pere.

Martin continued to brew in Manitowoc County for a few more years. The R. G. Dun and Co. representative reported in 1875 and 1876 that he was doing a nice business, but that by 1878 the property was in the hands of the sheriff and Schmidt was out of business.

Marathon *(Marathon County)*

Marathon City Brewing Co. (1881–89)
Frank R. Sindermann (1889–1896)
Stuhlfauth Bros. (1896–1900)
Marathon City Brewing Co. (1901–1965)
Marathon Brewing, Inc. (1965–66)
Pine and Second Streets

Frank R. Sindermann started his brewery on the banks of Rib River in 1881. At first he was in partnership with his brother August and Charles Klein, but Frank later bought out his partners. (Having family around may have worried Frank, especially considering a later incident in 1892 when his intoxicated brother Franz started shooting through a partition and one bullet grazed Frank's skull.) The capacity during the first two decades was listed variously in industry directories as between 500 and 1,000 barrels per year. Sindermann died sometime between 1896 and 1898, and the company was sold to the Stuhlfauth brothers, Oscar and George. The Stuhlfauths met with bad luck during their ownership: a new cellar they built shortly after purchasing the brewery collapsed from the weight of the ice, and the ice machine they purchased developed an ammonia leak which ruined the beer in storage. The brewery was foreclosed and the Stuhlfauths declared bankruptcy.

At this point, accounts of the ownership changes differ slightly. Most accounts have Nicholas Schmidt purchasing the brewery at this point, however an article in the *Marshfield Times* in January 1902 about the purchase indicates that Michael Duerstein had purchased the brewery at the sheriff's sale, and then sold it to Nicholas Schmidt and Fred Brand (Brandt). It appears that Duerstein did not operate the brewery, since the article reported these two men from Chicago were "practical brewers" and hoped "they

Marathon City Brewing used virtually identical labels for Tannenbaum Beer before and after Prohibition. This is pre-Prohibition; the 1930s version included the U-permit number and other required statements. COLLECTION OF TYE SCHWALBE.

will put the plant in shape" and "have it in full operation in a few weeks." Nicholas Schmidt ended up being elected to the State Assembly in 1906, and eventually sold his share of the firm. Among the other brewery officials in the early 1900s were Michael Duerstein and August Sindermann, both of whom were previous owners. The brewery's most popular beer was Tannenbaum—which originally was supposed to have been named after Richard Wagner's opera Tannhäuser. The labels and advertisements came printed with the wrong name, but the brand proved popular and the company never bothered to change it.

The brewery burned in 1912, and the directors considered rebuilding in Wausau, closer to the center of population in the county. However they built a new brick building on the original location and were back in production the next year. The first years in the new brewery were generally uneventful as the company struggled to pay off the debt, but the company began to turn a profit by the time of World War I—just in time to be put out of business by Prohibition. The company made near beer for a short time, but was closed by the government because their product was in excess of the ½ percent allowed by law.

Marathon City Brewing Co. was brewing again in 1933, and under Fred Brand re-established itself as a relatively successful local brewery. For the first decade production was typically around 10,000 barrels, though production reached 22,000 barrels in 1949. After this peak, it dropped back to the 10,000-barrel range, and remained there until the early 1960s. Marathon's Tannenbaum beer was a local favorite through World War II but later was replaced by Marathon Lager and other brands. Probably the most popular package was Wee Willie, the 8-ounce version of bottled Marathon Lager. Ironically, the name Little Willie was used for the larger picnic bottles. The brewery sponsored a semi-pro basketball team in the 1940s and 1950s that first was called the Marathon Lagers, but from 1946 to 1955 they were known as the Wee Willies and bottles of the namesake beer were sold at home games. (This was a strange name for a basketball team, especially for one that won about 90 percent of their games.) The brewery sponsored the usual bowling teams, and the more unusual Tannenbaum Beer hockey team. Marathon City also produced a wide variety of openers, pens, and other promotional items ranging from wallets to fly swatters.

Carl Lins, president and brewmaster since 1943, retired in 1956 and was replaced as brewmaster by Howard Ruff, former brewmaster at the recently defunct People's Brewing Co. of Duluth, Minnesota. (Ruff was best known for formulating the brand that would eventually be called Olde English 800.) Local sources suggest that the company's beer was not very consistent in the later years, and in some cases the brewery ran out of their own beer and had to fill draught orders with kegs filled at Oshkosh Brewing Co. with what was really Chief Oshkosh beer.

In 1965, the troubled brewery was sold to three local businessmen: Francis Rondeau, Philip Knauf, and Bernard Knauf (sometimes recorded inaccurately as Knaus). They had the task of reinvigorating a business that was only producing about 6,000 barrels a years in a plant capable of 20,000. They brought back Tannenbaum—packaged in green bottles they were able to obtain at a discount. The bottles proved popular, but they were unable to get any more of them, sales slumped again, and the brewery closed for good in 1966. The nearby Figi Brewing Co. in Marshfield purchased the Tannenbaum and Superfine brands and produced them for less than a year before it closed as well.

MARINETTE *(Marinette County; then Oconto County)*

Rodabaugh, Wesley & Co. (1867–68)
Rodabaugh & Anderson (1868–1869?)
G. Anderson & Co. (1869?–1872)
HALL AVENUE

Based on excise tax records, Rodabaugh, Wesley & Co. began brewing near the Traversy House in Fall 1867. By April 1868, Wesley was no longer with the firm and was replaced by Gustaff Anderson—one of the rare Swedish brewers of the era.

In the 1870 industrial census, G. Anderson & Co. reported production of approximately 425 barrels by his three employees. His partner at this point appears to have been Matthew Phillipps, a Prussian. The brewery burned on New Years' Day 1872, and the cause of the fire was "shrouded in mystery."

Swedish Brewing Co. (1898–99)
NEAR OGDEN AND BAY SHORE

In January 1898, newspapers around the state reported that a new brewery was planned for

This sign is most likely from the 1940s, based on the dress and hairstyle of the model and the shape of the pilsner glass. COLLECTION OF DAVID WENDL.

Marinette. The *Oshkosh Daily Northwestern* reported that "[L]ocal parties are preparing to build a $50,000 brewery at Marinette in the spring," and the *Weekly Wisconsin* indicated that Gustave Reinke was the leader of the enterprise. These appear to herald the creation of what became the Swedish Brewing Co. under its proprietors C. F. Bergenheim, Willliam Moe, and Fred Holt. Under the name of C. F. Bergenheim, the firm reported to the excise collectors that they brewed seventy-five barrels from May to October 1899. This report was in June 1900, and since no further production was recorded, it is likely that the brewery closed at this time. The 1900 census listed Bergenheim as a malt extract manufacturer, rather than a brewer, and Moe and Holt both had other occupations.

Rail House Restaurant & Brewpub (1994–present)
W 1130 Old Peshtigo Road (1994–97)
2029 Old Peshtigo Road (1997–present)

In 1898, Leisen & Henes Brewery of Menominee, Michigan, purchased a building in Marinette from the Chicago and Northwestern Railroad to use as a depot for the beer they were shipping into Wisconsin. In 1992, Paul and Courtney Monnette purchased the building and brought in their son-in-law, Rick Sauer, to start brewing in 1994. Rail House became so popular they needed a much larger space. In 1997 they built the current Rail House location.

Under current owner Ron Beyer and brewmaster Kris Konyn, Rail House typically has ten to twelve house beers on tap at a given time, including several that pay homage to beers brewed in the area in the years after Prohibition, such as Silver Cream, Oconto Premium, and Brewers' Best Pilsner. Several of these were bottled on a small scale beginning in 2006. Output is generally about 250–300 barrels per year.

Marion *(Shawano County)*

Pigeon River Brewing Co. (2012–present)
W12710 U.S. Highway 45 (2012–16)
1103 North Main Street (2016–present)

Pigeon River Brewing Co. opened for business on 18 July 2012, a date selected specifically to honor the feast day of St. Arnold of Metz, the patron saint of brewers. Nathan Knaack, Matt Wichman, and Brett Hintz came together over their love of homebrewing and decided, along with Nathan's wife Kayla, to start a brewpub in Marion, where Nathan and Matt both grew up (though somehow without ever meeting each other).

Pigeon River beers took a while to catch on with residents used to Bud Light, but after a couple of years became so popular that they installed a bottling line to sell several of the year-round beers at other establishments. However, the bottling line put too much of a strain on their original location, so in 2016 Pigeon River Brewing moved just across the street and around the corner to a spot inside NorthWinds Banquet Hall. The new location made it possible to use a forklift to move pallets of bottles around, and also provided increased kitchen space for the brewpub.

Markesan *(Mackford)* *(Green Lake County)*

John Hale (1856?–1868?)

John Hale appears as a brewer in the 1857 state directory, but could have been brewing earlier. The native of England operated his small brewery for at least a decade, probably with his son Edward as the only other employee. The only known production figures are for 8¼ barrels in August 1867. He is known to have been in business as late as 1868; in the 1870 census he is listed as a farmer, though this does not necessarily mean that he did not still brew occasionally.

Marshfield *(Wood County)*

Scheibe & Schneider (1890–93)
Marshfield Brewing Co. (1893–1966)
J. Figi Brewing Co., Inc. (1966–67)
509 North Pine Street

(While some sources list Mathias Bourgeois as a brewer in Marshfield in the late 1870s and early 1880s, his was the Mt. Calvary brewery in Marshfield Township, Fond du Lac County, and not in the City of Marshfield.)

The Marshfield Brewing Co. provides excellent examples of two periods in Wisconsin's brewing history: breweries started in the period after bottling became commonplace and therefore had to start at a relatively large size, and small breweries that survived more than a few years after the repeal of Prohibition. When it finally closed in 1967, the Marshfield brewery was believed to be the smallest left in the country, but its survival to that point must be considered a success.

In September 1889, two experienced brewers, Emil Scheibe and Albert Schneider, were in Marshfield looking for a site for a proposed 5,000-barrel brewery. They had recently lost their brewery in Centreville to fire, and after first considering rebuilding there, and later at Brillion, they decided that Marshfield presented a better prospect. On this the Marshfield newspapers agreed, since they had been agitating for a brewery in the city for nearly ten years (not just the four years claimed in an article in the *Marshfield Times*). The *Times* claimed a brewery would employ "a large number of men and keep within our own boundaries at least $60,000, which now finds its way into the hands of Milwaukee and other brewers." Perhaps because of their experience in Centreville, Scheibe and Schneider elected to build their new brewery out of brick, not wood. In addition, since the brewery was built after ice house technology had advanced, it was not necessary to dig lagering caves for the brewery. This meant they could select a site based on water supply and access to transportation rather than needing to include caves in their calculations. By April 1890 the beer was ready, and the proprietors sought to build a market by soliciting "trial orders from dealers everywhere" and by urging potential customers to "Visit our Brewery when in the city." A later account claimed that forty-one barrels were sold on the first day of business. Scheibe and Schneider offered top prices to farmers for barley, hoping to eventually replace the supplies they were buying from Konrad Schreier in Sheboygan.

For the first year or two, sales were strong and the brewery expanded to meet demand. The *Times* reported that the brewery was making thirty barrels a day and "find a ready market for all they can make." The same article noted that capacity had been expanded to 20,000 barrels per year, and claimed (quite incorrectly) "the brewery is now second to none outside of Milwaukee in size." Size mattered, because a high level of sales was necessary to recoup the investment. Furthermore, it would have been extremely difficult for any firm starting at the farm or household brewery size to survive in an era when customers expected their beer to come from modern plants. In the late summer of 1892 the company installed a new seventy-five-barrel brewkettle and a new sixty horsepower boiler to increase capacity. Scheibe & Schneider released their bock beer in late April 1892 with the usual colorful posters and other promotional activities associated with the spring specialty. the company also engaged in a price war with Leinenkugel of Chippewa Falls to attract saloon accounts in areas between their breweries.

However, all the expansion seems to have plunged the company into debt. In February 1893, Scheibe & Schneider assigned the assets of the brewery to their creditors "due to heavy expenditures for improvement." The creditors met and proposed a stock company to buy the brewery and operate it, with each creditor getting shares in the company proportional to the amount they were owed. Emil Scheibe remained with the company, though Schneider did not. Within two years the new company had dramatically reduced the debt, and the outlook for the future looked bright. One of the main creditors, August F. Backhaus (or Backus), who was a hop dealer from Kewaskum, bought the entire controlling stock in 1894 and later moved his family to Marshfield to operate the brewery.

While the company engaged in mundane tasks like buying new filters and releasing bock each spring, a series of events were to put Marshfield Brewing Co. on the front pages for reasons both dramatic and tragic. In November 1896, Marshfield's labor unions boycotted the brewery's product after the foreman had discharged a union man. This dispute was resolved quickly, but the next event left a lasting mark on the community. In May 1897, Chief of Police Alf Gerwing and brewery employee Fred Meyers were both stabbed to death by four tramps who had been asked to leave the brewery grounds. After capture, the tramps had to be transferred to jail in another city to avoid being lynched for the murders. The misfortune continued the next year when a July storm tore down the smokestack from the brewery. The company was forced to raise prices by one dollar per barrel when the excise tax was increased by that amount to pay for the Spanish-American War, though all brewers were affected to some degree by this development. Another concern for Marshfield was also shared by other brewers—loss of cooperage. In 1901 the brewery was forced to establish as system by which purchasers of quarter- or eighth-barrel kegs were required to pay an additional 25¢, which would be returned when they brought the keg and rebate check back. As if all this wasn't enough, in June 1900 the employees went on strike demanding an additional 55¢ per month. While the dispute was settled quickly in favor of the workers, it was yet another distraction in a fiercely competitive market.

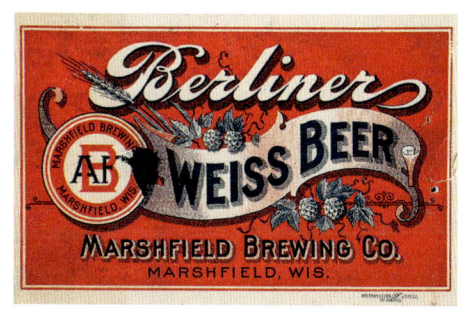

Weiss beer labels prior to Prohibition are rare, especially those designating the product as Berliner Weiss (ca. 1910). COLLECTION OF JOHN STEINER.

Under the ownership of A. F. Backhaus and his family, who had purchased all the stock in 1898, Marshfield Brewing Co. maintained the quality of its beer. The local press was quick to seize on any praise from outside sources, whether it was visitors to town who proclaimed the beer better than Pabst or a finding by the United States Health Reports (which was not a government agency) that claimed that the purity of Marshfield beer was excelled by none. After the brewery and the *Times* spun this report to read that their beer was of higher quality than that of Milwaukee, demand increased so much that the company decided to install a bottling house "to supply the goods ready for home use." Given the relatively large size at which the brewery started, it is somewhat surprising that they had not started bottling earlier. The new product met with success, and the brewery produced near its capacity of about 12,000 barrels for the next several years.

Unfortunately, tragedy continued to stalk Marshfield Brewing Co. In 1908 sales manager Otto Backhaus, son of the company president, was struck by a train and killed at age thirty-five. After A. F. Backhaus died the next year, the family decided to sell their stock to a group of investors, most of whom were "local capitalists and businessmen." However, there was an interesting subset of investors: representatives of Pabst, Schlitz and Miller each held $5,000 of the $65,000 capital stock. Unfortunately no documents exist to show why the Milwaukee breweries chose to invest together in a small brewery halfway across the state, but they must have thought the investment would give them either profit or control—though why three different breweries would make such an investment is not clear. Louis A. Hartl, a son-in-law of A. F. Backhaus, became president of the company and Herman C. Eiche, a former mayor of Marshfield who had been working for Blatz, returned to the city to take charge of operating the brewery.

The last years before Prohibition seem to have been much smoother for Marshfield

Brewing Co. The brewery continued to buy barley from local farmers, offering from 90¢ to $1.05 per bushel in 1911. The company remodeled the brewery in 1913 to double the capacity, and invited the public to an open house complete with brewery tours and refreshments. Eiche profited enough from his work that he could afford to buy a new five-passenger Buick in 1912. Eiche left the company in 1914, and management passed to Louis Hartl, who managed the brewery through Prohibition. In 1915 the brewery changed the name of its bottled brand to Preferred Stock, and introduced it with a newspaper advertising campaign.

During Prohibition, Marshfield Brewing Co. made a near beer called Preferred Stock brew, but as with most similar products, it was not a lucrative line for the company. The brewery also made malt products and soda water, but the brewery was raided in 1925 and 1927 for alleged violations of the Prohibition Act. Hartl considered selling the business to a dairy products company, but ended up holding on to the business.

Marshfield Brewing Co. was not among the brewers ready on 7 April 1933, but they were in operation shortly thereafter, which led to the most noteworthy tragedy in the brewery's history. On 5 August 1933, gangster violence reached Marshfield when reserve policeman Fred Beell was shot and killed while trying to thwart a robbery at the brewery. The burglars stole $1,550 in tax revenue stamps, which were sold at a discount to illicit bottlers who used them on beer from questionable sources including wildcat breweries. The tragedy was especially hard on the city because Beell was one of its most famous and popular residents, having won three world championships as a wrestler, and even had a move called the Beell

This flat Vitrolite glass sign was probably made by the Meyercord Company of Chicago around 1916. COURTESY OF NATIONAL BREWERY MUSEUM.

Throw named after him. (Beell is a member of the Wisconsin Athletic Hall of Fame and the stadium at Marshfield High School is named after him.) Two of the assailants were brought to trial and convicted, two others were believed to have died of injuries suffered in the shootout.

Despite the tragedy, Marshfield Brewing Co. continued to live the life of a typical small Wisconsin brewery. During the 1930s and 1940s, its production varied between about 10,000 barrels and 21,000 barrels per year. In 1939, Marshfield ranked twenty-sixth out of more than seventy Wisconsin breweries, though most of the breweries that produced less would close in short order. During the decade immediately after Prohibition, Marshfield was an active sponsor of community activities in the area, prominently advertised that the beer was union-made, and continued to offer bock beer in the spring until wartime restrictions put this tradition on hold. Marshfield also brewed a special beer during the winter, which was called Holiday Brew or Santa Claus Brew. After World War II, sales declined rapidly and after 1951 Marshfield never exceeded 10,000 barrels in a year. In the mid-1950s the main brand was Marshfield Premium, which was sold for a time with the same drawing of Paul Bunyan that was on the canned product of that name produced by Weber Waukesha. (Marshfield never produced canned beer.)

Louis Hartl passed away in July 1959, after fifty years at the helm of the company. His daughter Caroline Hartl Allen took over management of the brewery for the next six years until she sold it to John Figi Jr. in 1965. It remained the Marshfield Brewing Company for a year, but in 1966 changed its name to J. Figi Brewing Co. Figi acquired the Tannenbaum and Marathon labels from the nearby and recently closed Marathon Brewing Co. and launched a new brand, Figi's Certified Beer, which was distributed within a forty-mile radius. However, the timing was inauspicious, since between 1965 and 1967 nine of Wisconsin's twenty-four breweries closed. Figi's became one of the casualties in October 1967. At the time the brewery was reported to be the smallest in the nation, "with the possible exception of one in Honolulu." Figi turned his full attention back to "the world's largest mail order gift cheese business," and the brewing company became a distributor for Grain Belt beer from Minneapolis. The brewery was razed in 1981.

Central Waters Brewpub (2005–8)
Blue Heron Brewpub (2008–present)
108 WEST NINTH STREET

When Marshfield's brewpub opened, it was affiliated with Central Waters Brewing Co., then located in Junction City. When Central Waters moved to Amherst, the brewpub took the opportunity to create its own identity as Blue Heron. The brewpub is located in Parkin Place, the former headquarters of Parkin Dairy—locally famous for its fancy molded ice cream desserts.

Blue Heron beers range from simple lagers to barrel-aged ales. Blue Heron is noteworthy for its partnership with the Marshfield Area Society of Homebrewers (M*A*S*H), and features a rotating tap reserved for brews created at the brewpub in collaboration with club members.

This early coaster from Central Waters Brewpub was made of foam rubber. COLLECTION OF SCOTT REICH.

MARSHFIELD TOWNSHIP
(Fond du Lac County)

Carl De Haas (1848?–1850?)
WOLF LAKE

According to a county history from 1905, "The first brewery in this county was a small one built by Mr. De Haas, on the shore of Wolf Lake, in the town[ship] of Marshfield." To the annoyance of historians without time-traveling capability, he added, "Ex-Sheriff Kunz knows something about it." Wayne Kroll has identified Mr. De Hass as Dr. Carl de Haas, but almost nothing is known of his rustic brewery on what was then called de Haas Lake.

MAUSTON *(Juneau County)*

Maria Runkel (1868–1874)
Maria Runkel & Co. (1874–1886)
Runkel & Miller (1886–88)
Charles Miller (1888–1893)
Miller & Hauer (1893–1901)
J. Hauer Brewing Co. (1901–3)
John Hauer (1903–4)
J. Willems (1904–5)
Chas. Ellison, Mauston Brewery (1905–1914)
Mauston Brewery, Jos. Vogl (1911–16)
451 WINSOR STREET

The research of Richard D. Rossin Jr. is the definitive work on the Mauston brewery. Henry Runkel began to move his brewery from Germantown to the shore of Decorah Lake in Mauston in 1867, and by August of that year the cellars for lagering the beer were well under way. The first production reported in the excise records was twenty-three barrels in March 1868. Despite Henry Runkel remaining alive and well until 1905, the business and the property were in the name of his wife Maria. During the 1870s production was typically around 500 barrels per year, though they produced 630 barrels in 1872. The brewery had no malting facilities during the Runkel era.

In 1886, Maria Runkel sold a half share of the brewery to Charles Miller, who appears to have been a friend of the Runkels' son Philip. She sold the other half to Miller in 1888, who then ran the brewery on his own for about five years. In early 1893, he first advertised bottled beer for $1.80 a case. In 1893 Miller took on saloon owner John Hauer as a partner, and this partnership made significant improvements to the brewery. The most important addition was a malthouse, which would allow the brewery to make malt to its own specification, and also made the brewery a more significant part of the local economy.

The brewery then went through some financial trouble and several rapid ownership changes. It may have also been idle for a few years during Hauer's ownership, who seems to have concentrated on running his saloons. The brewery was subject to a sheriff's sale in 1904. The new proprietor Julius Willems was unable to sell enough beer to cover his investments in improvements, so the property went up for auction again in 1905. The next owner, Charles Ellison, brought some needed stability to the business. The brewery reportedly produced about 3,000 barrels of Special Brew and Pure Lager a year. Ellison sold the brewery to Joseph Vogl of South Germantown (and Vogl's Independent Brewery) in 1914. Vogl may have overextended himself by running two breweries, and he gave up both of them in 1916. The Mauston brewery ended up as property of the Juneau County State Bank. The brewery building was eventually purchased by the Hussa Canning and Pickle Co. of Bangor, and operated by them from 1918 until 1922 when the factory burned.

Instead of a delicate glass, Miller & Hauer offered customers this sturdy mug. A few breweries included the slogan "Farmers Friend" or "Workingman's Friend" on glassware. Very few artifacts from the Mauston brewery are known. COLLECTION OF TYE SCHWALBE.

MAYVILLE *(Dodge County)*

Benjamin Mayer (1853–55)
Martin Bachhuber (1855–1868)
John Henninger (1868–69)
Emeron Bachhuber (1869–1870)
Leonard Uhl (1870–1872?)
George Wurst (1872)
Matheus Ziegler (1874–1880)
Matheus Ziegler & Co. (1880–1892)
Matheus Ziegler Brewing Co. (1892–1920)
MAIN STREET

Benedict Mayer, a friend of Milwaukee founder Solomon Juneau, had worked as a brewer in Milwaukee, Theresa and New Fane (in Fond du Lac County) before moving to Mayville. Mayer started both a meat market and a brewery in 1853, but sold the brewery in 1855 to Martin Bachhuber.

Bachhuber's brewery was a small one, and since he was also a practicing veterinarian, he may have been a part time brewer. His two-person operation produced 300 barrels in 1860, beer that was sold at $6 per barrel. (Dodge County brewery historian Michael D. Benter indicates that Caspar Maedder was Bachhuber's brewmaster at this point, but the 1860 industrial census lists Maedder and Bachhuber as separate breweries with different statistics, which is strong evidence these were two different breweries.) In 1865 Bachhuber brought in as a partner John J. Kohl, a veteran of the 35th Wisconsin Infantry. The records of R. G. Dun & Co. suggest that Bachhuber remained in the background, since Kohl was the party listed in the credit reports (though with different initials). Kohl remained until 1867 or 1868, when he and Bachhuber sold the brewery to John Henninger, who had started another brewery in the city the previous decade. (Kohl would later start a brewery in Negaunee, Michigan, but would be shot and killed in the line of duty in 1885 while serving as deputy sheriff.) Henninger's ownership of this brewery only lasted about a year, before he sold it to Emeron Bachhuber, son of Martin. Emeron may not have been a trained brewer either, and it appears that Jacob Lehner (or Saemer or Sauner) was at least brewmaster, if not a full partner. (Jacob Lehner is listed in the excise reports in 1868 and 1869, and the timing and other entries suggest that he represents the Bachhuber brewery.) Benter reports that Leonard Uhls purchased the brewery in 1870, but he does not appear in the excise records until 1872, at which point local accounts say he had already sold it to George Wurst. There was a Leonard Uhl in Waukesha until 1871, but he may have purchased the brewery without making any beer until 1872. It is also possible that Wurst was unable to get the brewery going, because he does not appear in any government or industry records.

The brewery was revitalized when Matheusiegler and his sons Louis and Emil purchased the property in 1874. Ziegler owned a tavern in Mayville, and would retail his own beer for many years to come. Ziegler either had capital that his predecessors lacked, or was simply more willing to invest it in improving the brewery. Ziegler restored production to just over 300 barrels a year by the end of the 1870s, but then began to expand both production and retail. In 1879 he purchased a five-acre plot across the river from the brewery and established Ziegler Park. In 1889 the company built a three-story brick building including a tavern and beer garden on North Main Street where the old Ziegler saloon had been. Most importantly, in the summer of 1888 they tore down the old brewery and built a new steam-powered facility on the site of the old plant. To cement their position as Mayville's most modern brewery, the Zieglers added a bottling house in 1890.

When Matt Ziegler died in 1892, his sons were ready to take over the business. Louis and Emil, along with brother Eugene, incorporated the company in 1892 and retained the name of M. Ziegler Brewing Co. in honor of their late father. The brothers expanded the retail side of the business in Dodge County by establishing saloons in places like Brownsville and Rubicon. They also improved Ziegler Park, in particular by adding a footbridge from the brewery to the park that would make it easier to reach the new dance hall. Louis Ziegler expanded the family's reach even further in 1905 by purchasing the former Goeggerle brewery in Beaver Dam, and in 1912 by purchasing the Fox Lake Brewery (which he turned over to his son-in-law John Brodessor). Ziegler moved to Beaver Dam, but continued as president of M. Ziegler Brewing Co.

The Zieglers guarded their home territory jealously, especially since they were also in the saloon business. In 1894, another saloon owner brought in Milwaukee beer to serve at his establishment. Since the Ziegler's also owned Mayville's icehouse, they retaliated by refusing to sell the offender any ice. The dispute apparently divided the town for some weeks, and a traveling minstrel show even incorporated a joke about Eugene Ziegler into their act.

As prohibition seemed more likely, M. Ziegler Brewing diversified into distributing other products, including those of Pabst. When beer became illegal, Ziegler continued production of near beer at the Mayville plant for a brief time, but devoted most of his attention to his Beaver Dam operations. The brewery was used mostly as a warehouse for soft drinks and other product lines until Anna Ziegler, widow of Louis, sold the brewery in July 1933. It would then be purchased by the Mayville Brewing Co. and operate briefly after Prohibition

John Henninger (1855–1864)
Robert Kloeden or Kroesing & Co (1864–1877)
Funke Bros (1877–79)
Steger & Co. (1881–1918)
410 Short Street

John Henninger was a farmer and livestock dealer who opened the first butcher shop in Mayville. He also started a brewery around 1855 and ran it until 1864. (In 1868 he would briefly operate a different brewery in Mayville, covered under the M. Ziegler brewery.) Henninger's brewmaster was Florian Schmidt, an uncle of Henninger's wife Barbara. Henninger reported production of 500 barrels in the 1860 industrial census, which was the most of any of the three breweries in Williamstown, the township that contains Mayville (and the name by which this area was reported in the census through 1870).

Local historian Michael D. Benter has clarified much of the previous confusion of the next years of the brewery. Two brothers-in-law, Charles Kroesing Jr. and Robert Kloeden owned the brewery, and the changes between who was the proprietor of record in government documents or local sources do not actually indicate a change in ownership. This brewery is absent from the industry directories of the 1870s, and both proprietors had other business interests and were involved in local politics, so it is likely that the brewery was only a part time job. Eventually Kroesing and Kloeden rented the brewery to Ernest Funke Sr., who operated from about 1877 to 1879 as Funke Brothers Brewery.

The next owner, John Steger, was an experienced brewer who had the focus and ability to renovate and expand the brewery. Steger had worked at two breweries in Theresa and for

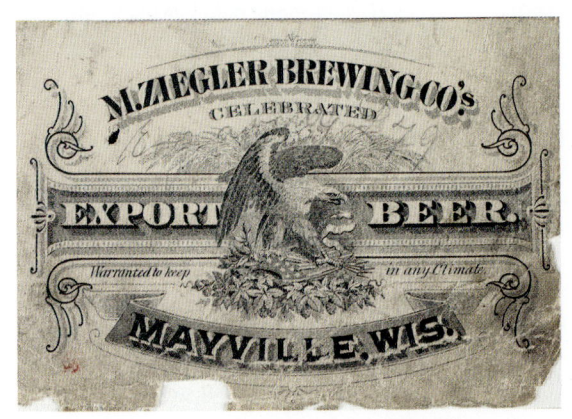

This Export Beer was simply a bottled product intended for local consumption. The label is likely from the early 1890s.
COLLECTION OF JOHN STEINER.

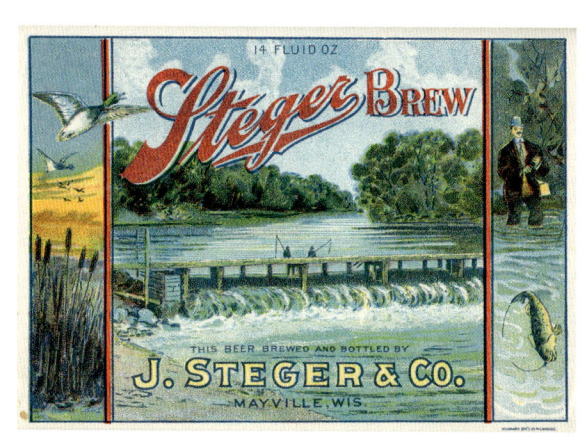

The Steger Brew label celebrated the good hunting and fishing to be found in Dodge County. (ca. 1910s) COLLECTION OF JOHN STEINER.

John Haas in Ripon, and with his new partner, Carl Anton Gerlach, Steger reinvigorated the Mayville plant. Brewery directories in the mid-1880s listed capacity between 1,000 and 1,500 barrels per year, and the new ownership added a malthouse early in their tenure. Gerlach remained with Steger until 1889, when he went into other businesses (including buying and selling the former Darge brewery).

Henry (Heinrich) Boehmer, Steger's father-in-law, replaced Gerlach in the brewery. Boehmer had been in the foundry and farm implement business, and brought business talent to the firm, though he seems to have come on board only briefly to help start the expansion, after which he returned to the foundry business. For the next several years the brewery was in a state of near constant expansion and improvement, including installation of steam power in the early 1890s. By 1912 the brewery consisted of seven buildings and a biergarten. That year, Steger added a bottling house with capacity of 15,000 bottles per day, though it is unlikely they ever ran at full production. As Benter has noted, this activity contributed to the local economy, as did the success of the business in general. Steger ordered beer wagons from local wagonmakers, advertising posters from local artists and, of course, barley from local farmers. John's son Henry trained to take over the business and became brewmaster at the family firm in the early 1910s. However, the advent of Prohibition brought an end to Steger & Co. John retired, and Henry went into other businesses.

The brewery, however, was not quite done. While parts of the brewery complex were used for other businesses, one group of entrepreneurs altered their wort manufacturing operation to make real beer, and the wildcat brewery was raided in 1927.

Caspar Maedder (1859?–1866?)
Fred Gutschow (1866?–1868)
Nagle & Cook (or Hook) (1868–69)

This group of brewers is something of a mystery. They are not covered in Michael D. Benter's comprehensive and well-documented book on the breweries of Eastern Dodge County, with the exception of Caspar Maedder, whom Benter includes as a brewmaster for Martin Bachhuber. However, Maedder had his own listing in the 1860 industrial census, which listed him as having brewed 180 barrels of beer to Bachhuber's 300. In addition, Maedder was listed as the proprietor of his own brewery in the R. G. Dun & Co. credit reports as late as 1866 (though his business prospects were considered bleak).

In addition, there are two other Mayville brewers in the excise records not yet accounted for. These are Fred (or Fritz) Gutschow, who was included in the 1867 and 1868 annual lists, and the firm of Nagle & Cook (or Hook), which was listed in special entries from November 1868 to March 1869 (when they produced a barrel and a half). While no clear link is yet established, the dates seem to work for these two businesses to have taken over Maedder's brewery for a few years.

William Darge (1866?–1885)
Louis Darge (1885–86)
EAST BANK OF ROCK RIVER, NORTH OF BRIDGE STREET

William Darge was a carpenter who built his own brewery along the Rock River sometime in the 1860s. He first appears in the excise records in the 1867 annual list, but may have been producing earlier. The few known production figures from include 428 barrels in 1878 and 385 barrels in 1879, which, at least in those two years, made his the largest brewery in Mayville. This assessment seems to be confirmed by a newspaper account of a fire at the "Darge Brewery, the largest brewery in Mayville," in July 1879. This was at least the second fire at the brewery, because the same article also recounted, "It was burned several years ago, and insurance rebuilt it, but this time it burned just the day before the insurance agent arrived from Fond du Lac."

Darge apparently rebuilt, since the brewery appears in industry directories through 1887 (though it seems they stopped brewing in 1886). William Darge died in 1885, and his son Louis, who took over the brewery, died in 1887 at age twenty-eight. Julia Darge, William's widow, sold the brewery to Carl Gerlach, formerly a partner in the John Steger Brewery, who converted the building to other uses.

Mayville Brewing Co. (1935–36)
331 SOUTH MAIN STREET

In 1933 a group of Fond du Lac-based investors purchased the former M. Ziegler brewery and began to prepare it for brewing again. The renovations took well over a year, and during that time many of the out-of-town investors cooled on the idea and sold their interests to Mayville residents. The brewery finally hired a brewmaster, Hugo Ogren, obtained its brewing permit, and began operations in January 1935.

The brewery chose to make Swedish-style porter and stout and English-style ale instead of lager. Whether this was because the Swedish-born Ogren was more comfortable with ale styles, or because they were trying to avoid direct competition with larger lager brewers, or a combination of the two, is unclear. Ogren proved to be particular about brewing with ingredients and equipment that were unavailable, and believed that his beers would find a ready market in his former home of Chicago. Production was miniscule—the few available figures show thirty-six barrels were made in April 1935 and thirty the following month. The delays in production and the failure to find a ready market once beer was available forced the brewery to shut down during the summer of 1935. The brewery spent several months trying to dispose of unsold stout and porter. By October the brewery was running again, but this time making lager essentially as the brewery for Gesell Brothers, beer distributors based in Milwaukee. Apparently the lager was no more successful in the market than the dark Swedish beers, and by February the brewery was closed, despite hopes that it could re-open later. The brewers' bond was terminated by Maryland Casualty Co., so the brewery was unable to operate legally. The building was eventually converted to a cheese factory.

Mazomanie *(Dane County)*

Peter Wirth, Mazomanie Brewery (1858–1868)
Pratt & Co. (1860?–63)
Wirth & Kuhn (1868–1870)
Hamm & Lenz (1870–71)
Alois Maier (1871–73?)
Tinker & Schlough, Mazomanie Brewery
    (1875–1880)
Ambrose Lang, Mazomanie Brewery
    (1880–1894)
Caroline Lang, Mazomanie Brewery (1894–97)
Edward M. Lang, Mazomanie Brewery
    (1897–1901)
J. A. Schmitz, Mazomanie Brewery (1901–2)
200 block Cramer Street on Shore of
Lake Marion

Peter Wirth (or Werth) started brewing in Mazomanie in 1858 in a small frame brewery. His brewery was too small to be included in the census of manufacturers in 1860, and given the frequent ownership changes it may well have been out of production for at least part of the year. Wirth apparently rented or leased his brewery to Edward Pratt shortly after opening it. The 1860 census lists the brewers in Mazomanie as Pratt and John Crotch—neither of whom possessed any real estate and so were unlikely to have actually owned the brewery. By 1861 Pratt had asked Edward Huggins to join the firm and provide financial backing for the brewery. The company was still in debt, and ceased operations sometime in late 1862.

Wirth apparently returned to brewing, and in 1868, John Kuhn joined him, but business was still not good enough to meet their obligations, and the capital-strapped partners sold out to John Hamm and Jacob Lenz by September 1870.

Hamm & Lenz had little more luck than their predecessors, including a fire in February 1871, and in late 1871 they turned the brewery over to Alois Maier, who ran it until mid-1873 when he too went out of business. Maier produced 236 barrels in 1871 and 303 the next year, but this may not have been enough to turn a profit. It is possible that Maier (or even Hamm & Lenz) did not own the brewery, since there are two other investors mentioned in connection with this brewery, Richard Block in the late 1860s and Herman Black in the early 1870s. Black is reported to be the person who bought the brewery from Wirth and in 1875 sold it to the next proprietors, Tinker and Schlough.

While Tinker was listed first in the business name, Charles Schlough (various spellings) was apparently the brewer, since it was he that the *Mazomanie Sickle* mentioned in reports about the renovation of the brewery. It is not clear what experience Schlough had as a brewer, but he had been arrested and fined in 1874 for running an illegal distillery. While he was in charge of the brewery in 1875, it apparently took him some time to return to production, since there was no evidence of brewing in 1876, and an 1879 report on the brewery said it had been finished "last spring." By the end of the decade Schlough had boosted production over 500 barrels per year, just in time for disaster to strike. In June 1879 the brewery was burned with a loss of about $3,000. The fire was blamed on straw in the ice house somehow igniting. As the 1880 county history put it in the style of the time: "Undaunted, he at once began rebuilding on a more extensive scale, erecting a stone structure" that was much larger than before, and estimated to cost $5,000. The new brewery was done within four months of the fire, but so was Schlough's money, and he was forced out of business.

The Mazomanie brewery had a poor reputation in the business community; the R. G. Dun credit reports said in 1880 "This brewery has always been an unfortunate piece of property." There appear to have been two reasons for this: strong temperance sentiment in the community, and stiff competition from breweries in the nearby capital city. The Dun evaluator noted: "The previous history of this brewery is not very flattering, owing principally to the competition in Madison. The saloon keepers here purchase their beer in Madison." However, the evaluator was high on the new proprietor, Ambrose Lang. Lang was a retired laborer who had built up some capital, and came from Madison to Mazomanie to invest in the brewery. While he knew little about brewing or business, his sons were considered quite capable, and he hired brewer Joseph Winnigs to run the operation. By the mid-1880s, Lang's brewery had a capacity of 1,500 barrels (and actually produced 1,000 barrels in 1885), was making its own malt and, interestingly, brewing ale as well as lager (which they still brewed as late as 1900). There was another fire in 1892, but this time the brewery itself was saved by prompt action by the fire company.

After Ambrose Lang died in 1894, his widow Caroline took over management of the

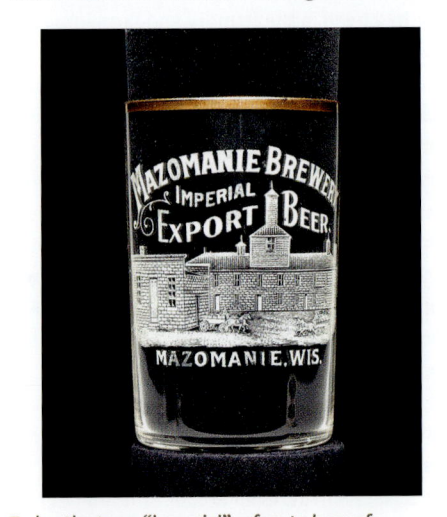

Today the term "imperial" refers to beer of particularly high alcoholic content, but here it almost certainly indicates a premium product. Even very small breweries could afford such attractive advertising pieces. COLLECTION OF JOHN STEINER.

business for a few years, then was succeeded by her son Edward. The Langs continued to improve the brewery, including converting the saloon into a bottling house in the late 1890s. The brewery was still modest in size with its thirty-three barrel brewhouse, but was doing a steady business and increased production to 1,200 barrels in 1895. In 1899, Edward Lang improved the malting operations by building a new cement malt cellar.

In 1901, J. A. Schmitz became proprietor of the brewery, and began advertising in the *Sickle* with an ad that featured a large picture of the brewery. However the brewery was destroyed by fire in January 1902, with a loss of $20,000 and insurance of only $10,000. The brewery did not return to production, though the ads in the *Sickle* continued to run until June, either because they were still selling existing stock, or because the editor just neglected to remove an ad that was already paid for.

Medford (Taylor County)

Carl Kuhn (1889–1890)
Kuhn Bros. Brewing Co. (1890–93)
Leo Kuhn (1893–94)
Medford Brewing Co. (1894–98)
William Kurz (1898–1900)
Estate of William Kurz (1900–2)
Medford Brewery Co. (1902–6)
Medford Brewery (1906–8)
Wm. Gehring (Gehring & Teuschel) (1908–9)
East Side of Third Street Between Taylor and Broad (Modern Lincoln)

Medford apparently seemed like a logical place to locate a brewery. There were very few breweries between Wausau and Chippewa Falls to the south and Superior to the north, and there was a thirsty population in the region. Starting in 1885, newspapers around the state announced rumors of a new brewery in the city every year or so, but until 1889 nothing much happened. Finally, in June 1889, the *Taylor County Star and News* announced that brothers Carl and Leopold Kuhn had started clearing land for their brewery. The reporter added "The proprietors are practical men, and will no doubt succeed." The most noteworthy incident in the early years occurred when a former employee shot Carl Kuhn at the brewery. John Heilemeir had only been employed two days, and had been dismissed the morning of the affray. Kuhn was hit by three of the four shots, but Heilemeir was intoxicated and probably not aiming particularly well, so none of the wounds were serious.

In 1894, Rosa and Charles Kuhn joined with Clinton Texter and Joseph Forst to incorporate the first version of Medford Brewing Co. The Kuhns sold their shares in the company a year later, though the terms of the sale carefully excluded the Kuhn's buggy and cutter, as well as a menagerie including a mare and colt, a cow, pigs, chickens, ducks and peacocks. The new owners apparently found a need to diversify their business, since an amendment to the articles of incorporation passed in 1897 allowed the company to, among other things, "sell and convey real estate, live stock and grain."

In 1898 William Kurz, of Plymouth, purchased the bankrupt brewery and planned the usual enlargements and improvements. Unfortunately Kurz passed away at in 1900 at age forty-one, and the frequent changes in management continued. Another corporation was founded in 1902, with Ida Kurz as one of the officers, but this also lasted only a few years. Often the name changes meant little more than an attempt to bring in new investors to keep the business alive, and some of the names were used interchangeably in different publications (the 1910 *Brewers and Bottlers Universal Encyclopedia* had both Medford Brewery Co. and Gehring & Teuschel). Even through the changes in ownership, the brewery provided work for eight to ten men of the community.

The Medford brewery suffered a massive fire "of unknown origin" in November 1909 that destroyed the brewhouse, refrigerator and power plant. Attempts to fight the fire were hampered by the fact that the city water main was under repair so the fire department had inadequate water. William Gehring, proprietor at the time, planned to rebuild "immediately," but funding proved elusive. By June, it was announced that Gehring & Henry Voss sold out to Minneapolis Brewing Co. It is possible that this sale was also just a rumor, since the 1913 Sanborn insurance map still lists Henry Voss as the owner of the property. In 1913, local businessmen Henry Voss, E. F. Giese and K. J. Urquhart formed Taylor County Brewing Co. *Western Brewer* announced in 1913 "Taylor County Brewing Co., Medford, newly incorporated, will, according to local newspaper reports, erect a complete new brewery to cost $40,000." However this new company never actually built the brewery, and Medford remained without locally brewed suds until 1935.

Medford Brewing Co. (1934–35)
Medford Brewing Co. (1940–48)
237 West Broadway (some sources say 132 North Wisconsin Avenue, but no brewery was there)

After legal beer returned in 1933, Medford was primarily a Blatz and Old Style town. But in September, "The city of Medford received the good news this week of the establishment of a brewery here within the next few weeks." The city donated the land for the new Medford Brewing Co., which was to be managed by W. F. Stauss of Chilton and Irvin Schwenzen and Richard Seuberdick, both of Plymouth. Construction of the all-new brewery started almost right away, with double shifts scheduled to work from 6:00 a.m. to 10:00 p.m. with lights set up on the site to work early morning and late night hours. Because such good jobs were scarce during the Great Depression, the name of each worker on the project was celebrated in the newspaper.

But while the early estimate of the time needed to put the brewery into production was six weeks, in reality brewing did not commence for more than a year. Local newspapers did not provide any reasons for the delays, which most likely were a lack of funding to finish the job. At the meeting of directors in January 1935, the three original officers were replaced by a slate of mostly Medford men. At least by this time, there was some beer in the aging tanks. The first batch of beer was started in mid-December 1934, after the federal permit

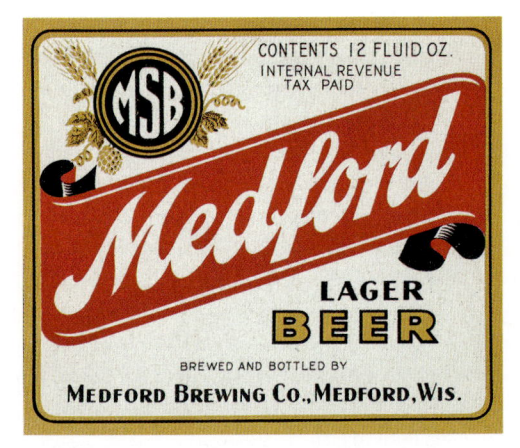

A label from the early 1940s—during the second attempt to resume brewing in Medford. COLLECTION OF JOHN STEINER.

was issued and the necessary supplies had been delivered. Hops came from Oregon, but malt was delivered from "one of the Manitowoc malting houses." The two-story brewery demonstrated the new world of brewery design in which gravity was no longer essential—the fermenters were on the second floor of the structure. The beer was aged in wooden vats and the kegs were all new northern oak cooperage that were lined in a pitch house on site. One piece of equipment was a particular nod to the past: one of the two keg washers had been used by the previous Medford Brewing Co. prior to Prohibition. Medford draught lager made it into taverns in early February 1935. But the brewery was unable to meet its financial obligations, and ceased production in June. The corporation continued to file annual reports in hopes that the business would continue, but hopes dwindled with each passing year.

In 1940, however, buyers appeared. E. J. Young, president of the Rice Lake Brewery, and George H. Lanswer of Portland, Oregon, purchased the building. Their purchase was dependent on local residents subscribing to $3,000 of preferred stock, but this happed quite quickly—$2,500 was sold in less than two weeks. The money was earmarked for a bottling house and a new office. But like the earlier incarnation of the business, the original leadership team was gone by the time the beer was flowing, replaced by Frank Mohr, former brewmaster at Marshfield, and Frank Kraut and Norbert Laabs. This time, it was only a matter of a few months before the brewery was readied for brewing. The new Medford Lager was in taverns on October 30, 1940, and the company announced that its roster of four employees would be expanded to twelve or fourteen when bottling commenced. Apparently the four did not include directors Kraut and Laabs, who were listed as truck drivers in the announcement that beer was back. But the brewery came on line just in time for World War II. While output peaked around 14,000 barrels during the war, it was generally less than 10,000 barrels per year, which was an inefficient use of a brewery built for a capacity of 25,000 barrels. The brewery languished, and by 1948 shut down again, never to reopen.

MEDINA *(Dale Township)* *(Outagamie County)*

Worth & Kuehn (1874?–1878?)
The firm of Worth and Kuehn appears first in November 1874, and earned acceptable reports from the R. G. Dun & Co. inspectors through June 1878. The reports note, however, "W & K are not [residents] of this place." While no clear link has yet been made, it is tempting to identify this Worth and Kuehn with the partnership who previously operated the brewery in Mazomanie.

MENASHA *(Winnebago County)*

Alanson K. Sperry (1850–51)
Sperry & Hall (1851–53)
Hall & Loescher (1853–1864?)
Hall & Lenz (1864–1871)
Mertz & Behse (1872–78)
Herman Mertz (1878–79)
Winz & Loescher (1879–1882)
Werner Winz (1882–88)
Menasha Brewing Co. (1888–1920)
NEAR MODERN 271 RIVER STREET AND WASHINGTON STREET (1850–56); NORTHEAST CORNER FIRST AND MANITOWOC STREET (1856–1920)

Recent research by Lee Reiherzer has uncovered new details about the early years of brewing in Menasha. Former Governor James Doty sold land to Edward O'Connell and Alanson K. Sperry, with the proviso that the partners "shall forthwith commence the erection of a frame building on said lots suitable for a brewery and proceed as fast as practical in the erection of same to completion and commence the business of brewing there within six months." Sperry soon sold a half interest to Orville Hall, and the other half to Fred Loescher, who arrived in Menasha from Oshkosh in August 1853. Loescher was a Bavarian immigrant, and Orville Hall was one of the rare pioneer brewers of Wisconsin not born in Germany—he hailed from New York.

In 1856, Hall and Loescher purchased land at First and Manitowoc and moved their brewing operations there. The horse-powered brewery was well established by 1860, when it reported 600 barrels produced to the industrial census of that year. Andrew Lemmel, who boarded with Loescher, was also employed by the brewery.

While some accounts have Loescher remaining with the brewery until 1871, he had in fact retired from active involvement in the mid-1860s and was replaced by John Lenz. Hall & Lenz produced one thousand barrels in 1870, about three times the amount of their cross-town competitors at Island City brewery. Hall & Lenz sold out in 1872 to Mertz & Behse (or Behre) who, according to the R. G. Dun credit reports, did a generally good business. However, Behse died in 1878, and Mertz was left with considerable debt and the affairs of the brewery in disorder. This is reflected in the production of the brewery, which dropped from 868 barrels in 1878 to only 615 the next year.

Werner Winz, a former Menasha resident and Milwaukee-trained brewer who had gone to Appleton to operate a brewery, returned to Menasha and purchased the brewery apparently with Frederick Loescher as a partner (though Mertz was still in the 1880 census as a brewer, and may have stayed on as an employee). Shortly thereafter, Loescher retired again and Winz ran the brewery on his own. The brewery maintained a capacity of about 1,000 barrels for the next several years, but during this period did not have its own malting or bottling operations. Winz incorporated the brewery with partners Peter Ducart and Julius Hartmann in April 1889 as Menasha Brewing Co.—the name it would keep through Prohibition.

In 1895 the Menasha Brewing Co. plant burned to the ground, but like several other fires in this era, it may have allowed the brewery to update the plant and equipment in a way they may not have without the urgent need. As built in 1895 the complex did not include a bottling house, but by 1900 this feature was present, along with expanded icehouses.

During Prohibition, the Menasha Brewing Co. continued to brew cereal beverages through 1921, but after that the buildings were converted to other uses. One of those uses was illegal distilling. An explosion in June 1930 exposed a massive operation with 120,000 gallons of mash, 2,500 gallons of alcohol and twenty-five tons of corn sugar seized by authorities. Authorities sought a padlock order, but another raid in 1931 found beer being made on the premises. The brewery would be reopened several years later as Fox Valley Brewing Co. The former location of the brewery is now Winz Park.

J. Dudler (1857?–1860?)

Dudler is mostly known from the not particularly reliable 1857 and 1858 state business directories, but there is also a Peter Dummet (or something similar) in the 1860 census, a brewer in Menasha who owned $300 of real estate. This business may also have been the predecessor of the Island City Brewery, but no link is yet confirmed.

Peter Caspary, Island City Brewery (1860?–68)
Joseph F. Mayer & Co., Island City Brewery (1868–1875)
Joseph Mayer, Island City Brewery (1875–79)
Habermehl & Mueller, Island City Brewery (1879–1882)
George Habermehl, Island City Brewery (1882–86)
Edward Fueger, Island Brewery (1886–88)
Walter Bros. & Fries, Island City Brewery (1888–1891)
Walter Bros. Brewing Co., Island City Brewery (1891–1920)
Walter Bros. Brewing Co. (1933–1956)
134–144 Nicolet Boulevard and Commercial Street

Peter Caspary (Caspari) was reputed to have started the Island City Brewery in 1860, but Lee Reiherzer' research suggests that Caspary was not in Menasha at that date, and did not purchase the land until 1866.

While Joseph Mayer's term as proprietor of the brewery was generally satisfactory, he decided to sell out at the end of 1879 for about $20,000 to "parties from Milwaukee," as the common phrase of the era put it. These parties were Habermehl & Mueller, who spent 1880 building a new brewery on the site. Early reports on their business abilities were favorable, but the new brewery evidently put them in significant debt—the brewery itself was estimated to have cost about $35,000 and the equipment another $15,000. The brewery had what the R. G. Dun & Co. credit evaluator called "a little bad luck with their beer for a time" but they apparently recovered. However, by 1883 Habermehl and Mueller had split, which caused the brewery even more financial difficulty.

In 1886 the Island Brewery was unable to pay its bills, and was sold at auction in order to pay the sums owed to Milwaukee malters. The purchaser was Edward Fueger, who at the time was with the Obermann brewery of Milwaukee. Fueger held the property for almost exactly a year until he too went bankrupt, and a group of Neenah men purchased the building. None of them were brewers, and they sought a buyer. The city had a near miss with notoriety when John Arensdorf of Sioux City, Iowa arrived to negotiate for the brewery. While he was an experienced brewer, he had also been charged with killing a temperance activist clergyman in Iowa, and though acquitted, the court of public opinion still held that he was guilty. Eventually this sale fell through and the brewery was purchased by Frank Fries of Appleton. Observers still seemed to think that the brewery could be profitable since a newspaper article argued that "[t]he property is a bargain at that price" which was $9,000.

Fries brought with him two partners who would provide generations of stability for the brewery: Christian and Martin Walter. The brothers, whose family also operated several other breweries in Wisconsin at various times, soon bought out Fries and created Walter Bros. Brewing Co. over the next decade, the Walters basically remodeled the entire brewery. A new malt house was in place by 1891, and soon after they added their own bottling plant and a warehouse that could store about 1,000 cases of beer. Walter Bros. made a strong effort to hold on to their home market, at one point winning a bidding war with Pabst over a prime piece of property on Broad Street. The Walters of Menasha also had sizeable financial interests in the Walter brewery in Pueblo, Colorado.

Walter Bros. continued brewing right up until the beginning of Prohibition, and in fact,

The slogan "It's in the Brewing" may have led Walter Bros. to depict a brew kettle on Gold Label labels. This metal sign uses the same shape and design as a pre-Prohibition label. Walter Bros. brought back similarly shaped labels after Prohibition for Gem pilsner and the return of Gold Label. Brewing equipment rarely appear as the centerpiece of a label, though mash paddles and malt shovels have been relatively common. COLLECTION OF RICHARD YAHR.

WISCONSIN BREWERIES AND BREWPUBS 497

somewhat past it. Walter Bros. was among the first companies to be charged with violating the federal Prohibition Act in 1920, and the brewery was also fined for a violation in 1923.

Walter Bros. Brewing Co. needed several months to repair the brewery and install new equipment when Prohibition ended, but they obtained their permit in May 1933 and had their GEM and Gold Label beers back on the market as soon as possible. As the company re-established itself in the market, it continued to expand the plant. In 1937 alone, the brewery set about rebuilding and expanding the malthouse, remodeling the cellars, adding new bottling equipment, and installing "the latest type of gas collector for saving the natural gas of the beer." In early 1938 the president of the company, Charles Kulnick, died, bringing to an end fifty years in the beer business that began with Schreihart's brewery in Manitowoc. At this point the brewery consistently produced about 13,000 barrels per year. During the 1930s, Walter Bros. advertised that it would buy barley from local farmers at "highest market prices," an ad much more common fifty or more years earlier. Kurbstor Gardens, a beer garden and beer retailer in Menasha, contracted with Walter Bros. to produce a special brand, Kurbstor Special Beer, which was introduced at the grand opening of the new garden in June 1937.

Walter Bros. Brewing was one of the few smaller post-Prohibition breweries that reached peak production in the early 1950s rather than the late 1940s. Some of this may have been due to a change in management in 1949, when several members of the Hopfensberger family took over the business (though Charles Lingelbach stayed on as brewmaster). The new management trumpeted the success of the Gem Pilsner 7-ounce package, which placed eighth in bottling and sales in the state in November 1950. Walter Bros. continued to brew bock beer, and was forced to increase production in 1950 after it sold out early in 1949. (In 1952 they brought out the bock at Christmastime, and under the Gem label.) But from a high of around 31,000 barrels in 1951 (about half of the 60,000 barrel capacity), production dropped slowly for a few years, to 25,301 barrels in 1953, and precipitously thereafter. The brewery's sales range was all within a fifty-mile radius of the plant, a zone which included several other breweries as well as agencies for many national brewers. The brewery closed in June 1956 and was razed in 1960. The malt house remained and was used by Chilton Malting Co.

Fox Valley Brewing Co. (1940–42)
501–505 Manitowoc Street (Brewery at First and Manitowoc)

Despite rumors that Menasha Brewing Co. would open soon after beer was legalized, it was several years before the old plant would be placed in operation. Fox Valley Brewing Co. filed articles of incorporation in 1936, but the first few annual reports could only report that they were "equipping and constructing plant to be used as brewery." The company had some initial difficulties with another business in Menasha called Valley Brewing Co. that wanted to force Fox Valley to change its name, but Fox Valley was allowed to use the name (and Valley Brewing never produced any beer that could be confused with Fox Valley's product). While initial predictions claimed production would begin in January 1937, remodeling the old plant at First and Manitowoc went at a slow pace. The local assessor for Wisconsin's Beverage Tax Division reported in 1938: "Contacted this brewery and found no activity there. No beer has been brewed. Doors of brewery were open but could find no one in the building. . . . in the past three years I have called at this place, and from all appearances no progress has been made." Despite the fact they received their federal permit to start brewing in July 1938, they were nowhere near ready.

The City of Menasha attempted to accelerate the process by debating a resolution exempting the brewery from taxes for three years if it was operated at full capacity during that time. John Feiner, brewmaster and point person for the business, urged the council to pass the resolution by noting that the firm would employ local labor ("except in the key posts") and that "reopening the brewery would be like securing a new industry" (and they would pay existing back taxes). The resolution passed with only one dissenting vote. Production finally started in April 1940, though no name had been selected for the beer and "Mr. Feiner plans to hold a contest to select a name for the new product." From appearances, Feiner won his own contest since the new beer was called Feiner beer. Bottled beer did not appear until November. The brewery produced 1,490 barrels in 1940, over 2,000 the next year, but only 140 in the first few months of 1942 before it went out of business for good.

Menomonie *(Dunn County)*

Virginia French (1856?–1858?)

The only contemporary reference for this brewery is the 1857 state business directory. There was indeed a Virginia French in Menomonie at the time, but she was the wife of a clerk—twenty-three years old and with an infant daughter—and unlikely to have been a commercial brewer.

Christian Fuss, Rock Brewery (1866?–1884)
Charles Diener (1885–?)
Weber & Werner (1888?)
Jacob Kiewel, City Brewery (1890?–1891)
Brewery Hill, west end of modern Twelfth Avenue

Clarifying the history of the Menomonie breweries is complicated not just by the multiple municipalities named Menomonie and the different versions of the spelling. It is further confused by brewers named Fuss in Menomonie or Menomonee in both Dunn and Waukesha counties. Making matters worse, the Menomonie newspapers never covered events at the brewery, including major fires and ownership changes.

Sometime prior to mid-1867, Christian Fuss established his brewery and beer garden on what came to be known as Brewery Hill. There are no known references to his brewery prior to his appearance in the 1867 excise records, but he may have been going prior to that time. Throughout the 1870s Fuss typically produced between 300 and 400 barrels per year, with a peak of 454 in 1877. However, at the end of 1877, his brewery was destroyed by fire. Insurance covered the loss, but as was often the case, he built a larger and better-equipped brewery and went into debt. The few records of the brewery suggest that Fuss was in debt at least sometime before and after the fire, since he was sued at least twice to recover payment on loans. Even so, the R. G. Dun & Co. credit reports suggest that he was doing a good business in the new brewery. However in 1884 he was bankrupt and sold the brewery. The first purchaser appears to have been Charles Diener, though it is possible that he did not actually operate the brewery since he is not listed in industry directories. (Research by Richard D. Rossin Jr. found that Diener was Fuss's son-in-law.) Some local accounts indicate that a G. Weber had the brewery around 1888, and the Sanborn map of that year showed the property owned by Weber & Werner, but also noted that the brewery was not in operation.

At some point prior to 1891, Jacob Kiewel of Fergus Falls, Minnesota, purchased the brewery. This is a bit of a mystery since Kiewel was still operating his brewery in Minnesota until 1892, but it is possible he purchased the Wisconsin business as a hedge because of the frequent dry votes in Fergus Falls. The end of the City Brewery came in February 1891, when it was destroyed by fire. Kiewel subsequently purchased a brewery in Little Falls, Minnesota, and Menomonie City Brewery was not rebuilt.

Christian Fuss came to a sad end. He died in 1894 at age sixty, and "died destitute in a brewery where he had for several years past worked for his board." Since his former brewery had not been rebuilt, he must have gone to work at the Burkhardt brewery.

August Geisert (1866?–1872)
Roleff & Wagner (1873?–1880)
Fred Wagner (1880–84)
Henry H. Brown (1884–85??)
Burkhardt Bros. (1888–1893)
Gottfried Burkhardt (1893–95)
Louis Burkhardt (1895–97)
G. Burkhardt & Son (1897–1912)
Josef Niedermair's Brewery (1912–16)

Hudson Road, Section 21, Township 28 North, Range 13 West

Sometime in the mid-1860s, August Geisert established a brewery west of Menomonie, though the date is not certain because he could have been in production prior to his first appearance in the excise records. Geisert was the only one of Menomonie's breweries to make enough money to be recorded in the 1870 industrial census: he made 400 barrels that sold for $8.00 each in his hand-powered brewery.

Geisert died in April 1872, and his brewery passed to the partnership of Roleff and Wagner (or Wagoner). The surveyor for R. G. Dun & Co. reported that the firm was not doing a very heavy business, perhaps because they "don't make very [good] beer." However, by 1881 Fred Wagner was sole proprietor, and the Dun reports noted that business had improved. In 1881, Wagner's brewery was destroyed by fire. He proceeded to rebuild, and apparently reestablished his reputation and credit. The new brewery had a capacity of between 1,5000 and 2,000 barrels per year, and while it is not known if Geisert had a malt house in his brewery, Wagner's new brewery did. *Western Brewer* reported in March that Henry H. Brown had succeeded Fred Wagner at the brewery,

This glass most likely dates from the late 1890s, during the early years of Burkhardt & Son. Collection of John Steiner.

but he never appears in any other industry publication, and may have purchased a bankrupt brewery and held it until he could sell it. (It is possible that neither Menomonie brewery was operating in 1887, since neither appears in the state industry reports for that year.)

The Burkhardt brothers from Minnesota were the next proprietors, and the brewery stayed in the family for nearly twenty-five years. During their time the brewery probably produced a few thousand barrels a year, though local accounts claim they were producing 10,000 barrels annually. (One of these articles also claims that the beer was 12–14 percent alcohol, which also was extremely unlikely.) Again, because the Menomonie newspapers did not report on events at the brewery, the operations of the brewery at this time are largely unknown. Josef Neidermair operated the brewery for the last few years. The reason for the closure of the brewery was not reported.

Das Bierhaus (2007–2016)
120 Sixth Avenue West

Robert Wilbers, a native of Germany and graduate of the Weihenstephaner brewing school in Munich, brewed a range of authentic German lagers at Das Bierhaus, a small German restaurant on the edge of downtown Menomonie. In addition to the standard year-round German styles, Wilbers brewed seasonals and specialties like roggenbier, rauchbier, and dunkel weizenbock. An occasional non-German style such as Belgian dubbel appeared on the beer menu.

Lucette Brewing Co. (2010–present)
910 Hudson Road

Mike Wilson had heard about the old Burkhardt brewery in Menomonie, and was intrigued by the idea of starting a brewery in the city. He and Tim Schletty, Tim's father Fred and Tim Drkula found a location along Hudson Road, the same road Burkhardt's brewery was on, and began brewing in 2010. Wilson, Tim Schletty and head brewer Jon Christiansen were the only employees at first, but by 2016 the company had twenty-five employees. The name Lucette comes from Paul Bunyan's sweetheart, and honors the lumbering industry

The earliest cans featured a Northwoods look suitable for Lucette's role as Paul Bunyan's sweetheart. Later cans (ca. 2018) had a flowery style. Photograph by Charles Walbridge. AUTHOR'S COLLECTION.

that was the source of Menomonie's prosperity.

The first beers were only available in kegs, but in 2012 Lucette added a canning line and offered their flagship beers in 16-ounce cans. The brewery has also introduced a series of Belgian-style beers, sour beers, and other small-batch projects, which have been available on draft or in 750 ml bottles.

In 2015 Lucette added a restaurant, the Lucette Woodfire Eatery, which specializes in pizza using locally sourced ingredients.

Real Deal Beer (2014–present)
603 South Broadway

The Raw Deal in Menomonie features raw, vegan, and gluten free food. In 2014, the Raw Deal asked Ryan Verdon to brew some house beers for the restaurant that matched their philosophy of locally sourced ingredients and a minimum of processing. Real Deal Brewery is a nanobrewery that only sells their beer in the taproom.

MEQUON (Thiensville)
(Ozaukee County)

Opitz & Zimmerman (1857–59)
Adolphus Zimmerman (1859–1876)
Franz Zimmerman & Co. (1876?–1887?)
August Gerlach (1887?–1900?)
Modern Highway 167 near Modern Industrial Drive

An 1881 county history is unusually clear (and accurate) about the early years of what was generally called the Mequon Brewery. Adolphus (Adolph) Zimmerman and partner William Opitz built the Mequon Brewery in 1857, and ran it under that name until Zimmerman bought out Opitz in 1859. It is possible that production did not start until 1858, since the R. G. Dun & Co. credit reports used the phrase "have been building a brewery" in February 1858, suggesting it wasn't quite finished. (Zimmerman was a four-term State Assemblyman and a nationally prominent Democratic politician; Opitz also served a term in the State Assembly.) By 1860, Zimmermann's production was already 1,200 barrels per year, making his the largest brewery in the county. This was in spite of the lingering effects of the Panic of 1857, which caused the Dun evaluator to note in February 1859 "business is very much curtailed this season" and in February 1860 that Zimmerman was doing well "despite the hard times." Throughout the 1870s his production was around 1,000 barrels per year, which required him to register as a "large" brewer for purposes of excise taxation (and pay an extra $50 per year). In 1876, likely to find the time needed for his political activities, Zimmerman rented the brewery to his son Franz (Francis) and son-in-law August Gerlach.

The new partnership, sometimes listed as F. Zimmerman & Co., continued the same level of production as before, and according to Wing's 1884 directory, had at least a small bottling operation (which was not listed in subsequent directories, but which does not necessarily mean they stopped bottling). Wing's 1887 directory was the first to note that Zimmerman & Co. had a malthouse, but that feature also could have been present earlier.

Sometime in the late 1880s August Gerlach became sole proprietor of the brewery (Wing's 1887 directory still has Zimmerman, though it may not have been up to date). Gerlach appears to have operated the brewery through 1900, since he disappears from directories after that year. Brewing was not done forever at the Mequon Brewery, but the final brewing was illegal. In 1926, prohibition agents raided the old brewery, "a landmark in this vicinity," and seized 1,000 gallons of beer and 2,000 gallons of fermenting wort. The wildcat brewers had constructed a loading dock for delivery trucks that "was concealed from the sight of passers-by."

Charles Engels (1859?–1860s?)
Engels & Runge (1860s)
Engels & Hadan (1860s?–67)
Manz & Goetz (1867–68)
Jacob Manz (1868–69?)

Since Charles Engels was already producing a substantial 850 barrels in 1860, it is likely that he started brewing at least a year or two before then. (Since Engels' oldest child was eight years old in 1860 and born in Wisconsin, it is possible that he could have started brewing in the early 1850s.) Engels was assisted in 1860 by Andreas Fleischmann, a twenty-two year-old brewer who boarded at the brewery. Later on, Engels took on partners, but stayed involved with the brewery until mid-1867. Manz & Goetz appear for the first time in excise records in September 1867, and this partnership seems to have lasted for about a year, after which Manz ran the brewery briefly on his own.

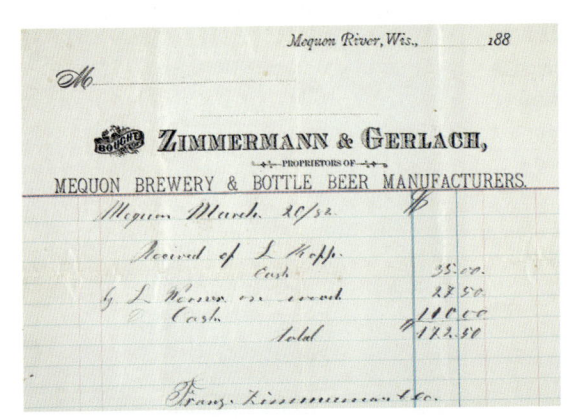

The Mequon brewery was also known as Zimmermann & Gerlach. This receipt indicates that bottled beer was sold as early as 1882—proof of how quickly bottled beer spread even to smaller breweries in the countryside. COLLECTION OF JOHN STEINER.

Jacob Harz (1859?–1869?)
Harz & Co. (1869?–1870)
Harz & Manz (1870–71)

Jacob Harz likely started his brewery prior to 1860, since he is listed in the 1860 industrial census as producing 350 barrels in the preceding fiscal year. Harz continues to make regular appearances in the excise records through 1871, occasionally under the name Harz & Co., and appears as Harz & Manz in the 1870 industrial census, though it is not clear whether Mr. Manz was John or Gottlob. That year, the horse-powered brewery produced 210 barrels, which sold for about $9.50 per barrel. Harz was fifty-eight years old in 1870, and owned land worth $8,000, so he may have simply retired.

MERRILL *(Lincoln County)*

Geo. Ruder (1884–88)
Geo. Ruder Brewery, Emil Ruder (1888–1894)
(Louis) Leidiger Brewing Co. (1896–1920)
Leidiger Brewing Co. (1933–1948)
1609 RIVER STREET (RIVER AND NAST STREETS)

Wausau brewer George Ruder, likely seeking additional capacity to satisfy customers who could not be supplied from his first plant, built a second brewery in Merrill in 1883, and brought the first beer to market the next year. This brewery was built to a capacity of about 3,000 barrels per year, and is believed to have produced that much as early as 1887. Wing's 1884 directory indicates that Ruder's brewery offered bottled beer, though the Sanborn insurance maps showed no separate bottling facility at that point (and did not until 1902). While sources disagree on precisely when, at some point in the mid-1880s George turned the brewery over to his son Emil, who ran the brewery until his untimely death in May 1894. (George had passed away only a few months earlier.) According to Emil's son George, his mother ran the brewery with her younger son William for about two years before selling it.

Brothers Louis and Ernest Leidiger had owned a brewery in Sturgeon Bay during the 1880s, but sold it in 1887 because Ernest was having health problems. However, they decided to get back into brewing, purchased the Ruder brewery in 1896 and incorporated Leidiger Brewing Co. the same year. An article in the *Merrill Daily Herald* looking back from 1934 probably overstated the rustic origins of the brewery: "Way back in 1896 Ernest, Louis, and Rudolph Leidiger began to brew their golden beverage in a small frame building on the corner of River and Nast streets," and continued to note that the 3,000 barrels the Leidigers brewed their first year was "hardly enough to take care of one good Liederkranz convention." While the joke about the consumption habits of Germans in song was no doubt appreciated, 3,000 barrels was hardly a small production total, and was more than many breweries in comparable cities. The brewery was already a modern one, equipped with steam power, and all the Leidigers had to do was continue to improve it. Most of the improvements were made by Ernest, since Louis died in 1900 and Rudolph provided financial support but remained in Milwaukee. Leidiger Brewing added refrigeration and a new bottling plant in 1901, and a new brewhouse followed shortly thereafter which increased capacity to 12,000 barrels. According to local tradition, Ernest Leidiger had a telephone in his first house in Merrill, but was so besieged by saloonkeepers calling him at all hours for more beer that when he moved into the former Ruder residence he refused to install a telephone in his new home.

The Leidiger family continued to improve the brewery until Prohibition, and longtime Leidiger brewmaster August Oppert continued to refine the beer. During Prohibition, the brewery turned to making cereal beverages and bottling soft drinks. However, Ernest Leidiger died in 1922, and in 1925 his son Louis G. Leidiger sold the brewery (but not the bottling plant) to Harry Hawley. The brewery was renamed the Merrill Brewing Co. for the rest of Prohibition.

In the early 1930s Louis G. Leidiger pursued a career in politics and was elected to the State Assembly in 1932 on a platform specifically calling for the return of real beer. The "Leidiger Bill" became the legislation that governed the sale of beer in Wisconsin, and Leidiger served out his term and returned to Merrill to take advantage of the changes he helped bring about. The newly renamed and reincorporated Leidiger Brewing Co. was not ready to distribute on the first day of legal beer, so the first beer in Merrill on 7 April 1933 was Chief Oshkosh. The capacity of the brewery was sometimes cited as 50,000 barrels, and while some sources claim the company reached this level, figures from the Wisconsin Beverage Tax Division show that was typically closer to 10,000 barrels per year. The company still had a solid reputation in the region, and Leidiger was known locally as a talented wrestler.

Even though the brewery still turned a profit at times during the post-Prohibition years, competition from breweries both near and far, and the death of Louis G. Leidiger in 1943 made it difficult for the brewery to carry on. The Leidigers sold the brewery to A. A. Wenzel of Milwaukee, but he died in 1944, and in

During peacetime, the three Vs stood for vim, vigor, and vitality. During World War II, the letters stood for Victory. The Morse Code symbol for V is near the bottom of the label. This label was for an 8-ounce bottle—against the wartime trend of larger containers to save bottle caps and other materials. COLLECTION OF TYE SCHWALBE.

1945 Alex Tankenoff of the Bloomer Brewing Co. purchased the brewery. Tankenoff wanted the Merrill plant more for access to its wartime grain quota than for any other merit of the plant. He used the brewery to increase production of his own Buckingham Ale and Beer brands but eliminated sales at the brewery, deliveries outside of Merrill and closed distributors.

In 1947 Tankenoff closed both the Bloomer and Merrill breweries. A group of local investors attempted to keep the brewery going and purchased it from Tankenoff against his advice. The new brand Lincoln Lager failed to sell and the company closed for good in 1948.

Nelson & Anderson (1904)
Erick Nelson (1904–1905?)
118 West First Street

In early 1904 the partnership of Nelson & Anderson started a small brewery in Merrill dedicated to producing Scandinavian-style ale. Their June advertisement in the *Merrill Advocate* announced: "Having decided to begin the manufacture of MALT ALE—SVAG DRIKA in the Sixth Ward, we desire to notify all who may desire to use this most healthful and invigorating beverage that I shall be pleased to deliver it to them upon order in person, by letter or telephone, at any time. We are now ready." Their "Malt Ale" was priced at $1.00 for a case of bottles or a mere 75¢ for an eighth-barrel keg. By August the advertisement only carried the name of Erick Nelson, and the ad was gone from the paper by mid-October. The latter is not necessarily proof that the brewery closed then, but there are no further references after the 1905 *Brewers' Handbook*.

Sawmill Brewing Co. (2017–present)

Sawmill Brewing Co. not only pays tribute to the logging heritage of the Merrill area, but it is located in a forest ranger station built in 1940–41. Most of the exterior was preserved, and local artisans and contractors created and installed most of the interior details and furniture. The beers include a variety of lagers and ales along with less common styles such as *bière de garde*.

Middleton (Dane County)

John and William Reeves (1859?–1860)
Reeves & Waddle, Middleton Brewery (1860–67)
Jones & Isaacson (1868–69)
L. T. Jones (1869–?)

According to an 1867 advertisement of the brewery's availability for purchase, John Reeves & James Waddle built the Middleton Brewery in 1860. However, newspaper notices from early 1860 announced the dissolution of the John and William Reeves partnership in February and the formation of the Reeves and Waddle partnership in March. The latter solicited "a continuence [sic] of the former patronage of the concern, and further favors from the public," and it is unlikely that a brewery that was not built until 1860 would already have any significant business worth continuing. (It is also possible that Reeves and Waddle built a second brewery in 1860.) Reeves had an established farm, and the brewery was merely one of his businesses. As early as 1861, Reeves & Waddle provided a testimonial in an advertisement for May's Patent Pumps, noting that the pump worked well by horse or hand power, and was used for stock and farm purposes as well as "large quantities for our Brewery."

Reeves and Waddle were Englishmen, and therefore brewed ales rather than lager. Their agent in Madison, E. Oswin, advertised "Pale, Amber and Bottled Ales! Brewed at Middleton . . . in Messrs. Reeves and Waddle's Completely Fitted Brewery." Their ale cost $1.25 per dozen pints, and bottles not returned would be charged for. Oswin added: "These Ales are brewed expressly for bottling purposes, and for purity and genuine excellence of quality cannot be surpassed by any imported Ales. Recommended by Drs. Joseph Hobbins, Brown, and Hayes, for those invalids requiring strengthening drinks."

Reeves and Waddle continued to operate the brewery until 1867, when they placed it on the market. The brewery included "all the appurtenances required for a first class brewery," and was "complete in all its parts, and will suit any person who desired to invest in the business." According to excise records, the brewery was purchased by Jones & Isaacson in mid-1868, though the business was going by the name of L. T. Jones the next year. Jones made sure to keep his product before the public by the tried and true method of providing the local editor with a keg. The reviews proclaimed the keg of Brown Stout Ale "a very superior article," with one taster claiming "it contained a very large amount of beer to the square inch."

John Wagner (1865–67)
Lenz & Hess (1867–1873)
Jacob Lenz (1871–72)
John Hess (1873–74?)
Hubert Bernard (1877–1880)
Bernard & Findorf (1880–82)
John Findorf (1882–85)
Brunkow & Mueller (1885–1905)
Brunkow & Mueller, Pheasant Branch Brewery (1905–1911)
Werten Bros., Middleton Brewery (1911–15?)

Pheasant Branch was a small community within the boundaries of modern Middleton. Despite the competition provided by breweries in nearby Madison, John Wagner started a small brewery in 1865. While the 1880 county history claims that Wagner operated the brewery until 1868, excise records show that Lenz and Hess had taken over the brewery by November 1867.

Jacob Lenz and John Hess made significant

The logo on this sticker is also on a large metal sign marking the entrance to the brewery from County Highway K. AUTHOR'S COLLECTION.

improvements to the brewery, and pushed production over the 500-barrel threshold separating large from small breweries in the eyes of the taxman. In fact, the brewery produced 1,078 barrels in 1871, which ranked them in the top thirty breweries in the state. However, the improvements helped Lenz accumulate more debt that he could handle. In May 1873, Lenz "absconded," leaving debts estimated (possibly exaggerated) between $100,000 and $200,000. Lenz had acted as a virtual banker for many Germans in the area, and his departure caused great hardship for many, especially John Hess, who was left holding the brewery and the debt. The First National Bank of Madison foreclosed on the brewery, and Hess eventually moved into Madison to operate a brewery there.

The brewery lay idle for nearly four years before it was acquired by Hubert Bernard. By 1878 he had started to turn the brewery around, and by 1879 production was back up to 760 barrels. He was still in debt, however, so he brought in wealthy farmer John Findorf to provide capital. The R. G. Dun & Co. credit reports had a high opinion of Findorf—the evaluator noted that while Bernard was the practical brewer, he had no capital, and it was Findorf that made the business "perfectly [good] and safe." Industry directories suggest that a malt house was added in the early 1880s, but it is possible it was there earlier. However, business itself was mediocre, and Findorf's term as sole proprietor ended after about two years.

John G. Mueller and August Brunkow, brothers-in-law from Racine, purchased the brewery in 1885 and established the business on a sound footing. According to the 1895 Wisconsin industrial census, the brewery produced 1,600 barrels the previous year, which was among the highest totals for a small town brewery that year. The federal totals for 1896 indicated production was nearly 4,000 barrels, which suggest the partners had enlarged the brewery in the interim. The brewery continued under Brunkow & Mueller until 1911, when they were succeeded by Wertin (Verten) Bros. The latter firm was still found in state gazetteers through 1915, but the Brewers' Handbook directory of 1916 lists the brewery with no officers or brewmaster, so it is likely that production had ceased by that point.

The old brewery, then in use as a slaughterhouse, was destroyed by fire in 1921.

This small tip tray (ca. 1900) is one of the few known breweriana items from Brunkow & Mueller's brewery. COLLECTION OF TYE SCHWALBE.

Capital Brewery (1986–present)
7734 TERRACE AVENUE

One of Wisconsin's most important breweries of the craft era was Capital Brewery, which started in 1986 in a former egg and produce processing plant in Middleton. (More on the origins of Capital may be found in chapter 10.) Original brewmaster Fred Scheer left for Hibernia Brewing Co. in 1987, and Kirby Nelson took his place. Nelson had experience in large commercial breweries including Heileman and a brewery in the Philippines—making him one of the few early craft brewers with international brewing experience. Nelson began to introduce new beers to the lineup, though most of them were either German styles or emphasized malt character over hoppiness. Ideas for beer styles came from everywhere—they could be inspired by random comments by sales managers or by the brewing staff looking at leftover ingredients and trying to decide what to make. Even so, pragmatic considerations still guided production decisions. Capital shied away from making smoked beers, because of questions whether they could sell 1,000 cases. But a number of the experimental beers such as Autumnal Fire became big hits, and the company heard from disappointed customers when beers such as Kloster Weizen or Wild Rice disappeared for more than just a season.

In 1997 the company began to retire GartenBräu name and simply used the Capital name in branding and on packaging. (In the mid-2010s, the GartenBräu name reappeared (though smaller) on labels of Special Pilsner and Munich Dark, celebrating their heritage as some of the earliest Capital beers). Capital made its first foray into canned beer in 1999 when Wisconsin Amber appeared in cans as a "seasonal package." In the early years of the twenty-first century, Capital's production slowly gradually approached 15,000 barrels, the industry threshold between microbreweries and regional breweries. An indication of Capital's increasing prominence came in 1999 when Coors threatened to sue over the use of the name Winterfest for Capital's holiday seasonal (Capital changed the name to Winter Skål).

The occasional experiments took more organized form through the Capital Square series, which were in four-packs of 12-ounce bottles when first introduced, but was converted to single twenty-two ounce "bomber"

The Oktoberfest bottle is from the early 1990s, the Wisconsin Amber label is from the early 2000s, and the Wild Rice and Tett Doppelbock labels are ca. 2010. AUTHOR'S COLLECTION.

bottles in 2015. Sometimes the experiments were about process as well as flavor: for the Capital Square Tett Doppelbock, the beer was given a hot water infusion of Tettnang hops six weeks into the lagering process. Other beers represented experiments with raw materials. Capital was among the leaders in developing beers that would focus on Wisconsin-grown ingredients, including Island Wheat, introduced in 2005, which featured wheat grown on Washington Island in Lake Michigan. The first batch had 15 percent percent Island wheat, but as the growers increased their crops and the beer found success, the percentage of Island wheat grew to 50 percent.

Capital also was an early supporter of collaboration between and among Wisconsin craft brewers—in fact Autumnal Fire was first brewed as a pilot batch at Great Dane (and served as "Octuple Bock"). Capital joined with Great Dane and Lake Louie to brew a Scottish ale as a stone beer (made by lowering hot rocks into the wort to caramelize the sugars), and the brewery has also been a regular participant in the Wisconsin Common Thread collaboration beers.

Capital was unusual for a brewery of its size in that it did not have its own bottling facilities. The brewery was landlocked and had little room to expand (without shrinking the popular beer garden), and packaging equipment was expensive and diverted funding from other priorities. For the first two years packaging was done at Huber Brewing Co. in Monroe, but after that an arrangement was worked out with Stevens Point Brewery in which beer would be shipped north in a special milk truck for bottling. The company launched plans in 2012 for a new brewery and packaging facility in nearby Sauk City, but development was delayed and the plans were shelved in 2016.

While the company had several management changes over the years, the most significant departures came in 2012 when president Carl Nolen and brewmaster Kirby Nelson left to start Wisconsin Brewing Co. in Verona. The most notable change (aside from the Sauk City plans) was a number of new hoppy brands in the portfolio. The first IPA brewed by Capital was called Mutiny—partially a reference to the history of the British merchant marine fleet that brought the beer to India, but perhaps also an expression by brewers who wanted a freer hand in recipe design.

As the company celebrated its thirtieth anniversary in 2016, Capital could look back on three decades of struggle, success and innovative beers. Production in the early 2010s was generally between 25,000 and 30,000 barrels per year, and the brewery continued to turn out creative and popular brands under the direction of head brewer Ashley Kinart-Short, the first woman in charge of brewing at a large Wisconsin brewery. (Additional illustrations of Capital products are found in chapter 10.)

MILWAUKEE *(Milwaukee County)*

Simon (Herman) Reutelshofer (1840?–41)
John B. Maier, Lake Brewery (1841–44)
Franz Neukirch, Lake Brewery (1844–48)
Neukirch & Melms, Menominee (Menomonee) Brewery (1848–1859)
C. T. Melms, Menominee Brewery (1859–1870)
Jacob Frey (1870)
Philip Best Brewing Co., South Side Brewery (1870–1886)

VIRGINIA & HANOVER (NOW OREGON) STREETS
The argument over whose brewery was the first in Milwaukee may have been colored by the Yankee or German sympathies of the chroniclers who awarded the prize. Even as early as the 1870s and 1880s claims were made for both Owens' brewery and the business that eventually became the South Side brewery of Philip Best. Simon (sometimes called Herman) Reutelshofer did not have a stable start at what was at least the first German-owned brewery in Milwaukee if not the first of all. According to one account, he tapped his first keg in May 1841, but business was slow and he got into financial difficulties. In a disputed transaction, Reutelshofer sold the brewery to baker John B. Maier, who, according to some accounts, proceeded to physically beat his predecessor from the brewery. Reutelshofer, who believed he had only signed a mortgage, eventually won damages from the courts, though not as much as he had sought, and by that point Maier had passed the brewery on to his father-in-law, Franz (Francis) Neukirch.

Neukirch steadied the business and soon brought in another son-in-law, C. T. Melms. Melms' first stay in Milwaukee was for a few months in 1843—he returned in 1847 after spending two years trapping in Minnesota Territory and making a trip back to Germany. He was credited with bringing scientific brewing techniques to the company; these launched the Menominee Brewery into the front rank of the city's lager makers. While obituaries following his death in 1869 claimed that he had the largest brewery in Milwaukee for twenty years, this was only true for a few years. Nonetheless, he was always close to the production of Best, Blatz and Schlitz, whose breweries were on the way to being among the largest in the nation. The brewery became a center of community activity: the first Sons of Hermann chapter in Milwaukee was founded at the brewery. Melms later opened beer gardens and saloons around the city. He was a master of promotion and found a way to get in the papers frequently. He sent a keg of "buck beer" (bock) to the printers of the *Milwaukee Sentinel*, which resulted in a column of thanks and praise. (He had apparently taken on for a time a partner named Schauss at this point in 1857.) Melms' bock earned rather fulsome (if ungrammatical) praise again in 1859 when a *Daily Sentinel* reporter enthused: "Buck Beer—when sold by Melms—is a nectarian tonic that tiltillates [sic] the olfactories [sic], rejuvenates the cellular membrane, animates the inner man, quickens the tympanum, and makes a man jolly and jovial. It partaketh [sic] of the nature of lager without it[s] deleteriousness, and Ale without its specific gravity; it is light, wholesome—elysian—provided Melms makes it...." A tour offered to a journalist in 1859 became a two-column feature article. Melms' position in the Milwaukee brewing firmament was well established. Several important brewers trained at his brewery, including Nicholas Klinger of Whitewater and Franz Falk—and

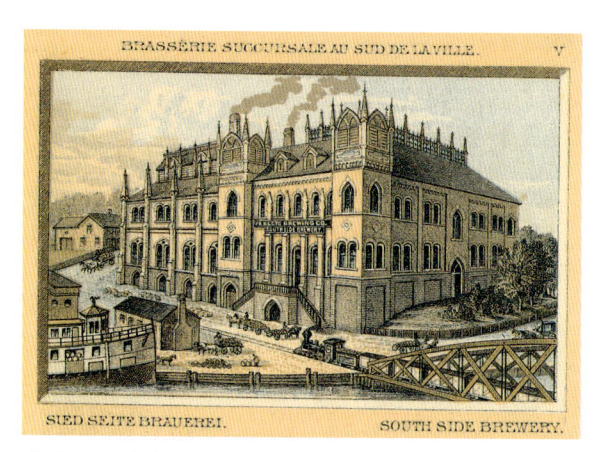

The brewery built by Melms in 1865 was occasionally mistaken for a cathedral by visitors. It is pictured here in a souvenir booklet from 1877, when it was Ph. Best's South Side Brewery. AUTHOR'S COLLECTION.

experience at Melms' was touted as a guarantee of skill. When praising the brewery of Charles Haertel of Portage, the *Daily Sentinel* could find no higher praise than to call him the "Melms of Portage."

Melms occasionally was in the papers for less fortunate reasons. In 1852, he offered a reward for the return of his dog, which had been stolen from the brewery. A new beer vault collapsed in 1857 inflicting a loss of more than $4,000, though all the beer had been removed because weakness had been detected earlier.

By the 1860 census of industry, Melms reported production of 15,000 barrels, almost twice as much as his closest competitor in the state and double what he had reported a year earlier. Melms built an impressive residence near the brewery to show off his wealth and the importance of his business. Despite appearances, research by Leonard P. Jurgensen has shown that Melms' financial position was precarious. He built a spectacular new brewery in 1865, and while writers claimed it was often mistaken for a cathedral, it may have placed him in more debt than his business could support. By the end of the 1860s, output had stagnated. The production in 1867 was just over 13,000 barrels, which was now about 5,000 behind Best and Blatz. Circumstances deteriorated further in 1868, when something went wrong with the brew and Melms had to dump about $48,000 worth of bad beer into the river. Melms died in February of 1869, and his brewery was put up for sale.

The brewery was first purchased in May 1870 for $80,000 by Melms' brother-in-law Jacob Frey, a brewer from Fond du Lac. Pabst historian Thomas Cochran claims was an attempt to save something from the estate for Mrs. Melms, but Jurgensen argues Frey simply may have been trying to buy and quickly sell the property at a profit. By November, Captain Pabst and Emil Schandein had completed the purchase of one of the best-equipped and situated breweries in the city for the Philip Best Brewing Co. at a cost of $95,000.

(For additional information on the Menominee Brewery, see Chapters 2 and 5 and the description of the Phillip Best/Pabst Brewing Co.)

Owens, Pawlett & Davis, Milwaukee Brewery (1841?–45)
Owens & Pawlett, Lake Brewery (1845–1850)
Richard G. Owens & Co., Lake Brewery (1850–1864)
M. W. Powell & Co. (1864–1875)
Powell's Ale Brewing Co. (1875–1880)
222 HURON STREET (MODERN CLYBOURNE)

Though one newspaper account erroneously claims a date of 1837, Richard G. Owens started Milwaukee's second brewery around 1841. (Further detail is found in chapter 2.) At some point in the early 1840s William Pawlett appears to have moved to the Eagle Brewery, but returned to work with Owens again within a few years. One point of confusion is when the name of the brewery changed from Milwaukee Brewery to Lake Brewery. There was another Lake Brewery during the 1840s, and advertisements from as late as 1851 name Owens' firm as the Milwaukee Brewery (with an address of 165, 167, 169 Washington Avenue). The brewery built its first expansion in 1845. The resulting complex included a two-story building sixty feet long and twenty-five feet wide, with another smaller but taller building of three stories behind it, both with cellars beneath.

The brewery prospered through its four decades of operation, maintaining a position among the leading ale brewers of the city—though its standing relative to the lager breweries declined steadily after the first ten years. Owens produced 4,000 barrels of ale worth $20,000 during the year recorded for the 1850 Census of Industry, and 2,000 barrels worth $12,000 ten years later. While this would suggest a decline in the market for British ales, M. W. Powell, a Chicago resident who rented or leased the brewery from Owens after 1864, was able to increase production to 2,891 barrels in 1865 and 3,095 two years later. Powell made the newspapers when he was unsuccessfully sued by a woman who fell down a hatchway while visiting the brewery to obtain yeast and spent grain.

Powell eventually bowed to local preferences and introduced lager in the summer of 1869. This was made possible by the erection of a brick brewery built the same year. Powell was able to keep production around 3,000 barrels for the next few years. By the end of the 1870s, this brewery, now operated by Powell's partner Owen Pritchard under the name Powell's Ale Brewery, was the only remaining producer of ale in Milwaukee. A correspondent for *Western Brewer* observed in 1877: "In the long list of breweries in Milwaukee, we find but one making ale–the A. B. Powell Brewing Co. Their product is well known, having won a good reputation in years past, which the proprietors are rigorously maintaining. It is good to find a little ale in the great ocean of Milwaukee lager." However, the days of the ale specialist were numbered. Still making over 2,000 barrels when *Western Brewer* visited, the next year production was cut in half and in 1879 it was down to 562 barrels. In May, 1880, the Milwaukee *Sentinel* reported that the "'old Lake'" was no longer in operation, blaming both lager and "shipment of bottled ales from the East. . . ."

Baker, Eagle Brewery (1841–42)
Miller & Pawlett, Eagle Brewery (1842–44)

Miller & Anson (also Miller & Knight) (1844–45)
Levi and Alonzo Blossom, Eagle Brewery (1845–1852)
NORTHWEST CORNER OF EIGHTH AND PRAIRIE (MODERN HIGHLAND)

Mr. Baker's Eagle brewery appears to have changed hands several times in its first few years of operation, and was for sale even more times. An ad which ran for many months in the Milwaukee Sentinel offered

> For Sale.—Those valuable premises situated in the town of Milwaukie [sic]–comprising a NEW BRICK BREWERY three stories high, 30 by 40 feet, cellar under the whole, with horse-mill attached for grinding all necessary grain—large malt-kill, cooling rooms, dwelling house, stable, and a never-failing stream of soft water which is introduced into the top of the brewery. Said buildings and fixtures are entirely new, and will be sold at a great bargain, with one or two acres of land attached to said premises.

Miller apparently had financial problems, since William Anson placed an ad in the Milwaukee Sentinel notifying the public that he was not responsible for Miller's debts, only those of the firm contracted by Anson himself. The real estate agent, Levi Blossom, eventually took over the brewery himself and ran it with his brother Alonzo for several years. Blossom evidently had difficulty retrieving all the brewery property, since he was compelled to run newspaper ads directing the public to return any kegs or other items of the Eagle Brewery to him rather than William Miller or his partners.

After this turmoil, the business settled down and prospered under the guidance of the Blossoms. The city directory of 1847 lauded the brewery, which was described as 175 feet long and three stories high, containing its own malting floors. The cellars were 100 feet deep with a masonry arch two feet thick that spanned twenty feet. Also on the property was a spring which was directed into a reservoir capable of holding 500 barrels of water. Blossom advertised Milwaukee, Eagle and Scotch Ale, which was available in casks or bottles. The latter appears to give the Eagle Brewery claim to having offered the first bottled Milwaukee beer, rather than the much-advertised later claim of Blatz. In the 1850 Census of Industry, the Blossoms' enterprise was the third-largest producer in the city (and the state) with 3,900 barrels, just behind the 4,000 sold by both Owens and Johann Braun. However, the building was "entirely consumed" by fire in November 1852, and Blossom seems to have left the brewing business.

Some accounts have Blossom selling the brewery to Middlewood, but evidence suggests that Middlewood & Gibson built a new brewery very close to the old Eagle Brewery, and the address given was sometimes different.

Conrad Muntzenberger (1842–47)

Conrad Muntzenberger was trained as a brewer in Germany, but also served in the German army in Algiers. He came to America in 1841, and was employed first in Cincinnati. The only early source specifically mentioning his Milwaukee brewery is Hermann Schlüter's 1910 work, which claims that Muntzenberger was the owner of the third brewery in the city. Nothing is known about Muntzenberger's operations in Milwaukee, and no documents have been found mentioning him. It is also possible that he was employed by another brewery for part of this time. He became much more prominent after he moved to Kenosha in 1847.

Johann Wolfgang Weise (1843)
David Gipfel, Union Brewery (1843–49)
Chas. W. Gipfel, Union Brewery, Weiss Beer (1849–1892)
Herman Schliebitz (1892–94)
417 CHESTNUT (MODERN 423–427 WEST JUNEAU AVENUE)

According to Albert Schnabel, secretary of the Milwaukee County Historical Society in the 1940s, David Wiese started a brewery at what was then 417 Chestnut street in 1843, though an unidentified account also found in the files of the Milwaukee Country Historical Society claims that the founder was named Wolfgang Weise, and that David Gipfel took over later that year. The research of Leonard P. Jurgensen clarifies that the founder was Johann Wolfgang Weise. Another unidentified account claimed that David Gipfel "was the richest Milwaukee brewery of his day, but not a close business man." In 1849, the brewery passed to David's brother Carl Wilhelm (Charles) who was in his mid-twenties. Most sources indicate that the first wooden brewery on this site was built in 1843, but a new brick brewhouse was added ten years later. While Gipfel's business is not included in the 1850 industry census, it is in the 1860 edition, where it was reported to have brewed 600 barrels the previous year. Interestingly, this census made particular mention of breweries producing "white beer" and Gipfel's was not included in this list. This supports Schnabel's claim that Charles switched to weiss beer in 1872—the earlier unidentified account gave no date but said he "later made white beer instead of brown, in a wooden addition at the rear." Gipfel also owned a farm on Green Bay Road (to which he retired in the 1890s) and a piece of property on a hillside which Jurgensen has concluded was used for lagering caves, given that the parcel was always owned by brewers.

Apart from imprecise reminiscences of

This Gipfel bottle, with a more graceful shape than many stoneware bottles, had a band of color and included the brewer's name in a design rather than simply stamping it on the bottle. Stoneware bottles were most popular in the 1870s, though they were used as early as the 1850s and as late as the 1890s. Their weight made them expensive to ship.
COLLECTION OF TYE SCHWALBE.

early residents, few details of Gipfel's operations exist. David Meyer, recounting the early breweries in 1925 at age ninety-three, declared that Gipfel had an old white horse that used to provide the power to grind the grain. Charles Gipfel was in the papers more often for his activities with the Second Ward Democrats or other government interactions than he was for brewing. He was drafted for military service in 1864, but his name does not appear in the regimental listings. He appears only intermittently in city and industry directories—suggesting that he did not brew consistently. His production in 1874 was only 100 barrels, though his 1875 output was reported as 5,211, a nearly impossible increase if this quantity is barrels, given the size of his plant and the smaller market for weiss beer. (It could have been gallons, cases or even bottles, since no other directory lists him with a capacity of more than 500 barrels.) By 1888, Gipfel's business was usually listed as a saloon, though it is possible that the wooden brewery in back was still used to make an occasional brew. Herman Schliebitz took over the business in 1892, and was listed as a weiss beer brewer in the city directory for a few more years. The building was subsequently occupied by the Marmon Soap Co., and then by the Elsner harness shop for several decades.

The Gipfel brewery may have more importance as a case study in the preservation of historic structures than for any merit as a brewery. The 1853 brick structure (which was the saloon rather than the brewery itself) was one of the few Federal-style buildings in the city to survive until the late twentieth century, and preservationists sought to keep the building from being razed. In 1998, the owners sought to demolish the building, contending that it was dilapidated and impossible to restore, but the city blocked the move. There was a proposal in 1998 by David Hansen of Ambier Brewing Group, Inc. to put a brewpub in the building, but that never came to fruition. In 2001, the building needed to be protected from damage when the Park East Freeway was being demolished. But since the building sat on a prime site in downtown near the Bradley Center, it was in the way of lucrative redevelopment opportunities. So, in March 2007, the building was uprooted and moved about a block to a new site on Old World Third Street. Two years later the city ruled that the structure was unstable and needed to be razed.

Best & Co., Empire Brewery (1844–1853)
Empire Brewery, Jacob Best, Jr. & Phillip Best (1853–1860)
Empire Brewery, Phillip Best (1860–64)
Phillip Best & Co., Empire Brewery (1864–1873)
Ph. Best Brewing Co., Empire Brewery (1873–1889)
Pabst Brewing Co. (1889–1920)
Pabst Corporation (1920–1933)
Premier-Pabst Corp. (1933–38)
Pabst Brewing Co. (1938–1996)
Pabst Milwaukee Brewery (2017–present)
917 Chestnut; 1037 West Juneau (2017–present)

While Pabst Brewing Co. eventually created a brewing empire on which the sun never set; early on the name Empire Brewery was more hope than reality. In fiscal 1850 John Braun produced nearly twice as much lager as the five-year old Best & Co., and Best also trailed both of the major ale breweries in the city. The area credit evaluator for R. G. Dun & Co. reported in February 1849 "Don't know them." Two years later he knew of them, but judged they were a poor credit risk. This opinion was to change quickly and dramatically.

The Empire Brewery was started in 1844 when Jacob Best Sr. and his four sons, Jacob Jr., Phillip, Charles and Lorenz started their small brewery on Chestnut Street. The brothers did not always get along, and Charles left in 1845 to return to making vinegar. Lorenz, the youngest, was apparently more like an employee than a partner of Jacob Jr. and Phillip, and he left in 1850 to join Charles in establishing the Plank Road Brewery (later Miller Brewing). Jacob Best Sr. withdrew from active involvement in the business in 1853, leaving his two eldest sons in charge. During the 1840s the Bests also distilled whiskey and produced vinegar as well as brewing their increasingly popular beers.

One of the earliest surviving signs from Best, probably from the early 1880s. Courtesy of National Brewery Museum.

The sons purchased more land, some of which was adjacent to the brewery and used to expand the plant, including a new brewhouse with additional cellars in 1857. Other land was used for beer halls, including a centrally located lot on Market Street between what is now East Kilbourn and East State. Best & Co. already was shipping beer to Chicago during the 1850s, and had established an office on Randolph Street by 1857.

Jacob Jr. retired from the partnership, receiving almost $10,000 and the Market Street beer hall as his share, and the fiery Phillip took full control of the company. The payout to Jacob Jr. as well as the economic depression of the late 1850s and the Civil War in the early 1860s meant that capital for expansion was scarce, and like most Midwest breweries, Best and Co. were forced to tread water while waiting for the business climate to improve.

The postwar expansion of Best & Co. was masterminded by its new leaders, Frederick Pabst and Emil Schandein. Both married daughters of Phillip Best: Pabst met Maria Best while he was captain of a steamer on Lake Michigan and married her in 1862, and Schandein married Maria's younger sister Elizabetha ("Lisette") in 1866. Best sought an opportunity to retire, and the appearance of two sons-in-law with business and technical ability and engaging personalities allowed him to turn over the family firm in 1866 with confidence. (Best died while visiting Germany in 1869).

The end of the war, the resumption of immigration from beer-consuming nations, and the recovery of the economy allowed Best & Co. to start growing again, and at a rate that outstripped breweries elsewhere in the country. Best & Co. had started shipping beer to Mexico in 1865, the expansion of the rail network opened markets to the West, and the Chicago fire of 1871 allowed Best and other Milwaukee brewers to move in to the Chicago market faster than they may have otherwise. In 1868 Best became the largest brewer in Milwaukee—a position it would not give up for the rest of the century. Part of the growth was likely due to the personalities of Schandein and Pabst (especially the latter; Schandein was less of a public figure), some due to their business ability and instincts. The most important move they made in the post-Civil War period was the purchase of the Melms brewery. The large, modern plant was subsequently known as Best's South Side Brewery, and not only gave the company more production capacity but also better access to railroad links, and thus more efficient shipping facilities.

Best had an office in Chicago in the early 1850s, and other breweries followed the lakeshore south. The importance of the Chicago market is indicated by the fact that the manager of Best's Chicago North Side branch, John S. Pierce, earned a higher salary than any other employee of the company other than the secretary and head brewmaster. While Chicago was too close and profitable to ignore, most of Best's first thirteen branches were in Wisconsin cities like Ashland, Eau Claire, Stevens Point, and Wausau. Other early expansions crossed the border to cities such as Peoria and St. Paul, along with Houghton and Calumet in Michigan's Upper Peninsula, which were reached more easily from Milwaukee than Detroit. The notable exceptions were the Kansas City branch, which was the first branch other than Chicago, and the Pittsburgh branch, established in 1884.

In 1873 the Phillip Best Brewing Co. was incorporated in Wisconsin with Pabst, Schandein and Charles Best Jr. as the only directors. The company was estimated to be worth $600,000, which ranked it among the largest manufacturers in the country. Frederick Pabst, known almost universally as Captain Pabst, held a majority of the shares for all but a brief period from incorporation until his death in 1904, which effectively made him the leader as well as the public face of the company. Emil Schandein died in 1888, and was replaced on the board of directors by his widow Lisette, who for the next several years was probably the only female vice-president of a major brewing company. Pabst orchestrated a few leadership changes at the beginning of the 1890s. He brought his son Gustave into the company as secretary when Charles Best Jr. retired due to ill health, and also appointed accountant Charles W. Henning as assistant secretary—the first non-family member to serve as an officer. Frederick Pabst Jr. and J. F. Theurer, superintendent of brewing, were both given a few shares of stock in 1892. Theurer's innovations in scientific brewing made him too valuable to lose to a competitor.

Phillip Best Brewing Co. changed its name to Pabst Brewing Co. in 1889, several months after the death of Emil Schandein, but the company maintained the logo of a capital B superimposed on a hop leaf in honor of the firm's beginnings. The firm was augmented by another major purchase in 1892, when Pabst acquired the equipment, good will and some of the property of the fire-prone Falk, Jung and Borchert Brewing Co. This also changed the composition of the ownership, since members of the Falk and Borchert family were given stock as part of the agreement. (Philipp Jung, who had been superintendent of brewing for Pabst from 1873 to 1879, went into businesses on his own, first in malting and later buying the Obermann Brewing Co.)

In the period from 1873 to 1893, the company led by Pabst developed into a modern multinational corporation. America's rapidly expanding population, especially urban industrial workers, created a huge new market for Best/Pabst and other brewers to supply. Best was an early adopter of bottled beer, and a series of brewmasters concluding with Theurer

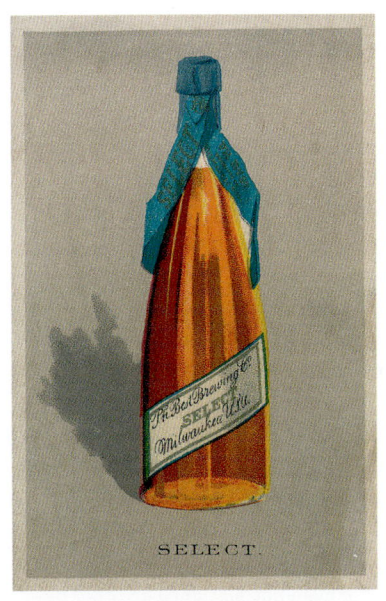

Legend has it that **Pabst Blue Ribbon** acquired its name after the 1893 Columbian Exposition, but the company had been tying blue ribbons on bottles of Best Select since the 1880s. This souvenir booklet was published in 1884. AUTHOR'S COLLECTION.

tinkered with the formula for the bottled beer until it was appealing in color, flavor, and stability. As Pabst Brewing Co., business was expanded into nearly every state by 1890 (New England was not an important market outside of the major cities in Massachusetts). In the mid-1880s the company began a concerted effort to start marketing beer overseas, instead of merely responding to special orders. While Best/Pabst only sent a few thousand barrels overseas in the years around 1890, this was still almost 30 percent of all U.S. beer exports.

Throughout this period, Best/Pabst continued to refine the marketing and promotion methods that would make the company one of the most important breweries in the world. The brewery celebrated the Centennial of the United States by producing a special Centennial Lager Beer, which was available on draught at selected locations. They also brought out Century beer near the turn of the twentieth century and supported it with strong advertising. Pabst, Theurer and other executives were well aware of the ability to attract attention

Commodore George Dewey and his flagship, the cruiser *Olympia*, are depicted to capitalize on American victories over Spain in 1898. It is not clear whether this label was used on any bottles of Pabst. COLLECTION OF JOHN STEINER.

by introducing new brands and harnessing the publicity for advertising. Red, White and Blue followed Century, and capitalized on the triumphant expansionism that followed the Spanish-American War. Advertising manager Joseph R. Kathrens came up with the idea of using a bottle with a shamrock instead of the usual logo for St. Patrick's Day. However, the company ended the label proliferation in the early 1900s and focused on their core brands. Pabst advertised extensively in newspapers and magazines, often with elaborate campaigns that stretched as long as three years. As early as the 1870s the brewery relied heavily on souvenirs for advertising, and this method of keeping the company's products in the public eye only increased over time.

Captain Pabst and his advertising teams were particularly adept at identifying events that could be used to publicize the brands and the company. Not only were the heroes of the Spanish-American War featured in advertising (see also Chapter 5), but Pabst made sure the heroes were well supplied with his beer. According to a newspaper article (that was probably really an advertisement rather than an authentic news story), Pabst

> sent an unlimited supply of his amber fluid to Manila to be given to the soldiers, and after each battle one barrel of the famous Milwaukee brand is sent to each company from the agency in Manila. That the soldiers appreciate the action of Col. [sic] Pabst is shown by the number of letters that are being received from them, in which they declare that the lives of many of the United States soldiers have been saved by the generous use of Pabst Milwaukee beer.

Of course, capitalizing on the awards from the Columbian Exposition in Chicago to relaunch Pabst Select as Pabst Blue Ribbon was the most enduring of these promotions (and is covered in more detail in chapter 5).

Pabst worked hard to position his beer as a luxury product that was worth spending extra to enjoy. The move into the New York City market depended on this tactic. Since the many established New York brewers already had the tied house saloons under control, Pabst focused on high-class restaurants who would not be serving Blue Ribbon exclusively, but where it would get exposure in a distinctive setting. In some cases, this meant building his own establishment, such as the Pabst Hotel on Times Square, or later the Grand Circle Restaurant at Columbus Circle. Pabst Brewing Co. exhibited a team of six "perfectly matched" dapple-gray Percherons at state fairs and international expositions, where they won numerous awards. Adding to the publicity value was the specially designed and brightly painted railroad car that brought the team to each event.

Pabst and other national brewers searched for every opportunity to place their name and logo in front of customers. This stein from this Coney Island hotel dates ca. 1905. COLLECTION OF JOHN STEINER.

As important as securing distant markets was to the company, it placed special emphasis on maintaining the home market—all the more difficult because so many of the nation's large brewers called the Cream City home. The Pabst Theater, the Whitefish Bay Resort, the Pabst Building, Pabst Park and the St. Charles Hotel all kept the brewery name before the public and associated it with quality and entertainment. The company also erected an enormous electric sign in 1910 at Grand Avenue and West Water Street in which the lights flashed so as to make appear that the hand pointing at the bottle of Blue Ribbon moved and the blue ribbon itself waved. As prominent as these monuments were, the brewery itself was the best advertisement, and nearly every visiting group or convention was invited to tour the plant and enjoy beer fresh from the brewery.

Growth continued through the 1910s, and worldwide expansion continued even during World War I, when some markets previously served by German or British breweries could no longer get those brands. Pabst could be found in nearly forty countries and was generally available in distant cities such as Shanghai. However, the omnipresent nature of Pabst made it one of the prime targets of the temperance movement, which finally triumphed with the passage of the 18th Amendment and the Volstead Act.

The Pabst brothers, Gustave and Fred Jr., decided against shutting down, and prepared to make the best of the situation until (what they believed would be) the eventual repeal of Prohibition. Fred took charge of marketing new products and did his best to retain longtime employees. The company produced a wide range of soft drinks, malt products, and cheese, and rented out portions of the brewery to other businesses. (More detail about Prohibition-era adjustments is in chapter 6.)

Pabst Brewing Co. was part of an unusual merger during Prohibition. The Premier Malt Products Co., successor to Decatur Brewing Co., had working capital that Pabst lacked, and Pabst had a national brand and reputation. Premier had also produced a brand of malt

WISCONSIN BREWERIES AND BREWPUBS   509

syrup called Blue Ribbon—Pabst protested the use of the name, but since they did not yet have a malt syrup under the name, they lost the suit. Premier's head, Harris Perlstein, led a talented group of executives, and Fred Pabst Jr. may have been looking toward his impending retirement. The new Premier-Pabst Corporation was formed October 1932, and within weeks Franklin D. Roosevelt had been elected president—at least in part because of his pledge to repeal Prohibition.

Pabst was one of several Milwaukee brewers that was ready to deliver beer as soon as it was legal on 7 April 1933. The brewery had plants in Milwaukee and Peoria Heights, Illinois, and began working to restore its position among the leading breweries. Premier-Pabst predicted that packaged beer would dominate the market, and the company emphasized both production and marketing of bottled beer, and in 1935, canned beer. The company also rebuilt its foreign trade, and by 1941 sold about 60 percent of all American exported beer.

In 1938, the stockholders voted to restore the name Pabst Brewing Co., though in recognition of the multiple plants the plural Pabst Breweries remained on the seal for several

Like many other brewers, Pabst encouraged support for the war effort in its advertising, as on this coaster. AUTHOR'S COLLECTION.

years. The years prior to World War II saw the brewery engage it the same tactics that brought it to the fore in earlier years. Starting with Blue Ribbon, the brewery introduced additional brands. Red, White and Blue was revived as the "popular price" beer (which at that time was 10¢ per bottle at retail compared to 15¢ for a premium beer). The Casino brand was another "popular price" brand that had a brief run in the wake of the popularity of the Pabst Casino at Chicago's Century of Progress exhibition in 1933 and 1934. Pabst also brought out two more flavorful beers: Old Tankard Ale in cans, and Andeker, an all-malt European-style premium lager, on draught only.

During World War II, Pabst was among the most vigorous supporters of the war effort: engaging in common activities like scrap metal drives and war bond drives, as well as unique activities such as supporting an essay contest on how to control postwar unemployment. (Two future chairmen of the Council of Economic Advisors, Herbert Stein and Leon Keyserling, won first and second prizes, respectively.) After the war, the company introduced a new slogan: "Thirty-three Fine Brews Blended into One

As canned beer became popular, breweries experimented with packaging. This unusual Pabst six-pack (ca. 1936) had two rows of three cans on top of each other rather than side by side. COLLECTION OF DAVID WENDL.

Great Beer," which may have had little meaning for the casual drinker, but was intended to highlight the consistency of the beer.

As the war drew to a close, Pabst began the territorial expansion that would characterize the growth plans of many of the large shipping brewers. In 1945, they purchased Hoffman Beverage Company in Newark, New Jersey, which gave them a modern brewery on the East Coast and access to a large distribution network. The growth on the Pacific Coast, caused in part by the booming military economy in the western states, made it imperative for brewers to enhance their presence, preferably in a way that would reduce shipping costs. To that end, Pabst purchased the plant of Los Angeles Brewing Co. in 1948. Pabst refrained from adding breweries in new regions until it built a new plant in Perry, Georgia, in 1971. The company attempted to purchase Blatz in 1958, but was blocked by anti-trust regulators. (Additional information about geographic expansion is in chapter 8.)

While Pabst Brewing Co. continued to grow in size and sales, it was unable to dislodge Anheuser-Busch and Schlitz from the top two spots in the national rankings after World

The lavish Pabst Blue Ribbon Casino at the south end of Northerly Island was a popular attraction at Chicago's Century of Progress Exposition of 1933–34. The casino seated 1,000, and the outdoor gardens accommodated 2,500 more. The Pabst Blue Ribbon radio program featuring Ben Bernie and his orchestra was broadcast from the casino on Tuesday nights. Three other bands regularly appeared on the circular revolving bandstand: Guy Lombardo and his Royal Canadians, Buddy Rogers and his Hollywood Music, and Tom Gerun and his Californians. The restaurant served Pabst-ett cheeses along with Pabst beers. COLLECTION OF JOHN STEINER.

War II. The sustained expansion program left the brewery with much more capacity than it needed by the 1970s. In a misguided attempt to boost sales, the company repositioned Blue Ribbon as a popular price brand, which worked for a few years but eventually devalued the brand and left the brewery without a true flagship premium beer. Pabst responded by buying even more breweries and labels, essentially following the lead of Heileman Brewing Co. in having a series of popular regional beers rather than a true national brand. Company annual reports adopted verbal gymnastics to place a positive spin on unsold beer, such as the claim: "By the end of 1979 we were able to reduce inventories of our products in the field to an absolute minimum."

In the 1980s, Pabst was the subject of a takeover attempt by Minneapolis-based financier Irwin Jacobs, who initiated a proxy fight to take control of the company. Infamous in the brewing community for his 1975 purchase and closure of Grain Belt Brewing Co. in Minneapolis, Jacobs had joined the board of Pabst in July 1981, allegedly to engineer a turnaround and avoid a proxy fight. However, the proxy fight began anyway in December, and continued until early 1983. During the conflict, Pabst sought a merger with C. Schmidt and Sons of Philadelphia (not to be confused with the Jacob Schmidt Brewing Co. of St. Paul, at this point part of the House of Heileman) in order to deter Jacobs. A proposed merger with Pittsburgh Brewing Co. failed because the Steel City firm tired of waiting for the drama in the Cream City to end.

Ultimately, Paul Kalmanovitz ended up purchasing Pabst Brewing Co., and the end of the Milwaukee company was not far away. In 1995, production of most of the brands was moved to Heileman's plant in La Crosse, and in October 1995 management announced that the 141-year old Milwaukee institution would close for good. The Pabst brands stayed alive, brewed under contract at Miller and other locations, and in the early twenty-first century Blue Ribbon saw a significant resurgence as a "hipster" beer, popular precisely because it wasn't a nationally advertised brand (and was often served in inexpensive 16-ounce "tallboy" cans).

Twenty years after the brewery closed, the Pabst name began to come back, and the brewery neighborhood was revitalized. The former brewhouse has been converted to the Brewhouse Inn & Suites, a hotel featuring a line of restored brewkettles in the lobby. Other buildings in the complex still await reuse. The Pabst brands were purchased by Eugene Kashper, an immigrant, who moved to America at age six. (Some headlines reporting Kashper's purchase erroneously reported that he was a Russian national, perhaps because of his holdings in Russian breweries.) Unlike several previous investors, Kashper was a beer industry veteran, and saw the opportunity to rebuild the Pabst brand. At this writing, Pabst has brought back Old Tankard Ale (reportedly brewed according to the 1937 recipe), recreated Ballantine's Ale and is considering reintroducing other classic recipes such as Doppel Braeu from the 1890s. In 2017, Pabst opened a small brewpub in a church that had been part of the Pabst complex since the nineteenth century—bringing back old recipes and offering creative new brews typical of many modern craft breweries.

John P. Engelhardt, Main Street Brewery (1845?–1861)

Elizabeth Engelhardt, Main Street Brewery (1861–62)

37 MAIN AND NORTH CHICAGO STREET (TODAY BROADWAY AND CHICAGO) (1845–);
1150 WINDLAKE AVENUE? (1857–1862)

The precise year in which John Engelhardt began brewing is unclear. An account from 1906 claims that he arrived in Milwaukee in 1845 and started the brewery shortly thereafter. However, it is likely that he was in the city by 1838, though he did not start brewing until later. By 1850 Engelhardt was among the larger brewers in town, employing four men and producing about 500 barrels per year. Engelhardt built a new facility in 1857 on Windlake Avenue. Even though the brewery was now operated by horse and hand power, the few statistics available suggest that he did not increase production much. The fact that city directories still listed the brewery at the earlier address suggests that the new location may have been a storage facility, and that brewing continued at the original site.

Unfortunately, Engelhardt was a passenger on the ill-fated steamer *Lady Elgin* which was wrecked on 8 September 1860 in a collision with the schooner *Augusta* on Lake Michigan. About 300 people died in what is still one of the greatest losses of life on the Great Lakes. Engelhardt's widow Mary Elizabeth continued to run the brewery for about two years, after which it was managed by Jacob Wind, who had been employed at the brewery since at least 1851. Albert Schnabel's history of city breweries indicates that Wind specialized in brown beer, as opposed to lager. after 1862 Wind (or Windt) is no longer listed as a brewer in city directories. The property remained in the Engelhardt family, and Elizabeth leased the building to Franz Ludwig and Charles L. Kiewert (later a dealer in brewery supplies), but the brewery no longer operated. The vaults on Windlake

Pabst introduced bottled Andeker, originally a draught-only product, in the early 1960s. Like other premium beers such as Michelob (Anheuser-Busch) and Erlanger (Schlitz), Andeker had a different bottle shape to emphasize it was a premium product. The name was from the monastic brewery of Andechs, near Munich. This bottle is from 1962.
COLLECTION OF JOHN STEINER.

Avenue collapsed in 1906, and Phillip Stephen Engelhardt sold the Main Street property in 1922, just before his death.

Johann Braun, Cedar Brewery (1846–47);
   City Brewery (1847–1851)
Valentin (Valentine) Blatz, City Brewery
   (1851–1889)
Val. Blatz Brewing Co. (1889–1891)
United States Brewing Co. of Val. Blatz
   (1891–1911)
Val. Blatz Brewing Co. (1911–1920)
Blatz Brewing Co. (1933–1959)
609 Broadway, later 1120 North Broadway

Johann Braun (John Brown) began producing beer in 1846 at his brewery at what was then Market Street between Martin and Division. First called the Cedar Brewery, in the 1848 city directory it was listed as the City Brewery, though it was sometimes still known by the former name.

Braun's production in the early years is confused by later accounts. The 1850 industry census listed Braun as producing 4,000 barrels, a figure that seems accurate given his revenue was $18,000. Val Blatz later claimed that he started by making 400–500 barrels in 1851, but his obituary in 1894 claimed that sales that year were only 150 barrels. It is likely there was a large drop in production due to the sudden death of Braun and the delay in restarting under Blatz. However, it is possible that the 150 figure was a downward exaggeration since that quantity was used in many articles and was applied to several of the early breweries and appeared to be the standard number used to dramatize the growth of a mighty brewery from humble origins.

Braun was the first in Wisconsin to own two breweries—in addition to the Cedar/City brewery in Milwaukee he was also a partner in the City Brewery of Racine with Fred Heck. Braun may not have been a trained brewer himself, since he employed several other brewers, including Louis Brauchle (later of Columbus) and Valentin Blatz. In fact, the 1851 city directory lists four "brewers" boarding with Braun. Unfortunately, Braun's multiple locations led to his demise—in March 1851, he was thrown from his buggy while traveling between the breweries and suffered injuries that proved to be fatal.

By this time, Val Blatz had started a small brewery of his own near the City Brewery. In December 1851, Blatz married Braun's widow Louise and took her two children, John and Louise, into his family. He then merged the two breweries and took the name of City Brewery for the new business. Blatz had been trained by his father as a brewer in his native Bavaria, and at eighteen had been sent on a tour of prominent breweries in Augsburg, Munich, and Würzburg to learn the trade. In 1847 his father paid for a substitute to take his place in the army, and later that year he emigrated to the United States. He worked for the Born Brewery in Buffalo, New York for about a year, and arrived in Milwaukee in 1848. Blatz was among the best trained of the early Cream City brewers, but he faced the same constraints as his local rivals. In an 1886 article in the *Sentinel*, he described the primitive conditions, and noted that most of the beer from this era was top-fermenting rather than lager and had to be consumed quickly (an 1892 article claimed that this so-called "present use beer" was entirely displaced by lager production at Blatz by 1855).

After Blatz took charge of the City Brewery, its growth kept it among the leading firms in the city. In 1856 he began working on plans for a significant brewery expansion, and in 1857 Blatz proposed a new seven-story malt house which was expected to cost between $15,000 and $20,000. (Sketches of the brewery from 1865 show no such structure.) By 1860 he ranked third in the city with 32,000 barrels, and would stay in that position for most of the rest of the century. His reach was expanding as well. In the summer of 1873, Blatz shipped about one thousand kegs a week to Chicago, and shipped out 300 to 500 a day to all points.

However, the growth was not uninterrupted. In 1865 Blatz was compelled to respond to allegations about a significant accident in his brewery:

To my greatest surprise I learn that it is rumored that a man had met with an accident by falling into a fermenting or mashing tub in my brewery. Hearing the report, at first I though it not worth while to pay any attention to such an absurd or malicious production; but learning that certain persons are making capital of this rumor, which was at first considered a bad joke, I declare said rumor an absolute falsehood, and offer ONE THOUSAND DOLLARS to any person, my workmen included, who will prove that any person has met with any such accident in my establishment.

Three years later Blatz himself fell seventeen feet through a trap door, and was badly bruised but recovered. After the disastrous fire of 1873 (see chapter 4) the brewery was rebuilt significantly larger and featured a brewing copper of 425 barrels capacity—large enough to brew in one batch about as much as Blatz had sold in his first year. Indeed, in the first full year after the fire, Blatz produced over 55,000 barrels—well behind Schlitz and Best, but almost 40,000 barrels ahead of the next largest firm.

Throughout the next decades, Val. Blatz Brewing Co. was as much an innovator as it was a leading producer. Blatz adopted electrical power throughout the building as well as other fire protection measures (see chapter 4). Blatz was one of the first in Milwaukee to offer

The reverse of this 1863 token advertises both the City Brewery and malt house of Val. Blatz. Tokens were common during the Civil War when shortages and financial uncertainty made U.S. coins hard to come by. Collection of Tye Schwalbe.

bottled lager, and for many years laid claim in advertising to being the very first to do so. Bottled beer enabled Blatz to increase their market across the nation, and their beer was on sale in San Francisco by 1877 (see chapter 5). In 1880 Blatz reached the 100,000-barrel mark, and could now be counted among the largest in the nation. In keeping with this status, Blatz advertised on a national level, sent elaborate exhibits to major fairs and exhibitions, and created a variety of souvenirs to keep the brand before the public.

As one of the leading Cream City businesses, Blatz was subject to the same labor unrest as its rivals (see Chapter 5). A few weeks after a maltsters strike in early 1888, there were a series of small explosions at the Blatz brewery, which the press was quick to sensationalize. The *Sentinel* claimed "there is now a strong feeling that they were not the result of any accident, but were the direct outcome of the recent troubles between the brewers and their employés [sic]." An anonymous brewery employee was quoted as saying that "There are men in the brewery who feel sore at being obliged to leave the union to retain their positions, and they are being watched now pretty closely." However, Albert Blatz claimed that allegations of dynamite were "a d—d lie" and a less dramatic article in the *Daily Journal* hypothesized that the bursts were small grain dust explosions and quoted Blatz reassuring the public that workers would have no reason to blow up a building in which they would themselves be killed."

As one of the largest businesses in an important industry, Blatz needed to keep up with financial trends as well as advances in brewing. Blatz incorporated his brewery as Val. Blatz Brewing Co. in September 1889, with his sons Albert C., Emil and Valentin Jr. and son-in-law John Kremer as partners. The new company produced 217,000 barrels in 1889, but was falling farther behind Pabst and Schlitz. Rumors of buyouts and syndicates were common at the time, and Blatz was the subject of several schemes. As was common, Blatz deflected any stories about deals, and in the fall of 1890 completed a striking new office building and announced plans for a significant expansion rather than selling the business. However, negotiations with a large syndicate had been underway since 1889, and in February 1891 a deal was confirmed in which Blatz and five Chicago breweries—Bartholomae & Leicht, Bartholomae & Roesing, Ernst Brothers, Michael Brand and K. G. Schmidt—joined under English capital to form the Milwaukee & Chicago Brewing Co. Some of the Chicago breweries had previously combined as the American-owned syndicate United States Brewing Co., and the new company took the latter name, though newspapers used both names during 1891 to refer to the combination. Blatz rejected the patriotic (though corporate-sounding) name, and continued to use its own name on labels and advertising materials, and officially changed its name back in 1911. The sale was expected to be especially beneficial to the Chicago firms, since they could use Blatz's marketing and distribution advantages to export more beer, but price wars during the mid-1890s limited the benefits and in some years the shareholders received no dividend.

Val Blatz himself became part of the syndicate and retained full control over the Milwaukee operations of the company. The sale was reportedly worth $3,000,000 to the Blatz family, which solidified their place among the wealthiest families in the state. However, Blatz did not enjoy the fruits of the sale for long. While stopping in St. Paul on the way back from a trip to California, Val Blatz died suddenly at a hotel in that city, aged sixty-eight. Milwaukee newspapers provided several days of coverage of his life and funeral arrangements, with articles praising his contributions to local charities, membership in civic organizations, and even his generosity to local waiters—who knew they could count on him for a (then) lavish 25¢ tip. Luckily, the family was ready to take over the business, and Albert Blatz became the new president. Like his father, Albert had learned the brewing trade in a variety of cities, and had traveled to the American brewing centers of Cincinnati, Rochester, New York, and Philadelphia. Val. Jr. had studied in Germany, though it appears that his studies were less in brewing and more in business. For a while starting in 1879, he ran a confectionary company and introduced a line of candy. He returned to the family business upon incorporation, and was vice president and superintendent of the company from 1891 until 1920. Val Jr. is credited with modernizing the brewery in the 1890s, and with diversifying its businesses. He was in charge of Alliance Investment Company, which handled the Blatz real estate holdings. He purchased the Blatz Hotel in Milwaukee, and in 1916 went back into candy, which turned out to be a good idea with Prohibition approaching.

At the turn of the twentieth century, Blatz remained one of the most important breweries in the nation. The slogan of the era, "It leads them all" was not accurate as far as volume was concerned, but Blatz products were shipped across the country and to Mexico,

This illustration of the Blatz product line is from a booklet published in 1899 to sell Blatz to wholesalers and retailers. After the introduction of the crown cap, Blatz continued to use corks for several years and touted this as a guarantee of authenticity. Unscrupulous operators sometimes obtained empty bottles, filled them with cheaper beer, and passed them off as the famous brand. AUTHOR'S COLLECTION.

South America, Australia, and Hawai'i. The company sang the praises of its product in a booklet intended for distributors just after the Spanish-American War, claiming "Complaints against the quality of Blatz are as scarce as Spanish victories in the Yankee-Spankee war," echoing the jingoistic and often racially tinged language of the era. Blatz Park was a popular resort on the Milwaukee River for those seeking escape from the city. However, as a national brewer, Blatz had already experienced financial losses due to the imposition of prohibition in several states, and was somewhat better prepared for national prohibition than other firms.

Blatz did more to keep the company name on products during Prohibition than most other breweries. The actually put some advertising support behind their near beer, Old Heidelberg, which proved popular enough that they kept the name for their flagship lager after Prohibition. The company manufactured a range of soft drinks, and continued to brew malt tonics. Blatz Bohemian Malt Syrup was available in plain and hop flavored varieties, and customers interested in ways to use it (for baking, not brewing, or so they claimed) could send for a free recipe book. In 1923 Blatz sought and was granted a charter to establish a warehouse in Kansas for its non-alcoholic products. This was remarkable not only for the simple fact of a brewery building new facilities during Prohibition, but also because Kansas had not granted a charter to any brewing company for any purpose for forty-two years (since Kansas became one of the first states to adopt prohibition).

Two important leaders took the helm at Blatz during Prohibition. Edward Landsberg, formerly of United States Brewing Co. and general manager of Blatz for that company, purchased the brewery from the syndicate in 1920 and became the president of the company, and his brother-in-law Frank Gabel became the secretary. The two would guide the brewery through Prohibition and through the decade of growth thereafter.

Since Blatz had continued to produce near beer throughout the dry years, the company was in a good position to make the conversion back to real beer. The *Journal* of 27 March 1933 featured a photo of Blatz's bottling line at work—they had started the day before to fill 600,000 bottles per day, the first of Milwaukee's breweries to bottle beer at the end of Prohibition. The Blatz plant was one of several where revelers camped out waiting for the first legal beer, and Blatz beer was among the bottles sent by air to President Roosevelt as soon as it was safe to fly through the stormy weather that day. In 1934 Blatz made what they rather immodestly called "the greatest advancement in the brewing industry in 20 years," placing the date of brewing on every bottle of Old Heidelberg. This feature was not entirely new, since perforated labels had been used for many years to indicate the bottling date. Contrary to late twentieth and early twenty-first century emphasis, however, the "Brew-Date" on Old Heidelberg was designed to show that the beer had been aged long enough, rather than to show how fresh the beer was. This was a reaction to the concern about insufficiently aged (or "green") beer being sold in the rush to capture the market in the wake of Repeal. Blatz began using "cone-top" cans in late 1935, making them the third Milwaukee brewery to offer canned beer (Pabst and Schlitz preceded them). The company erected a massive neon sign on top of the brewery in 1937 that was twenty-six feet high and thirty-three feet wide on all four sides and required 1,200 lineal feet of tubing. The brewery still held on to one pre-Prohibition practice for a few years, however—they continued to do some bottling at their branch in Prairie du Chien until 1937.

During the 1930s Blatz was able to rebuild much of its national market. Edward Landsberg died in February 1941, and Frank Gabel succeeded him as president. Shortly thereafter, in 1943, Schenley Distillers of New York purchased the brewery from the Landsberg estate for $6 million. Gabel remained as president to guide the million-barrel brewery through World War II, but retired in 1946. Gabel assured the 1,150 employees that no changes in operations were imminent.

For the next decade, the only changes were expansion-related. In 1945 the company announced a major building program to increase

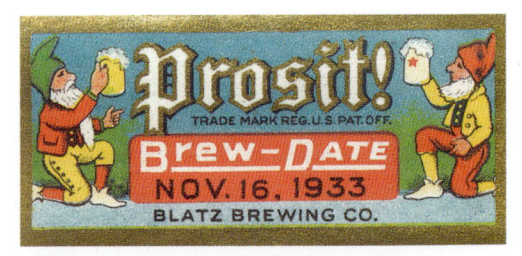

Today's "Born On" or brew date labels confirm the freshness of the beer, but in the months after Prohibition these neck labels assured customers that the beer was aged long enough. COLLECTION OF TIMOTHY HOLIAN.

Many breweries simply acted as jobbers for candy products of other manufacturers, but Blatz put its own name on chewing gum and supported it with extensive advertising. One campaign offered a set of twenty photographs of famous "Screen Stars" for ten Blatz gum wrappers and 10¢ in coin or stamps. This package is from the late 1920s. COLLECTION OF JOHN STEINER.

The Kork-N-Seal cap was used to reseal bottles, especially 64-ounce picnic bottles. These were not the original seal but were sold or given away separately. They were most popular in the decades immediately after Prohibition. COLLECTION OF TYE SCHWALBE.

514   THE DRINK THAT MADE WISCONSIN FAMOUS

For many years after Prohibition, the large Blatz sign above the Tower Restaurant was a landmark for travelers crossing the Wisconsin/Illinois border on U.S. Highway 41. COURTESY OF WISCONSIN HISTORICAL SOCIETY, WHI-90333.

capacity from 1.1 million to 2.25 million barrels. Blatz added a new bottle house and new guest facilities late in the 1940s (the bottle house is now part of Milwaukee School of Engineering). Finding the new additions still inadequate, in 1953 new president Frank Verbest started exploring the possibility of purchasing existing breweries, and was looking for facilities in California to the west, Louisiana, Texas or Georgia to the south, and New York, New Jersey or Pennsylvania to the northeast. However, no purchase was made, and Blatz was hit hard by the 1953 brewers strike. Because it settled with its workers before the other Milwaukee brewers, Blatz was kicked out of the Milwaukee Brewers Association and the Wisconsin State Brewers' Association. New product launches (such as Tempo, see Chapter 8), label changes and renewed advertising could not prevent production from slipping under one million barrels for the first time since 1943. In 1958, Pabst purchased Blatz, but the purchase was later ruled impermissible by anti-trust regulators, and Heileman acquired the Blatz brands. (See Chapter 8 for more details on the end of the brewery.)

Henry Stoltz, Union Brewery (1848–1850)
Stoltz & Schneider, Union Brewery (1850–1862)
Henry Stoltz, Union Brewery (1862–65)
Margaret Stoltz, Union Brewery (1865–68)
Knab, Sprey & Co., Union Brewery (1868–1870)
Paul Degan & Christian Fuss, Union Brewery (1870)
Paul Degan, Union Brewery (1870–73)
Joseph Fuss, Union Brewery (1873)
Jacob Stoltz, Union Brewery (1873–74)
Fred Borchert & Son, Union Brewery (1874–79)
Jung & Borchert, Union Brewery (1879–1884)
Jung & Borchert Brewing Co. (1884–88)
Falk, Jung & Borchert Brewing Co. (1888–1892)

110-123 OGDEN/CORNER OF OGDEN AND BROADWAY

While a few sources have claimed this firm dates back to the early 1840s under the management of Stoltz and Krell, the best documentation shows that the brewery could not have been that old. The research of Leonard P. Jurgensen indicates that Stoltz did not arrive in America until 1845, and that the lot he purchased in 1848 had no structures on it. Contemporary newspaper accounts place the construction no earlier than 1848. Michael Stoltz, most likely the brother of Henry, was in charge of building on the hilly site, which was selected so lagering caves could be excavated easily. By 1850, in partnership with Leonhardt Schneider, the business had grown to 1,600 barrels. Around this time he built a malt house, and replaced the brewery in the early 1850s. The brewery continued to grow along with the city and, by 1860, was producing 4,500 barrels. While this ranked sixth among the Cream City brewers that year, Stoltz & Schneider were in some ways still a second-tier brewery. They used horsepower unlike their main rivals who had switched to steam. Schneider died in 1862, and Stoltz purchased his share. Stoltz himself died in 1866 (though some sources inaccurately claim 1865), and his widow Margaret took over the management of the brewery for a few years. (Michael appears in the 1867 excise records, but he may simply have been paying the tax. He lived next door at 678 Main and was listed in the city directory as a distiller.)

In 1868, Margaret Stoltz rented or leased the brewery to David Knab and Matthew Sprey, who had limited success. Their first year of business saw production drop to 2,845 barrels, and by 1870, they turned the brewery over to Paul Degan, who had married Leonhardt Schneider's widow and had worked at the brewery during the 1860s. Sprey was subsequently employed at the Hartford brewery but was killed in 1873 in a railroad accident at Slinger (then Schleisingerville). The brewery was sold at a sheriff's sale to Charles Koefer, but Degan seems to have stayed on as brewer. The brewery continued to slip in the local rankings and sold only 178 barrels during September 1874.

In late 1874, Degan obtained a $6,000 mortgage on the property, but transferred it the next day to brothers Jacob and Joseph Fuss. But the brewery property was soon embroiled in a dispute between the Fuss family and Jacob Stoltz. The *Daily Sentinel* reported:

> *A quarrel about the ownership of the old Stolz [sic] Brewery resulted in a savage fight between the Fuss brothers and one of the Stolzes. It appears that the Fuss brothers purchased the property for $15,000, and have had some trouble in securing possession of the premises. Last week there was quite a squabble for the books, and, on yesterday, one of the Fuss brothers, a stepfather to young Stolz, got Fuss's thumb into*

This Blatz drummer backbar piece dates to the 1950s. The figure's arms moved to hoist the beer and clash the cymbals. COLLECTION OF SCOTT KOVAR.

The West Side Turners purchased beer from Borchert in 1878.
COLLECTION OF JOHN STEINER.

his mouth and bit it nearly off. . . . the quarrel is growing so bitter that the authorities will be obliged to bottle up the contestants.

This turbulent episode ended soon after when grain merchant Ernst Borchert bought the brewery with his brothers Charles and Frederick Jr. and named it after their late father.

Borchert took a few years to put the brewery "on a paying basis," but by 1879 had boosted production to an impressive 10,000 barrels—still firmly in the second tier of local firms, but respectable. In December of that year Borchert brought in a new partner, Philipp Jung, who had been a foreman (brewmaster) for Phillip Best Brewing Co. There were conspiracy theories that Captain Pabst had sent Jung to the Ogden Avenue brewery to control its operations as part of a cartel, but these were debunked—Jung was simply a rising foreman looking for a firm in which he could be a partner. Under this new management, the company expanded both its facilities and its reach. By the mid-1880s, the brewery had reached 60,000 barrels per year, just behind Miller, and had depots in cities around Wisconsin. In 1882 the company considered an expansion on land in the Chase Valley, but nothing came of these plans. During 1882 the brewery earned mention for using hops grown in nearby Wauwatosa. Jung & Borchert was among the breweries involved in the labor disputes of January 1888, and their work force of 160 abandoned the union to keep their jobs for about the same high wages as the larger breweries.

It was clear that the growth potential of this brewery was limited, at least in part by its location. It was in a crowded neighborhood, and could not expand. In October 1888, Jung & Borchert joined with the slightly larger Franz Falk Brewing Co. to create the new firm of Falk, Jung & Borchert. The plant at Ogden and Broadway was used briefly for storage, first by Falk, Jung & Borchert, and later by Pabst when that company took over the former in 1892. In 1896, Pabst took out a building permit for a "lithographic institution" which became the new facility for Gugler Lithographic Company, the creator of labels and advertising material for Pabst and other breweries. The rest of the firm's history is covered under the Falk, Jung & Borchert entry.

Green Bay Road Brewery
Christian Pfeiffer (1848–1851)
Pfeiffer & Conrad (1851–56)
William M. Middlewood (1856)
Rheude & Co. (1856–59)
Davis & Co. Albion Brewery (1863?–66?)
GREEN BAY ROAD AND THIRD STREET, THIRD BETWEEN GALENA AND WALNUT

According to Leonard P. Jurgensen, Christian Pfeiffer established the Green Bay Road Brewery in 1848. He was joined shortly thereafter by partner Valentin Conrad. The business was fairly small, since this brewery did not pass the $500 threshold to be included in the 1850 or 1860 census of industry. It was, however, significant enough to be mentioned in an 1853 survey of the industries of Wisconsin. Pfeiffer was sometimes listed alone in the city directories during the mid-1850s. Around 1856, Anton Rheude purchased the brewery from William Middlewood, who had acquired the property earlier.

The Green Bay Road Brewery had a beer hall at 217 East Water Street during the mid-1850s. A. Rheude "respectfully invited [his] friends and the public in general" to hear a "Grand Vocal Concert" at the hall in January 1858. However, by late March, the beer hall was under new management and serving the bock beer of Sauer & Muehlschuster's brewery. It may have been that Rheude got out of the brewing business around that time. The brewery was sold back to Middlewood at a sheriff's sale in 1859. In March 1860, he announced in the *Sentinel*:

> The subscriber having purchased the brewery late in the possession of Rheude & Meister, and not intending to carry it on as a Brewery, offers for sale the Plant, &c., of said concern, consisting of a first class Copper Boiler, Steam Engine, Malt Mill, Wort Pump and other fixtures; also a parcel of Puncheons and loose articles.

The language of the advertisement suggests that the brewery was not in operation at the time of the proposed sale.

It may have taken Middlewood some time to find someone to run the brewery, but by 1863, it was rented to John M. Davis, one of the partners in the original Lake Brewery. Davis operated under the name of the Albion Brewery along with partner John Dearsley and brewer Titus T. Luin. This company only lasted a few years, and the Green Bay Road Brewery was sold to Joseph Schlitz Brewing Co., which was using the facility by 1866.

August Krug (1849–1861)
Joseph Schlitz, Chestnut Brewery (1861–1874)
Joseph Schlitz Brewing Co. (1874–1920)
Joseph Schlitz Beverage Co. (1920–1933)
Joseph Schlitz Brewing Co. (1933–1981)
46–48 (LATER 420) CHESTNUT (MODERN JUNEAU) (1849–1868); THIRD AND GALENA STREETS (1868–1981)

August Krug arrived in Milwaukee in 1848, and the next year started a small restaurant and brewery on Chestnut Street. Krug may have been more of a manager than a brewer, since his first employee was apparently brewer Franz Falk, a fellow native of Miltenberg, Bavaria (as was Val Blatz). Later accounts claim his sales in the first year were either 400 or 500 barrels, but these numbers were often used to show how small a brewery once was, and may be imprecise. While the neighborhood around Krug's

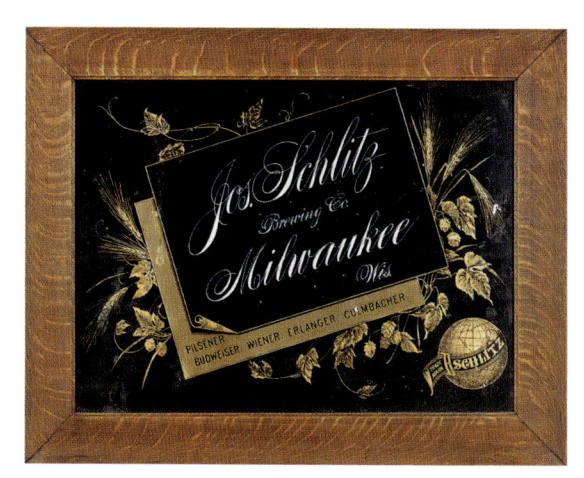

A Schlitz sign from around 1885 lists five beers: Pilsener, Budweiser, Wiener, Erlanger, and Culmbacher (also spelled Kulmbacher). COURTESY OF NATIONAL BREWERY MUSEUM.

brewery was filled with breweries and other businesses, Krug was wise enough to buy other land so he could expand his business after filling up the first lot.

As Krug's business expanded and he focused more on beer, he hired other employees, including bookkeeper Joseph Schlitz. (According to a later account, Schlitz had managed a brewery in Harrisburg, Pennsylvania prior to moving to Milwaukee.) When Krug died in December 1856, Schlitz took over management of the brewery. In 1858, Schlitz married Krug's widow Anna Maria (who was a member of the Hartig brewing family of Watertown), and later changed the name of the firm to Joseph Schlitz Brewing Co. By 1860, Schlitz was producing about 4,000 barrels of lager a year, which placed him among the second tier of Cream City breweries, behind Best, Blatz, and Melms. (The Census of Industry for 1860 also reports that he made 2,500 barrels of "young beer," which was probably another term for "present use beer," as distinct from lager.) Schlitz's Chestnut Street location was landlocked and did not allow for further expansion. (The brewery's original cellars, sometimes erroneously claimed to be the first in the city, were at Walnut and Third.) As a consequence, a new brewhouse was built in 1870 and 1871 near their existing beer vaults, which enabled the company to nearly triple its production. The new buildings, which cost $30,000, showed off the latest brewery architecture and equipment, and some of them stayed in use for several decades. The ice house and cellar could hold 7,000 barrels of beer. Water came from a spring at Fifth and Sherman and was brought to the brewery through cement pipes.

By the early 1870s, Schlitz had passed 50,000 barrels per year, and trailed only Best among Milwaukee's brewers. The brewery continued to expand rapidly. The company purchased the nearby Pfeiffer brewery at Third and Walnut in 1873. In 1874, Schlitz brewed over 9,000 barrels in September alone, and the *Daily Sentinel* remarked "The table shows that Schlitz's brewery is looming up in importance. It appears that the Best company have the largest home custom, and that Schlitz's beer is in great demand as an article of transportation." Indeed, by the next year Schlitz was shipping third and sixth-barrels to California. In November 1874, one of the vats collapsed, dumping three hundred barrels of beer into the offices below and causing $3,000 of damage or loss. Regardless, the year was a good one for the company, with production topping 70,000 barrels. Like many wealthy brewers, Schlitz occasionally traveled back to Germany to visit friends and family. On April 18, 1875, the *Milwaukee Daily News* published a note:

> Joseph Schlitz requests THE NEWS to announce that he hereby bids farewell to all friends and acquaintances whom he had not the opportunity to visit personally before his departure for Germany.

Tragically, this was his final farewell, for his vessel, the Eagle line steamship *Schiller*, was wrecked on May 8th off the Scilly Islands, with the loss of hundreds of passengers, including Joseph Schlitz. Schlitz left behind the now twice-widowed Anna Maria, and four step-nephews who had been living with him: August, Henry, Albert and Edward Uihlein (pronounced E-line). (The four boys were sons of August Krug's sister Katherina.) Schlitz had placed the four Uihleins in charge of the brewery while he was away, so the transition was smoother than it might have been. August Uihlein had worked as a bookkeeper at Schlitz's brewery and had also been general manager of the Uhrig brewery in St. Louis during the early 1860s, returning to Schlitz in late 1867 or early 1868. He became the secretary and chariman. Henry, the new president, had served an apprenticeship in Bavaria, but honed his skills as the manager of the Kunz brewery in Leavenworth, Kansas. Vice-president Edward joined the firm around 1871, and was responsible for spearheading the effort to capture the Chicago market after the fire, and for introducing and refining Schlitz's distribution branches. In some circles, Edward was better known for inventing an "improved wagon grease." Alfred became superintendent and brewmaster. Two younger brothers also came from Germany to Milwaukee and were brought into the firm: William became assistant superintendent and Charles was superintendent of the Schlitz bottling works (after they established their own plant). The company maintained the name Jos. Schlitz Brewing Co. for the next century, but contrary to popular belief there was nothing in Schlitz's will that required the name to stay the same.

Under the four brothers, the brewery continued to grow both in size and reach. The most important development in the years immediately after they took charge was the hiring of Voechting and Shape in 1877 to be the first official Milwaukee bottlers of Schlitz beer. (Bottled Schlitz beer was advertised by agents from Lincoln, Nebraska to Boston, Massachusetts in 1876.) In the first year alone, one million bottles of beer left the bottling works, and the demand forced Voechting and Shape to open new bottle houses multiple times while they held the Schlitz contract. After five years of Uihlein management the brewery was making more beer (139,154 barrels) with more employees (300) and distributing it in more places than ever before. Beer was being shipped to Mexico, Central America, and as far away as Brazil. Local trade was covered with thirty-eight teams of horses and thirsty patrons were entertained at Schlitz Park, (formerly Quentin Park) which the company bought in 1879 for $23,000.

The company experienced enormous growth in 1880, increasing production by fifty percent to top 210,000 barrels. Quality was not sacrificed—a shipment of Schlitz bottled beer was sent to Germany where it was analyzed and tasted and earned high praise for both purity and flavor. Shipping expanded to Australia, Japan and China. Bottles came from Germany (Milwaukee's glass industry was still in infancy) and $20,000 worth of corks were required. Despite the expansion of the nation's rail network, Schlitz still shipped to California via Cape Horn, since it was half the cost of rail shipment.

Over the next three decades, the story was one of steady and sometimes spectacular growth as Jos. Schlitz Brewing Co. moved into the ranks of the largest breweries in the world. The brewery expanded its bottling agencies in distant cities, built hotels in many cities and taverns in even more. (See chapters 4 and 5.) The *Milwaukee Sentinel* excerpted an article from *The Western Brewer* that called Schlitz "America's Boss Brewery" and detailed the extent of their operations:

> *There is a double track railroad entering the premises, with a loading capacity of fifty-two cars a day, and such are the working facilities of the establishment that it takes just fifteen minutes to load and pack one car of beer. The company manufactures all the fine grades of Bavarian and Bohemian beers, such as Salvator, Erlanger, Pilsen, Budweis and Wiener, for which they have been awarded the highest premiums for their brightness, pureness of taste and excellent flavor. Their brands are shipped all over America, Europe, South America, the West Indies, Australia and East India.*

About 150,000 barrels of the 1883 production of 339,000 barrels was bottled—testimony to how fast bottled beer was accepted after its introduction only a few years earlier. This volume made necessary an all-new bottling works on South Bay Street, which cost $100,000 to build. Since by law all beer had to be racked into barrels first, it was less of an inconvenience to ship the barrels from the brewery to the bottle house than it otherwise would have been. The success of the company brought great wealth to the owners. Several of the Uihleins built opulent mansions on what came to be known as Uihlein Hill. When Anna Maria Schlitz died in 1887, her will split up a fortune of half a million dollars. Henry could afford a six-month trip to Europe, and upon his return about 400 employees turned out with a band and a torchlight parade to welcome him home. The workers were not always this satisfied with management, and Schlitz was beset by several strikes (covered in earlier chapters). There were other occasional problems as well. In 1888, an agent of the company in Chicago had been caught forging the company's labels and doing his own bottling, while still representing it as the "brewery's own bottling." But in general, the brewery prospered, and the prosperity enabled the company to keep up with technological developments like artificial refrigeration—the brewery installed four ice machines in 1890 at a cost of $50,000. While this technology was available to smaller breweries as well, few could afford to make such a prodigious investment at one time.

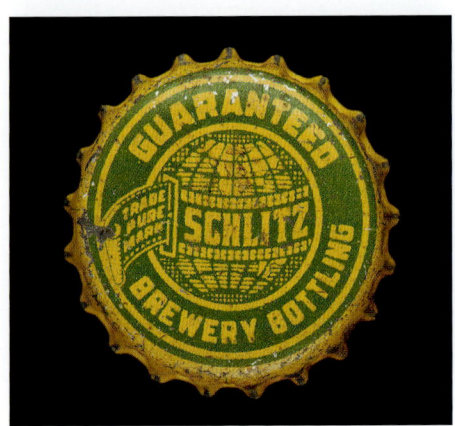

National brewers often advertised the merits of "the brewery's own bottling" before Prohibition, though they were often dependent on independent bottlers for a significant portion of their sales volume. COLLECTION OF TYE SCHWALBE.

The 1890s brought rumors of mergers and syndicates, but also plans for expansion. Schlitz had rival Pabst in its sights, and in 1892 planned an expansion that would eventually bring capacity to a staggering 1.7 million barrels per year, which the *Sentinel* called "the most colossal ever outlined by any brewing company."

To sell this much beer, the company had to promote it. Like several other brewers, Schlitz participated in the Columbian Exposition of 1893, and its pavilion was an architectural marvel. Around the same time, the slogan "The Beer that Made Milwaukee Famous" was introduced in Schlitz advertising. In 1896, the well-known Milwaukee solo sailor Adolph Frietsch announced that he planned to sail around the world alone in a twenty-eight foot schooner dubbed the *Schlitz Globe*. The voyage was to be sponsored by the brewery, the boat would be decorated with the Schlitz trademark, and he was to deliver samples of Schlitz beer "wherever he touches." "The company has agencies throughout the world," Frietsch proclaimed, "and I am going to visit most of them." However, the grand voyage apparently never took place, since an article from 1899 about Frietsch's next proposed adventure made no mention of the round-the-world trip. Schlitz joined Pabst in sending beer to soldiers and sailors during the Spanish-American War, and shipped beer to Teddy Roosevelt when he was hunting in Africa.

In the early decades of the twentieth century, the brewery focused its advertisements on the purity of the beer and the brewing process. Ads announcing Schlitz's presence at the St. Louis Exposition of 1904 not only described the several types of beers available (including Weiner draught and Export bottles at the Philippine exhibition) but also reassured readers "The doctor knows that malt and hops are nerve food and tonics."

Schlitz survived the Prohibition years by making malt syrup, near beer (Famo was the most famous brand) and many other products. The attempt to start a new line of candy products called Eline (after the phonetic

For the Columbian Exposition of 1893, Schlitz designed a souvenir booklet that pivoted open to display brewery scenes on one side and Schlitz beer being enjoyed around the world on the other (often reflecting the ethnic condescension of the time). The caption for this page reads: "The arrival of the famous Schlitz Milwaukee lager beer at Central and South American ports gives occasion for general rejoicing among the natives." COLLECTION OF JOHN STEINER.

pronunciation of the family name) was a financial disaster, but in general the Uihlein family (now mostly the second generation) invested wisely and were able to preserve the brewery in a state that could return quickly to producing beer when the time came. (See chapter 6 for more on the Prohibition-era operations.)

Schlitz Brewing Co. helped lead the celebrations in Milwaukee and nationwide on 7 April 1933, when beer became legal again. Schlitz also led in the adoption of new technologies: the steel beer keg and the beer can. Schlitz attempted to continue the pre-Prohibition practice of touting the purity of its beer, but claiming that Schlitz beer contained "Sunshine Vitamin D" was too much for regulators, even if true. Newspaper advertisements spoke of "enzyme control" and proclaimed "No Wild Yeast in Schlitz." Another advertisement advised: "Drink it freely. It flushes and tones the system. It is exhilarating by day and induces sound, restful sleep at bedtime. It is good and good for you." Schlitz also introduced a new "popular price" brand in the 1930s. Old Milwaukee wasn't a standard popular price brand, however: There were bock and winter beer versions, and it was sometimes bottled by agencies outside Milwaukee—a practice that continued for some time after Repeal.

The brewery continued to expand and modernize its plant during the years before World War II, spending millions of dollars on buildings and equipment. A notable addition in 1938 was the Brown Bottle hospitality room, which paid tribute to the importance of the brown bottle in pre-Prohibition advertising (though now brown was the industry standard). During World War II, the brewery joined the war effort and became a leading provider of beer to the armed forces. Schlitz emerged from the war as the largest brewery in the country, and expanded capacity further with its purchase of the former Ehret brewery in Brooklyn, New York in 1949. By 1950 Schlitz produced more than five million barrels, and in 1952 it set a record with 6.35 million barrels in a year. However the 1953 strike set the company back and Anheuser-Busch moved into the top spot in the rankings. Schlitz and Anheuser-Busch alternated in the top spot for the next few years, but a concerted push by the St. Louis company gave it the lead in 1957 and it has remained the largest brewery in the nation until this writing.

While no longer number one, Schlitz still expanded production, again by buying or building new breweries. Schlitz moved into California in 1954 with a brand-new brewery in Van Nuys. The company acquired the Muehlebach brewery in Kansas City, Missouri in 1956, just a year after Schlitz became the radio sponsor of the newly arrived Kansas City Athletics baseball club. The company started work on its new brewery in Tampa, Florida in 1957, and celebrated its opening in early 1959. Though foiled in its attempt to purchase Burgermeister Brewing Co. of San Francisco, Schlitz purchased the Hawaii Brewing Co. of Honolulu in 1963, and built a new brewery in Longview, Texas, that opened in 1966. Schlitz also attempted to one-up their crosstown rivals by proposing a brewery in Turkey, but these plans ultimately fell through.

Retaining market share required relentless advertising, both nationally and locally.

Budweiser was a style of beer originating in the city of Budweis before it became an Anheuser-Busch trademark. Schlitz brewed Budweiser in the late 1880s and early 1890s; Miller also produced one during the 1890s. In 1893 Anheuser-Busch sued Miller to drop the brand. A souvenir booklet from Miller ca. 1895 concluded: "For we have the full right to use / The names and brands of all our brews . . ." The judge disagreed, and Miller was forced to stop selling Budweiser in 1898. COLLECTION OF TYE SCHWALBE.

Before the federal government regulated beer packaging and advertising, Schlitz emphasized the vitamin D in its Sunshine beer (ca. 1936–37). COLLECTION OF DAVID WENDL.

WISCONSIN BREWERIES AND BREWPUBS

These two Schlitz items demonstrate both continuity and change in brewery artifacts: a cigarette lighter from the 1970s and a match safe ca. 1900. COLLECTION OF DAVID WENDL.

Slogans such as "Real gusto in a great light beer" (first used in 1962) and "When you're out of Schlitz, you're out of beer" were featured in catchy advertisements, especially on television commercials. Most Americans alive during the era, including this author, can and will break into song when the ads are mentioned. The company also took the unusual step of advertising its popular price beer, Old Milwaukee. The reason low-price beers were lower in price was the lack of advertising. But the move was successful at first, as Old Milwaukee became the fastest growing brand in the country in the 1960s. Schlitz also introduced Schlitz Malt Liquor during this period, and "The Bull" became one of the best-known and best-selling high strength beers in the nation. Locally, Schlitz sponsored the Circus World Museum's Fourth of July parade and Old Milwaukee Days, and the Uihlein family supported the Milwaukee zoo, museums, performing arts organizations, and donated land for the Schlitz Audubon Nature Center.

The 1970s started with Jos. Schlitz Brewing Co. enjoying spectacular gains, but ended with the business on the ropes. The company opened new breweries in Winston-Salem, North Carolina; Memphis, Tennessee; and Syracuse, New York. The first two had capacities of about 4.4 million barrels per year; the Syracuse plant was the largest in the world at the time, with capacity for brewing 5.8 million barrels in a year. In 1973, new capacity was seen as essential, since the company was producing at 98 percent capacity (21.3 million barrels). However, while this expansion enabled the company to sell $1 billion of beer in 1974, a series of setbacks harmed the company irreparably in the next few years. Robert A. Uihlein's death left the company without clear leadership, the federal government prosecuted Schlitz for illegal marketing activities, and the company's new Accelerated Batch Fermentation had resulted in quality control problems that forced the dumping of ten million bottles and cans of beer in Memphis and Tampa. Failed ad campaigns only harmed the brewery in the public mind, and continuing losses forced the company to close the Milwaukee brewery in 1981. The company was eventually purchased by Stroh Brewing Company of Detroit after a proposed deal with Heileman fell through. (More on the last years of Schlitz is found in chapter 9.)

Charles Best, (Best & Fine) Plank Road Brewery (1850–51)
Best Bros. Brewery, Plank Road Brewery (1851–53)
Best & Schultz (1853–54)
Best & Co. (1854)
Frederick Miller, Plank Road Brewery (1855?–1873)
Frederick Miller, Menominee Valley Brewery (1873–1888)
Fred Miller Brewing Co. (1888–1920)
Miller Brewing Co. (1920–2002)
SABMiller (2002–8)
MillerCoors (2008–present)
4000 BLOCK, WEST STATE STREET;
(CORPORATE HEADQUARTERS SINCE 2009: 250 SOUTH WACKER DRIVE, CHICAGO, ILLINOIS)

Prior to Frederick Miller's arrival on the scene, the history of the Plank Road Brewery was rather turbulent, and even the circumstances of his acquisition of the brewery were less crystal clear than his beer. In 1845, Charles Frederick Best left the brewery he helped start with his father and brothers. Four years later, he began to erect a brewery along the Watertown Plank Road, then under construction. While Cochran's history of Pabst claims that Charles didn't start until 1850, it is likely that he made at least some beer in 1849, as his production for the year ending in June 1850 was 1,200 barrels, which would have been an extremely high six-month total for a start up brewery. Best's first partner was Gustav Fine, a twenty-eight year-old German-born brewer. At some point in 1850 or 1851 Charles' brother Lorenz joined the business and Fine left, though it is not clear if Lorenz purchased Fine's shares or if Fine left later.

The partnership of Best & Brother, as the new firm was known, lasted only until the beginning of 1853, when Lorenz sold his shares to Otto Schulz and retired from the business. During 1854 Best & Co. opened a lavish "Summer Retreat" near the brewery (described in chapter 2). The new beer garden was successful, but Best ended up saddled with a partner who ruined the business. Schulz sold his share of the brewery to F. Tolber, who then sold it to Henry Wild. Wild, who had just moved to Milwaukee, posed as a sharp businessman, but was in fact a reckless speculator who lived extravagantly, lost money in real estate, and pulled the company into bankruptcy. The brewery was purchased at sheriff's sale by James Rogers, who then sold the brewery to Miller in 1856. Evidence seems to indicate that Miller was involved with the brewery in 1855, the date commonly given for the founding of Miller Brewing Co., perhaps as a renter, but the documentation is not conclusive.

Frederick Miller was among the best prepared of any of Milwaukee's pioneer brewers. Miller began his brewery training in 1839 with a two-year apprenticeship, followed by several years of working at different breweries in Germany and France. In contrast to most early immigrant brewers, some of the breweries where Miller worked are known, including the Horst brewery in Innestadt and the Schonich brewery in Augsburg. In 1849, Miller obtained the lease for the royal brewery of the Hohenzollern family at Sigmaringen, south of Stuttgart near the Swiss border. Miller built a solid reputation at Sigmaringen, and also developed experience in reviving an inadequately

Miller's brewery, ca. 1870—one of the earliest known photographs of a Wisconsin brewery. Up the hill to the left parts of Miller's beer garden can be seen. COURTESY OF MILLERCOORS BREWING CO.

equipped brewery, which would help him after his move to Milwaukee. Once he took over the Plank Road Brewery, Miller pushed the business with great energy, even in the face of the stiff local competition. In a December 1857 ad announcing the release of his "Buck Beer!" *[sic]* at the Plank Road Brewery Beer Hall, the proprietor modestly proclaimed "Miller expects to receive a call from all his friends and the rest of mankind today." A year later, the same hall featured "Munich Dopple Beer," which may have been similar to a doppelbock. Miller soon restarted Best's beer garden, and according to some secondhand accounts, was shipping beer to Chicago (which is likely) and New York (which would be more surprising). The evidence is better that Miller was selling his beer as far away as Memphis and New Orleans by 1860.

Despite Miller's efforts, his brewery remained in the second or even third tier of Milwaukee's breweries for many years. Its production in 1867 of 3,281 barrels was less than one-fifth that of leaders Blatz and Best, and in the same range of breweries little-remembered today: Enes & Co., Stoltz, and Maier & Hohl. Miller began to remedy this situation in 1870 by building an all-new steam-powered brewhouse and updating his equipment. He changed the name to the Menomonee Valley Brewery in 1873, established a branch office in Chicago, and over the next few years Miller was firmly entrenched in fifth place in Milwaukee (behind Best, Schlitz, Blatz and Falk). Miller joined the ranks of bottled beer sellers at the end of the decade, and by this time had a network of saloons and agencies all over Wisconsin and in the surrounding states. (A label from this period is pictured in chapter 5.) Miller's most ambitious expansion of this era was his attempt to start a branch brewery in Bismarck, North Dakota, a money-losing proposition that lasted for about five years (see chapter 4.) In addition to the Bismarck effort, Miller made significant expansions at the brewery the Menomonee River Valley and continued building icehouses and agencies around the Upper Midwest. They also built their own bottling department in 1884. Fred Miller insisted on pouring his profits back into the brewery, and generally was near the cutting edge of new brewing technology. The company's production in 1886 exceeded 62,000 barrels—still in fifth place.

Fred Miller died of cancer in June 1888, and his widow Lisette (his second wife, of the Gross brewery family of St. Martin) and his five children took over the business. The five children all served as president of the company at some point, including the girls. (The details of the Miller family are covered exhaustively by Tim John in *The Miller Beer Barons* and will only be summarized here.) Building continued almost constantly during the next decades, with new stockhouses, bottling plants, and other facilities being added on a regular basis. About the only subtractions were the beer garden on the bluff above the brewery, which declined in popularity and finally ended its run when fireworks destroyed the pavilion in 1891. The extensive cave system also fell into disuse with the rise of artificial refrigeration, and were totally abandoned by 1906. The turn of the twentieth century saw Fred Miller Brewing Co. now in fourth place among the city's brewers, partially because of its own growth but also because the brewery of Falk, Jung & Borchert burned and its remaining assets were purchased by Pabst.

The Miller of the 1890s joined its fellow Milwaukee brewers in producing a wide range of brands: an 1892 article listed Standard, Export, Pilsner, Muenchner, Culmbacher, and Budweiser, which at the time was still considered simply a style developed in the Bohemian city of Budweis (Budvar), just like the three preceding it in the list, rather than a unique trademark of Anheuser-Busch. And in what would be an interesting contrast for a company that would make globally famous pale beers in the next century, the article noted "In a few days the Malto Cream, we understand, the darkest beer ever sold in bottle form, will be placed on the market."

In the early years of the twentieth century, Miller Brewing was drawing closer and closer to its rival national shipping brewers. By 1910 it owned more than one thousand saloons around the country, many of them built by the company and identifiable by a seal with a large M in a sunburst displayed prominently on the building. The brewery increased

Water wagons often sprayed streets to keep the dust down. The term "on the wagon" for sobriety meant that one was drinking water rather than beer. This Miller postcard from around 1912 suggests that in Milwaukee the water wagon would be filled with Miller High Life. COLLECTION OF DAVID WENDL.

its advertising in all sorts of newspapers and magazines, mostly using the blunt but effective slogan "The Best Milwaukee Beer." This slogan was used on the earliest advertising for Miller's new flagship beer, Miller High Life, introduced in 1903. High Life was sold in a bottle with a tapered neck rather than the standard bottle with rather dramatic shoulders (which happened to serve the purpose of catching sediment present in all but the most carefully filtered beers). The bottle shape suggested a new slogan "The Champagne of Bottled Beers," first used in 1907. (The claim that Miller used clear glass to show the clarity of the beer may have been true but was not particularly innovative—many breweries used clear glass instead of brown glass at this point, a fact used in counter-advertising by Schlitz.) The new brand also had a striking symbol—the Girl in the Moon. (The girl originally was portrayed standing in a stylized Mexican equestrienne outfit, but she was placed on the crescent moon in 1907). The popularity of Miller High Life showed in increased sales: from an already impressive 260,000 barrels in 1903, production nearly doubled to 473,000 barrels in 1911. This turned out to be the pre-Prohibition high point because national consumption stagnated as more and more parts of the country went dry.

The company's success was due to a combination of solid management by the founder's sons Ernest, Frederick A., and Emil Miller, and a team of hired managers including Eugene Salbey, Oscar Treichler, and John Kraft, the brewmaster responsible for Miller High Life. The financial returns on the business were as impressive as the growth in production: net income was over $600,000 per year from 1902 to 1915, the value of the company's property (including saloons and fixtures) nearly quadrupled to over $12 million during the same period, and the dividends earned by the Miller siblings in 1916 were $800,000 each, which was a staggering sum in that era. The family built a grand new home at 3200 West Highland Boulevard (which was known as Sauerkraut Boulevard because of all the wealthy German residents in the neighborhood), and the family moved there in 1901.

When Prohibition arrived, Ernest Miller was extremely reluctant to switch to any business other than beverages. Miller made a near beer called Vivo, and an interesting companion product, a wheat beverage called Milo. Miller took the risky step of renaming its near beer Miller High Life Brew in 1920—most brewers were very reluctant to apply the name of a premium flagship beer to a product that was likely to have minimal acceptance. (A High Life Brew sign is pictured in chapter 6.) The numbers indicated that the beverage was not a consumer favorite: sales were just over 80,000 barrels in 1920 and dropped below 20,000 in just a few years. Sales of near beer dropped in part because of low customer satisfaction, but also because the bootleg and wildcat business had adapted and was ready to fill the vacuum with something approaching real beer. While the near beer, soda and malt product lines were generally money losers, the company continued to be profitable throughout the dry years because the family had invested wisely in real estate. The company was diversified enough to cushion the effects of Prohibition and leave the brewery in a good position to pivot back to making real beer in 1933.

The solid financial position of the family and the company stood in contrast to the drama in the Miller family. Lisette Miller died in 1920, and while she was no longer involved in day-to-day business operations, she was an intelligent and able manager of the family, and was in many ways she was the glue that held the family together. The brothers followed their own pursuits in the following years. Ernest resigned as president to devote much of his time to Catholic philanthropy—in 1925 he received a papal medal for his devotion. Frederick A. Miller preferred spending time on his estates and gardening, but was a capable successor to Ernest as president. Emil earned a reputation as a dissolute playboy, and was in frequent trouble with the law or his shady creditors. The family put the company up for sale in 1925, but when the only serious bidder was Emil, they

In the late 1930s Miller Bock was packaged in the new "steinie" bottle. COLLECTION OF DAVID WENDL.

took the property off the market and decided to ride out Prohibition.

Miller's brewery was a popular spot on 7 April 1933, like the other Milwaukee breweries that shipped out beer one minute after midnight. Even though the brewery had been producing near beer throughout the dry spell, much of the equipment was outdated. Frederick A. Miller approved a massive improvement program. Among the updates in 1936 was a canning line, making Miller the fourth Milwaukee brewery to adopt the new container. Miller decided to go with the flat top can rather than the cone top, which would ultimately be a money and time saver. Even though High Life was still the vast majority of production, the company had a few other brands that filled out the line, including Select, Export, and "Old Original."

The company was also quick to capitalize on two new forms of advertising. Miller became a leading proponent of neon signs, and launched a radio campaign in forty states. Distant markets were becoming lucrative and by the start of World War II, Miller was no longer a large regional brewer but a true national business.

Frederick A. Miller retired at the end of 1937, and control of the brewery passed to his youngest sister, Elise John, though older sister Clara Miller (married to Frederick J. Miller's nephew from his first marriage, Carl Miller) was still an active board member. The two sisters were sometimes at odds with each other, and this period through the end of World War II was marked by less aggressive expansion, stagnant sales, and the desire of some family members to increase their dividends at the expense of reinvestment. The brewery survived for a decade on a quality flagship beer, momentum, and talented management and employees. Sales dropped off during the later years of World War II due to raw material quotas and decreasing the number of states in which Miller was sold from forty-two to twenty-five. The refusal to change the formula during the war to produce more beer more cheaply was another cause of decreased production, but in the long run it maintained the reputation for quality which would help after the war.

In 1946, Elise John's only son Harry was installed as president of the company, but this experiment only lasted a year. While he was diligent about his work, his heart was in his devotion to the Catholic faith and a number of charities. He was replaced by Clara Miller's only son Frederick C. Miller, who led a period of dynamic growth for the company. Miller supervised the building of what was essentially an all-new modern plant, including a new brewhouse, a new bottling plant, a new office building and a series of new "Stockhouses"— fermenting and conditioning buildings full of enormous vats. The new buildings were all done in a modern style, in particular the administration building, which was designed by Milwaukee industrial designer Brooks Stevens (best known for the Oscar Mayer Wienermobile, but also for several other motor products, appliances, and the Miller High Life Cruiser). Stevens also created the "soft cross" logo introduced in 1954.

The new facilities were one of the key factors in both Miller's rapid increase in production and its climb up the national brewery rankings in the postwar years. In 1946, the brewery produced just over 650,000 barrels, but by 1949 had more than doubled that total,

and in 1950 reached the 2 million-barrel mark. In addition, the company climbed from twentieth place in 1947 to eighth in 1950 and into the top five by 1952 with more than 3 million barrels produced. Another factor in Miller's rise during this period was a concerted effort to expand abroad, especially into the Caribbean.

But the initiative that brought Miller the most national attention was its sponsorship of sports teams and events. Brewery sponsorship of sports was not new, and New York brewery owner Jacob Ruppert was responsible for bringing the Yankees to their dominant position in baseball. But Miller began to sponsor teams all over the country, especially NFL football teams. The sports connection, especially football, was logical for Fred Miller, who had been an All-American tackle for Knute Rockne's Notre Dame Fighting Irish in the late 1920s (and played in the famous "Win one for the Gipper" game against Army in 1928). During the early 1950s Miller sponsored radio broadcasts of the Green Bay Packers, the New York Giants and the Philadelphia Eagles, as well the telecasts of the Los Angeles Rams. (The Rams were a good choice not only because it gave the brewery exposure on the West Coast, but also because former University of Wisconsin standout Elroy "Crazylegs" Hirsch was a star for the Rams.) During the same period, the brewery also sponsored telecasts of the NFL championship game and all-star game. Fred Miller hired players to travel different regions on behalf of Miller during the off-season as representatives of their sport and the company, and was noteworthy for hiring African-American spokesmen in an era when that could have cost them business in some markets.

Fred Miller's efforts were critical to encouraging the Boston Braves National League baseball team to move to Milwaukee. Miller had been a leading booster of the Milwaukee Brewers of the American Association (who later moved to become the Toledo Mudhens), and led the drive to build Milwaukee's County Stadium, the first major league stadium to be built using public funding. Miller then worked with Lou Perini, owner of the Braves (and of

the Brewers) to bring the team to Milwaukee, where it set attendance records and brought a World Series championship to the Cream City in 1957.

Miller Brewing Co. suffered a major setback in 1953 when the Milwaukee brewery workers' strike shut the company down for seventy-six days during peak brewing season. Unlike rivals Pabst and Schlitz, Miller had no breweries in other locations that could fill the demand, and production dropped thirty percent. Much more tragically, Frederick C. Miller, his son Fred Jr. and two pilots were killed in a plane crash in December 1954. Norman Klug, a vice-president of the company, took over as president. (Lorraine Mulberger, daughter of Elise John, remained an important board member, and brewmaster Edward Huber was elected to take Fred Miller's place on the board.) Klug continued to build both the brewery and the brand. Miller Brewing purchased neighboring Gettelman Brewing Co. along with its brands in 1961, and used the brewery for extra capacity until 1970 when it was closed.

The end of family control of the company

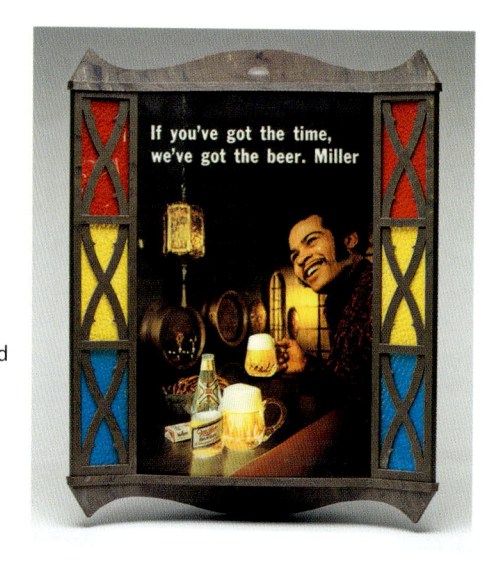

By the 1970s, national breweries included more people of color in their advertisements. On the bar behind the bottle of High Life is a pack of Marlboro cigarettes, a prominent product of Miller's parent company at the time, Philip Morris. COLLECTION OF DAVID SEARS.

came during the late 1960s. Peter Grace, the CEO of his family's firm, W. R. Grace & Co., had been brought onto the Miller board in 1960 by Harry John, but ended up owning the business. Norman Klug died and Lorraine Mulberger sold her majority interest in the company to W. R. Grace & Co. Harry John viewed Grace's move as a betrayal and refused to cooperate or sell his 47 percent of company stock. After a few years, Grace decided that it was impossible to run the business the way he wanted to without full control of the stock, so he sold his shares to tobacco giant Philip Morris in 1969. The next year, John sold his stake to Philip Morris for $96 million and the Miller descendants were no longer part of the company.

While Miller had been growing consistently since Fred Miller took over the company, Miller's most spectacular growth took place after the introduction of Miller Lite, a story recounted in chapter 9. Sales went from what had already been a record-breaking total of 12.8 million barrels in 1975 to 40.3 million in 1981. Miller built breweries in California, Texas, New York and North Carolina, another in California, one in Georgia and a final new brewery in Ohio. (The proliferation of breweries is covered in chapters 8 and 9.) Miller Brewing Co. was solidly established as the second-largest brewer in America, and one of the largest in the world.

Despite this success, Miller Brewing was stuck in second place, and the beer business was becoming less important to Philip Morris, the parent company. In 2002, the brewery was purchased by South African Breweries, and the new company became known as SABMiller, with headquarters in London. SAB had 4.8 percent of global market share (compared with 2.4 percent for Miller) though SAB had 108 breweries in twenty-three countries and over 40,000 employees worldwide. Miller's headquarters remained in Milwaukee (for the moment) and all seven breweries (nine counting the two operating under the Jacob Leinenkugel name) remained open.

But even bigger mergers were still to come. In October 2007, Miller and Molson Coors Brewing Co. agreed to combine their U.S. operations to compete more effectively with Anheuser-Busch. This combination of the second and third-largest breweries in the country was still not enough to vault them past Anheuser-Busch, which itself was bought out by InBev of Belgium in 2008. But while the drive to control American markets was still a priority, the American market for premium beers by large international brewing companies was stagnating, and emerging markets around the world showed greater potential for growth. In Fall 2015, the move that many industry observers believed was inevitable finally happened: AB InBev made an offer of approximately $110 billion for SABMiller. But anti-trust regulators let it be known they would only agree to the merger if the new company spun off its North American operations to another company. In October 2016, Molson Coors completed its acquisition of SABMiller's 58 percent stake in MillerCoors and all of the brands in the Miller portfolio. The company became the world's third-largest brewer (by enterprise value) and as of 2017 had not closed any of its breweries.

In fact, MillerCoors added breweries to its holdings, as did other multinationals concerned about the rise of craft beer and the potential threat it posed to their market share. Between September 2015 and August 2016, MillerCoors purchased majority interests in four craft breweries: Saint Archer Brewing Co. of San Diego, Terrapin Beer Company of Athens, Georgia, Hop Valley Brewing Co. of Eugene, Oregon, and Revolver Brewing of Granbury, Texas. These became part of the Tenth and Blake craft beer division, and as of 2017 industry analysts predicted additional acquisitions in the future.

William L. Hopkins & Co. (1849?–1855?)
MARTIN STREET (EAST STATE STREET) BETWEEN MARKET AND MAIN STREETS

William L. Hopkins probably started brewing sometime before 1850, since he appears in the industrial census of that year as a manufacturer of beer and soda. He had more employees than all but the two large ale brewers, Owens and Blossom, which probably means that several of his employees were involved with bottling (as was likely the case with Owens and Blossom). He appears in the city directory as a brewer in 1854, but not in any other year. The R. G. Dun & Co. records reported that he was still operating in Milwaukee in August 1854, but the next entry was not until 1859, by which time he had moved to Chicago.

Taylor & Brother (1849?–1851?)
Lake Brewery

John Taylor started a short-lived beer bottling operation with his brother Joseph that leased space in Owens' Lake Brewery. The few details available suggest that the Taylors did not brew their own beer, since their inputs in 1850 did not include hops or malt, though they were listed as producing small beer.

Henry Bevering & August Reimerdes (1849–1850?)
Nicholas Schunck (1850–56?)
Schunck & Hellberg (1856?–1860)
Peter Gerstner (1860–62)
NINTH AND WALNUT (MODERN NINTH AND GALENA)

Henry Bevering and August Reimerdes began brewing in 1849 at what was alternately called the Walnut Street Brewery and the Galena Street Brewery. The 1850 census of industry reported that the brewery employed five hands and produced 1,500 barrels of beer (which seems high, but is consistent with their revenue and raw materials used).

By 1851, Nicholas Schunck had taken over the brewery, and in that year had several employees boarding at the brewery. Louis Hellberg was not among these, but the distiller became a partner of Schunck at some point during the 1850s. When Schunck died in 1859, Hellberg ran the brewery with Schunk's widow Mary (Maria) for several months. Mary married Peter Gerstner in 1860, and he took over management of the brewery for the next two years. The couple closed the brewery in 1862, and after several transfers, the property was purchased by Louis Hellberg, who continued distilling but did not reopen the brewery.

Peter Gerstner met with a sad end. He had

aspirations of being an inventor, and became obsessed with perfecting a "water-wheel" which would convert a small flow into a considerable amount of power. His invention was a failure and that, combined with signs of mental aberration he had shown for several years, drove him to take his life in 1879.

Henry Nunnemacher (1849–1851?)
Bast & Nunnemacher, Wisconsin Brewery (1851?–52?)
Bast & Klingler, Wisconsin Brewery (1852?–1861)
Christopher Bast, Wisconsin Brewery (1861–69)
Wilhelmina Bast (1869–1871)
W. Manegold (Mangold) (1871?–72?)
Meeske Bros. & Hoch (1873?–75)
Meeske & Hoch, Wisconsin Brewery (1875–78)
Grisbaum & Kehrein (1878–1890)
91 Knapp Street (1849–1883)
607–613 Cherry Street (1883–1890)

Henry Nunnemacher, a Swiss-born distiller, was among the immigrants who reached Milwaukee through New Orleans rather than an East Coast port. Nunnemacher joined Christopher Bast in a brewery the latter founded in 1849. The brewery was at first called the Henry Nunnemacher brewery in the 1850 industry census, which is strange because the 1850 population census shows Bast as owning $2,000 of property and Nunnemacher with none. The brewery apparently got off to a quick start, since the partners sold about 800 barrels in their first full year of operation. The 1851 city directory indicated the name of the firm had been changed to Bast and Nunnemacher, and the Wisconsin Brewery name was appended (surprisingly no other brewery had taken advantage of that rather obvious name yet).

Nunnemacher sold his shares to John Klingler in 1852, and the name was changed to reflect the new ownership. The company ranked in the second tier of Cream City breweries: producing about 3,000 barrels per year by 1860. Klingler then sold his share in the brewery to Bast in 1861, and Bast became sole proprietor for the next several years. Production

This token from 1863 is one of the few artifacts from Bast's brewery. The reverse side features a six-pointed brewer's star. COLLECTION OF TYE SCHWALBE.

dropped in 1867 to only 1,244 barrels, but this may have been because of Bast's failing health. According to Milwaukee brewing historian Leonard P. Jurgensen, Christopher Bast died in 1867, though the brewery remained in his name in city directories through 1869.

Bast's widow Wilhelmina took over the brewery for a few years after her husband's death, and kept the business going. The R. G. Dun & Co. credit reports noted that Mrs. Bast was an "active woman" who was "doing a small but safe bus[iness]." In 1871, Mrs. Bast sold the brewery, but sources differ on the purchaser. Jurgensen, whose research is quite thorough, reports that she sold the brewery to John George Museweller, who then sold it to Val Blatz. Blatz then leased the brewery to Charles Meeske and Reiner Hoch. However, the excise records, Dun Co. reports, 1872 city directory and the 1873 Brewers' Register all list (Frederick) William Manegold (or Mangold) as the proprietor of the brewery at 91 Knapp. The brewery and property may have been sold separately.

By 1874, if not earlier, brothers Gustav, Otto and Charles Meeske and Reiner Hoch were operating the brewery and converted it to produce weiss beer. By 1875, Gustav and Otto left the firm and Charles continued with Hoch. Meeske & Hoch sold the brewery business to Joseph Grisbaum and Jacob Kehrein in October 1878. (Meeske and Hoch would own other breweries in the Upper Midwest, finally ending up at Duluth [Minnesota] Brewing and Malting Co.) Grisbaum and Kehrein were not considered to be particularly good businessmen at first, but they established a small local business and improved their reputations. In 1883 they moved their business to Cherry Street, and the original site became the location of the new Blatz bottling house.

Jacob Ziegler (1850–53)
Tamarack (Modern State Street) between Fifth and Sixth

The research of Leonard P. Jurgensen has revealed that Jacob Ziegler opened a small weiss beer brewery in 1850 and operated at this location until 1853 when he moved a few blocks down the road to his better known brewery between Eight and Ninth.

John Peter Weber (1850?–1853)
Michael Muehlschuster (Sauer & Muehlschuster) (1853–1860)
Thirteenth near Fond du Lac Avenue
South Side of North Avenue near Lisbon Plank Road and Thirtieth Street

On 4 July 1886, the Milwaukee Sentinel published reminiscences of Val Blatz about the early days of brewing in Milwaukee. Among the old time breweries he mentioned was one started by Weber on the Lisbon Plank Road that later became Muehlschuster's brewery. While Blatz implied the brewery was started in the mid-1840s, historian Leonard P. Jurgensen has discovered that this Weber was John Peter Weber and argues based on mortgage records that the date of founding was more likely around 1850. Records of the sale from Weber to Muehlschuster indicate that transfer happened in 1853 and the brewery was already on the property.

However, the history of the brewery is complicated by other accounts. Both Albert Schnabel and a 1926 Milwaukee Leader article indicate that Muehlschuster first had a brewery on Thirteenth near Fond du Lac Road (across from the West Hill/Cream City brewery site) and later moved to North Avenue. But Muehlschuster's only mention in Milwaukee city directories is in 1859 at the Fond du Lac Road location.

(Further confusion is caused by a note in the *Leader* article that Val Blatz had been a brewer for Muehlschuster, which does not work with the existing dates because Blatz had his own brewery by this point, and Blatz makes no mention of it in the 1886 article.) The brewery was not big enough to make either the 1850 or 1860 industrial census, but was large enough to capture at least some of the Milwaukee trade. An ad for John Schauss & Co.'s beer hall in 1858 indicated that their "Buck Beer" was provided by Sauer & Muehlschuster's brewery (which ads another player to the drama). Schnabel claims that Muehlschuster continued until 1861, but Jurgensen's research indicates that Muehlschuster left for St. Louis in 1860.

Valentin Blatz (1851?)
BROADWAY AND DIVISION STREETS

Val Blatz started his own brewery either late in 1850 or early 1851 at a location just down the street from that of his former employer, Johann Braun. Almost nothing is known about his independent operations at this location, since in April 1851 Braun died and Blatz took over the City Brewery and merged the two businesses.

Alois Gallagger, Washington Brewery (1851?–58?)
Mrs. Mary Gallagger (1858?–59?)
JOHNSON AND WATER STREETS (MODERN 207 EAST HIGHLAND)

Alois (sometimes given as Louis or Lewis) Gallagger (or Gallagher or other spellings) is reported to have started brewing around 1851. An account from 1926 relates that the Washington Brewery was begun on the side hill from Market to Main, along Johnson St., but eventually chose East Water St. As its head and front. It was a near neighbor to the Braun/Blatz brewery and just as large." The brewery was built in a Flemish architectural style, and was still in existence well into the twentieth century.

The claim that the Washington brewery was the same size as Blatz's brewery is surprising, but seems to be supported at least somewhat by advertisements in the late 1850s. There were several lager beer saloons that carried Gallagger's beer, including a saloon at the brewery operated by Lewis Drucker, which advertised with poems extolling the atmosphere:

> Uncle Sam spoke:
> 'There shall be light! and there was light!
> Lewis Drucker spoke:
> "There shall be night—then come the guests and all is right!'
> On every day—in every night,
> Until the sun comes pure and bright
> Shall be a concert mild and sweet
> And each one have the loveliest treat;
> There Humor flows in fullest stream,
> There sparkling with words the brightest beams.
> Your all World's Friend
> Lewis Drucker

Saloons elsewhere in the city advertised that they carried Gallagger's beer, which only would have been a useful advertising point if the Washington brewery had a large and solid reputation.

However, in the 1859 city directory Mrs. Mary Gallagger was listed as the proprietor of the brewery, and also as the widow of Alois. It appears that she did not continue the brewery long, because it is missing from the 1860 city directories, and one later account indicates the brewery "flourished" from 1851–60.

Felix Calgeer (1852–58)
Felix Calgeer, Phoenix Brewery (1858–1864)
Davis & Calgeer, Phoenix Brewery (1864–65)
Felix Calgeer, Phoenix Brewery (1865–69)
Louis Liebscher, (1871–1880)
189-195 SHERMAN STREET, SOUTH SIDE 200 BLOCK OF VINE STREET.

In 1852, Felix Calgeer started brewing at a site on the side of a hill at Sherman Street and Second. According to local accounts, he made both white and lager beer. One account has him selling the brewery in 1854 to D. Bauscheck who made malt at the site until 1868, but that does not square with other records. Calgeer bought the property in 1856, and added the name Phoenix to the brewery around 1858. Calgeer's production in 1860 was about 600 barrels, but it is not clear if this was a mix of white and lager beer.

Calgeer encountered financial difficulties,

A Liebscher stoneware bottle from the 1870s.
COLLECTION OF TYE SCHWALBE.

and in 1861 the brewery was sold at sheriff's sale to William Hensler and John Plankington, who appear to have bought it for speculative purposes. Calgeer remained as the brewer. John Davis joined as a partner in 1864, and was likely brought in as a source of funds rather than for his brewing experience. Calgeer continued brewing here for a few more years, but in 1869 he took a job in city government and ended his brewing career.

The brewery was not vacant long, since Louis Liebscher took over the Phoenix location after his partnership with John Berg dissolved. Liebscher's term in charge was marked by a series of misfortunes. In 1871, William Henig, a boy employed at the brewery, was drawn into the gearing of the horse power, which madly mangled his leg. Later that year Fritz Huster, a driver for Liebscher, suffered a crushed leg when his team of horses collided with another. In September 1877, the brewery withstood a fire that caused about $5,000 of damage; it did not interrupt business because the brewing equipment was spared. Liebscher converted the brewery to a malt house in 1880, but retained the Phoenix name.

Ludwig Bruel (1853–1856?)
CHERRY BETWEEN ELEVENTH AND TWELFTH

Old time histories of Milwaukee breweries include brief references to the brewery of Ludwig

Bruel on Cherry between Eleventh and Twelfth. He is listed in the 1854 city directory, but sources disagree on whether he went out of business in 1856 or 1858. (He is not listed in the 1856 city directory, but this is not conclusive.)

Christoph Schoepp (1852–55)
Phillip Knippenberg (1857?–1860)
Anton Korb (1860?–66?)
Knoblauch & Schreiber (Carl Knoblauch) (1866–68?)

THIRD STREET NEAR WILLIAMSBURG (NEAR SHOOTING PARK)

Christoph Schoepp's brewery near what was then the village of Williamsburg was unknown until uncovered by historian Leonard P. Jurgensen. Schoepp brewed from approximately 1852 until 1855, when the brewery burned. Philip Knippenberg (sometimes Knippenberger in city directories) first appears in Milwaukee's brewing scene as a partner of Jacob Obermann at Fifth and Cherry. Knippenberg sold his share to Obermann in 1856, and set out on his own. Several Milwaukee historians claim that Knippenberg started brewing at the Williamsburg location in 1857, though he did not actually purchase the property until 1858. Unfortunately, Knippenberg encountered financial difficulties and the brewery was sold at sheriff's auction in 1860 to Anton Korb, who held the mortgage.

It appears possible that the brewery was out of production for a few years—Anton Korb was listed as a saloon keeper in 1862, and though he was listed as a brewer in 1863 and 1865 in the individual listings, there was no brewery listed at this location in the business section. Carl Knoblauch, the next proprietor, was still serving as foreman at Blatz's City Brewery through 1865. The firm of Knoblauch and John Schreiber first appear in the 1866-7 city directory, and Knoblauch appears on his own the next year. Albert Schnabel reported that Knoblauch & Schreiber went out of business in 1868. However, other accounts claim that this site "finally became a weiss beer brewery, and a good one," or "eventually brewing some of the best Berlin weiss beer made here." It is never quite clear if it is Knoblauch and Schreiber who are brewing that beer, but no other brewery is ever listed in city directories at that location.

John Hess (1852?–1863?)
NORTHWEST CORNER OF TENTH AND CEDAR

John Hess has been mentioned in several sources as a brewer in the 1840s. However, research by Leonard P. Jurgensen shows that he did not buy his saloon property until 1848, and probably did not begin brewing until later. An article about the destruction of the building in 1909 reported that Hess had purchased the land in 1845, and claimed that brewing took place between 1852 and 1857. An advertisement for Hess's beer hall in the *Taglicher Volksfreund* in February 1852 does not specifically say that Hess brewed his own beer, but advertised a special wherein a quart of beer could be purchased for 6¢, and if a customer drank nine quarts the tenth was free (it did not say if that was in a single session). Historian Albert Schnabel argued that Hess was better classified as one of the many tavern owners that brewed his own beer than as a brewery, but by later standards he would have been classed as a brewer. Hess sold his property in 1863, which was likely the end of his time as a brewer. The combination tavern and grocery store was later known as the Crow's Nest, which was a popular establishment until it burned in 1909. John Hess was active in Milwaukee politics, first as a Whig and later as a Democrat.

Wehr & Forster, West Hill Brewery (1853–58)
George Wehr, West Hill Brewery (1858–1860)
Weber & Beck, West Hill Brewery (1860–62)
John Beck (1862–1877)
Jacob Veidt & Co. (1877–79)
Cream City Brewing Co. (1879–1920)
Cream City Products Co. (1920–1933)
Cream City Brewing Co. (1933–37)
490–510 THIRTEENTH STREET

It is a bit surprising that it took until 1879 for a brewery to adopt the Cream City name, given the imagery of the creamy head on the beer in addition to the cream-colored brick used so often in Milwaukee that was the actual source of the nickname.

According to a nineteenth-century account, George and Conrad Wehr and C. Forster started the West Hill Brewery in a residence and "after various vicissitudes" the company eventually became Cream City Brewing Co. By vicissitudes, the author apparently meant financial setbacks and changes of ownership. The first of these happened when George Wehr bought out his partners in 1858, the next when brothers-in-law Stephen Weber and John Beck (Johann Peck in the 1860 census) purchased the brewery in 1860. The brewery listed as Weber & Peck & Co. in the 1860 industrial census was one of the smallest listed in Milwaukee, with production of only 500 barrels. Weber sold his share to Beck in 1862, and moved west to take over a brewery in Waukesha that he also would name West Hill Brewery.

John Beck built up the business over the next decade. In 1867 production was over 1,000 barrels, and he reported 1,800 barrels for the 1870 industrial census. However, production dropped back under 1,000 barrels shortly thereafter, only to jump to 2,230 barrels in 1874. Such swings make it difficult to generalize either about Beck's business or the Milwaukee industry in general, though Beck was now facing local competitors who were much larger and were beginning to bottle their beer. At the end of 1875, revenue officials seized Beck's brewery and arrested Beck for reusing old revenue stamps on new kegs. This appears to have been just one symptom of financial difficulties, since the reports of R. G. Dun & Co. indicate that whereas Beck previously had been a safe risk, by 1876 he was in debt and was less creditworthy.

In 1877, Jacob Veidt moved from the once-mighty Rodermund brewery in Madison to lease the Thirteenth Street brewery. Veidt may have leased the brewery from a new owner, since most accounts claim that malter William Gerlach took over the brewery around this time. It is Veidt and not Gerlach that appears in the city directories, but it is likely that Gerlach took over the brewery from a bankrupt Beck especially if Beck was in debt to Gerlach for malt purchases.

In 1879, Gerlach, Charles Worst, and Veidt

incorporated the company as Cream City Brewing Co., the name it would use through the 1930s. The brewery shared offices with Gerlach's malting and milling operations at Eighth and Chestnut, but the brewery remained on Thirteenth. Under the new leadership, production blossomed from 3,245 barrels in 1879 to nearly 30,000 in 1884. William Gerlach died in early 1884, but the company was now on a sound footing. That same year the company increased its capital stock from $30,000 to $125,000—the type of move that typically heralded a major expansion. Unfortunately, Cream City Brewing was landlocked, so it was possible to modernize, but not to make a significant increase in capacity on that site. The company built a new brewhouse in 1886, a new cold storage facility in 1888, and new ice machines in 1884 and 1888. To conserve space, Cream City did not have its own malting on site, but since they were linked with Gerlach's malting company this was not necessary. Cream City contracted with Adam Dillman and Ignatz Morawetz to bottle their beer in 1882, though in 1884 this partnership broke up and the brewery took control of their own bottling in the facility just north of the brewery.

By the end of the 1880s Cream City Brewing was solidly established in the third tier of Milwaukee breweries: far behind Best, Schlitz and Blatz, but approximately the same size as Obermann or Gettelman. A profile of the company in 1892 reported that Cream City beer was sold in Wisconsin and "neighboring states," and listed seven different brands: Lager, Pilsner, Hofbrau, Edelbraeu, Extra Stock, Extra Pilsner and A-1 Cream (the last of which was only available in bottles). By the 1890s many of the directors were new and from different families, but unlike many of its rivals Cream City Brewing had never had a particularly strong family identity associated with its brand. Cream City had enough of a reputation to be the subject of merger or syndicate rumors: in 1889 it was believed to be a target of the ever popular "New York agents of English capitalists," and in 1892 it was rumored that Pabst would purchase the company. None of these came to pass, and Cream City remained independent for the rest of its existence. The brewery continued its modest export program, with depots or agents in several Wisconsin cities and a depot in Chicago at 13–15 West Ohio Street.

For the rest of the period until Prohibition, Cream City Brewing had a generally successful and steady business. They engaged in most of the same activities as other similar breweries, including sponsoring a baseball team. There were a few newsworthy items: An agent in Chicago was found to have embezzled $3,000; in 1913 a truck belonging to the company struck and injured an eight-year-old girl in Milwaukee, and another truck was struck by a train in 1914 and both employees were killed. Probably the most serious mishap was an explosion and fire in 1899 caused by an ammonia leak. While insurance covered the $10,000 of damage, one man died in the blaze. His death was not from the fire itself—after escaping the brewery he was struck in the street by a startled team of horses. Despite these setbacks, Cream City Brewing continued to brew until Prohibition forced them to change products.

Cream City Brewing changed their corporate structure to adapt to Prohibition somewhat earlier than many of their rivals. Cream City Brewing Co. dissolved its corporation in February 1919. After a few months as Regal Investment Co., the company emerged as Cream City Products in June. During Prohibition, Cream City made a variety of products, including malt tonic and soft drinks of various flavors. The company was one of the more aggressive in promoting a variety of different near beers, including one called Pilsnear. In addition, Cream City Products was one of the very few breweries that made private label cereal beverages.

Because Cream City remained functional throughout the dry years, they had to spend relatively little to retool for beer, though they expected to increase employment from twelve to seventy-five—welcome news during the Depression. The first two cases that left the

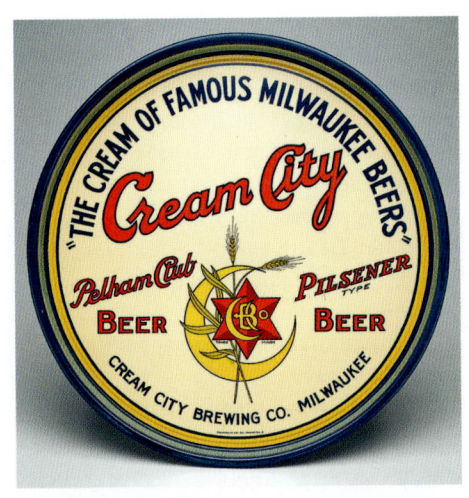

A post-Prohibition tray advertising the Pelham Club and Pilsener brands. COLLECTION OF DAVID WENDL.

brewery on "New Beers' Day" were part of a shipment flown to President Roosevelt, and the third and fourth cases were delivered straight from the plant to Governor Schmedeman in Madison.

Interestingly, Cream City was one of two Milwaukee breweries that continued to make 3.2 percent beer even after Prohibition was fully repealed and strong beer was legal again (Gettelman was the other). But Cream City had difficulty remaining competitive in the years after Prohibition. In just four years, the brewery went through several different brands and label styles, which is not a sign of a business with a stable, high-demand product. They also continued to brew beers under contract for bottlers and grocery stores, which is a sign of excess capacity that cannot be filled by the breweries' own brands. Production dropped rapidly through 1936 and by spring 1937 its production was well under 2,000 barrels per month—less than many small-town breweries. Cream City stopped production in May 1937, and the building was razed in 1943.

Western Brewery (1853–58?)
Maier & Winkler (Maier & Co.), Western Brewery (1858?–1862)
Maier & Hohl, Western Brewery (1862–68)
F. W. Manegold, Western Brewery (1868–69)

John Kargleder & Co., Western Brewery (1869–1875)
Milwaukee Brewing Association (1875–1882)
624 Cherry

City directories sometimes make the history of a brewery more confusing. Sometime in the late 1850s John Maier, formerly brewmaster for Stoltz & Schneider, started (or took over) a brewery at Seventh and Cherry which was called the Western Brewery. But in the 1859 directory, John Maier & Co. are listed at the corner of Cherry and Seventh, Meier and Winkler are listed on Cherry, corner of Seventh, but in the individual listing John Maier & Co. are listed not as brewers but as butchers, and the address is on Chestnut between Third and Fourth. On the other hand, the "Company" includes T. F. Hohl and T. F. Winkler, so at least the right personnel are present. In any case, Maier & Co. were established enough by 1860 to have produced about 2,000 barrels in the previous year. In 1862, (Joseph) Frederick Hohl's name was added, though it is not clear if he bought out Winkler's share (Winkler is not in the 1862 directory). By 1867, the brewery was one of several in town producing about 3,000 barrels per year. The partnership lasted until 1868, when William Manegold purchased the brewery (though Manegold never appeared in the excise records). He sold it the next year to John Kargleder, though Manegold continued with the company at least through 1871, when he appears to have taken over the Bast brewery for a time. (Fritz Hohl was still listed as part of the business in the 1870 industrial census.)

The note in the ribbon that this beer was "brewed expressly for [the] bottling department" supports the idea that the Milwaukee Brewing Association was at least in part a way for brewers to test the viability of bottled beer (ca. 1880).
Collection of John Steiner.

Kargleder (who was listed in the 1866 & 1867 city directory as Nepomuck Kargleder, previously a foreman for Val Blatz, increased production from about 4,000 barrels in 1871 to over 11,000 in 1872, and to a peak of just over 18,000 barrels in 1874. In 1871, Albert Blatz, brother of Valentin, purchased the brewery, though Kargleder's name remained on the business.

In 1874, the brewery was reorganized as Milwaukee Brewing Company, and a year later as the Milwaukee Brewing Association. An article from December 1879, seeking to debunk the rumors of a syndicate whereby the larger brewers were buying up and controlling the smaller ones, explained that "Kargleder was under obligations to the Second Ward Bank, and when he found himself unable to meet them, he turned the brewery over to the bankers, who, being brewers in the main, were conducting it to secure a fair return on the investment." In fact, the Milwaukee Brewing Association was a joint stock company led by president Emil Schandein of Phillip Best Brewing Co. Charles Gezelschap, a manager at Blatz, left that company to become secretary, and Captain Pabst was also interested in the company. Pabst Brewing Co. historian John Steiner contends that Milwaukee Brewing Association may have served as a way for Best and Blatz to experiment with bottled beer without putting the reputations of their own brands at risk if the products did not meet with popular approval.

Fire struck the Milwaukee Brewing Association plant in April 1882, and despite claims that the owner would "make strenuous efforts to have everything in shape to resume operations in about two weeks," the brewery did not return to production. Despite the attempt to claim independence for the Association, some papers referred to the plant as the "Best & Blatz brewing companies' brewery." Charles Gezelschap and Louis Knipp, one of the brewers, relocated to Janesville and purchased the Buob brewery. Charles Westhofen purchased the damaged property and entered a partnership with Jacob Froedtert to convert the facility into a malting plant. In 1884, Westhofen sold his share to Jacob's brother William, and this became the basis of Froedtert Malting Company.

Jacob Obermann, Germania Brewery (1854–1861)
Obermann & Caspari, Germania Brewery (1861–64)
J. Obermann & Co., Germania Brewery (1864–1880)
J. Obermann Brewing Co. (1880–1896)
Jung Brewing Co. (1896–1920)
502 Cherry Street

Jacob Obermann started to build his brewery in 1853 and sold his first beer in 1854. The company's advertising in the 1880s used the 1854 date of establishment. (The R. G. Dun reports of August 1854 noted the company had been in business about a year.) Obermann was fortunate to have a new line of business in 1854, since his grocery store on Chestnut Street burned in a fire that also destroyed Simon Meister's brewery and tavern. Obermann's brewery was apparently too small to be included in the 1860 census of industry, but he made several major improvements throughout the 1860s. In 1861 he received permission from the city council to build a sewer at his own expense to take brewery waste across Cherry Street to an alley for dumping. Obermann himself served on the city council for multiple terms, and invited the council to his brewery for refreshments at least once in 1863 (and it probably was not a one-time event).

In 1866 Obermann availed himself of the services of the best-known brewery architect in Milwaukee at the time, Leonard Schmidtner, to design a new brewhouse. The new facility helped him boost production over 1,700 barrels in 1867, which ranked tenth in the city. For a few years in the late 1860s, the company was listed in the city directories as Obermann & Fueger, recognizing the importance to the company of Max Fueger, former brewmaster for Phillip Best.

The early 1870s were a period of dramatic growth—Obermann & Co. jumped from around 2,000 barrels per year to over 7,500 by 1875. Obermann added a bottling house in 1877, which kept him among the leaders in this popular new package. Obermann was also an early adopter of artificial refrigeration. In February 1880 the company built a large icehouse on a railroad connection near Sutton's Lake in Ozaukee County, and added on to it the next year. In February 1882 he had eighty-two workers dedicated to the ice harvest, but at the end of the year he was putting in an ice machine—at the same time as the mighty Phillip Best brewery. While Obermann's brewery was never among the largest in the city, he was respected enough by his colleagues to be elected president of the Milwaukee Brewers' Association—a position he held in 1877 when the National Brewers Congress was held in Milwaukee. In addition to this task and his city council duties, Obermann was also treasurer for a time of Milwaukee Mechanics Mutual Insurance, which he co-founded in 1857, and was later president of Brewers' Protective Insurance Company of the West (later Brewers' Fire Insurance Company of America). The firm was incorporated as J. Obermann Brewing Co. in 1883, but this was more of a formality than an important change in business.

By the mid-1880s J. Obermann Brewing did a steady business of around 40,000 barrels a year—an impressive total except in Milwaukee. The company bought saloon properties and had branches or agencies in Racine, Janesville, Des Moines, Chicago, and elsewhere. An 1885 feature on the brewery celebrated the fact that Obermann "safely weathered the financial strain of 1857," and was a prosperous company. Exactly how prosperous Jacob Obermann was revealed after his passing in 1887, when his will was estimated at about half a million dollars. Obermann, like most Milwaukee breweries, was the subject of merger or syndicate rumors in the late 1880s and 1890s, though this was more because of the general trend than because of any relation to Jacob's death. Jacob's son George J. Obermann commented to the *Sentinel* that he thought the talk of English syndicates was more a matter of Americans trying to get rich by serving as agents for foreign parties rather than any genuine interest on the part of English investors in mid-sized American breweries. An 1892 article about the company and its directors George J., Frederick, Philipp and Herman Obermann suggested that the company did not export that much, only to Minnesota, Illinois, Iowa and Michigan, which was only "not much" by Milwaukee standards. Obermann Brewing's expansion had traditionally been conservative—the company refused to expand into the Chicago market after the Great Fire "because it would [have] necessitate[d] the purchase of additional beer kegs." When Obermann did move into Chicago, they did so during one of the many beer wars in the city, lost money, and abandoned the project in 1892.

While Obermann survived the Panics of 1857 and 1873, the financial crisis of 1893 brought the company down. Perhaps because of Jacob's ties to the insurance industry (which was closely tied to the banking system in Wisconsin dating back to Territorial days when banks were outlawed and insurance companies served as the financial clearing houses), Obermann Brewing Co. failed when Wisconsin Marine & Fire Insurance Co. Bank (known as the "Mitchell Bank") collapsed. The company remained in limbo for several months, but was reorganized in February 1894. Even the reorganization did little more than to allow the company to tread water. The next major change for the company came in June 1896, when Philipp Jung purchased the business at auctions for $230,000. Jung had been a brewmaster for Phillip Best, moved on to start his own brewery, and ended up back at Pabst briefly when Falk, Jung & Borchert Brewing Co. was acquired in 1892. He opted not to stay with Pabst, but Jung had a non-compete clause in his contract that enjoined him from working for

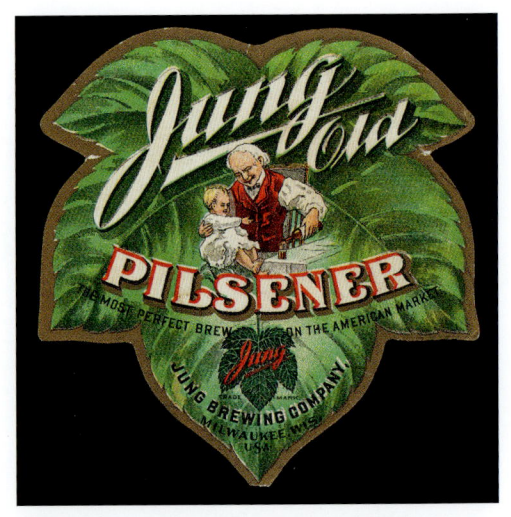

On this die-cut pre-Prohibition label, Jung proclaimed his beer to be "The most perfect brew on the American market." COLLECTION OF TYE SCHWALBE.

another brewery in Milwaukee for three years, so he spent his exile in the malting business. But the financial difficulties of Obermann gave Jung the opportunity to run his own business again. Jung soon renamed the company, and reestablished his business and the firm's reputation.

The most notable feature of Jung's twenty-four years was how uneventful they were. The brewery was seldom in the newspaper, but held a steady market in the region with its Pilsener, Cardinal, Jung Brau and Pale brands, along with a malt tonic. Philipp Jung died in 1911 at age sixty-five, but his sons, led by Philip Jr., continued the business through Prohibition. (Like Jacob Obermann, Jung was a wealthy man at his death, leaving an estate of over $2 million.) The company made a brief attempt to make alternative beverages during Prohibition, but was declared insolvent in 1922.

Colditz & Reitzenstein (1854)
George Schweickhart, Menominee Brewery (1855–1871)
Schweickhart & Gettelman, Menominee Brewery (1871–74)
Adam Gettelman, Menominee Brewery (1874–1887)
A. Gettelman Brewing Co. (1887–1920)

A. Gettelman Brewing Co. (1933–1961)
Gettelman Brewing Co. (division of Miller Brewing Co.) (1961–1970)
4400 STATE STREET

A case of similar names resulted in confusion about the origins of what would become the Gettelman brewery. The oft-repeated story was that Strohn & Reitzenstein started building the brewery in 1854, but died during a cholera epidemic that year. But the tobacconists Adolph Strohn and Guido (or Gustav) Reitzenstein were listed in city directories well into the 1860s, so they clearly did not perish a decade earlier. However, Leonard P. Jurgensen's work shows that Charles Reitzenstein and Frederick Colditz did start a brewery on the Watertown Plank Road, and they did die in the cholera epidemic, so apparently the last name of Reitzenstein caused the confusion.

The brewery remained unfinished for more than a year, until George Schweickhart took over the property and completed the plant. Later accounts related that Schweickhart produced the (standard) 300 barrels during his first year. He built his brewery up to about 1,000 barrels by 1860, and tripled this by 1870. The next year, he sold an interest in the brewery to his new son-in-law, Adam Gettelman. Gettelman was an experienced brewer who had worked for John Enes and Maier & Hohl prior to moving to his father-in-law's firm. After a brief drop under 2,000 barrels, Gettelman built the business up to more than 4,000 barrels per year during the last half of the decade. Often lost in accounts of this period is Charles Schunckmann, another son-in-law of Schweickhart, who was a co-owner of the brewery during this time. While Schunckmann transferred his half of the brewery to Gettelman in 1877, the actual deed was not transferred until Schunckmann died in 1887, and the R. G. Dun & Co. credit reports suggest that Schunckmann was still interested in the business in the early 1880s.

Gettelman suffered a setback in October 1877, when the brewery was badly damaged by fire. The distance of the brewery from central Milwaukee added to the difficulty because the plant was beyond the city fire limits, but the department saved what they could. While the brewery created their own ice field near the brewery, they replaced natural ice with artificial refrigeration in the 1880s. The company also added a side track to the Milwaukee Road railway in 1895, which not only made shipments to distant markets cheaper and more efficient, but also provided the inspiration for a celebration that featured six courses and five different Gettelman beers including "Golden Spike Extra Brew" bottled beer, brewed specially for the occasion.

Among the brews offered at the party was Gettelman's flagship beer, $1000 Lager Beer, which had been introduced a few years earlier. During the 1890s the company also introduced Gettelman's Hospital Tonic, which had much wider distribution than the company's beer: it was shipped throughout the Midwest and as far away as Los Angeles. In the 1890s, Gettelman was producing about 40,000 barrels per year—a drop in the growler compared to the millions brewed by Pabst or Schlitz, but consistent with Adam Gettelman's desire to produce a consistent, high-quality beer in a family brewery.

During Prohibition, the brewery produced near bear and malt syrup on a limited basis. There was also one attempt at brewing root beer, but the trial batch was dumped into the sewer on the orders of Fred (Fritz) Gettelman,

Gettelman's flagship $1000 Beer was advertised with its classic logo on this pre-Prohibition corner sign. COURTESY OF NATIONAL BREWERY MUSEUM.

Adam's son who had taken over management of the brewery. A more important innovation during this period had little to do with brewing, except that the lack of business allowed the inventive Fritz more time to tinker and draw on his beloved butcher paper. He designed an improved high-speed snowplow that was adopted widely throughout the snow belt.

Gettelman was ready to ship beer the minute it was legal, and Gettelman beer was included in the shipment to President Roosevelt from the Milwaukee breweries. Anticipating a shortage of wooden cooperage, Fritz designed a new steel keg which was put into production by the A. O. Smith Company. (Fritz also designed a new pasteurizing system and improved storage tanks, and helped refine the modern "church key" can opener.) In the 1930s, Fritz turned down the offer of American Can Company to purchase the brewery and use it for experiments with new types of beer cans. He preferred to pass the brewery on to his sons, Fred and Tom.

Throughout the 1940s and 1950s, Gettelman had a solid local following—over 90 percent of the beer was sold in Wisconsin. Their popular advertising figure "Fritzie," a Gettelman bottle with a head sporting a Tyrolian hat, appeared on walls all over the Milwaukee area. Because most of the prime advertising spots were already taken by larger companies, Gettelman settled for odd-shaped walls, but adapted the art to fit the particular setting. Slogans like "Let's have a Beer!" and "Get . . . Get . . . Gettelman" appeared along with Fritzie on the advertisements. The company also took advantage of advertising opportunities specific to the moment. The company repainted its sign on the Wisconsin Avenue viaduct to welcome home General Douglas MacArthur in 1951. Gettelman also used special neck labels for purposes ranging from welcoming the American Bowling Congress to Milwaukee in 1952 to encouraging people to vote in that year's election. Gettelman was also the first company in Milwaukee to sponsor a television show (in 1947), and was the first in the city to use one-way bottles (in 1949).

Gettelman's original one-way bottle was distinguished by its shape. It was sold in a six-pack carrier called a "Basket O' Beer." COLLECTION OF JOHN STEINER.

Fritz Gettelman passed away in 1954, and Fred and Tom took over. Fred was chairman of the board, and since he focused on production matters, he was known as "Mr. Inside." Tom dealt primarily with sales and public relations, and therefore was "Mr. Outside." Both were trained as brewers, which was unusual among the Milwaukee breweries in the post-Prohibition eras, where most top executives

The plastic sign displays the $1000 bottle of the late 1930s. The can is from the last years of the brewery. Collection of David Wendl.

were businessmen rather than brewmasters. Despite the numerous innovations by the brewery, Gettelman was still a very small plant in a large ocean of beer. The high point of production was 160,000 barrels in 1950, but few years were close to that figure. The Milwaukee brewers' strike of 1953 emphasized the high cost of doing business, even though Gettelman (and Independent Milwaukee Brewery) was granted a 10¢ per hour accommodation by the union based on their small size. The brothers began discussions about selling the brewery, but their preference was to sell to a company that would continue to operate the plant, rather than simply closing it.

The buyer turned out to be the most logical suitor—Miller Brewing Co. Miller was already a neighbor, and the larger company was looking for a premium beer and a popular price beer to round out their portfolio. Gettelman Milwaukee Beer (which was $2.98 a case in Milwaukee at the time compared to High Life's $3.13) took care of the "popular price" segment, and Gettelman's $1000 Beer (at about $4 a case) provided a high-end product for the lineup. (Also included in the deal was the brand Milwaukee's Best, which later became Miller's nationally-distributed popular price brand.) The sale was announced in January 1961, with the reassuring news that not only would the Gettelman plant stay in operation with its own employees, but those employees would now be on the higher Miller wage scale. The Gettelman brewery remained in operation until 1970, when it was closed and production of the Gettelman brands moved into the Miller plant.

Miller continues to brew Milwaukee's Best brands, and has brewed $1000 Beer for special events. As of late 2017, Miller Brewing proposed demolishing the offices and malt house of the brewery, but the 1856 homestead portion of the complex was granted permanent historic preservation status by the Milwaukee Common Council.

John H. Senne, Prairie Street Brewery (1854–58, 1860–61?)
Frederick Schwartz, Prairie Street Brewery (1858–1860?)
Prairie Street Brewery, John Enes (1861–62)
Frederick Schwartz (1862–63?)
SOUTH SIDE OF PRAIRIE STREET BETWEEN FIFTH AND SIXTH

John Senne is believed to have started a brewery at this location around 1854. A later account holds that the brewery was started in 1857 (which may refer to a beer hall rather than the brewery), but it did recount that Senne's "beer was so rich that glasses stuck to the tables if undisturbed for a few minutes." Frederick Schwartz became the proprietor of this brewery after leaving his previous brewery on Chestnut. Schwartz may not have owned the brewery or at least not for long, since the 1860 industrial census lists the brewery under the name of Johann Senne, and Senne was still listed as a brewer in the population census that year with $3,000 of real estate to his name. Senne may also have returned as proprietor of the brewery, which produced 800 barrels of beer in the 1860 fiscal year. John Enes served as brewmaster for Senne at one point, probably in the early 1860s, before moving to the State Street Brewery. Fred Schwartz returned to the brewery after Enes left, and appears to have operated the brewery at least until 1863, which marked his last appearance in city directories.

Jacob Ziegler (1854–1861?)
John Enes (& Co.) (1863?–1879)
TAMARACK BETWEEN EIGHTH AND NINTH (LATER 810 STATE STREET)

Jacob Ziegler moved from his earlier brewery to this location in late 1853 or early 1854. While Ziegler is still listed as a brewer at this location in the 1861 city directory, the research of Leonard P. Jurgensen has shown that Ziegler was in financial trouble, and the Fernekes brothers were the owners of the brewery. In November 1859, Anton Fernekes offered for sale "all casks, tuns, barrels and brewing kettles and oll other utensils vesels [sic] and appurtenances used in [the] brewery" as well as "the entire of beer malt and hops now in the cellar and building. . . ." Ziegler was still listed as a brewer owning $5,000 of real estate in the 1860 census. In 1862 the Fernekes brothers leased the

532 THE DRINK THAT MADE WISCONSIN FAMOUS

brewery to John Enes, who had previously been renting the Prairie Street Brewery.

Enes was an experienced brewer who had worked for Val. Blatz before going out on his own. Ziegler brewed around 800 barrels of beer in 1860, but Enes quickly expanded the buisness and brought it into the second tier of Cream City breweries. By 1868 he was producing over 3,000 barrels per year, and he kept that pace through the next several years. Existing data for the mid-1870s suggest that Enes was in business intermittently, since he reported no production in 1874 and only 300 barrels in 1875. The R. G. Dun & Co. credit reports indicate that his financial fortunes waxed and waned, and at the beginning of 1878 the sheriff was in possession of the property. While was back up over 3,600 by 1878, he would not be brewing in Milwaukee for long. During 1879, he traveled to Henderson, Minnesota to help his son Christian reestablish a brewery at that location. But Enes had obligations in Milwaukee that were not turning out well. He was supposed to be the guardian of a man suffering from mental illness, and was brought before the district attorney for allegedly neglecting his duties in this case. Enes also was in debt and traded the brewery to former employee Peter Kunz in lieu of the debt. In January 1880, Kunz took his life in the brewery dwelling just before it was to be turned into a malt house by John G. Krenzlein.

Enes returned to Henderson to join his son in the brewery. When Christian sold his share John took over the brewery, and eventually sold his share to another son, Hans, who operated the brewery until it closed in 1918.

Goes & Falk, Bavaria Brewery (1855–1866)
Franz Falk & Co., Bavaria Brewery (1866–1872)
Franz Falk, Bavaria Brewery (1872–1882)
Franz Falk Brewing Co. (1882–88)
Falk, Jung & Borchert (1888–1892)
EIGHTH AND HIGHLAND (1855); 29 SOUTH 29TH STREET (1856–1892)

Franz Falk was trained as a cooper in his father's shop in Bavaria, but after his apprenticeship was over, he took a job in a brewery in his hometown of Miltenberg-am-Main and began to learn that trade. In 1848 he was part of the flood of Germans that left the turmoil of revolution and sought new opportunities in the New World. Like many other Germans, he stopped for a while in Cincinnati, but then moved to Milwaukee, where he found a position in August Krug's new brewery. After six months, he was hired away by Charles Melms, and became the foreman (the term often used at the time for head brewmaster) of Melms' brewery for seven years.

Anxious to start his own brewery, Falk became partners with Frederick Goes, a storekeeper who was content to provide the money and let Falk run the brewery. According to Milwaukee brewery historian Leonard P. Jurgensen, the partnership actually started in 1855, a year earlier than normally stated, and the pair leased space in Blossom's Eagle Brewery for several months. (While the term was not in existence at the time, the arrangement at the Eagle Brewery resembles the alternating proprietorship practiced by some craft breweries that share a facility, and Jurgensen has hypothesized that Blossom brewed ale in the summer and Goes & Falk brewed their lager in the winter.) This arrangement lasted only briefly, as Goes & Falk soon leased and then purchased a site on 29th Street north of the Waukesha Plank Road (modern Pierce Street) along the Menomonee River. They called their new plant the Bavaria Brewery, and it produced about 1,000 barrels in the first year, though another source claims their inaugural production was only 300 barrels (the standard amount usually cited in later accounts). They may have been able to get to that level of production in the first year because of Falk's extensive experience, and also because the Milwaukee market was growing quickly. By 1860 production was up to 5,000 barrels, which ranked fifth in the city (and the state). Goes and Falk also acquired the malt house at the old Eagle Brewery, converted the entire old brewery into maltings and supplied the brewery from that site until Falk built a malt house on the brewery property in 1873. The Eighth and Chestnut location also housed the brewery office, since that location was much more convenient that the brewery itself, which was well out in the countryside at the time.

Falk bought out Goes' share of the brewery in 1866, though Goes continued in the malting business for several more years. Falk continued to expand production gradually, building a new brewery in 1870 and reaching 7,000 barrels in 1871. He launched a major expansion in 1873 that enabled him to push production to nearly 17,000 barrels in 1874. Falk was now one of the leading brewers of the city and he joined his rivals in adding bottled beer to his products in 1877, with bottling done by A. Gunther & Co. With the recent expansion of the Milwaukee Road tracks through the Menomonee Valley and a spur to the brewery, Falk was able to become one of the leading shippers of Milwaukee beer. Introduction of bottled beer helped expand production to 34,000 barrels in 1879, and to 60,000 by 1880. (Like most other brewers, Falk brought the bottling operations under his own roof after a few years.) While Franz Falk died in 1882, a few months after incorporating the business as Franz Falk Brewing Co., he left a brewery that was among the leaders of the industry, not just locally, but across the nation and the world. By the mid-1880s, Falk Brewing Co. had agencies in Chicago, Kansas City and Pittsburgh and two hundred employees at its home plant. In 1885, about 20,000 barrels worth of bottled beer were shipped throughout the United States, and to Mexico, Central America, and the Sandwich Islands (Hawai'i). Falk's beer could be found as far away as India and Singapore.

Part of the reason for the rapid growth of Falk Brewing Co. was the high regard the public had for the company and its products. In its 1879 exposé of the use of adjuncts (additives) in beer, the *Milwaukee Daily News* singled out Falk for praise as the only one of the major brewers who did not use rice or corn, and claimed "expert beer drinkers find his beer more palatable than the doctored stuff dispensed by other brewers." Falk employees and products regularly won contests of various types around Milwaukee, whether it was beer tasting or "most popular brewery foreman." Falk's beer also collected international accolades, earning top prizes in the early 1880s at the Industrial Exposition in San Francisco and the International Exposition in Sydney, Australia.

While the passing of Franz Falk was a loss noted in newspapers across the continent, his sons Frank and Louis proved to be more than up to the task, continuing to expand the brewery and dealing with the labor crises of the 1880s. Falk management typically had good relations with their workers, and when the Knights of Labor called the 1886 strike, Falk's employees stayed on the job until a special delegation of the Knights called them out. Likewise, during the labor disputes of 1888, the vast majority of Falk employees withdrew from the union rather than leave their jobs at the brewery.

In the fall of 1888, Falk Brewing Co. and Jung & Borchert Brewing Co. joined in the biggest change in the Milwaukee brewing scene since Phillip Best bought the Melms brewery almost two decades earlier. The new Falk, Jung & Borchert Brewing Co. combined the fourth and fifth largest breweries in the city, and brought the brilliant brewmaster Philipp Jung to the enterprise. Frank Falk was president of the new company, Jung was vice-president and superintendent of brewing, Ernst Borchert was the treasurer, and Falk brothers Louis, Otto, and Herman also held official positions. The new business picked up where the previous firms left off—with a strong reputation for quality beer and marketing that spread the word of that quality far and wide. Among their early successes was winning the contract to provide beer for the Milwaukee National Home (for Civil War veterans).

Unfortunately, the new company was pursued relentlessly by the "red demon" of fire. The brewery was destroyed by one of the most devastating fires in Milwaukee history to that point in July 1889, which caused well over half a million dollars in damage (early estimates were as high as $1 million). By the end of the month the company had started brewing again in temporary quarters, and preparations for the new brewery were under way. The new plant had a capacity of 400,000 barrels per year, and production in 1890 approached 200,000 barrels. However, a second fire struck in August 1892. Again, damages exceeded the amount of insurance, and though the company pledged to rebuild again, they were apparently weary of starting over another time. In October, Pabst Brewing Co. purchased all the assets of Falk, Jung and Borchert Brewing Co. for $500,000 in stock. Portions of the old Falk brewery were used briefly, but Pabst closed them in 1893 and the property was sold a few years later. Members of the Falk and Borchert families took positions on the Pabst board of directors, but Philipp Jung went into malting until his non-compete clause expired and he purchased the former Obermann brewery. Herman Falk decided to start a manufacturing company, beginning with wagon couplings and eventually gears. Falk Corporation was located along the Menomonee River on land that included the old brewery property. The company was a major producer of gears throughout the twentieth century, and remains in business as of 2017 as Rexnord Corporation.

Ludwig Conrad (1855–57)
Louis Arras (1858–1860)
FIFTH BETWEEN CHESTNUT AND POPLAR (MODERN JUNEAU AND MCKINLEY)

According to Albert Schnabel's history of Milwaukee breweries, Ludwig Conrad operated a brewery on Fifth Street from about 1855 to 1857, after which his cooper, Louis Arras, operated it for a few years. Arras appears in the 1859 city directory as both cooper and brewer, but Ludwig Conrad is more difficult to track. He is in the 1854 city directory as a brewer at another location (Fourth between Tamarack and Cedar) but not in other years.

Phillip Altpeter, Northwestern Brewery (1856–1883)
601–605 THIRD STREET AT SHERMAN (NOW VINE)

Phillip Altpeter, a veteran of the Prussian army who came to the United States in 1846, appeared in the 1854 Milwaukee city directory as the proprietor of a cooperage on the corner of Third and Sherman. In 1856, he started a small brewery at the same location. His brewery was listed as a "small beer brewery" in the 1870 industrial census and some other accounts describe his business as a weiss or white beer brewery. However, the 1870 census also noted that he made seventy barrels of lager beer, so it is possible that he was brewing lager off and on throughout his career.

Altpeter's brewery was never particularly large: The largest reported production was 781 barrels in 1874, but more often his sales were around 400 or 500 barrels per year. He built a new brewery in 1873, and even though the new plant was described as a "white beer brewery," Altpeter still stored ice during the winter of 1873-4, which would not have been necessary unless he was still brewing lager. He also donated two kegs of lager to the fundraiser held at Quentin's Park for yellow fever relief.

Altpeter was an alderman for the Sixth

This receipt (ca. 1890) shows the extent of the Falk, Jung & Borchert brewery along the Menomonee River. COLLECTION OF JOHN STEINER.

Ward, and his brewery was the site of many Democratic political meetings. Around 1883 he stopped brewing and turned the facility into a malt house the next year. Altpeter died in 1892 at age 73, but his family maintained a presence in the city's brewing business as his daughter Bertha married weiss beer brewer Eugene L. Husting and son Oscar had a short-lived bottling business in the 1890s.

J. Simon Meister, Weiss & Syphon Beer (1856–1867)
406 (or 408) Chestnut (modern Juneau) Street

John Simon Meister developed a larger reputation in Milwaukee than the size of his brewery would normally suggest. Historian Albert Schnabel recalled: "One of the most memorable [old breweries] was the Meister Brewery on Juneau near [f]ourth. It specialized in making heavy brown beer enjoyed by women and children." Another article written during Prohibition claimed that Meister "brewed some of the finest lager known to Milwaukeeans of that day." His brewery was a picturesque three-story structure on Chestnut Street with the brewery located in a brick addition at the back of the building. It is also possible that he was brewing at another site and used the address of his saloon for all his business. Meister died in 1867, and his brewery did not continue. The Meister building was remodeled several times, but lasted until 1966, when it was razed.

Syphon beer remains something of a mystery. It may have referred to the "young beer" of which Meister made 400 barrels in 1860.

Schwartz Brewery (1856?–1858?)
Louis Liebscher (1859)
Frederich Fritz (1863?)
Chestnut Between Fourth and Fifth

Fred Schwartz operated a brewery at this location for a few years before becoming proprietor of the Prairie Street Brewery. According to an account from 1926, Louis Liebscher took over this location for a brief period in 1859, before going to Fort Atkinson.

A Frederich Fritz has also been associated with a brewery previously owned by Schwartz, but confirmation is elusive. It is possible that this was a garbled rendering of Frederich ("Fritz") Schwartz.

Middlewood & Gibson (aka Pearson, Gibson & Co.) (1857–58)
Isaac Gibson & Co. (1858–59)
Sands' Spring Brewery (1859–1867)
Eighth between Chestnut and Prairie (now Juneau and Highland)

Located near the old Eagle Brewery, the Spring Brewery grew rapidly to become one of the largest breweries in the state, and faded just as fast.

William Middlewood and Isaac Gibson built a malt house in 1855 on the hill south of Chestnut Street, and added a large brick brewery in the fall of 1857. The *Sentinel* in 1858 described the "lofty" building and its network of cellars underneath. A separate report claimed the new brewery was to be used for lager beer, but all other accounts focus on the production of ale. The proprietors were still primarily concerned with the malting business, where they kept day and night shifts busy turning out 500 bushels per day. Later in 1858, Gibson & Co. took over the brewing side of the business, and Middlewood remained in charge of the now separate malting company.

The precise date of the purchase of the brewery by brothers J. J. And J. G Sands of Chicago is unclear, but it was in late 1858 or 1859. John G. Sands had previously worked in breweries in New York City and Albany, NY, and was placed in charge of the Milwaukee plant. Shortly after Sands took over the brewery, the *Daily Milwaukee News* published a lengthy column admiring the 225-foot long, four-story brewery and its business, which was said to extend into Iowa and Minnesota. They appear to have been among the earliest Milwaukee breweries to advertise heavily, since the *News* reported their expenditures for signs, trade cards, and photographs were over $4,000 in 1859. At this point, the capacity of the Milwaukee facility was 100 barrels a week, large by the standards of the day but dwarfed by that of the Chicago branch which claimed 100 barrels per day. The brewery returned a favor in December by sending the *News* a keg of Cream Ale to help them celebrate the New Year. The editor gushed "Indeed it was so gratifying that we have procured a photograph of Sands' Brewery, which we have hung up in our sanctum, that we may gaze upon the spot where such a delicious beverage is manufactured." Production was up to 5,000 barrels per year by the time of the 1860 census, and the brewery was adding to its product line. Advertisements in 1863 touted the firm's Stock Ale, Burton Ale, Cream Ale and Porter. In 1865, Sands advertised in Madison that their ale could be ordered from the brewery and shipped directly, saving the customer the additional dollar charged by the local agent. However, by 1867 production had dropped to 258 barrels, just enough to avoid being lumped under "other" in a January 1868 summary in the *Sentinel*. While the exact reason for ending the business is not clear, in 1868, the *News* announced that Sands' frame brewery and other property in Milwaukee were for sale.

William Grunert (1857?–1858?)
Mineral and North Jones (modern Barclay)

William Grunert operated a very short-lived weiss beer brewery near the corner of Mineral and Jones "in the latter 50s."

Zwietusch & Forster, Weiss Beer Brewery (1858–1862)
Otto Zwietusch (1862–64)
705–709 Chestnut Street (Modern Juneau)

Otto Zwietusch was better known as an inventor than a brewer. Zwietusch (sometimes spelled Zweitusch) came to Milwaukee in 1856 and was first employed as a machinist, which seems to have given him a foundation for many of his later inventions. In 1858 he joined with Christopher Forster, formerly of Milwaukee's West Hill brewery, to start a "white beer brewery." Their business was fairly large for a weiss beer brewery, reporting production of 500 barrels in the 1860 industrial census. In 1862 the partnership dissolved, but Zwietusch was still listed as a brewer in city directories for the next few years.

While he seems to have given up brewing

beer around 1864, he continued to make beverages of other types for many years, particularly soda water. In 1881 he created a display for the Milwaukee exposition and placed the following ad: "Otto Zweitusch [sic], the soda water manufacturer, it is said offers $500 for the most beautiful girl in Milwaukee to attend his fine fountain during the exposition exhibition this fall. The fountain is now under process of erection and will soon be finished." He also was president of the New Era Brewing Co., which was among the first companies to attempt to brew a palatable non-alcoholic beer. (See Kenosha)

But it was as an inventor and manufacturer of brewing equipment that Zwietusch made the biggest contribution to the industry. Among his nearly sixty patents were fermentation equipment, bottling equipment, and a beer preservation process. Zwietusch's name could be found in nearly every industry periodical for several decades, either in the news for having invented another device, or in advertisements touting their merits. Not only did he invent brewing machinery, but he also devised much of the machinery used to fabricate it. Otto Zwietusch died in 1903 at age seventy-one.

Plattz Bros. (1859?–1860?)
CORNER OF MAIN AND DIVISION

There are only a few fleeting references to the Plattz Bros. brewery: one in the city directory of 1859, and another in a manuscript history of Milwaukee's breweries which may have just taken the reference from the directory. The only Plattz actually listed in the directory is Albert, so it is possible the other brother lived elsewhere (or was simply omitted from the directory). A reference to a Mr. Platz building a new brewery in 1856 on Main Street at a cost of $40,000 is almost certainly supposed to be Mr. Blatz—if Platz had built a $40,000 brewery there would be much more information about his business.

Liebscher & Berg (1865)
Liebscher & Berg (1865?–1869?)
John Berg (1869?–1877?)
517 CHESTNUT STREET (1865); 936 WINNEBAGO (1865–1877?)

The cork in this John Berg stoneware bottle was held in place with a Putnam cork retainer. COLLECTION OF TYE SCHWALBE.

Louis Liebscher returned to Milwaukee from Fort Atkinson in 1865, and started a new brewery with partner John Berg. The 1865 directory listed their business at 517 Chestnut, but a year later the address was given as 936 Winnebago, suggesting they found temporary quarters to begin their business. This idea was supported somewhat by historian Albert Schnabel, who claimed that Liebscher and Berg moved their brewery from Sixth and Juneau to Winnebago (though the starting addresses don't quite line up). Milwaukee historian Leonard P. Jurgensen found that this partnership ended in 1869, but the business remained under both names in the 1870 industry census and in city directories until 1870. After Liebscher left for his own brewery at 189 Sherman, Berg continued at this location until about 1877, after which the brewery was no longer listed in the city directory.

William Aschmann (1858–1860)
NINTH AND CEDAR (MODERN WEST KILBOURN) STREETS

William Aschmann was piano and organ maker who had a small brewery from 1858 to 1860. The city directory of 1859 includes the brewery in the business list, but Aschmann is listed only as a piano maker in the individual section. (The 1926 *Milwaukee Leader* series on old breweries erroneously reported that William's brother was the piano maker.) It is not clear if he actually started this brewery or acquired it from someone else, but no previous brewery on this site has been discovered to this point. It is also unclear what happened to the brewery after it was foreclosed in 1860, though most likely it did not produce after that date.

Frederick Schwartz & Co. (1858–1864?)
CHESTNUT (JUNEAU) CORNER OF SIXTH

According to the *Milwaukee Leader* series of 1926, Schwartz & Co. moved from their location on between Fourth and Fifth Streets to a new location on Chestnut on the west side of the alley between Fifth and Sixth. But some of the dates he was listed in the city directory at this location conflict with dates when he was proprietor of the Prairie Street Brewery.

Ludwig (Louis) Mesow (1860?–66?)
SOUTH SIDE OF CHESTNUT (MODERN JUNEAU) EAST OF SEVENTH

Ludwig (sometimes Louis) Mesow (spelled several different ways in city directories) owned a grocery and general store during the 1850s. By the 1860 census he was listed as a brewer, suggesting that he had opened his small weiss beer brewery during the first part of that year. It disappeared from the city directories after 1863, though he may have continued brewing as late as 1866, when his brewery burned.

William H. & Joshua C. Gray (1863–65?)
WEST SIDE OF FERRY BETWEEN SOUTH WATER AND LAKE

The Gray brothers operated a small weiss beer brewery on Ferry Street around 1863. They may have brewed longer, but in the 1865 city directory they are listed as manufacturing root beer, so they may have switched entirely to soft drinks.

Anton Wahner (1867)
SHOOTING PARK

Anton Wahner is only known from a single reference in the excise records. He is not listed in the city directory in 1867 or 1868. It is possible he may briefly have rented or leased Carl Knoblauch's brewery near the Shooting Park.

John Foude (1868)
679 FIFTEENTH

John Foude is another elusive single-reference brewer. He is listed in the excise tax records in

September 1868, but never again. He may have paid his brewer's tax, but never produced.

F. Meixner, Lemon Beer Brewery (1872–77)
John F. Meixner (1878–79)?
1112 VLIET STREET

Francis (Frank) Meixner was listed as keeper of a boarding house in the 1870 census. He first appears as a brewer of "small beer" in the R. G. Dun & Co. credit reports in July 1872, though he may well have been in operation before then. According to the Dun reports, he had a small operation, and was of fair habits and character, but the business was struggling. In 1877 his lemon beer brewery was sold by the sheriff, and Meixner was out of business. *American Breweries II* contains a reference to John F. Meixner, who was a soda water manufacturer in Milwaukee at the time. The people who best fit this description were either Francis' much younger brother or his son, who were unlikely to have been in a position to take over the business. The only Frank or Francis Meixner in the 1880 census was a resident of the State Hospital for the Insane in Westport, and the age of this person suggests that it was the former brewer.

Louis Werrbach, Weiss Beer Brewery (1873–1908)
L. Werrbach & Co. (1908–1911)
88 MARTIN STREET (MODERN EAST STATE) (1873–76); 89 BIDDLE STREET (MODERN KILBOURN) (1876–1911)

Louis Werrbach operated a weiss beer brewery in Watertown in the 1860s before moving back to Milwaukee in 1869. (See Watertown) He worked for the Hickey soda factory before a brief partnership with John Mueller under Werrbach's name. Werrbach appears to have eventually taken over the former Hickey factory and operated it as the Werrbach Soda & Mineral Water and Weiss Beer Brewery.

In 1876, Werrbach went into significant debt to build a new brewery at 89 Biddle Street. While he appears to have had a large overall business, his brewing operation was still less than 500 barrels per year. His brewery was seldom in the news, though he did contribute some soda water to the large yellow fever

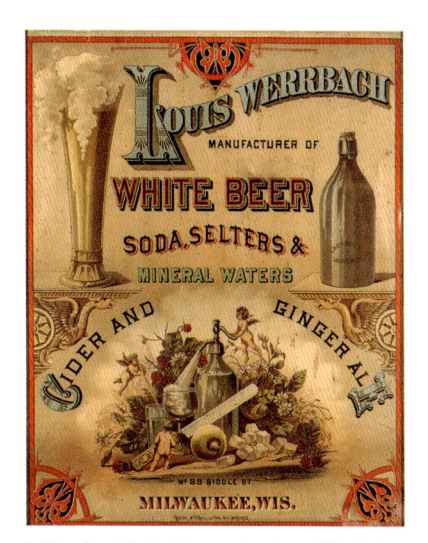

Louis Werrbach's striking poster (ca. 1882–83) features a stone bottle with a Putnam-style cork retainer. The foaming glass emphasized the effervescence of the highly carbonated beer. Below, cherubs serve cubed vegetables and seltzer water (spelled "selter"). COLLECTION OF JOHN STEINER.

fundraiser in 1878 in Quentin Park, and in 1896 a runaway horse became entangled with one of Werrbach's brewery wagons.

Louis Werrbach died in 1911, and though his son Louis Jr. carried on manufacturing soda until 1917, brewing weiss beer appears to have ended with the death of Louis Sr., as the 1912 Brewers' Hand Book no longer included L. Werrbach & Co.

John J. Graf & Co. (Graf & Madlener), Weiss Beer Brewery (1873–77)
Graf & Madlener, South Side White Beer Brewery (1877–1881)
John Graf, South Side Weiss Beer Brewery (1881–84)
John Graf Weiss Beer Brewery (1884–1913)
John Graf Co. (1913–1920)
380 GROVE (1873–76); 530 ELIZABETH (LATER NATIONAL) (1876–1884); 901–903 GREENFIELD AVENUE AND SEVENTEENTH (MODERN TWENTY-SECOND) STREET (1884–1920)

John Graf was probably the most important of Milwaukee's weiss beer brewers. He started in business with Philip Madlener in 1873, and remained in this partnership for eight years. They moved several blocks west in 1876, and the factory then was called the South Side White Beer Brewery. Graf and Madlener dissolved their partnership in 1881, and Madlener went in to the soda bottle and equipment business.

Graf continued brewing weiss beer and making soda water, and in 1884 constructed a much larger plant on Greenfield Avenue. The extent of the growth of his business was dramatized by a county history from 1909: "His plant, which originally employed but four people, now has a list of sixty employes {sic} and its product is valued at $120,000 per annum. It requires fourteen teams and wagons in constant use to transport the product to Mr. Graf's customers." Graf's products were distributed throughout the state, and Graf's slogan, "The Best What Gives," became famous. (A weiss beer glass is pictured in chapter 5.) The company also manufactured beverages for restaurants and retail establishments to sell under their own names. Graf continued to brew weiss beer until Prohibition, but he had such a well-established line of soft drinks that the loss of one product probably made little difference to his business.

John Graf died in May 1930, an event noted around the state. His son John Jr. had died

John Graf's 1910 letterhead not only pictured the founder and the brewery but also listed sixteen products other than weiss beer. This receipt from for sale of weiss beer to an account in Negaunee, in Michigan's Upper Peninsula, indicates that Graf had more than just a local trade. COLLECTION OF JOHN STEINER.

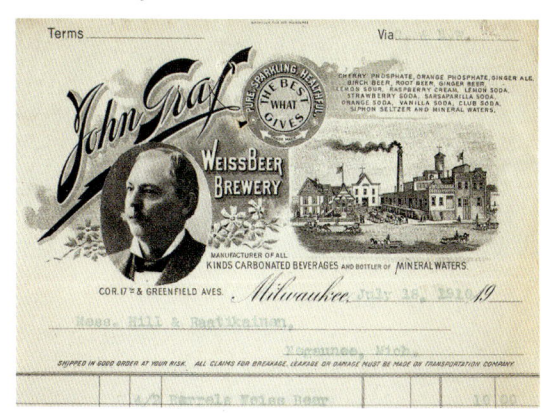

WISCONSIN BREWERIES AND BREWPUBS 537

the previous year, and John Jr.'s widow Sylvia succeeded to the business. The company remained in business into the 1980s under different names and the products remained popular through the 1970s.

Charles Goerke (1877?–1882?)

Charles Goerke owned saloons in Milwaukee, first at 293 Third (according to the 1878 city directory) and in 1880 at 324 Chestnut. There was also a William Goerke who was listed occasionally as a brewer residing at 1202 Chestnut. Goerke later leased the Shooting Park and certainly served beer there, but it is not certain that he actually operated his own brewery at any point. He does not appear in industry directories, and while a number of saloons brewed their own beer, most of them did so prior to the Civil War and the excise tax.

Joseph Wolf (1887?–1888)
Mary Wolf (1888–1889?)
759 NORTH RIVER

Joseph Wolf had a soda factory in Milwaukee since the late 1870s. At some point in the later 1880s he added weiss beer to his product lineup (though he never appeared in the city directory as a brewer). Their business ran into trouble with the federal government in 1888 when warrants were issued for both Joseph and Mary for reusing revenue stamps. The *Milwaukee Daily Journal* reported that the brewery had been in Joseph's name until 1 May 1888, after which it was in his wife's name. A few days later it amplified the importance of the offence, noting that the penalty for reusing stamps could be as much as $5,000 or ten years in prison. The government eventually dropped the charges, but the Wolfs also apparently dropped weiss beer brewing at the same time.

T. W. Falbe & Co., Weiss Beer Brewery (1878)
1312–1320 THIRD STREET

Anton (Toni) W. Falbe and partner Anton Czoernig were listed in the 1878 city directory as brewers of weiss beer. This was their only reference, and they did not appear in industry journals or other references. It is possible that they started the business and never began production or only produced for a very short time.

John Arnold (1881)
Ferd. Arnold (1881–82)
FOURTH AND CHESTNUT (NOW JUNEAU) STREETS (330 CHESTNUT)

It's not clear that the Arnolds actually owned a brewery. John Arnold was listed as a brewer in the 1881 city directory, but boarded at the address listed and may have worked for someone else. Ferdinand (or Fred) was listed as a butcher in 1881 and as a brewer in 1882 but was not in the brewery listings.

Eugene L Husting (1886?–1900)
E. L. Husting Co. (1900–1918)
CORNER OF FIFTH AND VLIET

Eugene L. Husting was one of the relatively rare natives of Luxemburg to operate a brewery in Wisconsin. His family moved to Dodge County in 1853 when he was five, and ten years later he moved to Milwaukee. After working as a wagon driver, he took a job at Philip Altpeter's brewery. Sometime in the mid-1870s he left (with Altpeter's daughter Bertha as his wife) to start his own business. Obituaries and company letterhead claimed the business was started in 1876, though he did not appear in city directories until 1878. (The 1877 directory listed an August Husting boarding at Altpeter's brewery, which is likely to have been a misreading of Eugene.) Husting did not make weiss beer right away, and was listed as a manufacturer of soda and mineral water for several years with no mention of beer. One account reports "[h]is beginning was humble, the business occupying originally only the basement of his dwelling house, and all departments of the work being performed by his wife and children."

Around 1886 Husting introduced weiss beer to his lineup, "which ... brought him the best returns as a selling product." (This date would fit with Husting's first appearance in brewing industry directories in 1887.) Husting continued to make weiss beer into the twentieth century, but directories indicate that he added ale and porter to his products in the early 1900s—a rare move for a weiss brewer and one that would have required additional facilities.

Husting died in November 1916, but his company continued brewing through Prohibition. Like compatriot John Graf, E. L. Husting Co. had a full line of established beverages to keep the business profitable. The company returned to the beer business after Prohibition ended, though this time as a distributor for G. Heileman Brewing Co. products. Eugene's brother John P. Husting was a brewer at several locations in Wisconsin.

Munzinger & Koethe (1892?–1895)
Munzinger & Gerlinger (1895–96)
Christian H. Munzinger (1897–99)
184–186 BURRELL STREET

Christian Munzinger started a small soda factory on Burrell Street in 1890, and the next year he partnered with Richard Koethe and built a weiss beer brewery at the same location. (Since the permit to build the brewery was not issued until late November 1891, it is possible that he did not begin production until the next year.) The partnership with Koethe lasted until 1895, though the company was sometimes listed under Munzinger's name alone. Munzinger then partnered with brewer Frederick Gerlinger, but this arrangement lasted only until the next year. Like most weiss beer breweries, this one manufactured and bottled a variety of other drinks. Munzinger continued to manufacture weiss beer under his own name for a few more years, and may have made soft drinks until 1901, when the business was foreclosed.

F. W. Brinkmeyer (1887)
530 NATIONAL AVENUE

According to Wing's 1887 industry directory, F. W. Brinkmeyer took over John Graf's old location. He is listed in the 1887 city directory as a soda water manufacturer at that location. His term as a weiss beer brewer was very short, since in 1886 he was listed in the directory as a cooper, and in 1888 as the owner of a saloon and restaurant at 297 Clinton.

Town of Lake Brewing Co. (1892–1893?)
Milwaukee Brewing Co. (1893–1901)
Milwaukee Brewing & Bottling Co. (1901-1)
Milwaukee Brewery Co. (1901–1919)
1091 EIGHTH AVENUE (NOW THIRTEENTH STREET) AT SOUTHWEST CORNER OF CLARENCE (NOW WEST ARTHUR STREET)

Several reliable sources indicate the Town of Lake Brewing Co. started at the corner of Eighth and Clarence in 1892. However, local newspaper accounts suggest that there was no brewery at this location prior to the construction of the Milwaukee Brewing Co. in 1893. An existing brewery on the site is never mentioned, though that is not conclusive. No brewery by that name appeared in the city directories, so any such brewery was very short-lived.

In March 1893, the *Journal* announced that a new firm called Milwaukee Brewing Co. had been organized. Among the founders were a few familiar names: Louis Liebscher, Charles Carstens (formerly a brewer in Eau Claire), and George Amann, who may have been the person of that name (spelled Aman) who formerly brewed in Beaver Dam. The company picked a site at Eighth and Clarence. The promoters claimed that they had already secured a guaranteed trade of 37,000 barrels, and planned to build a brewhouse sufficient to manufacture 40,000 to 50,000 barrels. The cornerstone of the brewery was laid in June, and construction proceeded fairly quickly, despite rumors of the collapse of the South Side Bank.

Breweries have manufactured "private label" brands for restaurants, retail stores, railroads, and steamship lines since well before Prohibition. The Milwaukee Brewing Co. bottled a beer for service aboard the Red D Line, the main steamship line connecting the United States and Venezuela between 1820 and 1936. COLLECTION OF TYE SCHWALBE.

By the end of 1893 production was underway, and the first beer was put on the market the following February. The company held a party on 8 February, which was described by a reporter: "It isn't every day, even in Milwaukee, that a new brewery is opened, as was very plainly shown by the multitude that crowded to the plant of the Milwaukee Brewing company yesterday. A 'beer test' had been announced and the prospect of free beer was enough to bring a crowd." The beer was apparently popular, since the crowd consumed fifteen barrels at the event.

The company went through a rapid series of management changes in 1901. The original company was dissolved and replaced by the Milwaukee Brewing & Bottling Co. for about two weeks, then succeeded by Milwaukee Brewery Co. Gustav Becherer headed the new company until the advent of Prohibition. The company continued to brew through 1918, but dissolved the corporation in December 1919.

Castalia Bottling Co. (1893–95?)
WAUWATOSA

Castalia Bottling Co. first appeared in city directories in 1893, with George Schweickhart Jr. and J. A. Eberhardt as the proprietors. This firm proclaimed in directory ads that Weiss beer was among their carbonated products and it was included in brewery listings for a few years. The last directory appearance was in 1895, and in May 1897 the *Weekly Wisconsin* announced that the company was bankrupt. Among the creditors was Charles Abresch, which suggests that Castalia had purchased wagons they were unable to pay for. The news of Castalia's bankruptcy was reported in newspapers from Ohio to Montana, but this seems to have been the result of a slow news day rather than an indication of the company's sales territory. Castalia was still listed in the Brewers' Handbook Directory of 1900, but this was almost certainly simply a case of failure to remove an old listing. There was a Castalia Bottling Co. listed in the Watertown city directory of 1897, which also had Schweickhart as the proprietor, but this business is not recorded elsewhere.

John Kohl (& Co.), Weiss Beer Brewery (1893–1900)
507 TWENTY-FIRST STREET

John Kohl's weiss beer brewery was located on an alley behind the dwelling at 507 Twenty-first Street. He appeared in a few directory listings and on the 1894 Sanborn Insurance map.

J. F. Gruszczynski, Excelsior Bottling Works (1895?–1896)
Oscar Altpeter, Excelsior Bottling Works (1896–97)
847 TENTH AVENUE (MODERN SOUTH FIFTEENTH AND WEST BECHER STREETS)

Joseph F. Gruszczynski (or Grusczynski) ran the Excelsior Bottling Works at the corner of what was then Tenth and Becher beginning in 1884. His products included weiss beer, but it is not clear if he even brewed it there or for how long. The 1894 Sanborn insurance map shows a saloon on the property with no brewing equipment, but it may have been added the next year. Oscar Altpeter (son of Phillip Altpeter of the old Northwestern brewery) is first listed in the 1896 city directory as proprietor of a weiss beer brewery on that site. Leonard P. Jurgensen contends that his business collapsed after a year at least in part because he was sold a shipment of bottles that were undersized, which put him at a disadvantage relative to his competitors.

A. H. Manske Brewing Co. (Manske & Co.) (1896–97)
Henry Fahl Brewing Co. (1897–98)
626 (ALSO 628 AND 629) EIGHTEENTH STREET

In November 1895, the *Sentinel* noted that A. H. Manske & Co. was planning a brewery at the corner of Eighteenth and Vine. Arnold Manske was a brewer from Germany, and Henry Fahl was listed as one of Manske's partners (George Gemeinhardt was also listed in the 1896 city directory). The same day, the *Journal* reported that the brewery "has been established." While the *Journal* was an afternoon paper as opposed to the morning *Sentinel*, it is not likely that the brewery was done already. The *Journal* report also scaled down the capacity from earlier in the day: it reported a capacity of 6,000 barrels per year as opposed to the 12,000 in the *Sentinel* account. The *Journal* also described the business as "[a] brewery for making the kind of beer brewed before lager beer was brought into the market...."

By the next year Manske was no longer with the business (and may have moved to Mazeppa, Minnesota and later to Pueblo, Colorado). Henry Fahl continued the business for about a year before it closed. Unlike some of the other short-lived breweries from this time period, Manske is known to have brewed beer, since bottles from his business exist.

Peter & Charles Anderson (1896)
281 South Pierce Street
Peter & Charles Anderson were listed in the city directory of 1896 as brewers of "malt ale." Very little is known about their operations, and it is not clear if they ever entered production.

Obermann Brewing & Bottling Co.
   (1896?–1900)
West Side Brewery (1900–1)
787 Twenty-fourth and a half Street and North Avenue
The Obermann name returned to Milwaukee brewing in 1896, when Obermann Brewing & Bottling Co. was incorporated in September 1896. It was clear this company would produce a variety of drinks from the start, since carbonated beverages were included in the articles of association. Gustav A. Obermann was the president, and Phil Obermann was the secretary and treasurer. It seems clear that they were in production at least for a while, since the firm appears in the 1900 Brewers' Handbook directory, and the Wisconsin Bureau of Labor Statistics reported in 1898–99 that they had nine employees (though they were listed as soft drink manufacturers).

Sometime in late 1900 or 1901, John H. Knothe took over the plant, and with the help of superintendent Emil Kohn operated it as West Side Brewery for a short time.

B. Roedel Brewing Co. (1897–99)
Badger Brewing Co. (1899–1901?)
Reservoir Avenue, northwest corner of Hubbard
Unlike many of the short-lived breweries founded near the turn of the twentieth century, the firm founded by Baptist Roedel, Philip Klein, and F. H. Kranpitz brewed lager beer. While they also proposed to bottle weiss beer and soft drinks in the articles of organization, the addition of an icehouse in early 1898, their listing as a lager beer brewer in the 1900 *Brewers' Handbook* directory, and the factory inspection records indicate the production of lager.

The successor firm, Badger Brewing Co. continued to appear in directories and brewing periodicals through 1901. The description in the factory inspection records of 1899 indicated that the brewery was a three-story building which employed nine men. According to the city directory of 1900, Badger Brewing Co. was I. H. Klein and O. H. Papke, but it is more likely that I.H Klein is a misprint of Philip Klein, who was listed in the 1900 census as a saloon owner. In 1901 *American Brewers' Review* printed a cryptic note that the firm of Badger Brewing Co. was succeeded by the firm of Badger Brewing Co., but this most likely referred to the transfer of the company to Hartwig Harders.

Ben Kornburger & Bro., Weiss Beer Brewery
   (1901–1911)
Ben Kornburger & Bros. Co. (1911–1920)
578 Twenty-third Street
Benedict Kornburger and his brother John began brewing in 1901. Though the city directory first only listed them as soda water manufacturers, *American Brewers' Review* of May 1901 listed them as brewers, as did subsequent industry directories.

Kornburger and Bro. (sometimes listed as Kornburger & Bros. when Louis and Fred joined the business in 1911) occupied several buildings on Twenty-third Street between Vine and Walnut, including the brewhouse, the bottling works, and a stable. In 1921 Kornburger & Bro. ceased to exist when the family sold the plant to Bright Spot Bottling Co.

George Zeiger, Zeiger Soda Water Co.
   (1901–8)
South Main Street
George Zeiger had a small weiss beer brewery and soda factory in South Milwaukee for a few years in the early 1900s. Little is known about his operations, but both soda and weiss beer bottles from the brewery are in private collections.

Independent Milwaukee Brewery (1901–1963)
2701 South Thirteenth Street
Independent Milwaukee Brewery was more than another of the breweries formed by businessmen who wanted an alternative to the tight control of the beer market by the big brewers, it was founded by Polish-Americans seeking to improve their status in the community. (Additional details about the beginnings of the brewery and a photo of opening festivities are found in chapter 5.) Emil Czarnecki, well-known in the Polish community as a banker and politician, was the first president and remained in charge through Prohibition. Charles Evers and William Jung were the other original incorporators, but the person who became most closely identified with the firm as it grew was its secretary, Henry N. Bills.

Bills previously had been employed as a salesman for Milwaukee Brewing Co., and when he moved to Independent, he brought his promotional skills with him. A later article claimed Bills "joined every club and society in sight" to promote his work. He was apparently skilled at the other, less above board methods of beer sales in the pre-Prohibition era: "It was not unusual for beer peddlers to present new suits to a saloon owner and his kids in order to get a two or three year 'exclusive' contract, or even offer gifts of as much as $500 in cash." Like many of his fellow Milwaukee brewery executives, Bills was fond of horses, and raced his trotting horses on what later became Layton Boulevard. At one point he owned the only two colts sired by the great trotter Dan Patch raised in Wisconsin.

In its earliest years, the brewery's brands bore uninteresting names on simple labels: Pilsener, Pale Beer, Export, and Select among them. However, in 1912 the brewery trademarked the Braumeister label, and the smiling brewmaster became a fixture of Milwaukee beer for decades to come. Braumeister was advertised with an "unusual... taste, like that

Two post-Prohibition seasonal Braumeister crowns for Bock and Holiday Special. COLLECTION OF TYE SCHWALBE.

of imported beers,"—in this case unusual was a good thing.

Independent Milwaukee Brewery employed around fifty people each year and continued brewing through Prohibition, but converted quickly to other products. When Emil Czarnecki moved on to banking industry Henry Bills took full control of the company, and many of the Prohibition-era products bore the Bills brand. Braumeister malt syrup became one of the best-known products of its kind. Ads proclaimed: "Folks know their malts in Milwaukee... To get the Purest, STRONGEST, Best Malt Syrup... demand Braumeister."

Because of its continued operations during the dry years, Independent needed relatively few changes to switch back to beer. Braumeister was among the beer shipped from Milwaukee on 7 April 1933. In the period after beer was legalized, many of the labels remained under the Bills name, and several contained the words "high power"—a claim that would soon be outlawed. Braumeister was only one of the brands manufactured after Prohibition— the company also brewed Deutscher Club, Log Cabin, and Independent brand beers. By this time the company was definitely a Bills family operation. Henry N. Bills Sr. was president, son Harry E. Bills was executive vice-president and younger son H. Newman Bills Jr. was the master brewer and chief chemist.

Independent was able to capitalize on the fame of Milwaukee beer and their own reputation in order to expand beyond their primary market in the Milwaukee area. Prior to World War II, Braumeister was available in Michigan's Upper Peninsula as well as markets in Iowa. After the decade after the war, Braumeister could be found in states from Arizona and New Mexico to Ohio and Florida, as well as Upper Midwest states such as Minnesota and Ohio. Even with the expanded territory, the company still sold most of its beer in the Milwaukee area. Like many other breweries, Independent sponsored radio programs to keep their name before the public. In the 1940s, they sponsored a ten-minute program on WIBU called "Pre-Game Dope" which preceded each Wisconsin Badgers football broadcast.

In the years after World War II, Independent Milwaukee Brewery continued to expand, though its relatively small size made it vulnerable to any changes in inputs or market conditions. After the brewery workers' strike of 1953, Independent was forced to raise prices in order to meet the salary increases gained by the workers. In 1960, capacity was listed at 300,000 barrels, though production never surpassed 187,000 barrels (in 1948). While the Braumeister brand still had a following, the company needed help. In 1963, G. Heileman Brewing Co. of La Crosse began negotiations to purchase the company, which at that point still had sales of "some 133,000 barrels in Ohio, Indiana, Michigan and New Jersey markets" in addition to their Milwaukee business. (Another article about the sale claimed the major markets were in "Ohio, Michigan and parts of Indiana and Illinois.") Production of Braumeister was moved to Heileman breweries at Sheboygan and La Crosse in October 1963, and on 12 December the sale was finalized. The sale included "brewing formulas, trademarks and copyrights, various pieces of equipment which could be used at the La Crosse and Sheboygan breweries, cartons, steel and aluminum kegs, certain inventories of raw materials and all inside and outdoor advertising signs." H. Newman Bills, Harry Bills, and longtime officer Fred Elsner retired, and some of the remaining employees were offered positions with Heileman.

Germantown Spring Brewery & Soda Co. (1915?–16?)
904 FIRST STREET (571 THIRD STREET IN 1916 CITY DIR)

Germantown Spring Brewery & Soda was reported to have been a successor firm to Vogl's Independent Brewery, though the addresses are different. This company produced some beverages, because bottles from the company exist. However, the bottles appear to be soda bottles rather than beer, and there is no definite mention of beer in industry publications. (See also the entry under Germantown.)

Banner Brewing Co. (1933–36)
2302–2312 WEST CLYBOURN STREET

Banner Brewing Co. was one of several firms to take advantage of the phenomenal enthusiasm for beer immediately after re-legalization. Incorporated 1 June 1933 by Albert W. Erdmann, David E. Beatty and Esther Erdmann, the company began brewing in September. The articles of incorporation reflected the changing technology of the industry, including a reference to any "appliances and things... such as are now or may hereafter be used for containing and transporting beer and the like."

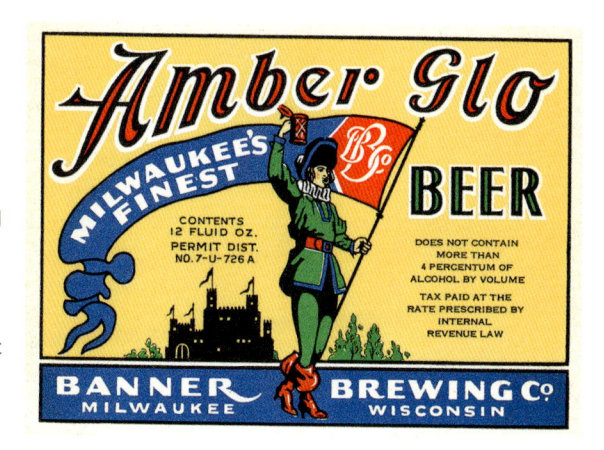

The Amber-Glo label was the most colorful of the known Banner Brewing labels. Banner also manufactured beer that was packaged by Fifty Grand Bottlers of Milwaukee. COLLECTION OF TYE SCHWALBE.

WISCONSIN BREWERIES AND BREWPUBS 541

Banner introduced a few different labels, but none caught on in the face of competition from well-established brands. Production was nearly 1,000 barrels per month in mid-1935, but it began to drop precipitously thereafter. After finishing up operations with a mere sixteen barrels in February 1936—the company went out of business.

Capitol Brewing Co. of Milwaukee (1933–1948)
3778 North Fratney Street

Breweries such as Capitol are relatively difficult to research since they generally operated outside the media glare that illuminated Pabst, Schlitz, Blatz, and Miller. Articles in newspapers and industry journals were few and far between, leaving an incomplete picture of operations.

The company was founded by Emil and Otto Fitterer, along with Edward and Elmer Keller. At least one of these men must have been based in St. Paul, as newspaper accounts at different periods noted the St. Paul ownership of the firm. They appear to have started production in the fall of 1933. Capitol's production surpassed 20,000 barrels by 1936, which suggests that they were building at least some following for their flagship beers Capitol and Commander.

Capitol worked hard to secure markets outside its hometown. In 1940, it launched a campaign in Sheboygan against the threat of being excluded from that market. Noting that its products outsold all others at Sheboygan Marsh, they argued

The public has decided and should continue to decide that by their particular taste preferences. There should be no trade barriers against Milwaukee beers. Sheboygan breweries sell in Milwaukee County without any interference. If they were to depend entirely on their own county for sales, their production would be far less, resulting in less employment and income. The brewers of Capitol and Commander Beers ask no special favors, only to be permitted to compete with all other beers on an equal basis.

How successful this campaign was is not known.

Capitol brewed bock and holiday beers at various points during their history, but also brewed a number of private label brands for beer distributors such as Kaschner's Beer Depot and the Conrad Private Beer Delivery. A significant portion of the beer was shipped out of state in later years.

In 1946, the Wisconsin Tavern Keepers Association voted to buy Capitol Brewing Co. About 180 tavern keepers subscribed $240,000 toward the purchase of the brewery, with more expected to join in time. The capacity of the brewery at that point was theoretically 35,000 cases under wartime restrictions, but was actually closer to 30,000 barrels. However, the sale fell through, and P. W. Heinrichs of Fergus Falls, Minnesota retained control for the time being. The brewery closed in 1948, just before the brewers' strike of that year.

Century Brewing Co. (1933–34)
Old Lager Brewing Co. (1934–38)
Milwaukee Beer Co. (1938–39)
2318–2332 North Thirtieth Street

Century Brewing Co. was incorporated a week before beer began to flow again in 1933. Milwaukeeans A. F. Schad, John B. Lange, Joseph A. Schaab, and Herbert Frisch were the original incorporators of the brewery, which was located in a former soap factory. By early 1934 William A. Gettelman was president of the company, but this firm was short-lived, and later that year it was superseded by Old Lager Brewing Co.

Peter Graf, Joseph Amrhein and Frederick Stahl were the principals of the new firm, which did not resume brewing until 1935. They ramped up production quickly, brewing a respectable 1,025 barrels in May 1935 alone. However production never rose to that level again, and dropped off significantly through 1938. The company was in nearly constant financial difficulty, and could only afford the necessary tax stamps by borrowing from their bank and leaving the stamps at the bank as collateral until needed for kegging. The entire output of the brewery was sold in Wisconsin. Old Lager Brewing Co. is not known to have bottled its own beer, though there is evidence that independent bottlers packaged some of the output. (See Chapter 7 for a photo of an Old Lager tap knob.)

By late 1938 Old Lager was no more, and the successor firm was Milwaukee Beer Co. Like Old Lager, Milwaukee Beer Co. was a draught-only producer, and like Old Lager, production was very limited. Total sales in 1939 were only 1,563 barrels, and the company was out of business before the end of the year.

Fischbach Brewing Co. (1933–36)
3045 West Walnut Street

Walter and Lydia Fischbach incorporated their brewery in June 1933. The articles of

Some breweries ordered grocery bags that were just large enough for six bottles. Collection of Tye Schwalbe.

Century Special Beer was bottled by Schallitz Beverage Company because the brewery was a draught-only plant. The W.B. numbers indicated permits issued to Wisconsin bottlers until the late 1930s. Collection of John Steiner.

Fischbach was a small brewery that brewed "private labels." These helped boost production and build a market, though they were not a long-term solution for struggling breweries. Bloomer Brewery and Plymouth Brewing Co. also made Big Boy Beer for Hanover Bottling. COLLECTION OF TYE SCHWALBE.

organization were unusual in that they authorized the company to "... conduct the business of manufacturing, brewing, bottling, buying, selling and generally dealing in all kinds of beer, ale, weiss beer, porter and other beverages...." While several breweries included a long list of beer styles in their founding documents, most of these were prior to Prohibition, and the Fischbachs were among the few actually to brew something other than lager. Fischbach Brewing apparently expected that weiss beer would be as popular after the dry years as it had been before. (See a label in chapter 7) Unfortunately, soft drinks had replaced weiss beer with drinkers looking for something light and effervescent. While the company occasionally brewed as much as 500 barrels in a month, production was usually much smaller. Even brewing a lager and manufacturing some beer under the Big Boy label for Hanover Bottling Works was not enough to sustain the company. Fischbach Brewing made a mere twelve and a half barrels of beer in November 1936 as it closed up operations.

Sprecher Brewing Co. (1985–1994)
730 WEST OREGON STREET

Randal Sprecher (no relation to nineteenth-century brewer Adam Sprecher of Madison) learned the brewing business at Pabst, where he rose to be superintendent of brewing operations. After Pabst eliminated his job as a result of corporate contraction, he worked with a partner to convert an old tannery chemical factory into the first brewery startup in Milwaukee since 1933. Sprecher made a deal with the company that owned the building to make improvements to the building instead of paying rent to keep costs down. By January 1986, the first kegs of Special Amber and Black Bavarian appeared in Milwaukee area bars and restaurants. (Additional information about the company is in chapter 10.)

Sprecher Brewing grew quickly, and by 1991 was brewing some draught beer at Capital Brewing in Middleton in order to fill orders. In 1993, the company purchased a site in the suburb of Glendale and moved there in early 1994. (The rest of the brewery history is covered under Glendale.)

Lakefront Brewery, Inc. (1987–present)
818A EAST CHAMBERS STREET (1987–1998);
1872 NORTH COMMERCE STREET (1998–PRESENT)

Lakefront's story helped set the pattern for many of the craft breweries that followed it both in Wisconsin and around the nation. Brothers Russ and Jim Klisch got their start by homebrewing, and eventually decided to turn professional. They originally planned to brew at their home in the Riverwest neighborhood, but found a better site in an old bakery at 818 East Chambers Street. They sold their first keg in December 1987 to the Gordon Park Pub. Production figures from the early years were reminiscent of the output of startup breweries in the previous century: seventy-two barrels in 1988; 125 in 1989. The brothers started with two lagers: Klisch Pilsner and Riverwest Stein Beer. They soon broadened their line up, but did not include ale styles for several years, contrary to the nationwide trend in craft beers. After about a decade in their original location, the brothers moved their operation to the historic building at 1872 North Commerce Street that once housed the Milwaukee Electric Railway and Light Company power plant. (Additional information about the early years of Lakefront is found in chapter 10).

Lakefront was at the forefront of much of the diversity that marks the craft beer industry in the modern era. They were among the nine participants in the first Wisconsin Microbrewers' Beer Fest at Chilton in 1992. Tours of the brewery quickly became popular, and as of this writing continue to be among the most popular regular events in Milwaukee. Visitors to the new brewery on Commerce Street could marvel at the faces of Stooges Larry, Moe, and Curly painted on 1,000-gallon fermentation tanks. (The three are no longer in operation, but the portraits were preserved and were still at the brewery at this writing.) Lakefront's interest in history goes beyond locating in an old building—they have a prominent section on their website devoted to historic preservation. The company saved Bernie Brewer's Chalet from the demolition of Milwaukee County Stadium, they rescued light fixtures from the old Plankinton Hotel and have been notable among craft brewers for keeping samples of nearly all their old packaging and souvenirs.

While deeply rooted in tradition, Lakefront has developed a reputation for exploring nearly every style of beer and for major innovations both in product and production. New Grist was the pioneering gluten-free beer, and helped make Lakefront's reputation in new markets around the country. Lots of breweries make some kind of pumpkin ale, but Lakefront is one of the few ever to try a pumpkin lager, which has become their most popular seasonal. In 1996, Lakefront became the first certified organic brewery in the United States, and began brewing Organic ESB (Extra Special Bitter). Many years later, a much stronger beer (12.5 percent abv), Beer Line Barleywine, was converted to an organic recipe and in 2015 Lakefront released a limited edition Beer Line aged in organic whiskey barrels. In 2015, Lakefront introduced Growing Power, a USDA-certified organic hoppy farmhouse-style pale ale in cooperation with Growing Power Inc., a Milwaukee-based non-profit and land trust that focuses on community farming and health food.

New Grist may have been the first beer with mandatory nutrition facts on its package—required because it was gluten free. AUTHOR'S COLLECTION.

With the increased interest in and availability of locally-grown ingredients, Lakefront introduced Local Acre in 2009, made using only Wisconsin grain and hops. Three years later, Lakefront got even more local with Wisconsinite, which is the first known beer to be made with a native Wisconsin yeast strain, and is believed to be the first in North America to use a native local yeast. In an unusual move, Lakefront made the yeast strain available to other brewers and even to homebrewers.

A dedicated collector could fill a long shelf with Lakefront bottles, not just with the year-round beers and seasonals, but also with distinctive one-time-only offerings. To celebrate their 25th anniversary, they brought out three seasonals marked by silver labels: A Belgian-Style Apricot Ale, an Imperial Pumpkin, and an Imperial Stout. A barrel-aged version of the Imperial Pumpkin was released the next year. In addition, Lakefront was one of the first craft brewers to make commemorative beers for community organizations and special occasions, and has continued to do so.

Lakefront's brewers have collaborated with brewers near and far, a recent example being a "hopfenweizen" (hoppy wheat beer) brewed with Great Lakes Brewing Company of Cleveland. They also worked with Bettina Arnold, a professor in the archaeology department of University of Wisconsin-Milwaukee, to create a braggot (a beer and mead hybrid) that would evoke the ales possibly made in Iron Age Europe.

Lakefront's rapid growth in the past decade (it jumped from 6,300 barrels in 2005 to 23,0000 in 2011, then to 33,000 in 2012 and to nearly 47,000 in 2015) has created a capacity problem. In order to maintain its shipments to thirty-six states, Canada, Japan and Israel (though some markets come and go), the company has been looking for a local for a second production facility. In 2014 it acquired an option on 9.3 acres of land on Canal Street in the Menomonee Valley area for the possible location of a new brewery, but shortly thereafter acquired a parcel of land adjacent to the existing brewery for a future expansion. Through the rapid growth, the company has kept its sense of humor: An April Fool's Day press release in 2016, reported with tongue firmly in cheek that Lakefront had become "one of those extreme metal breweries" and changed the logo and several beer styles to reflect the new identity. During the summer of 2016, Kristin Hueneke, chef at Lakefront's Beer Hall, created "beersicles"— frozen beer treats featuring Lakefront beers in three flavors: orange creamsicle, strawberry fudgsicle and pineapple basil.

Water Street Brewery (1987–present)
1101 North Water Street

Milwaukee's oldest brewpub, and the oldest still operating in Wisconsin, was founded in a historic brick building on Water Street. The same architects designed the Milwaukee Public Library and the Pabst Mansion. George Bluvas III, brewmaster since 1999, oversees brewing for all four Water Street locations, and the same beers are typically featured at each. (Beer writer Michael Agnew has detected slight differences in the beers from location to location, probably because of the local water characteristics.) Bluvas typically has between eight and twelve beers on tap at each location, representing a variety of lager and ale styles. In 2017, the original brewing system was removed and replaced with a new system fabricated by Quality Tank Solutions of Oconomowoc.

Owner R. C. Schmidt uses all four locations to display the Water Street Brewery Beer Memorabilia Collection, including many spectacular metal and neon signs, brewery lithographs, backbar pieces, openers and several thousand cans. The love of breweriana is reflected in

Lakefront's My Turn series features the creations of its employees: brews ranging from a Kölsch to a Maple Vanilla Doppelbock have been designed and brewed by the packaging manager, the head of tours, and other members of the team. Each beer bears the name of the employee who created the recipe. AUTHOR'S COLLECTION.

Since 1997, Water Street Brewery has issued a set of special anniversary coasters every five years, often paying tribute to historic poster or tray designs. COLLECTION OF SCOTT REICH.

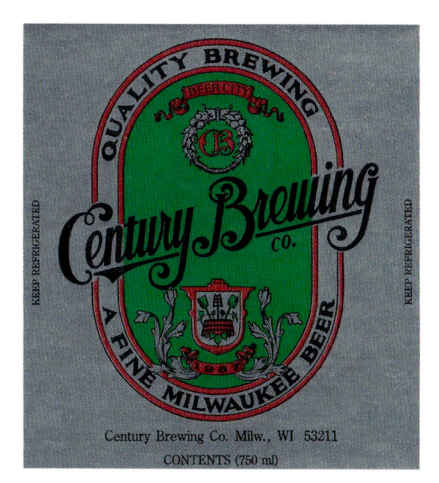

A rare label from Century Brewing Co. COLLECTION OF SCOTT REICH.

the anniversary coasters, which pay tribute to great beer logos and signs of the past.

Century Brewing Co. (1987–88)
2340 North Farwell Avenue

Century Brewing Co. was the second brewpub established in Milwaukee, and was located in Century Hall, which was a nationally known music venue that hosted concerts for important bands of the 1980s such as Hüsker Dü and Sonic Youth. It was also the second brewery in Milwaukee to use the Century name. Unfortunately, it survived about the same length as the earlier business. In April 1988, Century Hall was destroyed by an arsonist. The brewery did not resume business after the fire.

Wisconsin Brewing Co. (1995–98)
1064 North Eighty-second Street, Wauwatosa

Wisconsin Brewing Co., the third business to take that name, was among the many breweries to open and close during the "shakeout" of the late 1990s. However this brewery closed due to double misfortune, rather than because of problems with the beer or the business plan.

Mark May started homebrewing in the late 1970s, and later moved to Milwaukee where he worked at Lakefront Brewery and started selling homebrewing supplies. One of his customers was Mike Gerend, who had earned his MBA at University of Wisconsin-Madison. Gerend drew up a business plan for a microbrewery, but neither of them was ready to put it into effect at the moment. The two met again in Minneapolis in 1995, where Gerend was now a business analyst for Northwest Airlines (currently Delta). They started the brewery later that year in a former food production facility for Big Boy restaurants with an investment of $655,000. The first batch of Rainbow Red Ale was brewed in April 1996, and the brewery soon added Silver Fox Vienna lager, Whitetail Cream Ale, Wood Duck Wheat and Badger Porter. May worked as the general manager of the brewery and the founders hired Gary Versteegh to be the head brewer. (John Harrison, who would soon become head brewer at Delafield Brewhouse, was assistant brewer.) Wisconsin Brewing was experimenting with cask versions of their beers at Milwaukee bars, and even at this early date the brewery had a website.

The late 1990s were a difficult time to start a brewery, since the industry was overcrowded at the time, and breweries desperate to survive engaged in price-cutting to hold on to market share. This made it difficult enough for Wisconsin Brewing to turn a profit in its first year, but disaster struck in June 1997, when the brewery was devastated by a massive flood in the Menomonee River Valley that filled the brewery with six feet of water. While they had almost every other kind of insurance, the company had no flood insurance, so had to absorb the entire loss. All the raw materials were destroyed and the muck had to be painstakingly shoveled out of the brewery. All the equipment had to be completely disassembled and sanitized before it could be used again. One consolation was the support of local business and other area microbrewers. A group of businesses and brewers joined together to sponsor a FloodFest to benefit the damaged brewery, and other breweries lent equipment or offered space in their brewery while Wisconsin Brewing tried to recover.

During the recovery Mike Gerend took a leave from Northwest Airlines and devoted himself to rebuilding the business full time. The brewery was shut down completely for about a month, but by early 1998 was back on track to produce at pace that would allow the company to break even for the year. Wisconsin Brewing Co. beers were available in the Twin Cities as well as Milwaukee, largely because Mike and Julie Gerend lived in St. Paul and had connections there. Mike's airline connections also helped place Whitetail Cream Ale as one of two beer offerings on flights of Mesaba Airlines (a subsidiary of Northwest Airlines).

Unfortunately, another flood struck the brewery in August 1998, and this time the business was unable to recover. The company was closed by the end of the year, and the labels were sold to Pioneer Brewing Co. of Black River Falls (which would later become Sand Creek Brewing Co.) Badger Porter was still being brewed as of 2017.

Milwaukee Ale House (1997–present)
233 North Water Street

Jim McCabe and Mike Bieser were homebrewers who opened Milwaukee Ale House in 1997. Jim's brother John had experience in the restaurant business, so a brewpub was a logical choice. It now occupies several floors of the Saddlery building (which in addition to housing a saddle maker, was also occupied by a sailmaker and the inventor of the Hula Hoop). The location in the Historic Third Ward quickly built a reputation for good beer and attracted large crowds. The lower floor was developed into the Hopside Down. Because it is at river level, the Ale House is one of the few brewpubs

Badger Porter bottle and six-pack. AUTHOR'S COLLECTION.

accessible by water. Hopside Down has six slips to accommodate those arriving by boat.

Many of the popular beers had interesting stories behind their names. Louie's Demise was inspired by a nineteenth-century photo of a group of men drinking. Jim and Mike repeatedly toasted these men, but eventually discovered that the men were at a wake for their relative Louie, who was killed in an argument over a woman.

The success of Milwaukee Ale House led to the opening of Milwaukee Brewing Co. a short distance away. Milwaukee Ale House also opened a second location in Grafton in 2008, offering most of the same beers as the Third Ward location.

Rock Bottom Brewery (1997–present)
740 North Plankinton Road

The Milwaukee location of Rock Bottom Brewery was the thirteenth in the nationwide chain to open. Rock Bottom has been able to employ talented brewers by allowing them some freedom within the corporate guidelines for beer styles and names. Rock Bottom typically has at least one cask conditioned beer available along with eight or nine year-round or seasonal beers.

Stout Brothers Brewing Co. (2000–3)
777 North Water Street

Dave and Bob Leszczynski opened Stout Brothers Brewing in an 1874 building that was originally a bookbindery. Brewmaster Al Bunde offered a variety of ales and an occasional lager. The brewery was located, according to the 2003 Great Taste of the Midwest festival program "... in the shadow of a corrupt City Hall...." The same paragraph announced its imminent closing in September 2003.

Onopa Brewing Co. (2001–6)
Stonefly Brewing Co. (2006–2014)
Co.mpany Brewing Co. (2015–present)
735 East Center Street

A single building in Milwaukee's Riverwest neighborhood has housed three different iterations of brewpubs. The first was Onopa Brewing Co., which was open for about five years and offered a selection of ales created by Marc "Luther" Paul and his successor Jacob Sutrick. Onopa also experimented with barrel-aged beers.

In 2004, Milwaukee restaurateur Julia LaLoggia purchased Onopa, and renamed it Stonefly in 2006. Sutrick remained on as brewer, and the nature of the establishment was little changed—a local gathering place that was probably more famous as a music venue than as a brewery.

LaLoggia decided in 2014 to focus on her other restaurant, and the location was taken over (at first) by the team of restaurateur Karen Bell and brewer George Bregar. However, Milwaukee ordinances prohibited Bell from holding two licenses, so Rosy Rodriguez replaced her. (This was the same rule that originally forced Like Minds Brewing Co. to open in Chicago.) The new ownership changed the name to Co.mpany, but continued to feature live music.

Milwaukee Brewing Co. (2007–present)
613 South Second Street

The most recent business to be named Milwaukee Brewing Co. is the production brewery that grew out of the Milwaukee Ale House brewpub. The first beer was kegged in November 2007, and since then a full range of regular and seasonal beers were bottled and later canned at the brewery. The brewery made use of new technologies to reduce water, fuel and electricity use. Milwaukee Brewing Co. installed the first "micro-canning" system in Wisconsin to reduce energy use at all stages in the process and to make the product more acceptable at outdoor activities. The facility was also used to brew beer under contract for others, such as the early batches of Big Bay Brewing Co.

Milwaukee Brewing has made its mark with ales rather than lagers, and has also introduced several series worth of special beers. The Herb-In Legend Series is devoted to beers infused with tea from Rishi Tea company of Milwaukee including the "monster wheat beer" O-Gii, which clocks in at an extremely high 9.2 percent abv. The Destination Local Series are all high-alcohol beers whose labels are designed to resemble old airline luggage tags. (The brewery's logo contains the airport code for Milwaukee—MKE.) Many of these beers were piloted at the brewpub, and the favorites became packaged brands.

In 2016, the Second Street location was operating at full capacity and production was running at 30 percent above 2015 levels (when the company manufactured 10,702 barrels). To relieve the pressure, Milwaukee Brewing Co. leased space in the former Pabst Brewing Co. complex to expand its business. The company started using the building at 1311 North Eighth Street for storage, but plans include brewing facilities and public spaces including a rooftop beer garden.

The only known coaster variety from Stout Bros. Public House. Collection of Scott Reich.

The early bottles and cans of Milwaukee Brewing Co. (ca. 2007–11) hints at the range of styles brewed. Author's Collection.

Horny Goat Hideaway (2009–2015)
2011 South First Street

Jim Sorenson, a beer industry veteran, established Horny Goat Brewing Co. in 2008 with the idea that craft beer should be fun and not take itself so seriously. The original bottled beer was produced at Stevens Point Brewery (production later moved to City Brewing Co. in La Crosse). In 2009, Sorenson and his partners opened Horny Goat Hideaway, a large brewpub on the Milwaukee waterfront. The beer served on draught at the Hideaway was brewed on-site, and helped test recipes for potential wider distribution. By 2013, Horny Goat products were available in nineteen states. Many of the brands had names that fit the Horny Goat theme, and several of the more popular beers included non-traditional flavors, such as Chocolate Peanut Butter Porter. The company closed the brewpub in October 2015 to concentrate on their brewing operations, which included continuing the pilot brewery at the brewpub location.

Brenner Brewing Co. (2014–2017)
706 South Fifth Street

Brenner Brewing Co. was started by Mike Brenner, who designed the business plan while working on his MBA at University of Wisconsin-Milwaukee. Like many aspiring brewers in the modern era, Brenner undertook formal brewing studies, first at Siebel Institute in Chicago, and then at Doemens Akademie in Munich. The brewery was funded in part by a Kickstarter on-line fundraising campaign which raised over $25,000—well over the $10,000 goal.

Mike Brenner was a member of the Milwaukee arts community as a musician and art gallery owner for many years, so his plan was to create and "Art-Centered Brewery" which would incorporate an adjacent gallery and commission local artists to create labels for the beers. The first labels were created by Sue Lawton for Star Baby IPA, by Erin Paisley for City Fox Pale Ale, and by James Demski "Jimbot" for Bacon Bomb Rauchbier.

Brenner Brewing also allowed MobCraft Brewing to use their brewhouse while MobCraft was under construction. A combination of financial factors caused the brewery to close in November 2017.

District 14 Brewery and Pub (2014–2018)
2273 South Howell Avenue

District 14 (D14) opened in the Bay View neighborhood in September 2014. Owner and brewer Matt McCulloch quickly diversified his beer lineup to include different takes on standard styles. He released his first sour beer in 2017, but the brewery closed in October 2018.

Black Husky Brewing Co. (2016–present)
909 East Locust Street

Tim and Toni Eichinger moved their brewery from the northeastern village of Pembine to the Riverwest neighborhood of Milwaukee in 2016. The building was the former home of Manyo Motors, which relocated elsewhere in the city. The new location included an outdoor patio and a Northwoods-themed bar, as well as much more production space. The Locust Street location is also closer to their primary customers in southeastern Wisconsin.

Enlightened Brewing Co. (2014–present)
2018 South 1st Street

Tommy Vandervort started as a homebrewer and in 2014 started Enlightened Brewing Co. in the Bay View neighborhood of Milwaukee. He brought in James Larson to serve as "Heady Brewer"—Larson is one of the relatively few brewers working in the Upper Midwest to have studied at Heriot Watt University in Edinburgh, Scotland. By 2016, Enlightened beers were available in several dozen taverns and restaurants around the Milwaukee area, as well as in the brewery tap room.

Good City Brewing (2016–present)
2108 North Farwell Avenue

Brewmaster and co-founder Andy Jones is a graduate of the Master Brewers Program at University of California-Davis. The motto of the brewpub is "Seek the Good," which encompasses their approach to using locally sourced ingredients and creating an "open concept brewery."

MobCraft (2016–present)
505 South Fifth Street

MobCraft likely has the most unusual business proposition of any Wisconsin brewery.

The small batch sizes at Mob Craft make it economically feasible to experiment with unusual ingredients. The creator of each recipe is immortalized on the label. Photograph by Charles Walbridge. AUTHOR'S COLLECTION.

MobCraft is a crowdsourced brewery—which means that anyone can submit a recipe to be voted on by potential customers. Voting is done by placing a pre-order for the beer, and the one with the most pre-orders wins. Henry Schwartz came up with the idea while in a business class at University of Wisconsin-Whitewater (the idea was actually tested during the class). Meanwhile, lead brewer Andrew Gierczak was studying microbiology at UW-Madison. Schwartz, Gierczak and two other friends launched the idea in 2013, brewing their first batches at House of Brews in Madison.

After a few years, the team wanted more control (and a taproom) and decided to build a brewery in Milwaukee. They took a very modern American step—an appearance on the celebrity investment show *Shark Tank*, but did not succeed in winning any investors. The company also used more traditional funding sources, such as government loans, and was one of the first to use a new Wisconsin law permitting equity crowdfunding.

The site MobCraft selected for its new brewery was a former parking garage which had also been used to service the city's road salt spreading trucks. Nearby Brenner Brewing Co. offered MobCraft use of their brewery during the build out period. The new brewery and taproom celebrated a soft opening in June 2016 and ramped up over the course of the next several months.

While there are some flagship beers available year-round, most of the beers brewed at MobCraft are single thirty-barrel batches of the crowdsourced winners. These beers have ranged from an all malt lager to Señor Bob, which was an imperial cream ale brewed with agave syrup and aged in tequila barrels. Many of the recipes submitted by would-be recipe designers involve barrel-aging and non-traditional ingredients. Flagship beers are sold in cans and contest winners are packaged in 22-ounce or 500 ml bottles. Originally the winning beers were shipped only to those who had pre-ordered, but soon the beers started appearing on shelves from Madison to Milwaukee. In 2016, MobCraft began a wild and sour beer program and by 2017 there were already several such beers available.

Urban Harvest Brewing Co. (2016–present)
1024 SOUTH FIFTH STREET

Urban Harvest Brewing Co. opened its taproom in the Walker's Point neighborhood in 2016. Brewer Steve Pribek features a variety of regular and seasonal beers made on his two-barrel system in this nanobrewery.

City Lights Brewing Co. (2016–present)
2200 WEST MT. VERNON AVENUE

City Lights Brewing Co. grew out of the 4 Brothers Blended Beer company. This business, started Jimmy, Andy, Robin, and Tommy Gohsman in 2013, hoped to fill a gap in the beer market that offered full-flavored but more sessionable beers. Beers like Prodigal Son and Sibling Rivalry blended characteristics of multiple beers—in the case of Prodigal Son, a hoppy IPA and a smooth cream ale. The beers were brewed and canned at Sand Creek Brewing in Black River Falls.

The brothers planned to eventually open their own brewery, and in 2014 they began searching for an appropriate site and expanded the business beyond the family. They settled on the former West Side Water Works, which was a complex created to use coal gasification to provide gas for the city street lamps. Robin Gohsman became the brewery president, Jimmy (who had done most of the recipe formulation for 4 Brothers) became the brewmaster, and Dr. David Ryder was brought in as "Chief Innovation Officer." The brewery opened in 2016.

Third Space Brewing Co. (2016–present)
1505 WEST ST. PAUL AVENUE

Andy Gehl and Kevin Wright met at summer camp, which they referred to as their "third space." Wright graduated at the top of his brewing class from University of California, Davis in 2009, after which he spent seven years at Hangar 24 in Redlands, California.

Wright and Gehl planned a production brewery in their hometown of Milwaukee, so needed a spacious building. Abandoned industrial buildings often have a lot of space at a relatively affordable price, so they settled on a former metal stamping plant that had been abandoned for more than thirty years.

Like Minds Brewing Co. (2016–2018)
823 EAST HAMILTON STREET

Like Minds founders Justin Aprahamian and John Lavelle finally ended up with a brewery in the Cream City—after a detour to Chicago. The partners were originally looking for a location in their hometown of Milwaukee, but soon discovered they would not be able to get a brewing license in Wisconsin because the James Beard Award–winning chef Aprahamian already had a liquor license for Sanford Restaurant. They soon selected a location in Chicago and opened Like Minds in 2015.

The Wisconsin Department of Revenue made a "change in determination" and allowed the food-centric brewery to open in Milwaukee after all. (The Chicago location was sold to Finch's Beer Company.) The new brewery and restaurant opened in October 2016, but in December 2016 Aprahamian stepped back to focus on Sanford and his family. The restaurant closed in April 2017 to make way for additional space for foeders and barrels.

Beer names such as Ellison, Doctorow, Sendak, and Holden took their inspiration from noted authors or literary characters. After selling the Hamilton Street location, the partners could not agree on a direction for the brewery and the business closed.

Eagle Park Brewing Co. (2016–present)
2018 SOUTH FIRST STREET (2016–18); 823 EAST HAMILTON STREET (2018–PRESENT)

Jack and Max Borgardt were part of the band Eagle Trace and enjoyed drinking good beer. They decided that they had a better path to fame making good beer than recording a hit song. Along with Jake Schinker, they began brewing commercially in 2016 in a location vacated when Enlightened Brewing moved to a larger space in the Lincoln Warehouse. Brews on the one-barrel pilot system were supplemented by contract brews made at Octopi Brewing in Waunakee. In 2018 they moved into the restaurant and brewhouse previously occupied by Like Minds Brewing Co.—a former garage for the Gallun Tannery whose plant still dominates the view. Eagle Park focuses on IPAs, but also brews styles ranging from stout to Berliner weisse. Several of the beers are available in cans.

MINERAL POINT *(Iowa County)*

John Phillips Brewery (1835–1850?)
EAST END OF HIGH STREET

John Philips's brewery "near the old Mineral Point mill" was the first commercial brewery in Wisconsin, though little is known of its operations. A map of Mineral Point ca. 1840 does not show Phillips (sometimes spelled Philips) as a landowner, so it is possible that he was renting or leasing the premises. It was still in operation in 1845 and possibly into the 1850s, but the precise date of closing is not known. The only brewers listed in the 1850 population census were Thomas Julia and Thomas Williams, but there is not enough information to indicate whether they were actually brewing in Mineral Point at the time. It is possible one or both of them had taken over Phillips's brewery. (See also chapter 2.)

William Terrill (1851–53)
Jacob Roggy (1853?–1854)
Gillman Bros, Wisconsin Brewery (1854–1874)
Charles Gillman, Wisconsin Brewery/Tornado Brewery (1874–1898)

Ballo Bruetting (1898–1902)
Mineral Springs Brewing Co. (1903–1920)
Mineral Springs Products Co. (1920–1936)
Mineral Springs Brewing Co. (1936–1961)
272 Hoard Street (Shake Rag Street)

William Terrill was listed in the 1850 census as an innkeeper, and contemporary maps show that his property was located along the Dodgeville Road (modern Hoard Street). Terrill may have been brewing in a small way at his tavern, but later in the year he erected a separate brewery. The *Wisconsin Tribune* of Mineral Point reported in February 1851 "The new brewery of William Terrill, in this village, we understand is completed. The building is one of the first class, principally of stone, and reflects much credit upon those involved in its creation." However, almost exactly two years later Terrill advertised his brewery was for rent. There appears to have been little interest in the enterprise, since the brewery was still was on the market in November. Jacob Roggy operated the plant for less than a year before it was purchased by Charles and Frederick Gillman (sometimes spelled Gillmann).

Both the county history accounts and excise records indicate that Charles Gillman was not devoting his full time to the brewery, as he was mayor of Mineral Point and county treasurer at various points. The brothers took on other partners: Jacob Spielmann from 1855 to 1868 and William Muser from 1872 until 1874. At that point Charles Gillman purchased the entire business and became sole proprietor. By 1870, the brewery was employing eight hands to brew 2,500 barrels of beer. At this point the brewery was still powered by horse, but the establishment represented an investment of $25,000—two and a half times the value of rival Argall. The brewery shipped its beer around the region, and an 1871 map of Mineral Point shows a beer garden run by J. Jenck just across Hoard Street from the brewery.

In 1878, the brewery was struck by what is considered one of the most destructive tornadoes in Wisconsin history. On 23 May, the twelve people then on the premises heard the roar of the approaching storm and took refuge in the brewery cellar, along with the driver of the Arena stagecoach "who confiding in the stability of the brewery, had hurried thither with his vehicle in search of shelter." The roof of the brewery was torn off and shattered in the air, the stone walls were knocked down, two barns were flattened and Gillman's residence totally destroyed. None of those hiding in the cellar were harmed, though the brewery incurred $20,000 of damage, which was far more than any other property in the area. While unfortunate, the disaster gave Gillman a chance to rebuild with modern equipment. The new brewery was steam powered and more than doubled the previous capacity to 6,000 barrels per year. The new plant was often referred to as the Tornado Brewery, especially in the area. According to the 1884 Sanborn insurance map, the new brewery had a twelve-horsepower engine, a malt house, and several outbuildings but no bottling facilities. In the mid-1890s, a bottling house was added on Hoard Street.

In 1898, Charles Gillman retired from brewing, and the brewery passed to the management of Ballo Bruetting, a German immigrant who had previously worked at Blumer's brewery in Monroe. Bruetting worked to expand the market of his new brewery and bought a saloon in Monroe to introduce his new product in his former home. He operated the brewery for about four years until it was damaged by fire. In March 1903, brothers-in-law Felix Unterholzner and Otto H. Lieder moved to Mineral Point to restore the damaged brewery to production. Lieder was an experienced brewery manager, having worked for Ruhland Brewing in Baraboo for more than twenty years. While they changed the name of the company to Mineral Springs Brewing Co., the logo featured the initials U and L in honor of the owners. The new brewery had a capacity of 10,000 barrels per year, but distribution was still limited to the counties surrounding Mineral Point.

In 1918 Otto's son Raymond J. Lieder (sometimes spelled Leider in contemporary newspaper articles) returned from a stint in the U.S. Navy to become brewmaster at Mineral Springs—a position which seemed to have little future with Prohibition on the horizon. However, he ended up staying with the firm until he retired in 1960, eventually owning the company. Mineral Springs continued to operate for a time during the dry years but in 1926, Mineral Springs was fined for a violation of Prohibition laws.

The Unterholzner and Lieder families started brewing quickly after beer was legalized in 1933. (It is not clear how quickly—they were reported to have obtained their brewers' license in May, but an ad in the *Mineral Point Democrat* on 6 April 1933 advertised Mineral Springs beer.) During the following years, production averaged about 6,000 barrels per year, with a surge during World War II to around 11,000, in a brewery with a reported capacity of 12,000 barrels. This surge encouraged the owners to expand capacity to 15,000 barrels, though the company never approached the higher levels of production again. The brewery had only one major brand, Mineral Spring, though it occasionally released a bock or holiday beer in the appropriate season.

After the death of Otto Lieder in 1949, his widow Mary took over as president and Raymond remained as brewmaster, eventually becoming president in 1958. His son Raymond Jr.

Stereoscopic photographs were popular in the late nineteenth century, and natural disasters were frequent subjects. Gilman's brewery was damaged by a tornado in 1878 and had to be almost entirely rebuilt. Courtesy of New York Public Library.

"Feature Matches," issued by breweries and other businesses, were most popular during the 1930s and 1940s. COLLECTION OF TYE SCHWALBE.

joined the firm as assistant brewmaster. Sales declined precipitously in the last years of the 1950s, and in May 1961, Raymond J. Lieder Jr. Announced that the brewery had ceased operations. In 1968, local preservation advocate Kenneth Colwell purchased the old brewery with the intent of restoring the brewery as a crafts shop, and by 1972 the brewery was the site of weaving classes which continued until 1990, when the building was sold and used for a time as a winery. Since then, the brewery has continued to be used as a residence and for other purposes including a pottery studio.

James Argall, Garden City Brewery (1854–1884)

James Argall & Co. (1884–86)

Maurice J. Minor (1886–1898)

EAST END OF NICHOLS STREET NEAR BREWERY CREEK

It is possible that James Argall took over the brewery of John Phillips sometime in the 1850s. Nichols Street is essentially an extension of High Street toward Brewery Creek, so the location seems to fit, and Wayne Kroll concludes that Argall's business was a continuation of Phillips's. However, Phillips's building was apparently inadequate, since Argall built a large new stone brewery in 1854.

Argall was apparently well off, and had a good reputation in the city. Argall was primarily a brewer of ale and porter, though he was listed in the R. G. Dun & Co. credit reports as a lager beer brewer. (All references to the brewery in industry directories listed only ale and porter.) Argall installed steam power before his rival Gillman—the 1870 census of industry indicated that he had a five-horsepower boiler at that point. The 1884 Sanborn Insurance map shows that there was a dwelling on the second floor of the rear of the building, and that the brewery did its own malting. Argall seems to have made small improvements during the 1880s since capacity increased from 1,000 barrels in 1884 to 1,500 barrels. An 1881 county history claimed "For a number of years, Mr. Argall paid considerable attention to bottling beer; but of late years, has abandoned this branch of the business." While this would have made him an early bottler of lager beer, it was already common for ale brewers to bottle their product.

In 1886, Maurice Minor took over the brewery and operated it for the next twelve years. Industry journals indicate that he continued to brew draught ale and Sanborn maps show few changes to the brewery. These maps list the building as "dismantled" in 1900, but the plant was not torn down for many years.

Brewery Creek (1998–present)

23 COMMERCE STREET

Brewery Creek may have the most picturesque and historic location of any of Wisconsin's brewpubs. The creek from which the establishment takes its name is where John Phillips started the first brewery in Wisconsin. Brewery Creek is housed in an 1854 building that was originally a railroad warehouse and was later used for agricultural implements and a veterinary surgery. When Deb and Jeff Donaghue and their daughter Nelle purchased the building in 1995 it had a dirt floor and a lot of boarded up windows and doors. By 1998, they had converted the space into a restaurant, brewery, and bed-and-breakfast inn.

Jeff Donaghue started homebrewing in 1967—well before it was legal. His brews at

The stonework of Brewery Creek's building is typical of the historic section of Mineral Point. Photograph by Robert Fogt.

Brewery Creek represent a range of historical styles and classic ales. He has brewed a porter based on an 1750 recipe, and other creations like a Scottish stout. His shandies are among the most popular of his "cracking good beers."

MINOCQUA *(Oneida County)*

Minocqua Brewing Company (1998–present)

238 LAKE SHORE DRIVE

Minocqua Brewing Company began brewing in 1998. The building was originally a Masonic Lodge (it also served as an Evangelical Free Church) and is located on the shore of a peninsula that juts into Minocqua Lake. The first iteration of the brewpub was founded by five partners who developed a taste for craft beer on their western hunting trips. Under brewmaster Rick Mayer, Minocqua Brewing developed a strong local following with a variety of beer styles. In early 1999, the brewery hosted the first-ever Ice Cold Beer Fest, a fundraiser for local charities (and which has become an official festival of the Wisconsin Craft Brewers Guild). Minocqua began bottling some of its beers later that year, beginning with Northern Wheat Ale and Pale Ale under the Island City brand—making them the first bottled beers from Oneida County since Rhinelander Brewing Co. closed in 1967. Early on, the beer was packaged in liter and half-liter bottles, but the Minocqua purchased the assets of Far Superior Brewing Co. (of Colorado) which provided them with bottling equipment for 12-ounce bottles.

Ryan White had no previous experience when his family bought Minocqua Brewing after a fire in 2004. He trained at South Shore and Stone Cellar and then took over the brewing reins in Minocqua when the brewpub reopened in 2006. Minocqua Brewing has itself been a training ground for brewers, including Deb Loch, who co-founded Urban Growler in St. Paul—Minnesota's first all-female-owned brewery.

MISHICOT (Manitowoc County)

Vierth & Fick (1867?–1868?)
Julius Linstedt (1868?–1884)
John George Scheuer (1884–1904)
Mishicot Brewing Co. (1904–1921)
3 ROCKAWAY STREET, SOUTH SIDE OF TWIN RIVER

Vierth & Fick are only known from a single excise tax entry in December 1867. It is possible that this business was taken over by Julius Linstedt, though it may have been a separate location. The *Manitowoc Pilot* confirmed that a brewery was in operation by October 1867, but did not name the proprietors.

Julius Linstedt (spelled a variety of ways) first appears in the R. G. Dun & Co. credit reports in early January 1869, so it is likely that he was in possession of the brewery prior to that time. (The transfer is not confirmed in the excise records.) An account from 1935 claims that Linstedt built the brewery in 1864, and if this was the case, Vierth and Fick may have rented or leased the brewery for a short period. Linstedt's brewery was small—only producing 400 barrels with two workers in 1870, but the proprietor was highly regarded. The Dun reports included notes like "[good] man in all respects," and "first class man." He was also chairman of the County Board in 1880, and "held most of the local offices." Toward the end of the decade, Linstedt was able to increase production to more than 700 barrels a year, which was respectable for a small-town brewery at the time. However, Linstedt fell ill in 1883, and died in early 1884.

Area farmer John George Scheuer purchased the brewery in 1884, and continued to develop the brewery. His capacity remained between 500 and 1,000 barrels during the 1880s, and industry directories indicate that he added a malt house sometime during the 1890s. Early in the twentieth century, Scheuer added a bottling plant, though it is not clear when. The first mention of bottling in annual reports was in 1911, though breweries often made no special mention of bottling in these very minimal reports. The brewery was incorporated in 1904 with an infusion of Milwaukee capital, and while Scheuer was not among the original incorporators, he was still with the firm as brewmaster and became a director a few years later. The brewery continued to operate through 1918, but the 1919 annual report indicated that the company did not conduct business that year. A note on the 1920 report indicated: "We have reduced the value of our capital stock, since our business is obsolete and our property has decreased in value through enforced idleness." The corporation dissolved in July 1921, but Scheuer's sons stayed in business making soft drinks for a while under the name Scheuer Beverage Co.

An attempt was made to restart the brewery after Prohibition. The Scheuer family sold the business to Chicago investors led by Albert Diamond, Benjamin Bortz and Philip Heller, but they ran short of funds after starting extensive improvements and were unable to meet their obligations. Gertrude Scheuer sued to get the brewery back, and then sold it to the firm of Stelzer & Schmidt, but the brewery was never restarted.

A pre-Prohibition embossed quart bottle with a lightning stopper, ca. 1906. COURTESY OF NATIONAL BREWERY MUSEUM

MONROE (Green County)

Bissinger (1845–48)
John Knipschilt (1848–1857?)
Esser & Hermann (1858–1861)
John Hermann (1861–66)
Ruegger & Kolb (1867–68)
Ed Ruegger & Co. (1868–1871)
Ruegger & Hefty (1871–74?)
Jacob Hefty (1874?–1890)
Hefty & Son (1890–91)
Hefty & Blumer (1891)
Adam Blumer, Monroe Brewery (1891–1906)
Blumer Brewing Co. (1906–1920)
Blumer Products Co. (1920–1933)
Blumer Brewing Corp. (1933–1943)
Blumer Brewing Co. (1943–47)
Joseph Huber Brewing Co. (1947–1985)
Jos. Huber Brewing Co. (1985–89)
Berghoff-Huber Brewing Co. (1989–1990)
Jos. Huber Brewing Co. (1990–2006)
Minhas Craft Brewery (2006–present)
102 EMERSON/MODERN

Very little is known about the founder of the founder of this brewery, including the first name of Mr. Bissinger, or exactly when he started the brewery. Some accounts from the period suggested that his brewery supplied customers up to ninety miles away. German immigrant John Knipschilt (or Knipschild) acquired the business around 1848. The 1850 industrial census reported his output as 360 barrels, which sold for about $5.00 each. In February 1855 the jail across from the brewery caught fire, but the flames were reportedly doused "with the contents of some large vats inside" the brewery. While it is possible that the vats contained water rather than beer, the story that a fire was put out with beer was certainly more appealing. Knipschilt operated the brewery and its malt house until at least 1857, when he offered to pay Janesville prices for barley. When George Esser and John Hermann purchased the business in 1858, Esser claimed "it had not been in operation for some time and was in a rather neglected state, necessitating extensive repairs on the brewing kettle, and a number of other improvements, such as two cellars, a malt mill and a malt drier. By the end of October we were ready for operation and by mid-November we sold our first beer."

Esser made great claims for the expanded market of the brewery: "Gradually our business extended, until finally only a very negligible amount of beer was shipped into our territory from outside breweries." While he claimed his delivery range extended twenty-three miles from the brewery including three locations in Illinois, production in 1860 was 400 barrels—only ten percent more than a decade earlier. A dispute between the partners in 1861 resulted in John Hermann staying in Monroe and Esser returning to the Madison area. Hermann operated the brewery until 1866, when he went out of business.

The next owner, Captain Edward Ruegger, took over the brewery sometime prior to May 1867. His first partner was Abraham Kolb, who also owned a hotel and saloon in Monroe but was in financial trouble. In 1869 Ruegger found a new partner, Jacob Hefty, though Hefty's name did not appear on the business until 1871. With Hefty's arrival, the brewery began to grow rapidly—jumping from 858 barrels in 1871 to 1,122 the next year and over 1,300 two years later. Ruegger sold out to Hefty in 1874 and went into the grocery business in Monroe. Hefty's brewery suffered a disastrous fire in late December 1875. The total loss including building and contents was nearly $20,000. What was left of the thirty-foot wall of the brewery fell onto the Hefty residence a few days later, though the family had feared this outcome and had evacuated the premises. Ten years later the brewery was struck by fire again—this time believed to be arson because kerosene was found on the site.

In 1885 Hefty brought his brother-in-law Adam Blumer on as a partner, and sold his share of the brewery to Blumer in July 1891. (Hefty was married to Catherine Blumer, and Adam was married to Margaret Hefty). Once he became sole proprietor, Blumer immediately began an expansion program which featured a new warehouse designed by Chicago architect August Maritzen. Blumer also installed a ten-horsepower steam engine in the brewhouse that year. In 1895, the *Monroe Evening Times* carried a front-page feature with extensive details of the installation of a new Vilter ice machine, and at around the same time the company added a bottling plant. Despite the ice machine, the brewery continued to harvest ice (8,000 tons in 1898-9), mostly for shipment to its saloons. The business continued to prosper, and advertisements appealed as much to customers' sense of business as flavor:

We Don't Play Marbles. We get right down to business every day in the week. We run our business in a business-like manner. We don't descend to any trickery in order to gain a few pennies. We think more of the life long trade of a customer before we do of an extra ten per cent. profit on each sale. We believe we are going to last much longer than the other man. If you like this way of duing busines [sic] send us your order for a case of beer.

Though under different owners, this brewery definitely outlasted "the other man."

The year 1899 was a busy one for Blumer's brewery. The company continued to expand its

This gold and black tin sign from the 1890s, now flattened out, was originally a corner sign. COLLECTION OF TYE SCHWALBE.

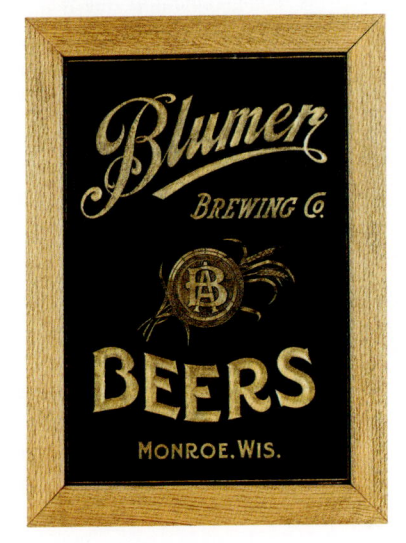

plant, building new stables to accommodate increased shipments. Output reached nearly 9,000 barrels, though the *Monroe Weekly Times* noted that while production was up over 800 barrels the amount paid for revenue stamps more than doubled to $17,636, mostly because of the extra tax imposed to fund the Spanish-American War. Blumer brought in a new foreman (brewmaster), Conrad Haberstumpf, formerly of Detroit, who remained through 1905. The company also purchased two railroad boxcars painted yellow and with the same monogram and lettering as used on the labels for shipping to outside markets, which now included Darlington and Mineral Point.

The company incorporated in 1906 and continued to grow steadily in the years preceding Prohibition, with the most noteworthy addition being a new bottling plant in 1907 to meet the still increasing demand. Adam Blumer also prepared for the future by giving increased responsibility to his sons Fred J., Jacob C. and Adam Jr. When Adam Sr. died in 1918, Fred took over the brewery, but could only shepherd the brewery into the dry years and oversee the conversion to other products. In addition to soft drinks and near beer, the company also made ice cream and was a distributor for farm and road machinery.

The Prohibition years were difficult for the Blumer family as well as the brewery. Fred Blumer originally leased the plant to a group of Chicago investors, but when one of them was found to have gang ties, Blumer took control again and reorganized the company with Ripon-based investors Charles Storeck and A. E. Wells joining the company. Blumer Products was raided in March 1925, and the officers were charged with violating the Prohibition Act by "flooding southern Wisconsin with high grade beer." While the charge of "flooding" may have been a press exaggeration, the "high grade" was not because two cases seized were found to be eight percent alcohol. A much bigger crisis came in April 1931, when Fred Blumer was kidnapped in front of his residence. The case became a national sensation, and was only resolved a week later when Blumer was released in Decatur, Illinois without payment of the $150,000 ransom which the kidnappers had demanded. (The ransom demand was reduced to $50,000 after it became clear that Blumer was not the wealthy beer baron the kidnappers had thought.) The Blumer family was traumatized by the event, and seldom spoke of it in subsequent years. Fred even refused to identify the suspected kidnappers after arrests were made.

When it became clear that real beer was on the way back in 1933, Blumer Brewing made a swift conversion and already had 3,000 barrels of real beer aging by mid-March. Golden Glow returned to its former designation as beer rather than "special brew" as an estimated 350,000 bottles left the plant on 7 April—headed for points as distant as Champaign and Urbana, Illinois, and Minneapolis. Fred Blumer remained in charge of the brewery until 1937, when he resigned in the midst of financial struggles at the brewery.

The company was taken over by Carl O. and Robert F. Marty (along with other investors), who were much better known as owners of cheese factories and developers of vacation properties than for their brewing. The brothers maintained control until 1941, when a group of employees leased the brewing operations, though the Monroe Marty Corp. continued to own the building and equipment and to store and cure cheese in a portion of the factory. The employee group was headed by Joseph Huber, who served as president and general manager. Huber, a Bavarian immigrant, had arrived in Wisconsin in 1923 and worked at Schlitz for four years before taking a position at Blumer Brewing. The new management decided to scale back production to 25,000 barrels and the distribution range to fifty miles in order to have a more manageable and profitable business. In 1947, the company made slight alterations to the business and changed the name to Jos. Huber Brewing Co.—a name that would remain until the next century. While most of the management team remained the same, the company planned two big changes: introducing a new product called Huber Beer and installing canning equipment. At this point, the company was producing over 30,000 barrels per year and distributing the Golden Glow and Hi-Brau brands in Illinois, Indiana, Iowa, North and South Dakota, and Minnesota as well as in Wisconsin.

Despite the original plan to focus on the local market, Jos. Huber Brewing Co. expanded significantly and became the largest of Wisconsin's small-town breweries. (The story of Huber's rise and transformation is covered in detail in chapter 10.)

Huber was successful with its own brands, but was also an important brewer of beer for other companies. Some of these, like Vienna Brewing Co.'s Vienna Style lager, were critically acclaimed and fairly successful. After first being brewed at Hibernia in Eau Claire, Vienna shifted production to Huber in 1986, and shortly thereafter was available in eight states, including craft beer hotspots Colorado and Oregon as well as several in the Upper Midwest. Not all contract brews were as noteworthy. The typical store brands were undistinguished, and one label caused several headaches. The brewery had been in discussions with Wilde's Brewing Co. of Sacramento, California, to brew a brand called Wilde's that was to be marketed to homosexual men. When negotiations broke down in early 1986, Wilde's claimed that Huber backed out of the agreement fearing backlash from conservative heterosexual male drinkers, and hired renowned California attorney Melvin Belli to recover damages. Huber countersued, claiming there had never been a contract and therefore the company had no liability.

Berghoff beer emerged as the salvation of the business after a very 1980s-style financial deal soured. In 1985, Fred Huber was burned out and looking for relief. The answer appeared to be a sale to MTX Co., Inc., a holding company founded by former Pabst executives William Smith and R. Craig Werle. For a couple years, all went well. But the brewery had been purchased through a leveraged buyout, and as was the case with many similar deals, the load of debt forced the new owners to sell off assets to meet obligations. The most important asset of Huber Brewing was the Augsburger label, and in 1988 it was sold to Stroh Brewing Co. of Detroit (and was subsequently brewed at the former Hamm Brewing Co. plant in St. Paul, Minnesota). At the same time, Smith and Werle wound down operations at the Monroe brewery, ceasing production in November. (The return of Fred Huber and the eventual sale to the Minhas family is covered in chapter 10.)

Leuenberger & Co. (1867–1879)
G. Leuenberger (1879–1880)
G. Leuenberger & Co. (1880–83)
JEFFERSON & RACINE STREETS

Civil War veteran Gottlieb Leuenberger started the second brewery in Monroe sometime in 1867, since his first appearance in the excise records was in September of that year. During 1868 Leuenberger had a partner named Schuler, and starting in 1872 the "Co." was John Somer. The brewery grew gradually from over 800 barrels per year in 1871 to 1,365 in 1879. While a few hundred barrels smaller than neighbor Jacob Hefty's brewery, Leuenberger still had one of the larger small-town breweries

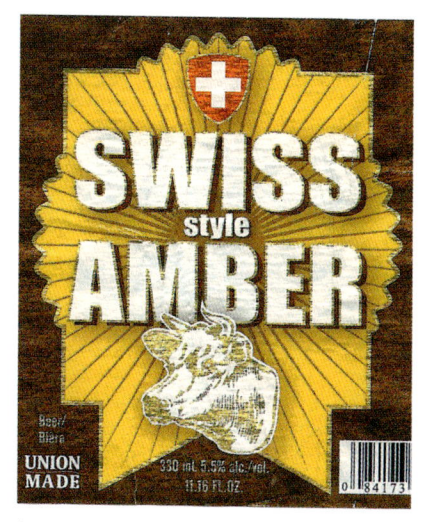

Swiss Style Amber pays tribute to the Swiss heritage of Monroe. Minhas is one of few craft breweries able to advertise "Union Made" on its labels. Minhas exports a significant portion of its beer to Canada, so this label has the bilingual designation Beer/Bière and the standard Canadian volume of 330 ml instead of 12 ounces. COLLECTION OF SCOTT REICH.

in the state. Leuenberger did not suffer as heavily from fire as Monroe's other brewery, though small fires hit both the brewery and his residence in the late 1870s.

Despite the promising growth, the brewery had underlying financial problems. In 1883 the brewery failed, and the R. G. Dun & Co. reported "[t]he failure was a surprise to everyone." Many investors in the business lost their entire stake. Leuenberger later moved to the Pacific Northwest in 1891.

Montello (Marquette County)

H. Wild (1856?–1858?)
Joseph Boreshcake? (1859?–1860?)

H. Wild was included as a brewer in the 1857 and 1858 Wisconsin state business directories. Joseph Boreshcake, a Hungarian immigrant, was listed as a brewer in the 1860 population census, though not in the industrial census. He owned $300 of real property, which suggests that the brewery was a small one.

Mount Calvary (Fond du Lac County)

Matthias Bourgeois (1875–1883?)
Henry Michels (1883?–1887)
John A. Wirth, Mount Calvary Brewing Co. (1887–1890)
John A. Wirth & Co. (1890–1900)
Neis Bros., Mt. Calvary Brewery (1900–1914)
Mt. Calvary Brewing Co. (1914–16)

Matthias (Mathew) Bourgeois moved to Mount Calvary (often listed as Marshfield Township) in 1875, and soon after started a brewery. Some sources suggest that Bourgeois purchased the brewery from an unnamed previous brewer. He also kept a general store and owned sixty acres of land in the city. During the late 1870s he produced over 900 barrels of beer each year. While some sources indicate that he kept the brewery until 1884, the R. G. Dun & Co. records report that he had sold the brewery to Henry Michels by February 1883 (and the sale was probably earlier). Michels (spelled Michel later in Eau Claire) made the Mount Calvary brewery one of the shorter stops in his career that started with Phillip Best and ended at the Eagle Brewery in Eau Claire. He built the business quickly and doubled production from his first year to his second.

In 1887 Michels purchased the Ehrgott brewery in Neenah, and the Mount Calvary brewery was acquired by John Wirth with the support of the Neis brothers, John and Mathias. Wirth remained with the firm until 1900 when he retired to his farm, and the Neis (Neiss) brothers took over. The 1900 census lists the older brother Mathias as a beer peddlar [sic] and John as a beer brewer. As of 1910, the brewery included three buildings, was powered by a relatively small twenty-horsepower boiler, and employed three men. The brothers continued the brewery until 1916, when it was sold to Plymouth Brewing Co. and used as a depot.

Mount Horeb (Dane County)

Mount Horeb Pub & Brewery (1998–2000)
Grumpy Troll (2000–present)
105 South Second Street

Mount Horeb Creamery and Cheese Company built a creamery in 1916, and later added another building to manufacture Swiss cheese. Starting in 1945, Ryser Brothers Cheese Company operated the plant for more that forty years. After it closed, the building remained vacant until Pat and Gail Proposom purchased it in 1996 and undertook a two-year remodeling project and opened Mount Horeb Pub & Brewery. They sold it two years later to a group of local businessmen who wanted to make sure the city still had a destination restaurant. After additional remodeling in 2000, the brewpub reopened as Grumpy Troll, to emphasize Mount Horeb's reputation as "Troll Capital of the World."

The brewpub has been through multiple ownership changes and multiple brewmasters, but has maintained a solid reputation for both food and beer. It is a very rare brewpub that considers its flagship to be a Russian imperial stout, as was the case for many years with Spetsnaz Stout. In recent years, Grumpy Troll has added some sour beers. Grumpy Troll was also among the first Wisconsin brewpubs to develop a relationship with local homebrewers. Winners of the Grumpy Troll Challenge (co-sponsored by the Madison Homebrewers and Tasters Guild) were given the opportunity to brew their beer at Grumpy Troll.

Mukwonago (Waukesha County)

J. K. Silver Brewing Co. (1996–99)
621 Baxter Drive

J. K. Silver Brewing Co. was a short-lived microbrewery located in Mukwonago, just southwest of Waukesha. The first beer to be released was an amber ale, followed by a premium lager and a wheat beer. J. K. Silver products were available on draught and in bottles in a seven-county area.

Muscoda (Grant County)

Joseph Roggy & Co. (1856?–1865)
John D. Pfiester (1865–67?)
Meyer & Pfiester (1867?–69)
Meyer & Postel (1869–1870)
Postel & Hüppeler (1870–1884?)
John Postel (1874?–1886)
Phillip Geiser (1886–1894)
Lampe & Kaiser (1894–98)
William Lampe, Muscoda Brewery (1898–1904)
George Lampe, Muscoda Brewery (1904–6)
Muscoda Brewing Co. (1906–7)
West of Wisconsin Avenue on the Wisconsin River

In 1851, Bavarian brewer Joseph Roggy arrived in Muscoda and several years later built

A rare coaster from the Mount Horeb Pub & Brewery.
Collection of Scott Reich.

This postcard has *Boscobel* written on it, but the brewery has been identified as that of Muscoda, perched precariously on the banks of the Wisconsin River. COLLECTION OF JOHN STEINER.

a brewery along the Wisconsin River. By 1857, Roggy's brewery had a reputation for being "a good and quietly conducted brewery"— apparently referring to the lack of incidents on the premises.

In the 1860 census the only brewer listed appeared to be (in very poor handwriting) Frederick Fouty, a native of Wurtenberg. While he had no property, he owned $1,000 of personal property, which may well have included brewing equipment. Since Roggy was not included in that year's census, he may have leased the brewery to Fouty for a time.

Excise taxes record several ownership changes in the late 1860s and early 1870s. John D. Pfiester (Pfleisterer) left the Muscoda brewery for the St. Charles Hotel in the same city. John Postel was the one common figure—remaining at the brewery from 1869 through 1886 (though he was given several middle initials, probably due to transcription errors). In 1870 the brewery employed three men year-round to make 500 barrels of beer (which sold for $8.00 per barrel). Production advanced from 605 barrels in 1871 to 834 the following year. In 1874 Postel & Hüppeler (various spellings) "made valuable improvements" which increased capacity. The partnership dissolved in December 1874: Hüppeler sold his share to Postel for $6,000 who continued alone. The enlarged brewery was struck by fire in May 1877, but rebuilding began immediately. By the end of the decade the firm was well established, with production approaching 1,600 barrels per year. Hüppeler apparently returned to the business at least once and maybe twice, since the R. G. Dun & Co. records report the partnership dissolving again in 1880, and some accounts report another split after the 1884 fire.

Phillip Geiser purchased the brewery in late 1886 or early 1887. He apparently ran into financial trouble within a few years, and in January 1894 attempted to take his own life over these concerns and family matters. Milwaukee brewery supplier Emil Kiewert purchased the brewery, and Lampe & Kaiser took a mortgage and prepared to operate it. The brewery was scheduled to be sold a few days later. It burned in July of the same year, causing between $10,000 and $15,000 of damage, but was rebuilt with improvements.

Between 1899 and 1904, George Lampe built a small bottling house on the property. But once again, the brewery fell victim to fire, this time in August 1907. While Lampe and his partners filed articles of incorporation that year, they did not rebuild and the brewery remained vacant for several years before being torn down.

NAMUR *(Door County)*

Charles Marchant (Mexime) (1872?–1876?)
During the early 1870s, Charles Marchant (though his first initial often appeared to be something else in some records) ran a very small brewery in Namur, in Union Township. He first appeared in the excise records in 1872, and Schade reported his production in 1874 and 1875 as forty and twenty-five barrels, respectively. This brewery is sometimes listed under the name Charles Mexime, who may have been the same person with a garbled spelling. While Marchant is still in the 1876 state business directory, he may have closed either earlier or later. It is not clear when he stopped brewing.

NEENAH *(Winnebago County)*

Loyal (Harvey?) Jones (1846?)
"BANK OF RIVER"
The origins of the first brewery in Neenah are colorful but unclear. (They are also somewhat complicated by the tendency of accounts to blend or confuse Neenah and Menasha.) According to a 1908 history of Winnebago County drawing on the account of early missionary Rev. O. P. Clinton:

In an early day one Jones, of Welsh extraction, or some other honorable nationality, dropped into our settlement and proposed to start a respectable brewery. Some questions arose between the proprietors of the soil and the would-be brewer, as to the site of such an institution. John Kimberly, Esq., [a founder of the company that would later become the paper giant Kimberly-Clark] had chosen Neenah as his home and he was thought to be a competent adviser in this grave matter. The question was therefore proposed in a business-like manner: "Mr. Kimberly, where do you think would be the best site for a brewery?" The characteristic reply was, "In h—l, sir!" But this opinion of Mr. Kimberly's was overruled by other counsel, who thought the machine could be run more successful [sic] in Neenah. And so it was erected upon the beautiful banks of the Fox river, in full view of Mr. Kimberly's residence.

This Jones was most likely Loyal Jones, brother of one of the early investors in the city. (A different account claimed that Kimberly said "In Hades, sir, in Hades," and that the brewery was not built.) There were no further reports of Jones' brewery, and he was not listed as a brewer in the 1850 census.

Jacob Lachmann (1856–1872)
Frank Ehrgott (1872–74)
Ehrgott Bros. (1874?–79)
Adam W. Ehrgott, Neenah Brewery (1879–1901)
Henry Angermeyer, Neenah Brewery (1901–5)
Estate of Henry Angermeyer, Neenah Brewery (1905–6)

WISCONSIN BREWERIES AND BREWPUBS 555

Neenah Brewery, Oscar Doerr (1906–1910)
Neenah Brewing Co. (Louis Sorenson)
 (1910–11)
129 NORTH LAKE STREET
Traditional sources recount that Jacob Lachmann may have started brewing in Neenah as early as 1856, though the R. G. Dun credit report from 1868 claimed he had been in business for eight years to that point. Research by Lee Reiherzer found that Lachmann purchased the property in 1856 and by the next January the brewery was already present. In 1870 he appears to have had a junior partner, Christian Ernst, and the industrial census reported their production at 400 barrels, sold at the prevailing local price of $8.00. Lachmann remained in charge of the brewery until 1872, when he sold the brewery to Frank and Adam Ehrgott.

While Adam's name is most commonly associated with the business, it appears that Frank made the original purchase. According to Dun, Frank came from Titusville, Pennsylvania, and "invested pretty much his pile in this purchase. [He was] [p]retty sharp but lacks experience." In late 1874 he deeded part of the brewery to Adam and the firm was then known as Ehrgott Brothers. Adam left the business for a time in 1877 after he "got in a 'scrape' with a woman," but eventually returned. In 1879 he took over the brewery from Frank. Production seems to have remained around 400 barrels, though several industry directories listed Ehrgott's capacity as between 500 and 1,000 barrels. Henry Michel purchased the brewery in 1887 for $10,000, leaving his brewery at Mount Calvary to be in a larger market. However, he soon left for Eau Claire, and Ehrgott resumed operation of the brewery. Ehrgott improved the brewery over the years: building a new brewhouse in the mid-1880s and adding icehouses as needed. While the brewery had malting facilities, according to Sanborn insurance maps they were out of use by the 1890s (though they were still listed in industry directories). In addition, insurance maps and industry directories differ on whether the brewery bottled beer. The maps do not show any bottling plant, though the directories indicate they offered bottled beer (possibly packaged by an independent bottler).

Very little is known about the operations during the last years of the brewery. The company did little that made the newspapers or industry journals and appears to have produced only a limited quantity for a local audience. Henry Angermeyer purchased the brewery in November 1901, but drowned in Neenah Slough, near the brewery, in 1905. Oscar Doerr, former brewmaster at White Eagle Brewery in Chicago, bought the brewery from the estate in 1906. He operated it until 1910 when he sold it to Louis Sorenson. Sorenson was in possession for just over a year before selling it to Walter Bros. Brewing Co. of Menasha. The new owners apparently had no interest in the brewery itself because they soon replaced it with the Lakeside Hotel.

Lion's Tail Brewing Co. (2015–present)
116 SOUTH COMMERCIAL STREET
Alex Wenzel left chemical engineering for brewing and opened Lion's Tail Brewing Co. in November 2015. It is housed in the former Equitable Reserve Association Building, and the old vault once used for cash and securities is now available for small private parties. The building presented some difficulties in the build out—because there was no cargo entrance, all the brewing equipment had to be designed to fit through a large window opening.

Wenzel's beers include traditional ale and lager styles, as well as a few rarities. In 2016, he offered Custom Pale Ale, which was an American Pale Ale which customers could dry-hop themselves at the bar using a French coffee press and hops they selected.

NEILLSVILLE *(Clark County)*

Neillsville Brewery
William Neverman & Co. (Lewis Sontag)
 (1869–1880)
William Neverman (1880–82)
John Forster (1882–85)
Ernest (Ernst) Eilert (1885–1898)
Kurt Listemann (1898)

Neillsville Brewing Co. (1898–1920)
STATE AND SECOND (MODERN SIXTH) STREETS
Like several other brewers of his generation, William Neverman was a veteran of the Civil War, having served in the 14th Wisconsin regiment. He had a wide-ranging business in the late 1860s: he operated a grocery store and a saloon, was a carpenter and joiner, and, in 1869 opened the first brewery in Clark County. He and his partner, Lewis Sontag (the 1870 census erred by two days and called him Freitag), gave up the carpentry part of the business in 1873 to focus on the brewery in what was then sometimes called Pine Valley.

Neverman and Sontag made steady improvements to their property during the 1870s, boosting production from about 250 in 1870 to over 600 barrels five years later. The partnership dissolved in 1880 (some sources say 1879) and Neverman carried on alone. However, the next owner of the brewery was already employed there—John Forster, who took over after Neverman suffered financial setbacks in 1882. Forster ran the brewery until 1885.

Since at least 1883, there had been rumors that Ernest Eilert, the brewer in nearby Humbird, was interested in the Neillsville property. In 1885, Eilert moved from Humbird to Neillsville to take over the smaller brewery in the bigger city. Eilert quickly moved to expand the plant, and by 1887 the Sanborn insurance map claimed the capacity of the brewery was 5,000 barrels. Throughout the next decade he continue to improve his brewery so that by 1897 the brewery was powered by steam, was hooked up to the city water supply, and the old cooper shop was converted into a bottle house.

In 1898 Kurt Listemann became the new brewmaster and one of the incorporators of the Neillsville Brewing Co. The brewery had a strong local trade but remained modest in size, employing only four men in 1908. The brewery remained in production until Prohibition, when it closed. The plant was converted to the Clark County Canning Co., and while there was discussion of bringing brewing back after Prohibition, these plans did not materialize.

Neosho *(Dodge County)*

Frank Keoline (1869–1875)
Jacob Binder, Neosho Brewery (1875–1912)
Neosho Brewing Co. (1912–14)
Sebastian Niedermair, Neosho Brewing Co. (1914–16)
Neosho Brewing Co. (1934–37)

Frank Keoline (spelled various ways) first appears in the excise records in March 1869. He appears to have run the brewery until about 1875, when he sold it to Jacob Binder. Binder came to Neosho from Theresa, where he had been employed in the brewery of his late uncle, Benedict Weber. Binder operated the brewery for nearly forty years, mostly by himself until the 1890s when his son Joseph was old enough to help. Binder's brewery usually produced less than 500 barrels per year, though excise records reveal that during a few years in the early 1900s he produced more than that amount and had his tax reassessed.

Sebastian Niedermair (or Niedermaier) acquired the Neosho Brewing Co. in 1914 and operated it for a short time before encountering financial difficulties. The pre-Prohibition story of the Neosho brewery is difficult to research since the business appeared only rarely if at all in the usual sources such as industry journals, newspapers or maps.

During Prohibition, Milwaukee resident Henry Bully purchased the brewery with the intent of making malt syrup. After the return of beer, Bully incorporated a new Neosho Brewing Co. with his wife Margaret and Paul Floss. By 1934 beer was flowing, but not very fast. Production was usually around 200 barrels per month, and only occasionally exceeded 300 barrels. Neosho Brewing bottled mostly in 12-ounce containers, though they occasionally packaged a few cases of 64-ounce picnic bottles. By mid-1937 production dipped below 200 barrels, and brewing ceased in October. In the meantime, the company was in trouble with both state and federal officials for failure to file required documents or to pay taxes. Ultimately the U.S. Attorney decided not to prosecute since the disposition of the case could not possibly cover the time and expense it would take.

This only known pre-Prohibition label from Niedermair's brewery featured an attractive landscape surrounded by American Indian crafts. Collection of Tye Schwalbe.

The original sketches for the design of the Neosho Brewing Co. logo and sign are in the National Brewery Museum in Potosi, Wisconsin. This light is the only one known to exist. Courtesy of National Brewery Museum.

Newburg *(Washington County)*

Robert Schwalbach (1871–1893)
Henry Schwalbach (1893–99)
315 Main Street

Robert Schwalbach (spelled various ways) probably started brewing sometime in 1871, though he first appears in the excise records in May 1872. He had prior experience in the hospitality industry, since the 1870 census lists him as a hotel keeper in nearby Trenton. In the early years, Schwalbach's brewery brewed less than many early twenty-first century nanobreweries and even some dedicated homebrewers: only seventeen barrels in 1874 and thirty-six barrels in 1875. He boosted production to 132 barrels in 1879, but does not appear to have ever produced much more than 200 barrels per year. (An incomplete record in the 1895 Wisconsin industrial census suggests he brewed between 150 and 200 barrels at that point.)

It is likely that most of the beer he brewed was served at his own saloon, and in many records the saloon and brewery were mentioned together. According to the R. G. Dun & Co. records, Schwalbach had a good reputation as a businessman in the late 1870s and early 1880s. In 1880 he had one employee, John B. Mayer. The excise reference in 1872 noted that Schwalbach was manufacturing weiss beer, but later industry directories listed him as a brewer of lager beer. Surprisingly for a brewery of this size, he not only bottled beer but also malted his own barley (according to industry directory listings). In later years, Robert's son Henry took over the business and operated it for a few more years.

New Cassel *(Auburn)* *(Fond du Lac County)*

John J. Langenbach (1865?–1870)
John P. Husting (1870–1890)
Hill and River Streets

John J. Langenbach appears to have begun brewing in New Cassel sometime in the mid-1860s. The 1865 state gazetteer lists the firm of Langenbosh [sic] and Bro. in Auburn, and he first appeared in the Dun & Co. reports in 1867 and the excise records in 1868. The 1868 Fond du Lac county gazetteer lists the business as Langenbach and Co., with John P. (Jean Pierre) Husting as Langenbach's partner. (The same directory also listed F. Hochgrasle as a brewer with the firm.) The Dun reports indicated business was good, but by 1870 Langenbach had left the area and Husting was now proprietor.

Wisconsin Breweries and Brewpubs 557

The 1870 census lists fifty-four year-old brewer Thedor [sic] Husting as the owner of the property, but John's name is in all other records.

Husting's brewery appears to have remained below the 500-barrel threshold for small breweries throughout his ownership. The high points were in the early 1870s, when he approached 500 barrels, and in 1885, when the Wisconsin state industrial census reported his production at 450 barrels. The lowest recorded figures were in the late 1870s, when he made just over 200 barrels. Husting does not appear to have malted his own barley.

In February, 1890, Husting's brewery was destroyed by fire. Newspaper accounts noted that the village had no fire department beyond a volunteer bucket brigade, making it difficult to fight the fire effectively. Husting's loss was more than twice his insurance, so he did not rebuild the brewery. Some sources suggest he remained in business as a beer distributor for a time after the fire.

New Fane (Auburn Township) (Fond du Lac County)

Benedict Mayer (1852?–1868?)

Benedict Mayer left his position with Ulrich Oberle's brewery in Theresa to start a brewery in New Fane. Dodge County brewing historian Michael D. Benter states that Mayer only stayed in New Fane for about a year before moving to Mayville and starting a brewery there. He then sold that brewery to Martin Bachhuber. Mayer appears to have returned to New Fane at some point, since he was included in the 1857 state business directory as a brewer at this location. He was listed as a brewer residing in Auburn Township in the 1860 census, and as a brewer and a butcher in an 1868 county directory. By the 1870 census, Mayer had moved to Williamstown (Mayville) in Dodge County, had given up brewing and become a full-time butcher.

The 1860 census also lists H. A. Hebner as a brewer and owner of $1,500 worth of property in Auburn Township, in a reference eight pages from Mayer. This is the only reference to Hebner (or Heberer) as a brewer, but hints at the tantalizing possibility of another brewery in the area.

New Glarus (Green County)

H. Temperlie?/Dr. Samuel Blumer? (1867–68)
Hefty & Elmer (1869–1870)
Jacob Hefty (1870?–1894)
Gabriel Zweifel, New Glarus Brewery (1894–1913)
New Glarus Brewing Co. (1913–17)
Northeast Corner of Mollis & Diesback (Modern Third Street and Fifth Avenue)

While most sources claim that brewing in New Glarus began at various dates with Jacob Hefty, the excise records suggest the first brewer in the village was actually H. Temperlie, who first appeared in December 1867. It is possible that this is simply a really poor rendering of Hefty, and Temperlie does not appear in any other records. The county history of 1884 makes matters no better. At one point it claims that Dr. Samuel Blumer built the brewery, at another point it says the brewery was built by Blumer and Hefty, and gives several different dates for the arrival of the proprietors in the same volume. Hefty was certainly on the scene in the late 1860s: one R. G. Dun & Co. report places him there as early as 1866, though another dates his business to 1870 (though this may have been the beginning of his sole proprietorship). Dr. Blumer left New Glarus in 1868 or before, so his role in the operation of the brewery was minimal. In the 1870 census, Jacob Hefty and Werner Elmer were both listed as brewers owning $2,000 worth of property, so Elmer may have been brought on board to replace the capital previously provided by Blumer.

By early 1871, Hefty was on his own, and was one of two brewers in Green County of that name (the other was at Monroe). His business grew steadily from 147 barrels in 1871 to 800 barrels by the mid 1880s.

In 1894, Gabriel Zweifel purchased the brewery and began to expand it with the addition of a malt house and a bottling plant. The company was incorporated in 1913, with mostly Zweifel family members as officers. The company generally stayed out of the newspapers, though in 1914 a driver for the brewery was arrested and fined for selling beer in Dane County in violation of excise laws.

New Glarus stopped brewing in 1917, and the corporation dissolved effective 1 January 1918. The brewery lay idle through Prohibition, though the plant was sold in 1924 to a Kenosha company that hoped to manufacture cereal products. As with many other pre-Prohibition breweries, 1933 brought rumors that the brewery would be restarted. The *Wisconsin State Journal* reported "Chicago interests now owning the brewery plant plan to rehabilitate it and start the manufacture of 3.2 beer. Employment for a number of local people is foreseen." It appears that remodeling was started, because the new company was sued in 1934 for payment for some of the work. The plans were soon abandoned, and brewing would not return to New Glarus for six decades.

New Glarus Brewing Co. (1993–present)
119 Elmer Road (County Road W and State Highway 69)

Entrepreneur Deb Carey wanted to start her own brewery as a present for her husband Dan, an experienced brewmaster and brewery engineer. They decided on New Glarus over several other locations, and began to brew in 1993. During the first year of operation, New Glarus Brewing

This cloth pennant, about two feet tall, features a bottle of Alpen Bräu (ca. 1915). Courtesy of National Brewery Museum.

The thumbprint in the Wisconsin outline logo adorns New Glarus crown caps and some labels. The green crowns are for year-round and some seasonal beers; the red crowns are for specialty beers. The slogan "Drink Indigenous" encourages the consumption of local craft beers. PHOTOGRAPH BY CHARLES WALBRIDGE. AUTHOR'S COLLECTION.

sold 2,446 barrels in a market limited to Green and Dane counties.

Within three years of opening, Dan Carey had given full vent to the creativity that had been bottled up while a production supervisor at Anheuser-Busch's Fort Collins brewery. New Glarus had up to ten beers on the market at any given time, ranging from traditional Bavarian styles to Belgian-inspired fruit beers that earned international accolades. They purchased a set of used brewing equipment from a defunct Bavarian brewery to keep up with production without burning out the employees. By 1996 their Wisconsin Belgian Red had won gold at the Brewing Industry International Awards, and the next year they introduced Spotted Cow, which soon became a fixture in Wisconsin taverns. Soon, Spotted Cow became the prized acquisition for beer seekers traveling through Wisconsin. A short experiment with exporting to the Chicago, Rockford, and Peoria areas was not satisfactory for the Careys, so they returned to Wisconsin and thereafter limited their market to their home state. (This has not stopped people from trying to sell the beer elsewhere: in 2015 a Minnesota bar was fined for illegally serving Spotted Cow on draught, and Deb Carey cited two earlier occurrences in Illinois and New York.)

(Additional information about the early years of New Glarus Brewing Co. is found in chapter 10.)

Production grew slowly and steadily at first, but by the mid-2000s growth became almost exponential. In 2002, Deb Carey joked in 2002 that she would quit if New Glarus brewed more than 30,000 barrels in a year. In three years the company was already over 40,000, but Carey found "nobody will accept my resignation." In 2008, New Glarus shipped over 75,000 barrels, they passed the 100,000 mark in 2011, and in 2015 was just six thousand barrels short of 200,000—making it the eighteenth largest regional brewery in the country and the only one that distributed exclusively in its home state.

The success of the company was (and is) a combination of good management, creative yet understated marketing, and outstanding beers. In March 2011 Deb Carey was named Wisconsin Small Business Person of the Year, and that summer she was honored as first runner-up for National Small Business Person of the Year as well as being named an Upper Midwest Entrepreneur of the Year. She also met with President Obama and Vice President Biden as a member of the White House Business Council and was invited to sit in the First Lady's box during the 2013 State of the Union address. Later in 2013, she was a recipient of the Wisconsin Women of Achievement award. Deb has been active in Wisconsin Brewers Guild Activities including lobbying and political contributions (to both parties). Deb's management of the brewery included overseeing numerous large expansions—all of which required working with the municipal government to remain a good corporate citizen. The Hilltop Brewery, completed in 2008, included a wastewater treatment system that reduced the pressure on the local sewer system. Both Deb and Dan have spoken about the importance of fostering a talented and dedicated workforce who sense that the management believes in them and are willing to embrace the mission of the company. The Careys were among the earliest craft brewers to offer full health care coverage to their employees, and a statement about the company's support for universal health care has been a fixture on the company website FAQ section—right next to more typical questions about beer prices and merchandise. The company is especially proud of their employment record, and takes satisfaction from the fact that employees have stayed with the company long enough to have retired from there—a rare occurrence in the early decades of craft brewing.

New Glarus Brewing has opted for a more subtle marketing strategy. The company has not made any neon signs, and most of the signs they have are small and simple in design.

Dan Carey's path to brewing was different from many of the Wisconsin craft brewers who followed him—rather than starting as a homebrewer and turning professional he earned a degree from University of California, Davis, was valedictorian of his class at Siebel Institute in Chicago and worked as a production supervisor for Anheuser-Busch in Fort Collins, Colorado. He apprenticed at the world-renowned Ayinger brewery outside Munich and was the first American in more than a decade to pass the Master Brewer examination of the Institute of Brewing and Distilling in London. While his background is deeply rooted in the brewing traditions of Europe and America, he has little interest in recreating old recipes. Rather, his goal is to take inspiration from classic styles and brew the best version that modern equipment and raw materials (especially Wisconsin-sourced where possible) will produce. One

The New Glarus brewhouse blends the traditional look of copper brew kettles with the latest modern technology. PHOTOGRAPH BY ROBERT FOGT.

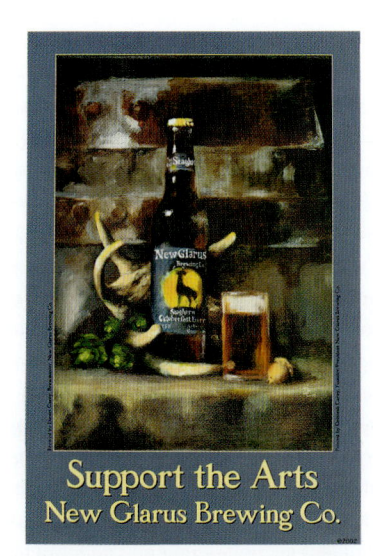

In addition to managing the brewery, Deb Carey is an artist and has designed the labels and packaging for New Glarus. This still life featuring Staghorn Octoberfest was released as a poster in 2002.
AUTHOR'S COLLECTION.

example of this was the Old English Porter, brewed in the early 2010s. The beer featured the "intense vinegar-like sourness" that was typical of this style in the 1870s, without being based on any particular recipe. (Many drinkers were expecting a porter with more pronounced malt sweetness, so it did not sell particularly well at retail outlets. The company recalled it and sold it at the brewery gift shop with a special notation that it was a sour beer. It sold out in a few weeks.) Dan has taken inspiration from photographs of old brewhouses, figuring out why brewers of the past set up their equipment as they did and what characteristics these brewhouses would produce in the beers.

Dan strives for a marriage of drinkability and complexity, but insists on incorporating passion into the beer. He has often compared making beer to making music—where the brewmaster is the conductor who directs all of the elements from raw materials to equipment to the brewing team. But Dan argues that in some ways we know less about brewing and its results than did brewers of some earlier generations because brewing often now uses techniques like dry-hopping and barrel-aging, as well as new varieties of grain, hops and all sorts of yeast strains.

New Glarus has been among the leaders of developing the craft beer movement, but has earned somewhat less credit because their beer is not distributed outside Wisconsin. This also informs how New Glarus views collaboration brews. Deb explained that collaboration beers are often inspired by brewing partnerships, but also with a goal of introducing a brewery to a new market, which was not a concern for New Glarus. The ability for Dan to work with skilled brewers like Randy Thiel, who came to New Glarus in 2008 after several years at Brewery Ommegang in New York, is a collaboration in its own way. Another beer that the Careys consider a collaboration is Two Women, which represents the productive relationship between New Glarus Brewing Co. and Weyermann Malting of Bamberg, Germany (the two women are Deb Carey and Sabine Weyermann, head of the German firm). In 2014 New Glarus finally worked with Sierra Nevada Brewing Co. of Chico, California on a multi-brewery collaboration—an English-style bitter called There and Back, created for Sierra Nevada's Beer Camp Across America program. More recently, New Glarus teamed with Dirk Naudts of De 'Proef Brouwerij in Lochristi, Belgium, to brew a dark Belgian ale called Abtsolution. Since it was sold through the Belgian firms importer, it was the first New Glarus beer many fans were able to buy without traveling to Wisconsin.

While best known among casual beer lovers for Spotted Cow or the fruit beers, over more than two decades New Glarus has offered nearly one hundred different brands of all types. Many of these beers were limited seasonal offerings, since Dan points out "beer is food, and you don't eat the same things in February as you do in August." A large number of these beers were inspired by Belgian styles and brewing processes. Production of these beers, which typically involve organisms that could contaminate the brewing equipment, became much less risky after the building of the Hilltop Brewery in 2008. The old brewery, now known as the Riverside Brewery, was dedicated to fruit beers and sour styles. The sour beer area is often referred to as "the ebola room" because of the need to decontaminate everything (and everyone) that comes out of the facility. In order to increase production of these unique beers (which despite their fame only amounted to about 4 percent of output in 2013) New Glarus built a new "wild fruit cave" in 2014, designed by the Careys' architect daughter Katherine. The cave features a coolship, which is an open cooling vessel which chills the wort slowly and allows wild yeasts to enter. The aging beer is stored in large foeders—oak tanks more commonly used in wineries with a capacity of approximately 90 barrels each (2,800 gallons). New Glarus was the first U.S. brewery to use foeders in the 1990s, so this program was more of an expansion than an innovation. The first beers released from the cave were an Oud Bruin (old brown) and a gueze—both of which were used as base beers for other products such as Cran-bic.

As of this writing, the most recent development for New Glarus Brewing was the introduction of canned beer to the lineup. The first brand in cans was Moon Man pale ale, followed by Spotted Cow. The canned product exemplified the New Glarus commitment to locally sourced inputs with the cans themselves being made in Fort Atkinson and the 12-pack boxes made in Menasha.

(Additional photographs of the New Glarus Brewing Co. and its products are found in Chapters 1 and 10.)

NEW LISBON *(Juneau County)*

Joseph Hausmann (1857–59)
Bierbauer & Fauerbach (1859–1862)
Henry Bierbauer (1862–1902)
Henry Bierbauer Estate (1902–1911)
Bierbauer Brewery (1911–14)
H. Bierbauer Brewing Co. (1914–16)
Christmann Brewery (1933–37)
Million Brewery, Inc. (1937–1941)
8 MONROE STREET

The precise point at which Joseph Hausmann started brewing in New Lisbon is not clear, though it could not have been much before

1857 since he was in Portage for several years. He is included in the 1857 state business directory at New Lisbon, and ads that began in the *Juneau County Argus* in August 1858 proclaimed that Hausman {sic} was "Manufacturing the well known excellent New Lisbon Beer, [a]t his brewery near the Depot."

At some point in 1859, Hausmann transferred control of the New Lisbon brewery to Peter Fauerbach and Henry Bierbauer (who was married to Barbara Fauerbach). The date the new partners took over is confused by advertisements in the *Argus,* which first feature their names in August, but revert to Hausmann in October for some reason. By the time of the 1860 census, Hausmann was in Madison working as foreman of the Sprecher brewery. Bierbauer came from a formidable brewing family: he worked for a time at the brewery of his brother Charles in Utica, New York, brother Louis operated a brewery in Canajoharie, New York, for many decades, and brother William operated a brewery in Mankato, Minnesota (in which brother Jacob was interested for a short time). In July 1862, Fauerbach sold his share in the brewery, and purchased a hotel in New Lisbon (though he later took over for Hausmann at the Sprecher brewery in Madison). An 1892 county history lauded Bierbauer's "prophetic eye seeing the future of New Lisbon,"

A glass from the later years of Bierbauer's ownership (ca. 1890s). COLLECTION OF TYE SCHWALBE.

but claimed "the building purchased of Mr. Hausmann was an unpretentious structure," though it was large enough to produce nearly 800 barrels in 1871. Bierbauer built a substantial new brewery in 1878 and by 1885 the property also featured a barn, a shed and a wagon house. Bierbauer also had a saloon associated with the brewery, and he advertised that "[G]entlemen will find my brewery open at all lawful hours and are cordially invited to give me a call when in New Lisbon." The county history account claimed that by 1892 he had expanded capacity to 10,000 barrels, but the 1895 industrial census showed production of only 150 barrels. A bottling house was added between 1900 and 1902.

In 1894, a proposal to adjust the tariffs on certain imports resulted in a unique glimpse into Bierbauer's operations (as well as those of several dozen other breweries around the country). In response to request for comment by the U.S. Senate Finance Committee, a number of brewers sent in revealing responses to the circulated questions. Bierbauer was among the most complete, providing full production figures from 1874 through 1893 (while noting that "the books before 1874 were destroyed"). While production remained below 1,000 barrels from 1875 to 1882, average production in the following decade averaged about 1,200 barrels per year (it had been over 1,300 in 1874). Bierbauer also commented on the beer market, noting that "[w]e are not doing as much business [in 1894] as in 1892 on account of the competition of large breweries. Bierbauer was politically active (including time as mayor of New Lisbon) and also offered his theory about the "present depression" (the Panic of 1893), which he attributed to "the Sherman silver bill and the present tariff law." He also reported that the brewery employed three skilled workers at $1.50 to $2.00 per day for skilled labor and two unskilled laborers at $1.00 to $1.25 per day. The work week at his brewery in 1894 was sixty hours.

Bierbauer continued to prosper, and later partnered with Enoch Smart in a flour mill. Bierbauer died in March 1903, but the brewery continued to operate under the direction of Henry's son Carl, first under the title Henry Bierbauer Estate, but starting in 1914 as the H. Bierbauer Brewing Co. (Industry publications used these names interchangeably for several years.) The business did not survive to the start of Prohibition, closing near the end of 1916.

During Prohibition, the Christmann family bought the brewery and made near beer (as Christmann & Sauer), and later made brewers' wort under the Juneau Products Co. name. The New Lisbon brewery was at the center of a local bootlegging ring with ties to Chicago during the later years of Prohibition. District Attorney Clinton G. Price and Sheriff Lyall T. Wright were both accused in 1930 of operating a protection racket that had involved both small local moonshiners and the New Lisbon brewery, which was employed to produce beer for shipment to Chicago. (Some newspaper accounts held that the beer was only distributed locally, but Chicago and Milwaukee residents were also indicted.) Price was acquitted, but was murdered a month later in what was believed to be a mob-related killing.

After Prohibition, the Christmanns changed the name of the company to Christmann Brewing Co., but in a move unusual for a small Wisconsin brewery, incorporated the business in Delaware rather than Wisconsin. The company had some initial success with Wisconsin Select Lager Beer, which was available in La Crosse and even shipped to other states. Wisconsin Select was a draught-only product at first, but in 1934 Christmann installed equipment to package the beer in 64-ounce "picnic" bottles. The brewery averaged about 7,000 barrels per year but was not a financial success, and in 1936 a federal judge appointed temporary trustees to manage the firm though the bankruptcy. At that point, the plant had capacity for about 30,000 barrels more than it was selling each year, and parties on all sides of the reorganization accused the other of bad management.

In 1937, the brewery was acquired by B. M. Million and renamed Million Brewery, Inc. The new ownership wanted to host a party

This sign, issued just after the end of Prohibition, was made of cardboard instead of the usual tin.
COURTESY OF NATIONAL BREWERY MUSEUM.

to celebrate their new bottling plant (which could fill 12-ounce bottles) in March 1938 and give away a free lunch, but was told by state officials that they could only give away beer, and nothing else. The new company kept the Wisconsin Select brand, but they produced only a few hundred barrels each month, and sales showed no sign of increasing. The company went bankrupt in early 1941, and production ceased.

(The Henry Bierbauer mansion still stands in New Lisbon, and was rehabilitated in the 2010s by its new owners.)

NEW LONDON *(Waupaca County)*

Joseph Lechner (1860?–1870)
Becker, Beyer & Knapstein (1870–75)
Theodore Knapstein & Co. (1875–1908)
Knapstein Brewing Co. (1908–1920)
New London Products Co. (1927–1933)
Knapstein Brewing Co. (1933–1959)
505–511 EAST COOK STREET

Sometime prior to 1860 Joseph Lechner began brewing in Hortonia Township, with the nearest post office at New London. He operated the small frame brewery for about a decade, though it is not clear how much or how often he brewed since he does not appear in the excise records. In the 1870 census of industry he reported producing 110 barrels of beer, which sold locally for $9 per barrel.

In 1871, Lechner sold the business to two brewers from Appleton, Edward Becker and Anton Beyer, and Theodore Knapstein, a farmer's son from Greenville Township. (Some later accounts have Knapstein taking over in 1869 or even as early as 1861, but in 1861 he would have been twelve years old.) The brewery cost the partners $5,000, of which Knapstein contributed $1,500 borrowed from his father. The partners expanded production to nearly 500 barrels in 1872. In 1875 Anton Beyer died and Knapstein bought out Becker's share. The business was renamed Theodore Knapstein and Co., though according to the R. G. Dun & Co. reports, Beyer's widow Mary retained a share in the business. Theodore Knapstein brought his brother Henry into the business, and the two continued as partners until 1908, when Henry sold his shares and Theodore brought his son Mathias into the firm. The Knapsteins pushed production to 900 barrels a year by the end of the 1870s, with the aid of extensive improvements. The brewery malted its own barley for many years, and built a new malt house in 1892 to take advantage of new technology and to meet increased demand. The company did a steady business through the turn of the twentieth century. They built a new brewery in 1902 and added their own bottling works in 1908 (their beer had been bottled previously by City (later New London) Bottling Works, which was right across the corner from the brewery (and operated by Edward Becker, son of the former brewery partner). The brewery employed a dozen men in 1910 and contributed almost as much to New London as the Knapstein family, several of whom served in the State Assembly, as mayor, or as other civic officials.

Knapstein Brewing Co. ceased brewing when Prohibition arrived, and the company went bankrupt in the mid-1920s. The bottling plant was sold to the Wolf River Ice Cream Co. (later Verifine Dairy Products) in 1922, and in 1928 the malt house was converted to a wort manufacturing plant under the ownership of Theodore's son William M. Knapstein, William's cousin William H. Knapstein of Greenville, and John Haug. One later account reports that no beer was brewed, but while that was true for the brewery, the family's brewing career continued. In October 1927, William M. was arrested for operating "an alleged home brewery" in New London. One account reported ". . . federal officers declare that the Knapstein establishment was one of the largest home-brewery establishments ever raided, and that it was also one of the cleanest, everything being in immaculate condition. A complete brewery equipment was discovered *[sic]* including an eighteen-pint bottle washer . . ." Four men were working at the Knapstein home (not the old brewery plant), though the raid occurred while Mr. And Mrs. Knapstein were on a trip to Milwaukee. Knapstein was subsequently fined $250 and sentenced to six months in the workhouse, and his four employees were each fined $100.

As Prohibition drew to an end, Knapstein announced plans to invest $40,000 in renovating the building and sold its first beer in July 1933. It also moved to re-establish its position in the crowded central Wisconsin market by sponsoring and participating in community events. In 1937, the brewery won the prize for the best commercial float in the New London Labor Day parade. Knapstein advertised regularly in area newspapers, though the early ungrammatical slogan "The Beer for Select" eventually became the awkward though more

A classic pre-Prohibition bock label from a stock design.
COLLECTION OF TYE SCHWALBE.

plausible "The Beer Select" (Select Beer was a brand name prior to Prohibition). The brewery generally gave the beers easily identifiable names such as Knapp's, though they also revived the old pre-Prohibition Red Band brand for a time. Like many other small breweries, Knapstein offered a wide array of promotional items, including signs, trays, thermometers, coasters and other small items. One of the most striking was a mirror produced during the 1950s featuring President Eisenhower and advertisements for Knapstein's Old Lager and Bohemian Style brands with the slogan "Let's Keep America Great!"

Knapstein Brewing Co. benefitted from the same World War II-era surge as many other Wisconsin breweries, though the company also had problems adjusting to new regulations. In 1947, William Knapstein was fined $1,000 for using 25,294 pounds of grain above their brewing quota in 1946. In 1951, Knapstein Brewing Co. was ordered to change its waste disposal practices to avoid polluting the Wolf River. While Knapstein continued to upgrade his equipment and was still able to exceed 10,000 barrels per year a few times even after these setbacks, increasing competition from larger breweries resulted in decreasing sales and profits. In 1957, sales dropped to about 5,000 barrels, and in 1958, William M. Knapstein died. His son Paul took over the brewery, but was only able to continue brewing for about two more years. The company ceased brewing in 1959 and the buildings were sold for other purposes. Berlin Brewing Co. bought the Knapstein labels, some of the equipment and a delivery truck. The brewery was razed in 1970, though the former bottling house/dairy still stood as of 2016. An obituary for Paul Knapstein reported that the brewing company was sold to Anheuser-Busch in the 1960s, and that Knapstein took a job with that company in Miami, but these stories had no basis in fact.

Edward Becker, City Brewery (1875–1898)
MAIN & SOUTH WATER STREETS (MODERN ALGOMA & WOLF RIVER STREETS)
In 1875, Edward Becker left the partnership with Anton Beyer and Theodore Knapstein, and started his own brewery in New London. The R. G. Dun & Co. reports noted that he was "making money" and "Stands well here," and the approving reports continued through 1883 (when Dun & Co. abandoned this reporting method). Becker got off to a fairly quick start, and was brewing over 500 barrels by 1878 (which qualified him as a "large" brewer by the standards of the era). Industry directories indicate that he did not malt his own barley, but between 1884 and 1887 he began to sell bottled beer, even though Sanborn insurance maps show no bottling works on the premises. (It is likely that his beer was bottled by City Bottling works, which the Becker family owned for several years.)

In general, local accounts generally ignored Becker's brewery in favor of Knapstein's, likely because the latter were more active in the community. In 1898 Becker sold the brewery to Knapstein Brewing, which used the premises for storage and keg pitching for a few years, before razing them.

NEWPORT *(Sauk County)*

Theo. Hoffman (1854?–1862?)
Theo. Hoffman operated a thriving brewery in the boomtown of Newport, though the accounts are piecemeal at best. According to the reminiscences of W. S. Marshall, who visited Newport in 1854, ". . . Hoffman was building what was, in those days, a mammoth brewery. . . ." An article in the *Daily State Journal* from September 1858 describing the rivalry between the settlements of Kilbourn and Newport noted that while Newport was generally still on the decline, it still had a brewery. The 1860 census of industry includes Hoffman, locating him in New Buffalo Township, and reports that he made a very respectable 1,000 barrels during the previous twelve months. The R. G. Dun & Co. credit reports locate Hoffman at Newport through early 1862 and indicate that he was doing a good business there. However, Newport was doomed when the railroad went through Kilbourn instead, and most residents and businesses either moved to Kilbourn (later Wisconsin Dells) or went somewhere else altogether. The brewery cave remained for many years, rechristened the "Robbers' Den," but Hoffman was among those who moved to Kilbourn (covered under Wisconsin Dells).

NEW RICHMOND *(St. Croix County)*

Brady's Brewhouse (2011–15)
230 SOUTH KNOWLES ROAD
Chris Polfus founded Brady's Brewhouse in 2010, but the brewery did not receive its brewing license until March 2011. Industry veteran Rick Sauer was the first brewer, and his assistant Luke Nirmaier took over when Sauer left. The brewpub featured a range of house beers, most of which were sessionable styles.

Barley John's Brewing Company (2015–present)
1280 MADISON AVENUE
John Moore had been running a successful brewpub in the Minneapolis suburb of New Brighton for nearly fifteen years when he decided he wanted to open a production brewery and sell his beers at retail establishments. Unfortunately, Minnesota law did not permit him to operate both a brewery and a brewpub within the state, so he looked across the river to New Richmond.

Ground was broken for the new brewery in September 2014, and brewing commenced the next year. Bob McKenzie, an experienced brewer and native of Scotland, was the brewmaster. The brewery is a separate company from the Minnesota brewpub, and while the regular lineup is the same at both establishments, the brewers at each location create their own seasonals and experimental beers.

NORTH LAKE *(Waukesha County)*

Frederickson & Hanson (1866–67)
Rasmus Frederickson, North Lake Brewery (1867–1910)
Carl Hanson (1910–18?)
N76W31364 HIGHWAY VV (MAIN STREET)
Rasmus Frederickson was one of the rare immigrants from Denmark to own a brewery in Wisconsin. Family accounts hold that Frederickson was on his way west to start a brewery

Local newspapers praised the qualities of Frederickson's porter, claiming support from national medical experts. COLLECTION OF TYE SCHWALBE.

when he passed through North Lake, whose residents prevailed upon him to remain and start his brewery there. He founded the brewery with fellow Dane Christian Hanson in 1866, but in 1867 Frederickson bought out his partner and continued to operate the brewery until his death in 1910.

In the early 1870s, Frederickson only produced about seventy barrels per year, though by the end of the decade production averaged about 100 barrels per year. (Several local accounts suggest he produced 500 barrels a year, but this is most likely drawn from industry journal indications of capacity rather than production.) Entries in industry journals indicate several unusual features of Frederickson's brewery. Around 1882 he was producing weiss beer in addition to lager, and as early as 1884 he was malting his own barley as well as bottling his beer. He may have had a malt house considerably earlier, since some accounts suggest that part of the reason he located the brewery in North Lake was to provide a more convenient market for area barley farmers. In the early twentieth century, Frederickson began to produce porter, which was not common for rural Wisconsin breweries, but was popular in Denmark. Being a producer of porter may have given Frederickson access to one unusual export market. According to local tradition, some of the porter was shipped to Chicago hospitals because of its healthy properties, and even as far as Florida. Several local accounts claim that one of Fredrickson's beers (probably a version of the porter) reached 12 percent alcohol, which would have made it one of the strongest of its era.

Running a small brewery and saloon may seem like a romantic way to live, but it was not always lucrative. The credit reports of R. G. Dun & Co. from 1871 to 1883 indicate that Frederickson was generally in financial trouble, though not from any particular shortcomings on his part. As owner of one of the few businesses in the small community, Frederickson had to wear multiple hats, including that of postmaster from 1872 until 1908. Local tradition holds that many wives were not pleased that the post office was in the brewery saloon, since their husbands went to check the mail much more often than they would have otherwise, and felt an obligation to drink a beer while there. As one of the few public facilities in town, the building also served multiple purposes, and Frederickson built a dance hall behind the brewery (and two others in the area around North Lake). Another section of the brewery was a small hotel, the Angler's Inn.

As Frederickson aged he needed help running the brewery, but had no children to take over. He wrote back home to Denmark and invited his nephew, Carl Hanson, to come to North Lake and take over the brewery. Hanson's eldest son Fred recalled bottling beer by hand during the last few years before Prohibition arrived and the brewery closed.

During and after Prohibition, the Hanson family engaged in a number of businesses in the old brewery to make a living. They installed gas pumps, sold soft drinks, and provided minnows for any anglers visiting the area. After Prohibition ended, the Hansons reopened the tavern, and Fred and Albert continued it after Carl's death in 1936. Photos of the tavern show the changing brands advertised for sale: Weber Waukesha for a while, later Pabst Blue Ribbon. The tavern is still open as of this writing—owned by descendants of the Hansons—and has many artifacts from the brewery on display.

OAK CREEK (Milwaukee County)

Titus T. Luin (1855–57)

Titus T. Luin brewed at a number of breweries in the Milwaukee area during his career, including the pioneering Lake Brewery. For a short time in the late 1850s he was proprietor of his own brewery near the railroad station in Oak Creek, just south of Milwaukee. A public notice of the sheriff's sale of the property indicated that Luin had purchased the property in February 1855. The brewery was advertised for sale in 1857, it also indicates that the business was "in working order with 200 barrels on hand." It appears that the business was not sold to another brewer, since this brewery disappears from the records after the 1858 state business directory (likely compiled in 1857).

Water Street Brewery (2015–17)
140 WEST TOWN SQUARE WAY

The fourth location of Water Street Brewery opened in 2015. The restaurant was designed to resemble the industrial buildings that once occupied the neighborhood. (See also under the Milwaukee location.)

OAKFIELD TOWNSHIP (Fond du Lac County)

John Cooper (?)

Historian Wayne Kroll discovered that John Cooper had a short-lived farm brewery in Oakfield Township.

OAK GROVE (Dodge County)

Dexter S. Woodworth (1857?–1858?)

Dexter S. Woodworth moved to Dodge County in 1853 and purchased a farm in Lowell Township. Two years later he traded his farm for a hop yard with which he had only limited success, and traded this in for a parcel of land in the village of Oak Grove. A county history stated: ". . . he began the manufacture of small beer and soda water, which he peddled in the villages of the surrounding county. He later became a very prosperous merchant. . . ." It does not say if he became prosperous from these beverages or another product. He was listed in

564 THE DRINK THAT MADE WISCONSIN FAMOUS

the 1860 population census as a grocer, though he may have continued brewing on a small way in his store.

Oconomowoc
(Waukesha County)

City Brewery
Peter Binzel (1868–1912)
Philip Binzel (1912–18)
Oconomowoc Brewing Co. (1933–36)
Binzel Brewing Co. (1936–1942)
219 Fowler Street

During the early 1860s John Philip and Peter Binzel had a brewery in Waupun, but after it burned they moved to Beaver Dam. Peter then left for Oconomowoc to open his own brewery. A notice published upon his retirement reported that he sold the first barrel of beer made in Oconomowoc in November 1868. Business was good for the Milwaukee-trained brewer, and he increased production from just under 500 barrels in 1871 to over 1,300 barrels by 1878, with the help of a new brewery built in 1877. The 1884 Sanborn insurance map listed the plant's capacity at 150 barrels per month. Binzel leased a local farm to grow barley and he purchased at least some of his hops from local growers. Binzel improved the brewery bit by bit over the years. In the late 1880s he built a new ice run to Lake Fowler, and in the early 1890s he converted from horsepower to steam. While Binzel had been bottling for many years, he built a new bottling works around the turn of the twentieth century, and built a new tile bottling facility about ten years later.

Binzel retired from brewing in 1912 and turned the operation over to his son Philip, who continued the program of careful expansion. In August 1917 the brewery was damaged badly by fire, causing about $30,000 of damage with only partial insurance. This financial setback was compounded by the approach of prohibition, and Philip ceased production in August 1918 and sold the business to Andrew Fischer, a former brewmaster for Leinenkugel Brewing of Chippewa Falls.

The Oconomowoc brewery had one of the most colorful Prohibition-era stories of any Wisconsin brewery. Fischer got in trouble with state authorities almost immediately, and was ordered closed in 1921 for violating the dry laws. Fischer's political connections resulted in the brewery being reopened the next year, and he sold it shortly afterward to George Sipple of Chicago. (Fischer would later serve as mayor of Oconomowoc from 1932-4.)

In 1924, Sipple sold the brewery to Chicago racketeer Walter A. Ross, who was quoted in the local newspaper gloating that he could "make a killing in this rinkey-dink town." He advertised malt extract and near beer, but authorities began investigating Ross in February 1925, after a truck carrying real beer overturned. Ross avoided prison for a while through fancy legal footwork and such techniques as using kegs that were divided so that the top half had near beer for the inspectors to sample, while the real beer was in the bottom of the barrel. Ross was arrested in 1930 for operating a distillery at the brewery, and was eventually captured and sentenced to eighteen months at Leavenworth Prison. (Labels from the Prohibition-era business are found in chapter 6.)

After Prohibition ended, Ross's old foreman, George Bucher, restarted the brewery as Oconomowoc Brewing Co. In the years immediately after repeal, the company introduced several brands including Piccolo, Kellermeister (advertised as "Wisconsin's Finest Beer"), and Old Hollander Lager—A Health Beer. Company letterhead of 1936 proclaimed that the company's products were "The Beers that Contain Vitamins for Your Health." Despite the burst of activity and early production that sometimes approached 1,000 barrels per month, the brewery was in financial difficulty more often than not, and sales declined significantly after the summer of 1935. Attempts to build a market in Illinois, Iowa, and even North Dakota were to no avail. The company was reduced to imploring the Wisconsin Beverage Tax Division to lend them $49.10 of tax stamps so they could sell enough beer to pay existing tax arrears. Their plea, "We do not think that the State of Wisconsin intends to force anybody out of business," was not persuasive. Oconomowoc Brewing Co. sold its last beer in November 1936, and the company went bankrupt.

Following the collapse of Oconomowoc Brewing, the Binzel family took one last shot at operating the brewery. Peter Binzel Jr. took over the brewery in 1937, sold his first beer in July, and moved to update the brewery. Unfortunately, Peter Jr. died in 1939, and Clarence Binzel took his place. (Andrew Fischer returned as brewmaster for a time.) While Peter Binzel was able to boost production back over 1,000 barrels per month in the summer of 1938 with new brands such as Esquire, sales slipped again and Binzel Brewing Co. made its last beer on 18 April 1942, ending more than seventy years of brewing on the family land. The buildings were used for cold storage until the 1960s, when they were razed and replaced with apartments.

LaBelle Brewing Co. (1994–96)
Oconomowoc Brewing Co. (1998–2006)
750 East Wisconsin Avenue

LaBelle Brewing Co. opened in late 1994 in a location not far from Binzel's former brewery. Their beers were available both in bottles and

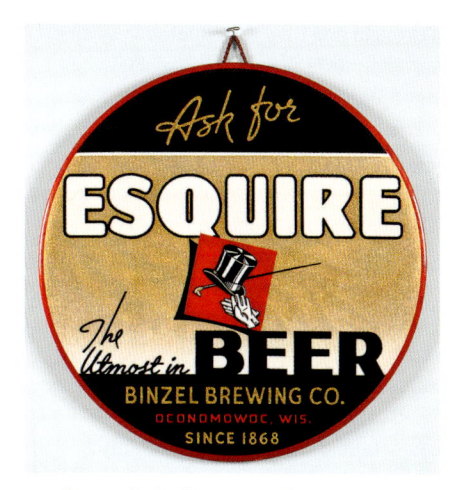

Sometimes called a "button sign" (though they were much too large to wear), this style was popular in the late 1930s and early 1940s. Courtesy of National Brewery Museum.

on draught and they participated in several beer festivals in the area. La Belle Brewing closed after a couple of years, but in 1998 homebrewer Tom "Julio" Miller purchased the location and some of the equipment and redesigned the brewery. Miller produced several well-regarded beers, including his German-Style Alt and chocolate cherry porter Winter Brew, and distributed them mostly on draught to area establishments. Miller began bottling in 2004, first offering Black Forest Gold and Amber Rye Lager. Oconomowoc Brewing Co. closed in 2006.

Sweet Mullets Brewing Co. (2012–18)
Brewfinity Brewing Co. (2018–present)
N58W39800 Industrial Road Suite D
Longtime brewer at Grumpy Troll (and other locations) Mark Duchow founded Sweet Mullets on the outskirts of Oconomowoc in 2012. The name came from the fact that Mark "... had a really sweet mullet [haircut] back in the 80s...." The brewpub building was once an auto body repair shop, but Duchow and partner Barbara Jones remodeled the space using about 90 percent reused or "upcycled" materials. Duchow used his new brewery to create unusual beers such as a buckwheat ale, a medieval gruit beer, and a steinbeer, in which the wort is heated and caramelized by immersing hot stones in the liquid.

In January 2016, Chad Ostram bought the brewery and took over as brewmaster. He continued some of the popular beers of previous years, but also introduced new recipes from his twenty years of homebrewing experience. In 2017, Sweet Mullets made the transition from brewpub to brewery. This meant they had to surrender their Class B liquor license, so they could no longer serve anything other than beer. This business changed its name to Brewfinity Brewing Co. in March 2018.

Oconto *(Oconto County)*

Anton Link & Co. (1858–1863)
Louis P. Pahl, Oconto Brewery (1863–1890)
Oconto Brewing Co. (1890–1920, 1933–1966)
Van Merritt Brewing Co. (1966–67)
1009–1023 Superior Avenue

Louis Pahl's story was like many German immigrants of his era. Upon arriving in America in 1854, he spent time in New York City, Albany, Milwaukee (where he worked briefly for Schlitz and Blatz), Green Bay and Two Rivers (also employed in breweries in those cities), and Chicago. In the middle of all this, he worked in the lumber business for about fifteen months. Finally, in 1858, he arrived in Oconto where he joined Anton Link in founding a brewery. Link and Pahl were advertising in the *Oconto Pioneer* by 1859 that they were prepared to furnish the citizens of the county "with some excellent Lager Beer, which, for a healthy beverage, can't be beat." By 1860 they had already pushed their output to 800 barrels a year, making it one of the largest breweries in northern Wisconsin. Production appears to have remained fairly steady, with the next reported totals in 1870 being 700 barrels. (This census reported that Pahl had three employees, one of whom was female—a rarity at that time, though it is likely that this was Pahl's domestic servant who may have helped in the brewery, rather than a female brewery laborer.) During the dry autumn of 1871 Pahl's plant was damaged by fire—nine days before the historic Peshtigo fire, and Pahl was injured after being thrown from his wagon while driving to get help.

Pahl continued to improve and expand his business after recovering from the fire and his injuries. He had become an important member of the community as well, and a newspaper report sang his praises:

Our enterprising German friend, Lewis P. Pahl, not only keeps the funds in the city treasury all right, but he also sells piles of lager beer, and makes large sums of money from the sale thereof, and what is still better for our city, spends the money in our midst. He is now building extensive improvements to his brewery—having place there in [sic] an engine and boiler, and now operates the same by steam.

Pahl's local market was limited, so he began seeking customers elsewhere. He was shipping beer to Green Bay by 1873 if not earlier, since his bock beer was being praised in the *Green Bay State Gazette* that year. However, he appears to have moved in and out of prosperity, like many small business owners. The R. G. Dun & Co. credit reports on Pahl's business varied from year to year, sometimes praising his creditworthiness, but in early 1883 going so far as to report "Makes poor beer + [doing] a poor bus[iness]." Pahl was bottling beer by the mid-1880s, and possibly earlier. The year 1887 was unfortunate for Pahl and his business: in April burglars broke into his saloon, and in November his brewery burned as a result of a fire in the pitch heater. Pahl had just installed new vats and lost a large stock of beer as well as the building. He rebuilt almost immediately, and the new building was completed in the autumn of the following year. Pahl was active in local politics, serving as city treasurer, township and county supervisor, and in 1876 as a member of the State Assembly (as a member of the Reform Party).

Louis Pahl died in 1891, but a few months before he had sold the brewery to George Vager, Gregor Ruth, and several other investors, who incorporated the business in December 1890 as Oconto Brewing Co. In 1893, the new firm was the intended beneficiary of a short-lived ordinance of the Oconto city

In 2012, a few Wisconsin brewpubs and taprooms created coasters from recycled cardboard boxes hand-stamped with a brewery logo. Tribute Brewing Co. and One Barrel Brewing Co. "mass produced" these items. One Barrel Brewing made at least twenty different coasters before ordering commercially made coasters in 2014. Collection of Scott Reich.

This Elk Brand label is unusual in listing the officers of the company: Ph. Lingelbach, president; Chas. Lingelbach, vice president and treasurer; and C. H. Roenitz, secretary.
COLLECTION OF JOHN STEINER.

council prohibiting brewers located outside of Oconto from selling beer in the city. Outside observers suspected this move was to boost the fortunes of the company and the profits of some councilmen who were stockholders, but the law was ultimately deemed unenforceable.

Jacob Spies purchased the brewery in the mid-1890s, but he soon sold to the Lingelbach family, who would manage the operation until Prohibition. In 1901 Oconto Brewing was rumored to be part of the large brewing trust in Northern Wisconsin that never came to pass. The Lingelbachs continued to add to the brewery with a new bottling house and office, and by 1910 all of the machinery was operated by electric power. They also continued to expand their market for its Eagle beer during the early twentieth century: Charles Lingelbach opened a branch office in Sheboygan and Oconto beer was sold in Michigan's Upper Peninsula. Despite this success, World War I fuel restrictions created difficulties for Oconto Brewing. In 1918, Oconto ceased brewing, and consolidated their operations with Rahr Brewing of Green Bay.

During Prohibition, the Lingelbachs reincorporated the business to manufacture soft drinks, and operated through 1925, but went out of business the next year. In 1927, H. F. Muehrske, a prominent Republican politician, purchased Oconto Brewing "expressing the belief that the sale of real beer is coming back soon." However, his move was several years premature, and he made no attempt to restart the business.

In 1933, when real beer actually returned, the Lingelbachs again took control of the brewery, and proposed to spend $10,000 modernizing the brewery with hopes of employing fifty men. But financial troubles forced them to dissolve and reform the company in June 1933 while already in receivership. They were insolvent and in receivership again in 1935, and the company was finally sold in 1938. The sale notice painted a desperate picture:

All assets of the Oconto Brewing company, including good will, will be sold, or leased with option to purchase on terms, at a sale to be held on the premises at 10 a.m. Tuesday, July 19 . . . Creditors were warned that sale on this date is imperative, and that unless an advantageous bid is offered there can be no hope of anything being realized except taxes and administration expense. . . .

The firm was first sold to R. E. Evrard of Green Bay, who then sold it to the Kolocheski family of Green Bay. George Kolocheski had been a shareholder in an earlier version of the corporation, and was prepared to make the business a success.

By April 1939, Oconto Brewing Co. was ready with a new brand called Arrowhead Beer, which replaced the revived Eagle Beer. Kolocheski sought to make Green Bay the primary market for Oconto beer and ran full page ads linking Oconto to the Green Bay Packers, which was a fortuitous choice since the Don Hutson–led team won the NFL championship that season. By 1941 the Arrowhead brand was dropped in favor of Oconto Pilsener, which remained the flagship beer for nearly two decades. Oconto Pilsener was advertised on tap in numerous area establishments, and in late 1941 was also available in the new 8-ounce "Buddy" bottle. However, wartime material shortages required the brewery to emphasize their "Full Quart Victory Size" package, which would save on crowns and therefore tinplate. At one point, Oconto proposed offering reusable rubber stoppers on their half-gallon bottles, but the Wisconsin Supervisor of Food Inspection shot the idea down because of the potential for contamination of the stoppers (to say nothing of the need to conserve rubber as well as tinplate). The brewery also limited its distribution area to northeastern Wisconsin and upper Michigan to make sure they could provide their regular customers with enough beer.

After the war ended, Oconto Brewing began a remodeling and expansion program including replacement of all kettles, vats, and the mash tun as well as new storage cellars which was intended to double the brewery's capacity to 60,000 barrels per year. By 1948 Oconto products could be found in over 2,500 establishments in their territory, though over 60 percent of sales were in the Green Bay area. During this period the company also made changes to the packaging: the "Buddy Bottle" was reduced from 8 ounces to 7 ounces, and in 1949 Oconto shifted from wooden to cardboard cases.

As the 1950s progressed, Oconto Brewing solidified their claim to be the one of the most important breweries in the northeast part of the state. In 1953 the company was fortunate to be able to hire Adolph Grahammer as brewmaster. Grahammer's path to Oconto was at least as complicated as Louis Pahl's. Grahammer apprenticed in northern Germany, but his career was interrupted by service in World War I. After that he worked for Löwenbrauerei in Munich, than for either Pschorr Brau or Spaten Brau (depending on the account), but after hearing Adolf Hitler speak in 1924 and seeing the swell of support for him in Bavaria, Grahammer decided to move to America. He worked at Berghoff Brewing Co. in Fort Wayne, Indiana, then at Vernon Brewing Co. in Los Angeles, and finally made it to Wisconsin where he worked at Gettelman in Milwaukee for twelve years before relocating to Oconto. Grahammer provided Oconto with a link to the upper echelons of the brewing world, and he routinely toured the hop yards of Hallertau and the Pacific Northwest to personally select hops for his beer. Production in his first year was 26,927 barrels, about 15,000 behind

Rahr–Green Bay. Grahammer introduced Oconto Premium in flat top cans in August 1954. The company earned a Gold Award at the Brewers' Association of America convention in 1956 for their increased sales, quality, and industry service. By 1957, they claimed to be the seventh-largest brewery in Wisconsin and continued to update the brewery and their fleet of trucks. Oconto Brewing also purchased the first color page ever in the *Green Bay Press-Gazette*, an ad featuring their bright blue cans. The brewery continued to sponsor community events (for example, sponsoring a float in Sheboygan's Bratwurst Day parade in 1957) and radio programs (like "Melody Inn" Sunday afternoon on WOMT of Manitowoc.) Oconto employed sixty-five people, all of whom were offered Asiatic flu serum in 1957 in an early example of employer-provided health care.

Unfortunately, the 1960s were not as favorable to Oconto Brewing as the previous decade had been. The company built a new bottle house in 1960, which was said to be the largest facility north of Milwaukee and which increased capacity to 240 bottles per minute. However, more than thirty workers of Local 299 went on strike in May 1961, demanding higher wages and increased benefits. During the strike, an Oconto truck required a police escort all the way to Beloit after the driver reported his brake lines had been slashed during a confrontation at a filling station just south of Oconto in Pensaukee. The strike lasted just over two weeks, and the employees settled for an increase of 20¢ per hour and paid insurance and health plan. Even after the strike, the brewery continued to expand its territory, moving into northern Minnesota. In 1963, Oconto became one of the first "regional" breweries to adopt the "tab-top" can, which was primarily used by national brands. Oconto had acquired some of the labels of the defunct Menominee-Marinette Brewing Co. and was packaging beer for Fox Head of Waukesha and Monarch Brewing of Chicago. But the biggest development came in April 1966, when Oconto Brewing merged with Van Merritt Brewing Co. of Chicago. All production was to be moved to Oconto, and "additional supervisors and production employees are being hired and trained to place the plant on an around-the-clock production basis." The new brewery had distribution in ten states, up from Oconto's four. Originally the business was supposed to remain the Oconto Brewing Co., but the name was changed to Van Merritt later in 1966. The new firm was unable to overcome underlying financial problems in both companies, and in February 1967 Van Merritt Brewing Co. closed its doors for good. Unlike some breweries that maintained hope of restarting, the receivers started selling equipment within the year—such as the tanks which were sold to Freeman Industries in Minneapolis for use in making soaps and detergents. The remainder of the brewery assets were sold in 1970 and the building was razed.

Oconoto Brewing Company (1994–98)
1200 West Main Street
Oconto Brewing Co. was a very small brewpub established in 1994 in the Main Event Sports Bar & Grill. They brewed once a week (in 1995, on Thursdays) in a half-barrel system.

Oconto Falls *(Oconto County)*

Falls Brewing Co. (2004–9)
782 North Main Street
Falls Brewing Co. opened in 2004, using a self-fabricated seven-barrel system in a former restaurant property. The brewery switched from labels with a drawing of a waterfall and style names for the brands to photographs of women and more provocative names such as Dirty Blonde.

Onalaska *(La Crosse County)*

Gabriel Knecht (1856?–1866?)
Mrs. W. Knecht (1867?)
Milford G. Moore (1867–1881)
Adolph Knecht, Onalaska Brewery (1881–84)
Onalaska Brewing Co., Adolph Knecht (1885–1891?)
Second Street (Modern Rose Street) South of Modern Oak Forest Drive
According to one county history, Gabriel Knecht, an immigrant from Baden, started building his brewery in Onalaska as early as 1856. By the time of the 1860 census, Knecht owned $2,000 of property, which could represent an established brewery. In October 1865, the weight of grain in the loft caused the brewery to collapse (which included Knecht's home). Two were killed and seven injured in the disaster. Knecht rebuilt soon after, and records from 1867 and after indicated that there was a hotel connected with the brewery. Knecht died in 1867, and his widow soon married Milford G. Moore, a native of Maine who carried on the brewery and hotel.

The Onalaska brewery seemed disaster prone regardless of who owned it. In 1879, robbers removed the safe, blew it up outside, and escaped with about $1,000 in cash. In 1881, Adolph Knecht, son of Gabriel, took over management of the brewery but Moore's name still was used to identify the brewery. In 1884 the complex caught fire and both the brewery and hotel were destroyed, along with the contents of the buildings. The malt house was saved, but the loss was between $15,000 and $20,000 with no insurance. Moore rebuilt the brewery, but only operated it for a few years before abandoning the brewing business. Local accounts indicate that the brewery lay idle for many years, but not exactly how long, and the last appearance in a state business

Falls Nut Brown Ale is from the early years of the brewery; Hot Tail ale is from later years. Author's collection.

directory was in 1891 (though these were often out of date).

In 1894, a group of La Crosse citizens attempted to reopen the brewery. Some early accounts indicated that the purchasers were "reported to be Knights of Labor from La Crosse," though no additional information links those who incorporated the brewery to the Knights. (Emil Kohn was an employee of Gund Brewing, and William Wudtke was employed by Heileman, though the city directories do not indicate in what capacity.) The new investors were not able to restart the brewery, so it remained dormant. To add further confusion, on the May 1894 Sanborn map, the brewery was listed as being owned by Mrs. Fruber.

In 1899, brewer Franz Bartl of La Crosse purchased the property, but it was sold again in 1901 to John Gedney of Prairie du Chein and was converted into a pickle factory. One local newspaper joked, making a comparison to the old metal growlers which were often called "cans": "We notice that a brewery at Onalaska is being converted to a canning factory. Isn't this rushing the can on rather a large scale?"

Two Beagles Brewpub (2016–present)
910 Second Avenue North

Despite all the discussion of reopening the Onalaska brewery in the 1890s, it took until 2016 for Onalaska to have a functioning brewery again. Steve Peters was a long-time homebrewer and a former supervisor and manager at City Brewing in La Crosse who always wanted to have his own brewery. Peters and his wife Christie purchased the former Seasons by the Lake restaurant which, as its name suggested, had panoramic views of Lake Onalaska and the Mississippi River valley. The view persuaded the Peters to put the brewhouse in back, where it could still be seen, but would not block the view of the valley. The beers tend toward lighter styles, but there is also a barrel-aged version of the Chocolate Beagle Amber. They have also brewed a Belgian dubbel with maple syrup and Caramel Apple Bock, which is aged on local Honeycrisp apples.

Skeleton Crew Brew (2016–present)
570 Theater Road Suite 100

Skeleton Crew Brew is the beer division of Lost Island Winery. They obtained their federal brewery permit in February 2016 and tapped their first beers in May. Since then, they have increased the number of beers on draught at the taproom to eight.

Osceola *(Osceola Mills)* *(Polk County)*

Veit Geiger (1867–1884?)

According to E. D. Neill's 1881 history of the St. Croix Valley, Veit Geiger, a native of Wurtemburg, established his small farm brewery in 1867, a year confirmed by excise records indicating production in November of that year. The first brewery was a small frame building of 20 x 30 feet, but in 1872 he built a two-story stone structure 23 x 50 feet. Geiger also had small cellars excavated into the rock behind the brewery. Neill claims that Geiger produced between 150 and 200 barrels per year, but the known production figures are substantially lower—usually less than one hundred barrels per year. Excise records suggest capacity was likely no more than ten barrels per month. In the 1880s (and possibly earlier) he had a small saloon that probably sold the majority of his beer.

Despite the size of his operation, Geiger was listed as a brewer rather than a farmer in the 1870 census, and the R. G. Dun & Co. reports indicate that he was at least a modest success. He had generally good credit ratings and was described as a "Good honest Dutchman" (Dutchman was a common corruption of Deutschman or German) who was "making money slowly, does but little bus[iness] but makes it pay." These positive reports continue through the end of 1883, and Geiger appeared in the 1884 reports of Dun's then-rival Bradstreet, but he was not listed in Wing's 1884 brewers' directory or thereafter, so he likely retired from brewing around that time.

Oshkosh *(Winnebago County)*

Lake Brewery
Jacob Konrad (1849–1854)
Anton Andrea (1854–1862)
Leonhardt Schwalm (1862–65)
Gottlieb Ecke (1865–69)
South of Ceape Avenue and Lake Street

Jacob Konrad earned the distinction of brewing the first beer in Oshkosh by a matter of a few months. He leased the land for his brewery in July, and soon after constructed his brewery. Ron Akin and Lee Reiherzer, the leading historians of Oshkosh brewing, suggest that Konrad may have left Oshkosh in 1854 because of a provision in the new city charter that allowed for a tax on alcohol sales. He moved to Weyauwega and established a new brewery there.

"Major" Anton Andrea (sometimes misspelled Andrae), who purchased the brewery from Konrad, had an adventurous life both in Europe and in Oshkosh. A veteran of the Hungarian Hussars, he fled in 1848, served a partial term on the Oshkosh city council, and went through several business failures. While the Lake Brewery was not a failure, he was not a brewer and hired Casper Haberbusch and Louis Keller to run the brewery for him. Apparently unable to focus on any business too long, Andrea leased the business to Leonhardt Schwalm, who remained for three years before starting his own brewery. The new brewer, Gottlieb Ecke, remained at this location for about three years, until demand compelled him to build a new brewery just to the west. (That new location is covered under the Gambrinus Brewery)

Schussler & Freund, Oshkosh Brewery (1850?–51)
Schussler & Tillmans, Oshkosh Brewery (1851–52)
South Side of River (modern Bay Shore) between Frankfort and Bowen

In March 1850, newspapers in Wisconsin reported that Oshkosh was to erect a second brewery during the next building season. This brewery became the Oshkosh Brewery of Joseph Schussler and John Freund. (Oshkosh historians Akin and Reiherzer date this brewery to November 1849 when Schussler purchased the land, but it is unlikely that they were in production before 1 January 1850.) Schussler was the experienced brewer (with a stop in

Milwaukee as well as training in his home of Baden) and Freund was the financial backer. By September, they advertised that they were

> ... prepared to supply Taven [sic], Grocery, and Saloon keepers of the surrounding country with good ale and beer. From a long experience in the business, they feel confident in warranting a superior article—better than is obtained from abroad under the title of "Detroit Ale," "Milwaukee Beer, &c."

In addition to ads offering their beer for sale, they typically had nearby advertisements offering to buy barley from local farmers. Even before 1850 was over, Freund was experiencing financial difficulties and backed out of the partnership. At the beginning of 1851, Schussler brought in Francis Tillmans as a new partner, but this new venture was no more successful than the first, and by June 1852, Schussler was out of business. Schussler returned to brewing as an employee of one of the Oshkosh firms in the late 1850s, went to the Frey brewery in Fond du Lac in 1861 (after the death of his son who had been apprenticed there) and ultimately opened the West Hill Brewery in Fond du Lac.

George Loescher, Oshkosh Brewery (1852–1880)

Ruety and Walter (1880)

George Loescher, Oshkosh Brewery (second location) (1880–84)

William M. Loescher, Oshkosh Brewery (1884–88?)

90 RIVER (MODERN BAY SHORE) BETWEEN FRANKFORT AND EVELINE (1852–1880); NORTHEAST CORNER OF FRANKFORT AND BAY SHORE (1880–88)

The second business to be named Oshkosh Brewery was established by brothers George and Frederick Loescher in autumn 1852. Frederick left in 1853 to start a brewery in Menasha, and George continued on his own.

Loescher's Oshkosh Brewery was unusual among the breweries of Winnebago County in that it produced ale and lager and advertised both equally. Akin and Reiherzer contend that this had the dual purpose of allowing Loescher to continue brewing during the summer months when lager could not be aged properly, and also to supply the increasing numbers of Yankee, English and Irish settlers who were used to ale. Loescher (which was spelled a number of different ways in various sources) was also a malster (as it was spelled in some ads), which provided area farmers with a local market for their barley.

While his business seems to have done well, the investigators for R. G. Dun & Co. were wary of George Loescher, who apparently enjoyed the fruits of his labors to a great extent throughout his career. However, they reported that "his wife and boys run the concern ... [and] watch him close," so the business was considered perfectly safe.

The Oshkosh brewery was destroyed by fire in October 1871, though about half of the $7,000 loss was covered through East Coast insurance companies. Early in the rebuilding process he apparently partnered with Andrew Ackerman, perhaps to obtain help with funding, since the company is referred to as Ackerman & Co. in excise records and an 1873 industry directory. Unfortunately, the rebuilt brewery was burnt out again in April 1878. At this point, he appears to have abandoned the site at 90 River, which was landlocked and did not allow for expansion to meet the increasing competition in Oshkosh. Newspaper accounts suggest that another firm tried to revive the business in 1880. The *Daily Northwestern* reported in August that John Walther [sic] and Bernard Reidel of New London had purchased the Luscher [sic] brewery and planned to move in the next month. However, in October the paper followed up the story:

> John Walter, of the firm of Ruety & Walter, proprietors of the brewery in the Second Ward, has been missing since last Friday and no trace of him can be found. The only explanation now entertained for his unexpected absence is that he has absconded. Ruety & Walter bought out Loescher's brewery some three months ago, and since running the brewery have quarreled among themselves, each trying to sell out to the other. A few days ago they mortgaged the personal property in the brewery for $300 and Ruety now claims that Walter has run away with this $300 and with all the money he could collect from saloon keepers to whom the firm had sold beer. At least Walter has not been seen since Friday and this is the explanation given. Herman Scherck has taken possession of the brewery by virtue of the chattel mortgage of $300 he holds against the personal property in the building and it is now in charge of an officer.

While the newspaper does not confirm his identity, it is most likely that this is the same John Walter who had recently dissolved his partnership with Lorenz Kuenzl.

By 1880, the Loeschers were established at their new site a block away on the other side of River (Bay Shore). The new horse-powered brewery was not much larger than the previous facility, and was still smaller than the local competition (but no longer brewed ale). George Loescher died in 1884, and his widow Regina took over the business while son William ran the brewhouse. The brewery closed sometime between 1888 and 1890. About a decade after the Loeschers closed the brewery, a group of saloon owners proposed reopening the brewery, in hopes that they could produce beer for about $4 per barrel, which would undercut Chicago ($6), Milwaukee (up to $9) and other Oshkosh beer ($7.40). While this plan came to nought, a similar scheme would bear fruit some years later with the establishment of Peoples Brewing Co.

Fischer & Weist (1856–57)

NEAR SOUTHWEST CORNER OF HIGH AND NEW YORK AVENUES

Tobias Fischer & August Weist purchased land for a new brewery in the Fifth Ward in October 1856. Both were experienced brewers, but this partnership lasted for less than a year. Weist moved to Princeton and started a brewery there, and Fischer entered a partnership with Christian Kaehler to develop another brewery in the Fifth Ward.

Fischer & Kaehler, Busch Brewery (1857–58)
Christian Kaehler, Fifth Ward Brewery (1858–1880?)
166 Algoma Street (Southeast corner of Algoma and Vine)

After Tobias Fischer and August Weist dissolved their partnership, Fischer joined with another newly landed brewer, Christian Kaehler, to build a new brewery in the Fifth Ward on Algoma Street. They brewed lager beer, and at least one batch of Salvator, which was sometimes used as a generic name for a doppelbock. Their partnership in the Busch Brewery was brief, since Fischer left for St. Louis in 1858, leaving Kaehler as sole proprietor.

Kaehler did a good business for nearly two decades, and invested his profits in lucrative real estate. In 1870 he produced 500 barrels, and peaked at 749 barrels in 1872. However the next recorded figures (from 1878 and 1879) were 140 and 178 barrels, respectively, so it is possible that Kaehler was either paying little attention to the brewery in favor of other enterprises, or he may have been in financial trouble. The R. G. Dun & Co. credit reports state that foreclosure proceedings began in 1880, and the *Daily Northwestern* reported that the sheriff's sale was in June 1881. The property ended up in the hands of C. W. Davis, who planned to move the buildings and erect a large house. The site of the building is now part of the campus of the University of Wisconsin-Oshkosh.

Leonhardt Schwalm (1858–1862)
Brooklyn neighborhood

Prior to building the much larger Brooklyn Brewery (later Horn & Schwalm) Leonhardt Schwalm operated a lager beer saloon that offered both food and his "excellent Lagerbier." In 1862 he leased the Lake Brewery from Anton Andrea to gain more brewing capacity. (Schwalm's other breweries are covered separately.)

Rudolph Otten (1865?)
Oxford Street

Rudolph Otten's brewery is known only from a stray page of the 1865 excise tax records uncovered by Akin and Reiherzer in their research. It is most likely that Otten's brewery was a slightly larger homebrewing system designed to brew for a few local accounts.

City Brewery
Charles Rahr & Bro. (August Rahr) (1865–1883)
Charles Rahr (1883–1897)
Charles Rahr, Jr. (1897–1904)
Rahr Brewing Co. (1904–1920)
The Rahr Company (1920–1933)
Rahr Brewing Co. (1933–1956)
91–103 Rahr Avenue

City Brewery/Rahr Brewing Co. had one of the longest tenures of family ownership of any brewery in Wisconsin. Charles Rahr was a nephew of William Rahr, brewer of Manitowoc, and younger brother of Henry, brewer of Green Bay. Charles worked at both of his kinsmen's breweries prior to his service with the 9th Wisconsin Infantry in Indian Territory (Oklahoma) and neighboring states during the Civil War. He returned to Green Bay in December 1864, and married Caroline Hochgreve, daughter of his brother's business partner, in an unusual midnight wedding at the turn of the new year of 1865. The new couple moved to Oshkosh and joined with Charles' brother August to start the Charles Rahr & Brother brewery that same year.

Rahr's new brewery had the advantage of being built on the edge of the city, which meant it had more room to expand than his pre-Civil War rivals. It briefly would be the largest brewery in Oshkosh, though several of the other postwar breweries would soon pass it. By the end of the 1870s, the Rahrs' brewery had settled into fourth place in Oshkosh, behind Glatz & Elser, Horn & Schwalm and Kuenzl & Walter. The Rahrs appear to have settled comfortably into their status as a small local brewery and did not engage in the expansion wars which ultimately led the three larger breweries to merge. The City Brewery had a taproom that was a popular destination for local residents, though it sometimes got the brewery in the news for unsavory reasons. In 1872, Charles Rahr and his brewery (called the Washington Street Brewery in one newspaper story) were sued by a woman for serving beer to her drunken and abusive husband. In 1878, he was apparently offering more than just his beer, since he was fined for selling liquor at the brewery without a license. Rivals Horn & Schwalm also accused Rahr of holding on to two of their kegs, and went so far as to demand a search warrant.

While Charles was in charge of brewing, August was the sales manager of the brewery, and the firm was sometimes referred to as the August Rahr Brewery. In 1883, August left the brewing partnership and formed his own company, which bottled the beer of his brother at a location next to the brewery. (Newspaper accounts suggest that the brothers had already been bottling beer for some time.) While the City Brewery did steady business, it was still small, and when Oshkosh Brewing Co. was formed in 1894, City was dwarfed by the new concern. However, the Rahrs had a devoted local following, and the elevation of Charles Jr. (Charlie) to brewmaster and proprietor kept the quality high. The cautious Charles Sr. finally bowed to the inevitable and approved construction of a new brewery in 1896. The new facility had twice the capacity of the original brewery, but even that was not enough. After Charlie took full control of the company in 1908, he began another modernization program which cost about $50,000 and rebuilt or expanded everything in the factory. Despite the expanded plant, Rahr still did not bottle his own beer, even well into the 1900s. After August left the business, Neumueller Bros. took over bottling for several years. Rahr brought bottling back to the brewery itself in 1915, apparently because of problems with their contractor. An ad announcing the change admitted:

> *In connection with this announcement we wish to say that we realize that this department of our business has not delivered the service that the public has the right to expect, but we assure those who wish Rahr's bottling that in the future strict*

attention will be paid to this department and that every order received will be delivered promptly to any part of the city. Our brewery phone number is 2394. A call will bring our wagon at once.

Despite the move to in-house packaging, Fred Neumueller was hired to work at the new bottling house. Perhaps to emphasize the change, in mid-1916 Rahr changed the name of its major bottled beer from Special Brew to Elk's Head.

Rahr continued to support their beers with heavy newspaper advertising, sometimes using patriotic imagery, other times touting the health-giving purity of the product. In one 1913 campaign, Rahr responded directly to the Schlitz campaign of the time which criticized other breweries for using clear bottles (see La Crosse—C. & J. Michel Brewing Co.) Rahr ads acknowledged the truth about brown bottles "that this certain Brewing Co. has evidently just discovered" and noted that Rahr had used brown bottles for forty years. However, they continued: "But when you get down to brass tacks the bottle plays a mighty small part in the production of good beer," which was an attack on the perceived cheapening of Schlitz, a major rival in Oshkosh. Rahr continued the brown bottle references in advertisements until Prohibition. Rahr was also one of the very rare brewers to encourage customers to obtain their beer from a tavern in a growler—a different 1913 ad urged patrons to "[A]sk for Rahr's in any kind of bottle, tin pail or keg. . . ."

Unlike his fiscally conservative father, Charlie was willing to spend some of his increasing earnings on luxury goods. He bought a new car and enjoyed sailing—including ice sailing on his ice yacht *Blanche,* named for his eldest daughter (who would soon be running the brewery office). The biggest decision Charlie had to make, however, was whether or not to sell his brewery in 1912 to the newly formed Peoples Brewing Co. The new company was not willing to meet Rahr's asking price, so the brewery stayed in the family. Charlie himself turned the brewery over to his three children, Blanche, Carl, and Lucille, though he stayed on to advise them and help guide them through the difficult transition to Prohibition.

While Rahr Brewing Co. still applied for renewal of its liquor license in August 1919, it was already evident that they would not get a full year's use of it. To stay in business, the Rahrs switched to a line of soft drinks with more variety than other converted breweries. In addition to standard flavors like grape, ginger ale, and root beer, they offered wild cherry and loganberry sodas as well. As in the beer era, households could call for delivery of any of these products. Later on, they made the unusual decision to attach the name of the former flagship beer to a non-near beer product: Elk's Head Chocolate Malted Milk. While the value of the company declined during the dry years and Charlie died in 1925, the family was able to persevere and return to brewing beer when it became legal in 1933.

Because it had stayed in business throughout the dry years, it was relatively easy for Rahr Brewing Co. to convert back to beer. It already had a near beer permit, and making real beer was the essential first step to making near beer. All they had to do was skip the dealcoholizing step and start aging beer in their cellars. Rahr started doing so as soon as it was clear that beer was coming back, and a company spokesman said in March 1933 "'We're not saying how much we've got, but we've got all we can legally have stored, under our near-beer permit.'" Rahr also ceased production of near beer, which would have been a "'no sale' product when real beer [returned]." An article in late March proclaimed that Rahr was to hire twelve to fifteen men and would purchase 50,000 bushels of grain per year—both major boons to the local economy.

Rahr continued to advertise in local newspapers after the return of beer, and continued the emphasis on quality and traditional process. While some limited modernizations were adopted after Prohibition, Rahr Brewing never made significant additions to its capacity and remained a small local brewery. Other than a brief wartime boom, production was typically less than 10,000 barrels per year. Rahr's reputation for quality remained high, and new brewmaster Charles (Chuck) Rahr III insisted on an old-fashioned hands-on approach to brewing. In 1952 Rahr introduced their own version of the 7-ounce bottle, making special note in advertisements that the company had "no connection with any outside firms"—emphasizing the local nature of the business. Even this new package did not help sales, and Rahr could not survive as a draught-beer oriented business in a bottled (and canned) beer world. The brewery survived long enough to brew and bottle a special all-malt pilsner in 1953 for Oshkosh's centennial celebration, but after a brief surge during the Milwaukee brewers strike later that year, sales plummeted over the next two years. Matters were made worse for Rahr by a one-day strike by Oshkosh brewery workers of CIO Local 90 in June 1955. Output in 1955 was 3,660 barrels and the family decided to close the brewery in June 1956. Customers were warned that the

The Elk's Head brand was brought back after Prohibition. It was briefly advertised as a "High Test Beer," claiming "Rahr's New Elk's Head Does Not Sacrifice Taste for High Power." Exactly how high power Elk's Head and similarly advertised beers were is not clear, but they were likely no more than 6 percent. Claims of high alcoholic strength were banned shortly thereafter. COLLECTION OF TYE SCHWALBE.

deposit would not be refunded on any cases returned after 1 August, though the brewery was in sufficient financial health to actually refund the deposits. The old brewery building was razed in 1964.

Leonard & Andrew Schiffman (1865?–1870s)
Leonard Schiffman (1870s–1880?)
MAIN STREET (1865–1870s)
79 DOTY STREET (1870s–1882?)

Leonard and Andrew Schiffman operated a saloon and apparently brewed weiss beer at their Main Street location during the 1860s and 1870s. They are seldom included in government or industry publications, so they may have brewed only intermittently, and certainly not in any large volume.

Leonard Schiffman appears to have brewed more seriously at his Doty Street location during the late 1870s and early 1880s, since he was listed as a brewer in the 1880 census (he was listed as a carpenter in 1870), was included in the 1879 city directory and was evaluated in R. G. Dun & Co.'s credit reports in the early 1880s. By early 1883 his brewery was out of business, and he appears to have focused on other lines of work after this time.

Brooklyn Brewery, Horn & Schwalm
    (1866–1894)
Oshkosh Brewing Co. (1894–1912)
1631–1642 DOTY STREET

In 1865, Leonhardt Schwalm purchased land in the Brooklyn neighborhood and built a new brewery that would allow him the ability to expand that his previous Lake Brewery lacked. Shortly after getting underway, he sold half a share to August Horn for $4,500 and brought him into the firm to handle the business side. Horn had joined Schwalm in a previous investment in a farm, and had married Schwalm's sister Amelia. Early accounts sometimes listed the brewery under Schwalm's name alone, though eventually the Brooklyn Brewery name became the popular title.

The Brooklyn Brewery quickly pushed to the front of the Oshkosh brewing community. It appears to have been the first brewery to produce more than 1,000 barrels in a year, a total reached in 1872. Like many proprietors, Horn & Schwalm offered room and board to their employees in a room above the brewery, though the conditions were crowded with the eight Horn children and seven Schwalm offspring. Unfortunately, one of the employees died from injuries suffered when he fell into a vat of near-boiling wort while attempting to cross over the vat on a plank in a dimly-lit room. Leonhardt Schwalm himself died just over a year later, and the brewery began to prepare the next generation for management.

August Horn sought to keep the Brooklyn Brewery among the local leaders by the force of his engaging personality. However, Akin and Reiherzer contend that two tragedies actually helped Horn move the brewery forward. The first was the passing of Leonhardt Schwalm who, while an experienced brewer, was definitely of the old school and may not have been prepared to follow the rapidly improving technology of brewing. The other was a catastrophic fire in March 1879 that destroyed the entire brewery complex except for part of the icehouse. The fire started around the brewing kettles, and the employees put out the flames with a bucket of water. However, the embers smoldered and reignited later that night and the conflagration soon enveloped the brewery. Workers who still lived upstairs were barely able to escape with their lives. The loss was a rather heavy $18,000, only half of which was covered by insurance. (It was typical of the times that even this amount of insurance was divided among nine different companies, including several foreign firms.) Akin and Reiherzer suggest that the fire forced the Schwalm family to agree to a risky but necessary expansion program. Whatever the case, August Horn embarked on a rebuilding project that resulted in a brewery that rose to three stories of brick, with a stone cellar and foundation. The brewery was as fireproof as Horn could make it, and equipped with a new steam engine and other modern equipment. The next generation— Theodore Schwalm and Henry, Otto and Charles Schwalm—moved into positions of responsibility at the brewery, even though they were either teenagers or in their early 20s.

The brewery continued to grow over the next two decades, and so did the business. The R. G. Dun & Co. credit report of 1883 noted that Horn & Schwalm were "[doing] the best bus[iness] in their line here" and were making money. However, the report also warned that "on [account] of the high price of hops and Barley will prob[ably] not make much $ this year." This success came despite the alcoholism of Theodore Schwalm, who was made a ward of the court in 1883 at age twenty-five, and who died of liver disease only five years later. The brewery also withstood a major tornado in July 1885, which caused $2,000 worth of damage but left the new brewery unscathed. The company also had to deal with smaller accidents such as an incident in January 1884 when a brewery sled (used during the winter instead of the standard brewery roll) collided with a streetcar with such force that it knocked the streetcar off its tracks and spun it around. Fortunately, August Horn was still present to guide the business, this time with the help of Sophia Schwalm, Theodore's widow.

The brewery continued to grow into the 1890s, and was the largest brewery in Oshkosh at the time of the formation of Oshkosh Brewing Co. in 1894 (which is covered below). The plant on Doty Street continued to brew until the construction of the new brewery in 1912.

Lake Brewery
Gottlieb Ecke (1869–1871)
Ecke & Neumann, (1871–75)
Gambrinus Brewery
Kuenzl & Louis Ecke (1875–76)
Kuenzl & Walter (1876–1880)
Lorenz Kuenzl (1880–1894)
Oshkosh Brewing Co. (1894–1902?)
1200 BLOCK OF HARNEY AVENUE

Gottlieb Ecke moved from his first Lake Brewery location and built a new brewery one block west. The new brewery suffered a significant fire in August 1869, but most of the loss was covered by insurance. Ecke produced 600 barrels in 1870—below the capacity of 3,000 but a respectable amount nonetheless. This start was marred by the death of Gottlieb Ecke in November 1871, from what circumstantial evidence suggests was suicide. His widow, Charlotte, boldly took up the business with the help of businessman Phillip Neumann. There may have been some delay in restarting production, since the *American Brewers' Guide* of 1873 lists no production for 1871 or 1872 (though it may have been referring to production under that business name). Ecke lost the brewery to foreclosure in 1874, but her brother, Henry Timm, purchased the brewery for her. Oshkosh historians Akin and Reiherzer suggest that running the brewery and managing her family was too difficult for Ecke, and she dissolved her partnership with Neumann and closed the brewery, though Timm remained owner of the property in trust for his sister.

While Ecke offered to sell the brewery, she was content to lease it, and in September 1875 she found a suitable occupant in Lorenz Kuenzl (Kuenzel), a trained brewer from Bohemia. Kuenzl first partnered with Louis Ecke, a brother of Gottlieb who likely called the availability of the brewery to Kuenzl's attention. However, Ecke returned to his previous career as a butcher in Stevens Point less than a year later, and Kuenzl brought in his brother-in-law, John Walter, as his new partner. The ownership of the brewery remained fluid for a few more years: John Walter left the partnership in 1880, and Kuenzl was finally able to purchase the brewery in 1883 from Henry Timm after considerable difficulty and an eviction notice.

Akin and Reiherzer described noteworthy features of the Gambrinus brewery in *The Breweries of Oshkosh*. Kuenzl's brewery appeared to be significantly overstaffed for its size and equipment—perhaps because he was committed to employing members of his family and some Ecke descendants as well. In addition, Kuenzl seems to have kept brewing traditional German and Bohemian recipes longer than most of his rivals, rather than converting to Americanized versions. Ultimately, he began to revise his recipes to reflect the reality of American-grown ingredients and American tastes, but he was unusual in his choice of rice as an adjunct grain rather than corn.

After Kuenzl purchased the brewery, he made some minor improvements and added bottled beer in the late 1880s. (Their beer had been bottled previously by John Sitter.) But for the most part, he settled into the second tier of Oshkosh breweries—behind Glatz and Horn & Schwalm, but larger than Rahr and the other rapidly disappearing competitors. When Oshkosh Brewing Company was formed in 1894, the Gambrinus plant brewed weiss beer for a couple of years, but the building was used mostly as a bottling plant for the new combination. Beer was brought in barrels from the Horn & Schwalm division to be bottled. Lorenz Kuenzl was named director of brewing operations for the new company, but died in 1897 of complications from edema. The Gambrinus brewery was torn down after the completion of the new Oshkosh Brewing plant.

Franz (Frank) Wahle (1867?–1869)
Union Brewery
Glatz & Elser (1869–1879)
John Glatz (1879–1888)
John Glatz & Son (1888–1894)
Oshkosh Brewing Co., Glatz & Son/Union Brewery (1894–1912)
31–34 DOTY STREET

Franz Wahle moved to Oshkosh in 1867, ten years after starting the Stevens Point Brewery. He started a small brewery on his new farm, but appears to have done little brewing before he leased it to John Glatz and Christian Elser in September 1869.

Glatz and Elser could hardly have been better prepared to run a brewery. Glatz had served twelve years at Charles Melms' South Side Brewery in Milwaukee, rising to the level of foreman/brewmaster. Elser worked for Franz Falk in Milwaukee, and his sister Louise married John Glatz in 1861. Both had experience with modern industrial brewing, which they would soon bring to Oshkosh. The conversion came about more abruptly than they may have planned—Glatz and Elser were among the many proprietors to have the fortunate misfortune of having their brewery burn down at a propitious moment. The fire in December 1871 enabled the partners to build a new modern brewery, which, by the end of the decade, passed the 1,600-barrel mark and was the largest brewery in the city. Oshkosh historians Akin and Reiherzer described the new Union Brewery as "the first truly American-style" modern brewery in the region. It was the first steam-powered brewery in Oshkosh and incorporated an efficient design for handling materials that drew on the layout of large breweries of Milwaukee. Glatz & Elser, in their limited advertising, claimed their beer was "as good as Milwaukee beer and much cheaper."

Glatz & Elser also took advantage of other modern innovations, including bottled beer. They appear to have been bottling by 1878 if not before, at least in part to fend off competition from Milwaukee. They sold at least some of their beer through Dichmann's Grocery Store, which enabled them to reach customers unwilling to patronize area saloons. While this tactic was used elsewhere in Wisconsin, it was not particularly common in the 1870s. In 1879, the partnership dissolved and Christian Elser specialized in beer bottling while Glatz stayed with the brewery. To replace Elser, John Glatz gave his son William increased responsibility and authority in the brewery, and in 1886 turned over management of the business to him. In May 1888, the firm was renamed J. Glatz & Son, and continued in business under that name until the formation of Oshkosh Brewing Co. in 1894. The Glatz brewery remained in production until the new plant was built, and was razed in 1915. The site today is the Glatz Nature Preserve.

Leonard Arnold (1875?–1876?)
CORNER OF SIXTEENTH AND KANSAS

Leonard Arnold was primarily a manufacturer of vinegar, but he also brewed some beer at his vinegar works. He appeared in the 1876 city directory (one of the few extant from the era) but was no longer in the 1879 edition.

Frederick Voelkel (1876?–1882?)
DOTY STREET NEIGHBORHOOD

Frederick Voelkel was a butcher who also owned a beer hall and occasionally manufactured weiss beer during the late 1870s and early 1880s. While his brewing business is included in the R. G. Dun & Co. credit reports, they were not always specific about his various ventures. It appears that he was brewing at least on and off from about 1876 to 1882. His other businesses were clearly more important, since he was not listed in city directories or the census as a brewer.

Oshkosh Brewing Co. (1894–1971)
1631 Doty Street

In May 1893, John Glatz, August Horn and Lorenz Kuenzl met to formulate a response to the combined perils of increased temperance agitation in Oshkosh and growing competition from outside breweries. At first, their agreement was limited to setting the terms upon which they would compete. But they quickly realized that this was not enough to save their breweries from the decrease in demand and their combined overcapacity. In March 1894, they merged into a new corporation called Oshkosh Brewing Co. The new business remained very much a family affair: August Horn and Sophia Schwalm controlled forty-four percent of the new concern, John and William Glatz thirty-one percent, and Lorenz Kuenzl twenty-four percent. (Horn & Schwalm bookkeeper Frank Schneider held the other share, and he was brother to Sophia Schwalm and related to the Glatz family by marriage.)

Oshkosh brewing historians Ron Akin and Lee Reiherzer have argued that the first few years showed little increase in efficiency and a substantial amount of independence by the proud members of the company. Only one brewery was closed, Kuenzl's Gambrinus Brewery, and that was used for bottling—which necessitated transporting the beer from plants on the other side of the Fox River. Some efficiency was forced on the company when William Glatz took over his father's position upon the latter's death and applied his strict business methods to the firm (mostly to the detriment of the free-spending August Horn, who in one week bought more than 300 beers for patrons during saloon visits).

Oshkosh Brewing Co. began using the image of Chief Oshkosh in advertising almost immediately. Chief Oshkosh was "ruler and hero of the Menominee Indians" and was one of those who ceded the territory to the U.S. government. The famous image of him in a "'plug hat'" was taken in 1855, but at that point, myth overwhelms discernable fact. A century later, it was claimed that the chief was a frequent visitor to the brewery, that the hat had been given him by August Horn, even that the picture was taken at the brewery—all either unlikely or impossible since Chief Oshkosh died in 1858.

After a few years, the brewery began to increase sales and profits. Upon the death of Lorenz Kuenzl in 1897, the company hired Frank Menzel as the new brewmaster—one of the few non-family members in a key position. The next year, the company found itself between a rock and a hard place after the U.S. government increased the excise tax on beer by $1 per barrel to help fund the war against Spain. While customers may have sympathized with the plight, the article in the *Daily Northwestern* referred to Oshkosh Brewing as "controlling all the breweries in this city," treating it more like a trust or holding company rather than a single business. Since the company controlled more than 75 percent of the beer trade in Oshkosh, it may have seemed like a combination in restraint of trade rather than a simple hometown brewery. The competitive nature of the market forced occasional cooperation from the brewers and major bottlers. They made a joint statement about the rise in prices in 1898, and in 1904 all agreed on a standard deposit for eighth-barrel kegs (and a joint discontinuation of giving beer as Christmas presents).

Oshkosh Brewing did little newspaper advertising during its first decade, confining notices to a listing among the city's manufacturing enterprises and an occasional announcement that bock beer was available. A typical notice of the latter appeared in March 1902 and indicated that the seasonal specialty would be on draught only on the coming Saturday, Sunday and Monday, but that it also would be for sale by the case. (This schedule also indicates the failure of earlier attempts to close saloons on Sundays.) Some later advertisements are interesting indicators of the position of the brewery in the community. In 1906 the company advertised for boys to work at the bottling department (at the former Kuenzl plant) and urged them to "Apply at once." The next year, the company placed ads in the spring seeking 3,000 bushels of choice barley and in the fall seeking any amount. Such ads were ever-present decades earlier, but

As bottled beer became more popular, breweries purchased delivery wagons designed specifically for beer cases. A. Streich & Bro. built this wagon prior to Prohibition for the Oshkosh Brewing Co. The back doors of the wagon advertise weiss beer. COURTESY OF WISCONSIN HISTORICAL SOCIETY, WHi-5217.

Branding was the most common way to mark the head of a wooden barrel. Loss of cooperage was a constant problem for breweries—even marking it did not guarantee a keg's return. COURTESY OF NATIONAL BREWERY MUSEUM.

very rare in the twentieth century. One advertisement for Oshkosh beer claimed: "Doctors declare that the great prevalence of typhoid fever in the city at present is due to impure water. We therefore recommend you to drink beer." This was the beginning of a series of ads touting the health-giving properties of Oshkosh beer, which may have been at least in part a response to the federal Pure Food and Drug Act of 1906. The level of advertisement in 1907 seems less directed at local competitors and more of a bulwark against Miller, Pabst and Schlitz, who continued to pursue the lucrative Oshkosh market. One hint of this was a short ad that proclaimed "Beer may have made some cities famous, but, THE OSHKOSH BREWING CO. makes famous Beer. Try it." While touting their scientific brewing processes in some ads, others made an appeal to simple traditions. The 1908 ads for bock beer simply read "Nothing New. Same Old Reliable Bock Beer You Have Always Called For." Later ads in 1908 included the invitation "You are invited to inspect our brewery," which was designed to show off the purity of the brewing process as much as it was to build goodwill through free beer samples.

The growth of the company from 1905 to 1909 provided the capital necessary to build the first all-new brewery in the city in more than three decades. Ads soliciting bids from contractors appeared in newspapers in April 1911, and the brewing press announced that the new plant "will represent the most advanced ideas of brewery construction, the result of years of labor on the part of Mr. [William] Glatz." The new brewery was designed by Chicago brewery architect Richard Griesser, and was typical of the grand designs of the first years of the twentieth century. An unusual ad in 1913 explained the benefits of the new brewery and also gave rare insight into ingredients and other inputs:

> A year ago, realizing the fact that some of the old ways and methods of brewing could be vastly improved by the application of later scientific principles and that for perfect sanitation and for other reasons, a new plant was necessary, we abandoned our old brewery and at the cost of many thousands of dollars built an entirely new plant on the latest and most scientific principles know to the brewers art.
>
> All vats, kettles and tanks are new. The storage rooms are built on the most sanitary principles, in place of the wooden tanks of our old brewery we use glass enameled steel tanks for storing our beer; the good housewife will appreciate this when she considers her granite and earthen ware as against the old time wooden household utensils.... Another sanita[r]y process we have adopted—one that no other brewer in this vicinity uses—is what is called the Government Cellar for bottled beer. By this process the beer does not come in contact with the air.... thus avoiding the contaminating influences of the air, such as dust, insects, odors, etc.

The same advertisement also addressed the fraught topic of brown versus clear bottles:

> Regarding brown bottles, we will say we have used brown bottles for years, because it is a recognized fact that light has a damaging influence on beer, as it has on all beverages that contain any organic matter. We also use light bottles where they are demanded but always they, [sic] are wrapped to protect their contents from the rays of light.

It is noteworthy that a brewery of this size would make an effort to offer multiple colors of bottles, but also interesting that they believed the color of bottle was a matter of consumer or distributor demand rather than a simple scientific question (and one which would continue through the twenty-first century). While in many ways the plant utilized the newest technology, the company still hired temporary workers to "put up ice" during the winter.

Oshkosh Brewing also provided information on the inputs:

> ... we have a purchasing agent of 29 years' experience who selects and buys everything that goes into our brew. None but the best Wisconsin barley is used in our plant. German hops, the best hops grown in the world, are used in making our bottled beer. Oregon hops, the choicest hops grown in the United States, are used for our keg beer. West India Rice, the finest rice in the world, the kind that mother serves on the family table, is also used in connection with barley malt in the brewing of our bottled beer.

Why different hops were used in the draught and bottled versions is not clear, though it is likely that the bottled version had more hop flavor and aroma, similar to the difference between a modern German pilsner and lager. While a few brewers, including Anheuser-Busch, have made a virtue of their use of rice, few went so far as Oshkosh as to link it to mother's cooking. Throughout the full-page advertisement, there were several appeals to the housewife, who was not just an icon of purity but increasingly often in charge of ordering beer for the household. The customer had two choices: Oshkosh beer at 80¢ per case or Oshkosh Old Special Lager at $1.40 per case. Bock beer was available for a week in late February, also at 80¢. In order to ward off the competition, in 1914 the company had a promotion in which customers could try three bottles from a case free and return the rest for a full refund if not satisfied.

While the brewery made an initial splash, profits fell for the next several years, partially because of the appearance of a new rival, Peoples Brewing Co., and partially because of increased temperance agitation. In an attempt to answer prohibitionists, Oshkosh Brewing conducted an essay contest in 1915 in which entrants could receive $50 in gold for the best essay on the value of beer. Sales and profits declined through the late 1910s, until Prohibition finally shut down the brewery in 1919.

Oshkosh made several products to get through Prohibition. The first beverage was Pep, "A Temperance Drink with SOME Pep to it." This was sold both in bottles and on draught, but Akin and Reiherzer suggest that it is likely that some of the saloon owners injected alcohol into the kegs to give it even more pep. They also brewed root beer and manufactured malt syrup. The ads for Pep and root beer still made many of the same claims for sanitation and health that the 1910s beer ads contained. The brewery was still producing a significant amount of spent grain, since even during the midst of Prohibition it was offering grain as feed to farmers at a low price. Oshkosh Brewing tried to kick start the near beer market again in 1928 with Chief Oshkosh Brew, but this fared little better and the company continued to lose money until beer was relegalized in 1933.

Oshkosh Brewing Co. had beer for sale on the first day beer was legal again, but it was later developments that helped Oshkosh prosper during the 1930s. The next generation of owners, led by Arthur Schwalm, Earl Horn and Lorenz "Shorty" Kuenzl decided to put more emphasis into the bottle trade, even if this was less popular with local tavern owners. It helped improve sales for a time, but sales started to fall again in 1938, a condition exacerbated by shortages during World War II.

The 1950s proved to be a much better decade for Oshkosh Brewing. The flagship beer was reformulated, and Chief Oshkosh Supreme Pilsner turned out to be a hit. However, the first attempts at canned beer were underwhelming. The crowntainer and conetop cans had both technical and marketing problems, and even the launch of flattop cans in 1955 did little to excite the public. Despite this, sales were increasing overall, driven in part by aggressive marketing by the brewery. When the city of Oshkosh first installed parking meters downtown in 1952, Oshkosh Brewing Co. gave away key ring coin holders complete with a new penny to the first 750 "customers" of the city's new meters (1¢ bought twelve minutes of parking time). In 1953, the brewery urged local residents to "look for these lovely girls in Indian Headdress! They'll have a Valuable Gift for you!" from the makers of Chief Oshkosh. The company produced a wide range of branded items and sponsored events and programs as did most other breweries of the period. Oshkosh Brewing threw a large party to commemorate its 90th anniversary in 1956 (counting from the founding of Horn & Schwalm in 1866 rather than Kuenzl's brewery in 1864). The

Daily Northwestern ran a special supplement that included stories about the brewery and congratulations from Wisconsin dignitaries, including controversial senator Joseph McCarthy. The brewery produced over 60,000 barrels of beer in 1958, which would prove to be the most ever in a year.

However, the third generation of leaders was ageing, and the next generation of children were not interested in taking over the company. In August 1961, David V. Uihelin purchased the brewery from the founding families. While Uihlein was a member of the family that owned Schlitz, he was not at that time directly involved in brewing but instead devoted most of his effort to running Banner Welding in Milwaukee. He was, however, a graduate of the U.S. Brewers' Academy in New York, and had worked in many capacities at the family brewery. To counter falling sales and profits, Uihlein attempted to cut costs by replacing corn grits with a corn syrup, but the reformulated beer went over poorly. Uihlein then redesigned the label in the summer of 1962 to capture the Northwoods imagery, but this was no more successful. Uihlein tried to generate interest in the brewery through his interest in antique vehicles: first adding a vintage 1930 Ford delivery truck named "Old Hank" to the brewery fleet, and later made the term fleet literal when he had a replica riverboat built for occasional deliveries up the river. The boat proved unworkable, and eventually it was donated to the city.

Uihlein also tried to boost sales by shipping beer to Ohio and Pennsylvania and expanding the Wisconsin market beyond the traditional one hundred mile radius. He also acquired brands from the defunct Two Rivers, Effinger, and Rahr of Green Bay breweries, but these brands were only available because they were not able to command their home markets. It is not clear whether Uihlein's management accelerated the decline of Oshkosh Brewing Co., or if the market forces that struck most small breweries caused a slide that Uihlein could not stop. Production dropped from 55,000 barrels in 1961 to 41,000 in 1969, though the latter number was still respectable among

Wisconsin's smaller breweries. In 1969, Uihlein sold the brewery to a group of local investors led by Harold Kriz and Roger Zilleges. Several former employees, including secretary Audrey Ackerman and John Vandermolen joined with them to create Hometown Brewery, Inc., which operated the brewery at a loss until September 1971. In that year production had dropped below 20,000 barrels—less than half of the total two years before. The brewery and its labels were sold to Theodore Mack of Peoples Brewing Co. The brewery building was razed in 1987, though the large terra cotta emblem was salvaged and later moved to the Oshkosh Public Museum.

Peoples Brewing Co. (1913–1972)
1506–1513 SOUTH MAIN STREET
Peoples Brewing Co. in Oshkosh was one of several breweries around Wisconsin to have been founded by a group of tavern keepers fighting back against what they saw as abuses by monopolistic breweries. Joseph Nigl, first president of the brewery, and Rheinhold Thom both had been retailers of Oshkosh Brewing Co. beer, but objected to the company's attempts to make tied houses of all saloons in the city and drive independent operators such as themselves out of business.

While plans to create a rival to Oshkosh Brewing years earlier had fizzled, the group that met in May 1911 was in deadly earnest. They had the advantage of an associate with experience in actually operating a brewery: William C. Kargus, who had fallen out with William Glatz after more than a decade in the front office at Oshkosh Brewing Co. The public announcement of the proposed brewery, made provocatively soon after the announcement of the plans for the new Oshkosh Brewing plant, argued that a cooperative brewery could be profitable and pointed to a large brewery in Duluth, Minnesota and nearly sixty others around the country as proof. By the end of 1911 the Oshkosh concern had taken the same name as the older Duluth business—Peoples Brewing Co.

The new company originally sought to purchase the Charles Rahr brewery, but Rahr refused to sell on terms agreeable to the cooperative. At one point in December 1911, there were rumors that Peoples and Oshkosh Brewing were to merge, but these were denied immediately by Kargus.

The next year, the company broke ground for its new brewery at a location less than a block south of Oshkosh Brewing Co. across Main Street. Whether intentional or not, Glatz and Oshkosh Brewing Co. took the formation and location of Peoples as a personal attack as well as an attack on the beer business of Oshkosh. In a large advertisement celebrating the opening of the new Oshkosh Brewing plant, the management could not resist taking a shot at the "so-called People's Brewing Company," alleging that it "has brought into this city an outside beer which is offered for sale for less money than the actual cost of producing high grade beer, so do not be deceived." In fact, Peoples was not yet in production at this point. Oshkosh Brewing also claimed that the city could not support multiple breweries, though it would do so for almost sixty years. Peoples Brewing Co. announced its opening just over a year later, but with a more celebratory, less defensive ad. It introduced its two brands: Standard, available in bottles or on draught, and Asterweiss, which was a premium bottled product.

Most of Peoples' early newspaper advertisements followed the same pattern as those of its neighborhood rival: touting the health benefits of the beer and the sanitary conditions under which it was brewed. Despite the prominent advertisements for bottled beer, Oshkosh brewing historians Ron Akin and Lee Reiherzer have argued that Peoples depended for its reputation and success on its draught beer business with saloons. The company suffered a setback in October 1915 when William Kargus died of cancer at age 38, but brewmaster Joseph Stier added management to his brewing duties. The company continued to manufacture beer until November 1918, when it ceased operations and sold off its remaining stock of real beer.

Peoples stayed in operation throughout Prohibition, attempting many product lines to pay the bills. Nigl and Stier wandered farther from beer than some of their compatriots— engaging in businesses ranging from dehydrated fruit to oleomargarine. None of these had any success, and they returned to bottled goods. Various near beers were placed on the market, but with little luck, even with attempts to expand the market beyond Winnebago County. In 1927 the company reinvigorated its line of soft drinks with new equipment and a new ad campaign. One ad touted no less than thirteen different products, including regular and premium ginger ales. Another ad devoted to Royal Aster, the premium ginger ale, contained the unfortunate phrase: "In connection with our complete line of Sodas and Soft Drinks our Pale Dry Royal Aster Ginger Ale stands out like a sore thumb." Peoples Malt Tonic was also marketed throughout the period, but with much less advertising splash.

When beer returned in 1933, Peoples wasted no time in getting real beer back on the market. In addition, when many other breweries waited to test the market for specialty products they brought back Holiday Beer right away in 1933 and bock in 1934. Holiday Beer came out after Prohibition was fully repealed, so it could exceed the 3.2 percent alcohol limit, and was advertised as "high test." Even higher test was Old Derby Ale, brewed first by Ripon Brewing Co. and distributed by Peoples, which reached an astounding 12 percent alcohol. After Ripon closed, Peoples acquired the brand and brewed it into the 1950s, though at a much lower alcohol content. The brewery went so far in 1935 as to offer a free case of Special Holiday Brew (note the name change) to the mother of the first baby born in Oshkosh that year.

Unlike many breweries that increased production during the war years only to see it shrink in the 1950s, Peoples continued to grow. Akin & Reiherzer attribute some of this to the diffuse leadership structure that the original cooperative model established, meaning that Peoples was not as dependent on any one individual as many of their rivals. In addition, Peoples continued to sell more than fifty percent of its beer on draught in loyal local taverns, giving it a market that proved harder for outside beers to crack. Credit is also due to the leadership of Richard Haidlinger, a noted local baseball player and bowler who took over as general manager and added the sales and advertising portfolio in 1951. Haidlinger was responsible for the new arrow and target logo, which broke from the traditions of agricultural scenes and script names and created a modern new look. Peoples was able to control losses in sales throughout the 1960s, dropping just 16 percent in a difficult market for small breweries compared to about 50 percent for Oshkosh Brewing Co.

The final chapter of Peoples Brewing Co. was even more historically significant than its cooperative origins. Theodore (Ted) Mack, an African American who was a former employee of Pabst, purchased the brewery in April 1970, making it one of the first Black-owned breweries in the nation—second only to Sunshine Brewing Co. of Reading, Pennsylvania. (The story of the purchase and last years of Peoples is covered in more detail in chapter 8.) When it closed, Peoples was distributed in Wisconsin, Indiana and California, but was not able to compete against larger national brands.

An early lighted sign features the new arrow and target logo. Old Derby Ale was still being brewed.
COLLECTION OF DAVID WENDL.

Fox River Brewing Co./Fratello's Waterfront Brewery & Restaurant (1995–2015)

Fox River Brewing Company & Taproom (2015–present)

1501 Arboretum Drive

The Supple brothers, Jay, Joe, and John, had been restaurateurs in Oshkosh for nearly three decades prior to opening Fox River Brewing Co in 1995. They decided they wanted a location on the water, and selected a site near Congress Avenue on the banks of the Fox River. The Supples consulted with Rob LoBreglio of Great Dane to help establish the brewing side of the operation, and LoBreglio recommended Al Bunde as the first brewmaster. The Supples and Bunde elected to challenge local taste preferences right away with a roster of full-flavored beers right from the start rather than changing tastes gradually. Oshkosh brewing historian Lee Reiherzer credits the presence of a growing group of craft beer lovers in Oshkosh, particularly the Society of Oshkosh Brewers homebrew club, with providing a good reception for Bunde's beers.

The Supples looked to expand beyond their walls in Oshkosh right from the beginning. In 1997, they contracted with Green Bay Brewing Co. (later Hinterland) to bottle their Golden Ale for sale in stores. They also built another Fox River brewpub in Appleton (see Appleton).

Fox River Brewing Co. is one of several craft brewers that cooperate with local homebrew clubs to brew beers created by homebrewers. Collection of Scott Reich.

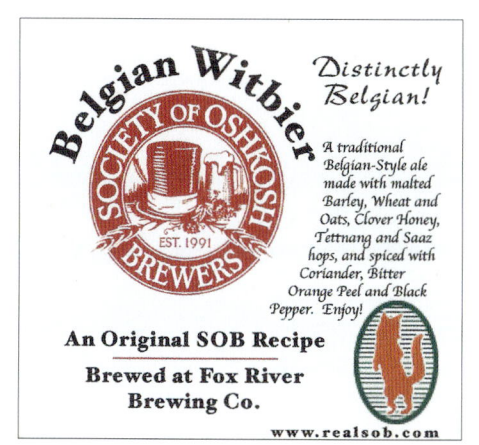

In 1998, Al Bunde left to take over brewing at Stout Brothers in Milwaukee, and Steve Lonsway, who had been in charge of brewing at the Appleton location, assumed duties at Oshkosh as well. Both locations brewed the same beers—a practice which continued for many years, through Brian Allen and Kevin Bowen's terms as brewmaster.

In 2007, the Supples decided to emphasize the Fratello's restaurant brand at the expense of the brewery, so they cut back on distribution of Fox River beer. However, in 2012 they refocused on the brewery and brewed beers under contract for Appleton's Old Bavarian Brewing Co. Seeking to reassert their presence on the shelves, Fox River returned to the wholesale market in 2014 featuring a series of draught beers under the Bago Brew name, which by the end of the year were also available in bottles. In 2015 they installed a bottling line at the Appleton location, and to further focus on the beer, the Oshkosh location dropped the Fratello's name and became Fox River Brewing Company & Taproom. In recent years, Fox River has continued to brew imaginative beers—such as a brandy-barrel-aged Belgian abbey ale (Abbey Normal—a reference to the Mel Brooks classic *Young Frankenstein*) which earned a silver medal at the 2012 World Beer Cup. Bowen also worked with Lee Reiherzer to create a reproduction of 1950s era Chief Oshkosh beer to celebrate the release of *The Breweries of Oshkosh* by Reiherzer and Ron Akin.

Bare Bones Brewery (2015–present)

4362 County Road S

Despite the size of Oshkosh and its importance in Wisconsin brewing history, nearly twenty years elapsed between the opening of the city's first new brewery since before Prohibition and its second. Bare Bones Brewery opened for business in 2015 after Dan and Patti Dringoli decided that a brewery and taproom would be a more exciting business to operate at their location near the Wiouwash Recreational Trail than their previous business, PuroClean (a water and fire damage clean up business).

Many of the beers' names have some sort of canine reference. Bare Bones developed a mix of classic styles and experimental beers, including one of the first fresh hop beers to be brewed in the area. In 2017, Bare Bones began canning some of its beers.

OSSEO (Trempealeau County)

Northwoods Brewpub and Grill (2015–present)

50819 West Avenue

Northwoods Brewpub was running out of space in its Eau Claire location, especially since they were hoping to expand their packaging operations. Since prices for the type of space they needed were prohibitive in Eau Claire, Jerry Bechard began to look elsewhere. Nels Gunderson, a Chevrolet dealer in Osseo, had been interested in starting a banquet center in an old milk condensary in that city about twenty-five miles southeast of Eau Claire. Gunderson approached Bechard, whose Norske Nook restaurants started in Osseo, and asked if he would be willing to bring the brewpub to Osseo (and which would hold the liquor license for the event center). Bechard and his team looked over the massive building, and soon agreed to the move. About three months after beginning renovations, the new brewery was ready to go.

While brewpub traffic was similar to if not better in the new location, the biggest advantages were in the packaging. The first canning had been done on a hand-operated system that filled two cans at a time—the new system had a capacity of 100 cans an hour. As of 2017, Northwoods was phasing out their 16-ounce cans and moving to 12-ounce cans. With the new space, brewer Eddie Rogers introduced barrel-aging and sour beer programs.

OTTAWA TOWNSHIP (Dousman) (Waukesha County)

David Link (1860?–1873?)

David Link (or Lenk) was brewing on his farm in Ottawa Township at least by 1860, since he is listed as a brewer in the census of that year. As owner of $5,000 of real estate spread out over several parcels, and $600 of personal property, he was fairly well-to-do. Excise records indicate he brewed regularly during the late

1860s and early 1870s, though the 1870 census lists him only as a farmer. The few production statistics indicate that he brewed for local consumption—thirty-five barrels in 1871 and twenty-one in 1872 were not enough to spread his reputation much beyond Dousman. David's son John later became a brewer in neighboring Summit Township. Link's brewery disappears from tax records and industry publications after 1873.

Paddock Lake (Kenosha County)

The Benjamin Beer Company (2014–15)
24425 75th Street

Jim Kennedy first opened the Benjamin Beer Company in September 2014 in Paddock Lake, west of Kenosha. The company was named after Benjamin Franklin. The site proved too small, and closed in July 2015. Kennedy looked for another Kenosha County site, but instead decided to move to downtown Racine, where it reopened in May 2016.

Palmyra (Jefferson County)

John Buzzell (1856?–58?)
John Buzzell appears to have had a brewery here in the late 1850s.

J. F. Smith (1856?–1858?)
Like Buzzell, Smith's existence as a brewery is known from a single directory reference. Given the questionable accuracy of these early directories, it is possible that these two could have been saloonkeepers who brewed their own beer, farmers who had a small brewing operation, or they may not have brewed at all.

Paris Township (Kenosha County)

John C. Custer (Custus) (1850?)
John C. Custer was listed as a brewer in the 1850 population census. While not definite proof that he owned a brewery, he was unlikely to have declared is occupation as brewer if he were not engaged in the trade, and there were no other breweries in the vicinity at which he could have been employed.

Pembine (Marinette County)

Black Husky Brewing Co. (2010–present)
W5951 Steffen Lane

In 2010 Tim and Toni Eichinger started one of Wisconsin's first nanobreweries in Pembine, near the Michigan border. The rural location was also the home of their rescued sled dogs, and each label bore a picture of one of the dogs. When possible, the beer was selected to match the personality of the dog. Howler was used for bold beers; Rinki Dinki was the label dog for Pembiner: a small beer, named for a small town and a small dog. The remote location created difficulties not encountered by many other breweries. All ingredients needed to be ordered by mail, and the local market was very supportive but small. Much of the beer was shipped to Milwaukee, and since all beer was self-distributed, this made for a lot of long drives.

While the early brews were well-brewed interpretations of classic styles, over time the brews became much more distinctive, particularly the "Beware of the Dog Series." Offerings included a Belgian Tripel, Smoke Monster Smoked Beer, Big Buck Brown Ale (with maple syrup) and the signature Sproose II IPA, made with spruce tips. Howler Imperial Pale was brewed with honey, and often with different hop varieties. Twelve-Dog Imperial Stout was available in regular and barrel-aged versions.

In 2010, production was about 100 barrels per year. But as the popularity of the beers grew beyond what the space in their log brewery could handle (production approached 300 barrels in 2015), the Eichingers decided to move to their brewery to Milwaukee to be near their son Jacob and his family, and to be nearer to their principal market.

Pepin (Pepin County)

August Geisert (ca. 1860)
August Geisert moved from Pennsylvania to Wisconsin sometime in the late 1850s. He was listed as a brewer located in the Village of Pepin's First Ward in the 1860 population census, but based on the fact that he had only $200 of real estate and $35 of personal property, his operation was undoubtedly a small one. Sometime after, he moved to Menomonie and started a larger brewery. His sons August and Louis later operated a brewery in Rice Lake.

Peshtigo (Marinette County)

Ferdinand Hoppe (1872?–1875)
Ferdinand Hoppe is believed to have started brewing near Peshtigo in the early 1870s. The brewery was mostly likely established after the fire of 1871, since it does not appear in any accounts of the damage from the blaze. This brewery burned in late May 1875 and was not rebuilt.

Pewaukee Township (Waukesha County)

Fox River Brewery, Jacob Goettelman (1854?–1862?)
Fox River, Pewaukee

Jacob Goettelman operated a modest brewery in Pewaukee Township in the 1850s. The first known mention of the brewery appears in 1854 and was not directly related to brewing—constituents of Democratic State Senator George R. McLane met at the Fox River Brewery "to consider whether he acted properly by supporting" the Kansas-Nebraska Act. Goettelman's listing in the 1860 industrial census

The Beware of the Dog series features several beers with higher alcohol content as well as a few with unusual ingredients—or both, such as Sproose II IPA, a double IPA brewed with spruce tips. Later labels read Sproose 2 IPA. Photograph by Charles Walbridge. Author's collection.

indicates that he brewed just over 100 barrels in the previous year, but more interestingly, that he employed one woman at the brewery. No one other than his wife Gertrude was listed in his household in the 1860 population census, so she may have helped in the brewery (for which she or the other female employee was paid $10 per month). Since Goettelman had no real estate listed in the population census, it is likely that he did not own the land the brewery was on, though he purchased some property in the area in 1861 with J. A. Wirth. Goettelman sold his share of the land to Wirth in 1862, which may have marked the end of his brewing at this site.

PIERCE TOWNSHIP (Kewaunee County)

John Frazier (Feezier, Vaser) (1876?–1879)
John Vaser of Pierce is listed in Salem's directory of brewers as producing 110 barrels in 1878 and 47 barrels in 1879—figures that suggest he was running a small farm brewery. Wayne Kroll has identified Vaser as John Frazier, whose address was sometimes listed as Ryan's Corners. The *Manitowoc Pilot* reported in 1879 that "Feezier" had built a small brewery "a few years ago" but since had fallen on hard times and "of late he had few customers besides himself." An incident in which he, while drunk, dipped his young daughter's legs into hot keg rinse water, after which he attempted to poison himself, was probably the end of his brewing career.

PLAINFIELD (Waushara County)

D. Wilson (1856?–1858?)
Wilson's Plainfield brewery was included in the 1857 directory but he was not listed in the 1860 census, so his brewery was most likely small and short lived.

PLATTEVILLE (Grant County)

J. F. Gluck (1851?–1852?)
"NORTHEAST PART OF TOWN"
The *Platteville Independent American* began running an ad placed by J. F. Gluck in February 1852 noting: "The subscriber is making and keeps constantly on hand a first rate article of Beer at his Brewery in the north east part of the town of Platteville." If this represents his earliest sales, he probably began construction of the brewery during the previous year. However, in April the brewery burned with a loss of $1,500. It is unclear whether Gluck rebuilt or not, since the ad remained in the *Independent American* until June 1852, but no further references to his business have been found to date.

Platteville Brewery
Centlivre (& Muesey) (1865?–1867)
Centlivre & Beyer (1868–69)
Denis Centlivre (1869–1871)
John Kemler (& Hein) (1871–74)
Briscoe & Rehmstedt (1874–78)
H. F. Rehmstedt (1878–1882)
Wedel & Helberg (1882–84)
George T. Wedel (1884–86)
John Kemler (1886–89)
Hoppe & Mueller (1890–92)
Fritz Hoppe (1892–1913)
List Brewing Co. (1913–1920)
Platteville Brewery, Inc. (1938–1941)
1001 EAST MINERAL STREET

The story of the Platteville Brewery was one of nearly constant ownership changes. Only Fritz Hoppe had his name on the business for more than ten years, and other owners came and went in various configurations.

Denis Centlivre was one of the very few Wisconsin brewery proprietors to have been born in France. (His brother Charles Louis started the Centlivre Brewing Co. in Fort Wayne, Indiana.) Newspaper reports suggest that his brewery was open as early as December 1865, though most local histories place the opening date later. He had a short-lived partnership with Joseph Muesey, which ended in late 1867, according to newspapers and excise records. Excise tax records indicate Centlivre remained on his own until he took on a partner named Beyer in late 1868. Beyer only stayed until September of the next year.

In 1871, local businessman John Kemler acquired the brewery through foreclosure, and ran it with partner John P. Hein. Kemler's first stint as an active partner was disrupted by a massive fire in September 1871, which caused damage estimated between $10,000 and $20,000. The brewery was rebuilt as a more impressive stone structure, along with an ice house, a barn and dwelling. Production of the new brewery reached 420 barrels in 1872 (the *American Brewers' Guide* made specific note that the previous year's records had burned). In late 1874, Richard Briscoe and H. F. Rehmsted took over the brewery. While the 1881 county history reports that they purchased the brewery in 1875, the excise records place them there in October 1874 (though they may have been renting or leasing at first). Production surpassed 700 barrels in 1878, but they ultimately succumbed to the same fate as Centlivre, and Kemler took control of the property again. Rehmsted was retained as the brewer for a few years and the 1881 county history reported that production was around 1,600 barrels per year with a crew of eight men (at a combined monthly wage bill of $350). In 1882, George Wedel took over the operations and expanded capacity to around 2,000 barrels per year. Sometime prior to 1884 he added malting and bottling facilities, and while subsequent industry directories do not include these features, they are shown on the 1885 Sanborn

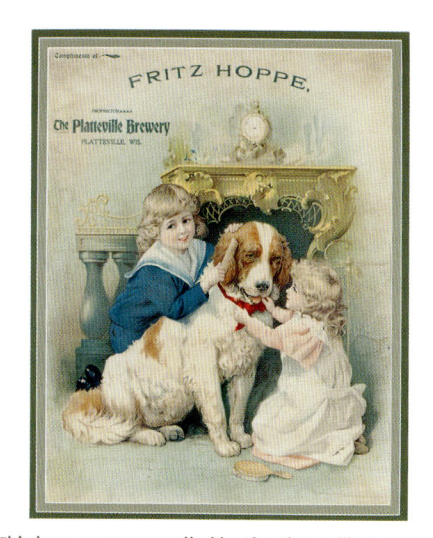

This large poster supplied by the Platteville Brewery has little to do with beer or brewing but was a stock image that could be used by any business.
COLLECTION OF TYE SCHWALBE.

Insurance Map. (The bottle house was located inconveniently across the creek that ran across the northwest side of the brewery, but it was on Mineral Street.)

Kemler became the proprietor of the brewery for one more spell, but he died in January 1889. This set the stage for the longest period of stability in Platteville Brewing history. Fritz Hoppe owned the brewery for nearly a quarter of a century, during which he improved the brewery by adding steam power, and also replaced the ice house which was washed away in a September 1894 storm. Hoppe apparently also engaged in fish farming: in 1895 he requested one hundred carp from the state fisheries commission which were most likely stocked in a pond near the brewery. In the early twentieth century Hoppe built a new bottle house that was on the same side of the creek as the brewery and continued to upgrade the brewery equipment. Hoppe had a pigpen on the brewery property, making him one of the few brewers to continue to house livestock on the premises during the twentieth century—but they provided a ready way to dispose of at least some of his spent brewery grains.

In 1913, John A. List purchased the brewery, and ran it with his son Louis as brewmaster until Prohibition.

When Prohibition ended, William Brey, his wife Jeannette, and R. J. Brachman sought to bring brewing back to Platteville. They incorporated Platteville Brewery, Inc. in July 1933, but the business did not produce beer until the beginning of 1938. However, the brewery never produced enough beer to be viable. Some of the amounts were ludicrously low: production seems to have peaked in 1939 at 1,580 barrels, which compares poorly with nearby Potosi's nearly 37,000 barrels the same year (not to mention Schlitz's 1.6 million barrels). The brewery had a tiny market outside Wisconsin—in July 1941 they sold $12.11 worth of beer in other states. The brewery closed for good in 1941, though the structure still remains and has been repurposed as a cheese factory.

Pioneer Haus Brew Pub (UW-Platteville Dining Services Brewpub) (2004–2010)
1 University Plaza
One of the more unusual brewpubs in Wisconsin, though fitting for the state, was Pioneer Haus Brew Pub, located in the Pioneer Student Center at University of Wisconsin-Platteville. It was believed to be the only commercial brewery owned by a university, and gave students in the University's homebrew club and biological science classes a chance to help brew the beer. The fact that the brewery was owned and operated by a university caused some delays with federal and state permits, since there was no precedent for such an arrangement. Brewer Tom Nickels, an experienced homebrewer, typically brewed a batch on the fifty-liter system every two or three weeks. The entire output, typically around ten barrels per year, was sold on campus at the Pioneer Student Center. For a while, the two Pioneer Haus brews—1866 Lager and Pioneer Pale Ale—outsold Miller Lite. Pioneer Haus was one of the smallest breweries in the country during its existence, and perhaps the smallest that brewed on a regular schedule. The brewery sold enough beer to cover expenses, but after several years the University decided to discontinue the experiment.

PLOVER *(Portage County)*

O'So Brewing Co.
1812 Post Road (2007–2011); 3028 Village Park Drive (2011–present)
Marc Buttera and his wife Katina started Point Brew Supply in 2003. The store outgrew two locations, after which they moved to a location where they could act on their plan to establish a brewery. The name O'So comes from an old Polish exclamation, and is a tribute to the Polish heritage of the region. The brewing equipment, acquired from a variety of sources, was jammed into the space of the original brewery in a small suburban strip mall. While production in the first year was only 350 barrels, wide acceptance of several excellent beers helped the brewery grow much more quickly than

O'So has produced a wide variety of beers. Its barrel program included Wease the Juice—a cherry sour fermented with brettanomyces. Photograph by Charles Walbridge. AUTHOR'S COLLECTION.

they expected. In 2012 they moved to a much larger location in Plover. The new brewery still featured some hand-me-down equipment, including some horizontal fermenters previously used by Lakefront Brewery which O'So painted with large representations of characters from children's shows: Big Bird, Oscar the Grouch, and Barney.

With more space in the new facility, the O'So brewing team began to experiment with barrel-aged and sour beers. They aged their sour blonde ale on blueberries, cherries, peaches, and a combination of kiwis and cranberries. Other offerings in the Extreme Beer line included IPAs fermented with brettanomyces. They also created a number of "one-off" beers that were intended to let the brewing team experiment and have fun, though a few of them, like Black Scotch, were so popular they were brewed again.

O'So Brewing has made a concerted effort to be responsible members of the community. They shipped waste effluent to Stevens Point Brewery to be converted into methane, which significantly reduced run-off from the brewery. In 2012 they introduced Memory Lane, a pilsner dedicated to Marc's grandfather who suffered from Alzheimer's disease, and from which a

PLYMOUTH (Sheboygan County)

Sander & Schneider (1856?–1864)
Andrew Schneider (1864–1884)
A. Schneider & Sons (1884–1890)
MILL STREET NORTH OF DIVISION

Adam Sander and Andrew Schneider started brewing in Plymouth in the mid-1850s, early enough to be included in the 1857 state business directory. An 1862 map of Sheboygan County listed them as brewers in Quitquioc—the name at the time for the eastern part of modern Plymouth. By 1860, Sander and Schneider had built production to 300 barrels, which sold for a local price of $4.00. In addition to 600 bushels of barley and 300 pounds of hops, the partners reported using 400 pounds of rosin for pitching their kegs. In 1864 Sander left to start his own brewery in Fond du Lac, and Schneider carried on alone. Schneider's production was somewhat larger than his rival Weber, though Weber had a larger brew kettle according to the 1870 census of industry (eight barrels to fourteen barrels, respectively). Production in 1870 was just under 500 barrels, which would represent slow but steady growth (though intermediate figures are not available). The evaluators for R. G. Dun & Co. had high praise for the business, noting in 1865 "The brewery is doing g[oo]d bus[iness], has the reputation of making g[oo]d beer," and reviews were equally good throughout the 1870s. Production was typically around 500 barrels per year throughout the decade.

During the 1880s Schneider brought his sons Otto and Richard into the business. Otto had already been working in the brewery for several years; Schneider also typically had at least one hired hand living with him. At some point during the mid 1880s the Schneiders added a malt house (it was listed for the first time in Wing's 1887 directory).

After it closed, the former Schneider brewery served as the local agency for Miller Brewing of Milwaukee, but the malt house remained in business under the name Schneider Brothers into the twentieth century.

Buckle & Brahmer (Brewer) (1861–68)
Gottfried Weber (1868–1882)
Ferdinand Streblow (1884?–86)
Plymouth Brewing Co. (1886–1894)
Anton Schreiner, Schwanstein Brewery (1894–1902)
Plymouth Brewing Co. (1902–1913)
Plymouth Brewing & Malting Co. (1913–1920)
Plymouth Brewing Co. (1920–23)
Curtiss Co. (1923–1933)
Plymouth Products Co. (late 1920s)
Plymouth Brewing Co. (1933–37)
2–16 EAST MAIN STREET

One account from 1913 claims that this brewery was originally built as a hotel and was sold to August Buckle (Buckel) and a variously named partner in 1868 or 1869, but this contradicts other sources, including excise records. Gottfried Weber acquired the brewery in 1868—his first appearance in excise records is in October of that year. There is a discrepancy with the R. G. Dun & Co. credit reports, which have "Brewer and Buckle" "[D]oing well" as late as June 1869, but they also have Weber brewing at this time. There is little likelihood that Weber worked for the others, since data in the 1870 census shows him to be a wealthy man, with real estate of $4,500 and $2,000 of personal property. The 1870 industrial census was unusually precise about the Plymouth breweries, reporting that Weber had a fourteen-barrel brew kettle in his hand-powered brewery, with which he produced 150 barrels of "lager" and 300 barrels of "beer." The latter sold at a lower price, but given the German brewer and market, it was unlikely to have been an English-style ale, but simply a lower-grade beer in the lager family. This is even more likely since he was only in business for seven months of the year, so was not taking advantage of summer months to brew ale.

Production ranged from about 250 barrels to about 450 barrels during the 1870s, and Weber's reputation remained high through the 1870s—though he appears to have come upon financial difficulties near the end of the decade. The Dun reports indicate that he was out of business by late 1882, perhaps due to illness as he died in 1883. The brewery appears to have lain dormant for a number of months until it was reopened by Ferdinand Streblow in late 1883 or early 1884. He was sole proprietor only briefly, since in 1887 the brewery was incorporated as Plymouth Brewing Company. Streblow was one of the original incorporators, as was Anton Schreiner (and James Cavner, who signed the documents with his "X" mark). This version of the brewery had a capacity of between 1,000 and 1,500 barrels per year, and had its own malt house. Plymouth Brewing dissolved in 1894, and Anton Schreiner became sole proprietor for the next several years. Schreiner apparently had a good reputation among his fellows, since was elected vice president of the Wisconsin State Brewers' Association when it was formed in 1900. Schreiner sold his share of the newest incarnation of Plymouth Brewing Co. in 1903 but remained an important member of the Plymouth business community. (He returned to Germany in 1916, where he lived until 1921.) Plymouth Brewing changed the name of the business to Plymouth Brewing & Malting in 1913 and made several major alterations to the plant that year, tearing down

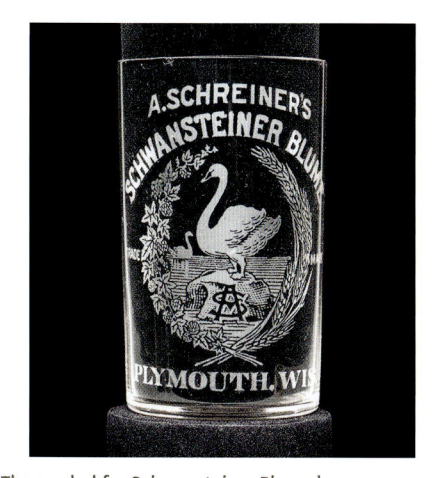

The symbol for Schwansteiner Blume beer was a swan perched on a stone. This glass is from the late 1890s. COLLECTION OF JOHN STEINER.

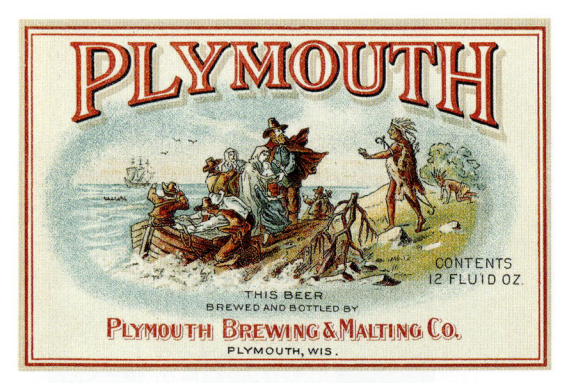

The vignette on this label shows a traditional view of the Pilgrims' arrival at Plymouth, Massachusetts (though this depiction has no basis in historical fact). COLLECTION OF TYE SCHWALBE.

some of the older outbuildings and replacing them with more substantial structures. J. E. Curtiss was president of the new company, and he remained an important leader through Prohibition.

In some ways, Plymouth Brewing was treated as part of the Sheboygan brewery community. In 1915, Plymouth joined with Gutsch and Schreier of Sheboygan (and P. Schoenhofen Brewing Co. of Chicago, which had a presence in the area) to establish a common deposit for cases, bottles, and kegs. The brewers claimed this was necessary to protect against lost or damaged containers.

During Prohibition, the brewery continued to make beverages for a few years, though they were not advertised heavily. The contemporary newspapers contradict the incorporation records, which show that the name of the business was changed to Curtiss Company in 1923, while newspapers in the late 1920s referred to the brewery as Plymouth Products Co. It made malt syrup for a time, but the brewery lost its smokestack to a storm in 1928, and when the boilers were in operation the smoke caused complaints in the neighborhood, so the city council prohibited emission of smoke from the factory until a new structure could be built. This may have encouraged the company to find a new line of business, so in 1929 the company began cultivating mushrooms in the old cellar.

When beer became legal, Plymouth moved quickly to convert back to brewing. While it was announced at first that the Schaller Brewing Co. would take over the old Curtiss business, this company decided to go into distilling instead. But a new business under the Plymouth Brewing Co. name formed and on 13 July 1933, a large ad in the *Sheboygan Press* announced "The finest fully aged Beer that it is possible to brew is now on tap for you at your favorite tavern." Bottled beer, it added, would be available in a few days.

The ad included a large photo of the brewery (complete with new belching smokestack) and a picture of the label for Plymouth Beer, which emphasized "Our Own Well Water Used Exclusively." For the rest of the year, the newspaper ads used the label as the ad design, with a bit of extra information about local distributors squeezed into the lower right. By early 1934, Plymouth was advertising its "High Power 5 percent Beer," which sold for $1.65 per case or eighth barrel. Production usually exceeded 600 barrels per month during 1936, and sometimes approached 900 barrels. Sales continued at this pace until June 1937, when they suffered a precipitous drop to less than 300 barrels per month. At this point, government auditors reported that the company's records were "all balled up." After dropping to just over one hundred barrels a few months later the brewery was unable to remain in business, and discontinued operations in October 1937. The building was sold in 1943 to S & R Cheese Corp., which by the 1970s was the largest producer of Italian cheeses in the United States.

Plymouth Brewing Co. (2013–present)
222 E. MILL STREET (2013–PRESENT); 207 E. MILL STREET (2016–PRESENT)

Joe and Nancy Fillion moved to Plymouth because they liked the area, but Joe also saw potential for small-scale brewing in the city. They opened their brewery and taproom in 2013 in a building dating to the 1870s that had previously served as a hotel, a small manufacturing business, a hardware store, a pizza place and several other businesses. The taproom is decorated with breweriana from the earlier Plymouth Brewing Co. (Joe contacted a descendant of the Curtiss family to get personal as well as legal approval for use of the name.)

When it became clear that demand had outgrown their original brewhouse, they acquired the former Reinhold Meyer building across the street for use as a production brewery and installed a fifteen-barrel system. This enabled Plymouth to increase production from about 130 barrels in 2106 to a projected total of about three times that volume in 2017. To date, Plymouth has done only limited bottling of varied brands—filling both 12-ounce and 22-ounce bottles by hand.

PORT WASHINGTON
(Ozaukee County)

John Arnet (1844?–1850?)
John Arnet (who was listed in a later history as Leonard) was probably the first brewer in Ozaukee County, which in the 1840s was still part of Washington County. An 1881 county history claims "his was the only establishment of its kind then known outside of Milwaukee." The brewery near his cabin "consisted of some half dozen posts driven into the ground, on these rested several cross-beams to which clamp-hooks were fastened, upon which were suspended two large iron kettles, in which he brewed his hops and other ingredients necessary to the manufacture of the foaming beverage." He sold his beer for 3¢ a pint and is reported to have done a good business. Few details are known about his production levels, but he was still listed as a brewer in the 1850 population census, though not in the census of industry. (He was not recorded in Washington County during the 1840 census).

Lakeside Brewery
Jacob Moritz (1847–1874)
Nicholas Welter (1874)
Welter & Mallinger (1874–76)
Henry Dix & Co. (1876–1881)

Gottlieb Biedermann & Co. (1881–1903)
Port Washington Brewing Co. (1903–1920)
Old Port Brewing Co. (1933–1947)
419 LAKE STREET

Jacob Moritz appears to have commenced business around 1847. By 1860 he was producing 1,000 barrels per year, which made him one of the larger brewers outside Milwaukee. A decade later, output was up to 1,500 barrels, and he had added horse-powered grinding and pumping equipment to increase efficiency. The R. G. Dun & Co. credit evaluators reported several times that he was a good brewer and an honest man, but he was sometimes in financial trouble: once after the Panic of 1857, other times due to problems collecting bills (because of the "scarcity of money"). Production dropped off in the early 1870s, and the brewery passed to new owner Nicholas Welter. He had little time to profit from his brewery before it was destroyed by fire in December 1874. The report of the blaze in the *Milwaukee Daily Sentinel* indicated that Welter was out of town at the time and was unaware of the disaster—hopefully his first information was not from a brief sentence in the newspaper.

Welter apparently relied on partners to finance his brewery—even more after the fire. In 1874 W. A. Tholen provided backing, and in 1875 John Mallinger (or Wollinger) sold his farm to enter the brewery business. Unfortunately, the Lakeside Brewery was now deeply in debt, and Mallinger assigned all his property to Nicholas Kemp, owner of a malt house in Port Washington. For the next few years the brewery did business under several different names. In April 1876, Frederick Knoepple returned to brewing and operated the business until the summer of 1878. It was subsequently called H. Dix & Co., though the Dun records indicate that while Henry Dix had a half interest and operated the business, Kemp and Co. continued to own the brewery. This ownership team dissolved in 1881 and the brewery was sold to Gottlieb Biedermann and J. M. Bostwick, a local jeweler who provided financial backing.

Biedermann rebuilt the business, and by 1883 the Dun representative praised Biedermann as "the best here." He also expanded the facility, and by 1895 the steam-powered brewery had its own bottle house (and a brick barrel-pitching house to avoid further fires). The Biederman home was on land south of the brewery, across the creek, but a catwalk enabled Biedermann to cross over to the plant on Lake Street. The grounds also contained a lagoon into which all the spent grain and other waste was dumped, which reportedly "was only occasionally flushed out into the lake."

Local histories give conflicting accounts of events after Biedermann left the business. However, the articles of incorporation indicate that Ludwig and Charles Labahn and George Blessing incorporated Port Washington Brewing Co. in June 1903. Under the new management team, the brewery added weiss beer to its list of products around 1906, and continued to brew it for about ten years.

George Blessing left for the Grafton brewery prior to Prohibition, and the Labahns amended their articles of incorporation to allow manufacture of non-intoxicating beverages and industrial distilling, in addition to "all business pertaining to a first-class brewery." Apparently they were serious about the brewery part, because Port Washington Brewing was one of the first to be raided by Prohibition agents during the dry years. The business was accused in 1921 of manufacturing and selling "large quantities of beer containing more than one-half of 1 per cent alcohol" and therefore the "brewery has become a public and common nuisance." The *Sheboygan Press* reported of the enforcement campaign:

> The relentless dry agencies of the government are reaching out along the west shore of Lake Michigan... grasping and crushing lawlessness, slowly moving north like a tidal wave smothering all opposition. The crest of the wave reached Port Washington yesterday. The Port Washington Brewing company plant was closed. Port Washington has been passed. The inexorable doom of the wets north of Milwaukee is sealed.

The company returned to business later under the name Premo Products Co., and remained operational until 1933.

Despite the trials of the dry years, the Labahn family held on to the business and was rewarded when beer returned in 1933. The company initiated a $35,000 remodeling program which included new bottling equipment and upgrades that resulted in the usual claim that it was "one of the most modern breweries in Wisconsin." Thirty years to the day after Ludwig Labahn purchased the brewery, his son Herbert saw that Old Port Lager and Premo were on draught in time to mark the July Fourth holiday of 1933. Release of bottled beer was delayed twice: first until the end of July, but that announcement came in an ad which featured a photo of a row of new fermenters commissioned from Dunck Tank Works of Milwaukee. The second delay was announced in early August, this time in an ad featuring an illustration of the new Vilter ice machine at the brewery. Yet another ad showed the brewery's new fleet of trucks. The company was emphasizing its modern equipment, apparently in an attempt to compete with larger breweries, though all this technology wasn't helping them get the beer to market. All of the ads made a virtue of the delay, pledging that only fully-aged beer would reach customers—appealing to those worried about breweries trying to

This shoe shine brush (an unusual brewery promotional item) featured a stretched-out version of the Old Port Lager label used both before and after Prohibition. COLLECTION OF TYE SCHWALBE.

cash in by releasing "green" beer. The company promoted their beer in part through sponsorship of a fifteen-minute radio program on WHBL featuring German music and the comedy of Putzelheimer and Bummelfritz. The also sponsored both a baseball team and a football team under the name Old Port Lagers. (Admission to games in the Badger football league was 40¢ in 1934.)

All the new equipment seems to have tested the finances of the company. In 1934, Old Port Brewing advertised a public sale of stock with newspaper advertisements including a clip out form which potential investors could request information about the sale. The brewery also reintroduced its bock beer in 1934, and made a point in advertisements of proclaiming that the beer was made by "100 percent Union" labor.

Old Port sought to expand their markets beyond state lines in order to stay profitable. Some beer was shipped to Illinois in the late 1930s. In August 1943, P. W. Heinrichs of Fergus Falls, Minnesota, purchased Old Port Brewing, and operated it for three years. He installed new bottling equipment, and most of the beer was shipped out of state, primarily to Washington and Texas. (Heinrichs also owned Capitol Brewing of Milwaukee.) In May 1946 Heinrichs sold the brewery to a group of distributors from Utah led by Stanford Kershaw, who planned to ship most of the production to their state to alleviate the postwar beer shortage. But Kershaw died in May 1947, and in August the brewery was offered for sale. The City of Port Washington purchased the building the next year and used it for storage until electing to raze the structure in 1958.

John Wittmann (1859?–1865)
Margarethe Wittmann (1865–1880s?)
George Wittmann (1867–1877)
John Wittmann (Jr.) (1877–1894?)
532 North Harrison Street

John Wittmann (spelled variously) began brewing sometime prior to 1860. By that year he was producing 600 barrels in a horse-powered brewery—not unheard of for a first-year brewer, but it is likely that he had been brewing for at least a year before this. The $4,000 he had invested in the business also suggests he had more than one year to build up the plant. He was not likely in operation too much before then, because an 1880 report states that the family had been in business for about twenty years at that date.

In 1865, Wittmann died, and his widow Margarethe took over the business. While she would delegate management of the brewery to her sons as they came of age, sources indicate that Margarethe was in charge of the business. It is possible that the brewery lay dormant for a period after John's death, but the R. G. Dun reports give conflicting accounts: first claiming that business was "carried on by his wife same as before," but a year later said the business was "not doing much." Eldest son George was only fifteen when his father died, but appears to have begun operating the brewery soon after (though none of the family were listed as brewers in the 1870 population census). The 1870 census of industry reported production of 550 barrels, which indicates the family business had recovered well. In fact, under George's management, production climbed to 1,209 barrels in 1875 before dropping back to around 600 barrels in the last years of the decade.

In 1878, George moved to Kansas, and John Jr. took over managing the brewery for his mother. According to Sanborn maps and industry directories, Wittmann's brewery apparently never had a bottle house or a malt house. The company was usually listed under John's name until the brewery closed in the early 1890s. By 1895 the brewery lay dormant, but the buildings stood for at least a decade and were used for storage.

John Eggerer (1859?–1860?)

John Eggerer had a small brewery in Port Washington in the late 1850s and early 1860s. The $500 he had invested in the brewery was one of the smallest amounts recorded in that year's census. During the year prior to May 1860, he produced one hundred barrels of beer at his hand-powered brewery.

Frederick Knoepple (1859?–1860?)

Frederick Knoepple was listed as a brewer in the 1860 population census. The fact that he owned $1,500 of real estate and $1,200 of personal property suggest he was not an employee of another brewer. However, he was not included in that year's census of industry, which suggests that he brewed on a scale too small to be recorded in those listings. Knoepple (or Knipple) would later return to brewing as an owner of the Lakeside Brewery from 1876–1878.

Harbor City Brewing Co. (1996–2007)
535 West Grand Avenue

Jim Schueller worked at New Belgium Brewing Co. of Fort Collins, Colorado before moving to Port Washington to found Harbor City Brewing with his father Rod and brother Bob. When New Belgium co-founder (and Schuller's cousin) Jeff Lebesch expanded his brewery, Schueller bought the redundant equipment and installed it in a former ice factory. Harbor City brewed a few mainstream ales, but also offered Raspberry Brown Ale, a version of Main Street Brown Ale that featured Oregon raspberries. Harbor City brews were distributed in most of eastern Wisconsin, parts of central Illinois, and Bloomington, Indiana. The company also experimented with selling Mile Rock Amber Ale in Florida, though this version was contract brewed at Joseph Huber Brewing in Monroe (and was pasteurized to withstand

The scene of a barley harvest is accompanied by the statement "Brewed in small batches so we can keep an eye on the process and anyone trying to sneak a keg off the production line." Collection of Scott Reich.

shipping). The Harbor City labels were acquired by Sand Creek Brewing Co. after the Port Washington brewery closed.

Port Washington Brewing Co. (1996–2002)
100 North Franklin Street

Port Washington Brewing Co. was located in space leased from Smith Brothers Brewpub. Port Washington Brewing sold beer to Smith Brothers and distributed kegs to other accounts in Wisconsin. The brewery boasted of having the first complete brewery installation in the state by the W. M. Sprinkman Corp. of Waukesha and Elroy. In 1999, Port Washington Brewing contracted with what was then Pioneer Brewing in Black River Falls to produce their bottled beer.

Portage *(formerly Fort Winnebago)* *(Columbia County)*

Fort Winnebago Brewery
John M. Hettinger (1849–1867)
Feiss & Jaeger (1868–69)
E. L. Jaeger (1869)
M. Hettinger & Co. (1869–1871)
Nauer & Gloeckler (1871–75)
John Hettinger (1875–76)
Winnebago Brewery, Henry Epstein (1876–1901)
Epstein Bros. (1901–1918)
Jefferson & Canal (modern Edgewater)

The 1880 *History of Columbia County, Wisconsin* was unusually precise about the origins of the first brewery in what would become Portage:

> On the 12th day of May, 1849, John M. Hettinger, with his family, arrived in Portage from Freeport, Ill. His first work was the building of a shanty, to protect his wife and children from the storms; then he built a brewery, and painted it red; and although he insisted upon calling it the Fort Winnebago Brewery, the people disregarded his wishes, and persistently styled it the Old Red Brewery. By the latter name it has ever since been known.

Whatever the name, the brewery was operated with success for many years, until Hettinger's death.

It appears that the Hettinger family rented or leased their brewery in the late 1860s, because they disappear from the excise records for a few years. The firm Feiss & Jaeger first appear in the excise records in September 1868. The brewery was sometimes referred to as F. A. Feiss & Co. in the existing monthly records. In May 1869, Jaeger took over the brewery and operated it for a few more months. Under their proprietorship the brewery typically produced between ten and thirty barrels per month. Michael Hettinger reappears in the records in October 1869, and placed an ad that month that announced: "Having again taken possession of the well known Hettinger Brewery, I shall soon be prepared to supply customers with a Superior Article Lager Beer [sic]. The Highest Price for Barley will be paid, and a large quantity is wanted forthwith. Famers, bring it along and get your cash." Brother Matthias was also involved in the brewery for a time around 1870, when it produced 500 barrels, but after his death, the brewery went back to Frances, widow of John Sr.

Mrs. Hettinger retained the brewery only briefly, and sold it in late 1871 to Caspar Nauer and Barnard Gloeckler. Gloeckler was an experienced brewer, and "the new firm expects to manufacture a superior article of beer." Misfortune struck in 1874 when fire took the saloon and ice house, though not everyone was disappointed. A report noted that the saloon was "the only drinking resort in the Second Ward, and had long been an eyesore to residents of that ward, there was more interest manifested in saving the shade trees than the building." "Through some cause the property reverted again" to Frances Hettinger, and her son John Jr. ran the brewery until 1876, when the family sold the brewery to Henry Epstein.

Epstein moved to Wisconsin in 1866, and first was employed at the brewery in Pheasant Branch, then one in Madison, and finally as foreman of a Baraboo brewery before moving to Portage to take over the Red Brewery. The brewery Epstein acquired was the smallest in Portage by a large margin, producing less than a tenth of what rival Haertel brewed in a year.

The east end of the Wauona Trail was in Portage, so it was fitting for a brewery there to depict portaging the Wisconsin River on a label (ca. 1915). Collection of John Steiner.

But he made small improvements to the brewery over time and built up the business.

Increasing demand by the 1890s forced Epstein to plan an expansion that would bring his capacity to fifty barrels per day. The *Wisconsin State Register* reported: "Epstein's brewery is well underway, and will be completed on contract-time [sic]. Brewing does not seem to suffer from stringency in money and the general trades depression," referring to the Panic of 1893. The new brewery was steam powered, and was part of a series of modernizations that included adding a bottle house in the early 1900s. Epstein Bros. remained in business until the approach of Prohibition. The company was sold at sheriff's sale in 1920, and the site became the Purdy Rootbeer Co.

City Brewery
Charles Haertel (1851–1876)
Charles Haertel Estate (1876–1880)
Chas. Haertel Brewing Co. (1880–84)
Eulberg Bros. (1884–1907)
Eulberg Brewing Co. (1907–1920)
Eulberg Products Co. (1920–1933)
Eulberg Brewing Co. (1933–1958)
Ziegler Brewing Co. (1950–53)
112–122 West Conant and Clark Streets

Charles Haertel began brewing at the northeast corner of Cook and Clark streets in 1852. His initial production of twelve barrels per week was insufficient to meet demand, so he built a three-story brick structure in 1855, and expanded it again shortly thereafter. By 1860 he was producing 2,000 barrels per year at his horse-powered brewery, making it one of the largest in the state outside Milwaukee.

In 1862, Haertel began construction of a new brick brewery, since his existing plant was "becoming somewhat dilapidated." He built yet another major structure in 1865, with the help of Milwaukee architect Leonard Schmidtner (see chapter 4). The new brewery allowed him to expand production significantly. A visitor to the city reported:

> The brewery of Mr. Haertel is worthy of especial mention. Mr. Haertel is the Melms of Portage, manufacturing some 2,500 barrels per year of a beverage which certainly approaches quite closely to the Milwaukee standard of lager. His brewery and store are large, ornamental buildings, and a source of just pride to the Portaguese [sic].

The store mentioned in the passage was the building known as Haertel's Block, an impressive retail and office building next to the brewery. Haertel made an important addition in the late 1860s—an 1869 announcement indicated that he had bottled beer for sale, making him one of the very first lager brewers to do so. Haertel's brewery was an important stop for rising brewers. Among the most important of these was Peter Fauerbach, who married Haertel's daughter Mary (Maria).

Charles Haertel Sr. died in 1876, and his son-in-law Jacob Best (not to be confused with the founder of the Milwaukee brewery) took over management of the brewery, though it remained under the Haertel name. Best added a new bottling plant that could package ten barrels a day (though as noted above this was not the first bottling of Haertel beer). Best was also among the first Wisconsin brewers to use paper labels on bottles, since an example is known that likely dates to the late 1870s. Even with the death of the founder, the Haertel brewery produced an average of about 3,000 barrels per year during the latter part of the 1870s—among the largest in the state outside the Cream City.

Charles Haertel Jr. left brewing in 1884 and went into the hardware business, which he pursued until his death in 1888. Haertel leased the brewery to Adam and Peter Eulberg, who operated it as tenants until October 1892, when they purchased the brewery and the Haertel Block commercial building for $27,000—reputed to be "the largest real estate deal ever consummated in this county." Peter Eulberg trained as a brewer in Dubuque, and while Adam had been trained as a tailor, he had been a tavern owner in Dodgeville. (Descendant Dave Eulberg has chronicled the history of his family's business.)

The Eulbergs paid close attention to the quality of their water. In 1890 they experimented with several different brewing waters—sending samples from the Wisconsin River, the city well, and the brewery well to Chicago for analysis. Peter died in 1895, and Adam's side of the family took over the brewery, though Adam himself died in 1901. His eight children incorporated the company in 1907, by which time it was one of the largest businesses in the city (its only rival was Portage Hosiery Co.) During this period the brewery, under the direction of president and brewmaster John Jacob Eulberg, had a fifty-barrel

Mildred was the name of the beauty on this tray produced by the American Art Works of Coshocton, Ohio (ca. 1910s). COLLECTION OF LARRY BOWDEN.

This decorated glass dates to the 1890s. COLLECTION OF LARRY BOWDEN.

brewhouse with a capacity of about 15,000 barrels per year. During Prohibition the family kept the business going by making malt syrup and near beer. They also purchased the nearby Crystal Bottling Works in 1918 and bottled soft drinks until they sold this business in 1940. The family diversified by owning and operating the Portage Opera House for several years. However, the main focus of the family was still the brewery, though the brewery also became the focus of federal officials. The Eulbergs were fined $1,000 in 1924 for selling real beer. The fine and loss of their near beer permit did not deter them, and in 1931 the brewery was raided again. This resulted in a major haul for the feds, who turned up more than 300 barrels of beer still fermenting, along with numerous kegs and about 4,000 bottles of finished brew. The Eulberg product was shipped as far as Madison, and they supplied so much of the capital's market that it was expected "to cause a temporary 'drought' [there]." Julius and Joseph Eulberg were both convicted, and while Julius' sentence was suspended, Joseph lost his appeal to President Hoover and served a six-month sentence.

When beer returned, the Eulbergs returned to production. The family announced plans

588   THE DRINK THAT MADE WISCONSIN FAMOUS

to recondition the plant, and started making Crown Select again, which found a market in Portage and nearby cities such as Wisconsin Rapids, Milwaukee and Madison. The brewery sponsored multiple bowling teams—the Crown Selects and the Eulberg Brews. But the company ran into financial trouble almost immediately, and in November 1934 went into receivership. One consequence of the difficulties was the decision to hire a consultant, an unusual move for a small brewery at this time. James Thorson was tasked with building a new sales organization, but it appears that the brewery did not adopt all of his recommendations and sales continued to fade. The brewery was only selling four or five thousand barrels a year in the early 1940s, and in 1944 the family sold the brewery to Alvin Bardin for $55,000.

Under Bardin's ownership, Eulberg Brewing took advantage of the wartime surge in demand and pushed production up to approximately 16,000 barrels for a few years, but it then dropped again after the war. Part of the drop may have been due to the legal troubles Bardin encountered. Eulberg Brewing was charged in 1946 with selling beer at more than ceiling prices, though the Portage brewery avoided the charges of watering and underfilling that were leveled against Bardin's brewery in Denmark. Bardin was also sued for breach of contract by a Milwaukee distributor who claimed that Bardin failed to fulfill a deal to provide 200,000 cases of beer, though this case was dismissed. (Additional information about Bardin's legal woes is found under Denmark Brewing Co.) The tax claims were finally settled in 1957, but the expense of $7,933 for the brewery (reduced from $398,280) and another $79,916 for Bardin himself was probably more than he could absorb. In 1958, he closed the brewery and moved what was left of his brewing operations to Waukesha. The brewery had been producing between 10,000 and 12,000 barrels in the years before closing. The brewery had also served as a branch of Ziegler Brewing Co. from 1950 to 1953. One building on the corner of Wisconsin and Clark remains and contains offices as of this writing, other portions were razed and a supermarket was built on the site.

Barnard Gloeckler (1865–1871)
Farm Brewery in Fort Winnebago Township
Barnard Gloeckler (or Gloeggler) entered the brewing business in Wisconsin when he worked for Charles Haertel for about seven years (approximately 1856–1862). He then moved to Minneapolis and operated a small brewery there from mid-1862 to late 1863. He returned to Columbia County, where he bought a farm in Fort Winnebago Township (most likely in Section 32, though the spelling of the owner's name on the map is different). A county history from 1901 reports that "[H]e devoted himself to [the farm's] cultivation with much enthusiasm, but still followed his trade in the winter seasons. He was not listed as a brewer in the 1870 census, nor did he appear in the excise records at any point, so his production was likely very small indeed. In 1871 he purchased the former Hettinger brewery with his father-in-law Casper Nauer, so he most likely ceased brewing on his farm.

Potosi *(Grant County)*

Albrecht & Hail (1852?–1872)
Gabriel Hail (1872–1884)
Adam Schumacher (1886–1905)
Potosi Brewing Co. (1905–1920, 1933–1972)
South Main Street

According to most local accounts, Gabriel Hail came to Potosi in 1845 as a farmer, and by 1852 was brewing small amounts of beer for two local taverns. However, recent research suggests that Hail did not arrive in Potosi from Dubuque until 1854 or 1855. Around that time, Hail and partner John Albrecht began construction of a two-story brewery near a spring with clear water for brewing. The structure, valued at $1,100, took advantage of caves in the adjacent bluffs as a cellar for lagering the beer at sufficiently cool temperatures. By 1860, the census of industry reported that Hail and Albrecht had $5,000 invested in the brewery and equipment and produced 900 barrels of beer which sold for $6.50 per barrel (slightly more expensive than most of their rivals in the region). Their output ranked them among the larger rural breweries in the era, and compared favorably to the breweries in the larger city of La Crosse approximately one hundred miles away.

During the next few decades, the brewery grew steadily. John Albrecht left the partnership in 1872, and Gabriel's brother John joined the company and became brewmaster a few years later. At its peak in the mid-1870s, the brewery employed eight hands and produced about 1,250 barrels annually. However, the Hail family suffered business and personal problems later in the decade. The population of the town declined and so did business, and Gabriel Hail died in 1879. Local tradition has long had it that Gabriel took his own life, but more recent research has called this conclusion into question. John Hail took over the brewery for a few years, but production continued to decline, and the property was transferred either by sale or foreclosure to John Schreiner in 1882.

Adam Schumacher came from Bavaria to southwestern Wisconsin in 1879. He was employed by the Hail family at the Potosi brewery for the next few years, but when the brewery was sold Schumacher moved to the one owned by Joseph Vogelberg at nearby British Hollow. Sensing opportunity in a revitalizing Potosi, he moved back in 1886 and leased (and later purchased) the Potosi Brewery from Schreiner.

A rare tin sign with Adam Schumacher listed as the proprietor (ca. 1896). COURTESY OF NATIONAL BREWERY MUSEUM.

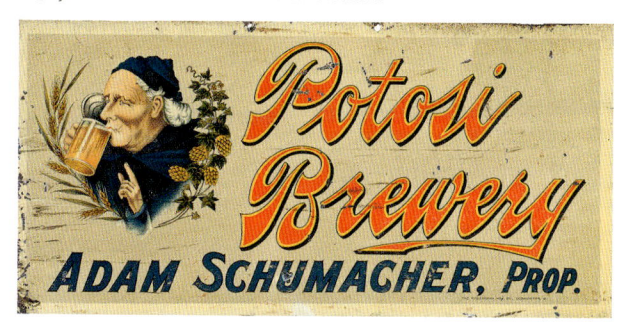

Adam brought his three brothers, Nicholas, Henry, and George, to Potosi and enlisted them in the business. The Schumachers expanded by adding a bottling facility and embraced advances in technology that some of their smaller rivals were unable to afford.

Throughout the early years of the twentieth century, the brewery expanded both its physical plant and its market area. Since the local market had a small population, the Schumachers sought customers throughout the region—eventually reaching markets in Iowa and Illinois as well as in southwestern Wisconsin. The company built a refrigerated storage depot in East Dubuque, Illinois to handle the southern portion of their market. Increased markets also required expansion of the brewing and packaging facilities at the brewery. From 1911 to 1916, the company added an office building, a tavern, a blacksmith shop, stables, a new ice house, and the brewery itself grew taller and bigger to accommodate a new 100-barrel copper brew kettle and other equipment. Little is known about the architects or the construction during this period—the structure gives a sense of economical additions rather than an attempt to advertise the wealth of the company.

The timing of the expansion, while similar to programs at other breweries in the region and essential to keeping up with them, was poor by the politics of the era. Potosi Brewing Co. lost part of its market when neighboring Iowa went dry in 1917, and the Schumachers began preparing for the worst. They started ice, coal, and dairy businesses, and purchased a dealcoholizer to produce near beer. Unlike most breweries that offered the non-alcoholic beverage, Potosi's Near Beer seems to have expanded the company's market, introducing the Potosi name to Kansas, Nebraska, and Minnesota. Like many other breweries during Prohibition, Potosi was accused of continuing to produce real beer during the dry years. Prohibition officers trying to stem the flood of illegal beer in Grant County inspected Potosi several times a month from 1922 to 1926. Eventually, agents received a tip that the beer was actually coming from the Cassville brewery.

The end of Prohibition in brought increased prosperity to Potosi Brewing Co. While Potosi was not one of the twenty-some Wisconsin breweries that were shipping on 7 April, they were ready about a week later, and re-established their market quickly. In addition to the local market, Potosi trucks carried beer to all neighboring states, and rail cars brought beer as far south as Texas and as far west as California and Arizona. In order to meet this demand, the company once again built new facilities and modernized equipment. The brewery increased staffing to fifty year-round employees, augmented by another twenty or so during the peak summer months. Interestingly, Potosi Brewing Co. was relatively late to adopt one of the most important innovations in American brewing—the beer can. Cans did not become part of Potosi's package mix until 1949, and even then they started with the cap-sealed "crowntainer," which could be filled on existing bottling lines.

Potosi's survival through the decades after the repeal of Prohibition was based on a combination of careful management, geography, and luck. While they were able to compete against large shipping breweries by depending on the devotion of Wisconsinites to their pitchers of tap beer, Potosi punched far above its weight class as a shipper of packaged beer. During the 1950s and 1960s, Potosi Brewing Co. purchased the right to a number of brands from defunct breweries, several of them from Chicago. One brewery employee recounted how different bottles would be shipped to the brewery, would be filled with Potosi's regular Holiday beer, given a different label, and shipped to Chicago. Potosi also followed the practice of several larger breweries by making special labels for chains of stores in Milwaukee, Chicago and other cities. Several students of the Potosi Brewing Co. contend that the brewery encouraged its employees to be represented by a union not so much for fair labor practices (because there were few complaints) but so that the union label would allow the beer to be accepted in the heavily unionized cities of the Upper Midwest.

All the pages have been torn off this calendar, but the story of the brewery printed underneath proclaims that the brewery was established seventy-five years earlier, meaning the calendar was likely from 1937 or 1938. COLLECTION OF MIKE KRESS.

Holiday Beer was a year-round product, but this cardboard advertising piece from the 1960s portrayed a winter scene—which could also evoke a refreshing cold beer during the summer. COLLECTION OF DAVID WENDL.

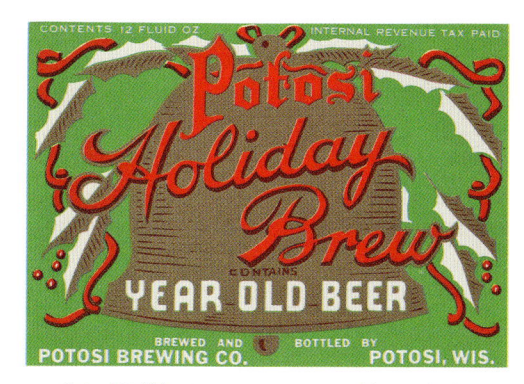

Potosi Holiday Brew was an unusual beer: the label indicated it contained "Year Old Beer." Many large brewers blended their beer, but few advertised it (except Pabst, during its "33 into 1" campaign). Those blends were to improve consistency, rather than create a different flavor, which seems the case here. COLLECTION OF TYE SCHWALBE.

While luck is hard to quantify and analyze, there are several factors that are inherent to a small family business that can determine success or failure. Potosi Brewing Co. was fortunate to have multiple generations of Schumacher family members who were able and willing to run the business, and who had the necessary training to do so. They were also able to attract skilled brewmasters from outside the family—no small task for a brewery far from an urban center with a limited labor budget. The position of the brewery in the local economy remained critical, as it did in the social life of the region. The brewery was still the largest employer in the area, and the brewery and its regional distributors sponsored teams and other activities around the region.

However, the continued consolidation of the industry and the end of some of their advantages marked the ultimate doom of the Potosi Brewing Co. The large shipping brewers increased their price-cutting promotions, many of which were designed to lower prices to a level the small breweries could not match for a sustained period. The market as a whole was shifting to non-returnable bottles, which either required new packing equipment or costly alterations to existing machines. New or even secondhand equipment could be much more expensive than a brewery could afford. In 1972, the company estimated that it would take nearly one million dollars to properly equip the plant for the next quarter century. The company did not have the cash on hand, and since production and market were both shrinking, banks were uninterested in making a loan likely to end in default.

Finally, time was running out for members of the Schumacher family and other key employees. President Adolph Schumacher was 81, cousin Rudolph had returned to run the bottling plant after having been retired for ten years, and all the other Schumachers were over 70. The next generation had little to no interest in continuing the business—Rudolph had returned because his son had left to take a job with John Deere in Dubuque, Iowa. Replacing longtime brewmasters became harder as the generation of German brewers retired. Small brewers were confronted with not just a lack of qualified individuals—few brewers were willing to work in a small town for lower wages than they could get at a major brewer or for a company in another field. While the brewery was still making a small profit, it was clear that there was no future for the company. "'It is hard to think that a business that never lost money should be closing,' Rudolph Schumacher lamented. 'I guess you could say that old age is creeping up on the Schumachers. And when you are old, you have to give up and quit.'"

The closing of the brewery cast a pall over the village. PBC was the only industry in town, and residents feared not just unemployment for many of the forty-five remaining workers, but loss of the tax base as well as water and sewer receipts for the village. The ripple effects were felt throughout the community. With the brewery gone, railroad business at the depot dropped significantly. Local businesses that supplied the brewery and its workers closed, forcing residents to leave town to get many of their needs. Even with these more urgent concerns, a few residents were also concerned about the loss of a local product. One employee of a tavern and beer depot complained "'while we will still be able to get it [Holiday and some other labels were purchased by Huber Brewing Co. in Monroe, Wisconsin], it just won't be the same. It won't be a local beer.'"

The brewery remained standing for the next three decades, though in a dilapidated state. The restoration of the brewery and the return of brewing are covered in chapter 10.

PRAIRIE DU CHIEN
(Crawford County)

Schumann & Georgii, Prairie Brewery (1855–1868)
Schumann & Kappel (1868–1870)
Schumann & Menges (1870–72)
Schumann & Menges, City Brewery (1872–1891)
Schumann & Menges Brewing Co. (1891–1909)
Schwarz Bros. Brewery (1909–1911)
Schumann & Menges Brewing Co., Gronert & Biittner, props. (1911–16)
Prairie du Chien Brewing Co. (1916–1920)
CHURCH STREET NEAR BLUFF STREET

Most accounts report that Theodore Schumann & Otto Georgii founded the Prairie Brewery in 1855. Schumann immigrated to Ohio in 1849 and farmed briefly before finding work in a Cincinnati brewery. He then brewed for two years in Guttenburg, Iowa, prior to moving to the east bank of the Mississippi. (Early state business directories list a brewery owned by Schibb, which is most likely a misreading of Schumann.) The brewery was already a significant business by 1860, producing 1,500 barrels that year with four employees at their horse-powered brewery. In the 1860 population census, Schumann was listed as a brewer and Georgii as a "dealer in beer," a division of labor seldom seen in the census. This apparently referred to Georgii's saloon "at the head of Bluff st.," where he advertised that "Lager Bier fsirom the single glass to any number of barrels can be had." He and Schumann "invite[d] their friends and customers to give them a call." In 1868 Georgii sold his share in the brewery to Fred Kappel, who remained for two years, after which he sold out to Michael Menges. Menges was trained as a carpenter, and was a contractor and builder in Prairie du

Chien. In 1871, Schumann & Menges began to sell bottled beer, using the services of independent bottler Andrew Bosch. The brewery at this time operated nine months of the year, and was still powered by horse.

It turned out to be useful to have a man of Menges' profession in the business, because fire destroyed the brewery in 1872. (Menges later became fire chief of Prairie du Chien, and started a fracas when he sprayed another citizen with the fire hose while testing it. Menges ended up the loser in the fistfight that followed, though editorial opinion held that both parties were at fault.) The partners began rebuilding almost immediately, and the new stone structure was named the City Brewery. The new brewery was substantially larger than the old plant, had a separate engine house for the boiler, and produced more than 3,200 barrels in 1878. By 1884, capacity was reported to be between 6,000 and 8,000 barrels, and the beer found "market in Wisconsin and Iowa, where eight salesmen are constantly employed." The brewery now had its own small bottle house located just south of the brewhouse. The brewery malted over 12,000 bushels annually, but was still forced to purchase a few thousand additional bushels each year. Cooling the beer required 1,800 tons of ice per year.

In 1894, the City Brewery was destroyed by a fire that also consumed the neighboring Garvey Block. The fire reportedly started in the barrel-pitching area, and spread to the brewery. The blazing malt created a particularly hot fire and ironically the fireproof iron roof prevented the firemen from reaching the conflagration. The building was insured for just over half the $22,000 loss, and as was common at the time, insurance was with several different companies—though it was unusual for a brewery of that size to use thirteen different insurers. They rebuilt immediately, and produced 5,000 barrels in 1895, though another fire in 1896 endangered the brewery. This one, believed to have been started by tramps sheltering in the brewery barns, was extinguished before it could spread to the brewery, but still

"A Close Game" was a popular sign by the Meyercord Company. Despite the wood-grained background, these signs were made of tin. This sign is from around 1912, when Gronert & Biittner were the proprietors of the brewery (which still kept the Schumann & Menges name). COURTESY OF NATIONAL BREWERY MUSEUM.

caused $3,000 of damage. A different misfortune struck just over a week later, when John Groenert, who had been a cellarman at City Brewery for two decades, drowned in a fifty-barrel cask. The brewery's own fire department proved to be of service when the nearby Prairie du Chien Woolen Mills burned in 1902—the Schumann & Menges fire engine provided one of the few effective streams played on the fire.

Founder Theodore Schumann died in 1905, though the brewery retained its well-established name even while others were leasing or operating the business. George Gronert and Franz Biittner leased the brewery for a few years in the late 1900s, and after the Schwarz Bros. operated it for a few years around 1910, Gronert and Biittner returned to management again. The brewery was put up for sale in 1915, and the ad in *Western Brewer* noted that the owner was selling on account of old age (presumably Michael Menges, who was 82). George Schwarz purchased the brewery and incorporated Prairie du Chien Brewing Co. in 1916, though by the next year Louis Silberschmidt was owner and president of the brewery.

The brewery stayed in operation through the first years of Prohibition, manufacturing cereal beverages and soft drinks they started producing in 1918. However, the brewery was raided in 1922, and appears to have lost its near beer license. Annual reports from 1924 and 1925 recorded only jobbing of soft drinks, and the 1926 document reported the brewery was closed. The company made an attempt to reform after Prohibition, but never went into production and the corporation dissolved in 1936.

PRESCOTT *(Pierce County)*

C. Haefner, Washington Brewery (1856–1861?)

Christian Haefner established the Washington Brewery in 1856. He continued to improve the brewery over the next two years, but offered it for sale in April 1858. The ad claimed: "It is well calculated for the brewery business or for any kind of business establishment." It is not clear if Haefner sold the brewery or not, but an 1861 newspaper article referred to "'A. Knoblauch, the brewer,'" without indicating what brewery he was associated with. There was an Adolph Knoblauch who in 1861 was in transition between breweries in Brownsville, Minnesota and Owatonna, Minnesota, but he would have had little time to either own or be employed by a brewery in Prescott.

Cook & Husting (1866–1870)
Nicholas P. Husting (1870–1891?)

Jacob Cook announced that he was starting a brewery in Prescott in 1865. The next year he was joined by Nicholas P. Husting, and they built a brewery near Lake and Hilton Streets that was in production by the end of the year. By 1870 they were making approximately 700 barrels of beer in nine months. Cook withdrew from the partnership in late 1870 and Husting continued alone. The evaluators of R. G. Dun & Co. made consistently good reports, affirming Husting was "Doing well [,] making money." Husting's profitable business enabled him to survive when in 1874 a vandal broke into the brewery and drilled a hole into a vat and destroyed about twenty barrels of beer.

Husting expanded his brewery in the late 1870s, and boosted production to around 800 barrels per year, which was mostly sold in Prescott and "in the country back from the river." Husting also raised livestock at his brewery, which he fed on spent grain from the brewery. The Wisconsin Industrial Census of 1885 reported production of 950 barrels, near the upper limit of the capacity reported in industry directories. After 1887 his business in Prescott seems to have languished. He may have worked for a time in Moorhead, Minnesota, but in 1891 he moved to nearby Ellsworth, Wisconsin to start a brewery there.

PRINCETON (Green Lake County)

August Weist (1857–1873?)
William Forster (1873?–76?)
Lutz & Messing (1876?–79)
Messing & Ernst (1879–1894)
John Ernst (1894–96)
John Ernst Estate (1896–1901)
John Ernst Brewing Co. (1901–1913)
Princeton Brewing Co. (1933–37)
36 FARMER STREET & HARVARD STREET

August Weist had been trained as a brewer in Hirschberg, Germany, before coming to America and Wisconsin in 1856. He started a brewery in Oshkosh with Tobias Fischer, but after less than a year he moved to Princeton to start his own brewery. The brewery was too small to appear in the industrial censuses of 1860 or 1870, a supposition supported by the relatively low $600 worth of real estate Weist reported in the 1860 census. The first reliable figures show production of just over 100 barrels per year in 1871 and 1872.

The transfer of ownership in the mid-1870s is not well-documented. Weist disappeared from the industry records after 1873, and William Forster is known only from an 1876 state directory. Sometime after this, John Lutz and Jacob Messing took over the brewery. John Lutz was son of brewer Andrew Lutz of Stevens Point, and the R. G. Dun reporter indicated that John's financial health depended on his father's wealth. In early 1879, Lutz returned to Stevens Point, and John Ernst took his place.

A "schnitt" glass produced between 1894 and 1896, when John Ernst was sole proprietor of the brewery. COLLECTION OF JOHN STEINER.

Ernst learned how to brew in Germany, and after arriving in America in 1875 worked at Philip Best Brewing in Milwaukee and for Schumann & Menges in Prairie du Chien. In a notable example of how intertwined Wisconsin's brewing families were, both Jacob Messing and John Ernst married sisters of John Lutz. Messing left brewing in the mid-1890s, and Ernst carried on alone until his death in 1896. A publication that came out just after Ernst's death praised his work:

> Mr J. Ernst, the owner of the brewery, has been engaged in manufacturing beer here for the past twenty years. He learned the trade of brewer in the old country. His beer is noted for its purity, brilliancy of color and richness of flavor so it is well liked by those who are judges of good beer. His plant which consists of a brew house, ice house, malt house, office, stables, etc., is located on the banks of the Fox River. The product consists of about seven hundred barrels per year which is sold in this and near by places. Mr. Ernst is one of the successful men of the village and has a large circle of friends both in the village and county.

The company continued in business under Ernst's name until it closed in 1913, under the supervision of Ernst's son-in-law Michael Gesse. The brewery continued to make modest improvements of plant and equipment throughout this period. The brewery's major brand at this point was Pure Health Beer—one of several named in a way to deflect claims of prohibitionists. The 1914 Sanborn Insurance Map lists the buildings as the John Haas Brewing Co., which seems to indicate that John Haas of Ripon purchased the plant either for expansion or storage, but the brewery was not in operation.

During Prohibition, the brewery made malt extract as Princeton Products Co., and apparently made no near beer nor wildcat beer during the dry years. After beer came back, John and J. Wilson Boyle, both of Fond du Lac, and Guy Johnson Jr. of Princeton restarted the brewery. The plant was in operation by September 1933, but production was modest at best: it approached 200 barrels per month in the summer of 1935, but dropped below 100 barrels at the beginning of 1937 and never exceeded that mark again. The company, at this point headed by J. W. Laper with Theo Radtke as brewmaster, ceased brewing in July 1937.

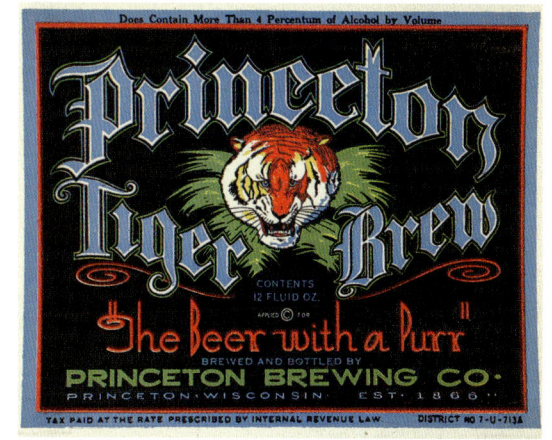

Princeton University's mascot is a tiger, and the brewery may have hoped this association would promote their beer. This label for "The Beer with a Purr" is probably from 1933, given the U-permit number at lower right and the fact that the beer was less than 4 percent abv (3.2 percent by weight)—all that was allowed until December 1933. COLLECTION OF JOHN STEINER.

WISCONSIN BREWERIES AND BREWPUBS 593

After the brewery closed, it served several purposes: a cheese factory, a warehouse, a Halloween haunted house, a mushroom growing operation and an antique mall.

RACINE *(Racine County)*

City Brewery
Heck & Braun (1848–1851)
Gnadt & Green (1851–57)
John Gnadt (1857?–59?)
Mary Gnadt (1859?–1862)
Fleisher & Zirbes (1862–66)
Philip Erhard Schelling (1868–1877)
Schelling & Klinkert (1877–78?)
Ernst (E. C.) Klinkert (1878–1904)
Ernst Klinkert Brewing Co. (1904–1920)
Belle City Products (1923–24)
EIGHTH STREET AND WESTERN PLANK ROAD (MODERN 828 WASHINGTON)

Racine's first brewery was founded by Frederick Heck and Johann Braun (John Brown) in 1848. Heck described his previous experience as "having brewed in France, Germany, Philadelphia and Milwaukee." Braun was proprietor of the City Brewery in Milwaukee. The 1850 industrial census reported that they had brewed 1,200 barrels in Racine, which sold at a local price of $5 per barrel. Braun died in 1851 from injuries sustained in a driving accident, and Heck sold the brewery to John Gnadt and Thomas Green. (Valentin Blatz took over Braun's Milwaukee brewery.)

According to Racine historian Gerald Karwowski, Green and Gnadt operated the brewery for several years, though it is not clear how long in partnership. Green was no longer in the city directory by 1858, and the brewery was listed in Gnadt's name only. In addition, by the 1860 census John Gnadt was gone and the brewery was in the name of Mary Gnadt. A brewer named David Lackman from Sweden was boarding with her, and was presumably taking care of brewing operations. At this point production at the brewery was down to 100 barrels, which probably was due to the frequent changes of proprietor.

In 1862, the brewery passed to Adolph Fleisher and Peter Zirbes, who ran the business until around 1866, when it was purchased by Phillip Erhard Schelling. The instability seems to have continued for the first several years of Schelling's ownership. R. G. Dun & Co. records indicate that Schelling sold out at some point in early 1869 (but did not indicate to whom). This might account for why a brewery that Karwowski and John Smallshaw claim had a capacity of 3,000 barrels was not included in the 1870 industrial census. However, by 1872 Schelling produced over 1,200 barrels and was not far behind Fred Heck's new brewery as the largest in the city. Production remained over 1,000 barrels per year for several years, and Schelling had improved his financial situation.

In 1877, Schelling took on a new partner, Ernst Klinkert, who had previously worked for Blatz in Milwaukee and Fred Heck in Racine. Klinkert soon bought out his partner, and from that point on the brewery bore his name. Over the next decades, Klinkert expanded the brewery on a regular basis and increased its market to the point where it was an important regional company. By 1879 he had already passed Heck to become the largest brewery in the city and would never again relinquish that status. By 1880 Klinkert had bottled beer for sale through his agent John Hartwig, though the advertisement did not make it clear if Hartwig was the bottler or merely a sales agent. Industry journals suggest that Klinkert also added his own malt house in the early 1880s. He undertook a $40,000 building project in 1884, and the new brewery was fully powered by steam, featured its own bottling house (and a soda factory) and had a capacity of 20,000 barrels per year. Klinkert soon had a railroad spur extended to the brewery, which would facilitate his shipping business. As early as 1887, he was shipping two carloads of beer to Milwaukee each week, at which the *Oshkosh Daily Northwestern* remarked: "This would appear like carrying coals to Newcastle."

Klinkert's moves into markets outside Racine drew the ire of the established brewers of those locales. In 1896, Klinkert was the target of a three-month-long "beer war," originally launched by Bohemian Brewing Co. of Chicago, but soon joined by Pabst, Schlitz, Obermann and other Milwaukee brewers. While the intent was to "crush Klinkert's home [Racine] trade," he lost little or no business, and "the local brewer, on whom the big brewery combine has been endeavoring to wreak vengeance for several months past, comes out of the scrimmage on top." On the other hand, in 1907, Klinkert's firm was rumored to be among the breweries involved in "a gigantic beer trust" that would consolidate "nearly all the beer manufacturers in the United States into a billion dollar corporation . . ."—a plan which never came to fruition.

Klinkert made regular appearances in industry journals noting the company's continuous improvements. The July 1909 issue of *Western Brewer* had two separate notes, one for installing new machinery, and the other for paving the brewery yards and roadways with brick—an expensive step worthy of a major regional brewer. The next year, *Ice and Refrigeration* announced that Klinkert was drawing up plans for a new power house (with a chimney that was among the tallest in the city), offices, and bottling works. The company's advanced

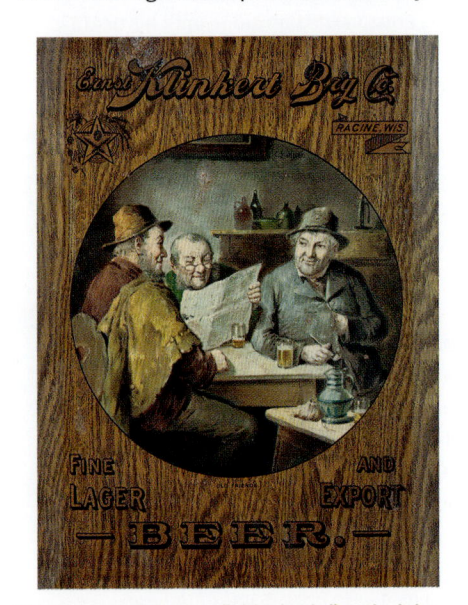

This Meyercord tin sign, "Old Friends," evoked the relaxed atmosphere that brewers hoped to associate with their product. COURTESY OF NATIONAL BREWERY MUSEUM.

equipment was sometimes used as a model for the entire industry: the Eureka Water Softener installed at Klinkert was featured in the September 1906 issue of *Power and Transmission*. Klinkert was also involved in other investments such as a hotel in nearby Corliss, in addition to a number of tied house saloons in Racine and the surrounding area. While Klinkert had a strong local following, Racine's location between Milwaukee and Chicago made it an attractive market for brewers in both cities. Klinkert's advertising argued for the loyalty of his local patrons with claims like "Your home brewery uses correct, old-time principles."

When Prohibition arrived in 1920, Klinkert Brewing attempted to continue brewing by taking advantage of some of the unclear features in the laws, but an injunction was issued in June 1920, and operations stopped, at least for the time being. (The brewery was fined in 1922 for violating the order.) The company briefly manufactured a malt beverage called Klinko, but like most others, it was not a success.

Belle City Products was incorporated in 1923 by George Lavin, Walter Smolenski and L. R. Larson and began operations the following June. However, it did not stay open long since it was raid a few months later and was ordered closed again. Thirty vats and 3,500 barrels of beer were ordered destroyed. This marked the end of brewing in the plant. A new Klinkert Brewing Co. was incorporated in October 1933, but plans never got past filing paperwork.

Henry Frey, Racine Brewery (1851?–1866)
Star Brewery
Goehring & Steiner (1866–68)
Jacob Goehring (& Co.) (1868–1877)
Engel & Co. (1879–1880)
George Hardweg (1880–83?)
Dorus Lyman (1883?)
Wedemeyer & Maas (1883?–85)
John Maas & Co. (1885–87)
Joseph Bezucha (1887–89)
Vincent Bezucha (1889–1891)
620 Stannard Street between Sixth and Water Streets

While most histories of Racine claim that Frey opened his brewery in 1852, evidence indicates that it was probably open the year before. In fact, in 1852 Frey (then spelled Fry) was trying to sell his brewery, an offer "made because the proprietor thinks his health injured by the climate...." The brewery at this point consisted of four buildings (one brick) with three cellars, as well as a horsepower and a twenty-five barrel brew kettle. This large establishment, as well as the fact that he had ale on hand which was included in the sale, suggests that he had already been in operation for some time. Apparently he abandoned his attempts to sell the brewery within a matter of months, because he was soon advertising that he had opened "a Summer House and Garden" where he could "offer to his friends the best Beer in Wisconsin, from a cool cellar, with a Spring of the softest and best water in the state."

Despite this auspicious start, his business was too small to make it into the 1860 industrial census, and he may not have been in continual operation (or residence in Racine) since he does not appear in the 1858 city directory or the 1860 population census. Frey left the business in 1866, after which it was taken over by Jacob Goehring and Ferdinand Steiner, who renamed it the Star Brewery.

Goehring had other partners in the brewery: the company was listed as Gehring and Elsner in the excise records from 1868–1870, and was listed later as Goehring & Co. (by various spellings). In 1870, with the one employee (and one horse), Goehring produced 450 barrels of beer, a total he boosted to nearly 800 barrels in 1872. While the brewery was in good financial shape during the late 1860s, the R. G. Dun & Co. evaluators reported that Goehring was deep in debt by 1873, perhaps because of expansions to the brewery. At the end of 1873, the Dun reports indicated the brewery had failed. Goehring had a personal mishap in 1873 as well: while leading one of his horses into the stable, the horse drew back and the halter caught Goehring's hand, pulling off part of one of his fingers. He walked to the doctor, had the finger taken off at the second joint, and was "doing well." Mrs. Goehring buried the part of the finger that had been torn off in a box." The ownership for the next few years is not clear. Karwowski indicates that Goehring continued to operate it until 1877, which is certainly possible, though he is not found in Dun records after 1873. He is also not in Schade's Annual of 1876, though other brewers are missing as well, nor is he in the 1876 Racine city directory. *American Breweries II* lists George Schlenk as the proprietor of the Star Brewery, but this is unlikely since the only brewer matching this description was brewing in Beloit at the time and there is no evidence he owned both breweries.

The next recorded owners of the Star Brewery were Valentine Engel and George Hardweg, known as Engel & Co. Excise records indicate that this firm started selling beer in January 1879, and Salem's list records production of 194 barrels in the first part of that year. In 1880, Dun & Co. reported that Engel had sold out and that Hardweg was now sole proprietor (the later Engel & Co. references are to his next brewery). Dorus Lyman was the owner of this brewery for much of the 1880s, though it appears that he leased it out to others much of this time. The 1882 city directory listed him as operating the brewery saloon at 620 Stannard, and the Dun reports of 1878 say he did not actually run the brewery (though he may have owned the property and operated it later). The 1883 city directory lists the proprietors as Henry F. Wedemeyer and John Maas. Wedemeyer owned a saloon at 1100 St. Clair, and Maas appears to be the partner who did the actual brewing. The same firm was still listed in the 1885 directory, but by 1887 the directory listing was John Maas & Co. Lyman's name was still listed on the highly reliable 1887 Sanborn maps.

The Star Brewery was struck by fire in March 1884, but the fire was confined mostly to the malt house and damage was only about $500. (A *Milwaukee Sentinel* account of the fire confirms that Wedemeyer and Maas owned the stock of beer but that Lyman owned the building.) A few years later, a chimney collapsed, but again the damage was only a few hundred dollars.

The 1888 city directory featured an ad for Joseph Bezucha, who was a lager beer brewer at the Stannard address. However, the 1890 directory listed Vincent Bezucha as the brewer at the Star brewery. Joseph appears to have moved to Hillsboro at this point, and Vincent had been a brewer in Racine at least since the 1880 census listed him as a brewer there (though it is not clear at which brewery he worked, and he was listed as doing other jobs in city directories in the 1880s). Either way, he was only at the Star brewery briefly, as the brewery closed in 1891.

Heck & Beebe (1852–58)
Fred Heck (Heck & Co.)(1858–1882)
EIGHTH AND CENTER STREETS

After Fred Heck sold the City Brewery, he started a new one with F. Beebe just over a block to the east. By 1858 Beebe sold out to Heck, and the new firm, Heck & Co. was comprised of Frederick and Philip Heck. Two other family members, Christian and Wilhelm, boarded at a house a block away while working at the brewery. Heck's brewery soon became the largest in the county, and in 1860 he produced 1,800 barrels. Heck occasionally had partners in his business: Dun & Co. records of early 1860 listed Heck & Schmidt as the name of the business, and noted that Emil Schmidt "was one of the guards of the State Prison at Waupun." This combination dissolved in 1860 and Heck carried on alone. In 1873 they reported that the firm was now called Heck & Wurst, though there was only one entry under that name.

In 1853, Heck wrote a letter in defense of pure lager beer to the *Racine Daily Advocate*, in response to allegations that the poison *coculus indiens* was being imported into the country for use in lager. In his reply, he offered to "any gentleman, however, (a chemist) who will analyze my lager beer, and find any other articles than the four above mentioned, I will pay the sum of one hundred dollars." This may be the earliest American example of the cash reward for proof of impurities (later $1,000) that became common in the early twentieth century.

Production peaked in 1870 at 2,300 barrels, though they surpassed 2,000 barrels again in 1878. Heck was arrested for violating the revenue act, but the *Racine County Argus* was of the opinion that an employee must have been responsible for the mishandled tax stamps since Heck "was not that kind of a man." The reporter's confidence was apparently vindicated, since the next year the paper enthused

> Heck is the proprietor of one of the most extensive establishments in this vicinity wherein is manufactured the best quality of Sage beer. The city brewery has 5 cellars, 2 for fermenting purposes and three for lager beer or stock. The number of men employed will average six—teams two. The business extends to Illinois and throughout Wisconsin.

(It is not clear what is meant by "Sage beer." It may have referred to the Sagetown neighborhood.)

Unfortunately, Heck began to have financial problems. By 1878, the Dun reports indicated that this "old resident" had been having bad luck, but was coming back. By 1882 his difficulties had returned, and he was out of business around the end of that year.

Buhler & Wolf (1856?–1858?)
Charles Wolf (1858?–1882?)
Casper Bertram (1883?–1884)
HARRIET STREET AND RAPIDS ROAD (MODERN NORTHWESTERN AVENUE), MT. PLEASANT

Racine historian Gerald Karwowski places the opening of the Buhler & Wolf brewery in the mid 1850s. By the publication of the 1858 city directory, the business was under Wolf's name alone. (Buhler may have been Edward Buhler, who was listed in the 1858 directory as a cooper.) The history of Wolf's brewery is more obscure than others of similar size, because for some reason he was not included in the industry directories of the time. The 1870 industrial census reported his production in the preceding year as 1,200 barrels, which made his brewery the second largest in the Racine area. Despite this status, and the popular beer garden behind the brewery which was a favorite of the local German community, Wolf could not sustain his success. By 1881, the R. G. Dun & Co. credit reports showed that he was doing only a small business, and that he was having trouble meeting his obligations. In May 1882, his brewery was closed on attachment to satisfy a claim of what several state newspapers reported was a claim of $56,908—a staggering amount for a business of that size. Indeed, the reports were corrected soon after to indicate the amount was actually $569.08. The Dun records suggest he continued to operate the business for at least another year even though he longer owned it, but it went out of business shortly thereafter. According *Western Brewer*, Casper Bertram took over the brewery for a short period, but he seems to have been out of business by 1884.

Badger Brewery
John Dearsley & Orrin Baker (1856–1860?)
John Dearsley (1860?)
STATE STREET IN SAGETOWN

At the end of December 1856, a new advertisement appeared in the *Racine Daily Journal*:

> Good News! Something for the Public! Pure Home-Brewed Ale! Manufactured at the Badger Brewery! John Dearsley & Co. Having recently established a brewery in this city, where they manufacture none but the Purest of Ale! Would call the attention of the public to this fact. They pledge themselves to make none but the pure article.

Dearsley's ale could be found on draught at the Empire Saloon on Main Street, which was also where orders could be placed for larger quantities. (Their business was also listed in the 1858 city directory as a "porter house," emphasizing the English character of their beers.) R. G. Dun & Co. reported in early 1857 the company was Dearsley & Barker *[sic]*, but by 1860 Dearsley was on his own and still apparently brewing (though he was listed as a saloon-keeper in the 1860 census). The same records indicate that Dearsley had moved to Milwaukee by 1862, and Gerald Karwowski dates the closing of this brewery to 1860.

The story of the Badger Brewery is complicated by another business of that name in Racine that operated at the same time.

Phillip Zirbes (1857–1861?)
Chippewa (later Park Avenue) & Sixth Streets

Phillip Zirbes started a grocery store in Racine in 1851. Around 1857, he added a brewery to his operations. While he expanded his grocery business by buying out a competitor in 1860, he apparently extended himself beyond what his assets could support. The R. G. Dun & Co. reported in 1861 that he was insolvent, "but still brews and sells beer." He appears to have stopped brewing in the early 1860s, but his wife continued in the grocery business and his son Peter took over the company in 1876.

Service & Co., Racine Brewery (1858)

The Racine Brewery of Phillip Service & Co. is known only through the 1858 city directory. Peter Service was the partner in this business, which was located near the Racine and Mississippi Railroad roundhouse, on Water Street between Center and Campbell. It is possible that they had leased or rented Henry Frey's Racine Brewery for a year, which would explain Frey's absence from the city directory that year. The location described is within a block of the Racine (later Star) Brewery on Stannard.

Badger Brewery: Shepherd & Co. (1859–1860)
Erie Street, Near the Ship Yard

In March 1859, a second business with the name of Badger Brewery started business in Racine. Shepherd & Co. advertised that "the Badger Brewery is in full blast, and is now turning out a good supply of the best English Home-Brewed Ale, Treble XXX and Double XX Stock Ale. . . ." They also sold yeast and grains at the brewery (presumably spent grains for livestock feed) and indicated they were willing to exchange ale for wood. Ads for this Badger Brewery continued through early 1860, after which it disappears from the records.

William Williams, Hope Brewery (1859?–1868)
Fourth Street (Opposite J. I. Case) (1860?–61?); Chippecotton Street (Modern Mound Avenue) South of Liberty (1861?–68?)

William Williams appears to have started either in early 1860 or before, since by the time of the 1860 industrial census he had already brewed 430 barrels of ale. An advertisement in July 1860 for his brewery on Fourth Street announced that Williams was "now prepared to furnish Pale, Amber and other Ales, and Porter of a superior quality highly recommended be [sic] the medical faculty to invalids &c.," which was "put up in large and small casks to suit purchasers."

The 1862 city directory listed the address of the Hope Brewery as Chippecotton Street, south of Liberty, so Williams may have needed a larger plant to supply the demand. The teaser in an ad from April 1866 referred to a major technological feat of the era when it proclaimed: "The Atlantic Telegraph Not in Operation! Williams' Brewery in Full Blast." Clients were informed that orders could be left at John Kimber's store, and would be delivered to railroad depots free of charge. A later ad announced that bottled porter and ale were always on hand, as well as the draught article.

Williams' new brewery appears to have extended him beyond his means, even though he was doing a fair business. The R. G. Dun & Co. credit investigator reported in July 1868 that "It is rumored he has run away and his [property] has been attached." A later entry clarified: "A few days ago he silently slipped off at Chicago [,] he wrote to some friends that he had started for England." Williams absence from excise records after 1868 seems to confirm that he left Racine at this time.

Adolph Weber (1868–1870)

Adolph Weber (or Webber) first appears in the excise records in 1868, and remains through June 1870 (though may have been in business longer). Weber's brewery was a small facility (with only $1,000 invested as of 1870), but produced enough beer to be reclassified from small to large in 1870 as it reached 500 barrels. Weber does not appear in other records, so it is difficult to locate his brewery or confirm these dates. It is also possible that he leased or rented another brewery—and the years and size of the brewery suggest it could have been Erhardt Schelling's second brewery.

John Heath (1868)

John Heath made a single appearance in the excise records in 1868. Heath was a businessman in Racine who may have simply been the partner who paid the excise tax for another brewer, but it is not clear who this would have been.

Lakeshore Brewery
Robert Grant (& Co.) (1870–74)
George Paradis (1875–76)
Edmund Dotten (1876–78)
William H. Weber (1878–1902)
William H. Weber Estate (1902–4)
Weber Brothers (1904–1912)
78 (later 1501–1509) North Michigan Street

According to excise records, Robert Grant & Co. appears to have sold his first beer in April 1870. The 1870 population census lists sixty-nine-year-old Joseph Grant (presumably the father of forty-one-year-old Robert) as a worker in the brewery. Their brewery was a small one—production was only seventy-eight barrels in 1871 and 137 the next year. French-Canadian immigrant George Paradis was the next owner, but production under him remained small—just sixty-five barrels in 1875. Paradis sold out to Edmund Dotten (or Dutton) in 1876, and he only held the brewery a short time before selling it to William H. Weber.

Stoneware bottle use peaked in the 1870s, so this one likely dates to the early years of Weber's ownership. Collection of John Steiner.

Weber took over the brewery in May 1878, and put it on a sound footing for the rest of the century. An 1888 city directory ad proclaimed W. H. Weber to be the brewer of "the celebrated White Lager Beer," and added that bottled beer "for family use" could be delivered to any part of the city. Industry directories indicate that Weber made both lager and weiss beer, so it is not clear if White Lager Beer was a hybrid style or a brand name.

After Weber's death in 1902, his sons Charles and Ernst took over the brewery and renamed it. It remained in business until 1912, specializing in weiss beer during the last few years of operation. In 1912 a fire destroyed the brewery, but the brothers had sold the property to the city some months earlier. Both brothers went into other occupations, and made no attempt to rebuild the brewery.

Jens Stephenson (1871–1875?)
Jens Stephenson & Hans Anderson (1875–77)
Northside Brewery
Anton R. Deinken (1877–79)
Deinken & Schad (1879–1880)
Deinken & Reiplinger (1880–81)
Deinken & Biwer (1881–83)
Deinken & Engel (1883–85)
Valentine Engel (1885–1890)
Branch of Klinkert Brewing Co. (1890–92?)
1627 DOUGLAS AVENUE

Jens Stephenson first appeared in the excise records in September 1871. Around 1875 he was joined in business by Hans Anderson. The evidence of the R. G. Dun & Co. records indicates that Anton Deinken joined in late 1877, but Stephenson stayed with the firm for a time. Deinken went through a series of partners, looking for financing, though the Dun reports indicated that Deinken's mother may have been helping him with money. Deinken fell foul of the law in 1883, when he was convicted of "giving away" beer at his brewery on a Sunday.

Western Brewer reported in December 1883 that there was a new brewing firm in Racine under the name of Engel & Co., which appears to be another name for Deinken & Engel. The brewery was powered by horse throughout its existence, and there was no bottling house on the property. Engel, an experienced brewer, took over the business on his own in 1885. (One source listed the name as E. Henkel, which is almost certainly a misreading of Engel.)

At the end of 1890, Ernst Klinkert purchased the brewery (which was referred to in several accounts as the Eagle Brewery). The *Weekly Wisconsin* noted that "Milwaukee parties were after it, but Klinkert headed them off. He now owns all the breweries in the city." The latter claim was inaccurate, since Erhard Schelling still operated his brewery farther out on Douglas Avenue. A fire at a brewery in 1896 was reported as at Engel's brewery. Since local accounts say that Engel stayed on as an employee of Klinkert, it is possible that he continued to operate this plant for a time as foreman of that location. However, the 1894 Sanborn insurance map indicates that the brewery was not in operation at that point, and the fire may well have been in an empty facility.

P. Erhard Schelling (1894–1904)
OLD MILWAUKEE ROAD (LATER DOUGLAS AVENUE)

Several sources hold that Schelling started his brewery on the north edge of Racine immediately after leaving the City Brewery. However, there was a gap of more than a decade before his next brewing venture. After he sold his share in the City Brewery, Erhard Schelling (or Shilling) apparently took up religion with what could only be described as mania. The *Milwaukee Sentinel* reported in 1892: "Gerhard Schelling, an inmate of the county insane asylum, had a jury examination and was declared sane. Schelling was ten years ago one of the most prosperous citizens of Racine. He owned a large brewery and considerable other property, but he became eccentric, sold out his brewery, made large donations to the church and used his money lavishly. . . ." Another account said "The gentleman experienced religion and became insane on the subject." Yet another article inaccurately claimed he attacked his doctor with an axe (it was actually Frank Schilling, who was not of the same family). However, an 1894 article in the *Sentinel* reported that he was "no longer under guardianship," and noted "he owns a lucrative brewery." This brewery appears to be his second brewery, located next to what was then Lincoln Park (now Douglas Park). According to another report on his restored health, the new brewery was producing about ninety barrels per week (which works out to an unlikely 30,000 barrels per year if that pace were maintained).

In 1900, a fire nearly destroyed the brewery, though quick action by the fire department stopped the blaze from spreading. Schelling (who was listed as Peter in this article, though there was no such person in Racine at the time) was burned about the face, but survived. The brewery went out of business around 1904, about the time of Schelling's death.

Christen Stephenson (1883?–1885?)
812 FOREST

Western Brewer first reported Christen Stephenson's brewery in November 1883. He was listed in Wing's 1884 directory as a small ale brewer, and the 1885 Racine city directory listed him as a brewer of "Danish ale" located at 812 Forest.

Belle City Brewing Co. (1895–1910)
Racine Malt Co.
Olsen & Feddersen (1910)
1210 STATE STREET (1895–1901); 1506–16 STATE STREET (1901–1912)

Hans C. Olsen formed Belle City Brewing Co. in 1895 and by July was advertising his non-intoxicating Crown Table Beer, which he claimed was "made exclusively from the best malt and hops." Ads in 1902 proclaimed that Crown Malt Ale was "delivered through the city at 70¢ for 12 quart bottles." In 1905, Belle City even advertised a Christmas Brew, which was "not only a flesh builder, but acknowledged as the most healthful of all malt brews." By 1907, Belle City had added a malt tonic—a more traditional product for a business focused on the health-giving properties of malt and hops. However, they still had a beverage as well as a medicine—this time called Health Table Malt, of which Belle City proclaimed "It is as much entitled to a place upon the table as bread."

Western Brewer reported that Belle City Brewing closed in late 1907, but the company

In 1907, Belle City Brewing advertised that Crown Malt Ale could be found "at all First-Class Saloons," suggesting an attempt to provide a beer alternative in places not usually receptive to the beverage. This label is from the brief period in 1910 when the firm was Racine Malt Co.
COLLECTION OF JOHN STEINER.

was still in other directories through 1910. Olsen and his partner Andrew Feddersen changed the name of the company to Racine Malt Co. to better describe the nature of their products, but this apparently did little to improve business. The company was declared bankrupt in January 1910, but was back in business selling a new product, Malt Marrow, later that year. This marked the end of manufacturing products locally, since Malt Marrow was a product of McAvoy Brewing of Chicago. When Olsen left the company, the stance on non-intoxicating beverages appears to have loosened, since Feddersen was listed as the Racine agent for McAvoy Brewing of Chicago. Malt Marrow was still offered, but the focus was now on McAvoy beers. On the eve of Prohibition, the company introduced Alpha malt beverage, but this was yet another product from McAvoy, rather than anything brewed locally.

The Prohibition-era Belle City Products Co. was located in the former Klinkert brewery, and was not an extension of this Belle City Brewing Co.

Benjamin Beer Co. (2016–17)
507 SIXTH STREET
This site in downtown Racine is the second location of Benjamin Beer Co. (the first was in Paddock Lake to the west). Founder Jim Kennedy and lead brewer Matt Jung sought to put an American twist on classic beer styles. This location closed in late 2017.

RANDOM LAKE
(Sheboygan County)

Charles Hamm, Silver Creek Brewery (1903?–1910)
Chas. Hamm Brewing Co. (1910–1920)
William G. Jung Beverage Co. (Products Co.) (1920–1933)
William G. Jung Brewing Co. (1935–1958)
CARROLL STREET NORTH OF FOURTH STREET

Many local accounts claim that Charles Hamm Sr. moved his brewery from Silver Creek to Random Lake around 1903, so it appears that this was not simply a case of Hamm listing a different post office as his address. In addition, the descriptions of the location are different enough to indicate this was not the same location. Typical of these was one in the *Sheboygan Press*: "This brewery . . . originally was located at Silver Creek adjacent to the old distillery. About twenty-five years ago Mr. Hamm had the building erected in the village of Random Lake."

Charles Sr. sold the brewery to his son Charles Jr. in 1910, and retired from business. The younger Hamm was looking to expand in 1911, and advertised in *American Brewers' Review* that he was in the market to purchase a "second hand brewery outfit, 50 bbls. Capacity." His new brewery was four stories high, included a new office and power house, and cost $30,000.

Charles and Joseph Hamm sold a majority share in the brewery in 1915, each ninth of a share realizing just over $5,000 at the sale. (The new buyer was not listed.) But the name of the brewery remained the same until Prohibition. (Joseph C. Hamm, son of Charles, moved west in 1912, and after Prohibition would serve as a brewmaster in Kalispell, Montana and Portland, Oregon.) The importance of Charles Hamm to the village was exemplified by the naming of the local American Legion Post after him. Shortly after this sale, William G. Jung leased the brewery. He was the son of William Jung of Milwaukee, and had been brewmaster at Star Brewing in Lomira. Through 1919 Jung was still making 2.5 percent beer, but had already introduced a variety of soft drinks. Believing this line of products showed promise, Jung installed new bottling equipment in late 1919. In 1921, Jung Brewing was shut down temporarily for selling beer with more alcohol than allowed, and for operating a de-alcoholizing plant without a state permit. The company eventually solved its legal problems, and produced under the Jung name throughout Prohibition, though Jung actually did not purchase the plant until late 1931. Jung paid $20,000 for the real estate and equipment and an additional $5,000 for the trade and trademarks of Charles Hamm Brewing Co.

Jung Brewing Co. had their brewing permit by May 1933 and planned to have beer on the market as soon as possible. Jung was one of several brewers who made a virtue of the fact that their beer was not available right away, claiming: "'We are going to give the beer plenty of time to age, realizing that the first impression they get of our beer will be a lasting impression. When our beer gets on the market, those who drink it will know they have had the real old brand.'" Jung added new bottling and refrigeration equipment, and made plans to employ fifteen men regularly. By November 1935, they were brewing a very respectable 2,000 barrels per month, and the next summer Jung manufactured 2,600 barrels per month. In 1939, Jung Brewing sold over 23,000 barrels of beer, and was making a small ($1,500) profit.

A 15-ounce bottle of Ideal Beer from around 1900.
COLLECTION OF JOHN STEINER.

WISCONSIN BREWERIES AND BREWPUBS   599

For several decades after Prohibition, mini-bottles were a popular brewery souvenir. Some were replicas of the full-size bottle, often filled with liquid to simulate beer. Others were salt and pepper shakers, and this example was a bottle opener. The Old Country Beer label was used around 1933–35.
COLLECTION OF DAVID WENDL.

The company usually was among the top thirty breweries of the roughly eighty in the state, and was among the very largest compared to the size of its home community.

Jung's product was received well in the vicinity, and the company promoted their Old Country Beer twice a week on the radio program "Beer Garden of the Air," broadcast on WHBL of Sheboygan. Jung was not large enough to stage a major promotion on their own, but in 1940 they teamed with several other area businesses in a contest that featured a grand prize of a 1940 Chevrolet. Labels from Old Country Beer (now in "steinie" bottles) and the reintroduced Jung Pilsener could be converted into "votes" in the contest.

The labor shortage of World War II apparently hit Jung Brewing hard. In May 1942, the company advertised for an experienced office manager, with the proviso that he "Must be married," presumably so he would not be subject to the draft. Other help wanted ads appeared during the war, and almost immediately after V-J day, the company advertised "steady employment" for several men in the brewery. In fact, Jung was one of the few breweries that survived World War II whose production dropped significantly during the war, though it recovered by 1945.

In 1952, Herman Sitzberger took over ownership of the brewery. Sitzberger started in brewing at Rahr Brewing of Oshkosh, came to work as brewmaster at Jung in the mid-1940s, left for a few years, but returned to Jung in 1950. Karl and Hugo Jung, sons of William, continued in their positions at the brewery. However, while the brewery once enjoyed "a large market at resorts and taverns in northern Wisconsin" as well as in Sheboygan County, rising costs and shrinking sales forced Jung Brewing Co. to cease production in April 1958. Kingsbury purchased most of the useable equipment and cooperage, and the building was converted to other uses. The bottling house served from 2008 to 2012 as the home of the Random Lake Area Historical Society.

READFIELD *(Waupaca County)*

Peter Grigger (1856?–1858?)

The brewery of Peter Grigger is known only from the 1857 and 1858 state business directories. Historian Wayne Kroll also includes it in his list of Wisconsin farm breweries, but there is no person that matches this description in the 1860 census, so Grigger's term as a brewery may have been a short one.

READSTOWN *(Vernon County)*

William H. Austin (1853–58)

The 1907 history of Vernon County claims that Austin settled at Readstown in 1853 and built a small brewery, which burned a few years later. "As the brewery had failed to supply a popular beverage, when a new building was constructed the business was changed to a distillery; but this also failed, and the building was washed away in the spring of 1857, never being replaced." But the *Richland County Observer* reported in September 1858: "The brewery of W. H. Austin, Readstown, Badax [sic] county, was consumed by fire on the 22nd—loss near $5,000. The dwelling house, and contents, and the dancing hall, in the same building, all being connected together, were burned, constituting a part of the loss." This seems to indicate that the brewery was still in operation at this date, and that the fire was later than the 1907 account claimed. This seems to have been the end for this brewery, since Austin became a lawyer and left the state.

B. S. Hale (1883?–1884?)

Bradstreet's credit reports for Wisconsin in 1884 list a B. S. Hale as a brewer in Readstown. Hale does not appear in other sources.

REEDSBURG *(Sauk County)*

Reedsburg Brewery
F. & F. Mechler (1870–73)
Frank Mechler (1873–74)
Mechler & Schroeder (1877–78)
Reedsburg Brewing Co. (1879–1920)
Reedsburg Brewery, Inc. (1933–1947)
The Reedsburg Brewing Co. (1949–1950)
401 NORTH WALNUT STREET

Considering that Reedsburg was in the center of the Sauk County hop-growing district, it is surprising there was not a brewery there in the 1860s. The brewery of Frank and Florian Mechler (various spellings) was clearly in operation by January 1870. They paid excise taxes that month, and had produced enough beer to be recorded in the 1870 census of industry. (However, the 2,400 "kegs" of production must have been pony kegs or similar small containers, since the value of inputs and beer sold fit better with production of about 300 barrels.) In early ads the Mechlers called their business the "Reedsburg Wholesale Brewery," which may have meant they did not have their own saloon on the premises.

The Mechlers dissolved their partnership in February 1873, and Frank continued the business on his own for a time. Mechler was in the process of making improvements to his "already extensive brewery," but in 1874 the brewery was destroyed by fire. The records seem to indicate that Mechler did not rebuild immediately, which would explain the absence of a Reedsburg brewery from Schade's directory of 1876. By 1877, Mechler was back in business with a new partner, Fred Schroeder. However, this partnership only lasted about two years, and by the end of 1878 Mechler was "busted" and he retired from brewing and took a farm at Loganville.

In 1879, the bankrupt business was purchased by Henry Geffert and John and Peter Hagenah. They "at once commenced the work of making additions and other improvements on a large scale," and were joined in 1880 by William Dierks. This group formed Reedsburg Brewing Co., which one of only a handful of Wisconsin breweries at that time to be officially named after the city rather than the founder. A feature of the brewery that drew special notice was

> ... the summer beer vault, situated a few rods northeast of the brewery. It was perfected at a cost of nearly $5,000 and is doubtless, the best vault in the State. Here the temperature is kept at 40° Fahrenheit, only 10° above the freezing point, and this, during the hottest of summer weather. It is a complete refrigerator, on a scale sufficiently extensive to accommodate nearly 10,000 gallons of beer.

The capacity of this new plant was about sixty barrels per week, which was more than many small town breweries in the early 1880s. The brewery also had a malt house, which provided an important market for the surrounding farm communities.

Reedsburg Brewing Co. continued to develop its local market over the following decades, with occasional changes in ownership. In 1895, the Wisconsin industrial census reported production of 3,000 barrels. By 1885 William Pahl had replaced the Hagenahs, and in 1896 Albert Fuhrmann purchased the brewery from Geffert and Pahl. Fuhrmann modernized the brewery, replacing horsepower with steam and adding a large water tower to the property. In 1904, this plant was destroyed by fire, giving Fuhrmann the opportunity to start all over. He erected a massive four-story brick building, this time oriented toward Walnut Street rather than Fourth Street. He also added a bottling plant and a separate pitch house,

"Compliments of" indicates that these small shell glasses (ca. 1900) were given to customers rather than sold to saloons. COLLECTION OF TYE SCHWALBE.

perhaps to eliminate a common cause of brewery fires. The brewery was threatened again by fire in 1916, though this blaze was stopped before it could do any significant damage. Ironically, the fire was first spotted by the local Baptist minister, Rev. J. Farrell, who notified the Fuhrmanns and helped organize a company of volunteers. This demonstration of civic duty from one whose faith called him to oppose strong drink earned nationwide news coverage. The business was incorporated in 1917, and continued to operate through 1919.

During Prohibition, the brewery lay idle for ten years, but in 1929 Hans Johnson of Milwaukee leased the brewery from Fuhrmann to make soft drinks. However, the drinks they produced were not as soft as the law required, and in February 1930, the plant of Reedsburg Products Co. was raided and "a quantity of alleged beer" was seized.

When beer returned, so did Reedsburg Brewing Co. Hans Johnson remained in charge, and he sought to expand business throughout southwestern Wisconsin and even into eastern Iowa. Robert Bechaud of Fond du Lac purchased the brewery in 1939, but had an unusual bit of legal trouble in 1940 for violating federal wage and hour laws. The company agreed to pay back wages to affected workers.

World War II also caused difficulties for the brewery. Supplies were short for all businesses and households, and the brewery had to make special application to get four new truck tires in 1942. The legal and wartime difficulties combined in 1944 when the brewery was charged with selling beer for more than was allowed by wartime price ceilings. Phillip Schweke sold the brewery "to Chicago parties" in 1946, but sales were nowhere near the brewery's 25,000 barrel capacity, and increased costs forced Reedsburg Brewery to file for bankruptcy in 1947. The brewery was offered for sale late that year by Albin Bill, the brewmaster and acting trustee. L. C. Dobbert and K. P. Graber purchased the shuttered brewery and re-opened it in 1949 featuring a new brand—Blue Wing beer. However sales remained around the 1,000-barrel per year mark, and the brewery closed for good in 1950. After being used for storage purposes for many years, the brewery was converted into apartments in the late 1980s.

In a strange epilogue to the Reedsburg Brewing story, Frank A. Weaner, who was associated with the brewery in the late 1940s,

Advertising Old Gold Lager Beer on a clock guaranteed that the brand would be noticed whenever a patron checked the time. The clock dates to the 1930s, when Old Gold was called a lager rather than a pilsner, as it was later. COLLECTION OF TYE SCHWALBE.

WISCONSIN BREWERIES AND BREWPUBS 601

formed a company in 1949 to sell "beer for use as hair champoo [sic]." The product was de-alcoholized and "decarbonized" and then had detergent added.

EndeHouse Brewery & Restaurant (1996–2002)
Corner Pub Brewery (2002–present)
1020 EAST MAIN STREET (1996–2002); 100 EAST MAIN STREET (2002–PRESENT)

EndeHouse Brewery was located in a historic Victorian house named for the Ende family that occupied it for more than a century. Pete Peterson first opened Pete's Supper Club, but by 1996 started using the restaurant to showcase recipes he had perfected as a homebrewer. After brewing at this location for about seven years, Pete Peterson moved his brewery about a mile west on Main Street to the Corner Pub.

The side of the Corner Pub facing Webb Avenue features a large mural commemorating the years when Reedsburg was the center of Wisconsin hop growing. Peterson divides his time between making fresh hamburgers and fresh beer. There are typically about ten beers on tap (some of which were on the menu at EndeHouse), covering the full range of beer styles—though the emphasis is on ales. Annual production is typically over one hundred barrels. In addition to housing a brewery, the Corner Pub is a classic small-town Wisconsin tavern that features live music several times a week. A peek under the raised stage provides a glimpse of the brewhouse below.

REESEVILLE *(Portland Township) (Dodge County)*

Philipp Jaeckel (1867?–1873?)

Philipp Jaeckel operated a tiny farm brewery in Portland Township (the nearest post office was Reeseville in Lowell Township) for several years. While some sources have him starting around 1860, his first appearance in the excise records was in December 1867. The only known production figures are from 1871 and 1872, when he produced thirty-one and thirteen barrels, respectively—little more than some twenty-first century homebrewers. He was still paying excise tax in February 1873, but after that disappears from the records.

RHINELANDER *(Oneida County)*

Rhinelander Brewing Co. (1893–1967)
1 OCALA STREET

Rhinelander Brewing Co. was the longest-lived and perhaps most successful of a later generation of breweries—those formed as corporations as opposed to those that grew out of a family business. Any brewery founded in the 1890s needed to start at least reasonably big to have any chance to compete against the established shipping breweries. Rhinelander was in an area with few local breweries, but that was no guarantee of success.

Like many breweries of this era, Rhinelander Brewing Co. was founded at least in part by investors from larger cities. In this case, Otto Hilgerman was a businessman from Minneapolis, which was about the same distance from Rhinelander as was Milwaukee. The first version of this business drafted its articles of incorporation in July 1893, and was in production shortly thereafter. The founders seem to have been thinking big, since the articles of incorporation authorized the company to "build or lease and own and operate a brewing plant or plants." The brewery began to build its market quickly—though a bit too quickly in one case, since the brewery driver was arrested and fined in May 1894 for driving too fast on the city streets. Rhinelander promoted its business in many of the typical ways, such as having a float in local parades.

Hilgerman, Henry Danner, and the other founders were able to start with a steam-powered brewery and modern beer storage facilities, unlike those breweries founded earlier that were forced to convert from horsepower and subterranean cellars. Unfortunately, the brewery was of frame construction, and they were not able to avoid the fiery fate of so many other breweries. The brewery was destroyed by fire in November 1897, and like many other breweries, was only insured for about half the amount of the damage. However, the paper in Hilgerman's former home, Minneapolis, reassured readers that "He had a good business and will probably rebuild." Luckily, several months worth of beer were saved, so there was some revenue coming in while Hilgerman rebuilt, this time in brick.

Throughout its history, Rhinelander Brewing advertised at rate more typical of much larger brewers. It had regular newspaper ads beginning in 1898 after the new brewery was finished, urging customers "Don't Let Beer Get the Best of You! Get the Best of Beer, which is Rhinelander Beer!" In 1900, the company ran a different newspaper ad every week for more than a year, including one just after the 1900 presidential election which claimed:

> *The Political Game of See-Saw has now ceased to interest the country, and the question of procuring the purest and best beer is agitating the people. All voters, as well as their wives and wives mothers, will agree that for strength, purity and exquisite flavor the beer made by Rhinelander Brewing Co. can't be beat....*

Another ad in the series pointed out that Rhinelander offered both light and dark beer, and seemed to indicate that both were available in bottles. Yet another, this with a Thanksgiving theme, advertised delivery of pints or quarts "upon personal, postal or telephone request." During Spring 1903, the brewery advertised both their bock beer and their new

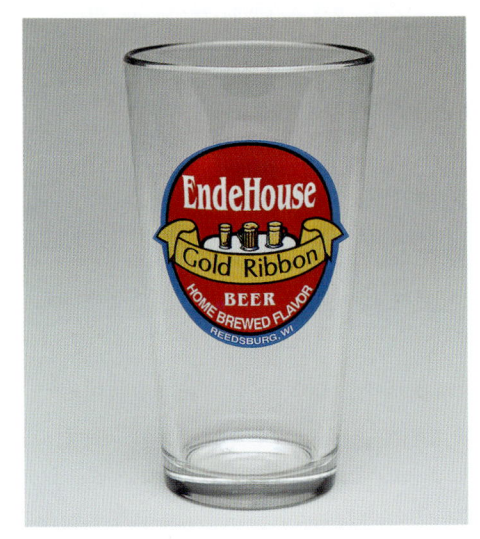

A "shaker pint" glass from the EndeHouse era.
AUTHOR'S COLLECTION.

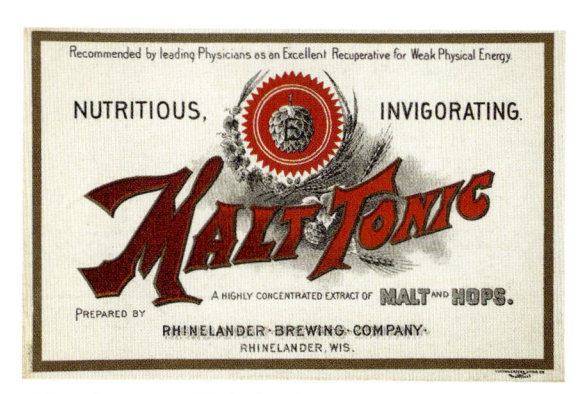

Malt Tonics were not limited to the major shipping breweries. Rhinelander Brewing Company produced this brand around 1910. COLLECTION OF JOHN STEINER.

malt tonic, which was a common enough product for major urban brewers at this time, but unusual for a smaller brewery in the countryside. This seems to be another indication that Rhinelander Brewing Co. planned to compete with the shipping brewers at least to some extent. Advertising slowed in the middle of the decade, and the newspaper ads followed the industry trend of making health claims for the beer.

Rhinelander Brewing Co. appeared to be well managed and profitable throughout the period prior to Prohibition. An article in 1911 about a routine board meeting added "It is understood the brewery will pay a substantial dividend."

Rhinelander's ability to produce anything during Prohibition was hampered by the fact that in 1921 "a company of Mexican capitalists" purchased the equipment of the brewery to be shipped to Mexico and installed in breweries there. Thus, when it was time to prepare for legal beer in 1933, the brewery had to be completely rebuilt with new equipment. Because the new owners, including Otto Hilgerman's son George, had enough capital (most of it from Minneapolis investors), this may have given them an advantage over other breweries of similar size that tried to make do with refurbishing old equipment rather than being able to start with the most efficient new brewhouse. The *Rhinelander Daily News* went into great detail about the plant, even mentioning the "Schlangen rocker" [racker] and the Yundt bottle washer. It drew a comparison between the old brewery "where the bottles... were cleaned with warm water and a handful of shot, the bottles in the new brewery will be cleaned with a massive and expensive machine operated by electricity and with heat-control units...." An equally important comparison was made with "a home brew outfit" which produced "cloudy, yeast-containing home brew." The brewery ran several ads urging potential customers to have patience while the beer aged properly, and by the end of November, the beer was ready for sale. Unlike some other smaller breweries, Rhinelander beer was ready both on draught and in bottles right away—others had to wait several months while bottling equipment was readied. In August 1934, they announced that "Good Old Rhinelander Beer" was available in pony kegs as well. Other ads adopted a theme common in the nineteenth century but less so after Prohibition, that Rhinelander was "A Local Product Deserving of Local Patronage." Another interesting feature of Rhinelander's return is that the beer was available to its Michigan accounts right away, rather than waiting to expand its market after reestablishing the home market. With a 50,000-barrel brewery in a sparsely populated region, Rhinelander would have to reach a broad market immediately. However, Rhinelander certainly did not neglect its home market. They encouraged tours of the brewery (again, unlike many of their small town rivals) and held contests where anyone who signed the guest register at the brewery was eligible to win a free case of beer.

Like many of its rivals, Rhinelander brought back bock beer: the first newspaper advertisements for it were in March 1937, though it is possible it was offered in previous years. Their bock was offered in "Willies" or smaller bottles (that year only), as well as the standard 12-ounce package and on draught. By 1937 the company had also begun using the slogan "Refreshing as the North Woods" to evoke the good memories of a hunting or fishing vacation. (During the late 1950s, the brewery placed flyers in cases of beer promoting vacationing in the Northwoods.) In 1939 the brewery had two different beers for sale: Rhinelander Beer and Export Beer.

But the line expansion the company would become best known for appeared in January 1940—the "Shorty" bottle. The 7-ounce package was an instant hit, and by August 1941 the brewery ran advertisements thanking "our friends in Northern Wisconsin, who have bought almost 5,000,000 Shortys." The brewery sponsored a baseball team named the Rhinelander Shortys, but was most famous for its advertising campaign. At first, they used simple text ads reminding readers that "Shorty Will Be There" at numerous events around town. As World War II was ending they hired Ross Lewis, cartoonist for the *Milwaukee Journal*, to create a series of cartoons which appeared on postcards, matchbooks, and other items. Wisconsin collector and historian Otto Tiegs has identified at least 128 different "Shorty" cartoons, some of which used wartime topics. Rhinelander Brewing also had their own airplane which was used for special events and once to transport Senator Joseph McCarthy from Milwaukee to a speaking engagement in Ashland.

During World War II, Rhinelander continued to produce between 20,000 and 30,000 barrels per year, and their advertising urged customers to buy war bonds and contribute to the Red Cross. Employees' productivity was critical to continued success during the war and after. In 1956, bottle house superintendent Charles Imwold figured out a way to adapt the bottle filler to fill flat top cans, which were displacing cone top cans in popularity with both brewers and the public. While cone tops were disappearing by the late 1950s, some smaller brewers continued to use them since they could be filled on existing equipment. Imwold's innovation made it possible to change packaging without needing to buy new equipment.

The last decade of Rhinelander Brewing echoed several of its small-town counterparts. Long-time owner Larry Henning sold the brewery in 1958 to Harold Bloomquist, a salesman with the company, and M. Wesley Kuswa, a Milwaukee lawyer who vacationed in the area. At this time, the brewery still employed thirty-five people and was one of the largest businesses in the city. The company introduced new packaging, such as the 12-pack of Shortys, which was promoted primarily on price and convenience: "12 ounces more than you get in a 6-pack." Even when selling a special beer, price seemed paramount. In 1959, ads for Rhinelander Dark Beer, released specially for the holidays, mentioned the expensive ingredients, but emphasized it was available "at no increase in price." In order to improve efficiency, the company remodeled the brewhouse in 1960 and added several new pieces of equipment at a cost of $30,000. At this point the brewery was still in the black, and had recently opened five new distributorships in Minnesota, in addition to the existing forty-one in Wisconsin, three in Northern Michigan, and two in the Chicago area. The brewery sold more beer in July 1959 than it had in any other single month in history, and the company clearly felt it was on the right track.

However, Rhinelander then made a decision which may have hastened the decline of the brewery. When Wausau Brewing Co. closed in 1961, Rhinelander acquired the Schoen's Old Lager, Adel Brau and Rib Mountain Lager brands. Long-time brewmaster Otto Dietz disagreed with purchasing these brands, though they apparently did not upset the brewhouse routine since the beer packaged under the various brands was simply Rhinelander. These brands were marketed as low-price beers, which was of limited benefit to the company. Production, which had been consistently above 20,000 barrels until 1961, began to drop considerably—and was near 12,000 by 1965. The brewery began to suffer financial reverses, and Dietz left Rhinelander for Oconto Brewing (and later for Hamm in St. Paul). The company ceased operations in June 1967, and was declared bankrupt in August of that year. The labels were purchased by Huber Brewing Co. of Monroe, so Rhinelander Beer continued to appear on store shelves for years to come.

Bugsy's Sports Bar/Brown Street Brewery (1998–2013)
16 North Brown Street
Bugsy's was started by brothers Earl "Butch" and Albert "Bugs" Meinen. They enjoyed vacationing in the area, and wanted to bring locally brewed beer to Oneida County. The bar and brewery occupied the former Fenlon Hotel building. In addition to the house beers, the bar carried a number of other commercial beers, which often diverted attention from the brands made on the premises. Brewing was intermittent through13, and Bugsy's closed in 2014.

Rice Lake *(Barron County)*

Lakeside Brewery
John Fuss & Charles Saile (1874–79?)
Charles Saile (1879?–1882)
Saile & Rudolf Arnstein (1882–83)
Charles Saile (1883–86)
Elizabeth Saile (1887?)
Southside Brewery
August Kuchera (1889–1890)
August Geisert (1890–91)
Rice Lake Brewing Co.
Geisert & Mueller (1891)
Mueller & Boortz (1891–92)
Mueller & Bernhardt (1892–96)
Richard Bernhardt (1896–97)
Jacob Dick (1897)
George Ruff (1897–98)
Joseph Dick & Co. (1898)
Adam & Joseph Baier (1898–1904)
Phoenix Brewing Co.
Jos. & Adam Baier, Adam Houck (1905–9)
J. Baier, Adam Houck, J. Hanzlik (1909–1917)
East Allen Street/119 East Freeman Street
The John Fuss who helped start the brewery in Rice Lake appears to be the same John Fuss whose Waukesha County brewery burned in February 1874. Charles Saile had brewed at multiple locations in Minnesota prior to moving to Rice Lake. Saile and Fuss apparently borrowed money to build the brewery and had trouble repaying their creditors at first, since Knapp, Stout & Co. (a lumber company and the largest business in the area at the time) sued Saile and Fuss for non-payment of a $100 note and for non-payment of almost $600 of lumber and supplies used in their building.

Fuss left the business prior to 1880. Rudolf Arnstein joined for about two years starting in early 1882, but by 1884 Saile was on his own again. A visiting correspondent reported in 1885 that Saile had produced "160 barrels of the amber beverage" in the previous year. Saile died on the last day of 1886, and his wife took control of the brewery for a brief period, though it may have lain dormant for some time around 1888. The next owner of the brewery, August Kuchera, left the brewery in October 1889, but in May 1890 "absconded" leaving his wife and creditors in the lurch. Shortly

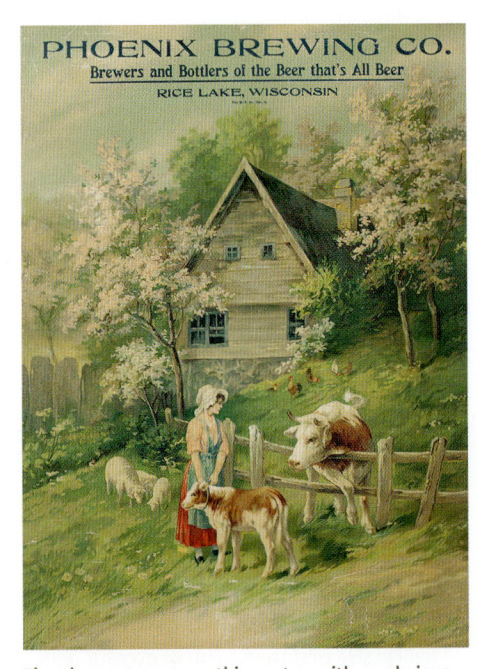

The pleasant scene on this poster, with no obvious connection to beer or brewing, was designed to draw the eye to the name of the Phoenix Brewing Co. Collection of Herbert and Helen Haydock.

thereafter, new owners, including Saile's son-in-law August Geisert, took over the brewery. The next decade saw frequent ownership changes, and while the arrivals and departures were duly recorded in local newspapers, the accounts said very little about the operations of the brewery. Adam and Joseph Baier provided a brief period of stability for Rice Lake Brewing Co., but this only lasted for about six years.

In 1905, the Baiers and Adam Houck formed a new corporation, Phoenix Brewing Co. In 1909 Joseph Hanzlik joined the firm, and shortly became president of the corporation. The brewery suffered a fire in the malt house in January 1916, and the company never quite recovered. Phoenix Brewing stopped making beer in June 1917, though it reopened in August 1918 to manufacture soft drinks.

Gottfried Beyrer, Brush Brewery (1892–95)
Scharbillig Bros. (1895–97)
Frederick Beyrer (1897–1902)
Schimmel & Glassbrenner (1902–5)
CUMBERLAND ROAD

Little is known about the operations of Rice Lake's shortest-lived brewery. Gottfried Beyrer started the business around 1892, but appears to have leased it to Scharbillig Bros. For a short time. Gottfried's son Frederick took over the brewery for several years. The malt house burned down in 1900. Joseph Schimmel and Leonard Glassbrenner acquired the brewery for a brief period after Frederick Beyrer left to revive a brewery in Long Prairie, Minnesota. The brewery closed in 1905, but a few years later was remodeled for a cheese factory.

Rice Lake Brewing Co. (1936–1974)
816 HAMMOND STREET

After legal beer returned, John G. Breunig first tried to resume brewing in Bloomer at his family's former plant. However, he had volunteered to serve by proxy a prison sentence for his father Jacob S. Breunig, who had been convicted of violating Prohibition laws in Bloomer. As a result, federal authorities denied his application for a brewing permit. He tried again in Rice Lake, and was successful, though Scott

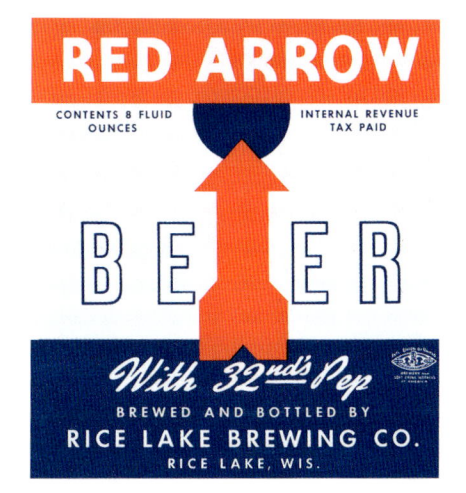

The 32nd Infantry Division ("Red Arrow") fought in World War I and in the Pacific Theater in World War II. It was later reorganized as a brigade comprised of National Guard units from Michigan and Wisconsin and fought in Operation Iraqi Freedom from 2004 to 2009. Only a few beers are known to honor particular military units. COLLECTION OF TYE SCHWALBE.

Thompson, a Breunig family member, suggests that the permit may have been submitted under the name of one of the other officers in order to evade detection.

Since the previous sites in Rice Lake were no longer available, Breuing and his backers acquired the former New Idea Potato Machinery plant in 1934 and began the process of converting it to manufacture beer. Like many new breweries, construction moved slowly, and brewing did not begin until the summer of 1936. The first draught beer was on the market in September of that year. The next year, 12-ounce and quart bottles were added to the mix. During the difficult economic times of the 1930s, brewery workers either were required to buy stock or were paid in stock. This was not necessarily a bad thing, as the brewery paid a 15 percent dividend to twenty-three local stockholders in 1938.

While Breunig's beer was normally found only within a sixty-mile radius of Rice Lake, the brewery shipped carload lots of 8-ounce bottles of special Red Arrow Beer to members of the 32nd Wisconsin National Guard, who had been mobilized in the early 1940s and were stationed in Louisiana and Texas.

The end of Rice Lake Brewing is better documented than many of the other small breweries that closed during the 1960s and 1970s. The brewery was still profitable during the early 1970s, but was the smallest brewery in Wisconsin and was reported to be the second smallest in the country. It was brewing a few private labels for markets in Minnesota and Wisconsin, as well as Breunig's Bock. However, the brewery was caught between price increases for supplies (malt jumped from $1.90 per bushel to $2.90 per bushel during 1973) and increased competition from low-priced beers of national breweries. The break-even point for Rice Lake Brewing was $2.45 per case, but other breweries were able to sell around $2.00 per case. The increasing scale of brewing also worked against a small business like Rice Lake—cans had to be bought in lots of 250,000 at a time, and near the end there was not enough beer in the vats to fill that many cans, nor anywhere to store them. The board of directors voted to dissolve the company in September 1973, and packaged the last beer early in 1974. Of the eighteen remaining employees one, 72-year-old Douglas McFarlane, was there when the brewery opened and when it closed. The labels were sold to Walter Brewing Co. of Eau Claire, which continued to make Breunig's Lager for a few more years. Jack Breunig was able to find a position at Anheuser-Busch—moving from one of the smallest breweries in the country to one of the biggest in the world. Portions of the brewery were razed, but part remains and as of 2016 housed a health club.

RICHFIELD *(Washington County)*

Jacob Gellner (1860?)

Jacob Gellner is only known from the 1860 population census. While it is possible that he was employed by another brewery, his location in the census is not near any of the other Washington County brewers. It is also possible that he was not practicing his trade at this point.

RICHLAND CITY
(Richland County)

W. E. Louis (1856?–1858?)

The brewery of W. E. Louis (various spellings) is known to have been in Richland City at least by 1856, since a visiting journalist reported: "This village in Richland county, containing over 500 inhabitants, has . . . 1 brewery . . . as yet it has no church." The local paper also carried advertisements for Louis' beer during much of 1856. Louis (as M. E. Lewis) remains in the 1857 and 1858 state business directories, but these were not always up-to-date, and it is unclear exactly when Louis started or ceased brewing. It is less likely that Aloix Fix purchased his brewery and continued the business.

Alois Fix (1859?–1861?)

Aloix Fix purchased land for his brewery in Richland City in 1857, and was probably brewing by the next year. He reported as brewing 50,000 gallons—around 1,600 barrels—in the 1860 industrial census. This seems like a very large quantity for such a remote brewery, but Fix was reported to have invested $3,000 in the brewery, and other breweries with similar or less value produced over 1,000 barrels in that census. It is not clear when he stopped brewing here, but he moved to Cazenovia in 1864. Richland City was largely abandoned as the Wisconsin and Pine rivers changed their courses.

RIPON *(Fond du Lac County)*

William R. Pierson (1856?–1872?)
JEFFERSON STREET

William R. Pierson appeared in the 1857 state business directory, but may have started brewing before then. By the time of the 1860 industrial census, he had $3,000 invested in his small hand-powered brewery. For this census, he reported the unusually precise total of 234 barrels of beer brewed in the previous twelve months (which sold at $6 per barrel). He remained in excise records through 1868, though his absence from later years as well as his absence from the 1870 industrial census is not conclusive, since several other breweries known to have been in operation at the time were not listed either. He is still listed in an 1869 history and directory of the region (which provides the Jefferson Street address—the street runs parallel to Silver Creek). He appears in the 1870 population census as "Agt—Patent Right *[sic]*," though this does not eliminate him from continuing to own a brewery at this point. Pierson's last appearance in public records as a brewer was in the 1872 state business directory. It is possible he ceased brewing before then.

Ripon (City Beer) Brewery
Haas & Fischer (1865–1870)
Haas & Klieforth (1870–72)
John Haas (1872–1907)
Haas Brewing Co. (1907–1915)
Ripon Brewing Co. (1933–37)
130 JEFFERSON STREET

The Ripon City Brewery was rather unusual for a brewery of its era, in that it took over a structure built for another purpose fifteen years earlier, rather than building a new plant. John Haas moved in to the former woolen mill and started brewing in 1865. His brewery grew at a measured pace, and by 1870 he was brewing 450 barrels per year in eight months of operation. However, he nearly doubled his production in the next two years, and by the beginning of 1873 he had bought out his most recent partner and was now sole proprietor. The R. G. Dun & Co. records gave Haas positive ratings, and at the end of 1873 noted that he had "never been burnt out," a rarity among breweries at that time.

By the end of the 1870s Haas' production was close to 1,300 barrels per year, and he was looking to markets beyond Ripon. During the summer of 1877 he built a stone bottling house, and within a few years it was reported that "Mr. Haas has large orders from surrounding cities" and that "Bottling and shipping beer is now one of the prominent features of his business." The local market was not neglected, however. In June 1878, it was reported that "John Haas . . . has given his annual 'treat.' It took 42 kegs of beer to go round."

The claim that Haas had "never been burnt out" was premature. The brewery suffered a catastrophic fire in June 1884 that started in the engine room and destroyed the new steam-powered equipment and about $5,000 worth of malt. As was typical, Haas had only $7,000 insurance to cover a loss estimated at $18,000. However, Haas rebuilt immediately, and on a greater scale than before. The *Milwaukee Daily Journal* took note of the construction and editorialized: "The ultra good people of Ripon jubilated *[sic]* when the local brewery burned down. The local brewer is preparing to rebuild upon a scale only exceeded in Milwaukee, and there is sadness in the tents of the faithful."

John Haas ended up being one of the longest-tenured brewery owners in Wisconsin, but in 1896 he considered selling his brewery to Gustav Kuenzel, who left the Obermann brewing company when it went bankrupt and changed hands. The deal was not consummated, and Kuenzel purchased the Lutz brewery at Stevens Point instead. After Haas' passing in 1907, his son C. (Conrad) John took over the brewery and operated it until around 1916. Some sources have the brewery closing as early as 1915, but in 1916 burglars blew open the brewery safe and absconded with $300 worth of revenue stamps—an unlikely haul

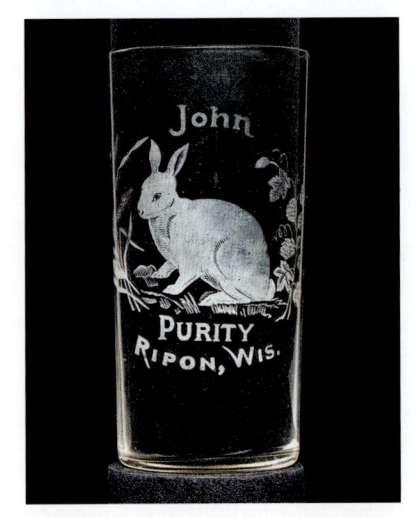

The name Haas means *hare,* so the proprietor put only his first name on this glass and let the picture of the animal stand for his family name (ca. 1890s). COLLECTION OF JOHN STEINER.

from a closed plant. C. John Haas died in Chicago in December 1918.

Charles Storck leased the brewery in 1920 for making ice cream and cereal beverages, however the brewery was raided in 1922 and 234 barrels of beer were seized and later dumped into Silver Creek. Shortly thereafter, Jacob Figi acquired the brewery, but was unable to obtain the necessary permits to manufacture near beer.

In 1933, the return of beer signaled welcome work for the tradesmen of Ripon, in addition to a remedy for local thirsts. New owners Louis Strong and Jack Wittstock employed dozens of men to rebuild the brewery, and by late 1933 the company had beer on the market again. While Ripon Beer was unremarkable except for its low price (it was by far the cheapest beer advertised at the Beer Depot in Sheboygan), Ripon Brewing became much better known for its Old Derby Ale. Seeking to attract younger drinkers or those who had gotten used to stronger beverages during Prohibition, Ripon's Old Derby Ale was advertised as having an alcohol content of 12 percent and was available either in bottles or on draught at select locations in the region (and was distributed in Oshkosh by Peoples Brewing Co.) Old Derby was typically sold at 10¢ per glass instead of the usual nickel, and was sometimes advertised as "mellow," which was apparently code for "strong." This was not enough to make the brewery profitable, and the company closed in April 1937.

Knuth Brewing Company (2015–present)
221 Watson Street

David Knuth was a homebrewer who decided to start his own brewery after being inspired by a trip to Washington D. C. and reflecting on the risks the founders took as entrepreneurs. He and his wife Marie co-founded Knuth Brewing Co. in a former bakery and restaurant site. The brewpub also features pizza baked in a wood-fired oven. Knuth sees the beer and pizza as related elements of gourmet cooking where he can create something from scratch.

Knuth began with two beers, but has since expanded the lineup to six or seven at a time, featuring his Red House Ale, named after the color of the house in which he made his first batch of homebrew. Knuth upgraded to a seven-barrel system in August 2016 to help him meet the local demand and to keep a bigger variety of house beers on draught.

River Falls *(Pierce County)*

Charles (Carl) Krauth (1860?–1877)
Hickey & Meyer (1877–79)
Charles Krauth (1879–1883)
Henry & Albert (1883–84)
John Schneider (Krauth & Schneider) (1884–88?)
Main Street South of Pine Street

Charles Krauth is listed as a lager beer brewer in the 1860 population census. His brewery was not large enough to be listed in the industrial census of that year, but since he reported $1,000 of real estate and $300 of personal property, it is likely that his brewery was already relatively large for the place and time. He built a "large addition to his brewery" in 1866, though it cannot have been particularly large, since the brewery's largest known production was 307 barrels in 1878, which was well above the usual average of around 180 barrels per year. While the business was small, it appears to have been profitable, since R. G. Dun & Co. gave the company good ratings through the 1870s and into the early 1880s, but noted that business was not as good in the summer of 1883. Around 1881 he brought his son Carl into the business, and the firm became C. F. Krauth & Son. Salem's list of brewers has Hickey & Meyer as the proprietors of this firm, so it appears that Krauth leased or rented the business for a few years (and Krauth is missing from the Dun records during these years).

In 1883 John Henry took over the brewery (with Mr. Albert for at least part of the time). The brewery was still powered by hand, but they malted their own barley. The Sanborn insurance map of 1884 shows a platform behind the brewery running along the Kinnickinnic River, which may have been used to load beer onto boats. After 1887, when the brewery was listed as Krauth & Schneider, it disappears from the records. The reason for the closure is suggested by the next use of the building, which was as a depot for Gund Brewing Co. of La Crosse.

S. T. Lobach (ca. 1870s)

The brewery of S. T. Lobach listed in *American Breweries II* has proved elusive to researchers. The business is not listed in known industry directories, state business directories or other sources. There was a farmer named Samuel Labach who lived in nearby Dunn County in 1880, but this appears to be the closest possible match.

Rush River Brewing Co. (2007–present)
990 Antler Court

Seeking larger quarters, Rush River Brewing Co. left their original site in Maiden Rock and settled in an industrial park on the outskirts of River Falls. The new facilities enabled Rush River to push production over 4,300 barrels in 2013 and to create special taproom-only beers. Additional special beers, often regular beers with fruit additions, were available at

Shortly after moving to its new location, Rush River redesigned its labels and gave each beer its own icon. Über Alt (showing the new design) is still available as a seasonal beer; Winter Warmer is no longer a regular bottled product. Author's collection.

Rush River draught accounts in Wisconsin and Minnesota.

Rush River also introduced a sour beer program, offering several different versions of Berliner weiss.

Swinging Bridge Brewing Co.
122 SOUTH MAIN STREET

Swinging Bridge Brewing Co. opened on St. Patrick's Day in 2017 as Wisconsin's second Community Supported Brewery. Members can join at three different share levels, with different discounts and benefits. The location is just a few blocks south of where Krauth's brewery was in the nineteenth century, and is named for the bridge in nearby Glen Park. The building was most recently a bike shop, and its small size presents some limits on the size and configuration of the brewhouse, and requires a lot of manual loading of ingredients and removal of spent grain. The 3 ½-barrel electric brew system is more energy efficient and reduced the need to cut more vents in the ceiling. Founder Dustin Dodge and brewer Mike O'Hara offer six to eight of their own brews in the taproom, including some special firkins.

ROBERTS *(St. Croix County)*

Bobtown Brewhouse and Grill (2016–present)
220 WEST MAIN STREET

Mike Christenson opened Bobtown Brewhouse and Grill with a former high school classmate, Katie Eells. Eells had been working for Northern Brewer homebrew supply in Minneapolis, and became the brewer for the establishment. Christenson purchased the former L&Ms Bar in Roberts ("Bobtown") and made only minor changes to the building to maintain the small-town Wisconsin feel. Eells maintains a draught list that includes five or six regular beers and a selection of rotating seasonals.

ROME *(Jefferson County)*

Gottlieb Tartsch (1866?–67?)
August Tartsch (1868–1871)
Henry Danner & George Foster (1871–72?)
WEST WATER STREET

Gottlieb Tartsch first appears in the 1867 excise records, though he may have started earlier since he purchased land in Jefferson county in 1855. In 1867, the seventy-year-old Gottlieb retired and turned the brewery over to his son August. The 1870 population census indicates that August had $3,000 of real estate and $3,000 of personal property, but since production was only one hundred barrels in 1870, it is likely that the brewery was only part of the property. In addition, the Tartschs seem to have had financial problems. The R. G. Dun & Co. credit evaluator reported in late 1868 that "They are hard up at present. They have sold ½ of the brewery to a Jefferson brewery who is to take charge as I understand . . ." The Dun records have Tartsch at this brewery into 1872, but according to excise records Henry Danner (Daumer) of Foster & Danner in Jefferson (apparently the brewery alluded to in the Dun report) was proprietor of the brewery. Production remained small—only thirty barrels were brewed in the year prior to May 1872, and apparently Danner and Foster shut down the Rome brewery to focus on their plant in Jefferson.

ROSHOLT *(Portage County)*

Kozy Yak Brewery (& Winery) (2012–present)
841 EAST MILWAUKEE

Rich Kosiec (roughly pronounced kozy yak) and Rose Richmond opened Wisconsin's first combination nanobrewery and winery in the small town of Rosholt, northeast of Stevens Point. (The winery actually preceded the brewery.) The brewpub, located in a converted residence, is typically open only a few days each month and output has generally been less than fifty barrels of beer per year. The winery was at first called Fresar Winery, but later changed its name to match the brewery.

Both businesses use non-traditional ingredients in some of their creations, such as a maple chardonnay wine. Kozy Yak also encourages customers and friends to bring in spruce tips and rhubarb for beer and wine, respectively. The brewpub serves a selection of gourmet pizzas.

ROXBURY *(Dane County)*

Foshenden/Adoph Fassbender (1856?–58?)
Mathias Leinenkugel (?)

A Mr. Foshenden is listed as a brewer in Roxbury in the 1857 state business directory. Historian Wayne Kroll has identified this brewer as Adolph Fassbender. Kroll also lists Mathias Leinenkugel as the successor to Fassbender at this business.

ST. CROIX FALLS *(Polk County)*

Miller & Bros. (1856?–58?)

Miller & Bros. are known only from the 1857 and 1858 state business directories. An extensive search of local records has so far failed to turn up additional information.

ST. FRANCIS *(Milwaukee County)*

See page 635

ST. LAWRENCE *(Washington County)*

Benedict Ziegelbauer (1857?–1893?)

Benedict Ziegelbauer was brewing near St. Lawrence in Addison Township at least as early as 1857, and possibly before. He brewed 500 barrels in 1860, but after that seems to have given more attention to his farm and blacksmith shop because the largest known production in his later years was eighty barrels in the 1870 tax year. It is possible that he did not brew every year, as his appearances in the excise records and industry directories are erratic. It appears that he continued to brew off and on until his death in 1893.

Nicholas Nenno (1855?–1864)
Schmid & Nenno (1864–1871)
Georg Schmid (1871–72)
Nicholas Nenno (1872–74)
August Fehlsdorf (1874–1875?)

According to the R. G. Dun & Co. records, Nicholas Nenno was brewing in Addison Township at least as early as 1855. He brewed about one hundred barrels in 1870, but does not appear in any other production records. Nenno was in frequent financial trouble: The Dun records noted that while he was doing considerable business he was "much encumbered." In 1864, he sold half of his interest to Georg Schmid of Farmersville (Dodge County), and in 1871 Nenno lost his entire brewery to Schmid through non-payment of another loan. Nenno was able to gain the brewery back after about a year, but his finances proved no more stable than before, and within a few years he lost the brewery again. The Dun records suggest that August Fehlsdorf acquired this brewery with the help of his father-in-law Mr. Keidel, but they do not specifically say Fehlsdorf directly succeeded Nenno as a brewer.

St. Nazianz *(Calumet County)*

St. Nazianz Communal Brewery

St. Nazianz was a socialist commune that flourished in Calumet County from the 1850s until the 1870s. Multiple sources indicate that there was a small brewery in the commune, and that its products were likely served at St. Gregorius Haus, a *gasthaus* built at the direction of Fr. Oschwald, the leader of the community. This may not have been a commercial brewery in the truest sence, and did not appear in excise records, but its presence is worth noting as a unique brewing effort in the state.

Sauk City *(Sauk County)*

Mathias Leinenkugel (1846–1871)
H. & F. Leinenkugel (1871–73)
F. L. Leinenkugel (1873–78)
George Schlenk (1878–79)
East of Water Street, South of John Quincy Adams Street

Mathias Leinenkugel, patriarch of one of the great Wisconsin brewing families, arrived in the United States in 1845 and by early 1846 was in Sauk City preparing to open a brewery. Some sources suggest that he started this brewery in 1845, but the research of Richard D. Rossin Jr. indicates that he did not purchase his land on the edge of the city until 1846, and it is very unlikely he would have had time to start a brewery on someone else's land in the meantime. Leinenkugel's brewery started small, and did not do enough business to be included in the 1850 industrial census. However, by 1860, Leinenkugel had boosted production to 1,000 barrels, and operated a relatively large brewery for a small city: it had two horse power and employed four men.

In the mid-1860s, Leinenkugel apparently intended to retire from the business, and briefly rented the brewery to Detlev Heick and Heinrich Berhens. Within a few months these two dissolved their partnership and Leinenkugel took the brewery back. Two years later, Leinenkugel sold the brewery to Christopher Luthrsen and John Esser for $6,000, but three months later the sale was "taken back and Mr. Leinenkugel is managing the brewery himself."

In April 1871, Mathias and his wife Maria Christina sold the brewery to their sons Henry Joseph and Frank Lambert for $5,500. During the early 1870s, the brewery produced between 400 and 500 barrels per year. Henry Joseph sold his share back to Mathias in 1873, but the brewery remained under Frank Lambert Leinenkugel's name (though some records misstated his initials as T. L.) Near the end of the decade, production dropped to near 300 barrels, perhaps because of deaths in the family. There is evidence that the Leinenkugel's rented the brewery to longtime employee George Schlenk in either late 1878 or early 1879, but it is not clear if Schlenk ever operated the brewery since no production figures exist. The property was eventually sold to Mary (Marie) Lenz, who owned another nearby brewery, and in 1905 Casper Roeser of the Sauk City Brewing Co. built an icehouse on the property.

Conrad Deininger (1851–1868)
Sauk City Brewery
William Lenz (1868–1881)
Mrs. Mary E. Lenz (1881–89)
Sauk City Brewing Co. (1889–1920)
1100 Water Street

The longest-lived of the Sauk City breweries was started by brothers George Conrad and Charles Deininger in 1851. The Deiningers reported production of 1,000 barrels in 1860, about the same as the slightly older Leinenkugel brewery just to the south. In 1859 Charles left the brewery to focus on his passion for natural history (particularly ornithology of the county) and Conrad continued on his own. The brewery was damaged by fire in 1867, and apparently Deininger saw this as a good time to leave the business. He traded properties with William and Mary (Marie) Lenz in 1868, who undertook the rebuilding of the brewery.

Even though he built an addition in 1869, the Lenz brewery appears to have had about the same capacity as under Deininger, though known production totals never reached the 1,000 barrels of 1860 (usually between 300 and 800 barrels). When William died in 1881, his widow Mary Elizabeth and eldest son Emil took over the brewery. A year later, Mary purchased the former Leinenkugel brewery for $3,500, though it is not clear if it was ever used for brewing under Lenz ownership.

In 1887, disaster struck the brewery. Sauk City had been without a major fire in ten years, but in February "The first fire of the season . . . broke out in Wm. Lenze's [sic] brewery . . . and consumed the kiln, malt-house, brewery, [horse]power, dwelling house, and most of the contents." The property was totally uninsured, and the loss was estimated at $10,000. The

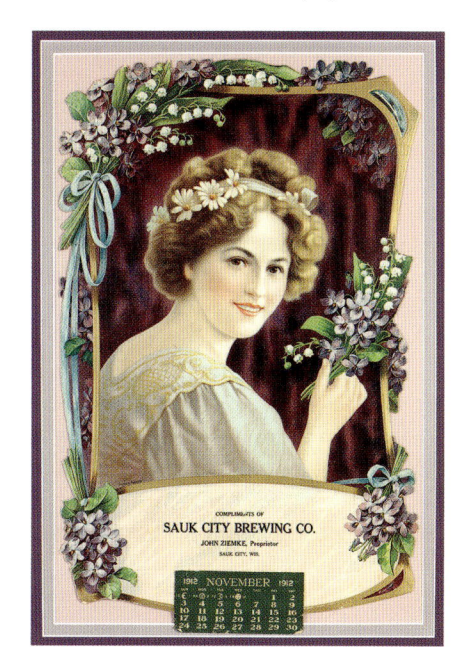

Calendars were probably intended for homes rather than saloons. This one is from 1912. Collection of Tye Schwalbe.

city fire department arrived, but the second-hand hand-pumped fire engine recently purchased from Madison "balked, and could not be made to work." The townspeople rallied around the Lenz family and put on a city fund-raising event which yielded $400 to help start rebuilding. The brewery was not done with misfortune, however. In July, *The Weekly Wisconsin* reported that William Lenz Jr. had been badly burned by falling into a vat of scalding water at his brother's newly operating brewery. In 1889, a thief broke into the brewery, drained brewing kettles and set the horses free. This loss, along with the illness of Emil in 1890, seems to have convinced Mary to give up the business. She rented the brewery to brewer Ferdinand Effinger of Baraboo, who sent one of his experienced employees, John Ziemke, to operate the brewery. At this point the business became Sauk City Brewing Co.

Effinger's five-year lease on the brewery expired in 1895, and Gustav Lenz returned to Sauk City from Chicago, where he had been in the malt business, to take over management of the brewery. He only remained a short time, during which he sold the brewery to John Ziemke for $4,500, and then returned to Chicago. Ziemke was involved with the brewery on and off for the next two decades. He sold a share of the brewery to Casper Roeser and Adam Nue in 1898, and sold out entirely in 1899. Nue sold out to Roeser in 1900, but in 1903 Ziemke returned as brewmaster. Ziemke then purchased the brewery in 1907 for $15,500. The increased purchase price since 1895 represented numerous improvements, including a new steam plant, brewhouse, and bottling plant. Ziemke stayed on as one of the original incorporators of Sauk City Brewing Co. in 1912, and this company continued to brew until 1919.

During Prohibition Sauk City Brewing Co. made cereal beverages from 1920 through 1925, but then stopped producing and the corporation dissolved in 1928. After Prohibition there were two attempts to start a brewery—one in the old Sauk City Brewing plant, the other by a new Sauk City Brewing Co., which planned to convert the former Wisconsin Farm Tractor Works building. Neither of these ever made any beer.

Frederick Frenzel (1851–1870?)
SOUTH SIDE OF POLK STREET BETWEEN JOHN ADAMS AND JEFFERSON STREETS
Frederick Frenzel's is the least well documented of the Sauk City breweries. Frenzel purchased land in 1851 in Sauk City, and appears to have begun brewing shortly thereafter. He reported that his hand-powered brewery (with one employee) manufactured 150 barrels of beer during the 1860 tax year—by far the smallest output in Sauk City.

It is possible that, like many small breweries, Frenzel did not brew year-around or even every year. He appears in the excise records from 1867 to 1870, though historian Richard D. Rossin Jr. has found that by 1870 Frenzel had essentially traded his Sauk City property for land in Troy Township to the west. He may have continued to pay the taxes on the brewery for a while, perhaps for beer brewed prior to the sale. Frenzel later built a new brewery in nearby Spring Green.

Max Stinglhammer (1855–1865)
Heinrich Schmitz (1865–1870)
Theresa Stinglhammer (1870–71)
Anna Rudolphi (1871)
R. A. Schraut & Co. (Theophil Rudolphi) (1871–74)
George Roeser (1878–1896)
Casper Roeser (1896–98)
George Roeser (1898–1900)
BRYANT STREET (MODERN PHILLIPS BOULEVARD (U.S. HIGHWAY 12))
While Max Stinglhammer moved to Sauk City in 1851, he did not start brewing right away. (He did, however, in 1851 sell Frederick Frenzel the lot on which the latter built his brewery.) Stinglhammer and his partner Anton Kaus ran a store for a few years, but in 1855 Stinglhammer purchased a new lot on what was then Bryant Street and built Sauk City's fourth brewery.

Stinglhammer's horse-powered brewery produced about 900 barrels of beer in 1860, just behind rivals Leinenkugel and Deininger. He also opened a summer-only beer garden near his beer cellars, which became a popular place for groups to gather. In 1865, Stinglhammer started a series of ownership changes when he sold the brewery to Heinrich Schmitz. Schmitz continued the brewery and beer garden for the next few years, though the brewery property appears to have been tied up in legal and financial difficulties after the divorce of Max and Theresa Stinglhammer. The brewery was offered at public auction in 1869, but since no bidder met the required $2,705, the property was returned to Theresa Stinglhammer. A lottery planned for 1870 to dispose of the property was postponed, and later that year the brewery was transferred from Theresa Stinglhammer (by way of the Sauk County Sheriff) to Anna Rudophi—the only known transfer of a brewery from one woman to another non-related woman prior to the craft brewing era in Wisconsin history. In the meantime, those who had purchased tickets for the brewery lottery were told different stories about who was responsible for the "swindle:" Schmitz or another person named Mr. Luening.

The confusion, which resulted in the brewery being out of production from at least 1870 to 1871, was not cleared up when Anna Rudolphi sold the brewery to her husband Theophil for the token price of $5.00. Rudolphi and his business partner R. A. Schraut made plans to reopen the brewery and brought in a "famous" brewer from Peru, Illinois named Peter Stein. Schraut & Co. apparently had the brewery running by December 1872, since they paid taxes on 15.5 barrels of beer. The R. G. Dun & Co. credit reports noted that the new firm "Appear to have plenty of means & I think understand the bus[iness]," while confirming that the brewery had been out of repair and closed for several years. Nonetheless, a few months later Theophil sold the brewery back to Anna, which appears to have been an indication of continuing financial troubles, since the Rudolphis missed a mortgage payment. Anna rented the brewery to one Fritz Crust of Mineral Point, but he does not appear to have run the brewery for long if at all. By 1876, the brewery was out of business again.

After a few more years of legal issues, soda bottler George Roeser was able to purchase the brewery in 1878 for a bargain price of $800. Roeser apparently was not a brewer himself, so he hired Robert Zapp to oversee production. (The brewery was sometimes listed under Zapp's name during this period.) Zapp got the brewery into production again, at a modest 300 barrels in 1879, but the new management made the brewery a paying concern for more than a decade. Roeser was able to upgrade equipment, build a new malt house and a new icehouse during the 1890s. In 1896, Roeser's son Casper took over the brewery and kept it going for a short time. However, Casper purchased an interest in Sauk City Brewing Co., and George took the brewery back until 1900, when he retired and closed the brewery.

Joseph Schorer (Schorer & Drossen)
   (1866–1871?)
Drossen & Molitor (1871?)
Nicholas Drossen & Co. (Drossen & Molitor)
   (1871–75)
Anna Drossen (1875–1882)
NORTHWEST CORNER OF POLK AND DALLAS STREETS

Joseph Schorer purchased the lots on which he would build his brewery in July 1865. Regional brewery historian Richard D. Rossin Jr. has observed that the land on the corner of Polk and Dallas Streets was an unusual location for a brewery, since the land was flat (and thus more difficult to excavate caves) and not near the river. Nevertheless, he built a brewery on that location, and in July 1866 he acquired Nicholas Drossen as a business partner (in a peculiar set of transactions in which Schorer sold a share in the brewery to Mathias Molitor who on the same day sold it for three times the price to Drossen). Molitor owned a saloon that almost certainly sold Schorer & Drossen's beer.

The brewery produced 420 barrels in 1870, just under the production of Mathias Leinenkugel's business, but only about half of Lenz's output. Joseph Schorer sold his share of the brewery to Nicholas Drossen in 1871, and moved to Merrimack to operate a saloon (and later to Elroy to start another brewery).

Throughout the 1870s, the brewery kept up a rate of production between 400 and 500 barrels per year. Drossen brought Mathias Molitor back into the business, and the partnership lasted until April 1875, when Drossen bought out Molitor.

Drossen's tenure as sole proprietor was brief, as he died in July 1876 at age 58. His widow Anna took over management and apparently operation of the brewery. She was listed in the 1880 population census as a brewer rather than a brewery owner (though she had two hired brewery workers and her son Nicholas Jr. living and working with her), and one local history claims she "tended the kettle, [and] sold the beer. . . ." The last years of the brewery are unclear. Anna Drossen appears in *Tovey's 1882 Brewers' Directory* and Rossin has found that the Drossen brewery had a liquor license in 1882, but this is the last known of the brewery.

SCOTT *(Brown County)*

Joseph Bress? (Bregs?) (1868)
Leopold Schilling (1872?)

Excise records list Joseph Bress (Bregs) as a brewer in Scott in 1868 and Leopold Schilling in 1872. Neither seems to fit with any of the other breweries in Brown County. Neither is listed in the 1870 census, and it is not clear that they operated the same brewery.

SHAWANO *(Shawano County)*

Godfried Keuhl (1868–1869?)
Godfried Keuhl & George Dengel (1870?)
George Dengel (1871–1884)

Godfried Keuhl started a small brewery in Shawano before the better known breweries were established. The *Shawano County Journal* announced in June 1868: "A Brewery will soon be established in this village. We understand that Godfried Keuhl, a cousin of Wm. Keuhl, will put up his brewery apparatus on Wm. K's premises in the course of a couple of weeks. He calculates to get to work and manufacture good beer by the first of October." The brewery was never large, and the early reports by R. G. Dun & Co. indicate that Keuhl had already taken on George Dengel as a partner. Dun claimed their "Means [were] not large" but they were honest. The 1870 population census places Dengel in Richmond Township, so it was likely that his brewery was on the west side of Shawano. By 1871, Dengel was on his own (Keuhl appears in the 1870 census in Oshkosh), and he was in a similarly precarious financial situation for several years, but by the end of the 1870s he was more stable. The only known production figures for his brewery are 250 barrels in 1878 and 292 barrels in in 1879. In 1880 the brewery was still a relatively small operation: brewer George Klaber lived with Dengel, and Dengel's son Herman may also have worked in the brewery. Dengel had a malt house, and presumably provided a good market for local farmers. Dengel remains in business and industry records through 1884, but disappears after this point. Dengel died in 1899 at the age of seventy-six.

E. Raddant & Bro. (1883–86)
Emil T. Raddant (1886–1898)
Emil T. Raddant Brewing Co. (1898–1920)
Shawano Specialty Co. (1928–1933)
Shawano Brewing Co. (1933)
Milwaukee-Shawano Brewing Co. (1933–34)
NORTH SIDE OF FIFTH STREET BETWEEN LINCOLN AND ANDREWS

In February 1883, Emil T. Raddant arrived in Shawano "with exactly 40 cents in his pocket" and announced his intent to build a brewery in Shawano that spring. His two-story frame brewery included a malt house, though this was the site of the first reported accident at the brewery—the malt house floor gave way in March 1885, sending 1,500 bushels of barley into the ice house below. Raddant recovered from this mishap and expanded his brewery rapidly, until it was praised (with the standard, exaggerated claim) as "one of the largest breweries north of Milwaukee, worth perhaps $15,000. . . ."

By the mid-1890s, Raddant's brewery was powered by steam, and included an ice house with a slide from the adjacent mill pond. Raddant continued to improve his plant, though in one case it almost cost him his life. While superintending construction of a new brick brewery in 1898, he was steadying a load of brick when the hoist lifting the brick caught "a heavy gold ring he wore" and hoisted him fifteen or twenty feet off the floor. The barrow of bricks then tipped and dropped Raddant to the floor with the bricks on top of him. Luckily, he escaped with only a broken ankle and a lot of bruises. He recovered enough to run a losing campaign for mayor of Shawano the next year as an independent candidate, part of what was described as "a sharp dash by the beer interests to defeat the mayor...."

In 1905, the Raddant family sold out to a corporation headed by August Anderson, though Raddant remained as brewer. (Anderson's company also owned and operated the brewery at nearby Cecil.) As usual, newspaper accounts praised the new ownership while implicitly criticizing the former proprietor, claiming "Within a short time a large corporation, with ample capital to handle the business satisfactorily, will be organized." The next year Emil T. Raddant "retired from business," and moved to Portland, Oregon, "where he will engage in business..."—a strange definition of retirement! Raddant was also reported to be starting a brewery in Tuscon, Arizona, though this projected business never came to fruition. William Buche came over from the now-defunct brewery in Cecil to assume brewmaster duties at the Raddant brewery.

The brewery continued to develop during the next decade. While the company eliminated its own malt house in the 1898 remodeling, they soon added bottling facilities, and by 1912 the company was important enough that the Wisconsin & Northern Railroad was granted permission to build a spur into the city to serve the brewery and the municipal power plant. The company was making soft drinks well before Prohibition as a way to broaden their product line. In 1910 Raddant installed a grain-drying plant to make livestock feed from the spent grain. Raddant Brewing also appears to have had at least some other real estate interests, including the Hotel Gillett in the village of that name. The company purchased a four-wheel-drive truck for deliveries in 1913—during its test run the truck carried a six-ton load sixty-four miles in less than seven hours. The advent of Farmers Brewing Co. as a local rival made these improvements critical. Raddant Brewing Co. was forced to engage in a beer war and to make a rival offer of stock to purchase tanks to increase capacity.

During Prohibition, Raddant Brewing received a license to brew near beer, however the brewery was raided in 1924 and the license was revoked. The plant was then purchased by a company who proposed to turn it into a candy factory. However, this plan did not go through and starting in 1928 William Buche and Paul Schardt used the brewery to manufacture soft drinks and operated as wholesalers of candy and gum under the name Shawano Specialty Company.

After Prohibition, two attempts were made to restart the brewery. The first, under the name Shawano Brewing Co. was led by Paul and Alma Schardt and former brewmaster William Buche. This company did not go into production, and denied that it had been sold to outside investors, but a new firm, Milwaukee-Shawano Brewing Co. incorporated in 1933 and actually began brewing late that year. This company went out of business in May 1934, and the managers were sued in 1936, in part on the grounds that one of the managers was in prison at the time and had defrauded investors.

Farmers Brewing Co. (1914–1920)
Farmers Brewing Co. (1934–1948)
Van Dyck Brewing Co. (1948–1950)
713 South Main Street

In 1913, local investors began seeking investors to start a second brewery in Shawano. The *Shawano County Advocate* was skeptical, noting: "It is not known that Shawano needs another brewery, but people seem to believe that there is considerable money to be made in conducting a brewery, so another company is to be organized and a brewery built in the near future." While the new firm was to be known as Farmers Brewing Co., there was no indication in any of the press reports or company statements that the brewery would be substantially owned by farmers, or conducted for their particular benefit. However, there were more than 150 shareholders of the $50,000 worth of shares, which suggests that a fairly large number of them made relatively modest investments.

Farmers Brewing Co. was an example of the last generation of pre-Prohibition breweries: rather than starting as a small family business it started as a relatively large brewery financed by a corporation founded by diverse stockholders. This method was the only way in which a new business could be competitive quickly enough to make a profit. While production figures are not available, it seems to have established a local market for its beer, and built a bottling facility in 1914 to meet the demand. (Labels for Farmers Brewing are also pictured in Chapters 3 & 4.)

When Prohibition arrived, Farmers, like local rival Raddant Brewing, obtained a license to make near beer as well as soft drinks. The brewery was raided in 1922 after strong beer was found in circulation. The company's defense was that the strong beer had left the brewery by mistake, and that they

During its brief time in operation, Milwaukee-Shawano Brewing Co. offered Unser Brau (Our Beer) in 11 ½-ounce bottles. These may have been the cheapest available bottles, which may not have contained a full 12 ounces. COLLECTION OF JOHN STEINER.

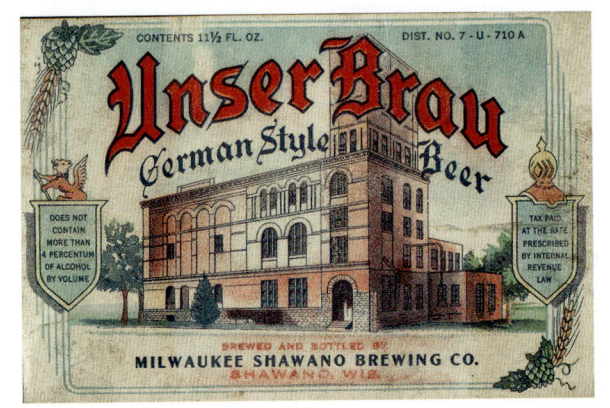

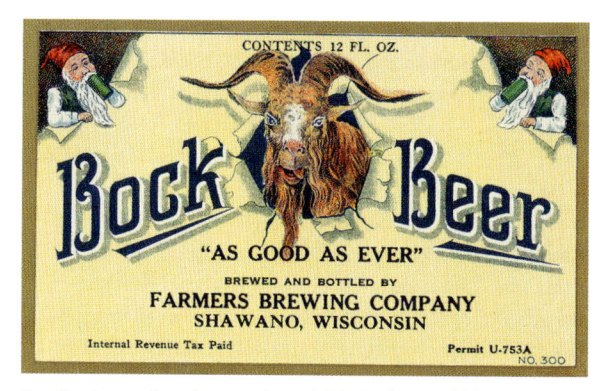

Smaller breweries often used stock labels that could be overprinted with name, slogan, volume, and other information. Many breweries around the country, including at least eight in Wisconsin, used Bock label No. 300. Although more common after Prohibition, Franz Bartl of La Crosse used it before Prohibition.
COLLECTION OF TYE SCHWALBE.

kept beer of "pre-Volstead strength for the use of employes [sic] who were working, in the belief that the law did not prohibit this practice." Somehow Farmers retained or regained its brewing permit, since it had a valid permit when the plant was raided again in 1932. Conrad Vollant, president and brewmaster, was arrested while loading six cases of beer into an automobile, and a truck driver from Green Bay was arrested with twenty-seven half-barrels of beer in his truck. At the time the brewery was one of the largest wildcat operations in northern Wisconsin, and supplied markets around the region with real beer. Newspapers in several cities reported the raid with more than passing interest, such as the *Manitowoc Herald-Times,* which claimed "It is known that trucks from that company have made periodical visits to Manitowoc for many months." The resulting padlock order delayed the plans of Farmers to return to making real beer, since the order remained in place for several months after beer was relegalized. As a consequence, Farmers Brewing did not return to brewing real lager until 1934. During the 1930s, the company typically produced between 7,000 and 10,000 barrels per year, with sales noticeably higher during the summer months. The most dramatic event during this period occurred in 1939, when burglars "chiseled through a brick wall a foot thick" to steal $400 in cash and checks from the vault of the brewery.

After World War II, production slipped, and the brewery sought new ways to increase their market. In 1948, the brewery entered a contract with Van Dyck Beer Company, a beer sales company in Chicago, to provide beer for the company, and changed the name of the brewery to Van Dyck Brewing Co. However, the Chicago firm cancelled the contract in 1949, allegedly because the Shawano brewery "failed to meet specifications of the so-called 'Holland formula.'" The Chicagoans moved their business to Rahr Green Bay Brewing, and attempted to prevent the Shawano brewery from using the Van Dyck name. The brewery actually owned the Van Dyck label, though, so they obtained an injunction and were allowed to continue temporarily to operate as Van Dyck Brewing. However, in 1950 a federal judge ruled that the Shawano brewery was no longer allowed to use the name. In addition, brewmaster and general manager Kurt Gaida was charged with piping beer to a different building for bottling to avoid federal taxes, as well as reusing tax stamps. The brewery in Shawano ceased making beer in late 1949, and was in bankruptcy proceedings in 1950.

As of 2017, the main building of Farmers Brewing was still standing on Main Street in Shawano.

SHEBOYGAN *(Sheboygan County)*

Gutsch Bros. (1847–1878)
Leopold Gutsch (1878–1885)
Adolph F. Gutsch (1885–88)
Gutsch Brewing Co. (1888–1920)
   (A. O. Gutsch Co.) (1912–1920)
Gutsch Products Co. (1920–26)
Manitowoc Products Co. (1926–1933)
Kingsbury Breweries Co. (1934–1962)
G. Heileman Brewing Co. (1962–1974)
1012 NEW YORK AVENUE

Twin brothers Leopold and Francis Gutsch came to Sheboygan in 1847 after working for a year or two at a brewery in Cincinnati (though another source claims they came straight to Sheboygan). They started a brewery that year, which is generally considered the first in Sheboygan. Their brewery developed a strong reputation for quality and integrity early on. The reports of the R. G. Dun & Co. credit evaluators were filled with phrases like "Busy, hardworking, money making little Dutchmen," and "Hardest working little Dutch devils in the County" ("Dutch" and "Dutchmen" were common corruptions of the term "Deutsch" or German). Evidence indicates that Gutsch was shipping beer on Lake Michigan during the early 1850s, because an 1853 newspaper item reported that most of the output of the Gutsch and Binz breweries was intended for the Chicago market. It appears that their export market extended to the west by the late 1850s, since an article discussing the beer situation in Superior noted that a brewery in that village would "be the means of keeping much money among us, that otherwise would go to Milwaukee or Sheboygan." The Gutsch brothers had a permanent presence in Chicago at least as early as the mid-1860s—their brother Anton, who had worked with them for a while in Sheboygan, moved to Chicago and opened a branch office which he conducted until his death in 1867. The brewery was a large one by standards of the place and time: The 1860 census of industry reported that the brothers had $15,000 invested in the brewery, employed seven men, and produced 3,000 barrels in the previous year.

The early years did not pass entirely without hardship. The Gutsch brewery was destroyed by fire in April 1860—insurance was about one third of the estimated $10,000 loss. Some temperance advocates rejoiced, and the *Fond du Lac Weekly Commonwealth* exulted that "A ten thousand dollar Brewery was destroyed in Sheboygan by fire, a few days since. We accept it as another evidence of the fact that a good Providence reigns, and the he is still not unmindful of the true welfare of the

Sheboyganders." During the 1860s Konrad Schreier passed Gutsch Brothers as the largest brewery in Sheboygan and was soon almost twice the size of the older brewery. Gutsch's production apparently did not return to 1860 levels until the 1880s.

The Gutsch brothers were interested in expanding their market, and were selling beer in Milwaukee at least as early as 1872. By 1874, their trade extended "throughout Wisconsin, Minnesota and Iowa." One laudatory article praised their lager, "the recipe for which has been handed down at great expense and trouble from the time [of] King Gambrinus." Some of the beer was shipped by boat from a warehouse near the Pennsylvania Avenue Bridge. Attempting to join the ranks of the major shipping breweries carried risks, however. In 1890, Gutsch Brewing got caught up in the beer war in Chicago, and at one point was accused of starting the war by cutting prices to $4 per barrel, an allegation denied by company president C. B. Henschel. Gutsch was one of the signatories to an agreement to sell beer for $8 per barrel (though with an allowable discount of no more than 25 percent). The most distant market for Gutsch Brewing appears to have been Puerto Rico, where the brewery shipped fifty cases of Liebotschaner in 1898—presumably for the enjoyment of U.S. troops occupying the island. Shipments to the South apparently continued at least through 1910, based on an unusual circumstance reported in *American Brewers' Review*:

> A [railroad] car which was recently received from the south by the Gutsch Brewing Co. of Sheboygan, Wis., contained a negro who had made the ten-day trip with nothing to exist on but a case of bottle beer. It seems that the car was sealed while the negro was sleeping inside. He has been sent back to the south.

After Adolph F. Gutsch bought out his father Leopold in 1885, the company went through several ownership changes in the next decades, while still retaining the Gutsch name. The Gutsch Brewing Co. was incorporated in 1888, and Adolph's father-in-law Charles B. Henschel (Henschell) bought a share in the company. Gutsch Brewing was targeted by a strike and boycott in 1891 (as was Konrad Schreier). Workers demanded an eight-hour day and a closed-shop provision in their contract. Brewers settled for a $5 per week wage increase but demanded workers leave the union. Gutsch fired men who refused to leave the union, which earned them the condemnation of the Federated Trades Council. In 1894, Gutsch Brewing made a voluntary assignment for bankruptcy protection, even though assets far exceeded liabilities. Henschel reported that the $100,000 "failure" resulted when Wolf Refrigerator Co. of Chicago "failed to furnish cooling apparatus," and $25,000 worth of beer spoiled. But it was also reported that Henschel wanted to get out of the beer business, and that this was simply a way to sell the company. (Since Henschel remained with the firm until 1909, this was ultimately not the reason.) Even though production in 1894 was a modest 9,332 barrels, it was an indication of the importance of Gutsch Brewing that the failure was noted in newspapers from New York to Montana. However, this was merely a temporary condition, and the company was reorganized in 1895 with no perceptible change in business. (Another label from this period is pictured in chapter 4.)

Like many other larger breweries, Gutsch Brewing controlled properties other than their brewery. One example was Standard Hall, which the company purchased in 1908 for $7,000. They also held a number of saloon properties, and in 1909 added to their Sheboygan holdings by purchasing some of the Oconto Brewing Co. saloons in Sheboygan when the latter company left the market. Gutsch Brewing opened a new branch office in Chicago in 1910, solidifying their market in the Windy City, and was one of the largest out-of-town breweries operating in Milwaukee. Owning saloons brought other problems, however. In 1915, a saloon at 1501 South Eighth Street owned by the brewery was the site of a murder, which exposed other corruption at the establishment. Gutsch Brewing took control of the saloon and pledged to run a clean house under new management.

One feature that Gutsch shared with a few other breweries was an inventive owner. Alfred Gutsch was responsible for several small innovations at the brewery, but in 1911 he devised a system to cycle the unburned gasses from boiler exhaust through the system again to provide additional fuel and reduce emissions. His system first was placed in use at the brewery, but was intended for wider use on railroad locomotives.

Gutsch Brewing Co. was unusual among breweries of comparable size in that it did not do its own malting. They had a malt kiln which seems to have been used briefly during the mid-1880s, but it appears that when the brewery converted to steam power in the late 1880s the malt kiln was abandoned shortly afterwards. While the boiler house did not replace the malt kiln, the brewery was landlocked and had little room to spare, so a malt house sufficient for the size of the brewery was not feasible on the site.

Kottbusser (as it is now usually spelled) was a wheat beer brewed with oats, honey, and molasses. These ingredients were unacceptable in Germany due to strict regulations *(Reinheitsgebot)*. Few U.S. breweries brewed the style until craft brewers resurrected long-lost recipes. An advertisement for Gutsch's version did not mention oats, honey, or molasses but simply stated it was "brewed similar to the old Hanovarian process" (ca. 1900). COLLECTION OF JOHN STEINER.

In 1909, C. B. Henschel and his son retired from the business and A. O. "Allie" or "Ollie" Gutsch took control of the family business again. Ollie Gutsch, grandson of Leopold, had been brewmaster for the previous ten years and was respected in Sheboygan as a businessman as well as a brewer. The brewery employed around one hundred people at this point, with a minimum wage of $15.25 per week, which was relatively high for the time. In an article opposing prohibition, it was also noted that the company also employed from time to time "contractors, carpenters, masons, tinsmiths and machinists. In addition there is [sic] a large amount of wagons to be kept in repair and new ones added every year." In 1909, Gutsch Brewing Co. made a public offering of bonds bearing five percent interest, creating yet another link with the community. The company was not ready, however, to expand their line into soft drinks, and at one point in 1910 placed an announcement in the *Sheboygan Press* indignantly and firmly denying that any such plans were in the works.

Like many breweries of similar size, Gutsch Brewing had regular newspaper ads in their market, and like their rivals, ads often focused on health claims. In 1910, ads for Gold Schaum bottled beer proclaimed it "An invigorating tonic for a tired brain. A tonic that immediately dispels that tired feeling. Something to build you up after a hard days work." That fall, Gutsch launched a campaign for its Liebotschaner premium beer, but these ads concentrated instead on the quality ingredients and brewing traditions—the labels proclaimed that this brand had been made since 1848. In late 1910 Gutsch introduced yet another label, Lifestaff, and purchased a new wagon for delivering this brand. Lifestaff would later be advertised as "The Long Storage Beer," though why that was considered a benefit was not said.

The most noteworthy piece of pre-Prohibition advertising by Gutsch Brewing Co. was the installation of an "automatic electric sign" in Sheboygan on Eighth Street. Proposed in late 1910, it consisted of "a large bottle which is turned in a pouring position with is contents running into a glass," with hundreds of electric light bulbs creating the pouring motion. However, the sign was damaged by fire shortly after being installed when the motor that controlled the light switches burned out. The sign was apparently short-lived since the Sheboygan street car company placed a sign in that location in 1912. Gutsch also advertised its products by way of a new delivery truck—custom built by the Kissel Kar company.

It seems that all the expenditures may have been more than the company could afford. In 1911, Gutsch Brewing Co. was again in financial trouble, and shut down for a time. The name mentioned most often as a potential buyer was a familiar one, C. B. Henschel. Henschel was still the principal bondholder, and in January 1912 he took control of the company again, though A. O. Gutsch was one of the incorporators and the company retained his name. A new brewmaster, Fred Blust, was brought in from Pocatello, Idaho, and Gutsch Brewing had its own beer back on the market in April 1912. Later that year, the company embarked on an expansion program to boost capacity and improve the bottling department. (The new bottling equipment was the first of that model to be installed, and visitors from as far away as Amsterdam and Buenos Aires came to inspect the facility.) The capacity of the brewery at this point was 80,000 barrels per year, which was delivered over a range of about 200 miles—placing Gutsch Brewing as a regional brewery. However by this point the brewery was not controlled by Sheboygan residents anymore—President Alfred Henschel lived in Chicago and Secretary Robert Heysen (C. B. Henschel's son-in-law) was from Milwaukee. The brewery continued to have multiple beers on the market: in 1913 they offered both Easter Brew and bock beer during March.

Gutsch continued to supply spent grain to farmers, but in 1915 they installed a drying machine and offered dried grains for sale both at the brewery and at feed stores. The brewery emphasized the benefit to farmers, since dried grain could be stored and farmers would not have to get wet malt from the brewery daily.

During World War I, Gutsch Brewing contributed to the war effort, and in June 1918 sponsored an advertisement encouraging donations to the local War Chest with the vaguely Marxist slogan "From every patriot according to his ability—to every worthy cause according to its needs." But of greater concern both to Gutsch Brewing and Sheboygan was the brewery closing order and approach of Prohibition. At the end of 1918, Gutsch Brewing employed thirty-five men full time and owned about fifty saloon properties. An article in the *Sheboygan Press* noted that not only would the brewery be nearly impossible to convert to other purposes, but the closing of the saloons would lower real estate prices and rental rates throughout out the city. Breweries also faced the loss of experienced skilled employees. Fred Blust, brewmaster at Gutsch, was said in early 1919 to be leaving to take charge of the Brahma brewery in Rio de Janiero (though this move was not as remarkable as it may seem because Blust had worked in Rio prior to coming to the United States). However, he was prevailed upon to remain in Sheboygan. During Prohibition he continued his training, and returned to Germany for three months for postgraduate studies in Berlin. The *Sheboygan Press* hoped he might "return with some salvation formula for Sheboygan, which will comply with the prohibition laws of the country." (He later left Sheboygan, but only as far as Milwaukee.)

Shortly after the brewery shut down order took effect, Gutsch began to advertise Gutsch Special, a near beer which was supposed to be "refreshing and invigorating." However, both Gutsch and Schreier continued to make some real beer and made hesitant deliveries of it as the lawyers worked out exactly how Prohibition was to be enforced. The respite was brief, and Prohibition shut down business in Sheboygan as it did elsewhere. There was a brief period when it appeared that beer could be sold for medicinal purposes in 1921. Gutsch was prepared to start brewing again and to sell the 2,000 barrels they still had on hand, but this too came to nought.

Gutsch Brewing sought to survive Prohibition with a number of enterprises. In 1921 they purchased equipment for a large ice manufacturing operation, which was heralded as a source of jobs as well as pure ice. They continued to make near beer, including special editions for most major holidays. (A Gutsch Root Beer bottle is pictured in chapter 6.)

In 1924, they launched a competition to name a new cereal beverage in an attempt to create publicity for the new product. (The winning name was "Tipper," but no labels are known for this product.)

Gutsch was one of the rare breweries to suffer a strike during Prohibition when half of the thirty employees walked out over a dispute involving the discharge of one of their members.

One of the most important brewery ownership changes of the Prohibition era, a period which saw very little investment or merger activity at all, occurred in 1926, when Manitowoc Products purchased Gutsch Brewing. The owners of Manitowoc Products represented three of the most important families in the brewing history of that city: Daniel C. Bleser, Guido R. Rahr, and Otto H. Senglaub. Manitowoc Products faced increased demand for their "exceptionally good grade of near beer" (Kingsbury Pale) from as far west as Wyoming, and needed the additional capacity that the Gutsch plant would provide. A new company called Gutsch Products was created, though it was completely controlled by Manitowoc Products. Even more unusual was the need to expand the brewery during Prohibition, but in 1930 Manitowoc Products erected a new warehouse for bottled beer the corner of North Tenth and Wisconsin. The new facility was needed because of increasing demand for Kingsbury Pale, which was now sold in thirty-nine states, and "a carload of Kingsbury Pale was shipped to Hollywood, leading moving picture stars demanding this particular beverage." The popularity of Kingsbury Pale also meant that one hundred men were employed in Sheboygan at what was still locally referred to as Gutsch Brewing—as many as at any previous point in the company's history. (Additional information about Manitowoc Products may be found in the Manitowoc breweries section.)

The return of real beer was a boon for Gutsch Products, as the Kingsbury label made a smooth transition to Kingsbury Pale Beer and Old Style beer was added (briefly) to the product mix. By mid-1934, Gutsch employed 115 people and had eleven delivery trucks, and claimed production of 300,000 barrels per year. While the company name was changed to Kingsbury in 1933, the Gutsch Products name was still used locally for a few more years. The name change became effective in July 1933, and the company planned to list its stock on the Boston, Chicago, and New York stock exchanges. (Additional information about of kingsbury Breweries, Inc. is found under the Manitowoc listing.) After the company filed for bankruptcy in 1936, a group of Manitowoc and Sheboygan investors led by brothers William H. and Felix T. Pauly purchased a large block of shares in the company to keep the ownership local. William Pauly would eventually be elected chairman of the board and Felix would become treasurer. (Felix's great-grandson Grant later opened 3 Sheeps Brewing Co. in Sheboygan.)

Despite the fact that plans for breweries on the east and west coasts fizzled, the Kingsbury name continued to have a nationwide presence after repeal. In 1941 the company named Larcade Distributing Co. its agent in Corpus Christi, Texas, and the beer was distributed throughout the Upper Midwest.

During World War II, breweries were limited in the number of miles that trucks could drive and the number of deliveries allowed in any one week. However, to meet demand during the Christmas season of 1943, Kingsbury resurrected one of the old Gutsch brewery wagons and brought in a team of prize-winning Belgian draft horses to make deliveries in the city.

After World War II, Kingsbury continued to be one of the most important regional breweries in the Upper Midwest. Sales grew from over 84,000 barrels in 1952 to an estimated

The label on the bottle on this beautiful lighted sign is from the mid-1960s after Kingsbury was purchased by G. Heileman. The neck label includes a tear-off coupon that could be redeemed for merchandise. COLLECTION OF DAVID WENDL.

255,000 in 1959. In March 1959, Kingsbury purchased Sioux City Brewing Co. of Iowa, which was at the time the largest brewery in Iowa with a capacity of 160,000 barrels. (A label from the Sioux City branch is pictured in chapter 8.) O. H. "King" Cole said that this purchase would allow Kingsbury to expand its distribution in portions of Iowa, Nebraska, the Dakotas, and Minnesota that were "not previously reached." However, in January 1960, Kingsbury itself was purchased by Heileman Brewing Co. of La Crosse. Heileman acquired 51 percent of the shares by purchasing the holdings of the Pauly family for nearly $400,000. Heileman left the management of Kingsbury intact, and the takeover was a friendly one. Heileman's main reason for the purchase was to acquire the well-established Kingsbury Pale and use it as the company's popular price beer, rather than trying to develop and market a new brand at the La Crosse brewery.

Unlike many brewery buyouts, Heileman intended to use the Sheboygan brewery at full capacity, rather than just acquiring the labels and razing the brewery. Heileman proposed multiple expansions of the brewery, including one in 1969 to move production of its newly-acquired Blatz label to the Kingsbury plant.

The only known gallon can produced by a Wisconsin brewery contained Kingsbury beer. These were on sale only during the second half of 1965. A Madison liquor store sold them for $1.29 per can (approximately $10 in 2018). COLLECTION OF DAVID WENDL.

However, the brewery was threatened with closure in 1970, as the expansion was not as successful as hoped, and a maintenance shut down put ninety-three of the breweries 140 employees out of work. Union leaders alleged that the shut down was simply a measure to "'scare' workers in advance of new contract talks and to avoid payment of holiday overtime pay." Local 277 of the Brewery Workers and Malsters Union went on strike for eleven days in 1971 during a contract dispute, but the brewery stayed in production until 1974, making Kingbury products as well as Blatz and Drewry's beers. In February 1974, Heileman announced that it was closing the 127-year old brewery for good. (Additional information on the last years of Kingsbury in Sheboygan is found in chapter 8.)

Christopher Hoberg (1847?–1854?)
"River Street Between Fourth and Fifth"

Christopher Hoberg is believed to have started a brewery (and a general store) in Sheboygan around 1847. Some sources claim that his brewery was the first in Sheboygan, though the precise date is disputed and other sources give the honor to the Gutsch brewery. While his brewery was reported to be on River Street, the 1850 population census recorded his residence in Lyndon Township, well to the west of Sheboygan proper. Son John Hoberg founded Hoberg Paper Company, which would later give the world Charmin toilet paper.

Jacob Muth (1848–1850?)
Muth, Binz & Bros. (1850?–52)
Binz Bros. (1852–1861)
August Binz (1861–67?)
Koepl & Gruebner (1867–68)
Henry Gruebner (1869)
Thomas Schlachter (1870–1880)
Thos. Schlachter & Co. (1880–83)
Michigan Avenue between Fourteenth and Fifteenth

Jacob Muth started his brewery around 1848, and by 1850 it was large enough that he had three other brewers boarding with him (though not large enough to have production recorded in the 1850 industrial census). The Binz brothers, August and Jacob (sometimes listed as Joseph) joined him in 1850. Though many sources claim the Binz brewery dates to 1856, this refers to their brewery built after the 1855 fire. The Binzes apparently joined the firm just after the 1850 census, since an August 1850 advertisement in the Dutch-language *Sheboygan Nieuwsbode* for 3,000 bushels of "Garst" (barley), for which the usual highest prices would be paid, was placed in the name of "Brouwerij van Muth, Binz & Gebroeders." (The Gutsch brothers requested 6,000 bushels at the same time.)

Muth appears to have left for Burlington in 1852, and the Binz brothers carried on. In 1853 they purchased a lot near their brewery to build a malt house and a beer cellar. Their business must have been fairly extensive at this point, since an article in 1853 claimed that the combined output of Gutsch and Binz was worth about $25,000 per year, much of which was shipped to Chicago (presumably on Lake Michigan). Their brewery and residence were destroyed by a fire in October 1855 which started in the malt house and spread to other buildings. While the fire department was called, it did not reach the scene until it was too late, and one of the firemen was run over by the engine and killed on the way to the fire. There was no insurance at all on the property, and the only item of value saved was a small trunk belonging to Mrs. Binz, which was believed to have been stolen after the fire. August and Jacob rebuilt immediately, though it is possible that they rebuilt on a new location, since some of the accounts place their brewery on Ontario near Twelfth Street at the time of the fire. However, sources agree that the rebuilt Binz brewery was on the site of what eventually became Born's Park on Michigan Avenue.

The new brewery prospered, according to the reports of R. G. Dun & Co., which said they were "... able men, do a g[oo]d bus[iness] and may be set down as entirely safe." Interestingly, the brothers had no real estate listed in their names in the 1860 population census, nor did they appear in the industrial census of that year. By 1861, Jacob had left the business, and August carried on alone. However, at this point the business ran into financial difficulties, and by 1863 the brewery was placed in the name of August's father. The Dun investigator reported in 1867 that Binz was "Busted & gone to Chicago."

The next few years of the business sometimes called the Sheboygan Brewery are less well documented. A city directory of 1868 lists Frank Koepl and Henry Gruebner as the proprietors of the brewery at this address, and the excise records seem to support their acquisition of the brewery sometime in early 1867. (However, the 1867 excise record appears to read Goldener, and a 1930 obituary for one of Gruebner's sons indicates that Henry sold his share in the brewery to a Mr. Gildner) Gruebner appeared in the census records on his own in 1869, but in 1870 the brewery passed into the hands of Thomas Schlachter. The Dun records claimed he had "quite an extensive brewery," but in the early years he struggled financially before "striving away" and becoming more stable in the middle of the decade. His highest known production was around 800 barrels in 1870, but he usually brewed between 200 and

500 barrels, depending on whether he had a full year of brewing or not. The brewery burned in 1872, and yet again in 1878, but Schlacter was now in good enough shape to rebuild the brewery in brick. However, it appears that the continued expense of rebuilding took its toll on Schlachter's finances, and by 1880 he was considered a poor credit risk. By 1883 he was out of business. According to one account, the brewery equipment was moved to Chicago where it was used in the Keeley brewery.

After Schlachter left the business, the land on which the brewery stood was incorporated into Born's Park, and the brewery became a recreation hall. The hall served as an armory during the Spanish-American War and was used as a sanitarium in the early twentieth century based on the claim that the waters from the mineral waters contained radium (considered a remedy at the time). The building later became 99 Hall, hosted a variety of dances and other events and finally became a tavern and social center under a number of names until finally being destroyed by fire in 1988.

Schlicht & Wellhoffer (1854–56?)
Schlicht & Schreier (1856–1872)
Konrad Schreier (1872–1895)
Konrad Schreier Co. (1895–1930)
Sheboygan Brewing Co. (1930–34)
1504 NEW JERSEY AVENUE

The origin stories of the brewery that would eventually become Konrad Schreier Co. vary as to the year of founding and the original founders. Most sources give the date of 1854 as the founding, though a few claim 1856. Some of the confusion appears to be related to when Konrad Schreier joined the firm. One history from 1912 held that Schreier did not arrive in Sheboygan until 1856, and a reminiscence published in 1921 holds that Leonard Schlicht built the brewery, and brought in George Wellhoffer (Wellhoefer) as a partner before Schreier joined the business in 1856. Schlicht's brewery was already an important community center: when the city of Sheboygan announced the building of a new road in 1856, the contracting for the grading was organized at the brewery. By the 1860 industrial census, Schlicht & Schreier had increased production to 500 barrels, which at the time was third most in the city.

The prosperity of Schreier & Schlicht suffered a setback in 1866. Their new steam-powered brewery was destroyed by fire less than a month after completion, with the insurance of $2,000 nowhere near enough to cover the estimated $20,000 loss. The insurance seems not to have been updated to cover the value of the new brewery. Schlicht & Schreier rebuilt quickly, and bigger and better than before. Their new brewery was one of the very few steam-powered breweries in Northern Wisconsin, and by 1870 they had passed Gutsch Brothers for the largest brewery in Sheboygan—producing 3,200 barrels to the Gutsch's 2,500. The establishment employed many hands: four additional brewers boarded with Schlicht and a few more with Schreier. In 1872 the partnership dissolved, and Leonard Schlicht took over management of the brewery's saloon until his death in 1875. By 1876, the R. G. Dun & Co. credit evaluator described Konrad Schreier as the "Beer King of the City" and affirmed that the brewery was making money.

Schreier began offering bottled beer at least as early as 1877, when the contract was given to Adolph Lebermann, who continued to serve as Schreier's bottler for at least the next sixteen years. (Lebermann was also Sheriff of Sheboygan County during the 1890s.)

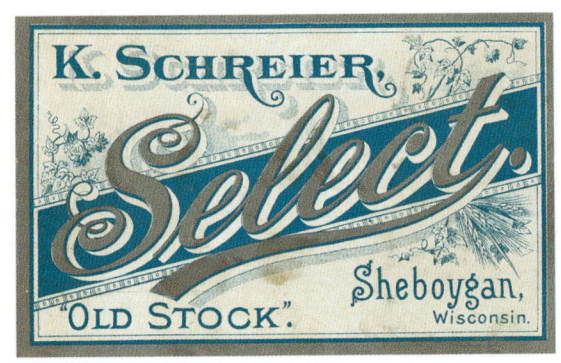

A simple yet elegant label from the early 1890s. COLLECTION OF TYE SCHWALBE.

The constant improvement of a regional brewery was not always easy. In 1895, Schreier Brewing sought a new source of brewing water. Their attempt to drill a new artesian well cost thousands of dollars, and was not successful until they finally struck a "copious stream of water at the depth of 1,800 feet."

The result of all the improvements was a brewery that was important to the health of the local economy. In an article answering calls for prohibition, the Sheboygan Press argued Konrad Schreier Co. was

> . . . operating a brewery and a malting house, and employing a hundred men, all at prices equally as high as paid by the other brewery [Gutsch, which had a minimum weekly wage of $15.25]. This concern with a reputation of sixty years has gone forward increasing each year. The men employed there have built their homes and it can be said that no enterprise in Sheboygan has done more for this city than this same company. The money is invested here at home and the growth of these institutions means a great deal to Sheboygan.

In 1896, Konrad Schreier Co. was incorporated, with Konrad Schreier and his sons-in-law A. P. Steffen and Louis Testwuide as the officers. The absence of "Brewing" from the name indicated that the malting operation was at least as important as the brewery, if not more so. Schreier malt was distributed throughout America, and the *Sheboygan Press* occasionally noted shipments to new or distant markets, as in 1900 when Schreier shipped three carloads to Pennsylvania. Konrad Schreier remained at the head of the company until his death in 1903, when his son Herman then took over.

In order to maintain the local market against strong competition, Konrad Schreier Co. needed to produce a variety of brands, and to advertise them. In 1907, Schreier advertised four regular brands of bottled beer: Edelbrau, Perfection, Select and Pilsiner [sic], as well as "Our Celebrated Bohemian," which was only available around the Christmas holidays.

Schreier also brewed bock beer (which they called Pilsener Bock). In 1908 sales were limited to three days in early June—rather late for bock season.

Like most brewers of the era, Schreier also depended on pseudo-medical testimony in their advertisements. In 1908, an ad proclaimed:

Medical men always display a decided preference for Edelbrau. Long practical experience of human diet has taught them its healthful superiority. They know it is a true and most delicious liquid extract of the farmer's hops and barley; that it is always properly aged and sterilized; hence cannot hurt them or ferment in the stomach. They are also well aware that hop juice calms the nerves, and acts as a tonic; while the alcohol is an efficient digestive and a generator of energy.

While overstated, these ads made no claims not being made by other brewers. Other ads of the time period urged customers to choose Schreier's beer because "it is a home product, made by home labor."

Schreier took advantage of the interest in modern technology in their advertising. In 1911, the brewery ordered 500 "transfer pictures" from the Meyercord Company of Chicago, which depicted a night scene of the East Side of Sheboygan, with "a modern air ship" (dirigible) with a search light trained on "a huge bottle of Edelbrau in the foreground."

One of the largest disasters in Sheboygan history struck the malt house of Konrad Schreier Co. in June 1911. A fire that started in a malfunctioning fan spread throughout the eight-story malt house and the enormous elevators, causing more than $250,000 damage. Luckily the local fire department, augmented by crews from Manitowoc, was able to protect the brewery and the downtown business district, so the catastrophe was limited to the malting complex. Insurance covered about 90 percent of the loss, and rebuilding started immediately. The rebuilt malt house had a capacity of 1,500,000 bushels per year, to go with a sizeable brewery with capacity to brew 75,000 barrels of beer each year. The brewery had its own electric plant, and the brewery was "fitted with all the latest appliances and improved machinery," in the common claim of the era.

Schreier Co. also took the lead in building concrete roads in Sheboygan, partly to beautify their section of the city, but also to make sure that the roads would be strong enough to support the new, heavy trucks the company was using for deliveries.

The approach of Prohibition threatened all breweries, but those with significant malting operations were doubly vulnerable. By 1918, Konrad Schreier Co. was brewing 42,000 barrels of beer and malting approximately 800,000 bushels of barley each year, most of which came from farmers in the vicinity. Schreier employed sixty men in brewing and malting, and the *Sheboygan Press* pointed out that many of these were older men who had worked their entire lives in this industry, and who would have a harder time finding work in a new field. Schreier continued to bottle beer into 1919, using up the stock on hand. However, as Prohibition approached, Schreier Co. bowed to the inevitable and began advertising "New Edelbrau," a non-intoxicating malt beverage. The company continued to market this beverage for several years, but ads in 1923 seemed to recognize the limits of this product by urging customers "Don't be skeptical or doubtful. It's Great." Edelbrau seemed to have become an accepted product, and Schreier decided in 1926 to introduce a dark "Muenchner Style" near beer, which was advertised as "made from a full 5 percent brew." By August 1920, the company had refitted the brewery to manufacture and bottle soft drinks, which were on the market in mixed cases in time for the Christmas holidays. The company offered the usual ginger ale and root beer, as well as Grape Smash, Cherry Blossoms, and Green River, "the Original Snappy Lime Drink. In 1922, Schreier added Choc-Lo, a chocolate soda product." It added numerous other flavors throughout Prohibition, though the most unusual was probably Hop-Blossoms, which appeared in 1924 and was advertised as a tonic to be served with meals. The company continued to experiment with new labels throughout Prohibition, introducing Brewmaster Special in 1928, which was packaged in pint bottles rather than the standard 12-ounce or 7-ounce bottles.

Because Konrad Schreier Co. had emphasized malting for many years, it had options during Prohibition that brewery-only businesses did not have. The company built a flour mill to the west of the elevators, and began to make "cereal products." In 1925, Emil Mohr Bakery of Sheboygan advertised a new whole wheat bread that was made "out of the improved whole wheat flour made by the Konrad Schreier Co." Like many breweries, the company also turned portions of its plant into cold storage: in 1928 Herziger Sausage Co. leased enough space to store and dry 75,000 pounds of sausage.

While the company diversified its product line, it also started to sell off its many saloon properties in the city, despairing that beer would return anytime soon. It also sold its beer warehouses in outlying villages such as Kiel. Schreier Co. even had occasional supply bottlenecks during the Prohibition era: in November 1926, they advertised asking customers with empty cases and bottles to arrange to return them to the factory "as we are in urgent need of cases and bottles."

In 1930, Manitowoc Products, which already owned the former Gutsch brewery in Sheboygan, needed even more capacity to meet the continually expanding demand for Kingsbury Pale near beer. They sale of the brewery portion of Konrad Schreier was closed in October 1930, and the Schreier plant began to brew Kingsbury Pale and Lifestaff (a Gutsch label that Manitowoc Products continued) and continued producing Dublin Dry and Lemon Dry soft drinks. Konrad Schreier Co. continued to control and operate the malting portion of the business. Later that year, a new company was formed, Sheboygan Brewing Co., which took over the malt and soda business of Schreier Co. and had its offices in the Schreier complex. This business was not simply another name for the Manitowoc Products-owned brewery, since Sheboygan Brewing continued to brew Edelbrau and Muenchner rather than Kingsbury Pale. However, the incorporators of this company included Daniel Bleser and O. H. Senglaub, who were directors of Manitowoc Products. Confusing the issue further was the fact that a number of soft drinks continued to be advertised under the Schreier brand for a few months, but eventually the products were converted to Sheboygan Brewing labels.

Upon the return of beer, Sheboygan Brewing Co. converted the Edelbrau label back to real beer, and by mid-1934 the company was employing forty people and operating seven delivery trucks. However, the plant's capacity of 150,000 barrels was much more than this company could possibly use. But Kingsbury needed the capacity, and on 1 July 1934, Kingsbury Breweries Co. officially took over the Sheboygan Brewing Co. plant. Occasional advertisements or mentions of Sheboygan Brewing Co. continued even into 1935, but the company ceased to brew under that name in 1934. Brewing did not continue at the former Schreier facility very long, as Kingsbury focused on upgrading the former Gutsch plant instead.

Rheinhart Able (1860?)
FOURTH WARD

Rheinhart Able is so far known only from the 1860 population census. Since he had real estate of $1,000 it is unlikely he was employed by the Binz brewery (also in the Fourth Ward).

Ernst Ninmann (ca. 1860)
FOURTH WARD

Like Rheinhart Able, Ernst Ninmann appears in the 1860 population census as a brewer, but nowhere else. He does not have any real estate listed (but neither did Binz). His son Rudolf was listed as an apprentice brewer, which suggests that he may have worked for his father, but they both may have been employed by one of the other Sheboygan breweries.

Wellhoffer & Buckle (1856?–1867?)
George Wellhoffer (Wellhoefer) (1867?)
Wellhoffer & Keanitz (1867–68)
George Wellhoffer (1868–1870?)
Edmund Ohse, Sheboygan Brewery (1870?)
Ohse & Runkel (1870)
Kleiber & Runkel (1870–71)
Kroos Brewery
William Kroos (1872–74)
Richard Weidenser (1874–75?)
Kuhl & Koppert (1875?–77)
Martin Kuhl (1877–79)
CALUMET ROAD AND TWENTY-FOURTH STREET

George Wellhoffer (spelled various ways) and August Buckle began brewing near the toll booth on the Calumet Plank Road sometime prior to 1857, since they were included in that year's state business directory. Their brewery grew quickly and in 1860 they produced 700 barrels of beer. The mid-1860s are poorly documented, so it is not clear at what point Buckle left the business, though he was at a brewery in Plymouth by 1867 at the latest. The excise records indicate that Wellhoffer was on his own by May 1867, though he had a partner on and off during the late 1860s. However, the R. G. Dun & Co. records indicate that that Wellhoffer was being foreclosed in late 1870, which fits with his last appearance in the excise records. Wellhoffer stayed in the brewing industry even after leaving his brewery—in the 1875 Sheboygan city directory he was listed as the brewer for Frank Tasche's small white beer brewery.

In the 1870 industrial census, the brewery appeared under the name of Edmund Ohse, and was a significant operation. The brewery represented an investment of $8,000, employed three men and one youth, and produced 900 barrels of beer (as well as 3,000 bushels of feed and 100 gallons of yeast). Again, the transfers of management are not clear during the early 1870s, and it is not clear whether Runkel and Kleiber purchased shares in the brewery or were leasing from another owner.

William Kroos purchased the brewery in 1872, and was considered to be a reliable businessman who was also in the produce business. Kroos' time at the brewery appears to have ended about the same time as a fire that destroyed the brewery in March 1874. The fire department was never called to the scene, but the insurance of $4,000 was estimated to be enough to cover the damage—a rarity among breweries of that time.

Richard Weidenser (various spellings) may have owned the brewery for a brief period after the fire. In October 1875 the *Milwaukee Daily Sentinel* mentioned that this veteran of Milwaukee's South Side Brewery had purchased the "Dickson" (presumably Dick) brewery in Sheboygan Falls. While there is little other documentation of this move, it seems to indicate the point at which he left the brewery on Calumet Road.

The next documented owners were Kuhl and Koppert, who took over sometime prior to 1877. In 1877 this partnership dissolved and Martin Kuhl took over the business on his own. The final appearance of this brewery in the news was in September 1879, when the *Milwaukee Daily Sentinel* reported that "Kull's [sic] brewery, owned by C. M. Limprecht, just outside city limits, burned. . . ." The building was reported to be unoccupied at the time, though whether this means that no one was in the building, or that the building was vacant is not clear. The R. G. Dun & Co. reports confirm that Kuhl was out of business by the end of 1879.

August Thamer (1872–76?)
ONTARIO AVENUE AND TWELFTH STREETS

August Thamer first appeared in the excise records in June 1872, though through a transcription error was listed as Robert. The 1875 city directory corrected the first name, but gave different last names in the business and personal listings (Thamur and Thomas, respectively). His business was described as a "small beer manufacturer" and Schade's listing of brewers recorded his production in 1875 as twenty barrels—a small producer of small beer.

Frank Tasche, Weiss Beer Brewery & Saloon (1874?–77?)
EIGHTH STREET NORTH OF NIAGARA AVENUE

Frank Tasche first appeared in the excise records in April 1874. His small weiss beer brewery and saloon also appeared in the 1875–76 Sheboygan city directory. The evaluators for R. G. Dun & Co. in December 1876 considered his business too small to be extended much credit. His business disappears from the records after 1876, though he may have operated through 1877, given the date of the Dun report.

Augustus Goebel (1875?–76)
SUPERIOR AVENUE AND TWELFTH STREET
The R. G. Dun & Co. credit reports are the only source so far for the brewery of Augustus Goebel. The evaluator reported in June 1875 that he had "very [small] means." At the end of 1876 he added that Goebel had "Played out and moved away." The 1875 Sheboygan city directory included a listing for Augustus Goebel, but with a pottery at Superior and Twelfth. He may have shifted into brewing with little success (but could have made his own beer bottles).

Hops Haven Brewhaus (2003–2010)
1327 NORTH FOURTEENTH STREET
Hops Haven, opened in 2003, brought brewing back to Sheboygan after a nearly thirty-year absence. Owner and brewer Jeff Kolar refurbished the 100-year old Wigwam Mills building to create a 70,000-square-foot pub. Some of the sub floor removed during the renovation was reused for tables in the bar. Kolar previously was the brewer at Port Washington Brewing Co., and he brought several of the PWBC brands with him to Hops Haven. The restaurant featured a collection of breweriana, much of it donated by local collectors. In addition, the restaurant was the site of many local meetings and hosted live music. The business closed due to financial difficulties in 2012, but the brewery part became 3 Sheeps Brewing Co.

Three Sheeps Brewing Co. (2012–present)
1327 NORTH FOURTEENTH STREET (2012–16);
1837 NORTH AVENUE (2016–PRESENT)
Grant Pauly was not excited by his family's concrete business and found more fulfillment in homebrewing experiments. Brewing was in his blood, as his great-grandfather Felix Pauly had been an owner and officer of Kingsbury Brewing Co. for many years. So when Hops Haven Brewhaus went out of business, Pauly arranged to take over the brewery portion of the building and 3 Sheeps Brewing began operation in 2012. As with many new breweries, for the first several months they produced only draught beer, but were bottling by the end of 2012.

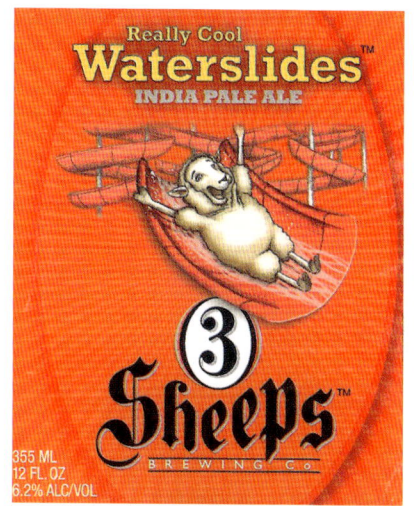

Really Cool Waterslides took its name from a T-shirt Grant Pauly owned that showed a choice between two paths: one led to fame, fortune, power, and success, the other to "really cool waterslides." The original labels featured cartoon sheep; the rebranding in 2017 focused on different design elements. COLLECTION OF SCOTT REICH (TOP); COURTESY OF 3 SHEEPS BREWING CO. (BOTTOM).

Pauly's approach to beer was described in the original company slogan—"One off of Normal." The beers are designed to be enjoyable, but with some difference in ingredients or process. The original beers included Enkel (a Belgian table ale), Baaad Boy Black Wheat, Rebel Kent (an amber ale) and Really Cool Waterslides IPA (now called simply Waterslides). Over time, 3 Sheeps introduced new seasonal beers, barrel-aged beers, and the Nimble Lips, Noble Tongue series of experimental beers.

The enthusiastic reception for 3 Sheeps beers eventually forced the company to seek larger quarters. In 2016 they opened a new brewery with a spacious taproom on North Avenue. This made it possible to introduce canned beer, which they did in 2017 with three brands: Waterslides, 3 Sheeps Pils, and Fresh Coast Pale Ale. In 2017, 3 Sheeps also embarked on a rebranding campaign including new label designs (in which sheep were less prominent) and a new slogan: "Brewed with Heart & Science."

8th Street Ale House (2013–present)
1132 NORTH 8TH STREET
The 8th Street Ale House had a reputation as a great craft beer bar before they decided to start brewing their own beer in 2013. Brewer Eric Hansen started brewing on a five-gallon system in the prep kitchen in the basement. As the beer became more popular, they moved the brewery into the building next door and expanded to a one-barrel system.

Brewing for a beer bar presents special challenges. While 8th Street currently reserves eight taps for Hansen's beers, he has to be able to justify why the bar manager should choose his beers over a popular "guest tap." When the Ale House hosts a special event like a "tap takeover," some of the house beers may be taken off line temporarily. Some guest taps will duplicate styles like Scotch Ale or Amber that are brewed in house, but Hard Roll Hefe has replaced all other outside hefeweizens. Seasonal styles range from New England IPA to Russian Imperial Stout.

SHEBOYGAN FALLS
(Sheboygan County)

Charles Osthelder (1853–1863)
Joseph Osthelder (1864–1874)
NEAR BROADWAY STREET AT FOOT OF BUFFALO STREET
Charles (or Carl) Osthelder moved to Sheboygan in 1851, and worked for a time

as a cooper. In 1853 he moved to Sheboygan Falls, and started a brewery there. (Though a 1915 remembrance by Joseph Osthelder claimed that Charles rented a brewery owned by Michael Rothmann.) In December 1855 the brewery was destroyed by fire, though the stables and the family dwelling were saved. Apparently he was not only sufficiently insured but received excellent service from Aetna Insurance Co.; he was featured in an ad endorsing the company the following March. The brewery was modest in size, producing 400 barrels in 1860. Charles' son Joseph worked in the brewery, and two hired brewers lived on the premises. According to one rather flowery biography, "After putting aside his text-books [Joseph] became identified with the brewing business, in which he was interested at the time of his enlistment...." One of his duties was delivering the beer, which was often done with teams of oxen. He was often armed during his trips, for protection from wolves and to safeguard the cash used to pay local farmers for barley—once as much as $500. Joseph served as part of General Butler's army that occupied New Orleans until 1864, when he received an honorable discharge and returned to Sheboygan Falls, "interesting himself again in the brewing business, in which he continued until 1874." Charles Osthelder had died in 1863, and it is unclear if the brewery had continued to operate while Joseph and his brother Charles Jr. were absent. Charles Jr. also worked in the brewery but later went to Milwaukee with Fred Muth to work as a beer bottler. (Osthelder advertised that he bottled beer for Best, Blatz, Melms, and Lill in the 1867 Milwaukee city directory, though Sheboygan sources claim he did not move to Milwaukee until 1868.)

The brewery burned again in September 1869, though insurance covered the majority of the $5,000 loss. Production during these years was typically between 100 and 200 barrels per year. One unusual note is that the 1870 industrial census listed one female employee, though this person cannot be identified from the population census. Joseph continued to operate the brewery until 1874, when he closed it and opened a saloon in downtown Sheboygan Falls which later became Koene's Korner and still later Ye Old Corner Tavern.

Henry Dicke (1860?–67?)
Margaret Wissman (1867?–68)
Liebner & Ortmayer (1868–69?)
Ortmayer & Kappelbaum (1870)
S. Ortmayer (1870–71)
Henry Dicke (1871–75)
Richard Weidenser (Wiedensen) (1875)
Durow & Herber (1875–78)
David Durow (1878–79)

The origins of Henry Dicke's brewery are not as clear as its well-documented ending. Henry Dicke (or Dick) is listed in the 1860 population census as a wealthy wagon maker, but his son Frederic was listed as a brewer, and may have run his father's brewery at the time. According to an 1862 map of Sheboygan County, Henry Dicke appears to have abandoned the wagon business and moved into brewing full time. This appears to have been temporary, however, because by the 1870 census he is again recorded as a wagon maker, and seems to have leased the brewery to a series of proprietors. The excise records do not include Dicke from 1867 to 1871, but during that time Wissman, Liebner, Ortmayer and Kappelbaum all appear in Sheboygan Falls. Evidence that this was all the same brewery is suggested by a 1921 retrospective which lists this brewery as Dix & Luebner, which is likely an alternate spelling of Dicke and Liebner. The entry in the 1870 industrial census was listed under Ortmayer and Kassebaum, and produced 340 barrels with the aid of one employee and two horsepowers.

Henry Dicke appears to have taken the brewery back in 1871, since he reappears in the excise records in September. He operated the brewery for a few years until selling it to Dick Weidenser "until recently of the South Side Brewery" in Milwaukee. However, Weidenser's apparently managed the brewery only a short time, since the firm of Durow and Herber soon took over the brewery, and the R. G. Dun & Co. credit report of September 1877 noted that they had been in business about two years at that point. The Dun evaluator did not recommend the business for credit, since both proprietors drank "too much of [their] own [manufacture]. Herber left the business in 1878, and Durow continued on alone.

The brewery came to an ignominious end in 1879. The *Milwaukee Daily Sentinel* reported "An important seizure was made by the internal revenue officials Saturday [11 November]. A few days since it was reported that the large brewing establishment of David Durow, of Sheboygan Falls ... not making proper entries in the brewer books; with buying stamps that had been once used, and with retailing beer without a license. A warrant for the arrest of Durow was placed in the hands of the United States Marshal. Durow had considerable reputation in business circles where he is known."

A month later, Durow pled guilty, and the property was sold early in 1880. The sale of the stock netted only $71.53, since the beer was "a bad brew and only fit for hog feed." Since no buyer was willing to bid enough for the beer to pay for the revenue stamps, forty barrels were dumped "into the purling waters of the Sheboygan River."

SHULLSBURG *(Lafayette County)*

Shullsburg Brewery
Philip Marx (1851?–1867?)
Miller, Marx & Co. (1867?)
Marx & Wagner (1870?)
Wagner & Mahoney (1871?–1872)
Thomas Mahoney (1872–1874?)
Mahoney & Stephens (1874–1880)
Jacob Blotz (1882–85)
John Schock (1885–1890)
Carl Steiner (1890–93)
Wm. Buexton (1893–95)
Moritz Hoffmann (1895–1902)
Fred W. Langenberg (1902–3)
Shullsburg Brewing Co., Louis Zimmerer (1903–5)
Shullsburg Brewery (Shullsburg Brewing Co.)
Michael Littel (1905–1910)
Gustav Varrelmann (1910)
Fred W. Goetz (1910–12)

Frank O. Moesmer (1912–14)
Ludwig Meindl (1914–16)
North of Shullsburg on Modern County Road O

As early as the founding of the Shullsburg Brewery was, it was still a relative latecomer in the mining region where Mineral Point had a brewery in 1835 and Elk Grove in 1836. Philip Marx may have started brewing as early as 1850, but he was clearly functioning by 1851 at the latest. His brewery produced 500 barrels with the aid of three men in 1860. The reports of the R. G. Dun & Co. credit evaluators provide the most detailed records of these early years. A report in early 1857 claimed he had been "in the brewery business about 6 years," and as early as 1853 he was said to be "Doing a good bus[iness]." The evaluators duly noted that Marx was "a large consumer of his own beer," and that he was "still making beer and drinking it" but that he was still an honorable and "economical[,] industrious German." As late as 1862 the evaluator confessed that "'Lager' has not killed him yet." Perhaps the most noteworthy feature of the early years of this brewery was that, according to Dun & Co., he had gone out of business in late 1862 or early 1863 "on account of Govt. Tax"—making him one of the very few brewers in the Upper Midwest who can be documented as having been pushed out of business by the excise tax imposed to fund the Civil War.

The Shullsburg Brewery changed hands more often and at a faster rate than all but a few Wisconsin breweries, and these changes are poorly documented or even conflicted. Marx appears to have returned to brewing after the war, since he appears in the excise records with various partners. However the brewery seems to have gone in and out of business frequently over the next several decades, and the plant sat idle several times during ownership changes. Thomas Mahoney was associated with the brewery for almost a decade, but lost the business in late 1879 or early 1880, perhaps in part because, according to the Dun Co. records, the U.S. government seized the brewery for making illicit whiskey. The Dun & Co. evaluator also noted that "The old brewery they are running is not first class."

The frequent ownership changes continued through the next decades, though Mortiz Hoffmann provided several years of continuity. Louis and Anna Zimmerer and Fred Langenberg filed articles of incorporation for Shullsburg Brewing Co. in September 1903, but this version of the company lasted only about two years. In June 1910, *American Brewer's Review* reported that Michael Littel had sold the property to Gustav Varrelmann, formerly brewmaster at Wainwright Brewing of Pittsburgh. It noted that the brewery had been closed for about eight months, but that Mr. Varrelmann planned to "run the brewery on modern lines." Varrelmann incorporated the company, along with Millicent Varrelmann and F. C. Mueller, but he did not stay long. Varrelmann's name has not been found in local sources, and the next known proprietor is Fred Goetz.

Shullsburg Brewing Co. served a local market, and had to fight to keep that. The company purchased an advertisement on a 1904 map of Lafayette County in which the brewers of Pure Pilsner and Bohemian Lager announced "Bottle Beer a Specialty," but nearby ads touted the products of Mineral Spring Brewing Co. and Blumer's Monroe Brewery—and Blumer's ad even included a sketch of the brewery.

The brewery closed sometime in 1916, which was announced in *American Brewers' Review* in December. As of 2017 the brewery building still stands.

Schmidt & Schulte (1867–68)
Severin Schulte (1868?–1875?)
Schulte & Lauterbach (1876–79?)
Rosalie Schulte (1879?–1887?)

Excise records and the credit reports of R. G. Dun & Co. indicate that there were two breweries in Shullsburg, though occasions when both were in full operation at the same time were rare. Severin Schulte first appears in the excise records in July 1867 with a partner named Schmidt, he then operated the brewery on his own for several years. According to the Dun records, he started well and did a large business. (The 1870 industrial census reported that he made 1,000 barrels of beer, and perhaps an additional 100 barrels of "cream" ale, though this section is barely legible.) However, by 1870 he was "heavily in debt but is persevering and hard at work." The evaluator opined in 1872 that Schulte would have trouble getting out of debt "unless … the RR [railroad] is built thro' here." He still managed to pay his bills, but in 1876 opted to sell a half share in the brewery to [Peter?] Lauterbach.

Lauterbach was a local farmer who "sold a farm" in 1876 and put the money into the brewery. However, the partners were unable to eliminate the debt, and in July 1879 their brewery was seized "for making illicit whiskey. 'Exploded.'" Production had already dropped to 303 barrels in 1878 and a mere 159 the next year.

Rosalie Schulte appears to have taken over the brewery in 1879, or perhaps the brewery was placed in her name to avoid creditors. This business change somehow was not reported in *Western Brewer* until 1885. Her brewery was still listed in the 1887 Wing's Brewers' Annual, but this is the last appearance of this brewery in the records.

This tray is from the period when Fred W. Langenberg was proprietor. Weiss beer is advertised as a brewery product, though industry journals suggest it was brewed only intermittently. Collection of Tye Schwalbe.

Sigel Township
(Wood County)

John Pelisell (?)

Historian Wayne Kroll lists John Pelisell as the operator of a farm brewery in Sigel Township in *Wisconsin's Farm Breweries*. He was listed as a farmer in both the 1860 and 1870 population censuses (spelled Peliselle), but it is not clear how long or how often he brewed.

Silver Creek *(Sherman Township) (Sheboygan County)*

Herman Seifert & Co. (1866?–69?)
Herman Seifert (& Bro.) (1870–72)
Seifert Bros. (1872–73?)
Julius Seifert (1874–1881)
Charles Hamm (1881–1903)
Near Modern State Highway 144 and Camp Awana Road

Local tradition holds that Herman Seifert started his brewery in Sherman Township "toward the end of the Sixties," which is supported by his appearance in the excise records in January 1867 (which suggests he started operations late in 1866). Seifert made 180 barrels of lager and 222 barrels of "beer" in 1870—enough to supply a local market but much smaller than the breweries of nearby Sheboygan and West Bend. The "& Co." appears to have been Herman's brother Julius, who lived next door to Herman and was also listed as a brewer in the 1870 population census.

The changes in business name seem to be mostly cosmetic or meaningless, since both Herman and Julius were active in the business during the early years. Production remained modest: 316 barrels in 1871 and 259 the next year. However after Julius became sole proprietor in 1874, production gradually increased until he manufactured 672 barrels in 1878. However, it appears that any expansion of the brewery at this time caused him financial difficulty.

In 1881, Seifert sold the brewery to Charles Hamm, who the R. G. Dun & Co. agent rated as "Honest and attentive, a good brewer." Industry directories from the 1880s list Seifert and then Hamm as both producing weiss beer, which may also have been the cheaper "beer" listed in the 1870 industrial census. Both the 1884 and 1887 Wing directories claim Hamm was also bottling, which would have been essential for weiss beer, but he may also have been bottling lager at this point. Sometime in the late 1880s Hamm also added a malt house, which he continued to operate into the 1900s.

Around 1903, Hamm built a new plant just to the east in Random Lake, and moved the equipment to the new site. It is clear from maps and local descriptions that Hamm actually built a new brewery in a new location, and this was not simply a change in the mailing address for the same location, (even though he kept the name Silver Creek Brewery at the new site).

Slinger *(Schleisingerville) (Washington County)*

Jules Schleisinger (?)
August Lehner (1856?–1861?)
John Klingler (1861?–1873?)

The early years of the first brewery in the region of Schleisingerville (later Slinger) are not well documented. Wayne Kroll has identified Jules Schleisinger and August Lehner as early brewers in this location. August (or Andreas) Lehner (Leinhardt, Lekner) appears in several sources as a brewer in Cedar Creek from the mid-1850s through the early 1860s. He produced 300 barrels in the tax year ending in 1860 and sold them for $2,000.

Kroll also indicates that John Klingler was the next brewer at this site. Klingler is slightly better documented. He appeared in the excise records from 1867 through 1872, and the 1870 industrial census reported that he sold 200 barrels of beer. The brewery was still a small one, with one horsepower and three employees, though one of these was reported as a "youth." While it was common for younger family members to work in the breweries, it was not often reported in the census, which means this may not have been a relative. John Klingler left his brewery in Polk Township around 1873, but he remained in the industry, since the 1880 population census indicated that he was employed as a brewery worker in Milwaukee.

Benedict Kornburger (1868–1870)
Lehman Rosenheimer (1870–77)
Storck & Hartig (1877–1884)
Chas. Storck & Co. (1884–88)
Chas. Storck (1888–1895)
Chas. Storck's Brewery (1895–1903)
Estate of Chas. Storck (1903–4)
Storck Brewing Co. (1904–1912)
Storck Cooperative Brewing and Malting Co. (1912–13)
Storck Brewing Co. (1913–1920)
Storck Products Co. (1933–1953)
Storck Brewery, Inc. (1953–58)
201 South Storck Street

The research of Otto Tiegs has helped clarify the ownership changes in the early years of what became the Storck Brewing Co. Benedict Kornburger built a brewery on the south side of Schleisingerville (later Slinger) in 1868, selecting a site near the La Crosse Railroad line. In the early years the brewery did not operate year-round. The 1870 industrial census reported that the brewery had been in production for seven of the previous twelve months, and had produced 130 barrels of beer—about two thirds as much as John Klingler's nearby older brewery.

In late 1870 Kornburger sold the brewery to local businessman Lehman Rosenheimer. (Kornburger's name remained in the excise records through 1871.) This new acquisition was only one of Rosenheimer's many enterprises—a business directory on a county map from 1873 lists "L. Rosenheimer, Prop. of Brewery and Saloon, Manuf. of Harness, and Dealer in Country Produce, Dry Goods, Groceries, Clothing, Crockery, Boots and Shoes, Agric. Implements, Lumber." Rosenheimer put his son John in charge of the brewery, and Tiegs argues that the access the Rosenheimers had to materials and markets helped build their brewery. The brewery was still a small one by standards of the area, with a capacity of around 500 barrels per year and production in 1875 of 208 barrels.

The *Milwaukee Daily Sentinel* added confusion to the story of this brewery in January 1872 when it reported "Kronenbergers brewery, at Schleisingerville, has passed into the hands of Mr. John Enes, of this city [Milwaukee]." This announcement was either premature or erroneous, since no other source indicated that Enes in fact took over this brewery.

H. Charles Storck and William Hartig met while employed at Val. Blatz's brewery in Milwaukee, and in 1877 purchased the Schleisingerville brewery for $5,000 from Rosenheimer, whose health was deteriorating. Storck and Hartig began to improve the brewery and increase capacity. Around 1883 they added a malt house to the complex. However, Hartig wanted to own his own brewery, so in 1884 he sold his share of the business to Charles Ehlert for $6,000. The parting between Hartig and Storck was friendly, and the families remained close for many decades. Storck also wanted to own a brewery outright, so he worked for four years to buy out Ehlert's shares.

Storck continued to expand his brewery, and the 1895 Wisconsin industrial census reported that Storck produced around 6,000 barrels, some of which was shipped as far as Stevens Point. H. Charles Storck died in 1903, and his sons took over the brewery. They incorporated the company as Storck Brewing Co., built a new brewhouse and bottle house, and began a modest expansion to their advertising program to compete against the Milwaukee breweries and other local firms. One noteworthy form of advertisement was at the local movie house, where the theater projected a promotional slide for Storck's beer on the screen during intermissions. Like most other brewery owners in small cities, the Storcks were all active in other local business and municipal government. It was during August's term as village president in 1921 that the name Schleisingerville was changed to Slinger.

Business was strong through the beginning of World War I, but the Storck brothers anticipated Prohibition and began to develop other product lines to survive the dry years. Storck Products Co. became well known for their ice

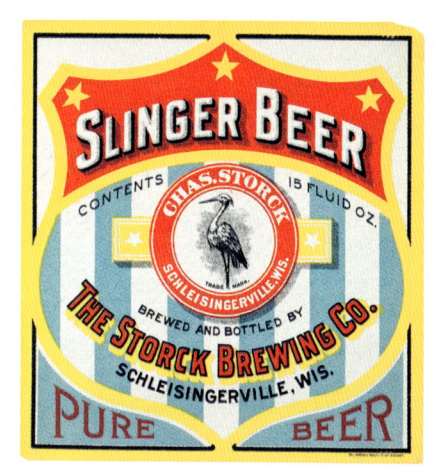

The name of the proprietors inspired a distinctive logo. This pre-Prohibition label also appeared as a die-cut shield-shaped version. COLLECTION OF TYE SCHWALBE.

cream, which was produced both in Slinger and at a branch plant in Beaver Dam that was formerly R. H. Martin Bottling Works.

The Storcks did not give up brewing completely, however. While they never marketed a near beer, they continued to make real beer. (The company had been denied a near beer license several times.) Brewing equipment was hidden among the ice cream vessels, and serving equipment in the brewery taproom could be hidden quickly. While some of the beer was served locally, some was shipped to Hartford and Milwaukee. Eventually the size of their operation caught up with them, and the brewery was raided in March 1926. Agents confiscated 2,348 gallons of beer, and claimed "the chief source of Milwaukee's real beer has been stopped." In July the brewery was padlocked for one year, which prevented them from using the premises at all during that time. The Storcks took an even bigger risk during 1922, when they allowed (if that is the correct word) Chicago mobsters to use the brewery for three weeks as a "gypsy" distillery. Henry Storck was ordered to keep family and employees away from the brewery during that time, but at the end of the three weeks the equipment had all been replaced and there was no sign of the temporary distillery.

Storck's legal troubles delayed their brewing permit when beer was re-legalized, but they were soon back in business, and began to seek markets in Milwaukee as well as the local area. During World War II the company reached a more unusual market: Storck supplied beer to German prisoners of war confined at the camp near Hartford. Wartime shortages required the brewery to recycle many inputs, and to use high school students to take the positions of other employees who were working in war plants or serving in the military.

After World War II, Storck Products continued to have strong sales in Milwaukee until a falling out with one of the larger beer depots in the city led to a loss of business. However, it was Milwaukee beer depots that ultimately provided the cash necessary for badly needed upgrades. The postwar beer shortage left many retailers without sufficient stock to meet demand, and some Wisconsin breweries were being purchased by out-of-state distributors and the production was shipped to distant markets. Elmer Keller, a member of the Uihlein family and former manager of Capital Brewing in Milwaukee, headed a group called Associated Beer Depots, which purchased Storck Products in 1946 for $175,000. The new owners retained Ray Storck as manager, but made significant upgrades in the equipment, especially in the bottling house.

However, by emphasizing the Milwaukee market, the new management alienated residents of Slinger, who had supported the brewery for decades. Local residents could not buy Storck beer even for special occasions, and when sales in Milwaukee started to slide after the shortages eased, Slinger customers refused to buy the beer again. New brews and labels also flopped and the company was in financial trouble. Matters were made worse in 1951 when a fire caused $30,000 of damage to the boiler room and adjacent buildings. The brewery's new brand—Storck Club beer, not only earned legal action from New York's Stork Club, the red ink on the labels dissolved in the rinse water, coated the insides of the bottles, and resulted in a red-tinted beer. Ray Storck left the company in 1952 after a disagreement with management, ending the family association with the brewery that stretched back to 1877. Storck Products was well placed to benefit from the 1953 brewers strike in Milwaukee, both because of its proximity and because it already had distribution channels in the city. Storck ran double shifts, produced a record 30,000 barrels of beer, and even sold beer in Milwaukee County Stadium at Braves' games. However the return of Milwaukee beer precipitated the breakup of Associated Beer Depots, and the brewery was sold back to local owners. Gene Schall had been working in the brewery and as a delivery driver, and he and his partners worked to rebuild the company's reputation in its home town. The brewery rathskeller was reopened, the company hosted numerous events at the brewery, and even considered packaging beer in cans (which did not come to pass).

However, old equipment and limited capital eventually caught up with Storck Products. In 1953, one of the old cypress aging tanks was put under too much pressure and exploded, killing employee Norbert Nineck and injuring Jake Mergenthaler. In 1954, old equipment resulted in a bad batch of beer which was not only shipped by the brewery, but was also resold after being returned by retailers. This caused permanent damage to the company's reputation around Wisconsin, which was exacerbated when Storck was forced to withdraw from its Illinois markets because of a dispute over inspections. The company also alleged that other brewers were sabotaging shipments of Storck beer by skunking it. The company went bankrupt in 1958, with production down to about 800 barrels a month. Sales in Slinger were not enough to compensate for discount pricing used to remain in more distant markets. Portions of the brewery building still remain, and parts of the brewery were used in other structures—such as the top of the brew kettle which was converted into a fireplace shelter at Slinger's Little Switzerland ski hill.

Soldiers Grove
(Crawford County)

Driftless Brewing Co. (2013–present)
Rural Excelsior (2013–14)
102 Sunbeam Blvd E. (2014–present)

Chris Balistreri and Michael Varnes-Epstein observed that "We [Driftless Brewing Company] were born in a barn, literally," in what they lovingly referred to as "the rural middle of the middle of nowhere." Balistreri began homebrewing in 1987 with a friend who was trying to found a homebrew club. However, the distance between members and their need to concentrate on their farms and other businesses made it difficult to keep the club active. But Balistreri kept brewing, and with Varnes-Epstein and co-founders Scott Noe and Cynthia Olmstead decided to move to the next level. They started brewing in a barn in rural Excelsior between County Highways F and X. Their twenty-gallon brew system made just enough to have some bottles on sale in the Gays Mills and Viroqua co-ops, but they did not want the dead end road their brewery was on to become a metaphor for the business.

In 2014, Driftless Brewing Co. moved to a former grocery store in Soldiers Grove. The village offered a loan for Driftless to acquire a one-barrel brewing system, and the brewery began a period of gradual but sustained growth. From fifty-one barrels in 2014, they grew to 102 barrels in 2016 and project 125 for 2017.

The brewery takes its name from the "Driftless Region" (which escaped glaciation in the Ice Age). In recent years, the region has become a magnet for people interested in organic farming, solar energy, and local sourcing of everything from food to building materials. The owners of Driftless Brewing share these values, and have made a special effort to source not only their ingredients but also other inputs and contracting from as close to the brewery as they can. The idea of local beer has been embraced by the community, and while the population of the area is not dense enough on its own to support a larger brewery, enough visitors come through the area that Driftless has not been able to make enough beer to supply the demand. They are planning for a new brewhouse with a fifteen-barrel system that will enable them to take care of their local markets and eventually expand distribution to larger cities along Interstate 90. The beers brewed so far by Driftless range from seasonal lagers to saisons brewed with local fruit, and from sessionable blonde ales to Solar Town barrel-aged stout. The latter took its name from a project undertaken by Soldiers Grove in 1979 when the village mandated that all twenty new downtown buildings use solar power. Many of the beers are brewed with certified organic ingredients, though they have not yet sought organic certification for the entire brewery.

Somerset *(St. Croix County)*

Oliphant Brewing (2014–present)
350 Main Street #2

Oliphant Brewing's eye-catching graphics and name were designed to start conversations, and the beer brewed by Trevor Wirtanen and Matt Wallace encourages the discussion. The pair brewed their first batch of homebrew in 2010, and the next year they decided to start their own brewery. They were able to lease a former 7UP bottling plant in Somerset, which meant that some of the design features required for breweries, such as a drainage system, were already present.

The beers produced by Oliphant represent the major beer styles and then some. Some beers, like Prizza Demon, are styles less commonly seen in America (in this case an English-style mild ale suitable for enjoying "after a spin in the tardis"). Others incorporate unusual ingredients into traditional styles like Hobotown 2.0 (a gose aged in tequila barrels with sea salt and lime). Some simply transcend style, like Milkman Manbaby—a "German-style milk stout," whatever that is. (These three examples were consecutive entries on the taproom list in August 2017—showcasing the variety of styles.) Crowlers of Oliphant beers became available in beer stores in 2016, and in 2017 Oliphant began selling beer in four-packs of 16-ounce cans.

South Grove *(Sharon Township) (Walworth County)*

William J. Arnold (1856?–58?)

Historian Wayne Kroll includes William J. Arnold in his list of Walworth County farm brewers, and Arnold is listed in the 1857 state business directory.

Sparta *(Monroe County)*

Ignatz Furst (1857–58)
Shaw & Nye (1858–1861)
Nelson Nye (1861–62)
Loomis Parrish (1862–63)
Louis Whipple (1863–66)
Merrill & Walsath (1866?–67)
A. W. Lynn & Bro. (1867?)

Montgomery and Court Streets

Ignatz Furst has traditionally been listed among the brewers of La Crosse in the mid-1850s, based on a listing in the 1857 state business directory. However the research of Richard D. Rossin Jr. so far has failed to turn up any evidence of Furst owning property or a business in La Crosse. Rossin's research has, however, shown that Furst purchased property in nearby Sparta and built a brewery in 1857. Furst's tenure was brief, since he sold the brewery in December 1858 to Nelson J. Nye and Spicer Shaw for $1,000. Nye appears to have been the brewer while Shaw provided the most of the initial capital. The brewery attracted notice from visitors, and a correspondent to the *Daily Milwaukee News* reported that "Shaw and Nye have an extensive ale brewery in successful operation [in Sparta]."

Shaw sold his share of the brewery to Nye in 1861 for $4,000, which seems to indicate that the brewery had been improved in the previous three years. The R. G. Dun & Co. credit evaluator praised Nye as "economical and attentive to bus[iness]. However, Nye's turn as sole proprietor would also be short, since he died in February 1862 of consumption (though the Dun & Co. reports claimed he died by drowning in June!). Following his death, Loomis Parrish, a native New Yorker like Nye, purchased the brewery for just under $1,500. Parrish took on a partner later that year, D. J. Matteson, who actually managed the brewery. However, a few months later Parrish sold the brewery to another New Yorker, Louis Whipple. Whipple apparently stayed in Otsego County, New York, and let his son-in-law Matteson manage the brewery. The brewery was known as Parrish and Whipple for a while during 1863, so either Whipple had a share in the brewery before purchasing it outright, or Parrish maintained a share in it for a while longer. The new owners expanded the brewery in 1863 with a new cellar and other improvements including their own cooperage. Whipple advertised his "Celebrated Sparta XXX Cream Ale" with orders to be addressed to Matteson at the brewery. But the revolving door of management continued, and in March 1864 Parrish leased the brewery again and Matteson left for Idaho, possibly for the small mining rush occurring at that time. Whipple put the brewery up for sale in early 1865, advertising the brewery as "one of the best located breweries in the state, with everything convenient, and has gained a good reputation. A rare chance is offered for a good Brewer."

However, the proposal drew no purchasers, and Parrish continued to lease the brewery until 1866, when he moved to Baraboo to start a brewery there. Management then passed to H. A. Merrill and Mr. Walrath, who appear in excise records as soon as existing records begin in 1867, but were there at least by October 1866, when the *Sparta Eagle* reported a runaway accident "near Merrill's brewery." In April 1867, Alexander W. and James H. Lynn leased the brewery and continued to brew and bottle ale for a brief period under the name A. W. Lynn & Bro. The brothers advertised enthusiastically, calling their product "The Best Ale West of the Lakes," though in one ad they placed their brewery at the corner of Maine and Montgomery streets, which Rossin has pointed out do not meet. They produced thirteen barrels of ale in May and twenty-six in June, but disappear from the records after that point. The property was turned into a soap factory in 1870, and at this writing the property is occupied by the local Masonic Temple.

Sparta City Brewery, John N. Wagoner (1866–1875)

Northeast Corner of Benton and Main Streets

In 1865, saloon owner John Wagoner purchased land at Benton and Main Streets on which he began constructing a brewery. In 1866 the brewery was completed and he sold his saloon to concentrate on brewing. By April 1868, the evaluator of R. G. Dun & Co. reported that Wagoner was making money. The 1870 industrial census indicated that Wagoner had made 650 barrels of beer in his horse-powered brewery with the assistance of two employees. He claimed to have $10,000 invested in the brewery, which was relatively high for a brewery outside an urban center.

However, the 1870s were less kind to Wagoner. Production began to drop: to 392 barrels in 1871 and 351 in 1872. These were still respectable totals for a brewery in his situation, but the Dun records indicate that Wagoner was starting to have financial difficulty. The evaluator noted that he "manages to get along all the time, is naturally a good bus[iness] man but drinks too much beer. . . ." Wagoner placed occasional ads in local newspapers, but since he served a local market, additional advertising was probably not necessary. Wagoner's setbacks soon became more dramatic. In December 1873, the upper floor of his brewery collapsed from the weight of 1,500 bushels of barley, injuring two workers. The final blow came in April 1875 when his brewery was "almost entirely destroyed" by fire. The fire department was called and arrived, but was unable to save the brewery. The *Sparta Herald* reported that there had been no fire in the brewery for several days, and drew the usual conclusion that arson (or "incendiarism") was the cause of the blaze. This account also notes that Wagoner's windmill was among the structures destroyed, which suggest that he was using wind power for at least some of his needs. This fire also indicates the perils of researching from newspapers of the era. The *Herald* reported that damage was between $10,000 and $12,000 with insurance of $3,500 from the Hartford company and $2,500 with Ætna. However, papers from Eau Claire to Milwaukee added a zero to the insurance amounts and estimated the loss at $60,000—an impossible figure for a small brewery at that time.

Wagoner attempted to rebuild, but did not have the funds to revive his business.

SHERMAN TOWNSHIP
(Spencer) (Clark County)

Joseph Mayer (1878-79)
Eichert & Frothinger (1879)
Kuethe & Eichert (1879–1881)
Kuethe & Walter (1881–82)
JOHN WALTER (1882–89)
NORTHEAST CORNER OF SECTION 12, SHERMAN TOWNSHIP (SOUTH OF MODERN STATE HIGHWAY 98 AND WEST OF FAIRVIEW AVENUE)

The earliest known mention of the Spencer brewery (which was actually located just west of Spencer across the Clark-Marathon county line in Sherman Township) appeared in the *Stevens Point Journal* in December 1876, which announced "Two Germans have recently completed a brewery near the village [of Spencer] and will shortly be turning over barley in a liquid state at 5 cents per glass." It is not clear exactly who these men were or how soon they went into production. They likely included Joseph Mayer, who was listed at Sherman in Salem's directory as having produced 234 barrels in 1878 and 207 in 1879.

The brewery is much better documented during the 1880s. The R. G. Dun & Co. creditor assessor reported that the firm of Fred Kuethe and John Eckert (Eichert) were doing a good business, but that in 1881 the firm had dissolved and Kuethe's new partner was brewer John Walter. In 1882 Walter became sole proprietor, but ran into trouble almost immediately. In September 1883, federal agents seized Walter's brewery for reusing tax stamps. Some newspaper reports provided the confusing information that the brewery was "owned and operated by Philip Scheiffer," which is inconsistent with local and industry sources. In spite of rumors that the brewery would be confiscated and sold, Walter paid the fine and made a rapid recovery.

The Spencer brewery was situated in an area with few breweries, and was able to develop markets in larger cities such as Marshfield that had no brewery. The *Marshfield Times* lamented that fact:

> The brewery at Spencer, with a capacity of about 1,200 barrels yearly, and which has been in existence for several years has proved a paying investment to the proprietors, a valuable acquisition to the town and put hundreds of dollars in the pockets of farmers in that vicinity.

The Wisconsin industrial census of 1885 reported that production was actually 1,300 barrels, and much of that was in fact shipped to Marshfield, where Walter had a saloon near the Clarke House billed as the "Headquarters for the Spencer Brewery." Spencer beer was also available at celebrations such as the Marshfield Fourth of July picnic.

Unfortunately, Walter's time in Spencer came to an end in February 1889, when his brewery, malt house and residence were destroyed by fire. The *Milwaukee Sentinel* reported that the insurance of $5,000 would only cover half the $10,000 loss, and claimed (inaccurately) that "It was the only brewery between Stevens Point and Ashland, and was doing a large business. It will undoubtedly be rebuilt as soon as possible." However, Walter elected to move rather than rebuild, and took over the Theresa Leinenkugel brewery in Eau Claire.

SPRING GREEN *(Sauk County)*

Frederick Frenzel (1872–1882?)
SOUTH SIDE OF WEST MONROE STREET AT WOOD STREET

Frederick Frenzel moved to Spring Green from his farm outside Sauk City in 1872. Later that year, he purchased three lots near the intersection of West Monroe and Wood Streets, where he built his new brewery (following the one he owned in Sauk City). Excise records show Frenzel produced about three barrels of beer per month from February to May 1872, so he either was still producing some beer on the farm, or had begun brewing in Spring Green before he owned the property (the excise entry listed his location as Spring Green). The former is more likely, since the purchase price of $40 per lot seems to indicate there were no structures on the properties when Frenzel purchased them. Frenzel was listed in the 1873 *American Brewers' Guide* at Spring Green, but with no reported production prior to May 1872.

Frenzel's brewery was not listed in any of the brewing industry directories of the 1870s, nor does he appear in the excise records after 1872. However, he was still listed as a brewer in the 1880 population census. Local brewing historian Richard D. Rossin Jr. suggests that Frenzel probably continued brewing off and on until he retired in 1882. The brewery remained as a private dwelling until the 1960s, and local accounts claim that the cellars were used for illegal distilling during Prohibition. The building was demolished in the late 1960s or early 1970s and the remaining tunnels were filled.

STEPHENSVILLE
(Outagamie County)

Geo. Wunderlich (1866–67)
Charles Graetz & Co. (or R. Graetz & Co.) (1868–1877?)
Anton Fischer (1881?–1889?)
NEAR PEW ROAD AND TREMONT STREET

The R. G. Dun & Co. credit reports indicates that George Wunderlich had a new brewery erected by November 1866, and was in production close to that time. His business was modest, but he was doing well enough to receive a positive credit rating. However, by the next year, the Stephensville brewery was operated by brothers Rheinhard and Charles Graetz (or Gratz). Their brewery was a small one, and produced about 115 barrels in the 1870 tax year.

The 1872 state business directory lists both Wolf, Wunderlich & Co. and Graetz & Co. as brewers, however it is unlikely that there were two breweries in operation at the same time. It is more likely that Wolf & Wunderlich briefly resumed control of the brewery during 1871 (perhaps for financial reasons) and that the Graetz brothers were able to return the next year. There is no indication in the Dun records that Wunderlich returned to active management of the brewery for any significant length of time, and these records also indicate that Graetz & Co. were still operating the brewery at least through 1876. A map of Outagamie County from 1873 lists the Graetz brothers as proprietors of the brewery, and shows the Wunderlich family focused on their lumber business and other enterprises (a state supported by the 1870 population census). The fact that the 1873 *American Brewers' Guide* directory shows no production through May 1871 and only fifty-seven barrels the next year also seems to indicate that the Graetz brothers were not operating the brewery in 1871.

It is not clear when Graetz family control ended, but it was sometime prior to 1880 since they were not represented in the census of that year, and neither was the next proprietor of the Stephensville brewery, Anton Fischer. He was included in Tovey's 1882 directory, suggesting he may have been open at least part of 1881. He was listed as a new firm in the May 1885 issue of *Western Brewer,* but these listings often lagged behind events. Fischer was still in Wing's 1887 directory (as a brewer of less than 500 barrels) and in the 1888 state business directory, but disappears from the records after this.

Sterling Township
(Bad Axe P.O.) (Vernon County)

Justus Groh (1867–69)
Wacker & Groh (1869–1871?)
Section 20, Sterling Township

Justus Groh built a brewery in Sterling Township in 1867, and it appeared in the excise records that December. The same records indicate that Reinhard Wacker joined the business sometime between May and October 1869. The brewery was never large: its production in 1870 was only about 200 barrels. The fact that Wacker & Groh had only invested $900 in the brewery and it didn't even have horsepower support the idea that it was a small operation. A county history from 1907 recounted: "Justice [sic] Groh and Reinhard Walker [sic] erected a brewery in the town, on the Lidie branch of the Bad Ax river, in 1870 [sic], but after being in use about two years it was allowed to go to decay." The last appearance of this brewery in the excise records is in 1871, but it may have operated for a few months in 1872.

Stevens Point
(Portage County)

Frank Wahle & George Ruder (1857–59)
Frank Wahle (Wahle & Smith?) (1859–1867)
Lutz & Ellinger (1867)
Andrew Lutz & Bro. (1867–1880)
Andrew Lutz (1880–1897)
Gustav Kuenzel, Stevens Point Brewery (1897–1901)
Gustav Kuenzel Brewing Co. (1901)
Stevens Point Brewing Co. (1901–1924)
Stevens Point Beverage Co. (1924–1958)
Stevens Point Brewery (1958–present)
2617 Water Street (street numbers have changed over time)

The first newspaper references to a brewery in Stevens Point came in 1856, when a report announced: "A brewery is being built there [Stevens Point] for the accommodation of the Pineries. They now obtain their regular supply of lager from Fond du Lac." There is some historical question as to precisely when the brewery started operations—long historical tradition says 1857, but local historian Kevin Knitt suggests that it may have been in business before then. (A brewery ad from 1938 cited 1855 as the year Wahle built his brewery.) They apparently built a following quickly, since the *Stevens Point Pinery* reported on Christmas Day of 1857:

> There is a Stevens Point institution which is probably not so generally known as it should be: we allude to the 'Stevens Point Brewery' of Messrs. Ruder & Wahle, some half mile out of town on the Plank Road. Commencing in a small way at first, these gentlemen have extend'd their works, and furnished them with apparatus and skillful hands till their Establishment is quite respectable, producing a really first-rate article of Lager. They are contracting for a further extension of their cellars and other rooms. Those fond of this delightful drink can be assured they now have no need to go abroad for their supplies.

The description of their expansion above seems strange if it was all done in one year. Perhaps in the excitement over their prospects, one newspaper reported inaccurately that Wahle and Ruder had purchased the brewery in Weyauwega. The brewery advertised their "Stock Ale, Lager Beer, Malt, Hops & Yeast. All orders from abroad promptly attended to. All kinds of Grain good for cattle and hogs always on hand." George Ruder left the firm in 1859 and founded his own brewery in Wausau, though he was still listed in Stevens Point in the 1860 population census.

According to some listings, Wahle brought in one Mr. Smith as a partner, though the timing is not clear. Advertisements in the *Pinery* in 1861 named Wahle as sole proprietor, as did an article about the business, yet Wahle & Smith appeared in a state business directory as late as 1872, long after Wahle sold the brewery. It is possible that the Smith listings were a misprint.

In 1867, Frank Wahle sold the business to Frederick Ellinger (or Illinger) and Jacob Lutz. According to an 1895 history, Lutz had worked at the brewery for five years before he took a share in the ownership. Ellinger only remained in the business for a few months, sold his share to Andrew Lutz, and by the beginning of the next year the firm was known as Lutz and Bro. (though both Jacob and Andrew were each sometimes given top billing, depending on the source).

By 1870 the Lutz brothers maintained a narrow lead over local rival Adam Kuhl—296 barrels to 274. The brewery was in operation year-round and employed four men (and one horsepower). While Kuhl passed Lutz Bros. in the early 1870s for a few years, the Lutz brothers responded by expanding their brewery and by the end of the decade were producing several hundred barrels a year more than Kuhl.

The census of 1880 showed that the Lutz household in Stevens Point was large—and confusing. Andrew and his wife Elizabeth shared their home with four hired servants (two of whom were listed as brewers) and several family members: brother Jacob, sons John and Jacob and nephew Jacob. The presence of three Jacobs sometimes made it difficult to tell which a newspaper article was referring to. H. B. Phillen, who was apparently a federal revenue collector as well as a correspondent for the *Grand Rapids Reporter,* gave this whimsical account of a visit to the brewery:

> . . . *we struck Lutz' Brewery where Uncle Andrew and the infant hold for the edification of the inner man. . . . He [Jacob] kicks the beam at little less than 300 pounds, . . . in any position he is a boy of the right stamp, and never travels* inkegnito *[sic]. His jollity and good nature are proverbial, and he pays Uncle Sam about $100 a month for keg plasters . . .*

The situation became a bit less crowded and complicated when brother Jacob sold his share to Andrew and moved to Grand Rapids (now Wisconsin Rapids) where he and brother David purchased the brewery of Nicholas Schmidt. The Stevens Point brewery was occasionally called A. Lutz & Son or A. Lutz & Bro., but local sources simply called it Lutz's brewery for the next seventeen years.

Andrew continued to add to his brewery, and added other businesses as well. In 1881 he purchased "the pop manufacturing apperatus *[sic]* of John Knauf and the machinery has been removed to the building near the brewery, where George Lutz [Andrew's son] will run the pop business in connection with the beer trade." Thus the production of soft drinks by the modern Stevens Point Brewery has a tradition nearly as old as the brewery. Lutz also had a smokehouse on the brewery property (which was broken into in 1896 and a large quantity of ham and bacon was stolen).

By 1895 Andrew Lutz was in his seventies, and was looking for a way to retire. Apparently none of his children wanted to take over the brewery, so he sought a buyer. The first rumor of a sale occurred in March 1895, when the brewery was reported sold to Louis Leidiger of Milwaukee for $21,000. However, this sale did not go through (reasons were not published) and Leidiger purchased the Ruder brewery at Merrill instead. Two years later, Lutz finally found an appropriate buyer. Gustav Kuenzel of Milwaukee, who was reported to have "held responsible positions in some of the largest breweries in that city" purchased the brewery and related property for $14,000. The brewery was producing approximately 3,000 barrels per year at the time of the sale. Kuenzel started improving the property almost immediately, building a new barn the same month. He completely rebuilt the storage cellar over the winter of 1897-8 so there would be enough capacity for the beer to lager for a full three months and so that the water from melting ice would drain better. The brewery did not install artificial refrigeration until 1908, so prior to this beer was "hauled to an underground storage plant at McDill" southeast of Stevens Point. There was also a saloon and beer garden near the caves, and these were popular destinations for area residents, and some customers walked all the way from Stevens Point for a fresh beer.

Gustav Kuenzel was unable to work for a while during the summer of 1901, which may have influenced his decision to sell the brewery that October. Michael Littel of Green Bay was the head of a group which purchased the brewery for $14,000, with the usual plans to "greatly improve the plant." The new owners filed articles of incorporation for the Stevens Point Brewing Co. within a month. They then closed the brewery for repairs and improvements, and began to produce beer again the next spring, though beer was not ready for sale until the end of June. Some of the stock was held by employees of the company, and occasionally this stock was offered for sale. Because the brewery was such an important part of the community, meetings of the board of directors were big news, and the minutes and remarks of the president were sometimes published verbatim.

The new company continued to make soft drinks as well as bock beer, which typically was released around Easter. The increasing demand for the company's product and the profits earned therefrom encouraged the company to launch a complete overhaul of the brewery in 1907. Chicago brewery architect Richard Griesser drew up the plans for the remodeled brewhouse, and Stevens Point Brick Company was asked to supply 250,000 bricks for the expansion. Among the improvements was a new power house twice the size of the existing structure, artificial refrigeration, and a new loading platform along a new side track of the Green Bay & Western Railroad. The additional capacity enabled the brewery to lager its bock beer for six months in the new glass-lined tanks, though it was still available only in limited quantities. In 1908, the brewery introduced two new flagship beers: Pink's Pale and Pink's Crystal, both available in bottles. These two brands were named after brewery manager Nicholas Gross, who was known as "Pinky." For a brief period the company used rhomboid shaped labels similar to those of Schlitz, with the slogan "The Beer that Made Milwaukee Furious," but Schlitz sought an

This was the non-controversial Pink's Crystal label. The label "that made Milwaukee furious" is in chapter 5. COLLECTION OF TYE SCHWALBE.

injunction and forced Stevens Point to change the labels. A Milwaukee columnist reprinted the label in the *Sentinel* with a poem describing the supposed anger of the Milwaukee beer community over the competition from Stevens Point, concluding

> The men who open bottles
> And the can [growler] brigade penurious
> Would die before they'd drink the beer
> That made Milwaukee furious.

The concern expressed by Milwaukee breweries seems misplaced since Pink's was not distributed outside the Stevens Point area.

Stevens Point Brewing had a quality control scare in 1909, when several batches of beer with an off flavor were released. Dr. John E. Siebel came up from Chicago to examine the premises, and found the culprit to be a leak in the brine-filled cooling coils in the keg racking room. The company ran front-page ads explaining the problem, and imploring customers to continue their patronage.

Throughout the 1910s, Stevens Point Brewing continued to increase their advertising and to modernize their operations. In 1914, Point purchased its first delivery truck, a three-ton four-wheel-drive model built at Clintonville, Wisconsin. In order to make the transition, teamster Ed Lutz went to the factory for two weeks to learn about the mechanics and operation of the truck prior to becoming the driver. The truck was nearly wrecked the same month it arrived when it proved too heavy for a section of road that collapsed under it. The truck was towed out and continued on. Another truck was purchased from a Milwaukee manufacturer in 1915, and these vehicles were likely the reason for an ad placed by the company in 1915 offering for sale eight horses. Some horses remained in use, especially in winter when some beer was delivered by sleigh. One team of horses took fright and took flight, dumping off the sleigh box with a shipment of case beer. It is a testimony to the durability of the cases and bottles of the era that only a few bottles were reported broken. Also in 1914, the company built another expansion, this time a new "fireproof" office and bottling plant.

When the United States entered World War I, Stevens Point Brewing led the way in demonstrating patriotism by purchasing $5,000 of Liberty Bonds. The company sponsored a full-page ad in April 1918 to back the Third Liberty Loan. However, the brewery was subject to the same restrictions as other businesses, and was forced to close for a time in January 1918 when an order limiting the use of coal went into effect. The brewery returned to production, but was forced to cease brewing again in December when wartime prohibition went into effect. The board of directors reported at the 1919 annual meeting that enough product remained to supply customers for several months, but the fate of the brewery and its twenty employees after that was unclear. The company converted to making near beer, and in 1921, the shareholders voted to purchase new equipment for soft drink manufacture. Stevens Point Brewing was one of many firms that was ready to make real beer again when Secretary of Treasury Andrew Mellon issued regulations which appeared to allow beer to be sold for medicinal purposes by prescription, but this proved to be a false alarm and no such market developed.

Even though most of the company's production was in soft drinks, the name of the business was not changed until March 1924, when new ownership changed the name to Stevens Point Beverage Co. The new president, Ludwig Korfmann, and vice president, Chris Kurth, were both from Milwaukee, though other Stevens Point residents retained their positions or their stock. Korfmann spoke highly of the prospects for the city and the company, and had special praise for the water from the Plover Hills basin, which he claimed was an important factor in his investment. The corporate entity Stevens Point Brewing Co. was not officially dissolved for a few more years, but all the business was conducted under the Beverage Co. name. The new company sponsored softball and bowling teams throughout Prohibition (and after) to build goodwill in the community.

Stevens Point Beverage was raided by federal agents in June 1928, and forty-eight half-barrels of beer were found in the keg racking room. This appears to be the only time that this brewery fell afoul of the law during the dry years.

With the election of President Franklin D. Roosevelt, Stevens Point Beverage began to prepare the brewery for the imminent return of real beer. The company had not been making its own near beer for the previous three years, but had "handled near beer under the name 'Point Special' as a jobbed product." (Special was brewed at Stevens Point when it was first introduced in 1929.) However, Point Special was slated to be the name for the new bottled beer, rather than returning to the "Pink's" brands from before Prohibition. The company expected to spend several thousand dollars reconditioning the brewery, as well as buying raw materials and containers for the new product. The return of jobs was also welcome during the Great Depression—the company employed only five men at the end of 1932, compared with twenty-four during the peak years of 1916 and 1917. When Roosevelt signed the Cullen Act, brewmaster George Eggenhofer and Calvin L. Korfmann took turns blowing the steam whistle at the brewery. Eggenhofer also shaved off his beard, which he had been growing for three weeks "asserting he would not cut off his whiskers until the president signed the beer bill." Even when beer came back (see chapter 7), the company purchased advertisements to remind customers that they were continuing in the soft drink business. Point bock returned in 1934, and later that year Eggenhofer brewed special light and dark beers for Thanksgiving (which could be purchased in cases of half light and half dark). The "Big Charlie" package (normally ½ gallon, though one gallon labels exist) was first advertised in 1935, and was named after brewery manager Charles Schenk. In 1937, ads began proclaiming that Point beer was "Union Made and Union Delivered."

Stevens Point Beverage was profitable enough in 1939 to purchase new pasteurizing and bottling equipment, as well as a system to capture carbon dioxide given off during fermentation and use it during bottling. Point also

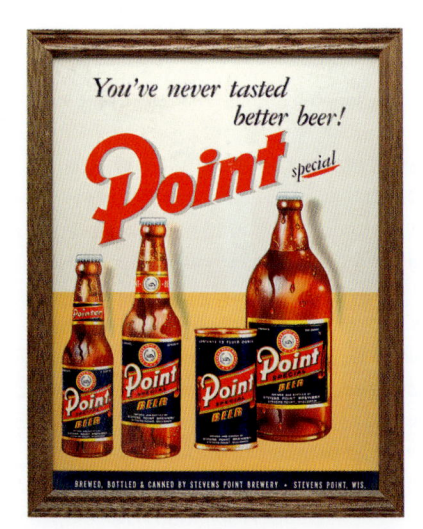

Stevens Point Brewery had only one year-round beer but produced 7-ounce, 12-ounce, and 32-ounce bottles and 12-ounce cans (ca. 1950s). COLLECTION OF DAVID WENDL.

introduced a new beer that year to show off the new brewing processes using a new formula, and launched a contest to come up with a name for it. Anyone could enter, provided they sent in seven labels of what was tentatively called "Prize Beer" with each proposed name. More than 3,000 entries were submitted, and the winning entry was Amber Cream. However, company officials decided to alter the name to Amber Prize (though the original contest winner was still paid). Amber Prize appeared in "Steinie" bottles, as did Point Special.

Stevens Point Beverage installed equipment to package beer in cans in May 1953. Rather than using cone-top cans, Point started with flat-top cans, and general manager Phil Shibilski noted that this "installation was the second of its kind to be put in service in this country in a small brewery." Canned beer did not begin to appear in newspaper advertisements until early 1955. In the late 1950s, the company identity started to re-emphasize brewing. An ad celebrating its "leap day" anniversary in February 1956 stated that the firm was "now known as the Stevens Point Brewery or Point Brewery," though that name had been used in ads since 1954. However, the Beverage Co. name remained in use on labels until 1960.

From 1947–1973, output never fell below 30,000 barrels per year, but never exceeded 41,000. Point continued to survive by supplying its Central Wisconsin market with a single brand of beer (not counting bock during the spring). In 1973, Point Special was the top-rated American beer in a taste test sponsored by Chicago columnist and personality Mike Royko. In the following years, Point Special became a national cult, the brewery expanded production and capacity, and eventually developed into an important regional brewer. (Additional information on this period is found in chapter 10.)

With its capacity and market expanding, the brewery increased the number of products offered. The soda line expanded with Diet Root Beer, Vanilla Cream Soda, and Black Cherry Cream. As of this writing, Point has added Kitty Cocktail, which has a ginger ale base with maraschino cherry and lemon-lime flavors. Meanwhile, the beer offerings were burgeoning as well. In 2004, Point acknowledged the trend toward hoppier craft beers with their new Cascade Pale Ale. Four years later, Point created a series of seasonal beers, ending decades during which Point Bock was the only true seasonal beer. The seasonal that gained the most national attention was the summer wheat beer Nude Beach, which featured a label with beach goers shielded by conveniently placed surfboards, coolers and towels. Novelty aside, the beer went on to earn medals at important beer competitions. By the early 2010s, Point had expanded into Alabama, Georgia, Texas and North Carolina, and was the second-largest craft brewery based in Wisconsin.

Expanding markets led to even more expansions of the brewery. In 2013, Point launched its fourth expansion in four years; this one included a second brew kettle in addition to additional fermenting capacity. This boosted capacity from 120,000 to 150,000 barrels per year. Point also brought back the "Big Charlie," though the 2012 version was a 16-ounce can rather than a half-gallon bottle. Other Point beers, including Nude Beach Summer Wheat also came out in the 16-ounce cans, which were popular with craft beer drinkers. The Whole Hog line grew to five beers (though some earlier brands were phased out), and new summer, harvest and winter variety packs were introduced containing creative beers not otherwise available. The James Page label purchased from a defunct Minneapolis brewery was renamed JP's to produce "adventurous brews with a twist" such as Yabba Dhaba Chai Tea Porter and Casper White Stout (seemingly a contradiction in terms). Much of the credit for Point's continued success was due to longtime brewmaster John Zappa, who guided the brewhouse through the changes from a single-beer brewery in 1977 to the IPA-filled product line of 2015.

As of 2017, Stevens Point Brewery was the twenty-fourth largest craft brewing company in the United States, and the thirty-second largest brewery overall, with production in 2017 of 125,000 barrels (after a high of 142,000 in 2015).

Haertel & Kemmeter (1864–1865?)

Rumors of a new brewery in Stevens Point began in 1863, when *The Pinery* reported that plans were underway. It was more than a year

Nicholas C. Point is the brewery's mascot. This root beer label is ca. 2007. AUTHOR'S COLLECTION.

later that *The Pinery* was able to report that Hartel & Kemmeter had opened a new brewery on Main Street. This would be a different location than the later Kuhl brewery, and it is possible that Kemmeter joined Kuhl later at the Prentice Street site. A 1958 history of brewing in the area claims that Hartel & Kemmeter was in fact a different business.

J. Kemmeter & A. Kuhl (1866?–67)
Adam Kuhl (& Estate) (1867–1885)
Illenberger & Ritter (1886–88?)
Stanley E. Kellar (1890?–92)
Charles & Fred Kuhl (1892)

Brown and Prentice Streets

The firm of J. Kemmeter and Adam Kuhl first appears in the excise records in January 1867. Since they were taxed on nineteen barrels that month, it is possible that they were in full operation late in the previous year. This partnership dissolved in May 1867, and Adam Kuhl became sole proprietor of the brewery. By 1870 Kuhl was well established and was making nearly as much beer as the much older Lutz brewery. Kuhl only employed three men, but he had two horsepower to Lutz's single horse. Kuhl's production generally remained between 500 and 800 barrels per year during the 1870s, and his brewery was a popular gathering place in Stevens Point.

After the death of Adam Kuhl in July 1883, his widow Christine leased the brewery to experienced brewers rather than turn the business over to her sons right away "to give her sons an opportunity to attend school." By 1884, Kuhl's brewery was a significant steam-powered plant. The Kuhl estate started building a soda water factory across Prentice Street to the east of the brewery in 1883 which was also available for bottling beer. The first lessees were George Illenberger and Mr. Ritter of Milwaukee, who took possession on New Years' Day 1886. However the story gets confusing here, because in March 1886 the *Stevens Point Daily Journal* reported that John Sheer and George Ellenberger [sic] had purchased land "south of 4th street between Prentice and Smith streets for a new brewery." However, there was no 4th Avenue at Prentice and Smith, and the existing Kuhl brewery was between Smith and Prentice. Whatever the case, no new brewery was built on that site, though Illenberger later built a new brewery on Michigan Avenue. Mrs. Kuhl continued to improve the property, and in 1886 built a large new residence on the lot to the south of the brewery. It is not clear if Illenberger held the brewery for the entire period of his lease since the Kuhl brewery was still mentioned in occasional newspaper accounts in the late 1880s, though this may have been casual use of a recognized local name. Illenberger appears in Wing's directory of 1887, and the size given for his brewery suggests it was the larger Kuhl plant rather than his Michigan Avenue enterprise, and his obituary said he operated the Kuhl brewery for about three years. In 1890, Mrs. Kuhl leased the brewery to insurance agent Stanley E. Kellar, who operated it for two years. By 1891, some of the grain storage and lodging facilities on the Prentice Street side had been converted to an office and an attached saloon. Kellar also dug a new cistern to contain waste from the brewery "thus entirely dissipating the disagreeable order [sic] that had of late been complained of in that vicinity." In August 1891, Kellar was accused by the local W.C.T.U. of selling beer to a minor, though there was no evidence and the case was thrown out.

In February 1892, Kellar left the brewery business and the brewery lay dormant for about a month. In March, Charles and Fred Kuhl announced plans to restart the plant. Fred had been working for Falk, Jung & Borchert in Milwaukee, and returned to Stevens Point with a fine reputation as a brewer. However, in August the brewery burned down. Fred Kuhl and David Lutz, who were sleeping in the building, managed to escape. While estimates of the damage varied from $12,000 to $18,000, insurance only covered about one third of the damage, and the Kuhls decided not to rebuild.

George Illenberger (1890?–93)
Neuberger & Ritter (1893–95)
Frank Michalski, Neuberger & Ritter lessees (1895)

522 Michigan Avenue

George Illenberger built a new brewery prior to 1891 on the east side of Stevens Point. While the building was of brick construction, in other ways the brewery was rather basic—it did not use steam power which was in common use by then, and did not have a malt house. The date of construction has been difficult to pin down. Illenberger apparently was still leasing the Kuhl brewery until at least 1888, though one much later history claims that he started the Michigan Avenue brewery in 1888, but the brewery was completed and in operation before the publication of the 1891 Sanborn insurance map in October.

Illenberger only operated the brewery for a short time. In November 1893, Neuberger and Ritter took over the brewery, and Steve Neuberger moved his family from Minneapolis to Stevens Point. Illenberger (or Ellenberger) stayed in the industry at the Lutz/Kuenzel brewery until his retirement in 1900, though he returned briefly in 1901 when Gustav Kuenzel was laid up and ended up working until a few months before his death in 1906. The new proprietors apparently added a malt house, since they advertised their business in early 1895 as "Neuberger & Ritter, Brewers & Maltsters." They adopted the name "Central City Brewery" for their business, which had a capacity of fifteen barrels per day, and proclaimed their motto was "Purity and Strength." In early 1895, Frank Michalski purchased the brewery, but Neuberger stayed on to operate the brewery. The new management appeared to be moving aggressively into the void created by the destruction of the Kuhl brewery, and Michalski installed a new boiler to power the brewery in 1895. They also staged promotions like entering a large float in the *Eintrachts Verein* parade, "with the proprietors and assistants seated thereon, and there seemed to be no lack of homemade beverage to quench the thirst of the inner man."

A catastrophic fire struck the Central City brewery in late June 1895. Four men, including Neuberger, were in the brewery and managed to escape, but the brewery, two houses and a barn were destroyed, together with all the contents including a new delivery wagon. The fire department was late to the scene because "[A]n attempt to turn in an alarm by telephone proved fruitless, the night operator claiming that she was unable to understand what was wanted. After the fire had been burning for some time, Albert Kostush mounted a bicycle and rode to engine house No. 2, and No. 1 was given the alarm from there." Michalski's insurance was less than $5,000, and the damage was considerably more, and he decided not to rebuild. Stone from the foundation of the brewery was later used for the Curran & Wiesner building.

Polish Brewing Co. (1908–1913)
National Brewing Co. (1913–17)
CORNER OF WISCONSIN AND WOOD

There had been only one brewery in Stevens Point since 1895, and the possibility of a second brewery was tempting to investors. In this era, saloonkeepers were looking for options to paying prices they considered too high demanded by large breweries. In addition, members of the growing Polish American community were seeking more economic influence. Portage County and Stevens Point had a large community of Polish immigrants, and in 1907 they were approached about buying stock for a new brewery. The first attempts drew little support: in January Frank Boyanski of Grand Rapids (now Wisconsin Rapids) held a meeting to assess interest in a new brewery. Boyanski had been associated with Grand Rapids Brewing Co., but left in a dispute and had sued that business, and had also been at a brewery in Antigo. Only eight people attended the first meeting and only one was prepared to commit to buying a share for $100. A subsequent meeting encouraged more interest, and between sixty and seventy people purchased stock in Polish Brewing Co., which was incorporated in March 1907. The company selected a site at the corner of Wisconsin & Wood, convenient to the Wisconsin Central and Green Bay & Western tracks as well as to the city sewer.

The company did not actually start production until 1908 according to annual reports. Some of the delay was caused by the inability to attract bids for construction that were within the parameters set by the company. However, building eventually commenced and the brewery was in operation. Unfortunately, they had only produced for a few months before the brewery was struck by a destructive late-season tornado in November 1908. The newly built bottling works was demolished, and a portion of the brewhouse roof was found near the corner of Main and Prentice, about a mile away.

Polish Brewing Co. rebuilt, though they had trouble keeping brewmasters in Stevens Point. In March 1911, Jaroslaw Ondracek left to take over as manager of Hillsboro Brewing Co., in which he was already a stockholder. His brother Frank moved back from Chicago to take over brewing duties, but he then moved back to Chicago in May 1912. Polish Brewing hired Reinhardt Ernest Eggert from (appropriately enough) Warsaw, Illinois. Eggert was married in June 1914, and in November short ads for the brewery announced that a new brewmaster (later identified as A. Wismeth) had arrived from Marshfield. Wismeth himself left in 1916, and a third Ondracek, Garry, came from Antigo to assume brewing duties.

In 1913, shareholders met to consider changing the name of the company from Polish Brewing Co. to National Brewing Co. While descriptive, the former name may have limited the market, which the latter certainly did not. The final vote was 267 shares in favor of the change and three against. The new name did not protect the company any better from wind damage. In April 1913 a new seventy-foot smokestack was installed to replace the previous stack which had been damaged by a heavy wind storm. The change did not help business enough and by early 1916 a committee was appointed to oversee reorganization of the company. In March, the stockholders met to decide whether to close the brewery or to raise an assessment to keep the business going. The business continued, but the lack of capital caused delays in maintenance, and this resulted in a loss that the struggling brewery could not absorb. In August 1916, the company was forced to dump 523 barrels of beer that had spoiled, most likely because they aging vats had not been coated properly with shellac in three years—a process that was recommended every year. The condition of the vats was exacerbated by the hot weather and the fact that the refrigeration plant had not been working properly for some time. The loss was estimated at $3,556.40 (at a prevailing price of $6.80 per barrel) which the company could ill afford. The event provided some humor for others: The *Daily Journal* waggishly noted "Wisconsin river fish below Stevens Point cannot complain of being 'dry' for a day or two at any rate, in view of the 523 barrels of beer dumped into the stream by the National Brewing Co. Wonder how a fish looks when he is 'tight?'" Another 150 barrels were dumped later in the week, and it was reported at that time that the vats would have to be replaced entirely.

In February 1917, the stockholders met and decided to close the brewery and turn the plant to other uses, considering the recent decline in business and the fact that the brewery could not turn a profit at such a small scale, as well as the likelihood that prohibition was on the way. Some stockholders also alleged

Natural disasters were often depicted on postcards. Here the Polish Brewing Co. is shown after the 1908 tornado. AUTHOR'S COLLECTION.

that the brewery had been mismanaged from the beginning, even though sales started well. After closing, the brewery was used as a bakery and for storage, and was razed in 1994.
Isadore Street Brewing (1998-2000)
The Keg (2000-4)
200 ISADORE STREET
Isadore Street Brewing opened in 1998 in downtown Stevens Point, near the university campus. In 2000, new owners changed the name to The Keg to suggest more of a college-town bar atmosphere. Ronald and Carol Gorski produced just under 200 barrels in 2001, but despite the local popularity of the beer, the brewpub closed in 2004.

ST. FRANCIS (Milwaukee County)

St. Francis Brewing Company (St. Francis Brewery & Restaurant) (2009-present)
3825 SOUTH KINNICKINNIC AVENUE
St. Francis Brewing Co. began brewing in 2009 in a suburb southeast of Milwaukee and on the northeast corner of General Mitchell International Airport. St. Francis took advantage of their saintly name by naming their beers after the seven deadly sins: lust, wrath, greed, envy, sloth, pride, and gluttony. (Pride and Gluttony are both rotating seasonals.) Other special and seasonal beers are named with religious themes as well. (The brewery's rewards program/pint club equivalent is called the Frequent Sinner Card.) In 2013 St. Francis began bottling their beer—brewed and packaged at Sand Creek Brewing in Black River Falls. In 2015, St. Francis was considering expanding to a site in the Menomonee Valley for a new brewery with packaging capabilities, but cost proved prohibitive and they decided on a more modest plan adjacent to the brewpub.

The most interesting initiative by St. Francis Brewing to date is their partnership with Milwaukee County Parks in Milwaukee's Craft Beer Garden at Humboldt Park in the Bay View neighborhood. The beer garden, established in 2014, features St. Francis beers, though in 2017 each Friday was devoted to a "tap takeover" by a different Wisconsin craft brewery.

STOUGHTON (Dane County)

Vik'ing Brewpub (2015-present)
211 EAST MAIN STREET
'Vik'ing Brewpub opened in 2014, at first with beers made at House of Brews in Madison, then in 2015 added beer made on their own 3.5 barrel system. While 'Vik'ing features a fanciful representation of a Viking ship as the bar, the name actually comes from the name of co-owner, Vik Malling. Stoughton celebrates its Norwegian heritage, but was also a stronghold of "drys" throughout much of its history, so it not surprising it took until 2015 for a brewery to open there. Among the regular beers is Soot in My Eye Black Rye IPA, which is based on Malling's problems pronouncing Syttende Mai, the Norwegian national holiday.

STURGEON BAY (Door County)

Hugo Seidemann & Bro. (1867-?)
Hermann Seidemann (1872-79)
Leidiger Bros. (1879-1887)
Hagemeister Brewing Co. Branch (1887-1920)
Schonbrunn Brewing Co., Inc. (1933-38)
3879 BAY SHORE ROAD AND GEORGIA STREET
The first positive evidence of a brewery in Sturgeon Bay is in the excise records of October 1867, when Hugo Seidemann was listed as a brewer in Sevastopol, the township just north of downtown Sturgeon Bay. Seidemann is listed as a beer brewer in the 1870 populations census (unfortunately the 1870 industrial census for Door county is unreadable, so it is not clear if he brewed enough to be listed or not). It appears that Hugo sold the brewery to brother Hermann in 1872. Hermann is listed in Schade's 1876 directory as having brewed 475 barrels in 1874 and 339 the following year. Production kept declining, since Salem's records for (the misspelled) Lindemann show 225 barrels in 1878 and 207 in 1879.

The R. G. Dun & Co. records state that Seidemann rented his brewery to George Brockford in 1878 for a period of five years, but either this arrangement was cut short or never came to pass, since in 1879 Louis Leidiger and his brother Ernest rented the brewery. Louis was an experienced brewer, who had started brewing at age thirteen in Sheboygan, worked for several years in Milwaukee, later in Omaha and Sioux City, and finally back in Milwaukee, where he remained until moving to Door County in 1879. While some sources suggest that the Leidigers took over the brewery of Arnold Wagener, both the location of the brewery and the fact that the Leidiger brothers were listed as brewers boarding with farmer Herman Seidermann [sic] in the 1880 population census support the conclusion that the Leidigers purchased the brewery in Sevastopol.

The Leidigers purchased the brewery within a few years, and by 1884 were "doing a large business" according to the Dun & Co. evaluator. They produced just under 700 barrels in the 1881-2 tax year, which was twice as much as the other brewer of Sturgeon Bay, Arnold Wagener.

In 1887, Hagemeister Brewing Co. of Green Bay purchased the Leidiger brewery for $5,000 to acquire extra brewing capacity. Louis Leidiger later took over the former Ruder brewery in Merrill. Al Hagemeister moved to Sturgeon Bay to take over management of the plant, which operated under the Sturgeon Bay Brewing Co. name. The plant does not appear ever to have had its own malt house, and probably brought in all the necessary grain from the Green Bay branch. By 1907, capacity of this branch was

This bock poster is from about 1900. COURTESY OF NATIONAL BREWERY MUSEUM.

10,000 barrels, and it supplied "the trade in the northern country up as far as Houghton. A wind storm struck the brewery in 1910 and caused $5,000 of damage to the boiler house, the brewhouse and several out buildings.

In 1917, Hagemeister Brewing was looking into alternative beverages, and decided that cherry juice would be a profitable alternative to grape juice—especially given the importance of cherries in Door County. The company was prepared to invest more than $10,000 in creating and promoting the new drink, but the company ultimately decided not to pursue this product. During Prohibition, the company operated briefly as the Sturgeon Bay branch of Hagemeister Products Co., but Hagemeister dropped this business completely within a few years and the Sturgeon Bay branch seems to have shut down even earlier (perhaps as early as 1921).

After Prohibition, several parties showed interest in restarting the brewery. In July 1933, the *Manitowoc Herald-Times* reported that the brewery had been sold to Robert Seider of Chicago, despite the fact that "a group of Door county men" held an option on the property. A few days later, the sale was closed and Robert Schoenbrunn, attorney for Seider, announced that repairs were already underway and that he hoped to have beer on the market in at most two months. One question that was unanswered at this point was whether the new company "expects to cater principally to the local trade or is brewing for the Chicago thirst." (The Door County tavern owners who lost out on the Hagemeister plant planned their own brewery "in the heart of the city" with a capacity of 150 barrels, but these plans did not come to pass.) Seider (or Seiter) was a police officer in Chicago, and along with police Sgt. John Orgel, he quit the force to operate the brewery. Why the brewery was run under Schonbrunn's name (and misspelled) suggests Seider was unable to get a license to operate in Wisconsin.

In fact, the brewery sent nearly all its production to Illinois, but the brewery operated only intermittently. (The Fort Dearborn brand

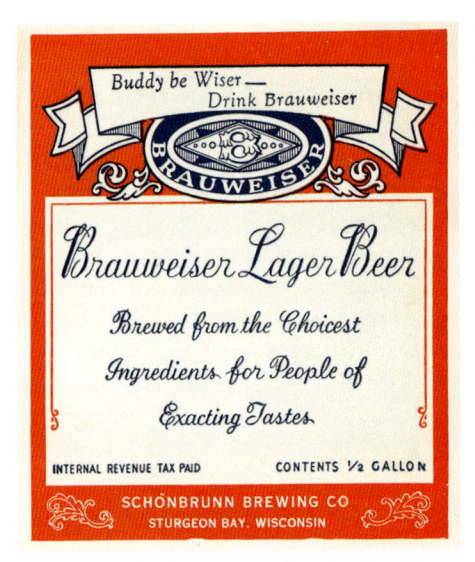

The design of this label (ca. 1936) strongly suggests another attempt to trade on the fame of Budweiser while avoiding lawsuits. COLLECTION OF TYE SCHWALBE.

would have much more appeal in Chicago, where the historic fort had been, than in Door County.) Brewing historian John Steiner argues that much of the beer sold under the Schonbrunn name was actually produced in Chicago. Despite reports that the company changed its name to Sturgeon Bay Brewing Co., the name was never changed and all official records still used the Schonbrunn name. At one point the Sturgeon Bay brewery occasionally produced over 400 barrels per month in 1936, but by 1937 and 1938 it was rare for the brewery to produce more than 100 barrels in a month. The last recorded sales were in October 1938, and the brewery appears to have gone out of business at that time.

Wagener Bros. (1874–1882?)
MAIN STREET NEAR SPRUCE (MODERN FIRST AVENUE NEAR NEBRASKA STREET)

The Wagener Brothers, William and Nicholas A., started their brewery in 1874, just too late to be included in the surviving excise records. Nicholas (sometimes called Arnold, his middle name) served in the 5th Wisconsin Infantry during the Civil War, and afterwards went to Nebraska to work in a brewery there. He then traveled throughout the west, but returned to Wisconsin, where in 1873 he took a position in the Blatz brewery before moving to Sturgeon Bay. William was a veteran of the 16th Infantry, suffering wounds at Murfreesboro but returned to carry the regiment's colors at Lookout Mountain. Their brewery was a small one, brewing just sixty-two barrels in 1875. The brothers increased production during the next few years, reaching 469 barrels in 1879. However, the brothers did not have a smooth path to prosperity. In 1876, the brewery was raided and D. M. Whitney, the U.S. Marshal, "arrested Arnold Wagener, and looked around for his brother, who was not to be found. He also seized their brewery. They are charged with selling 'crooked beer.' They are sons of the crooked whisky Wagener of Mishicott." Despite this brush with the law, both brothers served as sheriffs of Door County, first William and then Arnold. William died in November 1878, though the firm continued to be known as Wagner Bros. since his widow was part of the business.

This brewery continued through at least 1881, since Arnold is still listed in the 1880 population census as a brewer and is still in Tovey's 1882 directory (which was sometimes a year behind). The R. G. Dun & Co. credit reports indicate he was out of business by July 1882, and may have been some months before. However, federal records indicate that Wagner Bros. *[sic]* purchased tax stamps sufficient for 333 3/8 barrels in the year ending April 30 1882, so they may have been in business into 1882.

Some accounts claim that Leidiger Bros. took over this brewery. However, this clashes with the fact that Leidiger and Wagener were both listed as brewers in the 1880 population census and the 1882 Tovey directory, as well as the 1882 revenue stamp records. In addition, Leidiger was listed in Sevastopol and Wagener in Sturgeon Bay, which seems to indicate that Leidiger took over Seidemann's brewery, not Wagner's. The Seidemann/Leidiger/Hagemeister brewery was clearly north of the city and on the bay, but there had to be another brewery in downtown Sturgeon Bay, which was probably Wagener's. The existence of a brewery on Main Street comes from a passage in a 1917 history of Door County, which related this tale:

> Just across the street from the *Advocate* is the site of the first county courthouse. Adjoining this on the southeast was Leidiger's brewery. The courthouse was a two-story building with a basement. The basement was used for a saloon, which was very convenient for the court and jury. However, it was customary for the jury to provide itself with refreshments in another manner. After O. E. Dreutzer had harangued the jury into a real bellicose attitude, the jury would retire into its sanctum sweating under the collar. A rope would then be dropped to a side door of the brewery and a keg of beer hauled up. After due investigation of the contents of the keg the verdict would be returned.

The location does not appear to fit Leidiger's brewery, which was nowhere near the old courthouse. It is possible that Leidiger had a brewery saloon at this location, but it seems more likely that this was Wagener's brewery, and the account from forty years later confused the names of the two brewers.

Cherryland Brewery (1987–1998)
Cherryland Brewpub (1998)
Sturgeon Bay Brewing Co. (1998)
341 North Third Avenue or 560 Gordon Road

In 1987, Tom Alberts and Mark Feld brought brewing back to Door County when they founded Cherryland Brewery in the 1914 Oliver Station railroad depot on the Green Bay and Western line. Cherryland was typically classified as a brewpub since it was associated with Del Santo's Restaurant. In keeping with its setting, Cherryland's most notable beer was Cherry Rail, a lager made with cherry extract that garnered a silver medal at the 1991 Great American Beer Festival. All of the lagers were brewed at Dubuque Brewing Co., but the ales were made in Sturgeon Bay, as were the beers intended for consumption on the premises.

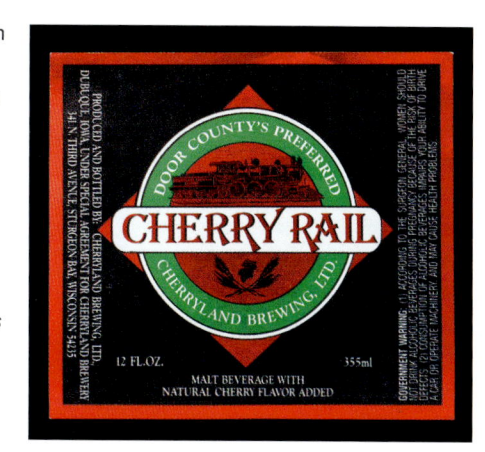

Glossy labels for Cherry Rail and other Cherryland beers stood out in coolers and on store shelves. Later labels abandoned the glossy paper. AUTHOR'S COLLECTION.

The attention brought by Cherry Rail made Cherryland an attractive partner for a venture that proposed creating a "beer-of-the-month club" selling American craft beers in Japan. (This plan never came to pass.) At its peak, Cherryland sold about sold about 3,000 barrels of beer per year. However, starting in 1998, the brewery was sold and Cherryland contracted the brewing of all its beers, first to Dubuque Brewing in Iowa, then to Hinterland, though the beers were still sold at the restaurant in Sturgeon Bay.

Starboard Brewing Co. (2014–present)
151 North 3rd Avenue

Amanda and Patrick Surfus wanted to bring a local brewery to Sturgeon Bay, and opened Starboard Brewing Co. in October 2014. As Starboard employee Steve Rice put it: "[A] town should have certain things, its butcher, its baker, its candlestick maker, and its brewery. Sturgeon Bay is finally complete again." In 2016 they produced 95 barrels on their one-barrel system. Starboard does not have any particular flagship beers, but produces a variety of different styles. In August 2017, the beer list included everything from an American pale ale to a rhubarb saison and Wood Stock Ale, brewed with sap and spruce tips.

Summit Township *(Dousman/Golden Lake) (Waukesha County)*

Jacob Grubb (1858–1871)
Adam Grubb (1871–74)
Michael Silverling (1874–75)
John Link (1875–1881)
Mrs. Margaret Link (1881–82)
Louis C. Kuhry (1883–88)
Section 31, South of Modern U.S. Highway 18.

Jacob Grubb appears to have started brewing around 1858 just south of Golden Lake in Summit Township. He appears in the 1870 census of industry as a brewer of sixty barrels. This earned him $480, which was actually below the $500 threshold required to be listed in the census. His small brewery was powered by hand, and he was the only employee. His son Adam took over in the fall of 1871, according to excise records and the 1873 industry directory, which listed him as brewing eighty barrels in the year prior to May 1872. Little is known about Michael Silverling's tenure at the brewery. By 1875 John Link had acquired the brewery. Link expanded production significantly—producing 368 barrels in 1878 (but only 238 the next year). He operated it until his death in 1881, after which his widow Margaret took charge of the brewery. A few years later she either sold it or leased it to Louis C. Kuhry (Kouhry) who continued to run the brewery for a few more years. The entry in Tovey's 1882 directory indicates that the brewery had a malt house, but subsequent entries in Wing's directories do not include a malt house.

Superior *(Douglas County)*

Louis Kiichli (1859–1869)
Klein & Co. (Klein & Decemval), Superior City Brewery (1869–1875?)
346 West Second Street (1859–61)
Central Park, Third Street and Sixth Avenue (also given as L Street and Third Street) (1861–1875?)

Louis Kiichli (various spellings) is believed to have started brewing in the Twin Ports around

1859. Local historian Tony Dierckins has uncovered the earliest mention of Kiichi's brewery: he advertised as a "'manufacturer and wholesale and retail dealer in lager beer'" in August 1859. He moved to a new location in 1861, though unfortunately the newspaper article that announced the beginning of production did not indicate the location. It did, however, confirm: "The beer made there is of much better quality than the last two brewings at the old place." Kiichli's location is confused by his listing in the 1860 population census as a resident of Duluth. The commute in 1860 would have been much more difficult than in the modern era.

His new brewery still may not have been large enough, since an ad that ran from 1864 through 1868 noted that Kiichli "keeps constantly on hand and will furnish to order Old, New and all kinds of Beer and Ale, *Usually* manufactured in this vicinity." (Emphasis added.) Where any beer not "manufactured in this vicinity" came from was not stated. Kiichli also had a butcher shop in Superior, and was later elected county clerk. The R. G. Dun & Co. credit evaluator reported that Kiichli worked hard and made money despite not having much capital. His wife helped out in the saloon, and "they work well together in making & saving money." The last entry for Kiichli in the Dun records was in 1868 but he may have continued after that. In 1933, old settler John Bardon described Kiichli's beer as "'a fine product—with plenty of body to it.'"

In 1869, Kiichli sold the business to Jacob Klein and Klein's brother-in-law Victor Decemval (or Descimval). They enlarged and improved the brewery, including a new beer cellar. Advertisements in the *Superior Times* announced that they would deliver their beer "around the head of Lake Superior or along the Northern Pacific Railroad," though at that time the Northern Pacific was still in the very early stages of construction so this did not enhance their delivery range very much. Production at their renamed Superior City Brewery dropped from 469 barrels in 1871 to 167 the following year, but ads for the brewery continued to run in the *Superior Times* through October 1875.

Thomas Shiels (Shiels & Sizer) (1865?–1870)
John Walbourne (Walbram) (1871–72?)
Thomas Shiels (1873?)

Nemadji River near Modern Thirty-first Avenue and Second Street

The R. G. Dun & Co. reports indicate that Thomas Shiels, recently of Buffalo, New York, was building a brewery in Superior. His first appearance in the excise records was in May 1870, and the next month he paid tax on seventeen barrels of beer. However, historian Tony Dierckins suggests that the "Nemadji Brewery" may have been open as early as 1865. Henry Sizer was associated with Shiels in the business, apparently as the bookkeeper. Long-time area resident John Bardon recalled in 1933 that Shiels' "'beer was wonderful. The red iron[-] impregnated waters of the Nemadji imparted to this beverage health giving qualities rivaling "Ayres' Cherry Pectoral," "Vinegar Bitters," or Lydia Pinkham's vegetable compound.'" The Dun records indicate that Shiels "sold out" in late 1870 and the company was out of business for a few months.

In late 1870 John Walbourne came from Detroit and leased the brewery. The article in the *Superior Times* announcing the change reported "Mr. W. has made many valuable improvements in and about the establishment," suggesting that he had been in possession for some months. He is listed (as Walbram) in the excise records starting in April 1871, and was reported to have made "'many valuable improvements in and about the establishment, and those who know prounounce his beer first class.'" Walbourne does not appear in any other records after 1871, and Dierckins found that Walbourne died in a duck hunting accident in October 1872. Shiels took control of the building again, though may not have resumed brewing. Bardon reported that the equipment from a Superior brewery was sold to the Kreimer brewery in Duluth, and the timing appears to fit the Nemadji brewery better than the Superior City brewery. In June 1873, Shiels offered a $10 reward for information "lead[ing] to the arrest and conviction of the parties that removed the plank platform from my Brewery on Left Hand river," suggesting that he was at least interested in maintaining the plant at this date. A passing reference in the *Superior Times* indicated that it was still standing in 1877. Some sources suggest that this plant was in operation as late as 1884, but this appears unlikely.

West Superior Brewing Co. (1891–1901?)

215 Hammond Avenue

The West Superior Brewing Co. was established in 1889, though it does not appear to have begun production until 1891. Its founders were Bernard Schwanekamp and Johan Joseph Hennes, who were brothers-in-law. The plant consisted of one three-story frame building and two single-story frame buildings and employed seven men, of whom three slept on the premises in 1892. The Rascher insurance map of that year listed the capacity of the brewery as 9,000 barrels per year, though there is no evidence production ever reached that level. West Superior Brewing "signed the scale of the Breweryworkers Union No. 158" in 1898, and contributed two half-barrels of beer as prizes for the Superior Labor Day games in 1899 (for the winners of the "running high jump" and "running hop, skip and jump.") Other than that, this business was seldom in the newspapers, and very little is known about its operations. The company last appeared in the city directory of 1900, and historian Tony Dierckins discovered that West Superior was absorbed by Northern Brewing Co. in 1901.

Klinkert Brewing Co. (1890–98)
L. Rueping Co. (1898)
Northern Brewing Co. (1898–1920)
Northern Brewing Co. (1933–1967)

702–724 North Eighth and Catlin

John A. Klinkert was an experienced brewer who had graduated from the Brewers Academy at Frankfurt, Germany, and worked for fifteen years in Milwaukee, including six years as foreman at Best. He then sought his fortune as a partner in Red River Valley Brewing Co.

in Fargo, Dakota Territory, where one of his partners was Louis Rueping. Rueping's family owned a malt house and other businesses in Fond du Lac, Wisconsin. When North Dakota became a state and wrote prohibition into its constitution, the partners decided to move to Wisconsin and start a new brewery in a place more hospitable to beer.

Klinkert Brewing's market extended beyond the Twin Ports. The company had an agency in Fargo, North Dakota, which was logical because of Klinkert's ties to the area. However, since North Dakota was a dry state, this arrangement could yield only limited revenue.

There were apparently disputes between the partners prior to the dissolution of the partnership. In 1894 Rueping sued to have a receiver appointed for the company, but this suit was discontinued in 1895. Klinkert ultimately sold the brewery to Rueping in January 1898. Mayor Louis Erhart of Fond du Lac was reported to be involved as well, and indeed Erhart was one of the incorporators of the new Northern Brewing Co., along with Louis, Frederick R., and Fred J. Rueping. (The brewery was known as L. Rueping Co. for the brief period prior to incorporation.) The early newspaper reports claimed that Klinkert planned to retire, but this was clearly intended to mask the differences of opinion as he proceeded to start Klinkert Brewing and Malting in February. Erhart was mayor of Fond du Lac in 1897, but left after one term to become manager of Northern. Erhart remained manager of the company until he retired in 1917, at which point Louis McKinnon, who had worked his way up through the company by managing the Fond du Lac branch and the Fond du Lac malt house, took over.

Because Northern started as a larger corporate brewery rather than a small family business, it had the advantage of obtaining up-to-date equipment relatively early. They purchased hand-me-down glass-lined storage tanks from Anheuser-Busch in 1909, and installed modern bottling and kegging equipment. The brewery was located on a railroad

Once common, the prevalence of brewery ashtrays has declined along with smoking. This Northern Brewing Co. ashtray dates to the late 1950s or early 1960s. COLLECTION OF DAVID WENDL.

line, which made shipping much easier. By the mid-1910s, the brewery's capacity was increased to 20,000 barrels, fifty men were employed, and Northern's flagship Blue Label beer was popular throughout the region.

Northern Brewing signed on with Breweryworkers Union Local 158 in 1898, and continued to identify as a union shop thereafter. Northern sometimes acted more like a regional brewery than a small local firm, such as when it opened a branch in Virginia, Minnesota. The Virginia office was open just over a year, however. Northern also had a branch office in Fond du Lac, which made sense given the Fond du Lac roots of the officers of the company.

When Prohibition arrived, Northern closed down, and the Fond du Lac-based management moved back south. The new owners applied for a near beer permit in 1922, and started production that November. The company made near beer and root beer for the local market. Northern Brewing was raided in July 1924, when a brewery worker was stopped with five kegs of beer in his car. Northern's brewing permit was revoked that November, and the brewery remained out of commission until 1933.

In 1933, Northern Brewing Co. reopened under the management of Rudolph Peterson, who began to remodel and upgrade the brewery. Among the new additions was a pasteurizer, brought in to comply with a short-lived Wisconsin law which required package stores to sell beer at room temperature. Pasteurization increased the shelf life so the stores could compete with taverns. Northern was not ready to sell beer on New Beer's Day, partially because the company could not acquire the federal permit right away. However since Peterson was not involved with the company when it was raided in 1924, the permit was granted in July.

Northern brought back its Blue Label brand, though Premier-Pabst forced Northern to change the label. The company kept Blue Label for a few more years, but eventually decided to call the flagship beers Northern Select and Northern Pale. The company suffered a more serious setback in July 1936 when Rudolph Peterson died of heat prostration while at the brewery. Without his leadership, the brewery became insolvent and was reorganized in 1938. New owner Victor Nelson was credited with running an efficient business and getting the company back on firm footing. Vic's Beer, which came in screen-printed shorty bottles, was named after Nelson. The brewery introduced cone top cans in 1948 and continued to use them until flat top canning equipment was installed in 1953.

The new ownership invested in improvements, but still had difficulty growing. Part of the problem was retaining skilled employees. Northern had six different brewmasters between 1933 and 1943, which caused inconsistent brews. Finally, Joseph Hartel joined the company in 1943, and remained until 1961. Hartel was given credit for improving the recipes and using high quality ingredients. There were few labor problems, but Northern was shuttered briefly by a strike of Brewery and Soft Drink Workers Local 133 in June 1946, a walk-out that also affected the three Duluth breweries. The brewery also found trouble with state revenue officials, who in 1940 insisted that Northern stop using labels and advertisements which used the word "strong." The brewery was sold to Robert R. Rooney in December 1955,

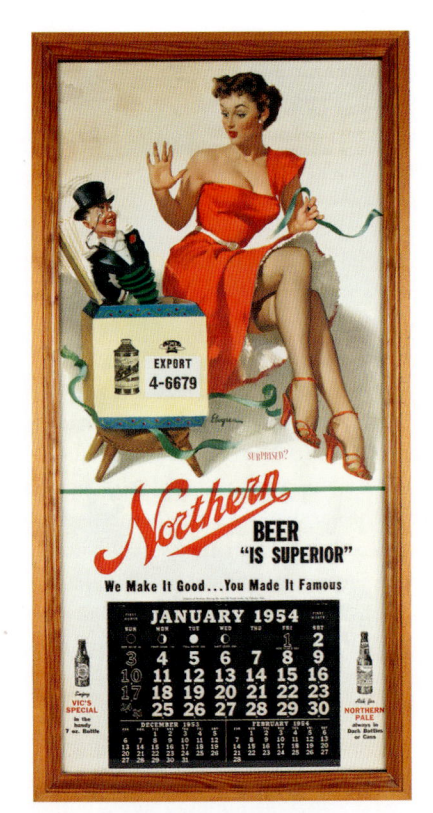

Gil Elvgren was a well-known illustrator and painter of pin-up girls. This 1954 calendar features a painting titled "Surprised?" and advertises 7-ounce bottles of Vic's Special as well as Northern Pale. COLLECTION OF DAVID WENDL.

and Rooney encouraged Hartel to make flavorful beers with high quality ingredients. Rooney also wanted a beer with his name on it, so the company packaged the regular Northern beer in bottles with Bob's Beer labels. However, new owners and managers in the early 1960s began to focus on cost cutting. Quality suffered and sales decreased, a trend made worse when a bad batch of Northern beer was shipped, causing many accounts to stop carrying Northern. Sales were still about 20,000 barrels per year through 1960, but after that they declined annually. The brewery closed in February 1967.

After closing, Cold Spring Brewing Co. of Minnesota acquired the trademarks and distribution rights of Northern Brewing, and continued to brew Northern for several more years.

Since closing, the remaining portions of the building have been used for a variety of light industrial purposes.

Klinkert Brewing and Malting Co. (1898–1908)
TWENTY-FOURTH STREET AND SCRANTON AVENUE

The Twin Ports were a good market for beer, and several investors thought there was room for more breweries than were already in operation. In 1893, reports spread that Phillip Altpeter and his sons were making plans for "the erection of a large brewery at the east end" of West Superior reported to cost between $60,000 and $70,000. While nothing came of these plans, an established brewer soon built a brewery in West Superior.

After John Klinkert left his brewery on North Eighth Street, he formed a partnership with Frank Pabst and started a new brewery on Twenty-fourth Street and Scranton Avenue. The articles of incorporation were filed in February, and production started later that year. The brewery had some brief problems with the brewery workers union in 1900, when the union declared the beer was "unfair." However the company disputed the claim and the union removed the unfair label. Klinkert's relations with the union clearly improved, and his beer was one of the few local options available to saloons that wanted to serve union beer.

The brewery closed in 1908, and the Great Northern Railroad and the Northern Pacific Railroad purchased the site because it was between their lines and both companies wanted to expand their rail yards.

Twin Ports Brewing Co. (1996–2006)
Thirsty Pagan Brewing (2006–present)
Choo Choo Bar & Grill
5002 EAST THIRD STREET (1996–99); 1623 BROADWAY (1999–PRESENT)

Rick and Nancy Sauer established Superior's first brewery since 1967 in the Choo Choo Bar & Grill in 1996. Sauer was already brewing at Rail House in Marinette, but he moved to Superior and commuted back to Marinette to continue brewing. In 1999, they moved from the Choo Choo to a location closer to downtown

A growler from the Twin Ports era, acquired around 2004. AUTHOR'S COLLECTION.

Superior, in the 1910 Russell Creamery building. The brewpub also served as a mini-museum for Duluth and Superior breweriana, largely from the collection of Pete Clure.

In 2006, Susan and Steve Knauss purchased Twin Ports Brewing, and soon changed the name to Thirsty Pagan Brewing (which maintained the TP initials). Rick Sauer remained as brewmaster at first. Thirsty Pagan continued its reputation as a great place for a pizza and a beer, but also became more family friendly. In 2012, Allyson Rolph replaced Nate MacAlpine as head brewer, making her one of the few female brewmasters in the state. (In 2017 Rolph was named one of the lead brewers at the new Earth Rider Brewery in Superior.)

SUSSEX *(Lisbon Township) (Waukesha County)*

Weaver & Sims (1849?–1853)
Stephen Stone & Co. (1854–57)
Weaver & Stone Brewery (1857–1861)
Ephraim Boots (1861–1878)
Boots & Co. (1878–1880)
Jos. Dvorak (1880–84?)
MODERN W239 N6638 MAPLE AVENUE

The research of Michael R. Reilly of the Sussex-Lisbon Area Historical Society has cleared up much of the confusion about the early years of this brewery. James Weaver and Edward Sims first appear in the Lisbon tax and assessment records in 1849, and a brewery was recorded in the same records in 1850, suggesting that it was built in 1849 or perhaps late 1848. Around 1853, Stephen Stone replaced Sims, and James Weaver turned over his hops and brewery interests to his son Richard. The property was listed under several different combinations of the proprietors' names during the late 1850s.

In 1861, Ephraim Boots became proprietor of the brewery, though Reilly's research indicates that Boots did not actually own the property until 1864. Boots built up the business throughout the decade, and by 1870 was brewing around 350 barrels per year with three employees working year around. Boots maintained this level of production through the 1870s, and even increased it to 463 barrels in 1879.

It is most likely, given the English heritage of the proprietors, that the Sussex brewery produced ale for the first two decades. However, in November 1869 the *Waukesha Plaindealer* announced: "Mr. E. Boots, of the Sussex Brewery, is now furnishing lager beer to severel [sic] retail dealers in this village, and all pronounce it a first-class article." This seems to indicate a switch to lager, though it is possible he had been brewing lager earlier but was only just now shipping to Waukesha establishments.

The last years of the brewery are less clear. The R. G. Dun & Co. records indicate that Boots (or Boots & Co.) were still in operation through 1880, but by 1881 Boots was renting the brewery. The renter appears to have been Joseph Dvorak, who appears in Tovey's 1882 brewery listing as the proprietor of the brewery in Lisbon. However, the Dun records claim that by December 1881 the brewery was closed and Boots was "busted." Boots left Sussex for Janesville, where he became a beer distributor, first for Schlitz, then for Blatz, and finally for Miller. It is unclear how much longer Dvorak operated the brewery. Most references claim that he continued through 1884, though there is scant industry or local support for any date past 1882. Opening and closing notices in periodicals such as *Western Brewer* were sometimes published a year or more after the actual event.

Bernard W. Hephen (1856?–1858?)

Bernard Hephen was listed as a brewer in the 1857 state business directory, but extensive research by Michael R. Reilly has failed to unearth any additional proof of his brewing operations or land ownership. Because his brewery was listed at the same time as Weaver & Stone's business, it seems possible that Hephen was neither a predecessor nor successor to the other brewery.

Taycheedah
(Fond du Lac County)

Hauser & Dix, Spring Brewery (1856?–1864)
Paul Hauser (1864–68)
Hauser & Bechuad (1868–1871?)

The brewery of Paul Hauser and his various partners is not well documented. The county histories refer to it in vague but sometimes picturesque ways, such as the A. T. Glaze history from 1905, which recounted:

> People who have passed through Taycheedah and up the ledge on the Sheboygan road have not failed to notice the ruins of a stone building near the road. The structure was erected for a brewery by Hauser & Dix, of Fond du Lac, with the intent to use the water from a beautiful spring across the road, and was named the "Spring Brewery." The buildings now used by the Harrison Postal Bag Rack Co. at Sheboygan and Portland streets, were erected by the same firm as a place to store and handle the beer. But this business venture proved a failure, as the spring water at Taycheedah could not compete with the fountain water in Fond du Lac in making and selling beer.

Glaze's account overstates the degree to which the business was a failure, since Hauser was there for at least fifteen years.

Hauser was listed as a brewer at Taycheedah in the 1857 state business directory, though a Fond du Lac directory from the same year list Hauser & Dix as proprietors of a lager beer saloon in the city of Fond du Lac. Hauser and Dix appear in the records of R. G. Dun & Co. in 1861 with indications that they were making money through 1864. In 1864 Dix left the business, and Hauser carried on alone, but with equally good credit ratings through 1866. In 1867 the Dun evaluator reported that Hauser had been "burned out," but that he was well insured and was still worthy of credit. The excise records indicate that Adolph Bechaud joined the business and remained until he started his own brewery in Fond du Lac. In 1871 Hauser & Bechaud appear to have started a brewery in Fond du Lac, since the entries from the excise records show a changed location, supported by later city directories. (The history of the business in Fond du Lac is under the entries for that city.) However, newspapers reported that the "extensive" brewery at Taycheedah burned in April 1872 with a loss of $14,000—an unlikely total for an abandoned brewery. The fire brought a conclusive end to brewing at this location.

John W. Whinfield (1856?–1876?)
Fred Schroeder (1873?)

John Whinfield (Winfield) appears off and on in the records. He was listed in the first state business directory of 1857, and in a Fond du Lac directory as late as 1876, when he would have been well advanced in years (while the 1860 census lists him as 60, the 1870 version has him at 78). The 1870 census specifically mentions that he brewed ale, though it was probably not a full time occupation. He does not appear in excise records from 1867–1874, and the 1860 census lists his occupation as civil engineer. The 1870 census further confuses matters by placing his residence in the First Ward of Fond du Lac proper, though he may well have had a residence there and maintained his brewery in Taycheedah.

Fred Schroeder is listed as a brewer of weiss beer in the 1873 excise records. There is no evidence specifically linking him to Whinfield's business, but it is possible that Schroeder rented or leased from Whinfield, explaining some of the gaps in the latter's record. Schroeder may have had a short-lived brewery of his own. He does not appear to fit well as a successor to Hauser, whose brewery in Taycheedah made lager beer.

Moritz Krembz (1867?–1868?)
TAYCHEEDAH ROAD

Mortiz Krembz appears as a brewer in an 1868 county gazetteer, with his brewery on Taycheedah Road east of the tollgate. By the 1870 census he is listed as a druggist, and in an 1872 city directory he was also listed as a chicory manufacturer, at the same address as his old brewery. The fact that Krembz was still occupying the same building in 1872 makes it less likely that Peter Severin took over the Krembz brewery in 1871.

F. Peter Severin (1871?–1883?)
Stamm & Severin (1871)
TAYCHEEDAH ROAD

Peter Severin first appears in the excise records in May 1871 as a brewer of weiss beer, and he remains in the records for the next decade or so as either a brewer of weiss beer or as a bottler. The R. G. Dun & Co. credit evaluator listed him as a beer bottler in 1880 and 1881, and recommended against extending credit. Philip Stamm had a weiss beer brewery in Fond du Lac, though it is possible that that Severin worked with Stamm for a while, or that Stamm had some of his beer made at Severin's brewery. (See Philip Stamm under Fond du Lac.)

THERESA *(Dodge County)*

Ulrich Oberle (1849–1854)
Benedict Weber (1854–1864)
Maria Weber (1864–1867?)
Gebhard Weber (1867?–1906)
G. Weber Brewing Co. (1906–1920)
G. Weber Brewing Co. (1934–1961)
NORTHEAST CORNER OF MENOMINEE AND HENNI STREETS

Ulrich Oberle built the first brewery in Theresa in 1849. The settlement had become a popular stopping place on Wisconsin's pioneer trails, and had an abundance of hotels and taverns for a small community. According to local tradition, the thick, stone walls of the brewery provided safety for the townsfolk during an Indian attack in the early years, though it appears more likely that this was an account of rumored attacks inspired by the Dakota War of 1862 hundreds of miles to the west in Minnesota rather than any real attack. Benedict Mayer was employed at the brewery (or may have been a partner in the business) from 1850 to 1852. If he was a partner, he may have sold his share of the brewery to Benedict Weber before leaving for New Fane in Fond du Lac County to operate a brewery and store.

In 1853, Benedict Weber became a partner in the brewery. A year later, Weber bought out Oberle, and took control of the company. Two accounts claim that when Weber took over the company he incorporated it and named it G. Weber Brewing Co. after his son Gebhard. However, the company still appears under Benedict's name in the 1857 state business directory and the 1860 industrial census, and this would have been the earliest incorporation of a brewery in Wisconsin by more than twenty years—an unlikely step for a family business to take prior to the Civil War. Weber's brewery employed two men (probably both family members) and produced 450 barrels of lager beer in 1860, making this the largest of Theresa's breweries by a slight margin.

The 1860s was a difficult decade for the Webers. The brewery was destroyed by fire in 1860, and Benedict rebuilt the brewery using stones from the burned out structure. While the building was still under construction, a tornado wrecked the foundation, but Weber persevered, and eventually completed the brewery and new malt house. Benedict Weber died from injuries sustained in a horse riding accident in 1864, and his family took over the brewery. According to several sources, Gebhard did not take full control of the brewery until 1873 or 1874, and his mother Maria Josephine Weber directed the business. Mrs. Weber hired experienced brewers to help run the business, including John Steger, who later had a brewery at Mayville, and Benedict's nephew Jacob Binder, who later purchased the brewery at Neosho. The brewery is absent from the 1870 industrial census and the brewery directories of the early 1870s, which make it difficult to assess production. However, by 1878 Weber's brewery produced almost 1,400 barrels of beer, making it by far the largest brewery in Theresa and the nearby communities. The brewery grew some of its own hops on Weber farmland.

During the decades after the Civil War, Gebhard Weber upgraded the primitive, hand-powered brewery and around 1880 built a new brick brewhouse. In 1890, Weber added a new icehouse and the next year built a new storage cellar. Business appears to have expanded rapidly, since in 1894 Weber replaced the 1890 icehouse with a larger facility and remodeled much of the brewery. In addition, Weber bought the former Nenno brewery in Addison and used its cellars and saloon. The Webers incorporated the business at the end of this flurry of growth in 1896.

G. Weber Brewing Co. installed bottling equipment in 1907, which was necessary to compete with breweries in West Bend and other cities that were moving into the territory. The upgrades continued in the 1910s, when Weber added more bottling equipment, a new

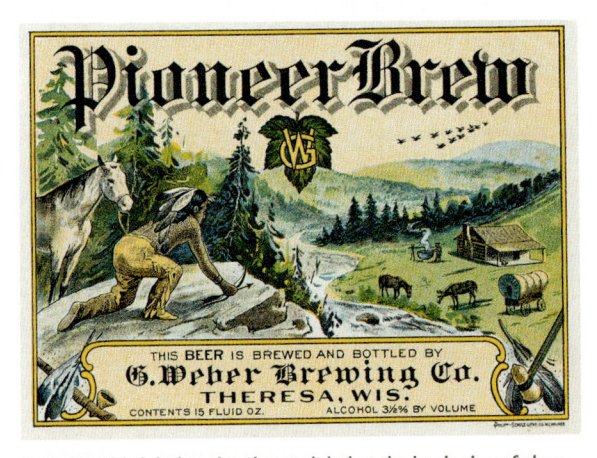

Compare this label to the Pioneer label at the beginning of chapter 2. This label was designed for a 15-ounce bottle and includes alcohol content (3.5 percent abv). COLLECTION OF TYE SCHWALBE.

mash tun, and took advantage of the arrival of electric power in Theresa to run some of the equipment.

Gebhard Weber died in 1917, after more than half a century of involvement in his family's brewery, and just before the arrival of prohibition. The brewery made malt syrup during Prohibition, but there were rumors that the tunnel that carried steam pipes under the road to heat the Weber house was also used to transport bottles of real beer from the brewery to the house. The bottles would then be packaged and shipped within the area. The Weber brewery was never raided during Prohibition, so either they were very good at concealing the operations, or the rumors were nothing more than that.

After Prohibition, Bert and Victor Weber sought financial help from two Milwaukee investors, Sam Chemer and Mark C. Hanna. Cornelius (Cornie) Weber, who still owned a share in the brewery, negotiated with the Milwaukeeans, and brought in Hanna as secretary and general manager of the business. With the new financial support, brewmaster Bert Weber was able to get the brewery going again by July 1933. The brewery was upgraded, and some of the upgrades were developed and built by Cornie, who was an electrical engineer, and Chemer, who was a mechanic. The workers at the brewery belonged to Brewery Workers Local 9-Branch 5, demonstrating the trend of workers at even the smallest breweries to be unionized in the post-Prohibition era.

The remodeled brewery generally produced between 5,000 and 10,000 barrels per year during the years after Prohibition. Weber's production was fairly consistent, but these totals continued to slide down the rankings of Wisconsin's breweries as smaller business closed. Weber's business suffered a blow in 1945 when Mark Hanna was killed in a car accident. His hard work was responsible for the consistent level of sales, and he even shipped beer into Milwaukee for a few years. Hanna had been educated at the Boston Conservatory of Music, and in Theresa formed the Theresa Pioneer Band, which played at events in the area.

During the last years of the brewery owner Cornie Weber spent most of his time in Milwaukee, but made sure that the brewery was properly maintained. He also trained cellarman Gilbert Radtke to be the new brewmaster—at the time the youngest brewmaster in the United States. The brewery continued to be a gathering place for local residents who stopped in for a free beer, and Radtke made occasional special batches of beer for the American Legion and the firemen's annual picnic. G. Weber gained some extra sales during the Milwaukee brewery strike of 1953, but sales were generally flat or declining. In 1958 Cornie Weber and Sam Chemer sold their interests in the brewery to Nathaniel Lemke and David Kincaid. Nathaniel's wife Alice was appointed president of the company and held that post until the brewery closed in 1961. The new ownership changed the formula of Pioneer beer, and made some possibly ill-advised decisions about investments and expenditures. In 1960 the brewery was down to three employees: Radtke, bottling room superintendent Gebhard Weber (son of Victor) and driver and brewery hand Walter Zastrow. The brewery made less than 1,000 barrels, and was unable to compete in the modern beer market. The brewery was closed in March 1961, and was later converted into a distributor for Braumeister beer until Independent Milwaukee Brewing Co. closed in 1963. The Weber family got the property back in 1962, and kept the brewery intact until 1978, when it was sold to pay off past due property taxes. As of this writing, portions of the brewing equipment were on display at the Spring Green tourist attraction the House on the Rock, and a fermenter was brought to the Milwaukee Ale House and used as the centerpiece of the bar area.

Hussa Brewery (1850?-?)
Miller & Hartman (1856?-58?)
Alois Heischmidt (1859?-1860?)
John Embs (1867)
Berthold & Co. (Berthold & Hartzhein) (1868-1870)
M. Hartzhein (1870)

There are two Theresa breweries listed in the federal census of industry prior to the Civil War that do not fit well with the known chronologies. But census of industry records were generally accurate, so these need to be accounted for. The Hussa Brewery was listed in the 1850 census as producing 500 barrels of beer with three employees and $1,000 of capital. Unfortunately there are no relevant Hussa listings in the population census to support this entry. This was the only Theresa brewery listed in the industrial census that year. The brewery of Alois Heischmidt was one of three Theresa breweries included in the 1860 industrial census. Heischmidt's brewery represented an investment of $1,200 and produced 400 barrels of lager beer with two employees. Neither Hussa nor Heischmidt fits with the Oberle or Weber timelines, but it is possible that Hussa could represent an earlier stage in the Miller & Hartman brewery and Heischmidt a successor. Three breweries was already a lot for a village of this size, and a fourth or fifth brewery would have been unlikely (though still possible).

Miller and Hartman were included in the 1857 state business directory as brewers in Theresa. Stephan Miller was listed as a brewer in the 1860 population census, but Heischmidt could have owned the brewery that Miller worked in since the census indicated that Heischmidt owned $850 worth of real estate and $75 of personal property, and Miller had nothing in either category.

The connection between Miller's business and that of John Embs, who appears in the 1867 excise records is not clear in the documents, but is supported by historian Wayne Kroll. Berthold and Hartzhein replace Embs in the excise records in March 1868, and M. Hartzhein (spelled Hartzheim) appears alone in 1870.

Ulrich Oberle (1856?-1861?)
John Quast (1867?-1889)
Luhn & Asenbauer (1893-94)
Gustav Luhn (1894-95)
Luhn & Bandlow, Union Brewery (1895-96)
Fred W. Bandlow, Union Brewery (1896-1910)

WEST ROCK RIVER STREET

Local brewery historian Michael D. Benter concludes that Ulrich Oberle remained with Weber

Few artifacts from Bandlow's Union Brewery survive. This sentimental scene of a dog protecting a young girl from danger near a cliff has little to do with brewing. COLLECTION OF RICHARD YAHR.

as brewmaster for several years after selling the brewery, since he is still listed as a brewer in the 1860 census at a location near or next to Weber. However, the 1857 state business directory lists the two as separate business, and while this source is sometimes questionable, the much more reliable 1860 census of industry also lists the two as separate businesses with different valuations and output totals. The brewery that later became the Bandlow brewery was located just west of Weber's business, so it appears that Oberle started a new brewery after selling out to Weber. (Unfortunately the R. G. Dun & Co. credit reports which are often quite helpful in clearing up these cases either never evaluated the Theresa breweries or those records have been lost.)

If this is the case, Oberle may have started his new brewery a very short time after selling out to Weber. It is not clear when Oberle sold out for a second time, this time to John Quast. Quast appears in the first available excise records in 1867, and continued to run the brewery until his death in 1889. Industry directories show Quast produced around 350 barrels per year in the late 1870s. Quast did not have his own malt house, and there are no records of whether he purchased any supplies from his neighbor Gebhard Weber. According to a descendant of the Weber family next door, "Quast was about the only customer of his brewery." The Weber family considered buying the property, but decided that there was no threat to their business and let the brewery lay idle for several years without purchasing it.

In 1893, carpenter Gustav Luhn purchased the brewery in partnership with Vinzent Asenbauer. In 1894 Luhn bought out Asenbauer, and ran the brewery on his own for a year. In 1895, Luhn brought in his brother-in-law Frederick Bandlow, and the new company became known as the Union Brewery. Bandlow took over the brewery on his own in 1896, and operated it until 1901 when the brewery was badly damaged by fire. The fire spread to the east and damaged several other buildings, but the wind kept the blaze away from the Weber brewery. Bandlow repaired the brewery and was in business soon afterwards.

In 1905, Bandlow considered starting a brewery in Lomira in 1905, but apparently the expansion of the Sterr malting operation into the brewing business persuaded Bandlow to stay in Theresa. He continued to brew until 1910, and then worked as a distributor for Gutsch Brewing of Sheboygan for a few years. The brewery was demolished in 1913 and a residence was built on the property.

TOMAH *(Monroe County)*

Ignatz Gondrezick (1871–1889)
(MODERN) 502 GLENDALE AVENUE.

Ignatz Gondrezick moved from Humbird to Tomah in 1871, and started a new brewery soon after arriving. He was in operation by September, and by the end of April 1872, he had produced 120 barrels of beer. In 1874 he produced 458 barrels, but by the end of the decade he was typically making about 200 barrels per year. According to industry directories he did not have his own malt house, and never offered bottled beer. He appears to have stopped brewing around 1889, and went into the ice business.

LogJam's six-pack holders were made of corrugated cardboard. AUTHOR'S COLLECTION.

TOMAHAWK *(Lincoln County)*

LogJam Microbrewery (1999–2008)
N10096 KINGS ROAD

LogJam Microbrewery was founded in 1999 by father and son Jerry and Bob Cook in the former Tomahawk Power and Pulp Mill. The brewery was intended to be part of a much larger complex that would include a restaurant and dance hall. Brewer Art Turnquist produced some well-regarded beers for a few years before brewing was suspended in 2004. The brewery reopened in 2010 in Unity.

TREMPEALEAU *(Trempealeau County)*

Jacob Melchoir (1859–1881)
FIRST STREET AND HIGH STREET (SOUTH OF MODERN HASTINGS STREET)

Jacob Melchoir moved to Trempealeau in 1859 and immediately started work on his brewery and saloon. By the time of the 1860 industrial census, his small brewery had already produced 200 barrels of beer. The money for the business came from the family of his wife, and the property was in Wilhelmina's name. According to the R.G Dun & Co. records of 1862, another reason Melchoir placed the property in his wife's name was so he could avoid paying a local tax, but his wife paid it anyway. The Dun records then noted "Is shrewd and smart," but it was not clear if this was about the husband or the wife. In 1864, the Dun evaluator observed: "Like all Germans, he takes the world and lagerbier easy." However, the Dun Co. records also reported that the business was doing well and making money, to the point where Melchoir was able to build a new stone brewery in 1866.

According to local lore, both Jacob and Wilhelmina were large individuals, and she apparently liked to joke that they were each 400 pounds. However, the pair were also reputed to be good dancers despite their weight. Jacob was also known for his strength—one resident recalled Jacob lifting a beer barrel over his head and drinking from the bung.

In 1868 and 1869, Melchoir was part of the firm of Melchoir and Tamish, which had a saloon with a small brewery in Galesville. (See the Galesville entry.) This venture appears to have been supported by Wilhelmina's family, with money coming from Prussia on a yearly basis.

Melchoir probably brewed mostly for his own tavern and a few other local accounts, but the market was still good because, as the Dun evaluator reported: "Lager flourishes here as in Milwaukee." Jacob had three caves behind his brewery in which he could lager his beer: one thirty-six feet long, another fifty, and the longest was 110 feet long. He brewed about 350 barrels per year in the early 1870s, though this total dropped to around 150 barrels per year later in the decade. Part of this drop may have been because he had to convert his saloon into a hotel after he was refused a liquor license in 1874. The hotel started well, but even though it was a popular stop for travelers, it did not make money. Jacob died in April 1881, and Wilhelmina originally planned to convert the brewery into an addition to the hotel. However, she and her adult children soon moved to Illinois and the brewery was left vacant. In 1896 the brewery was converted to a private residence and was used for this purpose for several decades. As of 2017, the ruins of the brewery still stand on First Street.

Two Creeks (Manitowoc County)

Robert Trottman & Co. (1864?–1868?)

While *American Breweries II* lists Trottman as a partner of Lutz in Kewaunee as early as 1864, the R. G. Dun & Co. credit reports locate the Trottman & Co. brewery in Two Creeks, about twelve miles south of Kewaunee. (Lutz may have been in Two Creeks briefly, but was clearly back in Kewaunee by 1866.) The credit evaluator listed Trottman & Co. as a safe investment in 1867, but in January 1869 reported "All I can learn is that they dissolved and broke up in a row."

Two Rivers (Manitowoc County)

City Brewery
Edward Mueller & Valentine Kaufmann
    (1848–1851?)
Edward Mueller (1851?–1871)
Richard E. Mueller (1871–1895)
Mueller Bros. (1895–96)
Mueller Bros. Brewing Co. (1896–1920)
Two Rivers Beverage Co. (1933–1966)
1608 Adams Street

Some local accounts claim that the brewery of Mueller & Kaufmann supplied the first beer in Manitowoc County, though it is likely that one of the breweries in the city of Manitowoc did so earlier. Because the brewery made more than the small community of Two Rivers could consume, they reportedly shipped beer to Manitowoc by rowboat in the summer and overland during the winter. Mueller & Kaufmann were clearly brewing by 1848, and by 1850 they sold $3,330 worth of beer (while the volume was not given, it was likely around 750 barrels). The brewery had a saloon which was a popular gathering place, though in 1850 Mueller was assaulted by "a gang of toughs" when he refused to give them beer.

In the early 1850s, Kaufmann left the partnership to start his own brewery, and Mueller carried on alone. His brewery seems to have remained about the same size throughout the decade—his production in 1860 was around 600 barrels.

Edward Mueller died in 1871, and his son Richard Edward Mueller took control of the brewery. He soon began to expand and improve the brewery, and production reached 1,000 barrels in 1875. By 1882, he was producing more than 1,400 barrels, which ranked him among the largest brewers in the county outside of the city of Manitowoc. R. G. Dun & Co. reported that he was making money and rated Richard "a first class man." In 1882, Richard's brother Edward opened a bottling works, which sold the family's bottled beer until the brewery opened their own bottling plant in 1902, after Edward died. Sales of bottled beer helped the brewery grow to nearly 4,000 barrels in 1891, and while one local history enthusiastically claimed sales would top 7,000 barrels the next year, actual production appears to have remained in the 3,000 to 4,000 range, according to the 1895 state industry census. The brewery malted much of its own barley, using the traditional floor-malting method. Richard's sons Charles and Edwin helped their father run the brewery, and took over the business when Richard died in 1894. They changed the name to Mueller Bros. Brewing and introduced a new flagship beer, Golden Drops.

The Mueller brothers sold the brewery in 1914 to Frank Lieblich and his father-in-law John Eisenbeiss. According to his obituary, Eisenbeiss was a partner in the Ahnapee brewery for a few years, but "as his ability became known he received offers to affiliate himself with larger firms and he went to Chicago where he became a national figure in his profession. He sent his son Andrew, a former brewmaster at Miller, to become president and brewmaster of the company, which kept the Mueller Bros. name until brewing ceased on 28 November 1918.

During Prohibition, Mueller Bros. Brewing changed its name to Two Rivers Beverage. In addition to reformulating Golden Drops as a near beer, the company distributed Bellevue ice cream from Hagemeister Food Products (formerly Hagemeister Brewing). Two Rivers Beverage also sold soda waters. It occasionally introduced other products such as "Old Fashioned Chocolate," and in 1926 they became the

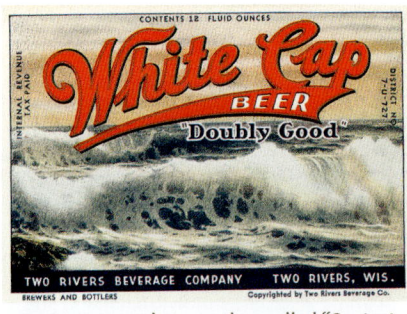

This rare set of labels depicts the process of naming and labeling White Cap beer. The first label announced the contest to name what was then called "Contest Beer"; the contest ended December 31, 1935. The winning name was White Cap, with the winning slogan "Doubly Good." Contest winners for both name and slogan were women, Mrs. Milton W. (Bonnie) Zuehl and Mrs A. R. Naidl. The second label was a temporary design. Mike Kazar, an art teacher at Two Rivers High School, designed the final label. COLLECTIONS OF JOHN STEINER AND TYE SCHWALBE.

first Coca-Cola bottler in Manitowoc County. In April 1927, Two Rivers advertised "Bock, an Aged Brew," making it one of several breweries to offer seasonal near beers. In 1929, the company introduced a new near beer, with the question "Do you remember 'way back when Wisconsin was the brewing capital of the world?" However, the brew that was supposed to bring back memories of old Wisconsin was strangely named Old Manhattan. Old Manhattan was the sponsor product for a radio program of the Meister Singers of Two Rivers on radio station WOMT in Manitowoc.

One interesting feature of this period was that Two Rivers Beverage was still harvesting ice for their ice house on Sixteenth Street as late as 1929—well after artificial refrigeration was the norm in the industry. Even with this historic anachronism, Two Rivers was profitable enough to install an all-new bottling plant in October 1929, which earned banner headlines in the *Manitowoc Herald-Times*. However, most of the newspaper coverage of Two Rivers Beverage during the dry years was of the company's baseball and bowling teams. The baseball team made headlines around the state in 1930 when pitcher Clarence Bantle struck out the first seventeen Manitowoc Judge Cigars players he faced and a total of twenty-four for the game.

After the election of Roosevelt, Two Rivers Beverage began immediate preparations to resume production of beer. Andrew's younger brother George, who was now in charge of the business, directed the improvements which included new concrete floors and new tanks. Two Rivers was one of more than twenty Wisconsin breweries that were able to ship beer at 12:01 a.m. on 7 April 1933. The brewery was allowed to begin bottling three days before, and to rack kegs on 6 April. Two Rivers was soon advertising the revived Golden Drops brand, with the claim "Easter will be much more cheerful with the old time hospitality."

Later in 1933, Two Rivers became one of very few Wisconsin breweries to offer an ale. Bobbie Ale continued to be flagship beer for the company until the 1960s, and remained one of the few ales made in Wisconsin. The next new brew was introduced in late 1935, and Two Rivers created a contest to name the beer. Eventually, White Cap displaced Golden Drops as the flagship lager. Two Rivers also brewed bock (which returned in 1936) and Holiday Brew (1937) in their seasons. The company also continued to manufacture soft drinks, including the new "Kreme-Puff" which debuted in 1938.

Two Rivers Beverage was in the news in 1938 when one of their salesmen, George Otis, reported that he had been kidnapped and robbed when leaving the brewery. After an investigation, it turned out that Otis had faked the kidnapping in order to take enough money to cover the amount that he was behind in his payments to the brewery.

Throughout the 1940s and 1950s, Two Rivers Beverage typically brewed between 15,000 and 24,000 barrels per year, in a brewery with a capacity for 35,000 per year. In 1948, the company used some of its excess capacity to be one of about a dozen breweries around the country that made Brewers' Best, an attempt to create a national brand that was brewed by small local producers. (The label is pictured in chapter 8.) However, the tactic that worked with some other products like ice cream (Sealtest) was unsuccessful with beer, and the brand only lasted a few years. Two Rivers Beverage also became one of the first union shops in Two Rivers, but according to George Lieblich (son of Frank), labor peace was the general rule.

Sales slipped below 10,000 barrels per year in the 1960s, and even the introduction of a new flagship beer, Liebrau, could not stop the slide. While owner Harold Lieblich predicted "We look for an even better year in 1965," it was not to be. Sales continued to fall, and the brewery closed in 1966.

Forty years later, Carl and Chris Lieblich, children of Harold Lieblich, worked with John Jagemann, owner of the Courthouse Pub in Manitowoc, to bring back White Cap beer. Harry's brother George found the original recipe, and the beer was offered at Courthouse Pub in a version modified for the Pub's brewing system.

Valentine Kaufmann & Frederic Krause
  (1852?–54)
Valentine Kaufmann, Twin Rivers Brewery
  (1854–1863?)
Fred Kaufmann, Twin Rivers Brewery
  (1863?–1873?)

Valentine Kaufmann left his partnership with Edward Mueller sometime in the early 1850s, and started a new brewery with Frederic Krause. The brewery was partially destroyed by fire in 1853 but was rebuilt. In 1854 this partnership dissolved, and Kaufmann carried on the business. The Panic of 1857 appears to have hit his business hard. The R. G. Dun & Co. credit reports stated that while he had always been good about paying his debts, in 1858 he could not "get money in these times from anybody in this Co[unty]." The 1860 industrial census showed that Kaufmann produced about 500 barrels at his brewery, which was powered by horse and had a single employee.

Kaufmann appears to have kept brewing for at least a few more years, since R. G. Dun & Co. credit reports list him as a brewer and beer seller through 1863, with continued positive references to his good habits "except Beer drinking." After this, Kaufmann's brewery disappears from official and industry records, but is mentioned in passing in the obituary of Fred Kaufmann. Upon his death in 1884, the *Green Bay State Gazette* reported, "Until eleven years ago he attended to the business of a brewery in Two Rivers, left by his deceased father." It is possible that this business did not involve actually brewing, which was why it did not appear in production statistics or excise records.

John Hullman (1871?–1872?)

John Hullman (or Huppmann) operated a brewery in Two Rivers in the early 1870s. It is not clear whether he took over the Kaufmann brewery or built his own plant. His only appearance in the excise records was in May 1872, but he had clearly been brewing for some months before then since the 1873 *Brewers' Guide* reported that he had produced 138 barrels in the previous year.

UNITY *(Marathon County)*

LogJam Microbrewery at Monster Hall Campground (2010–12)
B4864 COUNTY HIGHWAY F

In 2010 LogJam Microbrewery moved to Monster Hall Campground. It produced through 2012, when it suspended brewing.

VERONA *(Dane County)*

Gray's Tied House (2008–2011)
950 KIMBALL LANE

While it primarily serves beer produced by Gray Brewing Co. in Janesville, Gray's Tied House in Verona had a small brewing system and brewed seasonal and specialty beers for the restaurant. The restaurant opened in 2006, but brewing did not start until almost two years later. The brewpub hosted the Fauerbach Challenge (in cooperation with the Madison Homebrewers and Tasters Guild) to replicate a 1940s era bock recipe from Fauerbach Brewing Co. in Madison.

Wisconsin Brewing Co. (2013–present)
1079 AMERICAN WAY

Wisconsin Brewing Co. is rare among production breweries in the craft beer era—it started with a "destination brewery" rather than working its way up by scavenging equipment to put in a converted but inexpensive space. After leaving Capital Brewery (and having his bid to take over Capital rejected), Carl Nolen decided to start his own brewery. Nolen brought in his brother Mark to help raise $8 million to start Wisconsin Brewing Co. (Mark remained as chief financial officer.) Nolen explained his reasoning: "If you are undercapitalized out of the gate, you are probably going to be screwed." Nolen sought to position Wisconsin Brewing as one of the leaders in the Wisconsin craft industry, arguing "If Wisconsin is to emerge as a powerhouse state of craft brewing, there needs to be a significant number two player [after New Glarus]. We think that slot is wide open and we intend to shoot for it." Nolen's former brewmaster at Capital, Kirby Nelson, joined him at the new company, the brewhouse was completed on time and brewed the first batch in September 2013.

Unlike many start-up breweries, Wisconsin Brewing met its initial projections. Nolen hoped to produce around 14,000 barrels in the first twelve months, and was within a few barrels of that goal. The very first beer was an amber lager, but that was followed by a bold American IPA—a style Nelson avoided while

In 2015, Inaugural Red was Wisconsin Brewing's best-selling beer, accounting for about 3,000 of the total of 13,000 barrels. Photograph by Charles Walbridge. AUTHOR'S COLLECTION.

at Capital. (Wisconsin Brewing beers bear the number of the recipe on the neck label, so historians and collectors know in what order the beers were initially released.) The lineup of beers now includes a range of year-round beers, the in and Out Series of seasonal beers, and the Conspiracies Series of experimental recipes. Wisconsin Brewing has also brewed beers on contract for other companies, including Old Tankard Ale for Pabst.

Perhaps the most innovative series of beers brewed at Wisconsin Brewing is the Campus Craft Brewery series. In 2014, Nelson and students at University of Wisconsin-Madison's College of Agricultural and Life Sciences (CALS) hatched a plan to allow teams of students to design recipes for a particular style of beer, and the winning beer would be brewed at Wisconsin Brewing to be sold on campus and statewide. Teams brew their pilot batches on a thirty-liter brewing system in Babcock Hall on campus. Students also select the name and design the packaging. The first beer, Inaugural Red from 2015, has remained in the WBC lineup. Subsequent years introduced new Campus Craft brews: S'Wheat Caroline American wheat ale (2016) and Red Arrow American pale ale (2017)—which is named after Wisconsin's famed 32nd Infantry Division of World War I (the Red Arrow Division).

Hop Haus Brewing Co. (2015–present)
231 South Main Street

Owners Phil and Sara Hoeschst opened the Hop Haus brewery and taproom in 2015, while both were working other jobs and while they were raising two small boys (one then three years old and the other five months old). Phil, who was born in Germany, designed Hop Haus to have the atmosphere of a German beer hall, where beer and conversation could be the focus. As the name suggests, Hop Haus Brewing Co. emphasizes hoppy beers, but also produces less hoppy but still flavorful styles such as hefeweizens, Scotch ales, and blonde ales. In fact, the Plaid Panther Scotch ale was a winner in the Grumpy Troll homebrewing contest.

VIROQUA *(Vernon County)*

Sebastian Baltz & H. D. Chapman (1866?–68)

The excise records paint a confusing picture of this brewery. H. D. Chapman appears for the first time in February 1867, with a note that he brewed four barrels of beer. The next month Chapman brewed another two barrels, but Sebastian Baltz is also listed as having brewed nine and one half barrels in March. It appears that these were not separate breweries, since there is a note on the first Chapman entry that he was "Successor to L. Battz." Chapman does not appear ever to have brewed more than a few barrels per month. It is possible that Baltz still owned the brewery, because when the brewery burned in January 1868, it was described as the "Baltz brewery." While the loss of $300 was insured, Baltz and Chapman apparently decided not to resume brewing, as they disappear from the records after this point.

WASHBURN *(Bayfield County)*

Washburn Brewing Co. (1890–99)
Washburn Brewing Associaion (1899–1904)
Pure Beer Brewing Co. (1904–1913)
Southwest Corner of Third Avenue West and Fifth Street

A family from Ashland decided to build a brewery in Washburn, a promising site a few miles to the west. John, Mary Madelaine, and George Waegerle filed standard boilerplate articles of incorporation for Washburn Brewing Co. in December 1889. The new brick brewery was estimated to cost $24,000 and went into production in 1890. The next year they added an ice house, and another ice house a few years later. Perhaps the most interesting event in the history of this brewery occurred in 1892. Washburn and nearby Bayfield were locked in a battle to move the county seat to Washburn. However the injunction Bayfield had obtained could not be served on the county clerk, who "hid in the attic of the brewery until it had expired." The Waegerles experienced financial trouble in 1893, which local historian Lars Erik Larson suggests was because of the Panic of 1893. The company went into receivership, but a long legal battle ensued and the brewery was sold in 1896.

The next proprietor of the brewery was Charles H. Flynn, also from Ashland. In 1899, Flynn, William H. Irish Jr. and George Waegerle changed the name of the corporation to Washburn Brewing Association, though the articles of incorporation gave no indication of anything in the corporate structure that would make the name change significant. The Association added a bottling house sometime prior to 1904. However, during this period Schlitz Brewing Co. purchased the goodwill of Washburn Brewing Association (though not the property) in an apparent attempt to drive the company out of business and capture more of the Washburn market. Indeed, the annual reports of Washburn Brewing Association show that no business was conducted in 1906, and that the business of the company in 1908 was "farming." In answer to the question of whether the company engaged in business in 1911, the secretary answered "not that I know of," and business in 1912 consisted wrapping up affairs of the company and selling real estate. There was another brewing company incorporated in Washburn in 1903, Home Brewing Company, which appears to have been an attempt by Washburn residents to save the brewery for local interests. However, the company never filed an annual report and it appears that this company never actually operated the business.

Yet another company was formed in December 1903, but Pure Beer Brewing Co. actually brewed for a few years. The company made a small addition to the bottle house, but fared little better than any of the previous businesses. Charles Flynn, who still owned the brewery, sold his interest to Ed Borgan, who said it was "his aim to build the brewery up to what it was in former years." Pure Beer Brewing stopped brewing in 1913, and the equipment was sold to Fitger Brewing Co. of Duluth. The building remained on the site until it was torn down in 1941, and replaced with a school.

South Shore Brewing Co. Taphouse (2016–present)
532 West Bayfield Street

The increased demand for South Shore beers meant it was impossible to remain competitive in wholesale distribution packaging in the basement of the Ashland location. Bo Bélanger acquired a former bowling alley in nearby Washburn to expand brewery operations. The first batch of beer was brewed at the end of November 2016. The Washburn location includes a taproom and a larger brewhouse.

WASHINGTON HARBOR *(Door County)*

Peter Bridham (1856?–58?)

Peter Bridham's small brewery is listed in the 1857 state business directory, and in Wayne Kroll's survey of farm breweries in Wisconsin.

WATERFORD *(Racine County)*

B. A. Linke (1859?–1860?)
Waterford Brewery
John Beck & Bro. (1866?–1880)
John Beck (1880–1890)
Jefferson Street

The first known report of a brewery in Waterford appears in the 1860 industrial census. The brewery of B. A. Linke was a small one, representing an investment of only $500 (though it was powered by two horses instead of the usual one). Linke brewed just over 200 barrels of beer, which appears to have been of two different grades: he sold 156 barrels of a beer that sold for $6.00 per barrel, and fifty barrels at a price of $8.00 per barrel.

Linke's brewery disappears from the records, and the next known brewery in Waterford was that of John Beck and Brother (Paul), which appears in the excise records for the first time in 1867, but since that is the first year for which records exist, he may have started earlier. (It is also possible that he built a new brewery rather than purchasing Linke's.) Production jumped from 172 barrels in 1871 to 315 the next year, and for the next few years production remained above 300 barrels, though it slipped back to around 200 per year by the end of the decade. Beck had his own malt house, and the R. G. Dun & Co. credit evaluator in 1875 referred to the brothers' brewery as "a good sized one." The brothers also owned a sixty-acre farm nearby. The brewery went out of business around 1890 for unknown reasons and John Beck turned to farming full time.

WATERLOO *(Jefferson County)*

Abendroth & Co. (1866?–1872?)
Theodore Menk (1870)

William Abendroth was sometimes listed as a brewer at Lake Mills, though he appeared in many more records at Waterloo. He appears in the 1867 annual list of the excise records, which generally means that he was in business at least by 1866 if not before. While he does not appear in the 1870 census of industry, he was included in the 1873 *Brewers' Guide* directory, with production of 320 barrels in 1871 and 404 the next year. He appears to have retired briefly from brewing, since he was listed as a farmer in the 1870 population census, and was not included in the 1870 annual excise collection. The *Watertown Republican* reported in April 1870 "Abendroth has sold his brewery to Theodore Menke [sic] of our place [Waterloo]." But it appears that this was short-lived, since Abendroth appeared in the excise rolls again in October. Abendroth died in 1872, and his heirs did not continue the business.

Theodore Menk (1866?–1869)
Charlotte Menk (1870)

Theodore Menk first appeared in the R. G. Dun & Co. records in late 1866, and the evaluator considered "Menck" to be of good habits and character. However two years later the reporter noted that Menk was careless about paying his bills, and that he was out of business in March 1869.

Menk was listed in the 1870 industrial census, but this may represent the brief period when he operated William Abendroth's brewery. The data indicate that he had $5,000 invested in the brewery, employed two hands, and judging by the inputs, brewed a relatively hoppy beer (though no production or revenue totals were listed). Theodore was still listed as proprietor in the 1870 industrial census and was still in the population census of that year. The brewery was in the name of his wife Charlotte starting in May 1870, but again this may have been the Abendroth brewery. The Menks disappeared from the excise records after 1870, but in August 1873 Theodore Menk started a soda factory in Watertown in which he also bottled lager and weiss beer.

Andrew Handschiegl & Co. (1866?–69?)
Schwager & Helmes (1869–1870)
William Schwager (1870–1880)
Monroe Street near Madison Street

Andrew Handschiegl (& Co.) was also probably brewing at least in 1866 if not before, based on excise records. In March 1869, Handscheigl sold the business to William Schwager and Mr. Helmes. The R. G. Dun & Co. records appear to claim that the firm was worth $7,000, but if so, they must have had more businesses than the brewery, or they did not use the brewery to its fullest extent. The 1870 census of industry states that $3,000 had been invested in the brewery, but only employed one person. He was hardly overworked, since in the six months the brewery was in operation that year he brewed forty-two barrels of beer and seventy of "lager." This appears to have been the high point, since Schwager only brewed twenty-two barrels in 1871 and twenty the next year, though he brewed ninety-nine in 1874. The Dun reports indicate he owned a saloon along with his brewery, and it is likely that most of his production was sold in-house. He disappears from the records after 1880.

WATERTOWN *(Jefferson County)*

Watertown Brewery, William Anson (1846–1855)
Foot of South First Street, South Side of Bailey Street

William Anson started what was probably Watertown's first commercial brewery in 1846. He planned a large business for the winter of 1847, since he advertised his need for 10,000 bushels of barley. Watertown brewing historian William F. Jannke III reported that Anson brewed ale, and cites an 1868 account that claimed that Anson's product tasted like weak coffee and "half the town became ill from drinking it." This may have been exaggeration (and perhaps an insult of ale intended for a German audience), but the size of Anson's brewery suggests that he must have done reasonably good business at least for a while. Anson put his brewery up for sale in 1854, but no record of a successful sale has been found. The point became moot in July 1855, when the brewery was struck by lightning and destroyed by fire. A newspaper account estimated the total loss of what was called "the brewery at the Railroad Hotel" at between $1,200 and $1,500, though this was later updated to nearly $4,000.

John Jacob Hoeffner, Red Brewery (1847–1854)
City Brewery
Joseph Bursinger (1854–1883)
Hartig & Manz (1884–1896)
William Hartig (1896–1920)
The Hartig Co. (1933–1947)
100 Cady Street

Watertown's longest-lived brewery lasted for almost exactly a century. The *Watertown Chronicle* provided an unusually precise date (for breweries of the 1840s) for the opening of the business in November 1847. His brewery was described as "a substantial and handsome building, 24 by 34 ft, and three stories high. It is expected to turn out from eight to ten barrels of beer per week, of a quality second to none made in the territory." In a separate ad, Hoeffner sought to buy barley "for which cash or beer will be paid, at the new red Brewery, a short distance above the bridge." While Hoeffner apparently was not fond of Red Brewery as a name for the business, it stuck and residents referred to it as such for many years. The Red Brewery was visited by the "Red Demon" within a month of opening, but Hoeffner was able to put out the small fire himself. Hoeffner appears to have had excess space at the brewery, since the *Chronicle* reported in 1848 that the firm of Frohne & Averbeck were making two barrels of whiskey per day at the brewery. Hoeffner continued to operate the brewery until 1851, when he rented the brewery to William and Charles Bieber for about six months. Hoeffner returned for a few years, but in 1854 he sold the brewery to Joseph Bursinger.

Bursinger, who had a partner named Mr. Laur for a brief time, developed the brewery by 1870 into the largest in Watertown, and one of the largest in the state outside Milwaukee. He excavated a system of cellars which would provide increased lagering and storage capacity in 1860, a year in which he produced about 1,700 barrels of beer, still behind Fuermann, but growing rapidly. Bursinger built an extensive new brewery in 1866 overtook Fuermann in the late 1860s, and while Fuermann edged back in front in 1872, Bursinger was still larger than any brewery outside Milwaukee except Fuermann and Gund & Heileman. The new brewery was powered by steam, and had modern safety devices. However, these were not always effective—in 1868 lighting struck the chimney, but the lightning rods did not divert all the current and some traveled down the chimney and blew apart the boiler. Bursinger produced between 3,000 and 8,000 barrels during the 1870s, and in 1877 began to offer bottled beer through the bottling firm of S. M. Eaton. After using the services of Eaton for a few years, Bursinger started his own bottling plant in 1880. Bursinger joined Fuermann in Chicago by opening an agency there in 1872. As modern as his brewery was in many ways, the *Wisconsin State Register* reported in 1876 that Bursinger "was cutting peat on the marsh for his brewery," presumably for fuel.

It is possible that the expansions forced Bursinger to spend beyond his means, because in November 1883 he was deep in debt and the brewery was turned over to his creditors to be sold at Sheriff's sale in April 1884. (The R. G. Dun & Co. evaluator seems to have missed some warning signs because Bursinger was given a clean bill of financial health in 1883.) Henry Mulberger purchased the brewery at auction, and a few months later sold it to William Hartig of Schleisingerville (now Slinger) and Carl Manz of Milwaukee. Manz was well connected in the brewing world—he was a nephew of Mrs. Joseph Schlitz, who provided the money for the purchase of Bursinger's brewery.

The new owners continued to make the renamed Hartig & Manz brewery a modern, competitive business. In 1888, they purchased the bottling plant of Paul Hoppe for $4,000 so they would have an in-house packaging operation. An advertisement in the 1895 Watertown city directory, listed three brands of bottled beer: Export and Loewenbrau, both available in quarts and pints, and Lager,

The Hartig & Manz brewery, about 1895. Note the ice ramp reaching down to the Rock River. COURTESY OF NATIONAL BREWERY MUSEUM.

Brewers developed beers of 2.75 percent alcohol (the lowest percentage for a stable and palatable beverage) to try to be acceptable to temperance and prohibition advocates. This bottle has a Hartig label, but it is embossed with the name of Heger's brewery in Jefferson. Breweries sometimes purchased bottles from other breweries or used whatever was returned to their bottle houses (ca. 1918). COLLECTION OF JOHN STEINER.

available in pints and half-pints. In 1896, Manz sold his interest in the brewery to his partner, and the new business was renamed William Hartig Brewing Co. The company generally stayed out of the news during the late pre-Prohibition period—even the industry journals had few references to the brewery.

During Prohibition, the name of the business changed to the Hartig Co. and the nature of business changed to ice cream. (The company continued to make ice cream until 1936). There appear to have been no attempts to brew wildcat beer at the Hartig brewery during Prohibition, perhaps because the needs of the community were met by a wildcat brewery operated by the Ryan brothers at 317 North Montgomery Street. According to local tradition, that brewery survived for many years with minimal harassment from law enforcement because the chief of police was a regular customer. William Hartig did not live to see the return of legal beer—he died in March 1923.

The renamed Hartig Co. received its permit

650   THE DRINK THAT MADE WISCONSIN FAMOUS

to brew beer in June 1933, and began to brew Hartig's Select again. However, the company was faced with a very competitive market and an out-of-date brewery. Production was well under capacity and the company was losing money.

With production declining, the Hartig family decided to get out of brewing, and sold the business in June 1945 to Harvey Roscoe of Minneapolis. At this time the brewery's capacity was reported as 40,000 barrels per year, but production had been less than 8,000 barrels per year throughout the 1940s. Almost immediately, the company was charged with selling beer above wartime ceiling prices. Roscoe and company president Harold McEvoy were unable to restore the business, and the situation continued to deteriorate. In November 1946, Hartig Co. was forced to destroy over 1,700 cases of Wisconsin Premium that had become adulterated because the use of molasses in the brewing process resulted in an acid by-product. Unfortunately, because some of this beer was shipped across state lines, the issue ended up in federal court. Like many small Wisconsin breweries, Hartig was shipping beer to distant states because of the nationwide beer shortage. Molasses was used as a shortcut to meet demand, but beer distributors in Alabama and Texas sued the company for breach of contract. Matters were made worse in April 1947 when McEvoy and the company were fined $8,000 for exceeding their wartime grain quota. The company was unable to meet its obligations, and closed in later that year. The building was torn down in 1953 and a grocery store was built on the site.

Charles M. Ducasse (1848–1850?)
EMMET STREET

According to some old histories, the brewery of Charles Ducasse was the first in Watertown, but better evidence exists for other breweries. His was described as "a rude and diminutive establishment located about four miles north of the village. He made weekly trips to Watertown, with a few kegs in a cart drawn by a yoke of oxen." The beer was described as "'so dark you couldn't see a frog in it.' It is not disputed, however, that a great many persons were very fond of looking for one . . ." Another recollection claimed that Ducasse's quality control and consistency left much to be desired:

Bad as was the beer, the drinkers of that day made liberal concessions, but they balked at the worst kind, so that where it was undrinkable the brewer fed it to his hogs on the farm. When the brewer's hogs lay on their backs pawing the air and squealing in riotous glee, the passing pioneer farmers, patiently driving their oxen to town, knew that another brew had miscarried. The brewery went bankrupt, and its principal asset, a thirty-five gallon copper kettle, came into the possession of Joe Miller, the local coppersmith. In 1861 an orchestra was formed in Watertown to assist the choral society in performing Haydn's 'Creation.' Kettledrums were quite necessary but not available. So E. C. Gaebler, the conductor, commissioned Miller to build a pair. Miller utilized the old brewing kettle for the body of the larger one, and it was a success.

Ducasse does not appear as a brewer in either the population or the industrial census of 1850 (though much of the census for Watertown is illegible), so he may have ceased brewing by that time. Ducasse was still in Watertown until at least 1869, running a saloon and tobacco shop.

August Fuermann (1848–1853)
Empire Brewery
August Fuermann (1853–1885)
A. Fuermann Brewing Co. (1885–1897)
100 JONES STREET

August Fuermann made Watertown beer famous throughout the region—to the point where his brewery was rumored to be a takeover target of British capitalists. He founded the brewery in 1848, and expanded at a rapid pace, though he apparently did not own the land under the brewery until 1853. By 1860 he was producing 2,500 barrels per year, third-most in the state outside Milwaukee (behind Rodermund of Madison and Gutsch of Sheboygan). Fuermann continued to grow throughout the 1860s, but so did rival Joseph Bursinger, and Fuermann slipped to second place in the city. Both breweries were modern, steam-powered plants capable of producing several thousand barrels per year.

Fuermann Brewing built a large addition to the brewery and opened a branch office in Chicago (at 9 West Ohio Street) in 1871. The R. G. Dun & Co. credit evaluator noted at one point that the "loc[al] trade there is not suff[icient] to support 2 large breweries," and the Chicago venture helped Fuermann push back in front of Bursinger. The *Watertown Republican* reported in 1872: "Mr. Fuerman's [sic] business in Chicago has become so extensive that it requires the constant supervision of his son to attend to the shipments at this point." In 1872 Fuermann sold 4,047 barrels of beer, more than any brewery outside of Milwaukee other than Gund & Heileman's fast-growing La Crosse business. Fuermann's expansion accelerated, and in 1874 his brewery produced over 11,000 barrels—more than any brewery outside of Milwaukee by a large margin. In 1878, Fuermann brewed just a few hundred barrels less than Fred Miller's brewery.

In 1877, bottled beer came to Watertown. S. M. Eaton began to bottle beer for Fuermann and Bursinger, and in November, Charles Fuermann opened a bottling plant in the city. However Miller and Schlitz also established agencies in Watertown that year, which meant that the competition was stiffer than ever.

A. Fuermann Brewing Co. was incorporated in April 1885—one of the earliest known incorporated breweries in the state. The articles of incorporation gave the company authority to "manufacture . . . malt, lager beer, porter and ale," though no evidence has been found so far of porter or ale for sale. Shortly after, the company commenced a large addition to the brewery, estimated to cost $5,000. Not everything went smoothly for Fuermann, however—in February 1888 the ice house collapsed from the weight of snow on the structure, though fortunately no one was injured. (A sign from this period is pictured in chapter 3.)

In 1889, the wave of international syndicates and mergers reached the shores of Watertown.

In October, newspapers reported that A. Fuermann Brewing had "disposed of its brewery to an English brewing syndicate, the consideration being $500,000." Milwaukee papers reported that the new owners planned to double the capacity of the plant (then at 20,000 barrels per year), which was a mild threat to Cream City brewers. The *Sentinel* noted: "This is the largest of the two Watertown breweries, and had had a good paying business, shipping large quantities of beer to the Chicago market." The reported purchase price was many times what the brewery was generally reported to be worth—about $100,000 in the 1870s, but may have been correct because many syndicate builders bid high to make sure of acquiring the property. However, no further indications of English ownership have been found and the Fuermann family remained in charge of the brewery, so it appears that this story was one more example of the overheated excitement over business mergers during the Gilded Age.

In the mid-1890s, Fuermann Brewing advertised Imperial $1,000 Beer, which was one of the first beers to use the $1,000 guarantee as an advertising feature. An ad in the Watertown city directory proclaimed "The Sum of $1,000! Is on deposit in the Merchants Bank of Watertown, Wis., as a guarantee that it is Strictly Pure."

August Fuermann Sr. died in August 1894, less than a year after his son August Jr. passed away. Sons Albert, Gerhard, and Henry took over management of the brewery. Perhaps the sons were not up to the task, the brewery had underlying financial weaknesses, or competition from local and Milwaukee breweries finally became too much for Fuermann Brewing. Whatever the cause, A. Fuermann Brewing Co. went bankrupt in 1897 and was taken over by the bank. Because they were right across the street from his plant, William Hartig purchased the buildings at auction and used them for storage, though articles at the time of the sale suggested Hartig would also use the malt house. Albert Fuermann started a new company, Watertown Bottling Co., at 1026 North Second Street and for about three years was sole bottler for his former competitor, William Hartig, as well as for John Graf's weiss beer from Milwaukee. Some early reports indicated that Albert Fuermann was planning to brew weiss beer in a portion of the old family brewery, but there is no indication that he ever did more than bottling. The Fuermann brewery was dismantled in 1915–1916 and the bricks were used for the new Watertown High School. In the 1920s the property was converted into Memorial Park, but in the 1960s the park was replaced by a new municipal building.

William Buchheit & Charles Riedinger (1852–57)
Charles Riedinger (1857?–1860?)
Plank Road Brewery, Fred Schwartz & Co. (1865–67)

West Main, near Railroad

William Buchheit and Charles Riedinger began brewing in the crowded Watertown brewing market in 1852. According to William F. Jannke III, Buchheit was hurt badly in the Panic of 1857, and left brewing. Riedinger was still in the 1860 population census as a brewer, but there are few references to the Plank Road Brewery compared with the larger breweries of Watertown. An element of confusion was added when the *Watertown Democrat* announced in 1859 that Francis Belrose was the new proprietor of the Plank Road Brewery, though the same ad was altered a month later indicating that Belrose was with the City Brewery instead. Since Joseph Bursinger was well established at City Brewery at this point, the change of brewery for Belrose is baffling. It would make more sense for him to have remained at Plank Road for a while.

In 1865, Frederick Schwartz and his partner Louis Werrbach, both of Milwaukee, began brewing weiss beer in the former Buchheit brewery. Schwartz had operated the Prairie Street Brewery in Milwaukee prior to moving to Watertown, and Werrbach would become a famous weiss beer brewer in Milwaukee after leaving Watertown. The market for weiss beer in Watertown apparently did not meet the expectations of Schwartz and Werrbach because they remained only a few years. The R. G. Dun & Co. credit reports indicate that they were in good financial condition in June 1867, but that by March 1868 they were out of business. Excise reports included Schwartz & Co. in 1867, but not in 1868 or any year thereafter, and Jannke confirms that they closed their brewery in November 1867. The buildings burned in 1871.

Joseph Hussa (1851–54)
Frederick Raasch (1854–1866?)
Kading & Strehlow (1866?–68)
Rock River Brewery
Fred Strehlow (1868)
Gottfried Thiele (1868–69)
Thiele & Habhegger (1869–1870)
John & Ulrich Habhegger (1870–72)

Oconomowoc Avenue Near East Water Street

Watertown historian William F. Jannke III found that Joseph Hussa began operating his brewery "in the Bohemian section of Watertown" in 1851. Hussa remained only a few years, before selling the brewery to Frederick Raasch and leaving to brew elsewhere in the state.

Raasch was proprietor of the brewery for several years, but according to the 1860 population census he owned no real estate, so he may have been leasing the brewery from the landowner. Little is known about the brewery during his term. At some point prior to 1867, the brewery passed to Fred Kading and Fred Strehlow. Jannke suggests that they may have been in possession by June 1866, and the fact that their first listing in the excise records is the 1867 annual list seems to confirm that they were operating the brewery before 1867. The business was also known as Kading, Strehlow & Bro. in early 1868.

According to some sources, Strehlow bought out Kading in 1868, but Kading remained in the excise records through January 1869, where he is listed along with Gottfried Thiele, who rented the brewery in December 1868 for a term of nine months. But before Thiele's term was over, H. P. Seibel bought Fred Strehlow's shares in the brewery and almost immediately sold a half interest to John

U. Habhegger Sr. and his son Ulrich. The next year, the Habheggers purchased the rest of the brewery from Seibel. The Habheggers sold 739 barrels in 1871 and 610 the next year, which were respectable totals but a mere fraction of the much larger Bursinger and Fuermann breweries. The brewery burned in May 1872, and the Habheggers returned to other businesses.

Frederick Herman (1860?)
SIXTH WARD

Frederick Herman was listed as a brewer in the 1860 population census. He owned $600 of real estate and $350 of personal property. Because he was the only brewer listed in the Sixth Ward it is at least reasonably likely that he owned his own business rather than being employed at another brewery.

Woodward & Bro. (1864?-65?)

Woodward & Bro. were listed as brewers in the 1865 state business directory. However, this particular directory is even less reliable than most, particularly since this is the only Watertown brewery listed. More reliable sources, including Jannke and Dun, have no record of this firm, and they did not last long enough to be included in excise records. It is possible that this company briefly owned the Plank Road Brewery before Schwartz or the Rock River Brewery between Raasch and Strehlow.

Langenberg & Kypke (1874?-76?)

The firm of Langenberg & Kypke was included in Schade's directory of brewers, and produced 155 barrels of beer in 1875. However, this brewery was not listed in other industry or government sources.

Bellows Brew Crew/Bellows Brewpub
(2001-7)
201 EAST MAIN STREET

The second location for John Bellows' brewery was in one of the most historic buildings in Watertown, the J. W. Cole building, built in 1841. The new location may not technically have been a brewpub, since they did not have an associated restaurant. The brewpub continued to brew highly regarded beers and had good initial support, but lasted only a short time in Watertown.

WAUKESHA (Waukesha County)

John M. Heisleutner (1849?-1863?)
Mrs. Myers (1864?-66)
Weber & Schock (1866-68)
Matthias Schock (1868-1876)

Waukesha's first brewery was established prior to 1850, though the execrable writing in the 1850 population and industrial censuses make it almost impossible to determine the name of the proprietor. In the population census it appears to be spelled J. M. Huplenstein, and in the industrial census it looks more like S. M. Klieptubner. It is likely that this was actually the brewery of John M. Heisleutner whose name was spelled several different ways even in newspaper ads. By whichever name, the brewery produced 200 barrels of beer in 1850 with three employees, one of whom appears to have been son John Jr., who was a clerk. In 1851, Heisleutner opened a bakery in connection with his brewery. He proclaimed:

> In erecting my BREWERY, I was always desirous of producing a clean, wholesome drink, without any intoxicating substances, knowing by experience that Beer, produced in that way never can undermine the health of any body. Good Beer and Good Bread are after my opinion two articles which nobody can spare, than what can better refresh the laborer after a hard day's work than a glass of Beer and a piece of Bread.

Heisleutner also dealt in ice, which he advertised for sale in any quantity at his brewery in 1855. He apparently built an addition to his brewery or an all new building in 1856, since the *Plaindealer* reported that "Heiselhutner [sic] is going to erect a large Brewery in the rear of his Hall."

Heisleutner was still brewing at least through the end of 1862. R. G. Dun & Co. reports note that he ran a saloon as well as a brewery. According to the evaluator, "He is considered a responsible man, is intemperate and trusts mostly to others in carrying on his business, is a German some advanced in life, & when sober is a very intelligent man." Among those he counted on to run his business was Jacob Engmann, his brewer, who had been employed previously at Goetter's brewery in West Bend. However, by the beginning of 1864, he was dead, and his daughter Mrs. Myers carried on the business through 1866. At that point she sold the business to Stephen Weber and Matthias Schock (spelled Schaub in the record).

It is possible that this brewery is the one that Schock was running in 1867, rather than the Henry Meyer brewery and saloon that he purchased in 1866. In 1868, Weber sold his share of this property, specifically described in the notice as Heisleutner's old brewery, to Schock for $2,500. This may be the brewery that was called the Fountain Brewery as early as 1871, though there is question about the location. Schock was not listed in excise records or industry journals at any point, so it is possible that he did not actually brew until the new Fountain Brewery was built in 1876.

Henry A. Meyer (1854?-59?)
West Hill Brewery, Stephen Weber
  (1862?-1885)
Bethesda Brewery
Weber & Land (1885-86)
Wm. A. Weber (1886-1899)
Estate of Wm. A. Weber (1900-1904)
Weber's Brewery, Stephan F. Weber (1904-7)
Weber Brewing Co. (1907-1920)
Weber Waukesha Brewing Co. (1934-1958)
220 EAST NORTH STREET

While the precise date that Henry A. Meyer started to brew in Waukesha is open to debate, at least one piece of circumstantial evidence places it as early as 1854. In an article on how well the local economy was doing, the *Waukesha Plaindealer* listed as evidence "Our breweries are using up all the barley they can find." The use of the plural implies that there was another brewery other than that of Heisleutner. Additional evidence that this second business was Meyer's comes from his application in May 1855 to sell beer at his brewery.

Meyer may have stopped brewing and left the vicinity in the late 1850s, since he was not listed in the 1860 population or industrial censuses. The property was not sold until 1862, when Stephen Weber, until then a partner in

West Hill Brewery of Milwaukee, purchased the old Meyer property. Weber retained the West Hill name from the Cream City business, and applied it to his new brewery.

Weber began putting the brewery back in order, and began to develop his local market. He was successful enough to be able to build a large dwelling on the north side of the brewery in 1869. By 1870 he was producing 900 barrels with three employees, which appears to have been the capacity of the brewery since he brewed just under 900 barrels the next two years as well. In 1873 Weber decided to build an all-new brewery to meet the increasing demand. Weber drew on his Milwaukee connections to hire an architect to draw up the plans but contracted with local builders to erect the structure. The new plant appears to have more than doubled his capacity, since in 1875 he topped 2,100 barrels. Though production declined the next few years, it still was well over 1,000 barrels per year. To deliver the beer to his customers, Weber purchased a new brewery wagon "'of the latest pattern.'"

Patrons in Waukesha had previous access to bottled beer, and the breweries in nearby Milwaukee were embracing the bottle as a way to conquer new markets. As a forward-looking brewer, Weber introduced his own bottled product in 1878, calling his customers' attention to his use of bottles "with patent Lightning Stoppers, which require no corkscrew to draw them...." He continued to expand his plant as well, building a new ice house in December 1878 which could hold 175 tons of ice. The bottled beer was quite popular: in 1881 the *Waukesha Freeman* reported that "Mr. Weber is receiving orders for West Hill Brewery beer in such quantities that he is unable to obtain bottles fast enough to supply the demand."

In 1883, Stephen Weber transferred the brewery to his son William and his son-in-law John Land. William had already been foreman (brewmaster) at the family business for about five years, and Land was a photographer who had married Stephen's daughter Barbara in 1881. The *Freeman* described the transfer thus:

> *Wm. Weber and John Land received a present on Thanksgiving day that must have made their mouths water. It was nothing less than the West Hill Brewery, one of the most flourishing institutions here. They will begin their partnership business January 1st. Mr. Stephen Weber was the donor. He has grown old and rich in the brewery business and is willing to giver the 'boys' a chance now. Waukesha beer is excelled by none.*

A few months later, the new owners renamed the business "Bethesda Brewery," in recognition of Waukesha's growing importance as a resort for those seeking health at the local mineral springs. Reports of the change made the usual claim that the new owners "expect to make some notable improvements in the general management of the business." The brewery was capable of producing 3,000 barrels per year, but the "improvements" included plans to double the capacity.

The Weber and Land partnership lasted only three years, most likely because the two did not get along. On 22 August 1887, the *Waukesha Republican* reported that Land had purchased Weber's interest in the brewery for $21,500. However the next day the *Republican* was forced to run a correction:

> *Yesterday it was mentioned that Mr. J. C. Land had purchased Mr. Weber's interest in the Bethesda Brewery, which, at the time, was a correct statement. But within the past twenty-four hours an understanding was reached whereby Mr. Weber became the purchaser of Mr. Land's interest in the property, and the papers were prepared to-day. The price agreed upon is about $21,000 for the half interest."*

It made much more sense for Weber to keep the brewery, since he had trained as a brewer, whereas Land had not. Land appears to have kept some share in the brewery until 1900, and was briefly appointed guardian of the brewery during the late 1890s while William and Stephen were incapacitated.

It appears that one of the first things Weber did after becoming sole proprietor was to convert the brewery from horsepower to steam. This change is indicated on the Sanborn insurance maps, and in September 1887 Weber offered "A horse power for sale ... cheap." In 1889, he commissioned a new barn and new brick smokestack. Weber brewed three regular brews: Standard, Pilsner, and Export, as well as a regular bock beer. The *Waukesha Journal* exulted: "If Bethesda beer keeps growing in popularity it will not be long before it will attain the reputation of that already had by Bethesda water." Weber was sometimes forced to protect his brand—in 1893 he published a notice that two local bottlers, Charles Minick Sr. and his son Lewis, "have no connection whatever with the Bethesda Brewery... the beer they are bottling is manufactured in some brewery outside Waukesha...." (A receipt from this era is pictured in chapter 6.)

All went well for the brewery until the end of the 1890s, when William Weber contracted pneumonia in 1897. His health appeared to be permanently damaged, and he died in 1900. A year later, founder Stephen Weber died, leaving the brewery in the hands of William's widow Julia Weber and her sons Killian and Stephan. According to family tradition, Julia was very much in charge of the business, and the sons cleared all decisions with her.

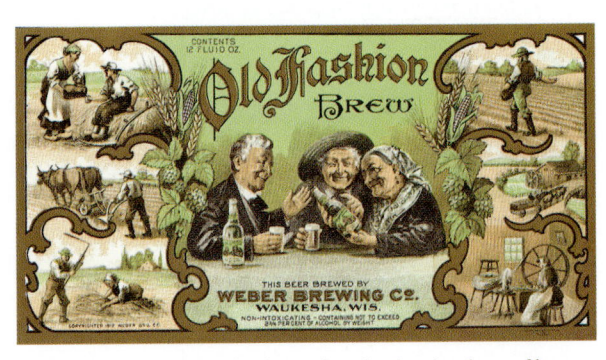

Old Fashion Brew claimed to be nonintoxicating, by virtue of its 2.75 percent alcohol by weight. Label copyright 1912. COLLECTION OF TYE SCHWALBE.

Stephan F. Weber became manager of the brewery (and of the estate) and Killian eventually became the brewmaster. The company made some name changes that had little impact on the business.

Weber Brewing Co. introduced two new beers in 1912: Weber's Old Fashion Beer and Weber's Superb Beer. These two served as the flagship brands until the advent of Prohibition.

With the advent of Prohibition, the Webers attempted to market a near beer version of Old Fashion Beer as New Fashion Brew, but this product was unsuccessful. Killian converted the brewery into Waukesha Dairy Company with the help of local dairyman Howard T. Green. They continued in this business throughout the dry years, but abandoned it as soon as it was clear that real beer would be returning.

In 1933, the Webers remodeled the brewery with the financial assistance of Hawley W. Wilbur, owner of a lumber company in Waukesha. They purchased an all-new stainless steel brew kettle (said to be the first of its type ever built in America), new bottling equipment, and hired a new brewmaster, William Neumann. Neumann had worked for Hamm Brewing in St. Paul and Birk Brothers of Chicago, so was an able superintendent. Production at the renamed Weber Waukesha brewery did not start again until June 1934, but the opportunity for work was welcomed by the forty employees and the return of Old Fashion Beer was welcomed by the community. (A lighted sign is pictured in chapter 8.)

The early 1940s brought sad changes. Julia Weber died in August 1941, and Killian died in November 1942. Stephan F. Weber assumed the presidency of the company, and along with new brewmaster Andy Schnell (another St. Paul veteran, though this time from Jacob Schmidt Brewing), the new leadership boosted production from about 30,000 barrels in 1942 to 75,000 barrels in 1948. Much of this increase probably came from increased demand during the war and the beer shortage after the war, but Weber and Schnell were able to capitalize on the conditions where other brewers were not able to do so. While many of Wisconsin's smaller breweries sought to increase production by shipping to distant markets, Weber Waukesha products were sold only in southern Wisconsin during the late 1940s. In addition, Weber Waukesha gained no advantage from the Milwaukee brewers' strike of 1948 since they were only able to supply existing customers. The continued strong business led the company in 1948 to convert the Weber home into offices for the company.

In the early 1950s production started to drop drastically. Part of this may have been due to the failing health of Stephan Weber, but members of the Weber family were uninterested in maintaining the business. Elliott Johnson of Milwaukee purchased a large block of Weber stock in 1950, and by the end of 1951 he completed the sale and took over as president of the company. After Stephan F. Weber died in 1952, Johnson purchased the rest of the family's stock, ending ninety years of family ownership. While Johnson was an experienced brewery executive, and Weber Waukesha was regarded as "one of the strongest and soundest small breweries in the United States," industry conditions were against him. Even so, Johnson made several changes that gave Weber Waukesha a fighting chance. In 1952, he hired designer William Johnson of Milwaukee to redesign all the brewery's packaging and advertising. The large red W was credited with giving the brand increased visibility and won a design award. The company also introduced flat-top cans that year.

Not every move was as successful. In 1953, Weber Distributing Co., a subsidiary of the brewery, attempted to fill the gap during the Milwaukee brewery strike of 1953 by bringing in beer from Mitchell Brewing Co. in El Paso, Texas. Unfortunately, the beer sold poorly, and Elliott Johnson explained: "the Mitchell beer is a good beer but nobody here ever heard of it." In 1954, Weber Waukesha purchased the former Van Merritt brewery in Burlington to produce the first canned soft drinks in Wisconsin. However, after initial success the cans proved unsuited to the acids produced by some flavors, and customers complained of leaky cans, so the project was abandoned. (Weber Waukesha also acquired two brands from Van Merritt: Wisconsin Premium and Paul Bunyan, which they brewed for a few years.) In 1955, Johnson formed a separate company to produce Sassy—perhaps the first in a line of what later would be called "malternatives" or "malt beverages." Sassy debuted in 1957, and while it poured with a head and was 6 percent alcohol, it didn't taste like beer and did not leave "beer breath." Sassy's short life was probably caused by poor consumer acceptance and resistance from other brewers, as well as consumer activists who perceived Sassy as an attempt to sell alcohol to youth. (A four pack of Sassy is pictured in chapter 8.)

Though adept management, Elliott Johnson had managed not only to help Weber Waukesha to survive, but even to thrive. By the mid-1950s, the brewery was producing over 100,000 barrels per year, though this was still only about half of what crosstown rival Fox Head was selling. But in 1957, Elliott Johnson died of a heart attack. The loss of Johnson's

After Prohibition, the brewery's new design for packaging and advertising (an American Indian at a spring) was similar to the Waukesha city seal. This can is from the 1950s. COLLECTION OF DAVID WENDL.

leadership, cost-cutting that resulted in unacceptable changes in the flavor of the beer, and a one-week brewery workers strike in September 1958 spelled doom for Weber Waukesha. Two weeks later, the two Waukesha breweries began merger talks, and the deal was closed in October. Weber management was in charge of the company, which used the Fox Head plant and name. The Weber brewery was shut down in November 1958.

H. A. Meyer, Waukesha Brewery (1864–66?)
Matthias Schock (1866?–1870?)
MAIN STREET NEAR BROADWAY

H. A. Meyer returned to Waukesha in 1864 and began brewing again, his time at a new location on Main Street. The announcement of his return to business in the *Waukesha Freeman* proclaimed: "The undersigned, having again commenced to Brew, is ready to fill all orders for Beer with promptness and despatch [sic], at the market price. Bottle Beer constantly on hand." Stoneware bottles marked H.A.W. confirm that his beer was packaged at this early date. (An article accompanying the advertisement referred to "Capt. Meyer"—the only officer that appears to fit this description is Herman A. Meyer of the 28th Wisconsin Infantry. This creates a problem, however, because the earlier brewer in Waukesha was Henry A. Meyer. Previous brewing by Herman is not recorded.)

In April 1866, Meyer sold his saloon to Matthias Schock, but held on to the brewery for at least a few months. Meyer announced:

Having disposed of my property and given possession of the saloon to M. Schock, I take this opportunity of returning my thanks to the public for the very liberal patronage bestowed upon me, hoping the same will be extended to my successor. I shall continue, as heretofore to sell Beer by the Keg.

He does not appear in the excise records which start in 1867, so he appears to have ceased brewing in late 1886.

While Matthias Schock is not in the excise records either, he is included in the R. G. Dun & Co. records in 1867 as the operator of a brewery and saloon, so it appears that he had by that point acquired the rest of the property. He brewed at the saloon for a few more years, until he built the Fountain Brewery in the 1870s.

Uhl & Kreiner (1868–1871)
Kreiner & Pappenheimer (1871–73)
Plate & Pappenheimer (1873–74)
EAST MAIN STREET AND HARTWELL AVENUE

Leonard Uhl and Christoph Kreiner purchased part of Hickory Grove, a picnic area on the edge of the city, in 1867, and proposed to "erect on it immediately an extensive brewery, with a garden, etc. connected with it." They had the brewery in operation by January 1868, and produced between 175 and 200 barrels in each of the years for which figures are available.

In September 1871, Uhl sold his share of the property to John L. Pappenheimer for $2,100, a change confirmed in the excise records. Kreiner sold his share to John J. Plate in 1873, but new ownership did not bring new fortune to the business. The R. G. Dun & Co. evaluator reported the brewery was out of business in June 1874, though they may have stopped brewing prior to that time. Hickory Grove remained a popular resort for many more years.

Fountain Brewery, Matthias Schock (1876?–78)
Fountain Brewery, John M. Schock (1878–1887)
NORTH STREET

In addition to the family saloon on Main Street, Matthias Schock had a separate brewery in Waukesha. However, accounts differ on when he acquired it and which brewery site it was. Some evidence suggests that for a while he brewed in the former Heisleutner brewery. In addition, Waukesha brewery historians John Schoenknecht and David Kapsos found an advertisement for the Fountain Brewery (and its bottled and keg beer) in the *Waukesha Democrat* in 1871. (It is also possible that he only brewed at the saloon, or possibly not at all, since he does not appear in excise records or industry directories during the early and mid-1870s.)

What is clear is that Schock built a new brewery in 1876 at the Almanris mineral spring and called it Fountain Brewery. Matthias Schock died in 1878, but his family continued the brewery for several years. John M. Schock, brother of Matthias, appears to have operated both the brewery and saloon for much of the time. The brewery made bock beer (which in 1877 was released on New Year's Day—much earlier than usual), and reintroduced bottled beer in 1882. The Fountain Brewery Grove was a popular setting for picnics and concerts, especially after a bridge was built across the Fox River near the brewery. (The bridge was not absolutely necessary, since there were reports of revelers rowing boats across to get to the brewery.) John Schock closed the brewery in 1887 and returned to operating saloons downtown.

Waukesha Spring Brewing Co. (1893–96)
Waukesha Imperial Spring Brewing Co. (1896–99)
Milwaukee-Waukesha Brewing Co. (1899–1920)
Fox Head Beverage Co. (1920–1933)
Fox Head Waukesha Corp. (1933–1947)
Fox Head Brewing Co. (1947–1962)
227 MAPLE AVENUE

With health-giving water and only one brewery, as well as its proximity to Milwaukee and Chicago, Waukesha was a tempting market for potential brewers. Indeed, rumors of a new brewery started in late 1890, with vauge references to "Chicago parties." In March 1891, the current rumor was that Mitchell Brewing Co. of Chicago was to buy property on Arcadian Heights in Waukesha, provided Arcadian Spring was large enough to supply their needs. A year later, the brewery was to be built by White Rock Mineral Spring Co. with plans drawn by eminent brewery architect August Martizen. This company also proposed to make ice from the White Rock Spring for "table use." The *Milwaukee Journal* claimed that this business started with $1 million in capital and "the brewery will be one of the largest in the country"—which was claimed by nearly every similar project at the time. Despite numerous and occasionally breathless updates on the project, construction did not start until June 1893. The cornerstone was laid in August, with lots of Chicagoans on hand to witness the event and to present at least the appearance of significant financial support.

Finally, in April 1894, brewing operations commenced, with the grand opening scheduled for 15 May. The first barrel of beer was auctioned for charity, and realized $75, to which the company pledged to add $25 to the (unnamed) charity. The opening of what was called Waukesha Spring Brewing Co. did not stop rumors of additional breweries in the area—another was proposed for Acme Spring, and other groups of Chicago and St. Louis investors were still looking at sites or trying to buy Weber's Bethesda Brewery. Elk Spring Brewing Co. went so far as to file articles of incorporation, but never actually built a brewery.

Waukesha Spring Brewing Co. was founded by a consortium of Chicago saloonkeepers who hoped a cooperative brewery would help them obtain beer at a lower price. Matthew Thome was head of this group, and became the first president. The company was focused on the Chicago trade and advertised heavily there, proclaiming in one 1895 ad that its beer was available "at 500 resorts in Chicago." Waukesha Spring owned thirty-two saloons in Milwaukee including the saloon at Milwaukee Garden. It also owned property in Dubuque, Rockford, and South Bend. The Maritzen-designed, 100,000-barrel capacity brewery had an imposing brick tower with a cupola, and had a unique spring house in front shaped like a twenty-foot tall beer bottle. Located near the Northwestern Railroad Depot, it was ideally placed to attract visiting tourists. However, the company ran into financial problems almost immediately, perhaps because of the effects of making a major investment during the Panic of 1893. The company's saloons were reportedly sold in August 1895 to Peter Schoenhoefen Brewing of Chicago, and the brewery itself went into receivership in November. The extent of the company's spending on advertising is indicated by the fact that American Fine Art Co. of Milwaukee sued Waukesha Spring for unpaid lithography work in the amount of $249,538.38—more than the assets of the company. The *Milwaukee Journal* editorialized: "The fate of the Waukesha brewery is another proof of the fact that a successful business has to be started on a small scale and expanded with the growth of years."

After several disputes over reorganization, a new company, Waukesha Imperial Spring Brewing Co., was formed in June 1896. (The articles of incorporation had unusual provisions allowing the company to purchase devices to produce electrical power and to "furnish and supply the same to consumers.") the new brewery continued to seek distant markets, and established a branch office in the already crowded Minneapolis market in 1897. However, the new owners were not successful in reducing the debt, and in 1899 yet another company formed, Milwaukee-Waukesha Brewing Co. This concern was headed by Milwaukee brewing supplies merchant Charles Manegold (one of the principal creditors of the previous businesses) and his son-in-law August Lindemann.

Throughout the pre-Prohibition era, whatever entity was operating the brewery focused on the health-giving properties of their beers, and used the Health Beer brand on several products. The brewery produced a variety of lagers and ales, and while some of these may have been well suited to the water supply, few drinkers outside Chicago were interested in porter or old stock ale, and perhaps not even enough Chicagoans to make the brands profitable. Waukesha Imperial Spring letterhead listed three different bottled beers, three draught beers and a malt tonic. Milwaukee-Waukesha increased the number of ales, but decided to replace the German two-headed eagle on the label with the fox head used on the original Waukesha Spring labels. The fox head would provide the company with an identity for the next six decades.

The company continued to expand its plant and its market during the pre-Prohibition era. They built a new bottling plant in 1902, but had to expand it further in 1905. An ad placed by Frank Fenolio, Milwaukee-Waukesha's agent in Fort Smith, Arkansas, advertised the company's Club House Beer, Health Beers, Stock Ale, Porter, Malt Tonic, Ginger Ale and Club Lithia Water—giving an idea both of the scope of the product line and its distribution range.

When Prohibition arrived, Milwaukee-Waukesha was in a good position to make alternative beverages. It had several on the market already, and could trade on the fame of Waukesha water. During the early years of Prohibition, the company reorganized as Fox Head Spring Beverage Co., and then changed its name again to Fox Head Waukesha Corp by 1929. Fox Head had a variety of sodas and malt products for sale during Prohibition, and the ability to keep the brewery functioning during the dry years made it easy to return to brewing in 1933.

In 1928, Charles Manegold died, and his daughter, Emilie Lindemann, became president of the company—one of the few female brewery heads in the country. Lindemann was the subject of an article in the *Chicago Tribune* in 1937 when she was the only woman at the convention of the American Brewers' Association. The article pointed out that she was particularly interested in laboratory testing. Because she had been raised in the brewery supply business it was not surprising that she would be an expert rather than a figurehead.

Fox Head Waukesha was among the breweries ready to deliver beer on 7 April, and was already advertising in Chicago suburbs that day. Soon, Fox Head beers were advertised in Michigan's Upper Peninsula, Indiana and Nebraska as well. When the 21st amendment was passed, Fox Head returned to brewing ale, and at the 6 to 7 percent strength used prior to Prohibition. The company's most popular beer, Fox Head 400, was introduced in September 1936. By 1940, Fox Head Lager, 400, and Ale were on sale in New Jersey. Fox Head routinely produced over 100,000 barrels per year and was in the top six breweries in Wisconsin: exceeded only by the four Milwaukee giants and Heileman (and sometimes Kingsbury, but the latter had two breweries).

During World War II, Fox Head increased production each year, despite a fire in January 1944 that destroyed the bottling works and shipping depot, along with a large stock of labels and crowns. Fox Head was also among the breweries fined by the Office of Price Administration for selling beer above ceiling prices. Just after the war, Fox Head was involved in a four-man carpenters' strike that had national implications for jurisdictional disputes between unions. (The four wanted to work as members of the carpenters' union rather than the brewery workers' union.)

In 1947, the company changed its name to Fox Head Brewing Co., a name change that made little difference in marketing. A change which did make a difference in marketing was their move into television advertising and program sponsorship from 1953–1955—a venture that indicated Fox Head was more than a local or regional brewer, as only larger breweries could afford even limited television advertising. Another indication that Fox Head was no longer a family brewery was the fact that its stock was traded on the American Stock Exchange.

In 1955, Fox de Luxe Brewing Co. of Chicago acquired a "'substantial interest'" in Fox Head Brewing—a logical merger based on the company names. (Canadian Ace Brewery of Chicago also was interested in acquiring Fox Head.) Production of Fox de Luxe beer was moved to Waukesha, which helped the Fox Head plant exceed 200,000 barrels for the first time in 1956. However the new management resulted in bitter infighting, and in late 1957, Arthur Feicht and Frank Huber were ousted as officers by a group of directors headed by Joseph Antonow and Alexander Morse. An indication of how little connection the directors had to the local community was that none of the directors was from Waukesha, and Morse was from New York. Sales declined from $5.4 million in 1956 to $5 million in 1957 (though the *Chicago Tribune* erroneously wrote that they had declined *by* $5 million). Just after the leadership fight, the two Waukesha breweries combined, pushing the production at the Fox Head facility over 200,000 barrels again.

However the leadership fight turned out to be related to another, more serious problem. In 1958, it was revealed by a U.S. Senate committee that Fox Head had paid reputed Chicago gangster Tony Accardo almost $43,000 through a distributor for no apparent work. Investigations showed that Accardo was using this business to avoid taxation. During testimony, Accardo cited the Fifth Amendment 172 times to avoid answering questions about ties to Chicago's crime syndicates. In July 1959, one of the distributors involved in the case was gunned down in a gangland-style assassination. Fox Head cut its ties with Premium Beer Sales, but the case had become national news and Fox Head's reputation was tarnished.

Fox Head also tried to capture part of the nonalcoholic malt beverage market, shipping its new Fox Brew to Saudi Arabia in 1961 to attempt to create a market in a hostile environment. Early sales were promising, and president Howard Hartman claimed that a freighter picked up 2,000 cases for an "emergency order" for Saudi Arabia that winter, but the expected production of 300,000 barrels per year of the new beverage never materialized.

During the early 1960s, Fox Head Brewing attempted to diversify its interests. In November 1960, it acquired a share in a new brewery in Managua, Nicaragua. Executive vice president (and former Weber Waukesha brewmaster) Andrew Schnell went there to supervise the beginning of production. In November 1961, the company acquired the Marrakesh hotel in Jamaica, at that time the largest on the island. While both of these acquisitions could be tied to the company's core business, the purchase of Illinois Felt Corp. was less logical. To reflect the more diverse nature of the company, in January 1962 stockholders agreed to change the name of the business to Noramco, Inc. (short for North American Consolidated).

The end of Noramco's brewing business came in June 1962, when G. Heileman Brewing Co. of La Crosse acquired the brewery and its brands. While Heileman president Roy Kumm initially said that the purchase of Fox Head would provide the company with additional capacity, production of Fox Head brands was soon moved to Sheboygan and La Crosse and the brewery was shut down in late 1962. Much of the building was demolished, but part of the complex still stands and has housed various light industries and artists' studios, and during the late 1990s was home to RWS Brewing/Watson Brewing Co.

Fox Head's Old Waukesha Ale was one of few canned ales in the Upper Midwest during the 1950s. COLLECTION OF DAVID WENDL.

In the late 1950s, Fox Head made an early attempt to create a brand of beer for female drinkers—but provided minimal advertising to support the brand, which was an unnecessary product. COLLECTION OF JOHN STEINER.

Supreme Bottling Co. (1904–1920)
237 Delafield

While weiss beer bottles from Supreme Bottling Co. exist, none of the city directory entries or advertisements located so far give any indication that this business actually brewed weiss beer. Several Wisconsin bottlers packaged weiss beer of other producers like John Graf of Milwaukee, and that may have been the case with Supreme. Since weiss beer production was not complicated and required relatively little equipment, it is possible that Supreme could have brewed at some point, but they do not appear in any industry directories or publications during the pre-Prohibition era.

RWS Brewing (1994–99)
Watson Brewing Co. (1999–2000)
223 Maple Avenue

Brewing returned to the former Fox Head Brewing complex in 1994, when three homebrewers: Brett Remington, Scott Watson, and Steve Smith, opened Remington-Watson-Smith Brewing. A six-month search for a site led them to the building at 223 Maple, which had the advantage of good insulation and a floor suited for drainage. However the old building required almost entirely new gas, electricity, plumbing and drains. The three, along with their wives and girlfriends, did much of the rehabilitation along with the mountains of required paperwork. While expenditures ballooned past expectations, Remington explained their reason for perseverance in a 1994 *Milwaukee Journal* article: "'We're all young. If we didn't do this now, we would say we should have tried it. You have to be an optimist about any small business, especially this one.'"

RWS Brewing specialized in English-style ales, offered on draught and in 16-ounce bottles. Several of the beers earned good reviews, but the brewery was not financially stable and was probably a bit before its time. When owned by Dick and Vaune Cooper, they introduced the Barrelmaker Brewing Company line of beers, as a reference to their name. After several ownership changes it closed in December 2000.

Fixture Brewing Co. (2013–16)
716 Clinton Street

Fixture Brewing Co. began brewing in Waukesha in 2013. Owner Steve Fix planned to have its own beers on tap in 2012, but parts for the boiler were delayed because Hurricane Sandy destroyed one of the warehouses of the supplier. The name was partially inspired by the owner's last name, and by hopes that the establishment would become a "fixture" in downtown Waukesha, which it was for a few years. Fixture closed in 2016 after state revenue agents seized the brewery assets for failing to have a valid brewpub permit and failing to pay malt beverage taxes.

Raised Grain Brewing Co. (2015–present)
2244 West Bluemound Road

Two local doctors and homebrewing enthusiasts, Scott Kelley and Jimmy Gosset, had an argument over which nation made better beer, Scotland or Belgium. The compromise beer they made inspired them and two other founders to start the brewery (and as Paradocs Red IIPA the beer became a gold medal winner at Great American Beer Festival in 2016). The name was inspired by co-founder Nick Reistad, who grew up helping in his father's woodworking shop, where "raising the grain" is an essential step to finishing the surface—and which evokes the idea of raising the grain in beer to a high level of craft. (The other founder was area entrepreneur Kevin Brandenburg.) The taproom was finished with rustic wood details to emphasize the theme.

Raised Grain describes its products as "Boldly Brewed Beers," which is an apt description. Most of the beers tend toward the higher end of the alcohol scale for each style, and there are some bold experiments as well. The most noteworthy of these is Les Trois Docteurs, a barrel-aged Belgian quadruple brewed with grapes from a fellow doctor's vineyard in Oregon. Several of the regular beers and some additional specialties were available in 22-ounce bottles. Within a year, Raised Grain went from having one employee to nineteen, jumped from one local draught account to fifty, began bottling, and built their own food truck. The rapid growth of interest in Raised Grain beers made it necessary to consider significant expansion almost immediately, and in 2017, Raised Grain announced plans to establish a production brewery with a canning line at 1725 Dolphin Drive in Waukesha. The original brewery and taproom would remain, and would serve as a pilot brewhouse for testing new recipes.

WAUNAKEE *(Dane County)*

Bellows Brew Company/Whistle Stop Tavern (1999–2001)
101 East Main Street

John Bellows established a small brewery inside the Whistle Stop Tavern in Waunakee. He brewed his first beers in December 1999 and had them on tap a month later. Business grew steadily for more than a year, but an ownership change at the Whistle Stop encouraged him to close shut down his brewery there and move it to a new location closer to his home in Watertown. His Irish Stout brewed at this location won Silver at the Great American Beer Festival in 2001.

Octopi Brewing Co. (Third Sign Beers) (2015–present)
1131 Uniek Drive

Octopi Brewing Co. was formed with a different business plan than any other brewery in Wisconsin's history—to brew beers for other labels. Founder Isaac Showaki, who was also co-founder of the innovative 5 Rabbit Cerveceria in Chicago, designed a state-of-the-art 65,000 barrel per year brewery to brew high end beers for other breweries with insufficient capacity in their existing breweries or whose breweries were not yet in production. Octopi also provides a range of services to its clients, including consultation, recipe formulation, merchandising and design, and equipment and supply selection. The name Octopi was chosen because the shape-shifting character of an octopus was a metaphor for the ability of the company to take multiple forms to provide different beers and services for its clients.

In addition to the contract brews, Octopi also produced a range of beers under its own label, 3rd Sign Brewery. The third sign of the

3rd Sign beers had the slogan "Dually Brewed" to emphasize that they were released in related pairs. AUTHOR'S COLLECTION.

zodiac is Gemini, the twins, and the 3rd Sign beers were released in pairs to show off differences in ingredients, such as Castor and Pollux (the original Gemini twins)—a hoppy wheat and a Belgian wit, respectively. One purpose of these beers was to demonstrate the capabilities of the brewhouse and brewing team to potential contract clients. The 3rd Sign beers were discontinued in May 2017 due to distribution difficulties.

Lone Girl Brewing (2016–present)
114 EAST MAIN STREET, SUITE 101

Co-owners Kevin and Kerry Abercrombie and Paul and Tammi Kozlowski had a total of seven children between the ages of four and ten, but only one was a girl. The lone girl inspired the name of their brewpub in a new building between Main Street and the railroad tracks in downtown Waunakee. The couples owned the bar Matilda in Chicago, and wanted to bring a "brewery with food, not a restaurant with good beer," to their adopted (and much quieter) home of Waunakee. Brewer John Russell, whose full-time job is scientist at UW-Madison School of Medicine, has created a mix of classic and experimental beers. Among the latter is Harry's Coconut IPA, inspired by a song by Harry Nillson, which combines lime flavor from the hops with coconut. The Double Trubbel series of Belgian Dubbels features the malty base beer used as a platform to introduce other ingredients, ranging from pumpkin spice to apricots.

WAUPACA
(Waupaca County)

Waupaca Brewery
Leonard Arnold (1860?–1889)
Arnold Bros. (1889–1892)
Mrs. Amelia Padgham (1892?–95?)
WAUPACA RIVER AT MODERN INTERSECTION OF ELM STREET AND STATE HIGHWAY 49

Leonard Arnold was trained as a brewer and cooper in Bavaria. Upon arrival in the United States, he moved from Boston to Milwaukee and "thence to Oshkosh, where he followed his trade for five years." He then went to Weyauwega to work in Jacob Konrad's brewery for two years before starting his brewery in Waupaca. While local tradition holds that he started his brewery in 1858, the years he spent at each location as reported by the 1881 *History of Northern Wisconsin* mean he can not have moved to Waupaca until 1860 at the earliest, and the 1860 population census places him in Weyauwega living next door to Konrad.

The 1881 history provided a vivid account of his pioneer brewing:

> . . . he cleared the trees and grubs away so that the building could be erected, and put up a small building 20x40, and opened his brewery; he made all his kegs and casks and ground his malt by hand. It was a hard and feeble beginning, but he has prospered and now owns twenty-four acres of land, and his brewery is 20x100, with an addition 14x40 for machinery and cooling rooms.

While this book described his brewery as "good sized," it was in fact a small brewery. It was not included in the 1870 industrial census, and the largest known production figures show 300 barrels brewed in 1885. He brewed much less in other years—fifty-three barrels in 1878 and thirty-nine in 1879. The Sanborn insurance map of 1885 shows the brewery as a small horse-powered operation, with the family dwelling right in the middle of the building. In many ways the operation was a true farm brewery: A pig pen, feed mill and summer kitchen either shared the brewery building or were a few steps away.

Arnold's ability to brew was limited by an accident he suffered around 1868, when his left hand was blown off by the premature discharge of a cannon during a political celebration. Like many German brewers, he enjoyed his own product, but never to an extent that would harm his business, at least according to the R. G. Dun & Co. credit evaluators. While he was apparently not a first-class businessman, his eldest daughter Frances was quite accomplished and was admitted to the bar in 1880 as "the third lady lawyer in the state."

Leonard Arnold died in 1889 and his two sons Leonard Jr. and Albert ran the brewery for a few years as Arnold Bros. The 1895 state business directory lists a Mrs. Amelia Padgham as a brewer in Waupaca. Since Amelia was the daughter of Leonard Arnold Sr., it is possible that she operated the brewery for a short period. However, the Sanborn map of June 1895 shows the building as Arnold Bros. Beer Depot, which was the local agency for Schlitz Brewing Co.

WAUPUN *(Fond du Lac County)*

John M. Schroeck (Schroeck & Reinhard) (1855?–1859?)
August Hauf (Valentine Konrad, lessee) (1859?–1863?)
Philip Binzel (1863–66)
August Hauf (1867–69)
Bucher & Seifert (1870–71)
Wisconsin Brewery, Peter Seifert (1871–1894)
John Skala (1894–96)
Augusta Skala (1896–1902)
Waupun Brewery, John Skala (1902–1911)
Waupun Brewing Co. (1911–17)
FRANKLIN STREET AT BREWERY STREET (MODERN ZIMMERMAN STREET)

Just before Christmas 1856, a visitor from Beaver Dam traveled to Waupun and

> . . . took the opportunity to call on our German friends, J. M. Schroeck and Reinhard, and to visit their extensive beer establishment, and test by actual trial the virtue of their sparkling Lager beverage. They have a

very large brewery, and are prepared to do a heavy business, and to manufacture as good an article of beer as can be found east or west. The large cellar is 28 feet underground, and will hold one thousand barrels. They have two other cellars that will hold five hundred barrels apiece. They have a well sixty feet deep, and a cistern that will hold five hundred barrels of soft water. Their malt floor is 60 by 20 for growing the malt.

The report does not make it clear how long the brewery had been in operation, though articles of this sort during the era typically mentioned if a business or structure was new.

It is also not clear how long Schroeck & Reinhart remained at the brewery, though a passing reference in a newspaper article indicates that Schroeck was still brewing there in May 1859. By the 1860 industrial census the brewery was under the name of August Hauf. While the cellars may have been capacious, the output in 1860 was not worthy of the space—a mere fifty barrels. Hauf appears to have owned the property but was not a brewer. The only brewer listed in Waupun in the 1860 population census was Valentine Konrad, but since he owned no property it is quite likely that he rented the brewery and operated it. (Actually, Konrad was not the only brewer living in Waupun that year, but he was the only one at liberty to work—since fellow brewer Franz Berire was confined to the nearby state prison.) Konrad is also listed on an 1862 map of Fond du Lac County as a brewer in Waupun.

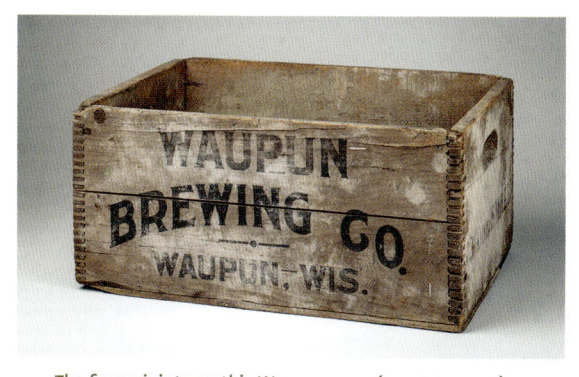

The finger joints on this Waupun case (ca. 1905–1910) were seldom seen on beer cases. COLLECTION OF JOHN STEINER.

Hauf's status as a landlord rather than brewer seems to be confirmed by an account of the brewery fire in 1866, which referred to the business as "Heniff's [Hauf's] brewery, occupied by [John] Phillip Bensell [Binzel]." The brewery was destroyed, and two employees escaped, though one was burned. There was no insurance to cover the estimated $5,000 loss. Hauf rebuilt, but Phillip Binzel and his brother Peter left for Beaver Dam, and Peter then moved to Oconomowoc to start his own brewery. Hauf appears to have been fire-prone, since in 1868 he and "a girl living in his family were arrested for arson for trying to burn down his house for the insurance money." Hauf's financial problems extended to the brewery, which appears to have been idle during early 1870 and was auctioned at a sheriff's sale in June. The winning bidder, J. Leary, soon sold the brewery to Bucher & Seifert. Peter Seifert soon bought out his partner, and brought much needed stability to the Waupun brewery.

Seifert ramped production up quickly, from 299 barrels in 1871 to 677 the following year. Unfortunately, Seifert's production is missing from most listings, but Wing's 1887 directory listed his capacity as between 500 and 1,000 barrels per year. In 1894, Seifert sold the brewery to John Skala, who continued the same production level. The 1895 Wisconsin industrial census placed output around 1,000 barrels. (For a few years, the brewery was in the name of Skala's wife Augusta.) Around 1903, Skala built an all-new brewery, this time powered by steam and built of brick and stone. The new facility also had a modern bottling plant and an old-fashioned hog pen.

The Skala era ended in June 1911, when he sold the brewery to Henry Storm and George Kueneth. They changed the name of the company to Waupun Brewing Co. and incorporated the business that June with a mix of local and Milwaukee investors. The brewery continued to operate until early 1917, when it closed for good. After the brewery closed, the property still known locally as Brewery Hill passed to Anna Skala, who sold it to the First Reformed Church of Waupun four decades later.

WAUSAU *(Marathon County)*

George Vetter (1856?)
Crowley & Brothers (1856?–1859?)
623 FOREST STREET

According to a county history from 1913, the first brewery in Wausau was built by George Vetter sometime in the 1850s, "and the place was long known as the Vetter Cellars." He was apparently a part-time brewer who spent the rest of the time at his farm. Unfortunately, there is no other known documentation of Vetter as a brewer. The only brewers listed in the Wisconsin state business directory of 1857 are Crowley & Brothers, who may have purchased or leased the brewery from Vetter. (It is also possible they built their own brewery.) The *Wausau Central Wisconsin* included a brewery in the list of Wausau's businesses in February 1859, so either Vetter or the Crowley brothers appear still to have been in operation at that date.

George Ruder (1860–1888)
George Ruder Brewery (1888–1892)
Geo. Ruder Brewing Co. (1892–1920)
American Brewing Co. (1920–25)
American Products Co. (1933–34)
Mathie-Ruder Brewing Co. (1934–1955)
504–516 GRAND AVENUE

After leaving his partnership with Henry Wahle in Stevens Point, George Ruder moved to Wausau and started work on his new brewery in 1860. By October, he was ready to announce

to the inhabitants of Marathon and surrounding counties, that his New and Extensive Establishment has just been completed, and is now in operation for the Manufacture of Beer and Ale. He will keep constantly on hand a large supply of Beer of All Kinds, and will also deal extensively in Malt, Hops, and Yeast. Grain and Feed for Cattle and Hogs always on hand. . . . the superior facilities of fitting up, and the supply of pure water, and excellence of stock on hand warrants Mr. Ruder in saying that he will furnish a better article of Beer than ever before manufactured in the Central part of the State.

An article accompanying the ad proclaimed "All who have tasted Ruder's beer unite in pronouncing the best they ever drank in the West" and added, "Mr R. is an experienced brewer, having been, as he says 'born in a brewery' and has been his whole life engaged in the business. . . ."

While little is known about his operations in the 1860s, by 1870 he was brewing around 600 barrels per year. His brewery represented an investment of $14,000, which was one of the largest in northern Wisconsin. Production dropped in 1871 and early 1872, perhaps as a result of Ruder's decision to leave brewing and go into the lumber business. Ruder sold the brewery to Zastrow & Loeffler, who took possession in early 1872. The *Central Wisconsin* reported "the Brewery pleasure grounds is [sic] being fixed up by the lessee, A. Zastrow, who intends to make it a first-class place of amusement." But this arrangement lasted only a few months, and in July the *Central Wisconsin* reassured readers (with several references that were presumably local jokes): "The great beer trouble is ended, and Mr. Geo. Ruder is back in possession. Mr. Loeffler retired yesterday from the business. We presume both thought it unprofitable to leave the business in the hands of the Sheriff, as that gentleman's capacity for using up the profits is questionable—we doubt not he is a Greeley man." With Ruder back in charge, production returned to around 800 barrels per year by the end of the decade. When Ruder first offered bottled beer, it was packaged by George Forster, located two blocks away at Grand and Plummer Streets, and later at Star Bottling Works, rather than at the brewery.

In 1881, Ruder decided to take advantage of the brewing talents of his sons and open a second brewery in Merrill. This made a relatively small business in Wausau one of the very first Wisconsin brewers to build a new branch brewery from the ground up rather than buying an existing business. George sold this plant to his son Emil in 1886, and retired from active involvement in the Wausau brewery in 1887. (See the Merrill section for more on this brewery.) Another building project became necessary in Wausau when the Ruder Brewery was destroyed by fire in 1892. The fire originated in the "sleeping rooms" of the brewery and spread "with alarming rapidity." All the structures, including the brewhouse, malt house, engine house, three ice houses, the office and the Ruder residence burned to the ground—with a total loss estimated at $90,000. The fire was one of the most disastrous in Wausau history, and several other buildings were destroyed and others damaged, including Frank Mathie's brewery next door. The structure and contents were woefully underinsured and Ruder considered merging with Frank Mathie after the fire, but instead started construction on a larger and more modern brewery. The new brewery was all-brick, as were several of the other buildings. The business was also incorporated as the new brewery was built. Unfortunately, George Ruder died in December 1893, before he could enjoy the results of his new brewery.

Geo. Ruder Brewing built a solid business, and was seldom in the news during the pre-Prohibition years. The only noteworthy event prior to the dry years was the merger in 1918 of the Ruder and Mathie breweries under the name American Brewing Company. A resolution passed by stockholders of Frank Mathie Brewing Co. cited the need to conserve fuel and other inputs due to wartime restrictions. Production moved to the Ruder plant, and the company continued to brew beer until Prohibition. American Brewing attempted to brew a near beer for a few years, but it was unsuccessful and the company shut down brewing operations in 1925.

When beer returned, the company was reorganized and renamed American Products Co.—an unusual decision as this was the type of name usually used during Prohibition, not after. In February 1933, Pure Food Products Company of La Crosse attempted to buy American Products and make it one of the fifteen breweries it planned to control (they already

This label was from the brief time when the brewery was American Products Co. In the alcohol content statement, "weight" is blacked out and "volume" added. COLLECTION OF JOHN STEINER.

had nine at this point). However this sale did not go through and the company led by Louis Silverschmidt was forced to look elsewhere. Because substantial remodeling was necessary, the brewery was not ready immediately, and American Products advertised in the *Wausau Daily Herald* its desire to borrow $30,000 to rehabilitate the buildings and buy new equipment. In August, American Products launched its flagship Red Ribbon beer on draught, and bottled beer followed a few weeks later. In April 1934, American Products began selling Old Lager in both light and bock versions in half-gallon picnic bottles. Even at this point, the ads contained the clarifying note "(Mathie-Ruder Breweries)," and soon the company decided to make the common name the official one. In May, the company provided official notice of the name change. The leadership of the new company included members of both the Mathie and Ruder families.

Mathie-Ruder Brewing followed the path of most other medium-sized Wisconsin breweries in the years after Prohibition. They introduced a wide range of brands and package sizes. In 1952 the company introduced Red Ribbon in cone-top cans, but in 1955 moved to a modern flat-top canning line. In one interesting way,

A Red Ribbon tray from the early 1940s. Collection of David Wendl.

the company revived a nineteenth-century practice: advertising for local farmers to sell their barley directly to the brewery. They urged farmers to "bring your barley samples to our office. We operate the only malting plant in Central Wisconsin, and we wish, if possible, to buy all our requirements locally." Also as in previous years, Mathie-Ruder sold spent grain and malt sprouts to local farmers, who were advised to "bring your own sacks."

The crowded Wisconsin beer market encouraged Mathie-Ruder to offer special promotional items for customers. In 1934, they offered a choice of a solid copper mug or a set of six platinum banded crystal glasses to anyone bringing in a coupon from a case of beer "with a small cash consideration." The company's solid sales enabled them to invest in improved equipment, including a new filter and an electric refrigeration system along with several new storage tanks in 1935. Later that year, they expanded the malt house so the company could manufacture all the malt needed for brewing as well as some extra for sale. To encourage improved barley culture, the brewery sponsored a prize for the best barley at the Wisconsin Valley Fair and Exposition. Mathie-Ruder also signed a contract with Local 226 of the International Union of United Breweries, Flour, Cereal, and Soft Drink Workers of America, and thereafter proudly advertised that their beer was union made.

Like many other smaller Wisconsin breweries, Mathie-Ruder enjoyed a surge in production immediately after World War II, but sales dropped precipitously from an average of over 32,000 barrels from 1944 to 1947 to 20,000 in 1948 then to 10,000 barrels in 1949 and only 6,000 in 1950. This may have been due in part to the departure of longtime brewmaster Peter Etzweiler and the last family officer, Otto Mathie, in 1948. The brewery began to have quality-control problems, and several bad batches of beer were shipped to customers. Sales never recovered, and the company ceased brewing in August 1955. The property was offered for sale that month, and the remaining beer was shipped out over the remainder of the year. Most of the brewery structures were torn down during the 1960s and 1970s.

Mathie & Huebner (1869)
Frank Mathie (1869–1888)
Frank Mathie Brewing Co. (1888–1892)
Mathie Brewing Co. (1892–1918)
408–416 Grand Avenue

Frank Mathie came to Wausau as a blacksmith, and later started a brickyard. In 1869 he decided that the city had room for two substantial lager breweries. He and partner Frank Huebner selected a site just to the north of George Ruder's established brewery. Since access to pure water, rail and road transportation and hillsides in which to excavate caves was so important, it was common for brewers to cluster together rather than to spread out in an attempt to serve different markets. To meet the inevitable competition from his neighbor, Mathie had to start big. As a brickmaker, he was able to make many of the bricks for his own brewery. The 1870 industrial census indicated that Mathie had invested $14,000 in the brewery, $6,000 more than Ruder. Mathie also had horse power rather than hand power, and took advantage of these to produce about 600 barrels during his first full year of production (almost twice as much as Ruder). Mathie was in operation by May 1869, when he sent a keg of beer to the staff of the *Wausau Central Wisconsin* who "tried it and pronounce[d] it excellent both in taste and flavor. That success attend his business and industry, is the wish of the whole force of the *Central*."

While Mathie started with a seven-barrel brew kettle, over time he built his capacity (though not up to 40,000 barrels per year in "a few years" as one later account claimed). He brewed 916 barrels in 1879, which put him about one hundred barrels ahead of Ruder.

In June 1892, a fire that started at the Ruder brewery spread to Mathie's brewery. The three-foot thick brick wall of the ice house helped slow down the fire. The cupola on top of the brewery caught fire and threatened the brewhouse until the cupola was cut down. While the Ruder brewery was destroyed, the Mathie plant was only damaged, but the damage was severe. The original estimate of $75,000 was later raised to $100,000. In the aftermath of the fire, the two companies considered combining. The *Milwaukee Journal* reported that the two facilities were to be "connected and rebuilt, . . . making one of the largest brewing plants in the state, outside Milwaukee." However, by late July they had decided not to combine, and both were rebuilt separately.

During the rebuilding process, Frank Mathie Sr. retired and sold the brewery to his sons Otto, Frank Jr. and John. The new owners

In 1908, the Mathie Brewing Co. received a shipment of one million labels for its Weisnesteiner beer. The *Wausau Daily Herald* noted that if these labels were placed end to end they would stretch for forty miles. Collection of John Steiner

incorporated the business as Mathie Brewing Co. They continued to improve the brewery with new equipment and expanded facilities. In 1896 they installed two new "refrigerating machines," which they proudly announced were "the same as used at the Pabst brewery in Milwaukee." Many smaller breweries were able to buy the same equipment and use the same supplies as the Milwaukee giants, which suggests that common economic theories claiming that large, successful companies reached that status because they could afford more modern equipment are flawed. Mathie built a bottling house in 1893, but offered bottled beer even before that year through Daniel Boehm Bottling Works. They built an expansion to the bottling house in 1902 to meet the demand for their flagship Weisensteiner beer. In 1906, the company introduced a new label, Red Ribbon Beer. Red Ribbon was also the flagship brand of the Mathie Brewing Co. of Los Angeles, which was owned by another of Frank's sons, Edward.

In 1918, the Mathie and Ruder breweries finally merged, driven by decreasing availability of raw materials during the war and increasing costs and prohibitionist sentiment. (The story of the merger is covered in more detail in the Ruder Brewing Co. section.) After the merger the Mathie plant was closed down and later used for light industrial purposes until the last remaining sections were torn down in 1977.

John Williams (1883–1884?)

In October 1883, *Western Brewer* reported that John Williams had opened a new brewery in Wausau. Wing's directory of 1884 listed him (spelled Willems) as a brewer and bottler of weiss beer. His business was apparently short lived, and does not appear in other records.

Wausau Brewing Co. (1913–1923)
Chief Wausau Co. (1925–26)
West End Malt Co. (1933)
Wausau Brewing Co. (1933–1961)
622–644 Seventh and Porter Streets

Wausau Brewing Co. was one of several new plants built during the brewery building boom of the pre-Prohibition era. Nicholas Veeser of Wausau had toured a new brewery in Pennsylvania (which one is lost to history) and decided that a modern brewery in Wausau could help supply a growing market which was buying more beer from out of town with Mathie and Ruder no longer expanding. In February 1913, a meeting was held to propose the project and fifty-four prospective stockholders turned out "and it was announced that there had already been a gratifying demand for the stock." The stockholders appointed a site committee which included Fred W. Krause, a local politician and president of Wausau Iron Works. Krause served as general contractor, had the staff at the Iron Works draw the plans for the brewery, and his company supplied the steel for the frame of the building. The directors filed articles of incorporation in March 1913, and building started within a few months. While the 1914 annual report stated that production began 1 May 1914, Wausau Brewing Co. had bock beer for sale in May 1914, which suggests that they had been brewing for at least a few months prior to this—no self-respecting brewer would release bock beer that had lagered less than a month. By the next year, Wausau had a lineup of three regular beers: Old Settlers' Brew, Cloverbelt, and West Side Brew.

Wausau Brewing had to cope with a variety of problems during its few years of production before Prohibition, some caused by internal strife, and others by world conflict. The breweries that were formed by a collection of unrelated stockholders were sometimes less stable than family businesses, and Wausau was plagued by corporate infighting for several years. U.S. entry into World War I forced breweries to make due with fewer quantities of inputs of all kinds. In addition to restrictions on the use of grain, the breweries of Marathon County were faced with a bottle shortage. The four county breweries placed a notice in newspapers in May 1917, announcing "Owing to the fact that the bottle factories have sold their entire output for 1917, we cannot buy any new bottles and must conserve those we have." The four breweries implemented a policy requiring a deposit on each case of bottles and charged 5¢ for each missing bottle.

As Prohibition approached, Wausau Brewing converted to producing near beer. The 1920 annual report indicated that the nature of the company's business in 1920 was "Brewing of Beer + Dealcoholizing same." Wausau offered a Special Christmas Brew in 1920, but apparently it was not worth repeating. By the next year they had added root beer to the line up, but by 1923 the company was merely acting as a jobber for the cereal beverages and soft drinks of other manufacturers. In 1923 the company changed its name to Wausau Produce and Storage Co., which better reflected the nature of its business.

In 1925, the company tried again, this time as Chief Wausau Co., but fared little better. The company had two problems that forced its closure in 1926. One was simply not doing enough business to pay the bills. Another was suspected Chicago mob involvement with the brewery. A shipment of three carloads of real beer arrived in Chicago from Kelly, a small station east of Wausau. While it is not certain that Chief Wausau Co. was involved, they were the only brewery in the area with the facilities to produce that much beer. The regional chief of Prohibition agents, Edward C. Yellowley, suspected Joe Saltis of being behind the Wausau brewery, especially since Saltis had a resort at nearby Winter. When he became the District Permit Supervisor for the Great Lakes region after Prohibition ended, he made sure through careful investigation that no brewery associated with Joe Saltis could get a permit.

James Fernock purchased the Chief Wausau property in 1926 at a sheriff's sale, but did little with the property until 1932, when Franklin Roosevelt's election made Repeal seem certain. He reopened the company as West End Malt Co., though he quickly readopted the Wausau Brewing name, and prepared to make real beer again. Given Yellowley's concerns about Saltis, and the fact that Fernock was from Chicago, the brewery was subject to frequent inspections by agents. Fernock reintroduced the brewery to Wausau residents in June with Adel Brau, which customers could have delivered to their home for $2.25 per case or could pick up at the brewery for $2.00. The ads noted in parentheses under Wausau Brewing that this was the former West End company. Wausau Brewing made an unusual move in December 1933, when full-strength beer became legal after the passage of the 21st amendment. It advertised that it would continue "old Adel Brau" for people who "prefer a lighter beer with a much lower percentage" but for those who wanted "a full bodied, rich, creamy beer, with that old-fashioned flavor and strength of the 'before the war days" they produced "New Adel Brau" at "Pre-War Strength."

In 1934, Fernock brought two experienced beer people in to give the business additional credibility: distributor George D. Wolff and brewmaster Louis Schoen. Schoen left G. Heileman Brewing of La Crosse in 1934 over a dispute over lagering times. Schoen insisted that all his beer be lagered for nine weeks, and Heileman was trying to speed up production to meet the post-Prohibition demand. Schoen introduced the brewing techniques he used at Heileman to Wausau, most importantly kreusening. Wausau continued to brew Adel Brau for a while and the brewery released its bock beer under the Adel Brau name. In 1936, the advertisements began to announce that Wausau beers were union made. The brewery introduced Rib Mountain Lager in 1938 to give the company three regular beers. Wausau Brewing shipped beer to Chicago and as far west as Portland, Oregon, though a claim by the *Daily Record-Herald* that the beer was sold "throughout the United States" was more boast than reality.

During World War II, Wausau Brewing added a Pepsi bottling business to the company, though the operation was not moved to Wausau until 1947. The brewery also faced a suit by Heileman over the label for Schoen's Old Lager. In 1943, Wausau agreed to pay an undisclosed amount to Heileman and to alter the label.

The 1950s were difficult years for Wausau Brewing, as they were for many other smaller breweries. While the brewery introduced Schoen's Old Lager in cans in 1953, this was a small victory. Louis Schoen retired in 1950, and his son Henry took over. However, Henry attempted to cut the cost of the beer by using more corn and rice, and quality suffered. When two bad batches of beer were allowed to leave the brewery, Schoen left the company. James Fernock died in 1956, and George Wolff passed away in 1960. George Wolff Jr. decided the brewery was getting in the way of the family trucking business and Pepsi bottling. Furthermore, the brewery union wanted wage increases more appropriate to a large Milwaukee brewery than to a struggling small brewery. Production slipped from a postwar high of around 48,000 barrels in 1948 to about one-third that total in the late 1950s—an unsustainable level in a brewery with 50,000 barrels capacity. In early 1961, Wolff closed the brewery. Newspapers at first reported that the shut down was temporary, but the brewery never reopened. The labels were sold to Rhinelander Brewing Co. where they were brewed for a few more years. The boiler house was later sold to University of Wisconsin Marathon County and used to heat buildings on the campus.

Hereford & Hops (2000–2008)
Great Dane Pub & Brewing—Wausau (2009–present)
2201 East Center Street

Hereford & Hops was a small brewpub chain that had restaurants near Pittsburgh and in Escanaba and Bay City, Michigan in addition to their location in Wausau. The Wausau restaurant was the third to be established, after the two in Michigan. (As of 2017, only the Escanaba location remains in business.) An unusual feature of the restaurant was the opportunity for patrons to select and grill their own steaks. Kevin Eichelberger moved from Great Dane to become the brewmaster in Wausau. Eichelberger stayed for more than six years before leaving to start Red Eye Brewing Co.

In 2008, Hereford and Hops filed for bankruptcy, but the restaurant remained empty for only a few months before Great Dane opened their first location outside of the Madison area. The Great Dane management and brewing staff made a few changes to the restaurant and brewhouse and brewed a few beers specific to the Wausau location. Great Dane's Rob LoBreglio noted that Wausau had soft city water which was particularly well suited to brewing lagers.

Production at the Wausau Great Dane is typically just over 1,000 barrels per year. Some of the Great Dane bottled beers have been packaged at the Wausau location.

Bull Falls Brewing Co. (2007–present)
901 East Thomas Street

Mike Zamzow got started in brewing when his wife, Mary, gave him a homebrew kit for Christmas in 1998. His passion eventually took him to Siebel Institute in Chicago for training, and in 2007 he established Bull Falls Brewing Co. with his father, Don. The name of the brewery is derived from the original name of the city, Big Bull Falls. (Zamzow was threatened with legal action by the producer of Red Bull energy drink, but they were able to come to an agreement.) Bull Falls demonstrates the early dependence of the craft brewing business on hand-me-down brewing equipment: while still in the early planning stages they bought the system from the old Loaf & Stein brewery in Eagle River (which they never actually used),

The Party Pig was a 2.25-gallon container designed primarily for homebrewers. Hereford & Hops was one of few commercial breweries to sell party pigs to customers. Collection of Scott Reich.

and the ten-barrel system they actually used when the brewery opened came from the defunct Isadore Street Brewery/The Keg in Stevens Point.

When Zamzow released his Oktoberfest in 2007, it met with an enthusiastic reception. Bull Falls beers were so popular that the taproom was often out of beer, inspiring the mayor of Wausau to remark that the most popular beer in the taproom was "Available Soon Beer." Bull Falls sold growlers in stores and had more than eighty regular draught accounts in a few years. The brewery built an expansion with a larger brewhouse and a canning line in 2013, and the cans became available around northern Wisconsin. Production jumped from just under 1,000 barrels in 2012 to nearly 3,000 in 2014. (The inaugural brew in the new thirty-barrel brewhouse was also Oktoberfest.)

Bull Falls Brewing focuses on German beer styles, though they brew some English and Irish styles as well. Most of the beers are named after the beers' styles with a few exceptions, such as Five Star Ale, an English-style amber ale named after Mike Zamzow's five daughters. Among the beers available is Marathon Lager, which is based on a 1954 recipe from Marathon Brewing Co. Bull Falls beers are solid examples of classic beer styles, rather than experiments with unusual ingredients or processes (except for Crossroads Coffee Lager introduced in 2017, but by that point coffee was not an unusual beer ingredient). A few special editions, such as Ubernacht doppelbock, were released in large, swing-top bottles. Bull Falls sponsors a variety of events and hosts live music at the taproom, including an annual Jazz Fest.

Red Eye Brewing Co. (2008–present)
612 Washington Street

Kevin Eichelberger left Hereford and Hops in 2006, and a year later began working on his own brewpub, Red Eye Brewing Co. Eichelberger's inaugural beers were bolder than many being brewed at the time in Central Wisconsin, including Thrust! IPA and Scarlet 7, a Belgian Dubbel. He has also experimented with ingredients such as lemongrass, cranberries, and caramelized figs (the latter in Scarlet 7). In addition to these varieties, he has many beers designed to refresh cyclists after a long ride. (Bicycles and bike parts adorn the walls and hang from the ceiling at Red Eye.)

Among the more noteworthy beers was Green Sky wheat—which was the first brewed using energy from Red Eye's solar panels. Red Eye received a federal grant to install additional solar panels in 2013, which were installed over the parking lot like a carport due to a lack of space elsewhere.

Wauwatosa *(Milwaukee County)*

Big Head Brewing Co. (2013–present)
6204 West State Street

Just a few miles west of Miller Brewing Co. is a brewery making less beer than Miller did before the Civil War. Big Head Brewing was founded by Andrew Dillard, who took the name from the fact that many people said he had a big head, but which also described a characteristic of a well-made beer. Dillard planned to brew diabetic-friendly beer and gluten-free beer. These beers were never brewed, and Dillard moved away within a year of starting the business. The brewery was purchased by four area beer lovers, led by head brewer Steve Parkhill. Big Head beers often represent experiments with flavors and ingredients, as Parkhill noted, "Our mission is to bring unnoticed and untasted styles out to the public."

Wayne Township *(Wayne and Kewaskum P. O.'s)* *(Washington County)*

Philip Pies (1859?–1876?)
Philip Pies & Sons (1876–79)
Kreutzer & Groeschl (1879–1880)
John Bertram (1880–82)
Wenzel Beisbier & Co. (1882–84)
Wenzel Beisbier (1884–1887?)

Philip Pies appeared as a brewer in the 1860 industrial census, and since his production was 500 barrels for the previous year, it is likely that he was in operation in 1859 if not earlier. (He was in Wisconsin around 1850, though not necessarily in Wayne.) This seems to have been the peak of his production, since the known production figures from the 1870s were all less than 200 barrels per year. Pies also was a farmer, and his real estate was valued at $8,000 in the 1870 census. It may be that he devoted less time to brewing and more to farming as he aged. In the mid-1870s he brought his sons into the business (though the records do not indicate if all four sons (Adam, Louis, Philip Jr., and Peter) or just some of them took up brewing.

Pies rented the brewery in 1879 to Ambrose Kreutzer and John Groeschl, who operated it for about a year. Pies took the brewery back briefly, and then rented it to John Bertram in 1882. Wenzel Beisbier was the next proprietor, and he operated the brewery through 1887, after which it disappears from the records.

Wequiot *(Brown County)*

John Mason (1856?–58?)
Joseph Marchant & Joseph Brys (1868?)

John Mason appeared as a brewer in the 1857 state business directory, but was not listed in the 1860 census. Wayne Kroll also lists the firm of Joseph Marchant & Joseph Brys at this location, but very little is known about this brewery. Joseph Brys appeared in the excise records once, in February 1868, but never again (he was listed in Scott Township for that entry).

Red Eye Growler, acquired 2010. Author's collection.

West Allis (Milwaukee County)

Westallion Brewing Co. (2017–present)
1825 South 72nd Street

Erik and Kim Dorfner opened West Allis' first brewery in 2017. Most beers have names that evoke local history, though the references are subtle. Lillehammer Gold honors Olympic champion speed skater Dan Jansen, and Mustang American Pale Ale honors the mascot of the now-closed West Milwaukee High School.

West Bend (Washington County)

Balthasar Goetter (1847?–1850?)
Christopher Eckstein (1850–51)
Mayer Bros. (Mayer & Bro.), West Bend Brewery (1851–1875)
Stephen F. Mayer & Co., West Bend Brewery (1875–1882)
East Side of River Street (Modern Main Street) between Ash and Beech

A traveler to West Bend reported in 1847 that there was a brewery in the village, which was most likely the brewery of Balthasar Goetter, though this is earlier than the date traditionally given for its founding. Goetter, who had trained as a cooper and brewer in Germany, worked at Levi Blossom's brewery in Milwaukee when he first came to Wisconsin. He operated his brewery for a few years, though old accounts differ on what happened next. Goetter was injured when a wood splinter struck his eye, and around 1850 he leased the brewery to Christopher Eckstein. Eckstein ran the brewery for a year, but in 1851 Goetter sold the brewery. However, one account claims he sold it to his brothers-in-law, Charles (or Carl) and Stephen Mayer, and another claims that Stephen Mayer bought the brewery and invited Eckstein to be a partner in the business for three years. In this version, Charles Mayer bought Eckstein's share in 1854, and the business became known as Mayer Brothers.

The Mayer brothers' brewery grew quickly. By 1860 they were producing 1,400 barrels with a team of six men and one horsepower. While production figures are not available for the mid-1860s, the R. G. Dun & Co. credit evaluator reported at different times that the Mayers were "thriving" and "This firm is wealthy." In 1868, Charles Mayer rebuilt and expanded the brewery, but without his brother—Stephen died in 1867 at age forty-seven. The new brewery was still powered by horse, but produced 1,800 barrels in 1870. Charles managed the brewery until 1871, when he died at the young age of forty-five. For the next four years the family continued the business "under the old style [name]" with the widows of the Mayer brothers in charge. The 1873 *American Brewers' Guide* listed Marie Mayer (widow of Stephen) and Susan Mayer (of Charles) as the proprietors—probably the only brewery in the nation at the time to be run by two women. They managed it well and increased production to nearly 2,500 barrels by 1872. Marie and Susan (or Susanna) were assisted by their sons and, according to the R. G. Dun & Co. report, "the young men manage well."

In 1875, the company was reorganized and Charles' eldest son Stephen F., a student at Notre Dame, made the trip north from South Bend to West Bend to take over the family business. The new S. F. Mayer & Company inhabited a steam-powered brewery with a capacity of 3,500 barrels that employed seven men. The brewery also operated a malt house and in 1876 began an ice business that shipped ice to Chicago and elsewhere. Both the Mayer brewery and the Eagle brewery across the street were doing good business: The *West Bend Democrat* reported in 1875: "West Bend 'amber juice' is in high flavor. The breweries here are making extra exertions to furnish a superior quality." The reputation of West Bend beer apparently reached the East Coast: The *Democrat* alerted readers in March 1876 that "The West Bend Brewing Co., S. F. Mayer & Co., have contracted to furnish 1,000 barrels of lager beer to quench the thirst of centennial visitor [sic] to Philadelphia."

Eventually, the West Bend and Eagle breweries decided that it would be more efficient to merge their operations. In 1882, the companies combined and became West Bend Brewing Co., with S. F. Mayer as president and Adam Kuehlthau as treasurer. To make the best use of their properties, they decided to build a new brewery on the east side of what was then River Street (modern Main Street) on the old Eagle Brewery site. The Mayer plant was converted into a malt house. The business was incorporated under the same name in 1889.

The former Mayer plant continued as a malting business until Prohibition, first under the S. F. Mayer name, and later as West Bend Malting Co. The building burned in 1921 and the remnants were razed in 1937.

Christoph Eckstein (1856–1860)
Rudolph E. Kotien (1860?)
Adolph Arzbacher, Eagle Brewery (1860–1874)
Kuehlthau & Janssen (1874–1880)
Adam Kuehlthau (1880–82)
West Bend Brewing Co. (1882–1911)
West Bend Lithia Brewing Co. (1911–1920)
West Bend Lithia Co. (1933–1972)
415–459 North Main

After leaving Mayer's West Bend Brewery, Christoph Eckstein moved across the street to start his own brewery in 1856. His brewery did well right from the start, and the R. G. Dun & Co. examiner reported he was "doing [a] large bus[iness]. He advertised in January 1860 that he brewed "Lager, Bock, and Winter Beer," (as did Mayer & Bro. across the street). Eckstein continued to brew until May 1860, when he traded the brewery to Adolph Arzbacher for a share in the West Bend Mills. The 1860 industrial census adds a bit of confusion to this transfer, because it lists the proprietor of the business as Rudolph E. Kotien (who is not listed as a brewer in the population census). This clearly refers to the Eagle Brewery and not another firm, since it produced 2,000 barrels in the previous year, and no other brewery of that size existed in West Bend at the time.

Arzbacher got off to a shaky start, despite having acquired the larger of West Bend's breweries. The Dun examiner reported in 1860 that he did "not understand the brewery bus[iness] and has but little cap'l [capital]...." (This suggests that Kotien may have been a brewer hired by Arzbacher.) Two years later

WISCONSIN BREWERIES AND BREWPUBS   667

the report stated he "Makes g[oo]d lager, but is hard up" and was heavily mortgaged. However, by 1865 he had improved the business and was stable through the mid-1870s. Despite this, the Mayer brothers passed Arzbacher to become the largest brewery in the city. The Eagle Brewery produced a still-respectable 600 barrels in 1870, and increased to over 1,000 barrels by 1872. The fact that Arzbacher "[made] good lager" was borne out by a stunt pulled by a Milwaukee beer hall in 1873. They ordered several kegs of Eagle Brewery beer and for a week passed the beer off as imported from Erlangen. The customers all fell for the ruse until they were shown the empty kegs.

In 1874, Arzbacher rented the brewery to Adam Kuehlthau and Peter Janssen. Kuehlthau had worked in the brewery since 1870 (it is not clear what Janssen's background was). The new proprietors did not act like mere renters, and immediately installed a steam engine and made other improvements in the plant. In September 1875, the *West Bend Democrat* compared the neighboring breweries:

> West Bend has two large breweries where "amber juice" is manufactured that cannot be excelled. The not only supply a large home trade, but ship to every section of the state. The largest buildings for the manufacture of beer are those of S. F. Mayer & Co., while the Eagle brewery has the largest vat. The Eagle brewery is operated by Kuehlthau & Janssen, and their vat has a brewing capacity of 45 barrels per day. The vat at Mayer & Co. is of a capacity of 35 barrels. Each brewery is supplied with steam apparatus, the Eagle having just introduced the same.

Like the West Bend Brewery, the Eagle Brewery provided beer for the Centennial Exposition in Philadelphia. Kuehlthau & Janssen purchased the brewery from the bankrupt Adolph Arzbacher in 1879, but Janssen left the business in 1880 and Kuehlthau continued alone, though not for long. While both breweries on River Street were doing well, inefficiencies of the businesses were clear to both Stephan Mayer and Adam Kuehlthau, so they merged in 1882. Because the Eagle Brewery plant was smaller, the new West Bend Brewing Co. decided to build an all-new brewery on that site. The new brick brewery had an initial capacity of 6,000 barrels per year. The company bottled beer at the bottling house located across the road at the old Mayer brewery (which strongly suggests that Mayer was bottling prior to the merger, since the location of the bottle house was not convenient for the new brewery). Eventually the company built a new bottling house on the east side of the street.

In 1893, a massive electrical storm caused a lightning strike on one of the company's barns, which destroyed the barn and seven horses and spread to the brewery. The fire department and other citizens were able to save the brewery, though the damages still amounted to about $4,000. Adam Kuehlthau sold his share in the company in 1900 to Andrew Pick, husband of Stephen Mayer's sister Emma. West Bend Brewing continued to upgrade their equipment throughout the early 1900s, and bought a delivery truck in 1910. However, the management of the company was struck by the same early deaths that the Mayer brewery had suffered. Andrew Pick, who was also mayor of West Bend, died in August 1910 of complications from typhoid at age fifty, and Stephen Mayer became ill, so the owners put the company up for sale. Martin Walter, son of George Walter of Appleton, purchased the business. Martin and his brother Charles moved from Appleton to take over management of the plant in West Bend (making it the fourth Walter-owned brewery in the state).

With the approach of Prohibition, West Bend Brewing began to prepare for the worst. They put their two Kissel delivery trucks up for sale, adding that they were "Going out of business." That notice was premature, since the company reformed as West Bend Lithia and attempted to survive Prohibition by manufacturing beverages that featured the local water with its high lithium content. (The composition of the water had been used to promote the beer in the pre-Prohibition era.)

While none of the dry-era products became particularly popular, they enabled the brewery to stay in operation, which made it much easier to convert back to beer when Roosevelt's election heralded an end to Prohibition. Lithia also managed to avoid being raided for violations of the Prohibition Act, so they were one of the first Wisconsin breweries to obtain their federal license. The *West Bend News* detailed the preparations at the brewery:

> Last fall, following the election when the return of beer seemed assured the manufacture of beer was started and instead of once a week brewing, two and three times a week became a habit, until at the present time the cellars of the company are filled with good aged beer, ready to serve the customers of this well established brewery. . . . the brewery is at present working 18 hours a day, and bottling of the beer will begin next Friday, March 30, so that it is expected that about 10,000 cases will be on hand by April 7th. Between 4,000 and 5,000 barrels of well aged beer is on hand for the early comers.

When the first deliveries were made on 7 April, the honor of receiving the first case went to Stephen F. Mayer, who had survived his earlier illness and became one of the founders of West Bend Aluminum Co., (now West Bend Corporation, makers of kitchen appliances). As one of the few breweries in operation in the early days of real beer, Lithia was swamped with orders—which came from as far away as Puerto Rico.

The years after repeal were generally un-

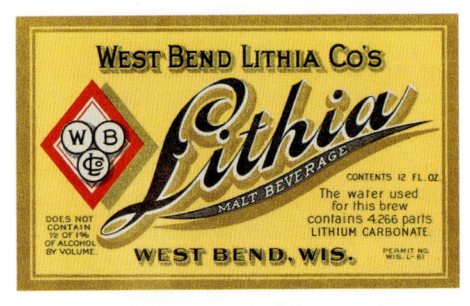

West Bend Lithia made much of the mineral content of its water, stating that the water contained 4.266 parts of lithium carbonate. This label for Prohibition-era near beer was similar to beer labels before Prohibition. COLLECTION OF TYE SCHWALBE.

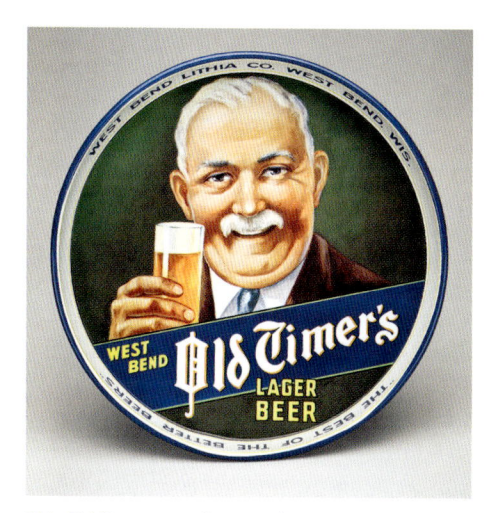

This Old Timers tray dates to the 1950s. COLLECTION OF DAVID WENDL.

eventful, but profitable for the company. Production in the late 1930s was around 30,000 barrels per year, but during the late 1940s and early 1950s Lithia expanded both capacity and production. The brewery had an estimated capacity of up to 75,000 barrels per year, and by 1948 reached an impressive 58,000 barrels. Old Timer's Lager beer was popular throughout the region, and the company seemed to be well positioned to survive increased competition.

Sales began to slip in the mid-1950s, and 1954 saw a precipitous drop to 38,000 barrels from 49,000 the year before. In 1955 Lithia introduced canned beer, but this did little to improve sales. The last time Lithia exceeded 30,000 barrels was in 1963, and while they were producing more than many other small breweries, they were also producing less as a percentage of capacity than most of their rivals. In 1969 the company reached an agreement to brew Black Pride Beer for a company headed by NAACP leader Edward J. McClellan. This product did not meet expectations, and was not sufficient to save the brewery. (More about Black Pride Inc. is found in chapter 8.)

In 1972, the directors voted to dissolve West Bend Lithia Co. The labels were sold to Walter Brewing Co. of Eau Claire, so they at least stayed in the Walter family. Most of the brewery still stands as of 2017, and is used for a variety of business and light industrial purposes.

Andreas Fetsch (1860?)

Andreas Fetsch was listed as a brewer in the 1860 census. He owned a mere $100 of real estate and (a very precise) $53 of personal property. He is not listed particularly near the other breweries, but it is possible that he worked for one of the other breweries in West Bend.

Riverside Brewery (2005–present)
255 SOUTH MAIN STREET

Wayne and Dana Kainz founded Riverside Brewery hoping to provide an "upper casual" dining experience. From the original three house beers, the menu has expanded to seven house beers and two house sodas. Under several different brewers, the beer menu has focused on classic beer styles for both the year-round and seasonal beers. Riverside is just a few blocks south of the former West Bend Lithia brewery.

WESTPORT *(Dane County)*

Parched Eagle Brewpub (2015–present)
5440 WILLOW ROAD #112

The Parched Eagle Brewpub was originally going to be located in the Sauk City area and called Driftless Brewpub. However, owner Jim Goronson discovered the Driftless name was already taken, and also decided to locate closer to Madison in the community of Westport. However he decided to retain the second name devised for a Sauk City location—Parched Eagle, derived from the area's popularity with eagle watchers. Goronson liked the business model of a brewpub better than a production brewery with a taproom, so with business partner Tom Christie, Parched Eagle opened in April 2015. In May 2017, Parched Eagle opened a taproom in Madison at 1444 East Washington.

Goronson's approach to beer is to be creative within the classic styles using the highest quality ingredients. The brewery featured a one-barrel brewing system, but additional beer was brewed under contract at House of Brews, where Goronson had interned after completing his brewing course at Siebel Institute in Chicago.

WEYAUWEGA *(Waupaca County)*

Jacob Konrad (1855–1865)
Consalus & Crocker (1865–67)
Kissinger & Schneider (1867–68)
Kissinger & Schaetzel (1868–1874)
Kissinger & Laisy (1874)
Walter & Laisy (1874–75)
Louis Herzinger (1875–79)
George Griel (1879–1883)
Louis Herzinger (1883–84)

Jacob Konrad left Oshkosh for Weyauwega in 1854, and soon established another brewery in his new home. His brewery was destroyed by fire in 1857, but Konrad had insurance for about two-thirds of the $1,500 loss, and was able to rebuild. According to the 1860 industrial census (which lists him in Dayton), he brewed 1,500 barrels of beer the previous year with the help of two men in one of the few breweries in the state powered by water.

After Konrad sold the brewery, it went through a confusing series of proprietors. The research of local historian Kevin Knitt has been essential in untangling the sequence of brewers and separating the two Weyauwega breweries. William Consalus and Jerome Crocker operated this brewery for two years before Kissinger and Schneider took over. The credit evaluators of R. G. Dun & Co. reported them to be of good character and habits, honest and prompt. This partnership dissolved in 1868, and Kissinger and Schaetzel became the new owners. Unfortunately, the Weyauwega breweries were not included in the 1870 industrial census or the early 1870s brewery directories, so little is known about the scope of their business.

In 1874, John Laisy purchased a share in the brewery. The Dun report noted that he had "but little exp[erien]ce + will be in competition with an active energ[etic] man." Laisy apparently attempted to remedy this by bringing in H. Walter from Milwaukee. The Dun evaluator claimed in May 1875 that "they make g[oo]d beer and will likely do well." However, by the

WISCONSIN BREWERIES AND BREWPUBS   669

end of the year they had encountered financial difficulties and were out of business.

Louis Herziger purchased the brewery in 1875 and restored some stability. The Dun reports indicate he was an "active and alert man." In 1879 he sold the brewery to George Griel and focused his energy on his farm. Griel started well, was "energetic and doing fair bus[iness]," (570 barrels in his first year) but the brewery suffered a fire in late 1881. Griel apparently had more debt than he could afford, and the fire made matters worse. In 1883, Herziger took the property back, but Griel continued to run the brewery. The brewery was struck by fire again in March 1884 and was not reopened.

Jacob Konrad (1870–74)
Joseph A. Duerr (1874–1891)
Loos & Quade (1891–93)
Quade & Schoenick (1893–1900)
Northeast Corner of North and East Streets (North Street no longer extant)

Jacob Konrad returned to brewing in Weyauwega in 1870, when he built a new brewery at the end of East Street near the Waupaca River. In 1874 he sold the brewery to Joseph A. Duerr, who owned it for longer than any of any of Weyauwega's brewers. The R. G. Dun & Co. credit evaluator called him a "V[er]y thrifty German, [making] money all the time. . . ." He produced 338 barrels in 1878 and 415 the following year, and the brewing directories of the 1880s generally listed his capacity around 500 barrels per year. (Wing's 1884 directory listed the capacity over 500 barrels, but the 1885 state industrial census reported that Duerr had brewed 800 barrels.) His plant was modest in size, and did not have its own malt house or bottling plant. The research of Kevin Knitt has shown that in 1891 Duerr sold the brewery to Loos and Quade, who operated it for two years before William Quade and Gustav Schoenick took over in 1893. The 1894 Sanborn map shows a small horse powered brewery with a small malting room, but still no bottling house. The 1895 state industrial census reported that Quade & Schoenick brewed 480 barrels in the previous year, so they clearly had not done much to expand the brewery since Duerr's tenure. The brewery burned in January 1900, and the estimated loss of $6,000 to $8,000 was much more than the $1,000 insurance covered and the brewery was not rebuilt.

Wheatland *(Kenosha County)*

Frederick Spencer (1860?)

The 1860 population census listed Frederick Spencer as a brewer. Since he owned $1,500 of real estate and $600 of personal property, it was unlikely that he was employed by another brewery, and at age forty-two it was unlikely he was retired.

Whitewater *(Walworth County)*

William Marshall (& Co.) (1855?–1858?)
George Streng (1859–1861?)
Marshall & Rundle (1861?–62?)
William Marshall (1862–64)
Nicholas Klinger (1864–1905)
Finke-Hoheisel Brewing Co. (1905–6)
Whitewater Brewing Co. (1906–1916)
Whitewater Brewing Co. (1933–1942)
Southwest Corner 200 Jefferson and East North Street.

In April 1856, the *Whitewater Gazette* reported that Marshall's brewery employed five persons and made 1,500 barrels of beer a year, which indicates that it was open well before the 1860 date given in the 1882 county history. However maps of Whitewater prior to 1860 show no structure at the Jefferson and North location, so it is possible that Marshall's first brewery was the one in Cold Spring Township which was later operated by Edward Roethe (and which burned in 1860). Some sources including *100 Years of Brewing* connect George Streng (or Strang) with this brewery around 1860, but that year's census has him listed as a saloonkeeper (though this does not rule out a connection with the brewery). The only brewer residing in Whitewater at the time of the census was John Wildersman, who was boarding in the city, though not with Streng. By 1861, Marshall had taken on a partner, one Mr. Rundle, and the two operated the brewery together for a year or so. The *Whitewater Register* in 1861 claimed this brewery had been built two years ago, which may have represented a new brewery building rather than a new business, and would fit with the county history account. William Marshall resumed sole proprietorship shortly thereafter, and in 1864 sold the business to Nicholas Klinger.

Nic Klinger had refined his brewing skills at Charles Melms' South Side Brewery in Milwaukee and had the ability to make the Whitewater brewery an important area brewery. His 1870 production was 800 barrels, which he increased over the course of the decade to nearly 1,500 barrels. His production was apparently not impaired significantly by a disaster in 1877 when his brewery and ice house collapsed. While most of his production was lager, he made some ale as well, and by the early 1880s was bottling some of his beer (though the 1884 Sanborn map does not show a bottling house on the premises). Klinger was popular in Whitewater, and so was his brewery, which in 1877 featured a "full orchestra" each night in the beer hall. Klinger's hospitality occasionally got him in trouble with the law. Around Christmastime in 1878, Klinger found himself without sufficient stamps to sell beer, however he did so anyway in the holiday spirit and was arrested for his cordiality. The R. G. Dun & Co. credit evaluator reported that Klinger was "indust[rious] but drinks a good deal of beer. . . ." In 1879 Klinger acquired a brewery in Fort Atkinson, but that enterprise was not profitable so he returned his attention to his Whitewater plant. (See Fort Atkinson)

While Klinger rebuilt his brewery in the late 1880s, it remained horse-powered and dependent on ice for cooling. In 1891, Klinger shared a tramway to bring ice from Cravath Lake with a produce company. There was some irony in this: "The wags of the town are exhausting their wit on the subject as the senior member of the Produce company is a Prohibitionist and has been one of Klinger's liveliest antagonists in times past." Klinger built yet another new brewery in 1893, increasing capacity from 1,800 to 2,400 barrels per year and this time adding a boiler house for steam power, though he still used ice for cooling. The bottling house remained across North Street from the brewery.

In 1905 Klinger retired after a long career in brewing and sold the brewery to William Finke and J. Hoheisel. Finke had been part of Finke-Uhen Brewing Co. in Burlington, and Hoheisel came from Arcadia Brewing Co. This new firm controlled the brewery for just over a year before they sold it to a group led by William Klann Sr., who incorporated it as Whitewater Brewing Co. This group operated the brewery until sometime in 1917, when it closed in advance of Prohibition. The company dissolved in July 1918 and did not operate during the dry years.

A group led by Olaf Martens, Emil Logemann and William Hesselman incorporated a new version of Whitewater Brewing Co. in September 1933. After refurbishing the plant, the company started brewing in October of that year. However, there was much more to the story. This group was at first refused a license because Martens, George Howlett and others involved with the brewery were "all former bootleggers and wild-cat brewery operators." An agent for the Wisconsin Beverage Tax Division reported in 1937 that the company spent between $70,000 and $80,000 remodeling the brewery, which was an extraordinary amount for a brewery of that size. The money came from Chicago, through "a man named McQuin" who was "the brains of the corporation" and was known a representative of racketeers who paid off officials for protection. The same company also owned Manhattan Brewing Co. of Chicago, which was also suspected of mob connections. Whitewater Brewing was actually making spirits as well as beer, and distributing it to wildcat operations in the countryside.

The brewery's primary market was the Chicago area, and about two thirds of the product was shipped there. This led to additional problems with taxes and permits. The brewery shut down briefly in October 1937 and again in October and November 1938, at least in part because of pressure from government agents. To make matters worse, the company was charged with misrepresenting the nature of one of its products, Badger Beer. Many of the labels featured a badger and an outline of the State of Wisconsin, but the beer was actually made in Chicago at Manhattan Brewing. The brewery officially closed in October 1942.

Whitewater Picnic Beer may have been brewed in Chicago but represented as made in Whitewater. COLLECTION OF JOHN STEINER.

H. R. Melster (1899?–1900?)
H. R. Melster had a short-lived weiss beer brewery in Whitewater for a few years around 1900.

Randy's Restaurant & Fun Hunters Brewery (1994–present)
841 Brewhouse (2015–present)
841 EAST MILWAUKEE

In 1972, Randy and Pat Cruse purchased a popular Whitewater supper club location that had been in business since the 1930s. After a full remodeling in the late 1980s, the restaurant was burned down by the owner of a competing supper club. While rebuilding, Randy decided to install a brewing system to make their restaurant stand out. By the early 1990s, he was able to find brewing equipment that would fit in the restaurant, and he brought in legendary brewing consultant Karl Strauss to help set up the brewhouse and recipes.

When the Cruses retired after more than forty years, the new owners changed the name to 841 Brewhouse. They kept the brewing system in place and maintained the same approach to brewing—make solid examples of basic styles that go well with food.

Second Salem Brewing Co. (2014–present)
111 WEST WHITEWATER STREET

The city of Whitewater acquired the nickname Second Salem early in the twentieth century because of the alleged presence of witches and demons in the area. (The legend probably grew out of the presence in town of the Morris Pratt Institute, a spiritualist organization, but was renewed through the years by other curious phenomena.) Many of the beers are named after local legends, and its Beast of Bray Road earned Bronze in the 2016 World Beer Cup. Christ G. Christon grew up washing dishes in his father's restaurant, which he purchased in 2010, and began converting the restaurant into a brewpub. Unlike Christon, a first-generation immigrant, business manager Thayer Coburn is a fourth-generation Whitewater native. The first beer from the brewpub was sold in 2014.

WILSON (St. Croix County)

Dave's BrewFarm (2009–present)
2470 WILSON STREET

Dave Anderson didn't start brewing on a farm, he bought the farm so that he and partner Pam Dixon could have a true farm brewery that used crops grown on the land for his brews. While there are a few beers that make regular appearances on the tap list like Mocha Diablo (a sweet stout with peppers), AuBeXXX (a golden strong ale with spices) and Matacabras, many beers on the "Labrewatory" list represent one-time experiments with spices, botanicals, and other ingredients. Honey used in some of the beers came from an apiary on the farm.

The first tap room was in the brewery (and the lower floor of the farmhouse), but an

Cream Top, the flagship brand of Whitewater Brewing Co. before Prohibition, returned after the dry years (ca. 1934). COURTESY OF NATIONAL BREWERY MUSEUM.

Anderson began contract brewing two of his brews to gain wider distribution. BrewFarm Select was an all-malt lager that debuted in late 2009, brewed and canned at Stevens Point Brewery. The Belgian-style strong ale Matacabras (from the Spanish word for a wind strong enough to kill goats) was bottled at Sand Creek Brewing and was on sale in early 2010. COLLECTION OF DAVID ANDERSON.

expanded tap room was completed in 2014. Energy to run the brewery is provided by a twenty-kilowatt windmill, giving rise to the slogan "Wisconsin's Wind-Brewed Beer." A geothermal heating system provides much of the heat for the building. Production at the BrewFarm is typically between 100 and 200 barrels per year.

WINDSOR *(Dane County)*

Archelaus Hobbs (c. 1857)

The brewery of Archelaus Hobbs is recorded in the 1857 state business directory, and Wayne Kroll includes him in his list of farm breweries.

WINNECONNE
(Winnebago County)

Theodore Yager (1866?–1882)
Mrs. Katherina Yager (1882–84)
ON EAST BANK OF WOLF RIVER NEAR END OF WATER STREET (MODERN 500 BLOCK OF SOUTH FIRST AVENUE)

The research of Lee Reiherzer has added considerable detail to the story of the Yaeger brewery. Theodore Yaeger was trained as a brewer in his native Baden, and left Germany following the turmoil of the late 1840s. In 1860, he and his wife Katharina moved to Winneconne, where Theodore worked as a cooper before enlisting in the 19th Wisconsin Infantry. After returning from the war, Yager purchased a lot along the Wolf River in 1866, and soon began building a brewery. The R. G. Dun & Co. credit evaluators noted in 1875 that Yager had been in business for ten years, and while technically possible, these figures were sometimes approximate. The evaluators praised his character and habits, but cautioned that he was beginning to have financial problems and owned little other than the brewery.

Yager's brewery was never a large one. The 1870 industrial census reported that he had produced 350 barrels of beer during the previous year, but since his revenue of $1,280 works out to only $3.66 per barrel, it is more likely that these were smaller kegs since the prevailing area price per barrel at the time was between $8 and $10. A newspaper ad from 1871 proclaimed that he offered "Lager Beer, Ale, and everything in the line made in the best manner, and furnished to customers at living rates." He also offered to perform "All kinds of tight barrel work," which indicates he was still working as a cooper. He was not listed in the 1873 *American Brewer's Guide* directory, nor Schade's 1876 listing, but according to Salem, Yager produced a mere seventy-eight barrels in 1878 and eighty-three the next year. A history of Northern Wisconsin published in 1881 claimed that Yager brewed 400 barrels of beer annually, but this is much more likely to have been his capacity rather than his production.

Reiherzer has argued that the decline in Yager's fortunes paralleled those of Winneconne, which was losing population after the end of the lumber boom. Yager was still listed in industry directories through 1884, and the R. G. Dun & Co. reports in 1883 suggest that his prospects were better but a year later tempered this by noting he was still hard pressed. Yager appears to have ceased brewing around 1884, and by 1885 he had disappeared from the records. (*American Breweries II* lists the brewery under Katherina's name from 1882–1884, though local sources do not support this change. It is possible that the brewery was put in her name for financial reasons.) The brewery building burned in 1893, and had been "idle for years."

WIOTA *(Lafayette County)*

Peter Ede (1866?–1884)
NEXT TO THE MAYNE HOTEL

After brewing for a few years at Cadiz, Peter Ede moved to Wiota and started another brewery. He first appears in the excise records in June 1867, though the R. G. Dun & Co. first evaluated his creditworthiness in May 1866.

Ede's brewery was a small operation—the only known production figures are ninety barrels in 1878 and seventy-four in 1879. The Dun examiner reported that he was making money and his "wants are small." These evaluations remained consistent through the end of the reports in 1883. Tovey's and Wing's brewery directories listed Ede as a brewer of ale, and Wing's 1884 directory noted that Ede offered bottled beer, which was less remarkable for a small ale brewery than it would have been for a lager brewery of that size.

John Glicker (ca. 1876)

John Bluker is listed as a brewer in the 1876 state business directory, but Wayne Kroll corrects the spelling to Glicker. Since Peter Ede does not appear ever to have leased or rented his brewery, this seems to be a separate brewery, albeit one about which nearly nothing is known.

WISCONSIN DELLS
(Kilbourn City) (Columbia County)

Mechler & Leute (1858–1861)
Leute Bros. (1861–67?)
C. A. Leute & Co./Julius Leute, City Brewery (1867?–1891)
Julius Leute Sons (1891–1895?)
Paul Keller (1898–99)
BROADWAY AND OAK STREETS

According to the 1880 *History of Columbia County*, W. Mechler and Andrew Leute started their brewery in 1858. (The 1860 population census listed the Magler [sic] family and their boarder Leute as living in Newport, but since they were recorded in Columbia County, this indicates they were on the Kilbourn City side of the river.) When Andrew Leute died in 1861, his brothers Julius, Charles and Thaddeus purchased the brewery from Mechler and Andrew's heirs. They appear to have adopted the name C. A. Leute & Co. around 1867, though for most of the period after 1870 Julius was sole proprietor because Charles died in 1872 and Thaddeus sold his share to Julius in 1874.

The Leute brewery was modest in size—about 400 barrels per year in 1870 was about right for its home market but dwarfed by Haertel's much larger Columbia County brewery in Portage. Like many breweries in the immediate post-Civil War era, he did not brew all year long: the 1870 census indicated he was only in production for eight months during the previous year. Production remained over 300 barrels for most of the 1870s, but dropped under 200 barrels per year by the end of the decade. Industry directory listings for Leute's brewery showed that capacity was less than 500 barrels per year, and that he did not have his own malt house. Leute died in 1891, after which the estate ran the brewery. (References listing Philip Klenk as proprietor of the City Brewery from 1891 to 1893 do not appear to be supported by local sources. He may have been a brewer employed by the Leute family.) The brewery still appeared in the 1895 state business directory under Julius Leute, though these volumes had a tendency to be a year or two behind. In 1898, Paul Kellar acquired the brewery, though he only owned it for a few months before it was destroyed by fire in October 1899. While some source report Keller was still in business through 1904, he sold the property in 1900 to Milwaukee brewery supply dealer Charles Kiewert. The state industrial and labor reports of 1901 and after do not include the City Brewery among the industries of Kilbourn City, confirming that Kiewert did not restart production.

Theobald Hoffman (1865?–1870)
Broadway between Eddy and Superior Streets

Theobald Hoffman appears to have hedged his bets on the race between Newport and Kilbourn City to become the principal port on that stretch of the Wisconsin River. Though he already had a brewery in Newport, in 1860 he purchased land across the river on which he would eventually build a brewery. Brewery historian Richard D. Rossin Jr. has found a mortgage that Hoffman took out in 1862, which may have been to raise money to start building his Kilbourn brewery. While little documentation exists, it seems that that he was brewing in this location by 1865, when he was listed in the 1865 state business directory. It appears that he was expanding his brewery in 1867, but this did not go well because when workers were blasting in his cellar a charge misfired and four German laborers who were excavating the cave were injured.

Hoffman's brewery was modest in size—producing an average of about twelve barrels per month in 1869. While he was listed as a brewer in the 1870 census, he did not produce enough to be listed in the industrial census that year. It also appears that Hoffman quit brewing sometime in late 1870, since he stopped advertising his saloon in August and sold his saloon to his brother-in-law Frederick Bauer. The R. G. Dun & Co. records suggest that Hoffman was still in business in early 1871, though these records were occasionally several months behind. Hoffman died in 1872 at age forty-seven, and his brewery was converted into a machine shop in 1878. The building still stands as of this writing, and is part of a much larger building in the middle of the Wisconsin Dells downtown tourist district.

Dells Brewing Co./Moosejaw Pizza (2002–2012)
Wisconsin Dells Brewing Co. (2012–present)
110 Wisconsin Dells Parkway South

Dells Brewing Co. is the official name of the brewpub located within the giant Moosejaw Pizza restaurant in Wisconsin Dells. Moosejaw (named after the city in southern Saskatchewan) was the first in a series of restaurants opened by Mark Schmitz and his partners (others include Buffalo Phil's and Kickers).

Dells Brewing is known in the brewing world for hiring Wisconsin's first female brewmaster, Jamie Baertsch (Jamie Martin when she was hired in 2005). She studied biotechnology in college, and became hooked on brewing after a class project involving brewing and yeast manipulation. She has been active in the Pink Boots Society (a group of women in the brewing industry) and has presented at brewing conferences.

Running a brewery in a restaurant catering mostly to tourists means that most of the beers need to be accessible to a broad audience. There are typically ten different beers on tap and since 2012 some beers have been available in bottles and cans, beginning with Rustic Red. Baertsch has developed some more adventurous beers, such as the two she brewed to celebrate the births of her children: Betty's Breakfast Stout and Wyatt's Barleywine.

Port Huron Brewing Co. (2011–present)
805 Business Park Road

Port Huron Brewing Co. became the first production brewery in Columbia county in more than fifty years. The name is not from the city in Michigan, but rather from a 1917 Port Huron tractor that Tanner Brethorst's family worked on restoring for many years (the tractor was made in the Michigan city). Brethorst studied brewing in Chicago and Munich and worked at several breweries in Wisconsin prior to

Port Huron Engine #8009 is featured on the brewery's labels. Collection of Scott Reich.

following his dream of starting his own brewery. Brethorst began brewing pilot batches in late 2011 and sold the first kegs in April 2012.

Port Huron Brewing offers a mix of German and English-inspired beers, with seasonals like Million Dollar Smoked Maibock, a collaboration beer with One Barrel Brewing Co. of Madison.

GRAND RAPIDS
(Wisconsin Rapids) (Wood County)

Apfel & Smith (Schmidt) (1859?–1862?)
Nicholas Schmidt (1866?–1880)
Jacob Lutz & Brother (1880–1891)
NORTH FIRST STREET

The 1860 industrial census includes a listing for the brewery of Adam Apfel and Smith. This is the earliest reference to the brewery of Nicholas Schmidt. In 1860 the partners produced 150 barrels of beer, a fair total considering how remote their location was at that time. They began to advertise in the *Wood County Reporter* in 1861, touting "the very best quality of BEER and ALE—none better in the state."

Schmidt appears to have made some modest expansions to the brewery during the 1860s, since he reported producing 350 barrels of beer in the 1870 industrial census. Schmidt's production fluctuated significantly throughout the 1870s, jumping from 171 barrels in 1872 to 618 in 1874 and back below 200 barrels a year at the end of the decade. While the reason for the increase is not clear, the R. G. Dun & Co. credit reports indicate the reason for the decline at the end of the decade was extreme intemperance. In 1880 Schmidt found capable buyers for the brewery and sold out.

Jacob and David Lutz moved from their family's brewery in Stevens Point to take over the Schmidt brewery in 1880, and immediately began to improve the plant. Throughout the 1880s they made continual improvements, though they do not appear to have added malting or bottling capacity. The 1885 Wisconsin industrial census reported their production at 1,400 barrels, which sold for $8.00 per barrel.

The Lutz brewery came to a disastrous end in July 1891 when it was destroyed by fire. The *Centralia Enterprise & Tribune* reported: "The structure was composed of wood, was in a dry condition, and consisted of wings and additions extending over an area of ground at least one hundred feet long and eighty feet wide. It was an extremely difficult place in which to fight fire. . . ." Even after the fire appeared to be put out, it broke out again the next day. The *Enterprise & Tribune* lamented:

> The destruction of this property is a serious loss not only to the owners, but to the city as well. It occurs at a time when business is at its best, and as the stock on hand was all consumed, they are unable to supply their customers. J. Lutz & Bro are regarded in commercial circles as men of the strictest integrity, and in business as enterprising and wide awake. It is not in the best interest of any city to see such people crippled in business, even though the fire should result in the building of a much better plant than the old one. The origin of the fire remains a mystery. . . . It can hardly be the work of an incendiary, for the gentlemen have but few if any enemies in town.

While this brewery was not rebuilt, Jacob Lutz would eventually become manager of Twin City Brewing Co., which was built nearby.

Schenck & Eberle (1863–)
Jackel & Winkel (1866?–1867)
Michael Eberle (1867–1875)
WATER STREET

The *Centralia Enterprise & Tribune*, eulogizing local pioneer Ulrich Schenck in 1899, claimed:

> Mr. Schenck's first undertaking, when he came to this country about forty-five years ago, was in partnership with the late M. Able, who established a small brewery at the upper eddy and tried to supply the local trade with a little beer. There was no railroad within a hundred miles of here at that time. Some years afterward he sold his interest to his partner and moved onto a wild piece of land . . .

If the dates are accurate, this creates a much earlier start for the brewery of Michael Eberle than is usually given. However, the *Wood County Reporter* noted the near completion of Schenck's brewery in November 1863, much later than the above account.

Very little is known so far about the early years of the brewery. The excise records also include the firm of Jackel & Winkel from January to May 1867, which suggests that this partnership leased the brewery for a period. (It is also possible that they leased Nicholas Schmidt's brewery, but the production levels in the excise records seem to fit Eberle's smaller brewery. It is unlikely Jackel & Winkel had a third brewery in Grand Rapids.)

Eberle does not appear in the R. G. Dun & Co. records, which often clarify transfers in ownership as well as the prosperity of a business. Eberle is first listed in the excise records in June 1867, after Jackel & Winkel's term. Eberle's brewery was destroyed by fire in April 1869, but he rebuilt soon after. The 1870 industrial census reported that Eberle had produced sixty barrels in the previous year, though he was only in operation for eight months. Production does not seem to have been hampered by the fire, since Eberle only brewed fifty-seven barrels in 1871 and sixty-one the next year. In the mid-1870s he boosted production above one hundred barrels for a few years, but does not appear in the records after 1875. A delinquent tax notice in the *Wood County Reporter* in 1880 indicated that the buildings on the property were still being occupied as a dwelling and a brewery, but do not indicate whether Eberle was actually still brewing.

Twin City Brewing Co. (1892–95)
FIRST STREET NORTH

Frank Stahl and Richard Sheibe organized a new brewery in Grand Rapids in 1892. They operated it for about a year before going bankrupt and "its interests were assigned to other parties." (Former sheriff Stahl's reward for this money-losing venture was to be elected to seven consecutive terms as city treasurer.) These other parties turned out to be a who's who of Wisconsin brewing. Brewer Jacob Lutz was specifically designated in the articles of incorporation of the new company as the general manager—the other incorporators included maltster William Froedert, brewing supply specialist Charles. L. Kiewert, and New London

674 THE DRINK THAT MADE WISCONSIN FAMOUS

brewer Theodore Knapstein. The *Centralia Enterprise & Tribune* had hoped

> to see Mr. Knapstein move here and take an active part in the management of the brewery, but we have learned since the sale that he simply represented some of the heaviest creditors of the firm, and that it was their purpose to form a stock company, put in enough money to place the concern on its feet and run it for all there is in it. We understand further that the Lutz Bros. are to have the management of its affairs, which means that the undertaking will be a success beyond peradventure.

However, before the brewery could fulfill its promise it was destroyed in 1895 by a fire that was caused by a fire in the boiler room which "blew out that side of the addition." In the aftermath of the fire, the federal revenue agent was called to Grand Rapids to deal with complaints of residents

> who state that free access has been afforded the boys of the city to the stale and damaged beer at the recent burned [sic] Twin City brewery, and that full advantage of this access was being taken by the boys from 8 to 15 years of age. Groups of boys and young men have been seen to wander in the direction of the brewery at about dusk ever since the fire, and to return soon after in an intoxicated and hilarious condition.

The revenue agent concluded this was a local problem, not a federal case.

Jacob Lutz, having now lost two breweries to fire, decided not to rebuild. Lutz died in May 1901, but his son Jacob Jr. would soon help start a brewery of his own.

Grand Rapids Brewing Co. (1905–1920)
WEST SIDE OF NORTH FIRST STREET AT LAVIGNE

After the turn of the twentieth century, Grand Rapids residents heard rumors that another brewery was proposed for the city. At first, Stevens Point brewer Gustav Kuenzel was supposed to be interested in taking over the former Lutz brewery site, but later reports indicated that Jacob Lutz Jr. and Kuenzel were looking at another property on High Street. Apparently the arrangements were not attractive enough for Kuenzel, since he purchased a brewery in Hastings, Minnesota instead.

In 1904, Jacob Lutz partnered with Frank Boyanowski to locate a brewery in Grand Rapids. The *Grand Rapids Tribune* believed a brewery "would be a paying institution in this city," and argued that money spent on beer "might as well remain here at home and be distributed to a certain extent among our local tradesmen." The site of the building was referred to as "the old court house site" (which was right next to the former Lutz brewery), and construction began during the summer of 1904. The brewery officially opened on 17 March 1905, "at which time the public [was] extended an invitation to visit the place and sample the product." The brewery promoted their beer in surrounding communities and offered bock beer during their first year of operation. Like most breweries, Grand Rapids had trouble getting their cooperage back, and regularly offered a reward of a keg of beer "to the farmer bringing in the largest number of our empty kegs. . . ." A few years after founding the company, Boyanowski left to help start Polish Brewing Co. in Stevens Point, and sued Grand Rapids Brewing for $2,235 that he claimed was "due him for services rendered in promoting and superintending the buildings of the company."

Within a few years, Grand Rapids Brewing Co. became an important part of the local business community. A rather effusive sketch of the company in 1914 proclaimed:

> The firm sells thousands of bottles of their 'Grand Rapids Special' bottled beer every week. They also sell large quantities barreled.
>
> Their big auto trucks can be seen daily delivering their goods. Practically every bar in the city sells their beer. . . .

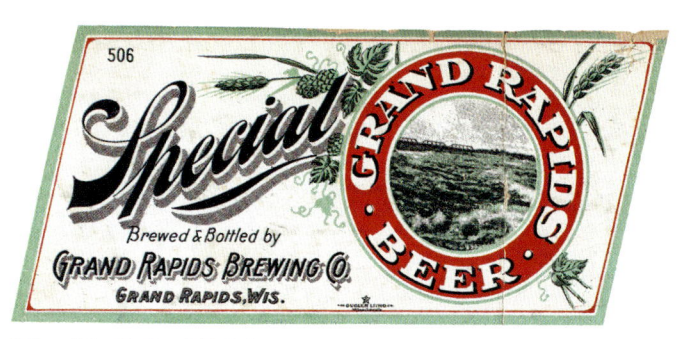

A Grand Rapids Special label ca. 1905. COLLECTION OF JOHN STEINER.

> They have one of the best brewmasters in the state, and their plant covers two acres of ground. Their brewery is up-to-date in every respect, and they have an annual capacity of 16,000 barrels, while 20 skilled men are employed. They use pure spring water only. They also manufacture soft drinks and carbonated waters.

The account closed with praise for the integrity of the company and its "good business basis."

Grand Rapids Brewing continued to operate until the arrival of Prohibition, after which it continued to manufacture soft drinks and began canning beans. The manufacture of drinks only lasted a few years, and in 1923 the business changed its name to Wisconsin Rapids Canning Co. No attempt was made to restart brewing after legal beer returned.

WOODMAN (Grant County)

Woodman Brewery (Whistle Stop) (2010–16)
401 MAIN STREET

The small Whistle Stop Restaurant and Woodman Brewery shared a building with a deer registration station and the local post office—restaurant co-owner Leslie Erb served as postmaster. Leslie's son Dennis started making beer in 2010 to add some distinctiveness to the establishment. He was a self-taught brewer, who constructed his own half-barrel system in the basement.

Erb liked to say that his brewery was like "Dogfish Head on a smaller scale," claiming kinship with the famous experimental brewery in Delaware. Erb experimented with nearly any ingredient that inspired him—nuts, fruit, peppers and one of his more noteworthy creations, Arctic IPA infused with mint. He noted in a 2012 interview "Most people do it [brewing] to make a living and make money. I just want to make crazy stuff and have fun." Starting in 2011, Erb bottled some of his brews and had them on sale in a limited number of stores from Janesville to Wisconsin Dells. At its peak, production reached about 570 barrels per year.

WOODRUFF *(Oneida County)*

Rocky Reef Brewing Co. (2015–present)
1101 FIRST AVENUE

Rocky Reef Brewing Co. was named after the street address of owner Christie Forrer's grandparents cabin in the north country. She and her husband Tyler Smith opened the brewery and taproom in June 2015. They began brewing on a half-barrel system, but after a year were able to upgrade to a ten-barrel system. As of 2017, their beer was distributed in a limited area in northern Wisconsin, as well as a few select locations in counties north of Milwaukee. Rocky Reef offers a selection of barrel-aged and sour beers in addition to their regular lineup and seasonal beers.

WRIGHTSTOWN *(Brown County)*

Fox River Brewery
Gutbier & Mueller (1868–69)
Gutbier & Mangold (1869–1870)
Gutbier & Mueller (1873–79)
Henry Kaufman (1882–1884?)
E. N. Seifert (1887?–1889)
WEST SIDE OF FOX RIVER, NEAR MODERN HICKORY STREET

Otto Gutbier and Carl G. Mueller built the first brewery in Wrightstown during the summer of 1868. Gutbier was an experienced cooper and brewer—which was only appropriate since his name translates as "good beer"—and Mueller was an important local businessman. While Mueller apparently helped start the brewery, by 1870 the firm was Gutbier and Mangold. According to the 1870 population census this was John Mangold, who owned $3,000 of real estate (compared to Gutbier's $4,000). One newspaper account from 1870 credits Mangold with being a founding partner of the brewery:

> Gutbier and Mangold, who started a brewery on the west side of the river, about two years since, have grown into an extensive business and the past summer could have disposed of double the quantity of beer they have sold had their facilities been greater. They are now making additions to their establishment.

However other reports specifically mention Mueller as a partner in the brewery in 1869, so Mangold must have taken his place later that year.

Unfortunately, Gutbier & Mangold's promising business was destroyed by fire in October 1870. The fire started in the malt house, and spread to the rest of the brewery. The partners had insurance for only a fraction of the loss, and decided against rebuilding, at least for the moment. Gutbier moved to Kaukauna where he operated a hotel for a few years, but soon returned to Wrightstown and built a new brewery on the spot of the previous structure. Carl Mueller again provided financial support for the new business, which was operational no later than 1873. The business was sometimes referred to as Mueller & Co., but Gutbier was still in charge of brewing operations. Gutbier produced 203 barrels in 1878 but only sixty-four in 1879—probably indicating that he retired from brewing that year to build another hotel. Gutbier was "a devoted follower of the dog and gun, and stands prominent in the State as a crack shot on woodcock." He was also an amateur painter, specializing in local landmarks.

The brewery appears to have been vacant for about three years until Henry Kaufman of Milwaukee (listed as George in some records) purchased the brewery from Charles Redeman of Green Bay for $2,500. Kaufman put the brewery back into production, purchased a new delivery wagon in Green Bay, and operated the brewery for a few years. While the precise ending date is not clear, he was still listed in the Bradstreet credit report guide of 1884. At some point Redeman purchased the brewery again, and leased it to E. N. Seifert of Milwaukee. In December 1889, the brewery burned again, and was not rebuilt.

In 1912, a group headed by Len Valk and Hugh Freeman proposed a $50,000 brewery for Wrightstown, but these plans never came to pass.

YUBA *(Greenwood) (Vernon County)*

Ludwig & Stovey (1889?–1890?)
Ludwig & Norz (1890?–1897)
Joseph Bulin (1897–1902?)

Carl Ludwig, who had been brewing in Wisconsin since the 1850s, started another brewery when he was in his late 50s. This one was located a few miles south of his home in Hillsboro. The first time it appeared in the news was in 1890, when the brewery ran into trouble:

> Carl Ludwig, one of the most prominent residents of Hillsboro, and his partner, Frank Stovey, were arrested yesterday for selling beer in unstamped kegs. They ran a brewery at Yuba, Richland County. They waived examination and gave bail at $300 each. The case will be passed upon in the fall by a grand jury. It is the general belief that Ludwig was simply careless. He is regarded as thoroughly honest by all who know him.

The tone of this article suggests that the brewery was not a new one, but it is not clear when it was established.

Sometime in the 1890s Frank Stovey left the brewery and Mr. Norz took over. The 1895 Wisconsin census of industry did not report the volume produced in Yuba (listed as Greenwood) but included the revenue total of $700, which appears to represent production of around 150 barrels.

Carl Ludwig retired from brewing sometime prior to 1897. The next reference (found so far) to the brewery was a note in the *Hillsboro Sentry* that longtime local saloonkeeper Joseph Bulin had "purchased an icebox of Frank Travernick which he will use in his brewery." Bulin's "Greenwood Beer" was available on tap in several locations near Hillsboro, but his market was strictly local. He was included in a 1900 industry directory, but little is known about when he ceased production.

NOTES

CHAPTER 1. FROM BARLEY TO BARSTOOL

1. This discussion of brewing history draws on several sources: Stanley Baron, *Brewed in America: A History of Beer and Ale in the United States* (1962; repr., Cleveland: BeerBooks.com: 2006); Michael Jackson, *Michael Jackson's Beer Companion: The World's Great Beer Styles, Gastronomy, and Traditions*, 2nd ed. (Philadelphia: Running Press, 1997); Randy Mosher, *Tasting Beer: An Insider's Guide to the World's Greatest Drink* (North Adams, Mass.: Storey Publishing, 2009); Richard W. Unger, *Beer in the Middle Ages and the Renaissance* (Philadelphia: University of Pennsylvania Press, 2004); *One Hundred Years of Brewing* (supplement to the *Western Brewer*) (repr.; New York: Arno Press, 1972). In addition, the author thanks the University of Minnesota Press for permission to draw heavily upon his previous book, *Land of Amber Waters: The History of Brewing in Minnesota* for this section.

2. The section on beer styles and the brewing process is indebted to many authors and experts: Jackson, *Beer Companion*; Charles Bamforth, *Beer: Tap into the Art and Science of Brewing*, 3rd ed. (New York: Oxford University Press, 2009); Garrett Oliver, *The Brewmaster's Table: Discovering the Pleasures of Real Beer with Real Food* (New York: HarperCollins, 2003); Lee W. Janson, *Brew Chem 101: The Basics of Homebrewing Chemistry* (Pownal, Vt.: Storey Communications, 1996); Randy Mosher, *Tasting Beer: An Insider's Guide to the World's Greatest Drink*, 2nd ed. (North Adams, Mass.: Storey Publishing, 2017), and *Radical Brewing: Recipes, Tales and World-Altering Meditations in a Glass* (Boulder, Colo.: Brewers Publications, 2004); John Palmer, *How to Brew*, http://www.howtobrew.com; Charlie Papazian, *The Complete Joy of Home Brewing* (New York: Avon, 1984); Gordon Strong et al., *Beer Judge Certification Program 2015 Style Guidelines for Beer*, https://www.bjcp.org; issues of the periodicals *Brew Your Own*, *Brewers Digest*, and *Zymurgy*. The contributions of numerous professional brewers, as well as members of Minnesota Homebrewers Association, St. Paul Homebrewers Club, Beer Barons of Milwaukee, Society of Oshkosh Brewers, and other homebrewers were also helpful.

3. *Milwaukie Sentinel*, 25 January 1843 (online, n.p.).

4. *Janesville Gazette*, 3 February 1872, 1; 1 September 1875, 3.

5. *Sheboygan Press*, 3 October 1927, 11.

6. John Henry Ott, ed., *Jefferson County Wisconsin and Its People* (Chicago: S. J. Clarke, 1917), 173

7. *Sheboygan Press*, 27 March 1918, 7.

8. *Milwaukee Daily News*, 20 July 1879, 6; *Eau Claire News*, 24 January 1885, 1.

9. *Milwaukee Journal*, 22 March 1933, 1.

10. Judy Newman, "MillerCoors Decries Water Rate Proposal," *Capital Times and Wisconsin State Journal*, 20 May 2010, C4.

11. *Milwaukee Sentinel*, 27 June 1952, pt. 1, 5.

12. *Sheboygan Press*, 24 August 1916, 2.

13. *Watertown Chronicle*, 8 September 1847, 3.

14. *Monroe Sentinel*, 28 January 1857, 4. The ad was first placed in October.

15. Proportions taken from *Wing's Brewers' Handbook 1884* (where 87 of 176 listed breweries had maltings), *Tovey's Brewers' Handbook 1891* (74 of 160), and *Brewers' Hand Book 1912* (64 of 139).

16. *Juneau Daily Alaska Dispatch*, 16 July 1906, 4; *Pawtucket (R.I.) Evening Times*, 26 July 1906, 4.

17. *Sheboygan Press*, 7 April 1933, 19.

18. *Sheboygan Press*, 27 March 1935, 3.

19. *Winona (Minn.) Republican-Herald*, 5 August 1949, 10.

20. *Stevens Point Daily Journal*, 8 April 1933, 1.
21. *Sheboygan Press*, 2 August 1935, 17.
22. Milwaukee County Historical Society, Beer Label Collection, label 020.100; *Milwaukee Sentinel*, 26 November 1873, 8.
23. *Milwaukee Sentinel*, 10 December 1875, 8; *Sheboygan Press*, 27 March 1935, 3.
24. The brewing publications of the era did not use these terms with precision, and newspaper advertisements tended to use whatever term was most familiar to the local audience. See M. L. Byrn, *The Complete Practical Brewer* (1852; repr., Chagrin Falls, Ohio: Raudins Books, 2002).

Chapter 2. Pioneer Brewing

1. *The Young Woman's Companion & Instructor, in Grammar, Writing, Arithmetic, Geography, Drawing, Book-Keeping, Chronology, History, Letter-Writing, Cooking, Carving, Pickling, Preserving, Brewing, Wine Making, &c. &c.* (Manchester, UK: J. Aston, 1806), 468–80.
2. Peter T. Harstad, "Sickness and Disease on the Wisconsin Frontier: Malaria, 1820–1850," *Wisconsin Magazine of History* 43, no. 2 (Winter 1959–60): 96.
3. *Minneapolis StarTribune*, 6 July 2000, T2.
4. Elizabeth Krynski and Kimberly Little, eds., "Hannah's Letters: The Story of a Wisconsin Pioneer Family, 1856–1864," *Wisconsin Magazine of History* 74, no. 3 (Spring 1991): 190.
5. "Some Recollections of Thomas Pederson," *Wisconsin Magazine of History* 2, no. 1 (September 1973): 29.
6. Henry Herbst, Don Roussin, and Kevin Kious, *St. Louis Brews: 200 Years of Brewing in St. Louis, 1809–2009* (St. Louis: Reedy Press, 2009), 4–5.
7. Fort Winnebago Orderly Book, Order No. 40 (16 May 1835), in *Wisconsin Historical Collections*, vol. 14 (1898), 111, http://content.wisconsinhistory.org/u?/whc,6275.
8. "La Pointe Letters," *Wisconsin Magazine of History* 16, no. 2 (December 1932): 207, http://content.wisconsinhistory.org/u?/wmh,8999.
9. Robert C. Nesbit and William F. Thompson, *Wisconsin: A History*, 2nd ed. (Madison: University of Wisconsin Press, 1989), 103, 106–7, 110–11.
10. Unger, *Beer in the Middle Ages and the Renaissance*, 11–13.
11. Nesbit and Thompson, *Wisconsin*, 100.
12. George Crawford and Robert M. Crawford, eds., *Memoirs of Iowa County, Wisconsin* (Northwestern Historical Association, 1913), 195.
13. *History of Iowa County, Wisconsin* (Chicago: Western Historical Company, 1881), 660.
14. *History of La Fayette County, Wisconsin* (Chicago: Western Historical Company, 1881), 603.
15. Nesbit and Thompson, *Wisconsin*, 91–93, 150–53. The term *Yankee* did not carry any pejorative connotations at the time, and Nesbit and Thompson report that "the informal appellation Yankees of the Lake came into common use."
16. Jerome A. Watrous, ed., *Memoirs of Milwaukee County*, vol. 2 (Madison, Wis.: Western Historical Association, 1909), 214; "The History of Brewing and Its Meaning to Milwaukee" (unidentified manuscript), Breweries Collection MSS 2200, box 1, folder 12, Milwaukee County Historical Society (MCHS); H. Russell Austin, *The Milwaukee Story: The Making of an American City* (Milwaukee: Journal Company, 1946), 81. The story of the early brewing vessels is in other anonymous, undated sources in the MCHS collection; the earliest of them likely date from the 1890s.
17. *History of Washington and Ozaukee Counties, Wisconsin* (Chicago: Western Historical Company, 1881), 547.
18. *The Wisconsin*, undated article (ca. 1892) in Miscellaneous Brewery Clippings, microfilm roll 257, MCHS; United States Bureau of the Census: United States Census Schedules for Wisconsin, Industry Schedules for 1850 and 1860.
19. Watrous, *Memoirs of Milwaukee County*, 214.
20. *Milwaukee Daily Sentinel*, 30 December 1859, 1.
21. *Milwaukee Daily Sentinel*, 24 January 1860, 1.
22. *Milwaukee Sentinel*, 16 October 1895, special section, n.p.

23 *Milwaukee Sentinel,* 16 October 1895, special section, n.p.

24 Maureen Ogle, *Ambitious Brew: The Story of American Beer* (Orlando, Fla.: Harcourt, 2006), 14–15; Leonard P. Jurgensen, *Milwaukee Beer Barons, Brewers, Bottlers and Others Buried at Forest Home Cemetery* (Milwaukee: privately published, 2011), 50, 54; Jurgensen, interview by author, 12–13 August 2013.

25 *Milwaukee Sentinel,* 16 October 1895, special section; *Milwaukee Sentinel,* 9 December 1887, 5; Albert Schnabel, "History of the Milwaukee Breweries," 1943, Breweries Collection MSS 2200, box 1, folder 12, MCHS.

26 *One Hundred Years of Brewing,* 224.

27 *Wiskonsin-Banner* (Milwaukee), 15 March 1845, 3; also in Thomas Cochran *The Pabst Brewing Company: The History of an American Business* (New York: New York University Press, 1948), 21–22.

28 *Milwaukee Journal,* 21 June 1890, 8

29 Rich Wagner, the leading historian of brewing in Philadelphia, has researched the John/Ferdinand Wagner question and has found support for the claim that Wagner ended up in Milwaukee from an address by Frederick Lauer, a brewer of Reading, Pa., given in 1877 in Milwaukee in which he lamented that "the secret of brewing beer with stock yeast was stolen from Bavaria by one Wagner, and he ran away and came to Milwaukee. That's how Milwaukee got the start of us and now makes the best beer in the world." *Western Brewer,* 15 June 1877, supplement; Rich Wagner, correspondence with author, 8 February 2012. Ads for Phillip Best's beer hall did not mention lager specifically either in 1847 or 1852. An account purportedly written in 1850 (published in 1853) describes lager as the well-established preference of the city; John Gregory, *Industrial Resources of Wisconsin* (Chicago: Langdon & Rounds, 1853), 293–94. The "first lager" question is made even more complicated by the discovery of an advertisement in a German-language newspaper for Weickert & Schemmer's Menomonee-Lagerbier Halle in Madison, Wis., in 1837. *Atlas* (Milwaukee), 29 August 1837, 3.

30 *History of Washington and Ozaukee Counties, Wisconsin,* 513.

31 *Southport Telegraph,* 24 January 1843, 3.

32 Blesch was listed in the 1850 population census as a brewer, but it is not clear whether his brewery was in operation yet. *Commemorative Biographical Record of the Fox River Valley Counties of Brown, Outagamie and Winnebago* (Chicago: J. H. Beers, 1895), 160–61.

33 *History of Washington and Ozaukee Counties,* 529, 533.

34 *The History of Sauk County, Wisconsin* (Chicago: Western Historical Company, 1880), 598

35 Otto Kerl, "58 Years in Dane County: The Experiences of a German Pioneer" (unidentified translator), Manuscript Collection SC 2834, Wisconsin Historical Society, Madison, 10.

36 *History of La Crosse County, Wisconsin* (Chicago: Western Historical Company, 1881), 440.

37 *Vermont Gazette* (Bennington), 21 July 1847, 3.

38 *Milwaukie Sentinel,* 25 January 1843, 2.

39 *History of Columbia County, Wisconsin* (Chicago: Western Historical Company, 1880), 635.

40 *Kenosha Tribune and Telegraph,* 27 May 1858, 3.

41 *History of Columbia County, Wisconsin,* 687.

42 *One Hundred Years of Brewing,* 86.

43 *Milwaukee Sentinel,* 4 July 1886, 11.

44 John Gurda, *Miller Time: A History of Miller Brewing Company, 1855–2005* (Milwaukee: Miller Brewing, 2005), 5–6.

45 *One Hundred Years of Brewing,* 152.

46 *History of Columbia County, Wisconsin,* 957.

47 *Commemorative Biographical Record . . . Brown, Outagamie and Winnebago,* 612.

48 George Esser, *A Pioneer Life: Memoirs of My Life and Autobiography,* trans. Herman Eisner (Cross Plains, Wis.: privately published, ca. 1954), 13–25.

49 Nesbit and Thompson, *Wisconsin,* 184–87; Alice E. Smith, "Banking without Banks: George Smith and the Wisconsin Marine and Fire Insurance Co.," *Wisconsin Magazine of History* 48, no. 4 (Summer 1965): 270–71.

50 *Janesville Gazette,* 1 August 1846, 8; *Watertown Chronicle,* 10 November 1847, 2. These are just two examples among many.

51 *Janesville Gazette,* 4 November 1854, 6.

52 Cochran, *The Pabst Brewing Company,* 15; U.S. Census of Industry, 1850, various pages. Not every brewery reported the amount of fuel used; most of those that did were smaller breweries in rural villages.

53 *Racine Daily Journal,* 1 March 1859, 3

54 *Milwaukee Sentinel*, 24 July 1847, 2; 18 December 1847, 2.

55 Nesbit and Thompson, *Wisconsin*, 151.

56 *History of Columbia County, Wisconsin*, 688.

57 Kerl, "58 Years in Dane County," 25; *Umberhine's Milwaukee City Business Directory and Advertiser for 1861* (Indianapolis: D. W. Umberhine, 1861), 30.

58 Esser, *A Pioneer Life*, 22.

59 *Milwaukee Sentinel and Gazette*, 10 April 1850, 2.

60 *Winona (Minn.) Republican-Herald*, 26 July 1936, 6.

61 Cochran, *The Pabst Brewing Company*, 31–32.

62 Folder: La Crosse Businesses—Breweries: Bluff Brewery (several sheets of MS), Special Collections and Area Research Center, University of Wisconsin–La Crosse.

63 *Milwaukee Sentinel*, 2 June 1854, 3.

64 *Milwaukee Sentinel*, 4 January 1848, 3.

65 *Oshkosh Democrat*, 6 September 1850, 3.

66 *Weekly Democratic Standard* (Janesville), 17 November 1856, 3. The name of the Chicago firm was spelled Lill & Diversey later in the century, but while Michael Diversy was alive, it was spelled Diversy in directories, advertising matter, and newspaper articles. It is also spelled Diversy on his memorial in Chicago's St. Boniface Cemetery. The brewery burned in the Chicago fire of 1871. Neil Gale, "The Digital Research Library of Illinois History Journal," 2 December 2017, http://drloihjournal.blogspot.com/2017/12/lill-and-diversey-brewery-chicago.html.

67 *Milwaukee Sentinel*, 21 December 1847, 2. The name Tennent's was spelled with one *n* in the ad.

68 *Richland County Observer*, 28 September 1858, 1.

69 *History of La Crosse County, Wisconsin*, 663.

70 *Sheboygan Journal*, 24 July 1856, 3.

71 Schnabel, "History of the Milwaukee Breweries," 5; also in Austin, *The Milwaukee Story*, 82; and Cochran, *The Pabst Brewing Company*, 35.

72 *History of Rock County, Wisconsin* (Chicago: Western Historical Company, 1879), 565, 571.

73 Nesbitt and Thompson, *Wisconsin*, 235–38.

74 *Southport Telegraph*, 6 January 1846, 2.

75 *Wisconsin Express* (Madison), 26 February 1850, 2.

76 *Wisconsin Free Democrat* (Madison), 6 March 1850, 2.

77 *Stevens Point Pinery*, 8 June 1860, 3.

78 *Fond du Lac Weekly Commonwealth*, 2 May 1860, 2.

79 *100 Years of Brewing*, 225; Tim John, *The Miller Beer Barons* (Oregon, Wis.: Badger Books, 2005), 34.

80 Cochran, *The Pabst Brewing Company*, 30–31.

81 Nesbit and Thompson, *Wisconsin*, 267.

82 *Milwaukee Weekly Wisconsin*, 25 March 1857, 5.

83 *Wisconsin Weekly Free Democrat*, 28 July 1858, 3.

84 *Milwaukee Sentinel*, 11 June 1855, 2.

85 *Milwaukee Daily Sentinel*, 12 April 1859, 1.

Chapter 3. Encouraging Home Industry

1 *[Wausau] Central Wisconsin*, 1 November 1860, 2.

2 *Racine Weekly Journal*, 17 December 1862, 3.

3 Esser, *A Pioneer Life*, 26.

4 *Portrait and Biographical Record of Sheboygan County, Wis.* (Chicago: Excelsior Publishing, 1894), 721.

5 *Milwaukee Sentinel*, 15 August 1862, 1

6 Kerl, "58 Years in Dane County."

7 Esser, *A Pioneer Life*, 26.

8 Nesbit and Thompson, *Wisconsin*, 210; *Milwaukee Sentinel*, 23 August 1862, 1.

9 *Milwaukee Daily Sentinel*, 16 July 1860, 1.

10 *Milwaukee Sentinel*, 15 October 1863, 1.

11 *Wisconsin Daily Patriot* (Madison), 24 September 1864, 4.

12 *Wisconsin State Journal*, 14 May 1864, 1; Nesbit and Thompson, *Wisconsin*, 249.

13 Baron, *Brewed in America*, 213.

14 Some authors have written that the rates were $50 and $100, but the rate guide from 1862 and the actual amounts paid support the lower figures. The fees were doubled later in the decade.

15 *100 Years of Brewing,* 540–43. The USBA met in St. Louis in 1866, and Chicago in 1867.

16 *One Hundred Years of Brewing,* 215; *Yearbook of the United States Brewers' Association* (New York: USBA, 1909), 11–12.

17 *Oshkosh Daily Northwestern,* 4 March 1876, 4.

18 *Racine County Argus,* 16 December 1875, 2.

19 *Milwaukee Daily News,* 18 December 1875, 4.

20 Baron, *Brewed in America,* 217.

21 *Whitewater Register,* 26 April 1861, 2. It is also possible that Streng was not the proprietor but the construction contractor. Early county histories were not always clear about this.

22 *Beaver Dam Argus,* 26 August 1863, 3.

23 *Waukesha Freeman,* 6 December 1864, 2, 3.

24 Franklyn Curtiss-Wedge, ed., *History of Buffalo and Pepin Counties, Wisconsin* (Winona, Minn.: H. C. Cooper Jr., 1919), 367.

25 Esser, *A Pioneer Life,* 26. Victorian-era county histories often mentioned Civil War service by brewers (and other community leaders), but they often omitted the regiment, and sometimes the service was with regiments from other states.

26 The opening (and closing) dates of breweries cannot always be determined with precision. When possible, they are drawn from contemporary local newspaper accounts or from tax records. While the tax records are more complete for Wisconsin from 1866 to 1873 than from 1862 to 1865, other sources document the direction and trend of brewery growth even if future research shows a few breweries to have been founded earlier than heretofore recorded.

27 *100 Years of Brewing,* 608–9.

28 Ron Akin and Lee Reiherzer, *The Breweries of Oshkosh* (Oshkosh: privately published, 2012), 18, 43–45, 55–56, 68.

29 *Wisconsin State Journal,* 17 November 1865, 1.

30 *History of Columbia County, Wisconsin,* 688.

31 *Janesville Gazette,* 6 October 1866, 1.

32 *Janesville Gazette,* 11 August 1871, 6.

33 Ralph G. Plumb, *A History of Manitowoc County* (Manitowoc: Brandt Printing and Binding, 1904), 40.

34 *Janesville Gazette,* 12 August 1871, 1.

35 *Janesville Gazette,* 5 January 1876, 4; 4 February 1876, 8; 22 March 1876, 4.

36 *Marshfield Times,* 17 July 1885, 1.

37 *Oshkosh Daily Northwestern,* 28 September 1883, 4.

38 *Memorial and Biographical Record and Illustrated Compendium of Biography containing a compendium of local biography including biographical sketches of hundreds of prominent old settlers and representative citizens of Columbia, Sauk and Adams Counties, Wisconsin* (Chicago: Geo. A. Ogle, 1901), 239.

39 Satterlee, Tifft, and Marsh, *Clark County: The Garden of Wisconsin* (Neillsville, Wis.: Satterlee & Tifft, 1890), 70.

40 John M. Ware, ed., *A Standard History of Waupaca County, Wisconsin* (Chicago: Lewis Publishing, 1917), 282, 554, 565–67.

41 Michael J. Keane, "Those Who Served: Wisconsin Legislators 1848–2007," *Wisconsin Blue Book 2007–2008* (Madison: State of Wisconsin, 2007), 108, https://docs.legis.wisconsin.gov/misc/lrb/blue_book/2007_2008/300_feature.pdf. Since brewing was such a time-consuming operation, brewers would have had much less time available to travel to Madison than some other occupations unless they had employees who could run the business in their absence.

42 *Milwaukee Sentinel,* 10 March 1882, 4.

43 *Milwaukee Sentinel,* 2 April 1884, 4.

44 *Appleton Post-Crescent,* 25 January 1960, 4.

45 *Stevens Point Journal,* 21 June 1913, 6.

46 *Wisconsin State Journal,* 21 December 1870, 4. A similar problem caused by a brewery in Racine was reported in the *Racine Daily Argus,* 4 September 1880, 4.

47 *Sheboygan Press,* 31 January 1976, 13.

48 *Minneapolis Star Tribune,* 10 April 2015, B2.

49 *Milwaukee Daily Republican Sentinel,* 25 September 1882, 4.

50 *Milwaukee Journal,* 22 October 1890, 10.

51 *Milwaukee Journal,* 26 February 1891, 1.

52 *Milwaukee Sentinel,* 11 January 1891, 15.

53 *Milwaukee Journal,* 22 July 1892, 6.

54 *Stevens Point Journal,* 14 January 1911, 8.

55 *Necedah Yellow River Lumberman,* 3 April 1884, 1. The ad was first placed in 1882.

56 *Milwaukee Sentinel,* 2 February 1877, 2.

57 *Milwaukee Sentinel,* 1 July 1874, 4.

58 *Janesville Gazette,* 24 October 1870, 1.

59 *Milwaukee Journal,* 23 March 1891, 8; 10 September 1892, 4.

60 *Milwaukee Daily Republican Sentinel,* 5 December 1882, 4.

61 *Milwaukee Daily Sentinel,* 12 September 1871, 4.

62 *Milwaukee Daily Journal,* 29 August 1889, 1.

63 *Milwaukee Journal,* 16 October 1895, 15.

64 *Wisconsin State Register* (Portage), 14 July 1893, 4.

65 *Oshkosh Daily Northwestern,* 11 June 1887, 3.

66 *Marshfield Times,* 23 December 1882, 1.

67 *Chicago Herald,* 15 March 1891, 35.

68 *Milwaukee Sentinel,* 4 October 1896, 24.

69 *Wisconsin State Journal,* 1 February 1889, 2; *Sunday Inter Ocean* (Chicago), 10 March 1890, 9.

70 *Milwaukee Journal,* 18 February 1891, 2; 19 February 1891, 3.

71 Akin and Reiherzer, *Breweries of Oshkosh,* 76–80, 83–84.

72 *Milwaukee Journal,* 15 November 1901, 2.

73 Cochran, *The Pabst Brewing Company,* 139–42, 146, 225–26. In Chicago, prices sometimes went as low as two dollars per barrel; 149.

74 *Milwaukee Journal,* 13 January 1893, 4.

75 *Shawano County Advocate,* 13 May 1913, 1; 24 June 1913, 1; 1 July 1913, 1.

76 Akin and Reiherzer, *Breweries of Oshkosh,* 128–34.

77 *Stevens Point Journal,* 13 February 1909, 3.

78 Paul Koeller and David DeLano, *Brewed with Style: The Story of the House of Heileman* (La Crosse: University of Wisconsin–La Crosse Foundation, 2005), 6–9, 16.

79 *Commemorative Biographical Record . . . Brown, Outagamie and Winnebago,* 612; *Milwaukee Sentinel,* 3 December 1884, 8.

80 *Wisconsin,* vol. 51, R. G. Dun & Co. Collection, Baker Library Historical Collections, Harvard Business School, 20.

81 *Wisconsin,* vol. 49, R. G. Dun & Co. Collection, Baker Library Historical Collections, Harvard Business School, 204z.

82 Michael J. Goc, *Lives Lived Here: A Walk through the History of Sauk City,* comp. Myrtle Cushing (Friendship, Wis.: New Past Press, 1992), 37.

83 Unidentified newspaper, 21 May 1903, n.p. Misc. brewery clippings, microfilm roll 257, Milwaukee County Historical Society.

84 Curtiss-Wedge, *History of Buffalo and Pepin Counties, Wisconsin,* 159–60.

85 State of Wisconsin Corporation Records (Madison), series 356, box 245, folder 115.

86 State of Wisconsin Corporation Records (Madison), series 356, box 329, folder 494.

87 State of Wisconsin Corporation Records (Madison), series 356, box 513, folder M1534.

88 *Milwaukee Journal,* 22 May 1891, 1.

89 *Milwaukee Journal,* 23 May 1891, 5.

90 *Milwaukee Sentinel,* 23 May 1891, 8; *Sheboygan Press,* 31 January 1976, sec. 2, 13.

91 *Milwaukee Sentinel,* 18 December 1891, 3.

92 *Eau Claire Daily Telegram,* 21 November 1903, 1; 14 December 1903, 5.

93 *Milwaukee Daily Journal,* 5 February 1892, 3.

94 *Minneapolis Journal,* 2 November 1896, 3.

95 *Minneapolis Morning Tribune,* 6 April 1912, 1.

96 *Stevens Point Journal,* 2 April 1910, 4.

97 *Winona Daily Republican,* 25 September 1894, 3; *La Crosse Morning Chronicle,* 25 September 1894, 1.

98 *Winona Daily Republican,* 24 September 1897, 3.

99 *Winona Daily Republican,* 31 March 1913, 2.

100 *La Crosse Morning Chronicle,* 20 September 1894, 1; *Milwaukee Sentinel,* 21 September 1894, 10; *Milwaukee Journal,* 22 September 1894, 8.

Chapter 4. The Leading Industry

1. *100 Years of Brewing*, 604.
2. *Milwaukie Daily Sentinel*, 10 December 1844, 3.
3. *100 Years of Brewing*, 588, 596.
4. *Daily Milwaukee News*, 24 November 1869, 4.
5. *Milwaukee Sentinel*, 21 July 1946, B5.
6. *Milwaukee Journal*, 27 September 1897, 7.
7. *100 Years of Brewing*, 595–99; "About Briess—History," http://www.briess.com/food/About/history.php.
8. *Milwaukee Sentinel*, 23 June 1970, 10; *Jefferson Banner*, 7 August 1902, n.p., http://jeffersonhistoricalsociety.org/database/show_date.php?date=1902-08-07.
9. *Milwaukee Journal*, 26 June 1899, sec. 2, 4.
10. Fred L. Holmes, "Craze for Hops Held Wisconsin; Disaster Came," Wisconsin Historical Society, Wisconsin Local History and Biography Articles; *Milwaukee Sentinel*, 16 January 1921, https://www.wisconsinhistory.org/Records/Newspaper/BA3929; *Sparta Eagle*, 17 July 1867, 2.
11. Examples include reprints of "Emmet Wells Weekly Hop Circular," *Weekly Wisconsin* and *Semi-Weekly Wisconsin* (Milwaukee), and regular articles by local correspondents in the *Reedsburg Free Press*.
12. Wisconsin Historical Society, Wisconsin Local History and Biography Articles; *Baraboo News*, 26 October 1911, http://www.wisconsinhistory.org.
13. *Reedsburg Free Press*, 15 August 1873, 3.
14. *Western Brewer*, November 1876, 90.
15. *Wisconsin State Register* (Portage), 2 May 1868, 1; 8 August 1868, 1.
16. *Baraboo News*, 26 October 1911.
17. *Reedsburg Free Press*, 31 October 1873, 3.
18. *One Hundred Years of Brewing*, 96–97.
19. Undated, anonymous article, Kurth Company, misc. items M-96-093 MAD 3M/58/A2, Wisconsin Historical Society, Madison.
20. *Milwaukee Sentinel*, 27 January 1873, 4.
21. Susan K. Appel, "Artificial Refrigeration and the Architecture of 19th-Century American Breweries," *Journal of the Society for Industrial Archeology* 16, no. 1 (1990): 25.
22. *Milwaukee Sentinel*, 3 February 1882, 6.
23. Baron, *Brewed in America*, 231.
24. *Milwaukee Daily Republican Sentinel*, 12 December 1882, 6.
25. *Milwaukee Sentinel*, 27 January 1895, 7.
26. *New Orleans Times*, 16 September 1875, 5.
27. Baron, *Brewed in America*, 259.
28. Cochran, *The Pabst Brewing Company*, 162.
29. *Chicago Herald*, 6 July 1890, 16.
30. *Minneapolis Tribune*, 31 January 1906, 7.
31. Cochran, *The Pabst Brewing Company*, 107–10.
32. *Milwaukee Sentinel*, 7 August 1874, 4.
33. Francis X. Murphy, "Brewing Was Once a Sizable Industry in County," *Manitowoc Herald-Times*, 23 November 1953, sec. 2, 1.
34. *Milwaukee Sentinel*, 6 February 1872, 4; 28 February 1872, 4.
35. *Milwaukee Sentinel*, 9 June 1873, 8; 10 June 1873, 8.
36. *Milwaukee Sentinel*, 26 August 1873, 8; 29 August 1873, 8; 31 August 1873, 8.
37. *Milwaukee Daily Sentinel*, 4 August 1866, 1.
38. *Milwaukee Daily Sentinel*, 6 March 1866, 1.
39. *Milwaukee Journal*, 3 September 1892, 1.
40. *Milwaukee Sentinel*, 13 November 1876, 8.
41. *Milwaukee Sentinel*, 6 April 1877, 8; 11 January 1877.
42. *Milwaukee Sentinel*, 23 February 1877, 8.
43. *Memorial and Biographical Record and Illustrated Compendium . . . Columbia, Sauk and Adams Counties, Wisconsin*, 239.
44. *Eau Claire Daily Free Press*, 25 June 1883, 3.
45. *Commemorative Biographical Record . . . Brown, Outagamie and Winnebago*, 612.
46. *History of Crawford and Richland Counties, Wisconsin* (Springfield, Ill.: Union Publishing, 1884), 661.

47 *Western Brewer,* June 1877, 209; January 1881, n.p.

48 *Western Brewer,* June 1877, 168.

49 "Vilter History," http://www.emersonclimate.com/en-us/Brands/Vilter/Pages/VilterHistory.aspx; *American Brewer* 40–44 (April 1927): 38.

50 *Milwaukee Sentinel,* 24 January 1893, 5.

51 *Catalogue [of engravings of brewery plants and beer bottle labels]* (Milwaukee: Milwaukee Lith. & Engr., ca. 1900), 14–15.

52 Milwaukee County Historical Society, http://www.milwaukeehistory.net/museum/exhibits/online-exhibit/unlocking-the-vault/gugler-lincoln-lithographic-print-text.

53 *Bock Beer Posters* (Milwaukee: Gugler Lithographic, ca. 1905); *Interim Historic Designation Study Report: Gugler Lithographic Company Building, 1333–1339 N. Milwaukee Street* (City of Milwaukee Historic Preservation Committee, 2004), http://www.city.milwaukee.gov/ImageLibrary/Groups/cityHPC/StudyReports/vticnf/GuglerLithographicCoBuilding2004.pdfm 3–6.

54 Undated, unidentified article, Kurth Company, misc. items M-96-093 MAD 3M/58/A2, Wisconsin Historical Society, Madison. The document claims that the wagon maker was Chas. Albresch, which was presumably a misspelling of Charles Abresch.

55 Cochran, *The Pabst Brewing Company,* 112–13; *American Brewers' Review* 17, no. 5 (20 November 1903): 205; 17, no. 3 (20 September 1903), advertising supplement 47, 57–58.

56 *Letters on Brewing,* July 1900, 12, 14; *Milwaukee Journal,* 5 June 1895, 2.

57 *Oshkosh Daily Northwestern,* 9 June 1887, 2.

58 *Eau Claire News,* 4 October 1884, 3.

59 *Milwaukee Daily Republican-Sentinel,* 23 July 1882, 8.

60 *Commemorative Biographical Record . . . Brown, Outagamie and Winnebago,* 592.

61 Undated, unidentified article, Kurth Company, misc. items M-96-093 MAD 3M/58/A2, Wisconsin Historical Society, Madison.

62 *Sheboygan Daily Press,* 4 April 1908, 1.

63 All data come from Sanborn Insurance Maps, various cities and dates.

64 *Sheboygan Press,* 5 December 1913, 5; 5 March 1914, 8.

65 *Milwaukee Sentinel,* 1 August 1879, 1.

66 *Milwaukee Sentinel,* 6 February 1872, 4.

67 *Milwaukee Sentinel,* 15 July 1893, 1.

68 *Stevens Point Journal,* 12 February 1916, 1.

69 *Sheboygan Press,* 22 January 1918, 8.

70 Murphy, "Brewing Was Once a Sizable Industry in County."

71 *Sheboygan Press,* 18 September 1915, 8.

72 *Wisconsin State Journal,* 12 December 1943, 12.

73 *American Brewers' Review* 31, no. 7 (July 1917): 225.

74 *Reading (Pa.) Eagle,* 19 February 1920, 13.

75 *Milwaukee Sentinel,* 26 May 1918, 18.

76 *American Brewers' Review* 30, no. 1 (June 1916): 222; *American Brewers' Review* 31, no. 7 (July 1917): 223. The first electric truck to be used by an American brewery was built by General Vehicle Company for Central Brewing of New York City. *Western Brewer,* February 1912, 86.

77 *Milwaukee: A Half Century's Progress, 1846–1896* (Milwaukee: Consolidated Illustrating, 1896), 210–11.

78 *Milwaukee Journal,* 19 September 1891, 3.

79 Mark Theobald, "Charles Abresch Co.," *Coachbuilt,* 2013, http://www.coachbuilt.com/bui/a/abresch/abresch.htm.

80 Harry S. Houpt, "Making Chauffeurs of Teamsters," *Western Brewer* 38, no. 2 (February 1912): 85.

81 "The Brewery Motor Truck," *American Brewers' Review* 31, no. 7 (July 1917): 223–25; William C. Hunt, "Motor Trucks in Brewery Business," *American Brewers' Review* 31, no. 7 (July 1917): 225–26; J. W. McDowell, "The Electric Truck in Brewery Service," *American Brewers' Review* 31, no. 7 (July 1917): 226–28.

82 Curtis A. Wessel, "The Brewery Motor Truck," *American Brewers' Review* 31, no. 5 (May 1917): 143–47. Statistics in this article were consistent with those in the July articles but drew on evidence from different breweries.

83 John F. Dutcher, "The Potosi Steamboat," *American Breweriana Journal* 132 (November–December 2004): 21.

84 *Oshkosh Daily Northwestern,* 4 June 1888, 4.

85 *Racine Daily Journal,* 18 April 1866, 2.

86. *Superior Times*, 15 April 1871, 4.
87. *Atlanta (Ga.) Constitution*, 10 August 1887, 5.
88. *Green Bay Semi-Weekly Gazette*, 8 May 1912, 7.
89. Susan K. Appel, "Building Milwaukee's Breweries: Pre-Prohibition Brewery Architecture in the Cream City," *Wisconsin Magazine of History* 78, no. 3 (Spring 1995): 165–66. Appel's is the most thorough work on American brewery architecture, and any discussion in this book of brewery buildings draws heavily on her work and assistance.
90. *Milwaukee Journal of Commerce*, 14 May 1873, 2.
91. *Milwaukee Daily Journal*, 27 July 1865, 2.
92. Appel, "Building Milwaukee's Breweries," 169.
93. Appel, "Building Milwaukee's Breweries," 171–72, 175.
94. Appel, "Building Milwaukee's Breweries," 177–80; Jurgensen, *Milwaukee Beer Barons, Brewers, Bottlers*, 61.
95. *Milwaukee Daily Republican Sentinel*, 10 December 1882, 3.
96. *Milwaukee Sentinel*, 5 July 1889, 1.
97. *Milwaukee Journal*, 18 December 1891, 3.
98. *Milwaukee Sentinel*, 31 July 1892, 6; 23 July 1896, 5.
99. Louis Lehle, "Notes on Brewery Design," *Western Brewer* 38, no. 1 (January 1912): 10–14.

Chapter 5. Milwaukee

1. Nesbit and Thompson, *Wisconsin*, 333, claims that brewing was only ranked first in 1890, but the *Milwaukee Sentinel* (1 January 1893) reported that brewing was the biggest industry in the city in 1892 by $2 million. Data for 1879 from *Milwaukee Sentinel*, 2 January 1880, 8; data compiled by the *Western Brewer* for 1890 placed Milwaukee fourth with 1.5 million barrels, just behind third-place Chicago and second-place St. Louis, but well behind New York City, which made more than 4.2 million barrels. Cited in Herbst, Roussin, and Kious, *St. Louis Brews*, 14.
2. *Milwaukee Sentinel*, 31 July 1892, 6.
3. Cochran, *The Pabst Brewing Company*, 46.
4. Cochran, *The Pabst Brewing Company*, 56.
5. *Milwaukee Sentinel*, 22 November 1870, 1.
6. *Milwaukee Sentinel*, 16 September 1873, 8.
7. *Milwaukee Sentinel*, 6 June 1873.
8. *Milwaukee Sentinel*, 18 May 1870; Cochran, *The Pabst Brewing Company*, 57–60.
9. Production statistics are from *Milwaukee Sentinel*, 21 January 1868, 1. The assessment of industry concentration uses the Herfindahl-Hirschman Index; the index for 1868 (with estimated production for brewers listed as "other") was 1,395, which is considered "unconcentrated" by modern antitrust regulators. Andrew Chin, "Herfindahl-Hirschman Index Calculator," http://www.unclaw.com/chin/teaching/antitrust/herfindahl.htm.
10. Cochran, *The Pabst Brewing Company*, 53.
11. Bob Skilnik, *The History of Beer and Brewing in Chicago, 1833–1978* (St. Paul: Pogo Press, 1999), 22–24.
12. *Milwaukee Sentinel*, 30 December 1871, 1.
13. Cochran, *The Pabst Brewing Company*, 167–70.
14. Cochran, *The Pabst Brewing Company*, 123.
15. *Eau Claire Daily News*, 7 November 1885, 2; Gurda, *Miller Time*, 50–51.
16. "Milwaukee's First," souvenir pamphlet (Milwaukee, Blatz Brewing Co., 1949), front cover.
17. Cochran, *The Pabst Brewing Company*, 126; Baron, *Brewed in America*, 241–42; *Eau Claire Daily Free Press*, 21 December 1876, 1.
18. *Milwaukee Daily Sentinel*, 19 January 1875, 8.
19. John Steiner, interview by author, 23 March 2013; *Milwaukee Daily Sentinel*, 27 April 1882, 2.
20. Jurgensen, *Milwaukee Beer Barons, Brewers, Bottlers*, 40; "Milwaukee's First," 5.
21. Gurda, Miller Time, 43–44; Jurgensen, *Milwaukee Beer Barons, Brewers, Bottlers*, 35–36, 60.
22. Cochran, *The Pabst Brewing Company*, 123–24.
23. Jurgensen, *Milwaukee Beer Barons, Brewers, Bottlers*, 19.
24. *La Crosse Tribune Leader-Press*, 7 February 1932, 10.
25. *Milwaukee Directory for 1878* (Milwaukee: William Hogg, 1878), facing 90, facing 97, facing 173, facing 433.

26 *San Francisco Daily Evening Bulletin*, 30 May 1877, 3.

27 Cochran, *The Pabst Brewing Company*, 123–24; Jurgensen, *Milwaukee Beer Barons, Brewers, Bottlers*, 40, 67.

28 Cochran, *The Pabst Brewing Company*, 176.

29 *Milwaukee Sentinel*, 19 May 1888, 9.

30 *Milwaukee Sentinel*, 18 June 1895, 5.

31 Nicholas J. Hoffman, "Miniature Demons: The Young Helpers of Milwaukee's Glass Industry, 1880–1922," *Wisconsin Magazine of History* 91, no. 1 (Autumn 2007): 7–8.

32 *Milwaukee Journal*, 18 June 1895, 1.

33 *Milwaukee Sentinel*, 17 June 1895, 1.

34 *Milwaukee Sentinel*, 18 October 1895, 1.

35 *Milwaukee Daily Sentinel*, 3 May 1873, 4. This strike is not mentioned in Cochran, *The Pabst Brewing Company*.

36 Cochran, *The Pabst Brewing Company*, 272.

37 Hermann Schlüter, *The Brewing Industry and the Brewery Workers' Movement in America* (Cincinnati: International Union of United Brewery Workmen of America, 1910), 92; *Milwaukee Sentinel*, 16 February 1886, 2.

38 Cochran, *The Pabst Brewing Company*, 272.

39 Schlüter, *The Brewing Industry*, 254–61.

40 *Milwaukee Daily Sentinel*, 28 April 1871, 4; 12 September 1871, 4.

41 Schlüter, *The Brewing Industry*, 100–107; Cochran, *The Pabst Brewing Company*, 275.

42 Schlüter, *The Brewing Industry*, 110–12; Cochran, *The Pabst Brewing Company*, 274.

43 Cochran, *The Pabst Brewing Company*, 274.

44 *Milwaukee Sentinel*, 16 February 1886, 2; 29 March 1886, 2.

45 *Wisconsin State Journal* (Madison), 7 May 1886, 1.

46 Cochran, *The Pabst Brewing Company*, 280–81; *Wisconsin State Journal* (Madison), 7 May 1886, 1.

47 Cochran, *The Pabst Brewing Company*, 281.

48 *Milwaukee Sentinel*, 4 May 1886, 2; *Milwaukee Daily Journal*, 4 May 1886, 1, 5.

49 *Wisconsin State Journal* (Madison), 7 May 1886, 1.

50 *Milwaukee Sentinel*, 6 May 1886, 4.

51 *Milwaukee Daily Journal*, 5 May 1886, 1.

52 Cochran, *The Pabst Brewing Company*, 282.

53 Schlüter, *The Brewing Industry*, 113.

54 Cochran, *The Pabst Brewing Company*, 283.

55 *Milwaukee Daily Journal*, 9 November 1887, 1; Cochran, *The Pabst Brewing Company*, 283–86.

56 Cochran, *The Pabst Brewing Company*, 287–88; Schlüter, *The Brewing Industry*, 146–48.

57 *Daily Journal*, 25 January 1888, 1; 26 January 1888, 1; 27 January 1888, 1; *Milwaukee Sentinel*, 26 January 1888, 1; Cochran, *The Pabst Brewing Company*, 287; Schlüter, *The Brewing Industry*, 148. Cochran claimed the beer served at the ball was St. Louis beer, but Schlüter reported it was from Chicago.

58 *Milwaukee Sentinel*, 2 February 1888, 3; *Milwaukee Sentinel*, 9 February 1888, 1; *Milwaukee Daily Journal*, 9 February 1888, 1.

59 *Milwaukee Journal*, 15 December 1891, 2; *Milwaukee Sentinel*, 15 December 1891, 3.

60 Cochran, *The Pabst Brewing Company*, 296–301.

61 Schlüter, *The Brewing Industry*, 92–93.

62 *Milwaukee Journal*, 6 December 1895, 2.

63 *Milwaukee Sentinel*, 18 October 1895, 1.

64 *Milwaukee Sentinel*, 3 February 1895, 1.

65 *Milwaukee Sentinel*, 14 August 1891, 3.

66 *Milwaukee Sentinel*, 5 February 1893, 15. The Anakim were a race of giants mentioned several times in the Hebrew scriptures.

67 *Wisconsin State Journal*, 8 March 1881, 8.

68 *Milwaukee Sentinel*, 13 January 1888, 3.

69 *Milwaukee Sentinel*, 21 January 1881, 2.

70 *Milwaukee Sentinel*, 4 September 1893, 4.

71 *Milwaukee Sentinel*, 4 August 1890, 4.

72 Schlüter, *The Brewing Industry*, 261–63.

73 *Milwaukee Sentinel*, 30 March 1884, 6.

74 *Milwaukee Sentinel*, 2 January 1885, 5.

75 *Milwaukee Sentinel*, 5 February 1893, 15; 31 July 1892, 6.

76 *Chicago Herald,* 19 August 1891, 9; *Milwaukee Daily Journal,* 23 October 1889, 1.

77 *Milwaukee Journal,* 21 April 1893, 8; *Milwaukee Sentinel,* 4 September 1893, 4.

78 *Milwaukee Sentinel,* 13 January 1888, 3.

79 *Stevens Point Journal,* 29 October 1887, 1.

80 *Milwaukee Daily Journal,* 14 October 1887, 2; cited from *Janesville Recorder.*

81 Cochran, *The Pabst Brewing Company,* 136.

82 *Milwaukee Daily Sentinel,* 10 April 1879, 8.

83 *Milwaukee Sentinel,* 12 September 1884, 8; Cochran, *The Pabst Brewing Company,* 136.

84 *Yenowine's Illustrated News* (Milwaukee), 11 October 1891, 4. George Yenowine had been Best's advertising manager during the 1880s.

85 *Milwaukee Sentinel,* 15 January 1889, 7.

86 *Plain Talk and Hard Facts about Blatz* (Milwaukee: Blatz Brewing, ca. 1899), 2.

87 *Bock Beer Posters.*

88 Madelon Powers, *Faces along the Bar: Lore and Order in the Workingman's Saloon* (Chicago: University of Chicago Press, 1998), 12, 16, 30, 66–67.

89 *Milwaukee Journal,* 15 March 1961, pt. 4, 2.

90 Mike Reilly, "Joseph Schlitz Brewing Co.: Schlitz Waukesha Hotel History," http://www.slahs.org/schlitz/waukesha_hotel.htm; *Winona Daily-Republican,* 1 October 1892, 5. A Kenosha establishment called the Schlitz Hotel did not take that name until the 1930s. Diane Giles, "History Mystery: Schlitz Brewing Co. Globe Topped Maple House," *Kenosha News,* posted 16 April 2015.

91 Valerie Cranston, "Stately Hotel's Secrets Hidden in Ashes," *Carlsbad (N. Mex.) Current-Argus,* posted 14 September 2014.

92 Christopher White, "Washington Hotel & Other Albany Hotels," *Finding Your Past: Genealogical Gleanings in Albany,* http://findingyourpast.blogspot.com/2015/01/washington-hotel-other-albany-hotels.html.

93 Jennifer L. Lehrke and Robert Short, *Village of Whitefish Bay, Wisconsin Architectural and Historical Intensive Survey Report* (Madison: Wisconsin Historical Society, Division of Historic Preservation, 2010–11), 156–57.

94 Cochran, *The Pabst Brewing Company,* 210–13.

95 Cochran, *The Pabst Brewing Company,* 211–12; "When Beer, *Milwaukee Style,* Was Introduced to New York," *Milwaukee Journal,* 30 May 1930, online facsimile at http://www.wisconsinhistory.org/turningpoints/search.asp?id=1269.

96 *Shanghai Mercury,* 10 July 1899, n.p., microfilm roll 257, Milwaukee County Historical Society.

97 *Milwaukee Sentinel,* 9 September 1878, 2.

98 *Milwaukee Sentinel,* 17 February 1871, 1; 13 October 1871, 4; 8 February 1872, 4; 16 February 1884, 3; *Milwaukee Daily Sentinel,* 26 October 1880, 8; *Wisconsin State Journal,* 24 January 1871, 2; 2 February 1870, 3; 3 November 1871, 3.

99 Katie Adams, "The Second Ward Savings Bank: One-Hundred Years of History," *MKEMemoirs,* https://milwaukeehistoryblog.wordpress.com/2013/02/04/the-second-ward-savings-bank-one-hundred-years-of-history; *Daily Milwaukee News,* 8 March 1866, 3.

100 *Milwaukee Sentinel,* 18 December 1891, 3.

101 *Milwaukee Journal,* 13 September 1895, 1.

102 *Milwaukee Journal,* 7 July 1890, 3; *Milwaukee Sentinel,* 8 July 1890, 3.

103 *Milwaukee Sentinel,* 9 February 1893, 1; 30 March 1893, 3. Another account claimed the balloon carried only fifteen passengers: James Wilson Pierce, *Photographic History of the World's Fair and Sketch of the City of Chicago* (Baltimore: R. H. Woodward, 1893), 354.

104 Cochran, *The Pabst Brewing Company,* 137–38; Ogle, *Ambitious Brew,* 126–33; *Milwaukee Sentinel,* 28 October 1893, 1; 3 November 1893, 2; 17 November 1893, 5; *Wedding Secrets* (Milwaukee: Pabst Brewing, ca. 1896), 1 and facing.

105 *Milwaukee Sentinel,* 3 November 1893, 2; 17 November 1893, 5; *Milwaukee Journal,* 16 November 1893, 1; 17 November 1893, 2; 18 November 1893, 6; Cochran, *The Pabst Brewing Company,* 177; Ogle, *Ambitious Brew,* 133.

106 *Perham (Minn.) Enterprise-Bulletin,* 30 October 1986, 7; Watrous, *Memoirs of Milwaukee County,* 2:965.

107 *Milwaukee Daily Sentinel,* 24 December 1874, 8; *Waukesha County Democrat,* 2 January 1875, 1.

108 *Milwaukee Daily News,* 19 January 1879, 6.

109 Cochran, *The Pabst Brewing Company,* 119–21.

110 *Milwaukee Sentinel,* 4 July 1886, 11.

111 Martin Stack, "Liquid Bread: An Examination of the American Brewing Industry, 1865 to 1940," part 2, *Brewery History* 154 (Autumn 2013): esp. 33, 41.

112 *Milwaukee Daily News,* 19 January 1879, 6.

113 *Milwaukee Daily Sentinel,* 20 November 1865, 1.

114 Stack, "Liquid Bread," esp. 33, 41, 55, 73.

115 *Semi-Weekly Wisconsin* (Milwaukee), 9 November 1867, 3.

116 *Milwaukee Daily Republican Sentinel,* 8 November 1882, 1; 9 November 1882, 2.

117 *Milwaukee Sentinel,* 3 November 1886, 6.

118 *Milwaukee Sentinel,* 26 January 1890, 1; 14 May 1890, 1; Cochran, *The Pabst Brewing Company,* 126–27.

119 *Milwaukee Sentinel,* 19 December 1890, 1.

120 *Milwaukee Journal,* 19 December 1890, 2.

121 Cochran, *The Pabst Brewing Company,* 164.

122 *Milwaukee Journal,* 25 February 1893, 2; Cochran, *The Pabst Brewing Company,* 199–200.

123 Charles H. Schmidt, "My Memories with the A. Gettelman Brewing Co. Starting April 1st 1890" (ca. 1940), Milwaukee County Historical Society, Breweries, box 1, folder 10.

124 *Milwaukee Sentinel,* 10 April 1879, 8.

125 *Milwaukee Sentinel,* 21 August 1879, 8; 22 August 1879, 3.

126 *Milwaukee Sentinel,* 28 October 1891, 4.

127 *Milwaukee Journal,* 21 June 1894, 1.

128 *Milwaukee Sentinel,* 24 June 1894, 11.

129 *Milwaukee Sentinel,* 17 June 1894, 1.

130 *Milwaukee Sentinel,* 7 June 1891, 6.

131 *Milwaukee Sentinel,* 15 March 1896, 19.

132 *Milwaukee Journal,* 29 February 1892, 4.

133 *Milwaukee Journal,* 29 February 1892, 4.

134 *Milwaukee Sentinel,* 25 August 1889, 1; Cochran, *The Pabst Brewing Company,* 133–34.

135 *Milwaukee Daily Journal,* 6 May 1890, 4; 3 July 1890, 3.

136 *Chicago Daily Inter-Ocean,* 1 June 1890, 7. Ironically, the 3 July 1890 page of the *Daily Journal* that announced the purchase of more acres for parkland also contained ads for both Schlitz Park and Whitefish Bay.

137 *Milwaukee Daily Sentinel,* 21 January 1868, 1; Cochran, *The Pabst Brewing Company,* 180.

138 Charles B. Harger, *Milwaukee Illustrated: Its Trade, Commerce, Manufacturing Interests, and Advantages as a Residence City* (Milwaukee: W. W. Coleman, 1877), 104.

139 *Milwaukee Daily Journal,* 16 November 1885, 10.

140 *Yenowine's Illustrated News* (Milwaukee), 7 April 1889, 16.

141 *Milwaukee Sentinel,* 29 September 1890, 1.

142 *Milwaukee Sentinel,* 29 September 1890, 1.

143 Eastberg, *The Captain Frederick Pabst Mansion: An Illustrated History* (Milwaukee: Captain Frederick Pabst Mansion, 2009), 41, 73–83.

144 "Alfred Uihlein House," *Historic Structures,* http://www.historic-structures.com/wi/milwaukee/uilein_house.php.

145 *Milwaukee Sentinel,* 17 October 1890, 3.

146 *Milwaukee Sentinel,* 13 September 1895, 1.

147 Cochran, *The Pabst Brewing Company,* 181.

148 *Milwaukee Sentinel,* 27 January 1895, 7.

Chapter 6. Oasis in the Dry Years

1 The general background of drink and the temperance movement is primarily drawn from Andrew Barr, *Drink: A Social History of America* (New York: Carroll & Graf, 1999); Mark Edward Lender and James Kirby Martin, *Drinking in America: A History; The Revised and Expanded Edition* (New York: Free Press, 1987); and Daniel Okrent, *Last Call: The Rise and Fall of Prohibition* (New York: Scribner, 2010).

2 Nesbit and Thompson, *Wisconsin,* 355.

3 Nesbit and Thompson, *Wisconsin,* 239.

4 *Janesville Gazette,* 16 July 1877, 1.

5   Lender and Martin, *Drinking in America*, 69.

6   *The History of Sauk County, Wisconsin*, 599–600.

7   Okrent, *Last Call*, 9–10.

8   *Sons of Temperance*, http://www.sonsoftemperance.info/history_us.htm (accessed 9 August 2014; now defunct). Although the Sons of Temperance still has a website, it is based in the United Kingdom and notes that "nowhere is the society still functioning in its traditional form."

9   *Wisconsin Enquirer* (Madison), 19 January 1839, 3.

10 Kate G. Berres, "The Temperance Movement in Fond du Lac, 1847–1878," in *Source of the Lake: 150 Years of History in Fond du Lac*, ed. Clarence B. Davis (Fond du Lac, Wis.: Action Printing, 2002), 70; C. W. Butterfield, *History of Green County* (Springfield, Ill.: Union Publishing, 1884), 945; *History of Dane County, Wisconsin* (Chicago: Western Historical Company, 1880), 741; *Sheboygan Press*, 17 June 1958, 16.

11 *History of Dane County, Wisconsin*, 908.

12 *History of Rock County, Wisconsin*, 655.

13 Ashland Commandery no. 22, Invitation to 1895 Easter Service, in Ephemera Collection PH2724, box 6, folder: Fraternal Orders: Knights Templar, Wisconsin Historical Society, Madison.

14 *History of Columbia County, Wisconsin*, 691.

15 *History of Dane County*, 862.

16 Nesbit and Thompson, *Wisconsin*, 356.

17 Butterfield, *History of Green County*, 692.

18 *Baraboo Republic*, 28 January 1858, 1. The *Mirror* referred to was not specified, but was most likely the newspaper of that name in Newport, which later became Kilbourn City and finally Wisconsin Dells.

19 *Wisconsin Chief* (Fort Atkinson), 1 April 1863, 7. Martin Huscher was listed in the 1860 population census as a brewer, but apparently did not own his own brewery in 1863. A seidel is a large glass for beer.

20 *Wisconsin State Journal* (Madison), 12 June 1883, 3.

21 Herman J. Deutsch, "Yankee-Teuton Rivalry in Wisconsin Politics of the Seventies," sec. 1, "Temperance," *Wisconsin Magazine of History* 14, no. 3 (March 1931): 273–75.

22 *Weekly Wisconsin* (Milwaukee), 4 February 1886, 4.

23 *Milwaukee Sentinel*, 6 May 1874, 5; Louis Schade, *The Brewers' Hand-book for 1876* (Washington, D.C.: Washington Sentinel, 1876), 150.

24 *Milwaukee Daily Journal*, 15 September 1885, 3.

25 *Milwaukee Sentinel*, 14 May 1886, 8.

26 *Janesville Gazette*, 31 March 1884, 4.

27 *Wisconsin State Journal*, 4 April 1884, 1.

28 *Chicago Herald*, 4 November 1891, 9.

29 Nesbit and Thompson, *Wisconsin*, 356.

30 Nesbit and Thompson, *Wisconsin*, 368, 370, 383; Deutsch, "Yankee-Teuton Rivalry," 267–78.

31 Powers, *Faces along the Bar*, 93–95, 102–3, 110–11; Nesbit and Thompson, *Wisconsin*, 356; *Janesville Daily Gazette*, 19 April 1881, 1.

32 *Duluth (Minn.) News-Tribune*, 16 April 1913; *Racine Journal-News*, 30 March 1917, 1.

33 Okrent, *Last Call*, 13–14; *Janesville Gazette*, 7 May 1874, 1; *Cincinnati Daily Gazette*, 5 June 1875, 4.

34 Okrent, *Last Call*, 16.

35 Okrent, *Last Call*, 16–19.

36 *Janesville Gazette*, 9 March 1874, 4; *History of Rock County, Wisconsin*, 637.

37 William H. Canfield, *Outline Sketches of Sauk County* (Baraboo: A. N. Kellogg, 1896), 38.

38 Canfield, *Outline Sketches of Sauk County*, 38.

39 Okrent, *Last Call*, 20–23.

40 Okrent, *Last Call*, 37.

41 David V. Mollenhoff, *Madison: A History of the Formative Years* (Dubuque, Iowa: Kendall/Hunt Publishing, 1982), 312.

42 Elizabeth Jozwiak, "Bottoms Up: The Socialist Fight for the Workingman's Saloon," *Wisconsin Magazine of History* 90, no. 2 (Winter 2006–7): 14.

43 Powers, *Faces along the Bar*, 32.

44 Powers, *Faces along the Bar*, 32.

45 Jozwiak, "Bottoms Up," 12, 14–15, 18, 22.

46 Mollenhoff, *Madison*, 312; Okrent, *Last Call*, 27.

47 Mollenhoff, *Madison*, 314.

48 Okrent, *Last Call*, 27.

49 Watrous, *Memoirs of Milwaukee County*, 2:771.

50 Wisconsin Legislature, Committee on White Slave Traffic and Kindred Subjects: Report and Recommendations of the Wisconsin Legislative Committee to Investigate the White Slave Traffic and Kindred Subjects (Madison, Wis.: The Committee, 1914), online facsimile http://content.wisconsinhistory.org/u?/tp,26592, 98–102; Milwaukee Hearings, part 1, July 13–18, 1914, Wisconsin Legislature, Investigations, 1837–1945, series 173, box 19, folder: Exhibits . . . Milwaukee, online facsimile http://www.wisconsinhistory.org/turningpoints/search.asp?id=1568, 118, 128, 130.

51 Mary D. Bradford, "Memoirs of Mary D. Bradford," chapter 15, "My Experiences as Superintendent of Public Schools," *Wisconsin Magazine of History* 16, no. 1 (September 1932): 64.

52 Okrent, *Last Call*, 36–37.

53 This congressman was Charles H. Randall of California, though Kittel Halvorson of Minnesota claimed the Prohibition label as well as the endorsement of the Farmers' Alliance (the latter was probably more important to his victory). Biography folder, Los Angeles Public Library, http://dbase1.lapl.org/webpics/calindex/documents/07/518077.pdf; Hoverson, *Land of Amber Waters*, 109.

54 Sean Dennis Cashman, *Prohibition: The Lie of the Land* (New York: Free Press, 1981), 7. The estimated $35 million the league spent by 1926 on trying to sway public opinion would have been equal to at least $388 million in 2016 dollars.

55 Okrent, *Last Call*, 58, 61.

56 *Minneapolis Journal*, 4 January 1907, 7.

57 *Spokane (Wash.) Spokesman-Review*, 21 October 1914, 7; *Schlitz Rhomboid* 1, no. 3 (Summer 1952): 12.

58 Okrent, *Last Call*, 63–66.

59 Norman K. Risjord, *Wisconsin: The Story of the Badger State* (Madison: Trails Books, 2007), 180–81.

60 Risjord, *Wisconsin*, 180–81; Nesbit and Thompson, *Wisconsin*, 444–45, 462; "The Enemy in Our Midst" (Milwaukee: Wisconsin Anti-Saloon League, 1918), Ephemera Collection, PH2724, box 3, folder: Alcohol and Brewing, Prohibition and Temperance, Wisconsin Historical Society, Madison.

61 *Milwaukee Journal*, 13 February 1918, 6.

62 *Appleton Evening Crescent*, 17 May 1918, 3.

63 Unidentified Milwaukee newspaper clipping, 13 December 1917, microfilm roll 257, Milwaukee Historical Society.

64 *Appleton Evening Crescent*, 2 May 1918, 3.

65 *Minneapolis Morning Tribune*, 6 October 1918, D2.

66 *Sheboygan Press*, 29 October 1919, 1.

67 *Milwaukee Journal*, 15 December 1919, 1.

68 *Statutes of the United States of America, 66th Cong., 1st Sess.* (Washington, D.C.: Government Printing Office, 1919), chap. 85, 1919: 307–8.

69 *Milwaukee Journal*, 30 June 1919, 1; Paul W. Glad, "When John Barleycorn Went into Hiding in Wisconsin," *Wisconsin Magazine of History* 68, no. 2 (Winter 1984–85): 131. Research by Richard Rossin Jr. indicates that a few breweries reopened during the confusion of the conflicting laws.

70 Glad, "When John Barleycorn Went into Hiding," 119.

71 *History of Iron County* (Hurley, Wis.: Iron County WPA Historical Project 6555, 1937–38), 342.

72 *Sheboygan Press*, 3 March 1919, 6.

73 Cochran, *The Pabst Brewing Company*, 325.

74 *Sheboygan Press*, 8 April 1920, 1.

75 *Sheboygan Press*, 26 June 1920, 1.

76 *Sheboygan Press*, 12 February 1925, 17; 20 March 1925, 12; 10 June 1925, 1; 1 July 1931, 21; *Appleton Post-Crescent*, 16 January 1925, 1.

77 *Sheboygan Press*, 7 June 1926, 16.

78 *Appleton Post-Crescent*, 26 September 1924, 1; 10 December 1924, 1.

79 Barbara Barquist, *Oconomowoc: Barons to Bootleggers* (Oconomowoc, Wis.: Barbara and David Barquist, ca. 1999), 245–50; *Sheboygan Press*, 23 January 1930, 1. Product valued at $51,000 in 1925 would have been worth at least $698,000 in 2016 (https://MeasuringWorth.com).

80 *Sheboygan Press*, 23 July 1926, 1; 10 October 1929, 1; 6 August 1931, 8.

81 *Sheboygan Press*, 22 January 1921, 1.

82 *Sheboygan Press*, 4 September 1926, 2.

83 *City of Antigo Diamond Jubilee, 1878–1953* (Sparks-Doernenburg Post no. 3, American Legion, 1953), 24, 42; *Sheboygan Press*, 23 March 1937, 20.

84 *Sheboygan Press*, 3 March 1919, 2.

85 *The Gate to Eline's* (Milwaukee: Eline's, ca. 1922), 2, 5, 6, 9.

86 "Business & Finance: Resurrection," *Time*, 3 April 1933, http://www.time.com/time/magazine/article/0,9171,753648-5,00.html#ixzz0n7TgpcBr; Michael R. Reilly, "Joseph Schlitz Brewing Co.: A Chronological History, 1907–1933" (Sussex-Lisbon Area Historical Society, revised 24 March 2013), http://www.slahs.org/schlitz/history4.htm.

87 *Sheboygan Press*, 3 March 1919, 2; Cochran, *The Pabst Brewing Company*, 332–33.

88 *Sheboygan Press*, 20 February 1928, 10.

89 Cochran, *The Pabst Brewing Company*, 335; *Pittsburgh Press*, 12 November 1929, 27; 25 July 1930, 29; 17 October 1945, 18; *Milwaukee Sentinel*, 10 November 1940, "American Weekly" supplement, 16.

90 Jim Widner, "Gildersleeve and the Pabst-ett Mystery," *Old Radio Times* 15 (February 2007): 6–7. The last advertisement found during this research for Pabst-ett was from 1952.

91 *Milwaukee Journal*, 7 July 1931, 9.

92 Richard J. Merrill, "Personal Remembrances of Ralph Lucas Merrill" (unpublished manuscript, September 2006, author's collection).

93 Tina Susedik, *Among the Prairies and Rolling Hills: A History of Bloomer Township* (Eau Claire, Wis.: privately published, ca. 2000), 148.

94 *Eau Claire Leader*, 28 July 1923, 12.

95 *Sheboygan Press*, 6 April 1931, 3.

96 *Sheboygan Press*, 13 April 1929, 10.

97 *Sheboygan Press*, 13 April 1926, 18.

98 *Sheboygan Press*, 14 March 1929, 19.

99 *Sheboygan Press*, 22 May 1931, 1, 2.

100 *Winona (Minn.) Republican-Herald*, 9 April 1932, 3; 12 April 1932, 3; 14 April 1932, 3.

101 *Sheboygan Press*, 23 February 1929, 1, 16.

102 Betsy Foley, ed., *The Green Bay Area in History and Legend: Green Bay Press-Gazette Articles by Jack Rudolph* (Green Bay, Wis.: Brown County Historical Society, 2004), 126.

103 One example was Fauerbach Brewing of Madison, which continued to sponsor bowling teams throughout Prohibition. *Capital Times*, 4 February 1927, 11.

104 *Sheboygan Press-Telegram*, 24 December 1923, 9.

105 *Milwaukee Journal*, 3 November 1926, 1.

106 Glad, "When John Barleycorn Went into Hiding," 135; *Milwaukee Sentinel*, 12 August 1930, 3.

107 *Sheboygan Press*, 17 November 1930, 7; *Appleton Post-Crescent*, 17 November 1930, 15.

Chapter 7. Back to Work, Off to War

1 *Sheboygan Press*, 5 September 1931, 20.

2 Minutes of Board of Directors Meeting, 7 September 1931, Effinger Brewing Co. Records (hereafter Effinger Records), MS 419, box 1, folder 2, Wisconsin Historical Society, Madison, 103.

3 While nine other states had a repeal measure on the ballot, Wisconsin had no such referendum to gauge more precisely how motivated voters were by repeal. *Racine Journal-Times*, 10 November 1932, 1.

4 House of Representatives, 73rd Cong., 1st Sess., Document No. 3, "Immediate Modification of the Volstead Act," original in Franklin D. Roosevelt Papers (hereafter Roosevelt Papers), Roosevelt Library, Hyde Park, N.Y., official file 761: Liquor, folder 1.

5 Baron, *Brewed in America*, 321.

6 Common Council of the City of Milwaukee, File Number 51283, 20 March 1933, in Roosevelt Papers, official file 761: Liquor, folder 1.

7 *Sheboygan Press*, 10 November 1932, 3.

8 *Sheboygan Press*, 24 March 1933, 4.

9 Minutes of Board of Directors Meeting, 7 September 1931, Effinger Records, box 1, folder 2, 104.

10 *Ripon Press*, 30 March 1933, 1, 2nd sec.

11 *Winona (Minn.) Republican-Herald*, 6 July 1934, 12; Sanborn Insurance Map, Arcadia, 1914: 3.

12 *Rhinelander Daily News*, 1 November 1933, 2.

13 *Sheboygan Press*, 20 April 1933, 3.

14 *Sheboygan Press*, 10 November 1932, 3.

15 *Sheboygan Press*, 24 March 1933, 4.

16 Jonathan Kasparek, "FDR's 'Old Friends' in Wisconsin," *Wisconsin Magazine of History* 84, no. 4 (Summer 2001): 18–21.

17 *Sheboygan Press*, 18 March 1933, 1.

18 *Sheboygan Press*, 6 April 1933, 2.

19 *Milwaukee Journal*, 6 April 1933, 10.

20 *Oshkosh Daily Northwestern*, 7 April 1933, 4.

21 *Milwaukee Journal*, 7 April 1933, 1.

22 *Sheboygan Press*, 7 April 1933, 1. The number of breweries open on 7 April in Wisconsin is unclear. Twenty-seven breweries had permits in time, and the *West Bend (Weekly) News* of 12 April 1933 claimed that "twenty-seven breweries are busy at the present time turning out their product," but it is not possible to confirm six of the breweries at this date owing to lack of coverage in local newspapers. In *Brewed in America*, Stanley Baron stated that "some 31 brewers" nationwide were back in operation by June 1933, but this number was reached on the first day in Wisconsin and Minnesota alone.

23 *Stevens Point Daily Journal*, 7 April 1933, 1. The beer sent to the president was forwarded to the National Press Club.

24 *Winona (Minn.) Republican-Herald*, 11 April 1933, 7.

25 *Sheboygan Press*, 28 April 1933, 4; 8 May 1933, 6; *Milwaukee Journal*, 7 April 1933, 3; 8 April 1933, 2; *Two Rivers Reporter*, 7 April 1933, 1.

26 *Milwaukee Journal*, 7 April 1933, 1.

27 *Milwaukee Journal*, 9 April 1933, 1.

28 *Sheboygan Press*, 17 June 1933, 8; *Green Bay Press-Gazette*, 23 June 1933, 3.

29 *Milwaukee Journal*, 7 April 1933, spec. sec. 8.

30 *Milwaukee Journal*, 7 April 1933, 3.

31 *Milwaukee Journal*, 7 April 1933, supp. 1–16.

32 *Milwaukee Journal*, 22 March 1933, 1; *Cleveland (Ohio) Plain Dealer*, 9 April 1933, 8.

33 *Milwaukee Journal*, 9 April 1933, 3.

34 *Berlin Evening Journal*, 5 April 1933, 2.

35 *Appleton Post-Crescent*, 6 April 1933, 7.

36 Michael D. Benter, *Roll Out the Barrels: Brewers of Eastern Dodge County, Wisconsin, 1850–1961* (privately published, 2004), 122–25.

37 Data on the number of breweries producing ale and bock and the approximate years they were produced are from John Vetter, *The New Who's Who in Brew* (Fairfax, Va.: privately published, 2000).

38 *West Bend News*, 12 April 1933, 1. An active search located only two other mentions of Wisconsin-made bock beer in 1933, for Sheboygan Brewing and Peoples Brewing of Oshkosh.

39 American Brewers' Association, bulletin no. 21, 23 March 1936, in Stevens Point Beverage Co. Records 1927–1979 (hereafter SPB Records), box 1, folder: American Brewers' Association, 1935–1936, University of Wisconsin–Stevens Point (UWSP).

40 Ted Marti, August Schell Brewing Co., Minnesota, interview by author, 8 July 2005.

41 *Mayville News*, 5 April 1933, in Benter, *Roll Out the Barrels*, 115.

42 Tom Lewis, "Small Brewery Decline Hits Breunig's," *Eau Claire Leader Telegram*, 5 October 1973, 7.

43 C. S. Tutton to Wm. M. Schneller, 26 September 1942, Register of the Wisconsin Division of Beverage and Cigarette Taxes General Correspondence, 1934–1944 (hereafter BTD), box 17, folder 56, Wisconsin Historical Society, Madison.

44 L. E. McKinnon to Robert K. Henry (state treasurer), 14 March 1935, BTD, box 3, folder 17, WHS.

45 Otto Tiegs, "Stork Brewery, Inc.," *American Breweriana Journal*, July–August 1995, 10.

46 Dale P. Van Wieren, *American Breweries II* (West Point, Pa.: Eastern Coast Breweriana Association, 1995), 388–423, for listings of breweries in Wisconsin, including those that acquired permits after 1932 but did not produce.

47 *Sheboygan Press*, 8 July 1933, 4; *Monroe Evening Times*, 6 April 1933, 1; *Milwaukee Journal*, 15 May 1946, B1; *Bloomer Advance*, 28 September 1933, 1.

48 *Sheboygan Press*, 28 July 1933, 17; *Wisconsin State Journal*, 24 May 1933, 4; *Milwaukee Sentinel*, 16 July 1933, B12; 15 June 1934, 17; *Milwaukee Journal*, 3 June 1933, 3; 2 December 1934, 2–5.

49 *Green Bay Press-Gazette*, 15 February 1936, 4.

50 American Brewers' Association circular, 5 April 1937,

SPB Records, box 1, folder: American Brewers' Association, 1935–1936, UWSP.

51 *Local Job Descriptions for Two Establishments in the Malt Liquor Manufacturing Industry,* Preliminary Job Study No. 5-113, Works Progress Administration and Minnesota Department of Education (St. Paul: United States Employment Center, 1939), 2–6. While the study used two unnamed St. Paul breweries as examples, the jobs described would have existed at any other similarly sized brewery.

52 *Winona (Minn.) Republican-Herald,* 23 June 1935, 14; 6 May 1936, 11; 3 April 1937, 12; 26 June 1937, 10; 29 October 1938, 12; 24 January 1941, 12; 16 April 1939, 14; 21 March 1941, 14.

53 *Rhinelander Daily News,* 1 November 1933, 2.

54 *Freeport (Ill.) Journal Standard,* 9 August 1935, 3; *Milwaukee Sentinel,* 27 August 1935, sec. 2, 18. The Freeport advertisement is the earliest found so far.

55 Cochran, *The Pabst Brewing Company,* 390.

56 *Fortune,* January 1936, 75, 80.

57 Otto Tiegs, "Merrill, Wisconsin's Own Leidiger Brewing Co.," *American Breweriana Journal* 77 (November–December 1995): 7.

58 Skilnik, *The History of Beer and Brewing in Chicago,* 121–201.

59 BTD correspondence with Prima Brewing, various dates, BTD, box 4, folder 3, WHS.

60 BTD to Wisconsin Brewing Co., various dates, BTD, box 5, folder 14; BTD correspondence with Smith & Wesson, various dates, BTD, box 4, folder 14, WHS.

61 *Stevens Point Daily Journal,* 8 April 1933, 1; SPB Records, box 1, folder: ABA, 1936–37, UWSP.

62 American Brewers' Association bulletin, 23 December 1936, SPB Records, box 1, folder: American Brewers' Association, 1935–1936, UWSP; *Code of Fair Competition for the Bottled Soft Drink Industry* (Washington, D.C.: Government Printing Office, 1934), in SPB Records, box 5, UWSP.

63 J. N. Dribben (La Crosse Breweries) to Robert K. Henry (BTD), 4 June 1935, and Henry to Dribben, 5 June 1935, BTD, box 2, folder 20, WHS; John W. Roach (BTD) to R. C. Zimmerman (Pabst), 26 January 1940, BTD, box 16, folder 26, WHS.

64 David S. Rouse, "Pages from My Past: The Civilian Conservation Corps," *Wisconsin Magazine of History* 71, no. 3 (Spring 1988): 208.

65 Mortimer M. Kassell, "Interstate Tax Conflicts from an Administrative Viewpoint," in *Federal-State-Local Tax Correlation* (Princeton, N.J.: Tax Institute, 1954), 147.

66 Foreword, *Tax Relations among Governmental Units* (New York: Tax Policy League, 1938), v; Mabel Newcomer, "The Federal, State and Local Tax Structure After the War," in *Symposium on Taxation and the Social Structure* (Philadelphia: American Philosophical Society, 1944), 50, 54.

67 *Brewers Almanac 1949* (New York: United States Brewers Foundation, 1949), 85.

68 *Brewers Almanac 1949,* 86–87.

69 John W. Roach to Arcadia Brewing Company, 3 February 1941, BTD, box 17, folder 56, WHS; American Brewers' Association Circular, 15 June 1937, SPB Records, box 1, folder: ABA 1936–37, UWSP. In the revisions of 11 June 1937, the Federal Alcohol Administration dropped its objections to the use of "refreshing," "digestible," and "wholesome."

70 Grain Belt Breweries Inc. Records (hereafter Grain Belt Records), box 14, folder 3, various documents from 1935 to 1939, Minnesota Historical Society, St. Paul. Minneapolis Brewing Company changed its name to Grain Belt Breweries Inc. in 1967.

71 BTD correspondence with *Modern Brewery,* 27 November 1936 and 2 December 1936: BTD, box 3, folder 12, WHS.

72 E. S. Horn to Robert K. Henry, 14 March 1936, BTD, box 3, folder 20, WHS.

73 Van Wieren, *American Breweries II.* Many of these would-be breweries have been confirmed by local accounts.

74 American Brewers' Association, bulletin no. 21, 23 March 1936, in SPB Records, PCHS Collection 59, box 1, folder: American Brewers' Association, 1935–1936, UWSP.

75 Arthur Pugh (BTD) to A. Gettelman Brewing Co., 25 March 1939; Fred Gettelman to BTD, 27 March 1939, BTD, box 14, folder 36; W. A. Franz (Miller Brewing Co.) to Pugh, 27 March 1939, BTD, box 16, folder 1, WHS.

76 "Wisconsin Beer Stamp Sales July, 1934," folder: Beer Stamp Sales—1934–1940, Wisconsin Division of Beverage and Cigarette Taxes, Series 1524 MAD 2M/5/G6.

77 Adam Scheidt Brewing Co. to Beverage Tax Division, 26 July 1937, BTD, box 11, folder 46; Cervecería Cuauhtémoc S.A. to Beverage Tax Division, 22 August 1939, BTD, box 14, folder 6, WHS.

The degree to which Hamm's beer penetrated the Wisconsin market by the 1960s is visible in the number of Hamm's signs still mounted outside Wisconsin taverns.

78 "List of Registered Out-of-State Brewers and Wholesalers of Fermented Malt Beverages, January 15, 1940," BTD, box 14, folder 40, WHS.

79 Cochran, *The Pabst Brewing Company*, 390. "The Army Calls for Beer" is the headline of an editorial by Jos. Dubin in *Modern Brewery Age*, July 1943, 9.

80 D. H. Prichard to Weber Waukesha Brewing Co., 29 July 1944, BTD, box 32, folder 9; Prichard to Carl Ebner Brewing Co., 28 July 1944, BTD, box 27, folder 9, WHS.

81 Baron, *Brewed in America*, 332–34; Barr, *Drink*, 335.

82 Lyle H. Nolop, memo to L. N. Weinberg, 18 August 1940, BTD, box 14, folder 33; E. S. Horn (Oshkosh Brewing) to Roach, 22 August 1940, BTD, box 16, folder 22, WHS.

83 *Modern Brewery Age*, June 1943, 18.

84 Application, 12 June 1945; Office of Defense Transportation to Stevens Point Beverage Company, 20 June 1945, in SPB Records, box 5, folder: Office of Price Administration, 1943; 1944–47, UWSP. A replacement vehicle was eventually approved a week after V-J Day.

85 Car Occupancy Report, 9 February 1945, in SPB Records, box 5, folder: Office of Price Administration, 1943; 1944–47, UWSP.

86 Undated circular, Capitol Brewing Co.; Kenneth M. Orchard (Wis. Dept. of Agriculture) to Capitol Brewing Co., 8 January 1942, BTD, box 22, folder 34, WHS.

87 *New York Times*, 30 April 1943, 31; R. C. Zimmerman (Pabst) to Roach (3 July 1942), BTD, box 23, folder 4, WHS (Zimmerman said the slogan "does certainly express a lot of good ideas").

88 *La Crosse Tribune and Leader Press*, 28 June 1942, 5.

89 "Notes on Estimates of Minimum Civilian Consumer Requirements," *New York Times*, 21 February 1942, 24; *Modern Brewery Age*, March 1943, 10.

90 *Brewers Digest*, October 1946, 29.

91 Kihm Winship, "Three Millennia of Beer Styles," *All about Beer* 21, no. 1 (March 2000): 31; Roland C. Amundson, "Listen to the Bottle Say Gluek, Gluek, Gluek," *Hennepin History* (Winter 1988–89): 7; *Index to Patents and Trademarks* (Washington, D.C.: U.S. Patent and Trademark Office, 1943, 1944).

92 Kihm Winship, "Malt Liquor: A History," *Faithful Readers*, 29 April 2012, https://faithfulreaders.com/2012/04/29/malt-liquor-a-history. American brewers generally define malt liquor as a high-alcohol, low-cost lager beer. Confusingly, some states, including Minnesota, applied the term to any strong beer, and governments also used the term to refer to any fermented malt beverage.

93 Tiegs, "Merrill," 8; Jos. Dubin, "Stop Transferring Malt Quotas," *Modern Brewery Age*, November 1943, 11.

94 *New York Times*, 5 May 1943, 33; 12 September 1943, S11.

95 *Brewers Digest*, March 1945, 59; April 1945, 33; July 1945, 60.

96 F. J. Luetscher (Blatz) to John W. Roach (BTD), 6 May 1942, BTD, box 18, folder 15, WHS.

97 George D. Wolff (Wausau) to Roach, 24 November 1942, BTD, box 25, folder 5, WHS.

98 *Brewers Digest*, August 1945, 33, 41.

99 *Winona (Minn.) Republican-Herald*, 31 January 1945, 4; *Waukesha Freeman*, 21 March 1944, 3.

100 *Brewers Digest*, June 1946, 32; *Winona (Minn.) Republican-Herald*, 14 May 1946, 3; *Rhinelander Daily News*, 6 December 1946, 2.

101 *Milwaukee Journal*, 1 May 1946, L6.

102 *Milwaukee Journal*, 15 May 1946, L1; 16 May 1946, L2.

103 *Manitowoc Herald-Times*, 21 October 1948, 5

104 *Milwaukee Sentinel*, 18 March 1952, sec. 2, 6.

Chapter 8. The American Way of Beer

1 *Brewers Digest*, February 1950, 30.

2 *Brewers Almanac: 1952* (New York: United States Brewers Foundation, 1952), 3.

3   *Brewers Digest,* April 1952, 59–60.

4   Bernie Erf, "To Make Out They're Pushing Carry-Out," *Brewers Digest,* July 1953, 40–41.

5   Ross M. Dick, "Blatz to Offer a New Beer," *Milwaukee Journal,* 15 August 1955, sec. 2, 1.

6   *Brewers Digest,* June 1946, 32; October 1946, 10.

7   *Omaha World-Herald,* 28 May 1967, in Grain Belt records, box 8, scrapbook 1964–68, Minnesota Historical Society, St. Paul.

8   *Wisconsin State Journal,* 2 April 1969, 4–7; *Capital Times,* 4 April 1969, 7; 12 June 1969, 5; *Schlitz Brewing Co. Beer Commercials* (Manitowish Waters, Wis.: American Breweriana Association Museum Foundation, 2012), DVD. The last print ads discovered for the brand were by suburban Chicago liquor stores selling their stock of leftover Encore goblets in early 1973. The brand was mentioned in an article about a new Schlitz plant in New York, but the author was apparently quoting from old company publicity material.

9   *Brewers Digest,* January 1957, 42–43; *Milwaukee Sentinel,* 3 January 1957, sec. 4, 2; *Oneonta (N.Y.) Star,* 15 March 1957, 3. Sassy was advertised as far away as New York and Pennsylvania, but the last ad found was from 1959, and the previous one had been a year earlier. It is likely that the 1959 product was old stock, since "one of the biggest selling points" was the shelf life of Sassy, which was more than a year.

10 William O. Baldwin, "Historical Geography of the Brewing Industry: Focus on Wisconsin" (Ph.D. diss.; Urbana: University of Illinois, 1966; Ann Arbor, Mich.: University Microfilms edition 1979), 102–7. Business analysts disagreed on which breweries belonged in the category of national shipping brewer (which was not the same as giant). Miller usually replaced Blatz in later periods, Falstaff and Hamm were sometimes included, and Ballantine was sometimes classed as a regional even though it was the only nationally distributed ale brand (the demand for ale was highest in the Northeast). Anheuser-Busch, Schlitz, and Pabst were the only three included in every study.

11 Douglas F. Greer, "Product Differentiation and Concentration in the Brewing Industry," *Journal of Industrial Economics* 19, no. 3 (July 1971): 202; Ira Horowitz and Ann R. Horowitz, "Firms in a Declining Market: The Brewing Case," *Journal of Industrial Economics* 13, no. 2 (March 1965): 130; *Brewers Almanac: 1973* (New York: United States Brewers' Association, 1973), 3.

12 Baldwin, "Historical Geography of the Brewing Industry," 108.

13 Horowitz and Horowitz, "Firms in a Declining Market," 131; Cochran, *The Pabst Brewing Company,* 376; A. M. McGahan, "The Emergence of the National Brewing Oligopoly: Competition in the American Market, 1933–1958," *Business History Review* 65 (Summer 1991): 270–71.

14 John Smallshaw, "History of Falstaff Beer," accessed 22 June 2014, http://www.falstaffbrewing.com/history-falstaff-brewing.htm; Baron, *Brewed in America,* 339–40.

15 Baron, *Brewed in America,* 339–40; Cochran, *The Pabst Brewing Company,* 376–77; McGahan, "The Emergence of the National Brewing Oligopoly," 265, 271.

16 "Pabst Buys L.A. Brewing Company," *La Crosse Tribune,* 13 May 1948, 13; *Manitowoc Herald-Times,* 24 October 1953, 3; 18 November 1953, T7; *Oakland Tribune,* 16 November 1953, 22; *Corona (Calif.) Daily Independent,* 28 October 1953, 3; "Big Brewers Move West," *Business Week,* 16 January 1954, 128; Baron, *Brewed in America,* 341 (Baron erroneously dates the opening of Pabst in Los Angeles to 1954).

17 *Sheboygan Press,* 18 March 1949, 2.

18 *Racine Journal-Times,* 6 August 1952, 6.

19 *Van Nuys News,* 25 January 1955, 11B.

20 *Schlitz Brewing Co. Beer Commercials.*

21 Gurda, *Miller Time,* 142.

22 *Brewers Digest,* November 1971, 55–56, 62–68.

23 *Oshkosh Daily Northwestern,* 3 November 1961, 7; *Brewers Digest,* March 1959, 20–21.

24 *Brewers Digest,* November 1969, 65.

25 *Brewers Digest,* February 1957, 12; June 1970, 26, 46; June 1972, 69.

26 *Sheboygan Press,* 7 January 1959, 4

27 *Racine Journal-Times,* 1 October 1960, 12.

28 *Stevens Point Daily Journal,* 5 May 1960, 7

29 *Capital Times,* 27 August 1960, 19; 24 November 1960, 4.

30 United States v. Pabst Brewing Co., 384 US 546 (1966); *Oshkosh Daily Northwestern,* 18 July 1966, 12.

31   *Capital Times,* 15 November 1960, 6; 9 February 1961, 4.

32   *Capital Times,* 20 February 1964, 2; *Sheboygan Press,* 9 October 1964, 9; *Capital Times,* 25 March 1965, 6; *Manitowoc Herald-Times,* 2 April 1965, 10T; 16 August 1965, T5; United States v. Jos. Schlitz Brewing Company, 253 F. Supp. 129—Dist. Court (N.D. Calif. 1966).

33   "108-Year-Old Brewery's Race Policy Pays Big Dividends in Beer Sales," *Our World,* April 1952; reprint edition published by Pabst Brewing, 2.

34   *Brewers Digest,* December 1969, 20–26; November 1970, 28; *Milwaukee Sentinel,* 8 November 1969, 2–5.

35   *Oshkosh Daily Northwestern,* 24 April 1970, 8. Despite claims that Peoples was the first black-owned brewery in the country, the title actually belonged to Sunshine Brewing of Reading, Pa., which preceded Peoples by seven months. *Brewers Digest,* November 1970, 38.

36   *New York Times,* 15 May 1971, 39; *Oshkosh Daily Northwestern,* 5 November 1971, 1.

37   *Milwaukee Journal,* 16 February 1971, sec. 2, 1.

38   *Sheboygan Press,* 19 June 1971, 7; 2 July 1971, 3.

39   *Milwaukee Journal,* 4 December 1972, sec. 2, 19.

40   *Milwaukee Journal,* 3 November 1972, sec. 1, 1.

41   *Sheboygan Press,* 14 November 1972, 10.

42   *Sheboygan Press,* 12 March 1973, 10.

43   Otto Tiegs and Bob Pirie, "Potosi Brewing Co.—Preserving the History and Tradition," *American Breweriana Journal* 132 (November–December 2004): 25; John Dutcher, interview by author, 8 August 2009.

44   *Working with Schlitz* (Milwaukee: Jos. Schlitz Brewing, 1946), 27.

45   *A Two-Way Street* (La Crosse: G. Heileman Brewing, 1946), 49.

46   *Appleton Post-Crescent,* 3 June 1961, 13; 5 June 1961, 30.

47   *Winona (Minn.) Republican Herald,* 22 June 1955, 18; 23 June 1955, 7; 6 July 1955, 1.

48   *Sheboygan Press,* 14 May 1971, 1.

49   *Sheboygan Press,* 17 May 1971, 2.

50   *Appleton Post-Crescent,* 5 April 1960, 2.

51   *Sheboygan Press,* 14 May 1953, 1.

52   *Sheboygan Press,* 20 May 1953, 25.

53   *Sheboygan Press,* 23 May 1953, 10.

54   *Sheboygan Press,* 29 July 1953, 20.

55   McGahan, "The Emergence of the National Brewing Oligopoly," 276; Herbst, Roussin, and Kious, *St. Louis Brews,* 22–26, 43.

56   Horowitz and Horowitz, "Firms in a Declining Market," 131; Greer, "Product Differentiation and Concentration," 203.

57   *Oshkosh Daily Northwestern,* 16 March 1957, 1; Baldwin, "Historical Geography of the Brewing Industry," 110–12.

58   *Sheboygan Press,* 1 July 1953, 16.

59   *Sheboygan Press,* 30 July 1953, 23.

60   *Sheboygan Press,* 30 July 1953, 23.

61   *Sheboygan Press,* 30 July 1953, 23.

62   *Sheboygan Press,* 10 June 1969, 15.

63   McGahan, "The Emergence of the National Brewing Oligopoly," 276.

64   *Appleton Post-Crescent,* 31 July 1965, A2.

65   *Sheboygan Press,* 11 February 1966, 10.

66   *Sheboygan Press,* 12 June 1969, 12; *Milwaukee Sentinel,* 3 July 1969, n.p., clipping in microfilm roll 257, Milwaukee County Historical Society.

67   *Sheboygan Press,* 15 July 1969, 1.

68   Doug Hoverson, "Brewing Returns to Good Old Potosi," *Brewery History,* no. 155 (2013): 110–12.

69   Koeller and DeLano, *Brewed with Style,* 34.

70   Koeller and DeLano, *Brewed with Style,* 33–40.

71   Jim Drager and Mark Speltz, *Bottoms Up: A Toast to Wisconsin's Historic Bars and Breweries* (Madison: Wisconsin Historical Society Press, 2012), 1, 66–67.

72   McGahan, "The Emergence of the National Brewing Oligopoly," 242; *Brewers Almanac: 1973,* 66–81.

73   Effinger Records, box 5, folder 18. Wisconsin law allows bars to sell unopened bottles to customers to take to another location for consumption. Bars, liquor stores, and grocery stores regularly sought legislation to restrict the sales of other types of retailers.

74   John Steiner, interview by author, 24 April 2013.

75   Otto Tiegs, interview by author, 8 July 2012.

76   Effinger Records, MSS 419, box 5, folder 17.

77 *Appleton Post-Crescent,* 12 November 1962, 20; 22 March 1964, 50.

78 *Eau Claire Leader,* 22 November 1967, 8B.

79 *Marshfield News-Herald,* 24 October 1967, n.p., in folder: Breweries Closed 1966–1970, Beer Institute, Washington, D.C.

80 *Oshkosh Daily Northwestern,* 23 December 1964, 29; Fred J. Effinger to Alcohol and Tobacco Tax Division, 12 March 1960, Effinger Records, box 5, folder 7.

81 *Marshfield News-Herald,* 24 October 1967, n.p., in folder: Breweries Closed 1966–1970.

82 *Duluth News-Tribune,* 16 February 1967, n.p., in folder: Breweries Closed 1966–1970.

83 Akin and Reiherzer, *The Breweries of Oshkosh,* 36.

84 *Brewers Bulletin,* 5 July 1962, n.p., in folder: Breweries Closed Prior 1966, Beer Institute, Washington, D.C.

85 *Wausau Record-Herald,* 31 December 1966, n.p., in folder: Breweries Closed Prior 1966.

86 *Brewers Bulletin,* 14 June 1965, n.p., in folder: Breweries Closed 1966–1970.

87 Unidentified newspaper clipping, ca. 1972, Potosi Brewing Co. Records, 1848–1977, Platteville MSS AG, box 84, folder 1, Area Research Center, University of Wisconsin–Platteville (hereafter Potosi Records).

88 Leo Holt, "The Regional Brewery," *Brewers Digest,* September 1955, 22.

89 "Blatz Advertising Figurines," http://www.slahs.org/history/brewery/blatz/figures.htm.

90 *Brewers' Association of America Bulletin,* no. 1848 (January 1972): 1–2.

91 William M. O'Shea to Edward R. Ragatz, 18 February 1972; Ragatz to O'Shea, 21 April 1972, Potosi Records, box 86, folder 5.

92 Adolph Schumacher to O'Shea, 22 September 1972, Potosi Records, box 86, folder 5.

93 Francis A. O'Brien to Fred J. Effinger, 11 May 1967; Effinger to O'Brien, 27 May 1967; Effinger Records, MSS 419, box 5, folder 10.

94 *Brewers' Association of America Bulletin,* no. 1682 (March 1965): 1. Punctuation and capitalization are in the original.

95 *Winona (Minn.) News,* 8 July 1965, n.p., in folder: Breweries Closed Prior 1966.

96 *Oshkosh Daily Northwestern,* 23 July 1956, 17; 26 July 1956, 13; 11 June 1956, 13; 14 September 1961, 23. The softball records were drawn from numerous papers during the era.

97 *Oshkosh Daily Northwestern,* 3 August 1960, 10.

98 Matthew Honer, "The Anchor of a Community: The Closing of the Potosi Brewing Company and the Town It Left Behind," *American Breweriana Journal* 170 (March–April 2011): 8; Tiegs and Pirie, "Potosi Brewing Co.," 30–31. Portions of this section on Potosi Brewing were adapted from this author's "Brewing Returns to Good Old Potosi."

99 R. W. Jaeger, "Closing of Potosi Brewery Spreads Gloom over Village," *Wisconsin State Journal,* 1 October 1972, sec. 4, 1.

100 Honer, "The Anchor of a Community," 8–9; Tiegs and Pirie, "Potosi Brewing Co.," 30.

101 Jaeger, "Closing of Potosi Brewery."

102 Jaeger, "Closing of Potosi Brewery."

103 Honer, "The Anchor of a Community," 9.

104 Jaeger, "Closing of Potosi Brewery."

Chapter 9. One Lite On, Other Lights Out

1 Steve Byers, "As Schlitz Sales Slump, Pabst May Edge Ahead," *Milwaukee Journal,* 21 October 1980, pt. 2, 9–10.

2 Koeller and DeLano, *Brewed with Style,* 25–26, 29.

3 Gurda, *Miller Time,* 142–45, 148.

4 *Moberly (Mo.) Monitor-Index and Democrat,* 22 August 1939, 3; *Lima (Ohio) News,* 26 October 1939, 14.

5 *Benton Harbor (Mich.) News-Palladium,* 26 January 1940, 7.

6 *Fitchburg (Mass.) Sentinel,* 5 May 1953, 8.

7 *Oakland (Calif.) Tribune,* 24 February 1953, D30.

8   *Portsmouth (N.H.) Herald,* 29 January 1954, 10.

9   *Syracuse (N.Y.) Post-Standard,* 6 September 1961, 7–8.

10 *Cedar Rapids (Iowa) Gazette,* 14 September 1961, 5A.

11 *Waunakee Tribune,* 23 October 1969, 2.

12 Frank Deford, *Lite Reading* (New York: Penguin Books, 1984), 29–30; Philip Van Munching, *Beer Blast: The Inside Story of the Brewing Industry's Bizarre Battles for Your Money* (New York: Random House, 1997), 29–31; Gurda, *Miller Time,* 150–51. Despite the generally accepted narrative of the allegedly insulting advertising, the early print ads featured headlines such as "It Doesn't Taste like It Doesn't Fill You Up" and the cans and bottles prominently featured the line "Doesn't Fill You Up." To emphasize its light nature, an eighty-ounce mug was offered in some markets as a premium with the line "When you really want to hoist a few." *Nashua (N.H.) Telegraph,* 28 September 1967, 11. Starting in 1968 the labels had to bear a large legend clarifying "Not a Weight Reducing Product," which was not particularly helpful. While many accounts suggest that Gablinger ads encouraged drinkers to consume less, 1971 ads touted it as "The First Beer Brewed to Be a Second Beer." *Nashua Telegraph,* 8 April 1971, 19.

13 Deford, *Lite Reading,* 26, 30–31.

14 Deford, *Lite Reading,* various pages; Bob Garfield, "Ad Age Advertising Century: The Top 100 Campaigns," *Advertising Age,* 29 March 1999, http://adage.com/article/special-report-the-advertising-century/ad-age-advertising-century-top-100-campaigns/140918.

15 Gurda, *Miller Time,* 152.

16 Gurda, *Miller Time,* 153–54.

17 Gurda, *Miller Time,* 167.

18 Gurda, *Miller Time,* 154.

19 Van Munching, *Beer Blast,* 48.

20 Gurda, *Miller Time,* 157.

21 Jacques Neher, "What Went Wrong," *Advertising Age,* 13 April 1981, 61.

22 Neher, "What Went Wrong," 62–63.

23 Neher, "What Went Wrong," 63. Sources differ on how much ABF cut fermentation time. Neher's article claims that it was cut from twelve days to four; others report that it was from nine days to seven.

24 Jeff Glynn, interview by author, 10 March 2012.

25 Jacques Neher, "Lost at Sea," *Advertising Age,* 20 April 1981, 49; Van Munching, *Beer Blast,* 42–43; Glynn interview.

26 Neher, "Lost at Sea," 50; *Wall Street Journal,* 16 March 1978, 16.

27 Van Munching, *Beer Blast,* 45.

28 *Wisconsin State Journal,* 19 August 1978, 1–3. Coburn later claimed that he had actually been paid $1 million, but that he had to say the words "400 or 500 times." He also quipped, "The commercials were effective, but the beer wasn't very good. . . . We had lots of initial sales, but no repeat sales." *Kenosha Sunday News,* 20 December 1981, B11. The fee would be in excess of $2.5 million in 2016 dollars.

29 Neher, "Lost at Sea," 50; Glynn interview; Ray Kenney, "Trying to Stop the Flight from Schlitz," *New York Times,* 1 March 1981, n.p., reprint in Schlitz folder, Beer Institute, Washington, D.C.; Carl Cannon, "Sellinger, a Miracle Worker, Has Schlitz on the Right Road," *Capital Times* (Madison), 16 March 1981, 22.

30 David A. Aaker, "Whatever Happened to . . . 'The Beer That Made Milwaukee Famous,'?" *Across the Board,* April 1992, 31.

31 Daniel Rosenheim, "Schlitz May Use Strike as Excuse to Leave Milwaukee," *Capital Times* (Madison), 23 July 1981, 1, 2; *Capital Times,* 28 July 1981, 13; *Capital Times,* 31 July 1981, 1.

32 *Wisconsin State Journal,* 28 November 1981, sec. 4, 1; *Milwaukee Journal,* 29 September 1981, 2–11.

33 *New York Times,* 6 April 1982, D4.

34 James Rowen, "Pain in the Heartland," *New York Times,* 8 July 1982, A19.

35 Victor J. Tremblay and Carol Horton Tremblay, *The U.S. Brewing Industry: Data and Economic Analysis* (Cambridge, Mass.: MIT Press, 2005), 148–49, 165.

36 *Pabst Brewing Co. 1980 Annual Report* (Milwaukee, 1981), 5–7; *Pabst Brewing Co. 1983 Annual Report* (Milwaukee, 1983), 1–2.

37 *Capital Times,* 29 July 1981, 19; 7 April 1982, 15; 14 November 1984, 17.

38 *Wisconsin State Journal,* 20 December 1984, sec. 1, 7; 3 January 1985, sec. 4, 3; *Milwaukee Journal,* 26 February 1985, pt. 3, 4.

39 Tina Daniell, "Pabst Wholesalers Fighting Bad Publicity," *Milwaukee Journal,* 9 April 1985, pt. 3, 4; John

Torinus Jr., "Pabst Gun-Fighting It, Smith Says of New Act," *Milwaukee Sentinel,* 11 August 1983, pt. 5, 2.

40 Torinus, "Pabst Gun-Fighting It."

41 John Steiner, Pabst Brewing Co., interview by author, 23–25 March 2013.

42 James E. Causey, "Pabst Faulted for Business Plan," *Milwaukee Journal Sentinel,* 19 October 1996, 8A; Torinus, "Pabst Gun-Fighting It."

43 James E. Causey and Rick Romell, "Taps for Pabst," *Milwaukee Journal Sentinel,* 18 October 1996, 1A, 12A; Alan J. Borsuk, "Brewer Has Gone from Rock Solid to Ground Down," *Milwaukee Journal Sentinel,* 18 October 1996, 1A, 12A.

44 Jesse Garza, "Workers Recall Concessions, Cry Betrayal," *Milwaukee Journal Sentinel,* 18 October 1996, 1A, 4A.

45 Georgia Pabst, "Pabst Shutdown Decision 'Deplorable,' Kleczka Says," *Milwaukee Journal Sentinel,* 18 October 1996, 4A.

46 Jim Chilsen, "Milwaukee Losing Fame in Brewing," *Daily Gazette* (Schenectady, N.Y.), 19 August 1995, E2.

47 Causey, "Pabst Faulted for Business Plan"; James E. Causey, "One Time Giant Pabst Falls Victim to Change," *Milwaukee Journal Sentinel,* 17 December 1995, 12–13D.

48 *Milwaukee Journal Sentinel,* 14 March 2001, D3; *Rome (Ga.) News-Tribune,* 20 September 2001, 6A.

49 *Reading (Pa.) Eagle & Reading Times,* 25 July 2001, A8.

50 Tom Daykin, "Pabst Looked at Return to Milwaukee," *Milwaukee Journal Sentinel,* 9 June 2006, 3D; Peter Lattman and David Kessmodel, "Pabst's New Owner Built Fortune on Old Brands," *Wall Street Journal,* 26 May 2010, B1.

51 Julie Wernau, "Sobering Move for Pabst Fans," *Chicago Tribune,* 14 May 2011, n.p.

52 Greg Kitsock, "Comrade Brewer," *American Brewer,* Fall 2014, 1.

53 John Cunniff, "Anheuser-Busch Is Battling with Miller over Löwenbräu," *Kentucky New Era* (Hopkinsville), 15 December 1977, 36; Van Munching, *Beer Blast,* 50–54; Gurda, *Miller Time,* 162–63; *Eugene (Ore.) Register-Guard,* 3 October 1999, 9D. Miller had acquired the exclusive rights to import German Löwenbräu in 1975. George Lazarus, "Miller Wins Lowenbrau Distribution," *Chicago Tribune,* 19 March 1975, sec. 4, 13 (no umlauts in original). Most accounts claim that Miller started to brew Löwenbräu in the United States in 1977, but a Miller spokesman admitted in 1977 in response to a lawsuit by a drinker that the domestic version had been brewed in Fort Worth since 1975. "Lowenbrau from Texas! He Sues Miller Brewing," *Des Moines Register,* 10 June 1977, 7S.

54 Steven R. Byers, "Schlitz Set to Unveil Top of the Line Beer," *Milwaukee Journal,* 1 February 1979, pt. 1, 1, 7; *Milwaukee Sentinel,* 8 January 1980, pt. 4, 2; Byers, "As Schlitz Sales Slump"; *Milwaukee Journal,* 17 April 1979, 6.

55 *Pabst Brewing Co. 1980 Annual Report,* 4–5.

56 Steve Byers, "Pabst to Sell 'Light' Dark Beer," *Milwaukee Journal,* 27 March 1979, pt. 1, 1.

57 Roger Stafford, "New Dark Beer from Pabst Puts Marketing Man in Brighter Mood," *Milwaukee Sentinel,* 4 June 1979, pt. 2, 11; *Milwaukee Journal,* 3 May 1979, pt. 3, 2; Steve Byers, "Miller's Latest: A Dark Light," *Milwaukee Journal,* 17 April 1979, pt. 1, 1, 6.

58 Gurda, *Miller Time,* 161–62; David I. Bednarek, "Miller Genuine Draft Makes List of Top 10 US Beers," *Milwaukee Journal,* 22 January 1990, 7C; Van Munching, *Beer Blast,* 94–98. Gurda claims that MGD was ninth in 1989; Bednarek cites sales figures placing it tenth.

59 Bamforth, *Beer,* 74.

60 David I. Bednarek, "Is the Dry Beer Market for Real?," *Milwaukee Journal,* 10 April 1990, 6–7C; Randolph Picht, "Infatuation with Dry Beer Could Be Passing Fad," *Hour* (Norwalk, Conn.), 26 August 1989, 16; Van Munching, *Beer Blast,* 232–36; Steve Byers, "Are We Ready for Dry Beer?," *Milwaukee Journal,* 22 January 1989, *Wisconsin* magazine, 14.

61 Bamforth, *Beer,* 73–74.

62 Lee Bergquist, "Miller Rolling Out Ice-Brewed Beer across the U.S.," *Milwaukee Sentinel,* 24 November 1993, 1D; Eric Gunn, "Miller Tries an Ice Beer," *Milwaukee Journal,* 21 September 1993, C1; Van Munching, *Beer Blast,* 244–48; Lee Bergquist, "Lite Ice: Miller to Offer Low-Cal Beer in February," *Milwaukee Sentinel,* 29 January 1994, 6B; Skip Wollenberg, "Will Ice Beer Craze Slowly Melt Away?," *Gainesville (Fla.) Sun,* 11 August 1994, 5B; Lee Bergquist, "Miller's Sales Rise the Most," *Milwaukee Sentinel,* 19 December 1994, D1, 8; *Modern Brewery Age,* 30 December 2014, 3.

63 Timothy J. Holian, *Over the Barrel: The Brewing History and Beer Culture of Cincinnati,* vol. 2, *Prohibition–2001* (St. Joseph, Mo.: Sudhaus Press, 2001), 315–16; "Nation's Brewers Test Marketing Low-Alcohol Beer," *Henderson (N.C.) Times-News,* 19 March 1984, 16; Helen Pauly, "Real Battle Brewing over Low-Alcohol Beer," *Milwaukee Journal,* 31 July 1984, pt. 2, 9, 12; "'LA' Fight Portrayed as Davids vs. Goliath," *Milwaukee Journal,* 26 September 1984, pt. 3, 9.

64 Ken Wysocky, "Miller, Heileman Win in L.A. Case," *Milwaukee Journal,* 5 January 1988, pt. 4, 3.

65 Van Munching, *Beer Blast,* 238–41; David I. Bednarek, "Pabst Hopes New Ads Build on Company's Progress," *Milwaukee Journal,* 12 April 1989, 10C; Ken Brekke, "Heileman Gets New Heat over Powerful Brew," *La Crosse Tribune,* 21 June 1991, n.p.; "Top Health Official Joins Brouhaha over Brew," *La Crosse Tribune,* 26 June 1991, n.p.; David Kraemer, "Priests to Meet with Heileman Officials," *La Crosse Tribune,* 29 June 1991, n.p.; Ken Brekke, "PowerMaster Is Dead," *La Crosse Tribune,* 2 July 1991, n.p.; Gayda Hollnagel, "Priest Says Changing Name Isn't Enough," *La Crosse Tribune,* 2 July 1991, n.p (these five *La Crosse Tribune* articles are all at Wisconsin Historical Society, La Crosse Area Resource Center, folder: G. Heileman: PowerMaster Controversy).

66 Van Munching, *Beer Blast,* 239–41, David Bauder, "Malt Liquor Ads Put Brewer, Rappers under Fire," *Milwaukee Journal,* 24 November 1991, E6; James E. Causey, "Stroh Signs Exclusive Deal on McKenzie River Beverages," *Milwaukee Journal,* 13 January 1997, 5D.

67 "New Crazy Horse Malt Liquor Insults Indians, Novello Says," *Milwaukee Journal,* 23 April 1992, C8–9.

68 "Victory for Crazy Horse: Minnesota Bans Sale of Malt Liquor Named after Sioux Leader," *Milwaukee Journal,* 11 May 1994, C7.

69 "Judge Rules in Favor of Crazy Horse Name," *Milwaukee Journal,* 14 April 1993, C9.

70 Elizabeth Stawicki, "Crazy Horse Dispute Settled," Minnesota Public Radio, 26 April 2001. Johnson was subsequently elected to the U.S. Senate.

71 Koeller and DeLano, *Brewed with Style,* 35.

72 *Barron's,* 3 July 1967, 1; *Dow Digest,* August 1968, 14, 16, 67.

73 Koeller and DeLano, *Brewed with Style,* 40–42.

74 Peter H. Blum, *Brewed in Detroit: Breweries and Beers since 1830* (Detroit: Wayne State University Press, 1999), 242. The Piels Bros. brewery of Brooklyn and Hampden-Harvard Breweries of Willimansett, Massachusetts, were not included in the sale.

75 Roger A. Stafford, "Heileman Closes Associated Deal," *Milwaukee Sentinel,* 1 August 1972, pt. 2, 5; "Heileman Agrees to Brand Cutbacks," *Milwaukee Journal,* 13 June 1973, pt. 2, 22; Koeller and DeLano, *Brewed with Style,* 45–46.

76 Tony Kennedy, "A Regional Brand's Boisterous Century," *Minneapolis Star Tribune,* 30 August 1993, 1D; "Brands Added by Heileman," *Milwaukee Sentinel,* 23 December 1975, pt. 2, 5; Koeller and DeLano, *Brewed with Style,* 44–46.

77 Koeller and DeLano, *Brewed with Style,* 46; "Heileman Purchases Company," *Milwaukee Journal,* 6 April 1977, pt. 2, 18. While Rainier was primarily a West Coast brand, it was later introduced in Milwaukee as a low-price brand. Chuck Doherty, "Heileman Trying a More-for-Less Strategy," *Milwaukee Sentinel,* 12 November 1991, 1D.

78 Koeller and DeLano, *Brewed with Style,* 49.

79 Steve Byers, "Heileman Charges into Brewing Elite," *Milwaukee Journal,* 9 March 1979, pt. 2, 15; Byers, "As Schlitz Sales Slump"; Carl Cannon, "Brewing '81: Anheuser-Busch Reigns 'King of Beers,'" *Milwaukee Sentinel,* 26 May 1981, pt. 6, 2; Koeller and DeLano, *Brewed with Style,* 54–58.

80 Koeller and DeLano, *Brewed with Style,* 103–8; Mike Ivey, "Heileman's Demise Had Its Roots in Takeover," *Capital Times,* 16 February 1999, 1C.

81 Koeller and DeLano, *Brewed with Style,* 135–41; Maxene Renner, "Same Brew Flows under New Owner," *La Crosse Tribune,* 29 March 1997, n.p., folder: La Crosse—Businesses: Breweries—General, Wisconsin Historical Society, La Crosse Area Research Center; "Stroh Brewery Agrees to Buy Rival Heileman," *Capital Times,* 29 February 1996, 1C.

82 Chris Roush, "Stroh Sells Brands to Miller, Pabst," *Pittsburgh Post-Gazette,* 9 February 1999, F8.

83 Koeller and DeLano, *Brewed with Style,* 143–46; Steve Cahalan, "Secrets of Success," *La Crosse Tribune,* 10 December 2001, D1.

84 Steve Cahalan, "On a Roll," *La Crosse Tribune,* 11 July 2010, H1.

85 Steve Cahalan, "Brewery Looks to Grow," *La Crosse Tribune*, 30 March 2011, B1–2.

86 Mike Tighe, "Old Style Returns to La Crosse," *La Crosse Tribune*, 22 July 2016, A1.

87 Van Munching, *Beer Blast*, 252–53; *Capital Times*, 6 October 1994, 11A; Mike Ivey, "Miller Seeks to Regain the High Life," *Capital Times*, 12 November 1996, 5C. In 1996 Anheuser-Busch and several other breweries sought federal rule changes that would prohibit the use of "fictitious trade names" like Plank Road Brewery. *Cedar Rapids Gazette*, 27 January 1996, 5B.

88 Gurda, *Miller Time*, 164–66; Chuck Doherty, "Miller Path to New Beer Wasn't Clear," *Milwaukee Sentinel*, 31 March 1993, 1D, 3D; "Miller's Clear Beer Goes the Way of the Edsel," *Fredericksburg (Va.) Free Lance-Star*, 29 September 1993, D7.

89 Tom Daykin, "U.S. on Tap," *Milwaukee Journal Sentinel*, 30 May 2002, 1–2D.

90 Gurda, *Miller Time*, 169–71; Daykin, "U.S. on Tap"; Tom Daykin, "Miller Will Be Sold for $5.6 Billion," *Milwaukee Journal Sentinel*, 30 May 2002, 1A, 14A.

91 Tom Daykin, "Miller, Molson Coors Deal Gets Closer," *Milwaukee Journal Sentinel*, 22 December 2007, 1–2D; MillerCoors, http://www.millercoors.com/who-we-are/locations.aspx.

92 MillerCoors, press release, 11 October 2016, https://www.millercoors.com/News-Center/Latest-News/molson-coors-completes-acquisition-of-full-ownership-of-millercoors-and-global-miller-brand-portfolio.

93 Tom Daykin, "Beer: Has Mainstream Lost Steam?," *Wilmington (N.C.) Star-News*, 2 December 2007, 4E.

Chapter 10. Return of the Local

1 Darlene E. Waterstreet, *Pre-Prohibition United States Beer Statistics 1934–2000* (Milwaukee: Badger Infosearch, 2003), 572.

2 David McAninch, "In Wisconsin Supper Clubs Open to All," *New York Times*, 23 November 2011, https://www.nytimes.com/2011/11/27/travel/wisconsin-supper-clubs-old-fashioned-and-open-to-all.html.

3 Van Munching, *Beer Blast*, 117–18.

4 Anchor Brewing Company, "Gold Rush to Earthquake," http://www.anchorbrewing.com/brewery/ourhistory.htm; Tom Acitelli, *The Audacity of Hops: The History of America's Craft Beer Revolution* (Chicago: Chicago Review Press, 2013), 3–4, 26–27,

5 *Monroe Evening Times*, 11 July 1957, 1; 3 June 1958, 1, 2; 3 July 1958, 6.

6 *Monroe Evening Times*, 6 April 1959, 2.

7 *Monroe Evening Times*, 6 April 1959, 2.

8 *Wisconsin State Journal*, 26 September 1972, sec. 2, 1.

9 Steve Hopkins, "House of Augsburger Has Taste of the Times," *Wisconsin State Journal*, 13 December 1987, sec. 2, 1.

10 *Capital Times*, 7 July 1979, 1.

11 *Wisconsin State Journal*, 13 December 1987, sec. 2, 1.

12 *Wisconsin State Journal*, 2 August 1987, 3, 1.

13 *Capital Times*, 17 May 1989, 12.

14 *Capital Times*, 2 November 1982, 10.

15 *Wisconsin State Journal*, 13 March 1983, sec. 4, 5.

16 *Wisconsin State Journal*, 25 January 1989, 1A.

17 Nathan Seppa, "Huber Brewing Bucks Trend and Rolls Out Barrels," *Wisconsin State Journal*, 19 June 1991, 8B.

18 Manjit Minhas and Ravinder Minhas, *Brewing Up a Damn Good Story* (Monroe, Wis.: Mountain Crest Publishing, 2009), 49; *Wisconsin State Journal*, 26 September 1982.

19 Minhas and Minhas, *Brewing Up a Damn Good Story*, 49.

20 *Capital Times*, 24 August 1995, 24

21 Minhas and Minhas, *Brewing Up a Damn Good Story*, 49.

22 Tere Dunlap, "Minhas Brewery Set to Break Record," *Wisconsin State Journal*, 17 August 2009, A5; Barry Adams, "Economies of Ale," *Wisconsin State Journal*, 21 November 2010, F1.

23 Minhas and Minhas, *Brewing Up a Damn Good Story*, 51–54; http://minhasbrewery.com/our-history.

24 *New Brewer,* May/June 2017, 57–58. Changes in the Brewers' Association's definition of craft beer allowed Minhas to be listed as a craft brewery for the first time in 2015.
25 *Stevens Point Journal,* 15 March 1989, 1; *St. Paul Pioneer Press-Dispatch,* 19 June 1989, 1B.
26 *Stevens Point Daily Journal,* 23 August 1962, 16; 13 May 1966, 16.
27 *Stevens Point Journal,* 10 December 1982, 6.
28 *Chicago Daily News,* 10 July 1973, reprint in UWSP Archives, folder: Stevens Point Brewery.
29 *Stevens Point Daily Journal,* 1 September 1973, 5.
30 *Stevens Point Daily Journal,* 1 September 1973, 5.
31 *Portage County Gazette,* 29 August 2003, in UWSP Archives, folder: Stevens Point Brewery; *Stevens Point Journal,* 10 December 1982, 6.
32 *Appleton Post-Crescent,* 3 October 1975, B1, B3.
33 *Wisconsin State Journal,* 24 August 1989, 1.
34 *Stevens Point Journal,* 15 March 1989, 1.
35 *Wisconsin State Journal,* 30 May 1990, 8B.
36 Mike Ivey, "Point Taps into Specialty Craze," *Capital Times,* 24 April 1996, 1C.
37 *Portage County Gazette,* 15 March 2002, 1.
38 http://www.pointbeer.com/point-nude-beach; http://www.pointbeer.com/history.
39 Stevens Point Brewery, press releases: 30 January 2013, 17 September 2012, 6 October 2015, 15 November 2105; James Page Brewing Co. website, http://www.jpbrewery.com/about.html.
40 Waterstreet, *Pre-Prohibition United States,* 375–76.
41 Waterstreet, *Pre-Prohibition United States*; "Leinenkugel's 125th Anniversary," commemorative supplement, *Chippewa Herald Telegram,* September 1992, 21, 28, 36; https://leinie.com/Heritage.aspx#.
42 *Modern Brewery Age,* 29 October 1973, n.p., clipping in folder: Breweries Sold, Beer Institute, Washington, D.C.
43 "Leinenkugel's 125th Anniversary," 36.
44 Mark Baker, "Merger with Miller Working Well: Jake," in "Leinenkugel's 125th Anniversary," 51.
45 *Wisconsin State Journal,* 26 March 1996, 8B.
46 *Wisconsin State Journal,* 11 January 2000, 8C.
47 Jacob Leinenkugel Brewing Co., https://leinie.com, Beers, Our Heritage—Brewery.
48 Waterstreet, *Pre-Prohibition United States,* 377–78.
49 Dan Bradford, "Hibernia Brewing," *All about Beer,* April 1986, 16–17; Bill Stokes, "A Brewer Takes a Stand to Beat the Bland," *Chicago Tribune,* 20 September 1985, Tempo sec., 1, 3.
50 Bradford, "Hibernia Brewing"; Stokes, "A Brewer Takes a Stand."
51 Bradford, "Hibernia Brewing"; Stokes, "A Brewer Takes a Stand"; Great American Beer Festival, http://www.greatamericanbeerfestival.com/the-competition/winners.
52 Fred Eckhardt, "Two Local Bock Beers Return to Traditional Brewing," *Oregonian* (Portland), 8 April 1986, FD12; Karin A. Wetzel, "Beer Made Old-World Fashion," *Columbus Dispatch,* 23 April 1986, 3E; Darel Jevens, "Hibernia's All Malt Gains Popularity in Chicago Market," *Eau Claire Leader Telegram,* 29 June 1987, 3A.
53 Stokes, "A Brewer Takes a Stand," 3.
54 *Wisconsin State Journal,* 21 September 1987, sec. 1, 9; 21 November 1987, sec. 4, 3.
55 Stokes, "A Brewer Takes a Stand," 3.
56 John Smallshaw, "Walter Brewing Co.—the Beer That Is Beer," http://www.falstaffbrewing.com/walter's.htm.
57 American Breweriana Association Brewery database.
58 Randy Sprecher, interview by author, 28 July 2012.
59 Kris Kodrich, "Brewery Owner Thirsts for Best," *Wisconsin State Journal,* 4 August 1988, 1D.
60 *Capital Times,* 15 August 1986, 11; Mike Ivey, "Sprecher Has Thirst for Survival," *Capital Times,* 19 March 1997, 1C.
61 *Midwest Beer Notes,* May/June 1994, 4.
62 *Wisconsin State Journal,* 27 August 1991, 5B; 23 July 1993, 7D.
63 Ivey, "Sprecher Has Thirst."
64 Mike Stamler, "Trio Gears Up to Produce Capital Beer," *Capital Times,* 12 January 1984, 10.
65 Al Perkins, "Brewer Talks Suds—Beer Suds," *Capital Times,* 2 August 1984, 10.
66 *Capital Times,* 29 October 1984, 10.

67 *New Brewer,* July–August 1985, 21.

68 *Wisconsin State Journal,* 6 April 2003, C1.

69 Jerry Apps, *Breweries of Wisconsin* (Madison: University of Wisconsin Press, 1992), 165–66.

70 *Capital Times,* 27 November 1998, C1.

71 Bob Paolino, "Lakefront Brewery Celebrates 20 Years," *Great Lakes Brewing News,* December 2007/January 2008, 15; Jim Klisch, interview by author, 28 July 2011.

72 Klisch interview.

73 Paolino, "Lakefront Brewery Celebrates 20 Years"; http://www.lakefrontbrewery.com/about.

74 http://www.lakefrontbrewery.com/about; Klisch interview.

75 Deb and Dan Carey, interviews by author, 11 August 2011; Lindsay Wettach, "Meet Our Neighbor . . . Carey Wants to Change Attitudes about Drinking," *New Glarus Post Messenger,* 13 June 2001, https://newglarusbrewing.com/brewery/headlines/page/11.

76 Carey interviews; *Midwest Beer Notes,* June/July 1996, 16; http://www.newglarusbrewing.com/index.cfm/beers/ourbeers/beer/wisconsin-belgian-red.

77 *Wisconsin State Journal,* 15 May 2005, C10.

78 Acitelli, *The Audacity of Hops,* 216, 265–68.

79 Acitelli, *The Audacity of Hops,* 84–85.

80 Ken Wysocky, "Century Hall Arsonist Used Natural Gas Blast," *Milwaukee Sentinel,* 29 July 1988, part 1, 5.

81 Rob LoBreglio, interview by author, 14 August 2010; Eliot Butler, interview by author, 12 August 2011; Robin Shepard, *Wisconsin's Best Breweries and Brewpubs* (Madison: University of Wisconsin Press, 2001), 42; *Capital Times,* 21 August 1994, 6B; 9 December 1994, 6B.

82 Shepard, *Wisconsin's Best Breweries,* 94.

83 Bob Paolino, *Great Lakes Brewing News* 12, no. 4 (August–September 2007): 35; Paolino, *Great Lakes Brewing News* 12, no. 6 (December 2007–January 2008): 34.

84 Acitelli, *The Audacity of Hops,* 265.

85 Acitelli, *The Audacity of Hops,* 245–54, 265–67.

86 Sig Pflagens, interview by author, April 2005.

87 John Dutcher, "A Visit to the University of Wisconsin–Platteville Micro Brewery," *Port of Potosi [Chapter] Newsletter* 3, no. 2 (Summer 2008): 4; John Dutcher and Thomas Nickels, interviews by author, 20 June 2008.

88 Jay Brooks, "Nano Breweries," *Brookston Beer Bulletin,* 11 February 2007; John Hall, "Nano-Breweries: Talk of the Craft Beer Nation," 2011, http://www.craftbeer.com.

89 Tim and Toni Eichinger, interview by author, 7 August 2010; http://www.blackhuskybrewing.com.

90 Robin Shepard, "MobCraft Beer Launching Crowdsourced, Community-Supported Brewing Operation in Madison," 8 May 2013, http://www.thedailypage.com.

91 https://www.mobcraftbeer.com/recipes/previous_winners.

92 Paul Graham, interview by author, 4 August 2010.

93 B. C. Kowalski, "Central Waters Brewing Co. Recognized for Environmental Energy Efficiency," 28 January 2011, https://Stevenspointjournal.com; http://centralwaters.com/about/renewable-energy.php.

94 Brad Bryan, "Midwest Hops and Barley Co-op," *Great Lakes Brewing News* 14, no. 3 (June–July 2009): 27.

95 Bob Paolino, *Great Lakes Brewing News* 16, no. 1 (February–March 2011): 39.

96 http://www.lakefrontbrewery.com/beer/seasonals/wisconsinite.

97 This section is based on dozens of interviews with Wisconsin craft brewers, whose individual contributions are not separated—often because they provided the information as background and not for specific attribution. Many provided similar stories. Also helpful in this section were many brewery websites, in particular the blogs or Facebook posts by Grant Pauly of 3 Sheeps Brewing and Tim Eichinger of Black Husky Brewing.

98 "Labor of Love," https://www.appletonbeerfactory.com/about; Mairi and Ben Fogel, interview by author, 31 July 2013.

99 Kyle Nabilcy, "Beers Called Bubbler," 17 May 2016, https://isthmus.com/api/search.html?q=Beers+Called+Bubbler+&sa=.

INDEX

100 Years of Brewing, 42, 48, 50
3 Sheeps Brewing Co., 310
4 Brothers Blended Beer, 548
841 Brewhouse, 671
8th Street Ale House, 621
AB InBev, merger with Miller, 309. *See also* Anheuser-Busch
Abendroth, William, 649
Abercrombie, Kerry, 660
Abercrombie, Kevin, 660
Able, Rheinhart, 620
Abrath, Henry, 386
Abresch, Charles, Co., 113–14
Abresch-Cramer Auto Truck Co., 114
Accardo, Tony, 658
accelerated batch fermentation (ABF), 287, 520
Ackerman, Andrew, 570
Ackerman, Audrey, 576
Ackermann, G. W., 382
Adams, Aaron, 396
Adams, Sandye, 396
Addison (Twp.), Wis. *See* St. Lawrence, Wis.
adjuncts, 22, 159, 240, 287, 329
Adler, Fred, 378
Adler Brau Pub & Restaurant, 365
advertising: cartoons, 269; expenditures on, 253, 285, 287; health and purity claims, 187, 188, 652; in magazines, 246, 252; in newspapers, 39, 43, 187, 195, 220–21, 226, 251, 253, 256, 270, 317, 458, 464, 466, 576; legal issues concerning, 247, 298, 302–3; on radio, 253, 317; on television, 5, 248–49, 252, 253, 274, 301, 531, 658; strategies, 247–48, 269–70, 293, 294, 302–3
African Americans: in advertising, 260, 301, 523; as brewery employees, 300; as brewery owners, 259–61, 374, n35, 578; marketing to, 259–61, 301, 302–3

agents. *See* branch offices; depots; distributors
Ahnapee, Wis. *See* Algoma, Wis.
Ahnapee Brewery (craft brewery), 360–61
Ahnapee Brewery/Brewing Co. (pre-Prohibition), 360
Aigner, Mathias, 385
Albany, N.Y., 95, 152
Albany, Wis., 176
Alberts, Tom, 637
Albion Brewery, 516
Albrecht, John, 589
alcoholism. *See* drunkenness
Aldrich, Hannah, 35
ale: characteristics of, 16, 17, 25, 27, 29–30, 128; imported into Wisconsin, 40, 53, 238; production of in Wisconsin, 21, 34, 35, 39–40, 41, 71, 136, 216, 217, 227, 249, 327, 438–39, 535, 578, 597, 646; as temperance drink, 170–72. *See also* beer: styles
Ale Asylum, 310, 351, 478
Alexis, Alexander, 423
Algoma, Wis., 360–63
Alix, Alberta, Rahr Malting facility in, 482
Allen, Brian, 579
Allen, Caroline (neé Hartl), 490
Allis, Edward P., & Co., 105, 114
Alma, Wis., 75, 87, 361-4
Alma Brewery, 362
Alma Brewing Co., 75, 361
alt beer, 41, 43, 327
Alt, Harold, 485–86
Alt Brew. *See* Greenview Brewing Co. LLC
Althans, Charles, 378
Altpeter, Oscar, 535, 539
Altpeter, Phillip, 123, 534–35
Altria Group. *See* Philip Morris
Aman, Edward, 434

Aman, George, 373, 539
Aman, George, 373, 374
American Bowling Congress, 531
American Breweriana Association, 290, 352
American Brewers' Association, 218, 219–20, 229, 657
American Brewing Academy, 48
American Brewing/Products Co., 662
American Can Co., 226, 531
American Federation of Labor, 143
American Fur Co., 34–35
American Homebrewers Association (AHA), 203, 329
American Indians, 52, 382; and advertising, 32, 557, 577, 655; and malt liquor protests, 303–4
American Malting Co., 95
American Sky Brewing Co., 436
American Temperance Society, 171–72
Amherst, Wis., 342, 344, 362
Amrhein, Joseph, 542
Anchor Steam beer, 111, 315
Ancient Order of the Mendotas, 174
Ancient Order of United Workmen, 72
Andeker beer, 235, 297, 298, 299
Anderson, August, 612
Anderson, Charles, 540
Anderson, Dave, 343, 671
Anderson, Gustaff, 487
Anderson, Hans, 598
Anderson, Peter, 540
Anderson, Will, 288,
Andrea, Anton, 569
Andrews, George M., 437
Angelic Brewing, 477
Angermeyer, Henry, 556
Angry Minnow, 310, 432
Angus, Charles B., 469
Anheuser-Busch Brewing Co. (St. Louis), 79, 100, 122, 143, 156, 235, 256, 275, 285, 291, 298, 302, 305, 308, 351, 482, 519; compared to

Wisconsin breweries, 1, 253, 264, 286, 309
Anson, William, 51, 506, 649
Anthony, Susan B., 188
Anti-Saloon League, 169, 185–86, 191
Anti-treating Law, 179–80
antitrust regulation and enforcement, 257–58, 281. *See also* Federal Trade Commission
Antigo, Wis., 77, 83, 178, 188, 197, 362–63
Antigo Brewing Co., 197, 362–63
Antonow, Joseph, 658
Anzinger, Wolfgang, 476
Apfel, Adam, 674
Appel, Susan K., 117
apples, in beer, 391, 569
Appleton, Wis., 51, 58, 62, 63, 74, 77–78, 80, 84, 89, 104, 191, 217, 219, 221–25, 274, 277, 363–66
Appleton Beer Factory, 347, 366
Appleton Brewing & Malting Co., 80, 191, 338, 363–64
Appleton Brewing Co. (brewpub), 337, 338, 365
Aprahamian, Justin, 548
Arcadia, Wis., 76, 210, 218
Arcadia Brewery/Brewing Co., 76, 210, 218, 220, 366–67
architects: of breweries, 116–19. *See also individual breweries*
Arensdorf, John, 497
Argall, James, 550
Arlen & Gut, 388–89
Arndt, J. Peter, 453
Arnet, John (Leonard), 44, 584
Arnold, Albert, 660
Arnold, Bettina, 544
Arnold, Ferd., 538
Arnold, John, 538
Arnold, Leonard, 574, 660
Arnold, Leonard Jr., 660
Arnold, William J., 627
Arnoldt, Louis, 104, 405
Arnstein, Rudolf, 604
Arras, Louis, 534
arsenic, as beer adulterant, 188
Arzbacher, Adolph, 667–68
Aschmann, William, 536
Asenbauer, Vinzent, 644
Ashland, Wis., 3, 4, 38, 174, 339, 368–69

Ashland Brewing Co., 4, 38, 368
Ashland Union Brewing Co., 368
Ashwaubenon, Wis., 369
Ashworth, Edmond, 398
ASL. *See* Anti-Saloon League
Asmuth Malt and Grain Co., 95
Associated Beer Depots, 625
Associated Brewing Co. (Detroit), purchased by Heileman, 304, 462
Association of Brewers, 329. *See also* Brewers Association
ATF. *See* Bureau of Alcohol, Tobacco and Firearms
Atlantic City, N.J., 152
Auburn (Twp.), Wis. *See* New Cassel, Wis.; New Fane, Wis.
Augsburger beer, 312, 316–17, 327, 553
Augusta, Wis., 109, 369
Austin, William H. (brewer), 53, 600
Austin, William H. (lawyer), 191
Australia, shipments to, 164
Avon Center, Wis., 369
Aztalan, Wis., 369

Bachhuber, Emeron, 492
Bachhuber, Martin, 491–92
Backhaus, August F., 489
Bad Axe (P. O.), Wis. *See* Sterling, Wis.
Badger Brewery (Racine), 596, 597
Badger Brewing Co. (Black River Falls), 377
Badger Brewing Co. (Hurley), 438
Badger Brewing Co. (Milwaukee), 540
Badger State Brewery (Eau Claire), 402
Badger State Brewing Co. (Green Bay), 310, 349, 349, 429–30
Badger State Brewing Co. (Janesville), 441
Baertsch, Jamie (neé Martin), 673
Baesemann, Elmer, 393
Bahr, Nate, 421
Baier, Adam, 605
Baier, Joseph, 605
Bailey, Charles, 412
Baileys Harbor, Wis., 369–70
Baines, Thomas, 423
Baireuther, Charles, 369
Baker (brewer in Milwaukee), 505–6
Baker, Orrin, 596
bakeries, in breweries, 425, 653
Baldwin, William O., 253
Baldwin, Wis., 370

Balistreri, Chris, 626
Ball (Bool), Nicholas, 394–95
Ballantine Ale, 238, 253, 283, 296, 695n10
Baltz, Sebastian, 648
bananas, in beer, 421
Band of Hope, 173
Bandlow, Frederick, 102, 644
Bangor, Wis., 18, 74, 370, 457
Banner Brewing Co., 233, 234, 541–42
Bantle, Clarence, 646
Baptists, 171
bar lights. *See* signs: lighted
Baraboo, Wis., 69, 72, 104, 106, 172, 176, 181, 268–69, 275, 370–72
Barclay, Perkins & Co. (London, England), porter, 40, 53
Bardin, Alvin, 399, 589
Bardin, Lawrence P., 399
Bare Bones Brewery, 579
Bark River Brewery, 432
barley, 3, 18–22; cultivation, 18–21; regulation of, 200–201, 229; malting by brewers, 19–20, 94–95; Oderbrucker, 20, 21; prices, 20, 159, 481; purchases by breweries, 44, 50, 51, 71, 442, 663; spent grains as livestock feed, 71–72; Wis. No. 38, 21; Wis. production, 18–21, 34, 94, 344–45, 364. *See also* malt; grain
Barley John's Brewing Co., 310, 349, 563
Barnes, Horace, 469
Baron, Stanley, 66, 99
Barre Mills (P. O.), Wis., 430
barrel-aged beer, 341, 347, 348, 353, 362
barrels, as measurement unit, 129, 145, 329. *See also* kegs
Barstow, William A., 58
Bartl, Edward, 457
Bartl, Franz, 456–57, 569
Bartl, Joseph, 457
Barton Beers Ltd., 321–22
baseball cards, 396
baseball teams: beer brewed for, 365, 478; sponsored by breweries, 396, 454, 459, 472, 519, 523, 528, 586, 603, 646
basketball teams, sponsored by breweries, 390, 487
Bast, Christopher, 525
Bast, Wilhelmina, 525
Bates, Albert J., 238

INDEX 705

Battle, Laurie, 247
Bauer, Gary, 327, 365
Bauer, William, 431
Baum, Daniel, 432
Baum, Jacob, 432
Baum, John, 432
Baumann, Anton, 395
Baur, Frank, 401
Bauscheck, D., 526
Bavaria Brewery (Milwaukee), 533–34
Bavarian Bierhaus, 421
Bavarian Brewery (Kewaunee), 454
Bay Brewery (Green Bay), 423
Bay City Brewery (Ashland), 368
Bay City Brewery (Green Bay), 424–25
Bay View Roller Mills, 142
Beatty, David E., 541
Beaver Dam, Wis., 62, 67, 174, 194, 242, 243, 372–74
Bechard, Jerry, 579
Bechaud, Adolph B., 412
Bechaud, Adolph G., 411, 641
Bechaud, August R., 412
Bechaud, Frank, 411
Bechaud, John, 411
Bechaud, Robert, 412, 601
Bechaud Brewing Co., 411–12
Becherer, Gustav, 539
Beck, John, 527, 649
Beck, Joseph, 375
Beck, Paul, 649
Becker, Edward, 109, 365, 562, 563
Becker, Philip (Calvary), 385
Becker, Philip, 368, 389, 438
Becker, Rich, 477
Beebe, F., 596
Beef Slough, Wis. *See* Alma, Wis.
Beell, Fred, 490
beer can collecting. *See* breweriana
Beer Can Collectors of America (BCCA), 289–90
beer cans. *See* cans
beer combs (foam scrapers), 289
beer competitions, 154, 156–58
beer festivals, 153
beer gardens, 52–53, 153, 163–64, 172, 326, 327, 345, 363, 467, 492, 498, 521, 549, 610, 630, 635
Beer Judge Certification Program (BJCP), 29, 203
Beer Line (railroad), 162

beer marketers. *See* contract brewers
beer tourism, 321
beer: allegations of impurity, 158–161, 186–87, 287, 596, 652; brand loyalty, 151, 163, 236, 312; draught, 3, 81, 218, 227, 234, 238, 267, 268, 294–95, 298, 313, 331; drinking and serving, 29–31; dumping of, 291; during wartime, 235–42; experimental styles, 231–32, 297–302, 308–9, 334–35, 348–49; health claims for, 187–88, 518, 519, 619; home consumption, 244, 246–47; legalization of, 208–15; prices of, 35, 37, 44, 237–38, 589, 604; public taps at breweries, 218; serving, 29–30; strength, 29, 30, 191, 192, 208, 231, 232, 302, 379, 572; styles, 22, 23, 29, 136, 227, 314, 315, 327, 348; wood/barrel aged, 341, 347, 348, 353. *See also individual breweries*
Behlmer, Henry, 415
Beireuther, Charles, 369, 448
Beisbier, Wenzel, 666
Beischel, Joseph, 446
Bélanger, Eugene (Bo), 344, 368–69, 432, 648
Belgian-style beers, 23, 29, 78, 328, 335, 337, 348, 349, 350, 480
Bell, Karen, 546
Belle City Brewing Co., 598–99
Belle City Products, 195, 595
Bellevue, Wis. *See* Green Bay
Bellevue Products Co., 427
Belli, Melvin, 553
Bellows, John, 653, 659
Bellows Brew Co./Whistle Stop Tavern, 659
Bellows Brew Crew/Bellows Brewpub (Watertown), 653
Beloit Steam Brewery, 374
Beloit, Wis., 374–75
Belrose, Francis, 652
Ben-Hur Mfg. Co., 412
Bender, Adolph, 371
Bender, Anna, 371
Bender, George, 69, 371
Bender, Henry, 387
Bender, Robert, 371
Benishek, John, 362–63
Benjamin Beer Co., 580, 599
Berens, Joseph, 445
Berens & Stephan, 445

Berg, John, 536
Bergen Twp., 375
Bergenheim, C. F., 488
Berghoff Restaurant (Chicago), 318
Berhens, Heinrich, 609
Berlin, Irving, 214
Berlin Brewing Co., 216, 271, 273–74, 276, 375–76, 563
Bernard, Hubert, 503
Bernhardt, Richard, 604
Berni, Stephen, 453
Berthold & Hartzhein, 643
Berthold & Schmidt, 374
Bertram, Casper, 596
Bertram, John, 666
Best, Maria (later Mrs. Frederick Pabst), 507–8
Best, Elizabetha (Lisette) (later Mrs. Emil Schandein), 507–8
Best, Charles, 52, 507, 520
Best, Charles Jr., 508
Best, Jacob (Portage), 588
Best, Jacob Jr., 52, 507
Best, Jacob, Sr., 41, 55, 294, 507
Best, Lorenz, 52, 507, 520
Best, Phillip, 40, 41, 42, 52, 351, 507
Best, Phillip, Brewing Co., 41, 63, 66, 98, 99, 101, 103, 104, 117, 123–24, 129, 139, 155, 156, 507–8, 529; advertising, 70, 505, 507; Empire Brewery, 41, 63, 102, 103, 110, 118, 123–24, 140, 507–8; Kansas City agency, 127. *See also* Pabst Brewing Co.
Best Tonic (Pabst), 150, 158
Bethesda Brewery, 188, 654–55, 657
Between the Locks Mall (Appleton), 338, 338
Betz, L., 463
Beverage Tax Division (BTD). *See* Division of Beverage and Cigarette Taxes
Beverage Testing Institute, 332
Beveridge, Albert J., 180
Bevering, Henry, 524
Beyer (brewer in Platteville), 581
Beyer, Anton, 365, 562
Beyer, Ron, 488
Beyrer, Frederick, 605
Beyrer, Gottfried, 605
Bezucha, Joseph, 434, 596
Bezucha, Vincent, 434, 596
Bichel (Pischell), J. F., 400

Biddick, Mike, 421
Biden, Joseph, 559
Bieber, Charles, 650
Bieber, William, 650
Biedermann, Gottlieb, 585
Bielerman, brewer in Boscobel, 380
Bierbauer, Henry, 73, 75-76, 85, 561
biergärten. See beer gardens
Biersach, Michael, 372
Bieser, Mike, 545-46
Big Bear Eatery & Brewery, 380
Big Bend, Wis., 377
Big Head Brewing Co., 666
Bill, Albin, 601
Bills & Mergener, 366
Bills, H. Newman Jr., 541
Bills, Harry E., 541
Bills, Henry N., 540-41
Biloba Brewing Co., 381-84
Binder, Jacob, 557, 642
Binz, August, 617
Binz, Jacob (Joseph), 617
Binz Bros. Brewery, 18
Binzel, Alvin, 374
Binzel, Clarence, 565
Binzel, Edward, 374
Binzel, (John) Philip, 373, 565, 661
Binzel, Louisa, 373-74-16
Binzel, Peter, 565, 661
Binzel, Peter Jr., 565
Binzel Brewing Co., 196, 242, 565
Bion, Christian, 366
Bion, John, 366
Birkhauser, J. Adolph, 418-19
Birkhofer, Conrad, 447
Bismarck, N.D., Miller brewery in, 127-28, 255, 521
Bissinger (brewer in Monroe), 45, 551
Bittner, Franz, 592
BJCP. *See* Beer Judge Certification Program
Black, Herman, 494
Black Creek, Wis., 377
Black Forest Dining & Spirits, 429
Black Hawk Brewery, 440
Black Hawk War, 35
Black Husky Brewing Co. (Milwaukee), 547
Black Husky Brewing Co. (Pembine), 342-44, 580
Black Pride, Inc., 259-60, 669
Black River Brewery & Pub, 466

Black River Falls, Wis., 14, 76, 81, 85, 109, 377-78
Blackwell, William, 452
Blaine, John J., 197
Blaser, Lon, 408
Blass, John, 380
Blatz, Albert C., 513, 529
Blatz, Emil, 513
Blatz, Val., Brewing Co., 2, 78-79, 102, 117, 118, 123, 124, 128, 129, 131, 132, 143, 214, 264, 282, 414, 512-57; acquistion by Pabst, 258, 260; advertising, 70, 131, 135, 148, 150, 155, 215; employees, 139, 141-42, 160-61, 242, 249, 251, 263, 266; non-brewery properties, 151, 152; products, 98, 159, 201, 217, 231, 249-51, 304; special events, 131, 144, 153, 155, 212, 214
Blatz, Val., Brewing Co. (1980s-present), 305. *See also* Tenth and Blake Brewery
Blatz, Valentin, 41, 43, 50, 79, 103, 123, 159, 160-61, 165, 512-13, 525, 526
Blatz, Valentin Jr., 513
Blatz Hotel, 513
blending, of beer, 510, 591
Blesch, Francis, 45, 66, 423, 679n33
Bleser Brewing Co., 485-86
Bleser, Daniel B., 483, 484
Bleser, Daniel C., 483, 485-86, 616
Blessing, George, 422, 585
Blitz-Weinhard Brewing Co. (Portland, Ore.), purchase by Pabst, 293
Block, Richard, 494
Bloesing, Frederick, 200
Bloomer Brewery/Brewing Co. (-1947), 378-79
Bloomer Brewing Co. (2013-), 379
Bloomquist, Harold, 604
Blossom, Alonzo, 506
Blossom, Levi, 52, 129, 506, 533
Blotz, Jacob, 622
Blue Heron Brewpub, 490
Bluff Brewery, 53
Blumer, Adam, 552
Blumer, Adam Jr., 552
Blumer, Catherine, 552
Blumer, Fred J., 552-53
Blumer, Jacob C., 552
Blumer, Samuel, 558
Blumer Brewing Co./Corp., 43, 45, 213

See also Huber, Jos. Brewing Co.; Minhas Craft Brewery
Blust, Fred, 192, 615
Bluvas, George, III, 544
Bobtown Brewhouse and Grill, 349, 608
bock beer, 6, 217-18, 237, 249, 250, 312, 313, 613; advertising of, 106, 110, 113, 149, 249, 299
Bodega Brew Pub, 466
Bodendorfer, Leonhardt, 418
Bodmer, Otto, 416
Boehmer, Henry (Heinrich), 493
Bogk, Frederick, 384-85
Bohman, Barbara, 454
Bohman, Joseph, 454
Bohman, Mary, 454
boilers. *See* breweries (buildings): steam power in
Boldt, Brent, 486
Bond, Alan, 305-6, 462
Bond Corporation Holdings, Ltd., 306
Bonduel, Wis., 379-80
Bonk, Edward, 389
Boortz (brewer in Rice Lake), 604
Boots, Ephraim, 641
Borchert, Charles, 516
Borchert, Ernst, 130, 153, 516
Borchert, Frederick Jr., 516
Boreshcake, Joseph, 554
Borgan, Ed, 648
Borgardt, Jack, 548
Borgardt, Max, 548
Borsche, Joseph, 435
Bosch, Andrew, 592
Bosch Brewing Co. (Houghton, Mich.), 323, 393
Boscobel Brewing Co., 380
Boston, Mass.: shipments to, 149
Bostwick, J. M., 585
bottle caps, 483, 514. *See also* Crown caps
bottled beer, 2, 25-26, 128-39, 159-60, 224, 518, 632; closures, 128, 129, 134-35, 231, 238, 567; early examples, 53, 128-30, 622; in homes, 137, 147, 244, 247, 269, 336; laws governing, 129, 132-33; popularity of, 126, 131, 298, 310, 313, 324; prices of, 227, 238; shipping, 113, 126, 129, 131-33, 136, 165, 518, 575;
bottlers: independent, 38, 79, 104, 127, 129-32. *See also individual breweries*

bottles, 25, 128–39, 149, 155, 195, 197, 199, 250, 251, 290, 297, 299, 301, 303, 348, 511, 522, 572, 576; large sizes, 83, 230, 238, 288, 567, 599, 631; non-returnable, 276–77, 531–32; returnable, 130–31, 319; small sizes, 30, 195, 249, 267, 269, 297, 487, 603; stoneware, 128, 506, 536, 597; supplies of, 68, 128, 134, 219, 272, 286, 319, 664. *See also individual breweries*

bottling houses (buildings), 44, 112, 138, 162, 210, 352. *See also individual breweries*

bottling lines (equipment), 101, 105, 119, 128–29, 137–38, 162, 167, 197, 204, 209, 211, 223–25, 226, 261, 294, 315. *See also individual breweries*

bottling process, 105, 108, 112, 131–33, 137–38, 145, 162, 228, 231, 232; by female employees, 137–39, 143, 144, 145, 226, 242; by hand, 34, 130–31

Bottomley, Edwin, 34
Boulder Junction, 380
Bourgeois, Matthias, 385, 488, 554
Bow, Edwin R., 371
Bowen, Kevin, 579
Bower, J. H., & Co., 384
Bower City Beverage Co., 439–40
bowling teams, sponsored by breweries, 589
Bowron-Murray Co., 4
Boyanowski (Boyanski), Frank, 634, 675
Boyce, Thomas, 438
boycotts, 88, 90, 142, 143, 161, 295, 327
Boyle, J. Wilson, 593
Boyle, John, 593
Brachman, R. J., 582
Bradford, Mary D., 185
Brady's Brewhouse, 563
Braitinger, Michael, 331
Branch, Wis., 110, 380–81
Brand, Fred, 486–87
Brandenburg, Kevin, 659
Brandes, Charles, 453
Brandes, Charles Jr., 454
Brandt, Herman M., 204
Brandt, Irene, 220
Brauchle, Agnes, 395
Brauchle, Alois, 47, 50–51, 395
Brauchle, Peter, 395

Braun (Brown), Johann (John), 51, 512, 594
Braun, Louise (later Louise Blatz), 512
Bray, Thomas, 37, 408–9
Brazil: shipments to, 165
Breckheimer, Mathias, 64, 67, 68, 471, 476
Breckheimer Brewing Co., 476
Bregar, George, 546
Breneman, Tom, 408
Brenner, Mike, 547
Brenner Brewing Co., 349, 547
Bress (Bregs), Joseph, 611
Brethorst, Tanner, 673–74
Breunig, Jacob S., 605
Breunig, Jacob, 379, 401, 445–46
Breunig, John G., 605
Breunig, John S. (Jack), 605
Breunig, Joseph, 446
Brew on Premises facilities, 479
Brewer, Richard, 409
Brewer, William, 380
breweriana, 288–90
breweries (buildings): architecture of, 47, 364; chimneys/smokestacks, 111, 163, 266; construction of, 46–47, 116–19, 123; dance/meeting halls at, 53, 55, 76; energy use, 344; environmental damage caused by, 74, 102, 162–63, 399; public meetings at, 55; renovation of, 116–19; steam power in, 47, 50, 71, 75, 109, 111–12. *See also individual breweries*

breweries (businesses): aggregate production levels, 68; bankruptcies of, 167, 261, 306–7, 316, 318–19, 340–41; benefits to local economy, 1, 51, 52, 71, 73, 74–75, 209, 220, 226, 247–48, 266, 273–74, 276–77, 618, 619; charitable contributions by, 153, 205, 275, 291, 321, 365, 583, 615; closures, 67–68, 80–81, 242, 266, 271–77, 336–37, 340–41, 605; consolidation of, 78–80, 123–24, 191, 240, 364, 594, 656, 662, 667, 668; controlled by organized crime, 195–96, 383; conversion during Prohibition, 192–99; cooperative, 84–85, 143, 219, 243; diversification of, 87–88, 270–71; expansion strategies, 84, 85, 254–58, 304–5; finances, 77, 281–82, 346, 615; incorporation,

69, 85, 86, 87, 166, 233, 282, 651; investors in, 71, 77, 422, 652; legal departments, 229, 287; number in Wisconsin, 233, 243, 253; operated by estates, 84, 85; production levels, 123, 124, 243, 253; raids during Prohibition, 194–97; sale of stock in, 79, 83–85, 86, 87, 276, 282, 315, 335, 350, 461, 616, 658; starting of, 67, 80; as temperance institutions, 57; violence/crimes at, 52, 64, 76–77, 382, 383, 439, 489, 490. *See also individual breweries*

brewers (brewmasters and proprietors): benevolences, 73–74; as community leaders, 163–64; hiring of, 71, 277; organizations, 49; as politicians, 73, 74, 398, 427, 500, 527, 612; residences of, 76, 165, 168, 522; training of, 47, 48–49, 92, 107–8, 346, 520. *See also individual breweries*

Brewers Association (BA), 49, 329
Brewers Journal, 48
Brewers' Association of America (BAA), 275
Brewers' Best (beer), 265, 646
Brewers' Fire Insurance Co. of America, 153, 530
Brewers' Protective Insurance Co. of the West, 153, 530
Brewery and Soft Drink Workers: Local 133, 639
Brewery Creek (brewpub), 339, 550
brewery employees, 221–25, 241, 261; accidents, 140, 512, 526; beer comsumption, 144, 145; benefits, 144–45, 220, 224, 263, 295, 568; during wartime, 235, 241, 242; employee handbooks, 262; pensions, 295; social events, 143, 144; stock option programs, 350; training of, 48–49, 50–51, 107–8, 346; wages, 89, 123, 138, 140, 263, 273, 275, 396; working conditions, 89, 137–44, 220, 221–25, 262–63, 273. *See also individual breweries*

brewery employees: union activity. *See* unions; individual locals; strikes
Brewery Malt Co., 200
brewery rolls. *See* delivery wagons
brewery saloons. *See* saloons
brewery tours, viii, 30–31, 68, 75, 122,

147, 163, 176, 322, 326, 331, 333–34, 576, 603, 615
Brewfinity Brewing Co., 566
Brewhouse Inn & Suites, 511
brewing equipment, 42, 45, 50, 52, 92, 234, 333, 336, 341, 346, 353; modernization of, 71, 104–5, 107, 111–12, 119, 128, 167, 210, 315, 443, 576, 603; purchases by breweries, 104–5, 209, 275, 346; sale of, 101, 119. *See also individual breweries*
brewing process, 16, 42, 50
Brewing Projekt, The, 310, 408
brewing schools. *See* brewers (brewmasters and proprietors): training of
brewmaster. *See* brewers (brewmasters and proprietors)
Brewmasters Pub–Parkside, 337, 452
Brewmasters Pub, Restaurant and Brewery, 337–38, 452
brewpub chains, 339–40
brewpubs, 314, 335–41. *See also* microbreweries; craft breweries
Brewster Bros. Brewing Co., 394
Brey, Jeannette, 582
Brey, William, 582
Brick House Brewery, 471
Bridham, Peter, 648
Briess Malting Co., 95, 203
Briggeboos, William, 362
Bright Spot Bottling Co., 540
Brillion, Wis., 388, 488
Brinkmeyer, F. W., 538
Briscoe, Richard, 581
British Hollow, Wis., 381
Brockford, George, 635
Brodesser, John C., 417
Brooklyn Brewery. *See* Horn and Schwalm Brewery
Brown, Henry H., 499
Brown, N. A., 451
Brown Bottle hospitality room, 25, 254–55, 256, 519 *See also* Schlitz, Joseph, Brewing Co.
Brown Street Brewery, 604
Brown's Ale Brewery, 451
Bruel, Ludwig, 526–27
Bruemmer, Louis, 360
Bruenig, Joseph, 446
Bruetting, Ballo, 549
Brunkow, August, 503
Brunster, Arthur, 51

Brush Brewery, 605
Bryan, William Jennings, 181
Brys, Joseph, 666
Bub, Peter, Brewery/Brewing Co. (Winona, Minn.), 326, 406
Buchanan, Page, 343–44, 479
Buchanan (Twp.), Wis. *See* Kaukauna, Wis.
Buche, E. W. (William), 387, 612
Bucher, George, 565
Bucher & Seifert, 661
Buchheit, William, 652
Buckle (Buckel), August, 583, 620
Budweiser beer, 154, 158, 255, 285, 293, 309, 519
Buena Vista (Twp.), Wis. *See* Richland City, Wis.
Buexton, William, 622
Buffalo, Wis., 382
Bugsy's Sports Bar, 604
Buhler, August, 375–76
Buhler, Edward, 375–76, 596
Bulin, Joseph, 676
Bull Falls Brewing Co., 310, 665–66
Bullesbach, Tobias, 402
Bully, Henry, 557
Bunde, Al, 546, 579
Bunster, Arthur W., 441–42
Bunster, Henry B., 53, 441–42
Bunyan, Paul (beer), 5
Buob, John, 17, 68, 438–39, 441
Buob, Mary, 441
Buob, Michael, 68, 182, 439, 441
Buob, William, 441
Buob & Brunbolt, 438
Burdick, Bill, 478
Bureau of Alcohol, Tobacco and Firearms (ATF), 302
Burge, Craig, 421
Burgermeister Brewing Co. *See* Schlitz, Joseph, Brewing Co.: Burgermeister purchase
Burkhardt, Gottfried, 499
Burkhardt, Louis, 499
Burlington, Wis., 62, 382–84
Burlington Brewing Co., 249, 264, 383–84
Burlington Cereal Products, 383
Burr Oak, Wis., 384
Bursinger, Joseph, 650
Burton ale (beer), 40, 53
Burton-on-Trent (England), 17, 53

Busch, Adolphus, 154, 158
Busselman, Louis, 393
Butler, Eliot, 338, 477
Butte des Morts, Wis., 384–85
Buttera, Katina, 582
Buttera, Marc, 582
Buzzell, John, 580
Byass, Robert B., Brewery (London, England), 53

Cadiz (Twp.), Wis., 385
Calaway, Nick, 360
calendars (advertising), 3, 50, 92, 137, 147, 150–51, 590, 609
Calgeer, Felix, 526
California: expansion of breweries into, 256–58
Calumet (Twp.), Wis., 385
Calumet Brewing Co., 195, 213, 218, 238, 389–90
Calumet Brewing Co. (brewpub). *See* Rowland's Calumet Brewing Co.
Calumet Sales Corp., 389
Calvary (village), Wis., 385
Calvert, Alfred, 401–2
Camp Hartford, 431
Campaign for Real Ale (CAMRA), 314
Campbell (P. O.), Wis., 467
Campus Craft Brewery, 647
Canada: exports to, 319; as source of malt, 21
Canadian Ace Brewing Co. (Chicago), 264, 658. *See also* Manhattan Brewing Co.
candy, 199, 200, 513, 514, 518–19, 612
canned beer, 220–21, 226–28, 235–36, 242, 327–29
canning lines. *See* cans: filling
cans, 220–21, 248, 289–90, 315–16; cone top, 2, 226, 227, 228, 289, 519, 655; filling, 226, 546; large sizes, 248, 255, 289, 292, 617; olive drab, 235–36; with opening instructions (OI), 226
Cantor, Eddie, 24
Capital Brewery, 8, 310, 312, 331–33, 348, 351
Capitol Brewing Co. of Milwaukee, 219, 238, 243, 267, 542
Carew, J. L., brewery (Detroit, Mich.), 53
Carey, Dan, 334–35, 558–59
Carey, Deb, 334–36, 558–59

Carey, Katherine, 560
Carisch, Christ., 360
Carisch, George, 360
Carling National Breweries: Fort Worth branch purchased by Miller, 257; purchased by Heileman, 305
Carlsbad, New Mexico, 152
Carlsberg Brewery (Copenhagen, Denmark), 27
Carlton (Twp.), Wis., 385
Carstens, Charles, 404, 539
Carter, Jimmy, 337
Carver Park. *See* Schlitz Park
Casanova, Christopher, 436
Casanova, Joseph A., 436
Casanova Brewing Co., 436
cases, for beer bottles, 110, 133, 137, 242, 288, 300, 465, 661
Cash, W. H. H., 434
Cashman, John, 21
Cask-conditioned ale, 27, 314
Caspari, Peter, 497
Casper, Henry, 393
Cass, Lewis, 65
Cassville Brewery/Brewing Co., 385–86
Castalia Bottling Co., 539
Castle Rock, 52
Caswell, Oscar B., 375
Cato, Wis. *See* Clarks Mills, Wis.
caves (brewery): converted to other purposes, 36, lagering (storing) beer, 3, 36, 37–38, 51, 55, 98, 100–101, 102, 104, 118, 140, 601, 630. *See also individual breweries*
Cavner, James, 583
Cazenovia, Wis., 386–87
Cecil, Wis., 387, 612
Cedar Brewery, 512
Cedar Creek, Wis., 388. *See also* Slinger
Cedar Falls, Wis., 388
Cedarburg, Wis., 45, 75, 342, 387–88
Cedarburg Brewery, 45
cellars. *See* caves
Centennial Exposition (Philadelphia), 100, 105, 131, 157, 667, 668
Centerville (Cleveland, Hika), Wis., 71, 388–89
Centerville Brewery/Brewing Co., 388–89
Centlivre, Denis, 581
Central Waters Brewing Co., 23, 341, 344, 347, 362

Central Waters Brewpub, 490
Century Brewing Co. (1933–34), 542
Century Brewing Co. (1987–88), 338, 545
Century Hall, 545
Century of Progress exhibition, 510
Cereal Products Co. (Cepro), 95, Rahr Malting Co.
Cervecería Cuahtémoc (Monterrey, Mexico), 235
Cezejaria Brahma (Rio de Janeiro, Brazil), 192
Chalupsky, Frank (John?), 362–63
Chameleon Brewing Co., 421
Chandelier Ballroom, 431
Chapman, Chandler P., 177
Chapman, H. D., 648
Charry, Robert, 424–25
Chatterhouse Brewery, 399
cheese, 215, 249, 271; made in breweries or converted breweries, 197, 198–99, 200, 363, 369, 494, 509, 553, 582, 584, 594
Chemer, Sam, 643
chemists, employed by breweries, 17, 18, 21, 26, 98, 108, 229, 441
Cherryland Brewery/Brewpub, 337, 637
Chestnut Brewery. *See* Schlitz, Joseph, Brewing Co.
Chewing gum, 514, 612
Chicago, Ill.: agencies in, 78, 113, 125; Fire of 1871, 1, 125, 474, 508; investors in Wisconsin breweries, 219, 243, 282, 378, 383–84, 406, 461, 552, 558, 601, 636, 656–57, 658, 671; shipments of beer from, 53, 146; shipments to, 59, 195, 214, 229, 262, 300, 305, 318, 320, 327, 335, 462, 474, 486, 517, 518, 521, 528, 530, 533, 559, 564, 590, 594, 604, 613, 614, 617, 636, 650, 651, 665
Chicago and Northwestern Railway, 58
Chicago, Milwaukee and St. Paul Railway, 162
Chicago, Rock Island & Pacific Railway, 450
Chicago Stock Exchange, 304, 461
Chicago White Sox, 90, 360, 396
Chief Wausau Co., 664
children: as brewery employees, 138–39, 538, 575

Chile: shipments to, 165
Chilton, Wis., 21, 95, 195, 213, 225, 337–38, 389–91
Chilton Brewery, 389
Chilton Malting Co., 21, 95
chimneys. *See* breweries (buildings): chimneys/smokestacks
Chippewa Falls, Wis., 73, 74, 82, 88, 112, 178, 216, 322–24, 391–94
Chitel, Ernst, 459
Chloupek, Anton, 455
Choo Choo Bar & Grill, 640
Christ, John, 398
Christenson, Mike, 608
Christiana (Twp.), Wis., 394
Christiansen, Jon, 499
Christianson, Christian, 432
Christie, Tom, 669
Christman, Peter, 471
Christmann Brewery, 561
Christon, Christ G., 671
Church & Kenworthy, 371
church keys. *See* openers
cider, 170, 181, 445
CIO. *See* Congress of Industrial Organizations
Circus World Museum, 520
Citizens Brewing Co., 363
City Brewing Co. (formerly Heileman), 307–8; Latrobe branch, 308, 462; Memphis branch, 308, 462. *See also* Heileman, G., Brewing Co.
City Lights Brewing Co., 548
Civil War, effect on labor, 63,
Civilian Conservation Corps, 230
Clarks Mills, Wis., 394
clear beer, 307, 308–9
Clear Lake, Wis., 395
Cleary, Russell, 263, 304–6, 308, 462
Clements, George, 302–3
Cleveland, Frances Folsom, 150, 151
Cleveland, Grover, 147, 148
Cleveland, Wis. *See* Centerville, Wis.
Clinton (village), Wis., 177
clocks, 601
Clydesdales. *See* horses
Company Brewing Co., 546
coal, 51, 191, 198, 224, 242
coasters, 43, 47, 215, 274, 290, 291, 294, 338, 490, 544, 566
Coburn, James, 291, 698n28
Coburn, Thayer, 671

Cochran, Thomas, 80, 107, 126, 140, 143, 152
coffee, in beer, 23. *See also individual breweries*
Coffey, Dean, 477, 478
cold filtering, 299
Cold Spring (Twp.), Wis., 395. *See also* Whitewater, Wis.
Cold Spring Brewing Co. (Cold Spring, Minn.), 375, 640
Cold Springs Brewery, 440
cold-filtered beers, 299
Colditz, Frederick, 531
Colish, Badger, 432
collaboration beers, 349, 350, 429–30, 560, 674
Collier's magazine, 246
Collins, John, 398
Columbian Exposition (1893), 154–58, 509, 518, 519
Columbus, Wis., 47, 50–51, 52, 90, 95, 98, 106, 109, 174, 175, 395–96
Colwell, Kenneth, 550
community-supported breweries, 343–44, 478, 608
competitions, beer, 155–57
cone top cans. *See* cans: cone top
Coney Island, 153
Congress of Industrial Organizations (CIO), 263
Connelly, Kane & Co., 400
Conrad, Ludwig, 534
Conrad, Valentin, 516
Consalus, William, 669
Considine, Bob, 283
Continental Can Co., 226
contract brewing, 260, 274, 295, 296, 303, 308, 314–15, 317, 318, 319, 322, 327, 331, 341, 343, 353, 365, 378, 528
Conway Pub & Brewing Co., 372
Cook, Bob, 644
Cook, Jacob, 592
Cook, Jerry, 644
Coolidge, Calvin, 427
Cooper, Dick, 659
Cooper, John, 564
Cooper, Vaune, 659
cooperages: on brewery premises, 102, 110. *See also individual breweries*
cooperative breweries. *See* breweries (businesses): cooperative

Cooperative Brewing Co. (Oshkosh). *See* Peoples Brewing Co.
coopers, 90, 94, 211; as brewery employees, 50–1, 52, 142. *See also individual breweries*
Coors, A. Brewing Co. *See* MillerCoors
Copper State Brewing Co., 430
corks, 34, 129, 130, 134–35, 513
corkscrews, 134
Corliss engine, 105
corn, 170; used in beer, 22, 159, 229, 240, 298, 334, 577
Cornell, Wis., 396–97
Corner Pub Brewery, 8, 602
Cottrell, William H., 375
county fairs, 54, 154, 181, 443
County Stadium (Milwaukee), 260, 333, 523, 626
Courthouse Pub, 486, 646
Courtney & Fricker, 366
craft beer, product naming, 349–50
craft breweries, 327, 331–52; definition, 329; employees, 331, 350; employees, 331, 350; expansion of, 350–51; financing, 331, 346; location of, 347; naming of, 349–50. *See also* microbreweries
Cramer, Robert, 114
Cramolini, Napoleon, 367
Crazy Horse malt liquor, 303–4
cream ale, 40, 280, 297
Cream City Brewing (Products) Co., 104, 130, 142, 166, 193, 209, 210, 211, 234, 527–28
creative destruction, 297
Crescent Commercial Corporation, 243
Croak, Frank, 439–40
Croak, William, 439–40
Croak Brewing Co., 439–40
Crocker, Jerome, 669
Cromaner, Jacob, 418
Cross Plains Brewing Co., 378
Cross Plains, Wis., 47, 51, 62
Crotch, John, 494
crowdfunding, of breweries, 346, 547–48
crowdsourcing, of recipes, 344, 547–48
crowlers (cans), 348. *See also* beer cans; canned beer
Crowley & Brothers, 661
crown caps, 127, 135, 197, 227, 231, 238, 251, 290, 541, 558

Crown Cork & Seal Co., 135, 228
crowntainer, 228. *See also* cans: cone-top
Cruse, Pat, 671
Cruse, Randy, 671
Crystal Bottling Works, 588
cub bottles. *See* bottles: small sizes
Cullen-Harrison Act, 208
Cummings, Matthew J., 394
Cunningham, Bernard, 371
Curran, Patrick J., 273–74, 376
Curtiss, J. E., 584
Custer, John C., 580
Czarnecki, Emil, 540–41
Czoernig, Anton, 538

Dahlke, Gustav, 469
Dahlke, Harvey, 469
Dahlke, Wayne, 469
Dahlke Brewing Co., 469
dairies, breweries converted to, 655
Dale (Twp.), Wis. *See* Medina, Wis.
Dallas, Wis., 397
Dalton, Andrew, 413
Dambruch, George, 365
Dangerfield, Rodney, 284
Daniel, Henry, 414–15
Daniels, Josephus, 186
Danner, Henry, 369, 446–47, 602, 608
Darge, Louis, 493
Darge, William, 493
dark beers. *See* specific styles
Darlington, Wis., 398
Das Bierhaus, 499
Dave's BrewFarm, 24, 343, 671–72
David, Denis, 352
David, Gary, 352
David, Madonna, 352
Davidson, F., 470
Davis, John, 516, 526
Davis, Paul H. & Co., 459
Dawes, Charles, 458
De 'Proef Brouwerij (Lochristi, Belgium), 560
De Haas, Carl, 491
De Pere, Wis., 399–400, 454
De Pere Brewing Co., 249, 288
de Sleutel Brewery (Dordrecht, Netherlands), 383
De Soto, Wis., 400
Dearen, Adam, 393
Dearsley (Dearsly), John, 516, 596

INDEX   711

Decemval (Descimval), Victor, 116, 638
Decker, Edward, 360
DeCleene, Ann, 435
DeCleene, Greg, 435
Deda, Charles, 453, 454
Deda & Wenger, 453
Dedrich, Peter, 448
Deegan, George, 485
Deep Water Grille, 369
Deerfield, Wis., 398
Degan, Paul, 515
Deierlein, Charles H., 434-35
Deierlein, John S., 434-35
Deierlein, Paul, 434-35
Deininger, Charles, 609
Deininger, Conrad, 419-20, 609
Deinken, Anton R., 598
Deitloff & Wenger, 453
Del Santo's Restaurant, 637
Delafield (city), Wis., 398
Delafield (Twp.), Wis., 398
Delafield Brewery, 398
Delafield Brewhaus, 339, 398
Delevan, Wis., 175
delivery trucks, 113-15, 212-13, 214, 215, 237, 263, 273, 363, 431, 631, 684n76
delivery wagons, 36, 106-7, 110, 113-14, 126, 144-45, 162, 169, 575, 616
Dells Brewery (Eau Claire), 104, 405
Dells Brewing Co., 13, 673
Democratic party, 64, 178, 179
Dengel, George, 611
Denmark Brewing (1999-2008), 399
Denmark Brewing Co., 206, 238, 243, 398-99
Denmark, Wis., 21, 219
Department of Defense, 261
deposit, on kegs, 572-15, 575, 584
Derichs Bros., 386
Dethier, Joseph, 365
Detroit, Mich., shipments of beer from, 53, 237
Deubig, Michael, 383
Deuhs, Greg, 308
Dewey, Nelson, 40
Dick Bros. Brewing Co. (Quincy, Ill.), 371
Dick, Jacob, 604
Dicke (Dick), Henry, 622
Diebenow, Julius, 409
Diedrich, Henry, 422
Diefenthaler, Fritz, 53, 467
Diener, Charles, 499

Dierks, William, 601
Dieter, Aric, 480
Dieter, Crystal, 480
Dietrick, Joseph, 398
Dietz, Otto, 604
Dikty, Alan, 311, 326-27-28
Dilba, Hathaway, 478
Dilba, Otto, 478
Dillard, Andrew, 666
Dillmann & Morawetz, 130, 528
Dillmann, Adam, 130, 528
Dimler, John, 17, 455
distilled spirits, made at breweries, 373, 394
distilleries: in breweries, 373, 394, 442, 565, 623, 625, 650, 671
distributors, 28, 47, 229, 254, 258, 260, 263, 270-71, 285, 290, 294, 306, 320, 322-23, 349, 373, 397, 399, 414, 420, 444, 457, 459, 460, 471, 483, 494, 542, 576, 586, 604, 625, 641, 651, 658
District 14 Brewery and Pub, 547
Division of Beverage and Cigarette Taxes (BTD), 228-29
Dix, Henry, & Co., 585
Dix, Richard, 410-11
Dixon, Pam, 671
Dobbert, L. C., 601
Dobert, Christian, 485
Doble, Joan, 430
Doble, Mike, 430
Dobler, Carl, 380
Dobler, Joseph, 380
Doc Powell's, 466
Dodge, Dustin, 608
Dodgeville, Wis., 400
Doerr, Oscar, 556
dogs: in advertising, 580, 644; at breweries, 580
Dolegal, Mathias, 455
Doll, George, 380
Doll, Joseph, 380
Donaghue, Deb, 550
Donaghue, Jeff, 550
Donaghue, Nelle, 550
Door County Brewing Co., 369-70
doppelbock, 324-25, 332, 571, 503, 504, 521, 544
Dorfner, Erik, 667
Dorfner, Kim, 667
Dortmunder beer (style), 136, 457
Dos Bandidos, 365

Dotten (Dutton), Edmund, 597
Doty, James, 496
Dousman (P.O.), Wis. See Ottawa (Twp.); Summit (Twp.)
Downer, Hiram, 470
Downing, Wis., 400-43
Downsville, Wis., 401
draft beer. See beer: draught
dram shop law, 57, 179. See also temperance
draymen. See drivers
drays. See delivery wagons
Dreher, Anton, 37
Dressendoerfer, Andrew, 87
Dreyfus, Lee, 292
Driftless Brewing Co., 626
Dringoli, Dan, 579
Dringoli, Patti, 579
drivers, 89, 110, 114, 140, 141, 144, 145, 196, 223-24, 271
Drkula, Tim, 499
Drossen, Anna, 87, 611
Drossen, Nicholas (Nic), 87, 611
Drucker, Lewis, 526
drunkenness, punishments for, 65, 170-71
dry beer, 299-300
dry-hopping, 25, 556, 560
drys. See prohibition; temperance
Ducart, Peter, 497
Ducasse, Charles M., 651
Duchow, Mark, 566
Dudler, J., 496
Duerr, Joseph A., 670
Duerrwaechter, Philip G., 420
Duerstein, Michael, 486-87
Dummet, Peter, 496
Dunck Tank Works, 107, 585
Dundas, Wis., 401
Duplainville, Wis., 401
Durand, Wis., 401
Durand Brewing Co., 401
Durow, David, 622
Durow & Herber, 622
Dvorak, Joseph, 641

Eagle Brewery (Eau Claire), 402-45, 406
Eagle Brewery (Fountain City), 415
Eagle Brewery (Janesville), 442
Eagle Brewery (La Crosse), 456
Eagle Brewery (Manitowoc), 482

Eagle Brewery (Milwaukee), 129, 505–6, 533
Eagle Brewery (West Bend), 667–68
Eagle Park Brewing Co., 548
Eagle River, Wis., 402
Eagleton, Wis., 378
Earl, Anthony, 332
Earth Rider Brewery, 640
East River Brewery, 425
East Troy (Twp.), Wis., 402
Eastern Coast Breweriana Association (ECBA), 289
Easton, Maureen, 480
Easton, Trevor, 480
Eaton, Hiram W., 413
Eaton, S. M., 650, 651
Eau Claire, Wis., 13, 18, 45, 52, 62, 76, 88, 101, 104, 200, 216, 270, 326–28, 339, 402–50
Eau Claire Brewing Co., 404
Ebel, Adolph, 452
Ebel, Jerome, 448
Eberhardt, J. A., 539
Eberle, Michael, 674
Ebner, Carl, 414
Ebner, Carl, Brewing Co., 236, 242, 243, 414
Ebner, William, 405
Ecke, Charlotte, 574
Ecke, Gottlieb, 569, 573–16
Ecke, Louis, 574
Eckel, Henry, 432
Eckhardt, Christian Ernst, 62
Eckhardt, Fred, 202
Eckhardt, George, 400
Eckhart, Philip, 414
Eckstein, Christopher, 667
Eclipse Brewing Co., 377
economies of scale, 80, 116, 268
Ede, Peter, 385, 672
Eder, Philip, 67, 415, 416
Eder, Valentine, 415
Eells, Katie, 608
Effinger, Ferdinand, 72, 104, 106, 197, 208, 209–10, 268–69, 271, 275, 371, 610
Effinger Brewing Co., 104, 371–72
Egan, Nick, 400
Egan Brewing, 400
Egg Harbor, 408
Eggenhofer, George, 631
Eggerer, John, 586

Eggert, Reinhardt Ernest, 634
Eggleston, William, 438
Ehlert, Charles, 625
Ehret, George, Brewery (New York), 256, 519. See also Schlitz, Jos.
Ehrgott, Adam W., 556
Ehrgott, Frank, 556
Eiche, Herman C., 489–90
Eichelberger, Kevin, 665, 666
Eichert (Eckert), John, 628
Eichinger, Tim, 342, 547, 580
Eichinger, Toni, 342, 547, 580
Eifert, Johann Heinrich Jr., 437
Eifert, Johann Heinrich, Sr., 437
Eighteenth Amendment, 192, 208
Eilert, Ernest (Ernst), 437, 556
Eisenbeis, John, & Co., 470
Eisenbeiss, Andrew, 645
Eisenbeiss, John, 645
elections, influence of beer and brewers on, 58, 74, 161, 179, 183, 531
Electric City Brewing Co., 243, 449
electricity, in breweries, 112, 117, 118, 344, 643
Eline Co., 197–98, 518–19. See also Schlitz, Joseph, Brewing Co.
Elk Grove, Wis., 37, 408–51
Elk Spring Brewing Co., 657
Ellenson, John, 47
Ellinger, Frederick, 629
Ellison, Charles, 491
Ellsworth Brewing Co., 409
Elmer, Werner, 558
Elroy, Wis., 409
Elser, Christian, 68, 574
Embs, John, 643
Emerson Climate Technologies. See Vilter Manufacturing Co.
Empire (Imperial) Brewery (Madison), 476–77
Empire Brewery (Eau Claire), 406
Empire Brewery (Fond du Lac), 411–12
Empire Brewery (La Crosse), 463
Empire Brewery (Milwaukee). See Best, Phillip, Brewing Co.
Empire Brewery (Watertown), 651
Encore beer (Schlitz), 251
EndeHouse Brewery & Restaurant, 339, 340, 602
Enes, John, 532–33
Engebos, Krystine, 428

Engel, Valentine, 595, 598
Engel, William, 450
Engelhardt, George Henry, 418
Engelhardt, Heinrich, 418
Engelhardt, John P., 511
Engelhardt, John, 451
Engelhardt, Laura, 420
Engelhardt, Mary Elizabeth, 511
Engelhardt, Philip Stephen, 512
Engels & Schaeffer, 45, 387
Engels Brewing Co., 485
Engels, Charles, 387, 500
English immigrants, as brewers, 374, 375, 385, 488, 641
Engmann, Jacob, 653
Enlightened Brewing Co., 547
Epstein, Henry, 77, 587
Erb, Dennis, 675–76
Erb, Leslie, 675
Erdmann, Albert W., 541
Erdmann, Esther, 541
Erhardt, Xaver, 415
Erhart, Louis, 639
Erickson, Jacob L., 466
Erie Canal, 35
Erlanger beer, 297, 298, 511, 517, 518
Ernst, Christian, 556
Ernst, John, 592
Esser, George H., 445
Esser, George, 47, 51, 62, 63, 67, 397, 551–52
Esser, Jacob, 397
Esser, John, 609
Esser, Larry, 47, 378, 397
Esser, Wayne, 47, 378, 397
Esser's Ale Brewery, 445
Etzweiler, Peter, 663
Eulberg, Adam, 482, 588
Eulberg, John Jacob, 588
Eulberg, Joseph, 588
Eulberg, Julius, 588
Eulberg, Peter, 482, 588
Eulberg Brewing/Products Co., 399, 588–89
Evans, Alex, 479–80
Evrard, R. E., 567
Ewe, Louis, 415
Excelsior Bottling Works, 539
excise tax. See taxation
Explorium, The, 430
explosions, in breweries, 94, 112, 143, 513

Export beer (style), 130, 131, 136, 227, 427. *See also individual breweries*

Faatz, John George, 395
Fabry, Andrew, 429
Fahl, Henry, 539–40
Falbe, Anton (Toni) W., 538
Falbe, T. W. & Co., 538
Falk, Frank, 505, 534
Falk, Franz, Brewery/Brewing Co., 117, 118, 124, 129, 130, 139, 141, 153, 159, 165, 533–34
Falk, Herman, 534
Falk, Jung & Borchert Brewing Co., 102–3, 163, 516, 534
Falk, Louis, 534
Falk, Otto, 534
Falk Corporation (Rexnord Corporation), 534
Falls Brewing Co., 568
Falstaff Brewing Copmpany (St. Louis), 235, 256, 264, 294, 695n10
Faltz, Michael, 385
Fardy, Matthew, 444
Farmer's Brewery (Beaver Dam), 68, 373
Farmer's Brewery (Columbus), 396
Farmers Brewery (LeRoy), 469–70
Farmers Brewing Co. (Shawano), 82, 84, 118, 210, 612–13
Farmersville, Wis., 409
Farmington, Wis., 409–52
Farwell & Co., 57, 473
Fassbender (Foshenden), Adolph, 608
Fauerbach, Karl P. (Prib), 472
Fauerbach, Louis, 472
Fauerbach, Maria, 471, 588
Fauerbach, Peter, 471, 561, 588
Fauerbach Brewing Co., 67, 68, 183, 209, 214, 331, 369, n103, 471–73
Feddersen, Andrew, 599
Federal Trade Commission, 257, 275, 298
Federated Trades Council, 88
Fehlsdorf, August, 609
Feicht, Arthur, 658
Feiner, John, 498
Feiss, F. A., 587
Feld, Mark, 637
fermentation, 26–28, 29, 67, 287
fermenteries, 478
fermenters, 107, 282, 285, 348, 393, 496, 582, 585

Fermentorium, The, 310, 387–88
Fernekes, Anton, 532–33
Fernock, James P., 265, 664–65
Fertig, John N., 366
Feser, Casper, 471
Fess Hotel (Madison), 338
Fetsch, Andreas, 669
Fick, Christian, 485
Fiedler, Henry, 415, 416
Figi, J. Brewing Co., 271, 272, 487, 490
Figi, John Jr., 271, 272
Fillion, Joe, 584
Fillion, Nancy, 584
Fillmore (P.O.), Wis. *See* Farmington, Wis.
filtering, 299
Findorf, John, 503
Fine, Gustav, 520
Finke, Anton, 383
Finke, Catharine, 383
Finke, William J., 383, 671
Finke-Uhen Brewing Co., 382, 383
fires: in breweries, 55, 58, 101–4, 110, 339; causes of, 55, 90, 94, 98, 101–4; insurance against, 104, 119, 153, 622; protection against, 55, 103–4, 119. *See also individual breweries*
Fisch (Fish), Albert, 362–63
Fischbach, Lydia, 542–43
Fischbach, Walter, 542–43
Fischbach Brewing Co., 233–34, 542–43
Fischer, Andrew X., 195–96, 417, 565
Fischer, Anton, 62, 629
Fischer, C. F., 458
Fischer, Tobias, 570
Fisher, Anton (John), 363
Fitchburg, Wis., 340, 410
Fitger, A. Brewing Co. (Duluth, Minn.), 235, 648
Fitterer, Emil, 542
Fitterer, Otto, 542
Five Star Brewing Co., 397
Fix, Alois, 386–87, 606
Fix, Dorothy, 387
Fix, Steve, 659
Fixture Brewing Co., 659
Flamon (Hannon/Annon), Philippe, 425
flat top cans. *See* beer cans
Fleck, Stephen, 68, 396
Fleischmann, Andreas, 500
Fleisher, Adolph, 594
Flemming, Bob, 398

Florence, Wis., 410
Floss, Margaret, 557
Floss, Paul, 557
Flynn, Charles H., 648
foam scrapers (beer combs), 289
Foast (Frost), Charles, 470
Fogle, Ben, 366
Fogle, Jeff, 366
Fogle, Leah, 366
Fogle, Mairi, 366
Fond du Lac, Wis., 410–13
football, teams sponsored by breweries, 523, 586
Ford trucks, 113
Forrer, Christie, 676
Forst, Joseph, 495
Forster, Christopher, 527, 535
Forster, John, 556
Forster, William, 593
Fort Atkinson, Wis., 36, 49, 176, 236, 242, 243, 413–15
Fort De Seelhorst, 37, 408–51
Fort Winnebago, 35
Fort Winnebago Brewery (Old Red Brewery), 46–47, 68
Fortune magazine, 227–28
Foster & Danner, 369
Foster, C., 527
Foster, George, 369, 608
Foude, John, 536–37
Fountain Brewery (Waukesha), 653, 656
Fountain City, Wis., 2, 52, 67, 87, 218, 274, 415–17
Fountain City Brewing Co. (Inc.), 2, 87, 218, 242, 268, 272, 416
Fouty, Frederick, 555
Fox, J. P., 404
Fox Classic Brewing Co., 366
Fox de Luxe Brewing Co. (Chicago), 658
Fox Head Brewing/Beverage Co. (Noramco), 252, 264, 267, 268, 272, 322, 658
Fox Head Waukesha Corp., 189, 232, 242, 657–58
Fox Lake Brewing Co., 417–18
Fox Lake, Wis., 234, 417–18
Fox River Brewery (Pewaukee), 55, 580–81
Fox River Brewery (Wrightstown), 676
Fox River Brewing Co. (Oshkosh), 579
Fox River Brewing II (Appleton), 366
Fox Valley & Western Railroad, 428

Fox Valley Brewing Co., 498
Francis Creek, Wis. See Kossuth, Wis.
Frank, Leos, 407–50
Frank, Maurice, 384
Frank, Theresa, 407–50
Frank, William, 431
Franklin, Wis. (Milwaukee Co.), 418
Franklin, Wis. (Sheboygan Co.), 418
Franz (France), Jacob, 456
Frase, August, 404
Fratello's Restaurant & Brewery, 366
Frazier (Feezier), John, 581
Fredericksen, Mike, 437
Frederickson, Rasmus, 563–64
Freistadt, Wis., 418
French, Virginia, 498
Frenzel, Frederick, 628
Freund, John, 569
Frey (Fry), Henry, 595, 597
Frey, Charles, 410
Frey, Jacob, 410, 505
Freyer, Albert, 389
Fricke, Carl (Charles), 484
Fricke, Theodore, 387, 485
Fricke, William, 484
Fricker, William, 366–67
Fries, Frank, 80, 363, 497
Fries, Michael, 364
Frietsch, Adolph, 518
Frings, Charles H., 450
Fritz, Frederick, 535
Froedert, William, 674
Froedtert Malting Co., 95, 144, 529
Froedtert, Jacob, 529
Froedtert, William, 529
Frommader, George, 445
fruit beers, 23, 27, 29, 280, 324, 331, 333, 334. See also individual breweries
Fryer, Albert, 446
Fuchs, Joseph, 476–77
Fueger, Edward, 497
Fueger, Max, 42–43, 530
Fuermann, A., Brewing Co., 78, 651–52
Fuermann, Albert, 652
Fuermann, August, 651–52
Fuermann, Gerhard, 652
Fuermann, Henry, 652
Fugina Bros. & Fertig, 366
Fuhrmann, Albert, 601
Fuller, Charles, 427
Fun Hunters Brewery, 313
Funk Factory Geuzeria, 480

Funk, Levi, 480
Funke, Ernest, Sr., 492
Furst, Ignatz, 463, 627
Furthermore Brewing Co., 23, 378
Fuss, Christian, 498–99
Fuss, Henry J., 418–19
Fuss, Jacob, 515–16
Fuss, John, 604
Fuss, John H., 418–19, 423
Fuss, Joseph, 515–16
Fuss & Baines, 418
Fussville, Wis., 418–19

Gabel, Frank, 514
GABF. See Great American Beer Festival
Gablinger's beer, 282, 283, 284, 698n12
Gaida, Kurt, 613
Galesville, Wis., 419
Gallagger, Alois (Louis), 526
Gallagger, Mary, 526
Galveston-Houston Breweries (Galveston, Tex.), 283
Gambrinus (King): depictions of, 70, 147, 308, 361, 464
Gambrinus Assembly, Knights of Labor, 141, 142
Gambrinus Brewery, 79, 573–16. See also Kuenzl, Lorenz
garages. See breweries: buildings
Garden City Brewery, 550
Gartzke, Edward, 388
Gartzke, Emil, 388
Gartzke, Otto, 388
Gary, Indiana, 261
Gataike, C., 418
Geary, Matt, 452
Gebhard (brewer in Chippewa Falls), 391
Gecman, Joseph, 424–25
Geffert, Henry, 601
Gehl, Andy, 548
Gehring, Jake, 461
Gehring, William, 495
Gehring & Teuschel, 495
Geiger, F. A., 210, 389
Geiger, Veit, 569
Geiser, Phillip, 555
Geisert, August, 499, 580, 604
Geisler & Hagen, 456
Geisler, Edward, 434
Geisler, Harry, 380
Gellner, Jacob, 605–6

General Beer Distributors (Madison), 319
General Brewing Co. (Azuza, Calif.). See Miller Brewing Co., Azuza brewery
General Vehicle Co., 684n76
Geneva (Twp.), Wis., 419
Geneva Lake Brewing Co., 468
Gentry, Peter, 479
Georgelein, John, 445
Georgii, Otto, 591
Gerend, Mike, 545
Gerlach, August, 500
Gerlach, Carl Anton, 493
Gerlach, William, 527–28
Gerlinger, Frederick, 538
German beers, imported to Wisconsin, 298, 320, 326–27
German immigrants, 1, 33, 38, 40–41, 45, 51, 52, 53, 54, 56, 58, 63–64, 68, 88, 117, 166, 172, 189–90; anti-German sentiment, 170, 172, 185, 190–91; political views of, 56, 63–65, 179; resistance to draft (1860s), 63
Germania Brewery, 529
Germantown, Wis. (Washington Co.), 419–21
Germantown (Twp.), Wis. (Juneau Co.), 419
Germantown Spring Brewing & Soda Co., 420, 541
Gerstner, Peter, 524–25
Gerwing, Alf, 489
Gesell (Brothers) (Distributing), 494
Gesse, Michael, 593
Gettelman, A., Brewing Co., 17, 99, 142, 144, 153, 160, 162, 163, 166, 232, 233, 240, 249, 263, 266, 531–32
Gettelman, Adam, 531
Gettelman, Fred (Fritz), 531
Gettelman, Fred, 531–32
Gettelman, William A., 542
Gettleman, Tom, 531–32
Gezelschap, Charles H., 178, 439, 529
Gibson, Isaac, 535
Gierczak, Andrew, 344, 547
Gierow, Herman, 389
Gierow & Hoch (Brewing Co.), 389
Giese, E. F., 495
Gilbert, Bill, 365
Gildenhaus, K. J., 394
Gillaume, Keith, 399

Gillman, Charles, 73, 432, 549
Gillman, Frederick, 549
Gillman, Phillip, 432
Gillman, William, 432
Gipfel, Charles W., 506-7
Gipfel, David, 41, 506
Giverson, John E., 242
Glass, Will, 408
Glassbrenner, Leonard, 605
glasses, 31, 37, 44, 73, 145, 147, 148, 149, 202-3, 270, 290, 561, 602
Glatz, John, 68, 79, 574, 575 Union Brewery (Oshkosh)
Glatz, William, 574, 575-18
Glendale, Wis., 331, 421
Glicker, John, 672
Gloeckler (Gloeggler), Barnard, 68, 587, 589
Gluck, J. F., 581
Gluek Brewing Co. (Minneapolis, Minn.), 240, 268, 281
gluten-free beers, 421, 480, 544
Gnadt, John, 594
Gnadt, Mary, 594
goats, 110, 113, 149, 312
Goebel Brewing Co. (Detroit, Mich.), 237
Goebel, Augustus, 621
Goeggerle, Frank, 373
Goeggerle, John, 372-73
Goeggerle, Julia, 373
Goehring, Jacob, 595
Goeltz, Adam, 368
Goerke, Charles, 538
Goerke, William, 538
Goes, Frederick, 533
Goettelman, Gertrude, 581
Goettelman, Jacob, 580-81
Goetter, Balthasar, 51, 667
Goetz, Fred W., 623
Gogebic Range Spring Brewery, 438
Gohsman, Andy, 548
Gohsman, Jimmy, 548
Gohsman, Robin, 548
Gohsman, Tommy, 548
Golden Lake, Wis. *See* Summit, Wis.
Golling, Joseph, 471
Gondrezick, Ignatz, 437, 644
Good City Brewing, 547
Good Templars. *See* Independent Order of Good Templars
Goronson, Jim, 669

Gorski, Carol, 635
Gorski, Ronald, 635
Gosser, Jay, 435
Gosser, Julie, 435
Gosset, Jimmy, 659
Gottfredson, Frederick J., 451
Gottfredson, Jacob G., 450-51
Gottfredson & Gunnermann, 47, 450-51
Gould Grain Co., 482
Govier, John, 442
Graber, K. P., 601
Grabner, Karl, 272, 276, 417
Grace, Peter, 524
Grace, W. R., & Co., 282, 524
Graetz, Charles, 628-29
Graetz, Rheinhard, 628-29
Graf, Hugo, 369, 447
Graf, John J., 144, 153, 537-38, 652
Graf, Peter, 542
Graf, Sylvia, 538
Graff, Julius, 485
Grafton Brewing Co., 193, 421-22
Grafton, Wis., 45, 193, 219, 340-41, 421-22
Graham Law, 179
Graham, Paul, 362, 448
Graham, William (Pabst employee), 259
Grahammer, Adolph, 567-10
grain quotas, violation of, 563
Grambrinus Assembly, Local 7953, 141
Grand Army of the Republic, 138, 152, 163, 164
Grand Rapids, Wis. *See* Wisconsin Rapids, Wis.
Grand Rapids Brewing Co., 675
Grand Valley Brewing Co. (Ionia, Mich.), 240
Granite City Food & Brewery, 478
Grant, Bert, 335
Grant, Robert, 597
Grant Distributing, 420
Granville, Wis., 43, 422-23
Grassmuck, William, 413
Gravesville, Wis., 423
Gray Brewing Co., 429, 445
Gray, Joshua C., 445, 536
Gray, William H., 536
Gray's Tied House, 445, 647
Great American Beer Festival (GABF), 326
Great Dane Bill, 340

Great Dane Pub & Brewing #2 (Fitchburg), 340, 410
Great Dane Pub & Brewing-Hilldale, 340, 478
Great Dane Pub & Brewing-Wausau, 340, 665
Great Dane Pub and Brewery, 338-39, 477
Great Depression, 205, 210, 220, 495, 631
Great Lakes Brew Fest, 203
Great Taste of the Midwest, 202-3
Green, Howard T., 655
Green, Thomas, 594
Green Bay Brewing Co. (Hinterland), 23, 310, 399, 400, 429, 579
Green Bay Packers, 426, 427, 429, 523, 567
Green Bay Road Brewery, 516
Green Bay, Wis., 16, 35, 36, 44-45, 68, 80, 85, 88, 112, 116, 195, 255, 290, 339, 350, 423-24
Greenfield, Wis., 430
Greenfield (Twp.), Wis., 430
Greenview Brewing Co. LLC, 480
Greenwood, Wis. *See* Yuba, Wis.
Gregory, Jared Comstock, 177
Gretzinger, Jerry, 337
Gridley, Russell A., 436
Griel, George, 670
Griesbach Brewing Co., 450
Griesser, Richard, 208, 406, 576, 630
Griffin, Michael, 451
Grigger, Peter, 600
Grignon, Augustin, 384
Grimm, Aloys, 386
Grimm, Hugo, 386
Grimm, William, 386
Grisbaum, Joseph, 525
grocery stores, beer sold by, 528, 570, 574
Groeschl, John, 666
Groessel, George, 425
Groh, Justus, 629
Groh & Henschel, 414
Gronert, George, 592
Gross, Elisabetha (Lisette) (later Lisette Miller), 418, 521, 522
Gross, Godfred, 418
Gross, Nicholas (Pinky), 630
Gross, Philip, 418
Grosskopf, John, 435

Grotch & Seidel, 482–83
growlers: glass, 336, 348, 408; metal, 184, 569, 572
Grubb, Adam, 637
Grubb, Jacob, 637
Gruebner, Henry, 617
gruit, 24, 566
Grumpy Troll, 554
Grunert, William, 535
Gruszczynski, Joseph F., 539
Gugler, Henry, 106
Gugler Lithographic Co., 106
Guinness Stout, 29, 158
gum arabic, 76
Gund, George, 463
Gund, Henry, 465
Gund, John, brewery (1854-8), 46, 53, 456, 457
Gund, John, Brewing Co. (1873-1920), 7, 19, 46, 89, 90, 134, 157, 463-66
Gund, John Jr., 465
Gund, John Sr., 457, 459, 463-65
Gunderson, Nels, 579
Gundlach, Jacob, 419
Gunlach, Jacob, 432
Gunnerman, John, 450-51
Gunther, A., & Co., 129, 130, 131, 533
Gustavson, John, 428
Gut, Ulbrich, 388-89
Gutbier, Otto, 676
Gutheil, Bernhard, 17, 454-55
Gutheil, Ferdinand, 454-55
Gutheil, Fred R., 389
Gutheil, Louis, 454-55
Gutsch, A. O. (Ollie/Allie), 615
Gutsch, Adolph F., 614
Gutsch, Alfred, 614
Gutsch, Anton, 613
Gutsch, Francis, 613
Gutsch, Henry F., 388
Gutsch, Leopold, 613
Gutsch Brewing/Products Co., 88, 109, 116, 119, 192, 197, 205, 584, 614-16. See also Kingsbury Breweries Co.
Gutschow, Fred, 493

Haak, William, 455
Haas, Conrad John, 606
Haas, John, 593, 606
Haberbusch, Casper, 569
Habermann, John, 386
Habermehl, George, 497

Habermehl & Mueller, 497
Haberstumpf, Conrad, 552
Habhegger, John U., 652-53
Habhegger, Ulrich, 653
Haefner, Christian, 592
Haertel, Charles Jr., 588
Haertel, Charles Sr., 47, 51, 63, 76, 117, 139, 505, 587-88
Haertel & Kemmeter, 632-33
Hagemeister, Al, 635
Hagemeister, Albert, 427
Hagemeister, Francis (Franz) Henry, 68, 426-27
Hagemeister, Henry, 427
Hagemeister, Louis, 427
Hagemeister Brewing Co., 75, 80, 195, 255, 426-27, 635-36, 645
Hagen, George, 484
Hagenah, John, 601
Hagenah, Peter, 601
Haidlinger, Richard, 578
Haiga, J., 440
Hail, Gabriel, 589
Hail, John, 589
Haines, Ralph, 367
Hale, B. S., 600
Hale, John, 488
Hall, Orville, 496
Hall, William H., 53
Halvorson, Kittel, 690n53
Hamilton, Robert D., 373, 414, 457
Hamlin, S. M., 371
Hamm, Charles, 599, 624
Hamm, Charles Jr., 599
Hamm, John, 494
Hamm, Joseph C., 599
Hamm, Theo., Brewing Co. (St. Paul, Minn.), 235, 264, 274, 553, 653, 695n10
Hammond, Wis., 430-31
Handschiegl, Andrew, 649
Hanhagen (Hauchung), Erik S., 398
Hanna, Mark C., 643
Hanover Bottling Works, 542
Hansen, David, 507
Hansen, Emil Christian, 27, 98
Hansen, Eric, 621
Hansen, W. R., 243, 449
Hanson, Carl, 564
Hanson, Christian, 564
Hanson, Todd, 366
Hantke, Ernst, 108

Hantke's Brewers' School & Laboratories, 92, 108
Hantzsch, Emilie, 405
Hantzsch, Ernest Robert (E. R.), 404-5
Hanzal, Frank, 362-63
Hanzlik, Joseph, 605
Harbor City Brewing Co., 586
Harders, Hartwig, 540
Hardweg, George, 595
Harrington, John, 451
Harris, Greg, 436-37
Harris, Molly, 436-37
Harris, Stuart, 329
Harrison, Benjamin, 148
Harrison, John, 398, 545
Harstoff & Stending, 401
Hart, William, 441
Hartel, Joseph, 639-40
Hartford, Wis., 431-32
Hartford City Brewery, 431
Hartig, William, 625, 650, 652
Hartig & Manz City Brewery, 81, 650
Hartig Co., 650-51
Hartl, Louis A., 489-90
Hartland, Wis., 432
Hartman, Howard, 658
Hartmann, Julius, 497
Hartwell, George, 394
Hartwig, Albert, 404
Hartwig, John, 594
Hartzhein, M., 643
Harvey, George, 442
Harz, Jacob, 501
Haskett, Jacob, 369
Hasslinger, Charles, 414, 448
Hauer, John, 491
Hauf, August, 661
Haug, John, 363, 562
Hauser, Paul, 410-11, 641
Hauser & Dix, 410-11, 641
Hausmann, Carl, 475
Hausmann, Joseph, 471, 474-75, 560-63
Hausmann, Otto, 475
Hausmann, William, 475
Hausmann Brewing Co., 64, 67, 68, 179, 397, 474-76
Haverkorn, Cindy, 429
Haverkorn, Mike, 429
Havliceck, Wenzel, 385
Hawai'i: shipments to, 165
Hayden Bros., 396

INDEX   717

Hayes, Rutherford B., 153
Haylofters (theater group), 382–83
Haymarket Affair, 142
Hayward, Wis., 432
Healy, Michael, 326–28, 406–49
Heath, John, 597
Hebner, H. A., 558
Heck, Frederick, 62, 66, 110, 594, 596
Heck, Philip, 596
Hefty, Jacob (Monroe), 552
Hefty, Jacob (New Glarus), 558
Hefty, Margaret, 552
Heger, R. Malt & Brewing Co., 32, 446–47
Heger, Rudolph, 369, 446–47
Heger, Rudolph, City Brewery, 17, 18, 446–47
Heibel Bottling Co., 445
Heick, Detlev, 609
Heid, Math., 85
Heid, Wallie. See Muench, Wallie
Heil Co., 209
Heileman, G., Brewing Co., 89, 90, 209, 213, 238, 241, 260, 265, 266, 272, 282, 292, 293, 302–3, 304–6, 459–5, 511, 665; advertising, 289, 301, 306; Baltimore brewery, 305, 307; Belleville, Illinois brewery, 306, 462; as contract brewer, 295, 302–3; employees, 89, 90, 262, 263, 265; Evansville, Indiana brewery, 304; expansion of, 268, 280, 293–94, 304–5, 658; Louisville brewery, 268; national rank of, 267–68, 304, 305; Newport, Ky., brewery, 268, 304, 462; Perry, Ga., brewery, 293, 307, 462; Phoenix, Arizona, brewery, 305; products, 193–94, 199, 201, 240, 280–81, 297, 299, 300, 301, 302, 304–7; San Antonio brewery, 307; Seattle brewery, 305; Sheboygan brewery, 268, 277, 304, 616–17; South Bend, Indiana brewery, 304; St. Paul brewery, 304, 306, 462. See also City Brewing Co.
Heileman, Gottlieb, 459
Heileman, Henry, 85, 459
Heileman, Johanna, 85, 459–60
Heimdal, Knut, 97
Hein, John P., 581
Heinrich, G. W., 434
Heinrich, M. W., 434

Heinrichs, P. W., 542, 586
Heinz, Hubert, 446
Heischmidt, Alois, 643
Heisleutner, John M., 653
Heitman, Clement, 451
Held, George, 447
Helf, Jacob, 449
Helf, John C., 449
Helf, Katie, 449
Helf, Peter, 449
Hellberg, Louis, 524
Hellenschmidt, John, 388
Hellman, Dave, 377–78
Hellman, Jim, 377–78
Hemming, William, 444–45
Hemming's Ale Brewery, 444–45
Hemrich, Alvin, 361
Hemrich, Fred, 361
Hemrich, John, 360
Hemrich, William, 360
Henig, William, 526
Hennes, Johan Joseph, 638
Henning, Charles W., 129, 508
Henning, Larry, 604
Henninger, John, 491–92
Henry, John, 607
Henschel, Alfred, 615
Henschel, Charles B., 614
Hensler, William, 526
Hephen, Bernard W., 641
Hereford & Hops, 340, 665
Heriot Watt University (Edinburgh, Scotland), 547
Herman, Frederick, 653
Herman, Marquart & Co., 435
Herman, Peter, 381
Herman (Twp.), Wis. (Dodge Co.). See Huilsburg, Wis.
Herman (Twp.), Wis. (Sheboygan Co.). See Franklin, Wis.
Hermann, John, 551–52
Herrick, Henry, 427
Herziger, Louis, 670
Hess, Frank J. and Sons Cooperage, 211
Hess, John, 477, 502–3, 527
Hess and Lohrer Brewery, 76
Hesselman, William, 671
Hettinger, Frances, 587
Hettinger, John, 46–47, 587
Hettinger, Matthias, 587
Hettinger, Michael, 587
Heysen, Robert, 615

Heyson & Son, 403
Hibernia Brewing Co., 6, 326–28, 406–49
Hickenlooper, John, 428
Hickey & Meyer, 607
Highland, Wis., 432–33
high license, 178. See also temperance: legislation
High Life beer (Miller), 522–24
Hika, Wis. See Centerville, Wis.
Hilgerman, George, 603
Hilgerman, Otto, 602
Hilldale (Great Dane location), 340, 477, 478
Hillsboro (Hillsborough), Wis., 433–34
Hillsboro Brewing Co. (–1942), 412, 434
Hillsboro Brewing Co. (2013–), 310, 434
Hinterland Brewery/Brewing Co., 23, 399
Hintz, Brett, 488
Hipler, Joseph, 360
Hirsch, Elroy "Crazy Legs", 523
Hispanic Americans, marketing beer to, 309
historic preservation, of breweries, 507, 532
Hobbs, Archelaus, 672
Hoberg, Christopher, 617
Hoch, John, 389
Hoch, Reiner, 525
Hochgrasle, F., 557
Hochgreve, Adolph, 424
Hochgreve, August, 51, 423–24
Hochgreve, Caroline, 423–24
Hochgreve, Chris, 424
Hochgreve Brewing Co., 423–24
Hochstein, Anton, 436
Hochstein, Joseph, 436
hockey teams, sponsored by breweries, 487
Hocking, Samuel, 68, 442
Hodson, Maria, 443
Hodson, William, 51, 55, 71, 438, 442–43
Hoeffner, John Jacob, 649–50
Hoeflein & Herley, 415
Hoeschst, Phil, 648
Hoeschst, Sara, 648
Hofer, A. W., 361
Hofer, John, 456
Hoffman, Theobald, 563, 673

Hoffman & Mill, 388
Hoffman Beverage Co. (Newark, N.J.), purchased by Pabst, 256, 510
Hoffmann, Mortiz, 623
Hoheisel, J., 671
Hohl, Joseph Frederick (Fritz), 529
Hohl, T. F., 529
Hoier, Charles, 435
Hoke, William, 415
holiday beers, 23, 326, 333, 541, 578, 581. *See also individual breweries*
Holinak, Thomas, 454
Hollander, Edward, 485
Holmen, Wis., 35
Holt, Fred, 488
Holub, Wenzel, 385
Home Brewery, 167
Home Brewing Co. (Washburn), 87, 648
"Home Life in America" advertisements, 244, 246, 247. *See also* advertising: in magazines
homebrewing: clubs, 202–3, 337, 387, 437, 579; nineteenth century, 34–35, 44; Prohibition era, 199–201, 204, 205, 367; since 1970s, 202–3, 328, 329, 337–38, 391, 648; supply stores, 204, 365
Honolulu, Hawai'i, Schlitz branch in. *See* Schlitz, Joseph Brewing Co.
Hoover, Harold, 220
Hoover, Herbert, 205, 588
Hope Brewery, 116, 597
Hop Haus Brewing Co., 648
Hopkins, Norman F., 413
Hopkins, William L., 524
Hopp, Charles, 454
Hoppe, Ferdinand, 580
Hoppe, Fritz, 582
Hoppe, Paul, 650
hops, 23–25, 35, 37, 160, 201, 202, 204, 229, 235, 249, 251, 252, 287, 576; cultivation in Wisconsin, 3, 96–98, 344–45; harvesting, 96–97, pests, 97; prices of, 97; purchases by breweries, 51
Hops Haven Brewhaus, 621
hop tea, 98
Hop Valley Brewing Co. (Eugene, Ore.), purchase by MillerCoors, 524
Horicon, Wis., 434–35
Horn, August, 68, 79, 573, 575
Horn, Earl, 577

Horn and Schwalm Brewery, 68, 71–72, 79, 115
Hornell Brewing Co., 304
Horny Goat Hideaway, 310, 547
horsepower, used in breweries, 47, 50, 109–10, 140
horses, 99, 106–7, 109–13, 114, 115, 121, 126, 145, 169; accidents involving, 110, 140
Hortonia (Twp.), Wis. *See* New London, Wis.
Hortonville Brewing Co., 17, 435
Hortonville, Wis., 17, 435
Hotels, owned by breweries, 371, 475
Hottelmann, Charles, 54, 482
Houck, Adam, 605
House of Brews, 344, 479, 669
House of Heileman. *See* Heileman, G., Brewing Co.
Houthmaker, August, 466
Howard, Wis., 435
Howards Grove. *See* Franklin (Sheboygan Co.)
howlers, 349
Howlett, George, 671
Hoyer, Joseph, 485
Huber, Edward, 523
Huber, Frank, 658
Huber, Fred, 317–18
Huber, Henry, 360
Huber, Jos., Brewing Co., 315–19, 553, 591; advertising, 317; as Berghoff-Huber, 318, 553; products, 312, 316, 318. *See also* Blumer Brewing Co., Minhas Craft Brewery
Huber, Joseph, 553
Huber & Neher, 391–92
Hucherheidt, Leo, 441
Hudepohl Brewing Co. (Cincinnati), 302
Hudson Brewing Co., 436
Hudson, Wis., 62, 436–37
Huebner, Frank, 405–48, 663
Huels, John, 431, 437
Hueneke, Kristin, 544
Huggins, Edward, 494
Hughes, J. M., 450
Hughes, Randy, 308, 463
Hughes, William, 419
Hughlett, Harold, 242
Huilsburg, Wis., 79
Hullman (Huppmann), John, 647
Humbird, Wis., 437

Hunner, John A., 361, 362, 404
Hunt, Mary Hanchett, 181
Hunt, William C., 113
Hüppeler (brewer in Muscoda), 555
Hurley, Wis., 192, 438
Huscher, Martin, 413–14
Hussa Brewery (Theresa), 643
Hussa Brewing Co. (Bangor), 18, 74, 197, 370, 491
Hussa, John, 370, 417
Hussa, Joseph, 370, 417, 652
Huster, Fritz, 526
Husting, Eugene L. (Co.), 144, 535, 538
Husting, John P., 557–58
Husting, Nicholas P., 76, 409, 592–93
Hustisford, Wis., 438
Huth, Charles, 360
Hutter Brewing Co., 434
Hutter Construction Co., 373
Hutter stopper, 135
Hydro Street Brewing Co., 396
hydrometers, 108

ice: for cooling, 3, 98–100, 140; harvesting, 99–100, 412, 646; made by breweries, 100–101; quantities used, 98–99; for shipment, 100, 133, 162, 165; trade in, 100
ice beer, 300–301, 324, 332, 337
ice cream, made or distributed by breweries, 645, 650
Icehouse beer, 300–301
icehouses, 98–100, 118, 123, 125, 126, 133. *See also individual breweries; breweries (buildings)*
IGOT. *See* Independent Order of Good Templars
Ihlenfeldt, Edward, 422
Illenberger, George, 633
Illing, Christian, 446
Imhoff, Anthony, 433
immigration, to Wisconsin. *See individual immigrant groups*
imperial beers, 29. *See also individual breweries*
Imperial Lithographing Co., 211
imported beers, 313
Imwold, Charles, 603
InBev. *See* AB InBev; Anheuser-Busch
incorporation. *See* breweries (businesses): incorporation; *individual breweries*

Independence Bottling Co., 457
Independent Milwaukee Brewery, 83, 166, 204, 209, 210, 231, 249, 263, 268, 338, 540-41
Independent Order of Good Templars, 57, 174, 175
India Pale Ale (IPA), 17, 444. *See also individual breweries*
Indians. *See* American Indians
Inquiry into the Effects of Ardent Spirits on the Human Mind and Body (Rush), 171
Internal Revenue Service, 213, 296. *See also* taxation
International Bitterness Units (IBUs), 25
Irish, William H. Jr., 648
Irish immigrants, 64, 172
Ironwood, Mich., 192
IRS. *See* Internal Revenue Service
IRTP. *See* labels: regulations concerning; taxation
Isadore Street Brewing, 635
Island City Brewery, 497
Israel, exports to, 255, 544

Jackel & Winkel, 674
Jackson (brewer in Darlington), 398
Jackson, Harold B. Jr., 260
Jacobs, Irwin, 293, 295, 511
Jacobson, Ole, 361
Jaeckel, Philipp, 602
Jaeckels, Jacob, 389
Jaeger, E. L., 587
Jaehnig, Ernst W., 410
Jaehnig, H. John, 410
Jaehnig (Klessig), Liberta, 410
Jagemann, John, 486, 646
James Page beers, 632
Janesville, Wis., 10, 17, 20, 40, 45, 51, 53, 55, 68, 71, 96, 109, 111, 112, 147, 174, 178, 180, 438-45
Janesville Steam Brewery, 111, 440
Janssen, Peter, 668
Janus, Ed, 331
Japan, shipments to, 165, 319, 378
Jefferson Brewing & Malting Co., 446
Jefferson Brewing Co., 448
Jefferson Junction, 95
Jefferson, Thomas, 34
Jefferson, Wis., 17, 18, 445-48
Jenkins Machine Co., 211
Jentsch, Frank, 455

John, Elise, 522-23
John, Harry, 523-24
John, Harry Jr., 282
Johnny O's (restaurant), 365
Johnson, Edward B., 368
Johnson, Elliott, 655-66
Johnson, Guy Jr., 593
Johnson, Hans, 601
Johnson, Harold C., Brewing Co., 471
Johnson, Tim, 303
Johnson, William, 655
Johnstown, Wis., 448
Jones & Isaacson, 502
Jones, Andy, 547
Jones, Arthur, 449
Jones, Barbara, 566
Jones, Harvey, 555
Jones, L. T., 502
Jones, Thomas C., 381
Julia, Thomas, 548
Junction City, Wis., 341, 448
Juneau, Solomon, 38, 491
Juneau Products Co., 561
Jung, Hugo, 600
Jung, Karl, 600
Jung, Matt, 599
Jung, Philip Jr., 530
Jung, Philipp, 159, 516, 530, 534
Jung, William G., 599
Jung & Borchert, 130, 141, 142, 389
Jung Beverage/Products/Brewing Co. (Random Lake), 232
Jung Brewing Co. (Milwaukee), 166, 530
Jungers, John, 337-38, 365
Jungers, Phyllis, 337-38, 365
Jungle, The (Sinclair), 187
Jussen, Jacob, 47, 395
Justice Department (U. S.), 258, 281, 291, 304
Justin, Joseph, 387

K Point Brewing, 408
Kading, Fred, 652
Kaeding, Frederick, 432
Kaehler, Christian, 571
Kainz, Dana, 669
Kainz, Wayne, 669
Kalkbrenner, Philip, 152
Kalmanovitz Charitable Foundation, 296
Kalmanovitz, Paul, 293-94, 295, 511
Kamlich, R., 438

Kamps, Greg, 429
Kane & Connelly, 400
Kansas City, Mo., 127
Kansas-Nebraska Act, 55, 58
Kappel, Fred, 591
Kappelbaum/Kassebaum (brewer in Sheboygan Falls), 622
Kappes, Peter, 456
Karben4 Brewing, 479-80
Kargleder, John (Johann Nepomuk), 129, 529
Kargus, William C., 84, 577-78
Karls, Joe, 429
Kashper, Eugene, 296, 511
Katchever, Joe, 467
Katchever, Tony, 467
Katler, Alois, 415
Kaufman, Henry, 74, 676
Kaufmann, Fred, 647
Kaufmann, Valentine, 645, 646-47
Kaukauna, Wis., 109, 243, 448-49
Kaukauna Brewery, 109, 448-49
Keg, The, 635
keg beer. *See* beer: draught; racking
kegs, 28, 52, 90, 94, 115, 128, 129, 137, 145, 196, 200, 219-20, 575; pitching, 101, 140; retrieval by breweries, 575, 675; to ship bottled beer, 130, 132, 133, 138; steel, 211, 229, 531; washing, 105, 225
Kehrein, Jacob, 525
Kellar, Paul, 673
Kellar, Stanley E., 633
Keller, Edward, 542
Keller, Elmer, 542, 625
Keller, Louis, 569
Kelley, Scott, 659
Kelly, Tim, 407
Kemeler, John, 448
Kemler, John, 581-82
Kemmeter, J., 633
Kemp, Nicholas, 585
Kennedy, Jim, 580, 599
Kenosha, Wis. (Southport), 42, 44, 46, 47, 57, 95, 105, 112, 116, 146, 185, 203, 229, 233, 336-37-38, 450-52
Kenosha Bidal Society, 203, 337
Kenosha Brewing Co., 451-52
Kenosha Malt House. *See* Pettit, M. H. & Co.
Kent, Rockwell, 481
Keoline, Frank, 557

Kerl, Otto, 52, 63, 376–77
Kershaw, Stanford, 586
Kersting & Co., 422
Kestler, Hans, 317
Keuhl, Godfried, 611
Kewaskum (P.O.), Wis. *See* Wayne (Twp.), Wis.
Kewaunee, Wis., 62, 85, 109, 452–54
Kewaunee Brewing Co. (post-1933), 214, 239, 267, 453–54
Kewaunee Brewing Co. (pre-1916), 454
Keyes, S. (John), 473
Keyserling, Leon, 510
Kick, Erhardt, 389
Kickstarter, 346
Kiel, Christian, 424
Kiel, Wis., 17, 454–55, 619
Kiesling, Christian, 446
Kiewel, Jacob, 499
Kiewert, Charles L., 450, 511, 673, 674
Kiewert, Emil, 555
Kiichli, Louis, 62, 637–38
Kilbourn, Byron, 38
Kilbourn City, Wis. *See* Wisconsin Dells, Wis.
Kimberly, John, 555
Kinart-Short, Ashley, 504
Kincaid, David, 643
Kingsbury Breweries Co., 54, 228, 237, 263, 266, 267–68, 269, 277, 283, 322, 483, 616, 620
Kinky Kabin Brewing Co., 370
Kippes, Andrew, 446
Kirsch, Nicholas, 365
KisselKar trucks, 113, 431, 615
Kissinger & Schaetzel, 669
Kissinger & Schneider, 669
Kitchen, Charles, 425
Klaber, George, 611
Klann, William, Sr., 671
Kleiber (brewer in Sheboygan), 620
Klein, Charles, 486
Klein, Francis G., 384
Klein, Jacob, 116, 638
Klein, Philip, 540
Klenk, Christoph, 384
Klessig (Klessing), Ernst, 409–10
Klett, Theodore, 454
Kline, Michael, 448–49
Klinger, Nicholas, 75, 76, 178, 414, 504–7, 670–71
Klingler, John, 525, 624

Klinkert, Ernst (Ernest), City Brewery, 75, 88, 116, 143, 193, 194, 594–95
Klinkert, John A., 638–39, 640
Klinkert Brewing & Malting Co. (1898–1908), 640
Klinkert Brewing Co. (Superior) (1890–98), 638–39
Klisch, Jim, 333, 543
Klisch, Russ, 333, 543
Kloeden, Robert, 492
Klogner, Pytlik, 360
Klug, August, & Co., 422
Klug, Norman, 282, 523–24
Knaack, Nathan, 488
Knab, David, 515
Knapstein, Henry, 73
Knapstein, Mathias, 73
Knapstein, Paul, 563
Knapstein, Theodore, 73, 562, 674–75
Knapstein, William H., 562
Knapstein, William M., 562–5
Knapstein Brewing Co., 249, 269, 562–63
Knauf, Bernard, 487
Knauf, Philip, 487
Knaus, Alex Jr., 222, 364
Knauss, Steve, 640
Knauss, Susan, 640
Knecht, Adolph, 568
Knecht, Gabriel, 568
Knights of Labor, 91, 141–43, 569
Knights of Pythias, 154
Knipp, Louis (Lewis) F., 439, 529
Knipp, William Philip, 439
Knippenberg, Phillip, 527
Knipschilt, John, 20, 551
Knoblauch, A., 592
Knoblauch, Carl, 527, 536
Knoepple, Frederick, 585, 586
Knothe, John H., 540
Know-Nothing Party, 172
Knowles, Wis., 409
Knuth, David, 607
Knuth, Marie, 607
Knuth Brewing Co., 607
Kobes, Joseph, 455
Koefer, Charles, 515
Koellner, A., 418
Koepl, Frank, 617
Koepp, J. F., 378
Koethe, Richard, 538
Koga, Ryan, 479–80

Koga, Zak, 479–80
Kohl, Anna, 470
Kohl, Elizabeth, 364
Kohl, John (& Co.), 539
Kohl, John J., 491
Kohl, Susan, 364
Kohl, William, 469–70
Kohlenborn & Quick, 405
Kohler, Walter J., Sr., 205
Kohn, Emil G., 466, 569
Kohn, Emil, 540
Koke, Henry, 403
Kolar, Jeff, 621
Kolb, Abraham, 552
Kolocheski, George, 567
Konrad, Jacob, 569, 669, 670
Konrad, Valentine, 661
Konyn, Kris, 488
Korb, Anton, 527
Korean War, 237, 242, 283
Korfmann, Calvin, 320, 631
Korfmann, Ludwig, 631
Kornburger, Benedict, 540, 624
Koschitz, John, 415
Kosiec, Rich, 608
Kossuth (Francis Creek), Wis., 455
Kotien, Rudolph E., 667
Kowalke, Tom, 479
Kozlowski, Paul, 660
Kozlowski, Tammi, 660
Kozy Yak Brewery, 608
Kraft Foods, 197, 199, 363
Kraft, John, 522
Kramer, Brittany, 477
Kramer, Mark, 477
Kramer, Nicholas, 441
Kramer, Trent, 477
Kranpitz, F. H., 540
Kraus, Allis, 388
Krause, Fred W., 664
Krause, Frederic, 647
Krause, John H., 432
Krause, Simon, 388
Kraut, Frank, 496
Krauth, Charles (Carl), 607
Krefertz & Wing, 365
Kreiner, Christoph, 656
Kreiter, Bryan, 480
Krembz, Moritz, 642
Kremer, John, 129
Krenzlein, John G., 533
Kretschmer, Emma, 454

INDEX 721

Kretschmer, Louis, 454
Kreutzer, Ambrose, 666
Krieger (brewer of Fountain City), 415
Kriz, Harold, 577
Kroesing, Charles Jr., 492
Kronschnabl, Peter, 367
Kronshage, Theodore, 158
Kroos, William, 620
Krueger, G., Brewing Co. (Newark, N.J.), 226
Krueger, Todd, 377-78
Krug, August, 123, 516-17
Kuchera, August, 604
Kuehlthau, Adam, 667, 668
Kueneth, George, 661
Kuenzel, Gustav, 469, 606, 630, 675
Kuenzl (Kuenzel), Lorenz, 68, 79, 574, 575
Kuenzl, Lorenz "Shorty", 577
Kuethe, Fred, 628
Kuether, William, Brewing Co., 395
Kuhl, Adam, 68, 633
Kuhl, Charles, 633
Kuhl, Christine, 633
Kuhl, Fred, 633
Kuhl, Martin, 620
Kuhn Bros. Brewing Co., 495
Kuhn, Carl, 495
Kuhn, John, 494
Kuhn, Leo, 494
Kuhn, Rosa, 495
Kuhry (Kouhry), Louis C., 637
Kulmbacher (Culmbacher) beer (style), 136, 517, 521
Kulnick, Charles, 376, 484, 498
Kulnick, James, 376
Kumm, Roy, 268, 304, 461-4
Kunz, Elizabeth, 110, 380-81, 482
Kunz, George, 457
Kunz, George, Co., 457
Kunz, Gottfried, 110, 380-81, 482
Kunz, Heinrich George, 54, 381, 482
Kunz, Louis, II, 482, 484
Kunz, Peter, 533
Kunz & Bleser, 484
Kunz-Bleser Co., 54, 482-83
Kurth, Chris, 631
Kurth, Christian, 396
Kurth, Co., 90, 395-96
Kurth, Henry, 52, 395-96
Kurth, John Henry, 396
Kurth, John Robert, 396

Kurth, LauRetta, 396
Kurth Co., 90, 95, 98, 106, 109, 171, 395-96
Kurz, William, 495
Kuswa, M. Wesley, 604

L-permits, on labels, 82, 194
Laabs, Norbert, 496
Labahn, Charles, 585
Labahn, Ludwig, 585
Labatt Brewing Co. (Canada), 258, 300
Labatt USA, 298
LaBelle Brewing Co., 565-8
labels, 131, 132, 231-32, 273-74, 514, 613, 646, 663; regulations concerning, 206, 218, 231-32, 434. *See also individual breweries*
laboratories, in breweries, 26, 92, 265
Lachmann, Jacob, 556
Lackman, David, 594
La Crosse, Wis., 46, 53, 62, 74, 85, 89-90, 91, 131, 176, 204, 243, 274, 282, 302-3, 304-8, 319, 455-67
La Crosse Bottling Works, 466
La Crosse Breweries, Inc., 230, 238, 263, 457-58
La Crosse Refining Co., 458
Ladies Temperance Union, 180
La Follette, Philip, 21
La Follette, Robert M., Sr., 162
lager beer, 3, 25, 27-28, 29-30, 37, 40-43, 78, 99, 122, 126, 128, 136, 172, 217, 283, 312, 333, 334; first American examples, 37, 43; first Wisconsin examples, 40-43, 679n30; manufacture of, 37-38, 42, 118, 251, 316, 327, 349; *See also individual breweries*
Laisy, John, 669-70
Lake Brewery. *See* Owens, Pawlett & Davis
Lake Delton, Wis., 467-68
Lakefront Brewery, 333-34, 345, 346 351, 543-44
Lakefront Brewery: products, 23, 336, 345, 543-44
Lake Geneva, Wis., 468
Lake Louie Brewing Co. LLC, 367-68
Lake Mills, Wis., 341, 468-69
Lakeshore Brewery, 597
Lakeside Brewery (Port Washington), 585
Lakeside Brewery (Rice Lake), 604

LaLoggia, Julia, 546
Lampe brothers, 433
Lampe, George, 555
Lampson, Leonard, 438
Lancaster, Wis., 469
Land, John, 654
Landgraf, John, 389
Landsberg, Edward, 514
Landsinger, Joseph, 433
Landwehr & Baier, 427
Landwehr, Sebastian, 427
Lane, Gordon, 381-82
Lane, James, 369
Lane, Jean, 381
Lane, Kathryn, 382
Lane, Kristen, 381-82
Lang, Ambrose, 494-95
Lang, Caroline, 494-95
Lang, Edward, 495
Lang, George, 407
Lang, Henry, 446
Lang & Miller, 476
Lange, Frank ("Seagan"), 396
Lange, John B., 542
Langenbach, John J., 557
Langenberg, Fred, 623
Langenberg & Kypke, 653
Langenkamp, Anton, 385
Langer, Joseph, 453
Langlade County Creamery, 197, 363
Lanswer, George H., 496
Laper, J. W., 593
La Pointe, Wis., 35
Larson, James, 547
Larson, L. R., 595
Larson, Rob, 341, 468-69
Lasche, Alfred, 108
Lauterbach, Peter, 409, 623
Laux, George, 360, 470
Lavelle, John, 548
Lavin, George, 595
Lavoisier, Antoine-Laurent, 26
Lawrence, Wis., 219, 469
Lazy Monk Brewing Co., 407-8
Le Roy, Wis., 409, 469-70
lead mining, 35
Lebermann, Adolph, 618
Lebesch, Jeff, 586
Lechner, Joseph, 562
Lederer, Kevin, 421
Lee, Ann, 397-98
Lee, Randy, 397-98

Legends Brewhouse, 339, 435
Legends of Ashwaubenon, 339, 369
Legends of De Pere, 339, 400
Lehle, Louis, 118-9, 465
Lehner, August, 624
Lehner, Jacob, 409, 469, 492
Leidiger, Ernest, 501, 635
Leidiger, Louis G., 228, 501
Leidiger, Louis, 501, 630, 635
Leidiger, Rudolph, 501
Leidiger Beer Bill, 228, 501
Leidiger Brewing Co., 240, 267, 501
Leidiger Bros., 427, 635, 636-37
Leihe, Charles, 378
Leinenkugel, Rose (later Rose Casper), 393
Leinenkugel, Susan (later Susan Mayer), 393
Leinenkugel & Miller, 112, 392, 405
Leinenkugel, Caroline, 404
Leinenkugel, Frank Lambert, 609
Leinenkugel, Henry Joseph Jr., 404
Leinenkugel, Henry Joseph, Sr., 404, 405, 609
Leinenkugel, Henry, 403
Leinenkugel, Jacob, 73, 178, 392-93
Leinenkugel, Jacob, Brewing Co., 2, 82, 88, 216, 265, 322-26, 392-93; advertising, 324; employees, 88, 195; market area, 322-23; products, 193, 228, 312, 323, 324-26; purchase by Miller, 393-94
Leinenkugel, Jake, 324
Leinenkugel, John, 324
Leinenkugel, Joseph, 402-45
Leinenkugel, Josephine, 392
Leinenkugel, Maria Christina, 609
Leinenkugel, Mathias (Eau Claire), 52, 101, 402, 404, 608
Leinenkugel, Mathias (Sauk City), 45, 609
Leinenkugel, Matt, 393
Leinenkugel, Theresa, 402-3, 405
Leinenkugel, William (Bill), 322-23
Leinie Lodge, 325, 394 brewery tours
Leissegger & Burns, 369
Lemke, Alice, 643
Lemke, Nathaniel, 643
Lemmel, Andrew, 496
Lemon Beer Brewery, 537
lemonade, hard, 378
Lenhardt, Michael, 416

Lennon, M. E., 438
Lenroot, Irvine, 197
Lenz, Bob, 284
Lenz, Emil, 609-10
Lenz, Gustav, 610
Lenz, Jacob, 494, 502-3
Lenz, John, 496
Lenz, Marie (Mary), 609
Lenz, William, 609-10
Lenz, William Jr., 610
Lepner, Michael, 409
LeRoy, Wis., 469-70
Leszczynski, Bob, 546
Leszczynski, Dave, 546
Letters on Brewing, 108
Leuenberger, Gottlieb, 553-54
Leute, Andrew, 672-73
Leute, Charles, 673
Leute, Julius, 673
Leute, Thaddeus, 673
Lever Food and Fuel Control Act (1917), 191
Lewis, G., 394
Lewis, George, 413
Lewis, Ross, 603
Liberty Bonds, 631
Liebenstein, Catherine, 417
Liebenstein, Frank, 370, 372, 417
Lieblich, Carl, 646
Lieblich, Chris, 646
Lieblich, Frank, 645
Lieblich, George, 646
Lieblich, Harold, 646
Liebner (brewer in Sheboygan Falls), 622
Liebscher, Louis, 87, 140, 153, 413, 526, 535, 536, 539
Lieder, Mary, 549
Lieder, Otto H., 549
Lieder, Raymond J. Jr., 549-50
Lieder, Raymond J., 549
Lies, Art, 410
Life magazine, 246
light (low-calorie) beers, 299, 305, 308; history, 282-86
lighters, 461, 520
Lightning stopper, 134-35, 415, 485, 551, 654
lightning strikes, at breweries, 55, 101, 110, 398, 438, 453, 463, 649, 650, 668
Like Minds Brewing Co., 548

Lill & Diversy (Diversey) brewery (Chicago), 53, 442, 680n67
Lima (Twp.), Wis., 470
Limprecht, C. M., 620
Lincoln, Abraham, 106
Lincoln, Wis., 77, 470
Lindemann, August, 657
Lindemann, Emilie, 657
Lindner, Andrew J., 386
Lingelbach, Charles, 498, 567
Link, Anton, (& Co.), 566
Link, David, 579-80
Link, John, 580, 637
Link, Margaret, 637
Linke, B. A., 648-49
Linn (Twp.), Wis., 470
Lins, Carl, 487
Linstedt, Julius, 551
Lion Brewery (Fountain City), 416
Lion's Tail Brewing Co., 349, 556
Lipschulz, A. L., 379
Lisbon (Twp.), Wis. *See* Sussex, Wis.
Liske, Franz, 380
Lissack, Ernest, 404
List Brewing Co., 86
List, John A., 582
List, Louis, 582
List, Sophie, 86
Listemann, Kurt, 556
Lite Beer (Miller): advertising, 278, 284-85, 297; origins, 129, 283-85; sales, 285-86
lithium, in beer, 668
lithographs: advertising, 537
lithographs: of breweries, 106, 148, 472
Littel, Michael, 623, 630
Little Chute, Wis., 77-78
livestock, kept at breweries, 447
Loaf & Stein Brewing, 402, 665
Lobach, S. T., 607
LoBreglio, Rob, 338, 477, 579, 665
locavore movement, 344
Loch, Deb, 551
Lock Haven, Wis., 470
Lockman, Almon W., 413
Lockwood, J. H., 412
Loeher, John, 477
Loescher, Frederick (Fred), 496-97, 570
Loescher, George, 570
Loescher, Regina, 570
Loescher, William, 570
Logemann, Emil, 671

LogJam Microbrewery, 644, 647
Lomasky, Selma, E., 420
Lomira, Wis., 470-71, 644
Lone Girl Brewing, 660
Longnecks Brew Pub and Restaurant, 377
Lonsway, Steve, 365-66, 579
Lonsway, Tom, 365-66
Look magazine, 246
Loop Hotel (Pabst), 153
Loos & Quade, 670
Lorain, Ohio, 113
Lorenz, Philip, 407
Lorenz & Jacoby, 401
Lorscheter, Mathias, 386
Los Angeles Brewing Co., purchase by Pabst, 510
Louis, W. E., 606
low alcohol beers, 301-2
low carbohydrate beers, 308, 309
Lowell, Wis., 471
Lowell (Twp.), Wis. *See* Oak Grove, Wis.; Reeseville, Wis.
Löwenbräu beer (Miller), 5, 298, 699n53
Loyal Temperance Legion of Wisconsin, 182
Lucette Brewing Co., 499-500
Lucid Brewing Co., 437
Lucky's 1313 Brewpub, 480
Ludwig, Carl, 376, 433-34, 676
Ludwig, Franz, 511
Ludwig, Heather, 428
Luhn, Gustav, 644
Luin, Titus T., 516, 564
Luse, Claude, 414
Luthrsen, Christopher, 609
Lutz & Wenger, 454
Lutz, Andrew, 74, 629-30
Lutz, August (& Co.), 440
Lutz, David, 633, 674
Lutz, Ed, 631
Lutz, Elizabeth, 629
Lutz, George, 630
Lutz, Jacob, 74, 629-30, 674-75
Lutz, Jacob Jr., 630, 675
Lutz, John, 593, 630
Lutz, Lorenzo & Co., 454
Lyman, Dorus, 595
Lynn, Alexander W., 627
Lynn, James H., 627
Lyons, Wis., 471
Lytle-Stoppenbach Co., 95

Maas, John, 595
MacAlpine, Nate, 640
MacArthur, Douglas, 531
Mach, Anton, 109, 453
Mach, Catherina (Katie), 85, 453
Mack, Theodore (Ted), Sr., 260-61, 577, 578
Macke, Henry, 381
Mackford, Wis. *See* Markesan, Wis.
Madden, Aran, 378
Mader's restaurant, 212
Madison, Wis., 45, 51, 62, 64, 67, 68, 74, 76, 110, 128, 139, 152, 177, 179, 184, 186, 203, 209, 211, 319, 331-33, 340, 343, 348, 350, 471-80
Madison Homebrewers and Tasters Guild, 202-3, 554
Madlener, Philip, 537
Maedder, Caspar, 493
Mahler, Cecelia, 386
Mahler, Zelley, 386
Mahoney, Thomas, 623
Maiden Rock, Wis., 480-81
Maier, Alois, 494
Maier, Ernest, 220
Maier, Henry, 292
Maier, John B., 41, 504
Maier, John, 529
Main Event Sports Bar & Grill, 568
Main Street Brewery, 511
Maine Law, 57-58. *See also* prohibition
Mairet & Schmidt, 394
Malling, Vik, 635
Mallinger, John, 585
Malt Duck beer, 280
malt liquor, 240, 280-81, 287, 293, 295, 301, 302-4, 305, 694n89; marketing, 302-3; protests against, 303-4
malt: production levels, 96; shortages, 239-40, 242. *See also* barley
malting: by breweries. *See individual breweries*
malting: equipment, 19, 94, 105; process, 19-21
maltsters, 20, 94-96; consolidation of, 95-96; independent of breweries, 20-1, 88, 95-6, 142; strikes, 141, 142
malt syrup, 199, 200-1, 202, 204
malt tonic, 136, 150, 158, 171, 483, 513, 603
mandioca (cassava), in beer, 240
Manegold, Charles, 657
Manegold, William, 525, 529

Mangold, John, 676
Manhattan Brewing Co. (Chicago), 229, 452, 671. *See also* Canadian Ace Brewing Co.
Manitowoc, Wis., 20, 44, 54, 69, 73, 95, 101, 348, 481-86
Manitowoc Breweries Co., 482
Manitowoc Malting Co., 482
Manitowoc Products, 216, 237, 483, 484-85, 616, 619-20
Manitowoc Rapids, Wis., 486
Manning, Scott, 477
Mansen, Herbert, 391-92
Manske, Arnold H., 539-40
Manz & Goetz, 500
Manz, Carl, 650
Manz, Gottlob, 501
Manz, Jacob, 500
Manz, John, 501
maple syrup, in beer, 399, 429, 569, 580
Marathon (City), Wis., 73, 272, 486-87
Marathon City Brewing Co., 272, 486-87, 666
Marchant (Mexime), Charles, 555
Marchant, Joseph, 666
Marinette, Wis., 339, 487-88
Marion, Wis., 488
Maritzen, August, 118, 552, 656-57
Markesan, Wis., 488
Markham, Pacey, 284
Marshall & Rundle, 670
Marshall, W. J., 441
Marshall, William, 395, 670
Marshfield, Wis., 61, 71, 77, 88, 271, 272, 488-90, 628
Marshfield (Twp.), Wis., 491
Marshfield Area Society of Homebrewers (M*A*S*H), 490
Marshfield Brewing Co., 82, 238, 489-90
Martens, Jon, 430
Martens, Olaf, 671
Martin, Frank, 477
Martin, William F., 451
Martin, Xavier, 425
Martinson, Brent, 467
Marty, Carl O., 552
Marty, Robert F., 552
Marx, Philip, 623
Mason, John, 666
Master Brewers Association of America (MBAA), 49, 210

matchbooks, 216, 240, 267, 550
Mathie, Frank Jr., 663-64
Mathie, Frank, Sr., 663
Mathie, John, 663-64
Mathie, Otto, 663-64
Mathie-Ruder Brewing Co., 662-64
Mattes, Charles, 418
Mattes, F., 446
Matteson, D. J., 627
Matzen, Charlie, 203
Mauston, Wis., 491
Mauston Brewing Co., 87
Mauz (Maus, Manz, Mautz), Barnhard, brewery, 74, 420, 476
Mauz & Little, 475
May, Mark, 545
Mayer, Benedict, 558, 642
Mayer, Benjamin, 491
Mayer, Charles (Carl), 667
Mayer, George, 364
Mayer, John B., 557
Mayer, John, 393
Mayer, Joseph F., 497
Mayer, Joseph, 628
Mayer, Marie, 667
Mayer, Rick, 550
Mayer, Stephen, 431, 667
Mayer, Stephen F., 667
Mayer, Susan (Susanna), 667
Maytag, Fritz, 315
Mayville, Wis., 218, 491-94
Mayville Brewing Co., 217, 233, 492, 493-94
Mazomanie, Wis., 494-95
Mazzuto, John D., 307
McAdoo, William Gibbs, 191
McCabe, Jim, 545-46
McCabe, John, 545-46
McCall's magazine, 246
McCann-Erickson agency, 284
McCarthy, Joseph, 577, 603
McCartny, H. A., 370-71
McCarty, O. W., 390
McClellan, Edward J., 259-60, 669
McClintic, Brian, 375
McClintic, BT, Beer Co., 375
McClintic, Tony, 375
McCulloch, Matt, 547
McElwain, Mike, 448
McEvoy, Harold, 651
McFarlane, Douglas, 605
McGeehan Bros., 438
McIntosh, Jonathan, 468

McIntosh, Pat, 468
McKenzie, Bob, 563
McKenzie River Brewing Co., 303
McKinnon, Louis, 639
McLane, George R., 55, 580
McMahon, Angie, 370
McMahon, Ben, 370
McMahon, Danny, 370
McMahon, John, 370
mead, 397, 544
Mechler, Florian, 600
Mechler, Frank, 600-601
Mechler, W., 672-73
Medford, Wis., 77, 495-96
Medford Brewery/Brewing Co. (1894-1908), 495
Medford Brewing Co. (1934-48), 233, 495-96
Medina (Dale Twp.), Wis., 496
Meeske, Charles, 525
Meeske, Gustav, 525
Meeske, Otto, 525
Mehls, Henry, 394
Meindl, Ludwig, 623
Meinen, Albert "Bugs," 604
Meinen, Earl "Butch," 604
Meister Brau, Inc. (Chicago), 283, 284, 316
Meister, J. Simon, 535
Meister, Simon, brewery, 63, 535
Meixner, Francis (Frank), 537
Meixner, John F., 537
Melchoir, Jacob, 86, 419, 644-45
Melchoir, Leopold, 419
Melchoir, Wilhelmina, 86, 419, 644-45
Melms, Charles T., 41, 59, 63, 65, 123-24, 125, 255, 504-5
Melster, H. R., 671
Menasha, Wis., 44, 79, 89, 196, 276, 496-98
Menasha Brewing Co., 497
Menges, Michael, 591-92
Menk, Charlotte, 649
Menk, Theodore, 649
Menke, Claus, 418
Menomonie, Wis., 140-42
Menominee Brewery. See Melms, C. T.; or Gettelman, A. Brewing Co.
Menominee-Marinette Brewing Co. (Menominee, Mich.), 235, 249, 288
Menomonee Valley Brewery. See Miller Brewing Co.
Menzel, Frank, 575

Mequon, Wis., 39, 196, 418, 500-501
Meredith, Lee, 278, 284
Mergener, Nick, 366, 369
Mergenthaler, Jake, 626
mergers. See breweries (businesses): consolidation of
Merrill, Wis., 228, 240, 267, 347, 501-2
Merrill, H. A., 627
Mertes, Nicholas H. (Nick), 401
Mertz & Behse, 496-97
Merz, Herman, 427
Mesow, Ludwig (Louis), 536
Messing, Jacob, 593
Methodists, 171
Metropoulos, C. Dean, 296
Metzer, George, 431
Metzer, Nic, 431
Mexico, shipments to, 125, 165, 508, 513, 517, 533
Meyer, C. H., 52
Meyer, George J., Manufacturing Co., 211
Meyer, Henry A., 653-54, 656
Meyer, Herman A. Jr., 67, 656
Meyer, John, 405
Meyercord signs, 182, 592
Meyers, Fred, 489
Michalski, Frank, 633-34
Michel (Michels), Henry, 88, 403, 554, 556
Michel (Michels), Henry Jr., 403
Michel, C. & J. Brewing Co., 89, 176, 457-58
Michel, Carl F., 458
Michel, Charles, 74, 457-58
Michel, John, 457-58
Mick & Hasslinger, 448
Mickey's Malt Liquor, 301, 302, 307
Micro-canning, 546
microbreweries, 298, 314, 327-28; definition, 329; origin of, 314-15; in Wisconsin, 327-28, 331-52. See also individual breweries; craft breweries
Middlebury, Wis., 191
Middleton, Wis., 332, 502-3
Middlewood, William M., 506, 516, 535
Midwest Hops and Barley Co-op, 344, 362
Miller, Charles, 491
Miller, Christoph, 448
Miller, Cindy, 396-97
Miller, Clara, 523
Miller, Emil, 522

INDEX 725

Miller, Ernest, 522
Miller, F. W., 368
Miller, Frank A., 482
Miller, Frank, 371
Miller, Frederick A., 522
Miller, Frederick C., 282, 523
Miller, Frederick J., 46, 50, 128, 165, 418, 520–21
Miller, John, 392
Miller, Joseph, 374
Miller, Mathias, 476–77
Miller, Roger, 396–97
Miller, Stephen, 643
Miller, Tom (Julio), 566
Miller, William, 47, 506
Miller, William, Brewery, 17, 47, 506
Miller & Anson, 506
Miller & Bros., 608
Miller & Co (Hortonville), 435
Miller & Co. (Ashland), 368
Miller & Hartman, 643
Miller & Knight, 506
Miller & Mohrenberg, 381
Miller & Pawlett, 506
Miller Brewing Co., 2, 22, 113, 114, 124, 129, 132, 153, 163, 168, 185, 209, 234, 253, 258, 271, 282–86, 294, 301, 302, 521–24; advertising, 70, 284–86, 298, 317, 521–24; Albany, Ga., brewery, 286; and antitrust actions, 258, 281; Azuza, Calfornia brewery, 257; Bismarck, N.D., brewery, 127–28, 255, 521; as contract brewer, 296; Eden, N.C., brewery, 286; employees, 139, 142, 144, 145, 210, 229, 231, 261, 263, 264, 265, 266, 295, 523; event sponsorships, 154; Fort Worth, Tex., brewery, 256, 257; Fulton, N.Y., brewery, 286; Irwindale, Calif., brewery, 285, 286; Plank Road Brewery (19th century), 52–53, 520–21; Plank Road Brewery (20th century), 300, 701n87; production and sales, 285–86; products, 132, 217, 284–86, 298, 299, 300, 301, 302, 307, 308, 309, 521–24; purchase by Philip Morris, 524; purchase by SAB 308–9, 524; purchase of Gettelman, A. Brewing Co., 523; purchase of Leinenkugel Brewing Co., 323–25, 393–96; Trenton, Ohio brewery, 286
MillerCoors, 18, 309

Miller Lite All-Stars, 3, 5, 278, 284–85, 309
Milleson, Jeff, 437
Million, B. M., 561–62
Million Brewery, Inc., 561–62
Milwaukee, Wis., 38–39, 40–43, 51–53, 55, 58, 59, 63, 70, 75, 78, 92, 103, 120–167, 170, 178, 183, 191, 192, 204, 205, 208–9, 210, 211, 213, 215, 263–65, 292, 295–96, 331, 346, 504–48, 685n1; advantages for brewing, 43, 58; German settlement and influence in, 38, 40–41, 43, 50; manufacturing industries, 52, 101, 105–8, 198, 211
Milwaukee Ale House (Grafton), 339, 422
Milwaukee Ale House, 339–40, 545–46
Milwaukee and Chicago Brewing Co. See Blatz, Valentine Brewing Co.
Milwaukee Beer Co., 542
Milwaukee beer, other beers compared to, 53, 73, 158
Milwaukee Braves (baseball team), 523
Milwaukee Brewers (baseball team), 1, 523
Milwaukee Brewers' Association, 158, 167, 191, 530
Milwaukee Brewery. See Owens, Pawlett & Davis
Milwaukee Brewing Academy, 108
Milwaukee Brewing Association, 129, 529
Milwaukee Brewing Co. (1874), 529
Milwaukee Brewing Co. (2007–), 310, 546
Milwaukee Brewing/Brewery Co. (1893–1919), 84, 101, 144, 166, 538–39
Milwaukee County Historical Society, 154
Milwaukee Industrial Exposition (1887), 147
Milwaukee Industrial Exposition (1895) (Semi-Centennial), 41, 139, 144
Milwaukee Lithographic Co., 106
Milwaukee Malt and Grain Co., 95
Milwaukee Malt Extract Co., 450
Milwaukee Mechanics Mutual Insurance, 530
Milwaukee public schools, 108
Milwaukee-Germantown Brewing Co., 420
Milwaukee-Shawano Brewing Co., 219, 612

Milwaukee-Waukesha Brewing Co., 188, 189, 657
Milwaukee-Western Malt Co., 96
Mineral Point, Wis., 35, 37, 73, 339, 351, 548–50
Mineral Springs Brewing/Products Co., 549–50
Minhas, Manjit, 319
Minhas, Ravinder, 319
Minhas Craft Brewery, 319, 329, 553. See also Huber, Jos., Brewing Co.
mini-bottles, 599
Minick, Charles, Sr., 654
Minneapolis, Minn.: investors from, 85, 293, 602
Minneapolis Brewing Co. (Grain Belt), 250, 447
Minoqua, Wis., 339, 550–51
Minocqua Brewing Co., 550–51
Minor, Maurice J., 550
Mishicot, Wis., 551
Mishicot Brewing Co., 551
Mitchell, John P., 392, 394
Mitchell Brewing Co. (El Paso, Tex.), 655
MobCraft (brewery in Milwaukee), 547–48
MobCraft Beer, 344–45, 349, 547–48
mobsters. See prohibition: and organized crime
Moe, William, 488
Moesmer, Frank O., 623
Moethwig (Mathwig), brewer of Fountain City, 415
Mohr, Frank, 496
Mohrenberg, William, 381
molasses, in beer, 651
Molitor, Mathias, 611
Molson Coors Brewing Co., 524
Molson USA, 300
Monitor Brewery, 466
Monnette, Courtney, 488
Monnette, Paul, 488
Monostori, Veronika, 265
Monroe, Wis., 20, 43, 45, 51, 62, 213, 277, 315–19, 551–54
Monster Hall Campground, 647
Montagne, William, 451
Montagne & Graff, 451
Montayne, R. D. L., 371
Montello, Wis., 58, 554
Montmann, William, 62, 436
Moon Ridge Brewpub, 396–97

Moore, John, 563
Moore, Milford G., 568
Moosejaw Pizza. See Dells Brewing Co.
Morawetz, Ignatz, 528
Moritz, Jacob, 585
Morrison, A. Cressy, 136
Morrison, D. S., 413
Mors & Becker, 365
Morse, Alexander, 658
Morshe & Wagoner, 439
Moser, Adolph, 477
Mount Calvary Brewing Co., 554
Mount Horeb Pub & Brewery, 554
MTX Co., Inc., 553
Muehlebach Brewing Co. (Kansas City, Mo.), 519
Muehlschuster, Michael, 525–26
Muehrske, H. F., 567
Mueller, Carl G., 676
Mueller, Charles, 645
Mueller, Edward, 52, 645
Mueller, Edwin, 645
Mueller, Emil T., 459
Mueller, F. C., 623
Mueller, Fred, 456
Mueller, Gustave, 484
Mueller, John G., 503
Mueller, John P., 370
Mueller, Richard Edward, 645
Mueller Bros. (Brewing Co.), 645
Muench, Carl (Charles), 51, 85, 363
Muench, George, 364
Muench, Wallie (later Wallie Heid), 85, 363
Muench, William, 363
Muench Brewing Co., 104, 363
Muesey, Joseph, 581
Mukwonago, Wis., 554
Mulberger Act, 192
Mulberger, Henry, 650
Mulberger, Louise, 282, 523–24
mules, 109, 110, 169
Münchner beer (style), 470
Munich, Germany: beers of, 37
municipal government, relations with breweries, 162, 176, 276
Muntzenberger, Adolph, 42, 105, 450
Muntzenberger, Conrad, 41, 44, 47, 112, 450, 506
Munzinger, Christian, 538
Murphy, John, 286
Murphy, Virginia, 265

Muscoda Brewing Co., 555
Muscoda, Wis., 554–55
Muser, William, 549
Museweller, John George, 525
music: written for breweries, 4, 167
Muskie Capital Brewery, 432
Muth, Jacob, Sr., 39, 62, 382, 617
Mutual Brewing Co., 166–67
Myers (Mrs.) (brewer in Waukesha), 653

Nagel, Otto, 463
Nagle & Cook (Hook), 493
Namur, Wis., 555
nanobreweries, 201, 330, 343, 379, 400, 452, 479, 500, 548, 608
Nash, Greg, 400
Nation, Carry, 172
National Brewers Congress, 530
National Brewery Museum and Library, 352–53
National Brewing Co., 634–35
National German–American Alliance, 191
National Labor Union, 140
National Microbreweries Conference, 336
National Recovery Administration (NRA), 229–30, 412, 485
National Register of Historic Places, breweries on, 352, 466
Naudts, Dirk, 349, 560
Nauer, Caspar, 587, 589
near beer, 82, 192–94, 196, 208, 209, 237, 280, 283, 483, 528, 590, 665; advertising, 70, 168, 193–94, 195. See also individual breweries
Neenah Brewery/Brewing Co., 556
Neenah, Wis., 555–56
Neher, Kaspar, (& Co.), 369, 391–92
Neher, Melchoir, 404
Neillsville Brewing Co., 72–73, 556
Neis, John, 554
Neis, Mathias, 554
Nelson & Anderson, 502
Nelson, Erick, 502
Nelson, Kirby, 332, 503–4, 647
Nelson, Victor, 639
Nemadji Brewery, 638
Nenno, Nicholas, 608–9
Neosho Brewery/Brewing Co., 557
Neuberger, Steve, 633
Neuer, Christian, 445

Neuer, Stephen, 445
Neukirch, Franz, 33, 41, 55, 504
Neumann, Philip, 574
Neumann, William, 655
Neumueller, Fred, 571–72
Neverman, William, 556
New Albion Brewing Co. (Sonoma, Calif.), 328
New Buffalo (Twp.), Wis., 563
New Cassel, Wis., 557–58
New Deal, 214, 229–30
New Era Brewing Co., 116, 450
New Fane, Wis., 558
New Glarus Brewing Co. (post-Prohibition), 21, 26, 27, 310, 329, 334–36, 349, 350, 558–60
New Glarus Brewing Co. (pre-Prohibition), 558
New Glarus, Wis., 219, 309, 334
New Lisbon, Wis., 73, 75–76, 560–62
New London Products Co., 562
New London, Wis., 73, 109, 274, 562–3
New Orleans: beer shipments to, 59, 100
New Process Fermentation Co., 67, 105
New Richmond, Wis., 563
New York, N.Y.: beer shipments to, 58, 126, 127, 153
Newburg, Wis., 557
Newport, Wis., 563
newspapers: advertisements in, 39, 43, 187, 195, 220–21, 226, 251, 253, 256, 270, 317, 458, 464, 466, 576; and temperance, 57, 71, 147, 176, 181, 185, 204
Next Door Brewery, 480
Nicaragua, breweries in, 318, 658
Nicholai, Gustavus, 456, 463
Nickels, Tom, 582
Nicolet Brewing Co., 410
Nicollet Brewery, 399–400
Niedermaier, Sebastian, 557
Niedermair, Josef, 499
Niehoff, Bernard, 374
Nigl, Joseph, 84, 577–78
Nineck, Norbert, 626
Ninmann, Ernst, 620
Nirmaier, Luke, 563
no license, 178. See also temperance: legislation
Noe, Scott, 626
Nolen, Carl, 504, 647

INDEX 727

Nolen, Mark, 647
Noramco. *See* Fox Head Brewing
Nordberg Manufacturing Co., 105
North Lake, Wis., 563-6
Northern, Rodney, 300
Northern Brewing Co., 218, 272, 639-40
Northern Lakes Brewing Co., 363
Northern Manufacturing Co., 363
Northern Pacific Railroad, 116
Northside Brewery, 598
Northwestern Railroad, 75, 428
Northwoods Brewpub (Eau Claire), 13, 339, 407
Northwoods Brewpub and Grill (Osseo), 310, 579
Norwegian immigrants, as brewers, 394
Nothhelfer, August, 395
Novak, Ken, 435
Novello, Antonia, 302, 303
Nue, Adam, 610
Nuhlicek, Frank, 453
Nunnemacher, Henry, 525
Nye, Nelson J., 627

Oak Creek, Wis., 564
Oak Grove, Wis., 564-65
Oakfield (Twp.), Wis., 564
Oasis Beverages, 296
oats, 240
Obama, Barack, 560
Obama, Michelle, 560
Oberle, Ulrich, 642, 643-44
Obermann, George J., 529
Obermann, Gustav A., 540
Obermann, J., Brewing Co., 99, 153, 529-30
Obermann, Jacob, 153, 166, 527, 529-30
Obermann, Philipp, 530
Obermann & Caspari, 529
Obermann Brewing & Bottling Co., 540
O'Brien, Marc, 402
Oconomowoc, Wis., 195-96, 198, 242, 565-66
Oconomowoc Brewing Co. (1933-6), 565
Oconomowoc Brewing Co. (1998-2006), 565-8
Oconto, Wis., 62, 566-10
Oconto Brewing Co. (brewpub), 568
Oconto Brewing Co., 79, 94, 238, 262-63, 566-68, 614

Oconto Falls, Wis., 568
Octopi Brewing Co., 548, 659-60
Oderbolz, Anna, 377
Oderbolz, Charley, 377
Oderbolz, Frank, 377
Oderbolz, Ulrich, 51, 76, 85, 109, 377
Odholek, Joseph, 423
O'Donnell, Tom, 195, 422
Oehlschlager & Kuehn, 394
Oehlschlager, Peter, 394, 416
Oertel Brewing Co. (Louisville, Ky.), 268
Oest, "Uncle" Ernie, 288
Office of Price Administration (OPA), 237
Oglethorpe, James, 171
Ogren, Hugo, 493
O'Halleran, James T., 413
O'Halleran, Mary, 413
O'Hara, Mike, 608
Ohse, Edmund, 620
Okrent, Daniel, 185
Old Bavarian Brewing Co., 579
Old Derby Ale, 578, 607
Old Hayward Eatery & Brewpub, 432
Old Lager Brewing Co., 232, 542
Old Milwaukee (beer), 271, 275, 287, 293, 519-20
Old Oaken Bucket (newspaper), 56, 177
Old Port Brewing Co., 585-86
Old Style beer, 5, 236, 289, 297, 299, 300, 302, 303, 305, 308, 460
Olen, Jim, 428
Oliphant Brewing, 310, 349, 626-27
Oliver, Edward, 405
Olmstead, Cynthia, 626
Olsen, Hans C., 598-99
Olson, Ole, 394
Olympia beer, 250, 293, 294
Olympia Brewing Co. (Tumwater, Wash.), 235, 295
Onalaska, Wis., 91, 393, 456
Ondracek, Frank, 634
Ondracek, Garry, 634
Ondracek, Jaroslaw, 634
Ondracek, Oscar, 434
One Barrel Brewing Co., 343, 479, 674
Onopa Brewing Co., 546
openers, 134-35, 226, 458, 481
opening instructions, on cans, 226
Opitz, William, 500
Oppert, August, 501
organic beers, 334, 543, 626

organized crime. *See* prohibition: and organized crime
Orgel, John, 636
Orth, A. V., 412
Orth, J.B., 360
Orth, John, Brewing Co. (Minneapolis), 464
Ortmayer, S., 622
Ortscheid, Andrew, 385-86
Osceola (Osceola Mills), 569
Oshkosh, Chief, 79, 575
Oshkosh, Wis., 53, 68, 71-72, 79, 84-85, 89, 113, 115, 212, 260-61, 274, 338, 569-79
Oshkosh Brewing Co., 79, 84-85, 89, 113, 199, 233, 238, 260, 268, 270, 272, 274, 426, 575-77
O'So Brewing Co., 349-50, 399, 582
Osseo, Wis., 579
Osthelder, Charles, 621-22
Osthelder, Charles Jr., 622
Osthelder, Joseph, 110, 622
Ostram, Chad, 566
Otis, George, 646
Ottawa (Twp.), Wis., 579-80
Otten, Rudolph, 571
Oudenhaven, Theodore, 368
Owades, Joseph (Joe), 295
Owener, Adam, 393
Owens, Richard, 21, 39-40, 52, 505
Owens, Pawlett & Davis, Lake Brewery, 40, 55, 505
Owens, Pawlett & Davis, Milwaukee Brewery, 39, 41, 505
oxen, 39, 110

Pabst, Frank, 640
Pabst, Frederick ("Captain"), 41, 66, 78, 101, 102, 103, 123, 126, 141, 143, 147, 154, 162, 163, 165, 166, 505, 507-9, 516
Pabst, Frederick Jr., 140, 198, 210, 508-10
Pabst, Gustave, 211, 508-9
Pabst Blue Ribbon beer, 4, 136, 158, 212, 227, 255, 265, 293, 294, 508-11
Pabst Brewing Co., 1, 2, 21, 41, 87, 98, 100, 113, 129, 132, 134, 135, 139, 158, 229, 231, 237, 281, 293-96, 304, 305, 508-11; acquisition of Blatz Brewing Co., 258, 260; advertising, 4, 136, 137, 147, 148, 150, 151, 152, 153, 154,

164, 167, 220-21, 238, 252, 253, 295, 302, 508-11; agents & depots, 79, 100, 113, 126, 127, 136, 149, 254, 258, 259; employees, 137, 139, 141, 142, 144, 145, 158, 162, 166, 210, 214, 235, 241, 242, 254, 258, 259, 260, 262, 263-64, 266, 294-96, 308, 328; exports, 165; Fogelsville, Pa., brewery, 296; Los Angeles brewery, 256, 265; Milwaukee brewery, 24, 28, 105, 132, 133, 138, 147, 162, 163, 294, 295; Newark brewery, 256; non-brewery properties, 149, 151, 152, 153, 154, 183, 198, 509; Peoria Heights, Ill., brewery, 255, 256, 264, 510; Perry, Ga., brewery, 257, 293, 510; Portland, Ore., brewery, 293; as Premier-Pabst, 226, 509-10, 639; production levels, 1, 146, 164, 256, 293, 296; products, 40, 149, 193, 198-99, 217, 220-21, 226, 235, 275, 292, 294, 296, 297, 298-99, 302; during Prohibition, 193, 197-99, 200, 205, 509-510; purchase of Stroh brands, 307; sale to Kalmanovitz, 293-94, 511; sale to Metropoulous, 296; sale to Oasis Beverages, 296, 511; San Antonio brewery, 295, 296; special events, 147, 153, 154, 156, 157, 158, 163, 509-510. See also Best, Phillip, Brewing Co.
Pabst-ett, 198-99, 200
Pabst Mansion, 156, 165, 166
Packard Motor Car Co., 113
Packer Chapter, 290
Paddock Lake, Wis., 580
Padgham, Amelia, 660
Pahl, Louis P., 566
Pahl, William, 601
Painter, William, 135
Palm Garden (Schlitz), 146
Palmyra, Wis., 579
Pan-American Congress (1889), 147
Panic of 1857, 58, 62, 647, 652
Panic of 1873, 97, 140
Panic of 1893, 77, 79, 154, 561, 587, 648, 657
Papazian, Charlie, 203
Papke, O. H., 540
Pappenheimer, John L., 656
parades, 88, 89, 113, 139, 141, 144, 166, 217, 568

Paradis, George, 597
Parched Eagle Brewpub, 669
Paris (Twp.), Wis., 580
Paris Exhibition (1878), 131
Parisian Exposition Universelle, 157, 464
Parkhill, Steve, 666
Parrish, Caleb, 371
Parrish, Loomis, 371, 404-5, 627
Party Pig, 665
Pasteur, Louis, 26, 128,
pasteurization, 27, 119, 128-29, 225, 228, 299
patent medicines, 456
Patterson, Leon, 427
Patzlsberger, John, 372
Patzlsberger, Joseph, 372
Paul, Marc (Luther), 546
Paulus, John, 389
Pauly, Felix, 616, 263
Pauly, Grant, 616, 621
Pauly, William, 616
Pautz, Freidrich, 482
Pawlett, William, 505
Pearl Brewing Co. (San Antonio, Tex.), 296
Pearl Street Brewing Co., 467
Pearson, Gibson & Co., 535
Peck, George W., 164
Peerless beer, 7, 268, 463-7. See also Gund, John, Brewing Co.
Pelisell (Peliselle), John, 624
Pelissier's Limited (Winnipeg, Manitoba), 483
Pelot, Catherine, 265
Pembine, Wis., 343, 580
Penn, William, 34
pennants, 558
Peoples Brewing Co., 84-85, 260-61, 274, 277, 577-78, 692n35, 696n35
Pepin, Wis., 580
Percherons. See horses
Perini, Lou, 523
Perks, Ian, 429
Perks, Sheila, 429
Perlstein, Harris, 510
Perplies, Emil, 447, 452
Perry, Clark M., 195
Perry, Ga. See Pabst Brewing Co.: Perry branch
Peshtigo, Wis., 580
Peters, Christie, 569
Peters, Steve, 8, 569

Peterson, Pete, 602
Peterson, Rudolph, 639
Pettit, M. H. & Co., 95, Pt2-5
Pewaukee, Wis., 55, 99, 580-81
Pfeiffer, Christian, 516
Pfeiffer, Curt, 434
Pfeil, Jacob, 387-88
Pfeil, William, 418
Pfestel & Steil, 371
Pfiester, John D., 555
Pfleger, Michael, 302-3
Pheasant Branch. See Middleton
Philip Morris Co. (Altria), 286, 309
Phillipps, Matthew, 487
Phillips, John, 37, 351, 548
Phoenix, Samuel F., 175
Phoenix Brewery (Janesville), 440
Phoenix Brewery (Milwaukee), 526
Phoenix Brewing Co. (Rice Lake), 604-5
Pick, Andrew, 668
picnic bottles, 135, 230, 288, 561-62. See also bottles: large sizes
Piel Bros., Inc. (Brooklyn, N.Y.), 283
Pierce (Twp.), Wis., 581
Pierce-Arrow trucks, 113
Pierce, DeWitt B., 381
Pierce, John S., 508
piers, at breweries, 75
Pierson, William R., 606
Pies, Philip, 666
Pigeon River Brewing Co., 488
Pilmire, Matthew, 418
Pilsen (Plzeň), Czech Republic, 17, 37
Pilsen Brewery (Kewaunee), 85, 453
pilsner (pilsener) beer, 17. See also individual breweries
Pink Boots Society, 673
Pioneer Brewing Co. (Black River Falls), 377-78, 545
Pioneer Brewing Co. (Fond du Lac), 412
Pioneer Haus Brew Pub, 342, 582
Pistorius, Mary, 415
Pistorius, Michael, 415
pitch houses, 101. See also breweries (buildings); coopers; cooperages
Pitchfork Brewing Co., 437
Pittsburgh, Pa.: shipments to, 13, 16, 127
placemats, 13, 16
Plainfield, Wis., 581
Plank Road Brewery (La Crosse), 9n, 463

Plank Road Brewery (Milwaukee). See Miller Brewing Co.
Plank Road Brewery (Watertown), 652
Plankington, John, 526
Plate, John J., 656
Platteville Brewery, Inc., 6, 582
Platteville, Wis., 581-82
Plattz Bros., 536
Platzer, Michael, 470
playing cards, 359, 464
Plover, Wis., 582-83
Plymouth, Wis., 21, 60, 76, 95, 350, 583-84
Plymouth Brewing (& Malting) Co. (1886-1937), 60, 554, 583-84
Plymouth Brewing Co. (2013-), 350, 584
Polakowski, Walter, 422
Polfus, Chris, 563
Polish Brewing Co., 75, 83, 634
Polish immigrants, 83-84, 166, 634
Polk (Twp.), Wis. (Washington Co.). See Cedar Creek, Wis.
Pollman, Noreen, 408
Pollman, Robert (Bob), 408
Ponsloff, Frederic, 400
pop. See soft drinks
popular price beers, 268, 275, 289, 293, 294, 519-20, 532. See also beer: prices
Port Huron Brewing Co., 673-74
Port Washington Brewing Co. (1903-1920), 585
Port Washington Brewing Co. (1996-2002), 587
Port Washington, Wis., 44, 75, 584-87
Portage, Wis., 35, 51, 63, 68, 76, 77, 117, 220, 243, 587-89
porter, 29, 34, 38, 40, 53, 68, 217, 315, 350, 426, 564, 596. See also individual breweries
Porter, Tom, 367
porter, imported to Wisconsin, 40, 53
Portland (Twp.), Wis. See Reeseville (P.O.), Wis.
Portz Brothers Malt and Grain Co., 95, 431
Portz, George, 431
Portz, Jacob, 431
Portz, Jacob, Brewing & Malt Co., 431
postcards, 434, 521
Postel, John, 555

posters, 106, 150, 537, 560, 604
potatoes, in beer, 240, 320-21
Potosi, Wis., 352-53, 589-91
Potosi Brewery Foundation, 352-53
Potosi Brewing Co. (1905-72), 115, 197, 228, 262, 270, 272, 275, 276-77, 316, 589-91
Potosi Brewing Co. (2008-), 310, 346, 352-53
Powderly, Terence V., 141
Poweleit, Cheryl, 398
Poweleit, John, 398
Powell, John, 360
Powell, M. W., 505
Powell's Ale Brewing Co., 505
PowerMaster malt liquor, 302-3
Prairie du Chien Brewing Co., 592
Prairie du Chien, Wis., 104, 514, 591-92
Prairie Street Brewery, 532
Pratt, Edward, 494
Premier Malt Products (Peoria Heights, Ill.), 509-510
Premier-Pabst. See Pabst Brewing Co.
Premo Products Co., 585
Presbyterians, 171
Prescott, Wis., 76, 592-93
Pressed Steel Tank Corp., 211
Pribek, Steve, 548
price ceilings, for beer, 237-38. See also beer: prices
Price, Clinton G., 561
Priestly, Joseph, 26,
Prima Brewing Co. (Chicago), 229, 235
Princeton Brewing Co., 593-94
Princeton Products Co., 593
prisoner of war camps, beer sold to, 236, 414, 625
Pritchard, Henry S., 36, 413
Pritchard, Owen, 505
private labels, 539, 590
prohibition: enforcement of, 194-97, 204-5, 613, 625; opponents (wets), 187, 190-91; and organized crime, 195, 204, 214, 383, 414, 422, 625, 658, 671; and politics, 185-86: repeal of, 197, 208-15, 230; and World War I, 188-89, 191-92; and World War II, 236. See also temperance
Prohibition Party, 185-86
Proposom, Gail, 554
Proposom, Pat, 554
proprietors. See brewers

prostitution, and saloons, 184. See also saloons: and women
Public Craft Brewing Co., 452
Puerner, Adam, 446
Puerto Rico, exports to, 614, 668
Pumphouse Pizza, 467-68
pumpkin beers, 321, 333, 391, 468, 480, 543, 544
punchboards, 270
Pure Beer Brewing Co., 648
Pure Food and Drug Act (1906), 187-88, 458, 576
Pure Food Products Company, 662
Pusch, Anthony (Anton), 433
Putnam, Henry W., 134
Putnam cork retainer, 134, 536, 537

Quade, William, 670
Quakers, 171
Quast, John, 644
Quenengasser, Charles, 421-22
Quentin Park. See Schlitz Park

R'Noggin Brewing Co., 452
Raasch, Frederick, 652
Rabenstein, F., 380
Rablin, Henry, 37, 408-9
Rablin, John, 409
Racine, Wis., 44, 51, 56, 62, 66, 75, 77, 88, 109, 110, 116, 143, 146, 177, 194, 203, 594-99, 681n46
Racine Malt Co., 598-99
racking (kegging) of beer, 294. See also kegs
Raddant, Emil T., Brewing Co., 84, 116, 611-12
radio programs, sponsored by breweries, 389, 510, 519, 523, 541, 568, 585-86, 600, 646
Radtke, Gilbert, 643
Radtke, Theo, 593
Radzanowski, David, 316
Rahr Brewing Co. (Green Bay), 112, 228, 425-26, 613
Rahr Brewing Co. (Oshkosh), 79, 272, 571-15
Rahr Malting Co./Rahr Corporation, 19, 20, 94-95, 482
Rahr, August, 571
Rahr, Blanche, 572
Rahr, Carl, 572
Rahr, Charles III (Chuck), 272, 572

Rahr, Charles Jr. (Charlie), 571–72
Rahr, Charles Sr., 68, 571–72
Rahr, Fred A., 426
Rahr, Guido Reinhardt, 481, 616
Rahr, Henry (Brewing Co.), 423, 67–68, 567
Rahr, Henry C., Brewing Co.: purchase of Calumet Brewing Co., 390
Rahr, Lucille, 572
Rahr, Maximilian, 482
Rahr, Natalie, 481
Rahr, Reinhardt, 482
Rahr, William Jr., 482
Rahr, William, 54, 73, 481–82
Rahr, William, Sons, 20, 388, 482
Rahte, Henry, 410
Raids, on breweries. *See* prohibition: enforcement of; wildcat breweries
Rail House Restaurant & Brewpub, 488
railroads: and beer shipments, 73, 75, 100, 116, 125–27, 162, 220, 277, 240–41; breweries located near, 116, 256; freight cars, 115, 133, 191
Raised Grain Brewing Co., 659
Ramlack, Gustave J., 127
Randall, Charles H., 690n53
Random Lake, Wis., 241–42
Randy's Restaurant and Fun Hunters Brewery, 671
Rank, Frank, 455
Rasmussen, Jason, 432
Rasmussen, Will, 432
rathskellers. *See* taprooms
Rattigan, Thomas, 302
Rauch, Raymond, 453
Readfield, Wis., 600
Readstown, Wis., 53, 600
Real Deal Beer, 500
Red Arrow Division (32nd Infantry), 605, 647
Red Brewery, 649–50
Red Brick Brewing Co., 432
Red Eye Brewing Co., 666
Redeman, Charles, 676
Reedsburg Brewery/Brewing Co., 220, 243, 600–602
Reedsburg, Wis., 8, 339, 340, 600–602
Reeseville (P.O.), Wis., 602
Reeves & Waddle, 502
Reeves, John, 502
Reeves, William, 502
refrigeration: household, 199, 215, 226, 228, 246; mechanical (artificial), 38, 100–101, 105, 108, 118, 141, 204; rail cars, 100, 133, 169, 214
Regenfuss, George, & Co., 420–21
Regenfuss, John, 449
Regenfuss, Mathias, 421
Reglein, John Christoph, 414, 417
Rehmsted, H. F., 581
Reidel, Bernard, 212
Reidenbach, Charles, 420
Reimerdes, August, 524
Reiner, George, 380
Reinertsen, Emma May Alexander (Gale Forest), 184
Reingrueber, A. H., 420
Reinheitsgebot, 16, 22
Reinke, Gustave, 488
Reistad, Nick, 659
Reiter, Charles, 400
Reitzenstein, Charles, 531
Reitzenstein, Guido (Gustav), 531
Remington, Brett, 659
Renzy, Jerry, 452
repeal. *See* prohibition: repeal of
Republican Party, 63, 73, 74, 147, 161, 197, 365
Reuss, Henry, 292
Reutelshofer (Reuthlisberger), Simon (Herman), 41, 43, 504
Revolver Brewing (Granbury, Tex.), purchase by MillerCoors, 524
Rezny, Jerry, 337
Rheingold Breweries, Inc. (Brooklyn, N.Y.), 282, 283, 284
Rheude, Anton, 516
Rhinelander, Wis., 100, 602–4
Rhinelander Brewing Co., 77, 210, 226, 267, 269, 316, 602–4
Rice Lake, Wis., 218, 604–5
Rice Lake Brewing Co. (1891–1904), 604
Rice Lake Brewing Co. (1936–74), 277, 406, 605
rice, in beer, 22, 159, 229, 332, 576
Rice, Steve, 637
Richards & Harrison, 131
Richardson & Barrett, 374
Richfield, Wis., 605–6
Richland City, Wis., 606
Richmond, Rose, 608
Richter, Frederick, 415, 416
Richter, J., 484
Riedel, George, 436
Riedinger, Charles, 652
Rindskoff (Rindskopf), Samuel F., 129
Ring, Frank, 417
Ripon, Wis., 606–7
Ripon Brewing Co., 578, 607
Rissler & Hemrich, 360
Rissler & Jung, 360
Ristau, Charles, 449
Ritter (brewer of Stevens Point), 633
River Falls, Wis., 607–8
Riverside Brewery (West Bend), 669
Riverview Brewing Co., 234, 485
Riverwest neighborhood (Milwaukee), 333, 346, 543, 546, 547
Roberts, Wis., 349, 608
Robinson, Norton B., 444
Robinson's Ale Brewery, 444
Rochester, Wis., 201
Rock Bottom Brewery, 339, 546
Rock Brewery, 498
Rock River Brewery (Janesville), 440
Rock River Brewery (Watertown), 652–53
Rockdale, Wis. *See* Clinton, Wis.
Rockenbach, George, 471
Rockford, Ill., 374–75
Rockhound Brewing Co., 480
Rockland (Twp.), Wis., 400
RockPere Brewing Co., 400
Rocky Reef Brewing Co., 314
Rodabaugh, Wesley, & Co., 487
Rodermund, John, 473–74
Rodriquez, Rosy, 546
Roedel, Baptist, 540
Roeffs, John, 484
Roehrl, Ignatz, 19
Roensch, Steve, 387
Roeser, Casper, 609, 610, 611
Roeser, George, 611
Roethe, Edward, 395
Roethinger, Anna B., 441
Roethinger, George, 441
Roethinger, John, 17, 71, 111, 440–41
Rogers, Anson, 68, 112, 438–39
Rogers, Eddie, 579
Rogers, James, 520
Roggy, Jacob, 549
Roggy, Joseph, 554–55
Roleff & Wagner, 499
Rolph, Allyson, 640
Romander, William, 413
Rome, Wis., 608

Rondeau, Francis, 487
Rooney, Robert R., 639–40
Roosevelt, Franklin Delano, 208, 209, 213, 214, 229, 390
Roosevelt, Theodore, 518
Root, N. A., Co., 129
Rosa & Bender, 440
Rosa, C., 440
Roscoe, Harvey, 651
Rosenheimer, Lehman, 624
Rosholt, Wis., 608
Ross, Walter A., 196, 565
Roth, George Frederick, 419–20
Rothaus Restaurant & Brewery, 432
Rothmann, Michael, 622
Roundhouse Brewing (Aurora, Ill.), as contract brewer, 375
Rowland, Bob, 337–38, 390–91
Rowland, Bonita, 337–38, 390–91
Rowland, Pat, 391
Rowland's Calumet Brewing Co., Inc., 337–38, 391
Roxbury, Wis., 608
Royko, Mike, 246, 320, 632
Ruder, Emil, 501, 662
Ruder, George, 62, 501, 629, 661–62
Rudersdorf, John, 400
Rudolph, Jack, 205
Rudolphi, Anna, 610
Rudolphi, Theophil, 610
Ruegger, Edward, 552
Rueping, Fred J., 639
Rueping, Frederick R., 639
Rueping, Louis, 639
Ruety & Walter, 570
Ruff, George, 604
Ruff, Howard, 487
Ruhland Brewing Co., 69, 371
Ruhland, George, 371
rum, 170, 394
Rundbogenstil, 117
Runge, August, 387
Runkel (brewer in Sheboygan), 620
Runkel, Henry, 419, 491
Runkel, Maria, 419, 491
Rush River Brewing Co. (Maiden Rock), 480–81
Rush River Brewing Co. (River Falls), 607–8
Rush, Benjamin, 171
rushing the growler, 184. *See also* growlers

Russell, Howard, Hyde, 185
Russell, John, 660
Rustic Rail Grill & Brewhouse, 429
Rustic Road Brewing Co., 452
Ruth, Gregor, 566–67
RWS Brewing, 659
Ryan's Corners, Wis. *See* Pierce (Twp.), Wis.
Ryder, David, 548
rye, 170, 240, 325

S & R Cheese Corp., 584
SABMiller. *See* Miller Brewing Co.
Sacket, H. S., 376
Saile, Charles, 401, 604
Saile, Elizabeth, 604
Saint Archer Brewing Co. (San Diego, Calif.), purchase by MillerCoors, 524
Saint Jerome Society, 174
Saint Joseph Society, 174
Salbey, Eugene, 522
saloonkeepers: and brewery ownership, 83–85, 243; and politics, 55, 88–89, 161, 183, 185
saloons, 80–83, 126, 140, 144, 146, 151, 192, 204; attacks on, 172–73; at breweries, 52, 69, 75–76, 335; as community centers, 64, 181–84; number of, 80, 146; owned by Pabst, 183; owned by Schlitz, 120, 186; regulation of, 74, 79, 177–78; tied houses, 87, 88, 146, 147–48, 151–52, 184–85, 186, 191, 218, 614; and vice, 167, 183–85, 246; and women, 148–49. *See also* taverns
Saltis, Joe, 664
San Francisco, Calif., shipments to, 14, 76, 131
Sand Creek Brewing Co., 370, 377–78, 400–401, 545
Sander Bros., 411
Sander, Adam, 411, 583
Sands, J. G., 535
Sands, J. J., 535
Sands' Ale Brewing Co., 535
Sands' Columbia Brewery (Chicago), 53, 535
Sands' Spring Brewery, 38, 40, 53, 535
Sänger-Bund, 190
Sapporo Breweries (Japan), 299
Sarbecker, George, 178
Sassy Brew, 251–52, 655, 695n9

Saudi Arabia, sales in, 658
Sauer & Muehlschuster, 516, 526
Sauer, Nancy, 640
Sauer, Rick, 488, 563, 640
Sauk City, Wis., 45, 52, 62, 87, 609–11
Sauk City Brewing Co., 609–10
Sauk County: as hop region, 96–97
Savage, J. T., 376
Sawmill Brewing Co., 347, 502
Sawyer, Philetus, 162
Saxon Brewing Co., 447
Saxton, F. B., 409
Schaab, Joseph A., 542
Schacttler (Schaettle), Charles, 382
Schad, A. F., 542
Schade, Louis, 180
Schaefer (Shaefer), Anthony, 402
Schaeffer, Lewis, 387
Schaeffer, Valentine, 401
Schaffra, John, 433
Schall, Gene, 625
Schaller Brewing Co., 584
Schandein, Emil, 102, 108, 126, 129, 162, 505, 529
Scharbillig Bros., 605
Schardt, Alma, 612
Schardt, Paul, 612
Scharmann, Heinrich, Sr., 437
Schatz, F. J., 448
Scheer, Fred, 503
Scheibe, Christian, 71, 388, 482
Scheibe, Emil, 388, 488–89
Scheibe, Gustav A., 388
Scheibl, George, 386
Scheibl, Mary, 386
Scheidt, Adam, Brewing Co. (Norristown, Pa.), 235
Scheiffer, Philip, 628
Schellhas, Kurt, 416–17
Schelling, Phillip Erhard, 594, 597, 598
Schenck, Augustina, 87
Schenck, George, 87
Schenck, Ulrich, 674
schenk beer, 451
Schenk, Charles, 631
Schenkel, Andrew, 411
Schenley Distillers, 514
Scherer (Scheer), Franz, 386
Scheuer, John George, 551
Schiffman, Andrew, 573
Schiffman, Leonard, 573
Schilling, Leopold, 611

Schimmel, Joseph, 605
Schinker, Jake, 548
Schirbe, Charles, 484
Schlacter, Thomas, 617–18
Schlegal, Charles, 422
Schleisinger, Jules, 624
Schleisingerville, Wis. *See* Slinger, Wis.
Schlenk, Augustina, 375
Schlenk, Frank, 375
Schlenk, George (Beloit), 371–72, 595
Schlenk, George (Sauk City), 609
Schleswig, Wis. *See* Kiel, Wis.
Schletty, Fred, 499
Schletty, Tim, 499
Schlicht, Leonard, 55, 618
Schlict, John, 420
Schliebitz, Herman, 507
Schlitz, Anna, 517–18
Schlitz, Joseph, 65, 153, 517
Schlitz, Joseph, Brewing Co., 2, 21, 80, 87, 98, 109, 114, 117, 129, 131, 133, 141–42, 143, 154, 158, 197–98, 229, 231, 256–58, 266, 281, 286–93, 648, 517–162; advertising, 1, 3, 25, 106, 117, 131, 135, 147, 148, 153, 154, 155–56, 158, 187, 227, 236, 251, 252, 253, 257, 271, 275, 291–93, 517–20; agents & depots, 79, 113, 125, 152, 271, 291; Brooklyn, N.Y., brewery (Ehret), 256, 519; Burgermeister purchase attempt, 257, 258, 519; decline of, 28, 286–93; employees, 51, 99, 138, 139, 141–2, 161, 262, 263–64, 266, 286, 292; exports and shipments, 100, 148, 162, 231, 255, 518; Honolulu, Hawai'i brewery, 257, 519; Kansas City, Mo., brewery, 257, 519; legal issues, 258, 275, 287, 291, 292; Longview, Tex., brewery, 519; Memphis, Tennessee brewery, 257, 308, 519–20; Milwaukee brewery, 63, 117, 118, 123, 213, 214; non-brewery properties, 146, 147, 152, 154, 186, 687n90; Palm Garden, 146, 334; production levels, 123, 124, 257, 264, 286–7, 291, 329, 518; products, 129, 131, 134, 193, 204, 227, 238, 251, 271, 285, 287, 298; during Prohibition, 193, 197–98; sale to Stroh, 292, 520; special events, 144, 147, 153, 155–56, 158; Syracuse, N.Y., brewery, 520; Tampa, Florida brewery, 257; and Turkey, proposed brewery in, 519; Van Nuys, Calif., brewery, 254–55, 256, 519; Winston-Salem, N.C., brewery, 257, 519–20
Schlitz Malt Liquor beer: advertising, 5, 287, 297, 301, 302, 520
Schlitz Park, 147, 153, 165, 518
Schlough, Charles, 494
Schlüter, Hermann, 142, 143
Schmedeman, Albert G., 215
Schmid, Georg, 409, 608–9
Schmidmeyer, F. X., 391–92
Schmidt, Adam, 448
Schmidt, Alexander P., 399–400, 486
Schmidt, C. & Sons Brewing Co. (Philadelphia, Pa.), 293, 462, 511
Schmidt, Cornils F., 393
Schmidt, Emil, 596
Schmidt, Florian, 492
Schmidt, Henry, 485
Schmidt, Jacob, Brewing Co. (St. Paul), branch of Heileman, 304
Schmidt, Martin, 399, 486
Schmidt, Nicholas, 73, 83, 486–87, 674
Schmidt, R. C., 544–45
Schmidt & Co., 448
Schmidt & Schunk, 376
Schmidt & Son, 394
Schmidt Brewing Co. (Detroit), 282–83
Schmidternecht, William, 423
Schmidtner, Leonard, 117, 529, 588
Schmieg, George, J., 471
Schmiling, Aric, 360
Schmiling, Brad, 360
Schmilling, Henry, 360
Schmitz, Heinrich, 610
Schmitz, Henry, 80
Schmitz, J. A., 495
Schmitz, Mark, 467–68, 673
Schmitz, William, 385
Schmitz & Ortscheid, 385–86
Schmitz & Weisse, 385–86
Schneeberger, Todd, 387
Schneider Brothers malting, 95, 583
Schneider, Albert, 488–89
Schneider, Andrew, 583
Schneider, John, 607
Schneider, Kurt, 394
Schneider, Leonhardt, 515
Schneider, Otto, 583
Schneider, Richard, 583
Schneider, Roger D., 263,

Schnell, Andrew (Andy), 655, 658
Schnell, Frederick, 434
Schnitt, 145, 441, 454–55, 593
Schock, John, 622
Schock, John M., 656
Schock, Matthias, 653, 656
Schoen, Henry, 665
Schoen, Louis, 665
Schoen, Valentine, 378
Schoenbrunn, Robert, 636
Schoenhofen, Peter, Brewing Co. (Chicago), 584, 657
Schoenick, Gustav, 670
Schoepp, Christoph, 527
Schonbrunn Brewing Co., 636
Schorer, Joseph, 409, 611
Schott, Saltzenberger & Co., 387
Schottmueller, Frank (Francis) X., 368
Schraut, R. A., & Co., 610
Schreiber, John, 527
Schreier, Herman, 618
Schreier, Konrad, 618
Schreier, Konrad, brewery/(Brewing) Co., 74, 88, 110, 584, 618–20
Schreihart, Henry J., 484
Schreihart, John, 482, 484
Schreihart, Peter, 484
Schreihart Brewing Co., 484
Schreiner, Anton, brewery (Schwanstein Brewery), 76, 583
Schreiner, John, 589
Schroeck, John M., 660–61
Schroeder Brewing Co. (Minn.), 158
Schroeder, Cory, 400–401
Schroeder, Fred, 601, 641
Schu, Jacob, 371
Schu, M., 371
Schueller, Bob, 586
Schueller, Jim, 586
Schueller, Rod, 586
Schuler, Frank, 380
Schuler, John, 52, 382
Schulkamp, Henry, 128
Schulkamp, John T., 128
Schulte, Rosalie, 623
Schulte, Severin, 623
Schultz, Charles, 263
Schultz, Clinton, 448
Schulz, Otto, 520
Schumacher, Adam, 381, 589–90
Schumacher, Adolph, 272, 277, 591
Schumacher, George, 589–91

INDEX   733

Schumacher, Henry, 589–90
Schumacher, Nicholas, 589–90
Schumacher, Rudolph, 277, 591
Schumann, Theodore, 591–92
Schumann & Menges, 104, 591–92
Schunck, Mary (Maria), 524
Schunck, Nicholas, 524
Schunckmann, Charles, 531
Schunk, Jacobina, 375–76
Schunk, Louis (Ludwig), 375–76
Schurz, Carl, 63, 189
Schussler, Albert, 412–13
Schussler, Arthur, 412–13
Schussler, Charles, 412
Schussler, Joseph, 411, 412, 569–12
Schuster, L., 463
Schutte, Charles, 373
Schwager, William, 649
Schwalbach, Henry, 557
Schwalbach, Robert, 557
Schwalm, Arthur, 577
Schwalm, Charles, 573
Schwalm, Henry, 573
Schwalm, Leonhardt, 68, 384, 569, 571, 573
Schwalm, Louis, 384
Schwalm, Otto, 573
Schwalm, Sophia, 573, 575
Schwalm, Theodore, 573
Schwanekamp, Bernard, 638
Schwanstein Brewery. *See* Schreiner, Anton
Schwartz, Andrew, 431
Schwartz, Cornelius, 378–79
Schwartz, Frederick, 532, 535, 536, 652
Schwartz, Henry, 344, 547
Schwartz, John F., 402
Schwartz, Joseph, 431
Schwartz, Joseph, Brewing Co., 431
Schwartz ballroom, 431
Schwarz, George, 592
Schwarzenbart, Peter, 485
Schweickhart, George, 531
Schweickhart, George Jr., 539
Schweke, Philip, 601
Schwenzen, Irvin, 495
scientific temperance instruction, 181
Scott (Twp.), Wis. *See* Wequiot, Wis.
Scott, Wis., 611
SDS. *See* Students for a Democratic Society
Sears, Jasper, 438

seasonal beers. *See* beer: styles; *individual breweries*
Second Salem Brewing Co., 671
Second Ward Savings Bank, 153–54
Sedlmayr, Gabriel, 37
Seibel, H. P., 652–53
Seideman, Frank, 418
Seideman, Gustav, 418
Seidemann, Hermann, 360, 635
Seidemann, Hugo, 635
Seider, Robert, 636
Seifert, E. N., 676
Seifert, Herman, 624
Seifert, Julius, 624
Seifert, Peter, 470, 661
Seigut, Peter, and Bros., 433
Seipp, Conrad, Brewing Co. (Chicago), 124
Seitz & Co., 385
Sellinger, Frank, 291
Semi-Centennial Exposition (Milwaukee), 144
Semrad-Pusch Brewing Co., 433
Semrad, Frank, 433
Semrad, John A., 433
Semrad, John V., 433
Semrad, Joseph, 433
Senglaub, Arthur, H., 486
Senglaub, Otto, 484, 616
Senne, John H., 532
Seresse, Nicholas, 410
Servais, Rob, 429
Servi, Mike, 429
Service, Phillip, & Co., 597
Seuberdick, Richard, 495
Severin, F. Peter, 642
Severson Act, 205
Shakman, James G., 242
Shakopee, Minn., Rahr Malting facility in, 482
shandies, 324–25, 550
Shankler Brewery, 418
shareholders. *See* breweries (businesses)
Sharon (Twp.), Wis. *See* South Grove, Wis.
Sharon, Amanda, 429
Sharon, Chad, 429
Shaw, Absalom, 419
Shaw, Spicer, 627
Shawano, Wis., 84, 116, 210, 611–13
Shawano Brewing Co., 193, 612

Shawano Specialty Co., 612
Shebert & Bion, 366
Sheboygan, Wis., 18, 55, 58, 62, 74, 88, 109, 110, 146, 192, 197, 208, 211, 212, 213, 263, 268, 304, 613–621
Sheboygan Brewing Co., 619–20
Sheboygan Falls, Wis., 621–22
Sheibe, Richard, 674
Sheibly, John, 401
Shepherd & Co., 597
Sherman (Twp.), Wis., 628
Shibilski, Felix (Phil), 320, 632
Shiels, Thomas, 638
Shipwrecked Brew Pub, 408
Shleip, John, 417
Shorewood, Wis., 199–200
shorty bottles. *See* bottles: small sizes
Shovenfelter, William, 371
Showaki, Isaac, 659
Shullsburg, Wis., 622–23
Shullsburg Brewing Co., 623
Sibley, Henry, 34–35
Siebel, John E., 631
Siebel Institute of Technology, 48, 559
Sieben, John, 421
Sigel (Twp.), Wis., 624
signs: indoor, 7, 148, 248, 301, 406, 616; lighted, 248, 390, 459, 461, 523, 557, 578; neon, 8, 378; outdoor, 60, 70, 81, 120, 121, 151, 185, 204, 216, 340, 343, 434, 509, 514, 515, 615, 693n73; reverse (painted) on glass, 17, 78; tin, 168, 182, 371, 372, 396; types, 70
Silberschmidt, Louis, 592
Silperson, E., 398
Silver Creek, Wis., 624
Silver Creek Brewery (pre-Prohibition), 599
Silver Creek Brewing (craft brewery), 342, 387
Silver Lake Brewery, 486
Silver, J. K., Brewing Co., 554
Silverling, Michael, 637
Silverschmidt, Louis, 662
Simon, Mathias, 360
Simons, Deb, 410
Sims, Edward, 641
Sindermann, August, 486–87
Sindermann, Frank R., 486
Singer, Jacob, 442
Singleman, Henry, 436

Sioux City Brewing Co. (Sioux City, Iowa), 266, 267, 616
Sipple, George, 196, 565
Sitzberger, Herman, 600
six-pack, 248; carriers/holders, 2, 248, 510, 544, 545, 644
Sizer, Henry, 638
Skala, John, 360, 661
Skarda, Mathias, 110
Skeleton Crew Brew, 569
Slab City Brewing Co., 379–80
sleds/sleighs, to transport beer, 110, 573
Slinger, Wis., 77, 624–26
Slow Food movement, 314
Smiley, H. F., 74
Smith, Henry, 375
Smith, J. (Burlington), 383
Smith, J. F., 580
Smith, John, 394
Smith, Steve, 659
Smith, Tyler, 676
Smith, William F. Jr., 293
Smith, William, 553
Smoko, Andrea, 402
Smoko, Brian, 402
Smolenski, Walter, 595
Snell, Matt, 284
Snoven, David, 413
Social Democratic Party, 183
Social Security, 229
socialists, 183
Society of Oshkosh Brewers, 579
soft drinks: made by breweries, 196, 197, 322, 331, 421, 578, 619. See also individual breweries
solar power, in breweries, 666
Soldiers Grove, Wis., 626
Somer, John, 553
Somerset, Wis., 349, 626–27
Sommermeyer, Henry, 405
Sons of Hermann, 504
Sons of Temperance, 56, 57, 173, 174, 175, 180, 689n8
Sontag, Lewis, 556
Sorenson, Jim, 547
Sorenson, Louis, 556
sorghum, in beer, 421
sour beers, 27, 560
South African Breweries (SAB), 309. See also Miller Brewing Co.
South Grove, Wis., 627

South Shore Brewing Co., 339, 368–69; Washburn taphouse, 648
South Side Brewery (Best). See Best, Phillip Brewing Co.
South Side Weiss Beer Brewery. See Graf, John J.
Southport, Wis. See Kenosha, Wis.
Southside Brewery (Rice Lake), 604
souvenir booklets, 99, 123, 127, 138, 146, 152, 164, 505, 519
Spaeth, William, 49, 414
Spanish-American War, 148, 150, 509, 518
Spany, John, 360
Sparta, Wis., 627–28
speakeasies, 204–5. See also prohibition: enforcement
Spehn, Peter, 422
Spencer, Frederick, 670
Spencer, Wis., 71. See also Sherman (Twp.), Wis.
spent grain, to farmers as livestock feed, 22, 71–72, 615
Sperry, Alanson K., 496
Spicer, Joseph (& Co.), 44, 450
Spielmann, Jacob, 549
Spies, Jacob, 567
Spillane, Mickey, 284
Spooner, John C., 162
Sporer, John, 375
Spotted Cow beer, 334, 559
Sprecher, Frederic (Adam), 51, 471
Sprecher, Margaret, 471
Sprecher, Randal (Randy), 328, 421, 543
Sprecher Brewery (19th century), 51, 64, 471
Sprecher Brewing Co. (1986–), 328, 331, 421, 543
Sprey, Matthew, 515
Spring Brewery (Taycheedah), 641
Spring Brewery, Milwaukee, 38, 40, 53
Spring Green, Wis., 628
Spring Lake Brewery, 382
spruce beer, 412, 413
St. Croix Falls, Wis., 608
St. Francis Brewing Co., 635
St. Francis, Wis., 635
St. Lawrence, Wis., 608
St. Louis Exposition (World's Fair) (1904), 17–18, 134, 447
St. Martins (P.O.), Wis. See Franklin, Wis. (Milwaukee Co.)

St. Nazianz, Wis., 609
St. Paul, Minn., 62, 77, 219, 235, 274, 304, 305, 306, 319, 327
Staats, John, 420
Staats, Valentine, 420
Staatsville, Wis. See Germantown, Wis. (Washington Co.)
stables, 55, 102, 103, 110, 114, 115, 123, 125, 465. See also breweries: buildings
Stahl, Frank, 674
Stahl, Frederick, 542
Stamm & Meyer, 129, 130, 131, 132
Stamm, Philip, 413, 642
Standard Brewing Co. (Rochester, N.Y.), 38
Star Brewery (Appleton). See Walter, Geo., Brewing Co.
Star Brewery (Racine), 595
Star Brewing Co., 470–71
Starboard Brewing Co., 637
Stauss, W. F., 495
steamboats: to deliver beer, 115
steam power. See breweries (buildings): steam power
steam whistles, 74
Stebbins, Pepper, 480
Steffen, A. P., 618
Steger, Henry, 493
Steger, John, 492–93, 642
Steidl, Jeff, 370
Steil, Frank X., 371
Stein, Herbert, 510
Stein, Peter, 610
Steiner, Carl, 622
Steiner, Ferdinand, 595
Steiner, Norman, 261
Steinmetz, John B., 45, 421
steins, 67, 215, 289, 306, 377, 509. See also glasses
Stending (Steiting), Gustav, 401–2, 403–4
Stephens, Samuel, 381
Stephenson, Christen, 598
Stephenson, Jens, 598
Stephensville, Wis., 628–29
Sterling (Twp.), Wis., 629
Sterr, Albert, 470–71
Sterr, August, 470–71
Sterr, Edward, 470–71
Sterr, Rudolph, 470–71
Stevens Point Brewery/Brewing/

INDEX 735

Beverage Co., 57, 74, 110, 158, 159, 213, 237, 274, 312, 319–22, 329, 353, 629–32
Stevens Point, Wis., 57, 68, 74, 75, 83, 97, 213, 629–35
Stevens, Bill, 377
Stevens, Brooks, 523
Stewart, Ethelbert, 138
stickers, 314, 344
Stieher, Leo, 441
Stier, Joseph, 578
Stillmank, Brad, 429
Stillmank Brewing Co., 310, 429
Stinglhammer, Max, 610
Stinglhammer, Theresa, 610
Stirn, Jim, 394
Stite beer, 240, 281, 383
stock. See breweries (businesses): sale of stock in
stockhouses, 118, 521, 523 breweries (buildings)
Stoddard (P.O.), Wis. See Bergen (Twp.), Wis.
Stofer, Xaver, 382
Stolt, Dan, 379
Stoltz, Henry, 515
Stoltz, Margaret, 102, 515
Stoltz, Michael, 515
Stoltz & Krell, 515
Stolz, Henry, 418–19
Stolz, Jacob, 423, 515–16
Stone Arch Brewpub, 365–66
Stone Cellar Brewpub/Brewery, 338, 365–66
Stone, Stephen, 641
Stonefly Brewing Co., 546
Storck, August, 625
Storck, H. Charles, 607, 625
Storck, Henry, 625
Storck, Ray, 625–26
Storck Brewery/Brewing/Products Co., 77, 197, 625–26
Storeck, Charles, 552
Storm, Henry, 661
Stoughton, Wis., 178, 635
Stout Brothers Brewing Co., 546
stout, 29, 31, 158. See also individual breweries
Stovey, Frank, 676
Strange, John, 191
Stransky & Swaty, 360
Stransky, Wyta, 360, 453

Strauss, Karl, 671
Strauss, W. F., 495
Streblow, Ferdinand, 583
Strehlow, Fred, 652
Streng, George, 67, 395, 670, 681n21
strikes, 3, 88–91, 140–43, 161, 243, 262–66, 291, 292, 305, 534, 568, 616, 658; violence during, 88, 140–42, 161, 263
Stringer (Stimger), John, 402
Stroh Brewery Co. (Detroit), 264, 292, 293, 295, 303, 306, 307, 317, 553
Stroh, Donald, 417
Strohn, Adolph, 531
Strong, Louis, 607
Strosell, Conrad, 393
Students for a Democratic Society (SDS), 266
Stueven, Richard, 395, 400
Stuhlfauth, George, 486
Stuhlfauth, Oscar, 486
Sturgeon Bay, Wis., 75, 219, 255, 337, 427, 635–37
Sturgeon Bay Brewery/Brewing Co., 75, 197, 255, 635–36, 637
Summers, Bill, 402
Summit (Twp.), Wis., 637
sumptuary laws. See temperance: legislation
Sun Prairie, Wis., 109
Sunday closing laws, 74, 79, 172, 177, 575. See also temperance
Sunday, Billy, 192
Sunshine Brewing (Reading, Pa.), 696n35
Superior, Wis., 62, 116, 218, 272, 338, 637–40
supper clubs, 313
Supple, Jay, 579
Supple, Joe, 579
Supple, John, 579
Supreme Bottling Co., 659
Supreme Court (of United States), 192, 258, 481
Supreme Court (of Wisconsin), 178, 179
Surfus, Amanda, 637
Surfus, Patrick, 637
Sussenguth, Theodore, 423
Sussex, Wis., 282–83
Sutrick, Jacob, 429, 546
Swedish Brewing Co., 487–88
"Sweet Adeline" (song), 215
Sweet Mullets Brewing Co., 566

Swellingrade, Ernst, 447–48
Swinging Bridge Brewing Co., 608
Swiss immigrants, 377, 436, 525, 553
Sylvan, Wis., 35
Symonds, Keith, 480
syndicates. See breweries (businesses): consolidation of
syphon beer, 535

Taft, N.D., Rahr Malting facility in, 482
Taft, William Howard, 186
Tampa, Florida. See Schlitz, Joseph, Brewing Co.; Pabst Brewing Co.
Tankenoff, Alex (Al), 379, 502
Tankenoff, M. B., 379
tap handles (knobs), 232, 233, 386, 393
taprooms, 218, 219, 342, 347–48, 350. See also individual breweries
Tartsch, August, 608
Tartsch, Gottlieb, 608
Tasche, Frank, 620–21
tavern culture, 1, 3, 55, 215, 218, 228, 233, 246, 248, 249, 267, 268–69, 294, 337, 339
taverns, 37, 151, 171, 216, 218, 272, 273, 275, 291, 312, 322, 335, 337–38. See also saloons
taxation,
taxation: amount paid by breweries, 215; effect on profits, 623; enforcement, 66, 129, 242; fraud by brewers, 66, 452, 527, 538, 596, 613, 622; methods, 129; rates, 65, 66 stamps, 65, 75, 129, 229, 234–35, 242; by states, 230–31; by U. S. government, 65, 66, 161–62, Pt2–7; by Wisconsin, 229, 230–31, 234–35
Taycheedah, Wis., 410–11, 641–42
Taylor & Son, 403
Taylor County Brewing Co., 495
Taylor, John, 524
Taylor, Terry, 399
tea, in beer, 408, 546, 632
Teasdale, Howard, 200–201
Teisch, Johnathan, 384
telephones, in breweries, 447, 464, 501
temperance, 4, 55–58, 171–185; in armed forces, 186; campaigns, 180; lectures, 174, 176; legislation, 58; meetings, 57; organizations, 4, 171–75; origins, 170–74; and schools,

181; in Wisconsin, 55–58, 172–83. *See also* prohibition
Temperlie, H., 558
Tempo beer (Blatz), 250, 251
Tenth and Blake Brewery, 393–94, 524. *See also* MillerCoors; Heileman, G. Brewing Co.
Terrapin Beer Co. (Athens, Ga.), purchase by MillerCoors, 524
Terrill, William, 549
Testwuide, Louis, 618
Tetzlaff, William, 72
Texter, Clinton, 495
Thamer, August, 620
Thamish & Melchoir, 419
Theresa, Wis., 102, 642–44
Theurer, J. F., 508
Thiel, Randy, 560
Thiele, Gottfried, 652
Thielke, August, 437
Thiensville (P. O.), Wis. *See* Mequon, Wis.
Third Sign Brewery. *See* Octopi Brewing Co.
Third Space Brewing Co., 548
Thirsty Pagan Brewing Co., 640
Tholen, W. A., 585
Thom, Rheinhold, 84, 577
Thomas, Nicholas, 389
Thome, Matthew, 657
Thompson, Eliza Jane Trimble ("Mother"), 180
Thompson, Tim, 478
Thompson, Tommy, 306
Thorp, Wis., 82
Thorson, James, 589
Thurm & Carl, 484
Tibbits & Gordon, 473
Tiechmann, Ray, 263
tied houses. *See* saloons: tied houses
Tiedemann, N. J., 111
Tillmans, Francis, 570
Timm, Henry, 574
Tinker & Schlough, 494
Tirade (P.O.), Wis. *See* Linn (Twp.), Wis.
Tisch Mills, Wis., 385
Titletown Brewing Co., 16, 339, 351, 428–29
Todd, John G., 68, 443–44
Toepfer, Wenzel, & Son, 105, 406
tokens, issued by breweries, 63, 233, 512, 521

Tolber, F., 520
Tomah, Wis., 644
Tomahawk, Wis., 644
Topp, John, 433
Torchiani & Kremer, 129, 131, 132
Tornado Brewery, 549
total abstinence. *See* prohibition; temperance
tourism: in Wisconsin, 275, 339–40
Town of Lake Brewing Co., 538–39
trays, 363, 370, 393, 406, 503, 528, 663, 669
Treatise of Lager Beers, 202
Treaty Beer (Hibernia), 327
Treichler, Oscar, 522
Trempeleau, Wis., 626–29
Trentzch, John G., 400
Tressler, Bill, 399, 429
Tressler, Michelle, 399, 429
Tribute Brewing Co., 310, 402
Troia, Giotto, 344
Trottman, Robert, 645
Troyer, Dominick, 423
trucks. *See* delivery trucks
trusts. *See* breweries (businesses): consolidation of
Tulif, William J., 383
Turners, 53
Turnquist, Art, 644
Turtle Stack Brewery, 349, 467
Twin City Brewing Co., 674–75
Twin Ports Brewing Co., 640
Twin Rivers Brewery, 646–47
Two Beagles Brewpub, 569
Two Creeks, Wis., 645
Two Rivers Beverage Co., 265, 645–46
Two Rivers, Wis., 52, 645–47
Tyranena Brewing Co., 341

U-permits, 230, 379
Udelhofen, Joseph, 381
Uecker, Bob, 285
Uhen, John, 383
Uhl (Uhls), Leonard, 492, 656
Uihlein, Albert, 517
Uihlein, August, 154, 166, 517
Uihlein, Charles, 517
Uihlein, David V., 577
Uihlein, Edward G., 125, 517
Uihlein, Erwin C., 256
Uihlein, Henry, 517
Uihlein, Robert A. (Bob), 287, 291, 520

Uihlein, William, 98, 517
Uihlein family, 161, 165, 198, 287
Ulrich, William, 360
Ulricker, Joseph, 453
Unger, Richard, 35
Union (Twp.), Wis. *See* Namur, Wis.
Union Brewery (Alma), 360
Union Brewery (Chippewa Falls), 394
Union Brewery (Green Bay), 426–27
Union Brewery (Milwaukee), 506–7
Union Brewery (Oshkosh), 79, 574
Union Brewery (Theresa), 644
unions, 3, 88, 89, 90, 139–43, 183, 221–25, 242, 262–66, 273, 292, 295, 317, 393, 513, 663. *See also* strikes
United Black Enterprises, 260
United Brewery Workers: (Local 9), 142, 143, 263, 264, 295, 643; (Local 81), 263; (Local 158), 638, 639; (Local 277), 208, 263, 617. *See also* unions; strikes
United States Brewers Foundation, 244, 246, 247
United States Brewers' Association (USBA), 65, 237
United States Brewing Co., 513. *See also* Blatz, Val., Brewing Co.
Unity, Wis., 647
University of California, Davis, 328, 334, 547, 559
University of Wisconsin Extension Service, 21
University of Wisconsin–Madison, 647
University of Wisconsin–Platteville, 342, 582
University of Wisconsin–Stevens Point, 321
Unmuth, Louis, 364
Unterholzner, Felix, 549
Urban Harvest Brewing Co., 548
Urquhart, K. J., 495

Vager, George, 566–67
Valentine, Louis & Co., 412
Valkyrie Brewing Co., 397–98
Van Allen, Mrs. H. L., 204,
Van Boxtel, Neal, 429
Van Dyck beer, 426, 613
Van Dyck Brewing Co. (Shawano), 612
Van Dycke, Constanz F., 428
Van Dycke, Emil, 428
Van Dycke, Louis, 427

Van Dycke, O., Brewing Co., 79–80, 85–86, 427–28
Van Dycke, Octavia, 85–86, 427–28
Van Merritt Brewing Co., 316, 383–84, 568
Van Nuys, Calif.. See Schlitz Joseph Brewing Co., Van Nuys brewery
Van Schaick, Charles, 81
Vandenburg, David, 413
Vandermolen, John, 577
Vandervort, Tommy, 547
Vanville, Wis. See Bloomer, Wis.
Vaplon & Saile, 401
Varnes-Epstein, Michael, 626
Varrelmann, Gustav, 623
Varrelmann, Millicent, 623
Vaser, John. See Frazier (Feezier), John
Veeser, Nicholas, 664
Veidt, Jacob, 474, 527–28
Venturini, Steve, 387
Verbest, Frank C., 515
Verbsky, Joe, 434
Verbsky, Kim, 434
Verbsky, Snapper, 434
Verdon, Ryan, 500
Verona, Wis., 351, 647–48
Versteegh, Gary, 545
Vetter, George, 661
Vienna, Austria: beers of, 37
Vierth & Fick, 551
Vik'ing Brewpub, 349, 635
Viking Brewing Co., 290, 397
Vilter Manufacturing Co., 101, 105
Viroqua, Wis., 648
Vistart, Edna Ann, 264
Vitamin D, in beer, 519
Vitrolite signs, 70, 490
Voechting & Shape, 129, 131, 132, 134, 517
Voegele, G. F., 465
Voelkel, Frederick, 574–75
Vogel, George "Dutch", 383–84
Vogelberg, Joseph, 381, 589
Vogl, John, 420
Vogl, Joseph, 420, 491
Vogl, Louis, 420
Vogl's Independent Brewery/Brewing Co., 78, 420
Vogt, Anton, 411
Voight, Carl William, 474
Volke, Tom, 477
Vollant, Conrad, 613

Volstead Act, 192, 197, 199, 205, 208
Voltz & Sitz, 385
von Kessel, Hans, 388
Von Steihl Winery, 360
Voss, Henry, 495

Waburton, Jack, 394
Wacker, Reinhard, 629
Waegerle, George, 648
Waegerle, John, 648
Waegerle, Mary Madelaine, 648
Wagener, Nicholas Arnold, 635–36
Wagener, William, 635
Wagner, Ferdinand, 43, 422, 679n30
Wagner, Fred, 499
Wagner, John, 37, 43, 502, 679n30
Wagner, Lewis, 43
Wagner, Marten, 447
Wagoner, John N., 627–28
wagons. See delivery wagons
Wahl-Henius Institute of Fermentology, 108, 252
Wahle, Franz (Frank), 68, 629
Wahner, Anton, 536
Walbourne (Walbram), John, 638
Walecka & Kulhanek, 385
Wales: immigrants from, 35, 555
Walker, Scott, 428
Walker's Point (Milwaukee), 41, 328, 346
Wallace, Matt, 626
Wallner & Deda, 400
Wallner, Fred C., 454
Walrath (brewer in Sparta), 627
Walter, Carlus, 406
Walter, Charles, 406, 668
Walter, Christian, 497
Walter, Edgar, 406
Walter, Geo., Brewing Co. (Star Brewery), 50, 79, 84, 191, 221–25, 249, 274, 277, 364–65
Walter, George M., 365
Walter, H., 669
Walter, John J., 326
Walter, John, 71, 406, 570, 574, 628
Walter, Martin, 406, 668
Walter Brewing Co. (Eau Claire), 200, 216–17, 219, 270, 289, 325–27
Walter Bros. Brewing Co., 44, 79, 276, 497–98
Walworth County, 175
war bonds, 238, 501
War Food Administration, 191, 241

War Production Board, 239
Warm, Adam, 455
Warm, Anna, 455
Warm, F. X., 401
Warninger, George H., 466
Warnke, Nate, 480
Warschauer, Arthur, 420
Washburn Brewing Co./Assoc., 648
Washburn, C. C., 179
Washburn, Wis., 87
Washington Brewery (Milwaukee), 526
Washington Brewery (Prescott), 592
Washington Harbor, Wis., 648
Washington, George, 34
Washingtonians, 57, 173
water power, breweries operated by, 473
Water Street Brewery (Grafton), 339, 422
Water Street Brewery (Milwaukee), 337, 339–41, 544–45
Water Street Brewery (Oak Creek), 340, 564
Water Street Brewery, Lake Country (Delafield), 339, 398
water, 3, 17–19, 37, 123, 127, 187, 188, 255, 465, 618; bottled by breweries, 17, 199; cleaning uses, 131, 137; conservation by breweries, 344; damage to breweries, 55, 545; fluoridation, 18; municipal supplies, 18, 159, 162, 215, 276, 277; refuse (waste water), 102, 162–63, 563, 633
Waterford, Wis., 648–49
Waterloo, Wis., 649
Waters, M. D., 448
Watertown, Wis., 45, 51, 78, 98, 649–53
Watson Brewing Co., 659
Watson, Scott, 659
Waukesha, Wis., 67, 112, 152, 174, 187–88, 189, 193, 232, 236, 242, 264, 272, 653–59
Waukesha (Imperial) Spring Brewing Co., 144, 188, 656–57. See also Milwaukee-Waukesha Brewing Co.
Waunakee, Wis., 659–60
Waupaca, Wis., 660
Waupun, Wis., 660–61
Waupun Brewing Co., 661
Wausau, Wis., 62, 85, 340, 661–66
Wausau Brewing Co., 83, 85, 242, 265, 604, 664–65

Wauwatosa, Wis., 666 *See also* Milwaukee
Wayne (Twp.), Wis., 666
WCTU. See Woman's Christian Temperance Union
Weaner, Frank A., 601–2
Weaver, James, 641
Weaver, Richard, 641
Webb-Kenyon Act, 186
Weber (Webber), Adolph, 597
Weber, Benedict, 557, 642, 643–44
Weber, Bert, 643
Weber, Charles, 598
Weber, Cornelius (Cornie), 643
Weber, Ernst, 598
Weber, G., Brewing Co., 642–43
Weber, Gebhard, 642, 643
Weber, Gottfried, 583
Weber, John Peter, 525
Weber, John, 387, 422
Weber, Julia, 654–55
Weber, Killian, 654–55
Weber, Maria, 642
Weber, Stephan F., 654–55
Weber, Stephen, 527, 653–54
Weber, Victor, 643
Weber, William A., 112, 188, 654
Weber, William H., 597–98
Weber, William, 422
Weber & Werner, 499
Weber Waukesha Brewing Co., 5, 193, 227, 236, 252, 384, 655–56
Weckwerth, Rudolph, 446
Wedel, George, 581
Wedemeyer, Henry F., 595
Wehle, Franz, 574
Wehr, Conrad, 527
Wehr, George, 527
Weidenser (Wiedensen), Richard, 620, 622
Weidig, Nic., 470
Weile, Rudolph, 375
Weise, Johann Wolfgang, 41, 506
weiss beer breweries, 67, 105, 123, 129, 144, 153, 166, 234, 485, 620, 641–42, 652
weiss beer, 489, 614. *See also* individual breweries; wheat beer
Weist, August, 570, 593
Weiter, Joseph, 367
Wellhoffer, George, 618, 620
Wells, A. E., 552

Welter (Wetter), Michael, 405
Welter, Nicholas, 585
Welton, Mike, 392
Wendland, John, 378
Wenger, Joseph, 453
Wenzel, A. A., 501
Wenzel, Alex, 556
Wequiot, Wis., 425
Werle, R. Craig, 553
Werner, William, 431
Werrbach, Louis, 153, 537, 652
Wertin Bros., 503
Wertz, J. A., 401
West Allis, Wis., 667
West Bend, Wis., 667–68
West Bend Aluminum Co./West Bend Corp., 668
West Bend Brewery, 667
West Bend Brewing Co., 668
West Bend Lithia (Brewing) Co., 119, 213, 217–18, 260, 269, 277, 406, 668–69
West End Malt Co., 664–65
West Hill Brewery (Fond du Lac), 411, 412
West Hill Brewery (Milwaukee), 234, 527–28
West Hill Brewery (Waukesha), 527, 654
West Side Brewery (Eau Claire), 404
West Side Brewery, 540
West Superior Brewing Co., 638
West Superior, Wis. See Superior, Wis.
Westallion Brewing Co., 667
Western Brewer, 48, 134, 357
Western Brewery, 528–29
Westfield (P. O.), Wis. See Lawrence, Wis.
Westhofen, Charles, 529
Westport, Wis., 669
Weyauwega, Wis., 629, 669–70
Weycker, Brent, 428
Weyermann, Sabine, 560
Weyhe, T. Frederick, 430–31, 436
WHBL (radio) Sheboygan, 212, 586, 600
wheat beer, 22, 27, 233, 324, 327, 345. *See also* weiss beer breweries, weiss beer
Wheatland, Wis., 670
Wheeler, Wayne B., 186, 192
Whinfield (Winfield), John W., 641
Whipple, Louis, 627

Whistle Stop Restaurant & Woodman Brewery, 675–76
white beer breweries. *See* weiss beer breweries
White Fish Bay Resort (Pabst), 149, 152, 509
White, James, 66
White, John G., 95
White, John L., 195, 386
White, Ryan, 551
White, T. H., 473
Whitewater, Wis., 67, 75, 76, 178, 670–71
Whitewater Brewing Co., 671
Whitham, Emmanuel, 409
Whitman & Metzer, 431
Whitney, Joshua, 427
Whitney's, J. T. Brewpub and Eatery, 477
WIBL (radio), 390
Wichman, Matt, 488
Wickersham Commission, 205
Wiechmann, Jim, 322
Wiedemann, George, Brewing Co. (Newport, Ky.), 268, 304
Wiener (Vienna) beer (style), 136, 484, 513
Wiesender, Jim, 378, 401
Wilbers, Robert, 432, 499
Wilbur, Hawley W., 655
Wild, H., 554
Wild, Henry, 520
wildcat breweries, 200–201. *See also* prohibition: enforcement of
Wilde's Brewing Co. (Sacramento, Calif.), 553
Wildersman, John, 670
wild rice, in beer, 332
Wiley, Harvey, 154
Willard, Frances, 4, 180, 181, 188
Willems, Julius, 491
Williams, Ezra, 74
Williams, Frank P., 444
Williams, J. C., 417
Williams, James A., 417
Williams, John, 664
Williams, Johnnie, 90, 396
Williams, Thomas, 548
Williams, William, 597
Willinger, Frank, 484
Willinger, William, 454
Wilson, D., 581

Wilson, Mike, 499
Wilson, Wis., 24, 343, 671–72
Wilson, Woodrow, 191, 192
Wind, Jacob, 511
Winding & Gezelschap, 105
windmills, at breweries, 343, 360, 378, 449, 628, 672
Windsor, Wis., 672
wineries, in conjuction with breweries, 569, 608
Winggen, Peter, 403–4
Winkler, T. F., 529
Winneconne, Wis., 672
Winona, Minn., 152, 220, 235, 326
Winsand, Bill, 379–80
Winston-Salem. *See* Schlitz: Winston-Salem branch
Winz (Wing), Werner, 364, 497
Wiota, Wis., 672
Wirtanen, Trevor, 626
Wirth (Werth), Peter, 494
Wirth, J. A., 581
Wirth, John A., 554
Wisconsin: as barley growing region, 3, 18–19; beer culture in, 3, 312–14; as malting center, 94–96
Wisconsin Aluminum Foundry, 348
Wisconsin Brewers Association, 191
Wisconsin Brewers Guild, 330
Wisconsin Brewing Co. (Burlington), 383
Wisconsin Brewing Co. (Kenosha), 451–52
Wisconsin Brewing Co. (proposed), 79–80
Wisconsin Brewing Co. (Verona), 310, 351, 647
Wisconsin Brewing Co. (Wauwatosa), 377, 545
Wisconsin Chief (newspaper), 176–77
Wisconsin Co-operative Brewery, 219, 422
Wisconsin Dells (Kilbourn City), Wis., 672–74
Wisconsin Department of Revenue, 203
Wisconsin Homebrewing Alliance, 437
Wisconsin Iron Works, 94
Wisconsin Marine & Fire Insurance Co. Bank, 530
Wisconsin Micro Brewers Beer Festival, 390–91
Wisconsin Rapids, Wis. (formerly Grand Rapids), 674–75

Wisconsin State Fair, 154, 333
Wisconsin state legislature, 58, 73, 75, 179, 192, 234, 306
Wisconsin Supervisor of Food Inspection, 567
Wisconsin Tavern Keepers Association, 243, 542
Wismeth, A., 634
Wissman, Margaret, 622
Witt, Kim, 398
Witt, Marvin, 416–17
Witt, Mary Ann, 398
Wittenberg, Albert, 484
Wittmann, George, 586
Wittmann, John, 586
Wittmann, John Jr., 586
Wittmann, Margarethe, 586
Wittstock, Jack, 607
Wolf, C., & Bion, 366
Wolf, Charles, 596
Wolf, Fred W., 117–18
Wolf, Joseph, 538
Wolf, Mary, 538
Wolff, George D., 665
Wolff, L., 398
Wolff, William, 385
Wolfram, Lawrence, 435
Wolle, Dana, 398
Woman's Christian Temperance Union, 4, 180–81, 185, 204, 214
Woman's Home Companion magazine, 246
women: used in advertising, 32, 137, 148, 150–51; as beer consumers, 252, 283; as brewery employees, 87, 89, 137–39, 143, 225, 226, 242, 264, 265–66, 458, 464–7, 538; as brewmasters, 350, 428, 504, 608, 640, 673; as hop pickers, 97; as proprietors of breweries, 85–87, 525, 609, 654–55, 657; and suffrage, 188, 190; as temperance campaigners, 58, 172–73, 175, 179–81, 184, 188, 204, 476; and wildcat breweries, 203–4. *See also* saloons: and women
wood: as building material, 46, 47, 347; as fuel, 51–52; purchases by breweries, 51; timber land owned by breweries, 154
Woodman Brewery, 675–76
Woodruff, Wis., 676
Woodward & Bro., 653

Woodward, Moses, 413
Woodworth, Dexter S., 564–65
World War I, 188, 631
World War II, 235–242, 510, 600, 601
World's Industrial and Cotton Centennial, 131
World's Largest Six-Pack, 303, 308
Worst, Charles, 528
Worth & Kuehn (Medina), 496
Wright, Kevin, 548
Wright, Lyall, T., 561
Wrightstown, Wis., 74–75, 676
Writenberg, John, 398
WTMJ (radio station), 212
Wudtke, William, 569
Wunderle, Frank, 380
Wunderlich, George, 628–29
Wurst, George, 492

Yager, Katherina, 672
Yager, Theodore, 672
Yanda, Sam, 429
Yankees (immigrants from northeastern states): as community leaders, 38, 56, 176, 178, 179; immigration to Wisconsin, 38, 56, 174
yeast, 16, 22, 26–27, 29, 34, 37, 38, 42, 44, 98, 159, 200, 326, 345, 349, 679n30
Yellowley, Edward C., 664
Yenowine, George, 687n84
Yoerg, Louis, 436
York, Greg, 452
Young Woman's Companion & Instructor, 34
Young, E. J., 496
Young, Thomas, 67, 374
Yuba, Wis., 676

Zamzow, Don, 665
Zamzow, Mary, 665
Zamzow, Mike, 665–66
Zapp, Robert, 611
Zappa, John, 632
Zastrow, Walter, 643
Zastrow & Loeffler, 662
Zeiger, George, Soda Water Co., 540
Zeisler, George, 463
Zenefski, Brian, 221
Zengel, Charles, 362
Ziegelbauer, Benedict, 608
Ziegelmaier, George, 380

Ziegenfuss, George P., 415–16
Ziegenfuss, John S., 415–16
Ziegler, Anna, 492
Ziegler, Emil, 492
Ziegler, Eugene, 492
Ziegler, Jacob, 525, 532–33
Ziegler, Louis, 373, 417, 492
Ziegler, Louis, Brewing Co., 194, 242, 243, 372–73, 374, 386, 589
Ziegler, Louis Jr., 373
Ziegler, Matheus, 492
Ziegler, Matheus, Brewing Co., 492
Zielke, Rich, 408
Ziemke, John, 610
Zilleges, Roger, 577
Zimmerer, Anna, 623
Zimmerer, Louis, 623
Zimmerman, Adolphus, 418, 500
Zimmerman, Franz, 500
Zimmerman, Julius, 453
Zimmerman, Valentine, 430
Zinn Malting Co., 95
Zinns, John F., 485
Zippemer, Alexander, 407
Zirbes, Peter, 594
Zirbes, Phillip, 597
Zirfass, H., 400
Zobel, Fred, 447
Zummach, Jack, 144
Zweifel, Gabriel, 558
Zwietusch & Forster, 535
Zwietusch, Otto, 67, 105, 153, 155, 450, 535–36

DOUG HOVERSON is the author of *Land of Amber Waters: The History of Brewing in Minnesota*. He has written about beer and brewing history for publications ranging from *American Breweriana Journal* to *The Growler* and *The Onion*. He has been a consultant on several documentaries about beer or related businesses and is a popular speaker on the history of beer. He teaches and coaches at Saint Thomas Academy in Mendota Heights, Minnesota.